MUSIC IN AMERICAN LIFE

Long Steel Rail

Long Steel Rail

The Railroad in American Folksong

Norm Cohen

Music edited by David Cohen

UNIVERSITY OF ILLINOIS PRESS

Urbana   Chicago   London

LIBRARY OF CONGRESS CATALOGING IN PUBLICATION DATA

Cohen, Norm.
Long steel rail.

(Music in American life)
Bibliography: p.
Includes index.
1. Folk-songs, American—History and criticism.
2. Railroads—Songs and music—History and criticism.
I. Title.
ML3551.C57   784.6′8385′0973   80-14874
ISBN 0-252-00343-8

Facing page constitutes an extension of the copyright page.

To
Carson
and
Alexa

They kept me going.

Contents

Preface

THIS BOOK IS the result of a project that began nearly fifteen years ago at the suggestion of Richard E. Lingenfelter. Lingenfelter, together with Richard A. Dwyer and David Cohen, had completed two song collections, *Gold Rush Songs* and *Songs of the American West*, and had begun initial research for a book of railroad songs. His wide-ranging interests took him along other paths, however, and he asked me if I would like to take his notebooks and carry out the plan. I discussed this with David Cohen, who agreed to serve as music editor, as he had for the previous volumes.

At the time we took over the project, it had been the general rule in published folksong collections that sound recordings were greatly underutilized compared to printed sources, and we resolved not to follow this unfortunate precedent. In particular, our interest in early hillbilly and blues recordings prompted maximum use of these resources—largely untapped at the time we began our work—in assembling an anthology of songs and ballads of the railroad.

A primary aim of this collection, then, has been the utilization, wherever possible, of commercial recordings as sources—especially hillbilly and blues (or "race") records of the period 1920–50. In a few instances, songs that had not been so recorded in those genres were too important to omit from the collection; in these cases we turned to noncommercial field recordings from the Library of Congress Archive of Folk Song or to "pop" recordings. In all cases, however, we have kept integral the text and tune of our source, eschewing a common practice of selecting text and tune from different sources. This necessarily meant that an example might feature a good tune but a garbled text, or vice versa. To overcome this drawback a supplementary text or tune is often provided, permitting the reader to perform his own musical graftsmanship if he is so inclined.

Two large classes of railroad music have been omitted from this collection: instrumental pieces—in particular, train imitations (usually on harmonica or fiddle); and worksongs—hammer songs, tie-tamping chants, and related pieces, which can be at once thrilling to hear and marvelous to behold in execution. Worksongs are almost completely absent from hillbilly and blues recordings. In Appendix I a short biblio-discography for both of these genres is provided. Apart from these exclusions, we have interpreted the phrase "railroad song" liberally, including pieces about trains, about railroaders, about railroad construction, and about railroad travelers. There are also songs that use railroad imagery metaphorically, as in the case of the religious songs in chapter 12.

Editorial method

The initial three chapters are introductory: the first offers a very brief history of railroading in the United States; the second, a history of American music—popular, folk, and related; and the third, an overview of American railroad songs from the 1830s through the 1970s. The purpose of these broad surveys is to provide background for discussions of the songs in the context of American history and social development. The songs are interesting not only for their own sake, but also for what they tell us about American railroads and attitudes toward them — in sum, about the impact of the railroads on American music.

Following these three chapters, the songs themselves are divided by types into nine chapters. The general introduction to each chapter offers musical and historical observations applicable to all the songs within the chapter. After each text/tune transcription is a discussion of the history and background of that particular song, of the performer whose version is transcribed, and of any other matters that might enhance the reader's interest in, or appreciation for the significance of, the particular song. Then comes a list of references (biblio-discography), divided into six sections: (A) principal versions; (B) other published printed versions; (C) other unpublished written versions (e.g., manuscripts in my own or other folksong collections, in particular, the Library of Congress Archive of Folk Song [LC AFS] or the Western Kentucky Folklore Archive [WKFA] housed at UCLA); (D) other commercial 78 rpm disc and cylinder recordings (or LP issues of commercial recordings made prior to ca. 1947); (E) other commercial 45 and 33 rpm recordings, including commercial releases of field-recorded material from the AFS and other archives; and (F) other noncommercial field recordings, either on disc or on tape. By "principal versions" I mean the version(s) transcribed in this book and versions of particular historical significance — for instance, original sheet music, first published version, first recording, most influential recording, and so on. Important items for which full information is given in the body of the discussion are not always included in the A section in the interest of brevity. The format of the entries in this section is loose, to permit as much information as is available and not already provided in the discussion itself. The entries in sections B-F are deliberately brief. Books and other printed sources are identified by a simple keyword and page number only; full bibliographic citations are given in the Bibliography at the end of the volume. Seventy-eight and 45 rpm records are identified by label and release number; LPs are identified by title as well, if that information is available (but see below). Manuscripts and field recordings are identified by an archive number, if there is one (in WKFA, for instance there is no numbering system for manuscripts). If a recording listed in D or E has been transcribed in a booklet (or liner notes) accompanying the recording, that booklet is not cited in B unless there is additional information making it important for future research.

With a few exceptions, I have striven for completeness in sections B-E of the biblio-discographies. The exceptions are (1) published or recorded collections intended for children; (2) secondary anthologies that are exclusively singing collections, of little historical importance and with no accompanying information useful to scholars or collectors; and (3) versions of pop songs taken directly from sheet music and of minimal interest from the perspective of folk music. In the first category are such songs as "I've Been Working on the Railroad," "Get on Board, Little Children," "New River Train," and "Rock Island Line"; in the second, many printings of "John Henry," "Railroad Bill," "Nine Pound Hammer," "Midnight Special," *"Wabash Cannonball,"* "Freight Train," "Jesse James," and "Paddy Works on the Railroad"; and in the third, printings of "Casey Jones,"

"In the Baggage Coach Ahead," *"Lightning Express,"* "Drill, Ye Tarriers, Drill," and a few others. I have by no means used these three grounds for exclusion liberally, as the nearly 125 published and more than 475 recorded references to "John Henry" attest. Generally, I have cited enough of the more common children's or general song anthologies to give a good idea of the extent of popularity.

I have heard most of the recordings cited, but not all; the parenthetical notation "possibly related" following a recording citation indicates that while I have not heard it, I assume that its inclusion is appropriate on the basis of title or some other information. That notation is not used in cases where I have not heard the recording but have taken the reference from a trade list, catalog, or other source, and the title (e.g., "John Henry" or *"Wabash Cannonball"*) is unlikely to be misleading. This does, however, open up the possibility of errors in the citation.

This raises another general problem—that of phonograph album titles. Discographers or bibliographers working with sound recordings in the areas of folk, pop, country, or blues music have doubtless found albums with one "title" on the front of the jacket, another on the back, possibly a third on the spine, and a fourth on the disc itself. A second printing or redesigned jacket can introduce further variations. Which is to be considered the "real title"? Unfortunately, the rewards that will accrue to the individual who solves this problem are few. I have usually favored the "title" on the disc label itself as primary, on the grounds that the jacket is not an intrinsic part of the recording. (I have abandoned this rule in cases where an album is commonly known by a different title. For example, the familiar title to Folkways FA 2951/52/53 is *Anthology of American Folk Music,* but all the disc labels, the front covers, and, in the case of FA 2952, the spine, are titled *American Folk Music* on some sets.) In some cases, this policy is not helpful, for example, if the label gives only the artist's name, but the jacket indicates another title. Another type of ambiguity in album titles involves the use of phrases such as *Martha Carson Sings* or *Folk Songs of Many Lands Sung by Martha Schlamme.* In the former case I take the full three-word phrase as the title, but in the latter, I assume "sung by Martha Schlamme" to be the artist credit and not part of the title. I dwell on these questions because they may confuse a prospective user or purchaser of a record; it is therefore best to rely on the album number as principal means of identification in any contemplated transaction.

For a number of years while record companies were simultaneously issuing the same album in monaural and stereophonic versions, it was frequently the custom to assign different release numbers to the different formats; where both are known, they are listed with the monaural number first. Sometimes only the prefix is different; this is indicated by a slash. Thus VRS/VSD means that VRS is the mono version and VSD the stereo; or DL/DL7 means that DL is the mono and DL7 the stereo. In some instances (particularly on the Folkways label) a recording was assigned a new release number but remained otherwise unchanged. In this case the old number follows the new in parentheses, for instance, FA 2951 (FP 251). The Kanawha label was originally Folk Promotions; therefore on some Kanawha releases the Folk Promotions release number appears in parentheses. Occasionally the reader may spot orthographic inconsistencies in the use of hyphens, slashes, and spaces in record release number citations. In a few cases this is due to the record company's own inconsistency; in others it simply reflects the inevitable difficulty of relying on secondhand notices in trade publications, advertisements, catalogs, auction lists, and discographies.

Three other brief annotations are occasionally given in the biblio-discographies:

"derivative piece," "related piece," and "parody." The first indicates a song somehow derived from the piece under consideration, whether in tune, text, or structure; the second, a song that is thematically but not structurally related (or vice versa); and the last, a song that is a fullfledged parody—though not necessarily humorous.

In section B, I have occasionally added to the citation a note that the version is taken verbatim from some other source. If the reference cited includes only a discussion and not a text, or is a checklist bibliography with only title and/or first line of the song, that fact is noted. In all sections, if the song title in the referenced work is significantly different from the title used as a heading in this book, it is included.

In the discography, all releases of a given song by a given artist separated by commas are taken from the same recording; different recordings are indicated by separate lines. Thus, in the discography to "The Wreck of the *Royal Palm*," we find the following:

> Vernon Dalhart—Brunswick 101, Brunswick 3470, Vocalion 5138, Super-
> tone 2001
> —OKeh 45086
> —Victor 20528
> —Cameo 1143, Romeo 350, Varsity 5059
> —Pathé 32380, Perfect 12459

This series of entries indicates five separate recordings by Vernon Dalhart: one was released on Brunswick 101, Brunswick 3470, Vocalion 5138, and Supertone 2001; another was released only on OKeh 45086; and so on. If a particular release uses a pseudonym for the artist credit, it is noted in parentheses following label name and release number.

A separate preface by the music editor follows these remarks; here it is appropriate to include a few words about the treatment of text transcriptions. In matters of punctuation I have been singularly unimaginative, generally using the standard sequence (, ; , .) for a quatrain of poetry. Stanzas are written as two, three, four, eight, or some other number of lines according to the musical phrasing. A new stanza begins each time the musical unit repeats. I have not tried to make the transcriptions at all phonetic, but have settled for standard English, except for such common editorial practices as replacing the final g in an -ing ending by an apostrophe if that pronunciation was obvious. In cases where a text was transcribed from an earlier printed source I have not meddled with the orthographic whims of the previous editor, but I will not vouch for full fidelity to archaic punctuation practices. It is always disconcerting, in transcribing a song for publication, to find that one cannot understand the words of the singer. Under ideal conditions this need never happen; but when one is listening to untrained singers who occasionally mumble, forget words, stumble over phrases, or employ regional dialect or now-obsolete slang, or when one is working from old recordings often distorted or obscured by poor initial recording technique or subsequent surface wear, lacunae are unavoidable. Occasionally, in such instances, the missing word could be conjectured on the basis of another text, and when I have done so, the editorial suggestion is noted in brackets. In a few cases where a singer accidentally used a wrong word I have left the transcription in agreement with what was sung, commenting editorially only if the error would not be obvious to the reader.

Acknowledgments

===

RECALLING THE MANY persons who graciously contributed their time or resources to aid me in this study is a pleasant task, marred only by the fear that I have failed to make the list complete. In most cases, I have cited, either in the text itself or in the notes or references, the specific contribution of this legion of helpers.

Among my most memorable hours on this project have been those spent with the singers, musicians, and writers who were responsible for some of the songs or recordings discussed here: Green Bailey, Cliff Carlisle, Bernice "Si" Coleman, Sid Harkreader, Clayton McMichen, Asa Martin, Doc Roberts, and Welby Toomey. I am likewise indebted to others with whom I either corresponded or conversed by telephone: Sara Carter Bayes, Gona Blankenship, Edward L. Crain, Buell Kazee, J. E. Mainer, Sam McGee, C. C. Meeks, Charlie Monroe, Dick Parman, and John V. Walker.

Of the many scholars and students of folklore and folksong who shared materials, ideas, or resources with me, the names of Roger Abrahams, Mac Benford, Ben A. Botkin, Jan Harold Brunvand, John Cowley, Harlan Daniel, Sam Eskin, David Evans, Lisa Feldman, Austin Fife, Edith Fowke, Alfred Frankenstein, Archie Green, Pricilla Herdman, Ed Kahn, William Henry Koon, Kip Lornell, Mack McCormick, Judith McCulloh, Guthrie T. Meade, Jr., Doug Seroff, Richard K. Spottswood, J. Barre Toelken, Ivan M. Tribe, John White, D. K. Wilgus, Charles K. Wolfe, and David Wylie come most easily to mind. To record collectors Joe Bussard, Eugene Earle, David Freeman, Robert R. Healy, Robert Hyland, Frank Mare, Donald Lee Nelson, Robert Olson, and Bob Pinson I owe thanks either for copies of recordings or for discographic and related data. Railroad song enthusiasts and rail historians C. Bruce Gurner, Clifton E. Hull, Freeman Hubbard, Ron Lane, B. W. Overall, Judge H. Leroy Pope, Paul Shue, Hugh F. Stephens, and Pick Temple similarly offered information on particular songs.

Through the pages of *Good Old Days, Old Time Songs and Poems.* and *Railroad Magazine* I exchanged songs or information with many correspondents across the country. Among those who contributed to this study were Laura Affolter, Nellie Allen, Mrs. Ercie Barrett, Marie A. Benson, Ruth Butcher, Arling R. Judd, William G. MacDonald, Ralph Oatley, Janice Page, L. K. Penningroth, Ronald Thurlow, Olive Whiteman, and Cora V. Wilkins.

My quests for information and illustrative matter brought me to the doors (sometimes figuratively, at other times literally) of many libraries and archives. The staff at these institutions made my searches enjoyable if not always successful. Many of the librarians and archivists who assisted me did not give their names, but I can acknowledge others: Josiah Q. Bennett of the Lilly Library, Indiana University, Bloomington; Ann Billingsly, Chicago Historical Society, Chicago; Harley C. Brooks, Jr., George Peabody College for Teachers, Nashville; Eslie E. Cann, Nevada Historical Society, Reno; Harry L. Eddy, Library of the Association of American Railroads, Washington, D.C.; Eric S. Flower, R. H. Fogler Library, University of Maine, Orono; Anne Hinckley, Interlibrary Loan Department, UCLA; Norma Jean Lamb, Buffalo and Erie County Public Library, Buffalo, N.Y.; Gerald Roberts, Berea College Library, Berea, Ky.; Mary Russo, Brown University Library, Providence, R.I.; Elizabeth R. Schubert, University of Virginia Library, Charlottesville; Charles A. Webbert, University Library, University of Idaho, Moscow; and Brooke Whiting, Special Collections Library, UCLA. To Joseph C. Hickerson, Alan Jabbour, and Gerald Parsons of the Library of Congress Archive of Folk Song, for spending literally dozens of hours on numerous searches among the dusty relics of our finest (though at times most frustrating) library, I am particularly grateful. Lester Levy and David Morton generously made available sheet-music covers from their private collections. At the end of the project, Linda Painter offered invaluable assistance indexing the book.

My greatest debt is to four of the individuals named above, not only for their specific help in the field of railroad songs, but especially for opening up for me the once esoteric subject of hillbilly folk music. Archie Green's own work on railroad folksongs preceded mine and aided me immensely. In addition to making available his vast files of unpublished information and materials, he has shared ideas constantly during the past ten years; he read and criticized and contributed extensively to this book during various stages of preparation, and set an unsurpassable model for me with his own parallel study of recorded coal-mining songs, *Only a Miner*. Eugene Earle has always shared his extensive collection of 78 rpm hillbilly records, one of the finest in the country, and has offered discographic and other data that would have taken additional years to assemble had he not been so generous. D. K. Wilgus has likewise opened to me not only his own collection, but also the holdings of the Western Kentucky Folklore Archive and other resources at his disposal at the Folklore and Mythology Center at UCLA. To Ed Kahn, who first taught me, both formally and informally, what folklore is all about, I am also indebted.

Two other persons deserve special acknowledgment. The first is Anne Cohen, whose love for and interest in folk music grew with my own. She endured hundreds of hours alone during the dozen years that this book was in preparation; she listened to my meditations, gave audience to my discoveries, and read and re-read numerous drafts. She on occasion infuriated me with her criticisms, but in the end I almost always acceded to her ear for language and her knack for lucid exposition. This book is much the stronger for her contributions.

The other is Judith McCulloh, who brought to this book an unusual combination of editorial and academic skills. One is rarely so fortunate and privileged to have the services of an editor who is also a recognized scholar in the field.

There are other thank-yous to be made, but they shall be done differently.

Music Editor's Preface

THE STANDARDS OF accuracy I aimed at in transcribing these songs were relatively high, with the following (admittedly large) qualification: the ubiquitous rhythmic anticipations, characteristic of American folk and popular music in general, and probably due to the influence of black musicians and singers, have not always been reproduced here. It seemed unnecessary to indicate what the reader will find himself doing unconsciously as he sings these songs, for such anticipations are still pervasive in American style. Furthermore, greater rhythmic precision would have made the transcriptions much more difficult to read.

For scholarly usage, I believe that the same reasoning holds. Our ability to grasp rhythm analytically seems to be considerably more primitive than our corresponding ability to deal with pitch and harmony. Our ability to comprehend rhythm visually is similarly undeveloped—not that we lack the means to notate accurately, but rather, that the product of such accuracy is less immediately meaningful to us than the notation of pitch or harmony. A scrupulously exact transcription would have to be painstakingly deciphered before it yielded a sense of the rhythmic character of the song or performance—a sense that could be arrived at sooner, in most cases, by reliance on one's intuitive understanding of style. Where I felt that such reliance might not suffice, I have attempted greater fidelity to the original.

The word *shuffle* is prefixed to many songs. As a useful convention for describing a rhythmic classification, this term comes from usage among professional pop musicians and arrangers. It is used to indicate a kind of "swing" in the rhythm. More precisely, it is a shorthand way of converting 4/4 into 12/8 or, what amounts to the same thing, continual triplets. Thus, a phrase such as

would be sung as if it were

or

Note values other than eighths are not affected. This, incidentally, is what is customarily meant, in notation of American popular, jazz and folk music, by the following dotted rhythm:

In matters of pitch, I took few liberties. Where a chord differs for any reason from the original, a note to that effect will be found.

DAVID COHEN

Long Steel Rail

1

"The Railway Cars Are Coming"

A Brief History of the Railroads in the United States

> The great Pacific Railroad, for California mail [?hail],
> Bring on the locomotive, lay down the iron rail;
> Across the rolling prairie, by steam we're bound to go,
> The railroad cars are coming, humming thru' New Mexico.
>
> We've got a million on the road, and who will dare beat that?
> Just said [?send] in your subscription now and down will go the track.
> The track's the one we read about, forever free from snow;
> The railroad cars are coming, humming thru' New Mexico.[1]

Nothing has so drastically altered the face of this continent as the web of parallel steel ribbons that Americans began to weave across it in the 1830s. Like lines of age, they multiplied as the nation matured; but the railroad cars that they bore back and forth hastened that maturing process more than any other single development. To many Americans, these same ribbons were lines of worry, for the growth of the railroads was not viewed unanimously with total approval.

The story of the development of the railroads and of their impact on American society has been told often and told well; in a book whose primary concern is railroad songs, it is appropriate to repeat the tale only in most abridged form. Readers who seek elaboration on the brief narrative of this chapter will find useful the references cited at its end.

Mankind has seen two great revolutions during the course of "history": the neolithic and the industrial. These developments were revolutions not in the sense of being precipitous events occurring at precise moments of time, but rather in that they transformed the quality of life profoundly. The earlier neolithic revolution was marked by the introduction of agriculture, a far less time-consuming means of food gathering than the previous practices of hunting and collecting wild vegetation. One quantitative way of

3

assessing the state of a society is to measure the energy consumed by its members. In a paleolithic hunting society, individuals consumed only slightly more energy than was represented by the food they ingested. In an advanced agricultural society, typified by fifteenth-century Europe, the average energy consumption was about eight times as much as was actually consumed in food.[2] The industrial revolution was marked by several changes, most noteworthy being the exploitation of sources of energy other than muscle, wind, or water, and, in particular, the introduction of mobile power sources. In 1875 in Britain, a classic industrial society, energy consumption amounted to more than twenty-five times the food intake. The single device that was most important in ushering in the industrial revolution was the steam engine, the prime example of a movable power supply that depended on combustion as its ultimate source of energy. The full potential of the steam engine was realized in two inventions early in the nineteenth century: the steam-boat and the steam locomotive. Of the two, the locomotive had by far the greater impact.

It is no accident of history that almost all the great cities of the world prior to the industrial revolution were built on rivers, lakes, or seashores. Cities that had to depend entirely on overland transportation and communication paid dearly for whatever benefits such isolation brought. In the 1750s it took three days by wagon from New York to Philadelphia, only some ninety miles away. In the early nineteenth century, shipments from Pittsburgh to New Orleans took three months by sea; transport by wagon over the mountains was too costly to be practical.

The steamboat and the early nineteenth-century canals did much to improve transportation, but still steamboats were restricted to existing waterways (or short extensions of them). Although today one thinks of trains as being seriously disadvantaged (with respect to motor buses and trucks) because they are confined to immovable tracks, a century and a half ago they were a wonderfully liberating innovation.

The precise date of the beginnings of railroading cannot be assigned without a preliminary digression on the word *railroad*. In the seventeenth century, the term *rail-road* seems to have been standard in England, and by the eighteenth century, both *railroad* and *railway* were in use there. Since the nineteenth century, the English have preferred *railway*, whereas in the United States *railroad* has become standard. An exception to this clear-cut regionalism was often found in the United States in corporate naming practice, when one company was dissolved and reconstituted as a legally distinct entity for any of several reasons. For example, if the Lock, Stock, and Barrel Railroad went bankrupt in January, 1895, and its assets were taken over by another group of investors, it might have been renamed the Lock, Stock, and Barrel Railway. A similar name change might have occurred if controlling interest in the line was acquired by another railroad company.

In the literal sense of a guiding rail along which vehicles with flanged wheels traveled, *railroad* was used to describe a European construction as early as 1556. In England, by 1630, horsedrawn vehicles were guided along wooden tracks near New-castle. Travel on rails in America was rare prior to 1800, although in 1764 British troops under Captain John Montressor built an inclined railway to transport supplies at a military camp in New York. Gravity provided the energy for the downhill trip, and manpower applied to a windlass brought the cars back to the top. Several American-built railways made their appearance early in the nineteenth century. Perhaps the best known was the Granite Railway built at Charlestown, Massachusetts, to transport the granite used to build the Bunker Hill monument. It depended on gravity and horse power to keep it operating along a three-mile stretch from the Quincy quarry to the Neponset River.

The railroad as we generally think of it involves not direct human or animal power, but some more modern means of propulsion, such as a steam engine. In this sense, the first railroad was invented by Britain's Richard Trevithick, who built his first rail-operating steam-powered vehicle in 1805. The earliest steam locomotive to run on a track in the United States was designed and built by John Stevens in 1825 and demonstrated on a 220-foot oval track at his home in Hoboken, New Jersey. The first American railroad to offer public transportation was the Baltimore and Ohio, chartered on February 28, 1827, and operating almost fourteen miles of track regularly in Maryland by 1830. However, although steam was tried early in its history, for several years the B & O relied on horse power for its regular runs. The first outfit to use steam regularly for its daily service was the South Carolina Canal and Railroad Company, whose schedule went into effect on Christmas Day of 1830. America was thus not far behind Britain, whose first railway, the Manchester and Liverpool, officially opened on September 15, 1830, its maiden run being marked by the first fatal railroad accident in history. One of the attending notables got in the way of a parading engine and was run over by a wheel; he died later that day.

Early experiences on rail in the United States were likewise marked by mishaps and discomforts. In 1831, the Mohawk and Hudson Rail Road Company, later to become part of the New York Central, completed its first stretch of road between Albany and Schenectady. The maiden jaunt took place on August 13, the small train being pulled by the famous locomotive the DeWitt Clinton. Years later, a writer recalled the trip:

> It is some fifty-three years ago since the first trip was taken on the Albany & Schenectady railroad. The cars were coach bodies from an Albany livery stable, mounted on trucks. The trucks were coupled with chains, leaving two or three feet slack, so that when the train started the passengers were "jerked from under their hats," and in stopping, they were sent flying to their seats. The locomotive fuel was pitch-pine, and a dense volume of the blackest smoke floated toward the train. Those on top of the coaches had to raise their umbrellas; but, in less than a mile the cloth was burned off, and the frames thrown away. The passengers spent the rest of the time in whipping each other's clothes to put out the fire, the sparks from which were as big as one's thumb-nail. Everybody had heard of the trip and came thronging to the track as though a presidential candidate was on exhibition. They drove as close as they could get to the railroad, in order to secure a place to look at this new curiosity. The horses everywhere took fright, and the roads in the vicinity were strewn with the wrecks of vehicles. . . . A Boston paper said that a railroad to that city would be as useless as one to the moon. . . .[3]

In the United States, growth after 1830 was steady and spectacular. By 1835 more than 200 railway charters had been granted in eleven states and more than 1,000 miles of rails were in service. Construction continued at an accelerating pace until 1872, in which year more than 7,400 miles of track were laid down. For the next thirty-two years construction varied between about 1,000 and 5,000 miles each year. After 1918, the quantity of new track laid down was slight. In 1881 the total mileage in operation exceeded, for the first time, 100,000. In 1930 a peak of 303,000 miles was in use; a steady decline occurred thereafter.[4]

From 1830, passenger traffic grew steadily until 1920, during which year each American traveled an average of 445 miles by train. After 1920 the volume of traffic declined, falling to 77 miles per person for the year 1969.[5]

Although passenger travel has steadily declined for some sixty years (except during World War II), freight traffic, on the other hand, has continued to increase. The result has been that the railroads' revenue has increasingly stemmed from freight. Whereas prior to 1910 about 25 percent of the railroads' revenues came from passenger service, since 1940 freight revenues have accounted for 90 percent or more of the total.[6]

Nevertheless, although the railroads' volume of freight has continued to grow, competition from bus, truck, and airplane has sharpened. From 1939 to 1962 the percentage of total intercity freight traffic carried by rail declined from 62 to 43. Similarly, passengers have turned to other modes of travel in increasing numbers. Passenger travel by bus, which first became measurable in 1922, has exceeded that by train in terms of numbers of passengers carried in every year since 1948. Air travel, first significant in 1930, exceeded rail travel for the first time in 1958 (in terms of passenger-miles), and has done so ever since.

In 1900 the total value of the railroads was approximately \$10.2 billion, or about 11 percent of the total national wealth. The actual value grew yearly to 1932, although not so rapidly as the gross national wealth, so that by 1929 the railroads represented 6 percent of the nation's wealth. By 1958, the share was down to less than 3 percent.

In 1890 the railroads employed 749,000 persons, or one out of every 44 persons between the ages of twenty and sixty-five. Many a young maid could proclaim, along with the heroine in Charles Graham's 1895 hit of the same title, "My dad's the engineer." In 1920, when the number of employees was largest (2.1 million), one out of 28 (between twenty and sixty-five years of age) worked for the railroads. Since then, both the total and the proportional number of employees have declined steadily. By 1969, the railroads employed only 590,000 persons, or one out of 170 persons (between twenty and sixty-five).[7]

These figures characterize some quantitative aspects of the growth and subsequent decline of the railroad industry. What is the significance of these data in terms of impact on the nation's history?

As indicated above, the growth of railroading in this country during its first few decades was considerable. The 1830s saw the first steam locomotive in regular service (1830), the first mail carried by rail (1831), the first American-built steam locomotive (1831), the first railroad periodical (1832), the first railroad fatality (1833), the first land grant to a railroad (1835), and the first locomotive whistle (1837). Thus, by the end of the first decade of public transportation by rail, the railroads had, at least qualitatively, exhibited most of the characteristics that are generally associated with them.

In this early period, according to P. Harvey Middleton, the public attitude toward the railways was almost unanimously approving. The inauguration of almost every new line was marked by receptions, welcoming speeches, and cannon fire at each station. Songs and musical compositions were composed for these auspicious occasions or while the railroad companies were still in their infancy. Delia B. Ward's "North Western Railway Polka" (1859) was dedicated to the officers of the Chicago and North Western Railway, organized two years earlier; C. C. Smith's "Northern Route March" (1876) was dedicated to Fred Taylor, president of the Burlington and Northern Railway; Jas. N. Beck's "The Fast Line Gallop" (1853) was inscribed "to the President & Directors of the great Pennsylvania Central R.R." Stephen C. Massett's "Clear the Way" (1856) was "dedicated to the pioneers of the Great Pacific Rail Road." What opposition there was came almost entirely from the threatened canal interests.[8]

The 1840s saw the rails push westward from the Atlantic coast, so that by 1852 the

MOTHERS LOOK OUT FOR YOUR CHILDREN!
ARTISANS, MECHANICS, CITIZENS!

When you leave your family in health, must you be hurried home to mourn a

DREADFUL CASUALITY!

PHILADELPHIANS, your **RIGHTS** are being invaded! regardless of your interests, or the **LIVES OF YOUR LITTLE ONES**. THE **CAMDEN AND AMBOY**, with the assistance of other companies without a Charter, and in **VIOLATION OF LAW**, as decreed by your Courts, are laying a

LOCOMOTIVE RAIL ROAD!

Through your most Beautiful Streets, to the **RUIN** of your **TRADE**, annihilation of your **RIGHTS**, and regardless of your **PROSPERITY** and **COMFORT**. **Will you permit this!** or do you consent to be a

SUBURB OF NEW YORK !!

Rails are now being laid on **BROAD STREET** to **CONNECT** the **TRENTON RAIL ROAD** with the **WILMINGTON** and **BALTIMORE ROAD**, under the pretence of constructing a City Passenger Railway from the Navy Yard to Fairmount!!! This is done under the auspices of the **CAMDEN AND AMBOY MONOPOLY**!

RALLY PEOPLE in the Majesty of your Strength and forbid THIS

OUTRAGE!

Warning poster from the 1830s circulated by canal, steamboat, toll road, and stagecoach interests.
Collection of the Louisiana State Museum, New Orleans.

Sheet music: "North Western Railway Polka." Author's Collection.

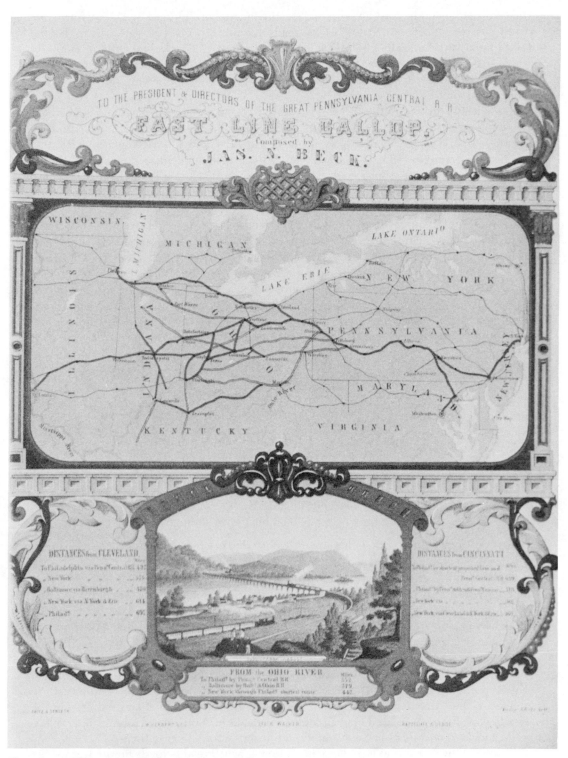

Sheet music: "Fast Line Gallop." Author's Collection.

first railroad from the East had reached the tiny hamlet of Chicago. By 1850, twenty-five of the nation's thirty-two states had railroads operating, with New York, Pennsylvania, and Massachusetts leading in track mileage in that order. Thanks to the railroads, postal rates dropped in 1851 from five cents for distances up to 300 miles and ten cents for greater distances to three cents for any distance up to 3,000 miles, which meant all of the country at that time.

As traffic and velocities increased, safety became a matter of concern. In 1852, 42 passenger deaths were due to accidents, and 120 employees were killed on duty. In 1853 there were 138 major accidents, 234 passenger deaths, and 496 passenger injuries. In a single derailment in 1859, 43 lives were lost. Out of such moments of tragedy some of the most enduring railroad songs, such as "Casey Jones" and "The Wreck of the Old 97," were born; several train-wreck ballads are discussed in detail in chapter 5. Disasters dating from before 1880, however, have left no record in the folk tradition. Songwriters of the mid-nineteenth century used the railroads as settings for ditties of romance and adventure, as in "The Charming Young Widow I Met in the Train" (late 1860s) or "Riding Down from Bangor in an Eastern Train" (1871). A decade or two later, the same backdrop was used, but then preferably for tales of pathos and woe, as illustrated amply in chapter 7.

During the 1840s and 1850s, as railroads became less of a novelty in some areas, enthusiasm began to cool. In the previous decade, rates were of secondary importance inasmuch as railroads were generally much faster and cheaper than their competitors, the older forms of transport. A minstrel song of the 1840s contrasted rail with waterway travel:

> Oh, de steamboat makes a mighty splutter,
> And when de biler bursts it lands you in de water!

and

> De hoss boat can trabel, if de wedder wet or dry,
> An noffin' can stop you if de ole hoss don't die;

but

> Railroad trabel's gettin' all de go,
> 'Kase de hoss boat an steamboat goes so might slow.[9]

But as rail competition stiffened, railroads resorted to pricing practices that aroused much public opposition, which reached its peak during the 1870s and 1880s.

The Civil War was the world's first war in which railroads played a major role. It has been written that railroads "largely determined the location of battles and to a great extent their outcome."[10] European military experts, watching the War between the States from across the Atlantic, compared the efforts of the North to subdue the South to Napoleon's attempt to take Russia, and prophesied that the Union, like the French emperor before, would not be able to wage war successfully so far from a base of operations and supplies. The railroads changed the odds dramatically. A major factor in the Union's victory was its superior use of railroads. The frequent observation that the defeat of the Confederacy was due to the concentration of the nation's industry in the North can also be translated in terms of the railroad: the North could rebuild and replace rails and locomotives as fast as Confederate troops could destroy them.

When the war was at last over, the railroads, which had helped win the war for the North, brought home the bodies of 140,000 Union soldiers who had died on the bat-

passed in response to these agitations was an 1869 Illinois statute limiting "just, reasonable and uniform rates." The railroads countered that states had to regulate public utilities; furthermore, they contended, the question of what a just or reasonable rate was a judicial rather than a legislative matter, so not Congress should pass any regulatory measures. Courts handed down contradictory [decisions] on these questions during the 1870s and 1880s, now supporting the railroad now attacking it. With the passage in 1887 of the Interstate Commerce Act and [the est]ablishment of the ICC, the question of who was to regulate the railroads was [settled] once and for all. The efficacy of the ICC in fulfilling its role, however, was another [matter.] Although the public generally regarded the act as a victory for antirailroad [interest]s, its passage was supported by the railroads themselves, and their confidence in the [weak]ness of its effects was justified during the next two decades. It took the Hepburn Act [of 1]906 and the Mann-Elkins Act of 1910 to strengthen the powers of the ICC to the point [w]here it could regulate rail traffic effectively.

Public attitudes toward the railroad remained predominantly negative until 1920. During World War I, the government took over operation of the railroads in order to expedite the handling of troops and supplies. Although the railroads were themselves incapable of providing the unified control necessary for the war effort, the government takeover was apparently very unpopular. When, at war's end, the question of the continued government operation of the railways was discussed, the public sided with private enterprise. With the Transportation Act of 1920, Congress returned the railroads to private control, but strengthened still further the regulatory powers of the ICC. From this point on, railroads enjoyed more public confidence than they had at any time in the previous seven decades. It was too late, however, to eradicate the popular image that had been conceived in the rapacity of railroads' robber barons and born out of the numerous hardships imposed on a generation of common folk.

Nevertheless, there were signs that the railroads were concerned with their public image and were consciously trying to improve it. In a booklet of the same period titled *The Immigrant* (the opening page and cover of which are reproduced here), the C & NW Railway advised the public of its efforts to help care for the newly arrived immigrants—yet could not resist the reminder that its actions were not simply humanitarian, but were dictated by "enlightened self-interest."

From the perspective of the twentieth century there is little doubt that the railroads fostered injustices and inequities; that fortunes were made ruthlessly; that lives were lost and miseries inflicted. Nevertheless, the enduring fact is that the development and expansion of more than half of this country was facilitated by those near-ubiquitous rails of steel and crossties of wood. We may well ask whether the same development could not have occurred in a more civil manner. But folksongs are born out of what was, and not what could have been; it is inappropriate—not to say too late—to propose a different script for the unfolding drama of the American railroads.

Today, it taxes the imagination of young people to appreciate the impact that the rails once had on their grandparents. In 1970, the average American rode less than one-sixth as many miles by train as his grandfather did in 1920, but this is only a small aspect of the diminishing role the railroads play in our developing technological society. For many towns in the Midwest and West in the late nineteenth century, the railroad was the major—if not the only—contact with the outside world. Not only passenger but also freight travel was dominated by the railroads. Furthermore, the trains represented the major mode of communication as well as of transportation. Today, the telephone carries

tlefield. "He's Coming to Us Dead," sometimes titled "The Boys in Blue," must have described a not uncommon homecoming that saddened many a parent's heart.

Although completion of the first transcontinental railway did not occur until 1869 with the driving in of the two now-famous golden spikes at Promontory Point, Utah, plans for a coast-to-coast railroad began long before the Civil War. As early as 1832 the idea for a rail from New York City to the Oregon Territory was proposed in print. In the 1840s and 1850s several bills were placed before Congress, generally backed by far-sighted industrialists and merchants who foresaw great economic benefits coming from a direct link with the far West. However, the factor that finally persuaded Congress to pass the Pacific Railroad Act, which President Lincoln signed into law in July, 1862, was the fear of how defenseless the western regions of the nation would be in the event of military invasion by a foreign power. The new law called for establishing the Union Pacific Railroad Company to build a line west from Omaha. The Central Pacific, chartered the previous year, was to build east from Sacramento to meet the UP. Great numbers of Chinese laborers were engaged by the Central Pacific to provide inexpensive manpower, while the rival Union Pacific hired as many sons of Erin as it could find. From the pens and lips of these Paddys came some fine songlore: "Paddy Works on the Railway," "Drill, Ye Tarriers, Drill," "Jerry, Go Ile That Car," and others; the more popular pieces from this era are displayed in chapter 11. As incentive for the speedy completion of this endeavor deemed essential to the national defense, Congress relied not on the patriotism of the chief officers of the various railroad companies, but on generous financial rewards. Subsidies, varying between $16,000 per mile for flat terrain and $48,000 for each mile of mountains, were offered to both railroads for the track they laid down. A dishonest state geologist employed by Governor Stanford declared that the Sierra Nevadas began to rise seven miles east of Sacramento, and President Lincoln was persuaded, thus entitling the CP to an additional $800,800 subsidy.[11] Furthermore, as a consequence of the railroad land-grant scheme, vast sections of public land along the tracks, varying from six to forty square miles for each linear mile of track, were given to the competing lines.

The significance of this action, as well as its propriety, has been argued for decades: opinions range from labeling it an outright giveaway to a segment of society that hardly needed it, to the contrary view that the incentive was necessary to compensate for the great financial risks involved.[12] In the 1860s Congress authorized charters and land grants to three other transcontinental railroads: the Northern Pacific, the Southern Pacific, and the Santa Fe, all of which had completed tracks to the Pacific coast by 1884. These five lines received the major benefits of the land-grant system, although smaller grants were made to other lines as well.

The subsidization of the Central Pacific Railroad, a giant that grew out of an agreement between Theodore D. Judah and Doc Strong in Strong's Dutch Flat drugstore in 1860, was the subject of an anonymous 1872 composition, "Subsidy: A Goat Island Ballad":

> There is a corporation within this Golden State,
> Which owns a line of railroads for conveying men and freight
> To the Mormon town of Ogden at an elevated rate,
> And which began in a very small way via the Dutch Flat swindle
> But by perserverance and bonds, including subsidies,
> Became both strong and great,
> For this Railroad Corporation is the deuce in subsidies.[13]

The way in which the extent of acreage given under the land-grant system is tallied differs with different authors. A probably reliable evaluation places the figure at 223 million acres given (in both federal and state grants), of which some 35 million were later forfeited because the railroads did not fulfill the conditions of the grants. In many states, the extent of the land granted to railroads by the federal government alone (and not forfeited) exceeded 10 percent of the total area of the public domain in those states. The land itself was of little value until it was developed, so the railroads embarked on an extensive campaign to bring people out west, offering enticingly low transportation rates and, more significantly, making available very cheap leases and sales of the land they had acquired. However, in many areas of outright sales, the railroads were careful to reserve for themselves those parcels of land with significant mineral or timber value. According to some historians, the sale of these lands in most cases more than compensated for the entire constructions costs of the railroads.[14] Jay Gould, Commodore Vanderbilt, and Jim Fisk were three financiers associated with various railroad scandals whose names found their way into bits of railroad folksong.

It was probably during the 1870s and 1880s that public hostility toward the railroads reached its peak. The responsible factors were many. Managers took the position that the railroads were above governmental regulation. Employees were often arrogant in their dealings with the public. Songs always depicted conductors as stern-faced and stone-hearted, men who would put off ticketless orphans but for the intercessions of merciful passengers, as in "The *Lightning Express*." In the West, farmers were antagonized by the high freight rates, and at times they burned their corn for fuel rather than ship it. Throughout the country there were complaints of discriminatory practices in rates, with blatant favoritism shown men of influence, legislators, powerful shippers, and other friends of the railroads.[15] These inequities were recalled years later in a 1907 election campaign song for Theodore Roosevelt:

> Not long ago the railroads owned the whole United States,
> Their rates were high to farmers, but a trust could get rebates;
> Who stopped this crime of freight rebates among the railroad men?
> Who fixed it so the railroads carry people now and then?
> It's Theodore, the peaceful Theodore,
> Of all the rulers great or small
> He is the greatest of them all.[16]

The financial scandal involving the Credit Mobilier that rocked the continent in the early 1870s did much to associate the railroads with greed and corruption in the public mind. The railroads became the faceless enemy, and small men secretly admired those brazen souls, like Jesse James and Cole Younger, who dared to challenge it. Hatred for the railroads made heroes of train robbers, a syndrome treated in chapter 4 and in the discussion of "Jesse James." Partly in response to what they perceived as abuses at the hands of the railroads, farmers, through their Granger Movement, pressed for state and federal regulation of railroad practices. One long-forgotten militant song of 1873, "Railroad Monopoly," captured the mood of the angry farmers:

> Farmers, haste defend your freedom, which the Railroads threaten now;
> Leave your flocks and herds, ye freemen, leave the mattock and the plow.
> Break ye th' oppressors hand, and joining hand and hand,
> Rid, rid our happy land of Railroad Monopoly.[17]

Advertisement in the 1867 *Tribune Almanac*. Courtesy of the Illinois Central Gulf Railroad.

STRANGERS WITHIN THE GATES

How the Chicago and North Western Railway
Takes Care of the Newly-Arrived Immigrant

THE LAND OF OPPORTUNITY

ONLY an American whose birthplace was overseas, or the child of such, can intimately realize how from every hamlet, every village, every city of Europe, longing eyes turn toward America as the land of opportunity. To the moderately well-to-do, as well as to the poor of every Old-World race, this promise of greater opportunity is a powerful lure. The Federal law excludes those whom it terms undesirable immigrants, but the hundreds of thousands who find welcome include persons possessed of every degree of refinement, education, and intelligence. The newcomers are stamped in the various molds of every race, and from this heterogeneous humanity is to be smelted a large part of the future citizenship of the United States.

Since these foreign-born home-seekers are to become fellow-citizens, self-governing units in our society, each with his voice in our affairs, the duty which the United States—its individuals, its communities, its public service corporations—owe to these "strangers within the gates" at the time of their arrival is not merely humanitarian, but the obligation is rather dictated by enlightened self-interest.

Opening page of the 1911 booklet *The Care of the Immigrant*. Collection of Arthur D. Dubin.

The Care of the Immigrant, front and back covers. Collection of Arthur D. Dubin.

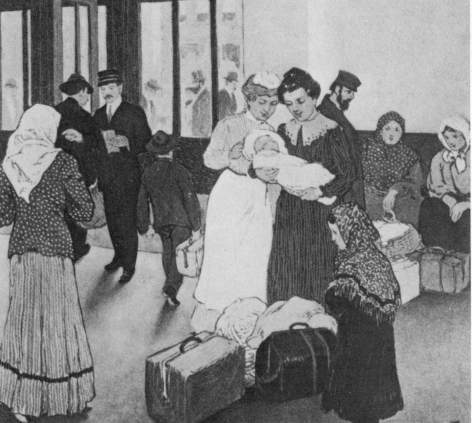

THE CARE OF THE IMMIGRANT

IN THE
NEW PASSENGER TERMINAL
CHICAGO AND NORTHWESTERN RY.
CHICAGO, ILL.

THE NORTH WESTERN LINE

more messages each year than does the postal system, but this was not the case prior to 1925. In 1896, six messages went by post for every one by telephone, and most of those six went by train.

Thus, in 1900, the average American relied on the railroad for most of his personal travel, his freight, and, via the mails, his communications. West of the Mississippi, especially in smaller towns, the odds were high that a typical resident was obligated to a railroad for some form of mortgage. Throughout the country, almost everyone had a close friend or relative employed by a railroad.

Many of the songs in this book reflect the concerns not of the railroader or the railroad construction worker, but of the ordinary citizen, whose life and language were permeated by trains, real and symbolic. Busy tunesmiths from both city and country fashioned an extensive garland of songlore that attested to the pervasive presence of the trains. Maids asserted their refusal to marry railroadmen ("I Would Not Marry a Railroader"); businessmen exchanged small talk in smoking cars ("Three Wishes"); fire-and-brimstone preachers preached allegories ("Black Diamond Express to Hell"); prisoners longed for the train to take them to freedom ("The Midnight Special"); widowers and orphans shared their sorrow with sympathetic passengers ("In the Baggage Coach Ahead," "The *Lightning Express*"); young swains courted comely maidens ("Ridin' in a Rail Road Keer"); and forsaken beaux lost their sweethearts ("The Train That Carried My Girl from Town").

Today, it is a different world. The financial ties between the small land- or property-holder and the railroads are few. Travel is dominated by the automobile, and the train has been supplanted by the airplane and the bus. Large-scale freight may still go by rail, but if an individual sends or receives a parcel, chances are it will go by truck. The Railway Express Agency, the result of an amalgamation of the few remaining express companies during World War I, changed its name to REA Express to de-emphasize the role of the railroads; it has since gone out of business. Communications media are dominated by television, radio, and telephone. The telegraph office is no longer at the town depot. And today, most of our personal mail is transported by airplane.

Railroad historians have written of the glorious age of steam, extolling the magnificent splendor of rail travel a half-century ago. They have lamented the decline of the iron horse, describing it in terms of the replacement of steam by diesel and electricity. They have bemoaned the disappearance of the splendidly appointed Edwardian coaches and Pullmans from the rails, and lamented the now-rundown, near-deserted state of the once bustling train terminals, in their day the center of town activity. All these observations may be true, but they point to effects, not causes, of the decline of the railroads' significance in American social life. The basic fact is that as a medium of transportation and communication, and as an instrument of finance, the railroad has been largely replaced by other institutions. Nevertheless, as I make these observations in the 1970s, I am confident that a recent development is going to revitalize the railroads as a mode of transportation in the coming decades: the sudden growing awareness that man's sources of energy are not limitless. The telling facts are these figures for the relative energy required for passenger and freight transport:[18]

Relative energy per passenger-mile		*Relative energy per ton-mile*
Railroad	1.0	1.0
Bus	.55	—
Truck	—	5.7
Automobile	1.2	—
Airplane	5.3	63

Thus, the rails will recover some of the transportation business they have lost to other modes, but not to the extent that they once dominated the scene. The media of transportation and communication are today, and doubtless will remain, quite separate and thoroughly diversified; it is inconceivable that any single institution can play the grand central role in the life of America that the railroad did thirty to a hundred years ago. [19]

NOTES

1. Collected by Harry Lee Ridenour from Luvera Payne Smith of Orwell, Ohio, in December, 1935. In *Folk Songs of Rural Ohio*, edited by W. Alwyn Ashburn (Berea, Ohio: Baldwin-Wallace College, 1973), vol. 10 (book 9), p. 78. Ridenour calls the song "The Great Pacific Railroad," but "The Railway Cars Are Coming" is the usual title. For a Mormon version of this song, and references to other variants, see Richard E. Lingenfelter, Richard A. Dwyer, and David Cohen, *Songs of the American West* (Berkeley and Los Angeles: University of California Press, 1968), pp. 67–68.

2. Earl Cook, "The Flow of Energy in an Industrial Society," *Scientific American*, 224 (Sept., 1971), 135.

3. *Bizarre Notes & Queries* (Manchester, N.H.), 7 (Mar.–Apr., 1890), 73.

4. These data are taken from *Historical Statistics of the United States: Colonial Times to 1970* (Washington, D.C.: U.S. Bureau of the Census, 1975), chap. Q, "Transportation." More complete figures are as follows:

Year	Miles of track built	Total miles of track in operation	Number of operating railroads
1830	40	23	—
1840	491	2,818	—
1850	1,261	9,021	—
1860	1,500	30,626	—
1870	5,658	52,922	—
1879	5,006	86,556	—
1890	a	166,703	1,013
1900	4,894	193,300	1,224
1910	4,122	240,300	1,306
1920	314	252,800	1,085
1930	460	249,000[b]	775
1940	19	233,700	574
1950	33	223,800	471
1960	21[c]	217,600	407
1970	80	205,800	351

[a]Figures are not available.

[b]The total mileage decreased in this and following years because the abandoned mileage exceeded the newly constructed mileage.

[c]Figures for this year include Alaska and Hawaii.

5. Ibid. Population figures are taken from chap. A. More complete data are as follows; those for 1970 and 1973 are based on *Statistical Abstract of the United States*, 96th ed. (Washington, D.C.: U.S. Bureau of the Census, 1975), table 974:

Year	Millions of passenger-miles	Passenger-miles per capita
1880	5,740	—
1882	7,700	143
1890	12,500	199
1900	16,000	210
1910	32,300	350
1920	47,400	445
1930	26,900	219

1940	23,800	180
1950	31,800[a]	210
1960	21,300	119
1970	10,800	54
1973	9,300	44

[a]In 1942 traffic increased sharply by 70 percent, presumably owing to the war, and continued to rise until 1944; then it slowly fell back, reaching prewar levels about 1954.

6. *Historical Statistics* (1970). Data are taken from chap. Q, sections 311 and 343.

7. Ibid. Population figures are taken from chap. A.

8. P. Harvey Middleton, *Railways and Public Opinion* (Chicago: Railway Business Association, 1941), pp. 18–20.

9. "Rail Road Trabeler," *Christy's Panorama Songster* (New York: William H. Murphy, 184–), p. 76; also in *White's New Illustrated Melodeon Song Book* (Philadelphia: T. B. Peterson, 18–), p. 66, titled "Rail Road Travel."

10. Hank Wieand Bowman, *Pioneer Railroads* (New York: Arco Publishing, 1954), p. 105.

11. Peter Lyon, *To Hell in a Day Coach* (Philadelphia and New York: J. B. Lippincott, 1968), pp. 32–33.

12. The literature dealing with various aspects of the railroad land-grant issue is extensive. Some useful articles are David Maldwyn Ellis, "The Forfeiture of Railroad Land Grants, 1867–1894," *Mississippi Valley Historical Review,* 33 (1946–47), 27–60; Paul W. Gates, "The Railroad Land Grant Legend," *Journal of Economic History,* 14 (1954), 143–46; Robert S. Henry, "The Railroad Land Grant Legend in American History Texts," *Mississippi Valley Historical Review,* 32 (1945–46), 171–94; John W. Johnston, "Railway Land Grants," *North American Review,* 140 (1885), 280–89; Ralph N. Traxler, Jr., "The Texas and Pacific Railroad Land Grants: A Comparison of Land Grant Policies of the United States and Texas," *Southern Historical Quarterly,* 61 (1958), 359–70.

13. Lingenfelter, Dwyer, and Cohen, *Songs of the American West,* pp. 69–70.

14. Samuel Eliot Morison and Henry Steele Commager, *The Growth of the American Republic* (New York: Oxford University Press, 1950), p. 112.

15. Frank Norris's novel *The Octopus: A Story of California* (1901), while primarily the story of growing and harvesting wheat in the central valley of California, provides an excellent picture of the encroachments of a giant railroad empire into various walks of life, and of the consequent widespread negative feelings engendered toward the railroad, especially among the farmers.

16. "Theodore," words and music by Vincent Bryan, copyrighted 1907 by Shapiro, Bernstein, New York. Cited in Lester S. Levy, *Give Me Yesterday* (Norman: University of Oklahoma Press, 1975), p. 122.

17. "Railroad Monopoly," by J. W. Carhart and Martin Towne, published by National Music, copyrighted 1873 by H. N. Hempstead.

18. E. Hirst, as quoted in *Science,* Dec. 8, 1972, p. 1080.

19. In addition to Bowman, *Pioneer Railroads,* Lyon, *To Hell in a Day Coach,* and Middleton, *Railways and Public Opinion,* the following sources used in the preparation of this chapter will provide the interested reader with further information: Charles Francis Adams, Jr., *Railroads* (New York: G. P. Putnam's Sons, 1879); C. Hamilton Ellis, "The Development of Railway Engineering," in *A History of Technology,* vol. 5, *The Late Nineteenth Century,* edited by Charles Singer et al. (London and New York: Oxford University Press, 1958), pp. 322–49; Harold Underwood Faulkner, *American Political and Social History,* 7th ed. (New York: Appleton-Century-Crofts, 1957); Steward H. Holbrook, *The Story of American Railroads* (New York: Crown Publishers, 1947); James F. Hudson, *The Railways and the Republic* (New York: Harper and Brothers, 1886); and Frank P. Morse, *Cavalcade of the Rails* (New York: E. P. Dutton 1940).

2

America's Music: Written and Recorded

ON FEBRUARY 19, 1636, a London broadside printer registered a new ballad entitled "The Coaches' Overthrow," a complaint about the large number of such new vehicles that were clogging the narrow streets of the town. Confident that coaches were but a passing fancy, the ballad writer ended his piece:

> But, to conclude, 'tis true, I heare,
> They'l soone be out of fashion;
> 'Tis thought they very likely are
> To have a long vacation.
>   Heigh, downe dery, dery downe,
>   With the hackney coaches downe!
>   Their term's neere done,
>   And shall be begun
>   No more in London towne.[1]

Although probably not the first ballad to rail against technological innovation, this early commentary does remind us that to complain about modernization is a venerable tradition. On the other hand, there were doubtless literary compositions in praise of the new devices, since novelties always have admirers as well as detractors.

From our vantage point three and a half centuries later, it appears that "The Coaches' Overthrow" left no discernible mark on oral tradition. This is not surprising; songs and poems dealing with topical matters are generally forgotten after the events that inspired them fade into history. Only if a song is so written as to have living significance to future generations can it be expected to survive. In other words, "The Coaches' Overthrow" is not a folksong in the twentieth century. Whether it was a folksong in the seventeenth century we do not know; our knowledge of what songs people were singing in the 1630s and under what circumstances is too incomplete for us to be able to call this item either folk or popular music.

An older definition of folksong would have it that such a composition "originated anonymously, among unlettered folk in times past."[2] According to such a restrictive view,

21

a composition from the pen of an identifiable author disseminated on a broadside could never be a folksong. As a consequence, whether or not a person consigned songs to that category would depend largely on the state of his knowledge. Scholars who adhered rigidly to the above definition generally believed that in principle the style of a song originating among unlettered folk was so distinct from that of a broadside ballad that one would never be mistaken for the other simply because the name of the author was lacking. In practice, however, even the writer of the above quotation admitted that it was difficult to draw the line between the two, that the distinction was "accidental rather than inherent."

The broadside press was perhaps the first communications technology to make a major assault on the pre-Gutenberg culture of European society. The first broadside, unlike the Gutenberg Bible, is not regarded as a major literary landmark, and its identity and precise date are not known. There were, however, broadsides that predated Gutenberg's celebrated production of 1456, and there were broadside ballads early in the sixteenth century. In the sixteenth century and later, the broadside ballads were newspapers in verse, offering both factual accounts of matters of current interest and editorial comments on them. Unlike books, which were generally printed and bound with care, and priced beyond the reach of all but a small elite, broadsides were crudely and hastily printed in remarkably large quantities and sold relatively inexpensively. Thus, their impact on the popular culture was probably much greater than that of books.[3]

But broadsides and other forms of cheap print were not an isolated innovation in an otherwise unchanging world; they were part of an extensive series of social upheavals that included the rise of the city and of Protestant capitalism, and the concurrent decline of the two dominant medieval institutions, feudalism and the church. The same technology that made possible the new mercantile class provided the machinery for cheap print. The new medium helped document some of the social changes that were taking place and provided an outlet for expressing the sentiments of those who were witness to such changes.

The broadside ballad, a single sheet of paper on one side of which the text of a song was printed, was succeeded by sheet music or the song sheet, which differed in the important property of including music as well as words. Chronologically, of course, the two forms overlapped for centuries; but in America sheet music did not come into its heyday until the nineteenth century, at a time when many families were affluent enough to possess pianos. In the early twentieth century, sheet music was supplanted by the phonograph, which, in turn, has been partly displaced by radio, television, and tape. Each of these innovations has its own implications for the survival of folk music. That each successive medium could be a source for folksong has required a new generation of folksong scholars to recognize. The generation that admitted broadside balladry as possibly relevant to folksong closed its eyes to the sheet music of Tin Pan Alley. The collectors who opened the canons to those nineteenth-century parlor ballads refused to accept hillbilly and blues music. Today, the folklorists who study hillbilly and blues records are slow to accept current radio- and TV-disseminated rock music.

Each of these new media has dealt a hard blow to the venerable mechanisms of oral tradition. Prior to broadsides, songs could be preserved only by manuscript or by memory. Both involved individual acts, necessarily repeated anew if a song was to be transferred from one possessor to the next. The frailty of human memory (along with native creativity) permitted textual and musical variation to flourish. In fact, many scholars have accepted the existence of variation as proof of currency in oral tradition—a position that reveals an inadequate understanding of both folk and popular song. The broadside relieved the memory of its responsibility for the text of a song, thus freeing songwriters of the stylistic constraints of older oral poetry that were conducive to easy memorization (e.g., repetition, and the use of a familiar catalog of clichés and formalisms). Tune transmission was handled differently. Generally, the broadside heading included the instruction "To the tune of . . . ," citing some familiar melody. In some cases, for example in rural America, the broadside writer/seller sang the tune over and over for his customers until they had committed to memory a reasonable facsimile of it. Of course, the main goal of the broadside printer was to sell as many broadsides as possible, and most of his ballads were fresh compositions. In some instances, he did print up versions of older, well-established folksongs. Anglo-Americans have apparently had great respect for the printed word—the fact that "it's in the book" conferred special authority on a text—and the broadside ballads often drove out the older versions transmitted memorially. Some folksong scholars viewed this as a musical analog of Gresham's law: bad music driving out good. Sheet music then did for the melody what the broadside had done for the text. Now text and tune, wedded together on quality paper, could outlast the life of the composer/ writer by centuries and not suffer casual adulterations.

The phonograph record relieved the individual of the need to make by himself the music he sought for entertainment. No longer did he need to rely on his own memory for text or tune of a favored composition. If it was available on record, it was his for the purchasing. With his wind-up phonograph and his treasured discs or cylinders he could hear his favorites at will. In the context of this succession of changes, the novelty of radio was that it took out of the listener's hands the power to program his own musical fare. Each of these four changes moved the listener a step away from his music; each permitted another degree of passivity on his part.

All of these media ought to be able to provide sources for folk music. And all do; but each successive one is a less likely source. The reason is inherent not in any stylistic or thematic changes in the music, but rather in the fact that each change makes it less likely that a person will make his own music. My own notion of folk music is broad enough to permit any source to contribute to the pot, but sufficiently conservative to require that in order to be a folksong a piece must be performed for self-enjoyment in a noncommercial act. If people do not sing for their own entertainment, there can be no folksong as the word is used here. A definition I find useful in the context of Anglo-American society is that a folksong is a song the survival of which does not depend entirely on commercial media. Thus a song need not be old in order to qualify, but it must outlive its vogue in sheet music and records. That is, antiquity is a de facto but not de jure requisite. Variation is another useful indicator. Respect for the printed word means that the existence of variation generally is proof that the printed authority has lost its influence. It should be noted, however, that at certain periods in our musical history it was not uncommon for different printed versions of the same song to exist side by side; examples are discussed elsewhere in this book. Oral transmission is by its very nature proof that the transmitted piece is not entirely dependent on commercial media; therefore, if we can convince ourselves that a single documented case of oral transmission is not unique, we can be satisfied that it indicates a folksong. In this book I use the phrase "entered oral tradition" to mean "became a folksong." Popular songs are often the forgotten siblings of folksongs, disappearing with the sheet music that first gave them life.

Not all folksongs originated on broadside, sheet music, or phonograph disc. Some never had a commercial aspect, coming rather from the lips of some local poet or balladeer who sought merely to entertain his own family and friends—or perhaps simply to gain relief from inner tension by the cathartic process of creating a song. These pieces meet the requirements of definitions of *folksong* more conservative than mine. However, one can still apply the test of oral transmission to such pieces. My own view is that if they fail that test, they may be considered folk-like songs (if they are in the style of folksongs), but not folksongs. This book is a collection of songs taken (with a few exceptions) from the medium of the commercial phonograph record, but songs that nevertheless can be regarded (by my definition) as folksongs (or, in a very few instances, as folk-like songs).

The particular classes of phonograph records that I draw upon are what have been designated—to the disapproval of many—as "hillbilly" and "race" records. These genres came from two of the many musical subcultures that record companies in the United States have explored and exploited since the 1920s. Popular music was the nationally distributed product with which the record industry saturated the nation's "middle-brow" listeners. It differed from "high-brow" or classical music in that it was danced to or sung along with or talked over, but never just listened to. Its audience was the entire nation; its performers were professional, often trained musicians and singers; its creators were likewise professional, often trained musicians, but usually they were not the performers.[4]

The musical subcultures to which I refer were mostly ethnic enclaves within the United States that were in contact with the popular culture but still maintained at least a partial separateness from it. These cultures included Polish-Americans of the Midwest, Finnish-Americans of Michigan, black Americans of Harlem and other urban ghettos, southern white Americans of Appalachia and the Ozarks, Yiddish-speaking Americans of the Jewish ghettos, Cajuns of the Louisiana bayous, Mexican-Americans of the Southwest, French-Canadians of the Northeast, and at least two dozen other foreign-language groups. For each of these groups the basic pattern was the same: the record company went to the well-established performers within the appropriate community, recorded them, frequently on-site, and advertised and sold the records in that same community. The content of the music varied greatly, from genuine folksongs to foreign-language popular songs to American popular music as modulated by the musical style of the given ethnic culture. Record companies were not very discriminating when they began these ventures; they did not ask if a particular number, rendered in, say, Lithuanian, was a translation of a current American pop hit, or was an Italian operatic aria offered in Lithuanian, or was an old Lithuanian hymn. Naturally, as the genres persisted, the more successful artists turned less and less to old standards and folk pieces, more to new, unrecorded selections, frequently of their own composition.[5] The two most extensive of these genres were those that had the largest audiences: hillbilly music, aimed at the rural white South, and race records, aimed at both the southern rural and the northern ghetto blacks.

According to this view, hillbilly music is solely a recorded phenomenon. However, a much broader connotation is sometimes meant. Some writers use the term to refer to the semiprofessional string-band and minstrel-singer (in the European sense) traditions that existed in the rural South alongside the domestic, noncommercial musical traditions.[6] The latter was home music, made strictly for private or near-private consumption. It was the tradition that has preserved, for centuries, our country's heritage of the old British folksongs and ballads. The former traditions catered to the local but not-so-private demand for entertainment—Saturday night dances or local concerts in the nearby schoolhouse. The latter preserved the unaccompanied older singing styles; the former provided a mixing pot for several styles: Anglo-American folk, Afro-American folk, and middle-American popular, always with instrumental accompaniment, often with vocal harmonization.

This sharply drawn distinction between the domestic and the hillbilly traditions was in reality often rather blurred. Indeed, there were a few unaccompanied singers who recorded commercial discs; there were a few nonprofessionals who found their way to the studios in response to requests for talent published in the papers. But by and large, the two traditions did remain distinct, especially after the first two or three experimental years of hillbilly recordings. With few exceptions, the hillbilly recording artists were men (and some women) who sought to make their livelihood solely through their music. With few exceptions, they were rural southerners steeped in the folk culture of their native county, whose first musical experiences were ballads sung by a mother, or banjo songs performed by a father, or fiddle tunes played by an uncle. In the first few years of recorded hillbilly music—1922 through 1925—the selections they brought to the studios included a generous share of pieces from oral tradition (or its instrumental analog); in the years that followed, they wrote an increasing proportion of their own material, in the style of the older traditional pieces.

The roots of both hillbilly and race music in older traditional Anglo-American and Afro-American folk musics have been carefully traced.[7] But it is also valid to view these developments in the context of America's popular music. Although songsters and other inexpensively produced songs and music were printed in this country well before the revolutionary war, it was probably not until the rise of the minstrel stage in the 1830s that American music broke out of the mold shaped by the styles of our European ancestors. The quantity of music published before the minstrel era was not large, even when allowances for the small national population are made. Sonneck and Upton's *Bibliography of Early Secular American Music*, a near-complete catalog of music published prior to 1800, lists some 3,000 items, mostly from 1760 to 1800. Wolfe's *Bibliography of Secular American Music (1801–1825)* cites 10,000 items, a good indicator of the quantity of material printed in the first quarter of the nineteenth century. The growth curve soared upward after the Civil War, as the surge in urbanization and industrialization provided both the means and the market for a mass-produced entertainment medium. In 1878, the first year for which detailed figures are available, almost 3,800 musical compositions were copyrighted. By 1890 the annual production exceeded 9,000 pieces.

While probably most of the popular songs of the period dealt with love, romance, and other tender sentiments, there were a remarkable number of pieces of a topical nature. Every major new technological achievement was commemorated in popular song. Consider, for example, "Atlantic Telegraph Polka" (1858), by A. Talexy; "The Ocean Cable Polka" (1858), by Fritz Kielblock; "The Telegraph" (1865), by W. J. Wellman, Jr.; "The Great Graphic Balloon Galop" (1873), by William H. Fitch; "Battle of the Sewing Machines" (1874), by F. Hyde; "The Wondrous Telephone" (1877), by Thomas P. Westendorf; "The Highway in the Air, or a Ballad of the Brooklyn Bridge" (1883), by Elf St. Moritz and John Vorsatz.

Although writers a half-century ago marveled at the survival of pre-nineteenth-century culture in the southern highlands—it was reported that Elizabethan English was still spoken in the Appalachians—the isolation was never so complete as such romanticized accounts suggested. Black and white rural southerners were always exposed to national popular music. Even what meager evidence we have is sufficient to prove that nationally distributed popular songs from every decade since the 1820s have entered oral tradition in that part of the country. Sheet music was obtainable almost everywhere, and even back in the mountains a surprising number of dwellings had pianos or small pump organs. However, probably of greater impact on rural southern life was the regular

procession of live entertainment that paraded through the countryside—traveling minstrel shows, circuses and other tent shows, and the ubiquitous patent-medicine doctor
and his medicine show. Many early hillbilly and race artists acquired their training in
such entourages in the years before World War I, and by watching them many more kept
up to date on the musical happenings of the nation. The formative years of hillbilly
records witnessed the recording of more songs traceable to the latter-nineteenth-century
minstrel and vaudeville stage than to older folk traditions.

Southern whites, predisposed through their Anglo-American folk heritage to the
narrative ballad, took a ready liking to the Tin Pan Alley balladry of the 1880s and 1890s.[8]
This congenial wellspring dried up after the turn of the century, as popular music turned
from the ballad to the dance craze, opening the curtain on ragtime, jazz, and other
instrumental forms. The ballad singers, left out, had to cling to the nineteenth-century
favorites. But the rural instrumentalists had their heyday. Musicians who got their first
calluses on their pappy's fiddle and banjo learned to play the guitar from black construction workers who were part of the railroad road gangs that laid the way for the steel rails.
Infiltrating the hills from the city were other strange instruments—mandolin, ukulele,
Hawaiian guitar, harmonica, autoharp. The older Anglo-American fiddle tunes and
dances gave way to rag-timey and jazzy numbers. Reels and hornpipes, carried across the
Atlantic by Scots and Scots-Irish fiddlers and played with double stops and drones, were
joined by relaxed and syncopated blues melodies accented with flatted thirds and
sevenths. This, more than the unaccompanied ancient ballads and solo fiddle pieces of
the eighteenth century and earlier, was the paternity of the hillbilly music that emerged on
record a decade or so later.

I would be embarrassed to describe in only a few paragraphs the complex and
fascinating histories of hillbilly and race music were it not that several fine studies have
already been published. Pioneering work by a small but dedicated band of folklorists,
record collectors, and historians has resulted in a thorough understanding of the beginnings of these industries, although many of the fine details—the stories of the individual
artists who contributed in no small measure to the success of those industries—are often
still lacking.[9]

Briefly told, the origins of the two genres of recorded race and hillbilly music were
similar, both resulting from almost chance encounters between industry and artist. Early
in 1920, Perry Bradford, a black, Alabama-born songwriter living in New York, took it
upon himself to convince the record industry of the merits of recording black talent for a
black audience. Prior to that time, few blacks, apart from comedians and singers of
Europeanized spirituals, had been given the opportunity to record. Bradford brought
Mamie Smith, a black singer who had achieved some success in a Harlem musical, *Made
in Harlem,* to Victor's recording studios; there, in January, test pressings were made of
her singing two of Bradford's compositions. The recordings were never released. When
Columbia refused to audition Mamie, Bradford was forced to appeal to the smaller record
companies. In February, he persuaded Fred Hager of the General Phonograph Company
to let Mamie cut a few numbers, but only after Hager had been dissuaded from his idea of
using Sophie Tucker for Bradford's pieces. The two selections, released in July, were
heralded in the black press, and sales were unexpectedly high. Mamie was called back to
the studio in August to record another pair of numbers, including "Crazy Blues."
Although her style was more that of a pop than a blues singer, and although blues songs
were nothing new in 1920, the event was noteworthy because it revealed to the industry
that there was a vast untapped market of black consumers willing to purchase recordings

by black artists. Other record companies were quick to follow the trail blazed by General and its label, OKeh records. The smaller outfits moved first: Arto recorded Lucille Hegamin in November, 1920; in March, 1921, Pathé-Frères waxed two sides by Lavinia Turner, and Emerson recorded two by Lillyn Brown. The Starr Piano Company recorded Daisy Martin for its Gennett label in April; the black-owned Black Swan brought Alberta Hunter into its studios in May; Paramount recorded Trixie Smith in September; and that same month, Columbia, one of the giants, braved a record session with Edith Wilson.

These were the trailblazers, but in the perspective of history they are seen to have been lesser luminaries. The styles of these early female performers were, broadly speaking, similar. All sang a mélange of jazz, pop, and classic twelve-bar blues songs to the accompaniment of a small jazz combo. Though mostly southern born, all were more pop than blues singers. The industry surged forward in 1923 with the recording of a funkier brand of classic blues (some prefer the term *Harlem blues*) singers: Paramount recorded Ida Cox and Ma Rainey that year, both of whom had begun their musical careers in black traveling minstrel shows early in the century; and Columbia found Bessie Smith, a one-time protégé of Ma Rainey, and Clara Smith, well established on the vaudeville circuits by 1918. These women proved to be giants, especially in terms of their commercial impact. Within a few years, however, their music, too, was supplanted by a rougher type of blues—the country blues, featuring (generally) male singers accompanied by their own guitars (or occasionally piano, banjo-guitar, or other instrument). OKeh recorded Atlanta guitarist Sylvester Weaver in 1923, and Ed Andrews, possibly the first country blues singer on wax, in April, 1924, in Atlanta. The Starr Piano Company recorded Johnny Watson (Daddy Stovepipe) and Sam Jones (Stovepipe #1) within a few days of each other in May, 1924. Paramount brought Papa Charlie Jackson to the studios in August, probably from New Orleans. In 1925 a Dallas music store employee recommended to Paramount officials that they record a local street-singer/guitarist known as Blind Lemon Jefferson. The following year that company found another star in Florida's ragtime guitarist Arthur Phelps, known better as Blind Blake. Columbia's first country blues singer was Peg Leg Howell from Atlanta, recorded in 1926. Not until 1927 did Victor make its first field trips to record local blues singers, visiting Atlanta, Memphis, Bristol, Charlotte, and Savannah. In the few remaining years before the Depression, the blues market was dominated by a handful of artists: Jefferson, Blake, Bessie Smith, Ma Rainey, Clara Smith, and Ida Cox headed the list. Each piled up more than forty releases—Bessie Smith, nearly eighty. Most early blues singers included in their recorded repertoires blues incorporating themes built around railroads and wandering. Jefferson's "Lemon's Cannon Ball Moan," "Bad Luck Blues," and "Easy Rider Blues"; Blind Blake's "Georgia Bound"; Bessie Smith's "Ticket Agent, Ease Your Window Down," "Dixie Flyer Blues," and "J. C. Holmes Blues"; Trixie Smith's "Freight Train Blues" and "Railroad Blues"; and Clara Smith's "Freight Train Blues" and "The L. & N. Blues" comprise only a partial roster.

Although country blues emerged as the main staple of race records in the latter 1920s, record companies did manage to wax a small but important number of pre-blues-styled folksingers, sometimes called songsters, the residue of an earlier black musical tradition. These men sang some blues, but their repertoires were also laden with older ballads and minstrel songs. Papa Charlie Jackson was the first of them to be recorded. In 1927 Vocalion recorded Furry Lewis in Memphis, beginning the session with "Rock Island Blues." Later sessions produced a never-released "Casey Jones Blues" and a two-part "John Henry," while for Victor he recorded "Cannon Ball Blues" and a two-part

"Kassie Jones." In the same city in 1927 Paramount struck pay dirt with Gus Cannon, but they lost him the following year to Victor, for whom he recorded "Big Railroad Blues" with his Jug Stompers. Vocalion recorded another old-timer, Jim Jackson, in Chicago in 1927. Along with some older minstrel pieces he recorded "Mobile-Central Blues." The following year two Avalon, Mississippi, hillbilly musicians recommended that OKeh record a local black guitarist/singer, John Hurt. His "Casey Jones" was never issued, but "Spike Driver Blues" was widely influential in later years. In 1921, the term *colored* was used to describe the new genre of recorded music, but in 1923 OKeh introduced the appellation *race*, and it soon became standard.

Country blues, the only form of Afro-American folk music to be commercially recorded in quantity, dominated the race market from Blind Lemon Jefferson's first recordings of spring, 1926, until the Depression. The first important suggestions of a new style were the recordings of Leroy Carr and Scrapper Blackwell, a piano/guitar combination whose more urbane and polished duets pointed the path away from the generally rougher and spontaneous country blues to a more city-influenced sound. In part, their popularity was due to the danceability and singability of their material. (Many country blues were hardly singable by typical record buyers.) Carr and Blackwell's first big hit, released in mid-1928, was "How Long Blues," a splendid example of the use of railroad lyrics in a blues song. Its immense success was responsible for their recording six separate versions of it in four years. Little music was recorded between 1930 and 1934, but after then, when activity picked up, a dominant blues style was that of Carr and Blackwell.

As 1940 approached, the black community began buying an increasing proportion of records in nonblues styles—performances by black artists that were much closer to the standard white popular music of the time than blues were. Vocal ensembles, both sacred (Golden Gate Quartet) and secular (Ink Spots), big bands (Duke Ellington, Count Basie, Lionel Hampton), and small combos (Louis Jordan) gained ascendancy.

The diversity of musical styles—as well as dissatisfaction with a terminology that bore unpleasant sociological implications to many consumers—led to a search for more appropriate labels. During the war Decca inaugurated its 8500 "sepia" series for black nonblues material, to parallel its 7000 "race" series begun in 1934. In 1942, *Billboard*, the leading trade publication, began charting popular hits by black artists under the title "Harlem Hit Parade." For a while, the editors switched to the label *race* again, but in 1949 they settled on *rhythm and blues*. Although blues recordings continued to constitute a portion of this heterogeneous field, in general, blues and nonblues R & B began more and more to reflect the fact that a growing proportion of performers and listeners were urban rather than rural dwellers.[10]

Recorded hillbilly music was slower to get off the ground than was the music recorded for "the race." Probably the first traditional rural white artists to record were Alexander "Eck" Campbell Robertson, a Texas fiddler, and Henry C. Gilliland, an Oklahoma fiddler, who decided to visit Victor's New York studios to cut some records before returning home from a Confederate Veterans' Reunion in Richmond, Virginia. Their initial waxings, made in June, 1922, were not released for almost ten months. In 1923, Henry Whitter, a cotton-mill worker and part-time musician from Fries, Virginia, went north on his own initiative to persuade OKeh's staff to record his voice, guitar, and harmonica. He was recorded, but the masters were not utilized for some time.

The event that opened industry's eyes to the potential market at hand was the recording, in June, 1923, of Atlanta's Fiddlin' John Carson. This came to pass because Polk Brockman, an Atlanta record distributor attending a business convention in New

Advertisement in the *Talking Machine World*, September 15, 1924. Courtesy of Archie Green and the John Edwards Memorial Foundation, UCLA.

York where sagging sales were discussed, was struck with the idea of recording local talent. Carson, a painter by trade but a prominent fiddler and entertainer in north Georgia, came immediately to mind. Carson's initial disc, recorded and released with great reluctance by OKeh's executives, reportedly sold in a frenzy in Atlanta, and a new industry was born. In 1924, OKeh recorded a host of talent in the Atlanta area. The Aeolian Company entered the new field in the same year with three Tennessee performers of local renown: Uncle Dave Macon, who later became the first featured star on the Grand Ole Opry; Uncle Am Stuart, a near-seventy-year-old fiddler; and George Reneau, known as the "blind minstrel of the Smoky Mountains." The Starr Piano Company made a few recordings of Kentucky artists that year, but did not get into hillbilly music in a serious way for another year. Columbia's initial ventures in the field were also in 1924, with Gid Tanner and Riley Puckett of Atlanta, Ernest Thompson of Winston-Salem, and Samantha Bumgarner and Eva Davis of Sylva, North Carolina—all well known in their home locales. Traditional folksongs figured heavily early in the recorded output of these pioneers, and railroad songs were well represented. Reneau's first session included "The Wreck on the Southern 97," "Life's Railway to Heaven," and "Casey Jones." Ernest Thompson's first session, spanning two days, produced "The Wreck on the Southern Old 97," "Life's Railway," "Jesse James," and "Lightning Express." Puckett's first two-day session saw the waxing of "Lightning Express" and "Casey Jones." Whitter's first recording was "The Wreck on the Southern Old 97." At his second session, Fiddlin' John Carson recorded "Casey Jones" and "Papa's Billy Goat," while later sessions produced "John Henry Blues," "The Baggage Coach Ahead," "The Lightning Express," and "I'm Nine Hundred Miles from Home."

A major landmark in hillbilly music was the career of Jimmie Rodgers. During his brief recording career, 1927 through 1933, he dominated the industry. He created a national style of country music, welding together the images of cowboy and railroad wanderer, the risqué classic blues lines and the sentimental ballads of Tin Pan Alley. He was the first major country performer to utilize unidentified studio sidemen: he was the star, they were the anonymous accompaniment. Rodgers popularized a form of white blues music—a pale imitation of the classic city blues—that made frequent use of railroad imagery. Following in Rodgers's footsteps trooped a retinue of country stars—Jimmie Davis, Gene Autry, Cliff Carlisle, Hank Snow, Wilf Carter—who perpetuated the themes of railroads, hoboes, and wanderers. For twenty years after Rodgers almost every major country singer had one or more hits in this vein: Goebel Reeves ("Railroad Bum," "Railroad Boomer," "Hobo's Lullaby"), Roy Acuff ("Wabash Cannonball," "Fire Ball Mail," "Streamlined Cannon Ball"), Harry McClintock ("Jesse James," "Hallelujah, I'm a Bum," "Big Rock Candy Mountain," "Jerry, Go Ile That Car"), Jimmie Davis ("Wild and Reckless Hobo," "The Davis Limited"), Gene Autry ("Railroad Boomer," "Waiting for a Train," "Hobo Bill's Last Ride," "Train Whistle Blues," "I'm a Railroad Man"), the Callahan Brothers ("Freight Train Blues," "Lonesome Freight Train Blues"), Bill Cox ("The Ramblin' Railroad Boy," "The Handcar Yodel," "Train Whistle Blues," "Runaway Train Blues"), Cliff Carlisle ("Box Car Blues," "Hobo Jack's Last Ride," "The Brakeman's Reply," "Brakeman's Blues," "Box Car Yodel"), Wilf Carter ("I'm Gonna Ride to Heaven on a Stream Line Train," "Rattlin' Cannonball," "The Midnight Train"), Hank Snow ("The Hobo's Last Ride," "I'm Moving On," "The Golden Rocket"), Hank Williams ("Pan American," "Lonesome Whistle"), Ernest Tubb ("Right Train to Heaven," "Waiting for a Train"), Eddy Arnold ("Casey Jones," "Wreck of the Old 97"), Tex Ritter ("Wreck of the Number Nine"), the Carter Family ("Wabash Cannonball," "Engine 143," "The Cannonball"), J. E. Mainer's Mountaineers ("The Longest Train," "John Henry Was a Little Boy"), the Delmore Brothers ("Blow Yo' Whistle, Freight Train," "Blue Railroad Train," "I've Got the Railroad Blues," "The Wabash Cannon Ball Blues"). When lesser artists are added to the account, the catalog of railroad songs in country music indeed appears immense.

As these titles indicate, older traditional folksongs continued to constitute part of country singers' repertoire through the 1930s, but newer compositions outnumbered them. Most of the latter cannot be classified as folksongs, at least on the basis of current available evidence; rather, they are best identified as folk-like pieces.

Through the 1930s and 1940s, the mainstream of hillbilly music—like that of race music—moved further and further from rural roots. And, as in the case of race music, dissatisfaction with the term *hillbilly* eventually led to a new rubric. In 1944, *Billboard* inaugurated a chart of "folk songs and blues" for hits not in the standard popular category. In 1949, it switched to the terms *country* or *country and western*.

So much for the broad outlines of these two genres of recorded music. What of their scope and significance? How many hillbilly and race recordings were made in the 1920s and 1930s? How many were issued? How many copies of each release were sold? Were sales national or regional? Finally, what was the impact of this music on the noncommercial folk music tradition? Most of these questions cannot be answered at present. The statistics that one would like to be able to examine are often not available. Record companies have, alas, not conducted their accounts with an eye to the future needs and interests of sociologists, folklorists, and historians. Old logs and ledgers, as well as old masters and original recordings, have been periodically destroyed to an extent that brings tears to the eyes of collector, fan, and scholar alike. Discography, the analytic tool that does for the recorded document what bibliography does for the written, is still a very primitive discipline. There is today no published work or collection of works to which one can refer to assay the recorded output of the thousands of hillbilly musicians who stood before microphones since the inception of the industry in 1922. And without even this basic knowledge of what was recorded and released, it becomes sheer fantasy to speculate on other matters, such as extent and distribution of sales, or analyses of thematic content. The state of affairs in the field of race records is considerably more advanced; Paul Oliver has made a notable beginning in the sociological analysis of blues lyrics.[11] Furthermore, we have a single volume of discographic data that purports to catalog all the blues and gospel recordings made prior to 1942.[12] Granting some subjectivity in the authors' decision of what constitutes sufficient "negroid" content to justify inclusion, the volume is a tool of first-order importance. For each recorded item, this reference gives, where known, recording date and location, personnel, title, master number, and the labels and numbers of the various releases.

It was not uncommon for the same master recording to be issued on different labels at different dates, often with different artist credits (or pseudonyms), and occasionally with different titles. Thus, an unsuspecting record purchaser might buy "Life's Railway to Heaven" by Welling and McGhee on Gennett 7156, by the Hutchens Brothers on Champion 15971, and by Harper and Turner on Supertone 9658 from the Sears catalog, without realizing that all three were the identical recording. A single recording made for the Plaza Music Company by Vernon Dalhart of "In the Baggage Coach Ahead" was released in the United States on Banner 1549, Regal 9847, Domino 3519, Clover 1694, Conqueror 7067, Banner 0826, Cameo 0426, Challenge 784, Domino 4643, Jewel 6076, Oriole 2076, Perfect 12644, Regal 10132, Romeo 1440, Oriole 421, Silvertone 2701, and

Lincoln 1520. In Canada, it was issued on Sterling 281104, Crown 81104, Minerva M902, and Apex 8345. In Australia, it appeared on Fossy 9847. Not only was the purchaser sometimes beguiled by this procedure; often the recording artist was not informed of leasing arrangements or releases on subsidiary labels. Usually this was justified by the now-obsolete practice of paying hillbilly and race performers a flat recording fee only, with no royalty payments. The reasons for this bewildering state of affairs lay in a tangled web of corporate relationships, transfers of ownership, and agreements to lease masters. For a brief overview of the problem, see the appendix to this chapter.[13]

It is apparent that if one is interested in some quantitative assay of the number of hillbilly recordings, he must be aware that the number of distinct performances issued could be very different from the total number of releases (after allowing for the fact that each release carries two selections).

From their extensive discographic researches in the area of race records (they prefer the term *blues and gospel*), Dixon and Godrich compiled figures on the number of releases for each year between 1920 and 1941.[14] Similar figures have not been published for hillbilly records, but they can be estimated from unpublished discographic data that are available. For the first dozen years of the hillbilly industry, the approximate figures are given below.

		Hillbilly records	*Race records*
		Number of releases	*Number of releases*
Year	*Total number*	*excluding overlap*	*excluding overlap*
1924	80	80	225
1925	225	225	250
1926	400	300	325
1927	1,050	675	500
1928	1,150	650	500
1929	1,250	800	500
1930	1,025	725	500
1931	975	575	400
1932	825	475	200
1933	850	275	150
1934	825	375	225
1935	975	375	350
1936	1,000	375	400

It should be stressed that these figures for hillbilly records are preliminary and subject to about 10 percent uncertainty. Nevertheless, they are sufficient to indicate some basic facts. One obvious inference is the profound effect of the Depression on record releases, augmented by the growing popularity of the competitive medium of radio. Recording activity slowed greatly in 1930; much of what was issued in the next three years was material that had been recorded earlier. A second conclusion is that after the first year or two, the figures for hillbilly releases and race releases were comparable. In the period of 1927–28, the total number of popular releases (including hillbilly and race) was approximately 8–10,000 records per year. Thus, at their peak, hillbilly and race records accounted for about 15 percent of the number of releases. This does not necessarily imply that they accounted for a like fraction of the total sales. Corresponding figures for more recent years are similar. During the 1960s, the number of singles released ranged from 6,000 to 7,000 records each year. Of these, about 10 percent were country and western, while rhythm and blues plus spiritual (the modern categories that are approximately equivalent to blues and gospel) releases ranged from about 5 to 9 percent.

Information on sales of individual records is very scarce, as record companies have always been tight-lipped about sales figures. In 1962, 210 million singles were sold, or an average of 31,000 copies for each of the 6,700 singles released. (This ignores the complication that some sales were for records released in previous years.) However, if one subtracts the 60 million-selling discs, the average of the remainder is less than 22,000. In 1927–28, approximately 100 million of the 8–10,000 singles were sold, or about 10,000 copies per single. Since few discs sold in very large quantities, this figure does not have to be corrected very much to obtain a median rather than average value.

Did the average hillbilly or race record sell as well as the average popular record? Based on currently available information, the answer would be no. On the Victor label, the industry leader, the most successful pop artists such as Paul Whiteman, Gene Austin, or Helen Kane occasionally hit 200,000 to 500,000 copies (very rarely more) before the Depression, but more typically sales were in the 30,000-to-50,000 range. Only one hillbilly disc, Vernon Dalhart's "Prisoner's Song"/"Wreck of the Old 97," sold in excess of 1,000,000 (and just barely). Jimmie Rodgers, the next most successful hillbilly artist, exceeded a quarter-million sales only three or four times; these hits included his "Waiting for a Train" and "Ben Dewberry's Final Run." The Carter Family, Victor's next-best-selling hillbilly group, sold more than 88,000 copies of "Engine 143," but the not quite 25,000 for their "Cannon Ball" and "Western Hobo" was more typical. Travis B. Hale and E. J. Derry, Jr.'s "The Dying Hobo" did surprisingly well at 58,000. Other hillbilly artists enjoyed considerably lower sales. Vernon Dalhart's "Jesse James" sold 13,300. Frank Luther's "Wreck of the Number Nine," another popular song by a popular singer, sold only 11,600, and Bob Miller's "Little Red Caboose behind the Train," fewer than 8,000. Blues artists sold comparably or slightly poorer. El Watson's harmonica instrumental "Narrow Gauge Blues" sold 17,000 copies, while Buddy Baker's "Boxcar Blues" sold 9,400.

The most successful artists recording for Columbia, the second largest firm at the time, tallied up fewer sales. Best-sellers by the Skillet Lickers, one of Columbia's most popular string bands, topped a quarter-million (though not often); their coupling of "John Henry" and "Wreck on the Southern Old 97" sold about 60,000. Smith's Sacred Singers, Columbia's best-selling sacred group, placed 52,000 of one of their singles, "Life's Railway to Heaven," in consumers' homes. These figures were exceptional. Even Vernon Dalhart, whose total hillbilly record sales over a period of several years undoubtedly exceeded those of any other artist, could often do no better than 6,000 or 7,000 copies with a Columbia release (and sometimes no better with Victor), even during the peak year of 1929.

Most other companies were dwarfed by comparison with Victor and Columbia. The popular team of Martin and Roberts, who recorded for the Starr Piano Company, offers a good example. In 1928 they recorded "Eastbound Train." It was released on the company's primary label, Gennett, as well as on their cheaper Champion label, and also on Sears's Supertone label. Fewer than 600 copies of the Gennett release were sold; Champion sales were under 5,000, and Supertone sales, under 6,000. These figures are typical of all their releases, and probably higher than for Starr's average hillbilly artists. During 1931–32 it was not uncommon for a disc to sell fewer than 500 copies. The Deep River Plantation Singers' 1931 recording of the spiritual "Train's a Comin'" for Starr was released on four labels; the Superior release, on sale for three months during 1932, sold 83 copies. Bernice Coleman's composition "The Wreck of the C & O *Sportsman*" was recorded for Starr and issued only on Superior; total sales for the ten months it was available in 1931–32 were only 370. Even sales on the Victor and Columbia labels dropped precipitously. Joe Steen's "Crazy Engineer," issued in January, 1932, sold a mere 500 copies, and the Burnett Brothers' "Countin' Cross Ties," issued in November of that year, sold fewer than 250 discs.

The biggest artists could do little better during the Depression. The Carter Family's Victor release "Wabash Cannonball," another November, 1932, issue, sold only 1,700 copies. The enormously popular Charlie Poole recorded "Milwaukee Blues" for Columbia; it was issued in September, 1931, but only 800 customers could be persuaded to buy it. One can only marvel at an industry that continued to issue records when the response was so slight; surely many releases were losing propositions financially. These figures document only a few scattered examples. While they are probably representative, a more extensive analysis must wait until complete data are available.

Little can be said about the geographic distribution of hillbilly and race record sales. Although the original premise on which these genres were initiated was that the industry could be stimulated by locally distributing recordings by locally known artists, by the mid-1930s distribution was essentially nonlocalized. How fast the transition occurred, we don't know. The energetic entry of Sears into the selling of hillbilly records in 1926 must have helped delocalize the distribution. Sears did have regional catalogs, but a comparative examination of several concurrent ones indicates a much more uniform series of releases than one might imagine. Virtually the same items were advertised in the catalogs for Los Angeles, Chicago, Philadelphia, and Kansas City.

What has also not yet been adequately assessed is the effect of hillbilly and race records on oral tradition. The qualitative features of the interaction are apparent. Hillbilly and race recordings—unbeknownst to the recording companies at the time—became the first major collection of traditional American folk music, preceding by several years any comparable extensive field recordings by professional folklorists.[15] Like broadside ballads, hillbilly records must have served to place the stamp of authority on some versions of traditional pieces at the expense of others. After a song was recorded by such popular artists as the Carter Family or Jimmie Rodgers or Roy Acuff, other versions appeared only rarely. At the same time, hillbilly recordings served to soften the distinctiveness of regional styles of music and gradually replace them with one nationalized style of country music; today the focal point of that style is Nashville. In contrast, the blues field was better able to sustain several distinct regional styles well into the World War II era. More interestingly, hillbilly records offered a market for new songs and ballads; and musicians and singers, ready for the opportunity, served up a fascinating collection of topical songs and ballads about a variety of current issues, both local and national. Just as the black-letter broadside ballads of the sixteenth and seventeenth centuries often served as newspapers in verse, spreading accounts of floods, monstrous births, hangings, and plagues, so can one find among the 78 rpm recordings of the 1920s and 1930s a wealth of material about train wrecks, air disasters, mine accidents, deeds of local badmen, Prohibition, Social Security, the Depression, women's suffrage, new hair styles, and many other topics. To many students today, the genre was most exciting when the discs served as the originators of the songs cut in their grooves, rather than simply as disseminators of older topical ballads that recounted affairs of a bygone age. Many of these songs, like the broadside ballads before them, outlived the currency of the physical medium itself and entered oral tradition for one or more generations. Some have since slipped out of oral tradition; every folksong eventually does. Hillbilly records were thus innovative in that they provided new songs and different styles to the community. But they were conservative in that—at least partially—they returned control of the music to the people, a control they were losing through the successive waves of sheet music, popular phonograph records, and radio. Some southern musicians found hillbilly music "newfangled"—too uptown for their own tastes. Others, finding it not modern enough, turned to some sort of jazz in a personal quest for respectability. What has been the net effect? Would rural folk music be more or less modernized had it not been for hillbilly music? This is another question that awaits an answer.

Earlier I distinguished between those folksongs that originated on broadsides or sheet music or other commercial media and those that never had a commercial life. Another dichotomy, not quite equivalent but perhaps more useful, distinguishes between those songs that originated within the folk culture and those that originated out of it, but in the mainstream of popular culture. According to this division, hillbilly and race songs created for the phonograph are generally within the scope of the folk culture, even though they are of commercial origin. With very few exceptions, the immediate sources of all the songs transcribed in this book are hillbilly and race recordings of the 1920s, 1930s, and 1940s. For many, however, the ultimate sources are commercial media outside the folk culture. Therefore, to improve the perspective of the survey of American railroad songs that occupies the following chapter, I include in the discussion both types: those originating without as well as within the folk cultures, and even those that apparently never entered oral tradition. The real concern of this book is with songs about the railroad, and what they tell us of social history. That almost all demonstrably entered oral tradition itself tells us something about what these songs meant to some people, but it is not the entire story.

The next logical question—Why do some songs enter oral tradition?—cannot be answered, for in no case can we be sure that a song did *not* enter oral tradition. Our current body of folksong is the residue left behind after two screenings: (1) it must have entered oral tradition, and (2) it must have been found there by some collector, academically trained or otherwise. Who is to deny that a song was not found there simply because no one looked long enough and carefully enough? Our quest for folksongs is made with a very coarse-mesh net. One of the most extensive state collections is represented in *The Folksongs of Virginia*. Some 3,200 items are reported, collected over a period of nearly four decades. During that time, probably 5 million people lived in Virginia; it would be conservative to estimate that 10 percent had some folksongs in their repertoires—typically a half-dozen songs. The collection thus would represent about 0.1 percent of the extant body of folksong. This would not be bad if we could be sure that it was a random sampling; but we know well that it was far from random. Many collectors have strong biases that tend to exclude entire categories of song in favor of others; and some regions are heavily canvassed, while others are completely overlooked. Today, some young folklorists are calling for more theory and less collecting. Alas, their arithmetic is faulty; the job of collecting is far from complete.

NOTES

1. *The Roxburghe Ballads*, edited by J. Woodfall Ebsworth and William Chappell (Hertford: printed for the Ballad Society by S. Austin & Sons, 1871–99), vol. 3 (1880), pp. 333–39.

2. Alexander H. Krappe, *The Science of Folklore* (1929; rpt., New York: W. W. Norton, 1964), p. 153.

3. An excellent introduction to broadside balladry is given by Leslie Shepard in *The Broadside Ballad: A Study in Origins and Meaning* (London: Herbert Jenkins, 1962). In the nineteenth century, English broadsides were typically priced at a penny each. A shilling seems to have been

typical payment to broadside ballad authors, with no royalties. Shepard cites one ballad on the execution of a murderer that sold 2.5 million copies.

4. My casual distinction between popular culture and high culture should not suggest that this subject has not been examined carefully by sociologists and historians in recent years. See Graham Vulliamy, "A Re-Assessment of the 'Mass Culture' Controversy: The Case of Rock Music," *Popular Music & Society,* 4 (1975), 130–55, for a useful review of some approaches to the problem of defining popular music vis-à-vis so-called serious music. Ray Browne identifies as popular culture "all those elements of life which are not narrowly intellectual or creatively elitist and which are generally though not necessarily disseminated through the mass media" ("Popular Culture: Notes toward a Definition," in *Popular Culture and Curricula,* edited by Browne and Ronald Ambrosetti [Bowling Green, Ohio: Bowling Green University Popular Press, 1970], p. 11). Using Browne's phrase "creatively elitist" as a springboard, I would suggest that popular music aims at quantitative success (i.e., mass approbation and, therefore, sales), while serious music aims at qualitative success (i.e., approbation by peers).

5. Little has been written about these ethnic series. An important beginning is Pekka Gronow, "A Preliminary Check-List of Foreign-Language 78s," *JEMFQ,* 9 (Spring, 1973), 24–31. One of the first reissue series in this country to feature some of this material is the Library of Congress *Folk Music in America* Bicentennial Series, edited by Richard K. Spottswood. For a fuller treatment see *Ethnic Recordings: A Neglected Heritage,* to be published by the American Folklife Center, Library of Congress. (For a complete list of abbreviations and short titles used in this book, see the Bibliography.)

6. "Domestic tradition" is the categorization D. K. Wilgus used in his *JAF* record reviews for many years. This concept is developed in Anne Cohen and Norm Cohen, "Folk and Hillbilly Music: Further Thoughts on Their Relation," *JEMFQ,* 13 (Summer, 1977), 50–57.

7. Some useful approaches to the development of the Afro-American commercial traditions (blues, jazz, etc.) from their folk roots are Marshall Stearns, *The Story of Jazz* (New York: Oxford University Press, 1956); LeRoi Jones, *Blues People* (New York: William Morrow, 1963); Harry Oster, *Living Country Blues* (Detroit: Folklore Associates, 1969); and Paul Oliver, *The Story of the Blues* (Philadelphia: Chilton Book, 1969). For a very early and particularly relevant study of how one hillbilly ballad grew out of folk tradition, see Alfred Frankenstein, "George Alley: A Study in Modern Folk Lore," *Musical Courier,* Apr. 16, 1932, p. 6, reprinted in *JEMFN,* 2 (June, 1967), 46. One of the first broad treatments of the subject was Fred G. Hoeptner, "Folk and Hillbilly Music: The Background of Their Relation," *Caravan,* No. 16 (Apr.-May, 1959), pp. 8, 16–17, 42, and No. 17 (June-July, 1959), pp. 20–23, 26–28. A more accessible and extensive survey is chap. 1 of Bill C. Malone, *Country Music, U.S.A.: A Fifty-Year History* (Austin: University of Texas Press, 1968).

8. See Norm Cohen, "Tin Pan Alley's Contribution to Folk Music," *WF,* 29 (Jan., 1970), 9–20.

9. The essential study of the formative years of hillbilly music is Archie Green, "Hillbilly Music: Source and Symbol," *JAF,* 78 (July-Sept., 1965), 204–28. He further examines the early years of both hillbilly and race records in *Only a Miner* (Urbana: University of Illinois Press, 1972), chap. 2. Several important books on country music have been published in the past few years, including Bill C. Malone and Judith McCulloh, eds., *Stars of Country Music* (Urbana: University of Illinois Press, 1975), and Charles K. Wolfe, *The Grand Ole Opry: The Early Years 1925–35* (London: Old Time Music, 1975).

10. See Barret Hansen, "Negro Popular Music, 1945–1953," M.A. thesis, UCLA, 1967.

11. Paul Oliver, *Blues Fell This Morning* (London: Cassell, 1960), published in the United States under the title *The Meaning of the Blues,* and *Screening the Blues* (London: Cassell, 1968).

12. John Godrich and Robert M. W. Dixon, *Blues and Gospel Records, 1902–1942,* rev. ed. (London: Storyville Publications, 1969).

13. See ibid., and also Robert M. W. Dixon and John Godrich, *Recording the Blues* (London: Studio Vista, 1970). For details on three individual companies (Columbia, Victor, Starr), see Dan Mahony, *Columbia 13/14000-D Series (Numerical Listing)* (Stanhope, N.J.: Walter C. Allen, 1961); Brian Rust, *The Victor Master Book, Volume 2 (1925–1936)* (Hatch End, Middlesex, England:

Brian Rust, 1969); and Norm Cohen, "Computerized Hillbilly Discography: The Gennett Project," *WF*, 30 (July, 1971), 182–93.

14. Dixon and Godrich, *Recording the Blues*, pp. 104–5.

15. My remarks are not intended to belittle the pioneering fieldwork by folklorists Robert W. Gordon and Frank C. Brown, both of whom had used portable equipment to record traditional singers prior to 1920.

Appendix

Record Companies Issuing Hillbilly and Race Material, 1922–41

From the inception of the hillbilly and race catalogs until the end of the Depression, more than 95 percent of the recordings were made by a dozen companies:

A. *Victor Talking Machine Company*. Its recordings were released on the Victor label even after 1929, when the company merged with RCA. Prior to that, hillbilly and race material had appeared in the general pop music series. In 1929 a 38500 series for race and a 40000 series for hillbilly were inaugurated. In 1931 these series were discontinued and replaced by a 23250 series and a 23500 series, respectively. In 1933 the Victor label was discontinued and the low-priced Bluebird label inaugurated. During the period 1931–34 some RCA recordings were issued on several subsidiary labels: Electradisc, Timely Tunes, Sunrise, and Gem. Also, during the Depression, RCA Victor leased material to Montgomery Ward for release on the Montgomery Ward label.

B. *Columbia Phonograph Company*. Formed in 1924 out of the old Columbia Graphophone Company, this firm issued material primarily on the Columbia label. From the end of 1923 to spring of 1933 race material was issued on a separate 14000-D series; hillbilly material was confined to the 15000-D series from November, 1924, to late 1932. In about 1928, some hillbilly material was also issued pseudonymously on three low-priced labels: Harmony, Velvetone, and Diva. Between 1931 and 1938 the company changed hands several times, being part of the Brunswick Record Corporation in 1934–38 and part of Columbia Broadcasting System after 1938. Some material was leased to Sears, Roebuck and Company for release on its own Silvertone label.

C. *OKeh Phonograph Corporation*. The OKeh label was originated in 1918 by the General Phonograph Corporation. In 1926 the record division was bought by Columbia and renamed OKeh Phonograph Corporation, which continued the OKeh label. From 1921 to 1935 race material was issued on a separate 8000 series; hillbilly material appeared in the 45000 series from 1925 to 1934. After about 1935 the label name was used for the release of ARC material (see below).

D. *Starr Piano Company*. Starr began recording hillbilly and race material in about 1924, issuing it on its primary label, Gennett, until 1930. A low-priced Champion label was initiated in 1927 and continued to 1934. Starr also pressed records from its own material for several other labels: Silvertone, Supertone, Challenge, and Conqueror were Sears owned; the Herwin label was owned by the Artophone Corporation of Saint Louis; the Superior label was probably marketed through chain stores. Some material was pressed for other independently owned labels: Bell, Gaiety, Black Patti, Paramount, and Montgomery Ward. For most of these labels, race and hillbilly material was interspersed in the general popular series.

E. *Brunswick-Balke-Collender Company (BBC)*. This unit began the Brunswick label in about 1918. Between 1926 and 1931 race material was issued on a separate 7000 series. Hillbilly material appeared on a parallel 100 series from 1927 to 1932. Some items were pressed for the Polk Furniture Company of Atlanta for the Polk label in 1931–32, and for the Aurora label, owned by a Toronto company, in 1931. In 1925 BBC purchased the Vocalion label from the Aeolian Company. Race and hillbilly material appeared on a 1000 series (1925–32) and a 5000 series (1926–30), respectively. Prior to the inauguration of those series the material appeared in the standard Aeolian Vocalion pop music series. The BBC phonograph and record division was purchased by Warner Brothers Pictures in 1930 and then in 1931 by Consolidated Film Industries.

F. *New York Recording Laboratories*. This subsidiary of the Wisconsin Chair Company initiated the Paramount label in about 1917 to supply records to promote the sale of phonographs. From 1922 to 1932 race material was issued on the 12000 series. Much less successful commercially was the hillbilly 3000 series, issued between 1927 and 1932. Some of the latter material also appeared on the subsidiary Broadway label.

G. *Edison Laboratories*. Although a pioneer in the invention and development of phonography, Edison's company paid little attention to the hillbilly field and even less to the race field. Some hillbilly material was issued between 1925 and 1929—on cylinders, discs, or both—in the regular popular series.

H. *Plaza Music Company*. This entity initiated the Banner (1921), Oriole (1923), Domino (1924), and Jewel (1926) labels, and purchased the Regal label in 1923. A 1929 merger made them part of the Regal Record Company. It recorded only a small quantity of race and hillbilly material.

I. *Cameo Record Corporation*. This firm began the Cameo (1922), Lincoln (1923), Romeo (1926), and Variety (1926) labels. Only a few hillbilly and race items were recorded.

J. *Pathé Phonograph and Radio Corporation*. Born in 1922 as a result of a reorganization of the older Pathé-Frères Phonograph Company, this corporation continued the Pathé and Perfect labels. Only a few hillbilly and race items were recorded. Cameo and Pathé were purchased by a single owner in 1927.

K. *American Record Corporation (ARC)*. This entity was created in 1929 as a result of the merger of Plaza, Cameo, and Pathé (H, I, and J above). It continued all the labels of its predecessor corporations. In 1930 ARC was bought by Consolidated Film Industries and in 1931 amalgamated with its Brunswick Record Corporation. At about this time several labels were discontinued, so that in the 1930s ARC recordings appeared on the following labels: Perfect, Oriole, Romeo, Banner, Melotone, Vocalion. After 1934, when the Columbia Phonograph Company was bought by the Brunswick Record Corporation, the same material appeared on OKeh. Most of the hillbilly and race recordings were also pressed for Sears's Conqueror label throughout the 1930s. During 1935–37, each new release appeared simultaneously on Banner, Perfect, Oriole, Romeo, and Melotone, with the same release number on each label. The first digit or pair of digits of the hyphenated release number indicated the year; the middle pair of digits, the month; and the last pair of digits, the order of the release in that month. Thus, ARC 7-06-69 indicates the sixty-ninth release in June of 1937. The distinction was that each of the five labels was marketed by a different chain store (Banner by S. S. Kresge, Oriole by McRory's, Romeo by S. H. Kress).

L. *Decca Records*. Begun in the United States late in 1934 as a subsidiary of the English Decca company, Decca helped bring the record business out of the depths of the Depression. A 7000 race series was launched in 1934 and terminated in 1944; a parallel 5000 hillbilly series ran concurrently. Decca purchased the rights to some Gennett and Paramount material and released it on a reactivated Champion label.

3

"Railroad March" to "City of New Orleans"

A Sesquicentennial of Railroad Songs

ON INDEPENDENCE DAY in 1828, ground-breaking ceremonies were held at Baltimore for the construction of America's first public railway carrier to be put in regular service: the Baltimore and Ohio Railroad Company. Charles Carroll, a prominent citizen of Baltimore and patriot of the revolutionary war, participated in the ceremony, declaring it to be his most important act since signing the Declaration of Independence. A song was specially written for the occasion:

> O we're all full of life, fun and jollity,
> We're all crazy here in Baltimore.
>
> Here's a road to be made
> With the pick and spade,
> 'Tis to reach to Ohio, for the benefit of trade;
>
> Here are mountains to be level'd,
> Here are valleys to be filled,
> Here are rocks to be blown, and bridges too to build.
>
> And we're all hopping, skipping, jumping,
> And we're all crazy here in Baltimore.
>
> And when the road is made,
> With the pick and the spade,
> In the locomotive engine, they will put a little fire,
> And while the kettle boils,
> We may ride three hundred miles
> Or go to bed in Baltimore and breakfast in Ohio.
> Where they're all waiting, hoping, praying
> For a quick way to come to Baltimore![1]

39

Thus, what was probably America's first railroad song came early in the history of railroading, actually preceding the first commercial run. In the next century and a half Americans were to see a great deal more of the parallel steel rails, the wooden crossties, the spark-throwing black locomotives, the little red cabooses, the stern old conductors, the whistle-blowing engineers, the lavishly appointed smoking cars, the bustling railroad stations, and the wayside watertanks. And those who joined in the festivities in Baltimore on the doubly historic date in 1828 doubtless had no idea of the number of railroad songs that would be written and sung in the years to come.

How many railroad songs *have* been written? This question is impossible to answer, not only because the documentation at hand is so scant, but also because the notion of a "railroad song" is ill defined. There are of course unquestioned claimants to the designation: songs of train wrecks, of railroad construction, of particular trains. At the other end of a subtly changing continuum are items that mention railroads only peripherally. Is the Anglo-American broadside ballad "The Boston Burglar" a railroad song because the protagonist is taken off to jail by train?

> They put me on an eastbound train one cold December day,
> And as I passed the station, I could hear those people say,
> "Yonder goes the burglar, for some great crime I know,
> For some great crime or other, to Frankfort town must go."[2]

Or what about George Reneau's recording "Railroad Lover" ("In Johnson City where I did dwell, that railroad boy I loved so well . . . "),[3] which is actually a variant of the familiar "Butcher's Boy"? My own tendency is to rule such items out if the appearance of the railroad is so slight as to be inessential—as it clearly is in "Railroad Lover." But in some cases, this principle is not easily applied. In scanning the literature of railroad songs, one can find some questionable inclusions. Because they robbed trains, Jesse James, Cole Younger, Harvey Logan, and other western outlaws remembered in song have found their way into many a discussion of railroad lore, and I have also succumbed to the temptation.[4] The figure of the wandering hobo is almost as much a part of American railroadiana as is the little red caboose; nevertheless, I have included in the chapter on hobos and bums only songs consistent with the principle that the appearance of the train must be more than just casual. For example, can the stanzas referring to trains in "The Great American Bum" be deleted without damaging the story?

> Oh, a-standing in the railroad yards
> A-waiting for a train;
> Waiting for a westbound freight,
> But I think it's all in vain.
>
> Going east they're loaded,
> Going west sealed tight;
> I think we'll have to get aboard
> A fast express tonight.[5]

I am inclined to think they can.

Ever since Sandburg wrote that "['She'll Be Coming around the Mountain'] spread to railroad work gangs in the midwest in the 1890s,"[6] it has been included in collections of railroad songs. As Lomax graphically described it, the song "catches the jubilation of the halcyon day when the first steam engine came whistling and snorting into a horse-and-buggy town on the prairies."[7] Nevertheless, I have resisted including it here because I do not consider it a railroad song; except during the very earliest years of railroading, no whistling, snorting steam engine ever puffed into town while "driving six white horses," as every version of the song states.

The notion that one can define railroad songs to include songs sung by railroadmen is misleading. My own experience with railroadmen who were also musicians—and therefore presumably sensitive to the musical interests of their fellow workers—leads me to conclude that railroadmen favored the same songs that nonrailroaders of the same social background liked.

John V. Walker, a fine fiddler from Corbin, Kentucky, who headed a string band called Walker's Corbin Ramblers, worked for the L & N Railroad for "fifty-one years, seven months, and five days," starting in 1909. He told me that "Casey Jones" and "Old 97" were popular with the railroadmen he knew—which is not surprising, as they were popular with almost everyone in their day.[8]

Bernice "Si" Coleman of Princeton, West Virginia, worked forty-four years for the Norfolk and Western Railway in various capacities from telegraph operator to assistant train-master. He also played fiddle, made several hillbilly recordings in the 1920s, and wrote some railroad songs as well. When I asked him what songs the railroaders liked to hear, he cited two train-wreck ballads, "The Wreck of the 1256" and "The Wreck of Number Nine," but he also recalled "Put My Little Shoes Away," "Letter Edged in Black," and "Santa Barbara Earthquake"—all hillbilly favorites during the 1920s.[9]

Dick Parman, also of Corbin, a switchman for fifty years for the L & N Railroad, enjoyed a brief recording career between 1927 and 1930. In response to my query for songs railroadmen liked, he wrote that they "never went out much for songs and music of any kind, they were interested most in old R.R. stories and smutty jokes. . . ."[10]

C. C. Meeks, who worked forty-five years for the Norfolk and Western Railway in Virginia and authored two of the train-wreck ballads included in this book, recalled that the railroadmen liked most any humorous or sentimental songs. "'Barney Google' was a big hit with RR men and no matter how busy they were you could hear their voices sound above the noise of air compressors as they would sing about Barney Google and his Goo Goo Googley eyes." "The Prisoner's Song" was also a favorite, he wrote.[11]

In 1914, *Railroad Man's Magazine,* a pulp periodical catering primarily to the interests of railroaders and rail enthusiasts, asked its readers to vote for their favorites of the poems and songs that had been printed during the previous six years. Three of the top seven listed were not even railroad songs: "The Face on the Barroom Floor," "Twenty Years Ago," and "Down in the Lehigh Valley." Another three are included in this book: "Casey Jones," "The Red and Green Signal Lights," and "The Dying Hobo." The seventh was Cy Warman's "Will the Lights Be White."[12]

These were the sentiments of railroadmen of the early twentieth century; I doubt that railroaders of a century earlier would have given a very different reply had the question been put to them. Consequently, we must rely most heavily on the content and theme of the song itself in deciding whether or not to include it in our survey of railroad songs.

The piece quoted at the beginning of this chapter, "The Carrollton March," by Arthur Clifton, was in all likelihood the country's first railroad song, copyrighted on July 1, 1828. Two days later, Charles Meineke copyrighted his "Rail Road March," dedicated "to the Directors of the Baltimore & Ohio Rail Road." We had, then, two railroad songs before ground was even broken for our first railroad. That same year Meineke composed another instrumental piece, "The Rail-Road." The illustration on the sheet-music cover bore a figure shouting to a traveler on the departing steam-drawn coach, "Don't forget to drop my letter in the Post Office at Wheeling so it may get to N. Orleans the next day." (One might vainly make the same wish today, a century and a half later.) The illustration for Meineke's earlier "Rail Road March" also depicted a steam-drawn train of cars. There is some irony here, inasmuch as the B & O relied on horse-drawn trains well into the 1830s.

Other railroads were soon commemorated in song, for example, "Syracuse Rail Road Quick Step" (1840), by I. P. Wind; "New Orleans and Great Western Railroad Polka" (1854), by Theodore La Hache; and "Fast Line Gallop" (1853), by James N. Beck, in honor of the Pennsylvania Railroad.

From the 1830s or 1840s was John Godfrey Saxe's "Rhyme of the Rail," sometimes titled "Railroad Rhyme," "Riding on a Rail," or "Rail Road Chorus." A broadside version with text only was published, without attribution, a few decades later under the title "Rail Road Song." Some of Saxe's passengers were quite nervous about the ride:

> Ancient maiden lady impiously remarks,
> That there must be danger from so many sparks,
> Roguish looking fellow turning to the stranger,
> Says its his opinion, she is out of all danger.

But the chorus betrayed an exuberant enthusiasm over the breathtaking twenty-miles-per-hour ride:

> Singing through the forest, rattling over ridges,
> Shooting over arches, dashing under bridges,
> Whizzing through the mountain buzzing o'er the vale,
> Bless me aint it pleasant riding on a rail.[13]

Other early songs and poems also suggest a mixture of some exhilaration but mostly terror on the part of railroad travelers. The British humor magazine *Punch* published a good example in the 1850s, a poem titled "The Railway Traveler's Farewell to His Family." In the third of the nine stanzas the loving father tells his children and wife:

> I'm going by the Rail, my dears, where the engines puff and hiss;
> And ten to one the chances are that something goes amiss;
> And in an instant, quick as thought—before you could cry "Ah!"
> An accident occurs, and—say good-by to poor Papa![14]

And a verse from "De Weschester Nigga Song," which appeared in minstrel songsters of the mid-1840s, claimed:

> De Harlem Rail Road Smashing Line,
> Dey start at four an stop at nine,
> An if you want to go to town,
> De quickest way is to foot it down;
> Sat'day noon we quit our work,
> An go to de depo for New York,
> And dere we wait till de stars do shine,
> For de Blow-shus-smo-shus-squindingjine.

> Den de agent tell you, O,
> Guv us your money or you can't go,
> We'll git to town 'bout seven or nine,
> Wid de Slowgo-nogo-squindingjine.[15]

Jacob P. Weaver wrote his "Rail-road Song" to the tune of "Jordan Am a Hard Road to Travel," probably in the 1850s. Echoing the sentiments of the above pieces, it is of particular interest in that it is a very early example of a song dealing in detail with all the key figures running the train—engineer, brakemen, and conductor:

> Rail road travelling is getting all the go,
> All you got to do is to get a board on,
> Fust they break your back, and then they throw you off the track,
> And they land you on the other side of Jordan.
>
> There's the engineer too, he's the best of the crew,
> He tries his water accordin',
> If his pumps work true, he's nothing more to do,
> For to land him on the other side of Jordan.
>
> Common brakesmen think they've a mighty good job,
> But that all depends upon the boarding,
> Nine dollars a week and not a bit of sleep,
> For to land them on the other side of Jordan.
>
> There's the hind brakesman too, he's nothing for to brag,
> If he can't make his premium accordin',
> They'll give him his time and they'll put him off the track,
> And they'll send him on the other side of Jordan.
>
> There's the conductor too, he's the worst of the crew,
> He's charged with the whole train accordin',
> If a car breaks down he's got to run around,
> For to land them on the other side of Jordan.[16]

Sometimes the criticism was not so good-natured. "The Song of the Engine" painted the picture of a demonic creature showering the landscape with destruction as it plunged relentlessly onward:

> Roaring o'er the trembling land,
> Mountains piercing, vallies crossing
> Right and left, on either hand,
> Glowing embers madly tossing;
> Like some fettered fiend of hell
> Speed I on my reckless way,
> Shouting aye, to wood and fell,
> My infernal roundelay.
> Over moor and pasture screaming
> Whilst the tired world is dreaming,
>   Ho! ho!
>   Away I go,
> With my train of weal and wo![17]

However, the most trenchant commentary on the destruction wreaked by the railroads was an unattributed song that appeared during the 1850s and 1860s on a broadside (reproduced here). "The Song of the Locomotive" began:

> Beware! beware! for I come in my might,
> With a scream, and a scowl of scorn;
> With a speed like the mountain eagle's flight,
> When he rides the breeze of morn.[18]

Notwithstanding such dissatisfaction with railroad safety, and in spite of the rapidly upward-spiraling rate of train wrecks and attendant fatalities, travelers continued to ride the railroads, and they continued to have romantic as well as dreadful experiences. "The Railroad Belle" appeared in several pocket songsters during the 1860s; it described the narrator's encounter with a charming maid who served refreshments on the train. As did many songs at that time, this one appeared in print in different versions. Compare the opening stanza from Tony Pastor's *201 Bowery Songster*:

> I traveled for Gallipot, Cork, & Co.,
> In the vinegar pickling trade;
> And never had cause for a moment's woe,
> Till meeting a fair young maid,
> Who served behind a first-class bar,
> On the Hudson River line—
> Refreshment-room I ought to say,
> But that mistake is mine.[19]

with a text from Fred Wilson's *Popular Comic Songs, No. 4*:

> I travel for a firm in Wonsockett,
> In the cotton and woollen trade,
> And never had cause for a moment's woe
> Till meeting a fair young maid
> Who served in a first class restaurant
> On the Chicago and Alton line,
> Refreshment room I ought to say,
> But that mistake is mine.[20]

The maid is attractive and popular, and the narrator seems to be making some headway with his courting until a rival appears who wins the girl's heart. In Pastor's version, he is a railroad guard:

> I try to be merry, but it is no use,
> My case is very hard;
> She left me as slyly as a farm-yard goose,
> When she married that railway guard.

In Wilson's text, the rival is a conductor:

> I try to be merry but it is no use,
> My heart's so full of pain;
> She left me and married that fine young man
> That conducted that rail-road train.

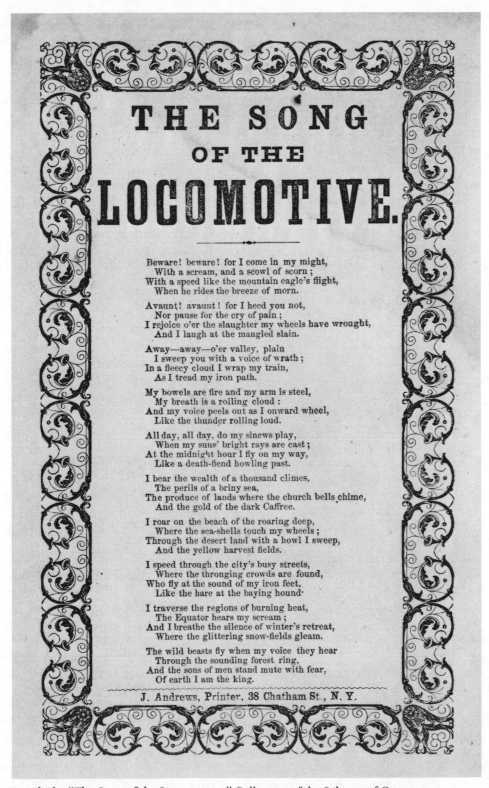

THE SONG
OF THE
LOCOMOTIVE.

Beware! beware! for I come in my might,
  With a scream, and a scowl of scorn ;
With a speed like the mountain eagle's flight,
  When he rides the breeze of morn.

Avaunt! avaunt! for I heed you not,
  Nor pause for the cry of pain ;
I rejoice o'er the slaughter my wheels have wrought,
  And I laugh at the mangled slain.

Away—away—o'er valley, plain
  I sweep you with a voice of wrath ;
In a fleecy cloud I wrap my train,
  As I tread my iron path.

My bowels are fire and my arm is steel,
  My breath is a rolling cloud :
And my voice peels out as I onward wheel,
  Like the thunder rolling loud.

All day, all day, do my sinews play,
  When my suns' bright rays are cast ;
At the midnight hour I fly on my way,
  Like a death-fiend howling past.

I bear the wealth of a thousand climes,
  The perils of a briny sea,
The produce of lands where the church bells chime,
  And the gold of the dark Caffree.

I roar on the beach of the roaring deep,
  Where the sea-shells touch my wheels ;
Through the desert land with a howl I sweep,
  And the yellow harvest fields.

I speed through the city's busy streets,
  Where the thronging crowds are found,
Who fly at the sound of my iron feet,
  Like the hare at the baying hound·

I traverse the regions of burning heat,
  The Equator hears my scream ;
And I breathe the silence of winter's retreat,
  Where the glittering snow-fields gleam.

The wild beasts fly when my voice they hear
  Through the sounding forest ring,
And the sons of men stand mute with fear,
  Of earth I am the king.

J. Andrews, Printer, 38 Chatham St., N. Y.

Broadside: "The Song of the Locomotive." Collection of the Library of Congress.

Another early courting song from the 1850s that appeared in several songsters and on broadsides was "Ridin' in a Rail Road Keer" (a broadside version is reproduced in this book):

> Suke Sattinet was a comely gal,
> And loved her parents dear,
> Till she met Slim Jim, the miller's son,
> A ridin' in a rail road keer.[21]

In this little romance Suke accepts Slim Jim's proposal, but when they confront her father to ask his permission, the old man snatches his gun from the shelf and runs Jim off the property.

Already by the 1840s the railroad was serving as an allegorical device in songs and poems; many of these are discussed in chapter 12, which deals with religious songs. One secular use of railroad symbolism deserves special comment because of its general historical interest: the singing Hutchinson Family's "'Get Off the Track!,'" an 1844 abolitionist song, the sheet-music cover of which is reproduced here. The first stanza reads:

> Ho! the Car Emancipation Rides majestic thro' our nation,
> Bearing on its Train, the Story, Liberty! a Nation's Glory.
> Roll it along, Roll it along, Roll it along, thro' the Nation Freedom's Car,
>   Emancipation,
> Roll it along, Roll it along, Roll it along, thro' the Nation Freedom's Car,
>   Emancipation.[22]

These early pieces have left no permanent mark on oral tradition. Whether they were at one time folksongs, we don't know; there is no evidence of it. It is probable that some of them, or similar pieces, did circulate in oral tradition for a time. In general, our knowledge of native American folksong prior to the Civil War is slender indeed. Two relatively early romantic ballads that have been collected in the twentieth century are "The Charming Young Widow I Met in the Train" and "The Harvard Student."[23] While they were interesting songs, they are not treated elsewhere in this book because they were not recorded commercially on hillbilly or race records.

"The Charming Young Widow I Met in the Train" is the title of at least two closely related ballads, both dating from the late 1860s. One, written by W. H. Gove, tells of a young man who receives a letter informing him that his uncle is dead and he is to appear in Boston to settle the will. On the train he meets a young widow, with a babe in arms; after chatting with him, she asks him to hold her infant while she disembarks for a moment to greet her late husband's brother, whom she espies on the platform. She never returns; he uncovers the swaddling clothes and finds no baby, only a dummy—and furthermore, he finds that he has been robbed of his purse, ticket, watch, and gold pencil-case. The London broadside printer H. P. Such published an almost identical text, but localized in England, in the 1870s; it is reproduced here. No author attribution is given. I assume that it followed rather than preceded Gove's American version.

The second ballad, which appeared unattributed in several songsters and on broadsides, commences with a similar narrative. However, after the widow leaves the train, the narrator finds a real but dead baby in his arms, with a note sewn to its garments requesting a proper burial for the poor creature. Pathetic in tone, it is quite different in mood from Gove's piece, although the opening stanzas of the two versions give no hint of the different conclusions. Gove's begins:

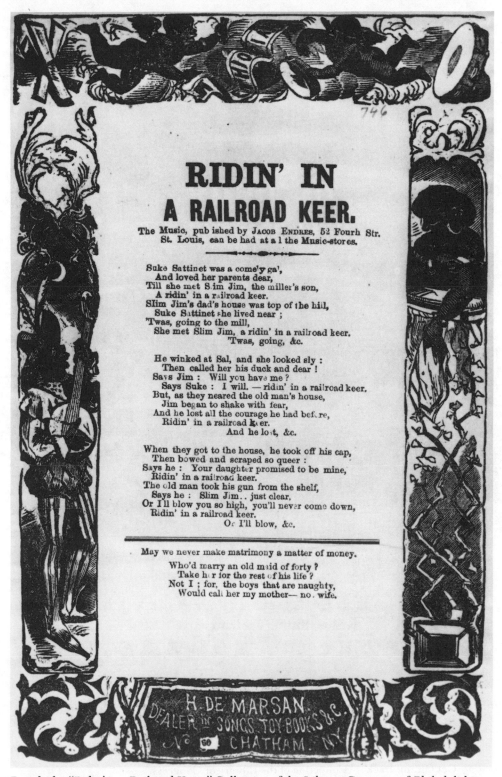

Broadside: "Ridin' in a Railroad Keer." Collection of the Library Company of Philadelphia.

Sheet music: " 'Get Off the Track!' " Collection of the Library of Congress.

Sheet music: "The Charming Young Widow I Met in the Train." Collection of the
Grosvenor Library.

> I live in Vermont, and one morning last summer,
> A letter inform'd me my uncle was dead;
> And also requested I'd come down to Boston,
> As he'd left me a large sum of money, it said.
> Of course I determin'd on making the journey,
> And to book myself by the "first class" I was fain,
> Tho' had I gone "second" I had never encounter'd
> The Charming Young Widow I met in the train.[24]

The second ballad opens:

> Whilst in New Jersey, a letter was sent to me
> From Boston, which bid me quickly repair
> To an uncle; it stated: fast he was dying,
> The wish had expressed to make me his heir.
> So, hurriedly packing a few things together,
> Wishing that Boston quickly might gain,
> By a first-class express went; in the same carriage,
> A charming young widow I met in the train.[25]

Gove's song was collected by Vance Randolph in Missouri in 1933, in a version remarkably similar in both text and tune to the original, but I have seen no evidence of the second ballad being in oral tradition.

The theme of deception and robbery by an artful young maid is an old one in Anglo-American broadside balladry, and "Charming Young Widow" was hardly the only composition to make use of it, even in the context of a railroad car. "Riding in the Cars" told of a traveler who met a coquettish maid on her way home from boarding school. Just when she had thoroughly beguiled him ("You are the nicest man I've met in these horse-railroad cars"), she dashed off with his purse.[26] The unique twist of "Charming Young Widow" was the use of the dummy child. Possibly this idea was taken from "Fooled in a Railroad Car," another song published in songsters in the 1860s. But in this case the lady really did leave a live baby in the arms of the unsuspecting narrator. The refrain of this piece,

> A black and a rolling eye, she wore a new poke bonnet,
> A nice little young thing, and just the one to woo,[27]

is strikingly reminiscent of a spicy sailors' song, "The Fire Ship," which tells of a sailor who picks up a saucy maid in port only to be deceived by her (in most versions, she gives him a venereal disease).[28] A companion piece to "The Charming Young Widow I Met in the Train" was "The Charming Young Lady I Met in the Rain," by J. G. Peters; it was sung to the same air as the former piece, according to the broadside instructions.[29] In this ballad, the female deceiver accompanies the narrator to a bar, plies him with drink, and robs him of his gold watch and chain. I have dwelt at length on these related pieces to show that many early railroad songs were no different from other contemporary romantic songs, except that the setting was moved from ship, tavern, or coach to railroad car.

The second romantic ballad referred to above, "The Harvard Student" (to use the title Vance Randolph gives it), is a lighter-hearted ditty about a bearded student and a blushing maiden who take adjacent seats on the railroad train "riding down from Bangor." When the train emerges from a long tunnel, one of the maiden's dainty earrings is tangled

THE
CHARMING YOUNG WIDOW
I MET IN THE TRAIN.

London :—H. P. SUCH, Machine Printer and Publisher, 177, Union-street, Borough, S.E.

I LIVE in North Wales, and one morning last summer,
   A letter informed me my uncle was dead,
And also requested I'd come up to London,
   As he'd left me a large sum of money it said ;
Of course I determined on making the journey,
   And to book myself by the " First Class " I was fain,
Tho' had I gone " Third " I had never encountered
   The charming young Widow I met in the Train.

The Widow and I side by side sat together,
   The carriage containing ourselves and no more,
When silence was broke by my fair companion,
   Who enquired the time by the watch that I wore ;
I of course satisfied her, and then conversation
   Was freely indulged in by both till my brain
Fairly reeled with excitement, I grew so enchanted,
   With the charming young Widow I met in the Train.

We became so familiar I ventured to ask her,
   How old was the child that she held at her breast?
" Ah ! sir," she responded, and into tears bursting,
   Her infant still closer convulsively prest ;

" When I think of my child I am well nigh distracted,
   Its Father ! my Husband ! O my heart breaks with
     pain !' "
She, choking with sobs lean'd her head on my waistcoat,
   Did the charming young Widow I met in the Train.

By this time the Train had arrived at the Station,
   Within a few miles of the great one in town,
When my charmer exclaimed as she looked through the
     window,
   " Good gracious alive ! why there goes Mr. Brown.
He's my late husband's brother ; dear sir, would you
     kindly,
   My best beloved child for a moment sustain ?
Of course I complied, then off to the platform,
   Tript the Charming young Widow I met in the
     Train.

Three minutes elapsed when the guard's whistle sounded,
   The train began moving, no Widow appeared,
I bawl'd out " Stop ! Stop ! " but they paid no attention,
   With a snort and a jerk starting off as I feared.
In this horrid dilemna I sought for the hour,
   But my watch ! ah ! where was it ? where, where
     was my chain ?
My purse too, my ticket, gold pencil-case, all gone !
   Oh ! that artful young Widow I met in the Train.

While I was my loss so deeply bewailing,
   The train again stopt and I ' tickets please ' heard,
So I told the Collector—while dandling the infant,
   The loss I'd sustained, but he doubted my word :
He called more officials, a lot gathered round me,
   Uncovered the child, oh ! how shall I explain,
For behold 'twas no baby, 'twas only a dummy !
   Oh that crafty young Widow I met in the Train.

Satisfied I'd been robb'd they allowed my departure,
   Tho' of course I'd to settle my fare the next day,
And I now wish to counsel young men from the country
   Lest they should get served in a similar way ;
Beware of young Widows you meet on the Railway,
   Who lean on your shoulder, whose tears fall like rain,
Look out for your pockets, in case they resemble
   The charming young Widow I met in the Train.

  468.

Broadside: "The Charming Young Widow I Met in the Train." UCLA Special Collections Library.

in the student's beard. Spaeth, remarking on the song's popularity during the 1890s, says that the correct title is "The Eastern Train" and that it was supposedly of Scots origin.[30] It is often titled "Riding Down from Bangor" and credited to Louis Shreve Osborne.[31] It was published in songsters of the 1880s as "On the Pullman Train."[32] The earliest printing I have found is in an 1871 issue of the *Harvard Advocate*, where the song was titled "In the Tunnel" and credited to "S.O.L." These initials are puzzling inasmuch as they are, in incorrect order, Louis Shreve Osborne's initials. There was a Louis S. Osborne at Harvard in 1871 who was a poet, but whether he was "S.O.L." I have not been able to determine. Nor do I know who was responsible for setting the text to music. Although the song was never recorded, it has sufficient merits to justify reprinting it here, as it appeared in the *Harvard Advocate* in 1871.

IN THE TUNNEL

Riding up from Bangor, on the Pullman train,
From a six weeks' shooting in the woods of Maine;
Quite extensive whiskers, beard, moustache as well,
Sat a "student feller," tall and fine and swell.

Empty seat behind him, no one at his side,
To a pleasant station now the train doth glide;
Enter aged couple, take the hinder seat,
Enter gentle maiden, beautiful, *petite*.

Blushing she falters, "Is this seat engaged?"
(See the aged couple properly enraged.)
Student, quite ecstatic, sees her ticket's "through;"
Thinks of the long tunnel,—knows what he will do.

So they sit and chatter, while the cinders fly,
Till that "student feller" gets one in his eye;
And the gentle maiden quickly turns about,
"May I, if you please, sir, try to get it out?"

Happy "student feller" feels a dainty touch,
Hears a gentle whisper,—"Does it hurt you much?"
Fizz! ding, dong! a moment in the tunnel quite,
And a glorious darkness black as Egypt's night.

Out into the daylight darts the Pullman train,
Student's beaver ruffled just the merest grain;
Maiden's hair is tumbled, and there soon appeared,
Cunning little ear-ring caught in student's beard.[33]

A song of the 1860s that combined elements of both of the compositions just discussed was "Riding in a Railroad Train."[34] In this piece the narrator is a young lady taken in by a handsome young gentleman with a moustache, of which he seems very vain. The train enters a tunnel, the young lady draws the man close to her because of her fear of the dark, and she feels his moustache tickling her lips. When they emerge from the tunnel, she finds that the false moustache is still sticking to her lips, to the amusement of the other passengers. To top off her humiliation, she later discovers that the young man had robbed her of her purse.

Most of the above early railroad songs are about travelers on trains and the adventures that befall them. One possible scheme for categorizing railroad songs would depend on who (or what) was the center of attention—traveler, nontraveler, railroader, or the train itself. In the case of either traveler- or railroader-oriented songs, the tenor of the piece could be either tragic or nontragic. "Travelers" would include paying and nonpaying (i.e., hobo) types; "railroaders" could be subdivided into railroad builders and railroad operators (mostly engineers and brakemen). Granting that there is not much evidence to go on, nevertheless it seems that prior to about 1870 most of the songs were of the "paying traveler" type. Even the earliest printed train-wreck songs—about the North Pennsylvania Railroad accident of 1856—are about passengers and not, as are many later wreck ballads, about the engineer. An important exception is the earliest broadside known to me describing an occupational accident on the railroads: "Mr. Pierce's Experience." This ballad print concerns a mishap on the Boston and Lowell Railroad in the early 1830s when the trains were still horse-drawn. A horse bolted from the path, and in trying to steer it, driver Pierce fell from his post and was run over by the wheels of the coaches.[35] An ambiguous case is that of the earliest railroad song known to have entered oral tradition: "Henry Sawyer," relating an 1848 accident that occurred on the Bangor and Oldtown Railroad in Maine. Sawyer was scalded to death when the train was derailed. He happened to be a superintendent on the railroad, and it is debatable whether the song is about him qua superintendent or qua passenger.[36]

In the 1880s much attention shifted to the engineers and brakemen on the railroads, and the dangers to which they were exposed. As noted in the introduction to chapter 5, the pages of the journals of the several railroad brotherhoods were filled with homiletic pieces about the tragic deaths and disfigurements of railroad employees. "The Brave Engineer" (1891), composed by Fred E. Reynolds, is an early example of a sheet-music song idolizing the brave man at the throttle, on whose skills the lives of so many passengers depend:

> Like a flash of light the through express, flies over the silvery line,
> And bearing its burden of human souls, on, on through the gay sunshine;
> See there at the throttle bar, brown and grim, his deep eyes looking ahead,
> The engineer in his oily clothes, stands firm and free from dread.

The concluding lines tell of the inevitable wreck:

> The engine turns upon the switch, ahead there stands the freight,
> He'll save the train if he keeps his post, for himself, ah well ask fate!
> Ah, God a crash the passengers saved, their faces white with dread,
> But under his engine crushed and torn, the brave engineer lies dead.[37]

The piece ends with a plea to "pray for the brave engineer."

The great decades of railroad expansion were those following the Civil War, and most ballads dealing with construction emerged in the 1870s and 1880s. These songs probably originated at the hands of Irish laborers, and some—in particular, "Drill, Ye Tarriers, Drill"—went on to become national hits. They are discussed further in chapter 11.

Another type of railroad song emerged in the 1870s, that in which the main figure was neither a passenger nor an employee, but someone else who did something for or to the train. One theme was prevention of disaster by an alert bystander who saw that some failure—such as a track washout—was about to cause an accident. "Bill Mason," given in chapter 6, is in this category. Perhaps the best-known story of this sort, however, is that of

Kate Shelly, the fifteen-year-old girl who, in 1881, braved the fury of storm and flood to warn the approaching train of a bridge washout on the Chicago and North Western main line across the Des Moines River.[38] Charles Graham's "The Train Was Saved" (1891) was a popular song recounting a similar, though doubtless fictional, episode. Also in the category of people doing things to trains are the train-robber songs. "Jesse James" and "Cole Younger" were the best known; they appeared in the 1880s and were followed by accounts of many later desperadoes.

Some of these themes continued through the nineteenth century and into the twentieth; others have died out. As railroad construction drew to a halt, so did the composition of new songs and ballads on that topic. As people's familiarity with trains grew, the early pieces betraying the inexperienced traveler's terror upon his first encounter with the iron horse fell into disuse. Other lyrical songs, using train images in a casual manner, indicated a comfortable familiarity with the sounds of the train's wheels and whistles. The 1890s, with their penchant for sentimental balladry, saw many new songs on the familiar subject of tragedies befalling both passengers and railroaders on the trains. The continued popularity of these themes in hillbilly music up through the 1930s insured the success of new ballads along similar lines. After the emergence of the style of black folksong called blues, singers often sang about the railroad—whether the train was a vehicle of escape or of wandering, or an agent bearing away a loved one. Writers of gospel songs were quick to build spiritual railroads into their homiletic harmonies. Most of these latter subjects are discussed in detail in separate chapters later in this book.

Since the early 1900s national pop music has moved away from themes of tragedy and disaster, and few train-wreck ballads or sentimental pieces of the "In the Baggage Coach Ahead" variety have achieved any success. "Casey Jones" was the last train-wreck song originating from Tin Pan Alley that achieved great popularity on a national scale—and it was regarded by its composers as comedy, not tragedy. From about 1920 to about 1960, the train songs were not ballads in either the folk-music or the pop-music sense; they are best described as novelty songs—light-hearted descriptive lyrics of little narrative content. The better-known titles are "Toot Toot Tootsie! (Goo' Bye)" (1922), by Gus Kahn, Ernie Erdman, and Dan Russo; "Alabamy Bound" (1925), by Bud De Sylva, Bud Green, and Ray Henderson; "Shuffle Off to Buffalo" (1932), by Al Dubin and Harry Warren; "The Atchison, Topeka and the Santa Fe" (1943), by Johnny Mercer and Harry Warren; and "City of New Orleans" (1972), by Steve Goodman.

"Railroad Chorus" and other songs from the early 1800s captured the vitality of a new phenomenon—one that set fire to a thousand imaginations as it exploded with showers of sparks across the American frontier. On the other hand, "City of New Orleans," more of a railroad song than most recent pieces that mention trains, cloaks the listener in wistful nostalgia for a bygone experience. It is the song of lonely footsteps echoing in a once-bustling railroad terminal. The celebrated Illinois Central's mainliner pleads, "Don't you know me, America, I'm your native son." A half-century of transportation history is succinctly summarized by Goodman's phrase "disappearing railroad blues."

For the most part, it seems, these songs of pop-music origin from the early twentieth century have not entered oral folk tradition. Rather, the source of railroad folksongs in this century—at least, since the 1920s—has been the hillbilly and blues traditions. "The *Wabash Cannonball*," though it originated much earlier, was given a new lease on life through the recordings of the Carter Family and Roy Acuff. Andrew Jenkins's composition "Ben Dewberry's Final Run" achieved popularity and entered oral tradition because of an influential recording by Jimmie Rodgers. "Bringing in the Georgia Mail" and

"Fireball Mail," written by the prolific songwriter-publisher Fred Rose, both show promise of becoming traditional—the former because of the influence of performer Charlie Monroe; the latter, Roy Acuff. Mississippi John Hurt's unusual hammer song, "Spike Driver Blues," has been given much exposure in recent years and has entered the repertoires of many young city guitar-pickers. Other songs that have already definitely entered oral tradition as a direct result of hillbilly recordings include "The Wreck of Number Nine," "The Railroad Boomer," "Hobo Bill's Last Ride," "Billy Richardson's Last Ride," and some versions of "The Little Red Caboose behind the Train."

Some songs clearly predate the hillbilly and blues traditions and are later than the minstrel era, yet seem not to have originated at the hands of professional Tin Pan Alley songwriters. These include such lyric folksongs as "New River Train," "A Railroader for Me," "Reuben's Train," "The Longest Train," "900 Miles," "Nine Pound Hammer," and "If I Die a Railroad Man." In general, these pieces are the most difficult to assign a period and place of origin. For the most part, I suspect such songs to have originated between 1875 and 1900, although reliable evidence prior to 1900 is often scarce. One and all, they escaped early capture on paper; yet most spread rather widely throughout the southern mountains before the era of recordings. And, as a class, they signal the casual familiarity with the railroads that makes a date much earlier than 1875 seem unreasonable.

Steve Goodman's hit "City of New Orleans" is sufficient testimony that a very popular song can still be written on the subject of the railroads. I see no reason not to expect more such hits in the coming years—especially if, in response to the economic factors discussed in chapter 1, the railroads recover some of their dwindling importance in passenger and freight traffic. A more speculative question is whether there will be any more railroad *folk*songs. Here I am convinced that the answer depends not so much on the economic future of the railroads as on the relative importance of the commercial media in providing Americans with entertainment. Americans in the 1970s sing for their own amusement a lot less than they did in the 1870s. They rely instead on records, radio, television, and other media. They are more the passive receivers of culture than the active creators of it. For these reasons, there are fewer folksongs of any sort in the 1970s than there were a century ago. There is no reason why this trend cannot be reversed in the near future. In fact, since the 1960s many more youngsters are learning to play guitars, banjos, and other instruments, and forming their own bands, whether to play rock music or bluegrass. If this movement continues to thrive, we will have the makings of a resurgent musical folk culture—not necessarily duplicating that of the last century, but by no means any less valid.

NOTES

1. Hank Wieand Bowman, *Pioneer Railroads* (New York: Arco Publishing, 1954), p. 23.

2. Hickory Nuts, "Louisville Burglar," OKeh 45169; reissued on County 522: *Old Time Ballads from the Southern Mountains*.

3. George Reneau, "Railroad Lover," Vocalion 15194 (1924).

4. See, e.g., Stewart H. Holbrook, *The Story of American Railroads* (New York: Crown Publishers, 1947), chap. 38; Eugene B. Block, *Great Train Robberies of the West* (New York: Coward-McCann, 1959), chap. 10; Frank P. Morse, *Cavalcade of the Rails* (New York: E. P. Dutton, 1940), chap. 15.

5. George Milburn, *The Hobo's Hornbook* (New York: Ives Washburn, 1930), p. 72.

6. Carl Sandburg, *The American Songbag* (New York: Harcourt, Brace, 1927), p. 372.

7. Alan Lomax, *The Folk Songs of North America* (Garden City, N.Y.: Doubleday, 1960), p. 406.

8. Telephone interview, Aug. 22, 1972.

9. Interview in Coleman's home in Princeton, W.Va., Sept. 18, 1971.

10. Parman to Cohen, postmarked Oct. 10, 1969.

11. Meeks to Cohen, Oct. 20, 1969.

12. *RRManM*, 23 (Apr., 1914), 957–60.

13. John Godfrey Saxe, *Poems* (Boston: Ticknor, Reed and Fields, 1849 and other editions), p. 55. A broadside version exists in the collection of the Library Company of Philadelphia; see Edwin Wolf II, *American Song Sheets, Slip Ballads and Poetical Broadsides, 1850–1870* (Philadelphia: Library Company of Philadelphia, 1963), no. 1953. Eugene Alvarez, in *Travel on Southern Antebellum Railroads, 1828–1860* (University: University of Alabama Press, 1974), p. 175, quotes a stanza of the song as it had appeared in the *Knickerbocker or New York Monthly Magazine*, 43 (Apr., 1854), 395. See also Sigmund Spaeth, *A History of Popular Music in America* (New York: Random House, 1948), p. 77. Sheet music versions have been published under the titles "Riding on a Rail," music by Charlie C. Converse (Boston: Ditson, 1853), and "Rail Road Chorus" (Philadelphia: J. F. Gould, 1854). Harry Lee Ridenour collected a four-stanza version titled "Railroad Song" in 1935 from Mrs. Luvera Payne Smith of Orwell, Ohio; she had learned it seventy-five years earlier. See Ridenour's *Folk Songs of Rural Ohio*, edited by W. Alwyn Ashburn (Berea, Ohio: Baldwin-Wallace College, 1973), vol. 10 (book 9), p. 77. This is the only evidence I have found for the song in oral tradition; even so, it deserves consideration as one of our oldest railroad folksongs.

14. Quoted in J. Parton, *The Humorous Poetry of the English Language* (New York: Mason Bros., 1857), p. 333.

15. *Book of 1001 Songs; or Songs for the Million* (New York: William H. Murphy, ca. 1847), vol. 3, p. 179. Words credited to Squintius Squintillian Squints Fobb.

16. Broadside, Los Angeles Public Library.

17. George Stuyvesant Jackson, *Early Songs of Uncle Sam* (Boston: Bruce Humphries, 1933), p. 43. Quoted from *Elton's Songs and Melodies for the Multitude; or Universal Songster* (New York: T. W. Strong, and Boston: G. W. Cottrell, ca. late 1840s).

18. Broadside, Library Company of Philadelphia, Wolf no. 2195.

19. *Tony Pastor's 201 Bowery Songster* (New York: Dick and Fitzgerald, 1867), pp. 27–28.

20. Fred Wilson, *Popular Comic Songs, No. 4* (Boston: Ditson, 1866).

21. Sheet music, "Ridin' in a Rail Road Keer," written and composed by W. J. Florence (St. Louis: Jacob Endres, 1859). A broadside version, reproduced here, is in the collection of the Library Company of Philadelphia, Wolf no. 2004. The text also appeared in songsters of the 1860s, e.g., *The Nightingale Songster, or Lyrics of Love* (New York: Dick and Fitzgerald, 1863), p. 61.

22. "Get Off the Track!," a "song for Emancipation," sung by the Hutchinsons, written by Jesse Hutchinson, Jr. (Boston: By the author, 1844).

23. See Vance Randolph, *Ozark Folksongs*, vol. 3 (Columbia: State Historical Society of Missouri, 1949), pp. 112–16. A fragment of "Charming Young Widow" was included in Gordon MS 329, from Mrs. F. N. Hoyt of New York City, May 5, 1924, who wrote that the song used to be sung by the older members of her family. A text collected in Wisconsin in 1941 appears in Harry B. Peters, ed., *Folk Songs out of Wisconsin* (Madison: State Historical Society of Wisconsin, 1977), p. 190. Another version, collected in Arkansas in 1953, is on deposit at the Library of Congress Archive of Folk Song (11890 B). According to Archive head Joseph C. Hickerson, texts of "The Harvard Student" collected from college students are on deposit in the Indiana University Folklore Archive.

24. Sheet music, n.p., n.d.

25. Broadside, Library Company of Philadelphia, Wolf no. 289.

26. *Bricktop's Songs, Recitations, and Parlor Dramas* (New York: M. J. Ivers, ca. late 1880s), p. 24.

27. *Paddle Your Own Canoe Songster* (New York: Robert DeWitt, 1868), pp. 28–30.

28. See, e.g., Stan Hugill, *Shanties from the Seven Seas* (London: Routledge and Kegan Paul, 1966), p. 171; or Ed Cray, *The Erotic Muse* (New York: Oak Publications, 1969), pp. 22–23, 185–89.

29. Broadside, Library Company of Philadelphia, Wolf no. 288.

30. Sigmund Spaeth, *Weep Some More My Lady* (New York: Doubleday, Page, 1927), p. 122.

31. See, e.g., Hazel Felleman, *The Best Loved Poems of the American People* (Garden City, N.Y.: Garden City Publishing, 1936), p. 515.

32. See *Bricktop's Songs*, pp. 40–41.

33. *Harvard Advocate*, Nov. 10, 1871, p. 40; reprinted in the *Harvard Alumni Bulletin*, Jan. 27, 1951, p. 331.

34. *Christy's Bones and Banjo Melodist* (New York: Dick and Fitzgerald, ca. 1865), pp. 48–49.

35. Helen Hartness Flanders et al., *The New Green Mountain Songster* (New Haven: Yale University Press, 1939), pp. 161–64.

36. Ibid., pp. 156–59.

37. Sheet music, composed by Fred E. Reynolds of Primrose and West Minstrels, "written for and sung with immense success by Mr. Fred. W. Oakland," copyrighted 1891 by Hitchcock and McCargo Publishing. The words were printed in *Railway Age*, Oct. 29, 1885, p. 689, titled "The Engineer," without attribution except the note that they were reprinted from the *Philadelphia News*.

38. See Freeman H. Hubbard, *Railroad Avenue* (New York: McGraw-Hill, 1945), chap. 9.

4

Heroes and Badmen

THIS CHAPTER RECALLS some of the best-known figures of American folk and popular musical lore. In the 1870s, John Henry, the steel driver, matched his skill and strength against a machine; his victory at the Big Bend Tunnel on the C & O Railroad cost his life. Heroic but reckless Casey Jones engineered the fast *Cannonball* to destruction one dark and cloudy night in 1900; his assignment, to make up ninety lost minutes, was all but completed when he lost his life and demolished several railroad cars. Jim Fisk, the robber baron, was closely associated with Jay Gould and the Erie Railroad in the years following the Civil War. He and Gould brought many a Wall Street wizard to financial ruin; yet he is remembered for sending a trainload of food to aid the survivers of the great Chicago fire. Jesse James and Cole Younger terrorized the Midwest in the 1860s and 1870s, robbing banks and trains at their fancy, and as often, of course, paying widows' mortgages. Railroad Bill was a notorious badman along the L & N route, burgling freight trains but—it was said—occasionally giving food to poor black families in Alabama. Lesser known are the D'Autremont brothers, who engineered the last great train robbery of the West but were singularly unsuccessful.

These are our railroad heroes and badmen. But which are the heroes and which the badmen? What is intriguing about this line-up of characters is that each can be regarded as both. The reasons for this paradox are discussed more fully in connection with "Jesse James." Basically, they stem from the tribal notion that the morality of an act depends on the allegiances of the persons involved, or—to be more specific in the case of robbery —that victimizing a tribal enemy is laudatory.

Casey Jones, like the many other engineers involved in the train wrecks discussed in chapter 5, is a typical occupational hero: the man who dies in the heroic performance of his duty because of a perverse universe. The line between bravery and foolhardiness is slender. Had Casey slammed his engine into a full Pullman car instead of an empty caboose, he might not have been treated so charitably by the public memory.

What of John Henry? Who would impute any but the noblest motives to his challenge of the steam drill? Who could fail to be moved by the tragedy of the heroic laborer who hammered his way to death? Perhaps one distant day, when society has learned to adapt the advantages of the technological revolution to the benefit of all its members rather than just some, then people will say of John Henry, "What a futile and senseless gesture, to oppose the very machine that would one day emancipate him from his demeaning labors."[1]

Discussions of heroes and heroism often prompt the question, How much of the legend that has been built up around the hero has to be true? It has been demonstrated that many of the tales involving such American heroes as Ethan Allen, George Washington, Henry Ford, and Davy Crockett cannot stand up under the careful scrutiny of the historian. The discussion of the songs about Jesse James, Cole Younger, Jim Fisk, and Railroad Bill implies that although the degree of these heroes' historicity is not of immediate concern to us, nevertheless much of their garb has been artificial padding over a rather slender historical frame.

In the cases of Allen, Washington, and Ford, the popular image can be traced to particularly overzealous biographers; Crockett was his own image-builder. In the cases dealt with in this chapter, no single person has been responsible for fleshing out the bones of the man to heroic proportions, although for James and Younger a handful of professional publicists were instrumental. In general, the people at large provided the necessary ingredients for apotheosis. The record thus suggests that there is precious little relationship between the height of the man and the length of his heroic shadow. John Henry, we must remember, may not have existed at all. It seems that a society will sculpt its pantheon of heroes whenever the need arises, and it will do so out of whatever material is at hand, however blemished the marble or knotted the timber.

Feelings toward the railroads ever since the 1840s have been so strong that needs for various kinds of heroes arose. In his *Machine in the Garden*, Leo Marx places the image of the railroad pervading the rustic quietude in the larger context of the impact of the industrial revolution on an agrarian and peasant society, especially as interpreted in Anglo-American literature of the past several hundred years.[2] The network of steel rails that crisscrossed the nation irrevocably altered the face of the land, bringing wealth and opportunity to many, but hardship and bitterness to others. As the great wheels clattered across the landscape, the dust they raised settled slowly on the pages of American literature, providing major themes for our writers for almost a century. Since 1844, when the sound of the locomotive intruded into Hawthorne's meditation as he sat in Sleepy Hollow inditing his impressions, there has been a persistent attitude that the railroads were rude invaders of the American panorama, bearers of wickedness and moral decay.

In the 1840s, proponents of the canal companies minced no words in castigating the threatening railroads:

> The railroad stems direct from Hell. It is the Devil's own invention, compounded of fire, smoke, soot, and dirt, spreading its infernal poison throughout the fair countryside. It will set fire to houses along its slimy tracks. It will throw burning brands into the ripe fields of the honest husbandman and destroy his crops. It will leave the land despoiled, ruined, a desert where only sable buzzards shall wing their loathesome way to feed upon the carrion accomplished by the iron monster of the locomotive engine. No, sir, let us hear no more of the railroad.[3]

After the Civil War, attitudes toward the railroad, catalyzed by the economic impact wrought by railroad activities and federal policies regarding them, crystallized into more specific complaints. This was the age that permitted a Jesse James and a Cole Younger to ride unrestrained. It was the era that Frank Norris chronicled in his muckraking novel of the San Joaquin Valley, *The Octopus*. The public created John Henry, the steel-driver, who resisted the technological invasion; Jesse James, the munificent train robber, who defied and dueled with the sprawling octopus; Jim Fisk, who tweaked the whiskers of the despised Commodore Vanderbilt; and Casey Jones, the brave harnesser of the iron horse's wildly destructive force. And then it willingly accepted the heroes it had molded. That John Henry may never have existed did not matter; that Jesse James terrorized sturdy citizens as well as railroads was shrugged off; that Casey Jones brought as much destruction as glory to the rails was forgotten; that Jim Fisk himself engineered his railroad to fortune over the toes of the helpless public was overlooked.

Today all that has changed. The public outcry over the railroads is still heard; but far from complaining of the monster's intrusion into our peaceful way of life, the voices are now begging that the iron horse not be led to the glue factory prematurely. An object of neither awe nor mistrust nor hatred, the steam engine is a kindly old friend. No longer does a Frank Norris write of the horrors wrought by the railroads; but a Lucius Beebe extols those glorious moments of the golden age of steam.

Today, the old heroes are still sung and talked about wherever the two parallel rails mean more than an urban streetcar. In 1933 the Southern Pacific experienced its fifty-ninth train robbery. Since then there have been no train robberies in the West. Nor have there been any new railroad heroes.

NOTES

1. Science fiction writer Arthur C. Clarke suggests that this has already happened: ". . . today, we should regard a man who challenged a steam hammer as merely crazy—not heroic" ("Are You Thinking Machines?," *Industrial Research,* Mar., 1969, p. 50).

2. Leo Marx, *The Machine in the Garden: Technology and the Pastoral Ideal in America* (New York: Oxford University Press, 1964). Related studies are Thomas Reed West, *Flesh of Steel: Literature and the Machine in American Culture* (Nashville, Vanderbilt University Press, 1967), and Herbert L. Sussman, *Victorians and the Machine: The Literary Response to Technology* (Cambridge: Harvard University Press, 1968).

3. Quoted without attribution in Stewart H. Holbrook, *The Story of American Railroads* (New York: Crown Publishers, 1947), p. 41.

John Henry

JOHN HENRY BLUES

*By using a C chord throughout, the performer will remain faithful to the harmonic implications of Carson's fiddle accompaniment.

John Henry was a very small boy,
Fell on his mammy's knee;
Picked up a hammer and a little piece of steel,
"Lord, a hammer'll be the death of me,
Lord, a hammer'll be the death of me."

John Henry went upon the mountain,
Come down on the side;
The mountain so tall, John Henry was so small,
Lord, he lay down his hammer and he cried, "Oh, Lord,"
He lay down his hammer and he cried.

John Henry was on the right hand,
But that steam drill was on the left;
"Before your steam drill beats me down,
Hammer my fool self to death,
Lord, I'll hammer my fool self to death."

The captain says to John Henry,
"Believe my tunnel's fallin' in."
"Captain, you needn't not to worry,
Just my hammer hawsing in the wind,
Just my hammer hawsing in the wind."

"Look away over yonder, captain,
You·can't see like me."
He hollered out in a low, lonesome cry,
"This hammer'll be the death of me,
Lord, this hammer'll be the death of me."

John Henry told his captain,
"Captain, you go to town,
Bring John back a twelve-pound hammer,
And he'll whup your steam drill down,
[?And] he'll whup your steam drill down."

For the man that invented that steam drill
.Thought he was mighty fine;
John Henry sunk a fo'teen foot,
The steam drill only made nine,
The steam drill only made nine.

John Henry told his shaker,
"Shaker, you better pray;
For if I miss this six-foot steel,
Tomorrow'll be your buryin' day,
An' tomorrow'll be your buryin' day."

John Henry told his lovin' little woman,
"Sick and I want to go to bed;
Fix me a place to lay down, child,
Got a rollin' in my head,
Got a rollin' in my head."

John Henry had a lovely little woman,
Called her Polly Ann;
John Henry got sick and he had to go home,
But Polly broke steel like a man,
Polly broke steel like a man.

John Henry had another little woman,
The dress she wore was blue;
She went down the track and she never looked back,
"John Henry, I've been true to you."
[*Answers this line with fiddle.*]

         Fiddlin' John Carson

DEATH OF JOHN HENRY

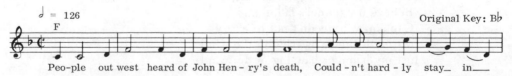

Peo-ple out west heard of John Hen-ry's death, Could-n't hard-ly stay_ in__

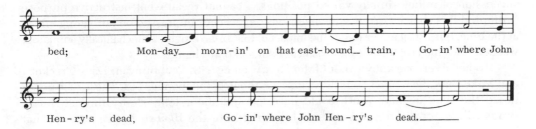

bed; Mon-day___ morn-in' on that east-bound_ train, Go-in' where John

Hen-ry's dead, Go-in' where John Hen-ry's dead._____

People out west heard of John Henry's death,
Couldn't hardly stay in bed;
Monday mornin' on that eastbound train,
Goin' where John Henry's dead,
Goin' where John Henry's dead.

Carried John Henry to the graveyard,
They looked at him good and long;
Very last words his old wife said to him,
"My husband, he is dead and gone,
My husband, he is dead and gone."

John Henry's wife wore a brand new dress,
It was all trimmed in blue;
Very last words she said to him,
"Honey, I've been good to you,
Honey, I've been good to you."

John Henry told a shaker,
"Lordy, shake while I sing;
Pullin' a hammer from my shoulder,
I'm bound to hear her when she rings,
Bound to hear her when she rings."

John Henry told his captain,
"I am a Tennessee man;
Before I would see that steam drill beat me down,
Die with a hammer in my hand,
Die with a hammer in my hand."

John Henry hammered in the mountains,
Till the hammer caught on fire;
Very last words I heard him say,
"Cool drink o' water 'fore I die,
Cool drink o' water 'fore I die."

Uncle Dave Macon

Years ago, while I was still in grammar school and long before I had any inkling of the concept "folksong," I remember seeing a movie about John Henry. The characters were puppets, and the animation was achieved by still photographs of the puppets in a succession of infinitesimally varied positions. I cannot recall what instructive purpose prompted this showing, or what conclusions our teacher impressed on our young minds at the time; but I shall never forget the impact of that bizarre sight: a mechanically animated, wooden black man contesting a mechanically animated machine.

Today, everyone knows about John Henry; along with Paul Bunyan, Davy Crockett, and Mike Fink, he is one of our illustrious pantheon of folk/pop heroes. Those who never heard the song in their youth could have learned about John Henry through Roark Bradford's fictionalized novel of 1931, *John Henry*; or the 1939 stage adaptation of that book; or any of the numerous accounts of John Henry that have appeared in books on America folk heroes; or in the various childrens' books based on the John Henry legend. In fact, much of the national awareness of John Henry stems from a revival of interest in the late 1920s, following the research of Guy B. Johnson, rather than from direct survival from the nineteenth century.[1] An admirable summary of the variety of literary and musical uses to which the John Henry story has been put was written by Richard M. Dorson.[2] His paper indicated that the legend of John Henry is able to stand up under a much heavier load than the real John Henry ever was subjected to—if there indeed was a real John Henry (a question to which I shall return).

The John Henry legend can be sketched in a few sentences. At some distant period in history, when thousands of laborers toiled to lay our nation's railroad tracks, human muscle was required to drill holes in solid granite for implanting explosives to blast out level passes through the mountains. One day a new invention was brought forward—a mechanical device, driven by steam, to do the hole drilling. The invention was controversially received: many argued that a machine could never adequately replace manual drilling. A contest was arranged between the steam drill and the best of the workers, a black steel-driver named John Henry. This trial was to determine whether men or machines made the better drillers, and on its outcome, therefore, depended the livelihoods of innumerable manual laborers. John Henry positioned himself on one side of the steam drill, and the go signal was given. By the time the steam drill had advanced nine feet, John Henry had progressed fourteen. He won the contest, but the superhuman exertion proved fatal, and he died shortly afterward.

Of course, the details of the story vary greatly from telling to telling. Some persons believe John Henry was driving railroad spikes into crossties, rather than drilling holes for explosives. Some claim the contest was associated with mine excavating rather than railroad construction. And, of course, there is disagreement regarding the railroad on which the incident occurred (the C & O, the L & N, the B & O, and the CC & O appear in different versions); the weight of his hammer (nine, ten, twelve, sixteen, twenty, or thirty pounds); the name of his woman (Mary Ann, Polly Ann, Julie Ann, Martha Ann, Delia Ann, Sary Ann, Nellie Ann, Mary Magdalene), whether the contest was at his or his captain's instigation, what locality he was from, where he was buried, and what the actions of his woman (or women) were after his death. But these are the types of variation that attest to the vigor of oral tradition in the dissemination of a ballad.

Some time after this contest supposedly occurred, John Henry's Pyrrhic victory was memorialized in ballad form. Whether there was any historical basis to the story, where and when it occurred if there was, and who authored the ballad or ballads—these were questions that occupied the attention of many folksong scholars from 1909 on.

Today, in retrospect, it is safe to assert that in recent decades no other ballad native to this country has been more widely known or more often recorded, has stimulated more printed commentary, or has inspired more folk and popular literature. In view of this abundance, it would be both hopeless and superfluous in this discussion to attempt a complete account of the migrations of the John Henry motif from fact to ballad to criticism to fiction. Much fine research has already been published on the story of the contest with the steam drill; my brief narrative borrows considerably from the pioneering studies of Guy Johnson and Louis Chappell[3] and from the more recent survey article by Dorson. These writings, as well as the others cited in section B, contain further details. My discussion summarizes what is known about the historical basis of the John Henry story and about the nature, style, and authorship of the ballads. The role of the John Henry legend in literature and culture in general is touched upon only briefly.

The John Henry theme first came to the attention of the folksong fraternity in print in a 1909 *Journal of American Folklore* article titled "Ballads and Songs of Western North Carolina." Anticipating for the moment the conclusion that the ballad deals with events of 1870–72, it might seem strange that no account of John Henry appeared for nearly four decades after his death. In 1909, however, the scholarly study of native American folksong was still in its infancy, and few articles on the subject had been published. The author of this one, Louise Rand Bascom, presented, with a patronizing air verging on contempt, several songs that she had acquired in the mountains of western North Carolina at some unspecified date. She concluded with a two-line fragment that she termed one of the most desirable of the mountain ballads, which had not yet come into her hands:

> Johnie Henry was a hard-workin' man,
> He died with his hammer in his hand.[4]

A more sympathetic and also much more extensive collector was E. C. Perrow, who lived as a child in the mountains of east Tennessee and was exposed to much traditional songlore there. Later in life he began to collect "such fragments of popular verse as I could remember or could induce my friends to write down for me."[5] His collections and recollections were published in a series of articles in the *Journal of American Folklore* between 1912 and 1915. Under the heading "John Henry," Perrow grouped five separate pieces. The oldest was a fragment that he had heard mountain whites sing in 1905 as they drove a steel drill into the rocks:

> If I could drive steel like John Henry,
> I'd go home, Baby, I'd go home.
>
> This ole hammer killed John Henry,
> Drivin' steel, Baby, drivin' steel.[6]

The longest of Perrow's recoveries was an eight-stanza ballad obtained from mountain whites of Kentucky by E. N. Caldwell, one of his most productive informants, in 1912. Although a note on Caldwell's manuscript stated "About half of John Henry here, very long," this ballad included most of the frequently recurring details about John Henry's premonition as a little boy, the contest itself, and the steel driver's loving wife. The concluding stanza localized the event to the C & O railroad, which runs through Kentucky.

Thus it early became apparent that the songlore concerning John Henry consisted of two distinct types of composition: ballad and worksong. The latter was a hammer song, a song used by workers to help them keep the rhythm of their hammering. Hammer songs are for steel drivers, gravel crushers, or road builders what chanteys are for sailors hoisting or lowering sails. Such worksongs serve important functions: not only do they provide a necessary rhythm, but they they can also help uplift the spirits of the workers, which heavy labor tends to drag down. The ballads, on the other hand, fall into the class of occupational song rather than worksong. Whereas the latter is actually a *part* of the work process, the former is generally *about* some aspect of the work: lumberjacks sing of log jams; sailors sing of girls back in port, either faithful or unfaithful; cowboys sing of fatal cattle stampedes; coal miners sing of mine disasters.

A full ballad version of "John Henry" was recovered by Josiah Combs in Knott County, Kentucky, about 1909. It was mentioned in Shearin and Combs's 1911 syllabus of Kentucky folksongs but not printed in full until 1925.[7] This text placed the contest at the Big Bend Tunnel on the C & O road. Located in Summers County, West Virginia, this tunnel was constructed between 1870 and 1872. Although officially named the Great Bend Tunnel after the nearby bend in the Greenbriar River, the name "Big Bend Tunnel" seems to have always been in use, even among railroad officials. Another early version was obtained by John Lomax and published in the 1915 *Journal of American Folklore* in a survey article titled "Some Types of American Folk-Song," the text of an address given at the annual meeting of the American Folklore Society in December, 1913.[8] The source of the ballad was not given. Textually, it resembled Combs's version; probably both came from white singers.

Between 1916 and 1925 several discussions of the ballad appeared in folklore and education journals and books, most notably by folksong collectors John Harrington Cox and Dorothy Scarborough.[9] Cox in particular championed the theory that John Henry was the same person as John Hardy, a West Virginia outlaw of verified historicity who was hanged in 1894, and the subject of a widespread ballad. Cox arrived at this erroneous conclusion partly because of the mistaken recollections of W. A. McCorkle, former governor of West Virginia, and partly because there were several early John Henry ballads that named the hero John Hardy and, conversely, several texts of "John Hardy" that included stanzas now known to belong to "John Henry." By 1919, Cox had established that the John Hardy of the ballads was a real person; and since reports suggested many close parallels between the careers of the two men, he concluded that John Henry was simply a corruption of John Hardy. However, in the 1920s, as much more evidence came to the fore, it became apparent that the instances of intermingling of the John Hardy and the John Henry stories were the exception rather than the rule. Folksong collectors writing in the period 1926–29 supported the view that Hardy and Henry were different men and that the ballads about them were in most instances distinct.[10] But Cox's influential 1925 collection, *Folk-Songs of the South*, had already disseminated the opinion that Henry and Hardy were the same; and that viewpoint persisted for some time among the nonscholarly readers of his book, as the accompanying letter from Galax folksinger Ernest V. Stoneman to musicologist Alfred Frankenstein illustrates. With Johnson's intensive study, *John Henry: Tracking Down a Negro Legend* (1929), the question of Henry/Hardy identity was laid to rest for nearly four decades, until MacEdward Leach reopened the problem of the origin of the Henry story (see below).[11]

The two principal investigations of the John Henry story were Johnson's 1929 monograph and Louis Chappell's investigation, published in final form in 1933. While Johnson's is the more readable work, Chappell's is the more persuasive because of its more extensive and better utilized data. Unfortunately, Chappell's otherwise fine study is distinctly marred—at least throughout the twenty-page introduction—by his apoplectic vituperations directed against Johnson. Chappell accused Johnson of borrowing, without credit, from a preliminary report he had made in 1927. Johnson never answered the claim, and the evidence that Chappell marshals on his own behalf is indeed compelling.[12] Considering that they worked from some of the same data, it is hardly surprising that Johnson and Chappell arrived at similar conclusions. Regarding the historicity of John Henry, Johnson summarized his findings: "Perhaps the wisest thing would be to suspend judgment on this question, but, after weighing all the evidence, I prefer to believe that (1) there was a Negro steel driver named John Henry at Big Bend Tunnel, that (2) he competed with a steam drill in a test of the practicability of the device, and that (3) he probably died soon after the contest, perhaps from fever."[13]

The chief alternatives for the locale of the John Henry incident were Jamaica, Alabama, and Kentucky. Chappell dismissed the Kentucky claim with little ado; the Alabama claim he rejected not because it was inherently weak, but rather because of the stronger evidence supporting the Big Bend Tunnel on the C & O as the site. The claim for Jamaican origin, which Johnson did not discuss, is more interesting, particularly in view of Leach's later resurrection of that theory. Chappell, however, had dismissed the Jamaican claim, which rested on a fragment collected by Jekyll in about 1900[14] and was supported by a living tradition in Jamaica as late as 1933. With Johnson's third conclusion, Chappell seemed less willing to agree, although all the trails of John Henry's whereabouts following the contest led to dead ends.

Chappell's convictions (and Johnson's, too, for that matter) were not based on primary historical documents: C & O documents had been either lost or destroyed years before his investigations began. (There was a strong belief that the documents were deliberately lost so as not to cast the C & O in an unfavorable light because of the inhuman working conditions the tunnel drillers endured in 1870–72 at Big Bend Tunnel.) In fact, no evidence could be found that steam drills had been used at all there, although both Chappell and Johnson searched diligently for positive information on that point. Hence the qualifier of Johnson's second conclusion: that the competition was one to *test* the practicability of the steam drill. Since the test failed, the steam drills were probably never used again in the tunnel, so that the one brief appearance in a contest of a few hours probably never occasioned a comment in contemporary documents. On the contrary, both the steam-drill company, who had lost the demonstration, and the railway, who had lost a man, would have discouraged any publicity.

Chappell's conclusions were based on the firsthand interviews he conducted in the Big Bend community in 1925 and the years following. He accepted the historicity of the John Henry contest because of the reports of reliable men who had been in the area during the years the tunnel was constructed. Although the evidence persuaded Chappell, it should be borne in mind that none of Chappell's informants actually witnessed the contest and that their testimonies all conflicted in nontrivial details.

It is regrettable that Chappell had not begun his investigations a decade earlier; then he might have found the trail significantly warmer. As it is, we shall probably never know for certain the circumstances of the alleged contest. Any future attempts to canvass the aged denizens of the area, as journalist Hank Burchard did in 1969, are doomed to failure.[15] Our only hope is that one day a contemporary printed account in some obscure journal or newspaper will be unearthed, and even that is unlikely, as Chappell was laudably industrious in scouring such records.

Needless to say, the name of the author of "John Henry" is not known to us. In the course of his research, Johnson obtained from a woman in Georgia a broadside version of "John Henry," signed by one W. T. Blankenship. The owner of the broadside could not

ERNEST V. STONEMAN

MANAGER DIXIE MOUNTAINEERS

RECORDING ARTISTS

GALAX, VA.

Agust 6 29

Mr Alfred.Frankenstein.
        4501.Ellis Ave.
                Chicago,
                        Ill.

Dear sir .
Rec your letter of the 2nd inst in regard to my records
and was glad to hear that you had enjoyed them.
and also we have plenty more coming that we recorded .
last November.28.which i hope you will greatly enjoy
and i will be very glad to answer your two Questions?
in regard to same?.
The Song called John.Henry was made in WestVirginia.
on the C&O. R.Road. the Man that the song was made about
was a negro who was a East Virginian.
he was a champion Steel driver on the Building of the
C&O.R.R. at the Big Bend tunnel as you will note in the
song.it was when the first steam drills was used and he
did run a race with the steam drill   but his real name
was John Hardy.later he killed two men in Shawnee W.VA.
and was hung in Welch,Mc.Dowell.County.W.Va.
he was a very large negro weighing over two hundred
pounds and the most handsome negro that could be found
at that time and was a reckless gambler and drunkard .
and a very fierce fighter when he killed those men over
fifty cents in a game of cards he first laid his gun
down and said to his gun that he would kill the first
nigger that tried to cheat he accused one of cheating
and when the other fellow said he would pay him back
he took the fifty cents he said he would not lie to his
gun and just picked it up and shot him.
i also have a song on this tragedy and it is called
John Hardy.recorded on Gennett.And Supertone records.
Sears Roebuck.& Co.Sells Supertone records.
but the two songs are about the same man.
and his Real Name Is John Hardy.

Ernest Stoneman letter. Courtesy of Alfred Frankenstein.

ERNEST V. STONEMAN

MANAGER DIXIE MOUNTAINEERS

RECORDING ARTISTS

GALAX, VA.

2

and i regard to the Fate Of Talmadge Osborne.

is a story about a young man from Grayson.county.Va.
the County in which i live who went to West.Va.
to work in the coal mines to pay for some land that he
had bought .
but he was given to drink and very oftenhe would
Hobo a ride on the trains around Williamson.W.Va.
and one night he was burning a ride and got killed
and was brought back home to Grayson county dead as
you will note in the song .

some of those song that i sing are known far and wide
ahd some are not known only by a very few and some i
compose myself and i am helping to make thaose old songs
that are almost forgotten known far and wide .
i am the first one that recorded The Sinking of the
Titanic   .
now one Question please tell me how you learned my
Address ?.

      Very truly yours.

      Ernest.V.Stoneman.

Ernest. V. Stoneman

date the purchase of the item; she stated only that it had been in the family for years. Typographers who examined the sheet could place an upper limit on its age—no earlier than 1862—but not a lower limit. A colleague of Johnson told him he recalled seeing a similar sheet in about 1900, and Johnson accepted 1900 as a probable date. An examination of Blankenship's text strongly suggests that the author was working from older material imperfectly remembered or understood; it is indisputable that the Blankenship ballad is not the original version of "John Henry." Furthermore, it seems clear that Blankenship's was a text in the Anglo-American rather than the Afro-American tradition.

In reviewing Chappell's book, Phillips Barry discussed three pieces of evidence that led him to believe that if "John Henry" was not actually written by a white person, the influence of white tradition was very strong.[16] The first piece was the Blankenship ballad; the second was the similarity of one stanza to a stanza in one text of the Scottish ballad "Mary Hamilton." Compare the opening stanza of Fiddlin' John Carson's song, transcribed above, with the following:

> Whan I was a babe, and a very little babe,
> And stood at my mither's knee;
> Nae witch nor warlock did unfauld
> The death I was to dree.[17]

One might strengthen Barry's argument with two stanzas from another Anglo-American ballad, "The Cherry Tree Carol":

> Then Mary took her babe,
> And sat him on her knee,
> Saying, My dear son, tell me
> What this world will be.
>
> O I shall be as dead, mother,
> As the stones in the wall;
> O the stones in the streets, mother,
> Shall mourn for me all.[18]

As his third piece of evidence, Barry identified the usual "John Henry" tune as a common tune of the British ballad "Earl Brand."[19] (One might add a fourth Anglo-Americanism, namely the "who's gonna shoe your pretty little feet" stanzas that occur in many versions and are closely associated with the British ballad "The Lass of Roch Royal.")[20] Without implying that I view this notion of the immediacy of white tradition with disfavor, I do wish to point out that refuting it is very difficult, since we lack any extensive collectanea of black secular tunes and texts of the Reconstruction era. The interchange of black and white folksong elements has been going on continually for a century or more, and we cannot assume that the appearance of the "Earl Brand" tune in an ostensibly black ballad was necessarily the first appearance of that tune in Afro-American folksong.

Perhaps a better argument for the influence of white tradition is simply the strength of the narration. What we know of early black folksong in the United States suggests that sustained narrative in the style of European balladry was rare; where it did occur, it was usually in songs sung by blacks for whites, as in minstrel and medicine shows. Of course, this still leaves room for the possibility of a skeletal song originated by blacks, celebrating the victory over a machine, fleshed out into a more elaborate ballad by later white singers. All we are left with for certain is that the earliest collected versions, the earliest printed version, and the earliest recorded versions (discussed below) were all by whites.

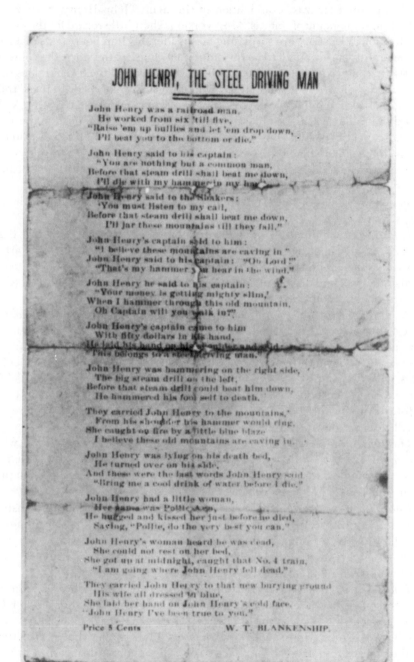

Broadside: W. T. Blankenship's "John Henry, the Steel Driving Man."
Reproduced from Guy Johnson, *John Henry*.

As for the structure of the ballad, although a detailed narrative can be pieced together from extant stanzas, examination of the many "John Henry" texts reveals an extremely fluid sequencing of stanzas. Most versions show little regard for the demands of sensible chronology. Even more surprising, a considerable number of texts make little or no mention of what surely ought to be the emotional climax of the story: the contest itself. Frequently, nothing is told of the outcome of the contest, and the listener does not learn from the ballad itself whether John Henry won or lost, lived or died. In these traits, the John Henry ballads fall into the category of native American folksong that D. K. Wilgus has termed the "blues ballad." Unlike the older ballads of Anglo-American tradition, the blues ballad expends itself in commentary on an implied event rather than in detailed report; it is to the older ballad style what the newspaper editorial is to the news story. Of course, its success depends on the audience's already knowing the "facts" of the story beforehand.

Most of the stanzas of the John Henry ballads can be classified according to the following scheme:

A. *Infantile premonition.* Young John Henry sees a hammer, or the Big Bend Tunnel, and prophesies that it will be responsible for his death. In an artistically interesting variation, John Henry takes his own little son on his knee, either encouraging the boy also to be a steel driver, or, more likely, admonishing him against it. (Compare the first stanza of Carson's text.)

B. *Preparation for the contest.* Some versions detail how the contest came about: who issued the challenge and so on. Then may follow John Henry's instructions to his captain to obtain hammers of specified weight. Sometimes the captain offers John Henry financial incentive to win the contest. A widely occurring stanza, and a most moving one, concludes with the couplet "The mountain was so tall, John Henry so small / He laid down his hammer and cried (died)." In another widespread and emotionally effective stanza, John Henry assures his captain that he will win, or die trying: "Before I let the steam drill beat me down / I'll die with my hammer in my hand."

C. *The contest.* Generally, the details are confined to couplets describing who stood where (Carson, st. 3), the relative speed of the contestants (Carson, st. 7), the power of John Henry's hammering (Carson, st. 4), and an admonition to the shaker to pray that John Henry not miss his hammer swings (Carson, st. 8).

D. *John Henry's last testament, death, and burial.* John Henry may give instructions about where he wants to be buried and what he wants done with his hammer. Other stanzas tell of people coming to the funeral, in particular his woman (or women). (Compare Macon's text, st. 3). These verses often become the core of a new secondary ballad, such as Uncle Dave Macon's song, transcribed above.

E. *John Henry's woman.* In addition to the behavior and attire of John Henry's woman at the funeral, we are often told of her own skill at throwing the hammer (Carson, st. 10). A frequent intrusion is the sequence of verses referred to above recounting a dialogue between John Henry and his woman: "Who's gonna shoe your little feet," "Where did you get your dress so fine," and so on. These stanzas float easily from folksong to folksong, occurring frequently in both black and white tradition. More rare, but recoverable with diligent searching, are bawdy verses that also have nothing to do with the basic John Henry story.

Of a quite different structure from the John Henry ballads are the John Henry hammer songs. Although they are discussed further in chapter 11, it is worth recalling here Johnson's hypotheses regarding the relationship between the two types of material:

The first songs about John Henry were simple, spontaneous hammer songs which did not go into the details of the John Henry story. Perhaps here and there someone made up a brief song of the ballad type. A short time later some person who was familiar with the tradition composed a ballad and had it printed on single sheets for distribution. . . . This was circulated in West Virginia and a few other states and was taken by the Negro laborers to various parts of the country. No copy of this hypothetical ballad has yet been found. Still later, one or more persons wrote and printed different versions of the ballad and sold them. One such version, that written by Blankenship, has come to light.[21]

Finally, I should like to return to the points raised in Leach's article on John Henry, the most recent scholarship concerning the ballad. Leach used important material he collected in Jamaica in 1957 to probe the weak points in the generally accepted theory of the ballad's origin (i.e., that it grew out of the Big Bend Tunnel construction in 1870–72 in West Virginia). Although he refused to accept any thesis of genesis as indisputable, he concluded that there most probably was a John Henry killed in construction work on the Kingston–Port Antonio Railroad between 1894 and 1896, and that a song about him was in oral circulation at that time. Leach's prime document was a map drawn in 1894, on the back of which was penciled a fragment of a song, one verse of which went:

> Ten pound hammer it crush me pardner
> Ten pound hammer it crush me pardner
> Ten pound hammer it crush me pardner
> Somebody dyin' every day.

His informant asserted that the song was known as "the John Henry song." On the basis of this item, Leach asserted that the earliest inditement of a Jamaican John Henry song predated by at least ten years the oldest objective data in the United States (the fragments collected by Perrow). The John Henry of Jamaican oral tradition died in construction work; there is no mention of a steam drill or a contest, or of a wife named Julie Ann; there is neither the epithet "steel-drivin' man" nor the death prophecy. Leach suggests three alternative hypotheses: (1) the Jamaican and American stories are separate, growing out of different but similar situations; (2) John Hardy was the original hero of the C & O construction and was replaced by John Henry from Jamaica about 1900; or (3) the John Henry story originated on the C & O and aas carried to Jamaica, where it was stripped of essential details and transformed into a different story.

Leach's second hypothesis rests on the assertion that John Henry did not appear in United States tradition before 1900, a claim I am most reluctant to accept. Although admittedly there is no concrete evidence to the contrary, there is ample circumstantial evidence to suggest that people were singing about John Henry in the early 1890s. Furthermore, there is no evidence that John Henry was sung about in Jamaica as early as 1894; and Leach's prize fragment does not mention John Henry by name.

The third of Leach's hypotheses seems unlikely (as he may have intended it to be). I suggest a modification of his first hypothesis. The Jamaican and American stories are indeed separate, both involving men named John Henry—a not uncommon name —killed in construction work on a tunnel. In both the United States and Jamaica, pre-existing hammer songs were modified to suit the incident. In the United States, a complete ballad, or series of ballads, grew out of the story.

If we are uncertain of the authorship of the "John Henry" ballads, we can assert confidently that the worksongs or hammer songs about John Henry are the product of black singing laborers. These songs are exemplified by "Nine Pound Hammer" and "Spike Driver Blues," discussed in chapter 11.

As Dorson demonstrated, the John Henry story has permeated all genres of American lore—prose fiction, drama, art, stage musical. The story lends itself to several interpretations. On the most direct level, it deals with an early episode in the American industrial revolution. John Henry is the hero representing resistance to technological innovations that threaten unemployment to those with the traditional manual skills. And since the lowest manual laborers were the blacks, the industrial revolution threatened them more than any other class. John Henry is therefore a black hero, the pride of his fellow Afro-Americans, who resists another advance in white domination. In both of these contexts, the song/story is a labor/protest piece in the best American tradition. Alternatively, we can subject the John Henry story to Freudian analysis and conclude that the sexual symbolism of a man hammering himself to death is the dominant motif. Archie Green has recently explored John Henry's appearance in graphic form and has compiled an extensive checklist of illustrations in books and journals, sheet music and record jackets, films and film strips, sculpture, and miscellaneous fine and folk art.[22]

John Henry's long and busy career on record began in late March of 1924 when Fiddlin' John Carson recorded the ballad in Atlanta for the OKeh Phonograph Corporation. Carson, born in 1868 in Fannin County, north Georgia, was a pioneer in the early days of hillbilly music on both radio and phonograph records. Notwithstanding his important contribution to the music of the 1920s, a detailed biography of Carson has yet to be published; however, my own recent account, with discography, lists articles about him,[23] and further information is given in the notes to "Papa's Billy Goat" (chap. 6). Carson's "John Henry," one of the few twelve-inch 78 rpm hillbilly discs made in the 1920s, features an unusually long text (transcribed above). The word *hawsing* in Carson's fourth stanza requires glossing. The *Oxford English Dictionary* gives *hawse* as an obsolete verb meaning 'to raise,' but only a transitive use is recorded.

The second recording was made by black musician Sam Jones on August 20, 1924, but it was never issued; nor was the third, by blind North Carolina minstrel Ernest Thompson, cut on September 9, 1924. The fourth recording of "John Henry" was made three days later by two acquaintances of Fiddlin' John's: fellow Atlantans Gid Tanner and Riley Puckett recorded the song for Columbia. There were no recordings of the ballad in 1925, but in 1926 two were made, and then four in 1927. The first issued recording by black artists was an instrumental version by Francis and Sowell in February, 1927. Thereafter a steady stream of renditions appeared; altogether, nearly fifty recordings were made on 78 rpm hillbilly and race records prior to 1948, and, as the discography shows, more than six times that number on LP discs in the next thirty years.

Carson's version is typical of a great many of the recorded renditions. A quite different ballad, both tune and text, is Uncle Dave Macon's "The Death of John Henry," recorded in April, 1927, for Vocalion. Because it provides an interesting contrast with the more familiar variants, and because it has much to recommend it musically, it also is transcribed here.

My final thoughts on John Henry return to the supposed significance of the song as a protest against industrialization. This is too narrow a view of the John Henry conflict. It is senseless to rebel against technological advances that can lighten man's burden. For each John Henry left unemployed there will be a job for a steam-drill operator—not to mention for the factory worker who makes the steam drill and the mechanic who repairs it. Just as the manuscript writer was once replaced by the moveable-type composer, who was in turn replaced by the linotype operator, who then was replaced by the photocompositor, so too will the steam-drill operator be replaced by another technological advance. The

First day cover. Author's Collection.

animated puppet that portrayed John Henry in the movie I recalled from my youth could as well represent the steam driller as the spike driver. The tragedy is not that the old ways of performing tasks are superannuated by newer ones, but that society finds it more convenient to discharge the old laborer than retrain him, or at least retire him in dignity. The fault of John Henry's era was that it lacked a sense of obligation toward the displaced common laborer. John Henry might as well die if he lost the contest, because he would surely lose his job, and in that age of Calvinist capitalism, that would have been tantamount to loss of life. Surely our society is capable of better.

NOTES

1. Guy B. Johnson, *John Henry* (Chapel Hill: University of North Carolina Press, 1929).

2. Richard M. Dorson, "The Career of 'John Henry,'" *WF*, 24 (July, 1965), 155–63.

3. Louis W. Chappell, *John Henry* (Jena: Frommannsche Verlag, 1933).

4. Louise Rand Bascom, "Ballads and Songs of Western North Carolina," *JAF*, 22 (Apr.–June, 1909), 249.

5. E. C. Perrow, "Songs and Rhymes from the South," *JAF*, 25 (June–Mar., 1912), 144.

6. Ibid., 26 (Apr.–June, 1913), 163.

7. Hubert G. Shearin and Josiah H. Combs, *A Syllabus of Kentucky Folk-Songs* (Lexington, Ky.: Transylvania Printing, 1911), p. 19, titled "The Steel-Driver"; Josiah H. Combs, *Folk-Songs du Midi des États-Unis* (Paris: Presses Universitaires de France, 1925), pp. 191–93; John Harrington Cox, *Folk-Songs of the South* (1925; rpt., Hatboro, Pa.: Folklore Associates, 1963), pp. 185–86.

8. John A. Lomax, "Some Types of American Folk-Song," *JAF*, 28 (Jan.–Mar., 1915), 1–17.

9. John Harrington Cox, "'John Hardy,'" *JAF*, 32 (Oct.–Dec., 1919), 505–20. This article contains Cox's most explicit statement about the ballads. An earlier mention appeared in *West Virginia Journal and Educator*, 44 (1915), 216–17. See also his *Folk-Songs of the South*, pp. 175–77, and Dorothy Scarborough, *On the Trail of Negro Folk-Songs* (1925; rpt., Hatboro, Pa.: Folklore Associates, 1963), pp. 218–19.

10. In addition to Johnson, *John Henry*, and Chappell, *John Henry*, see Newman I. White, *American Negro Folk-Songs* (1928; rpt., Hatboro, Pa.: Folklore Associates, 1965), pp. 189–90; and

Howard W. Odum and Guy B. Johnson, *Negro Workaday Songs* (Chapel Hill: University of North Carolina Press, 1926), pp. 221–24.

11. MacEdward Leach, "John Henry," in *Folklore and Society*, edited by Bruce Jackson (Hatboro, Pa.: Folklore Associates, 1966), pp. 93–106.

12. I do not know how the academic community received Chappell's accusation, but I imagine it was with considerable embarrassment or uneasy silence. Phillips Barry, in his review of Chappell's book (*BFSSNE*, No. 8 [1934], pp. 24–26), says nothing of the dispute. D. K. Wilgus (*Anglo-American Folksong Scholarship since 1898* [New Brunswick, N.J.: Rutgers University Press, 1959], p. 398) notes that Chappell's charges have never been satisfactorily answered. I am reminded of an incident that was hotly debated in 1973 among physical scientists, concerning an allegation of plagiarism in the field of nuclear physics in work performed some twenty-five years ago at the Lawrence Radiation Laboratory in Berkeley. The issues discussed included not only the basic question of whether one scientist's work had been utilized by others without his getting due credit, or what constituted the fair use of an idea or preliminary data, but also more diffuse ethical problems: how do scientists resolve such differences—among themselves, or by airing the issues in public? Such problems take us far afield from the immediate subject, but they do serve to remind us of the human side of research, and, therefore, of the fallibility of the results.

13. Johnson, *John Henry*, p. 54.

14. Walter Jekyll, *Jamaican Song and Story* (1907; rpt., New York: Dover Publications, 1966) p. 268.

15. Hank Burchard, "In Quest of the Historical John Henry," *Washington Post Potomac* (magazine section), Aug. 24, 1969, pp. 11–16, 22–24.

16. Barry, review of Chappell, *John Henry*.

17. Francis James Child, *The English and Scottish Popular Ballads* (1882–98; rpt., New York: Cooper Square Publishers, 1965), vol. 3, p. 391 (no. 173H).

18. Ibid., vol. 2, p. 2 (no. 54A).

19. E.g., cf. Bertrand Bronson, *The Traditional Tunes of the Child Ballads*, vol. 1 (Princeton, N.J.: Princeton University Press, 1959), pp. 106–27.

20. Child, *English and Scottish Popular Ballads*, vol. 2, p. 216 (no. 76A). For references to other American folksongs that contain this fragment, see George L. Kittredge, "Ballads and Songs," *JAF*, 30 (July–Sept., 1917), 304-5; Henry M. Belden, *Ballads and Songs Collected by the Missouri Folk-Lore Society*, 2d ed. (Columbia: University of Missouri Press, 1955), p. 480; *The Frank C. Brown Collection of North Carolina Folklore*, vol. 3, *Folk Songs*, edited by Henry M. Belden and Arthur Palmer Hudson (Durham: Duke University Press, 1952), pp. 299–300.

21. Johnson, *John Henry*, p. 85.

22. Archie Green, "John Henry Depicted," Graphics no. 46, *JEMFQ*, 14 (Autumn, 1978), 126–43.

23. Norm Cohen, "Fiddlin' John Carson—An Appreciation and a Discography," *JEMFQ*, 10 (Winter, 1974), 138–56. See also the manuscript by Gene Wiggins, "Fiddlin' Georgia Crazy: Fiddlin' John Carson, His Real World, and the World of His Songs."

REFERENCES

A. "John Henry, the Steel Driving Man," by W. T. Blankenship. Broadside ballad, probably printed in early 1900s. Obtained by Guy Johnson from Mrs. C. L. Lynn of Rome, Ga., in response to a want ad placed in five selected black newspapers of the South. Printed as frontispiece to Johnson's *John Henry* (Chapel Hill: University of North Carolina Press, 1929). Reproduced in this book.

"John Henry Blues," by Fiddlin' John Carson. Vocal and fiddle. Recorded late Mar., 1924 (OKeh master 8610), in Atlanta, Ga. Released on OKeh 7004 (12″ 78 rpm). This was the first commercial recording; transcribed in this book.

"Death of John Henry (Steel Driving
Man)," by Uncle Dave Macon. Macon,
vocal and banjo; Sam McGee, guitar.
Recorded Apr. 14, 1926
(Brunswick-Balke-Collender master
E2763–64), in New York City. Released
on Vocalion 15320 ca. May, 1926.
Reissued on Vocalion 5096, early 1927;
Brunswick 112, early 1927; Brunswick
BL 59001; Coral (Japan) MH 174:
American Folk Classics; County 502: *A
Collection of Mountain Ballads*;
Historical HLP 8006: *"Wait 'till the
Clouds Roll By"*; Vetco LP 101: *The
Dixie Dewdrop*. Transcribed in
Johnson, *John Henry,* pp. 117–18. Also
transcribed in this book.

"John Henry (the Steel-Driving Man)," in
Josiah Combs, *Folk-Songs du Midi des
États-Unis* (Paris: Presses Universitaires
de France, 1925), pp. 191–93;
reprinted as *Folk-Songs of the Southern
United States,* edited by D. K. Wilgus
(Austin: University of Texas Press,
1967), pp. 164–65. Also published by
John H. Cox, *Folk-Songs of the South*
(1925; rpt., Hatboro, Pa.: Folklore
Associates, 1963), pp. 185–86. Obtained
by Combs from Jesse Green of
Smithsboro, Knott County, Ky., ca.
1909. Possibly the first recovery of a
full "John Henry" text.

"John Henry," by Henry Thomas
(Ragtime Texas). Vocal, guitar, and
reed-pipes. Recorded ca. early July,
1927 (Vocalion master, number not
known), in Chicago. Released on
Vocalion 1094 in Dec., 1927. Reissued
on Origin Jazz Library OJL–3: *Henry
Thomas Sings the Texas Blues*; and
Herwin 209: *"Ragtime Texas" Henry
Thomas*. Probably the first commercial
recording by a black singer.

B. Asbell (discussion only)
Barry (1934) (discussion only)
Bascom, 249
Beard, 178–84
Boette, 55
Boni (1947), 170
Botkin (1944), 230–36
Botkin (1949), 748

Botkin & Harlow, 402
Bradford, *passim*
Brown II, 622, 624; V, 298
Buckley, 9
Burchard (discussion only)
Burton & Manning (1967), 48
Burton & Manning (1969), 27
Bush (1969), 53
Carmer (1934), 225
Carmer (1937), 122–28
Carpenter
Chappell (1933), *passim*
Chappell (1939), 179
Clifton, 34
Cohen (1967), 3 (discussion only)
Cole folios (all printed from the same
plate):
Blue Grass Roy (1933), 46
Hamlins Saddle Pals, 46
KFBI, 46
Play and Sing, 36
Robison (1930), 46
Tiny Texan, 46
WLW, 66
WSM, 6
Comstock, 4–6; 211; 322–36 (from Cox
[1925]); 338–481 (from Chappell [1933])
518–19 (from Carpenter)
Cooke (discussion only)
Courlander, 110–12, 280
Cowboy Songs #73, 19
Cox (1919), 505–20
Cox (1925), 175–88
Curtis-Burlin, 22–27
Davis, A. K., 294
Dickson (discussion only)
Donegan (1956)
Dorson (1966), 155–63
Downes & Siegmeister (1940), 270–73
Downes & Siegmeister (1943), 312
Duncan, 273–74
Emrich (1974), 657–59
Ewen (1947), 139
Fishwick, 77–85
Foley (1941), 27
Foley (1948?)
Folk Sing, 142
Folksong Festival, 22
Fowke & Glazer, 82
Friedman, 383–92
Frothingham, *Adventure*, Apr. 20, 1923,
p. 191

LC AFS:

"Bama" (convict at Mississippi State Penitentiary, Oakly, Miss.)—John A. Lomax MSS

WKFA:

Odell Alvey (fall, 1964)
Helen Arnold (May, 1957)
Viola Burgess family (fall, 1964)
E. N. Caldwell (E. C. Perrow Collection; 1913, N.C.)
Lawrence Cardwell (May, 1948)
Winford Claiborne (May, 1948)
Doyle Dockery (Apr. 22, 1961)
Nancy Frazer (Apr. 4, 1959)
Carl Hornback and the Green River Valley Boys (Feb., 1962)
Ewing Jackson (summer, 1949)
Mrs. Bird Lobb (spring, 1956)
Elvis Glenn Pace (spring, 1948)
Patrick L. Powers (Mar., 1961; parody)
Mrs. Terry Shanklin and Prudie Tillman (May, 1948)
Henry Smith (spring, 1964)
Bobby White (Dec., 1963)

D. Bill Bailey—Mercury 70080
De Ford Bailey—Victor 23336, Victor 23831; Herwin 201: *Sic 'em Dogs on Me*
Bailey Brothers—Rich-R-Tone 449; Rounder 1018: *Have You Forgotten the Bailey Brothers*
Arthur Bell—LC AFS 15; Library of Congress Archive of Folk Song L3: *Afro-American Spirituals, Work Songs, and Ballads*; Library of Congress Archive of Folk Song L50: *The Ballad Hunter*
Birmingham Jug Band—OKeh 8895; RBF RF 6: *The Jug Bands* "Bill Wilson" (related)
Callahan Brothers—Decca 5998; MCA (Japan) 3013–17: *The Fifty-Year History of Country Music*; Old Homestead OHM 90031: *The Callahan Brothers*
Blind Blues Darby—Decca 7816 "Spike Driver"
Richard Dyer-Bennet—Asch 4613; Asch-Stinson 461; Stinson SLP 35: *Ballads*
Tennessee Ernie Ford—Capitol 3421;

Capitol T/DT 700: *This Lusty Land*
William Francis and Richard Sowell —Vocalion 1090; Roots RL–320: *The Great Harmonica Players, Vol. 1* "John Henry Blues"
Fruit Jar Guzzlers—Paramount 3121, Broadway 8199 "Steel Driving Man"
Hank and Velma and the Dakota Ramblers—FM 461-M
(Sid) Harkreader and (Grady) Moore— Paramount 3023, Broadway 8114
Salty Holmes—Decca 24963, Decca 46116
Doc Hopkins—Radio 1411
Mississippi John Hurt—OKeh 8692; Folkways FA 2953 (FP 253): *Anthology of American Folk Music*; Biograph BLP-C4: *1928: His First Recordings* "Spike Driver Blues"
Burl Ives—Columbia 38733, Columbia (Australia) DO 3484; Columbia CL 1459: *Return of the Wayfaring Stranger*
Buffalo Johnson—Rich-R-Tone 1023
Earl Johnson and his Dixie Entertainers —OKeh 45101
Leadbelly (Huddie Ledbetter) and Sonny Terry—Asch 343–3 (in album 343: *Songs by Leadbelly*); Melodisc (England) EPM 7–77 (45 rpm); Melodisc 1187; Stinson SLP 17: *Leadbelly Memorial, Vol. 1*
—Elektra EKL 301–2 (from LC AFS 2503 A2)
Henry Levine and the Dixieland Jazz Group of NBC's Chamber Music Society of Lower Basin Street—Victor 27545 "John Henry Blues"
(Walter) "Furry" Lewis—Vocalion 1474 "John Henry (the Steel Driving Man) Parts 1/2"; Herwin 201: *Sic' em Dogs on Me* (part 1 only); Herwin 205: *Fillin' In Blues* (part 2 only)
Earl McCoy, Alfred Mang, and Clem Garner—Columbia 15622-D "John Henry the Steel Drivin' Man"
Black Bottom McPhail—Vocalion 04220 "John"
(J. E.) Mainer's Mountaineers—Bluebird B-6629, Montgomery Ward 7008;

Victor (Japan) RA 5220: *Blue Grass
Classics*   "John Henry Was a Little
Boy"
—King 550; King LP 666: *Good Old
Mountain Music*
New Orleans Blue Nine—Grey Gull
1263, Paramount 12003 (as by the
Harlem Harmony Kings), Nadsco 1263,
Radiex 1263   "John Henry Blues"
John Jacob Niles—Victor 2051
—Disc album 733
Novelty Blue Boys—Grey Gull 1465,
Grey Gull 7023, Radiex 7023, Madison
1920 (as by the Musical Trio)   "John
Henry Blues"
Riley Puckett—Columbia 15163-D; Old
Timey LP 101: *Old-Time Southern
Dance Music: The String Bands, Vol.
2*   "Darkey's Wail"
Ed Raper and his Carolina Mountain
Boys—Constellation 101
Paul Robeson—Columbia 17381-D;
Columbia M 610: *Spirituals;*
Columbia ML 4105: *Spirituals*
Earl Robinson—General 502, Timely 502;
General G-30
Shelton Brothers and Curly Fox—Decca
5173   "New John Henry Blues"
Spencer Trio—Decca 1873, Brunswick
(England) 02632, Brunswick (France)
A-505170
Ernest V. Stoneman—Edison 51869,
Edison 5194 (cylinder)
Wallace Swann and his Cherokee String
Band—LC AFS 10 (78 rpm); Library of
Congress Archive of Folk Song L2:
*Anglo-American Shanties, Lyric Songs,
Dance Tunes, and Spirituals*
Gid Tanner and his Skillet Lickers
—Columbia 15142-D
Gid Tanner and Riley Puckett—Columbia
15019-D, Silvertone 3262 (as by Gibbs
and Watson), Harmony 5144-H (as by
Gibbs and Watson); Rounder 1005:
*"Hear These New Southern Fiddle and
Guitar Records"*
Henry Thomas—Vocalion 1094; Origin
Jazz Library OJL-3: *Henry Thomas
Sings the Texas Blues*
Hank Thompson—Capitol 2553; Capitol
T-418: *Songs of the Brazos Valley*
Welby Toomey—Gennett 6005,

Silvertone 8146, Silvertone 5002,
Challenge 228 (as by Clarence Adams),
Herwin 75532, Supertone 9245,
Champion 15198 (as by Herb Jennings)
Merle Travis—Capitol 48000 (in album
AD-50: *Folk Songs of the Hills*); Capitol
T 891: *Back Home*; Capitol T/ST 2662:
The Best of Merle Travis; Capitol
(England) T 21010: *21 Years a Country
Singer*
Two Poor Boys (Joe Evans and Arthur
McClain pseudonym)—Perfect 181,
Romeo 5080, Oriole 8080, Conqueror
7876; Origin Jazz Library OJL-14:
Alabama Country, 1927/31   "John
Henry Blues"
Josh White—Keynote 541; Keynote K-125
—Decca A447
—Decca 23653; Decca DL 5082: *Ballads
and Blues*; Decca DL 8665: *Josh White*;
Decca 25627 (45 rpm); Decca DL/DL7
4469: *All Time Hootenanny*
Williamson Brothers and Curry—OKeh
45127; Folkways FA 2951 (FP 251):
*Anthology of American Folk
Music*   "Gonna Die with My
Hammer in My Hand"

E. Rich Amerson—Folkways FE 4471: *Negro
Folk Music of Alabama: Rich Amerson,
Vol. 1*
Ed Ames—RCA Victor LSP-3460: *It's a
Man's World*
Pink Anderson—Riverside RLP 12–611:
American Street Songs
Chet Atkins—RCA Victor LPM/
LSP-2025: *Hum and Strum Along with
Chet Atkins*
—RCA Victor EPA 4343 (45 rpm)
Chet Atkins and Jerry Reed—RCA Victor
CPL2-1014: *In Concert*
Hoyt Axton—World Pacific WP 1601
—Vee-Jay 1601: *Greenback Dollar*
Etta Baker—Tradition TLP 1007:
*Instrumental Music of the Southern
Appalachians*
James "Iron Head" Baker—Library of
Congress Archive of Folk Song L53:
The Ballad Hunter   "Little John
Henry"
Kenny Baker and Josh Graves—Puritan
5005: *Bucktime!*

Chris Barber—Everest 224: *Chris Barber*

Chris Barber and his Jazz Band—Decca (England) ACL 1037: *The Best of Chris Barber*

Harry Belafonte—RCA Victor LPM/ LSP-1022: *Mark Twain & Other Folk Favorites*

—RCA Victor LPC/LSO-6006: *Belafonte at Carnegie Hall*

Leon Bibb—Vanguard VRS 9058: *Tol' My Captain*   "This Is the Hammer That Killed John Henry"

Blind Thomas—Fonotone 611 (78 rpm)

Bluegrass Pals—Shawnee LPS 3: *Best of Bluegrass*

Blue Haze Folk Band—Ranwood 8132: *The Blue Haze Folk Band*

Blue Ridge Mountain Boys—Time 52083/2083: *Hootenanny n' Bluegrass*

Blue Ridge Partners—GHP (West Germany) 901: *Mountain Folks*

Dock Boggs—Folkways FA 2392: *Dock Boggs, Vol. 2*

Border Mountain Boys—Homestead 101: *Bluegrass on the Mountain*   "John Henry's Legend"

Bray Brothers and Red Cravens —Rounder 0053: *Prairie Bluegrass*

Brazos Valley Boys—Dot 10004: *The Brazos Valley Boys*

Lucius Bridges, Blind Snooks Eaglin, and Percy Randolph—Folk Lyric FL 107: *Possum up a Simmon Tree*

Marty Brill—Mercury MG 20178: *The Roving Balladeer*

Big Bill Broonzy—Mercury MG 20822/SR 60822: *Big Bill Broonzy Memorial*; Emarcy MG 26034: *Folk Blues*; Emarcy EM 36052: *Jazz Giants, Vol. 4, Folk Blues*

—Folkways FS 3864 (FP 86/4): *Folksongs and Blues with Pete Seeger and Big Bill Broonzy*

—Folkways FA 2328: *Big Bill Broonzy Sings Folk Songs*

—Verve MGV-3000-5: *The Big Bill Broonzy Story*; Verve MGV-3003: *Big Bill Broonzy's Last Session*

—Storyville (Denmark) SLP 154: *Portraits in Blues, Vol. 2*

—Storyville SEP 383

—Vogue (France) 118 (45 rpm); Vogue LDM 30037: *Big Bill Blues*; Vogue LD 524

—Vogue CLVLX 272: *Big Bill Broonzy*

—Crescendo GNPS 10004: *Feelin' Low Down*

—Crescendo GNPS 10009: *Lonesome Road Blues*; Scepter M/S 529: *The Blues*

—Joker SM 3608: *Blues/Folk Songs/ Ballads*

—DJM DJLMD 8009: *All Them Blues*

Buster Brown—Fire 1020 (45 and 78 rpm); Fire FLP 102

Don Brown and the Ozark Mountain Trio—K-Ark 6027: *Don Brown Live*

Fleming Brown—Folk-Legacy FSI-4: *Fleming Brown*

Gabriel Brown, Rochelle French, and John French—Flyright-Matchbox SDM 257: *Out in the Cold Again: Library of Congress Series, Vol. 3* (from LC AFS 335)

Hylo Brown—Rural Rhythm RR 176: *Hylo Brown*   "Little John Henry"

—Capitol F-4035 (45 rpm); CMH (West Germany) 301: *Four Sessions*

—Jessup Michigan Bluegrass MB 134: *Hylo Brown Sings His Bluegrass Hits*

Walt Brown—Warner Brothers W/WS-1568: *Walt Brown Show*

Bruce Buckley—Folkways FA 2025 (FP 23-2): *Ohio Valley Ballads*

Caffrey Family—TCAF 1075: *Country Thoughts*

James Campbell and his Nashville Street Band—Arhoolie F 1015: *Blind James Campbell*

Johnny Cash—Columbia CL-1930/ CS-8370: *Blood Sweat and Tears*; Philips (England) CBS-BPG-62015: *Blood Sweat and Tears*; Columbia GP 29: *The World of Johnny Cash*   "The Legend of John Henry's Hammer"

Bob Chapman—Scholastic CC-0630 (7″ LP): *Train Ballads*

Chicago String Band (Carl Martin and group)—Testament T-2220: *The Chicago String Band*

William Clauson—Capitol T-10158: *A William Clauson Concert*

—RCA Victor LPM 1286: *Folk Songs*

Paul Clayton—Folkways FG 3571:
Dulcimer Songs and Solos

Bill Clifton—Hillbilly (Switzerland)
HRS-001: *Wanderin'*

Bill Clifton and Paul Clayton—Bear
Family (West Germany) 15001: *A
Bluegrass Session 1952*

Fred Cockerham—songsheet in *Sing
Out!*, 21 (Nov.-Dec., 1972)

Michael Cooney—Folk-Legacy FSI-35:
The Cheese Stands Alone

Red Cravens and the Bray Brothers
—Five String 101 (45 rpm)

Kyle Creed and Fred Cockerham
—County 701: *Clawhammer Banjo*

Grace Creswell—Rebel RRLP 3064:
Grace Creswell

Crook Brothers—Starday SLP 182: *Opry
Old Timers*; Starday SLP 190: *Country
Music Hall of Fame, Vol. 2*

Dick Dale—Accent 5033: *Coast to Coast*

Jean Davis—Traditional 5117: *Old
Traditions*

Hazel Dickens and Alice Foster
—Folkways FTS 31034: *Won't
You Come and Sing for Me?*

Little Jimmy Dickens—Columbia CL
1478/CS 8269; Columbia CWS 1:
Country Music Festival

Lonnie Donegan—London 1650 (78 rpm),
London 45–1650 (45 rpm)

Dave Dudley—Mercury MG 20899/SR
60899: *Songs about the Working Man*
—Design DLP-620: *Country Music Hall
of Fame*

Richard Dyer-Bennet—Dyer-Bennet 5:
Richard Dyer-Bennet
—Archive of Folk Music AFM 203:
Richard Dyer-Bennet
—Remington RLP-199-34: *Folk Songs*

Easy Riders—Columbia CL 1272;
Columbia Special Products CSP 123

Duane Eddy—Jamboree J/ST-3011:
Duane Eddy Plays Songs of Heritage;
Jamboree J/ST-3021: *Million Dollars
Worth of Twang*

Jimmy Edmonds—Kanawha 319

Joe Edwards—Delmarti 102565
(demonstration album, no title)

Jack Elliott—Everest Archive of Folk
Music AFM/FS 210: *Jack Elliot*
[*sic*]   "Death of John Henry"

Bill Emerson and his Virginia
Mountaineers—Coronet CX-118: *Banjo
Pickin' n' Hot Fiddlin'*   "Fingers on
Fire"

Sam Eskin—Cook 1020: *Songs of All
Times*

John Fahey—Takoma C 1002: *Blind Joe
Death*
—Takoma C 1003: *Death Chants,
Breakdowns, & Military Waltzes*

Raymond Fairchild—Rural Rhythm
RR-256: *King of the Smokey Mt. Banjo
Players*

Frances Faye—Bethlehem BCP-6017:
Frances Faye Sings Folk Songs

Lester Flatt, Earl Scruggs, and the Foggy
Mountain Boys—Columbia CL 1564)CS
8364 and LE 10043: *Foggy Mountain
Banjo*; Columbia GP-30: *20 All-Time
Great Recordings in a Deluxe 2-Record
Set*; Columbia KG 31964: *The World of
Flatt and Scruggs*

Orval Fochtman—Weiser 19884: *National
Oldtime Fiddlers' Folk Music Contest
and Festival* (1964)

Folk Singers of Washington Square —
Continental CLP-4010: *The Folk Singers
of Washington Square*   "Brooklyn
John Henry"

Folksmiths—Folkways FA 2407: *We've
Got Some Singing to Do*

Frosty Mountain Boys—Rural Rhythm
RRFM-159: *Frosty Mountain Boys*

Jesse Fuller—Good Time Jazz
12051/S10051: *San Francisco Bay Blues*
—World Song EG-10-027: *Working on
the Railroad*; World Song WS-1
—Decca (England) LAG 574
—Topic (England) 12T134: *Move On
Down the Line* (part of "Railroad
Worksong")

Marty Garner—Stoneway STY-167: *On
the Rural Route*

Terry Gibbs—Time 52105/S 2105:
Hootenanny My Way

Bob Gibson—Riverside RLP 12-806: *I
Come for to Sing*
—Elektra EKL/EKS 7-197: *Yes I See*

Bob Gibson and Bob Camp—EKL/EKS
7-207: *Bob Gibson and Bob Camp at
the Gate of Horn*

Joe Glazer—Collector 1918: *Joe Glazer
Sings Labor Songs*

Arvella Gray—Heritage HLP 1004 "Railroad Songs and John Henry"
—Birch 60091: *The Singing Drifter*
—Gray 14

John Greenway—Wattle (Australia) C 1 (10″ LP): *Workin' On a Buildin'*

Bob Grossman—Elektra EKL-215: *Bob Grossman* "Legend of John Henry"

Woody Guthrie—Tradition 2058: *The Legendary Woody Guthrie—In Memoriam*
—Sine Qua Non 102: *An Anthology of Folk Music*

Woody Guthrie and Cisco Houston —Stinson 627; Stinson SLP 44: *Folk Songs, Vol. 1*; Everest Archive of Folk Music FS-204: *Woody Guthrie*
—Folkways FA 2483: *Woody Guthrie Sings Folk Songs with &c.*
—Olympic 7107: *The Immortal Woody Guthrie*

Ronnie Hawkins—R/SR 25120: *Folk Ballads of Ronnie Hawkins*

Walter Haynes—Mercury MG 20715/SR 60715: *Steel Guitar Sounds*

Charles Haywood—Charles Haywood (no number): *Program of Folk Songs from the Library of Marian and Allan Hancock*

Doc Hopkins—Birch 1945: *Doc Hopkins*

Shakey Horton—Argo 4037: *Soul of Blues Harmonica*

Cisco Houston—Verve/Folkways FV/FVS 9002: *Passing Through*

Frank Hovington—Rounder 2017: *Lonesome Road Blues*

Peg Leg Howell—Testament T-2204: *The Legendary Peg Leg Howell*

Max Hunter—Folk-Legacy FSA-11: *Max Hunter of Springfield, Missouri*

Mississippi John Hurt—Piedmont PLP 13157: *Folksongs and Blues* "Spike Driver Blues"
—Vanguard VRS 9148/VSD 79148: *Evening Concerts at Newport* "Spike Driver Blues"
—Vanguard VRS 9220/VSD 79220: *Mississippi John Hurt Today* "Spike Driver Blues"

Burl Ives—Columbia CL 1459: *Return of the Wayfaring Stranger*
—Encyclopaedia Britannica Films EBF 6: *Songs of Expanding America*
—Decca DL 8125: *Men*; Decca ED-2237 (EP): *Men*; Decca DXB/DXSB7-167: *Best of Burl Ives*; Brunswick (England) OE 9202 (EP); Ace of Hearts (England) AH 53: *Men*; Pickwick SPC-3393: *The Best of Burl Ives*

Carl Jackson—Capitol ST 11166: *Banjo Player* "James Louis Henry (Brother of John)"

Clarence Jackson, Charles Frye, Johnny Slack, and Bill Horney—Rural Rhythm RR-132: *Blue Grass Special*

John Jackson—Arhoolie 1025: *Blues and Country Dance Tunes from Virginia*

Tommy Jackson—Dot DLP 3580/25580: *Square Dances Played by Tommy Jackson*

Tommy Jarrell—County 748: *Tommy Jarrell's Banjo Album*
—Mountain 310: *Joke on the Puppy*

Snuffy Jenkins—Folkways FA 2314: *American Banjo: Tunes & Songs in Scruggs Style*

Doug Jernigan—Flying Fish FF 024: *Roadside Rag*

Henry Johnson—Trix 3304: *The Union County Flash!* (cante fable)

Eddie Lee Jones—Testament T-2224: *Yonder Go That Old Black Dog*

Tommy Jones—Ovation QD-14-20: *Tommy's Place*

Grandpa Jones (Louis Marshall Jones) —Monument SLP 18138: *Grandpa Live*; Harmony H31396: *Live*

Buell Kazee—Folkways FS 3810: *Buell Kazee Sings and Plays*

Kentucky Colonels—World Pacific WP/WPS-1821: *Appalachian Swing!*; World Pacific WPS-21898: *Bluegrass Special*

Fiddlin' Van Kidwell—Vetco LP 506: *Midnight Ride*

Pete Kirby. *See* Bashful Brother Oswald

Michael La Rue, Alex Foster, and the Drinking Gourds—Counterpoint CPT 566: *Follow the Drinking Gourd*; Esoteric ES-560

Laurel River Valley Boys—Judson J-3031: *Music for Moonshiners*; Riverside RLP 7504/97504: *Dance All Night with a Bottle in Your Hand*

Leadbelly (Huddie Ledbetter)—Folkways

FC 7533: *Negro Folk Songs for Young People*

—Playboy PB 119: *Leadbelly*

—Folkways FT 31030 S: *Shout On*; Xtra (England) 1017: *Shout On*

—Folkways FA 2941 (FP 241): *Leadbelly's Last Session, Vol. 1*

Leadbelly, Sonny Terry, and Brownie McGhee—Folkways FJ 2801 (FP 53): *Jazz, Vol. 1*

Jerry Lee Lewis—Sun 344 (45 rpm); Sun 121: *Old Tyme Country Music*

Ramsey Lewis Trio—Mercury MG-20536/SR-60213: *Down to Earth*

Walter "Furry" Lewis—Folkways FS 3823: *Furry Lewis*; Folkways FA 2691-D: *Music Down Home*; RBF RF202: *The Rural Blues*

—Asch 101: *The Blues*

—ASP 1: *At Home with Friends*

—Blue Star 80 602: *House of the Blues, Vol. 2: Fourth and Beale*

—Prestige Bluesville 1036: *Back on My Feet Again*; Prestige 7810: *Back on My Feet Again*; Fantasy 24703: *Shake 'em on Down*

—Sire SES 97015: *Stars of the 1969–1970 Memphis Country Blues Festival*

—Matchbox (England) SDR 190/Roots (Germany) SL 505: *Furry Lewis in Memphis*

—Barclay (France) 920.352T: *Beale Street Blues*

—Ampex A10140: *Live at the Gaslight at the Au Go Go* [sic]

Lilly Brothers—Event E-4272 (45 rpm); County 729: *Lilly Brothers and Don Stover*

Limelighters—RCA Victor LPM/LSP 2907: *The Limelighters*

—Elektra EKL/EKS7 180: *The Limelighters*; Legacy 113: *Their First Historic Album*

Jack Little—RCA Victor LPM/LSP 2840: *Porter Wagoner—In Person*

Living Guitars—RCA Camden ADL2-0292: *Bluegrass Special*

Richard Lockmiller and Jim Connor—Folklore (England) F/LEUT 5

Alan Lomax—Tradition TLP 1029: *Texas Folksongs* "My Little John Henry"

John Lomax, Jr.—Folkways FG 3508: *John A. Lomax, Jr. Sings American Folksongs*

Lost and Found—Outlet STLP-1006: *The Second Time Around* "John Henry Jr." (parody)

Bascom Lamar Lunsford—Riverside RLP 12-645: *Minstrel of the Appalachians*

Arthur Lyman—Hifi 1004: *Percussion Spectacular*

Bill McAdoo—Folkways FA 2448: *Bill McAdoo Sings*

Jim McCall—Vetco 3010: *"Pickin' and Singin'"*

Ed McCurdy—Riverside RLP 1419: *Everybody Sing*; Riverside RLP 12-601: *The Ballad Record*

—Prestige International 13002: *The Best of Ed McCurdy*

—Manhattan SR 044: *Canadian Folk Songs*

Charlie McCoy—Monument KZ 32215: *Good Time Charlie's Got the Blues*; Monument 25 7-8576 (45 rpm)

Fred McDowell—Biograph BLP 12017: *When I Lay My Burden Down*

—Milestone 93003: *Long Way from Home*

—Oblivion OD 1: *Live in New York*

Fred McDowell and Johnny Woods —Revival RVS 1001 and Rounder 2007: *Fred McDowell and Johnny Woods*

Bob McGhee—Sonora 147–171

Brownie McGhee and Sonny Terry —Choice LP 100; Sound of America 2001

—Folkways FW 2327: *Brownie McGhee and Sonny Terry Sing*; Verve/Folkways FTS 31024: *Preachin' the Blues*; Verve/Folkways FVS 9019; Topic (England) 12T29: *Brownie McGhee and Sonny Terry*

Uncle Dave Macon—Davis Unlimited DU-TFS 101: *At Home*

Maggie Valley Boys—Rural Rhythm RR 170: *Maggie Valley Boys*

J. E. Mainer—Blue Grass Special EP 601 (45 rpm)

Benny Martin—CMH 1776: *200 Years of American Heritage in Song*

Jimmy Martin—Decca DL/DL7 4643 and MCA 79: *Sunny Side of the Mountain*

Allison Mathis and Jessie Stroller
—Flyright Matchbox SDM 250
Memphis Slim (Peter Chatman)—United
Artists UAL 3137/UAS 6137: *Broken
Soul Blues*
—Candid CM 8024; Barnaby ZG 31291:
Bad Luck and Troubles
—Folkways FG 3535: *Memphis Slim and
the Real Honky Tonk*
Memphis Slim and Willie Dixon
—Folkways FA 2385: *Songs by
Memphis Slim & Willie Dixon*
—Verve V-3007: *The Blues Every Which
Way*
Merrill Jay Singers—Cabot CAB 503:
Songs of the Railroad
Paul, Vernon, and Wade Miles—Library
of Congress LBC 3: *Dance Music:
Breakdowns & Waltzes* (from LC AFS
4075)
Bill Monroe and his Bluegrass Boys—
Decca 45-31540 (45 rpm); Vocalion
VL 3702/73702: *Bill Monroe Sings
Country Songs* "New John Henry
Blues"
Charlie Monroe—Pine Tree PTSLP 528:
Live at Lake Norman Music Hall
Charlie Moore—Vetco 3011: *Charlie
Moore Sings Good Bluegrass*
"When John Henry Was a Little Boy"
Charlie Moore and Bill Napier—King
5050 (45 rpm)
—King LP 1021
David and John Morris—Kidtown 1FR69:
Music As We Learned It
Mountaineers—Cumberland SRC 69501:
Bluegrass Banjo Pickin'
Mountain Ramblers—Atlantic SD-1347:
Blue Ridge Mountain Music
Frank Necessary and the Stone Mountain
Boys—Old Homestead OHS 90010:
Cimarron Bluegrass
New Christy Minstrels—Columbia CL
2187/CS 8987: *Land of Giants*
"John Henry and the Steam Drill"
New Lost City Ramblers—Folkways FA
2395: *The New Lost City Ramblers,
Vol. 5*
New River Boys—Mad Bag MB 288–289:
Country Blue Grass Jamboree
Odetta—Fantasy 3-15: *The Tin Angel
Presents Odetta and Larry*; Fantasy

3252: *Odetta and Larry*; Fantasy 8345:
Odetta
—Vanguard VRS 9076/VSD 2072: *Odetta
at Carnegie Hall*; Vanguard VSD 17/18:
Greatest Folksingers of the Sixties;
Vanguard 43/44: *The Essential Odetta*
Milt Okun—Baton BL 1203: *America's
Best Loved Folk Songs*
Old Timey String Band—Blue Horizon
(Sweden) LP 500: *Tennessee
Travelers/Old Timey String Band*
Osborne Brothers—MGM E/SE 4090:
Bluegrass Instrumentals "John
Henry Blues"
Harry Oster—Folk Lyric LFS A2:
Louisiana Folksong Jamboree
Bashful Brother Oswald (Pete Kirby)
—Tennessee NR 4990: *Banjo & Dobro*
"Old John Henry"
—Rounder 0041: *That's Country*
Tom Paley—Elektra EKL-217: *Folk Banjo
Styles*
Peg Leg Sam (Arthur Jackson)—Flyright
(England) LP 507–508: *The Last
Medicine Show*
Peg Leg Sam and Louisiana Red—Blue
Labor BL105: *Going Train Blues*
George Pegram—Folkways FA 2435:
Galax Old Fiddlers' Convention
—Union Grove SS-1: *String Music*
—Rounder 0001: *George Pegram*
George Pegram and Walter Parham
—Riverside RLP 12–610: *Banjo Songs
from the Southern Mountains*
Virgil Perkins and Jack Sims—Folkways
FA 2610: *American Skiffle Bands*;
Folkways FE 4530: *Folk Music U.S.A.*
John Perry and group—Heritage 4: *Old
Time Hoedown Instrumentals*
Brock Peters—United Artists UAL 3062:
At the Village Gate "John Henry
Dead"
Cora Phillips—Physical PR 12–001: *Music
from the Hills of Caldwell County*
Billie Pierce, De De Pierce, Brother
Randolph, and Lucius Bridges—Folk
Lyric FL 110: *New Orleans Jazz*;
Arhoolie 2016: *New Orleans Music*
Pete Pike—Rebel 1473
Pine River Boys—Mountain 305:
Hoedown Time
Pinetop Slim—Kent KST 9004: *Anthology*

of the Blues/*Blues from the Deep*
South; Colonial 106

Fiddlin' Mutt Poston and the Farm
Hands—Rural Rhythm RRFT-157:
Hoedown, Vol. 7

Billy Preston—A & M 3507: *I Wrote a*
Simple Song

Wayne Raney—Starday SEP 133 (45
rpm); Rimrock EP 296 (45 rpm)   "John
Henry Blues"

Jerry Reed—RCA Victor LSP-3978:
Nashville Underground

—RCA Victor CPL2-1014: *In Concert*

—RCA Camden ACL1-0331: *Tupelo*
Mississippi Flash

John Renbourn—Reprise 2-6482: *John*
Renbourn; Transatlantic (England) TRA
135

Tony Rice—King Bluegrass KB 529

Larry Richardson, Red Barker, and the
Blue Ridge Boys—County 702: *Larry*
Richardson, Red Barker, and the Blue
Ridge Boys

Jimmy Riddle—Cumberland SRC 69511:
Country Harmonica

Rock City Singers—Cumberland MGS
29519/SRC 69519: *Classics*

Jimmie Rodgers—Dot 25496: *Jimmie*
Rodgers in Folk Concert

Will Rodgers, Jr., and Tom Scott—Judson
J 3013: *Great American Folk Heroes*

Art Rosenbaum—Kicking Mule KM 108:
Five String Banjo

Rube Rubin and the Westerners—Crown
CLP 5477

Carl Sandburg—Caedmon TC 2025: *Carl*
Sandburg Sings His American
Songbag   "If I Die a Railroad Man"

Booker T. Sapps, Roger Matthews, and
Willy Flowers—Flyright Matchbox
SDM 258: *Boot That Thing: Library of*
Congress Series, Vol. 4 (from LC AFS
371 B)

Tracy and Eloise Schwarz—Folk Variety
(West Germany) FV 12007: *Home*
among the Hills

Tom Scott—Signature Album S-5: *Sing of*
America; Coral CRL 56056: *Sing of*
America

Mike Seeger—Folkways FH 5273: *Tipple*
Loom & Rail   "Death of John
Henry"

Pete Seeger—Capitol W 2172: *Folk Songs*
by Pete Seeger

—Capitol DT 2718: *Pete Seeger*

—Columbia CL 1668/CS 8468: *Story*
Songs; Harmony HS 11337: *"John*
Henry" & Other Folk Favorites

—Columbia CL 2122/CS 8922: *All Star*
Hootenanny

—Columbia 32–16–0266: *3 Saints, 4*
Sinners, and 6 Other People

—Folkways FA 2319: *American Ballads*

—Folkways FN 2513: *Sing Out!*
Hootenanny

Brother John Sellers—Vanguard VRS
9036: *Brother John Sellers Sings Blues*
and Folk Songs

Shady Mountain Ramblers—Heritage 2:
Old Time Music from the Blue Ridge
Mountains

Ernie Sheldon and the Villagers
—Columbia CL 1515/CS 8315: *The Big*
Men—Bold and Bad

Jerry Shook—Somerset 18400

Virgil Shouse, Mike Lilly, and Wendy
Miller—Old Homestead OHS 80009:
Bluegrass

Jimmie Skinner—Decca 29179 (45 rpm);
Decca DL 4132: *Country Singer*
"John Henry and the Water Boy"

—Vetco 3027: *Jimmie Skinner Sings*
Bluegrass, Vol. 2

Bill Smith Quartet—Contemporary
M3591/S7591: *Folk Jazz*

Glen Smith—County 757: *Clawhammer*
Banjo, Vol. 3

Pinetop Smith—Colonial 106 (45 rpm);
Kent KST 9004: *Anthology of the*
Blues: Blues from the Deep South

Kilby Snow—Folkways FA 2365:
Mountain Music Played on the
Autoharp

Jo Stafford—Columbia CL 1339/CS 8139:
Ballad of the Blues

I. D. Stamper—June Appal 010: *Red*
Wing

Ralph Stanley—Jalyn JLP 118: *Old Time*
Music of Ralph Stanley

—Rebel SLP 1530: *A Man and His Music*

Stoneman Family—Folkways FA 2315:
Old-Time Tunes of the South

Win Stracke—Golden GLP 31: *Golden*
Treasury of Songs America Sings

Stringbean (Dave Akeman)—Starday SLP
215: *A Salute to Uncle Dave Macon*;
Nashville NLP 2100: *Hee Haw Corn
Shucker*

Joe Stuart—Atteiram API-L-1514: *Sittin'
on Top of the World*

Sykes Brothers—Laurel Leaf 2401314:
Twisting the Strings

Jimmie Tarlton—Testament T-3302: *Steel
Guitar Rag*

Earl Taylor and his Stoney Mountain
Boys—United Artists UAL 3049: *Folk
Songs from the Blue Grass*

Pick Temple—RCA "X" LXA-3022: *Folk
Songs of the People*

Sonny Terry—Riverside RLP 12-644:
Sonny Terry and His Mouth-Harp;
Washington WLP 702: *Talkin' 'bout the
Blues*

—Elektra EKL 14: *Folk Blues Sung by
Sonny Terry*

—Vanguard VRS 8523/4: *From Spirituals
to Swing* "The New John Henry"

Sonny Terry and Bull City Red—
Vanguard VRS 8523/4: *Spirituals to
Swing*

Sonny Terry and Brownie McGhee—
Fantasy 3317: *Shouts and Blues*

—Tomato TOM 2-7003: *A Tribute to
Leadbelly*

Sonny Terry and Pete Seeger—Verve
FV/FVS 9010: *Gettogether*

Hank Thompson—Capitol T/ST 1632:
Hank Thompson at the Golden Nugget

Hank Thompson's Brazos Valley Boys
—Warner Brothers W/WS 1679: *Hank
Thompson's Brazos Valley Boys*

Three from Nod—International M-103

Merle Travis—Shasta LP 517: *The Way
They Were Back When*

—Shasta LP 523: *The Guitar Player*

Happy Traum—Kicking Mule SNKF 111:
Relax Your Mind

Charles Trent—Smash MGS 27002/SRS
67002: *Sound of a Blue Grass Banjo*

Lucille Turner—Colonial C 17001

Willie Turner—Folkways FE 4474 (FP
474): *Negro Music of Alabama, Vol. 6*

Uncle Josh and Hoss Linneman—Starday
SLP 340: *That Dobro Sound's Goin'
'round*; Starday SEP 237 "John
Henry Breakdown"

Dave Van Ronk—Folkways FA 2383:
Dave Van Ronk Sings "Spike
Driver's Moan"

—Folkways FS 3818: *Dave Van Ronk
Sings Ballads, Blues, and a Spiritual*;
Verve/Folkways FV 9017: *Gambler's
Blues*

Howard Wallace—Jewel LPS 186:
Old-Time 5-String Banjo

Wandering Five—Somerset SF-18600:
We're Pickin' and Singin' Folk Songs

Fields Ward, Dr. W. P. Davis, and the
Virginia Bogtrotters—Biograph
RC-6003: *The Original Bogtrotters,
1937–1942* (from LC AFS 1362 B)

Washboard Band—Folkways FA 2201 (10″
LP): *The Washboard Band*

Doc Watson—Vanguard VSD 9/10: *Doc
Watson on Stage* "Spike Driver
Blues"

—Folkways FA 2426: *Jean Ritchie and
Doc Watson at Folk City* "Spike
Driver Blues"

—United Artists LA 601: *Doc and the
Boys* "Spikedriver Blues"

Bradley Wayne—Vee Jay VJLP 1079: *12
String Guitar Nanny*

Guitar Welch, Hogman Maxey, and Andy
Mosely—Louisiana Folklore Society
LFS A-5: *Prison Work Songs Recorded
in the Louisiana State Prison at Angola,
Louisiana*

Sally Wells—Pik 10 (45 rpm)

Billy Edd Wheeler and the Bluegrass
Singers—Monitor MF 367: *Billy Edd
and Bluegrass Too*

Josh White—Elektra EKL 123: *25th
Anniversary Album*; Elektra 701: *The
Story of John Henry and Ballads, Blues
and Other Stories*; Elektra EKS 75008;
The Best of Josh White

—Mercury MG 25014: *Strange Fruit*

—Crestview CRV/CRS7: *Hootenanny*

Red White and the Dixie Bluegrass
Band—Rural Rhythm RR-RW-172: *Red
White and the Dixie Blue Grass Band*

Paul Wiley—Voyager VHLP 302: *Comin'
round the Mountain*

Bill Williams—Blue Goose 2003: *Low and
Lonesome*

Connie Williams—Testament T-2225:
Blind Connie Williams

Wilson Brothers, Larry, and Joanna
　　—MRC MRLP 1093: *Stand Tall in
　　Bluegrass*
Stan Wilson—Cavalier CAV 6002;
　　Cavalier CAV 5001
George Winn—Major MRLP-2105: *Last
　　Train through (?Lunnburg) County*
Winnie Winston—Elektra EKL-276: *Old
　　Time Banjo Project*
Paul Winter—Columbia CL-2155/
　　CS-8955: *Jazz Meets the Folk Song*
Chubby Wise—Stoneway STY 146:
　　Sincerely Yours . . . ; Stoneway STY
　　157: *Grassy Fiddle*; Stoneway 1136 (45
　　rpm)
Willie Wright—Concert-Disc CS-45: *I
　　Sing Folk Songs*
Eldee Young—Argo 699: *Just for Kicks*
Martin Young and Corbett Grigsby
　　—Folkways FA 2317: *Mountain Music
　　of Kentucky*

F.　GORDON COLLECTION (Ga.):
　　A367 (MS 137)—A. Wilson
　　A372 (MS 140)—H. B. Oliver

　　GORDON COLLECTION (N.C.):
　　A7, A8 (MS 5)—Fred J. Lewey
　　A60 (MS 94)—G. S. Robinson
　　A182 (MS 271)—Henry Smith

　　LC AFS:

Joseph Aiken—AFS 13033 A2
Chester Allen and Joe Sharp—AFS 2943
　　A2 & B1
Richard Amerson—AFS 1305 B2
—AFS 4045 A2 & B1
Thomas Anderson—AFS 3636 A1 & A2
—AFS 3635 B2　　"John Henry Was a
　　Very Small Boy"
Ethel Arp—AFS 15070 A17
M. Asher—AFS 1519 A2
Bill Atkins—AFS 1989 B1 (10″)
William C. Bailey—AFS 13719-9
James "Iron Head" Baker—AFS 202 A1
　　"Little John Henry"
—AFS 224 B1　　"Little John Henry"
—AFS 1851 A3, B1, B2　　"Little John
　　Henry"
—AFS 1853 B　　"Little John Henry"
Leonard Bartlett and band—AFS 14768-2
Arthur Bell—AFS 2668 B1
Gabriel Brown—AFS 355 A & B

Joe Brown and Lonnie Thomas—AFS
　　2710 B1
Smith Brown—AFS 15067 B9
Luther Bryant—AFS 13718 B6
Ed Burkes—AFS 12045 B35
Harrison Burnette—AFS 12035 B
Jimmie Campbell—AFS 17021-6
Julius Clemens—AFS 689 A
Fred Cockerham—AFS 14161 A4
Calvin Cole—AFS 15060-16
Farmer Collett—AFS 1429 A2 & B1
Reese Crenshaw—AFS 259 A2
Rufus Crisp—AFS 8498I A2　　"Big John
　　Henry"
—AFS 8527 B　　"Steel Drivin' John
　　Henry"
Clovest Crotts—AFS 15067 A19
Bailey Dansley—AFS 13144 A1
John Davis—AFS 313 A1
—AFS 314 A1
—AFS 315 B1
Uncle Alec Dunford—AFS 1363 A3
Joe Edwards—AFS 743 A2
Leroy Gardner—AFS 11891 B
Hettie Godfrey—AFS 4049 B5
Charles Griffin—AFS 238 A
Vera Hall—AFS 1320 A2
Sherman Hammons—AFS 15545-1
　　"John Henry Blues"
Austin Harmon—AFS 2916 B2, 2917 A1
Gus Harper and group—AFS 883 B
Harold B. Hazelhurst—AFS 3143 A2
Sid Hemphill and his band—AFS 6673
　　A6
Jim Henry—AFS 743 A1
Aunt Molly Jackson—AFS 828 B3
—AFS 2551 A1
John Henry Jackson and Norman
　　Smith—AFS 3088 A2 & B1
Tommy Jarrell—AFS 14162-1
DeWitt "Snuffy" Jenkins—AFS 17109-26
Charley Jones—AFS 238 A
Albert Josey—AFS 2234 B3
Vera Kilgore—AFS 2939 A1
Huddie "Leadbelly" Ledbetter—AFS
　　2503 A2　　"Little John Henry"
—AFS 2503 B
—AFS 2504 A
L. M. Ledford—AFS 15571 A10
Addie Leffew—AFS 15062 B15
Bascom Lamar Lunsford—AFS 1814 A1
　　& A2
—AFS 3167 B1

—AFS 14768-11
—AFS 15054 B21
Jonesie Mack, Nick Robinson, and James Mack—AFS 1047 A2
Wade Mainer—AFS 4435 A2
—AFS 4490 A3
Allison Mathis—AFS 5158 B1
J. Paul Miles—AFS 4075 B2
Chapman J. Milling—AFS 3789 B
J. M. Mullins—AFS 1595 A1
David Northerton—AFS 13128 B13
J. Owens—AFS 730 A
Silas Pendleton—AFS 9059 A2
Sampson Pittman—AFS 4045 A2 & B1
Winnie Prater—AFS 1593 A3 & B1
Rufus Quesenberry—AFS 15053 B11
George Roark—AFS 1997 A
Booker T. Sapps, R. G. Matthews, and Willy Flowers—AFS 371 B

Ethridge Scott—AFS 14164 B24
—AFS 14650 B25
Glenn Smith—AFS 15053 A24
Hobart Smith—AFS 6742 A1 & A2
Pete Steele—AFS 1711 A2
Bernard Steffen and Charles Pollock —AFS 3304 A1
George Stoneman—AFS 4937 A3
David Thompson—AFS 14207 A4, A16, & B3
Fields Ward—AFS 4085 A1
Wade Ward—AFS 15055 A15
Oscar Wright—AFS 14093 A31
Group of Negro convicts—AFS 1865 A2
Group of Negro convicts—AFS 1867 B1
Group of Negro prisoners—AFS 174 B3
Skyline farms group—AFS 1629 A
Unidentified singer—John A. Lomax cylinder 13

WEST VIRGINIA UNIVERSITY
YEARS OF RESEARCH BY
LOUIS WATSON CHAPPELL
ENGLISH PROFESSOR AT
WEST VIRGINIA UNIVERSITY,
ESTABLISHED THE FACTUAL BASIS
OF THE JOHN HENRY LEGEND.
THIS PLAQUE HONORS PROFESSOR
CHAPPELL AND RECOGNIZES THE
WAYS IN WHICH UNIVERSITY
RESEARCH CONTRIBUTES TO MAN'S
UNDERSTANDING AND WELL-BEING.

Plaque honoring Louis Chappell. Courtesy of Archie Green.

Jim Fisk

JIM FISKE

*Stanzas 1 and 2 use this melody; the third stanza is different, as transcribed.
**The guitar chord is difficult to discern; the fiddle line implies this chord.

I'll sing of a man who's now dead in his grave,
A good man as ever was born;
Jim Fiske he was called, and his money he gave
To the outcast, the poor and forlorn.

We all knew he loved both women and wine,
But his heart it was right, I am sure;
Though he lived like a prince in his palace so fine,
Yet he never went back on the poor.

If a man was in trouble, Fiske helped him along,
He strove to do right, though he may have done wrong;
Though he lived like a prince in his palace so fine,
Yet he never went back on the poor.

Frank Luther

The backdrop for this vignette of class-conscious pulpit pounding is the vast canvas of the world of American finance in the 1870s. Two financial scoundrels swaggered back and forth before that canvas: Jay Gould and James Fisk. In a rash of brazen manipulations, they brought many speculators and financiers to ruin; their most audacious maneuver resulted from Gould's dream to corner the entire United States gold supply, and it ended in the panic of Black Friday, September 24, 1869. Involved in many of Fisk's and Gould's schemes was the Erie Railroad, which they gained control of in 1868. The two men had no interest in the railroad per se, but used it to further their shady operations on the stock market. Their attitude toward the Erie was neatly summarized in a little ditty written by a local wag and supposedly sung by Gould:

> O Jimmy Fisk, my Jo, Jim,
> We'll never, never weary
> Of squeezing every penny from
> The stockholders of Erie.
>
> And if by chance, Jim,
> We to the gallows go,
> We'll sleep together at the foot,
> O Jimmy Fisk, my Jo.[1]

The Erie could ill afford the treatment it received at the hands of Fisk and Gould and their cronies; rails, stock, and equipment were all in disgraceful condition at the time. (For the details of these events, see any of several available histories and biographies.)

Although they colluded in their Wall Street chicanery, Gould and Fisk were completely opposite in temperament. Gould was reserved, quiet, introverted, dyspeptic; he never seemed to gain any enjoyment from his millions—other than the pleasure of acquisition. Jubilee Jim Fisk, Prince of the Erie, on the other hand, was flashy, outgoing, and eager for publicity. And although he participated in schemes that bled millions from the Wall Street regulars, in his way he was a generous man. As Gilbert sentimentalized, "He probably had never heard of Robin Hood, but he was of that ilk—a one-man Tammany and Home Relief. He supplied coal and food to the needy, paid rentals for impoverished tenants, created sinecures for the halt. When the Chicago fire of October 8, 1871, left thousands destitute, Fisk sent a trainload of supplies to the stricken city."[2] This solitary act of charity was a stroke of genius in terms of gilding Fisk's tarnished popular image. It was apparently the idea of John H. Comer, Fisk's private secretary. Teams of the New York and Boston Express Company were used to gather clothing in New York. The track was cleared and every crossing had a guard to prevent accidents. "Much was said in the Colonel's praise by many newspapers in the west, who up to that time had been 'down on him.'"[3] Swanberg, one of Fisk's soberer biographers, recounted many instances of Fisk's charity, concluding that although the record may have been overembellished, still the basic thesis of Fisk's generosity was valid.[4]

Fisk, separated from his wife, lived a life of opulence and had a weakness for women. One courtesan to whom he became particularly attached was Helen Josephine Mansfield; he gave her a four-story residence not far from his Grand Opera House, servants, a carriage, a private box at the opera, Paris gowns, jewelry, and other accoutrements. Miss Mansfield was not entirely won over, however, and in 1870 she announced that she had fallen in love with Edward S. Stokes, a dashing young man Fisk had introduced to her. Fisk had also helped Stokes financially by favored treatment on the part of the Erie

Railroad with Stokes's oil refinery in Brooklyn. Josie Mansfield further demanded a $25,000 cash settlement from Fisk. Jubilee Jim took some revenge on Stokes by canceling all deals between the Erie and Stokes's refinery, thus ruining his business. The triangle of passions that engulfed Fisk, Stokes, and Mansfield was complex. Josie and Stokes threatened to publish Fisk's love letters to her if he did not pay the money she had demanded. Fisk publicly charged the two with blackmail; they brought a libel suit against him. The suit came to court on January 6, 1872, and the case was dismissed. When court adjourned, Stokes lunched at Delmonico's, where he shortly heard a report that he and Josie had been indicted for blackmail. Enraged at this abrupt reversal of fortune, Stokes armed himself with his Colt revolver, went to see Josie, and then left in search of Fisk. Learning that Fisk intended to visit some friends at the Grand Central Hotel, Stokes arrived there first and waited at the top of a staircase. He fired twice, wounding Fisk in his arm and stomach. Fisk was taken to a hotel room, where doctors tried unsuccessfully to probe through layers of fat to extract the bullet. Early in the morning, the Prince of the Erie died, his forgiving wife at his bedside.

Stokes was arrested and tried. In the first trial, the jury was hung; in the second, he was convicted, but the court of appeals set aside the verdict. Following a third trial in 1873, he was found guilty of manslaughter and sentenced to six years at Sing Sing. He was released in 1877 after serving only four years. Stokes lived until 1901, his career after leaving prison filled with a goodly share of double-dealing. It was said that he always slept in a lighted room for fear of Fisk's ghost.

The ballad "Jim Fisk, or He Never Went Back on the Poor" was published by W. F. Helmick of Cincinnati in 1874, with "J.S." (generally believed to be William J. Scanlan) credited as author. In songsters of the 1880s it appeared as "Stokes' Verdict." Because the first edition was signed simply "J.S.," Spaeth had some doubts that Scanlan actually authored the ballad in question, since he was born in 1856 and did not produce any other songs until 1881. In the eighties he achieved considerable popularity as a composer of lighthearted and Irish songs. "Jim Fisk" is quite unlike any of his other pieces. The similarity of the "Jim Fisk" ballad to an older piece, "Never Go Back on the Poor," the tune of which it borrowed, strongly suggests that the latter was a conscious model for the former. Henry Belden commented about a version collected in Missouri that "the author seems to fear that Stokes, because of his money and prominence, will not be convicted. As a matter of fact, he was not hanged, but was sentenced to life imprisonment. That ballad, then, we may suppose, was written before the outcome of the trial was known."[5] However, since Stokes was given only a very light sentence, it is reasonable that the ballad was written after the final trial, which accords with the publication date.

The noteworthy feature of both the ballad and the memory of Jim Fisk in oral tradition is that he had become a hero rather than a villain. Evidently the unscrupulous conduct of the robber baron in financial circles failed to impress the popular memory as much as did his generosity with a tiny fraction of his ill-gotten gains. Fisk had all the makings of an American popular hero. Just the circumstances of his death alone would have been sufficient to endow him with heroic dimensions: rejected by the woman he loved, betrayed by her and the man he had befriended and even introduced to her, assassinated in cold blood, forgiven at his deathbed by his wife (according to some accounts),[6] and done final injustice when his assassin was released from prison after only four years—this is the stuff that wins sympathy in America. But Fisk was a hero well before the events leading to his death: born a poor country boy who rose by his own talents, he typified the American success story. His frequent acts of generosity, his

Sheet music: "Jim Fisk, or He Never Went Back on the Poor." Collection of the Library of Congress.

deliberate use of rustic language and pronunciation, and his triumphs over the established bluebloods of the nation won him the support of the folk. As Swanberg wrote,

> Possibly in part because of this almost unanimous rejection of Fisk by the elite, the less privileged classes were inclined to view him with forgiveness and even fondness. Obviously he was a rascal, but he was the honestest rascal in sight. . . . Many humble citizens, sick of cant, thanked him because he beat rich impostors at their own game, carried on his larcenies without simultaneous resort to scriptures or hymns, and seemed comparatively free from one prevailing sin—hypocrisy. This socio-economic difference in attitude was reflected in the newspapers, the staid *Times* and *Tribune* always condemning him while the more earthy *Sun, Herald* and *World* as often as not found praiseworthy qualities in him.[7]

Fisk's career on commercial phonograph disc has been anything but princely. To my knowledge, only one prewar recording was made: by Frank Luther and Zora Layman, his wife, in about 1939. Luther, whose real name is Francis Luther Crow, began his musical career as an evangelistic singer. After a brief stint as a minister in Bakersfield, California, he joined the De Reszke Singers Quartette in 1926. When Vernon Dalhart and Carson Robison had a falling out, Luther became Robison's partner, and the team recorded prolifically in the late 1920s. In 1939 he recorded a series of historical, folk, and Gay Nineties songs for Decca; the Fisk recording was one of these. These items were issued in Decca's popular, rather than hillbilly, series. In more recent decades Luther has established a reputation as a narrator/singer on children's records.

Frank Luther's text is so abridged that I feel obliged to give here a fuller version, as the song appeared in the songsters of the 1880s. Most other versions lack the final stanza and chorus.

STOKES' VERDICT

Written and Sung by WILLIAM J. SCANLAN.
Air.—"Never Go Back on the Poor."

If you'll listen awhile, I'll sing to you a song
    About this "glorious land of the free,"
And the "difference" I'll show 'twixt the rich and the poor
    In a "trial by jury," you see
If you've plenty of "stamps," you can hold up your head.
    And walk out from your own prison door,
But they'll hang you up high if you've no friends or gold
    Let the "rich" go, but hang up the poor.

    In the trials for murder we've had now a days
        The rich ones get off swift and sure,
    While they've thousands to pay to the jury and judge,
        You can bet they'll go back on the poor.

Let me speak of a man who's now dead in his grave—
    A good man as ever was born—
Jim Fisk he was called, and his money he gave
    To the outcast, the poor and forlorn.

We all know he loved both women and wine,
    But his heart it was right, I am sure,
Though he lived like a "prince" in a palace so fine,
    Yet he never went back on the poor.

Jim Fisk was a man, wore his "heart on his sleeve,"
    No matter what people would say,
And he done all his deeds (both the good and the bad)
    In the broad, open light of the day.
With his grand "six in hand" on the beach at Long Branch
    He cut a "big dash" to be sure,
But "Chicago's great fire" show'd the world that Jim Fisk,
    With his "wealth" still remembered the poor.

    When the telegram came that the homeless that night,
        Were starving to death, slow but sure.
    His "Lighting Express" manned by noble Jim Fisk;
        Flew to feed all her hungry and poor!

Now what do you think of this "trial" of Stokes,
    Who murdered this friend of the poor?
When such men get free, is there any one safe,
    If they step from outside their own door!
Is there one law for the poor and one for the rich?
    It seems so, at least so I say;
If they hang up the poor, why—damn it!—the rich
    Ought to swing up the very same way!

    Don't show any favor to friend or to foe,
        The beggar or the prince at his door,
    The big millionaire you must hang up also,
        But never go back on the poor.

Oh shame on this "land of the free and the brave,"
    When such sights as this meet our eye!
The poor in their prisons are treated like slaves
    While the rich in their cells they live high
A poor devil "crazy with drink," they will hang
    For a murder he didn't intend,
But a wealthy assassin, with "political friends,"
    Gets off, for he's money to speed [*sic;* for *spend*]!"

    But if things go on this way, we'll stand it no more,
        The people will rise up in bands,
    A Vigiliance Commitee we'll raise on our shore,
        And take the law in our hands![8]

NOTES

1. Richard O'Conner, *Gould's Millions* (Garden City, N.Y.: Doubleday, 1962), p. 191.

2. Douglas Gilbert, *Lost Chords* (Garden City, N.Y.: Doubleday, Doran, 1942), pp. 100–101.

3. *Boston Evening Transcript,* July 9, 1910, "Notes and Queries" column, answer to no. 8693, asking for information on Fisk's train to Chicago. The answer was provided by Comer's son.

4. W. A. Swanberg, *Jim Fisk* (New York: Charles Scribner's Sons, 1959), pp. 116–19. The historical information in these notes is taken principally from Swanberg's book; from O'Conner, *Gould's Millions*; and from Willoughby Jones, *The Life of James Fisk, Jr.* (Philadelphia: Union Publishing, 1872).

5. Henry M. Belden, *Ballads and Songs Collected by the Missouri Folk-Lore Society*, 2d ed. (Columbia: University of Missouri Press, 1955), p. 415.

6. O'Conner, *Gould's Millions*, p. 121.

7. Swanberg, *Jim Fisk*, p. 170.

8. Hatfield Brothers, *Pride of Mayo Songster* (New York, n.d.), p. 52. The sheet music version differs from this songster text in several minor textual variations, but more importantly in lacking the final chorus.

REFERENCES

A. "Jim Fiske," by Frank Luther, Zora Layman, and the Century Quartet. Recorded in Mar., 1939 (Decca master 65198), in New York City. Released on Decca 2429 (in album 47: *Songs of Old New York [1650–1906]*).

B. Belden (1955), 415–16
Botkin (1947), 860–62
Burt, 48–50
Dean, M. C., 30–31
Delaney #16 (1898?), 25
Dorson (1973), 249
Ewen (1947), 146
Flanders et al., 213–15
Flanders & Brown, 75
Gilbert (1942), 97–102
Hatfield Songster, 52
Hubbard, L., 256–57
Laws, 200–201 (F 18; discussion only)

Luther, 225
Ridenour IX, 100–102
Ripley Songster, 50
Sandburg, 416–19
Shay (1928), 129–32; 195–97 in 1961 ed.
Silverman (1975) I, 80–81
Spaeth (1948), 178, 217 (discussion only)

E. Oscar Brand—Elektra EKL 16: *Badmen and Heroes*; Elektra EKL 129: *Badmen and Heroes and Pirate Songs*
Ronald Campbell and group—New World Records NW 267: *The Hand That Holds the Bread*

F. LC AFS:
J. C. Kenniston—AFS 3755 B
Archibald Spurling—AFS 10082 B14 (spoken)
Asel Trueblood—AFS 2332 B2

Jesse James

JESSE JAMES

♩ = 126   Original Key: C

How the peo-ple held their breath when they heard of Jes-se's death,

Won-dered how he came to die;___ For the big re-ward,

lit-tle Rob-ert Ford___ shot Jes-se James on the sly.

1st Chorus

Jes-se leaves a wife that-'ll moan all her life, The

chil-dren that he left will pray; For

Bob Ford, the cow-ard, that shot Mis-ter How-ard, And

laid Jes-se James in his grave._____ **2nd Chorus** Oh, they

laid poor Jes-se in his grave, yes, Lord, They laid Jes-se

James in___ his grave; Oh, he took from the rich and he

gave it to the poor,_ But they laid Jes-se James in his grave.___

How the people held their breath when they heard of Jesse's death,
Wondered how he came to die;
For the big reward, little Robert Ford
Shot Jesse James on the sly.

It was Robert Ford, that dirty little coward,
I wonder how he does feel;
For he ate Jesse's bread and he slept in Jesse's bed,
And he laid Jesse James in his grave.

> Jesse leaves a wife that'll moan all her life,
> The children that he left will pray;
> For Bob Ford, the coward, that shot Mr. Howard,
> And laid Jesse James in his grave.

Jesse was a man, a friend to the poor,
He'd never see a man suffer pain;
But with his brother Frank he robbed the Springfield bank,
And stopped the Glendale train.

It was his brother, Frank, that robbed the Gallatin Bank,
And carried the money from the town;
It was in this very place they had a little chase,
And they shot Captain Sheets to the ground.

> Jesse leaves a wife that'll moan [?mourn] all her life,
> The children that he left will pray;
> For Bob Ford, the coward, that shot Mr. Howard,
> That laid Jesse James in his grave.

They went to the crossin' not very far from there,
And there they did the same;
For the agent on his knees delivered up the keys
To the outlaws, Frank and Jesse James.

'Twas on a Saturday night, and Jesse was at home,
Talkin' with his family brave;
Bob Ford came along like a thief in the night,
And laid Jesse James in his grave.

> Oh, they laid poor Jesse in his grave, yes, Lord,
> They laid Jesse James in his grave;
> Oh, he took from the rich and he gave it to the poor,
> But they laid Jesse James in his grave.

Jesse went to his rest with his hand on his breast,
The devil will be upon his knee;
He was born one day in the county of Clay,
And came from a solitary race.

Now men, when you go out into the West,
Never be afraid to die;
They had the law in their hands, but they didn't have the sand,
To take Jesse James alive.

Jesse leaves a wife that will mourn all her life,
The children that he left will pray;
For Bob Ford, the coward, that shot Mr. Howard,
And laid Jesse James in his grave.

Oh, they laid poor Jesse in his grave, yes Lord,
They laid Jesse James in his grave;
Oh, he took from the rich and he gave it to the poor,
And they laid Jesse James in his grave.

Harry "Haywire Mac" McClintock

More interesting than the facts of the life and crimes of Jesse James is the process of his apotheosis. Of the former aspect of his career, much has been written, and some of that is accurate;[1] the latter question has been treated meticulously by William Settle in his excellent biography of James, and I recommend his study to readers who wish to pursue the subject further.

Jesse Woodson James was born September 5, 1847; and Alexander Franklin James, January 10, 1843, in Clay County, Missouri. Like Cole Younger (see my remarks on the following song), the James boys grew up in turbulent times, marked by border warfare, the Civil War, and then postbellum violence. Factors such as these are always invoked to explain why the Jameses turned to lives of crime. Similarly, the open approbation of the guerrillas who fought federal troops paved the way toward acceptance of the illegal activities of the ex-guerrillas after the war, particularly when those activities were directed against such disliked institutions as the banks and the railroads.

Social climate doubtless did have a great deal to do with the attitudes that made the Jameses and their associates heroes in the South, but this explanation is perhaps too easy; after all, hardly all of Clay County lived outside the law in those years, so there must have been other, perhaps personal, factors. Unfortunately, even today we cannot always explain why a criminal has become what he is; analysis of the criminalization of Jesse James must necessarily be speculative. Carl Breihan, in his biography of James, touches on the psychological aspect:

> Modern psychologists would categorize [Jesse James] quickly. His father had "deserted" him when he was four. His first stepfather had disliked him. The mother he worshipped showed a marked preference for his older brother, referred to him always as "Mister Frank." The second stepfather, of whom he was fond, was also partial toward Frank. Jesse had deep-set feelings of rejections, and he spent his childhood compensating for this by being wilder than his brother, and proving a superiority as a marksman and a rider.[2]

But if Breihan's assessment explains why Jesse developed an authority problem, it predicts quite the opposite for Frank, who hardly was Clay County's model citizen.

Breihan also stresses the significance of a single incident that occurred when Jesse was fifteen years old. Although Jesse was too young to join the army, Frank was not, and he had already established a reputation as one of William Clarke Quantrill's raiders—a band of Confederate partisans who had begun a civil war of their own well before Fort Sumter was fired upon and who continued their illegal acts of bravado afterward. Jesse and his stepfather, Dr. Samuel, were in the field when a band of Union soldiers came up looking for Frank. Attempting to extract information from the two, they beat Jesse and hoisted Dr. Samuel several times by a rope until he lost consciousness. It was said that after this Jesse was determined to kill as many Union soldiers as he could, and to that end he left home to join Quantrill.

But time blunts even the strongest emotions, and the feelings generated by an incident in 1863 could not motivate a career of violence and crime for nearly twenty years without other powerful contributing factors. So perhaps we must be content not with a "reason," but with only a list of contributing factors—psychological as well as social—that together created the criminal Jesse James.

James's life of crime, as distinct from his career of extralegal wartime activities, presumably began on February 13, 1866, when the Youngers and the Jameses robbed the Commercial Bank of Liberty, Missouri, of $58,000. Cole Younger and Frank James organized the raid, and it is assumed that Jesse was among the party. During the next ten years, Jesse was implicated in ten other bank holdups, but in most his involvement has not been proved beyond doubt. The last was the Northfield, Minnesota, bank robbery, which is discussed in connection with the song "Cole Younger."

In their first train robbery, on July 21, 1873, near Adair, Iowa, the gang stopped a Chicago, Rock Island, and Pacific Railroad train that was supposed to be carrying a large shipment of gold from the West. But the gold had been moved to a later train, so the robbers contented themselves with relieving the passengers of all valuables. Other train holdups that Jesse James was believed to have had a hand in were those on the Iron Mountain road near Gads Hill, Missouri, on January 31, 1874; on the Kansas and Pacific near Muncie, Kansas, on December 13, 1874; on the Missouri Pacific at Otterville, Missouri, on July 7, 1876; on the Chicago, Alton, and Saint Louis train at Glendale, Missouri, on October 7, 1879; on the Chicago, Rock Island, and Pacific near Winston, Missouri, on July 15, 1881; and on the Chicago and Alton Railroad near Blue Cut, Missouri, on September 7, 1881.

Jesse was in his thirty-fifth year when he was shot down by his cousin, Robert Ford. Ford had joined Jesse some months before, in a plan to betray him in return for the sizable reward on Jesse's head. A bank robbery was scheduled for the night of April 3, 1882, and Bob and Charley Ford had arranged an ambush with the law in return for the reward money. But that morning a rare opportunity presented itself. It was a warm, sunny day, and door and windows were open. A picture of Stonewall Jackson needed dusting and straightening. Jesse stood on a chair to do it, first removing his guns so as not to arouse suspicions on the part of any passersby. Unarmed, standing on a chair with his back to Bob Ford, Jesse was a perfect target.

As William Settle has pointed out, the process of building Jesse James into a hero began well within his lifetime. The argument followed two paths: first, most of the crimes attributed to the James boys could not have been committed by them (indeed, they were blamed for many more deeds than they perpetrated); and second, their boldness and audacity, and the fact that their wealthy victims had probably earned their money by means no more legal than those employed by the bank robbers, made the Jameses' activities actually laudable.[3] Similar reasons were usually given for the failure of the authorities to apprehend the criminals; legend has it that every poor farmer in Clay County would have been glad to hide the James boys and feed them, particularly since they always paid their hosts generously. While there may have been a kernel of truth to this argument, it should also be mentioned that the threat of revenge probably deterred many a Missourian from betraying their whereabouts. The characterization of Jesse James as a latter-day Robin Hood was made not long after his death. Kent Steckmesser's discussion of this from the folklorist's point of view concluded, not surprisingly, that most of the noble deeds attributed to James had no basis in fact.[4]

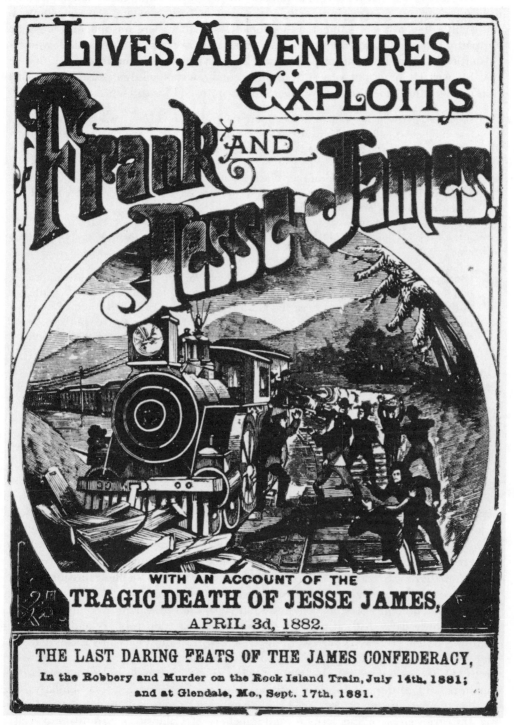

Frank and Jesse James: Lives, Adventures, Exploits, front cover of pulp novel. Author's Collection.

However, whether James did or did not pay the widow's mortgage need not concern us here; we are not primarily interested in the verity of such anecdotes. Two questions are especially relevant to the subject of this book: (1) whether there was indeed a feeling of antipathy toward the railroads that became a motive for train robbing, and (2) whether this attitude toward the railroads made robbery a virtue in the public eye.

Stewart Holbrook answers at least the second question affirmatively. The explanation for why the James-Younger gang went uncontrolled for so long, he writes,

> surely lies partly in the public attitude toward railroads in the 1870s. It was one largely of fear and hate combined. The roads had done a good deal . . . to bring about this state of affairs. Farmers who felt they had been cheated, either in land deals or in freight rates, were not prone to worrying much if other men preyed on the railroads. Still other men had lost their savings in wildcat railroad stocks and bonds. Many laboring men felt the roads were grinding them down—and in 1877 were to stage a strike and riots the like of which the country had not seen until then. . . .[5]

One history textbook characterized the polarization between farmer and railroads as follows:

> [Because] the farmer of the period after the Civil War . . . was quick to discern the danger to his own interests in the abuses of the railroad . . . the first great agrarian battle of the period was directed against the railroads. The early years of the railroad were characterized by the one great desire, that they be built at whatever sacrifice and cost. As time went on, however, and the abuses of unregulated expansion and competition developed, the attitude of the public became more critical. The railroads were, indeed, open to serious charges. They had been built at exorbitant expense by such construction companies as the Credit Mobilier and had often fallen into the hands of financial manipulators. . . . Bitter warfare at competitive points led to discrimination of various kinds among shippers, particularly in the form of rebates, and in charging more for a short haul under monopoly conditions than for a longer haul under stiff competition. This abuse bore heavily upon the farmer, who had no choice as to the railroad that would carry his products to the market, and the railroads were quick to make the farmer pay for the losses that he might sustain in carrying industrial freight between competitive points.[6]

There was, incidentally, also antipathy toward the banks. The rapid westward expansion in the decades following the Civil War and the expense of new machinery led farmers to borrow heavily, so that by the turn of the century more than 40 percent of the farms in the Midwest were mortgaged, generally to eastern moneylenders. The downward trend of agricultural prices in the 1870s left many farmers unable to pay mortgages.[7]

That there was good cause for strong feelings against both the railroads and the banks seems clear. Eugene Block, in *Great Train Robberies of the West*, suggests further that "in some ways, hatred of the railroads, then prevalent in some far western areas in those days, had an encouraging influence on train robbers and made their holdups popular crimes. Typical were the careers of the notorious Chris Evans and John Sontag, both railroad haters, who preyed on trains as much for personal revenge as for profit. Others relied on this feeling and were confident they could count on certain ranchers and cattlemen to side with anyone robbing trains. . . ."[8] Similarly, one of the sympathetic characters in Frank Norris's *Octopus*, an epic novel cataloguing the grievances of the farmers and ranchers of California's San Joaquin Valley against the railroad, was a train engineer who, after being fired and cheated by the railroad, turned to train robbery for revenge.

There have been few serious attempts, however, to make hatred for the railways a motive for the James-Younger band's train robberies, although occasionally their bank robberies were so explained. Cole Younger stated that the Northfield Bank was selected for robbery because General Benjamin Butler, noted for his ill treatment of southerners during the Civil War, was said to have large sums of money invested there.[9] However, there were other, better explanations for choosing Northfield's bank.

Settle concludes that the ex-guerrillas turned to crime because they were unable to adjust to postbellum tranquillity, that railroads and banks were logical targets for monetary reasons and did not represent any ideological commitments on the robbers' part.[10] But with regard to the apotheosis of the bandits, he notes that while no one factor was entirely responsible, the Civil War and its aftermath provided a good basis for other contributory social phenomena.[11] Thus it is interesting that the first and most important person to foster the James legend—and their most ardent defender while they were alive—was a newspaperman, Major John Edwards, who had also been a zealous defender of the Confederacy. Jesse James's assassination by a traitor, with the Missouri governor implicated as a conspirator, provided the final touch to the making of the hero.

It is useful to recall that we are dealing with a phenomenon that has cropped up elsewhere in the world at various times. In times of social unrest, particularly when there is one class of the populace who feel themselves at odds with the recognized authority, men whose illegal actions make them villains to the establishment are at the same time considered heroes by the opposing social class. From Saxon Robin Hood in Norman-ruled England to the Irish patriots of eighteenth- and nineteenth-century Britain to the Greek klephts resisting Turkish domination from the seventeenth through the twentieth centuries, history has witnessed similar confrontations, all of which gave rise to legendry and song that canonized men officially considered outlaws. To ex-Confederate Missourians, the one-time guerrillas were their own flesh and blood; the railroads and banks represented the industrialized North and subjugation by an alien element hostile to their own way of life. The continued popularity of all the outlaw heroes of past ages probably attests to the existence in each of us of a rebellious undercurrent directed against the authoritarian establishment mainstream.

A final factor that may have played some role in the antipathy toward the railroads was the conservative attitude that regarded them as modern, disruptive, and bearers of immorality—a notion already discussed in the introduction to this chapter.

Now let us turn to the ballads about Jesse James, with especial attention to the relationships and the historicity of the various extant versions. Jesse was shot on Monday morning, April 3, 1882, while living in Saint Joseph, Missouri, under the alias of Thomas Howard. He was buried at his mother's home in Kearney, and his grave became a shrine that attracted countless (paying) viewers. D. K. Wilgus recalls reading that Bob James, Frank's son, stated that Billy Gashade, a Liberty, Missouri, newspaper printer who was a friend of the James family, wrote the ballad about Jesse at the time of the funeral.[12] Although Bob James was only four then, this is a more credible explanation than Belden's unverified report, repeated by the Lomaxes (1947), that a black convict wrote the ballad. Still, it is difficult to believe that a friend of the James family would have written most of the familiar verses of the common version—particularly those implicating Frank James in any crimes, as his trials were still pending. (Frank James surrendered himself to the governor in October, and was placed in the Independence jail until he was tried at Gallatin in August, 1883.) The mention in one important text (Randolph E) of Frank being in the Independence jail suggests a composition date some months after Jesse's assassination.

Until recently, the earliest known printing of "Jesse James" was a broadside printed by New York publisher Henry J. Wehman (no. 1044). Though undated, it can be placed between 1888 and 1897 on the basis of Wehman's address given on the sheet. It has been reproduced by Finger (1927) and by Thede and Preece. In 1977, Guthrie T. Meade came across an 1887 pocket songster in the Library of Congress, *Comic and Sentimental Songs*; one of the texts, as sung by Robert Jones, is "Jesse James." Jones, born blind in east Tennessee, made his living after the age of fifteen by singing and playing the fiddle. Jones's "Jesse James" is a fine text, and since it has not seen the light of day in many years I reprint it here. The stanzas, originally in twelve lines, are given here in eight.

JESSE JAMES

Jesse James was a lad that killed many a man,
He robbed the Danville train;
But that dirty little coward that shot at Mr. Howard,
Has laid Jesse James in his grave.
It was little Robert Ford, that dirty little coward;
I wonder how he does feel;
For he ate of Jesse's bread and slept in Jesse's bed,
Then laid Jesse James in his grave.

Poor Jesse had a wife, to mourn for his life,
Children they were brave;
But that dirty little coward, that shot at Mr. Howard
Has laid Jesse James in his grave.

It was with his brother Frank, he robbed the Gallatin bank,
And carried the money from the town;
It was at this very place they had a little chase,
For they shot Capt. Sheets to the ground.
They went to the crossing not very far from there,
And there they did they same,
With the agent on his knees he delivered up the keys
To the outlaws Frank and Jesse James.

It was on Wednesday night, the moon was shining bright,
They robbed the Danville train;
The people they did say for many miles away,
It was robbed by Frank and Jesse James.
It was on Saturday night, the moon was shining bright,
Talking with his family brave,
Robert Ford came along like a thief in the night,
And he laid Jesse James in his grave.

The people held their breath when they heard of Jesse's death,
And wondered however he came to die.
It was one of the gang called little Robert Ford,
He shot Jesse James on the sly.

This song was made by Billy LaShade, as soon as the news did arrive,
As soon as the news did arrive;
He said there's no man with the law in his hand
Can take Jesse James alive.

While in this version the authorship is attributed to Billy LaShade, rather than Gashade, I am uneasy about building any hypotheses on this slender foundation. The text, early as it is, is not without factual errors, as noted below.

It is surprising that within twenty-five years after its composition a single ballad could have become so disjointed and diversified as the fragments collected in the first decade of the twentieth century indicate. On the other hand, there is no clear evidence of separate and distinct ballads having been penned in the 1880s. The evidence does suggest that a single ballad was written and later added to. Because of the large number of stanzas that exhibit carefully constructed internal rhyme, the hypothetical original ballad was undoubtedly written in that verse form; it taxes credulity to suppose that two independent ballads would have been written in the same somewhat unusual verse structure. The later additions could have been made haphazardly; the older ballad could also have been used as the core for a secondary recomposition. Because certain "corruptions" are so widespread, I feel that a secondary recomposition must have been made at some point:

(1) The second verse of the version transcribed in this book begins, as do almost all other variants, "It was Robert Ford, that dirty little coward, / I wonder how he does feel. . . ," which does not rhyme with the fourth line, "And he laid Jesse James in his grave." Gilbert's short fragment of two verses and chorus is the only text I have seen in which the corresponding verse begins "Oh, it was Robert Ford, the dirty little coward, / And how did he behave?" A version in the Combs collection has "I wonder what he did crave."

(2) Most versions have made a chorus out of what seems to me to have once been a verse:

Jesse had a wife to mourn for his life,
And three children, they were brave;
But that dirty little coward that shot Mr. Howard
Has laid poor Jesse in his grave.

Even the second half of the melody of this "chorus," as it is always sung, is the same as the second half of the melody of the verse. The song transcribed in this book has two choruses, the tunes of which differ from each other—and from the tune of the verses—up to the mid-cadence. The last two lines of each chorus and the verses are all sung to the same melody. Several versions have a chorus that begins "Poor Jesse James" and then lapses into the verse structure and meter.

(3) The almost invariable seventh verse of the version in this book must be a corruption. The second line, "The devil will be upon his knees," does not rhyme with the fourth line and makes questionable sense at that point. Randolph's E text has for that line "And there are many who never saw his face," which both rhymes and makes sense; in fact, there was some difficulty identifying the corpse with certainty because so few people, other than relatives, had seen Jesse James's face and known who he was.

(4) Northfield Bank has in our text become Springfield; but in a wide number of texts—even early ones from Missouri and Kentucky—it has become Chicago, which is not a likely substitution that one would expect to occur independently with such fre-

quency. Because all these corruptions appear in the Wehman broadside displayed by
Finger, it seems that the recomposed ballad was already in circulation by the 1890s.

It is tempting to speculate that Randolph's E text is close to the hypothetical original,
not only because of the distinctions already noted, but also because, with the exception of
two of the nine verses, nothing unfavorable is said about the James brothers; furthermore, the entire ballad is remarkably full of correct details that appear in no other
recovered texts. In fact, except for the universal internal rhyme scheme already mentioned, I would assume that the E text represents a different, independent ballad. The E
text dwells on the betrayal of Jesse by Bob and Charley Ford and is the type of song we
might expect a friend of the family to write a few months after the assassination.
Unfortunately for this hypothesis, this text does not bear the Billy Gashade attribution
of authorship.

Later additions to the factual original ballad can be spotted by their inaccuracies: for
example, the assassination is almost invariably placed on a Saturday night, whereas it was
actually a Monday morning. Some other details are correct. The Gallatin Bank was
robbed by two men, believed to have been the James brothers, on December 16, 1869,
and the bank cashier and owner, Captain John Sheets, was shot to death by one of the
bandits. The Chicago and Alton train was robbed at Glendale on Wednesday night,
October 8, 1879. The bandits rode up to the depot and held the agent at gunpoint while
the telegraph equipment was wrecked (could the "keys" the agent delivered up have
been a telegraph key?), the signal was changed to red, and rocks were piled on the tracks
in case the train did not stop for the signal. "Glendale" is corrupted in a wide number of
versions to "Danville" and sometimes to "Denver" or "Danfield."

Some of the errors are already engraved in the ballad as early as Robert Jones's 1887
text—a mere five and a half years after James's death. The circumstances about the
Gallatin bank robbery are correct, but the Glendale train has already been changed to
"Danville," and the day of James's assassination from Monday to Saturday. One gathers
that the song was already in oral tradition by the time Jones learned it.

One unusual stanza sent by a correspondent to Robert Frothingham in 1923 for his
Adventure magazine column, "Old Songs That Men Have Sung," is particularly interesting in its attempt to shape the image of Jesse James as industrious and impoverished,
driven by circumstances to a life of crime:

> Oh, Jessie and his wife have been toiling all their life,
> To keep starvation from the door;
> But Robert Ford's pistol ball brought old Jesse from the wall,
> They have laid Jessie James in his grave.[13]

The first printing of a "Jesse James" text in a collection of lasting influence was in
John A. Lomax's 1910 *Cowboy Songs and Other Frontier Ballads*. In that early compila-
tion, Lomax generally gave little information on his sources. When he and his son Alan
expanded the book in 1938, many citations and new texts were added. Furthermore,
some of the existing texts were altered. To the "Jesse James" of the 1910 and 1916 editions
the Lomaxes added two new stanzas (the fifth and the penultimate in the 1938 text) and
deleted one. To the final stanza of their first version in the 1938 edition, beginning "This
song was made by Billy Gashade," the Lomaxes appended the footnote "The last stanza
was made by a Missouri Negro." Because this remark has fueled an argument about the
origins of "Jesse James," it is worth reporting here some relevant documents among John
A. Lomax's papers at the Eugene C. Barker Texas History Center on the Austin campus of
the University of Texas.

One of the papers was a facsimile of page 28 of the 1910 edition—the second page of the original "Jesse James" text—on which Lomax had added in his own writing two stanzas and two footnotes. The footnote "The last stanza came from a Missouri Negro" was to refer to the new stanza (beginning "Jesse went down to the old man town") that was added, in the 1938 edition, just before the final "This song was made by Billy Gashade" stanza. Somehow, between the rough manuscript and the printing of the 1938 edition, both the meaning of the footnote and its referent were misinterpreted. That the meaning of the original manuscript version was correct is verified by another item among the Lomax papers, a transcription of a single "Jesse James" stanza—the one beginning "Jesse went down to the old man town"—with the annotation at the bottom "From a Missouri negro." Simply because of the ensuing transformation of this note, the possibility that the "Jesse James" ballad was of Afro-American origin has been seriously entertained.

The other added stanza in the 1938 edition, commencing "They rallied out West for to live upon the best," was, according to another of Lomax's papers, sent to him by Hubert Shearin of Lexington, Kentucky. This stanza fits the verse form the versions identified in the Shearin-Combs *Syllabus* (1911), but positive identification is not possible at this time.

The majority of the James ballad texts seem to be closely related to this internally rhymed ballad that, as I have argued, seems to have come in two successive versions. This family is designated E 1 in the Laws syllabus *Native American Balladry*. A completely distinct ballad that achieved fairly widespread popularity is Laws E 2, which begins:

> Living in Missouri was a bold, bad man,
> Was known from Seattle down to Birmingham;
> From Boston, Massachusetts, right across the States
> To Denver, Colorado, and the Golden Gate.

The chorus runs:

> Jesse James! We used to read about him,
> Jesse James! In our homes at night;
> Jesse James! We used to read about him,
> When the wind blew down the chimney we would shake with fright.

Because this song fits the "Casey Jones" tune and has occasionally been recovered with that melody, it has been assumed that it was originally composed to the "Casey Jones" tune. However, the ballad, as copyrighted in 1911 with words by Roger Lewis and music by F. Henri Klickmann, had a distinct tune of its own. (An unpublished version was copyrighted by Klickmann on April 3, 1911 [E 255136]; a published version was copyrighted by Will Rossiter on May 15 [E 257615].) While perhaps Lewis and Klickmann simply cashed in on an already circulating parody by writing a new melody and copyrighting it, the untraditional nature of the words strongly suggests that they were the product of a professional urban songwriter. In 1911 the play *The James Boys in Missouri* was enjoying a very successful rerun in Saint Louis, and it might have occasioned the new ballad.

A remaining handful of fragments and ballads do not fall into either the Laws E 1 or E 2 categories. A different ballad is suggested by three independent fragments all collected in Mississippi. The unusual verse they share includes a line something like "Mother, I am dreaming about Frank and Jesse James." The other verses that appear in these fragments are linked with E 1.

Sheet music: "Jesse James." Courtesy of David Morton and the Archives of Popular American Music, UCLA.

A complete and unique ballad collected by Belden exhibits a remarkable wealth of accurate historical details. Since it concludes with the murder of Robert Ford, it must have been composed later than February, 1892. It also has internal rhyme, but in a meter quite distinct from that of E 1, as the first stanza illustrates:

> Jesse James was one of his names,
> Another it was Howard;
> He robbed the rich of every stitch,
> You bet, he was no coward.

In about 1936, the hillbilly group the Vagabonds wrote a new ballad entitled "The Death of Jesse James." It was published in a few folios but does not seem to have entered oral tradition. Frank Luther's Grey Gull recording, transcribed in Fife and Fife (1969), is a separate and unique ballad.

The recorded history of "Jesse James" begins rather early compared to most of the other songs in this book. It was first recorded by Bentley Ball for Columbia in May, 1919, as part of a group of folksongs rendered in concert-hall style for "cultured" listeners. Between June, 1918, and June of the following year Ball recorded a series of thirteen such pieces, including English and Scottish songs, two American Indian pieces, and several American spirituals, folksongs, and ballads. His source for the "Jesse James" ballad was John Lomax's *Cowboy Songs*.[14] He made, however, a few minor textual changes; in particular, Lomax's "dirty little coward" has become, in Ball's rendition, a "mean little coward."

The first hillbilly recording of the ballad (E 1) was made in March, 1924, in Atlanta for OKeh by Bascom Lamar Lunsford, a lawyer from Marion, North Carolina, who was also a folksong collector and performer. It was the first song he recorded, and he had learned it in 1903 or before from Sam Sumner at Bear Waller, Henderson County, North Carolina. In September, 1924, Riley Puckett of northern Georgia recorded the ballad for Columbia in New York. Both his and Lunsford's versions had suggestions of the older E 1 variant, namely, part of the "poor Jesse James" chorus. At about the same time Puckett was in New York, another blind street-singer, George Reneau, was there recording for Aeolian. Reneau, who came from near Knoxville, Tennessee, made the only recording of E 2, on September 12; it was issued on the Vocalion label in December.

NOTES

1. The James literature is vast. William A. Settle, Jr., in *Jesse James Was His Name* (Columbia: University of Missouri Press, 1966), provides an excellent reference bibliography, which should be the starting point for any serious re-examination of the James saga; this work was the source of the factual details in my discussion, unless otherwise indicated. The reprint edition of Frank Triplett, *The Life, Times and Treacherous Death of Jesse James,* edited by Joseph Snell (1882; rpt., New York: Promontory Press, 1970, and Chicago: Swallow, 1970), is interesting and useful. Other generally reliable works are Robertus Love, *The Rise and Fall of Jesse James* (New York: G. P. Putnam's Sons, 1926); Homer Croy, *Jesse James Was My Neighbor* (New York: Duell, Sloan and Pearce, 1949); and Carl Breihan, *The Complete and Authentic Life of Jesse James* (New York: Frederick Fell, 1953) and *The Day Jesse James Was Killed* (New York: Frederick Fell, 1961).

2. Breihan, *Life of Jesse James*, pp. 23–24.

3. Homer Croy, in *Last of the Great Outlaws* (New York: Duell, Sloan and Pearce, 1956), p. 128, quotes Cole Younger as saying to the vice-president of a Minnesota bank that the only difference between the two of them was that the banker robbed the rich, and he, the poor. Settle, *Jesse James Was His Name*, p. 76, quotes the *Lexington Caucasian* (Dec. 12, 1874) as stating that the booty

seized by the bandits was "just as honestly earned as the riches of many a highly distinguished political leader and railroad job manipulator." Vance Randolph has expressed similar sentiments: "Of Frank James in particular it is said that he never left a mountain cabin without placing a goldpiece on the 'fire-board' to pay for his night's lodging, and some of his colleagues in derring-do were equally liberal. It is no wonder that the poverty-ridden hillfolk welcomed such men, concealed them when concealment was necessary, and helped them in every possible way." See *Ozark Folksongs*, vol. 2 (Columbia: State Historical Society of Missouri, 1948), pp. 11–12.

4. Kent L. Steckmesser, "Robin Hood and the American Outlaw," *JAF*, 79 (Apr.-June, 1966), 348–55; reprinted in *Folklore of the Great West*, edited by John Greenway (Palo Alto: American West Publishing, 1969), pp. 335–43.

5. Stewart H. Holbrook, *The Story of American Railroads* (New York: Crown Publishers, 1947), p. 373.

6. Harold Underwood Faulkner, *American Political and Social History*, 7th ed. (New York: Appleton-Century-Crofts, 1957), p. 544. For the railroads' point of view regarding short-haul rates, see E. P. Ripley, "Railroads and the People," *Atlantic Monthly*, 107 (Jan., 1911), 12–13. That strong, biased attitudes toward the railroads still persist is well illustrated by the land-grant controversy; see Robert S. Henry, "The Railroad Land Grant Legend in American History Texts," *Mississippi Valley Historical Review*, 32 (Sept., 1945), 171–94; and "Comments on 'The Railroad Land Grant Legend in American History Texts,'" ibid., 32 (Mar., 1946), 557–76.

7. Faulkner, *American Political and Social History*, p. 543.

8. Eugene B. Block, *Great Train Robberies of the West* (New York: Coward-McCann, 1959); p. 16.

9. *The Story of Cole Younger, by Himself* (1903; rpt., Houston: Frontier Press, 1955), p. 77.

10. Settle, *Jesse James Was His Name*, p. 32.

11. Ibid., p. 3.

12. According to Homer Croy, "Billy Garshade . . . lived in what was called the 'Crackerneck' section of Clay County, a few miles from where Frank and Jesse were born" (*Jesse James Was My Neighbor*, p. 242).

13. Frothingham MS 76, from H. J. Arthur of Portsmouth, Va. (Apr., 1923).

14. I am grateful to Richard K. Spottswood for obtaining information on Bentley Ball's recordings from the CBS archives in New York.

REFERENCES

A. "Jesse James," in *Comic and Sentimental Songs, Sung by Robert Jones. Also a Short Sketch of His Life* (Lost River, Ind.: By the author, 1887), pp. 4–5. Earliest known publication of the Laws E 1 ballad.

"Jesse James," Henry J. Wehman broadside no. 1044. Published in New York between 1888 and 1897. Reproduced in Charles J. Finger, *Frontier Ballads* (Garden City, N.Y.: Doubleday, Page, 1927), p. 57; and in Marion Thede and Harold Preece, "The Story behind the Song: The Ballad of Jesse James," *Real West*, 16, no. 119 (Sept., 1973), 10. (E 1)

"Jesse James," in Vance Randolph, *Ozark Folksongs*, vol. 2 (Columbia: State Historical Society of Missouri, 1948), p. 20 (E text). From a manuscript sent Randolph by Mrs. F. M. Warren, of Jane, Mo., Feb. 25, 1927; the song had been in her family "for about forty years." This version is probably close to the original. (E 1)

"Jesse James," by Bentley Ball. Ball, vocal; piano accompaniment. Recorded May 1, 1919 (Columbia master 90039), in New York City. Released on Columbia A 3085. The first commercial recording of the ballad. (E 1)

"Jesse James," by Harry McClintock. Vocal and guitar. Recorded Mar. 9, 1928 (Victor master 42073-2), in Oakland, Calif. Released on Victor 21420 in 1928. Reissued on RCA Victor

LPV 528: *Native American Ballads*.
Transcribed in this book. (E 1)

"Jesse James," sheet music. Roger Lewis,
words, and F. Henri Klickmann,
music. Published by Will Rossiter,
1911. Unpublished version copyrighted
by Klickmann on Apr. 3, 1911 (E
255136); published version copyrighted
by Rossiter on May 15, 1911 (E
257615). (E 2)

B. E 1 BALLAD:

Allen, 76
Barnes, 25 (from Lomax, J. [1916])
Bascom, 246
Beard, 128–30
Belcher, 30
Belden (1912), 17
Belden (1955), 401
Best & Best, 12–13
Big Roundup, 22
Boni (1952), 224
Botkin (1944), 107 (from Larkin)
Brown II, 557; IV, 282
Buford, 121–22
Burt, 191
Byrne (discussion only)
Cambiaire, 17
Chappell (1939), 192
Chimney Corner Songs, 9
Clifton, 44
Combs-Wilgus, 82 (discussion only)
Cousin Lee, 42
Cowboy Sings, 28
Cox, (1925), 216
Davis, A. K., 283 (title and first line only)
Downes & Siegmeister (1940), 267–69
Duncan, 256
Emrich (1958) (discussion only)
Family Herald, 44 (references only)
Fath, 46
Felton, 94–99
Fife & Fife (1969), 253
Finger (1923), 18
Finger (1927), 58
Folk Sing, 153
Folksong Festival, 32
Friedman, 378 (from Belden [1955])
Frontier West, 24
Gardner & Chickering, 339
Gilbert (1942), 190
Glazer (1964), 88

Gordon, *Adventure*, June 20, 1924,
p. 191
Grove, 9
Henry (1932), 150
Henry (1938), 321
Hudson (1928), 78
Hudson (1936), 236–37
Ives (1962), 198
Kennedy, C. O. (1952), 231–32
Koehnline, 108–11
Kolb, 49
Larkin, 154
Laws, 176 (E 1) (discussion only)
Leach, M., 177–80
Leach, MacE. (1955), 753–55
Leach, MacE. (1967), 148–49; 203
(discussion)
Leach & Beck, 278
Leisy (1966), 186
Levine, 416 (one stanza)
Lomax, A. (1960), 351; 346 (discussion)
Lomax, A. (1967), 112
Lomax, J. (1915), 15
Lomax, J. (1910 and 1916), 27–28
Lomax & Lomax (1934), 128
Lomax & Lomax (1938), 156
Lomax & Lomax (1947), 283 (discussion);
296
McGuire, 13
Mason, 103
Milburn, 191
Moore, 347
Musick, 35
Odell
Owens, W., 117
Pack, 53
Perrow (1913), 145
Pound (1913), 359
Pound (1915), 34
Pound (1922), 145
Randolph (1931), 195
Randolph II, 17
Redfearn, 124
Riddle-Abrahams, 12–13
Ridenour IX, 57
Robison (1931), 42
Robison (1936), 50
Rogers, 22
RVB, 15 (Apr., 1962), 11
Sandburg, 374, 420
Seeger, P. (1961), 36
Shay (1927), 84; 42 in 1961 ed.

Anna Gray (May, 1948)
Elmer Householder (Mar., 1960)
Cora Irvin (May, 1957)
Mrs. Luther Johns (Jan., 1961)
Lillian Koach (summer, 1949)
J. S. McClure (spring, 1953)
Wilma Pace (Nov., 1959)
Nannie Bell Parker (May, 1959)
Maggie V. Settles (n.d.)
Mary Shaw (California; Feb., 1963)
Ernest Street and band (California; Feb., 1965)
Lucile Tarry (spring, 1948)
Mrs. Carl Timmons (May, 1960)
Bobby White (Oct., 1963)
Edgar M. Wood (Mar., 1959)
Unidentified singers (Combs MSS; mentioned in Combs-Wilgus, 209)

D. Bill Bender—Varsity 5141, Asch 410-2; Stinson SLP 18: *Frontier Ballads and Cowboy Songs*
Fiddlin' John Carson—OKeh 45139
—OKeh 45402   "Times Are Not Like They Used to Be" (instrumental introduction)
Al Clauser and the Cowboys—Banner 7-11-63, Melotone 7-11-63, Oriole 7-11-63, Perfect 7-11-63, Romeo 7-11-63   "The Death of Jesse James"
Tom Cook—Madison 5073, Van Dyke 75073
Vernon Dalhart—Gennett 3143, Silvertone 4012, Herwin 75507, Challenge 503
—Champion 15546, Silvertone 4012, Silvertone 8132, Supertone 9229
—Edison 51621, Edison 5057 (cylinder)
—Victor 20966
—Golden Olden Classics, Vol. 1, 794: *Vernon Dalhart, 1921–1927* (reissue of one of the above)
Jad Dees—Crystal 117
Ham Gravy (Washboard Sam pseudonym) —Vocalion 03375   "Jesse James Blues"
Fisher Hendley, J. Small, and Henry Whitter—Victor 23528; County 515: *Mountain Banjo Songs and Tunes* "Shuffle Feet Shuffle" (tune only)
Grandpa Jones and his Grandchildren

—King 847; King 845: *Do You Remember*
Terrea Lea, Andy Parker, and the Plainsmen—Intro 6014
Leadbelly (Huddie Ledbetter)—Musicraft 310; Allegro Elite LP 4027; Allegro LEG 9025: *Goodnite, Irene*; Royale 18131: *Blues Songs by the Lonesome Blues Singer*; Sutton SSU 278: *Leadbelly Sings Ballads of Beautiful Women and Bad Men*   "When the Boys Were on the Western Plain"
—Disc 3002 (in album 660); Stinson SLP 19: *Leadbelly Memorial, Vol. 2*   "Out on the Western Plains"
Bascom Lamar Lunsford—OKeh 40155
Frank Luther—Banner 6433, Conqueror 7377, Domino 4364, Jewel 5642, Oriole 1621, Regal 8808   "The Death of Jesse James"
—Grey Gull 4133 (as by Luther and as by Jeff Calhoun), Radiex 4133, Supreme 4133, Van Dyke 74133 (last three probably as by Jeff Calhoun)
Clayton McMichen—Decca 5710
Brownie McNeil—Sonic (78 rpm album): *Ballads by Brownie McNeil*
Uncle Dave Macon and Sid Harkreader —Vocalion 5356; Folk Variety 12503: *The Gayest Old Dude in Town* "The Life and Death of Jesse James"
Massey Family—Vocalion 02850, Conqueror 8444 (as by the Westerners)   "If Jesse James Rode Again"
Masterpiece Male Quartet—Masterpiece 8600 (in album A-30)
Riley Puckett—Columbia 15033-D, Harmony 5146-H (as by Fred Wilson)
Rangers—Sonora 4041 (in album M-451)
George Reneau—Vocalion 14897, Vocalion 5050
Earl Robinson—General 502, Timely 502; General album G-30
Carl Sandburg—Decca 40023 (in album A-356)
Ernest Thompson—Columbia 145-D, Harmony 5121-H (as by Ernest Johnson)
Vagabonds—Bluebird B-5282, Victor 23820, Montgomery Ward 4443, Twin

(India) FT 1920   "The Death of Jesse
James"
Washboard Sam. *See* Ham Gravy
Westerners. *See* Massey Family
Whitey and Hogan—Cowboy CR 1301;
Rounder 1013: *The Early Days of
Bluegrass, Vol. 1*
Marc Williams—Brunswick 269
Woodruff Brothers—Bluebird B-8381

E. Albert Ammons—Storyville (Denmark)
670184
George Armstrong, Gerry Armstrong, and
group—Folk Legacy FSI-16: *Golden
Ring*
Eddy Arnold—RCA Victor LPM/LSP
2036: *Thereby Hangs a Tale*
Talking John Barry—Driftwood EP-1000
(45 rpm EP)
Smiley Bates, Rose Poirier, and Eddy
Poirier—Marathon (Canada)
MMS-76002: *The Best of Bluegrass*
Bergerfolk—Folkways FTS 32420: *Pack
Up Your Sorrows*
Bill Berry, Paul Chaney, and Blue Grass
Travelers—A.B.S. W/225/226 (7" EP)
Bluegrass Banjo Pickers—RCA Camden
CAL/CAS 2243: *Music for the Bonnie
and Clyde Era*
Bogtrotters. *See* Fields Ward
Bill Bonyun—Folkways FC 7402 (FP 2)
(10" LP): *Who Built America*
Pete Brady and the Blazers—ABC
Paramount ABCS-310: *Murder Ballads*
Henry E. Briggs—Library of Congress
Archive of Folk Song L49: *The Ballad
Hunter, Part 1*
Jack Casey—Rural Rhythm RRJC-206:
Jack Casey
Roy Clark—Dot DOS 26018: *Roy Clark's
Family Album*
Paul Clayton—Riverside RLP 12-640:
Wanted for Murder
Country Cooking—Music Minus One 185:
Bluegrass Guitar
Country Gentlemen—Folkways FA 2409:
Country Songs, Old and New
Jimmie Driftwood—RCA Victor
LSO-6070: *How the West Was Won*
Jack Elliott—Elektra EKL-BOX: *The Folk
Box*; Elektra EKL 129: *Badmen,
Heroes and Pirate Songs and Ballads*;

Elektra EKL 16 (10" LP): *Badmen and
Heroes*
Jimmy Gavin—Epic 5-0189 (45 rpm)
"The Ballad of Jesse James"
Goose Island Ramblers—Cuca K-1111: *A
Session with the Goose Island Ramblers*
Green Valley Singers—Diplomat DS
2422: *20 Golden Moments of Country
Music*
Jim Greer and group—Rural Rhythm RR
152: *Jim Greer and the Mac-O-Chee
Valley Folks*
Woody Guthrie and Cisco Houston
—Stinson SLP 32 (10" LP): *Cowboy
Songs*
Dickson Hall—MGM 3263
Bill Harrell and the Virginians—United
Artists UAL 3293/UAS 6293: *The
Wonderful World of Bluegrass Music*
Hootenairs—Crown CLP 535: *More
Hootenanny*
Doc Hopkins—Birch 1945: *Doc Hopkins*
Burl Ives—Encyclopaedia Britannica
Films EBF 6: *Songs of Expanding
America*
Johnny and Gerald and the Georgia
Mountain Boys—Atteiram API-1-1509A:
Bluegrass Hits
Louis M. "Grandpa" Jones—CMH 9007:
The Grandpa Jones Story
Jones Brothers—CMH 1776: *200 Years of
American Heritage in Song*; CMH
5900: *The World's Greatest Bluegrass
Bands*
Kingston Trio—Capitol T/ST 1642: *Close
Up*
Mike Lattimore Show—Rural Rhythm
RR-ML-169: *The Mike Lattimore Show*
Leadbelly (Huddie Ledbetter)—Capitol
T-1821: *Leadbelly*; Capitol EAP 2-369
(EP), Capitol (Netherlands) 369,
Capitol (England) LC 6597
"Western Plain"
Shorty Long—RCA BY-59 (45 rpm)
Norman Luboff Choir—RCA Victor LSP
3555: *Songs of the Trail*
Bascom Lamar Lunsford—Riverside RLP
12-645: *Minstrel of the Appalachians*
"Poor Jesse James"
—Library of Congress Archive of Folk
Song L20: *Anglo-American Songs and
Ballads*

Ed McCurdy—Elektra EKL 16 (10″ LP):
  Badmen and Heroes; Elektra EKL 112:
  Songs of the Old West; Elektra EKL
  205: *A Treasure Chest of American
  Folk Song*

—Riverside RLP 12-828: *Songs of a Bold
  Balladeer*

Joe McDonald—Vanguard 79348:
  Country Joe; Vanguard VSD 86: *The
  Essential Country McDonald*

Sam McGee—Arhoolie 5012: *Grand Dad
  of the Country Guitar Pickers*

John McManaman—Arc A-569: *Five
  String Banjo Jamboree*

Miller Brothers—Old Homestead 90039:
  *The Bluegrass Sound of the Miller
  Brothers*

Chad Mitchell—Cox CP/SCP 463: *In
  Concert . . . Everybody's Listening*

Chad Mitchell Trio—Mercury MG-20992/
  SR-60992: *Typical American Boys*

Leon Morris—Jessup MB 113: *Leon
  Morris Sings International Bluegrass*

Neil Morris—Atlantic LP/SD 1346:
  Sounds of the South

Mountain Ramblers—Atlantic LP/SD
  1346: *Sounds of the South*

Nitty Gritty Dirt Band—Liberty 7642:
  Uncle Charlie

Oddballs—Columbia 4-43024 (45 rpm)

Milt Okun—Elektra EKL KIT B: *Elektra
  Folk Song Kit*

Old Joe Clark—Vetco LP 3018

Jim Orange—MRC 2040: *Bluegrass
  Virginia Style*

Sonny Osborne—Gateway 3010 (45 rpm);
  Gateway LP 19; Deresco LP 19: *Five
  String Hi Fi*; Ultra Sonic LP-19;
  Gateway 31386: *The Early Recordings
  of Sonny Osborne, Vol. 1*

Osborne Brothers—MGM E/SE 4090:
  Bluegrass Instrumentals

Don Reno, Bill Harrell, and the
  Tennessee Cutups—Jalyn 108:
  Bluegrass Favorites

Will Rogers, Jr., and Tom Scott—Judson
  J 3013: *Great American Folk Heroes*

Pete Seeger—Folkways FA 2319:
  American Ballads

Pete Seeger, Jack Elliott, and Ed
  McCurdy—Columbia LS 1012: *The
  Badmen*

Sons of the Pioneers—RCA Victor
  LPM/LSP 3351: *The Sons of the
  Pioneers Sing Legends of the West*

Tom Spencer—Davis Unlimited
  DU-33034: *Old Time Singing*

Stone Mountain Boys—Old Homestead
  OHRC 90032: *Songs of the Pioneers*

Toby Stroud and the Blue Mountain
  Boys—New Star N100 (45 rpm?);
  Rounder 1014: *The Early Days of
  Bluegrass, Vol. 2*

Swagmen—Parkway P 7015: *Meet the
  Swagmen*

Tradewinds—Diplomat DS 2278: *The
  Tradewinds*

Charles Trent—Smash MGS 27002/SRS
  67002: *The Sound of a Blue Grass
  Banjo*

Van Dykes—Sutton 307: *A Hootin'
  Hootenanny!!*

Fields Ward, Wade Ward, and Glen
  Smith—Folkways FS 3832: *Bluegrass
  from the Blue Ridge*

Fields Ward and the Bogtrotters Band
  —Library of Congress Archive of Folk
  Song L49: *The Ballad Hunter, Part 1*;
  Biograph RC 6003: *The Original
  Bogtrotters, 1937-1942* (from AFS 1358
  A1)

Eric Weisberg, Mike Seeger, and Ralph
  Rinzler—Folkways FA 2314: *American
  Banjo Tunes and Songs in Scruggs
  Style*

Wellingtons—Disneyland ST-3921: *Walt
  Disney Presents Folk Heroes*

F. ACWF:
  Vern Partlow—T7-62-3
  Mary Shaw—T7-63-2

GORDON COLLECTION (GA.):
  A521, A522 (MS 298)—M. C. Mann

GORDON COLLECTION (N.C.):
  A50 (MS 81)—J. W. Dillon
  A114 (MS 171)—A. Williams
  A133 (MS 196)—W. R. Randall
  A155, A156 (MS 235)—J. D. Weaver

LC AFS:
  Joseph Aiken—AFS 13033 A5
  William C. Bailey—AFS 13719-12
  Wythe Bishop—AFS 5340 B1

E. A. Briggs—AFS 2641 A2

Henry E. Briggs—AFS L49

Luther Bryant—AFS 13718 B9

Cleophas Franklin—AFS 2892 A1

Mrs. Birmah Hill Grisson—AFS 2964 A2
& B1

Woody Guthrie—AFS 3412 B2 & 3413
B1

Austin Harmon—AFS 2917 A3

George Hastings—AFS 5361 B1

Sid Hemphill—AFS 6673 A1

Holly Hodges—AFS 13127 A14

Aunt Molly Jackson—AFS 73 A

Virgil Lance—AFS 11888 A

Leadbelly—AFS 119 B1   "Western
Cowboy"

—AFS 122 B   "Western Cowboy"

—AFS 135 B   "Western Cowboy"

Bascom Lamar Lunsford—AFS 1823

—AFS 7971 A1

May Kennedy McCord—AFS 5299 A2

Carroll Wayne Parker—AFS 11908 A

Houston Scott—AFS 13128 B22

Sharon Vergasons—AFS 11688 B10

Fields and D. C. Ward—AFS 4081 A1

Fields Ward and the Bogtrotters
Band—AFS 1358 A1, AFS L49,
Biograph RC 6003

Mrs. Vernie Westfall—AFS 3412 B2 &
3413 B1

Unknown singer—AFS 7887 A1

Harry "Haywire Mac" McClintock. *Radio Digest*,
November, 1930. Courtesy of David Freeman.

Cole Younger

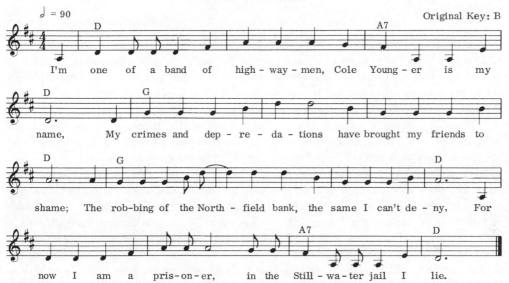

COLE YOUNGER

Original Key: B

I'm one of a band of high-way-men, Cole Young-er is my name, My crimes and dep-re-da-tions have brought my friends to shame; The rob-bing of the North-field bank, the same I can't de-ny, For now I am a pris-on-er, in the Still-wa-ter jail I lie.

I'm one of a band of highwaymen, Cole Younger is my name,
My crimes and depredations have brought my friends to shame;
The robbing of the Northfield bank, the same I can't deny,
For now I am a prisoner, in the Stillwater jail I lie.

'Tis of a bold, high robbery, a story I will tell,
Of a California miner who unto us fell;
We robbed him of his money and bid him go his way,
For which I will be sorry until my dying day.

And then we started homeward, when brother Bob did say,
"Now, Cole, we'll buy fast horses and on them ride away;
We'll ride to avenge our father's death and try to win the prize,
We'll fight those antiguerrillas until the day we die."

And then we rode towards Texas, that good old Lone Star State,
But on Nebraska's prairies the James boys we did meet;
With knives and guns and pistols we all sat down to play,
A-drinking of good whiskey to pass the time away.

A Union Pacific railway train was the next we did surprise,
And the crimes done by our bloody hands bring tears into my eyes;
The engineer and the fireman killed, conductor escaped alive,
And now their bones lie mouldering beneath Nebraska's skies.

Then we saddled horses, northwestward we did go,
To the God-forsaken country called Minnesote-o;
I had my eye on the Northfield bank when brother Bob did say,
"Now, Cole, if you undertake the job, you will surely curse the day."

But I stationed out my pickets and up to the bank did go,
And there upon the counter I struck my fatal blow;
"Just hand us over your money and make no further delay,
We are the famous Younger boys, we spare no time to pray."

                                                    Marc Williams

Like "Jesse James," the ballad about Cole Younger requires some justification for its appearance in a book of railroad songs. There is the one verse referring to a train robbery; more important is Younger's inclusion in most discussions of the notorious train robbers of the late nineteenth century—this even though he was implicated in four train hold-ups at most, participation in all of which he vehemently denied.

Because Younger's career, like that of his frequent companion, Jesse James, has been treated at length in numerous books,[1] I give here only a brief biography and discuss his career only as it relates to incidents described in the ballad itself.

Thomas Coleman Younger was born in Jackson County, Missouri, on January 15, 1844. His early youth was spent amid the constant turmoil and bloodshed of the Missouri-Kansas border skirmishes. During the Civil War he fought in Quantrill's guerrilla band, at which time he acquired a reputation for violence, bravado, and marksmanship. Although his hands were several times bloodstained, he apparently never considered his activities with Quantrill as extralegal, and when the war ended he had hopes for settling down and farming. However, the animosity built up against him and the others in Quantrill's band did not dissipate after the war, and he found it impossible to settle down peaceably.

On February 13, 1866, Cole, Frank James, and others engineered the first peace-time bank robbery in the United States, in Liberty, Missouri. Numerous bank robberies followed in the next few years, but the event that brought the group national notoriety was their first train robbery. Altogether, Cole Younger was accused of participation in four train robberies: (1) On July 21, 1873, at Council Bluffs, Iowa, a Chicago, Rock Island, and Pacific train was derailed and robbed; the engineer was killed and the fireman injured; (2) on January 31, 1874, at Gads Hill, Missouri, an Iron Mountain Railroad train was robbed; (3) between December 8 and 13, 1874—accounts vary—a Kansas and Pacific train with gold from Denver was robbed at Muncie, Kansas; and (4) on July 7, 1876, a Missouri Pacific train was held up near Otterville, Missouri. Throughout this period, no arrests were made for these crimes. Following the Iowa robbery, the gang was said to have spent some time in Texas.

On September 7, 1876, Cole, Bob, and Jim Younger, the James brothers, and three others rode into Northfield, Minnesota, to rob the First National Bank. Citizens outside the bank got word of what was happening, and in a few moments the town streets were full of men shooting at the eight robbers. Three outlaws were killed; the Youngers were wounded and later apprehended and taken to the Minnesota penitentiary at Stillwater. Bob Younger died there. Cole and Jim were paroled in 1901, largely due to the tireless efforts, for twenty years, of W. C. Bronaugh, a Civil War veteran whose life Cole Younger had saved in 1862.[2] Bronaugh's efforts were successful because Cole, from the moment he and his brothers pled guilty at their trial, comported himself as a model prisoner, and soon won the confidence and admiration of the prison authorities and all others with whom he came in contact.

For a while, after his parole, Cole traveled around with Frank James's Wild West Show. He frequently lectured on why a life of crime does not pay. He outlived Frank by a year, dying on February 21, 1916, not far from where he had been born.

The ballad about Cole Younger's exploits was probably composed and distributed on broadside in the late 1870s. The earliest printed reference is in John Lomax's 1910 collection, and he gives no source for his text.[3] Two of Randolph's informants claimed to have heard the ballad in the 1880s, but no printed versions are that early. Most of the other texts that have been collected, including the version transcribed in this book, are quite similar to Lomax's. The tunes, on the other hand, vary widely. Notably different are the two recordings by cowboy Edward L. Crain. Apart from lacking the verses about robbing the California miner and fighting the antiguerrillas, and from reporting the outlaws' playing poker instead of drinking whiskey to pass the time away, Crain's text is unusual in having three additional verses relating the death of the Northfield bank cashier and the subsequent flight, pursuit, and capture:

> The cashier, being as true as steel, refused our noted band,
> 'Twas Jesse James that pulled the trigger that killed this noble man.
>
> We run for life, for death was near, four hundred on our trail,
> We soon was overtaken, and landed safe in jail.
>
> Was there in the Stillwater jail we lay, a-wearing our lives away,
> Two James boys left to tell the tale of a sad and fatal day.[4]

There is thus no basis for the remark that "apparently Crain learned song word for word from the original edition of *Cowboy Songs*."[5] Nor does Crain's text match the one given by Lomax (1960), who cites Crain's recording as his source.

The ballad is written in the familiar broadside style called the "criminal's (last) goodnight." Such pieces purport to come from the pen of the criminal shortly before he is to be executed. "Cole Younger" is in some respects consistent with such an attribution, as the penitential attitude expressed in the text does mirror Younger's behavior after he was imprisoned. However, lest anyone actually believe that Cole wrote the ballad himself, such a notion is readily disproved: until his dying day Younger denied that the James brothers participated in the Northfield bank robbery, and further, he denied having had anything to do with any of the robberies the James boys perpetrated. There was, in fact, a good deal of mutual animosity between Cole Younger and Jesse James, and it is conceivable that they colluded a good deal less often than legend credits them.

The Union Pacific train robbery described in the ballad fails to match any of the robberies Cole Younger could have participated in. The James boys and others were suspected of robbing a UP train at Big Springs, Nebraska, in September, 1877, but Younger was already in jail at that time.[6] Furthermore, no one was killed in that robbery. Only in the CRI & P robbery of 1873 was anyone killed, and then only the engineer; the fireman was just injured. Evidently several robberies were confused in the ballad writer's mind.

In several other details the ballad disagrees with the historical record. I have found nothing about a robbery of a California miner in any of the Cole Younger biographies. The band of outlaws took the train to Minnesota and bought horses there; they did not ride horses all the way northward to "Minnesote-o."

Finally, the attribution of the murder of the Northfield cashier to Jesse James in Crain's long version revives a long-standing controversy regarding which outlaw committed that deed. Most later biographies left cashier Heywood's murderer unidentified. Younger, in his autobiography, quoted an account that named Charlie Pitts the murderer.[7] Several biographers and historians agreed that it was Jesse James, but more recent accounts by Breihan and Croy indicate that actually Frank James shot Heywood.[8]

The fact that Crain's text ends with the Youngers still in jail and the James brothers both alive suggests that the ballad was written before 1882, which is what we would expect.

The earliest commercial recording of "Cole Younger" was made in about November, 1930, in Dallas by Marc Williams, the "Cowboy Crooner." Between 1928 and 1930 he recorded nearly two dozen songs for Brunswick, most of which were traditional cowboy songs. The closeness of his "Cole Younger" text to Lomax's 1910 version suggests that popular volume as his source. In fact, all versions but one end, as does Lomax's, in the middle of the ballad—good evidence for the widespread influence of Lomax's collection. Cowboy Edward L. Crain recorded the ballad twice in 1931: in July for the American Record Corporation, and then in August for Columbia. The two recordings are virtually identical. His tune, transcribed in Lingenfelter, Dwyer, and Cohen's *Songs of the American West,* is quite different from Williams's, which is given in this volume.

Williams's background remains a mystery to record collectors, none of whom has been able to determine anything of his whereabouts either before or after his brief stint as a recording artist.[9] Of Edward Crain we know somewhat more. He was born in 1901 in Texas, about seventy miles west of Fort Worth. He learned to play guitar, violin, and mandolin early in his youth. In addition to radio work in Fort Worth, Dallas, and Longview, Crain spent time on a ranch and on cattle drives. He recalled that he learned "Cole Younger" as a boy of about ten or twelve, probably from someone's singing. In recent years he has been living in Ashland, Oregon.[10]

A 1972 article by the late folklorist John Q. Anderson discusses the various "Cole Younger" texts in detail and presents a new variant recorded by him in 1961.[11]

NOTES

1. The most reliable biography of Cole Younger seems to be Homer Croy, *Last of the Great Outlaws* (New York: Duell, Sloan and Pearce, 1956). The more recent *Younger Brothers* (San Antonio: Naylor Brothers, 1961), by Carl Breihan, is also useful. An important source is Younger's autobiography, *The Story of Cole Younger* (1903; rpt., Houston: Frontier Press, 1955). Other references, more often of interest for the legends they disseminate than for the facts they record, include Emerson Hough, *The Story of the Outlaw* (New York: Outing Publishing, 1907), of which chap. 20, "The Modern Bad Men," is devoted to the Youngers and the Jameses; William Ward, *The Younger Brothers* (Cleveland: Westbrook, 1908); George Huntington, *Robber and Hero* (1895; rpt., Minneapolis: Ross and Haines, 1962); J. W. Buel, *The Border Outlaws* (St. Louis: Dan Linahan, 1881); J. A. Dacus, *Illustrated Lives and Adventures of Frank and Jesse James and the Younger Brothers, the Noted Western Outlaws* (St. Louis: N. D. Thompson, 1882); A. C. Appler, *The Younger Brothers* (1892; rpt., New York: Frederick Fell, 1955). Most of the sources cited for Jesse James's biography in the notes to his song also contain material on Cole Younger.

2. Bronaugh's efforts are documented in his book, *The Youngers' Fight for Freedom* (Columbia, Mo.: E. W. Stephens Publishing, 1906).

3. D. K. Wilgus, *Anglo-American Folksong Scholarship since 1898* (New Brunswick, N.J.: Rutgers University Press, 1959), pp. 157–65, discusses the problems in tracing sources of Lomax's collectanea.

4. Edward L. Crain, Columbia 15710-D (see the discography). These verses also appear in South's text (Gordon MS 1091).

5. Alan Lomax, *The Folk Songs of North America* (Garden City, N.Y.: Doubleday, 1960), p. 350.

6. Breihan, *Younger Brothers,* p. 212, says this robbery was by Sam Bass and his gang.

7. Younger, *Story of Cole Younger,* p. 85.

8. Breihan, *Younger Brothers,* p. 98. Croy, *Last of the Great Outlaws,* p. 226.

9. A Williams discography was published in *Record Collector,* No. 7 (Nov., 1968), pp. 19–21.

10. Telephone interview, Mar. 25, 1970.

11. John Q. Anderson, "Another Texas Variant of 'Cole Younger,' Ballad of a Badman," *WF*, 31 (Apr., 1972), 103–15.

REFERENCES

A. "Cole Younger," in John A. Lomax, *Cowboy Songs and Other Frontier Ballads* (New York: Sturgis and Walton, 1910), pp. 106–7. No source is given for this. The first and most influential text printed.

"Cole Younger," by Marc Williams. Vocal and guitar. Recorded ca. Nov., 1930 (Brunswick master DAL 6748), in Dallas, Tex. Released on Brunswick 544 ca. 1931, and on Panachord (England) 25589. The earliest commercial recording of the ballad; transcribed here.

B. Anderson, J. Q.
Asch, 46–47 (transcription of Crain's Columbia recording)
Botkin (1951), 776 (transcription of LC AFS 3212 B1)
Brunvand, 238
Federal Writers Project, Cowboy Songs, Pt. 1 (Lincoln: WPA, 1937)
"Fiddler Joe's Corral," *Wild West Weekly*, July 2, 1932, p. 131
Finger (1923), 20–21
Finger (1927), 87 (discussion only)
Fife & Fife (1969), 261–62
Holbrook, 372 (discussion only)
Laws, 20, 177 (E 3) (discussion and references)
Lingenfelter, 321 (text from Lomax [1910], tune from Crain's Columbia recording)
Lomax, A. (1960), 345, 350 (conflation of Lomax [1910] text and that of Crain's Columbia recording)
Moore & Moore, 345–47
Ohrlin, 142–43
Randolph II, 12–16
Rosenberg, 18 (title only)
Silverman (1975) I, 82–83
Welsch (1966), 40–41

C. GORDON MSS:
1091—Walter R. South (1925)
3756—C. E. Roe (1929)

LOMAX PAPERS:
Mrs. Trantham (probably 1910, 7 stanzas)
J. B. Bourland, Marathon, Tex.
Mrs. W. O. Smith, Dallas, Tex.
Two other texts, sources not identified

D. Edward L. Crain—Columbia 15710-D; Folkways FA 2951 (FP 251): *Anthology of American Folk Music, Vol. 1* "Bandit Cole Younger"
Cowboy Ed Crane—Conqueror 8010   "Bandit Cole Younger"

E. Dock Boggs—Folkways FA 2392: *Dock Boggs, Vol. 2*
Paul Clayton—Riverside RLP 12-640: *Wanted for Murder*
Mary McCaslin—Philo 1024: *Prairie in the Sky*
Ed McCurdy—Columbia L2S 1012/L2L 1011: *The Badmen*
Glenn Ohrlin—Philo 1017: *Cowboy Songs*
Roger Welsch—Folkways FH 5337: *Sweet Nebraska Land*

F. ACWF:
Warde H. Ford (Dec. 25, 1938)
—(Dec. 26, 1938)—T7-66-136
Ollie Gilbert (July, 1965)—T7-65-31

LC AFS:
Oran Beasley—AFS 13142 A4
Wythe Bishop—AFS 5340 B2
Mrs. J. L. Davis—AFS 553 B
William Eden—AFS 12046 A32
Warde H. Ford—AFS 4197 B2
J. W. Green—AFS 2279 A
B. F. Head—AFS 3945 B1
Parker Johnson—AFS 11906 A
Mrs. Parker Johnson—AFS 11906 A
Virgil Lance—AFS 11887 A
George Lay—AFS 12050 A25
Vernon Light—AFS 901 B1   "Younger Brothers"
Mrs. Montie Martin—AFS 13134 B13
David W. Preece—AFS 911 A1
Ben Rice—AFS 3212 B1
Fred Woodruff—AFS 5348 B1

Railroad Bill

RAILROAD BILL

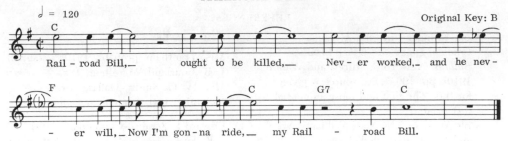

Rail - road Bill, — ought to be killed, — Nev - er worked, — and he nev -

er will, — Now I'm gon - na ride, — my Rail - road Bill.

Railroad Bill, ought to be killed,
Never worked, and he never will,
   Now I'm gonna ride, my Railroad Bill.

Railroad Bill done took my wife,
Threatened to me that he would take my life,
   Now I'm gonna ride, my Railroad Bill.

Going upon the mountain, take my stand,
Forty-one derringer in my right and left hand,
   Now I'm gonna ride, my Railroad Bill.

Going upon the mountain, going out west,
Forty-one derringer sticking in my breast,
   Now I'm gonna ride, my Railroad Bill.

Buy me a gun just as long as my arm,
Kill everybody ever done me wrong,
   Now I'm gonna ride, my Railroad Bill.

Buy me a gun with a shiny barrel,
Kill somebody 'bout my good-looking gal,
   Now I'm gonna ride, my Railroad Bill.

Got a thirty-eight special on a forty-four frame,
How in the world can I miss him when I've got dead aim,
   Now I'm gonna ride, my Railroad Bill.

When I went to the doctor, asked him what the matter could be,
Said, "If you don't stop drinking, son, it'll kill you dead,"
   Now I'm gonna ride, my Railroad Bill.

Gonna drink my liquor, drink it and win,
Doctor said it'd kill me, but he never said when,
   Now I'm gonna ride, my Railroad Bill.

If the river was brandy, and I was a duck,
I'd sink to the bottom, and I'd never come up,
   Now I'm gonna ride, my Railroad Bill.

Honey, honey, do you think I'm mean,
Times have caught me living on pork and beans,
    Now I'm gonna ride, my Railroad Bill.

Son, you talk about your honey, you ought to see mine,
She's humpbacked, bowlegged, crippled, and blind,
    Now I'm gonna ride, my Railroad Bill.

Honey, honey, do you think I'm a fool,
Think I'm gonna quit you while the weather is cool,
    Now I'm gonna ride, my Railroad Bill.

Honey, honey, quit worrying me,
It's going through the world in my [?]
    Now I'm gonna ride, my Railroad Bill.

[*Last stanza incomprehensible*]

Will Bennett

RAILROAD BILL

Railroad Bill, got so bad,
Stole all the chickens the poor farmers had,
Well, its tobacco [?too bad for] Railroad Bill.

Railroad Bill, went out west,
Shot all the buttons off a brakeman's vest,
Well, it's too bad, Railroad Bill.

Railroad Bill, got so fine,
Shot ninety-nine holes in a [?killer Shine],
Well, it's ride, Railroad Bill.

Railroad Bill, standing at the tank,
Waiting for the train you call Hancy Nank [*sic*],
Well, it's ride, Railroad Bill.

Railroad Bill, standing at the curve,
Gonna rob a mail train but he didn't have the nerve,
Well, it's too bad, Railroad Bill.

Railroad Bill, he lived on a hill,
He never worked or he never will,
Well, it's ride, Railroad Bill.

Railroad Bill, went out west,
Shot all the buttons off a brakeman's vest,
Well, it's too bad, Railroad Bill.

Frank Hutchison

In the mid-1890s, the phrase "railroad bill" was often seen in newspapers around the country. In the North and in big cities of the South, it referred to pending congressional legislation for railroad regulation; in the rural South, particularly along the L & N Railroad in Alabama and western Florida, it often referred to a "negro desperado by the name of Morris Slater, alias 'Railroad Bill,' who had been terrorizing the country generally throughout the South with his depredations."[1] Slater's activities first came to public notice in about 1894 and continued until March 7, 1897, when he was shot and killed in a grocery store in Atmore, Alabama.

The "official" version of Bill's activities and capture was published in the *L & N Employes' Magazine* in 1927 by J. B. Harlan, chief of the Louisville, Kentucky, police, who had been working for the L & N police in the 1890s and was in charge of the hunt for Bill after May, 1896. According to Harlan, Bill, who always was heavily armed with a rifle and two revolvers, robbed freight trains by tossing merchandise out along the tracks and later going back to gather up his booty. A succession of sheriffs, detectives, and railroad officers, both black and white, tried unsuccessfully to capture him. Deputy Sheriff Steward of Baldwin County, Alabama, was shot and killed by Bill on a raid. Black detective Stinson, who made friends with Bill and traveled with him waiting for the right moment to get the jump on him, disappeared one day and was never heard from again. In 1895, Sheriff E. S. McMillen of Escambia County announced his intention to capture Bill. Bill wrote him, "I love you and do not want to kill you so do not come after me."[2] Notwithstanding, McMillen set after him and was shot and killed on July 3.

In May, 1896, Chief Harlan was assigned to capture Bill. He and his assistants determined that Bill was confining his activities mostly to southern Alabama and Florida, and they directed the search to that area. On March 1, 1897, Henry Coldwell, Bill's partner, was captured near McDavid, Florida. Coldwell told the authorities all he knew of Bill's whereabouts, and they proceeded to Perdido, Alabama, where he was supposed to be hiding. While en route, Harlan received a telegram from Atmore stating that Constable McGowan had found and killed Railroad Bill there. McGowan had seen Bill sitting in a little grocery store on the outskirts of town eating crackers and cheese. He shot at him then and there. Bill drew his pistol and was about to return fire when he was shot by Bob Johns, the storekeeper.

Harlan's account naturally emphasized Slater's villainy, crediting him with little good. It would hardly have been appropriate for him to acknowledge that Railroad Bill was a folk hero in Alabama. Nevertheless, a few statements in Harlan's article did suggest more than he openly admitted: ". . . it was generally believed and talked by the negroes in that section of the country that 'Railroad Bill' was a superior being, possessed of super-human powers and, having been shot at so many times by different raiding parties, that he could not be killed with an ordinary leaden bullet; some of them claiming that the only bullet that would kill him was a solid silver missile."[3]

According to other accounts, Railroad Bill's image was even more fantastic. It was said he could change himself into various different animals to escape capture. The food he stole from railroad trains he gave to poor blacks, leaving it outside their cabin doors during the night.[4] Harlan also noted that local blacks were trying to protect and hide Bill, which suggests at least some approval of his conduct on the part of the local citizenry.

After he was gunned down, Slater's body was taken by Harlan and his colleagues to Brewton, Alabama, where the corpse was embalmed and photographed. Some three thousand persons came to see the remains. Later, the body was placed on exhibition in Montgomery, where viewers were charged a fee of fifty cents.

The official line, then, was that Morris Slater was a consummate villain who led a life of thievery and murder until he was cleverly apprehended. However, not everyone told

"The fight at the water tank" (*left*) and "The death of 'Railroad Bill' " (*right*). From J. B. Harlan, "Railroad Bill," *L & N Employes' Magazine*, May, 1927. Author's Collection.

the tale in the same manner. A quite contrary view was expressed by one of Robert W. Gordon's correspondents, W. B. Dinwiddie, whose family had moved into Escambia County in 1893:

> It was about three years later that two "smart alec" R.R. detectives who, being unable to run down some box car thieves first heard of a negro turpentine worker named Morris Slater, who being such a fast worker was called "Railroad Time." These detectives not waiting to learn anything about how he came by the name or the reason for it, broadcasted to the world at large that they were out to get this R.R. "Bill." How they got the names mixed no one knows but Railroad did know of their boast to take him dead or alive and being of the usual type of ignorant negro found around turpentine camps, only stopped long enough to get his Winchester .38 . . . and his old .45 cal. revolver, and took to the swamps. Nothing was heard from him for about a month when a country store was broken into and some few articles taken. This was the detectives chance and they let it be known that Railroad Bill was the culprit. . . . Slater wandered up and down the L & N R.R. for a couple of years and was never really known to bother anyone who did not start the ball rolling first and they usually got the worst of it. Slater was eventually killed in Tidmore and Ward's General Store at Williams Station (Atmore) by a shot in the back from a cowardly bystander. . . .[5]

According to Gordon's correspondent, Slater did not kill Sheriff McMillen; rather, when the sheriff took aim and shot at Slater, his gun misfired, killing him. Thus, in that informant's recollection of the events that took place more than a quarter-century before he wrote Gordon, Slater was almost completely harmless and deserved none of the persecution handed out by the law. Whether that point of view is accurate is of secondary concern here; the important fact is that Railroad Bill has emerged as not entirely a villain, but something of a martyr.

I don't know whether Railroad Bill still persists in the folk memory as a black hero who held his white oppressors at bay and stole from them to aid his fellow blacks. His memory is preserved in song, however. "Railroad Bill" is a good example of a "blues ballad," a narrative folksong with a rather loose organization rather than the temporally correct sequence of the broadside ballad.[6]

Some blues ballads seem to have acquired their present structure through years of oral transmission, with attendant imperfect memory or deliberate redaction. The Anglo-American "Pretty Polly," descended from a seventeenth-century British broadside, appears to be such a case.[7] Other blues ballads seem to have sprung forth in their loosely organized form, with little or no evidence for coherent and complete antecedent narrative ballads. In other words, blues ballads are not invariably the results of destructive processes, but testify to the existence in this country of a type of folksong that is persistent among both whites and blacks.

Three songs in this chapter are blues ballads. "John Henry" may once have been a more coherent narrative broadside type of ballad, but in most of the versions that still thrive, the order of verses is immaterial because the events are commented upon rather than recounted. "Casey Jones" is a blues ballad that has been recomposed into a formalized popular ballad of the narrative sort. Unlike either of these two, "Railroad Bill" is, I believe, a blues ballad that has never had a coherent structure. What is more, it is arguable that the ballad preceded the hero of the same name.

The earliest reports of songs about Railroad Bill came from Mississippi and Alabama blacks in the fieldwork of Perrow, White, and Odum. In 1912, Perrow reported four fragments that he had collected in 1909. One was a couplet that has since appeared in many "Railroad Bill" texts:

> Talk about yer five er yer ten dollar bill;
> Ain't no bill like de Railroad Bill.[8]

Another fragment, two couplets with refrain, included a part that has appeared in other blues ballads in black tradition, particularly about Casey Jones and Jay Gould and related songs:

> Railroad Bill said before he died,
> He'd fit all the trains so the rounders could ride.
>
> Railroad Bill cut a might big dash;
> He killed Bill Johnson with a lightning-flash.[9]

The reference in the second couplet has no historicity in the Slater affair, to my knowledge. In the third of Perrow's texts, Bill has "killed McMillan like a lightnin'-flash," a more accurate statement historically. The "ten-dollar bill / Railroad bill" rhyme appears in that version also.

In 1915–16, White obtained three fragments, one of which was reported sung by a construction gang in Mississippi in 1906. Two of his fragments included these lines:

> Railroad Bill did not know
> That Jim McMillan had a forty-fo'.[10]

Odum, in 1911, reported several longer texts (five, ten, and ten stanzas) and additional fragments, but identified no sources. However, two of his texts make an interesting contrast: one has no identifiable references to the historical outlaw at all, whereas the other is full of them. In the former, Railroad Bill is portrayed as lazy, thieving, and/or promiscuous:

> Some one went home an' tole my wife
> All about—well, my pas' life,
>   It was that bad Railroad Bill.

> Railroad Bill, Railroad Bill,
> He never work, an' he never will,
>   It was that bad Railroad Bill.
>
> Railroad Bill so mean an' so bad,
> Till he tuk ev'ything that farmer had,
>   It was that bad Railroad Bill.[11]

Verses such as these—and they comprise the bulk of the Railroad Bill ballad corpus—have little connection with Slater and could well have been sung before the events of the 1890s.

A plausible source for the Railroad Bill songs is the series of nineteenth-century black songs about various "Bill" characters: "Roscoe Bill,"[12] "Shootin' Bill,"[13] "Buffalo Bill,"[14] and "Nigger Bill," the latter including this couplet:

> I'se wild Nigger Bill, from Redpepper Hill,
> I never did wo'k, an' I never will.[15]

The universality of the latter verse form is suggested by the fragment of a children's rhyme reported from Peterborough, England:

> I'm Dirty Bill from Vinegar Hill,
> Never had a bath and never will.[16]

The most remarkable thing about Morris Slater and his activities is that he became known as "Railroad Bill," rather than "Railroad Moe" or something similar. In fact, in the few contemporary newspaper accounts I have seen, he was often nicknamed just "Railroad." Is the account of W. B. Dinwiddie, quoted above, correct? Can we attribute the name "Railroad Bill" to a bureaucratic error? The nickname is understandable to me only by assuming a pre-existing song tradition to which Slater's career was somehow appended. Furthermore, the extent of material that can unmistakably be traced to Slater's actions is slender indeed—not more than four or five verses.[17]

Although "Railroad Bill" became a standard showpiece for finger-picking guitarists in the urban folk music revival of the 1950s and 1960s, its early career on record was not vigorous at all. The first waxing was made on September 11, 1924, by Riley Puckett and Gid Tanner. Two months later, Roba Stanley and Bill Patterson of Atlanta recorded a handful of songs for OKeh, one of which was "Railroad Bill." None of the Patterson-Stanley performances recorded at that time was very strong musically, although their "Railroad Bill" text was noteworthy in containing a stanza referring to Cuba, thus probably dating it to about 1898:

> Two dice in Cuba, three tramps in Spain,
> Send all my money for gasoline,
>   Oh, drive on, you Railroad Bill.[18]

Roba Stanley took out the first copyright on "Railroad Bill" the following year, claiming credit for words and music (E unp. 605980, Feb. 21, 1925). Three more recordings were made in the latter half of 1929, including Will Bennett's, the first by a black artist (not counting Martha Copeland's related song, "Hobo Bill"). All but one of these early versions refer to Railroad Bill in only a few stanzas.

The recording responsible for the song's later popularity was Hobart Smith's rendition on the Disc label in the 1940s.[19] Smith's finger-picking virtuosity provided an oft-copied model for young city guitar players. Smith's was the first recording to use the now-standard refrain "Ride, ride, ride." (Sandburg's 1927 text was the first printed version with it.) Puckett's refrain was "Well, it's drive, drive, drive." Refrains prior to Smith's recording included "Lookin' for Railroad Bill," "That bad Railroad Bill," "Ride on, Railroad Bill," "I'm afraid of Railroad Bill." Frank Hutchison's finger-picking style on his OKeh recording is similar to Hobart Smith's in many ways. I have given Hutchison's text as a supplement to Will Bennett's version (the only prewar recording by a black musician) because Bennett's has so few references to Railroad Bill himself.

NOTES

1. J. B. Harlan, "Railroad Bill," *L & N Employes' Magazine,* 3 (May, 1927), 30–31, 69–70. This is the primary source of historical data used in these notes. Harlan's own narrative is also the source for other "official" accounts; see, e.g., Kincaid A. Herr, *The L & N Railroad, 1850–1940, 1941–1959,* enl. ed. (Louisville: L & N Magazine, 1959), p. 68.

2. Carl Carmer, *Stars Fell on Alabama* (1934; rpt., New York: Hill and Wang, 1961), pp. 122–25.

3. Harlan, "Railroad Bill," p. 30.

4. Carmer, *Stars Fell on Alabama,* p. 123, and *The Hurricane's Children* (New York and Toronto: Farrar and Rinehart, 1937), p. 115. These passages are reprinted in B. A. Botkin, ed., *A Treasury of Southern Folklore* (New York: Crown Publishers, 1949), p. 239.

5. W. B. Dinwiddie of Phoebus, Va., to R. W. Gordon, Sept. 21, 1929 (Gordon MS 782).

6. The term *blues ballad* was first proposed by D. K. Wilgus. The concept has been discussed in greatest detail in Marina Bokelman, " 'The Coon Can Game': A Blues Ballad Tradition" (M.A. thesis, University of California, Los Angeles, 1968). See also n. 18 following the discussion of "Casey Jones."

7. See, e.g., G. Malcolm Laws, Jr., *American Balladry from British Broadsides* (Philadelphia: American Folklore Society, 1957), pp. 268–69, for discussion and references.

8. E. C. Perrow, "Songs and Rhymes of the South" *JAF,* 25 (Jan.-Mar., 1912), 155, D text.

9. Ibid., B text.

10. Newman I. White, *American Negro Folk-Songs* (1928; rpt., Hatboro, Pa.: Folklore Associates, 1965), pp. 358–59.

11. Howard W. Odum, "Folk-Song and Folk-Poetry as Found in the Secular Songs of the Southern Negroes," *JAF,* 24 (July-Sept., 1911), 289.

12. Howard W. Odum and Guy B. Johnson, *Negro Workaday Songs* (Chapel Hill: University of North Carolina Press, 1926), p. 62.

13. Ibid., p. 63.

14. Ibid., p. 67. Here is a more interesting Buffalo Bill verse, possibly as old as the early 1870s:

> Buffalo Bill, Buffalo Bill,
> Never missed and never will;
> Always aims and shoots to kill,
> And the company pays his buffalo bill.

This verse, said to have been sung about William "Buffalo Bill" Cody at the time he first acquired his nickname, is cited in Marshall Fishwick, *The Hero, American Style* (New York: David McKay, 1969), p. 119, and Don Russell, *The Lives and Legends of Buffalo Bill* (Norman: University of Oklahoma Press, 1960), p. 90.

15. Thomas W. Talley, *Negro Folk Rhymes* (New York: Macmillan, 1922), p. 94.

16. Iona Opie and Peter Opie, *The Lore and Language of School Children* (Oxford: Oxford University Press, 1959), p. 20.

17. Alan Lomax has pointed out to me that southern blacks were often known to peers by nicknames that were not derived from their given names. This offers an alternative explanation for the nickname Railroad Bill.

18. I am grateful to Charles Wolfe, Peggy Bulger, and Gene Wiggins for publishing Roba Stanley's own transcription of her words to this song, since the original recording is very difficult to understand. See "Roba Stanley, the First Country Music Sweetheart," *Old Time Music*, No. 26 (Autumn, 1977), p. 18.

19. Transcribed in *New Lost City Ramblers Song Book*, edited by John Cohen and Mike Seeger (New York: Oak Publications, 1964), p. 164.

Roba Stanley. Courtesy of Charles Wolfe.

REFERENCES

A. ["Railroad Bill"], in Newman I. White,
    American Negro Folk-Songs (1928; rpt.,
    Hatboro, Pa.: Folklore Associates,
    1965), pp. 358–59. Text I was reported
    from Auburn, Ala., 1915–16, MS of C.
    C. Certain, as sung by a construction
    gang in Mississippi in 1906. Earliest
    report of the song in oral tradition.
    "Railroad Bill," by Riley Puckett. Puckett,
    vocal and banjo; Gid Tanner, fiddle.
    Recorded Sept. 11, 1924 (Columbia
    master 140023), in New York City.
    Released on Columbia 15040-D ca.
    Sept., 1925; on Silvertone 3258 (as by
    Tom Watson) ca. 1926–27; and on
    Harmony 5147-H (as by Fred Wilson),
    ca. 1928. Reissued on County 515:
    Mountain Banjo Songs and Tunes. First
    recording of the song.
    "Railroad Bill," by Will Bennett. Vocal
    and guitar. Recorded in ca. Sept., 1929
    (Vocalion master K-127), in Knoxville,
    Tenn. Released on Vocalion 1464.
    Reissued by accident on some pressings
    of Brunswick album B-1024: *Listen to
    Our Story*, ca. 1946. Reissued on
    Origin Jazz Library OJL-18: *Let's Go
    Riding*; Roots RL 318: *East Coast
    States*. First recording by a black artist;
    text and tune transcribed here.
    "Railroad Bill," by Frank Hutchison.
    Vocal and guitar. Recorded July 9, 1929
    (Columbia/OKeh master 402509-B), in
    New York City. Released on OKeh
    45425 on Mar. 25, 1930. Reissued on
    Rounder 1007: *The Train That Carried
    My Girl from Town*. The text is
    transcribed here.

B. *Alabama*, 126
    Beard, 201–2
    Botkin (1949), 239 (from Odum &
    Johnson [1926])
    Burt, 200
    Carmer (1934), 124
    Carmer (1937), 115–21 (discussion only)
    Colquhoun, 57   "Railway Bill" (New
    Zealand version)
    Gordon, *Adventure*, Oct. 20, 1924, p. 191
    Gordon, *Adventure*, June 23, 1926,
    p. 191

Harlan, J. B., "Railroad Bill," *L & N
Employes' Magazine*, May, 1927,
pp. 30–31, 69–70
Laws, 252 (I 13) (discussion and
references)
Leach, M., 175–76 (discussion only)
Leach & Beck, 257
Leisy (1966), 271
Levine, 410–11
Lomax, A. (1960), 568
Lomax & Lomax (1934), 118
NLCR, 164
Odum, 289
Odum & Johnson (1925), 198–203
Odum & Johnson (1926), 246
Oliver (1971)
Perrow (1912), 155
Sandburg, 384
Scarborough, 251
Shay (1927), 92; 48 in 1961 ed.
Silverman (1975) II, 342
Work, 240

C. LC AFS:
    C. C. de Gravelle, New Iberia, La.
    (June, 1934)—John A. Lomax MSS

D. Martha Copeland—Columbia 14248-D
    "Hobo Bill" (related piece)
    Otis Mote—OKeh 45389
    Hobart Smith—Disc 6081
    Roba Stanley and Bill Patterson—OKeh
    40295

E. Etta Baker—Tradition TLP 1007:
    *Instrumental Music of the Southern
    Appalachians*; Tradition TSP 2: *The
    Folk Song Tradition*; Sine Qua Non
    102: *An Anthology of Folk Music*
    Marilyn Bennett—Kiwi (New Zealand)
    SLC-102: *Song of a Young Country*
    "Railway Bill"
    Big Sky Singers—Dot DLP 3603: *The Big
    Sky Singers*
    Fleming Brown—Folk-Legacy FSI 1:
    Fleming Brown
    Guy Carawan, Peggy Seeger, Johnny
    Cole, and Sammy Stokes—Kapp KL
    1110: *Folk-Song Saturday Night*
    Cherry Hill Singers—Hi Fi Records L
    1020: *Cherry Hill Singers*

Paul Clayton—Folkways FA 2110 (FP
47/3) (10″ LP): *Folksongs and Ballads of
Virginia*
Jackie Dae—MPS (45 rpm) 11570
Lonnie Donegan—Mercury MG 20229:
*An Englishman Sings American Folk
Songs*
Jack Elliott—Prestige International 13033
and Prestige 7721: *Ramblin' Jack Elliott*
Gaslight Singers—Mercury MG 20848:
The Gaslight Singers
Frank Hamilton—Concert-Disc CS-54:
The Folk Singer's Folk Singer
Highwaymen—United Artists 3225/6225:
Encore
Homesteaders—Riverside RM 7537:
Railroad Bill
Cisco Houston—Folkways FA 2013 (FP
13): *900 Miles and Other Railroad
Songs*
—Vanguard VSD 2088: *Folk Festival at
Newport, 1960, Vol. 2*
Richard Lockmiller and Jim Connor
—Folklore F/LEUT 5
Alan Lomax and the Dupree Family
—Kapp KL-1316: *Raise a Ruckus and
Have a Hootenanny*
Lonesome River Boys—Battle BM 6128:
Bluegrass Hootenanny
—Riverside RLP 7535: *Raise a Ruckus*
J. E. Mainer and his Mountaineers
—Rural Rhythm RR 191: *The Legendary
J. E. Mainer and His Mountaineers*
—*More Old Time Mountain Music*
New Christy Minstrels—Columbia CL
1872/CS 8672: *Presenting—New
Christy Minstrels*; Harmony H 31180:
Songs of Our Wonderful Land
Tom Paley—Esoteric ES 538: *Shivaree!*

Richard and Jim—Capitol T/ST 2058:
Richard and Jim
Walt Robertson—Folkways FA 2330:
*Walt Robertson Sings American Folk
Songs*
Samplers—Kapp KL-1232: *The Samplers
in Person*
Hobart Smith—Prestige 25009: *Southern
Journey, Vol. 9, Bad Man Ballads*
—Vanguard VRS 9182/VSD 79182:
*Traditional Music at Newport, 1964,
Part 1*
—Asch AA 4: *The Asch Recordings
1939–45, Vol. 2*
Horace Sprott—Folkways FA 2652 (FP
652): *Music from the South, Vol. 3,
Horace Sprott* "One Dollar Bill
Two Dollar Bill" (related piece)
Stonemans—RCA Victor LSP-4431:
California Blues
Taj Mahal—Columbia KC 32600: *Oooh
So Good 'n Blues*
Chris Terrie—Custom CM 2085/CS 1085:
Ode to Billie Joe
Jim Wall and group—Rural Rhythm
RR-1168: *Old Time Songs*
Whiskeyhill Singers—Capitol T-1728:
*Dave Guard and the Whiskeyhill
Singers* "Ride on Railroad Bill"

F. LC AFS:

Vera Hall—AFS 1315 B2
—AFS 1323 A3
Blind Jesse Harris—AFS 1327 B2
H. D. Kinard—AFS 3039 B2
Bascom Lamar Lunsford—AFS 1801 B1
Luther Smith—AFS 6724 B2
—AFS 6725 A1
—AFS 6728 B2

Casey Jones

KASSIE JONES

I woke up this morn - ing, four o 'clock, Mis-ter
Cas - ey told his fire-man get his boil - er hot;___
Put on your wat - er, put on your coal,___ Put your
head out the win - dow, see my driv - ers roll;___ See my
driv-ers roll, Put your head out the win - dow, see my driv - ers roll._

I woke up this morning, four o'clock,
Mister Casey told his fireman get his boiler hot;
Put on your water, put on your coal,
Put your head out the window, see my drivers roll;
　　See my drivers roll,
　　　Put your head out the window, see my drivers roll.

Lord, some people said Mister Casey couldn't run,
Let me tell you what Mister Casey done;
He left Memphis, was a quarter to nine,
Got to Newport News, it was dinner time;
　　It was dinner time,
　　　Got [to] Newport News, it was dinner time.

I sold my gin, I sold it straight,
Police run to my woman's gate;
She come to the door, she nod her head.
She made me welcome to the folding bed;
　　To the folding bed,
　　　Made me welcome to the folding bed.

Lord, people said to Casey, "You're running over time,
You'll have nothin' losin' [?a collusion] with the one-o-nine."
Casey said, "This engine's mine,
I'll run her into glory 'less I make my time."
Said to all the passengers, "Better keep yourself hid,
I'm not gonna shake it like Chaney did;
  Chaney did,
  I'm not gonna shake it like Chaney did."

Mister Casey run his engine to a mile of the place,.
Number Four stabbed him in the face;
The deputy told Casey, "Well, you must leave town,"
"[I] believe to my soul I'm Alabama bound;
  Alabama bound,
  Believe to my soul I'm Alabama bound."

Missus Casey said she dreamt a dream,
The night she bought her sewin' machine;
The needle got broke and she could not sew,
She loved Mister Casey 'cause she told me so;
  Told me so,
  Loved Mister Casey 'cause she told me so.

There was a woman name Miss Alice Fry,
Said, "I'm gonna ride with Mister Casey or die;
I ain't good looking but I take my time,
A rambling woman with a rambling mind;
  Got a rambling mind."

Casey looked at his water, his water was low;
Looked at his watch, his watch was slow.
  On the road again,
  Natural born eas'man, on the road again.

Lord, the people tell by the throttle moan,
The man at the fire Mister Casey Jones,
  Mister Casey Jones.

Mister Casey said before he died,
One more road that he wants to ride;
People tell Casey, "Which road is he?"
"Southern Pacific and the Sancta Fee,
  Sancta Fee."

This morning I heard someone were dyin',
Missus Casey's children on her doorstep cryin';
"Mama, mama, I can't keep from cryin',
Papa got killed on the Southern Line,
  On the Southern Line,
  Papa got killed on the Southern Line."

"Mama, mama, how can it be?
Killed my father in the first degree."
"Children, children, won't you hold your breath,
Draw another pension from your father's death,
  From your father's death."

  On the road again,
  I'm a natural born eas'man, on the road again.

Tuesday morning it looked like rain,
Around the curve came a passenger train;
Under the boiler laid Casey Jones,
Good old engineer but he's dead and gone;
  Dead and gone.

  On the road again,
  I'm a natural born eas'man, on the road again.

I left Memphis to spread the news,
Memphis women don't wear no shoes;
Had it written in the back of my shirt,
Natural born eas'man, don't have to work;
  Don't have to work,
  I'm a natural born eas'man, don't have to work.

                                        Furry Lewis

The pop song that was to become one of the nation's favorites through much of the first half of the twentieth century was first given an audience at a small, now-long-defunct café in Venice, California. Today, more than six decades later, there are probably millions who can sing at least the chorus to "Casey Jones," but most of them are unaware that Jones was a real engineer, killed in an actual wreck on the Illinois Central Railroad in April of 1900. What we do know today of Casey Jones? Was the song true? Who composed it? How did it become so popular? These are a few of the questions that have been asked over and over by students of American railroad lore, folksong, and popular song. Some of the answers, at least, we can now provide.

Readers of the *Memphis Commercial Appeal* learned the details of a fatal wreck in the front page of the Tuesday morning, May 1, 1900, edition:

DEAD UNDER HIS CAB
THE SAD END OF ENGINEER CASEY JONES
ILLINOIS CENTRAL WRECK

Southbound Passenger Train No. 1 Crashes into the Rear of a Freight—Details of the Accident

Jackson, Miss. April 30—(Special)—A disastrous collision occurred about 4 o'clock this morning on the Illinois Central Railroad at Vaughan, a station eleven miles north of Canton. The Engineer, Casey Jones, was instantly killed and Express Messenger Miller was hurt internally, but not seriously.

The south-bound passenger train, No. 1, was running under a full head of steam when it crashed into the rear end of a caboose and three freight cars which were standing on the main track, the other portion of the train being on a sidetrack. The caboose and

Sheet music: "Casey Jones." Courtesy of David Morton and the Archives of Popular American Music, UCLA.

two of the cars were smashed to pieces, the engine left the rails and plowed into an embankment, where it overturned and was completely wrecked, the baggage and mail coaches also being thrown from the track and badly damaged. The engineer was killed outright by the concussion. His body was found lying under the cab with his skull crushed and the right arm torn from its socket. The fireman jumped just in time to save his life. The express messenger was thrown against the side of the car, having two of his ribs broken by the blow, but his condition is not considered dangerous.

The other employees and all of the passengers were more or less jolted by the shock, some of them receiving bruises and slight wounds, none of which, however, were serious.

Every effort was made to stop the speeding train, but without success. Two flagmen were sent down the track with danger signals and torpedoes were placed on the rails as a warning, but the engineer did not seem to take any notice of the signals nor to realize the situation until within a short distance of the caboose, when he made a violent attempt to put on the air brakes, but the distance was too short to avoid the crash. The freight boxes were loaded with bundled hay and the scattered coals from the engine soon set fire to the debris, and it was feared at one time that the whole mass of wreckage would be destroyed, but the fire was finally extinguished without doing very great damage.

The train was what is known as the New Orleans fast mail; it was running on time, and was in charge of Conductor Turner of Memphis. The indirect cause of the wreck seemed to be a lack of switching facilities at Vaughan's. Four long freight trains had gotten there and the siding was not sufficient to accommodate them. Traffic on the road has been unusually heavy since the recent floods, and the delay in freight transportation has caused much inconvenience. . . .

Engineer Jones had been in the service of the Illinois Central for many years, and was highly esteemed as one of the road's safest and most capable engineers. He lived at Jackson, Tenn., where his remains were shipped. He leaves a wife and three children.

To this summary—essentially correct in its details—can be added background information uncovered by later workers; in particular, two accounts by Freeman Hubbard, long-time editor of *Railroad Magazine* and author of *Railroad Avenue*, a fascinating collection of railroad lore, are highly recommended for supplementary reading, and I have drawn on them heavily.[1] Christened John Luther Jones, the hero of our story was born March 14, 1863—exactly where has been disputed—and reared in the town of Cayce, Kentucky. He adopted the nickname of his hometown, "Cayce," to distinguish himself from a legion of Welsh-American Joneses who also took to railroading as an occupation, and signed his name "Cayce Jones" on all but the most formal documents; it was newspapermen, according to Hubbard, who changed the spelling to "Casey" to match the pronunciation. While still in his teens he began his lifelong association with the railroads, working first as janitor, then on switching crew, then loading livestock, then as messenger, brakeman, fireman, and eventually, engineer—a post his three younger brothers also held. In 1886 he married his boardinghouse keeper's daughter, Jane Brady. Two years later he entered the employ of the Illinois Central Railroad, and in 1890 he moved from fireman to engineer. In January, 1900, he took over the most prestigious run of the railroad—the IC's *Cannonball Express*, the fast passenger train from Chicago to New Orleans. Casey brought with him his distinctive six-chime train whistle—in those days, engineers were permitted to install whatever type of whistle they wished—so that, indeed, as the ballad told,

> The switchman knew by the engine's moans
> That the man at the throttle was Casey Jones.

On Sunday, April 29, 1900, Casey and his fireman, Sim Webb, were due to take charge of the *Cannonball* in Memphis at a departure time of 11:35 P.M., southbound to Canton, Mississippi. However, the train was about ninety-five minutes late arriving in Memphis, so Casey and Sim left early Monday morning, Casey determined to make up the lost time in the course of the 188-mile ride. As Hubbard notes, even during his lifetime Casey had a reputation as a "fast roller," who never dawdled and who could be counted on to stick close to the schedule even if a few corners had to be cut. And nine times in his ten years of engineering for the IC he was cited for infractions of regulations, such as running through switches, or leaving them open behind him, or other negligences. Consequently, although the night was dark and cloudy, and the season had been rainy, early Monday morning found him highballing his engine southward in a race to recover lost time. He was nearly back on schedule when his train approached Vaughan, 175 miles south of Memphis. Here, because of an unusual combination of circumstances, the caboose of a southbound freight extended past the siding switch and was on the mainline in Jones's way. Jones was going too fast to stop. Sim Webb related that probably because the engine was on a sharp curve, the red lights were visible only on the fireman's side of the engine. Sim yelled, "Look out! We're gonna hit something." "Jump, Sim!" were Casey's last words, as he applied the brakes. Webb did jump, sustaining only slight injuries; but Jones died as his engine plowed into the caboose of the other train.[2]

These are the essential facts. One unsettled question is that of Casey's culpability in the accident. At the time of the tragedy, Casey's surviving fireman, Sim Webb, agreed with other railroadmen involved that all due precautions had been taken to warn the *Cannonball* of the mishap at Vaughan, that torpedoes had been placed on the tracks and the switch protected by a flagman. Years later, he altered his story, indicating that the crew at Vaughan had probably forgotten to send out a flagman to warn Casey. But the folk memory is uncluttered by such details; Casey, admired during his lifetime, was practically apotheosized in death. Whether he would still be remembered today is doubtful, had it not been for songlore that grew up around his name. Nine years after he met his death, one song in particular became a national rage: it was a pop song, "Casey Jones," written by two vaudevillians, T. Lawrence Seibert and Eddie Newton, and published in 1909. How did they find out about Casey Jones?

By 1911, different questions were being asked in many circles about the popular vaudeville song: Who was Casey Jones? Was the story of the ballad true?

In a November, 1910, letter to the editor of *Railroad Man's Magazine*, George L. Garnett of Birmingham recounted with reasonable accuracy the essential biographical details concerning John Luther Jones, except that the date of his death was given as March 18, 1900. Garnett also stated that "the song bearing his name was written and sung by an old roundhouse darky by the name of Wallace Sanders. . . .[3] Garnett may also have written a letter, signed "Railroader," to the *Kansas City Star* that was published on August 1, 1911. That newspaper had printed articles about Casey Jones and had received several letters from readers. "Railroader" supplied factual details similar to those of Garnett's 1910 letter. Along with his comments were three letters from other railroaders; each one claimed that a different person, killed in a different accident, was the inspiration for the ballad, and each quoted a different fragment of a ballad to prove it.

One writer, signing himself "A. Rounder," attributed the source to an accident near Mammoth Springs, Arkansas, in about 1902, in which engineer Peter Martin Jones, known as K. C. Jones, was killed on the old Kansas City, Fort Scott, and Memphis Railroad. He claimed that the ballad, which he first heard sung in the roundhouse at Thayer, Missouri, began:

Casey Jones, portrait in the Railroad Museum, Jackson, Tennessee. Collection of the Casey Jones Museum.

Grave marker, Mount Calvary Cemetery, Jackson, Tennessee. Collection of the Casey Jones Museum.

> Come all you rounders if you want to hear,
> The story of a brave engineer;
> K. C. Jones was the hero's name,
> He lived without fear and he died without blame.

Another writer claimed Casey Jones was in reality Harrison Stacey Jones, killed in an accident on the Northern Pacific Railroad near Billings, Montana, July 19, 1899. "One verse of the song," he wrote, "as originally sung, fixes beyond all doubt the place of the accident":

> Through Billings yards he let her rock,
> Fireman yelled, "You've passed the block."
> Stacey said as he threw her wide,
> "In another minute we're goin' to glide [?collide]."

Still another correspondent asserted that Casey Jones was killed on the B & O near Cumberland, Maryland, on December 18, 1895. His real name was Cassidy Jones, and his run was from Washington Junction to Connellsville: "There isn't a 'rounder' east of Pittsburgh who doesn't know the lines:

> Cassidy, 'twas known all through the gap
> Opened the throttle when he took a nap,
> And every town knew by the engine's blow
> When Cassidy went through on the B. & O.

In the August 21 issue a *Star* reader in Troy, Kansas, wrote that a man living there claimed to be Casey Jones; he railroaded on the Rock Island line from 1897 to 1907 and was slightly lame—from the famous wreck, the pretender explained.

One person who saw the August 1 letters was an itinerant hobo who went by the name of Kelley the Rake. The following day he wrote a fascinating letter to the *Star*, which was published on August 5. The essential part is as follows:

In the beginning I would say that after a sudden and unsought for exit from college when I was 16, and the ensuing wrath of my paternal ancestor, I took to the road and since have sought adventure in the realms of the unemployed. In this connection I am enabled to give authoritative and authentic information about this mythical Casey Jones, inasmuch as I was one of the progenitors of the original song.

Jay Gould, for reasons of economy, removed the platforms from the Missouri Pacific mail and baggage cars, thus eliminating a safe and comfortable means of transportation for "bos." A pal of mine, one Herkimer Hank, and myself were incited to some wrath by this action which resulted in the following effusion:

> Old Jay Gould said, before he died:
> I'll fix the blind so the 'bos can't ride.
> If they ride, they will ride a rod,
> And place their life in the hands of God.

This verse called for more so we added the following:

> Old Jay Gould said, as he was about to die,
> There's two more railroads I'd like to buy.
> We were wondering what they could be.
> He said, the New York Central and the Santa Fe.

These verses were afterward added one by one. My repertoire holds about fifty verses about Old Jay Gould.

And now for the Casey Jones part. Some years ago on the Rock Island between Herington and Kansas City was a freight engineer who was always good for a ride if we would heave coal. He said his name was James A. Michaels, and he was so known. He was a reckless runner, and verses began to be made to the tune of old Jay Gould. Here are six of them:

> Songs are sung about the heroes of old,
> I'll tell you of one that skins them cold.
> James A. Michaels was the eagle eye's name,
> And when he died he died dead game.

> James A. Michaels was a brave engineer;
> He told the tallow pot not to fear.
> Says he, all you got to do is to keep her hot,
> And we'll make it in about four o'clock.

> Just grab the shovel and heave the coal;
> Put your head out the window and watch the drivers roll.
> Then he looked at his watch and mumbled and said,
> We may make it, but we'll all be dead.

> They pulled out of ———— about forty minutes late,
> Dragging behind thirty-six cars of freight.
> The conductor didn't keep any tab,
> 'Cause James A. Michaels was in the cab.

> But when they got to the whistling post,
> James turned as pale as any old ghost.
> He had the tallow pot out on top,
> Helping the brakies to make the stop.

> The Cannon Ball come splitting the air
> He threw her over and unloaded right there.
> He yelled to the fireman, You'd better jump,
> 'Cause two locomotives is about to bump.

On railroads an engineer is an eagle eye, a fireman a tallow pot.

These verses chosen at random from among probably three hundred verses that I know.

I believe the way the Casey Jones song was started was thus: A small coterie of us were flopped under a bean tree in Arizona some time ago, singing this song. A guy asks if we would write some of it out. We did, and he said he was going to publish it. I think this is the real origin of the song. Yours respectfully,

Kelley The Rake

BS 8/2/11

In Camp, Near Porum, Ok., Aug. 2, 1911

In December, 1911, Peter Mulligan contributed a long article about Casey Jones to *Railroad Man's Magazine*. He discussed the various letters that the *Kansas City Star* had published, along with several other theories about the real Casey Jones, concluding with the story of John Luther Jones printed in a letter in the Nashville *Tennessean* (which contained the erroneous date of the accident). When Mulligan contacted Seibert and Newton regarding their song, they informed him that they wrote it "from an old negro song. . . . Nobody knows how many verses it had, and as near as we can trace it back it started about an old engineer named John Luther Jones. . . . We have searched back, and so far as we can learn, an old darkey by the name of Wallace Saunders, working in a roundhouse, started the first of the Casey Jones song. . . ."[4] The rest of the details quoted by Seibert and Newton (including the incorrect date of death) were as Garnett had given them in his letter.

Readers of the magazine were evidently still not satisfied, for in April, 1912, Mulligan published a follow-up article with another handful of theories and purported original ballads. An Ohio reader believed the real Casey Jones to have been Casey Shannon, an engineer who died on a switch engine from Marshfield to Myrtle Point, Oregon. He submitted a five-stanza ballad, the first and last stanzas of which were:

> Come all you dagos if you want to hear
> A story of a real good engineer;
> Casey Shannon was the hero's name,
> In a dinky line, boys, he won his fame.

> Casey said before he died,
> There were two more engines that he'd like to ride.
> Miller asked, "Which may they be?"
> "The nine-ninety-seven and the six-thirty-three."[5]

Another railroader claimed the hero of the wreck was really David Casey Jones, killed near Mammoth Springs, Tennessee, and insisted that he was the last person to talk to Jones before the bump. Yet another correspondent said Jones was an imaginary engineer, the subject of a song written in 1898 by a Minnesota baggageman. One "Red Mc.," a reader in Memphis, identified the correct accident but reported that the song was composed by a Negro named George Crockett, who was employed about the shop and roundhouse at Water Valley, Mississippi.

In sum, scarcely a dozen years after John Luther Jones was killed, and three years after the publication of the vaudeville hit about him, there were already handfuls of accounts identifying the Casey Jones of the song with numerous different railroad engineers on as many different railroad lines. But the preponderance of evidence favored John Luther Jones as the genuine article; and attribution of the source of the ballad to a black engine-wiper came from several corners. The next natural questions are these: What was the nature of the song Wash Saunders sang about Casey? How different was it from the Seibert-Newton song? Or, more generally, what do we know of Casey Jones songlore from before 1909?

To my knowledge, the first published reference to a song about Casey Jones appeared in the March, 1908, issue of *Railroad Man's Magazine*: "An engineer friend asks us to tell him the words of a song written in memory of Casey Jones, an engineer on the Southern, near Memphis, Tenn. . . ."[6] Two months later, a text was published, with the note that "Jones was an engineer on the I.C., between Memphis and Canton, Mississippi, and was killed in a wreck several years ago. The song is supposed to have been sung by his negro fireman."[7] This, hereafter referred to as the 1908 version, is the earliest published text of the ballad:

> Come all you rounders, for I want you to hear
> The story told of an engineer.
> Casey Jones was the rounder's name,
> A heavy right-wheeler of a mighty fame.

Caller called Jones about half past four;
He kissed his wife at the station door,
Climbed into the cab with his orders in his hand,
Says, "This is my trip to the holy land."

Through South Memphis yards, on the fly,
He heard the fire-boy say, "You've got a white eye."
All the switchmen knew, by the engine moan,
That the man at the throttle was Casey Jones.

It had been raining some five or six weeks,
The railroad track was like the bed of a creek;
They rated him down to a thirty-mile gait,
Threw the south-bound mail about eight hours late.

Fireman says, "Casey, you're running too fast,
You run the block-board the last station you passed."
Jones says, "Yes, I believe we'll make it through,
For she steams better than I ever knew."

Jones says, "Fireman, don't you fret;
Keep knocking at the fire-door, don't give up yet.
I'm going to run her till she leaves the rail,
Or make it in on time with the Southern mail."

Around the curve and down the dump
Two locomotives were bound to bump.
Fireman hollered, "Jones, it's just ahead;
We might jump and make it, but we'll all be dead."

'Twas around this curve he spied a passenger-train.
Reversing his engine, he caused the bell to ring.
Fireman jumped off, but Jones stayed on—
He's a good engineer, but he's dead and gone.

Poor Casey Jones was all right,
For he stuck to his duty both day and night.
They loved to hear his whistle and ring of number three,
As he came into Memphis on the old I. C.

Headaches and heartaches, and all kinds of pain,
Are not apart from a railroad train.
Tales that are in earnest, noble and grand,
Belong to the life of a railroad man.

This ballad text—or something very similar—was attributed to Wallace Saunders by two authorities on Jones's history. Fred Lee, in his somewhat fictionalized 1939 biography of John Luther Jones cited a similar text in an appendix discussing the genesis of the ballad.[8] Freeman Hubbard, in his book *Railroad Avenue*, quoted a text essentially the same as that given by Lee, but with a dozen or so minor textual differences—just enough to suggest that he had another, independent source.[9] Other texts have been attributed to Saunders. In 1910 John Lomax had received a letter from the mayor of Canton that

Saunders was the author of "Casey Jones" and was still living in that town. Not until 1933 did John and Alan Lomax reach Canton in search of Saunders, at which time they found that he had long since died. However, they did meet and interview seventy-year-old Cornelius Steen, who had worked in the Canton roundhouse at the turn of the century and had been a friend of Saunders. Steen told them that years before the accident, he had been visiting Kansas City and had heard a song called "Jimmie Jones," which he brought back to Canton with him. Saunders liked the song and added verses describing a wreck in which the imaginary Jimmie Jones was killed.[10] After Casey Jones died, Saunders changed the words to fit the circumstances of the April 29, 1900, wreck.

The Lomaxes' informant, Cornelius Steen, said he could recall only one stanza of the song he brought from Kansas City:

> On a Sunday mornin' it begin to rain,
> Around the curve he spied a passenger train;
> On the pilot lay poor Jimmie Jones,
> He's a good old porter, but he's dead and gone.
>   Dead and gone, oh he's dead and gone;
>   He's a good old porter but he'd dead and gone.[11]

Steen recalled three stanzas that Saunders sang:

> On a Sunday mornin' it begin to rain,
> Around the curve he spied a passenger train;
> Under the cab lay po' Casey Jones,
> He's a good engineer but he's dead and gone.
>   Chorus:
>
> Casey being a good engineer,
> Told his fireman not to have no fear;
> All I wan's a little water and coal,
> I'll peep out the cab and see the drivers roll.
>   Chorus:
>
> On a Sunday mornin' it begin to rain,
> Around the curve he spied a passenger train;
> Told his fireman he's better jump,
> Cause there's two locomotives that are bound to bump.
>   Chorus:[12]

In 1951 Sam Eskin collected a version from that fabulous character Harry "Haywire Mac" McClintock, in San Pedro, California (for a discussion of Mac's career, see "Jerry, Go Ile That Car" in chap. 11). Of the "Casey Jones" ballad, Mac told Eskin, "Well, I learned the song in 1909 when I was switching box cars in Memphis for the I.C. Railroad. And I heard Wallace Saunders sing the song myself. . . . All the Negro railroad men knew the song. A lot of 'em sang it and here is the original of 'Casey Jones'"[13] Mac's text follows:

> Casey Jones was an engineer,
> Told his fireman to have no fear;
> "All I want is water and coal,
> And my head out the window when the drivers roll.
>   When the drivers roll, when the drivers roll
>   And my head out the window when the drivers roll."

Through south Memphis yard on the fly,
The fireman hollered, "Ya got a white eye";
The switchman knew by the engine's moans
That the man at the throttle was Casey Jones.
　　Oh, Casey Jones, oh, Casey Jones,
　　That the man at the throttle was Casey Jones.

Well, the engine rocked and the drivers rolled,
The fireman hollered, "Lordy, save my soul!"
Casey said, "I'll roll her till she leaves the rails,
'Cause I'm way behind time with the Southern mail.
　　With the Southern mail, oh, that South bound mail,
　　I'm way behind time with the southbound mail."

Got within about a mile of the place,
A big old headlight stared him right in the face;
He told his fireman, "Boy, you'd better jump,
'Cause there's two locomotives that's a-goin' to bump.
　　That's a-goin' to bump, that's a-goin' to bump.
　　There's two locomotives that's a-goin' to bump."

You ought to been there for to see that sight,
The women stood cryin', both colored and white;
I was there for to tell the fact,
They flagged him down but he never looked back.
　　No, he never looked back, no, he never looked back,
　　They flagged him down but he never looked back.

Oh, Casey said, just before he died,
"There's lots more railroads that I'd like to ride";
But the good Lord whispered, "It is not to be,"
And he died at the throttle on the Y and MV.
　　On the Y and MV, on the Y and MV,
　　He died at the throttle on the Y and MV.[14]

One text that has been attributed to Saunders can be eliminated with confidence. B. W. Overall, in *The Story of Casey Jones* (a brochure published by the Casey Jones Museum), reported an interview with Jones's widow (who, incidentally, spent years publicly disclaiming the suggestions of infidelity in the final stanza of the vaudeville text): "She told this writer that the following is perhaps the most nearly correct version of the song originally intoned by Wallace Saunders. . . ." Possibly Mrs. Jones did not mean to imply that the version was an accurate rendition of what Saunders sang, but only that it was a historically correct recomposition of what he sang (it is factually correct). In any case, Mrs. Jones's version has stanzas unlike any reported elsewhere at any time. For example:

　　If I can have Sim Webb, my fireman, my engine 382,
　　Although I'm tired and weary, I'll take her through.
　　Put on my whistle that came in today,
　　Cause I mean to keep her wailing as we ride and pray.

> Casey's body lies buried in Jackson, Tennessee,
> Close beside the tracks of the old I.C.
> May his spirit live forever throughout the land
> As the greatest of all heroes of a railroad man.[15]

Finally, this survey of texts that might have been written by Saunders must take into account numerous shorter fragments collected in the field by folklorists E. C. Perrow and Howard W. Odum (in the period 1905–10) and John A. Lomax and Alan Lomax (in the 1930s or earlier).

In 1913, E. C. Perrow published several fragmentary ballads he had collected in Mississippi in 1909. He noted that during the winter of 1908–9, Mississippi was full of songs about Casey Jones.[16] All the verses that Cornelius Steen sang could be found among these fragments. In similar spirit was a ballad Odum published in 1911 that he had collected in Mississippi a few years earlier:

> Casey Jones wus engineer
> Told his fireman not to fear.
> All he wanted was a boiler hot,
> Run in Canton 'bout four o'clock.
>
> One Sunday mornin' it wus drizzlin' rain,
> Looked down road an' saw a train;
> Fireman says, "Let's make a jump;
> Two locomotives an' dey bound to bump."
>
> Casey Jones, I know him well,
> Tole de fireman to ring de bell;
> Fireman jump an' say "Goodbye,
> Casey Jones, you're bound to die."
>
> Went on down to de depot track,
> Beggin' my honey to take me back;
> She turn 'roun' some two or three times;
> "Take you back when you learn to grind."
>
> Womens in Kansas, all dressed in red,
> Got de news dat Casey was dead;
> De womens in Jackson, all dressed in black,
> Said, in fact, he was a cracker-jack.[17]

The problem facing us is that there are two different types of ballads that have been attributed to Saunders. On one hand we have the 1908 version and its relatives. From its opening "Come all you rounders" to the moralizing lines of the final verse, it is unmistakably in the Anglo-American "vulgar ballad" tradition; furthermore, it was written by and for railroad men, as evidenced by the constant use of railroad lingo. This ballad is related to numerous other ballads about railroad wrecks, but whether they preceded or followed the 1900 IC disaster is uncertain. If we can believe any of the accounts given by readers of the Kansas City newspapers or *Railroad Man's Magazine*, there must have been one or more similar ballads circulating before 1900.

The songs of the other group, many of them fragmentary, are more what one would expect from the blues ballad tradition (primarily but not exclusively a black tradition).[18]

This group includes Steen's verses, the fragments reported by the Lomaxes, Perrow, and Odum, and McClintock's song. Again, the fragments are clearly related to other songs (probably pre-1900) that had nothing to do with Casey Jones, and some doubtless had nothing to do with any accident; these are discussed below. If it were simply a matter of different versions of the same general style of ballad being attributed to Saunders, we could overlook textual variations as later developments; but the attribution of two completely different styles of song is vexing.

What are we to conclude about Saunders's original composition? First, it should be stressed that we have no reliable firsthand evidence of what Saunders did sing. All the imputations that ascribe to him some form of the 1908 text are further removed than secondhand. There are two purported firsthand accounts in favor of the second group of texts—Steen's and McClintock's—and both are suspect. In Steen's case, there is the unlikely chain of events that led to its recovery. The Lomaxes, twenty-three years after learning of Saunders's existence in Canton, went there to interview him. Saunders, as well as their correspondent, the mayor of Canton, had died. The mayor's daughter took them to see a friend of Saunders, Cornelius Steen. Steen told the Lomaxes that he taught Saunders the progenitor of the Casey Jones ballad. Lady Fortune is seldom so munificent to folklorists. Steen's story need not be summarily rejected, but it should be borne in mind that something is wanting in the evidence.

The search for Saunders's original composition has gone unfulfilled. No ballad claiming that role has impressive credentials. But my general experience with American folksong suggests at least a partial answer. If Wash Saunders was the uneducated black engine-wiper all accounts would have us believe he was, then the lament he put together after Jones's death was nothing like the 1908 version, but was rather in the spirit of "Joseph Michael," "Wreck of the Six-Wheeler," "Hobo John," and the other Afro-American fragments that were in oral circulation before the turn of the century. The 1908 ballad must have been a completely independent composition, probably by some other railroader along the route of the IC. And even that song, judging by the facts mentioned that do not square with the 1900 accident, and by the other reported independent ballads, must have been based on older material.

These "other Afro-American fragments" can be grouped in at least four categories according to their principal theme; probably separate ballad families at one time, by about 1900 they had already become commingled. One was the collection of verses about Jay Gould; the second, referred to above, was a closely related group of songs about hobos and ramblers; the third was a family of songs about train wrecks; and the fourth focused on rounders and men of loose morals. From the second group came the Jimmie Jones fragment that Steen recalled, analogs of which appear in more than twenty texts, only five of which mention Casey Jones. Also in this family is "Milwaukee Blues," which is transcribed in chapter 8; it, "Jay Gould," and other related songs are discussed there. In the third group is "Ben Dewberry's Final Run," which follows "Casey Jones" in this chapter. The discussion of "J. C. Holmes Blues," following "Ben Dewberry's Final Run," offers examples of the fourth group of pre–Casey Jones material, of which the Odum version quoted above is representative.

It seems clear, then, that by the time Newton and Seibert were inspired to write their vaudeville hit, there were two independent thriving traditions about Casey Jones; their song shows signs of having borrowed from both. Their first two quatrains, as well as couplets from the third and the fifth stanzas, are taken directly from the 1908 version (or something very similar to it). Stanzas 3, 4, and 6 are taken mainly from the blues ballad tradition. Note that in the central portion of the ballad (stanzas 3 through 5) there is no chronologically correct sequence of verses. Stanza 7 is the Jay Gould borrowing. The final stanza, " . . . you got another papa on the Salt Lake Line," is probably Newton and Seibert's own brilliant rewrite of the blues ballad verse " . . . you'll draw a pension at your daddy's death." The two vaudevillians probably also made the alterations that gave the ballad a western setting: "southern mail" becomes "western mail"; western localizations, "Frisco" and "Reno hill," are inserted; and all the railroad lines mentioned—Southern Pacific, Santa Fe, and Salt Lake Line—are western lines.

Unlike some of the other ballads discussed in this book, such as "Jesse James," the Casey Jones ballads defy neat compartmentalization into distinct and separate subgroupings. However, three texts have recurred often enough to be noted as standard forms, although when the mass of material is considered, there are more mavericks than standards.

The most widespread form, not surprisingly, is the Newton-Seibert version. This, or fragments of it, accounts for more than twenty of our recordings (Bernard, Collins and Harlan, County Harmonizers, Dalhart, Dixie Demons, Greene, Jones, Kaufman, Manhattan Quartet, Murray, Price, Reneau, Shannon Four, Straun's Pullman Porters, Varsity Eight, and Wilson). Instrumental versions of the vaudeville tune account for several more recordings (Jackson, Macon, Patterson, Griffin, Skiles, Military Band, Pitts, Scott and Wilkinson, unidentified performers on FS 3812). Of the field-collected versions, texts in Anderson, Brown, Buckley, *Colorado Folksong Bulletin*, Duncan (A text), Frothingham, L. Hubbard, Morris, and Neely and Spargo (A text) are derived from the Newton-Seibert song. Taken directly from that song rather than from informants in the field are the examples in Geller, *Good Old Days*, Lomax and Lomax (1947, II text), *Railroad Man's Magazine* (1910, 1914), Shay, Sherwin and McClintock, Spaeth, and Stein. In addition, fourteen texts in the Western Kentucky Folklore Archive, collected between 1948 and 1964, are essentially the Newton-Seibert text (no further identification is given for these items in the references), as are two items in the Gordon manuscripts (1179 and 1437).

The "1908 text" appeared in *Railroad Man's Magazine* for that year, and later Cohen (1973), Friedman, Gordon, F. Hubbard, Hudson, Lee, Mason (A text), Mulligan, Neal, Pound, and Shay. In all cases except three (Hudson, Mason, Neal) the source was a previous publication.

A third oft-quoted source is Sandburg's A text. It resembles the 1908 text except for two additional stanzas:

> Fireman goes down the depot track,
> Begging his honey to take him back,
> She says, "Oranges on the table, peaches on the shelf,
> You're a goin' to get tired sleepin' by yourself."

> Mrs. Casey Jones was a sittin' on the bed.
> Telegram comes that Casey is dead.
> She says, "Children, go to bed, and hush your cryin',
> 'Cause you got another papa on the Frisco line."

The same text appears in Kreimer, in the Robison and Lowery folios, and in *Popular Cowboy Songs* (the latter lacks two other stanzas). *Famous Old Time Songs* and the Rhinehart folio both credit the Sandburg collection as a source, but the text quoted is so abridged that it lacks the two stanzas that distinguish the Sandburg version from the 1908 version.

Nearly one hundred other texts defy simple classification. Because the songs peripherally related to Casey Jones range from those that are nearly the same ballad except for changing the names of the principals, to fragments that share only a line or a phrase with recognizable Casey Jones material, I have had to be arbitrary in drawing up the references. I have excluded the blues ballad fragments that share with "Casey Jones" only a single theme, such as the "natural born eas'man" verse. Related items listed in the references to "Ben Dewberry's Final Run," "Milwaukee Blues," or "J. C. Holmes Blues" are not repeated here.

Finally, nothing has been said about the effect of the vaudeville song on oral tradition. This song may have borrowed from the older traditions, but in turn it influenced both black and white folksong. Furthermore, the vaudeville tune provided the vehicle for a host of parodies and songs, from Joe Hill's railroad strike song[19] through a miner's version,[20] an Air Force parody,[21] a soldiers' song,[22] numerous bawdy offshoots,[23] a political satire about FDR,[24] "Sidney Allen" (Laws E 5), a KKK song,[25] and "Hellbound Train," to a Free Speech Movement song.[26] Few American ballads offer such striking confirmation of the interaction between folk and pop traditions as does "Casey Jones."

I conclude my lengthy remarks about "Casey Jones" with a few words on the recordings of the ballad, and the recording transcribed in this book.

Compared to other songs discussed in this volume, "Casey Jones" began its career on wax very early. By 1911 several recordings of the Newton-Seibert version were already on the market: Billy Murray on an Edison cylinder, Arthur Collins and Byron Harlan on Columbia, Gene Greene on Pathé, and others. The first recording by a hillbilly folk artist was made by Fiddlin' John Carson in New York, November, 1923, at his second recording session. A very similar but longer text was recorded by Riley Puckett on March 7, 1924; it has been transcribed and discussed in some detail elsewhere (Cohen [1965]). The first recording by a black artist was made by Walter "Furry" Lewis in Chicago in October, 1927, but it was never issued. Lewis recorded the ballad again in Memphis in August, 1928, for Victor; this remarkable version, closely related to several earlier songs, is transcribed here. Lewis's recording, in contrast to its interest later for folklorists and folk revivalists, was not very successful in its own day; fewer than 4,200 copies were sold. A second early recording by a black artist was that of Mississippi John Hurt in February, 1928; it, too, was never issued.

Born in Greenwood, Mississippi, in either 1893 or 1900—different interviewers have reported different dates—Walter Lewis fell in love with the guitar at an early age, and when still very young fashioned one out of a cigar box. By that time, Walter, nicknamed "Furry" by schoolmates, had moved to Memphis. As a teenager he played with medicine and tent shows, in W. C. Handy's orchestra, in taverns, dancehalls, and speakeasies, at picnics and all-night dances in the Memphis area. He was given to hoboing by train in his youth, but a railroad accident cost him a leg when he was seventeen and curtailed his rambling. In May, 1927, Jim Jackson, one of Memphis's best-known black musicians, took Furry to New York for a recording session with Brunswick's Vocalion division. Three more recording sessions with Victor and Vocalion were held in the next two years, and then Furry's career on wax came to a halt for three decades. In 1959, Samuel Charters found that he was still alive and well in Memphis, and recorded him again. Since that time he has made numerous records and appeared at many folk festivals and concerts.[27] Between 1928 and 1971, ten recordings of Furry's

"Casey Jones" were made and issued, so we have an excellent opportunity to study an artist's conception of one song in his repertoire over a considerable period of time. The evidence indicates that the ballad was extremely fluid in his mind: both the choice of stanzas (out of a total of eighteen) and the order are unique in each of his renditions. This is just what one might expect of a blues ballad: a collection of commentary verses on an implied incident with no chronologically correct ordering. The longest of his renditions was the 1928 version transcribed here; it occupied both sides of a single 78 rpm disc. Most of his other performances consist of only seven or eight stanzas. Lewis's refrain with the bawdy phrase "on the road again" is a clever insertion restoring the literal meaning of the phrase while still utilizing the slang of the Memphis Jug Band's "On the Road Again."

Of the new verses that Lewis incorporated into later renditions of the ballad, most have nothing at all to do with Casey Jones per se. For example, each of the six recordings made after 1968 includes this stanza:

> Now, if you want to go to heaven when you d-i-e,
> Put on your collar and a t-i-e;
> If you want to scare a rabbit out of a l-o-g,
> Just make a little stunt like a d-o-g.

One can say accurately that this stanza is now part of Furry Lewis's version of "Casey Jones." It is well to remember that what may start out as an obviously irrelevant intrusion into a blues ballad may, with the passage of time and an increasingly widespread provenance, become an accepted part of the whole. Perhaps Furry's stanzas 6 and 7 grew into the Casey Jones ballad in just such a way, the integration being helped by the insertion of Casey Jones's name where there was probably another name originally. This was almost certainly the case with his twelfth stanza, in recent recordings invariably rendered thus:

> I woke up this morning, was a shower of rain,
> Around the curve came a passenger train;
> Under the boiler lay hobo John,
> He's a good old hobo (rounder) but he's dead and gone.

I had also long wondered about his second stanza, with the couplet

> He left Memphis, was a quarter to nine,
> Got to Newport News, it was dinnertime,

and tried to interpret this as belonging to an older song about an engineer on some bizarre run from Memphis to Newport News (no single railroad line connects those two cities); but the verse was omitted from all subsequent recordings save one, and in that the city Newport News was replaced by New York City. Was Newport News a nonce insertion by Lewis in response to some one-time gig? (Newport News occurs in the 1936 recording by Jesse James, later copied by Bob Howard and his Boys, but there Memphis is replaced by Cincinnati; such a route is possible on the C & O railway.)

The text given here shares no verses with the 1908 version. One stanza (9) and parts of three others (5, 8, and 10) are very close to the Newton-Seibert standard text. Four of the stanzas (3, 6, 7, and 13) have nothing at all to do with a train wreck or Casey Jones; and two others (2 and 12), though they mention Jones, almost certainly have nothing to do with the historical accident of April, 1900, or with John Luther Jones. Much of Lewis's ballad, then, probably predates the accident under discussion, and belongs to that body of folksong referred to above that Wash Saunders must have drawn on in fashioning *his* Casey Jones elegy.

Furry Lewis's lyrics are by no means easy to transcribe; a comparison of the words given here with three previously published transcriptions shows considerable differences of interpretation.[28] In some instances, I have been influenced by Lewis's later recordings in which the pronunciation is more easily understood.

The tune to Furry Lewis's version is, like his text, quite different from the vaudeville song; however, it shares similarities with several other prevaudeville variants of "Casey Jones" and related songs—the versions by Cornelius Steen and Harry McClintock, and the songs "Milwaukee Blues" and "Ben Dewberry's Final Run." I suspect that the tune to Saunders's original ballad was similar to this group of melodies.[29]

NOTES

1. Freeman H. Hubbard, *Railroad Avenue* (New York; McGraw-Hill, 1945), chap. 2, and "The Real Casey Jones," *American Mercury*, 70 (June, 1950), 709–15. Other important writings on Jones's career and the beginnings of the vaudeville song are James J. Geller, *Famous Songs and Their Stories* (New York: Macaulay, 1931), pp. 231–32; B. W. Overall, *The Story of Casey Jones, the Brave Engineer* (Jackson, Tenn.: Casey Jones Museum, 1956); Carlton J. Corliss, *Main Line of Mid-America* (New York: Creative Age Press, 1950), pp. 301–11, reprinted in B. A. Botkin and Alvin F. Harlow, *A Treasury of Railroad Folklore* (New York: Bonanza Books, 1953), pp. 40–48; and Fred J. Lee, *Casey Jones* (Kingsport, Tenn.: Southern Publishers, 1939).

2. See Corliss, *Main Line of Mid-America*, for a detailed account of what went wrong at Vaughan.

3. The role of black engine-wipers as songwriters in American folklore needs to be further explored. Harry Bolser, in "Switchmen Knew by the Engine's Moans That at the Throttle Was Casey Jones," *Louisville Courier-Journal*, Apr. 27, 1950, writes that "Charley Antwerp, a Negro engine wiper at Canton, is believed to have written the original Casey Jones poem . . . [he] was the first person ever heard humming the tune." Two informants told John Harrington Cox that a black man (an engine-wiper in one report) who worked in the Hinton roundhouse wrote the ballad "The Wreck on the C & O"; see Cox, *Folk-Songs of the South* (1925; rpt., Hatboro, Pa.: Folklore Associates, 1963), p. 221. Furthermore, Saunders has been credited in print with composing another song about Casey Jones, this one more than ten years prior to the fatal wreck.

4. Peter Mulligan, "Casey Jones," *RRManM*, 16 (Dec., 1911), 397–402.

5. *RRManM*, 17 (Apr., 1912), 494–97.

6. Ibid., 5 (Mar., 1908), 384.

7. Ibid., p. 764.

8. Lee, *Casey Jones*, p. 285.

9. Hubbard, *Railroad Avenue*, pp. 18–19.

10. John A. Lomax and Alan Lomax, *American Ballads and Folk Songs* (New York: Macmillan, 1934), p. 37.

11. This text, which does not agree with the one given in Lomax and Lomax (1934) and credited to Steen, is taken from LC AFS 1866 A, "Casey Jones," singer unidentified. In the record jacket were some notes by Lomax: "Canton, Mississippi, August 1933. 'Original' version of 'Casey Jones,' sung by a friend of Wash Sanders, Negro, said to have composed the ballad." I assume the singer to have been Steen, although the discrepancy between the recorded and published texts remains unexplained.

12. Text from LC AFS 1866 A. Casey Jones was not the only engineer to tell his fireman to jump before an imminent wreck. "Billy Clark," a poem by S. W. Gillilan published in *LEMJ*, Sept., 1902, p. 580, has the line "He'd holler to his fireman, 'Jump.'" Clark dies in the ensuing wreck.

13. Sam Eskin to Cohen, Feb. 13, 1965.

14. Text from Folkways FD 5272: *Harry K. McClintock—"Haywire Mac."*

15. Overall, *Story of Casey Jones*, pp. 67, 69.

16. E. C. Perrow, "Songs and Rhymes from the South," *JAF*, 26 (Apr.-June, 1913), 165–67. Two

of these pieces are reprinted in Albert B. Friedman, *The Viking Book of Folk Ballads of the English-Speaking World* (New York: Viking Press, 1956), pp. 313–14.

17. Howard W. Odum, "Folk-Song and Folk-Poetry as Found in the Secular Songs of the Southern Negroes," *JAF*, 24 (Oct.-Dec., 1911), 352. This has been reprinted in Friedman, *Viking Book of Folk Ballads*, pp. 313–14; in Howard W. Odum and Guy B. Johnson, *The Negro and His Songs* (1925; rpt., Hatboro, Pa.: Folklore Associates, 1964), p. 207; and in Dorothy Scarborough, *On the Trail of Negro Folk-Songs* (1925; rpt., Hatboro, Pa.: Folklore Associates, 1963), p. 250.

18. Contemporary scholarship on native American balladry recognizes two distinct narrative styles. The "vulgar" ballad, often disseminated on broadsides and other cheap printed media in Great Britain and the United States through the eighteenth and nineteenth centuries, is characterized by its journalistic, chronologically correct exposition of events. It generally begins with a formulaic opening (an incipit) and concludes with a moralizing or sentimental commentary (sometimes termed an explicit). Unlike the vulgar ballad, which is primarily an Anglo-American phenomenon, the blues ballad is familiar in both Anglo- and Afro-American traditions. In the blues ballad, although there is a definite underlying narrative, the emphasis is on editorial comment rather than reportage. Thus the sequence of verses in a blues ballad is generally immaterial; in sharp contrast, if verses of a vulgar ballad were interchanged, the result often would be nonsense.

It is tempting to speculate that the blues ballad represents a merger of the journalistic style of the vulgar ballad with the lyrical approach of the Anglo-American banjo songs or Afro-American blues songs, but its origins are presently unclear. The labels "blues ballad" and "vulgar ballad" are easily applied to specimen texts of the American folksong corpus. But I am not prepared to claim that individual stanzas, taken out of context, can be identified as belonging to one ballad type or the other. What I do assert is that stanzas and verses can be classified on the basis of other ballads in which they occur. For further discussion see D. K. Wilgus, "A Type Index of Anglo-American Traditional Narrative Songs," *Journal of the Folklore Institute*, 7 (Aug.-Dec., 1970), 161–76, esp. the key references in n. 4.

19. William Alderson, "On the Wobbly 'Casey Jones' and Other Songs," *CFQ*, 1 (Oct., 1942), 373; Duncan Emrich, "Casey Jones, Union Scab," *CFQ*, 1 (July, 1942), 292.

20. Emrich, "Mining Songs," *SFQ*, 6 (June, 1942), 104–5; Wayland D. Hand et al., "Songs of the Butte Miners," *WF*, 9 (Jan., 1950), 33.

21. William Wallrich, *Air Force Airs* (New York: Duell, Sloan and Pearce, 1957), p. 31.

22. John Brophy and Eric Partridge, *The Long Trail* (New York: London House and Maxwell, 1965), p. 65.

23. Ed Cray, *The Erotic Muse* (New York: Oak Publications, 1969), p. 50.

24. James H. Forbes, *Railway Conductor*, 52 (July, 1953), 213.

25. "Casey Jones," singer unidentified, on 78 rpm Special K-1 (ca. 1924), produced by Rodeheaver Recording Laboratories, Chicago.

26. *"Free Speech Songbook: Songs of, by, and for the F.S.M.,"* mimeographed (Berkeley, 1964).

27. For further biographical information on Lewis, see the liner or brochure notes to the Fantasy, Folkways, and Blue Horizon LPs cited in the discography; Bengt Olsson, *Memphis Blues* (London: Studio Vista, 1970), pp. 72–78; and Samuel B. Charters, *The Country Blues* (New York: Rinehart, 1959), pp. 71–74.

28. Friedman, *Viking Book of Folk Ballads*, pp. 315–17; Eric Sackheim, *The Blues Line* (New York: Grossman Publishers, 1969), pp. 258–59; Moses Asch, Josh Dunson, and Ethel Raim, eds., *Anthology of American Folk Music* (New York: Oak Publications, 1973), p. 65.

29. The material in these notes overlaps my "'Casey Jones,'" *WF*, 32 (Apr., 1973), 77–103.

REFERENCES

A. "Casey Jones," in *Railroad Man's Magazine*, 5 (May, 1908), 764. Response to a reader's request in the March number, p. 384. The earliest publication of a full ballad.

"Casey Jones (The Brave Engineer)," sheet music, by T. Lawrence Seibert and Eddie Newton. Published by Southern California Music Company, Los Angeles. Copyrighted Apr. 7, 1909

(E 202519); copyright renewed in 1936 by Charles E. Seibert and Dorothy Elizabeth Newton, assigned to Shapiro, Bernstein and Co.; copyrighted 1937 by Shapiro, Bernstein and Co.

"Casey Jones," in Carl Sandburg, *The American Songbag* (New York: Harcourt, Brace, 1927), pp. 366–69. This version is the same as the 1908 ballad except for the addition of two stanzas.

"Kassie Jones," by Walter "Furry" Lewis. Vocal and guitar. Parts 1 and 2 recorded Aug. 28, 1928 (Victor masters 45431-2/45432-1), in Memphis, Tenn. Released on Victor 21664 in Nov., 1928. Reissued on Folkways FA 2951 (FP 251): *Anthology of American Folk Music, Vol. 1*; and on Roots RL 333: *Kings of Memphis Town*. Transcribed here and in three other collections (see n. 28).

"Casey Jones," by Fiddlin' John Carson. Vocal and fiddle. Recorded Nov. 7 or 8, 1923 (OKeh master S-72-014), in New York City. Released on OKeh 40038 in ca. Feb., 1924. First hillbilly recording of the ballad.

B. Anderson, G., 201
Asch, 64
Barnes, 22 (from Sandburg)
Barry (1912) (discussion only)
Beard, 168–71
Boni (1947), 142
Botkin (1944), 245
Botkin & Harlow, 456–57
Brown II, 510
Buckley, 8
Buford, 142
CFB, 2 (1963), 37
Chalker
Clifton, 30
Cohen (1965), 235
Cohen (1973), *passim*
Comic and Sentimental Songs (copy of text in WKFA)
Dew, *passim*
Dorson (1966), 23
Dorson (1973), 235–41, 244–46, 264–66
Downes & Siegmeister (1940)
Drake, *passim*

Family Herald, 35 (references only)
Famous Old Time Songs, 92
Friedman, 314–15
Frothingham, *Adventure,* May 10, 1923, p. 191
Geller, 231–34
Good Old Days, Oct., 1967, p. 8
Gordon, *Adventure,* June 20, 1925, p. 192 (from Gordon MS 61)
Gurner (from Lee)
Holbrook, 429–30 (discussion only)
Howse, 83–85
Hubbard, F., 18–19
Hubbard, L., 264–65
Hudson (1936), 214–15
Irwin, 214–15
Kansas City Star, Aug. 1, 1911
Kreimer, *RRM,* May, 1966, p. 35
Laws, 212 (G 1) (discussion and references)
Leach, M., 50–53 (discussion only)
Lee, 285
Loesser, 208–9
Lomax, A. (1960), 553–55, 564–65
Lomax & Lomax (1934), 34–39
Lomax & Lomax (1947), 248–50, 264–69
Lowery, 13
Mason, 107–8
Morris, 109–10
Morse, 307–10
Mulligan, *passim*
Mursell (Grade 6), 152
Neal, #38
Neely & Spargo, 168–69
Odum, 351
Odum & Johnson (1925), 207
Odum & Johnson (1926), 126
Overall, 67–69
Perrow (1913), 165–67
Popular Cowboy Songs
Pound (1922), 134, 250
Randolph (1945)
Rhinehart, 37
Robison (1931)
RRManM, 12 (July, 1910), 380
RRManM, 23 (Apr., 1914), 957–58
RRManM, May, 1918
Scarborough, 249–50
Shay (1927), 15
Sherwin & McClintock, 4–6
Spaeth (1926), 119
Stein

Styles (discussion only)
Wertz, 19

C. GORDON MSS:

37—Ruth A. Shannon
61—C. H. Street
407—O.D.W.
1170—Waller Crow
1175—W. C. Judd
1179—Bradford A. Shaw
1285—Dan Hepp
1420—Edw. Lane
1437—George Hirdt
1504—Hugh Manning
3261—Olive C. Kay
3266—Colletta Evans
3490—Alfred Frankenstein
3612—J. C. McDaniel
3779—Charles E. Roe

D. Al Bernard—Brunswick 178, Supertone
2044
California Ramblers—Pathé 36650,
Perfect 14831, Cameo 1255, Lincoln
2720
Blanche Calloway—Victor 26640, His
Master's Voice (France) K-6500, His
Master's Voice (England) B-6114, His
Master's Voice (Italy) R-14588
Fiddlin' John Carson—OKeh 40038
Jack Charman—Famous 90
Arthur Collins—Indestructible 3163
(cylinder)
Arthur Collins and Byron Harlan
—Columbia A-907, Oxford 4827
County Harmonizers—Actuelle 020670,
Perfect 11025, Silvertone 1201
Vernon Dalhart—Banner 1580, Regal
9878, Domino 3550 (as by Bob White),
Oriole 454 (as by Dick Morse)
—Edison 51611; Mark56 794: *First
Recorded Railroad Songs*
—Victor 20502, Zonophone (Australia) EE
47
—Grey Gull 4174, Radiex 4174, Van
Dyke 5085, Madison 5085 (last four as
by Jeff Calhoun), Madison 1923 (as by
James Ahearn)
Delmore Brothers—King 570   "Freight
Train Boogie" (related piece)
Al Dexter—King 875   "Blow That

Lonesome Whistle, Casey" (related
piece)
Dixie-Aires—Exclusive 116X (possibly
related)
Dixie Demons—Decca 5140
Five Birmingham Babies—Perfect 14831
Red Foley—Decca 46035   "Freight
Train Boogie" (related piece)
Four Showmen—Elite X27
Gene Greene—Pathé (England) 563
Ken Griffin—Rondo 45134
Hart and Ogle—Broadway 8303
Al Hopkins and his Buckle Busters
—Brunswick 177   "C.C. & O. No.
588" (related piece)
Bob Howard and his Boys—Decca
1958   "Southern Casey Jones"
Burl Ives—Decca 29129, Decca 9-29129
(45 rpm)
Jesse James—Decca 7213, Vocalion
(England) V-1037; Blues Classics BC-5:
Country Blues Classics, Vol. 1; Ace of
Hearts (England) AH 158: *Out Came
the Blues, Vol. 2*   "Southern Casey
Jones"
Jesters—Decca 24354 (in album A-639:
Railroad Songs)
Billy Jones and Male Chorus—Edison
50747-L
Irving and Jack Kaufman—Columbia
A-2809, Velvetone 7001-V, Diva
2480-D, Harmony 480-H, Velvetone
1480-H (last three as by Jack and Tom
Wilson); Harmony 5009-H
(unconfirmed)
Herb Kern—Tempo TR 1070
Fred Kirby of WBT's Briarhoppers and
the Mountaineers—Sonora 3040
Furry Lewis—Victor 21664; Folkways FA
2951 (FP 251): *Anthology of American
Folk Music, Vol. 1;* Roots RL 333:
Kings of Memphis Town; Yazoo L-1050:
Furry Lewis in His Prime 1927–1928
"Kassie Jones, Parts 1/2"
Uncle Dave Macon—Vocalion 5061
"Old Dan Tucker" (part of medley)
Manhattan Quartet—Champion 15521,
Montgomery Ward 4944
Wingy Manone—Bluebird B-10289,
Montgomery Ward M-8354, His
Master's Voice (England) B 9360, His
Master's Voice (Australia) EA 3280

Military Band—Scala (country of origin
and number not known)
Morland and Farland—Invicta 165
Billy Murray—Edison 10499 (cylinder)
Billy Murray and the American
Quartet—Victor 16483 (2 takes issued)
Billy Murray and the Peerless Quartet
—Victor 3575 (part of "Miniature
Concert")
Bibi Osterwald—Decca 22343 (in album
404)
Peerless Quartet—U.S. Everlasting 1106
(cylinder)
Stanford Price—Arrow (Germany)
(number not known)
George Riley Puckett—Columbia 113-D,
Harmony 5118-H (as by Fred Wilson)
Goebel Reeves—McGregor 855
(transcription recording)   "Main Line
Casey"
George Reneau—Vocalion 14813,
Vocalion 5032
Lou Reynolds' Recording Orchestra
—Flexo 133 (8″ 78 rpm)
Carson Robison—Regal Zonophone
(England) MR 645 (part of medley)
—Columbia (England) DX 365 (12″ 78
rpm) (part of medley)
Carl Sandburg—Musicraft 210 (in album
11)   "Mama Have You Heard the
News" (related piece)
Pete Seeger—Disc album 607: *America's
Favorite Songs, Vol. 1*
Terry Shand—Decca 3714
Shannon Four—Federal 5117, Silvertone
2117, Resona 75117, Supertone 9026
(as by Silvertone Quartet)
Bob Skiles' Four Old Timers—OKeh
45225
Eddie Stone—Banner 7-07-17, Oriole
7-07-17, Melotone 7-07-17, Perfect
7-07-17, Romeo 7-07-17, Vocalion 3576
(jazz parody)
Straun's Pullman Porters—Gennett 3005
Gid Tanner and his Skillet-Lickers, with
Riley Puckett and Clayton McMichen
—Columbia 15237-D; Vetco LP 103:
Songs of the Railroad
Charlie Troutt's Melody Artists
—Columbia 1030-D, Columbia (England)
4479, Columbia (England) 0724
"Transportation Blues, Part 1"

Varsity Eight—Cameo 1255, Romeo 489,
Lincoln 2720
Wilmer Watts and the Lonely Eagles
—Paramount 3210, Broadway 8248
"Knocking Down Casey Jones"
Byron Wolfe's Orchestra—Decca 2562
(part of medley)
Unidentified singer—Edison-Bell 20318
(cylinder)

E. Eddy Arnold—Victor 47-6001 (45 rpm);
RCA Camden CAL/CAS 897: *I'm
Throwing Rice*
Balfa Brothers—Rounder 6007: *J'ai Vu le
Loup, le Renard et la Belette*
Sidney Bechet—Crescendo 9012: *Sidney
Bechet*
Bluegrass Special—King Bluegrass 554
Jenks "Tex" Carmen—Sage LP C-9
Johnny Cash—Columbia CL 1930/CS
8730: *Blood, Sweat and Tears*; Philips
(England) CBS-BPG-62119: *Blood,
Sweat and Tears*; Columbia GP 29: *The
World of Johnny Cash*
Bob Chapman—Scholastic CC 0630 (7″
EP): *Train Ballads*
Percy Copeland—Rimrock LP 278: *The
Rackensack, Vol. 1*
Horace Crandall—Arizona Friends of
Folklore AFF 33-2: *Cowboy Songs,
Vol. 2*
K. C. Douglas—Cook 5002: *Blues and a
Guitar*
Frosty Mountain Boys—Rural Rhythm
RR-FM-159: *Mama Likes Blue Grass
Music*
Jule Garrish—Folkways FS 3848
Jim Glaser—Starday SLP 170: *Railroad
Special*
Joe Glazer—Folkways FA 2039 (FP 39):
The Songs of Joe Hill (labor union
parody)
—Collector 1924: *Singing BRAC* (labor
union parody)
—Collector 1925: *Union Train*
Joe Hickerson—Folk-Legacy FSI 58:
Drive Dull Care Away, Vol. 1
Mississippi John Hurt—Piedmont PLP
13157: *Presenting Mississippi John
Hurt, Folk Songs and Blues*
—Piedmont PLP 13161: *Worried Blues*
"Talkin' Casey" (related piece)

—Vanguard VRS 9181/VSD 79181: *The Blues at Newport, Part 2 (1964)* "Talkin' Casey" (related piece)

—Vanguard VRS 9220/VSD 79220: *Mississippi John Hurt Today* "Talkin' Casey" (related piece)

Burl Ives—Decca DL 8023

Tommy Jackson—Dot DLP 3085: *Square Dance without Calls*

Tommy Jarrell and group—Heritage 10: *Music from Round Peak*

Jubilee Four—Epic BN 26082: *The Jubilee Four on TV*

Bob Kames—King LP 612: *Songs I'm Sure You Remember*

Walter "Furry" Lewis—Adelphi AD 1007S: *On the Road Again*

—Adelphi AD 1009S: *Memphis Blues Again, Vol. l*   "Natural Born Eas'man #2"

—Asp 1: *At Home with Friends*

—Barclay (France) 920.352T: *Beale Street Blues*

—Biograph BLP 12017: *When I Lay My Burden Down*

—Blue Horizon (England) 7-63228: *Furry Lewis*

—Blue Star 80 602: *House of the Blues, Vol. 2: Fourth and Beale*

—Folkways FS 3823: *Furry Lewis*

—Matchbox SDR 190/Roots SL 505: *Furry Lewis in Memphis*

—Prestige/Bluesville BV 1037: *Done Changed My Mind*; Fantasy 24703: *Shake 'em on Down*

—RBF RF202: *The Rural Blues*

Harry K. McClintock—Folkways FD 5272: *Harry K. McClintock: "Haywire Mac"* (2 versions: traditional and labor union parody)

Ed McCurdy—Classic Editions CE 1045: *Frankie and Johnny*

—Riverside RLP 1419: *Everybody Sing*; Riverside RLP 12-807: *Barroom Ballads*

J. E. Mainer, with Red Smiley and the Blue Grass Cutups—Rural Rhythm 198: *The Legendary J. E. Mainer, Vol. 3*

Richard Maltby and his Orchestra —Roulette SR 25148: *Maltby Swings Folksongs*

Merrill Jay Singers—Cabot CAB-503: *Songs of the Railroad*

Charlie Monroe—County 538: *On the Noon-Day Jamboree*

New Christy Minstrels—Columbia CL 2187/CS 8987: *Land of Giants*

Milt Okun—Baton BL 1203: *America's Best Loved Folk Songs*

Dorothy Olsen—Bluebird WBY-95

Knuckles O'Toole—Grand Award GAS 68006: *Sing Along with Knuckles O'Toole, Vol. 1*; Grand Award GA 235 SD

Joe Patterson—Vanguard VRS 9182/VSD 79182: *Traditional Music at Newport, Part 1 (1964)*

Don Reno and Red Smiley—King 995: *Twenty-four Country Songs* "Freight Train Boogie" (related piece)

Jean Ritchie and the Manhattan Recorder Consort—Classic Editions CE 1043: *Music for a Child's World*

Earl Robinson—Folkways FG 3545: *Earl Robinson Sings* (labor union parody)

Carl Sandburg—Lyrichord LL-4 (10″ LP): *The American Songbag* "Mama Have You Heard the News" (related)

Pete Seeger—Columbia Cl 2503 (labor union parody)

—Folkways FH 5251: *American Industrial Ballads*; Olympic 7102: *America's Balladeer*

—Stinson SLP 9: *Folksay, Vol. 3*; Stinson SLPX 9: *Folksay, Vols. 3 and 4*

Pete Seeger and chorus—Folkways FH 5285: *Talking Union* (labor union parody)

Ernie Sheldon and the Villagers —Columbia CL 1515/CS 8315: *The Big Men—Bold and Bad*

Somethin' Smith and the Redheads —MGM E/SE 3941

Mike Stewart—Golden GLP-33

Win Stracke and the Arthur Norman Chorus—Golden GLP-31: *Golden Treasury of Songs America Sings*

Chubby Wise—Stoneway STY 146: *Sincerely Yours . . .* ; Stoneway 1119 (45 rpm)

Unidentified performers—Folkways FS 3812: *Music of the Ozarks* (2 renditions)

F. LC AFS:

Arthur Armstrong—AFS 3987 B4
Bessie Atchley—AFS 13131 B10
William C. Bailey—AFS 13719-20
Clyde Bland—AFS 13125 B2
Luther Bryant—AFS 13718 B28
Garland Claiborne—AFS 12044 A5
Ed Cobb—AFS 1330 B1
Byron Coffin (Byron Reno)—AFS 3823 B1
     & B2
Hiram M. Cranmer—AFS 11688 B33
—AFS 11688 B34 (bawdy parody)
Ambers Deaton—AFS 1551 B2
John Dell Duffy—AFS 9725
     B1   "Casey Jones on the S.P. Line"
Gilbert Fike—AFS 3186 A2
John Floyd—AFS 3076 B2
Rochelle French and Gabriel
     Brown—AFS 356 A
T. R. Hammond—AFS 10904 A
Holly Hodges—AFS 13127 A3
Jim Holbert—AFS 4136 A2
T. G. Hoskins—AFS 1461 B1
Aunt Molly Jackson—AFS 2573 A3 & B1
     (bawdy version)
Bascom Lamar Lunsford—AFS 1817 B2
Harry McClintock—AFS 10506 A2
Willie McCullough—AFS 13032 A15
Laura McDonald and Reba Glaze—AFS
     11904 A
James Maguire—AFS 11898
Raymond Martin—AFS 13128 A11
R. K. Moore—AFS 13130 B8
Ben Pitts—AFS 4225 A3
Daryl Price and Duane Price—
     AFS 13137 A24
Earl Robinson—AFS 1628 A1 (labor
     union parody)
Mrs. Ben Scott and Myrtle B.
     Wilkinson—AFS 4226 B1
Henry Truvillian—John A. Lomax
     cylinder 12
James M. Walden—AFS 11887 B
J. C. Warren—AFS 14650 B20
Friend of Wash Sanders [*sic*]—AFS 1866

MISCELLANEOUS HISTORICAL/BIOGRAPHICAL
     ACCOUNTS:

"The Ballad of Casey Jones." *Southern
     Living*, 3 (Apr., 1968).
Bolser, Harry. "Switchmen Knew by the
     Engine's Moans That at the Throttle

Was Casey Jones." *Louisville
     Courier-Journal*, Apr. 27, 1950.
"Casey Jones? I Knew Him." *Kansas City
     Times*, Feb. 24, 1911.
"Casey Jones of Song Fame to Get His
     Day in Court." *Knoxville* (Tenn.)
     News-Sentinel. Dec. 3, 1928.
Erie Railroad Magazine, 24 (Apr., 1928),
     13, 44. Reprinted in Botkin (1944),
     241–43.
Erie Railroad Magazine, 28 (Apr., 1932),
     12, 46. Reprinted in Botkin (1944),
     243–44.
Kincaid, Railroad. "Who Was 'Casey
     Jones'?" *RRManM*, 16 (Jan., 1912), 761.
Life Treasury, 262–63.
McKeown, Blanche. "Casey Jones."
     Yankee, May, 1955, pp. 38–41.
Mainer, M. L.
Mynders, Alfred. "Good Evenin'—Link
     with Casey Jones." *Chattanooga* (Ga.)
     News, Dec. 5, 1938.
Roark, Eldon. "Casey Jones's Fireman."
     RRM, 19 (Mar., 1936), 36–38.
Street, James H. *Look Away!* (New York:
     Viking Press, 1936), pp. 107–16.
Woo, William F. "Casey Jones—Mounted
     to the Cabin." *St. Louis Post-Dispatch*,
     Apr. 28, 1963.

PARODIES:

JOE HILL'S labor union parody, "Casey
     Jones on the SP Line":

Alderson
Emrich (1942b)
Joe Glazer—Folkways FA 2039 (FP 39):
     The Songs of Joe Hill
—Collector 1924: *Singing BRAC*
Harry K. McClintock—Folkways FD
     5272: *Harry K. McClintock: "Haywire
     Mac"*
Pete Seeger—Columbia CL 2503
Peter Seeger and chorus—Folkways FH
     5285: *Talking Union*
John Dell Duffy—LC AFS 9725 B1
Earl Robinson—LC AFS 1628 A1

MINERS' VERSIONS:

Emrich (1942a), 216
Emrich (1942c), 104
Emrich (1974), 682
Hand, 33

BAWDY VERSIONS:

Cray, 50

Hiram M. Cranmer—LC AFS 11688 B34

OTHER PARODIES (in chronological order of
publication/recording):

"Casey Jones Went Down on the Robert
E. Lee," sheet music, words by Marvin
Lee, music by Clarence Jones (Chicago:
Marvin Lee Music, 1912).

"Mrs. Casey Jones," poem by C. Herrick,
RRManM, 26 (Jan., 1915), 224.

"I'm the Man Who Fired for Casey
Jones," poem by H. C. Murdock,
RRManM, 26 (Mar., 1915).

"Mrs. Casey Jones," poem by Eddie
Newton, *RRManM*, 27 (June, 1915),
447; also sheet music, words and music
by Eddie Newton (Los Angeles: Hatch
and Loveland, 1915).

"Casey Jones," KKK song, on 78 rpm
Special K-1 (Chicago: Rodeheaver
Recording Laboratories, ca. 1924).

"The Stock Market Casey Jones," *Railway
Age*, July 6, 1929, p. 122.

"Casey Jones," parody on Franklin D.
Roosevelt, by James H. Forbes, *RC*, 52
(July, 1935), 213.

"Casey Jones," Air Force parody, in
Wallrich, 31.

"Casey Jones," British soldiers' song, in
John Brophy and Eric Partridge, *The
Long Trail* (New York: London House
and Maxwell, 1965), p. 65.

RELATED TRAIN-WRECK SONGS that do not
mention Casey Jones:

Newton Gaines—Timely Tunes C-1564
(as by Jim New); RCA Victor LPV 548:
Native American Ballads   "Wreck of
the Six Wheeler"

Blind Willie McTell—Melodeon MLP
7323: *Blind Willie McTell, 1940*
"Will Fox" (from LC AFS recording)

Ben Dewberry's Final Run

BEN DEWBERRY'S FINAL RUN

Ben Dewberry was a brave engineer,
He told his fireman, "Don't you ever fear;
All I want is the water and coal,
Put your head out the window, watch the drivers roll.
    Watch the drivers roll, watch the drivers roll;
    Put your head out the window, watch the drivers roll."

Ben Dewberry said before he died,
Two more roads that he wanted to ride;
His fireman asked him what could they be,
Said, "The old Northeastern and the A and V."
    "The A and V," he said, "the A and V,
    It's the old Northeastern and the A and V."

On the fatal morning it begin to rain,
Around the curve come a passenger train;
Ben Dewberry was the engineer,
With the throttle wide open and without any fear.

He didn't have no fear, he didn't have no fear;
He had her runnin' wide open without any fear.

Ben looked at his watch, shook his head,
"We may make Atlanta but we'll all be dead."
The train went flyin' by the trestle [*pronounced "trustle"*] and switch,
Without any warning then she took the ditch.
    Yeah, she went in the ditch, well, she took the ditch,
    Without any warning then she took the ditch.

The big locomotive leaped from the rail,
Ben never lived to tell that awful tale;
His life was ended and his work was done,
When Ben Dewberry made his final run.
    He made his final run, he made his final run,
    When Ben Dewberry made his final run.

Jimmie Rodgers

The plain facts in the case of "Ben Dewberry's Final Run" are that the song was written/composed by blind evangelist/singer Andrew Jenkins of Atlanta in 1927; it was copyrighted that year (Dec. 23, 1927; E 679537) and recorded on November 30 by Jimmie Rodgers. A reasonable conclusion, after examination of the text, would be that Jenkins had recomposed the Casey Jones story. However, I believe that Jenkins's ballad actually represents an older family of texts and tunes than does the popular vaudeville version of "Casey Jones." In discussing "Casey Jones" I referred to four families of blues ballads that provided one source for that popular ballad. One of these families includes the blues-ballad versions of "Casey Jones," among them the Furry Lewis rendition; Harry McClintock's "Casey Jones"; "Milwaukee Blues" (discussed separately in chap. 8); and "Ben Dewberry's Final Run." All these songs consist of eight-measure verses separated by six-measure refrains. (The vaudeville "Casey Jones" has a chorus the same length as the verses.) The refrain is constructed around repetitions of the fourth line of the verse immediately preceding it. The melody of the verse is hexatonic, lacking the fourth note of the scale. If we divide the eight measures according to the four lines of the verse, the first line ends on the octave; the second line ends on the dominant (midcadence); the third line repeats the first line; and the fourth line has a final cadence on the tonic. (By contrast, the lines of the vaudeville song end on the dominant, subtonic, dominant, and tonic, respectively.) Textually, the family is distinguished by such hallmarks as the "engineer/fear" couplet (rather than "engineer/hear" of the vaudeville song or of the 1908 "Casey Jones") and the "rain/train" couplet.

Andrew Jenkins, the author of "Ben Dewberry" as we know it, possessed a remarkable ability to compose songs and ballads in the folk idiom. One other song of his, "The Wreck of the *Royal Palm*" is transcribed in this book (see chap. 5). Jenkins was born in 1888 at Jenkinsburg, Georgia, on the outskirts of Atlanta. Almost blind from birth, he made a living during his early years selling newspapers. When he was twenty-one, he became a preacher and was thereafter addressed as the Reverend Jenkins. During the 1920s he wrote hundreds of songs, fairly equally divided between religious pieces and songs recounting contemporary tragedies and disasters. He composed to his own guitar accompaniment, while his stepdaughter, Irene, took down words and music.[1]

BLIND RADIO POET

REV. ANDREW JENKINS sells The Journal, preaches the gospel and writes and sings his own songs.

Andrew Jenkins hawks a newspaper headlined "Meet me in heaven, Dupre shouts to girl on way to gallows"—a story that prompted one of his own compositions, "Frank Dupree" (Laws E 24). *Atlanta Journal,* September 5, 1922. Author's Collection.

Years later, when Archie Green asked Irene Futrelle what she knew about Ben Dewberry, she could provide no clues either to the source of Jenkins's theme or to the date of the events described. She felt certain, however, that the ballad told a true story.[2]

In *Only a Miner*, Archie Green discusses another ballad that Jenkins is credited with authoring, and traces it back to older sources.[3] Andy Jenkins's stature as a great folk poet is not in the least diminished by noting that some of his songs closely parallel earlier pieces with which he was probably at least vaguely familiar. In the absence of any historical facts about a Ben Dewberry (Dubarry?), it is speculative to dwell on the origins of the ballad; yet I suspect that at the time he wrote "Ben Dewberry," Jenkins must have known some of the older blues ballads of the family discussed above.[4] The first three and a half stanzas were firmly in tradition prior to 1909; if Jenkins had any genuinely original contribution to the ballad apart from the selection and ordering of verses, it would be in the last three couplets, which I have not found elsewhere.

The song's popularity is doubtless due to Jimmie Rodgers's recording, the lead number at his second session. "Ben Dewberry" proved to be one of his most successful numbers—and indeed, one of the most successful of all hillbilly recordings of the 1920s, selling in excess of 275,000 copies. In the years following, it was recorded by Rodgers imitator Frankie Marvin for several labels. The song has not been reported in any of the published regional folksong collections, but it has been recovered, as unpublished collections such as the Western Kentucky Folklore Archive attest. The version given here is transcribed from the Rodgers recording, which differs in several ways from the usual Jenkins sheet music. Most notable differences are the substitution of "fireman" for "father" in the first two stanzas, and the phrase "trestle and switch" for "troublous switch" in the fourth stanza.

NOTES

1. For biographical information on Jenkins, see D. K. Wilgus, "Folksong and Folksong Scholarship," in *A Good Tale and a Bonny Tune*, edited by Mody C. Boatright (Dallas: Southern Methodist University Press, 1964), pp. 227–37; and Archie Green, *Only a Miner* (Urbana: University of Illinois Press, 1972), pp. 123–25.

2. Futrelle to Green, Nov. 29, 1957. My own attempts to establish the historicity of Ben Dewberry (or Dubarry) through correspondence with the B & O / C & O Railroad and the Brotherhood of Locomotive Engineers met with failure. Dallas Turner ("Nevada Slim"), a western cowboy singer and preacher who knew Jenkins fairly well, told D. K. Wilgus that he believed there had been a Dewberry in Jenkins's congregation at one time; I have been unable to trace this lead further.

3. Green, *Only a Miner*, pp. 123–30.

4. Plagiarism is a viable concept in our own society, in which the pervasive theme of private property is extended, in part through copyright and patent laws, to ideas, phrases, slogans, and devices, as well as poetry, prose, and music. But in a more tradition-oriented society, a song or poem or tale could be composed out of familiar older fragments without in any way impugning the creativity or originality of the composer/writer. The folk composer creates a new piece from older elements—sometimes just motifs or themes, sometimes words or phrases, sometimes whole sentences or stanzas. This calls to mind the old joke about the writer who shows his latest piece to a friend, who sourly notes that he has already seen every word of it in a book. Astonished, the writer asks what book, and receives the reply "The dictionary." Indeed, there is virtually nothing original in our words, but we do expect *groups* of words to be original. The unit of creativity in a folk culture, that is, is significantly larger than it is in a literary culture.

REFERENCES

A. "Ben Dewberry's Final Run," by Jimmie Rodgers. Vocal and guitar. Recorded Nov. 30, 1927 (Victor master BVE 40751), in Camden, N.J. Released on Victor 21245 on Apr. 6, 1928. Reissued on Bluebird B-5482, Montgomery Ward M-4224, Regal Zonophone (Australia) G 23117, Regal Zonophone (England) MR 2241, Regal Zonophone (Ireland) IZ 495, His Master's Voice (Australia) EA 1543, Twin (India) FT 8185; RCA Victor LPM 1640: *Train Whistle Blues;* RCA ANL 1-1052: *All about Trains;* RCA ANS 1-1052 (8-track tape): *All about Trains;* RCA Victor (Japan) RA 5459: *The Legendary Jimmie Rodgers' 110 Collections, Vol. 1;* RCA Victor (England) RD 27110; RCA Victor (England) DPS 2021. First recording of the song; this version is transcribed here.

B. Rodgers (1934a), 9
Rodgers (1934b), 5
Rodgers (1934c), 5
Rodgers (1943b), 2
Rodgers (1967b), 31

D. Frankie Marvin—Brunswick 253, Supertone 2055 (as by the Texas Ranger)
—Edison 20002, Edison 52436
Hank Snow—Victor 20-4096 (in album P-310), Victor 47-4096 (in album WP-310); RCA Camden CAL 514: *The Singing Ranger*
Joe Steen—Champion 16258
Frankie Wallace (Frankie Marvin pseudonym)—Banner 7179, Challenge 691, Conqueror 7164 (also issued as by Frankie Nelson), Jewel 5351, Oriole 1297, Regal 8605, Domino 0253

E. Johnny Bond—Starday SLP 354: *Hot Rodders I Have Known*
Jim Greer and group—Rural Rhythm RR-152: *Jim Greer and the Mac-O-Chee Valley Folk*
Bill Monroe—Bluegrass Special BS 3: *Bill Monroe*
Obray Ramsey—Prestige International 13009: *Jimmie Rodgers Favorites*

F. LC AFS:
Irene Sargent—AFS 13125 B17

J. C. Holmes Blues

J. C. HOLMES BLUES

Listen, people, if you want to hear
A story told about a brave engineer;
J. C. Holmes was the rider's name,
A heavy-weight wheelman with a mighty fame.

J.C. said with a smile so fine,
"Woman gets tired of one man all the time;
Get two or three, if you have to hide,
If the train go and leave, you've got a mule to ride."

In the second cabin sat Miss Alice Fry,
Going to ride with Mister J.C. or die;
"I ain't good looking and I don't dress fine,
But I'm a ramblin' woman with a ramblin' mind."

Just then the conductor hollered, "All aboard,"
Then the porter said, "We've got a load."
"Look-a here, son, we ought to (have) been gone,
I feel like riding if it's all night long."

J.C. said just before he died,
Two more roads he wanted to ride;
Everybody wondered what road it could be,
He said, "The Southern Pacific and the Santa Fe."

J.C. said, "I don't feel right,
I saw my gal with a man last night;
Soon as I get enough steam just right,
I been mistreated and I don't mind dyin'."

Bessie Smith

Like the preceding song, "Ben Dewberry's Final Run," Bessie Smith's "J. C. Holmes Blues" was first published in the 1920s, well after the vaudeville version of "Casey Jones" had crested in popularity; nevertheless, it also shows signs of being based on much older pre–Casey Jones material. The copyright claim credits Gus Horsley with authorship, but it is difficult to determine to what extent he refashioned older fragments. Probably we can credit him with the title of the song, clearly a parody on "Casey Jones."

"J. C. Holmes Blues" represents the several songs in the Casey Jones family that have no train wreck but focus on the fast-living rounder and his rambling female passenger. In fact, several stanzas strongly suggest that the entire imagery of the train, engineer, and rider is pure sexual metaphor. The woman, Miss Alice Fry, is also the other woman in some versions of "Frankie and Johnnie," and may at one time have represented the bad girl in a broader range of folk and popular lore. She also appears in the version of "Casey Jones" transcribed in this book.

Two later recordings are closely related to the J. C. Holmes song. Sloppy Henry's 1929 blues ballad, "Hobo Blues," includes four of the six stanzas of "J. C. Holmes Blues," together with three others. A 1937 Library of Congress field recording by Ed Cobb of Livingston, Alabama, is titled "Casey Jones"; but it consists mainly of elements from "J. C. Holmes" and "Hobo Blues," both of which include this stanza:

> Very last place I begin to sing this song,
> The hobos got 'rested last Sunday morn,
> The judge tol' me, I better leave town,
> Doggone my black soul, I'm Alabama bound.

This stanza also occurs in Riley Puckett's version of "Casey Jones," and the second couplet is in Furry Lewis's version transcribed in this book. This seems to have belonged originally to some other blues ballad, but its identification has eluded me. At any rate, it illustrates the complex way in which a variety of blues ballads are related by shared and borrowed stanzas, so that now it is almost impossible to sort out separate compositions.

Bessie Smith, the artist who immortalized J. C. Holmes on wax, is widely regarded as the greatest of the female blues singers. She was born in Chattanooga, Tennessee, probably in 1898. Family proverty and the loss of both parents by the time she was nine, together with her natural musical abilities, led to her early entry into the world of show buisiness. She was scarcely in her teens when she came under the tutelage of the legendary Ma Rainey and toured with the Raineys' Rabbit Foot Minstrels, a black vaudeville–tent-show troupe that entertained throughout the South. In February, 1923, she began a long and successful recording career with Columbia, and in the next eight years 156 recordings were issued. Although Bessie was nominally a blues singer, a large portion of her songs—including "J. C. Holmes Blues"—were not of the standard twelve-bar blues form, and many were strictly contemporary pop songs. An automobile accident took her life in 1937; but her career as a leading artist had ended years before because of alcohol, her own uncontrollable temper, and changing popular taste.[1]

NOTE

1. Several biographies of Bessie Smith have been written, the most recent and thoroughly researched of which is Chris Albertson, *Bessie* (London: Barrie and Jenkins, and New York: Stein and Day, 1972).

REFERENCES

A. "J. C. Holmes Blues," by Bessie Smith.
Smith, vocal; Louis Armstrong, cornet;
Charlie Green, trombone; Fletcher
Henderson, piano. Recorded on May
27, 1925 (Columbia master 140629–2),
in New York City. Released on
Columbia 14095-D on Sept. 30, 1925.
Reissued on Hot Jazz Clubs of America
HC67; Columbia CL 855: *The Bessie
Smith Story, Vol. 1*; Columbia
G 31093: *Nobody's Blues but Mine*.

D. Sloppy Henry (Waymon Henry)—OKeh
8683; Wax Shop 108   "Hobo Blues"

E. Erik Darling—Elektra EKL 154: *Erik
Darling*   "J. C. Holmes"

F. LC AFS:

Ed Cobb—AFS 1330 B1   "Casey
Jones"

Bessie Smith. Courtesy of Lawrence Cohn.

The Crime of the D'Autremont Brothers

THE CRIME OF THE D'AUTREMONT BROTHERS

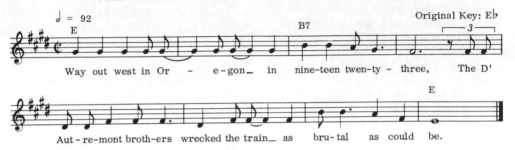

Way out west in Oregon in nineteen twenty-three,
The D'Autremont brothers wrecked the train as brutal as could be.

'Twas train number thirteen of the Southern Pacific line,
They just had passed through Siskiyou and were making regular time.

When going through the tunnel upon the engine they came,
Shot dead Bates and his fireman, and then they wrecked the train.

Then they killed the brakeman and the mail clerk, too,
And endangered all of the lives of the passengers and crew.

Then they fled to the mountains to hide their brutal crime,
Leaving death and destruction on the Southern Pacific line.

For nearly four long years they were sought in vain,
To pay for the lives and the wrecking of this train.

But God is always good and just, as we all know well,
They were finally caught at last as the time will always tell.

Now they are in prison for the lives they led,
Without any hope of pardon until they are dead.

Johnson Brothers

Unlike Jesse James, Cole Younger, Jim Fisk, and Railroad Bill, the protagonists of "The Crime of the D'Autremont Brothers" were thorough villains in the public eye, and did not inspire any romanticized accounts such as grew up around the other outlaws discussed in this chapter.

In the early afternoon of October 11, 1923, three brothers—Hugh, aged nineteen, and Ray and Roy, twins aged twenty-three—held up the Southern Pacific's *San Francisco Express* southbound just as it emerged from a tunnel south of Siskiyou, Oregon. They dynamited the mail car to gain access to the money and securities usually carried. The explosion resulted in a fire that burned the mail clerk to death in his car. When brakeman Johnson came running out of the tunnel to see what the matter was, he was told to uncouple the mail car from the rest of the train. He fumbled unsuccessfully with the coupling, then was shot without warning by the impatient and nervous bandits. The DeAutremonts—note the correct spelling—also shot the engineer, Bates, and the fireman, Seng. At this point the killers ran from the scene, their attempted robbery a failure.[1]

The identity of the killers was unknown for some days, until an abandoned pair of overalls near the scene of the crime was carefully examined and in a pocket was found a registered-mail receipt for a letter from Roy DeAutremont of Eugene, Oregon. The hunt for the three men continued unsuccessfully until February, 1927, when Hugh, living under an alias, was identified in a military base in the Philippines by an army sergeant who recognized his picture on the post office bulletin board.

In June, Roy and Ray were found in Steubenville, Ohio, where they had fled to escape detection. Hugh was brought to trial in Jacksonville, Oregon, found guilty, and sentenced to life imprisonment in the Oregon State Penitentiary at Salem. Ray and Roy confessed after Hugh's trial and were also sentenced to life imprisonment. Hugh was granted parole in November, 1958, after leading the life of a model prisoner (he started the prison newspaper and led it to excellence in competition with newspapers of much larger penal institutions). He died of cancer in March, 1959, after just a few short months of freedom. Roy was judged insane and transferred to a state asylum, where he still remained as of a few years ago. Ray was paroled in October, 1961, after serving thirty-four years. He, too, was a model prisoner, reading widely, learning several foreign languages, and contributing regularly to the inspirational column of the prison newspaper.[2]

Country-and-western singer and free-lance journalist Gary Williams interviewed Ray in November, 1973, about his life and his crime. Almost a half-century after the deed, Ray DeAutremont was still reluctant to discuss it: "There were many years of plain and fancy punishment that I had to suffer for the crime, and it makes me uneasy," he told Williams. "To recall it fifty years after is painful."[3] When Williams asked him if he had any regrets (referring to the many journalistic accounts that described the DeAutremonts as stubbornly unrepentant after their crime), Ray remarked cryptically, "Some wise man once said, those who find comfort in regret should regret a great deal . . . and when it comes to the task of regretting there is so much regretful in the past that the task is endless." Since his release from prison, Ray has been employed at the University of Oregon in Eugene, where he also is active in church work and teaches at the senior citizens' recreation center.

Charles and Paul Johnson recorded three times for the Victor company between May, 1927, and May 1928, and once for the Starr Piano Company in 1930. At their third Victor session, on May 24, the last song they recorded was "The Crime of the D'Autremont Brothers." It was copyrighted by Ralph Peer, crediting the Johnsons with authorship, on December 26, 1929 (E 148701). Set to a tune very similar to "Polly-Wolly-Doodle," their ballad told with reasonably accurate details the story of the crime and capture of the DeAutremonts. What prompted the Johnson brothers, who were probably from Johnson City, Tennessee, to commemorate this western robbery is not known. Nor is anything known about these two artists. When the copyright was renewed in 1957, their address was given simply as Tuco, Kentucky; but a thorough search of that state's placenames has failed to turn up any such locale. Their record sold close to 5,500 copies.

As far as I know, the song has not survived apart from the Johnson brothers' recording. It therefore can hardly be considered a genuine folksong, but the justification for its inclusion in this volume is the fact that it was composed by folk musicians in a folk style.

Stewart H. Holbrook, in *The Story of American Railroads*, concluded a brief account of the robbery: "Within six months of their incarceration some moron had composed a long ballad sentimentalizing them. I don't think it has survived, and am quite happy it didn't."[4] Since the Johnson brothers' ballad could hardly be said to sentimentalize the DeAutremonts, it is possible that another song about the crime circulated; if so, I have found no trace of it.

NOTES

1. Details of the crime vary in different accounts; this is the story given in the references cited in n. 2. According to the *Los Angeles Times*, Oct. 13, 1923, an SP agent was quoted as saying that the brothers probably did get some loot from the mail car before it burned up. Ray DeAutremont, in the Williams interview cited in n. 3, did not recall their getting any money.

2. The historical facts of the case are taken from Eugene B. Block, *Great Train Robberies of the West* (New York: Coward-McCann, 1959), chap. 17: "The Case of the Abandoned Overalls"; and from Richard M. Murdock, "Old Days at Dunsmuir Depot," *RRM*, 84 (Jan., 1969), 18–23. More recent accounts appear in George Dillon, "The Greatest Manhunt Ever Assembled," *Startling Detective*, 64 (May, 1974), 50, 52–55, 67, 69, 71; Gary Williams, "The Case of the Siskiyou Slayings," *Frontier Times*, Mar., 1973, pp. 38–40, 46–47; and Bert Webber, *Oregon's Great Train Holdup* (Fairfield, Wash.: Ye Galleon Press, 1973).

3. Ray DeAutremont, interviewed by Gary Williams, Nov. 27, 1973; tape made available to me by Eugene Earle.

4. Stewart H. Holbrook, *The Story of American Railroads* (New York: Crown Publishers, 1947), p. 387.

REFERENCES

A. "Crime of the D'Autremont Brothers," by the Johnson Brothers (Charles and Paul). Vocal duet; banjo and guitar accompaniment. Recorded May 24, 1928 (Victor master BVE-45206), in Camden, N.J. Released on Victor 21646 on Nov. 16, 1928. Reissued on RCA Victor LPV-532: *The Railroad in Folksong*.

5

The Fatal Run

IN THE 1890s, thousands of people attended the staged two-locomotive collisions that were featured at almost 150 different fairs. In other years, when such exhibitions were not available, the public voraciously consumed books, photographs, and newspapers documenting the loss of life and property on the rails. The age of the long steel rails hardly created a new interest in tales of mishap; it simply offered another wellspring to slake the public thirst.[1] The human appetite for accounts of tragedies and disasters has always seemed insatiable: with few exceptions, the staple fare offered by most of our newspapers for the past century or more has consisted of reports of murders, fires, shipwrecks, mine disasters, lynchings, and the like.

Folklorists have pointed out that folklore thrives where danger threatens. Miners had their tales and songs of mine explosions and tunnel cave-ins; cowboys sang of bronco busters and herders killed in stampedes or while fighting Indians; lumbermen recounted doleful ballads and tales of the brave lads who died in log jams or sawmill accidents; whalers and sailors sang of stormy maritime wrecks; and in this century, airplane pilots have fathered numerous tales of lucky scarves and amulets that warded off disaster. Railroadmen created tragic songs in the style of their predecessors. However, unlike the miners, cowboys, and loggers, the railroaders sang of disasters that involved innocent passengers as well as victims involved on account of their occupation. The opportunity thus arose for two types of poems and ballads, distinguished by whether the passengers or the crew were the primary object of lament. Not too strangely, the latter category far outweighed the former. Few poets wrote pieces that were long remembered about mass deaths; the human capacity for empathy seems to decrease as the number of deaths increases. Of course, it is only fair to point out that for every passenger killed or injured in a railroad accident in any given year there were approximately ten railroad employees killed or injured. (Still larger was the number of trespassers killed; this will be discussed in the chapter on hobo songs.) Nevertheless, even if passenger deaths outnumbered those of crew, one would still expect to find more elegiac poems written about the engineer killed on duty than about the trainload of passengers injured in the same accident. Fatal wrecks occurred every other day, but a brother engineer was killed only once. The typical train-wreck ballad or poem was not a journalistic account of the accident, but more likely a tribute to the crewmen who lost their lives, a memorial to the heroism of those who died in the course of duty.

One of the worst disasters in railroad history, the Chatsworth wreck of August, 1887, which killed eighty-one and injured 372, did give rise to a ballad that dwelt on passengers rather than crew. However, it has not been widely recovered in oral tradition, and I know of no recordings. Of the songs in this chapter, only one—"The New Market Wreck"— describes what can be considered a major accident; and it, too, is relatively rare. The C & O wreck took only one life; the Altoona wreck took two; the *Royal Palm,* nineteen; and the most famous ballad of all, about Old 97, described an accident that claimed only nine lives. The big takers of human life have not been immortalized in song, as if strength of numbers conferred silent anonymity to the victims. No ballad pays homage to the 101 killed in the worst wreck in American history, the collision of the Nashville, Chattanooga, and Saint Louis Railway on July 9, 1918; nor do we sing about the ninety-two killed on December 29, 1876, when the bridge over the ravine at Ashtabula, Ohio, collapsed; or about any of a score of other accidents that claimed fifty lives or more.

As I noted in chapter 1, just when railroading in this country began seems to depend on the definition of what constitutes a railroad; however, by 1830 the B & O had a daily scheduled run over fourteen miles of track, and nine more miles of track were in use elsewhere in the country. It was not long before railroading had its first notable accident: on October 8, 1833, the Amboy and Bordentown road experienced a "concussion" (the early term for a collision), and several passengers were killed and dozens more seriously injured.[2] During the 1830s and 1840s accidents were not a serious problem, mainly because of the low speeds at which trains operated, and also because there were few nighttime runs.

During the second half of the century, the situation worsened steadily, as each year saw more track laid and a constant increase in passenger and freight service. Eighteen fifty-three marked a sharp upturn in accidents and fatalities on the rails. Perhaps the riskiest job in railroading was that of the brakeman, who had to manipulate the old link-and-pin coupling that joined cars together and also operate the hand brakes from atop the cars. Although the automatic coupler was perfected in 1873, the relative cheapness of life compared to the cost of the new device kept the link-and-pin coupler predominant for more than another decade. Similarly, Westinghouse's air brake had to wait from 1869, when first patented, until 1893, when the Railroad Safety Appliance Act was passed, making its use mandatory.[3] This act reduced the employee accident rate by 60 percent, and significantly cut the passenger accident rate as well. From the turn of the century on, the number of passenger deaths relative to total passenger-miles traveled steadily declined.

The new law was greeted with enthusiasm by railroadmen. The *Railroad Trainman's Journal* editorialized:

> Sixteen thousand railroad employes were killed in the discharge of their duties in the seven years from 1888 to 1894. The awful record of the killed and injured seems incredible. . . . Few battles in history show so ghastly a fatality.
>
> The slaughter of American workmen is about ended. A national law . . . has called a halt to the heartlessness or heedlessness of railroad companies, and it has been decreed that an army of men shall no longer be offered up as an annual sacrifice to corporate greed. . . .
>
> A large percentage of these deaths were caused by the use of imperfect equipment by the railroad companies. There was not a city, village or hamlet in the United States but

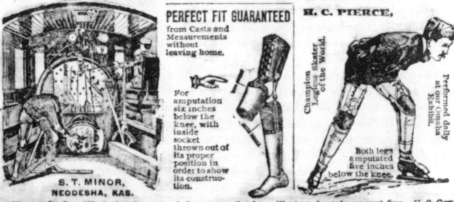

The Winkley Artificial Limb Co.

Largest Manufactory of Artificial Limbs in the World.

LOWELL E. JEPSON, M. S., PRESIDENT. (Incorporated under the Laws of the State of Minnesota.) J. H. JEPSON, SEC'Y & TREAS.

Inventors and Manufacturers of the - -

PATENT ADJUSTABLE DOUBLE SLIP SOCKET ARTIFICIAL LEG

WARRANTED NOT TO CHAFE STUMP.

PERFECT FIT GUARANTEED from Casts and Measurements without leaving home.

For amputation six inches below the knee, with inside socket thrown out of its proper position in order to show its construction.

H. C. PIERCE,

Champion Skater Legless of the World.

Performed daily at our Omaha Exhibit.

Both legs amputated five inches below the knee.

S. T. MINOR, NEODESHA, KAS.

Thousands of our Slip Socket Legs now being worn. Our large illustrated catalogue sent free. U. S. Government manufacturers. Received the highest awards at the World's Fair in '93, at the California International Exposition in '94, at the Atlanta International Exposition in '95, and at the Omaha Exposition in '98.

MINNEAPOLIS, MINNESOTA, U. S. A.

Advertisement in *Railway Trainman*, 1912. Note the fireman depicted at left. Author's Collection.

that numbered its maimed and killed. In thousands of homes widows and orphans mourned the loss of fathers whose lives had been crushed out beneath the wheels of railway cars.[4]

Many pages of that journal were regularly filled with advertisements for artificial arms and legs ("with rubber hands and feet"); and the very name Veteran and Railroad Men's Artificial Leg Manufacturing Company told which occupations of that day were liable to loss of limb.

Needless to say, although the Railroad Safety Act greatly helped matters, the crusading editor's ink did not dry up in his pen. The *Railroad Trainman's Journal* used the occasion of the Titanic's sinking in 1912 to excoriate the "incompetent steamship company that did not know enough properly to provide for their [passengers'] safety," and also to point out that the annual death toll on American railroads was far greater, but attracted less attention because "the casualties are spread over 300,000 miles of track" throughout the year. The article noted that each year one trainman was killed for each 194 employed, and one was injured for every 8 employed. Similarly, one switchman was killed for every 187 employed.[5] Another article quoted the *Army and Navy Journal* as saying that "the risk of life or limb among trainmen on the railroads in the United States is nearly four times as great as among the soldiers in the Philippines."[6]

Although the *Railroad Trainman's Journal* and other periodicals that served the employees' interests were forthright in condemning railroad management for allowing the use of shoddy and outdated equipment in callous disregard for the value of human life, journals that represented the employers' point of view often intimated that accidents were as likely to be the crewmen's fault. In a 1909 issue of *Railroad Herald,* W. L. Park, general superintendent of the Union Pacific Railway, cited four examples of accident investigations, carefully pointing out that at least two were the fault of the crew. The tone of the article clearly suggested that the blame could not always be fixed on the company.[7] An editorial in *National Car and Locomotive Builder* ("devoted to the interests of railway rolling stock") decried what was felt to be the "custom of juries to exonerate from blame on some ground or another every railroad man who is charged with crime when his neglect of duty results in loss of life. . . . Hundreds of people have been killed by accidents due to murderous carelessness on the part of railroad employes, yet we do not remember of any one having been properly punished for their crimes of omission and commission."[8]

The railroad companies were not totally indifferent to the loss of life and limb that followed the engine like a bloodstained red caboose. However, a short article in the *Birmingham News* suggested that financial rather than humanitarian motives prompted the Southern Railway to consider building three hospitals: "The object is to give more attention to people injured on the road and thereby reduce damage suits and other costs against the road. . . ."[9]

It might be pointed out that accidents have not decreased steadily in recent years —quite the contrary. A 1969 newspaper article noted that there were then almost a hundred railroad accidents a day, and that the year before, almost seven times as many persons were killed in railroad accidents as in airline accidents. The president of the Brotherhood of Maintenance of Way Employees stated that "rail and tie replacement work has been neglected and, as a direct consequence, railway accidents caused by track and roadway defects have increased." On the other hand, the president of the Association of American Railroads asserted, regarding the possible delegation to the Department of Transportation of the responsibility to establish safety regulations, that "safety can't be legislated."[10]

I do not wish to dwell on the historical facts surrounding frequencies of deaths and injuries; that subject has been treated exhaustively elsewhere and is not directly our concern. Comfortably removed from the argument by three-quarters of a century or more, we can say that probably neither side was blameless; yet the marked effects of the introduction of the Westinghouse air brake can hardly be explained by a magical transformation of previously negligent crewmen into highly conscientious employees. The articles quoted above are not necessarily objective, but the context of this discussion makes them all the more relevant. Folklore is born out of people's responses to their environment, whether or not those responses are justified in some objective sense. Therefore, I wish to pursue the question of attitudes toward train accidents and safety as revealed in the literature of the various brotherhood journals of the late nineteenth and early twentieth centuries.

Clearly, the feeling was rampant throughout the brotherhood journals of the turn-of-the-century decades that the public was indifferent to the deaths of trainmen—although it is difficult to find direct evidence for such callousness. Naturally, the relatives and friends of railroadmen felt differently; in view of the real danger always present, as indicated by the statistics quoted above, every death or injury to a fellow member of the brotherhood struck a responsive chord of sympathy. A letter to the editor of the Women's Section of *Railroad Brakemen's Journal,* signed simply "A Brakeman's Aunty," stated,

"Whenever I read of an accident, the brakemen, firemen, and engineers claim my earliest attention, then I get around to see to the passengers. . . . "[11]

A recurrent poetic theme of those decades was expressed in the phrase "only a brakeman," the title of many a poem the railroad journals published. Actually, the phrase was not confined to brakemen; a steady stream of similarly titled poems and ballads marched across the printed pages and into oblivion: "He's Only a Laboring Man,"[12] "Only a Navvy,"[13] "Only a Woman,"[14] and "Only a Tramp"[15] were but a few. However, the number of "Only a Brakeman" compositions is impressive. Two particularly popular ones were Constance Fenimore Woolson's "Only the Brakesman," which began:

> "Only the brakesman killed"—say, was that what they said?
> The brakesman was our Joe; so then—our Joe is dead!
> Dead? Dead? Dead?—But I cannot think it's so;
> It was some other brakesman, it cannot be our Joe.[16]

and Lydia M. Dunham O'Neil's "Only a Railroad Brakeman," which started:

> Only a railroad brakeman!
> Only a lump of clay!
> Only a soul that was pure and sweet,
> Freed from its prison to-day![17]

Less well known was Mrs. W. L. Ickes's "Only a Brakeman," dedicated to Elmer Ickes, her brother-in-law:

> Only a box secure and strong,
> Rough and wooden and six feet long,
> Lying there in the drizzling rain
> Waiting to take the south-bound train.[18]

Everett A. Budd's "Only a Brakeman" began:

> Only a brakeman! killed by the train;
> Only a brakeman! by accident slain.
> Onward, rush onward, no time for delay;
> Blow the shrill whistle and hasten away.[19]

The items above date from the early 1880s and later. An earlier poem on the same theme, but without the catch-phrase, was E. A. Clay's "Nobody Hurt!," which began:

> "Nobody hurt but the engineer!"
> The papers read to-day,
> Of a might-have-been horrible accident
> That happened over the way,
> "The Honorable Mr. So-and-so
> Was aboard the ill-fated train;
> What a fortunate thing for his State and friends
> He alighted unharmed again."[20]

A poem signed simply "Only a Brakeman's Wife," titled "Dedicated to All the B. of R.R.B.'s,"[21] and one by George Smith with the familiar title "Only a Brakeman"[22] differed from the others in that they did not concern specific accidents, but rather working conditions in general.

At least one "Only a Brakeman" was made into a song, with words and music by W. C. Hafley. The text, published by C. Tillman's Song Book Company in 1893, began:

'Twas only a poor dying brakeman
Simply a hard lab'ring man,
And the smoke and the soot of the engine,
Had covered his face of tan.

'Twas only a poor mangled being,
Nobody knew "What's his name,"
And they buried him out by the wayside,
In a rustic-like coffin and plain.

Only a brakeman, only a brakeman,
Out and away from his home;
And the loved ones to-night in their sadness,
Are waiting and watching alone![23]

To my knowledge, none of the above pieces entered oral tradition. One "Only a Brakeman" that did was a recomposition of an older cowboy song, "Only a Cowboy."[24] It was localized to an incident in Texas on the Texas and Pacific Line:

Only a brakeman, gone on before,
Only a brakeman we'll never see no more,
He was doin' his duty on the old Tee Pee train,
But now he is sleepin' on the old state plain.[25]

I have not found a printed source for this parody ballad.

Although Mother Jones, the editor of the Woman's Section of the *Railroad Train-man's Journal*, wrote in 1889 that "'Only a brakeman' is never heard any more; it is passed away among other slang words equally repulsive," she was too optimistic.[26] More than two decades later, L. R. McClarren complained:

One day not long ago a freight train was wrecked, and in the news report of the accident appeared the sentence, "Only a brakeman was killed." More attention to the description of what took place was given to the loss of property than to the human being who sacrificed his life in the discharge of his duty. . . . One of the mistakes of the age is the treatment of men in humble positions. Because a man is a brakeman, a laborer in any line that gives him a living, who makes an honest effort to pay his way the same as the man with unlimited means, ought to give him the right to more than passing notice. "Only a brakeman was killed" is a cruel way to refer to the passing of a mortal being. . . . The brakeman who was casually referred to in the wreck was at one time the idol of a loving mother, an object of her hopes and affections. . . . How about the widow and the little people he left? . . . Somewhere somebody is shedding tears for that brakeman. It is surely mother if she is alive and knows of his death. . . . A human being passed away. He had as much right to live as any of us. . . . In his worksuit he is just as human as the man in broadcloth.[27]

This summarizes a common sentiment during the decades when most of the better-known railroad wreck ballads originated. It is not meant, of course, to suggest that everyone shared such feeling. Historical facts indicate there was some justification; the pages of the periodicals that serviced trainmen's interests voiced continually the natural sentiments of those who never knew when they might be next.

If we pass over "Mr. Pierce's Experience," concerning a horse-drawn railroad line, the earliest song commemorating a railroad accident known to me dates from 1848. On June 9 of that year, Henry Sawyer was killed in a derailment of the Old Town Railway in Maine. The incident and its contribution to oral tradition have been documented by Phillips Barry.[28] Collectors in the Northeast have found only three persons who remembered the ballad or a fragment of it as of 1939. It is possible that by now the folksong has become extinct—that is, has vanished from oral tradition.

The earliest American broadsides commemorating a rail disaster that I have found were listed in Edwin Wolf's bibliography.[29] Item no. 1183, "The Killed by the Accident on the North Pennsylvania Railroad, July 17th 1856," was stylistically a kindred piece to the numerous street ballads printed on cheap broadsides and sold throughout the cities of the Old World and the New in the seventeenth through nineteenth centuries. Another song, no. 2453, "Verses on the Death of Miss. Annie Lilly, one of the victims of the accident on the North Pennsylvania Railroad," concerned the same accident, a collision at Camphill Station near Philadelphia involving an excursion train carrying more than a thousand Sunday school children. Sixty-six were killed and more than a hundred injured; it was the worst accident on the railroad prior to 1976. Both of these broadsides are reproduced here. Neither ballad seems to have left any mark on oral tradition.

There were apparently no train-wreck songs of any lasting popularity dating from the 1860s and 1870s. One early ballad that has enjoyed some currency in local oral tradition is "The Hartford Wreck," describing an accident on the Central Vermont Railroad in 1887. It is particularly effective at giving lifelike dimension to the tragedy by dwelling on one fatally injured victim and his young grief-stricken son. (The appendix to chap. 5 provides references for this and other ballads written by hillbilly and folk composers that never achieved widespread popularity.) The songs discussed in this book, which include the most widely known train-wreck ballads, all date from 1890 or later, ranging from "The Wreck on the C & O" (Oct. 23, 1890) to "The Wreck of the C & O *Sportsman*" (June 21, 1930).

Poems commemorating trainmen and yardmen who lost their lives in the course of duty filled the brotherhood journals from the 1870s on. In style, they generally were more rhetorical than the best of the ballads, but some could easily have been set to music. A relatively early fragment was recalled by a reader of *Railroad Man's Magazine*, who said it was written by James T. Dudley and printed in a New York newspaper following a wreck on the New York Central in the early 1870s. With only minor changes it could have been sung to the tune of "The Wreck on the C & O":

> "Jump, jump for your life!" the fireman cried,
> As he sprang from the fated train.
> "I'll stay by my engine," Doc replied,
> For he saw his duty plain.
> And there in his place he calmly stood,
> As he clutched the throttle lever;
> A fearful crash, and the brave man's soul
> Went back to God the giver.[30]

It is apparent that the wreck ballads of the 1890s and later were built upon an already traditional verse style that was used in early poems, if not songs. Another (untitled) poem in broadside ballad style that might easily have been set to music was written in 1889 by one who called himself "Tank Pin." It commenced:

THE KILLED BY THE ACCIDENT

ON THE

NORTH PENNSYLVANIA RAIL ROAD,

July 17th, 1856.

Rev. DANIEL SHERIDAN,
HUGH CAMPBELL,
ANNA LILLY,
JAMES McINTYRE,
BARNEY GREEN,
SARAH McGUIGAN,
JOHN DUGAN,
JOHN RINERS,
JAMES HICKEY,
JOHN BRADY,
WILLIAM BARNARD,
HENRY HARRIS,
JOHN DUDSON,
JAMES REY,
FRANCIS McCORT,
KATE McGURK,
JAMES CONGDON,
HENRY HARVEY,
EDWARD HALL,
ELLEN CLARK,
HUGH TRACEY,

HENRY CORE,
SALLY McGEE,
JOHN McGRAW,
JAMES CONLIN,
MARY O'DANIELS,
THOMAS BARNET,
JOHN DEVLIN,
EDMOND GILLEN,
PATRICK HICKEY,
JOHN SLOAN,
FRANCIS WALLS,
PATRICK FLANEGAN,
EDWARD FLANEGAN,
MICHAEL BURNES,
CATHARINE KROENER,
JAMES GALLAGHER,
LAWRENCE DILLON,
BRIDGET McCANN,
JOHN McVEY,

DANIEL MARLOW,
LEWIS RIVEL,

JOHN McGUIRE,
CATHARINE COKELY,

MARY McFARLEN,
MICHAEL O'BRIEN,

JOHN GREBBONS,
WILLIAM STREET,

Come all ye men and ladies, pay attention to these lines,
And think about your comrades you've seen so many times,
Their hearts were always with you wherever they did roam;
O think how we do miss them, and how they're missed at home.

But O poor souls they're gone, our hearts are sad and sore
To think that we are parted thus, to never see them more;
We saw them in the morning, their hearts were free and light,
How little then they thought they'd sleep in death 'ere night.

When they were in the burning cars, in sorrow and in fright,
With aching hearts and willing hands they worked with all their might;
But O! their time it was too short, their fatal hour had come,
For God their King knew all things best, and took them to his home.

We went into the ruins with hearts full of sad fears,
All for to find our comrades and save their parents' tears,
When our eyes met the sight, our hearts did ache with pain.
To see some in the ruins whose ashes none could claim.

Fathers and brothers did run mad, while mothers did run wild,
Around the burning cars they stood, crying "where, O where's my child?"
But those poor souls they called in vain, were with God in His bliss—
He took them to His Eternal Home where there is happiness.

As they were sitting in the cars, and thought no danger near,
With happy voices raised a song with hearts so full of cheer;
The chorus they all joined in, but to sorrow soon 'twas tuned,
When 'mid the wreck of burning cars, their bodies were entombed.

While in the blazing cars they laid, for mercy they did cry
"For God's sake come relieve us, or in the flames we die;"
Some did stay around them, with willing hearts and hands,
And would have assisted them, but the flames they could not stand,

O what a horrid sight was this for their poor friends to see,
To behold their dear relations in such painful misery;
We found them at the depot and took them to their homes,
But when their parents came to look, there was nothing left but bones.

O, dear children, you are gone, we are bidding you farewell,
But for how long there is none on earth that fatal time can tell;
Though to-morrow it might be, when called we must obey,—
For Death's a thing we cannot slight, nor from it turn away.

That smile is gone from off their face—the voice our hearts loved is still,
Oh! aching is the parents to think how their child was killed,
This world is is no more to them, of it they're unconcerned;
They went into a happy place, from whence no one returns.

That morning did the parents rise to see their children start;
Merry faces stood around, and many a gladdened heart;
Who could have dreamt or ever thought of that which all does know,
When not an hour from their sight, were in the midst of woe.

That smile has gone from off their face, that gladdened heart is still,—
The groans of some and awful cries their dying hearts did fill;
It's left mothers aching breasts, and father's are sore,
To think their children are gone from them, to see on earth no more.

Parents, do be satisfied, it was God's will, be content,
For years on earth soon pass by, time is only lent;
When our dying hour comes, so we are prepared
To meet our children's smiling faces, from sin and worldly care.

Broadside: "The Killed by the Accident on the North Pennsylvania Rail Road, July 17th, 1856."
Collection of the Library Company of Philadelphia.

VERSES
ON THE DEATH OF
MISS. ANNIE LILLY,
ONE OF THE
VICTIMS OF THE ACCIDENT
ON THE NORTH PENNSYLVANIA RAILROAD.

Kind reader, view this happy throng
Of merry children, bright and gay,
With teachers, parents, tender friends
Start to enjoy a holiday.
Their merry faces seem to say
The city has no power to-day,
But with our swings, our hoops, our play,
We'll spend a glorious holiday.
    And mid the laugh, the jest, the song,
    The whistle sounds, the train moves on.

But oh ! what means this sudden jar !
This wild confusion in the cars,
These shrieks that now assail the ear,
And fill the stoutest hearts with fear !
What flames are those, that now arise !
What horrid screams, and awful cries !
Those dying prayers, I'll ne'er forget,
"Have mercy, God !" the trains have met !

And our Annie was singing
"Do they miss me at home."
When the cars, by a sudden bound
Turned smiles into tears, and life into Death,
And strewed death and destruction around.
Five companions of her youthful heart
The mad'ning flames did brave,
And nobly did they strive in vain
Our darling's life to save.
    'Till forced by flames they must stand by
    And see our Annie helpless die.

Must see her burn and cannot save
Even her bones to fill a peaceful grave ;
Cut off in youth, so young, so soon,
With ne'er a coffin, grave, nor tomb.
But parents bow to Him above,
At whose right hand reclines your love—
No earthly pains distress her now,
No shade of care is on her brow.
    Yes, happy were her earthly days,
    She's now the object of the Angel's praise.

J. H. JOHNSON,
SONG PUBLISHER, CARD AND JOB PRINTER,
No. 5 NORTH TENTH ST.,
Three doors above Market, Philadelphia.

CARDS, CIRCULARS, BILL HEADs, &c., &c., NEATLY PRINTED.

Broadside: "Verses on the Death of Miss. Annie Lilly, One of the Victims of the Accident on the North Pennsylvania Railroad." Collection of the Library Company of Philadelphia.

> On the 5th day of December,
> Eighteen eighty-eight,
> When Bro. James Kennedy
> Met his awful fate.
>
> Twas in the morning early
> Brother Kennedy left the yard
> With engine 327,
> and Linsey pulling her hard.[31]

Typical of the elegies of a more stilted and formal style is the following written by Albert D. Thomas in 1880:

In Memory of Milton M. Gilbert, M.C.R.R. Engineer,
who was Killed While on duty at Jackson, Mich., Oct 10, 1879

> In memory of as brave a heart
> As ever beat with honest life,
> And in an effort to impart
> Condolence to his honored wife,
> These simple lines of our regard
> Are, sacred to his memory, penned,
> A tribute of the great esteem
> In which we held our martyred friend.[32]

The editors of *Railway Age* provided a contemporary evaluation of such poetasting in their comments on a wreck poem a reader had submitted, based on a true incident: ". . . the verses are quite as good as the average newspaper rhyming accounts of railway accidents, which we admit is not very high praise."[33] Thomas's poem, weighed in the muse's balance today, would be found equally wanting. Whether the editors of *Railway Age* would have had a higher opinion of Tank Pin's or Dudley's more folk-styled compositions is an unanswered question.

Such pieces, both "folk" and "pseudoliterary," appeared with doleful regularity in the issues of the *Locomotive Engineers' Monthly Journal* and the *Railroad Trainman's Journal*. They were often accompanied by notices that the brotherhood lodge to which the deceased had belonged had voted to express condolences to the survivors or had taken up a collection on their behalf.

One accident of some literary interest occurred on April 19, 1873, on the Stonington and Providence Railroad, when engineer William Guild's train was derailed. At least three poems were written in memory of Guild, of which the most significant, from a literary perspective, was Bret Harte's "Guild's Signal," published in the July, 1873, *LEMJ*.[34] The title derives from Guild's custom of blowing two low whistles as he passed his home in Providence to signal his wife that all was well.[35]

This chapter contains fifteen ballads (or ballad groups) recounting mishaps involving railroaders on their trains. The opening piece, "The Fatal Run," was awarded front position more for its wonderfully appropriate title than anything else. According to its author, Cliff Carlisle, the ballad is a fictional account with no basis in fact, although as the discussion points out, there is good cause to suspect that an older song about a factual incident was in the writer's mind. The chapter ends with another fictional ballad, "The Wreck of Number Nine," also by a hillbilly recording artist–composer of the 1920s. Its lilting air eases us gently out of a chapter of tragedy and disaster. The intermediate selections relate various kinds of mishaps that the railroader has cause to fear. Seven concern train derailments and three involve two-train collisions. "Billy Richardson's Last Ride" describes a freak accident in which the engineer's head strikes the mail crane. "The True and Trembling Brakeman," one of the few songs in this section that may not have evolved from a specific incident (although it has since come to be associated with more than one specific event), and one version of "Little Red Caboose" tell of brakemen who fall off the train to their deaths while discharging their duties.

Three songs in other chapters of the book also treat disasters that befall railroadmen: "Casey Jones" and "Ben Dewberry's Final Run" (chap. 4) and "Jim Blake's Message" (chap. 7). "Casey Jones" is included in the chapter on heroes and badmen because Jones's stature has outgrown the dimensions of an engineer killed in an accident and has approached the scale of a folk and popular hero. Furthermore, the song (as it is most widely known) is comic rather than tragic in its approach. The other two pieces could go equally well in their present locations or in this chapter.

This handful of train-wreck ballads, all similar in theme and style, almost forces on us the perplexing question of why some achieved such widespread and lasting popularity (e.g., "The Wreck of the Old 97"), whereas others got no further than the recordings of their composers (e.g., "The Wreck of the Virginian Number Three"). Part of the apparent great disparity must be due to the statistically minute sampling from the lips of American folksingers. Moreover, neither the persons approached nor the songs recorded from them have been randomly chosen. Strong biases on the part of most collectors have insured that certain items are systematically excluded from their collections while others are overcollected. This point is dicussed at greater length in chapter 2 and in the introduction to chapter 7.

This factor aside, however, there are still numerous variables that determine the popularity of a song. Some of the more tangible factors can quickly be ruled out in the case of the material under discussion. The verity of the train-wreck ballad seems totally irrelevant: truthful and fictional ballads rub shoulders at both the top and the bottom of the popularity roster. The role of the recording industry is at best ambiguous. Dalhart recorded both "The Freight Wreck at Altoona" and "The Wreck of the 1256" for Victor well before the Depression, so they had every opportunity of matching the popularity of "The Wreck of the Old 97"; but evidence shows they fell far short of it. The same examples rule out the artist himself as being the decisive factor in the ultimate survival of the song. We are left, then, with the most important—and probably least understood—factor: esthetics. And here we let the matter rest, save for a final observation: the immediate success of a popular song is neither a necessary nor a sufficient condition for a lasting niche in oral tradition. Folk and popular esthetics, that is, are two separate issues.

NOTES

1. Two outstanding examples of the continuing interest in train wrecks, and also good sources of information, are Robert C. Reed, *Train Wrecks* (Seattle: Superior Publishing, 1968), and Wesley S. Griswold, *Train Wreck!* (Brattleboro, Vt.: Stephen Greene Press, 1969). For an account of Crush City, which came into being for the sole purpose of exhibiting staged train wrecks, see Paul Norton, "Train Wrecks Made to Order," *Railway Progress*, 7 (May, 1953), 24–30, reprinted in B. A. Botkin and Alvin F. Harlow, *A Treasury of Railroad Folklore* (New York: Bonanza Books, 1953), pp. 354–56.

2. Hank Wieand Bowman, *Pioneer Railroads* (New York: Arco Publishing, 1954), p. 42.

3. Chap. 24 of Stewart H. Holbrook, *The Story of American Railroads* (New York: Crown Publishers, 1947), recounts the struggle to introduce the air brake and automatic coupler.

4. "Slaughter of Railroad Employees Stopped," *RTJ*, 13 (June, 1896), 423.

5. "It Was Necessary to Kill Fifteen Hundred at a Time to Get Action," ibid., 29 (June, 1912), 534.

6. "Railroading More Deadly than War," ibid., 17 (Oct., 1900), 885.

7. "Publicity for Railroad Accidents," *Railroad Herald*, 13 (Apr., 1909), 80.

8. "Unfair Investigations of Accidents," *National Car and Locomotive Builder*, 21 (Sept., 1890), 137.

9. "Railway Hospital for Injured Employes May Be Built by the Southern in Birmingham," *Birmingham News*, Mar. 15, 1897.

10. "Railroad Accidents Soar to Nearly 100 per Day, but Blame Is in Dispute," *Wall Street Journal*, June 26, 1969, p. 1.

11. *RTJ*, 6 (Apr., 1889), 168.

12. Ibid., 12 (Apr., 1895), 318.

13. Ibid., 29 (Dec., 1912), 1038.

14. Ibid., 10 (Feb., 1893), 205.

15. *RRManM*, 16 (Dec., 1911), 576.

16. See, e.g., *One Hundred Choice Selections*, No. 22, and *The Speaker's Garland*, vol. 6, no. 22 (Philadelphia: P. Garrett, 1885), p. 115.

17. *RRManM*, 17 (Apr., 1912), 575.

18. *RTJ*, 12 (Jan., 1895), 65.

19. *LEMJ*, 16 (Nov., 1882), 556.

20. Ibid., 11 (June, 1877), 253.

21. *RTJ*, 5 (Jan., 1888), 62.

22. Ibid., 12 (Aug., 1895), 742.

23. *Three Railroad Songs* (Atlanta: Tillman, 1893); *RRManM*, 13 (Jan., 1911), 764.

24. John A. Lomax, *Cowboy Songs and Other Frontier Ballads* (New York: Macmillan, 1916), pp. 124–25.

25. Vance Randolph, *Ozark Folksongs*, vol. 4 (Columbia: State Historical Society of Missouri, 1950), p. 126.

26. *RTJ*, 6 (May, 1889), 207.

27. Ibid., 29 (Aug., 1912), 665, reprinted from *Chicago World*.

28. *BFSSNE*, No. 9 (1935), p. 17.

29. Edwin Wolf II, *American Song Sheets, Slip Ballads, and Poetical Broadsides, 1850–1870* (Philadelphia: Library Company of Philadelphia, 1963).

30. *RRManM*, 6 (July, 1908), 382.

31. *RTJ*, 6 (Jan., 1889), 21.

32. *LEMJ*, 14 (May, 1880), 229.

33. *Railway Age*, Oct. 21, 1880, p. 551.

34. "Guild's Signal," by F. Bret Harte, ibid., 7 (July, 1873), 308; see also *Harte's Complete Works*, vol. 12: *Poems and Two Men of Sandy Bar* (Boston and New York: Houghton Mifflin, 1912), p. 217.

35. See F. L. Hildreth, "Love's Signal," *LEMJ*, 31 (Oct., 1897), 889; also ibid., 34 (July, 1900), 455. A feature article on Guild appeared in *RRM*, 15 (Oct., 1934), 89.

The Fatal Run

THE FATAL RUN

Shuffle ♩ = 168   Original Key: E

Frank-ie's moth-er came to him with his din-ner un-der her arm,_

Say-ing, "Frank-ie Lee,_ my_ dar-ling boy,_ be care-ful how you run;_

_____ There's a man-y poor man has lost his life,_ mak-ing up_ for lost

time, If you will run_ that en-gine right,_ you'll nev-er be be-hind

time." De yo-del lay-hee___ o - lay-hee o - de-lay-de lay-hee.___

*Falsetto.

Frankie's mother came to him, with his dinner under her arm,
Saying, "Frankie Lee, my darling boy, be careful how you run;
There's a many poor man has lost his life, making up for lost time,
If you will run that engine right, you'll never be behind time."
    Yodel:

Frankie said to his mother, a sad look on his face,
"Mother dear, my father's dead, I have to take his place."
"That is true, my darling boy, be careful and don't be late,
Your father didn't run his engine right, that's how he met his fate."

Climbing into his engine cab, and waving his mother goodbye,
Pulling the throttle wide open, to watch that engine fly;
He was headed round Dead Man's Curve, he looked into Forty-nine's face,
He thought of his mother and the folks back home; he'd run his final race.

Frankie's mother got the message, the tears streamed down her face,
To think that her only boy had run his final race;

"Mister engineer, take warning from the fate of that boy of mine,
There's a many poor man has lost his life by making up lost time."

Cliff Carlisle

Hillbilly musician Cliff Carlisle of Kentucky, who enjoyed considerable popularity on records, on radio, and in personal appearances throughout the 1930s, wrote "The Fatal Run," probably shortly before he recorded it for the Starr Piano Company (Gennett records) on April 18, 1931. It was never copyrighted. That first recording was not issued; instead, Carlisle re-recorded the song on September 8 of the same year, and that second master was utilized on the discs cited below in the references. On October 29, 1939, Carlisle recorded the song for the American Record Corporation, but that recording was never issued.

Although Carlisle wrote me that "the song is strictly fictional, it is based on nothing whatsoever of or in the past,"[1] a comparison of his lyrics with the text of "The Wreck on the C & O," following this song, indicates that the older ballad was at least an unconscious model for Carlisle's composition.

Carlisle's song, in slightly altered form, appeared in one hillbilly folio of the 1930s; apart from that item I know of no indications that his song will outlive the shellac on which it was disseminated. It is probably best to regard it as a short-lived descendant of the venerable "Wreck on the C & O," but still interesting as an example of how a creative folk artist refashions older traditional material to suit his taste.

Cliff Carlisle wrote and recorded two other train-wreck songs: "Wreck of the Happy Valley" and "Wreck of No. 52," the latter about an engineer named George Allen. He was also a prolific composer of hobo songs, and is discussed in that connection in chapter 8.

NOTE

1. Carlisle to Cohen, June 18, 1969.

REFERENCES

A. "The Fatal Run," by Cliff Carlisle. Carlisle, vocal and guitar; Wilbur Ball, guitar. Recorded Sept. 8, 1931 (Starr master N 18003), in Richmond, Ind. Released on Superior 2742 on Nov. 30, 1931 (as by Jimmy Boone); Champion 16447 in Aug., 1932; Champion 45162, Decca 5398, Melotone (Canada) 45208. This version is transcribed here.

B. Cowboy Jack, 10

The Wreck on the C & O/Engine 143

THE WRECK ON THE C & O

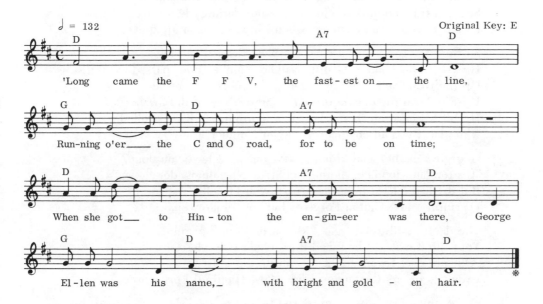

Stanzas 3, 5, 7, and 8 follow the melody of stanza 1. Stanzas 2, 4, and 6 are six lines each, rather than four. These lines are melodically similar to the lines in stanza 1 as follows: Stanza 2: lines 1, 4, 1, 2, 3, 4. Stanzas 4 and 6: lines 1, 2, 3, 2, 3, 4.

'Long came the FFV, the fastest on the line,
Running o'er the C & O road, for to be on time;
When she got to Hinton the engineer was there,
George Ellen was his name, with bright and golden hair.

And his pal Jack Dickenson was standing by his side,
Waiting for strict orders, both in the cab to ride;
George's mother said to him with a basket on her arm,
And gave to him a letter saying, "Be careful how you run.
For if you run your engine right, you'll get there just on time,
For many a poor man has lost his life by trying to make lost time."

"Yes, mother, your advice is good, to your letter I'll take heed,
I know my engine is all right, I'm sure she'll make speed;
O'er the road I mean to fly with a speed unknown to all,
And when I blow for the stock-yard gate, they'll surely hear my call."

George said to his pal, "Jack, a little more extra steam,
I mean to run old Number Four the fastest ever seen";
And Jack injected more water, they shoveled in more coal,
They climbed up in the cabin to watch the black smoke roll;

Up the road she went dashing, like an angry . . .
Sailing through the air, just like an aeroplane.

George said to his fireman, "A rock ahead I see,
I know that death's awaiting there to grab both you and me;
So from this cab now you must fly, your darling life to save;
I want you to be an engineer when I'm sleeping in my grave."

So from the cab poor Jack did fly, New River it run high,
He waved his hand to Georgie as Old Number Four passed by;
Up the road she started up, against the rocks she crashed,
Upside down the engine turned, against his head did mash;
He hit his head on the firebox door and burning flames rolled o'er,
"I'm glad I was an engineer to die on Number Four."

Georgie's mother said to him, "My son, what have you done?"
"It's too late, too late, mother, my [?race] is almost done;
But if I had a local train, it's true to you I'll tell,
I'd run her into Clifton Forge or bid you all farewell."

The doctor said to Georgie, "My darling son, lie still,
Your life it may yet be saved if it's God's only blessed will."
"Oh, no, doc, I want to die, I want to die so free,
I want to die by the engine's side, One Hundred Forty-three."

> Many a man's been murdered by the railroad, by the railroad, by
>   the railroad;
> Many a man's been murdered by the railroad, and sleeping in his
>   lonesome grave.

Charles Lewis Stine

ENGINE 143

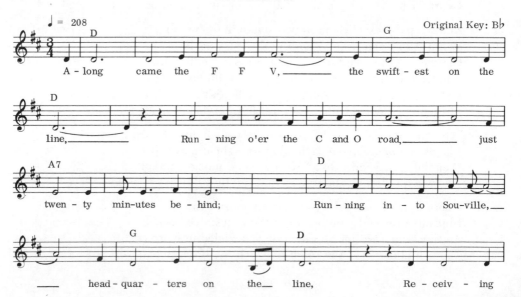

her strict or-ders____ from a sta-tion just be-hind._____

Along came the FFV, the swiftest on the line,
Running o'er the C & O road, just twenty minutes behind;
Running into Souville, headquarters on the line,
Receiving her strict orders from a station just behind.

Georgie's mother came to him with a bucket on her arm,
Saying, "My darling son, be careful how you run;
For many a man has lost his life in trying to make lost time,
And if you run your engine right, you'll get there just on time."

Up the road she darted, against the rock she crushed,
Upside down the engine turned and Georgie's breast did smash;
His head was against the firebox door, the flames were rolling high,
"I'm glad I was born for an engineer to die on the C & O Road."

The doctor said to Georgie, "My darling boy, be still,
Your life may yet be saved, if it is God's blessed will."
"Oh, no," said George, "that will not do, I want to die so free,
I want to die for the engine I love, One Hundred and Forty-three."

The doctor said to Georgie, "Your life cannot be saved."
Murdered upon a railroad, and laid in a lonesome grave,
His face was covered up with blood, his eyes you could not see,
And the very last words poor Georgie said was, "Nearer my God to Thee."

Carter Family

Upwards of seventy versions collected by folklorists or their commercial counter-parts, the A & R men for the phonograph companies, attest to the widespread popularity of this train-wreck ballad. The history of the accident behind the ballad is well known.[1] John H. Cox, who collected ten versions between 1915 and 1918, traced the historical incident and noted that, apart from the simple facts of the wreck on the C & O's Number Four train that killed the engineer while the fireman leaped to safety, most of the details of the ballad accounts were incorrect. Several years later, Alfred Frankenstein, in one of the earliest folksong case studies to use hillbilly recordings as source material, discussed the ballad versions sung by Ernest Stoneman and Roy Harvey and commented on the types of changes that had occurred from one version to the other. Currently, Ron Lane, a young railroad folksong enthusiast, has become interested in the C & O wreck ballads and promises a detailed case study of the wealth of material available.[2] All three of these researchers corresponded with engineer George Alley's surviving relatives and with railroad officials. In the following account I draw liberally from their findings.

George Alley, born in Richmond, Virginia, in 1860, was killed on eastbound Number Four, the FFV (officially, *Fast Flying Virginian;* but unofficially taken to signify, variously, *First Families of Virginia, Fast Flying Vestibule, Fuller's First Venture,* and several other combinations),[3] five hours after the engine struck a rock on the road on

THE CHESAPEAKE AND OHIO RAILWAY COMPANY

Clifton Forge, Va., November 21, 1929.

Mr. Alfred V. Frankenstein,
        1032 East 46th Street,
        Chicago, Ill.

Dear Sir:

Your letter of November 7th:

I enclose herewith copy of the poem on the death of My brother, Mr. Geo. W. Alley, as requested.

You are correct about **there being** nothing to the song so far as the actual facts are concerned. Mrs. Alley was at the opposite end of the run when the accident happened, so there is nothing to the dinner pail story, and the engine number, as well as the conductor's name, were wrong. In fact, I have never been impressed with the song, it being so far from the actual facts.

Incidentally, I might mention the fact that I have been in the service of the Railway Company for sixty-two years, being on the retired list in recent years.

Sincerely yours,

L. F. Alley

L. F. Alley letter. Courtesy of Alfred Frankenstein.

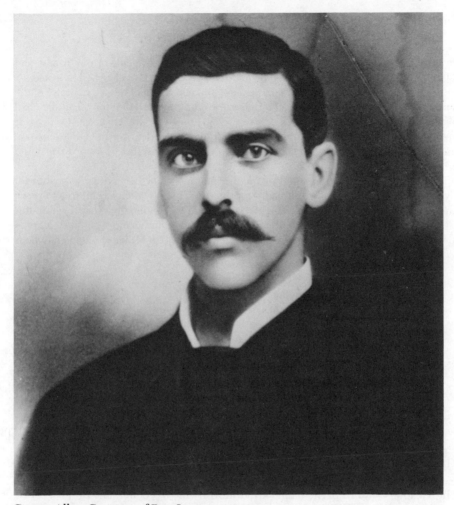

George Alley. Courtesy of Ron Lane.

October 23, 1890. Friday's edition of the *Clifton Forge and Iron Gate Review* was just going to press when word of the accident was received; a brief report was published, as follows:

FATAL ACCIDENT

As the vestibule train was coming east Thursday morning, it ran into a slide near Don, a short distance east of Hinton, resulting in the breaking of the leg and an arm of the engineer, Mr. George W. Alley, who resides with his family in this city, and also injuring the fireman. We have been unable to obtain particulars, further than that Mr. Alley was very badly hurt. His wife at once left on the west-bound train to minister to the sufferings of her husband.

P.S.—Further particulars as we go to press state that Mr. Alley died from his injuries before his devoted wife reached the scene of the accident at 10:30 a.m.; that the engine struck a rock and with it one car tippled over. Besides this, and the slight scalding of the fireman, no other serious damage was done. . . .[4]

The following week's paper provided readers with further details:

MR. GEORGE W. ALLEY

In the last issue of the Review, it briefly noted the death of our friend and fellow-townsman, Mr. George W. Alley, of this city. The sad news reached us just as we were going to press, but few of the particulars. Too much cannot be said in praise of the heroic conduct of this brave man. The facts are few but they tell the story. The slide had blocked the track—he saw the rock—he refused to jump—he stood to his post endeavoring to stop the train. The shock came and he lost his life, and a brave and noble christian spirit passed from earth leaving behind a noble example of unselfish devotion to duty and principle.

He lingered a few hours suffering intense pain, which he bore with great patience. Every effort was made by the railroad company to enable his wife and children to reach him before he died, but all was vain. He spoke of them continually every few minutes asking, "Are they coming! Are they coming?" which circumstance is touchingly alluded to in the following lines written by Mrs. Alexander McVeigh Miller of Alderson, who is an aunt of Mr. Alley:

In Memoriam

He is dying! Are they coming?
  Will he hear their last goodbye?
Last night when he passed from them
  Little did he think to die—
Die like this by dread disaster,
  Ending his young life so soon,
Ere the morning of existence
  Changed into life's fervid noon.[5]

The passengers on the train expressed their appreciation for his valor in staying at his post and risking his life to save others, and collected $103 in donations for his family.

This was the fourth serious accident on the FFV since the C & O inaugurated its first luxury "name" train on May 11, 1889.

The various versions of the ballad are uniformly incorrect in many details: (1) George Alley's mother did not come to him with a basket (or bucket) on her arm, as she had died years before; (2) George's hair was straight and black, not golden or curly; (3) Jack Dickenson was not on the engine at the time (and it has not been explained who he was and how he became implicated in the ballad); (4) the engine was numbered 134, not 143; (5) George's fireman did not have time to wave goodbye to him, nor did he jump into the river (as some versions assert); rather, he jumped out of the cab on the side away from the river; (6) George's mother did not come to his side as he was dying; (7) his last words were very likely "Are they coming?" rather than "Nearer my God to Thee."

The author of the ballad will probably never be revealed. Cox heard from two independent sources, one of whom was George's surviving brother, that the ballad was composed or "started on its way" by a black engine-wiper who worked in the Hinton roundhouse. Frankenstein interpreted Cox's phrase to mean that Cox felt that "the Hinton song was merely the germ out of which the ballad . . . developed in the process of folk circulation." Frankenstein himself, however, felt that the great similarity of all the versions Cox collected, twenty-five years after the accident, suggested that the original text could not differ greatly from them. I am inclined to agree with Frankenstein; furthermore, the story of the black engine-wiper, identical with an attribution of authorship in the case of "Casey Jones," may itself be folklore. In any case, the C & O ballad is hardly in the style of traditional Afro-American balladry, but rather suggests a composer/writer raised in the Anglo-American broadside ballad tradition. One of Cox's informants thought the ballad was composed by an engineer on the C & O—a more plausible statement.

An analysis of all texts at hand, with due weight given to the earlier versions, may permit construction of a hypothetical text that approximates the unavailable original. I believe, however, that the following text will prove to be close to the hypothetical original; it is possibly the earliest printed complete text, having been contributed to *Railroad Man's Magazine* in 1913. The ballad had been requested by a reader several years earlier.

THE WRECK ON THE C. AND O.

Along came the F.F.V., the fastest on the line,
A running on the C. and O. road, thirty minutes behind time.
As she passed the Sewalls it was quarters on the line;
And they received new orders to make up some lost time.

Many man's been murdered by the railroad, railroad,
Many man's been murdered by the railroad and lain in his
    lonesome grave.

When she arrived at Hinton the engineer was there,
His name was Georgie Alley, with bright and golden hair,
His fireman, Jackie Dickerson, was standing by his side,
Waiting to get orders, both in the cab to ride.

Georgie's mother came to him with a basket on her arm,
Saying "Georgie dear, my darling son, be careful how you run;
Many a poor man's lost his life trying to make up all lost time,
But if you hold your engine right, you'll get there just on time."

"Oh, mother, I know your advice is good, to the letter I'll take heed,
I know my engine is all right, I know that she will speed;
It's over this road I mean to fly with speed unknown to all,
And when I blow for the stock-yard gates they'll surely hear my call."

Georgie stepped into his cab, the throttle he did pull,
Off the engine darted like a fire in angry wool.
"It's o'er this road I mean to fly with speed unknown to all,
And when I blow for Big Bend tunnel they'll surely hear my call."

Georgie said to his fireman, "Jack, a little more extra steam,
I mean to pull old No. 4 the fastest you ever seen.
I mean to pull her through, my boy, with speed unknown to all,
And when I blow for Clifton Forge they'll surely hear my call."

Georgie said to his fireman, "Jack, a rock ahead I see!
I know that death is waiting there to grab both you and me.
From this cab now you must leap, your darling life to save;
I want you to be an engineer when I'm sleeping in my grave."

"Oh, no, George, I will not go, I want to die with you."
"Oh, no, Jack, I'll die for both me and you."
From the cab poor Jack did fly, New River it was high,
And as he kissed his hand to George old No. 4 flew by.

On the engine darted and against the rock she crashed,
Upside down the engine turned, her tender body mashed,
His head against the fire-box, the burning flames rolled o'er,
"I am glad I was born an engineer to die on 44."

Georgie's mother came to him, saying "Son, what have you done?"
"Too late, too late, mother dear, my race is almost run,
But if I had a local train, the truth to you I'll tell,
I would run her into Clifton Forge, or drop her into hell."

The doctor said to Georgie, "My darling son be still,
Your precious life may yet be saved if it be God's blessed will."
"Oh, no," said Georgie, "I want to die, I am ready now to go;
I want to die with the engine I love, and that's old 44."[6]

In a few respects I believe this text shows some deterioration from the original. The second line of verse 5 must be wrong; a better choice is the third line of verse 7 of Cox's A text: "Up the road she darted, just like an angry bull." The engine number, 44, in verses 9 and 11 is wrong: it should be either 4 (train number) or 134 (engine number). One additional verse appears in several texts and may have been in the original. A good example is stanza 8 of the text collected by Moore and Moore:

The people to this engine came to see this engineer.
Georgie said, "God bless you, friends; you'll surely find me here."
There never was a braver man than Georgie Allen born,
Who died upon the C & O road one reckless July morn.[7]

Similar verses appear in Cox's D text (st. 12) and his F text (st. 8); Kincaid's and Stoneman's recordings; one version cited in Davis's syllabus; and the version sent to me by Ralph Oatley of Lyons, Michigan, written from his memory.

One other verse, the final stanza of the Carter Family text transcribed above, sounds like a later accretion; it does not appear in the oldest texts or any of the versions that preserve the chorus. The two Florida texts cited by Morris both refer to a black cat crossing the engine's path, indicating another, more localized, accretion.

While much of this ballad was probably original with the author, there are lines that have a distinctly traditional ring. For example, the stanza about Georgie's mother coming with a basket on her arm is reminiscent of an early version of the blues ballad "Delia":

Death had proceeded, it wasn't so very long,
Till her mother come runnin' with a bucket on her arm.

"Delia" recounts a murder that supposedly occurred in Georgia in about 1900.[8]

I have noted the remarkable similarity among all of Cox's versions collected in 1915–18 (and the similarity of other early versions as well). What is more remarkable is that they all agree in reciting the same historical inaccuracies, enumerated above. How to account for this? One way would be to assume that the ballad was not written immediately after the accident, but rather several years later, when some of the details had been forgotten or become confused in the author's mind. Although we usually expect a ballad dealing with a specific local event to have been composed soon after the affair, this is not always the case, as my discussion of "Billy Richardson's Last Ride" indicates.

In this connection, there is a most interesting song that comes from the days of the Philippine Insurrection. Since it is not widely found, it is worth reprinting here for comparison:

THERE'S MANY A MAN BEEN MURDERED IN LUZON

Twas the emancipated race,
　That was charging up the hill
Up to where those insurrectors
　Were fighting fit to kill
The Captain bold of Company B
　Was fighting in the lead,
And like a true born soldier,
　He of bullets took no heed.
　　　For there's many a man been murdered in Luzon,
　　　In Samar, and in Mindanao,
　　　There's many a man been murdered in the Philippines
　　　And lies sleeping in some lonesome grave.

Now Private Alexander Green,
　Said to his Captain bold,
"They've got more men upon that hill,
　Than what we've been told.
So from this action we must hike,
　Our precious lives to save,
For I want you to be a Captain bold,
　When I'm sleeping in my grave."

"No! no! brave Green," says Cap,
　"Our duty lies right here,"
And with his trusty blade in hand,
　He led them with a cheer.
Up the hill, with a terrible yell,
　For he was working for a star,
And the Gu-Gus tell how he gave them hell,
　For he was U.S. REGULAR.

Now when that action was over,
　The wounded strewed the sod,
The Doctor came with the Hospital Corps,
　And a Chinese litter squad.
They found poor Alec where he lay,
　A-wallowing in his blood,
And they picked him up and took him where
　The dressing station stood.

"O never mind your Captain bold,"
   Says Doc to Private Green,
"You've got the worst wound in your head,
   I believe I've ever seen."
"O never mind my head," says Green,
   "I want to die, I do,
For the Captain needs his Alec Green,
   Beyond that pale of blue."

Now on that hill the Captain bold,
   In his last grave does reside,
And Private Alexander Green,
   Is sleeping by his side.
The wind a-sighing thru' the trees,
   Seems to whisper soft and low,
It's the Captain calling, "First Sergt. Green,"
   And Alec answering "Here-O!"[9]

While the melody of the verse has nothing to relate it to "The Wreck on the C & O," the melody of the chorus does; and the similarity in phrasing in several lines—and, of course, the chorus—is striking. The obvious conclusion would be that this soldiers' song, dating from 1900–1901, was based on the older "Wreck on the C & O." But what if the borrowing were in the other direction? That is, that our railroad song was not written until early in the 1900s, at least ten years after the accident occurred? That might explain the uniformly incorrect details of the account.

Can "The Wreck on the C & O" be pushed back farther than 1913, the date of earliest printing? Richard D. Burnett's songbook, which included a text, is not dated, but was probably printed in 1913. The version Shellans printed was sung by Ruby Vass from her father's old notebook, believed to have been written down around 1912. Shearin and Combs, in their 1911 syllabus, reported two versions (titles only); unfortunately, these texts have since been lost, but they must date to 1910 or earlier. Doc Hopkins learned his version in about 1909 from Blind Bill Cox, an itinerant balladeer. Allan Trout quotes a retired railroader who recalled a stanza from his days working on the C & O's Mud Valley Division in 1905–7. One of Gordon's correspondents, J. O. Hogan, submitted a text that he claimed he heard in Baltimore in 1896–97: "It was published in ballad form and sung in all the theaters."[10] Informants' memories of when they first learned songs are not always reliable, so there is the possibility that the last date is in error. In sum, we have no direct proof, and only hearsay evidence, that the ballad of the wreck predates 1900; and the relationship of "The Wreck on the C & O" to the song from the Philippines remains unresolved.

The earliest phonograph recording of "The Wreck on the C & O" was made on September 16, 1924, by George Reneau for the Aeolian Vocalion label in New York. It was a good text of ten stanzas that Reneau probably learned in his native Tennessee. In March, 1925, Charles Lewis Stine recorded a version for Columbia that was somewhat confused but nonetheless significant because it was the first version—and in fact one of only two—to preserve the chorus. It is transcribed here. Ernest Stoneman recorded the song twice: in August, 1925, for OKeh and in June, 1926, for Edison. Stoneman stated that he learned the song from Cox's book,[11] and his text is indeed similar to Cox's F text. Roy Harvey, an engineer for many years on various lines in the Southeast, recorded a ver-

Wreck on the C. & O. Railroad at Clifton's Ford, Va.

Along came the F. F. V., the fastest on the line,
Running over the C. & O. Road twenty minutes behind,
And when they got to Hinton they quartered on the line
Awaiting for strict orders for the crew so far behind.
When they got to Hinton the engineer was there,
George Allen was the young man's name with light and curly hair,
His Faithful fireman Jack Dickerson was standing by his side,
Waiting for the local train in a cab for two to ride.

CHORUS

There's many a man been killed by the R. R.
Many a man been murdered by the train
There's many a man killed by the R. R.
And sleeping in his lonesome grave.

George's mother came to him with his dinner on his arm
Saying George, Oh Goerge, my darling bok be careful how you run,
For many a man has lost his life making up lost time,
And if you run your engine right you'll seldom be behind.
Mother, your advice is good and later I'll take heed,
I know my engine is alright for she will surely speed
Down this road I mean to go with a record unknown to all,
And when I blow for the Big Bend tunnel the switchman will hear my call.

CHORUS

Said George to his fireman Jack, a rock ahead I see,
And death is awaiting there to pick up you and me.
Now from this cab you must leap your darling life to save,
I want you to be an Engneer when I am in my grave.
No, no George, I want to die, I want to die with you,
No, no Jack, my darling boy, I'll die for you and I.
And from the cab poor Jack did leap, the river was running high;
And as he kissed his hand to George old No. 4 flew by.

CHORUS

Now I have died a R. R. man, bury me on this line;
Because I missed old No. 4 I caught old No. 9.
His head and face is mangled, his eyes I could not see;
The last words poor George said was "Nearer, My God to Thee.

CHORUS

As sung by Bailey Briscoe, with Dakota Jack, the Cow Boy Medicine Man.

PRICE 10 CENTS

Broadside: Bailey Briscoe's "Wreck on the C. & O. Railroad at Clifton's Ford, Va." Courtesy of Ed Kahn.

sion entitled "The Brave Engineer" in September, 1926, which set the George Alley story to the tune of "The Wreck of the Old 97." Bradley Kincaid of Kentucky recorded a good text, one that preserved the chorus, in January, 1929, for the Starr Piano Company. The second version transcribed in this book was recorded in February, 1927, by the famous Carter Family of Virginia. Sara Carter had learned the song when she was young (she was born in 1898), and according to family lore, this is the song she was singing when, at the age of sixteen, she first met her husband-to-be, A. P. Carter. Sara's version is unusual in that it is one of the few recorded that is sung in 3/4 rather than 4/4 time. Although she grew up in Wise County, Virginia, within 150 miles of the section of the C & O line referred to in the song, and learned the ballad probably less than twenty years after the incident, her text has been considerably truncated and stripped of details; it makes an interesting epilogue to Frankenstein's study of the Stoneman and Harvey texts. Because of the great popularity of the Carter Family for the past forty years, this recording, like the others they made, has influenced many later singers, from both the city and the country.[12]

"Engine 143" was one of the Carters' best-selling records; their Victor release sold more than 88,000 copies, their Montgomery Ward reissue more than 5,400. In general, the Carter Family was Victor's second most valuable property in the hillbilly field, exceeded only by Jimmie Rodgers. Typically, the Carters and Rodgers sold five to ten times as many records as did Victor's other hillbilly artists at the same time.

NOTES

1. Details not given in John H. Cox, *Folk-Songs of the South* (1925; rpt., Hatboro, Pa.: Folklore Associates, 1963), pp. 221–30, and Alfred Frankenstein, "George Alley," *Musical Courier*, Apr. 16, 1932, p. 6, are taken from the *Clifton Forge and Iron Gate Review*, Oct. 21, 31, Nov. 21, 1890.

2. Lane to Cohen, Apr. 13, Aug. 14, 1968; July 9, Aug. 6, Nov. 2, 1969.

3. An article in *Railway Age*, Sept. 6, 1889, p. 584, discussed the mystery surrounding the name *FFV*, mentioning various meanings travelers had suggested for the initials, and explained that the name was given by general passenger agent Fuller of the C & O line. I am grateful to Ron Lane for making this item known to me.

4. *Clifton Forge and Iron Gate Review*, Oct. 24, 1890.

5. Ibid., Oct. 31, 1890.

6. *Railroad and Current Mechanics* [the title of *RRM* for 1913], 22 (Nov., 1913), 446–47.

7. Ethel Moore and Chauncy O. Moore, *Ballads and Folk Songs of the Southwest* (Norman: University of Oklahoma Press, 1964), p. 334.

8. Chapman J. Milling, "Delia Holmes—A Neglected Negro Ballad," *SFQ*, 1 (Dec., 1937), 3–8.

9. *The Book of Navy Songs*, collected and edited by the Trident Society of the United States Naval Academy (Garden City, N.Y.: Doubleday, Doran, 1926), p. 118. See also Edward Arthur Dolph, *Sound Off!* (New York: Cosmopolitan Book Corp., 1929), pp. 207–9, "The Emancipated Race."

10. Gordon MS 1232, J. O. Hogan of Galveston, Tex., to Gordon, Sept. 18, 1925.

11. Ernest V. "Pop" Stoneman, interviewed by Eugene Earle, at UCLA, Los Angeles, Mar. 27, 1964. See also *The Early Recording Career of Ernest V. "Pop" Stoneman—A Bio-Discography*, JEMF Special Series, No. 1 (Los Angeles: John Edwards Memorial Foundation, 1968).

12. For additional biographical information on the Carter Family, see the discussion of "Jim Blake's Message" (chap. 7), "Cannonball Blues"/"Whitehouse Blues" (chap. 9), and "Railroading on the Great Divide" (chap. 10).

REFERENCES

A. "The C & O," by George Reneau.
Reneau, guitar and harmonica; Gene
Austin, vocal (not credited on record
labels). Recorded Sept. 16, 1924
(Aeolian Vocalion masters 13698–99), in
New York City. Released on Vocalion
(Aeolian) 14897 in Dec., 1924; on
Vocalion (Brunswick) 5050 in 1927.
First commercial recording of the song.

"The Wreck on the C & O," by Charles
Lewis Stine. Vocal and guitar.
Recorded Mar. 19, 1925 (Columbia
master 140447), in New York City.
Released on Columbia 15027–D in ca.
June, 1925; on Harmony 5145–H (as by
Charles Lewis). First recording with
chorus.

"The Wreck on the C. and O.," in
Railroad and Current Mechanics [the
title of *Railroad Man's Magazine* for
1913], 22 (Nov., 1913), 446–47.
Contributed by O. M. Proehl of
Roanoke, Va., in response to a reader's
request a few months earlier. First
definitely datable printed version.

"Engine 143," by the Carter Family.
Sara, vocal and autoharp; Maybelle,
guitar. Recorded Feb. 15, 1929 (RCA
Victor master 49868–2), in Camden,
N.J. Released on Victor V-40089 on
July 19, 1929. Reissued on Bluebird
B-6223; Montgomery Ward M-4743;
Victor (England) RCX 7102 (EP);
Folkways FA 2951 (FP 251): *Anthology
of American Folk Music, Vol. 1*; RCA
Victor LPV 532: *The Railroad in
Folksong*; RCA Camden CAL 2473:
Lonesome Pine Special. Transcribed in
this book, as well as in Moses Asch,
Josh Dunson, and Ethel Raim, eds.,
Anthology of American Folk Music
(New York: Oak Publications, 1973),
pp. 62–63.

B. Anderson, G., 206
Asch, 62–63 (transcription of Carter
Family recording)
Boette, 71
Botkin (1949), 725 (Cox's D text)
Botkin & Harlow, 451 (Cox's D text)

Briscoe, broadside (n.d.) (original in
possession of Ed Kahn)
Brown IV, 356
Buck's Rock
Burnett, 3
Carlisle, I., 90–92   "George Allen"
Carpenter
Carter Family (1930?), 19
Carter Family (1937), 20
Carter, I. G., 41
Comstock, 553–54
Cox (1925), 221–30
Crabtree, 117   "Engine 143"
Davis, A. K., 293 (titles and first lines
only of two texts)
Emrich (1974), 660–61
Flatt & Scruggs
Frankenstein
Gainer (1963), 12
Gainer (1975), 116 (same as Gainer
[1963])
Gerould, 279 (Cox's F text)
Haun, 180   "Jack and George"
Lane, Pt. 5
Laws, 214 (G 3) (discussion only)
Lomax & Lomax (1934), 31 (Cox's D text)
Moore & Moore, 334
Morris, 111
Mynder, Alfred, *Chattanooga News*, Dec.
5, 1938
Perry, 209   "Engine 143"
Randolph IV, 129
Shearin & Combs, 20 (titles and first lines
only of two texts)
Shellans, 60
Silverman (1975) I, 137
Thomas, 115 (123 in reprint ed.)
Trout, Allan, "Greetings" column,
Louisville Courier Journal, Jan. 2, 1962
Watson, 58
Wilgus (1957), 98–99

C. Mrs. Burt Christian, unpublished sheet
music, copyrighted 1925

COHEN COLLECTION:

Laura Affolter (letter, June, 1968)
Mrs. Ercie Barrett (letter, Dec., 1968)
C. C. Meeks (letter, Oct. 20, 1969)
Ralph Oatley (letter, Sept. 29, 1967)

GORDON MSS:

332—Beulah Moses   "The F.F.V."
436—Virginia Berkeley   "The C & O Wreck, or Georgie Allen"
925—William F. Burroughs
1187—Frank Middleton   "Georgie Allen"
1232—J. O. Hogan (Sept. 18, 1925)
3447—Anonymous contributor

LC AFS:

Ruth Isom—WPA W11664 (Va., 1938–39)
Unidentified—WPA W12292 (Ark., 1936–37)

LOMAX PAPERS:

Nonie Peters, Griffith, Va.   "George Allen, or the Dying Engineer"

WKFA:

Troy Basil (1960)
George Disney (Apr., 1952; Aug., 1954)

D. Duke Clark—Superior 2687   "The Wreck of the F.F. & V."
Roy Harvey and the North Carolina Ramblers—Columbia 15174-D   "The Brave Engineer"
Bradley Kincaid—Gennett 6823, Champion 15710 (as by Dan Hughey), Champion 45098, Supertone 9350, Melotone (Canada) 45057   "Wreck on the C & O Road"
George Reneau—Vocalion 14897, Vocalion 5050   "The C & O Wreck"
Ernest V. Stoneman—Edison 51823, Edison 5198 (cylinder)
—OKeh 7011 (12″ 78 rpm)

E. John Allison—Ficker C10001: *Heroes, Heroines, and Mishaps*   "Wreck on the C and O Road"
Joan Baez—Vanguard VRS 9094: *Joan Baez, Vol. 2*   "Engine 143"
Talking John Barry—Driftwood EP 1000   "The F.F.V."
Alex Campbell—Society (England) SOC 960: *Folk Session*   "Engine 143"
A. P. Carter Family—Pine Mountain PMR-206: *A P. Carter's Clinch Mountain Ballads*   "The Fate of George Allen on Engine 143"

Lester Flatt, Earl Scruggs, and the Foggy Mountain Boys—Columbia CL 1830: *Folk Songs of Our Land*   "George Alley's F.F.V."
Austin Harmon—Library of Congress Archive of Folk Song L61: *Railroad Songs and Ballads*   "George Allen" (from LC AFS 2916A)
Doc Hopkins—Birch 1945: *Doc Hopkins*
Bradley Kincaid—Bluebonnet BL112: *Bradley Kincaid, the Kentucky Mountain Boy, Vol. 4*   "Wreck on the C & O Road"
Kossoy Sisters—Tradition TLP 1018: *Bowling Green and Other Folksongs from the Southern Mountains* "Engine 143"
Malcolm Price Trio—Decca (England) LK 4627: *Country Sessions*   "Engine 143"
Phipps Family—Starday SLP 195: *Old Time Mountain Pickin' and Singin'*; Starday SLP 170: *All Aboard! for the Railroad Special*; Starday SEP 159 (45 rpm)   "Wreck on the L & N"
—Vanguard VRS 9185/VSD 79185: *The Newport Folk Festival—1964: Evening Concerts, Vol. 2*   "Wreck on the L & M"
Romaniuk Family—Point PS-352: *Songs We Love to Sing*   "The Wreck on the C & O"
Dave Van Ronk—Folkways FA 2383: *Dave Van Ronk Sings*   "Georgie and the IRT" (parody)
Doc Watson—Vanguard VRS 9239/VSD 79239: *Home Again*   "The F.F.V."
Al Wood and the Smokey Ridge Boys —Rebel SLP 1519: *Sing a Bluegrass Song*   "Story of the F.F.E."

F. KAHN COLLECTION:

Lily Steele, Hamilton, Ohio (Aug. 17, 1958)

LC AFS:

Bradley Browning—AFS 1390 A1 "F.F.E.—The Fastest on the Line"
Maggie Gant—AFS 66 B1
Gladys McCarty—AFS 5313 A2 "Georgie the Engineer"

The Wreck of the Old 97

WRECK OF THE 97

Original Key: B♭

"May God bless you, For your dad must now go on his run."

Steve Brady kissed his loving wife,
By the rising of the sun;
And he said to his children, "May God bless you,
For your dad must now go on his run."

'Twas the twenty-second day of that November,
And the clouds were hanging low;
He took Old Ninety-seven out of Washington Station
Like an arrow shot from a bow.

I was standing on the mountain that cold and frosty morning,
And I watched curling smoke below;
It was steaming from Old Ninety-seven's smokestack
Way down on that Southern road.

Ninety-seven was the fastest mail train
Ever run the Southern line;
But when she reached into Richmond, Virginia,
She was twenty-seven minutes behind.

He received his orders at the Richmond station,
Saying, "Steve, you're far behind;
Now this isn't Thirty-eight, but it's Old Ninety-seven,
You must put her into Spencer on time."

When he read his orders he said to his fireman,
"Do not obey the whistle or the bell;
And we'll put Old Ninety-seven into Spencer on time,
Or we'll sink her in the bottom pits of hell."

He saw the brakeman signal and threw back his throttle,
Although his air was bad;
And the signalman said when he passed Franklin Junction
You could not see the man in the cab.

Steve looked at his watch and said to his fireman,
"Just throw in a little more coal,
And when we reach those Cumberland Mountains,
You can watch Old Ninety-seven roll."

He went over the grade making ninety miles an hour,
And his whistle broke into a scream;
He was found when dead with his hand on the throttle,
And was scalded to death by steam.

When the news went in o'er the telegraph wires,
This is what the Western said:
That brave, brave man that was driving Ninety-seven,
Is now laying in North Danville, dead.

The people waited at the depot,
Till the setting of the sun;
It was hours and hours the dispatch was waiting
For the fastest train ever run.

                                              Arizona Wranglers

Few folksongs have as interesting a history as the train-wreck ballad "The Wreck of the Old 97." Because much of the story, particularly as it relates to the accident itself, has been well told by Hubbard, Holbrook, Hamilton, Walsh, and Ulevich, and retold by Botkin and Harlow, in Brown, and by Friedman, my account will be relatively condensed.[1] However, even if I recounted every known detail, the story would be incomplete; some important links in the long ballad history have unfortunately still eluded discovery.

Number 97 was a fast mail train on the Southern Railway that ran between Washington and Atlanta from December, 1902, to January, 1907. On Sunday, September 27, 1903, because of various delays, Old 97 reached Monroe, Virginia, 165 miles south of Washington, about an hour late. At that station the crew was changed; the engineer who took command was Joseph A. Broady, nicknamed "Steve" after the vaunted daredevil Steve Brodie, who leaped from the Brooklyn Bridge on a bet in 1886 and lived to tell about it. Broady, who had been with the Southern Railway for only a month, having transferred from the Norfolk and Western, was unfamiliar with the route of Old 97, and highballed it trying to make up some of the lost time. From Monroe it was some eighty miles due south to Danville, a cotton-mill town on the southern bank of the Dan River and just north of the North Carolina border. Across the river from Danville was North Danville, then an unincorporated residential area that housed mills and millworkers' homes. The Southern's tracks approached the Dan River, then turned west, paralleling the river for some distance before actually crossing it and entering Danville. Where the tracks turned was Stillhouse Trestle, a wooden bridge spanning Stillhouse Creek, in a ravine some seventy-five feet below. Between the creek and the river was the Riverside and Dan River cotton mill. The trestle was preceded by the curve and a descending grade, a combination that made it a danger point.

Broady took Old 97 from Monroe south to Lynchburg, whence it traversed a rough section of road, including the White Oak Mountain grade, that took it to Lima Junction and then down another grade to Stillhouse Trestle. Broady approached the trestle too fast, and the locomotive, together with the five wooden cars behind it, flew off the rails some fifty feet before the trestle and hurtled into the ravine below, finally coming to rest

The wreck of Old 97. Courtesy of the Southern Railway Company.

when it struck the concrete viaduct that carried Stillhouse Creek beneath the cotton mill. The train was completely destroyed and nine persons were killed, including engineer, both firemen, conductor, and flagman; seven others were injured. It being a pleasant Sunday morning, many of the townfolk were outside on their porches and witnessed the whole tragedy. Some heard the dying words of engineer Broady as he begged to be put out of his misery; he was not killed instantly in the accident, but was very badly scalded, parts of his skin peeling off as rescuers tried to pull him from the wreckage.[2]

The history of the ballad, however, began long before Broady plunged Old 97 into a ravine beneath Stillhouse Trestle. It began in 1865, when Henry Clay Work, one of the leading popular composers of the 1860s and 1870s, wrote "The Ship That Never Return'd." Since the development of the later parodies (for want of a better term, I use this word in the classic sense of any literary imitation, humorous or otherwise) is more easily followed if Work's song text is available for comparison, I give here the original words, as published by Root and Cady in 1865:

On a summer's day when the wave was rippled
By the softest gentlest breeze,
Did a ship set sail with a cargo laden
For a port beyond the seas.
There were sweet farewells—there were loving signals,
While a form was yet discern'd,
Though they knew it not, 'twas a solemn parting,
For the ship—she never return'd.

Did she never return? She never return'd—
Her fate, it is yet unlearn'd;
Tho' for years and years there were fond ones watching,
But the ship—she never return'd.

Said a feeble lad to his anxious mother,
"I must cross the wide, wide sea,
For they say, perchance in a foreign climate,
There is health and strength for me."
'Twas a gleam of hope in a maze of danger,
And her heart for her youngest yearn'd;
Yet she sent him forth with a smile and blessing,
On the ship that never return'd.

"Only one more trip," said a gallant seaman,
As he kiss'd his weeping wife,
"Only one more bag of the golden treasure,
And 'twill last us all through life.
Then I'll spend my days in my cozy cottage,
And enjoy the rest I've earned;
But alas, poor man, for he sail'd commander
Of the ship that never return'd.[3]

Like many of Work's songs, including "Grandfather's Clock" and "Come Home, Father," "The Ship That Never Return'd" achieved widespread popularity, eventually entering folk tradition to enjoy a life that far outlasted the fifty-six years extended by the copyright law. The tune changed somewhat, although that does not alter our story. A sure indicator of a song's popularity is the occurrence of parodies, and several appeared based on Work's ballad in the 1880s, if not earlier. The only one for which the date and author are documented is "The Hand-Car That Never Returned," subtitled "A Parody on 'The Ship That Never Returned,'" copyrighted in 1888 by its author, Alexander Malin, and published on a 6-by-8½-inch broadside. The first verse of this parody, which describes a hand-car that leaves the rails at a trestle and hits a passing ship in the waters below, is as follows:

On a Winter's day, as the Train was whistling through the "Transcontinental" Gate,
A Hand Car started, with its burden laden, over Section seventy-eight.
There was many a joke among the "Jerrys," for their thoughts were unconcerned,
They little knew 'twas their last sad voyage on the Hand-Car that never returned.

Whether the author had created the first in a series of railroad parodies on Work's song, or whether he already had knowledge of an earlier train parody, we do not know. From an artistic point of view it might make a more interesting theory to suppose that there had already been train parodies and that Malin had composed a clever amalgam of the two themes in a kind of double parody.

Evidently, the earliest train parody of Work's song was "The Train That Never Returned." Although composer and date are unknown, if we can believe Stout's informant, it was current at least as early as 1888.[4] A disjointed text of this song was printed in

Railroad Magazine with the note that the song was reprinted "from a song sheet issued in about 1900 by the blind singer O. F. Saunders, Burlington Jct., Mo."[5] Other versions can, by virtue of various distinguishing textual features, be grouped into two categories distinct from one another and also distinct from the Saunders/Stout song, which for convenience I shall call "The Train That Never Returned (I)."

"That Train That Never Returned (II)" is a relatively stable group of texts all of which have three verses and a chorus and are localized to the C & O Railway.[6] Since the earliest of these was published in 1927, with no indication of the date of first appearance, we cannot be sure that version II predates "The Wreck of the Old 97." It is distinguished by the opening line, "I was going 'round the mountain one cold winter day," which is distinct from the opening lines of I and III, all of which are something like "On a cold winter night when the smoke was curling."

"The Train That Never Returned (III)" consists of several versions all of which have distinct localizations and not quite perfectly parallel verses; they seem to be more closely related to each other than to the other families.[7] All these songs have a distinctive line about painting the town red, although in different cases the town is Corbin, Somerset, or Pinole.

The other important member of the complex family of predecessors to "The Wreck of the Old 97" was probably titled "The Parted Lover," although it has also been remembered by the titles "The Face That Never Returned" and "Lovers Parted." We can be certain that it predated 1903 because Charles W. Noell, who wrote one of the ballads about Old 97, stated that he had set his poem to the tune of "The Parted Lover." The first seven stanzas of the song tell of a lovers' quarrel, on account of which the young man left his lover and rode (or sailed) away to a foreign country. His heart was still filled with pain; likewise crushed, she turned pale and bathed her pillow nightly in tears. Then the concluding moral:

> Now, young men and maids, from my song take warning
> Or your hearts will break with pain.
> Never speak harsh words to a faithful lover
> Or he'll leave you to never return.[8]

There were probably numerous other parodies of Henry C. Work's 1865 composition in circulation by 1903, but I will mention only one more, for it, too, is a train song. In 1927, Fiddlin' John Carson of north Georgia recorded "Did He Ever Return?," a fragmentary ballad that began:

> Oh, what did the bad boy say to his mother,
> When he swung to the side of a train?
> "Some day, I know, I will be a conductor,
> On that fast mail train."
>
> Did he ever return, no, he never returned,
> And the poor boy must be dead.
> His body was found on a cold iron railing
> And the snow had covered his head.[9]

Most singers learn the bulk of their repertoires in their younger years. Since Carson was thirty-five years old at the time Old 97 flew off the track at Stillhouse Trestle, it is likely that the ballad he imperfectly remembered predated that accident.

It is evident that half a dozen or more parodies on "The Ship That Never Return'd" were in oral circulation in the southern mountains in 1903; several of them involved trains. It is not unlikely, therefore, that different persons should write ballads about Old 97, all independently using the same tune—even though such an occurrence would generally be taken to indicate that the different balladists borrowed from one another.[10]

Precisely how many ballads were penned after the accident of September, 1903, and who the various authors were is not known; what facts we do have are largely due to Robert W. Gordon's researches. During the summer of 1923, while teaching at the University of California at Berkeley, Gordon took over the column "Old Songs That Men Have Sung," a regular feature of the pulp magazine *Adventure*. During the preceding February, his predecessor in charge of the column, Robert Frothingham, received a letter from a West Virginia correspondent requesting the words to "a railroad song about a wreck on the southern road. 'Old 97 pulled in to Monroe Virginia twenty minutes behind her time[;] they gave him his orders saying Stephen your way behind.'"[11] In his column for August 20, 1923, Gordon printed this verse and asked readers familiar with the song to submit the complete text. Soon he had received three responses, and in the January 30, 1924, issue he printed a composite text of fourteen stanzas that he had collated from the three versions.[12]

In 1925, Harvard University appointed Gordon a Sheldon Fellow for the collecting of folksongs. In October he was on his way to Asheville, North Carolina, to collect material, when he happened to see a Greensboro newspaper article recounting the story of the wreck of the Southern's fast mail in 1903. His appetite for information on the subject having been whetted by his earlier correspondence, Gordon stopped at the Greensboro newspaper office to search their files for further information. There he talked with newspapermen about the song and was referred to two men, Charles Noell and Fred Lewey, who, he was told, could give him more information. Gordon secured Noell's address in Greensboro and, on October 15, visited him and recorded his version of the song. Charles Weston Noell, seventeen years old at the time of the accident, told Gordon that he had written the song about the wreck.[13] That same evening Gordon drove to Concord, North Carolina, where he found and interviewed Frederick Jackson Lewey and recorded his version of the ballad as well. Lewey asserted that *he* had composed the ballad. Evidence Gordon later gathered led him to the conclusion that indeed Lewey had first begun the ballad about the wreck. To this point I shall return.

Early in the summer of 1925, before he went on his field trip, Gordon had opened negotiations with the Victor Talking Machine Company to see if they might be willing to underwrite part of his collecting in the hope of obtaining recordable material and if he might be able to act as folksong consultant to them. Gordon argued that Victor needed an expert to advise them in matters concerning copyrights and authorship of folksong material. He felt that "the company was treading on very dangerous ground in certain instances where copyright was, to say the least, extremely questionable. I knew that in a number of cases the firm was paying royalty to unscrupulous pretenders who had no [vestige] of right in the texts they sold; and I knew that in other cases there were ample grounds for suit for infringement if only the facts happened to fall into the hands of the right parties."[14]

Gordon's overtures to Victor were carefully considered but, by a narrow vote, turned down. A few days after this outcome was made known to him, Gordon received from Victor's legal department a request for "something of the history of the tune of the song 'Ships that Never Return.'"[15] Gordon, believing that Victor was trying "to obtain for a two-cent stamp what [the company] was not willing to pay for,"[16] ignored the query. A follow-up letter seven weeks later, bearing the notation "Re—'Wreck of the Southern Old 97,'" reiterated the request,[17] but Gordon still refused to reply. Not until November of the following year did Gordon find out, indirectly, that Victor's one hand did not know what the other was doing and that the request for information had come through channels completely separate from those that had decided upon his proposal to act as consultant. Gordon apologized to several of Victor's executives and was again on good terms with the company, but his involvement in the story of "The Wreck of the Old 97" and its court trial did not resume until 1929.

Why, one may well ask, was Victor, in July of 1925, suddenly concerned with the origin of "The Ship That Never Return'd"? The catalyst of the sequence of events that led to the inquiry was Henry Whitter. Born in Grayson County, Virginia, near Fries, Whitter made his living in the cotton mills. He also played banjo, violin, guitar, and harmonica. Whitter's role in the genesis of the hillbilly phonograph industry has been documented by Archie Green; suffice it to note here that in December of 1923 Whitter journeyed to New York and waxed, among other selections, "The Wreck on the Southern Old 97."[18] His recording was released the following January.

Not for very long was Whitter's recording the only one available describing the accident on the Southern Railway. In April, Ernest Thompson, a blind singer and musician from Winston-Salem, North Carolina, recorded the song for Columbia. Thompson's text included all five stanzas of Whitter's version but began with a different stanza—proof, if any was needed, that Henry Whitter was not the only person in 1924 responsible for keeping Old 97 in the public memory. Also late in April, George Reneau, a blind singer and guitarist from Knoxville, Tennessee, journeyed to Aeolian Vocalion's New York studios to make his first recording. It was a "cover" of Whitter's first disc, and his text of "Old 97" was the same as Whitter's.[19]

Whitter recalled that he was paid twenty-five dollars for each song he recorded in 1923 and a percentage in royalties. He did not recall how much he received in royalties, and we have no knowledge of how widely his first record sold. But one interested listener was Vernon Dalhart. Dalhart, one-time popular singer turned hillbilly recording star, was given a copy of Whitter's disc during the summer of 1924. He copied the words (as best he could understand them) and recorded the ballad for Edison on May 14, 1924. His rendition was released on Edison 51361 during the following July or August. What had prompted Dalhart, who had established himself first as a singer of light opera on stage and later as a recording artist of popular tunes, to turn to hillbilly music is still open to question. In any case, the Edison disc and then cylinder release sold sufficiently well to prompt Dalhart to persuade Victor to let him record the ballad for them. This was eventually agreed to and the song, waxed on August 13, was released on October 3, 1924.

Although "The Prisoner's Song," which was coupled with "Old 97," was the cause of that disc's phenomenal success, the fact remains that Victor 19427 sold more than one million copies in the next three years.[20] The record sold so well that in March, 1926, Victor called Dalhart back to the studio to re-record the songs on 19427 by the new electrical process. The new takes were issued on the same release number, 19427.

On October 1, 1924, just three days before the Victor catalog supplement announcing the new release, 19427, was issued, the song "The Wreck on the Southern Old 97" was copyrighted by F. Wallace Rega (a publishing house owned by OKeh's executive, Fred Hager), with words and music credited to Henry Whitter (E 600188). A second copyright was taken out on November 1 by the General Phonograph Corporation, parent company of the OKeh label, still with words and music credited to Whitter (E 602770). Some time later, OKeh filed a claim against the Victor company for copyright infringement. Doubtless in the hope of finding a way to circumvent any obligations to OKeh, Victor's agents began a search for antecedents to the song to invalidate the copyright.

Thus it came about that they contacted Robert W. Gordon, noted folk music authority at Harvard. Receiving no reply from him, they set about pursuing their own investigations in North Carolina, practically crossing paths with Gordon, who had just visited and recorded Noell and Lewey. Victor's fieldwork was less decisive than Gordon's had been. Their lawyers later claimed in court that Victor's representatives had scoured the countryside seeking information and publishing notices in newspapers that Victor was searching for the author of "Old 97" so they could pay him royalties. They found no one.

Therefore, they evidently decided to make peace with the OKeh people, and on April 8, 1926, Victor paid F. Wallace Rega $3,500 for all rights to the ballad. On April 26, 1926, Henry Whitter sold to Hager for $1,000 all his rights, including mechanical, to the song, except for a percentage of royalties on any discs sold by OKeh's new owner, the Columbia Phonograph Company. The sequence of these two transactions is, to say the least, curious.[21]

On March 1, 1927, a notice in the *Richmond News Leader* read: "The Wreck of the Old 97. When did the wreck of Old 97 happen and how many were killed? If we could locate an answer to this question we could win enough money to retire in peace."[22] The following day the editors summarized details of the wreck and noted, "Offers of money by the Victor Company, as royalty on the record, are said to have met with no takers."[23] Three days later, one David Graves George wrote to the *News Leader* a letter stating, among other things, "I with others composed the poetry of 97." The letter was published in the March 7 edition.[24] Some time thereafter, George appeared at the office of the *News Leader* and requested the loan of the letter, which he never returned. When it was demanded and handed over at the trial, it was seen that the phrase *with others* had been erased and replaced with the word *alone*. On March 16, George opened negotiations with Victor, claiming his rights to royalties; Victor refused to settle with him, and October 10, 1928, a bill of complaint was filed.

In April of 1929, Victor again turned to Gordon for help. In view of the evidence he had gathered, the company decided that Lewey and Noell had defensible claims to authorship and purchased from them their rights to the song for $100 each in March and May, 1929, respectively. Perhaps Victor felt that settling these accounts would be of value to them in the pending trial with George, and they were most anxious to obtain from Gordon documents substantiating the claims of Lewey and Noell.

On April 15, Gordon's services were officially requested to aid Victor in defending their suit against David Graves George, and for the next two years Gordon spent much of his spare time on the case. (Gordon was careful to write all his correspondence in the case from his residential address, rather than his business address at the Library of Congress.) He estimated that during that period he spent in excess of 1,000 hours in such work, more than 480 of which were spent away from Washington on specific requests of Victor.[25] The results of Gordon's labors formed the basis of RCA Victor's defense at the trial.[26] Here follows the early history of the ballad, largely as Gordon reconstructed it based on his own investigations and the results of pretrial testimony taken during 1929.

At the time of the wreck of Old 97, Fred Jackson Lewey was eighteen years old and was living in Danville; he was one of the first on the scene after the accident. A week or so

Sheet music: "The Wreck of the Old 97." Collection of the Library of Congress.

later he began writing a song about it. It took him about two months to complete the ballad, by which time he was living in Lynchburg. While in that city, he sang it in the presence of several men, including Charles Noell, at the home of Noell's fiancée, who lived next door to the residence where Lewey was staying. Lewey gave the words to the song three times during the investigations: on October 14, 1925, to Gordon; again on the following day, after Gordon had played Noell's recording for him; and in April, 1929, in Greensboro, North Carolina, at pretrial hearings. The texts of the three versions differed but slightly. Below is the text as transcribed by Gordon from the October 14, 1925, recording:

> Last evening I stood on a mountain
> Just watching the smoke from below;
> It was springing from a long slender smokestack
> Way down on the Southern Road.
> It was Ninety Seven, the fastest train
> That the South has ever seen;
> But she run too fast that fatal Sunday evening,
> And the death list numbered fourteen.
>
> Did she ever pull in? No she never pulled in,
> Though at one forty-five she was due;
> For hours and hours has the switchman been watching,
> For the fast mail that never came through.
>
> Well, the engineer was a brave, fast driver
> On that fatal Sunday eve,
> And his fireman leaned far out in Lynchburg
> Waiting for the signal to leave.
> When he got the board, well, he threw back his throttle
> And although his air was bad
> People all said when he passed Franklin Junction
> That you couldn't see the men in the cab.
>
> Did he ever pull in? No he never pulled in, *etc*.
>
> There's a mighty bad road from Lynchburg to Danville,
> And although he knew this well
> He said he'd pull his train on time into Spencer
> Or he'd jerk it right square into hell.
> When he hit the grade from Lima to Danville
> His whistle began to scream;
> He was found when she wrecked with his hand on the throttle
> Where he'd scalded to death from the steam.
>
> Did he ever pull in? No he never pulled in *etc*.[27]

The only significant change in later renderings was in the first line: on October 15 he sang "On a bright Sunday evening," while in court he recited "On a bright Sunday morning." Lewey recalled for Gordon one stanza that he said he had written but discarded because it was unsatisfactory:

> Did he ever come back? No, he never came back
> It's told with a soft, hushed breath—

> His poor little wife fell back and went crazy
> When the news came home of his death.[28]

Lewey stated that he set his poem to the tune of "The Ship That Never Return'd." Another of Gordon's informants recalled Lewey as a lad who spent much of his time sitting around singing and playing the guitar.[29]

Charles Weston Noell, seventeen at the time of the accident, was a cotton-mill worker until 1923, when he became a policeman. He played guitar, mandolin, banjo, and organ. He claimed to have written the song himself, but since it was reliably reported that as early as 1904 he and Lewey used to sing and play it together, it is easy to conclude that their respective versions could not have been completely independent.[30] According to his testimony, not long after the wreck he submitted a copy of his song to the *Mill News*, a Charlotte, North Carolina, newspaper, but it was not published, because the editor did not believe it was of sufficient interest to the mill workers.[31] The text Noell gave Gordon in 1925, the text submitted at the Danville pretrial hearings on April 4, 1929, and the version he recited orally at the hearings on April 5, 1929, all differ from one another considerably. I give here the first of these three, presumably the most reliable version of the early form of the song he composed or sang:

> Come all of you fellows and gather around me,
> And a sad sad story to hear;
> All about the wreck of Old Ninety-Seven,
> And the death of the brave engineer.
>
> At the Washington Station on that bright Sabbath morning,
> 'Twas just at the rising of sun;
> When he kissed his wife, said, "My children, God bless you,
> Your father must go on his run."
>
> Steve Broady was the engineer,
> And a brave, brave man was he;
> For a many poor man have lost his life
> For the railroad company.
>
> Ninety-Seven was the fastest train,
> That was ever on the Southern Line;
> All the freight trains and passengers had to hold for Ninety-Seven
> She's compelled to be at stations on time.
>
> At Monroe, Virginia, he received his orders,
> Saying, "Steve, you are way behind;
> This is not Thirty-Eight, but it's Ninety-Seven,
> You must put her into Danville on time."
>
> He climbed in his engine at Monroe, Virginia,
> Saying, "Fireman, it's do or die!
> I'll reverse the lever, throw the throttle wide open,
> We'll watch Old Ninety-Seven fly."
>
> Steve Broady he was that engineer,
> On that fatal Sunday eve;
> And his fireman was leaning far out at Lynchburg,
> Just waiting for the signal to leave.

When they gave him the board he threw back his throttle,
Although his airbrakes was bad;
And the people all said when he passed Franklin Junction
That it seemed like the engineer was mad.

Steve Broady he said to his black and greasy fireman,
"Just throw in a little more coal;
And when I turn over White Oak Mountain,
You just watch my drivers roll!"

Now it's a awful bad road from Lynchburg to Danville,
And from Lima it's a three-mile grade;
It was on this grade that his airbrakes failed him,
And look what a jump she made.

Falling down this grade at eighty miles a hour,
His whistle began to scream;
He was found in the wreck with his hand on the throttle,
Where he'd scalded to death from the steam.

When the news came slipping o'er the telegraph wires,
And this is the way it read:
"That brave engineer that pulled Ninety-Seven,
Is lying in North Danville, dead."

Did she ever pull in? No, she never pulled in,
At three forty-five she was due;
It was hours and hours dispatchers were waiting,
But that fast mail never came through.

Did she ever pull in? No, she never pulled in,
You could hear it in silent breath;
His poor little wife fell back and fainted,
When the news came home of his death.[32]

The principal difference in the version given on April 4, 1929, was the inclusion of two additional stanzas: one, after the fourth given above; the second, after the eighth:

Ninety-Seven was the fastest train,
That was ever on the Southern Line;
But when she pulled in at Monro Virginia,
She was Forty-Seven minutes behind.

The conductor said to the engineer and fireman,
"Don't neglect that whistle or bell;
For we must put this train on time in to Danville,
Or we will drop her right in to Hell."[33]

Noell told Gordon he had set his song to "the tune of 'The Parted Lover' and not into the tune of 'The Ship That Never Returned.' At the time of my writing this poem I did not know the tune of 'The Ship That Never Returned.' . . . you can well catch my voice on this record as being a little bit lower and a little bit slower and milder than the tune of 'The Ship That Never Returned' which is directly in accordance with the tune of 'The Parted Lover.'"[34]

As mentioned above, the tune of "The Ship That Never Returned" that has been traditional for fifty or possibly a hundred years is different from Henry C. Work's original melody. The familiar tune to "The Parted Lover," Noell's tune in 1925, is indistinguishable from that commonly used for "The Ship That Never Returned," "The Wreck of the Old 97," and all the other parodies in this family.

Noell's various texts suggest that he obviously was familiar with Lewey's song but changed and expanded it considerably. Although only a few of Noell's verses correspond to lines in Lewey's rendition, we do not know how much his original version utilized verses that Lewey had composed and later rejected: note, for example, Noell's final two stanzas. He told the court that the penultimate stanza he gave Lewey credit for writing, but the final one was his own. Lewey, in 1925, before he heard Noell's recording, spontaneously recalled that final stanza as one that he had written and rejected.[35]

Lewey's song (in its final form) had a slight debt to earlier versions of "The Train That Never Returned" (compare his first verse and chorus). Noell's ballad borrowed considerably from Lewey's but probably added much that was new. Gordon concluded that "Lewey started off the whole affair and that at a later date, perhaps about 1905–6, someone else made additions."[36] To Victor, Noell's claim was evidently as valid as Lewey's; whether a court of law would substantiate Noell's claim to authorship has never been critically tested.

As indicated above, Noell and Lewey frequently performed their song(s), either apart or together, in various towns they lived in, including Fries, Danville, and Lynchburg. In about 1904, Frank Burnett, another Virginia cotton-mill hand, heard Noell singing the song to Lewey's guitar accompaniment. In November, 1930, he recited for the court the song as, to the best of his recollection, he had learned it from Noell and possibly from Lewey:

> It was one bright Sunday morning, as I stood on the mountain
> I was watching the smoke from below.
> It was springing from a tall and slender smoke stack
> Way down on the Southern railroad.
>
> It was 97 the fastest mail
> That the south had even seen
> But she run too fast on the fatal Sunday morning
> And the death list was numbered fourteen.
>
> Did she ever pull in, no she never pulled in
> At one-forty-five she was due
> It was hours and hours have the switchmen been waiting
> For the fast mail never pulled through.
>
> 97 she runs from Washington to Atlanta
> She runs it rain or shine
> All freight trains and passengers take the side for 97
> She is bound to be at stations on time.
>
> They give him his orders at Monroe, Virginia,
> Saying "Steve, you are way behind time,
> This is not 38 but its old 97
> You must put her into Spencer on time."

He turned and said to his black, greasy fireman,
"Just throw me in a little more coal,
And when we cross the White Oak mountain,
You can watch old 97 roll."

It was a mighty bad road from Lynchburg to Danville
And Lima was a three mile grade,
It was on the grade that he lost his air brakes
Just see what a jump he made.

He went speeding down the grade making 90 miles an hour,
And his whistle began to scream,
He was found in the wreck with his hands on the throttle,
And scalded to death with the steam.

Now, young ladies, you must take warning
From this time now and on.
Never speak harsh words to your true loving husband
He may leave you and never return.[37]

Ten years later, Henry Whitter, a friend of Burnett's youth, heard Burnett singing it when they were both living near Fries, and thereupon learned it. Unlike Lewey, Noell, and Burnett, Henry Whitter was determined to make a career out of his music, and he kept the ballad of Old 97 active in his repertoire until the day in 1923 when he recorded it for the General Phonograph Corporation. However, he changed it from the way he had learned it; in about 1922, he testified, he made some slight changes and set the song to the tune of "The Ship That Never Returned," which meant making it "more peppy."[38] What the tune was like before these changes, we can only speculate. Evidently, Whitter also shortened the song considerably, stripping off several of the opening stanzas. According to Kelly Harrell, Whitter was the first person he heard who opened the song with the verse "They give him his orders."[39] Whitter's text, as he recorded it, follows:

They give him up his orders at Monroe, Virginia,
Saying "Steve you're way behind time,
This is not Thirty-eight, but it's Old Ninety-seven,
You must put her in Spencer on time."

Steve Brooklyn said to his black greasy fireman,
"Just shove on a little more coal,
And when we cross that White Oak Mountain,
You can watch old Ninety-seven roll."

It's a mighty rough road from Lynchburg to Danville,
And a line on a three-mile grade;
It was on that grade that he lost his air-brakes,
And see what a jump he made.

He was going down grade making ninety mile an hour
When his whistle begin to scream;
He was found in the wreck with his hand on the throttle
And was scalded to death with the steam.

> [So come] you ladies, you must take warning
> From this time, now and on,
> Never speak hard words to your true loving husband,
> He may leave you and never return.[40]

It is readily apparent that Whitter's text consists of the last five stanzas of Burnett's, with slight modifications. Burnett's differs from both Lewey's and Noell's, principally by the inclusion of the final stanza borrowed from "The Lover That Never Returned." Thus, if Burnett's recollection of the song he sang some two decades earlier is correct, Judge Avis was wrong when, in his decision, he attributed the addition of this stanza to Whitter. It might also be mentioned that Whitter's shortening of the text had nothing to do with the time restrictions of a ten-inch 78 rpm disc: his rendition consists of ninety seconds of singing and one hundred seconds of instrumental breaks.

One other commercial recording artist learned his version directly from Lewey or Noell. Kelly Crockett Harrell, who lived in Fries until 1925, worked in the textile mills from 1903, first as a weaver, then as a loom fixer, then as loom mechanic. Born in 1889, two miles from Max Meadows, Virginia, Harrell began his recording career in mid-1924 with the Victor Talking Machine Company. In August of the following year, for OKeh's recording team in Asheville, North Carolina, Harrell recorded, among other songs, "The Wreck on the Southern Old 97" to Henry Whitter's guitar and harmonica accompaniment. This recording was made at the request of the OKeh people, who, for some reason, wanted a twelve-inch-disc version of the song.[41] Harrell had first heard the song in 1904 in Fries from Lewey, and then from Noell. He testified that the two men sang different versions and that they kept changing their versions.[42] Since Harrell's version was intended for a twelve-inch 78 rpm disc, he was allowed time for a song longer than the other early recordings, all of which were issued on ten-inch discs. Except for the rearrangement of the verses, minor textual changes (especially in Burnett's fourth verse), and one additional chorus, Harrell's text was similar to Burnett's. The additional chorus, he insisted, was Lewey's:

> Did she ever pull in? No she never pulled in
> And that po' boy he must be dead;
> Oh yonder he lays, on that railroad track
> With the car wheels over his head.[43]

This chorus resembles that of Fiddlin' John Carson's "Did He Ever Return?" quoted earlier, which suggests that Lewey had borrowed it from oral tradition.

In the spring of 1931, after numerous delays, the trial of *George* v. *Victor Talking Machine Co.* finally came before the court. In retrospect, David Graves George could have sued Victor on two different grounds. He could have acknowledged that there was a song about Old 97 in public domain (or written by someone identifiable) but that he wrote another song or rearranged the one in public domain, adding sufficient original material to qualify for some copyright protection. In that case, the defendant (Victor) would owe him royalties if he could show that the Victor recording was based on his version (rather than on the underlying public-domain song). On the other hand, George could have claimed that he wrote the original song about Old 97, that the song had not previously been published, so that he owned common-law copyright, and therefore Victor's use of the song was an infringement of his common-law copyright. This claim would have some justice even if the recorded version was sufficiently different from

George's song to qualify as a new arrangement; George would have been entitled to compensation as original author.

Had George pursued the first alternative, Victor's defense likely would have been that it had had no possible access to George's unpublished song and therefore could not have used it as a basis for the recording. If George had chosen the second option, Victor could have responded either by proving that he could not have been the original author, or by showing that, even if he were original author, someone else had written an independent ballad on which the recording was based. As it happened, George claimed that he was the original author, and Victor chose to prove he could not have been, even though it probably would have exonerated the company simply to have shown that there was another independent version that it had used. The company's eagerness to obtain proof of Noell's and Lewey's claims of authorship, and its willingness to pay them for rights to the song, would have been consistent with either line of defense.

Victor's case against George rested on two types of evidence. The first, familiar enough in courtrooms, comprised inconsistent or perjured testimony. There was the matter of the altered letter to the *News Leader*, referred to above. There was the fact that George presented as evidence a sheet of paper on which he had traced, with carbon paper, the music from the sheet music of "The Ship That Never Returned" and then had written in the words to that composition. He claimed he had done this in 1903 and had witnesses to attest to that claim. But an analytic chemist demonstrated that the type of carbon paper employed was not in use until long after 1903. Furthermore, the same chemist, also a handwriting expert, testified that, based on samples of George's handwriting in 1901 and 1927, the words to the song were written in 1927. George's daughter testified that within a week of the wreck she had sung her father's song in the home of a friend who had just obtained a new organ and wanted to try it out. But it was established later that the friend did not have an organ in her home until May, 1907. A similar claim was made by another witness for the plaintiff, and again it was later shown by counsel for the defense that no organ was present in the home until November, 1907. Another acquaintance of George's testified that George had asked him to testify at the trial that the plaintiff had written the song for him on a certain day in a certain barbershop, but he had refused. "If I win, you'll get a piece [of the pie]," George assured him.[44] Such testimonies were very damaging to George's case.

Some of the above points were first suggested to RCA Victor's lawyers by Gordon (for example, the chemical analysis of the carbon paper). However, Gordon's primary role was to study the various versions of the ballad and to demonstrate, if possible, that on the basis of internal evidence George could not have composed, in 1903, the ballad he claimed he had. Gordon had suggested to Victor's legal department some time before the trial that he would "gladly chart and study the differences [among the various texts] in accord with a method which often brings surprising results. This method is *similar* to one now recognized as standard in all studies of folk-tales. (See an article by Archer Taylor in *Modern Philology*, 25, May 1928, entitled 'Precursers of the Finnish Method of Folk-Lore study.') The method is most delicate and not usable except by one trained in the subject. Also there are certain differences necessary in the study of songs as opposed to tales since the laws of growth and change tend to reverse somewhat."[45]

In court, when Gordon took the witness stand, he was asked, "Is there any accepted method used in the study of Folk Song text which enables the expert to determine the relative date of any given text?" He replied in the affirmative: "The text is examined entirely on internal evidence, not taking into consideration the testimony or alleged statements of the versions, but treating them all as possible. . . . They are examined internally for the presence or absence of verse, for changes or variation in phrasing, the presence of misunderstanding . . . or errors, and treated, in other words, as the philologist goes about the study of language."[46]

What Gordon did was present to the court an immense chart that represented comparatively all the important texts, designed to show differences, similarities, and borrowing. He established two major points. First, he noted that in four instances Dalhart had misunderstood the words on Whitter's recording, and consequently he rendered *Spencer, Steve, airbrakes,* and *begin to scream* as *Center, Pete, average,* and *broke into a scream,* respectively. The first three of these locutions have since served as benchmarks to determine that any collected or recorded version of the ballad derives from Dalhart's immensely influential recordings. In three of the four instances, George's manuscript followed the Dalhart version. There were, however, differences between the two texts apart from George's two additional stanzas. The two versions are compared below; those phrases or stanzas in George's text that are not in Dalhart's are enclosed in parentheses:

> (On a cold frosty morning in the month of September,
> When the clouds were hanging low;
> Ninety-Seven pulled out from the Washington station,
> Like an arrow shot from a bow.)
>
> They gave him his orders at Monroe, Virginia,
> Saying, "Pete, you're (you are) way behind time;
> This is (It's) not Thirty-Eight, but it's old Ninety-Seven,
> You must put her in Center (Spencer) on time.
>
> He looked round then to (looked at) his black, greasy fireman,
> "Just shove on (And said "shovel") in a little more coal;
> And (For) when we cross that White Oak Mountain,
> You can watch (see) old Ninety-Seven roll."
>
> It's a mighty rough road from Lynchburg to Danville,
> And a line on (Lima it's) a three-mile grade;
> It was on that (this) grade that he lost his average,
> And you see what a jump he made.
>
> He (They) was going down grade making ninety miles an hour
> When his whistle (Who when the whistle whistle whistle) broke
>   into a scream;
> He was found in the (a) wreck with his hand on the throttle,
> And a-scalded (scalded) to death with the steam.
>
> Now ladies, you must take warning,
> From this time now and on (time on);
> Never speak harsh words to your true love and (loving) husband,
> He (For they) may leave you and never return.
>
> (Did she ever pull in, no she never pulled in,
> . . . .
> For hours and hours . . . as watching,
> For the train that never pulled . . .)[47]

Gordon further demonstrated that, in several other respects, the texts of Whitter, Dalhart, George, and the other commercial recordings all differed from the "old versions—a group of four texts that seemed almost certainly to date from before 1910.[48] For example, in the "old" versions, the road from Lynchburg to Danville is described as "bad," while Whitter, Dalhart, George, and the post-Whitter phonograph records use the adjective "rough."

In one respect Gordon's argument was weak. Although it is reasonable to assume that the phonograph versions that have the same five verses as the Dalhart recording (the Skillet Lickers on Columbia, Jones and Hare on Brunswick) were based largely, if not entirely, on the Dalhart/Whitter text, it is not reasonable to make the same assumption for the texts of Harrell and Thompson, both of which included stanzas not found at all in the Dalhart/Whitter version. In fact, testimony established that Harrell had learned the song considerably earlier than Whitter had, although such evidence is not "internal" and therefore should not have been used by Gordon in his evaluation. Ernest Thompson was never located for interview; however, as a native of North Carolina he had probably also learned his version from oral tradition long before he recorded it. So, since Harrell said "rough road," it is very likely that the locution was in use well before the Whitter recording of 1923. An artist who has been singing a ballad for two decades is not likely to change his wording when he hears a different version.[49] In the last analysis, "internal evidence" alone does not offer a very strong defense one way or the other. For example, internal evidence could not refute the hypothetical claim that perhaps George had mailed Dalhart a copy of "his" text some time before either Dalhart or Whitter recorded it. Such a hypothesis is, of course, improbable to say the least: two years later, perhaps yes. By that time Dalhart was deluged by requests from his fans to sing this or that song, but "Old 97" was Dalhart's first hillbilly recording. He would not have received such a request in early 1924. So the imaginary hypothesis is refuted, but by external, not internal, evidence. Without the knowledge that Dalhart had copied Whitter's recording (external evidence) and the knowledge that Whitter had learned his text from Burnett, who in turn had learned it from Lewey or Noell (external evidence again), we could not rule out George's role as a link in the chain somewhere. I would not be surprised to learn that every folksong investigator who has pursued one song through all its meanderings has likewise encountered problems that could not be resolved on the basis of textual evidence alone, but required some external data: dates of recording or manuscript writing, a date of sojourn in a particular county, or a verification of who learned a particular variant from whom.

Gordon's zeal in executing his inquiry led him into many areas in addition to the collection of texts and interviews of informants. He searched thoroughly for all newspaper accounts, for train schedules, for weather reports from the day of the wreck, for interviews with survivors of the wreck. When these searches came to the attention of Victor's chief attorney for the case, Louis B. Le Duc, he wrote a letter to Gordon expressing his worry that Gordon's investigations were taking him into matters that were irrelevant to his responsibilities in the preparation of the defense.[50] Gordon's reply stressed the necessity of knowing what the actual facts were in order to date various versions—the assumption being that "a man who had at least heard a great deal of talk about the wreck would be closer to fact than a garbled version sung at a much later date by a man who had not been in the vicinity of Danville at the time."[51] Therefore, Gordon argued, he had to know the actual facts of the accident as well as what was commonly said and believed at the time.[52] Le Duc replied:

. . . if we propose to prove actual facts connected with the wreck, you would not be allowed to do this by repeated statements made to you by witnesses; the eye-witnesses themselves would have to be put on the stand. . . . the hypothesis on which your expert conclusions rest must be founded entirely in the evidence admitted at the trial. If such conclusions depend at all on facts which have not been regularly proved, your entire testimony would probably be ruled out and lost to the defendant. Your role on the stand, therefore, will be solely that of the expert dealing with hypotheses and not at all that of the fact investigator. The several versions of the song, their dates and places of publication and circulation—together with the newspaper stories of the wreck, if you deem these important—are the facts on which I have always expected your testimony would be based in its entirety.[53]

Thus, the very narrow type of case study, confined to purely textual matters, was all that would have been allowed in court; when Gordon attempted to make a more comprehensive study, taking external as well as internal factors into account, he was warned by the lawyers to desist.

On March 11, 1933, almost two years after the beginning of the trial, Judge John Boyd Avis of the circuit court handed down his decision that George had authored the ballad, as he had claimed, shortly after the wreck, and that the song on the Victor disc was essentially the same song, so that the company owed George appropriate royalties. In his decision, Avis first rejected the argument of the defense that George had copied his text from the Dalhart recording. The differences between the two texts were too great for that, he contended, regardless of the important similarities that were unique to those two texts. And he did not fail to notice that, for some unknown reason, when Noell recited his text on April 5, 1929, he used the word *average* instead of *airbrakes*. He rejected the argument that *whistle whistle whistle* indicated copying from the recording because it occurred at a point where two blasts of a train whistle sounded in the background behind Dalhart's singing. While he respected the able testimony of Gordon and of Melcher, the chemist and handwriting expert, he concluded that they "erred in their conclusions." Of the other arguments against George, he said nothing in his opinion. Avis acknowledged that Noell and Lewey could have composed songs about Old 97, but argued that the Victor song could not have been based either on one of their songs or even on some combination of both of them. Therefore, he felt there must have been a third text preceding the Victor one, namely, George's.

While I believe Avis was right in his conclusion that there must have been a third text, I believe the reasoning leading to his conclusion was faulty. His opinion was based largely on an insufficient understanding of the nature of oral transmission; he took permutations of single words as evidence for alternate sources. For example, he felt that Dalhart's "They give him his orders at Monroe, Virginia" could not have been derived from Noell's "He received his orders at Monroe, Virginia." Quite to the contrary, Avis decided that what similarities the texts of Noell and Lewey had with that of George were due to borrowings from George's prior text. Thus, ironically, Avis based his decision solely on his (incorrect) analysis of internal evidence and ignored the external data.

RCA Victor appealed the decision of the district court, and on January 3, 1934, the Third Circuit Court of Appeals at Philadelphia, in an opinion written by Judge J. Warren Davis, unanimously reversed the lower court's ruling. George's attorneys brought the case to the United States Supreme Court, which, on December 17, 1934, reversed the appellate court decision.

The successive court actions devolved upon the question of whether the decree of the district court was final or interlocutory; if it was an interlocutory ruling, the defendant (RCA Victor) had to appeal within thirty days; but if the decision was final, that time limit did not apply. Victor maintained that the ruling was final, whereas George's lawyers argued it was interlocutory. The circuit court upheld RCA; the Supreme Court, however, overturned that ruling and decreed that since the district court judgment was interlocutory the circuit court had no jurisdiction after thirty days. This reinstated Judge Avis's ruling in favor of George, which required RCA to present extensive evidence to enable determination of the extent of royalties due George. The district court, on September 15, 1938, awarded George $65,295.56. Again RCA appealed and took the case to the Third Circuit Court of Appeals, and on July 14, 1939, that court, this time with Judge Maris writing the decision, again reversed the lower court ruling. George appealed to the Supreme Court later that year for a review, but the petition was denied on November 13, 1939. A rehearing on the petition for rehearing was denied by the Supreme Court on December 11, 1939. Finally, a motion for leave to file a second petition for a rehearing was denied by the high court on January 29, 1940, thus ending ten years of litigation.

Today, four decades later, are we in a better position to pass final judgment on David Graves George's claim to authorship? The evidence presented in court does seem to have been predominantly against him, indicating clearly that he had assembled false testimony and perjured witnesses to back his claim. When the plaintiff has gone that far, one hesitates to give credence to any of his claims.

Yet, the opening stanza of George's version proves that he did know the song apart from the Dalhart and Whitter recordings. That stanza, claimed by neither Lewey nor Noell, strongly suggests that there was at one time a third ballad circulating about Old 97. We have nothing that can definitely be assigned to this hypothetical third ballad save for George's opening stanza. Everything else, except for the "parted lovers" moral, can be derived from Lewey's and Noell's texts. But this third ballad must have been well known at one time, as some variant of this stanza occurs in a half-dozen different renditions. The earliest appearance in print was in 1911, when a reader of *Railroad Man's Magazine* from Asheboro, North Carolina, requested a ballad beginning:

> On the twenty-first day of last September
> The clouds were hanging low;
> Ninety-seven pulled out from the station
> Like an arrow shot from a bow.[54]

A manuscript version given by Mrs. Lera McNeely Stephens of Lynchburg, Virginia, which she testified she had written prior to 1911, began:

> On a cool frosty morning in the month of September
> As the clouds were hanging low,
> 97 pulled out from the Washington Station
> Like an arrow shot from a bow.[55]

A similar stanza opened Ernest Thompson's 1924 recording. Two other versions, not available to Gordon in 1930, but probably both very old, begin with a similar verse. One was collected from millhand and hillbilly musician Dorsey Dixon, the other from black streetsinger and medicine-show performer Pink Anderson. Dixon reported he had learned his version in 1906 or 1907 from string-band musicians of Darlington, South Carolina. Anderson, born in Laurens, South Carolina, in 1900, may have had his version not long after. The date in Dixon's version was "one cold November morning"; that in Anderson's was "November 29."[56]

These facts are pertinent because of an interesting hunch Gordon had about the origin of this particular stanza. He had been bothered by the references to cloudy or frosty weather, because September 27, 1903, was an unusually warm and bright day. In checking through newspaper files, Gordon found that the most famous wreck that befell the Southern Railway occurred on November 30, 1906, when "Train 37, southbound, overtook and ran into Train 33, also southbound, ten miles beyond Lynchburg. . . . This was a cold frosty morning at the end of November."[57] Gordon also noted that in 1906 the government granted the Southern Railway a subsidy for fast mail trains, which was divided between 97 and 37, the latter being the fast mail train. Le Duc was at first impressed by this line of reasoning, but later he thought it would complicate the testimony excessively if it were brought up, and Gordon mentioned it only briefly while he was on the witness stand.[58] Gordon may not have noticed it, but it is intriguing that George's two witnesses who claimed to have played his new song on their new organs both obtained their musical instruments in 1907. Perhaps, then, George did write a ballad, but about this later wreck.

Whether or not this last speculation is correct, I am tempted to give credence to George's claim of authorship of a ballad about a train wreck. I suggest the hypothesis that George did write a ballad that was in circulation for a while—in either 1903 or 1906—but that later even he forgot it; so that when he heard the Dalhart record, he knew he had written something about Old 97 and concluded that Dalhart's song was his ballad. The rest was simply a matter of buttressing what he knew was a weak, though just, case. Many rural mountain folk have a different notion of what constitutes authorship of a new song. Collectors have encountered informants who asserted authorship of some song, when all they had done was alter other songs or other versions of the same song to produce a new version of the song for which they claimed authorship.[59] The alternative to this explanation, of course, is that George fabricated the entire story.

In this discussion I have cited and quoted from several of the early recordings of this famous train-wreck ballad. However, for full transcription in this book I have chosen a most unusual recording, the full circumstances surrounding which are unknown at present. The group featured is Sheriff Loyal Underwood's Arizona Wranglers, a popular cowboy-western singing outfit in the Southwest in the 1920s. They never made any commercial recordings; however, in August, 1929, or thereabout, they cut at least four tunes in the Freeman Lang studios in Hollywood for release on twelve-inch 78 rpm discs. Some of these were issued with plain white labels, others with a "Merry Xmas" label. Bob Pinson has suggested that they were intended as promotional giveaways for the 1929 holiday season.[60] Stanley Kilarr, of Rare-Arts Records, also believes that these discs were actually offered for sale in October, 1929.[61] One coupling was "Wreck of the 97," featuring the Wranglers' "cook," Hungry, backed with Curley Fletcher's "Strawberry Roan," sung by Nubbins, another member of the group. The text of "Wreck of the 97" is both long and unusual; according to Kilarr, it was Fletcher's own arrangement.[62] Whoever put the version together seems to have drawn upon several other texts.

"Old 97" is hardly ready to retire from old age. It has always been, and continues to be, a source for further parodies. Probably the earliest song about a truck accident, "Wreck on the Mountain Road," recorded by the Red Fox Chasers of North Carolina in 1928, used "Old 97" as inspiration.[63] In 1948, Bess Hawes and Jacqueline Steiner wrote "The MTA Song," a parody of "Old 97" that protested a proposed fare increase in Boston subways and at the same time campaigned for Progressive party mayoral candidate

Walter F. O'Brian.[64] More recent parodies have included Dave Dudley's "Wreck of the Old Slow Binder," a country-and-western trucking song,[65] and "The London Underground," an English take-off on "The MTA Song."[66]

NOTES

My earlier account of this song's history appeared as "Robert W. Gordon and the Second Wreck of 'Old 97,'" *JAF*, 87 (Jan.-Mar., 1974), 12–38.

1. Freeman H. Hubbard, *Railroad Avenue* (New York: McGraw-Hill, 1945), pp. 251–61; Stewart H. Holbrook, *The Story of American Railroads* (New York: Crown Publishers, 1947), pp. 430–32; Maxwell Hamilton, "Highball to Hell," *Cavalier*, June, 1959, pp. 38 ff.; Jim Walsh, *Hobbies, the Magazine for Collectors*, Sept., 1960, pp. 34 ff.; Neal Ulevich, *Washington Star Sunday Magazine*, Nov. 5, 1967, pp. 23–26; B. A. Botkin and Alvin F. Harlow, *A Treasury of Railroad Folklore* (New York: Bonanza Books, 1953), pp. 449–50; *Frank C. Brown Collection of North Carolina Folklore*, vol. 2., *Folk Ballads,* edited by Henry M. Belden and Arthur Palmer Hudson (Durham: Duke University Press, 1952), pp. 512–16; Albert Friedman, *Viking Book of Folk Ballads of the English Speaking World* (New York: Viking Press, 1956), p. 318. These last two references draw on the trial summary given by Judge John Boyd Avis, *Victor Talking Machine Co.* v. *George*, in the *Federal Reporter*, 2d ser., 69 (Apr.-May, 1934), 871–79; the same account was given in *Decisions of the United States Courts Involving Copyright: 1924–1935* (Washington: U.S. Government Printing Office, 1934), p. 754 ff.

2. I am grateful to Texas folklorist Mack McCormick for correcting the often garbled accounts of the geography involved in Old 97's wreck. In the late 1960s Mack interviewed Danville residents and Southern crewmembers and found several persons who had witnessed the accident. Parts of his findings are reported in the brochure notes to Library of Congress LBC 9, *Folk Music in America, Vol. 9: Songs of Death & Tragedy,* and he promises a fuller account elsewhere.

3. Henry Clay Work, "The Ship That Never Return'd" (Chicago: Root & Cady, 1865).

4. Earl J. Stout, *Folklore from Iowa* (New York: Stechert, 1936), p. 72. The informant's name was Oren Beck.

5. Barbara Kreimer, "Information Booth," *RRM*, Mar., 1967, p. 32.

6. In this family are the texts given in Brown II, p. 509; Richardson, p. 42; Spaeth (1927) p. 139; various song folios published by M. M. Cole of Chicago, such as Tiny Texan, p. 52; and Opal Burroughs, LC AFS 11873 A2.

7. In this family are the texts given in Anderson, p. 213; Lomax and Lomax (1941), p. 254, "The Wreck on the Somerset Road," a transcription of Justis Begley, LC AFS 1532; Wilma Pace, WKFA (Nov., 1959); Mrs. Darrell Pace, WKFA (May, 1962); E. N. Caldwell, WKFA (E. C. Perrow Collection, 1913); a recording by Clarence Greene, "Narrow Gauge Song" (Kahn Collection, Aug., 1961); a manuscript version sent me by John V. Walker of Corbin, Ky., entitled "Cumberland Valley Wreck" (Aug., 1972); and Tommy Jarrell, "Old 97," County 741: *Stay All Night and Don't Go Home.*

8. *Brown Collection,* vol. 2, *Folk Ballads,* p. 509.

9. OKeh 45176 (master W81728), recorded in Oct., 1927.

10. These songs were not only locally produced. William Jerome's "He Never Came Back" (1891) which seems to borrow at least the chorus structure from Work's original song, was very popular on vaudeville stages in the 1890s and, later, among hillbilly musicians.

11. Jack O'Connor to Frothingham, Feb. 12, 1923.

12. *Adventure,* Jan. 30, 1924, p. 191. For biographical information about Gordon, see Debora Kodish, "'Good Friends and Bad Enemies': Robert W. Gordon and American Folksong Scholarship" (manuscript). A selection of Gordon's field recordings was issued in 1978 in commemoration of the Archive of Folk Song's fiftieth anniversary; see Library of Congress Archive of Folk Song L68: *"Folk-Songs of America": The Robert Winslow Gordon Collection, 1922–1932,* edited by Debora G. Kodish and Neil V. Rosenberg. For a complementary account see Kodish, "A National Project with

Many Workers: Robert Winslow Gordon and the Archive of American Folk Song." *Quarterly Journal of the Library of Congress,* 35 (Oct., 1978), 218–33.

13. Gordon Collection (N.C.) 1; also cylinder recordings A1, A2, A3.

14. Gordon to J. E. Richards, Nov. 2, 1926. All letters to or from Gordon quoted in these notes are in the Robert W. Gordon Collection of American Folksong at the University of Oregon at Eugene. I thank Barre Toelken for making this material available to me.

15. John Paine to Gordon, July 2, 1925.

16. Gordon to Clifford Cairns, Victor executive, Nov. 2, 1926.

17. Paine to Gordon, Aug. 21, 1925.

18. Archie Green, "Hillbilly Music: Source and Symbol," *JAF,* 78 (July-Sept., 1965), 204–28. Green notes the problem in dating Whitter's first recording session. Whitter asserted, both in pretrial hearings in 1929 and in his song folio published ca. 1935, that he went to New York on Mar. 1, 1923, to record. At the trial, however, Ralph Peer, who had been employed by OKeh at that time, testified that the recording was made on Dec. 12, 1923. Perhaps a test recording in March proved unsatisfactory, requiring a second try. The issued master number is consistent with the later date.

19. The vocal on this and Reneau's other early numbers was provided by the young popular singer Gene Austin, probably because Vocalion executives found Reneau's singing too rough to suit them.

20. This sales figure is based on information given at one of the later trials. Elsewhere I have reproduced the sales statement and discussed the various claims that have been made, running as high as twenty-five million. See *JEMFQ,* 6 (Winter, 1970), 171–73.

21. The Victor-Hager bill of sale was reproduced in the court transcript. The Hager-Whitter bills of sale (one for $200, the other for $800) were in the possession of Whitter's son, Paul; they were copied and made available to me by Archie Green.

22. *Richmond* (Va.) *News Leader,* Mar. 1, 1927. Somehow, this paragraph was misquoted in the court transcript, the last word being rendered as "business." The author of this curious query was never identified; George, in court, denied he had written it.

23. Ibid., Mar. 2, 1927.

24. Ibid., Mar. 7, 1927.

25. Undated document in Gordon Collection, University of Oregon.

26. On Jan. 4, 1929, the Radio Corporation of America had concluded negotiations for the purchase of the Victor Talking Machine Company.

27. Gordon Collection (N.C.) 4, transcribed from recording A5.

28. Quoted from document in Gordon Collection, University of Oregon, titled "Statements of Fred J. Lewey, Concord, North Carolina, October 15, 1925," but possibly written later.

29. W. L. Plott to Gordon, Nov., 1926, quoted from a document ibid. titled "Statements Tending to Back Lewey's Claims."

30. Pretrial testimony of Kelly Harrell, Apr., 1929, at Danville; trial testimony of Frank Burnett. These trial and pretrial transcripts are all on deposit at the Federal Records Center, New York City.

31. According to Noell's pretrial testimony, Apr., 1929, at Greensboro, N.C.

32. From Gordon Collection, University of Oregon. Gordon retranscribed his field recordings A1, A2, and A3 for the trial; his original transcription (Gordon Collection [N.C.] 1), probably made shortly after his 1925 field trip, differs considerably from this text. Unfortunately, the cylinder recordings have deteriorated greatly with time, so that I am unable to resolve fine textual uncertainties. As far as I can tell, this later transcription is the more accurate.

33. From pretrial hearings in Danville; the text is given in *Federal Reporter* (quoted in *Brown Collection,* vol. 2, *Folk Ballads,* pp. 512–16).

34. Gordon Collection (N.C.) 1, transcribed from recording A3.

35. *Richmond* (Va.) *News Leader,* Mar. 2, 1927.

36. Gordon to E. H. Murphy, Victor Talking Machine Co., Mar. 6, 1929.

37. Trial transcript, p. 189; and from pretrial testimony of Burnett.

38. From pretrial testimony in Danville, Apr., 1929.

39. Ibid.

40. Transcribed directly from OKeh 40015. This transcription differs in several locutions, mostly minor, from Gordon's, which can most easily be found in *Brown Collection*, vol. 2, *Folk Ballads*, p. 513. This points out the difficulty in transcribing recorded songs, particularly from singers who occasionally mumble and swallow their words. (It is amusing to note that the *Brown Collection* transcription differs in two instances from that in the *Federal Reporter*, from which it was presumably copied *literatim et punctatim*.)

41. Testimony of Ralph S. Peer, trial transcript, p. 183.

42. From pretrial testimony in Danville, Apr., 1929.

43. Ibid. Harrell's version has been transcribed by Dorothy Horstman in *Sing Your Heart Out, Country Boy* (New York: E. P. Dutton, 1975), 336–37; and by Robert Nobley and Willard Johnson in brochure notes to Bear Family 15508: *The Complete Kelly Harrell, Vol. 1*. The latter transcription is the more accurate.

44. Pretrial testimony of Walter W. Rowles at Lynchburg, May 31, 1930. Also quoted in *Federal Reporter*, p. 876.

45. Gordon to Murphy, Mar. 6, 1929.

46. Trial transcript, p. 357.

47. From pretrial depositions.

48. This group includes the texts of Lewey and Noell; a manuscript sent Gordon by Ethel A. Bridges of Danville on Nov. 14, 1926, which she claimed was written "possibly 20 years ago or longer, by Mr. John Moore"; and a manuscript given at pretrial testimony by Lera McNeely Stephens of Lynchburg, which she testified she had written prior to 1911.

49. Noell's third rendition of the ballad, given in court on Apr. 5, 1929, uses the locution *lost his average*, not *air brakes*. This slip, probably prompted by the controversy over the terminology, was not unnoticed by Judge Avis.

50. Le Duc to Gordon, Sept. 19, 1930.

51. Gordon to Le Duc, Sept. 23, 1930; probably never mailed.

52. Ibid., Oct. 4, 1930.

53. Le Duc to Gordon, Oct. 6, 1930.

54. *RRManM*, 14 (Mar., 1911), 383.

55. From pretrial testimony in Danville, Apr., 1929.

56. Dixon's version can be heard on Testament T-3301; *Babies in the Mill*, recorded Aug., 1962; Anderson's is on Riverside RLP 12-611: *American Street Songs*, recorded May, 1950, and also on Prestige/Bluesville BV 1071: *The Blues of Pink Anderson: Ballad and Folksinger, Vol. 3*, recorded Aug., 1961. One long variant beginning with this stanza, the first line being "It was on the twenty-second of last December," seems to have been stabilized in print by the 1930s, if not earlier. The identical text appears in Lonnie E. Anderson and Raymond Anderson, *Red and Raymond's Song Book Featuring the Red Headed Briarhopper and His Yodelling Son Raymond* (ca. 1934); in Lillian G. Crabtree, "Songs and Ballads Sung in Overton County, Tennessee" (Master's thesis, George Peabody College for Teachers, 1936), p. 32; and in Marie A. Benson to Norm Cohen, July, 1968.

57. Gordon to Le Duc, Oct. 22, 1930.

58. Le Duc to Gordon, Sept. 19, 1930.

59. I am reminded of a scandal that rocked the world of pathology in 1973. A well-known and respected scientist, W. Summerlin, had reported remarkable results in trying to make skin grafts "take." Other workers were subsequently unable to duplicate his results; an intensive investigation revealed that Summerlin had touched up the grafts on experimental mice with a felt pen, thereby simulating dark skin grafts (which should have been rejected) on white mice. P. D. Medawar, reviewing a book on this scandal, *The Patchwork Mouse* (New York: Anchor Press, 1976), noted, "I believe that there is a fairly simple explanation of Summerlin's egregious folly. It is this: in his early experiments Summerlin did actually obtain, with mice, the results that later aroused so many misgivings. . . . If this is what happened then Summerlin would naturally have been

distraught when, on repeating his experiments with genuinely compatible mice, he found that they didn't work. Being absolutely convinced in his own mind that he was telling a true story, he thereupon resorted, disastrously, to deception." See *New York Review of Books*, Apr. 15, 1976, pp. 6–11.

60. Pinson to Judith McCulloh, Apr. 19, 1974.

61. Kilarr to McCulloh, Apr. 27, 1974.

62. Ibid.

63. "Wreck on the Mountain Road," by the Red Fox Chasers (A. P. Thompson, Bob Cranford, Paul Miles, Guy Brooks), issued on Conqueror 7256 and Champion 15484 (as by the Virginia Possum Tamers); reissued on County 502: *A Collection of Mountain Ballads*.

64. See *Sing Out!*, 8 (Winter, 1959), 8–9.

65. "Wreck of the Old Slow Binder," by Tillis and Burch; sung by Dave Dudley on Mercury MG 21028/SR 61028: *Truck Drivin' Son-of-a-Gun*.

66. In *Sounds like Folk, No. 2: The Railways in Song* (London: EFDS Publications, 1973), pp. 22–23.

REFERENCES

A. ["The Wreck of the Old 97"], by Fred Jackson Lewey. There are three separate renditions by Lewey: Gordon Collection (N.C.) MS 4, transcribed by Gordon from cylinder recording A5, recorded in Concord, N.C., on Oct. 14, 1925; this was retranscribed by Gordon at the time of the trial. Cylinder A6 was recorded in Concord on Oct. 15, 1925, and transcribed by Gordon. The third version was recited in Apr., 1929, at pretrial hearings in Greensboro, N.C. (pp. 307–8 of trial transcripts), and labeled exhibit D-1 at trial.

["The Wreck of the Old 97"], by Charles Weston Noell. There are three Noell renditions: Gordon Collection (N.C.) MS 1, transcribed by Gordon from cylinders A1, A2, and A3, recorded on Oct. 15, 1925, in Concord. The second text was submitted at the Danville pretrial hearings on Apr. 4, 1929; I do not know when it was written down. The third was recited orally at the hearings on Apr. 5, 1929 (pp. 292–94 of trial transcripts).

"Old 97," manuscript sent to R. W. Gordon by Ethel A. Bridges of Danville, Va., Nov. 14, 1926. Mrs. Bridges wrote in her letter, "I am sending you the words as it was written possibly 20 years ago or longer, by Mr. John Moore. He was the first person that sang this song in Danville, and wrote it for me 17 years ago, he said at that time he had been knowing it about three years. . . ."

[Wreck of the Old 97"], manuscript given at pretrial testimony by Lera McNeely Stephens of Lynchburg, which she testified she had written down prior to 1911 (pp. 12–13 of trial transcript). This and the preceding three texts constituted a group of four that Gordon considered "old" texts that almost certainly dated from before 1910.

"The Wreck on the Southern Old 97," by Henry Whitter. Vocal, guitar, and harmonica. Recorded Dec. 12, 1923 (OKeh master 72167-A), in New York City. Released on OKeh 40015 in Jan., 1924. The texts published in Whitter's 1924 sheet music and in his song folio, ca. 1935, both differ slightly from the recording and from each other. Whitter's version was copyrighted on Oct. 1, 1924 (E 600188), published by F. Wallace Rega; and again on Nov. 1, 1924 (E 602770), published by General Phonograph Corp. The copyright was renewed Dec. 10, 1951, by Paul Whitter (90342–43) and on Jan. 9, 1952, by Hattie W. Hader (91619–20) —Whitter's son and widow, respectively. This was the first recording of the song.

"The Wreck of the Southern Old '97," by

Ernest Thompson. Vocal, guitar, and harmonica. Recorded Apr. 26, 1924 (Columbia master 81742–1), in New York City. Released on Columbia 130-D ca. Aug., 1924; and Harmony 5120-H (as by Ernest Johnson) ca. 1928. The second recording of the song, and independent of Whitter's.

"The Wreck on the Southern Old 97," by Vernon Dalhart. Dalhart, vocal; guitar accompaniment. Recorded May 14, 1924 (Edison master 9514-C), in New York City. Released on Edison 51361 ca. July or Aug., 1924; and Edison cylinder 4898, ca. Sept., 1924. Dalhart's first recording of the song.

"Wreck of the Old 97," by Vernon Dalhart. Dalhart, vocal and harmonica; guitar accompaniment. Recorded Aug. 13, 1924 (Victor masters 30632-1, 3), in New York City. Released on Victor 19427 on Oct. 3, 1924. Re-recorded electrically on Mar. 18, 1926 (master 30632-4), in New York City, with guitar, harmonica, and viola accompaniment. Released on Victor 19427 ca. Apr., 1926; Bluebird B-5335, Feb., 1934; Sunrise 3416, ca. Feb., 1934; and Montgomery Ward M-4477, autumn, 1934; Victor (Canada) 119427, ca. Apr., 1926. Reissued on RCA Victor LPV 532: *The Railroad in Folksong* (from the electrical re-recording). The best-selling and most influential recording of the song.

"Wreck of the 97," by the Arizona Wranglers. Vocal by "Hungry." Recorded ca. Aug., 1929 (master L 949), in Freeman Lang studios, Hollywood, Calif. Released on unnumbered 12″ 78 rpm disc ca. Oct., 1929. Reissued on Rar-Arts WLP 1000: *Those Fabulous "Beverly Hill Billies."* Transcribed in this book.

B. Anderson, G., 203
Boos
Boston Evening Transcript, "Notes and Queries," May 23, 1931 (discussion only)
Boston Sunday Globe, "Everybody's Column," Sept. 10, 1933
Boston Sunday Globe Magazine, Mar. 11, 1928, p. 13.
Botkin & Harlow, 449
Brown II, 513–21
Burton & Manning (1967), 71

Cambiaire, 97
CFB, 2 (1963), 41
Clifton, 31
Coffin & Cohen, 88–89
Cohen (1974)
Comstock, 111–12 (from Cox [1939]); 219–20
Cowboy Songs, 19
Cox (1939), 118–21
Crabtree, 114
Davis, A. K., 293 (title and first line only)
Dawson (I), 22
Dew, 48–49
Downes & Siegmeister (1940), 244–45
Family Herald, 56 (references only)
Fath, 146
Fountain
Fox
Foy, 7
Friedman, 318
Gordon, *Adventure,* Aug. 20, 1923, p. 192 (1 verse)
Gordon, *Adventure,* Jan. 30, 1924, p. 191
Green (1966) (discussion only)
Hamilton
Heineman, *Railroad Stories,* Jan., 1934, pp. 37–41
Henry (1934), 79
Herbert, *Saga,* Dec., 1956, p. 13
Holbrook, 430
Horstman, 335–37 (transcription of Harrell recording)
Hubbard, F., 251
Irwin, 216
Johnson, M. R.
Kreimer, *RRM,* 86 (Nov. 1969), 29
Kreimer, *RRM,* 100 (May, 1976)
Laws, 213 (G 2) (discussion only)
Modern Railroads, 8 (Apr., 1953), 70 (discussion only)
OTS&P, 1 (Sept.-Oct., 1967), 32
Pack, 41
Prince, 128
Railroad Gazette, Oct. 2, 1903, p. 711 (discussion only)
Railroad Gazette, Oct. 23, 1903, p. 759 (discussion only)
Randolph IV, 132
Red & Raymond, 8
Reid (1964), 10–13 (discussion only)
Ridenour VI, 50
RRM, 14 (Mar., 1911), 383
RRM, 8 (May, 1932), 286

RRM, 59 (Dec., 1952), 63 (discussion only)
RVB, 10 (Jan., 1957), 2
RVB, 18 (Sept., 1965), 9
RVB, 34 (Nov., 1977), 9
Shay (1928), 131
Silverman (1975) II, 388
Spaeth (1945), 106
Spaeth (1948), 445 (discussion only)
Ulevich ·
Walsh, *Hobbies,* Sept., 1930, p. 34
West Virginia Hillbilly, June 15, 1974, p. 1
Whitter (Song #1)
Williams, 335

THE FOLLOWING newspaper and magazine articles deal principally with the story of "Old 97" in the context of the lawsuit:

Richmond (Va.) *News Leader,* Mar. 1, 1927.
Richmond (Va.) *Times Dispatch,* Sept. 12, 22, 1927.
New York Herald Tribune, Mar. 1, 1930.
Time, Mar. 2, 1933; Jan. 15, 1934; Dec. 31, 1934.
Washington Daily News, Mar. 6, 1930.
Federal Reporter, 2d ser., 69 (Apr.–May, 1934), 871.
Winston-Salem (N.C.) *Journal & Sentinel,* Feb. 9, 1941.

C. COHEN COLLECTION:
Marie Benson (letter, July, 1968)
Ruth Butcher (letter, June 1, 1968)

GORDON COLLECTION (N.C.):
1, 2—Charles Weston Noell
4—Fred J. Lewey
349—Lula Browning

GORDON MSS:
82—J. F. Hunt
138—L. O. Lineberger
3030—A. Stavinoha
3031—G. Hemkin
3033—E. Susee
3034—E. Phillips
3104—Mrs. J. O. Junturen
3126—G. M. Brooks
3260—C. M. Clark

ODUM-ARTHUR MSS:
79

WKFA:
Willard Neil Barry (May, 1960)
Thomas Burton (May, 1960)
Doyle Dockery (Apr., 1961)
Kenneth Duncan (July, 1959)
Carl Hornback and Green River Valley Boys (Feb., 1962)
Emily Irene Humphreys (Nov., 1956; ballet written 1925)
Nettie Jarboe (fall, 1964)
Mrs. W. L. Marton (May, 1957)
Nora Meisel (May, 1957)
Walter Pearson (May, 1960; ballet written Feb., 1929)
Edward Rold (Jan. 28, 1960)
Mrs. Meyer Smith (Mar., 1959)
Bill Veneman (May, 1955)
Neil C. Ward (n.d.)
Bobby White (Dec., 1963)
Jerry Lou Wunder (Apr., 1962)

D. Smilin' Billy Blinkhorn—Regal Zonophone (Australia) G 23883
Jenks "Tex" Carmen—Four Star 1230
Vernon Dalhart—Bell 340, Banner 1531, Regal 9829, Domino 3501, (as by Bob White), Oriole 325 (as by Dick Morse), Silvertone 2701, Conqueror 7067, Clover 1694; the following are all Canadian releases: Apex 8295, Apex 8428, Starr 10040, Leonora 10040, Microphone 22004 (as by Fred King), Domino 21121
—Gennett 5588, Gennett 3019 (1924 recording)
—Gennett 3019, Gennett 5588, Champion 15121, Herwin 75503, Challenge 161, Challenge 320 (1926 recording)
—Grey Gull 4131, Radiex 4131, Paramount 3018, Broadway 8053
—Champion 15121, Silvertone 8141, Gennett 6654, Supertone 9241 (1928 recording)
—Emerson 7348
—Davis Unlimited DU 33030: *Old Time Songs: 1925–1930* (reissue of one of the above)
Vaughn de Leath—Lincoln 2473 (as by Gloria Geer), Cameo 875 (as by Anabelle Lee)
Happy Dixon's Clodhoppers—Melotone

12052, Polk 9033, Aurora (Canada)
22030 (as by Yoder's Yokels)

Carl Fenton's Orchestra—Brunswick 2857
(Billy Jones and Ernest Hare, vocalists)

Arthur Fields—Grey Gull 4131, Radiex
4131, Van Dyke 84131, Madison 4085
(some copies of these were issued as by
Jeff Calhoun, Vel Veteran, and Mr. X)

Tex Fletcher—Fletcher 1782

Four Showmen—Elite X27

Kelly Harrell—OKeh 7010 (12″ 78 rpm);
Bear Family (West Germany) 12508:
The Complete Kelly Harrell

Henry and his Corn Poppers—Tops 250

Jesters—Decca 24355 (in album A-639:
Railroad Songs)

Danny Kaye—Decca 27050

Fred Kirby—Sonora 3038

Peggy Lloyd—Benida DB 2010

Clayton McMichen and his Georgia
Wildcats—Crown 3384 (as by Slim
Bryant), Varsity 5029, Homestead
23090, Asch 410-3

Johnny Mercer—Capitol 122

George Reneau (with Gene Austin,
vocal)—Vocalion 14809, Vocalion 5029

Dick Robertson and his Orchestra—
Decca 3125, Decca (Australia)
X 1891

Hank Snow—RCA Victor 20-4095 (in
album P 310: *Famous Railroading
Songs*); RCA Victor 47-4095 (in 45 rpm
album WP 310: *Famous Railroading
Songs*); RCA Victor EPA 310: *Famous
Railroading Songs*; RCA Victor
447-0560 (45 rpm); RCA Victor
LPM/LSP 2812: *More Souvenirs*; RCA
Camden CXS 9009(e): *The Wreck of
the Old 97*; RCA Camden CAL/CAS(e)
722: *One and Only*

Muggsy Spanier—Decca 4336, Brunswick
(England) 03530, Brunswick (France or
Germany) A-82713

Gid Tanner and his Skillet Lickers
—Columbia 15142-D

Charlie Troutt's Melody Artists—
Columbia 1265-D, Columbia (England)
01236   "Transportation Blues—Part
4: The Wreck of the Southern Old 97"

Sid Turner (Vernon Dalhart pseudonym)
—Pathé 032068, Perfect 12147,
Harmograph 970, Romeo 5050, Oriole
8050, Jewel 20050

E. Roy Acuff—Hickory LPM 125: *Great
Train Songs*
—Hickory LSP-162: *Why is Roy Acuff?*

Pink Anderson—Riverside RLP 12-611:
American Street Songs; Riverside 148

Eddy Arnold—RCA Victor LSP-2668:
Hits That Made Country Music History
—RCA Victor LPM 2036

Ed Badeaux—Folkways FG 3534:
American Guitar

Charlie Beverly—Starr SLP-1050: *Sounds
of the Dobro*

Johnny Bond—Starday SLP 354

Oscar Brand—Elektra EKL-168: *The
Wild Blue Yonder* (parody)

Paul Buskirk—Stoneway STY-158: *Good
Dobro Pickin'*

Johnny Cash—Sun SLP-1220: *Hot and
Blue Guitar*; Sun EPA-113: *Country
Boy, Vol. 2*: Sun SLP 1270: *All Aboard
the Blue Train*; London (England)
RE-1230: *Country Boy, Vol. 2*
—Sun 104: *Story Songs of the Trains and
Rivers*; Sun 106; Share SH-5002; Sun
2-126: *The Man, The World, His
Music*; Sun 127: *Original Hits, Vol. 3*
—Columbia CL 2190/CS 8990: *I Walk the
Line*; Philips (England)
CBS-BPG-62371: *I Walk the Line*;
Columbia (England) D363/DS363:
Legends and Love Songs
—Columbia CS-9827/CO-30961: *At San
Quentin*
—Pickwick JS-6201: *Rock Island Line*
—Everest Archive of Folk Music 278:
Johnny Cash

Lew Childre and friends—Starday SLP
153: *Old Time Get-Together*; Starday
SLP 170

Ken Colyer—London 1674 (45 rpm)

Stompin' Tom Connors—STC 2: *60 More
Oldtime Favorites*

Danny Davis, Nashville Brass—RCA
APL-1-0565: *Bluegrass Country*

Little Jimmy Dempsey—Plantation 10:
*Little Jimmy Dempsey Picks on Big
Johnny Cash*

Dorsey Dixon—Testament T-3301: *Babies
in the Mill*

Lonnie Donegan—Mercury MG 20229;
Nixa (England) NPT 19012

Jack Elliott—Prestige International 13045:
Jack Elliott Country Style: Prestige

7804: *Country Style*

Bob Ensign and the Stump Jumpers
—Rural Rhythm 180: *Bob Ensign and the Stump Jumpers*

Raymond Fairchild—Rural Rhythm RRRF
262: *King of the 5-String Banjo*

Hank Ferguson—Folk-Legacy FSA 13:
Behind These Walls

Lester Flatt—Flying Fish 015: *Lester Raymond Flatt*

Lester Flatt, Earl Scruggs, and the Foggy
Mountain Boys—Columbia CL 1951/CS
8751: *Hard Travelin'*

Frank George, Peter Gott, and Jim Cope
—Traditional FFS 528: *Folk Festival of the Smokies*

Goins Brothers—Jalyn JLP-131: *Bluegrass Country*

Goose Island Ramblers—Cuca K-1111: *A Session with the Goose Island Ramblers*

Woody Guthrie—Folkways FA 2484:
Woody Guthrie Sings Folk Songs, Vol. 2

Cisco Houston—Vanguard VRS 9107: *"I Ain't Got No Home"*; Vanguard SRV
3006: *"I Ain't Got No Home"*
—Folkways FA 2013 (FP 13): *900 Miles and Other Railroad Songs*

Jones Brothers—CMH 1776: *200 Years of American Heritage in Song*

Margie Lane and Sundown Pete
—Driftwood LPS-41429: *Treasures beneath the Shifting Sands of Time*

Mike Lattimore Show—Rural Rhythm
169: *The Mike Lattimore Show*

Clay Lewis—American Heritage Music
AW401-33: *Tall Shadows*

Little John and the Cochran Family
—Carpenters 20001

Living Guitars—RCA Camden CAS-924:
Living Guitars Play Music from the Country

Lucas and Harmon Brothers—Jaf-Tone
8644/5: *Sounds of the Mountains*

Hank MacDonald and the Roving
Brakemen—ARC 509: *One More Ride*

Maggie Valley Country Singers—Rural
Rhythm MVS 134: *Maggie Valley Country Singers*

Merrill Jay Singers—Cabot CAB-503:
Songs of the Railroad

Monte Mills—Horseshoe LP-2: *Second Album*

John Miracle and Virgil Joseph, with the
Tennessee Boys—Pine Tree PTSLP
515: *John Miracle and Virgil Joseph with the Tennessee Boys Sing Memories of Home*

David and John Morris—Kidtown 1FR69:
Music as We Learned It

Mountaineers—Cumberland SRC 69501:
Bluegrass Banjo Pickin'

George Pegram and Walter Parham
—Riverside RLP 12-650: *Pickin' and Blowin'*

Pete Seeger—Folkways FA 2320:
American Favorite Ballads; Folkways
FT 1017/FTS 31017

Patrick Sky—Vanguard VSD 79179:
Patrick Sky

Hank Snow—RCA LSP-6014(e): *This Is My Story*

—RCA Victor ANL1-1052; *All about Trains*;
RCA Victor ANS1-1052 (8-track tape):
All about Trains

Ernest Stoneman—Library of Congress
LBC 9: *Folk Music in America, Vol. 9: Songs of Death & Tragedy*

Stoneman Family—Folkways FA 2315:
Old Time Tunes of the South

Stonemans—CMH 6219: *On the Road*

Billy Strange—Crescendo GNP 2041:
Railroad Man

Stump Jumpers—Rural Rhythm RR 180:
Pickin' & Grinnin'

Earl Taylor and Jim McCall, with the
Stoney Mountain Boys—Rural Rhythm
RR 188: *Blue Grass Favorites*

Kenneth Threadgill—PSG Records 54:
Yesterday & Today

Traditions—Davis Unlimited 45001 (7"
45 rpm)

Uncle Leroy and the Pike County
Partners—Major MRLP-2105:
Star-Spangled Bluegrass

James Wall and Osbrine Cribb—Rural
Rhythm 2112: *Red Hot Country Instrumentals*

Wanderin' Five—Somerset SF-18600:
We're Pickin' and Singin' Folk Songs

Wear Family—Rural Rhythm RR 122:
The Great Wear Family

Larry Wilson—Eleventh Hour EH-1004-S:
*The Strawberry Hill Invitational
Bluegrass Festival*   "Casey Jones"

Mac Wiseman—Rural Rhythm 158: *Mac*

Wiseman Sings Old Time Country Favorites
—Dot 2543 (45 rpm); Dot DLP-3213; ABC ABDP-4009: *Sixteen Great Performances*
—CMH 9001: *The Mac Wiseman Story*; CMH 5900: *The World's Greatest Bluegrass Bands*
Unidentified artists—Folkways FS 3812: *Music from the Ozarks*

F. GORDON COLLECTION (N.C.):

A1, A2, A3 (MSS 1, 2)—Charles Weston Noell
A5, A6 (MS 4)—Fred J. Lewey

LC AFS:

Jesse Amburgey—AFS 10882 A7
Ethel Arp—AFS 15070 A18
William C. Bailey—AFS 13729-6
Leonard Bartlett and band—AFS 14768-4
Clyde Bland—AFS 13125 B4
Luther Bryant—AFS 13718 B29
Opal Burroughs—AFS 11873 A11
Ambers Deaton—AFS 1553 B2
Gilbert Fike—AFS 3189 A1
Lee Kilpatrick—AFS 10079 A8
Mrs. W. M. Klinger—AFS 11893 A32
Addie Leffew—AFS 15026 B16
Fred J. Lewey—AFS 13168 A (copied from Gordon cylinder)
Bascom Lamar Lunsford—AFS 1815 B1
—AFS 9509 A2
Vernon Lyons—AFS 9997 A9
Mrs. W. L. Martin—AFS 2747 B3
Silas Pardleton—AFS 9059 A1   "End of Old 97"
Mildred Ratcliff—AFS 11907 A26
Lillian Short—AFS 5327 A2
Pick Temple—AFS 8857 A2
Albert Vergasons—AFS 11688 A36
Sharon Vergasons—AFS 11688 B2
Claude Wolfenberger—AFS 15059 B9
Clarence H. Wyatt—AFS 10889 A4

"THE TRAIN THAT NEVER RETURNED" and other related train songs not specifically mentioning Old 97:

B. Anderson, 213   "The Reckless Conductor"

Brown II, 508   "Parted Lovers"
Brown II, 509   "The Train That Never Returned"
Cole folios (all using same plate), all titled "The Train That Never Returned":
Blue Grass Roy, 52
Hamlins Saddle Pals, 52
KFBI, 52
Robison, 52
Tiny Texan, 52
Lomax & Lomax (1949), 254   "The Wreck on the Somerset Road" (transcription of LC AFS 1532)
Alexander Malin broadside, 1888   "The Hand-Car That Never Returned"
Mountain Songs, 5   "The Train That Never Returned"
Perry, 200   "The Train That Never Returned"
Richardson, 42   "The Train That Never Returned"
RRM, Mar., 1967, p. 32   "The Train That Never Came In"
Sounds like Folk, 22–23   "The London Underground" (parody on "The MTA Song")
Spaeth (1927), 139   "The Train That Never Returned"
Stout, 72   "The Train That Never Returned"

D. KAHN COLLECTION:

Clarence Green (Aug., 1961)   "Narrow Gauge Song"

WKFA:

E. N. Caldwell (E. C. Perrow Collection, 1913) (no title)
Wilma Pace (Nov., 1959)   "The Train That Never Came Back"
Lasso Rose (1958)   "Last Trip of the Train"

E. Bruce Buckley—Folkways FP 23-2: *Ohio Valley Ballads*   "Rarden Wreck"
Tommy Jarrell—County 741: *Stay All Night*   "Old 97"

F. LC AFS:

Justis Begley—AFS 1532 A2 & B "Wreck on the Somerset Road"

The New Market Wreck

THE NEW MARKET WRECK

The South-ern Rail-way had a wreck at ten o'clock one morn, Near Hodg-e's and New Mar-ket ground, the place, the date a-dorned. The twen-ty-fourth of Sep-tem-ber, the year nine-teen and four, Was when that aw-ful wreck oc-curred of both the rich and poor.

The Southern Railway had a wreck at ten o'clock one morn,
Near Hodge's and New Market ground, the place, the date adorned.
The twenty-fourth of September, the year nineteen and four,
Was when that awful wreck occurred of both the rich and poor.

The conductor on the westbound train did make a grand mistake,
He never read his orders right and caused that awful fate.
He hurt one hundred and a half, and there were seventy dead,
I hope he has forgiveness now and lives without a dread.

The conductor on the eastbound train had kissed his darling wife,
And when he got on board the train he had to give his life.
I trust that he was pure in heart and now is with the blest,
And that his wife will meet him there and be with him at rest.

The trains were goin' east and west and speeding on their way,
They ran together on a curve and what a wreck that day.
The cars were bursted, torn, and split, and spread across the track,
You'll see a picture of the wreck just over on the back.

And oh, the men and women's cries did echo through the air,
Such cries were never heard before of human in despair.

The little children cried aloud for mercy to their God,
But now they all are dead and gone and under earthly sod.

George Reneau and Gene Austin

Two passenger trains on the Southern Railway met in a head-on collision on the forenoon of Sept. 24 near Hodge's Station, Tenn., with such force that both engines and several coaches were demolished, crushing to death no less than 62 persons, mostly passengers in the forward coaches of the eastbound train, besides injuring many others. The engineers of both trains were among the killed. No one in the sleepers was injured. Westbound train, No. 15, a local and eastbound train, No. 12, a heavy through train, carrying three sleepers, were directed by orders to meet and pass at New Market, a regular stopping point. The westbound train disregarded the order and went on toward Hodges, the usual meeting place, and the collision occurred about a mile and a half beyond New Market. The conductor of No. 15 is reported as admitted that he was responsible for the collision, having misread the order. The engineer, being dead, cannot explain his part in causing the calamity.[1]

Whether the number of dead was actually sixty-two or only fifty-six, as another source gives,[2] is a small discrepancy; in either case one can only speculate on the subsequent thoughts of the conductor whose negligence was responsible for one of the worst wrecks in the United States.

In the years following the accident, two ballads were composed about it. "The Southern Railroad Wreck," written by Charles O. Oaks, blind musician from Richmond, Kentucky, was printed and circulated in broadside form and was reprinted in the *Journal of American Folklore* in 1909, one of the first examples in its pages of a native American journalistic broadside ballad. Oaks's text, in whole or part, has appeared twice in print elsewhere; none of these items indicates a tune, although the broadside states "Written and composed by . . . ," which strongly suggests that a tune had been intended to accompany the poem.

A second ballad, titled "The New Market Wreck," words and music by Robert Hugh Brooks, of Whitesburg, Tennessee, was copyrighted on August 10, 1906 (C 127218). In 1915 it was published in *The Harmonic Praises*, a collection of shape-note songs. Brooks, said by Edwin C. Kirkland to have once been a teacher at Rutledge, Tennessee, credited a J. W. Cockreham with suggesting the subject of the song. The last line of the second verse, "You'll see a picture of the wreck, Just over on the back," suggests that the song had appeared in print on a broadside prior to its publication in the songbook. This was found to be the case when a copy of Brooks's song sheet (reproduced here) was discovered at the Library of Congress. That phrase also appears in the recording transcribed in this book, but in the fourth verse. All the other occurrences of this ballad —the three recordings and the three items recovered in folksong collections—can be traced to the Brooks version, text and tune. Brooks's tune, however, was not entirely original, but was strongly reminiscent of Will S. Hays's "We Parted by the River Side" (1866).

According to Mildred Haun, Nep Hollie, a preacher from Hamblen County who had lost an arm in the wreck, held revival meetings at which his favorite sermon was "The Last Run," the story of the wreck. Inspired by Hollie's effect on his hearers, Joshia Adams, an itinerant balladeer who wrote and adapted various songs, printed a broadside version of an old ballad about the wreck and sold it for ten cents throughout the countryside.

Adams's text was derived from Brooks's song, and may have been responsible for its survival in oral tradition in east Tennessee and southwest Virginia.

Two hillbilly recordings of "The New Market Wreck" appeared during the 1920s. The first, which is the version transcribed here, was recorded by George Reneau for Vocalion in New York on September 12, 1924, at his second session. Reneau grew up in the hills near Knoxville, Tennessee, and probably learned the ballad in his youth (he was about twenty-three when he recorded it). His text is close to Brooks's original, except that one verse and the chorus have been omitted. A second version was recorded in August, 1927, by Mr. and Mrs. Jim Baker of Virginia, and copyrighted October 10, 1927 (E 674615). Just over six thousand copies of this record were sold.

NOTES

1. *Railway Age*, Sept. 30, 1904, p. 480.
2. *The 1969 World Almanac and Book of Facts* (New York: Newspaper Association, 1968), p. 600. Data taken from Federal Railroad Association, Bureau of Railroad Safety.

REFERENCES

A. "The Southern Railroad Wreck," broadside, by Charles O. Oaks. Published between 1904 and 1908. No copies of this broadside are known to survive, but the text was reprinted by Beatty (see section B, below). Beatty's pages were reproduced in Archie Green, "Commercial Music Graphics: Number Twenty-seven," *JEMFQ*, 9 (Winter, 1973), 160–65.

"The New Market Wreck," sheet music, by R. H. Brooks. Published in 1906 by the author at Whitesburg, Tenn. Reproduced in Green (1973) and in this book.

"The New Market Wreck," by George Reneau. Reneau, harmonica and guitar; Gene Austin, vocal. Recorded Sept. 12, 1924 (Aeolian Vocalion master 13681), in New York City. Released on Vocalion 14930 in Feb., 1925. Reissued on (Brunswick) Vocalion 5054 in 1927. This recording is transcribed here.

ALL REFERENCES BELOW are to the Brooks ballad unless otherwise noted:

B. Anderson, G., 209
Beatty, 70–71 (Oaks ballad)
Davis, A. K., 293 (title and first line only)
Green (1966), 9–10
Harmonic Praises
Haun, 415
Kirkland, 4–7 (variants of both ballads given)
Rosenberg, 90 (title only; Oaks ballad)
Tennessee, 304 (fragment of Oaks ballad)

D. Mr. and Mrs. J. W. Baker—Victor 20863

E. Mike Seeger—Folkways FH 5273: *Tipple, Loom & Rail*

♫ ─ THE ─

NEW MARKET WRECK.

─ By ─

R. H. BROOKS,

─ of ─

Whitesburg, Tennessee.

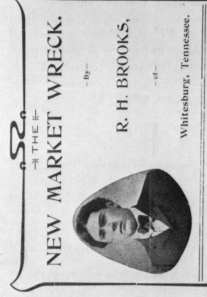

The Meeting of the Trains September 24, 1904.

The most disastrous wreck that has ever been in the South, occurred on the Southern line of railroad near New Market, Tenn., at 10 A. M., Sept. 24, 1904. And there was 70 lives lost, and 150 wounded. The writer feeling the impression that a discriptive song of the New Market wreck with illustrations and imitations, would be heartily welcomed by all music loving people, we offer you this copy carefully prepared.

Published by R. H. BROOKS, Whitesburg, Tennessee.

Price 25 Cents Each, $3 Per Dozen, Postpaid.

The New Market Wreck.

DIRECTIONS—For imitating the running of the trains, whistling, and explosion of the wreck, before playing the song, entitled "The New Market Wreck," by R. H. Brooks, Whitesburg, Tenn.

1 Have all the stops drawn to the right of the middle C, on the organ, except Diapason Forte, with only Diapason, Principal and Bass Coupler to the left.

2 Place that part of the left arm between the elbow and wrist on the black and white keys of the organ from the first key named C, above lowest key named F, on the bass.

3 Now press all the keys between the elbow and wrist. The keys at elbow must be pressed down as far as they will go. Those under wrist may not be pressed any.

4 To start the train, place your feet firmly on each pedal and give a stroke with great force, using right foot. Hold every position that is yet given. Then repeat the same act, making a stroke for each exhaustion, etc., then gradually increase, using right knee swell to aid, when the right foot has got to its highest speed, employ the left foot and let the right knee close gradually, to imitate the train leaving out. Both pedals can be used now to their fullest capacity. And raise the left arm just a little, and not press the keys so far down.

5 Then add the whistling, use the keys D, F sharp and A sharp, above middle C. Give the keys named a long stroke—then a quick stroke.

6 Then to imitate the other train, commencing use the keys A flat, B and E flat above middle C. Give these keys a long stroke, and two quick strokes. Don't press these keys over half way down.

7 Repeat the acts for about two minutes, then pull right knee swell out at an instant. And let it go itself with a "slam," taking up the left arm from the keys at the same time, thus stopping all noise. This will be the wreck.

8 Then give an introduction on the organ using the first eight measures of the song entitled, "The New Market Wreck," in the key of B flat, very mournfully. Then proceed with the song.

Yours truly,

R. H. BROOKS.

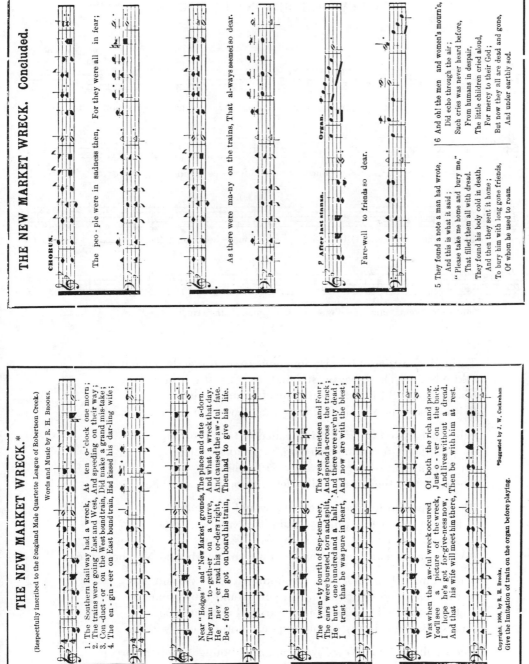

Sheet music: "The New Market Wreck." Collection of the Library of Congress and Archie Green.

Billy Richardson's Last Ride

BILLY RICHARDSON'S LAST RIDE

Through the West Vir-gin-ia moun-tains came the ear-ly morn-in' mail, Old Num-ber Three was west-bound, the fast-est on the rail; She pulled right in-to Hin-ton, a junc-tion on the line,___ With a Bald-win Moun-tain en-gine they made the run on time.

Through the West Virginia mountains came the early mornin' mail,
Old Number Three was westbound, the fastest on the rail;
She pulled right into Hinton, a junction on the line,
With a Baldwin Mountain engine they made the run on time.

Billy Richardson at Hinton was called to take the run,
To pull the fastest mail-train from there to Huntington;
His fireman he reported for duty on the line,
Then reading their train orders left Hinton right on time.

Then Billy told his fireman that he would happy be,
If he could die while pullin' a train like Number Three;
"I want to die on duty right in my cab," said he,
"While pullin' eastbound Number Four, or westbound Number Three."

The fireman then said, "Billy, you know you're old and gray,
Your name is on the pension list, you should retire some day."
But Billy said, "Dear fireman, the truth I'm tellin' you,
I must die right in my engine cab, and nothing else will do."

Then pulling down New River came westbound Number Three,
By Thurmond, then by Cotton Hill, no danger could he see;
His head then struck a mail-crane while pullin' down the line,
He'll never pull his train again to Huntington on time.

He pulled the fastest time freight, he pulled the U.S. mail,
He pulled the fast excursion to the music of the rail;
He lost his life on duty in his engine cab so free,
While pullin' in Montgomery on westbound Number Three.

Now ladies, if your husband is a railroad engineer,
You know he is in danger and death is ever near;
You know he loves you dearly when he is by your side,
Remember well that his next run may be his farewell ride.

Al Craver (Vernon Dalhart)

Although the public relations department of the C & O Railway Company, in response to my inquiry, assured me that their archives had no information at all about the hogger Billy Richardson,[1] he did indeed exist, and the ballad is a reasonably accurate account of how he was killed.

The story of the accident, along with a thumbnail sketch of William S. Richardson's career, was given by Thomas W. Dixon, owner and director of the Alderson Museum in West Virginia, in a 1968 issue of *Railroad Magazine*. According to Dixon, Richardson, born in 1848 in Hanover County, Virginia, was the best known of all C & O engineers, and pulled the westbound Number Three (the *Fast Flying Virginian*, or *FFV*) and eastbound Number Four almost daily for twenty-seven years.

On December 14, 1910, Richardson had taken the FFV out of Hinton as usual. At 12:30 P.M., as he approached the mail-crane at Scary, twenty miles west of Charleston, he blew the whistle for mail, leaned out of the cab to look back, and was struck on the temple by the crane. Fireman Cecil S. Lively took the train into Huntington, where an ambulance was waiting to take Richardson to the hospital, but all was in vain. Richardson died without regaining consciousness, shortly after entering the hospital. He had been railroading almost forty-six years.[2]

Although the accident occurred in 1910, the ballad was not written until 1926. That year Cleburne C. Meeks, who was a railroader for the Norfolk and Western from 1922 to 1967, heard Vernon Dalhart's recording of "Wreck of the Old 97." As Meeks tells it,

> . . . I bought a Victor recording of that song and liked it so well that I set out to learn the address of the singer as I thought I could write the words to a song, and if so, I might have Mr. Dalhart record it for me. I happened to think about an old engineer that I knew when I was a small boy. His train No. 3 passed by my home every other day, and I liked the idea of being in the yard where I could see him and wave at him when he passed by my home. His name was Billy Richardson. Sure enough, I did write the lyrics to that song and Vernon Dalhart accepted it and had his partner Carson J. Robison write the music.[3]

Meeks sent Dalhart a copy of his lyrics and on August 6, 1926, received the following reply from Dalhart:

> Your lyrics of "Engineer Billy Richardson" has been accepted. They are very good, and were approved by a big recording firm. The next thing now, is to write music suitable and copyright. My Pardner "Carson J. Robison" will write music first. First however, he will send you a contract giving you 10% of all mechanical royalties received by us for permission to use your lyrics to his music. He will then write the music, copyright same, and we will sell it on all records we can. If the above is *not* satisfactory, let me know and

I'll return your lyrics immediately. Kindly get the permission, or rejection, to me by return mail, as we want to get to work on it or something else. You may send your letter to Carson J. Robison %Hotel Knickerbocker 120 W 45th St New York City.

Very Respy Yours

Vernon Dalhart

P.S. Your name will appear as writer.[4]

Meeks, who incidentally later found out that fireman C. S. Lively was his cousin, was born in Fayette County, West Virginia, in 1902. He has worked for the N & W in various capacities including machinist, fireman, and hostler. During the 1920s and 1930s, he wrote five other songs, two of which pertain to the railroad. One, "The Wreck of the C & O Number Five," follows "Billy Richardson's Last Ride" in this chapter. The other, "The Wreck of the N & W *Cannonball*," was written in 1929 about an accident on June 27, 1903, at Dunlop Siding, Virginia.

On August 10, 1926, Carson J. Robison copyrighted "Billy Richardson's Last Ride" (E 643589; renewed in 1953, R 117841), with words credited to C. C. Meeks and music to C. J. Robison. In the following six months Vernon Dalhart recorded the song for Columbia, OKeh, Victor, Pathé, Plaza, Gennett, and Brunswick. This was a customary pattern of Dalhart's, and one we shall observe in the case of many railroad songs he recorded: evidently, as soon as he learned the song, he recorded it for every company that was interested. The version in this book is transcribed from Dalhart's Columbia recording.[5]

NOTES

1. C & O Railway Company to Cohen, Jan. 31, 1968.

2. *Hinton Daily News and Leader*, Dec. 14, 1910, p. 1.

3. Meeks to Cohen, Sept. 17, 1969.

4. Meeks gave Paul Shue two of his letters from Dalhart many years later. Shue was kind enough to send me copies of the letters in Sept., 1972.

5. For biographical information on Robison, see the discussion of "The Wreck of Number Nine."

REFERENCES

A. "Billy Richardson's Last Ride," by Vernon Dalhart. Dalhart, vocal and harmonica; Carson Robison, guitar. Recorded Sept. 14, 1926 (Columbia master 142617-3), in New York City. Released on Columbia 15098-D (as by Al Craver) on Oct. 20, 1926. This recording is transcribed here.

B. Carpenter
  Comstock, 7, 511–14 (from Carpenter)
  Dalhart & Robison, 24
  Dixon, Thomas W., *RRM*, 83 (Oct., 1968), 32–33
  Family Herald, 38 (reference only)
    "The Engineer"
  Kincaid #5, 38   "Old Number Three"

Kreimer, *RRM*, Mar., 1965, p. 46
Lane, Pt. 6
Railroad Stories, 20 (June, 1936), 23 (in column "The Sunny Side of the Track")
Red & Raymond, 21
RRM, 6 (Nov., 1931), 606
RVB, 34 (Nov., 1977), 9

C. SAN FERNANDO VALLEY STATE COLLEGE ARCHIVE:
  Harry Sikanek (1966)

D. Jeff Calhoun (pseudonym)—Grey Gull 4226, Radiex 4226
  Vernon Dalhart—Brunswick 102, Supertone 2003
  —Gennett 3378, Challenge 149,

Challenge 310, Gold Star 2005,
Silvertone 3839, Herwin 75527
—Edison 51856; Edison 5232 (cylinder);
Mark56 794: *First Recorded Railroad
Songs*
—OKeh 40685
—Victor 20538, Montgomery Ward
M-8063
—Banner 1879, Domino 3850, Regal
8190, Paramount 3048, Broadway 8063
—Cameo 1143, Romeo 350, Varsity 5059
—Davis Unlimited DU 33030: *Old Time
Songs: 1925–1930* (reissue of one of the
above)
George Goebel—Conqueror 8156
Bradley Kincaid—Gennett 7020,
Champion 15923 (as by Dan Hughey),
Supertone 9505, Superior 2788
"Old Number Three"

E. Cecil Goodman—Campus Folksong Club
(University of Illinois) CFC 201: *Green
Fields of Illinois*
Grandpa Jones—CMH 9015: *Grandpa
Jones' Family Album*
Eddie Nesbitt—Bluebonnet BL 103:
*Eddie Nesbitt Sings the Songs of
Bradley Kincaid*   "Old Number
Three"

F. LC AFS:
Irene Sargent—AFS 13125 B18

Billy Richardson

Uncle Billy Richardson (*third from left*) in 1908, in front of the engine on which he died two years later. Both photos courtesy of Thomas Dixon and the C & O Historical Society Collection.

The Wreck of the C & O Number Five

THE WRECK OF THE C & O NUMBER FIVE

From Washington to Charlottesville, then Staunton on the line,
Came the old *Midwestern Limited*, train Number Five on time.
She was a Cincinnati train, the fastest on the line,
Through the valley of Virginia into Clifton Forge on time.

The engineer at Clifton Forge, Dolly Womack was his name,
Was there to sign the register and pull the speeding train.
His fireman, Charley Poteet, was standing by his side,
And receiving their train orders they climbed in the cab to ride.

Then Dolly to his fireman said, "Oh Charley, well you know,
For years I've been an engineer to ride the C and O.
For many years I've had this run, just twenty-five in all,
And when I blow for Covington they will surely know my call."

For Covington to Jerry's Run, old Number Five did roll,
Through the Allegheny Mountains with a crew so brave and bold.
Then westward to the mountain state, White Sulphur Springs on time,
With orders to switch over there and take the east main line.

"I know my engine is all right, she's the U.S. Mountain kind,
One hundred thirty-seven she will put us there on time."
Said Dolly to his fireman, "We are running way behind,
But when I pull the Big Ben Tunnel I mean to be on time."

Just four miles farther down the line he hit a broken rail,
No more to pull old Number Five, no more to pull the mail.

The engine did not overturn but a steam pipe broke in two,
Two hundred pounds of pressure killed poor Dolly brave and true.

Until the brakes are set on time, life's throttle valve shut down,
Some day he'll pilot in the crew that wears the Master's crown.
With a clear block into Heaven's gate he'll pull his mighty train,
And there in God's own roundhouse he will register his name.

Vernon Dalhart

On October 6, 1920, the luxury passenger train known as the *Sportsman,* which ran daily between Cincinnati and Washington, left White Sulphur Springs, West Virginia, seven minutes late. There the crew had received an order directing their westbound train to run on the eastbound track to Ronceverte, because of a freight train on the westbound track with a derailed car. The train, pulled by engine 137, consisted of one mail car, one combination car (half baggage, half coach), two coaches, five Pullmans, and one business car; it pulled out at 10:27 P.M. Eight minutes later at Dickson, West Virginia, the engine struck a broken rail and was thrown into a bank. The coal car telescoped into the engine cab and filled it with coal, pinning the engineer, Dolly Womack, by the legs. Steam pipes broke and scalded him with live steam and boiling water. Rescuers tossed mail sacks into the cab to protect him from the steam and water, but their efforts were of no avail. The mail car was badly damaged, and one mail clerk was killed. Charlie Poteet, the fireman, leaped or was thrown clear of the wreck (accounts differ) and lived, suffering only a minor scratch on the back of his hand.

These details have been pieced together from the ICC accident investigation report;[1] information forwarded to me by Frieda Starkey of Covington, Virginia (see the discussion of "The Wreck of the 1256"), which she obtained from Mrs. John Paul Jones of Clifton Forge, Virginia, the daughter of engineer Womack;[2] and material made available to me by Pick Temple. Temple, who had learned the song in his youth from a schoolteacher and subsequently recorded it for the Library of Congress, made a vigorous attempt in the 1940s to learn the background of the ballad that in his youth had so captured his fancy. In January, 1948, he met a brakeman on the C & O who had been part of the rescue team back in 1920 when Number Five left the rails.[3] An article in the *Richmond Times-Dispatch* about Temple and his interest in this railroad ballad[4] served the further purpose of eliciting a letter from Cleburne C. Meeks, the author of the ballad, who was living in Colonial Heights and still working on the N & W Railway.[5] The knowledge of Meeks's whereabouts in 1950 was sufficient motivation for me to try to contact him in the same city nineteen years later (see my discussion of "Billy Richardson's Last Ride").

Meeks wrote "The Wreck of the C & O Number Five" in 1926, after he had written "Billy Richardson's Last Ride." His sources of information were two of his cousins, who had been engineers on the C & O, and also Charlie Poteet, the fireman who survived the wreck. At Dalhart's insistence, Meeks had written Poteet and asked permission to use his name in the song he was writing about the accident. According to Poteet, Womack was quite disturbed about having to run his train on the eastbound track. Womack's last words, spoken after they had lost some time making the switchover from the eastbound to the westbound track on the way out of White Sulphur Springs, were, "We are four minutes late."[6]

As a writer of disaster ballads, Meeks was unusual in that he dealt with accidents that preceded his compositions by many years. Tom Trautman, fireman on the Virginian line and brother-in-law of hillbilly singer Roy Harvey (see the discussion of "Bill Mason" in chap. 6) recalled "Billy Waumack," about an engineer killed when his train overturned, as an old ballad that was sung around 1917, many years before the advent of hillbilly phonograph recordings.[7] If we allow his memory a slip of a few years, this might have been another ballad about the wreck of Number Five that predated Meeks's composition.

Meeks concluded his first two compositions with the two favorite endings that grace tragedy ballads. "Billy Richardson's Last Ride" ends with a verse of warning to the wives of railroad engineers that death is always near. "I took a railroad man's view when I wrote the last verse of the song and wrote it with the widow in mind," Meeks explained, "also the vacant chair in that home that could never be filled again."[8] "The Wreck of the C & O Number Five" ends with a stanza about a spiritual railroad to heaven that will give railroaders their final ride. In other respects, the lyrics of this ballad are reminiscent of "Engine 143," given earlier in this chapter, about an 1890 wreck on the C & O.

"The Wreck of the C & O Number Five" was copyrighted on February 24, 1927 (E 660244), by Carson J. Robison, who set Meeks's words to music. Vernon Dalhart recorded the ballad a half-dozen times, the first being for Brunswick on March 12, 1927, and the second for OKeh five days later. Of the Columbia recording, issued under the pseudonym Al Craver (and transcribed here), more than sixteen thousand copies were sold. Aside from Dalhart's discs, few recordings or collections of this ballad have been made, and its position in oral tradition is insecure.

NOTES

1. *Summary of Accident Investigation Reports, No. 6, October-December 1920* (Washington, D.C.: Interstate Commerce Commission, Bureau of Safety, 1921), p. 5. See also *Hinton Daily News*, Oct. 7, 1920.

2. Starkey to Cohen, Feb. 27, 1968.

3. Pick Temple, liner notes to Prestige International 13008: *The Pick of the Crop*.

4. "His Songs Preserve Railroad History," *Richmond Times-Dispatch*, Apr. 2, 1950. See also "Railroad Balladeer," *Tracks*, July, 1950, p. 41.

5. "Railman, Still Alive, Is Composer," *Richmond Times-Dispatch*, Apr. 16, 1950.

6. Meeks to Cohen, Oct. 27, 1969.

7. Tom Trautman, interviewed by Archie Green and Eugene Earle in Beckley, W.Va., Aug. 15, 1962.

8. Meeks to Cohen, Oct. 5, 1969.

REFERENCES

A. "Wreck of the C & O #5," by Vernon Dalhart. Dalhart, vocal and harmonica; guitar and violin, probably by Carson Robison and Murray Kellner, respectively. Recorded Mar. 12, 1927 (Brunswick master E22016-17 [E4670-71]), in New York City. Released on Brunswick 117 in autumn, 1927, and on Vocalion 5140 and Supertone 2002. First recording of this song.

B. *Family Herald*, 56 (references only)
Lane Pt. 3, Pt. 12
RRM, 5 (July, 1931), 636

C. COHEN COLLECTION:
Laura Affolter (letter, May, 1968)
Ralph Oatley (letter, Sept. 29, 1967)

D. Vernon Dalhart—Brunswick 117, Supertone 2002, Vocalion 5140

—Champion 15907, Supertone 9240,
  Silvertone 8145
—OKeh 45102
—Cameo 8218, Romeo 598, Lincoln 2823
—Pathé 32270, Perfect 12349
—Banner 6113, Regal 8469, Domino 0209,
  Conqueror 7071, Conqueror 7169,
  Challenge 558, Challenge 733, Jewel
  5137 (as by Frank Evans), Oriole 1053 (as
  by Frank Evans), Apex (Canada) 8689,
  Domino (Canada) 21356

E. Pick Temple—Prestige International 13008:
      The Pick of the Crop
    Mac Wiseman—Hamilton HLP 167/12167:
      Songs of the Dear Old Days

F. LC AFS:
    Pick Temple—AFS 8857 A4
    —AFS 9132 B3

Paul Shue and C. C. Meeks. Courtesy of C. C. Meeks.

The Wreck of the 1256

THE WRECK OF THE 1256

On that cold and dark cloudy evenin',
Just before the close of the day,
There came Harry Lyle and Dillard,
And with Anderson they rode away.

From Clifton Forge they started,
And their spirits were running high,
As they stopped at Iron Gate and waited,
Till old Number Nine went by.

On the main line once more they started,
Down the James River so dark and drear;
And they gave no thought to the danger,
Or the death that was waiting so near.

They were gay and they joked with each other,
As they sped on their way side by side;
And the old engine rocked as she traveled,
Through the night on that last fatal ride.

In an instant the story was ended,
On her side in that cold river bed;
With poor Harry Lyle in the cabin,
With a deep fatal wound in his head.

Railroad men, you should all take warning,
From the fate that befell this young man;
Don't forget that the step is a short one,
From this earth to that sweet Promised Land.

Vernon Dalhart

The wreck occurred between 8:30 and 9:00 P.M. on January 3, 1925, on the James River Division of the C & O, eastbound out of Clifton Forge.[1] The night was bitter cold, and the ground was snow covered. About seven miles east of Clifton Forge the train approached Rock Allen Bluff. Here, around a left curve, a slide had occurred, which the engine's headlamp did not pick up until it was too late. The engine overturned into the James River and most of the cars left the track. Crewman Sydney Dillard found himself still in the cab but submerged in the icy water. Several hoboes who had been riding the cars helped pull him out of the river. They built a fire on the bank for warmth, not realizing that one of the overturned cars held a load of gasoline. The locomotive remained buried in the river for weeks, until special tracks could be laid up to the water's edge in order to extract it. The engineer, Harry G. Lyle, was thirty-nine years old at the time, and engaged to be married in a few weeks.

"The Wreck of the 1256" was copyrighted by Carson J. Robison on July 27, 1925, with words and music credited to Carlos B. McAfee, one of the many pseudonyms Robison used (E 617763). On June 22 Vernon Dalhart had recorded it for Columbia, and it was released late that year. Several more recordings by Dalhart followed in the next few months.

How Carson Robison learned about the accident is not clear; I have not found any contemporary newspaper accounts of it, nor have I found an ICC accident investigation report. A relative of the engineer wrote me that the song was written by John Van Buren of Selma, Virginia.[2] Whether Van Buren wrote the words to Robison's song or composed a completely independent ballad account is not certain. However, there is no reason to suspect that Robison would have accepted a poem from someone else and not given him due credit. Furthermore, "The Wreck of the 1256" is a perfect example of Robison's admitted formula for composing his tragedy ballads:

> First I read all the newspaper stories of, say, a disaster. Then I get to work on the old typewriter. There's a formula, of course. You start by painting everything in gay colors—"the folks were all happy and gay" stuff. That's sure fire. Then you ring [*sic*] in the tragedy—make it as morbid and gruesome as you can. Then you wind up with a moral. . . . These folks for whom we write and sing are finicky. They know the formula they like and they want no changes or improvements. . . . Take the story of The Wreck of the 12:56, which has sold half a million and is still going strong. There's a simple story and a simple tune. There are only sixteen bars of music to the whole thing, repeated over and over.[3]

The version transcribed in this book is Dalhart's Columbia recording, which was the first one made.

NOTES

1. I am indebted to several people for information on the background of this accident. My first lead came in a letter from Frieda Starkey, librarian of the Chas. P. Jones Memorial Library of Covington, Virginia (Feb. 27, 1968). Miss Starkey forwarded to me the account of the accident given her by Mrs. Harry G. Lyle of Clifton Forge, Virginia, whose husband is a cousin of the engineer, Harry Lyle, mentioned in the ballad. Further details were provided by Pick Temple of Potomac, Maryland, and Paul Shue, of Staunton, Virginia, both long-time railroad song enthusiasts. Shue had interviewed Sydney Dillard, the surviving crewman, several years earlier and had prepared a radio program on the accident for his regular series on train songs aired on Staunton's WTON. See Temple to Cohen, Oct. 13, 1970; taped copy of radio program received from Shue, Sept., 1972.

2. Mrs. Harry G. Lyle to Cohen, Apr., 1968.

3. Quoted by Hugh Leamy in "Now Come All You Good People," *Collier's*, Nov. 2, 1929, pp. 20, 58–59; reprinted by Linnell Gentry, *A History and Encyclopedia of Country, Western, and Gospel Music*, 2d ed. (Nashville: Clairmont Publishing Corp., 1969), pp. 6–13.

REFERENCES

A. "The Wreck of the 1256 (on the Main Line of the C & O)," by Vernon Dalhart. Dalhart, vocal, harmonica, and jew's-harp; Carson Robison, guitar. Recorded on June 22, 1925 (Columbia master 140708-1), in New York City. Released on Columbia 15034-D (as by Al Craver) in July, 1925. Reissued on Vetco LP 103: *Songs of the Railroad*. First recording of the song, and the version transcribed here.

B. Anderson, R. (discussion only)
   Burton & Manning (1967), 72

C. QDUM-ARTHUR MSS:
   78

D. Jeff Calhoun (pseudonym)—Grey Gull 4226
   Vernon Dalhart—Victor 19812
   —Edison 51620, Edison 5127 (cylinder); Mark56 794: *First Recorded Railroad Songs*
   —Gennett 3158, Challenge 231, Challenge 502, Silvertone 3812, Buddy 8012
   —Silvertone 8142, Supertone 9239
   —Cameo 869
   Curly Fox and Texas Ruby—King 716; King LP 840; King LP 869: *Railroad Songs*
   Guy Massey (Vernon Dalhart pseudonym)—Pathé 32139, Perfect 12218

Vernon Dalhart. Courtesy of the John Edwards Memorial Foundation, UCLA.

The Freight Wreck at Altoona/The Wreck of the 1262

THE ALTOONA FREIGHT WRECK

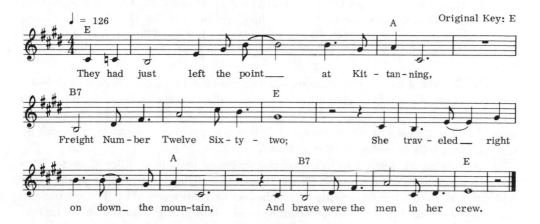

They had just left the point at Kittanning,
Freight Number Twelve Sixty-two;
She traveled right on down the mountain,
And brave were the men in her crew.

The engineer pulled at the whistle,
For the brakes wouldn't work when applied;
The brakeman climbed out on the car top,
For he knew what that whistle had cried.

With all of the strength that God gave him,
He tightened [?tied in] the brakes with a prayer;
But she kept right on down the mountain,
Her whistle was piercing the air.

She traveled at sixty an hour,
Gaining speed every foot of the way;
And then in a crash it was over,
And there on the track the freight lay.

They were found at their post in the wreckage,
Both had done their duty so well;
The engineer still held the whistle,
And the fireman still hung to the bell.

Riley Puckett

The wreck described in this ballad befell the eastbound freight train VL-4 hauled by engine 1282 on the morning of November 29, 1925, on the Pennsylvania Railroad. The train had reached a block station 3.3 miles from Altoona, Pennsylvania, and started down the grade, when it was stalled by an application of the brakes for some reason that was never determined. The engineer started the train up without checking that the air-brake system was working properly, and he never regained control. The train was derailed after it reached an estimated speed of sixty miles an hour on a downhill grade. The engineman and fireman were killed; most of the cars were demolished.[1]

The song about this disaster was copyrighted on January 30, 1926 (E 634286), by Carson Robison, who evidently set to music the words of Fred Tait-Douglas. I have been unable to learn anything about the life or career of this lyricist. The earliest recording of the ballad was made by Vernon Dalhart for Columbia on January 15, 1926, and released in March.

The melody of this ballad is more engaging than the preceding three that Robison produced, but it has not been significantly more popular. The song is less definitely tied to a specific incident, since names of individuals involved are not given. The engineer is praised as a brave man, as the train-wreck ballad genre normally requires, although he himself was partly to blame for the accident.

The version transcribed in this book was recorded in 1935 by Riley Puckett. Born near Alpharetta, Georgia, in 1894, Puckett was one of the most popular of the early hillbilly performers, highly regarded by audiences and musicians alike. His singing and guitar playing constituted the backbone of the music of the greatly admired Skillet Lickers string band. Though practically blind from birth, Puckett was always able to make his living by his music—first at dances, at parties, and on street corners, and later on radio, at fiddle conventions, and on records. He was featured on more than two hundred recordings between 1924 and 1941, apart from his work with the Skillet Lickers.[2]

Though he was able to read Braille, Puckett learned most of his songs from other singers and from recordings. He probably learned "Altoona Freight Wreck" from one of Dalhart's several discs. However, his version shortened the original nine stanzas to five and introduced one further significant textual change (in his last stanza). For comparison, here is the text as it appeared in Dalhart and Robison's song folio.

> She just left the point at Kittanning,
> The freight number Twelve Sixty Two;
> And on down the mountain she traveled,
> And brave were the men in her crew.
>
> The engineer pulled at the whistle,
> For the brakes wouldn't work when applied;
> And the brakeman climbed out on the car tops,
> For he knew what the whistle had cried.
>
> With all of the strength that God gave him,
> He tightened the brakes with a prayer;
> But the train kept right on down the mountain,
> And her whistle was piercing the air.
>
> And on down the grade she went racing,
> She sped like a demon from Hell;
> With the engineer blowing the whistle,
> And the fireman was ringing the bell.
>
> She traveled at sixty an hour,
> Gaining speed every foot of the way;

Riley Puckett (*center*), with Lowe Stokes (*left*) and Gid Tanner. Courtesy of the John Edwards Memorial Foundation, UCLA.

And then with a crash it was over,
And there on the track the freight lay.

The engine was broken to pieces,
The freight cars were thrown far and near;
And a mile up the track lay the wreckage,
The worst wreck in many a year.

It's not the amount of the damage,
Or the value of what it all cost;
It's the sad tale that came from the cabin,
Where the lives of two brave men were lost.

They were found at their posts in the wreckage,
They died when the engine had fell;
The engineer still held the whistle,
And the fireman still hung to the bell.

This story is told of a freight train,
And it should be a warning to all;
You should be prepared every minute,
For you cannot tell when He'll call.

The few later versions were based either on Dalhart's or Puckett's recordings, with one exception. The version by Grant Rogers was his own recomposition of the Robison song, written in about 1960. Rogers's song consists of Robison's first and last stanzas separated by four new and quite unfactual stanzas.

NOTES

1. *Summary of Accident Investigation Reports, No. 26, October-December 1925* (Washington, D.C.: Interstate Commerce Commission, Bureau of Safety, 1926), p. 42. See also *New York Times*, Nov. 30, 1925, p. 4.

2. For further biographical information on Puckett, see Norm Cohen, "The Skillet Lickers," *JAF*, 78 (July-Sept., 1965), 229, and "Riley Puckett: King of the Hillbillies," *JEMFQ*, 12 (Winter, 1976), 175–84. For more discographic data, see *Riley Puckett (1894–1946): Discography*, compiled by John Larsen, Tony Russell, and Richard Weize (Bremen: Archiv für Populäre Musik, 1977).

REFERENCES

A. "The Freight Wreck at Altoona," by Vernon Dalhart. Dalhart, vocal, harmonica, and jew's-harp; guitar and violin, probably by Carson Robison and Murray Kellner, respectively. Recorded Jan. 15, 1926 (Columbia master 141496-2), in New York City. Released on Columbia 15065-D (as by Al Craver) on Mar. 20, 1926. First recording of the song.

"Altoona Freight Wreck," by Riley Puckett. Vocal and guitar. Recorded Sept. 29, 1937 (Decca master 62631), in New York City. Released on Decca 5455. This version is transcribed here.

B. Burton & Manning (1967), 84
Cambiaire, 107   "The Wreck at Latona"
Dalhart & Robison, 6
Family Herald, 53 (references only)
Laws, 271 (dG 38) (discussion only)
Layne, 7
RRM, 5 (June, 1931), 478

D. Jeff Calhoun (Vernon Dalhart pseudonym)—Grey Gull 4172 "Freight Wreck at Altoona"
Vernon Dalhart—Victor 19999 "Freight Wreck at Altoona"
—Vocalion 15283, Vocalion 5090   "The Altoona Wreck"
—OKeh 40581   "Altoona Freight Wreck"

—Edison 51718, Edison 5122 (cylinder) "Freight Wreck at Altoona"
—Gennett 3260, Challenge 156, Challenge 317, Champion 15076, Herwin 75524, Buddy 8012   "Freight Wreck at Altoona"
—Pathé 32162, Perfect 12241 "Altoona Freight Wreck"
—Cameo 8218, Romeo 598, Lincoln 2823   "Altoona Freight Wreck"
—Banner 1741, Domino 3712 (some issued as by Bob White), Regal 8051, Conqueror 7070, Silvertone 2704, Paramount 3047, Broadway 8062, Apex (Canada) 8499   "Freight Wreck at Altoona"
Red River Dave (McEnery)—Musicraft 288 (in album 60: *Authentic Hillbilly Ballads*)   "Altoona Freight Wreck"

E. Lester Flatt, Earl Scruggs, and the Foggy Mountain Boys—Columbia CL 2686/CS 9486: *Hear the Whistles Blow* "Train 1262"
Grant Rogers—Folk-Legacy FSA 27: *Grant Rogers of Walton, New York* "Freight #1262"

F. LC AFS:

Grant Rogers—AFS 12309 B8   "The Wreck at Kittanning"

The Wreck of the *Royal Palm*

THE WRECK OF THE *ROYAL PALM* EXPRESS

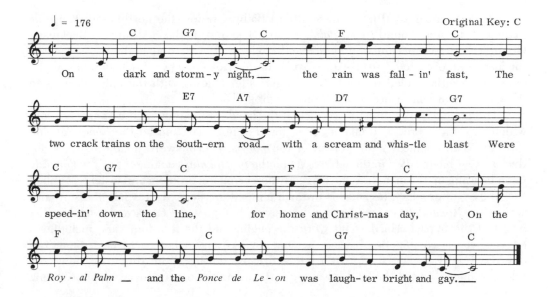

On a dark and stormy night, the rain was fallin' fast,
The two crack trains on the Southern road with a scream and whistle blast
Were speedin' down the line, for home and Christmas day,
On the *Royal Palm* and the *Ponce de Leon* was laughter bright and gay.

Then comin' 'round the curve at forty miles an hour,
The *Royal Palm* was makin' time amid the drenchin' shower;
There come a mighty crash, the two great engines met,
And in the minds of those who live is a scene they can't forget.

It was an awful sight, amidst the pouring rain,
The dead and dyin' lyin' there beneath that mighty train;
No tongue can ever tell, no pen can ever write,
No one will know but those who saw the horrors of that night.

On board the two great trains the folks were bright and gay,
When like a flash the Master called; they had no time to pray;
Then in a moment's time, the awful work was done,
And many souls that fatal night had made their final run.

There's many a saddened home since that sad Christmas day,
Whose loved ones never will return to drive the gloom away;
They were on the *Royal Palm* as she sped across the state,
Without a single warnin' cry they went to meet their fate.

We are on the road of life, and like the railroad man,
We ought to do our best to make the station if we can;

Then let us all take care, and keep our orders straight,
For if we get our orders mixed we'll surely be too late.

Al Craver (Vernon Dalhart)

On December 23, 1926, two Southern Railway trains, the northbound *Ponce de Leon* and the southbound *Royal Palm*, collided just outside the city limits of Rockmart, Georgia. Nineteen persons were killed and 123 injured. According to the ICC's analysis, the accident occurred because the "road foreman of engines who had relieved the engineman either failed to have a thorough understanding with the engineman as to the contents of a meet order or else he forgot it."[1]

The blame for the disaster was laid at the hands of the crew of the *Ponce de Leon*, which was under orders to take a siding south of Rockmart and let the *Royal Palm* on through. The engineer and fireman of the *Ponce de Leon* were unable to speak for themselves, having died in the wreck. When the *Royal Palm*'s engineer saw the *Ponce de Leon* heading up the main line, he correctly perceived the problem and instantly applied the brakes, after which he and his fireman jumped to safety. As a result of his prompt action, the *Royal Palm* escaped with relatively slight injury, the *Ponce de Leon* taking the brunt of the impact. Hardest hit were the engine and the first four cars, including a baggage car, a "combination baggage car and negro coach," a day coach, and a diner. The day coach was thrown up into the air and came down on the diner, crushing and telescoping it. Most of the fatalities were sustained in the diner, the accident occurring at 6:40 P.M.

As the engineer rolled down the embankment, he later recalled, he "heard the most awful noise I ever heard. It was the two trains coming together. I will never forget it. It sounded like the heavens had split open. I don't want to hear anything like it again."[2]

While memories of the disaster were still fresh, the Reverend Andrew Jenkins of Atlanta composed this ballad. Blind Andy Jenkins, an evangelist/newsboy, was a prolific writer of ballads and religious pieces, many of which have found their way into oral tradition, in addition to "The Wreck of the *Royal Palm*." This volume includes another of his compositions, "Ben Dewberry's Final Run." His career has been discussed elsewhere.[3]

Although Polk C. Brockman, OKeh's A & R man in the Atlanta area who worked with Jenkins, did not copyright the ballad in Jenkins's name until February 14, 1927 (E 653939; renewed Feb. 19, 1954, R 125910), Vernon Dalhart had already recorded it as early as January 14 for Columbia. This was not irregular: Brockman probably did not trouble to send in the copyright forms and fee until he knew that Columbia would actually issue the record (it was released Feb. 20). Thus, record buyers were able to purchase a ballad describing a wreck that had occurred less than two months earlier—an indication of how the hillbilly record industry was learning to gear itself to the rapid preparation and distribution of phonograph discs describing events that were still of current interest. Dalhart's Columbia recording is the version transcribed in this book. Some thirty-six thousand copies of it were sold.

Jenkins's words make an interesting contrast with the two ballads by C. C. Meeks given earlier in this chapter and with the one by Robison apparently modeled after Meeks's songs. Meeks, himself a railroadman, focuses attention on the engineer, fireman, and other trainmen, evoking listeners' sympathy by pointing out the tragedies in their lives and the lives of their families. The morals are directed to other railroadmen and their kin to be prepared for such accidents. On the other hand, Jenkins's ballad is concerned only with the tragedies of the passengers; there is no mention of railroadmen save in the metaphoric sense of the ultimate stanza. In this regard, the Jenkins ballad is unlike any of the other pieces of this chapter.

The most curious fact about Jenkins's ballad is the identification, both in the title and in the text, of the *Royal Palm* as the train principally involved in the tragedy, when in fact there were only slight injuries to that train and its passengers and crew; all the fatalities and serious injuries were to those on the *Ponce de Leon*.

NOTES

1. *Summary of Accident Investigation Reports, No. 33: Condensed Statement of Accidents Investigated during the Year Ended Dec. 31, 1926* (Washington, D.C.: Interstate Commerce Commission, Bureau of Safety, 1927), p. 47. Other information is taken from the *Atlanta Journal*, Dec. 29, 1926. See also Broadus McAfee, "Rockmart, Georgia Site of a Tragic Train Wreck, December 23, 1926," *North West Georgia Historical and Genealogical Society*, 4, no. 3 (July, 1972), 10–12.

2. *Atlanta Journal*, Dec. 24, 1926.

3. See, e.g., D. K. Wilgus, "The Rationalistic Approach," in *Folksong and Folksong Scholarship* (Dallas: Southern Methodist University Press, 1964), pp. 29–39, and Archie Green, *Only a Miner* (Urbana: University of Illinois Press, 1972), pp. 123–25.

REFERENCES

A. The Wreck of the *Royal Palm* Express," by Vernon Dalhart. Dalhart, vocal and harmonica; guitar and violin, probably by Carson Robison and Murray Kellner, respectively. Recorded Jan. 14, 1927 (Columbia master 143309-2), in New York City. Released on Columbia 15121-D (as by Al Craver) on Feb. 20, 1927. Reissued on Vetco LP 103: *Songs of the Railroad*. First recording and version transcribed here.

B. Brown II, 521
Emrich (1974), 662
Family Herald, 56 (reference only)
Green (1968) (discussion only)
Hamlins Singing Cowboy, 36
Laws, 273 (dG 51)
Peterson, 36–37
RRM, 6 (Sept., 1931), 316

D. Vernon Dalhart—Brunswick 101, Brunswick 3470, Vocalion 5138, Supertone 2001
—OKeh 45086

—Victor 20528
—Gennett 6051, Champion 15232, Challenge 243, Herwin 75540, Silvertone 5005, Silvertone 25005, Silvertone 8139, Supertone 9236, Vocalion (Australia) XA18019
—Cameo 1143, Romeo 350, Varsity 5059
—Pathé 32380, Perfect 12459
—Banner 1957, Domino 3927, Regal 8280, Oriole 860 (as by Frank Evans), Paramount 3016, Broadway 8050, Domino (Canada) 21464, Microphone (Canada) 22169, Lucky Strike (Canada) 24094
Frank Luther—Grey Gull 4200

E. Joe Glazer—Collector 1925: *Union Train*
Spark Gap Wonder Boys—Rounder 0002: *"Cluck Old Hen"*
Clarence Wyatt—Library of Congress Archive of Folk Song L61: *Railroad Songs and Ballads*

F. LC AFS:
Albert Vergasons—AFS 11688 A37

The Wreck of the Virginian Number Three

THE WRECK OF THE VIRGINIAN

*Chords supplied by the music editor.

Come all you brave, bold railroad men and listen while I tell,
The fate of E. G. Aldrich, a good man we all loved well;
This man was running on a road known as Virginian line,
He was a faithful engineer and pulled his train on time.

He was the oldest on the road, we always called him Dad,
He loved his engine very much, he was the best we've had;
Frank O'Neal was his fireman, he was faithful, true, and brave,
He stayed with Dad, he died with Dad, and filled a new-made grave.

It was a bright spring morning on the twenty-fourth of May,
The train crew was at Roanoke, they were feeling fine and gay;
Train Number Three had left Roanoke en route for Huntington,
These poor men did not know that they were making their last run.

Dad pulled his train, a pleasing smile on his bright face did beam,
He did not have to grumble, Frank sure kept him lots of steam;
At eleven-fifty-two that day they'd just left Ingleside,
An eastbound freight crushed into them, they took their farewell ride.

It seems that all good engineers to duty always sticks,
Dad entered into service in the year nineteen and six;
He did not have to work to live, they begged him to retire,
But Dad would not give his consent, to run was his desire.

Dear ladies, if your husband runs an engine on the line,
You may expect a message of his death most any time;
All railroad men should live for God and always faithful be,
Like Dad and Frank, they soon may pass into eternity.

Blind Alfred Reed

At 11:53 A.M. on May 24, 1927, at Ingleside, West Virginia, two Virginian Railway trains, a passenger and a freight, collided head-to-end, killing two and injuring twenty-nine. The accident was due to the passenger train crew's failure to obey a meet order.[1] The crew of the electric freight escaped serious injury, but engineer "Dad" Aldrich and fireman Frank O'Neal of the passenger train Number Three were scalded to death by steam from the bursted pipes. Aldrich had been with the railway since 1906 and lived not far from the Virginian's Roanoke yard office. It was said that he was financially able to retire, but the love of his engine kept him on active duty.[2]

Three separate ballad accounts of this accident were written and recorded by hillbilly musicians in 1927; two show a slender indication of having entered folk tradition.[3] The version transcribed above is musically the best of the three. Blind Alfred Reed, who probably composed the song, recorded it for Victor in Bristol, Tennessee, on July 28. Reed, a fiddler/singer born in Floyd, Virginia, in 1880, lived most of his life in West Virginia within thirty or forty miles of Ingleside. He recorded twenty-one songs for Victor between 1927 and 1929, many of which he wrote, with the help of his wife, Nettie. Reed played violin at numerous county fairs and in churches, and in later years he was a Methodist minister. "The Wreck of the Virginian" was the first song he recorded.[4] He wrote it shortly after the wreck, basing his information on radio news broadcasts and on newspaper accounts that his wife read to him. Not long after his record was issued, Victor withdrew it from the catalog at the request of the Virginian Railway.[5]

On July 26, Roy Harvey and the North Carolina Ramblers recorded their own ballad about the accident for Columbia. (See the discussion of "Bill Mason" for biographical data on Harvey). The third ballad was written by the Reverend John McGhee of Huntington, West Virginia, and recorded for the Starr Piano Company on December 27 of the same year.

Reed's ballad account, copyrighted September 15, 1927 (E 671400), is essentially correct as far as the details of the accident go. However, the overall impression the ballad leaves is that Aldrich and O'Neal, faithful and brave railroadmen, did their duty to the last and were innocent of the tragedy that befell them. Roy Harvey, born in Monroe County, West Virginia, was a railroader on the Virginian Railway for twelve years until he left during the Virginian Strike of 1923. Stanzas 5, 6, and 8 of his ballad, which was copyrighted April 14, 1928 (E 688812), clearly take the railroadmen to task for their negligence, and make that irresponsibility the point of the moral to all railroadmen. Since it is interesting to compare the three accounts of the accident, Roy Harvey's text and that of John McGhee are printed below.

McGhee's song, which was never copyrighted, has been recovered once by a folklorist. It is surprising that Reed's beautifully haunting melody, accompanied by his archaic fiddling, did not leave more of an impact on tradition. Perhaps the disc was withdrawn from circulation too soon for that. It is even more surprising that the North Carolina Ramblers, one of the most popular string bands in the Southeast, did not contribute their rendition to oral folk tradition. Their disc passed ten thousand sales, a typical number for hillbilly records of that period. Perhaps more intensive fieldwork in that part of the country will one day turn up evidence that the song has passed into tradition. This is how Roy Harvey sang it:

> On one Thursday morning, in the latter part of May,
> Old Number Three left Roanoke station, it was on their fatal day.
>
> The engineer's name was Aldrich, happy he always did feel,
> There with his young, cheerful fireman, his name was Frank O'Neal.
>
> Up through the Valley of Virginia, over Allegheny Mountains so high;
> But little did the men ever think of that day in the cab they would die.
>
> Dad Aldrich said to his fireman, who was riding by his side,
> "For twenty long years I've pulled this run, with Two Hundred and
>   Twelve, my pride."
>
> At Northcross they received their orders, eight-thirty-one it had to be;
> For they were to take a siding, and meet eastbound Hundred and Three.
>
> But they overlooked this order, at the station called Ingleside;
> For they failed to take a siding, side by side in the cab they both died.
>
> The engine climbed up on the motor, but she did not overturn;
> With all of the steam pipes broken, two hundred pounds, they did burn.
>
> Now railroad men, take this warning, heed your orders well;
> For how soon the Lord may call you, no human mind can tell.

Finally, here is the Reverend John McGhee's version:

> Just after the dawn of the morning, in the beautiful month of May,
> A farewell kiss had been planted on the cheeks of one who was brave.
>
> The morning was fresh in its glory, the sunlight was piercing the leaves,
> As they plunged their way through the mountains with Virginian Train
>   Number Three.
>
> The soft winds were laden with perfume, which swept o'er the green valley
>   wide;
> And onward they rushed toward the peril which awaits them at Ingleside.
>
> Some time at the dead hour of midnight, some prayers may be whispered
>   at home;
> For someone far out in the darkness may be crushed and dying alone.
>
> Jack Aldrich was proud of his engine, and fireman O'Neal of his run;
> For little they thought of approaching their final and last setting sun.
>
> Together they wended the mountains, together they watched for the slides;
> Together they looked for obstructions, together they perished and died.
>
> It's ever the same with the trainmen, their lives are in danger, we know;
> Through rain and through sleet and through darkness, wherever they're
>   called they must go.

NOTES

1. *Summary of Accident Investigation Reports, No. 34: Condensed Statement of Accidents Investigated during the Year Ended Dec. 31, 1927* (Washington, D.C.: Interstate Commerce Commission, Bureau of Safety, 1928), p. 41.

2. H. Reid, *The Virginian Railway* (Milwaukee: Kalmbach Publications, 1961), p. 197.

3. After RCA Victor LPV-532: *The Railroad in Folksong* was issued, Archie Green, who wrote liner notes for the album, received a letter from an anthropologist in California whose wife had learned the Reed ballad in the Bronx, ca. 1950, from a local fiddler who had lived in the southern mountains.

4. For further information see the Rounder Collective, "The Life of Blind Alfred Reed" *JEMFQ*, 23 (Autumn, 1971), 113–15, reprinted in the brochure notes to Rounder 1001: *How Can a Poor Man Stand Such Times and Live?*, a reissue LP of recordings by Reed, and in *Goldenseal*, 2 (Jan.-Mar., 1976), 20–22.

5. Brad McCuen of RCA Victor to Archie Green, Aug. 17, 1964.

REFERENCES

A. The Wreck of the Virginian #3," by Roy Harvey with the North Carolina Ramblers. Harvey, vocal and guitar; Charlie Poole, banjo; Posey Rorer, violin. Recorded July 26, 1927 (Columbia master 144520), probably in New York City. Released on Columbia 15174-D on Sept. 20, 1927.

"The Wreck of the Virginian Train No. 3," by John McGhee. Vocal, guitar, and harmonica. Recorded ca. Dec. 30, 1927 (Starr master GE-13330), in Chicago. Released on Champion 15467 (as by John Hutchens) on May 1, 1928; on Challenge 389 (as by George Holden); on Bell 1167 (as by Henry Graham); on Supertone 9257 (as by Jesse Oakley); and on Silvertone 8163 (as by Jesse Oakley).

"The Wreck of the Virginian," by Blind Alfred Reed. Vocal and violin. Recorded July 28, 1927 (Victor master 39725-2), in Bristol, Tenn. Released on Victor 20836, ca. Sept., 1927. Reissued on RCA Victor LPV 532: *The Railroad in Folksong*; and on County 502: *A Collection of Mountain Ballads*. This version is transcribed here.

B. Brunvand, 239 (title only; McGhee's song)

The Wreck of Number Four

THE WRECK OF NO. 4 AND DEATH OF JOHN DAILY

Come railroad men and listen to me,
A story you will hear,
Of a wreck on the line of the old L and E,
And the death of a brave engineer.

John Dailey was the engineer's name,
He rode through many, many years;
But little did he think on that fatal day,
That death was waiting so near.

Now from Neon old Number Four sped,
On her way with passengers and crew;
John Dailey was needed in the cab
As though he would pull her through.

The train left the rail as she rambled along,
And beneath the cart he lay;
He was pulled from the wreck by his fireman so true,
And was dead in an instant, they say.

Death came to him as an unseen foe,
In a moment he passed away;
As the train rambled on and a train rambled too
All seemed to be happy and gay.

We never know when death is near,
So a warning we should take
From the wreck on the line of the old L and E,
And engineer Dailey's fate.

Green Bailey

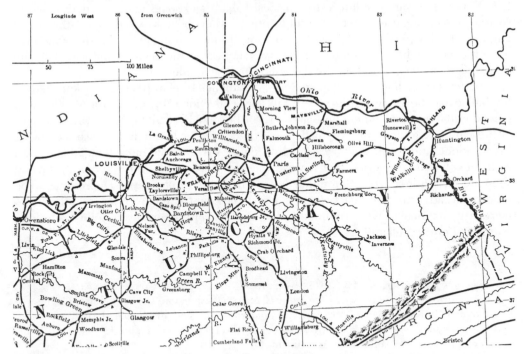

Shortline roads in eastern Kentucky. Author's Collection.

The history of railroading is filled with accounts of shortline roads whose existence, both spatially and temporally, was very limited. The Lexington and Eastern was brought into existence in October, 1894, for the purpose of reorganizing the older (chartered in 1872) Kentucky Union Railway. In November, 1910, the Louisville and Nashville Railroad purchased the stock of the L & E, acquiring rights to its ninety-three miles of track between Lexington and Jackson, Kentucky; but not until October, 1915, was the L & E actually transferred over to L & N hands.[1] Thus by the time of the accident recounted in "The Wreck of Number Four," although the ballad places the event on the L & E, that railroad had ceased to exist by that name almost two decades earlier. The L & E was a local company, however, regarded favorably by eastern Kentuckians as it wound in and out of the coal country, and the name stuck until the line was finally discontinued in the 1930s.

On December 31, 1928, at eleven o'clock in the morning, passenger train Number Four was derailed at Torrent, Kentucky, on the Eastern Kentucky Divison line running between Lexington and Neon via Winchester and Ravenna. The main line was blocked because of a freight derailment earlier that day, so Number Four was routed over the branch through Torrent to Lexington. Rounding a sharp curve, the engine left the rails and overturned. Engineer John Dailey, fifty years old, leaped from the engine, but his head struck a rock and he was killed—the only injury resulting from the accident. Dailey had been with the L & N for thirty years.[2]

On August 29, 1929, Green Bailey, then living in Powell County, recorded his composition "The Wreck of No. 4 and the Death of John Daily [sic]" for the Starr Piano Company's Gennett Record Division in Richmond, Indiana. Bailey was born in Owsley County, Kentucky, in 1900, and taught school beginning in 1921 in the region where the

L & E ran. He was very interested in local ballads and songs and recorded or wrote several concerning events in the part of Kentucky where he was reared.[3] His father knew engineer Dailey personally.[4] Details in the fourth stanza of Bailey's song are at variance with the facts I have recounted above, as taken from the account published in the *Louisville Courier-Journal* on the day following the accident.

Bailey's recording was issued on Sears's Challenge label in 1930. To my knowledge, his ballad has never appeared in any folksong collection. However, Asa Martin, who played guitar accompaniment on Bailey's recording and lived all his life in the same part of the country, told me that the ballad was quite popular locally in the years following the accident, and is still sung occasionally.[5] Bailey's record sold more than 5,800 copies in the twelve-month period that it was available (April, 1930–April, 1931)—not a bad showing for a minor artist on a minor label during the throes of the Depression.[6] The record was advertised in Sears catalogs across the country; one wonders whether sales were truly national or were confined to the locale where the names of John Dailey and Number Four were familiar.

NOTES

1. *Kentucky Engineer*, 7 (May, 1945), 3–12; *RRM*, May, 1972, p. 57.
2. *Summary of Accident Investigation Reports, No. 38* (Washington, D.C.: Interstate Commerce Commission, Bureau of Safety, 1929), p. 40; *Louisville Courier-Journal*, Jan. 1, 1929.
3. Green Bailey, interviewed by Archie Green and Norm Cohen in Trapp, Ky., May 27, 1969.
4. Telephone conversation with Asa Martin, Oct. 7, 1969.
5. Ibid.
6. Royalty statements in the possession of Doc Roberts.

REFERENCES

A. "The Wreck of No. 4 and the Death of John Daily," by Green Bailey. Bailey, vocal; Doc Roberts, mandolin; Asa Martin, guitar. Recorded Aug. 29, 1929 (Starr master GE-15532), in Richmond, Ind. Released on Challenge 425 (as by Dick Bell) in 1930.

Green Bailey. Courtesy of Archie Green.

The True and Trembling Brakeman

TRUE AND TREMBLING BRAKEMAN

Listen now while I tell you
Of a story you do not know;
Of a true and trembling brakeman,
And to heaven he did go.

Do you see that train a-coming,
Oh, it's [?through] old Ninety-nine;
Oh, she's puffing and a-blowing,
For you know she is behind.

See that true and trembling brakeman,
As he signals to the cab;
There is but one chance for him,
And that chance is to grab.

See that true and trembling brakeman,
As the cars go rushing by;
If he miss that yellow freight car,
He is almost sure to die.

See that true and trembling brakeman,
As he falls beneath the train;
He had not one moment's warning,
Before he fell beneath the train.

See that brave young engineerman,
At the age of twenty-one;
Stepping down from upon his engine,
Crying, "Now what have I done!

"Is it true I killed a brakeman,
Is it true that he is dying?
Lord, you know I tried to save him,
But I could not stop in time."

See the car wheels rolling o'er him,
O'er his mingled body 'n' head;

See his sister bending o'er him,
Crying, "Brother, are you dead?"

Sighing, "Sister, yes, I'm dying,
Going to a better shore;
Oh, my body's on a pathway,
I can never see no more.

"Sister, when you see my brother,
These few words to him I send;
Tell him never to venture braking,
If he does, his life will end."

These few words were sadly spoken,
Folding his arms across his breast;
And his heart now ceased beating,
And his eyes were closed in death.

Aulton Ray

In an earlier era of railroading, "brakies" ran along the tops of boxcars to strain at hand-brakes, or climbed down between the rocking cars to wrestle with the old link-and-pin couplers. Fingers and limbs were expendable then, and the life of such a brakeman was cheaper than the cost of installing more modern, safer equipment. "The True and Trembling Brakeman" would seem to be a fictional account of such a brakeman falling from a train to his death. However, the origins of our railroad songs are seldom established with such simple one-sentence pronouncements.

Although it is not apparent from the text transcribed in this book, some versions of the song place the action on a railroad running out of a coal mine. Orville Jenks, a local mining poet of West Virginia, told George Korson that he himself composed the song about an incident he had witnessed in 1915. Just what older material, if any, Jenks used as a model for his song we do not know; often folk composers feel justified in claiming authorship of a song if they have simply fashioned it out of fragments of diverse older songs. Most of the versions of "The True and Trembling Brakeman" recovered do not refer to mining, however; since there is no evidence for the song's appearance on paper or recording prior to 1927, we cannot say whether the railroad version derived from or preceded the more particularized mining version. In Jenks's text, titled "The Dying Mine Brakeman," as well as in some of the others, the engineerman is referred to as a motorman, implying that he was running an electrified train. This in itself does not preclude the possibility of the priority of the railroad version, since electric locomotives were introduced as early as 1895. One of the variants in the Western Kentucky Folklore Archive was contributed by a man who claimed it was written by his sister-in-law about the death of her husband at a Harlan County mine in 1938. The appearance of multiple claims of authorship indicates that the song, by its nature, is readily appropriated; thus each individual claim is somewhat weakened in the absence of incontrovertible evidence one way or another.

Six versions of the ballad were recorded on hillbilly discs between 1927 and 1938. The earliest, and the one transcribed in this book, was made by Aulton Ray in April, 1927, for the Starr Piano Company. Ray's title was used by three other hillbilly recording artists: Cliff Carlisle, Paul Mason, and Bradley Kincaid. Carlisle's and Mason's texts are very similar to Ray's, and they may have been learned from Ray's record. Carlisle was not positive but thought he might have been given the song by his A & R man, William R. Calaway (who could have taken it from Ray's record).[1] Kincaid learned his version from his uncle;[2] it is remarkably close to the version printed by Randolph, and may have been the source of the latter. The Carter Family recorded the only mining version of the six. They learned the song in southwestern Virginia; it was A. P. Carter's custom to collect material that he could rework for recording purposes, and their "Reckless Motorman" was learned on such a trip in 1937 or 1938.[3] It was recorded June 8, 1938, and copyrighted September 28, 1939 (E 205360).

On the basis of some similar lines, it has been suggested that the railroad/mining song was stylistically influenced by a much older piece, "The Dying Californian."[4] The latter, in turn, has been pronounced a derivative of William H. Lytle's poem, "Antony to Cleopatra" ("I am dying, Egypt, dying").[5]

NOTES

1. Cliff Carlisle, interviewed by Archie Green and Eugene Earle in Lexington, Ky., ca. 1960.

2. D. K. Wilgus, liner notes to Bluebonnet BL 112: *Bradley Kincaid—Album No. 4*.

3. Archie Green, brochure notes to Folkways FH 5273: *Tipple, Loom & Rail*, p. 9.

4. See, e.g., *New Lost City Ramblers Song Book*, edited by John Cohen and Mike Seeger (New York: Oak Publications, 1964), p. 108.

5. John H. Cox, *Folk-Songs of the South* (1925; rpt., Hatboro, Pa.: Folklore Associates, 1963), p. 232.

REFERENCES

A. "True and Trembling Brakeman," by Aulton Ray (or "Shine"). Vocal and guitar. Recorded ca. Apr., 1927 (Starr master 12749A), in Richmond, Ind. Released on Gennett 6129 in June, 1927; on Champion 15277 on July 1, 1927; on Challenge 269, Bell 1186 (as by Carl Bunch), Herwin 75552, and Superior 385. First recording of the song, and the version transcribed here.

"Reckless Mortorman," by the Carter Family. Sara and Maybelle Carter, vocals and guitars. Recorded June 8, 1938 (Decca master 64098A), in New York City. Released on Decca 5722. Reissued on Decca DL 4557: *More Favorites by the Carter Family*; Ace of Hearts (England) AH 112: *More Favourites by the Carter Family*. Best-known version of the song.

B. Carlisle, I., 93–94   "Dying Brakeman"
Crabtree, 116 (2 texts)
Cumberland Mountain Folks   "The Tragic Motorman"
Family Herald, 53 (reference only)
Green (1966), 9 (discussion)

Kincaid (1932), 28
Korson, 120 (discussion); 246; 447 (discussion)
Laws, 217 (G 11) (discussion only)
O'Day   "The Tragic Motorman"
Randolph IV, 146
Wilgus (1964?)

C. WKFA:
Maraget Patterson (Mar., 1959)
Zeb Ricketts (Feb., 1961) (no title)
Mrs. Raymond F. Wetzel (1955) "Reckless Motorman"

D. Cliff Carlisle and Wilbur Ball—Champion 16295 (as by the Lullaby Larkers), Champion 45029, Montgomery Ward 8036, Superior 2669 (as by Otto and Jim Fletcher)
Jess Johnson—Champion 16255
Bradley Kincaid—Conqueror 8091, Melotone 12184, Polk 9064, Vocalion 02683, Panachord (England) 25901, Panachord (Australia) P 12184
Paul Mason—OKeh 45479

Slim Smith—Vocalion 05178   "Lonely
   Little Hobo" (related piece)

E. Orville Jenks—Library of Congress Archive
   of Folk Song L60: *Songs and Ballads of
   the Bituminous Miners*   "Dying
   Mine Brakeman"
   Bradley Kincaid—Bluebonnet BL 112:
   Bradley Kincaid—Album Number Four
   New Lost City Ramblers—Folkways FA
   2395: *The New Lost City Ramblers, Vol. 5*
   Mike Seeger—Folkways FH 5273: *Tipple,
   Loom & Rail*   "The Reckless
   Motorman"

F. LC AFS:
   Arthur and Ralph Addington—AFS 2762
      B1   "Trembling Motorman"
   Lewis Bedingford—AFS 10824 A21
      "Dying Brakeman"
   Alice Begley—AFS 1457 B3   "Just a
      Wild, Reckless Motorman"
   Bradley Browning—AFS 1387 A1
      "True and Faithful Brakeman"
   Bert Martin—AFS 1497 A1
   Mary Trusty—AFS 1395 B1   "Wild and
      Reckless Motorman"

From *Scribner's Monthly*, November, 1888: ". . . an able-bodied brakeman could twist until
sparks shot from the wheels." Author's Collection.

The Little Red Caboose behind the Train (I)

LITTLE RED CABOOSE (I-A)

Conductor he's a fine old man, his hair is turning gray,
He works all day in sunshine and in rain;
And the angels all watch over as he rides upon the cars
In that little red caboose behind the train.

'Twas many years ago that his hair was black as jet,
It's whiter now, his heart has lonesome been;
And I'll tell you all his story, a story that is true,
Of that little red caboose behind the train.

He met her in September, she was so fair and sweet,
Ofttimes together they walked down lovers' lane;
Never was a girl more fair, no sweeter ever rode
In that little red caboose behind the train.

'Twas on a frosty morning, the cold north winds did blow,
The cold had frozen up the windowpane;
They were riding to the city, 'twas on their honeymoon,
In that little red caboose behind the train.

The engineer had ridden that line for many years,
He said the cold was driving him insane;
But he held on to the throttle, his pal was in the rear,
In that little red caboose behind the train.

The fast express came roarin' at ninety miles an hour,
The brakeman tried to see but 'twas in vain;
And his fingers were all frozen; he said a silent prayer
For that little red caboose behind the train.

'Twas after the collision, among the wreckage there,
They found her body crushed amid bloodstain;
Many were the tears and heartaches and many were the prayers
For that little red caboose behind the train.

They placed her in the graveyard beside the railroad track,
He still works in the sunshine and the rain;
And the angels all are sober as he rides all alone,
In that little red caboose behind the train.

Bob Ferguson (Bob Miller)

THE LITTLE RED CABOOSE (I-B)

Bill Jackson was a brakeman on number Fifty-one,
A member of a bold and daring crew;
An old hard working railroad boy, but full of life and fun,
A finer, braver lad you never knew.

His train pulled out of Corbin one wild December night,
Outside was ice and snow and sleet and rain;
The boys were gathered 'round the stove where all was warm and bright
In the little red caboose behind the train.
  Then say a prayer for railroad men when they're out on the run,
  Through the chilly winds and driving rain;
When they're called out you never know how soon they'll come back
  home
  In the little red caboose behind the train.

Dad Mendinhall was pulling old Fifty-one that night,
An old-time engineer with nerve and skill;
He kept his fireman bending down and everything went right,
Until he lost his brakes on Crooked Hill.
Rolling down the mountain they heard his whistle scream—
And what an awful sound that whistle makes!
The old conductor said to them, "Boys, you know what that means;
We've got to scramble out and set the brakes!"
  Chorus:

The runningboards were covered with snow and ice and sleet,
Bill was the first to hit them, on the run
The train went flying round a curve and threw him off his feet
And there before their eyes the deed was done.
They saw him sliding over that rocking boxcar rim,
They saw him when he took that fatal drop;
They clubbed those brakes and tied them down and said a prayer for him
As Fifty-one came jolting to a stop.
  Chorus:

They backed the train and took him in to the old caboose,
The boys they gathered round him one and all;
To do the best they could for him, but saw it was no use,
For poor old Bill had got his final call.
They took him on to Stanford, a message sent ahead,
Filled a poor old mother's heart with pain;
It told her that her only boy was coming to her, dead,
In the little red caboose behind the train.

                                                              John Lair

    Later in this book I discuss some of the other songs that share the title "The Little
Red Caboose behind the Train." Two of the most recent items both concern various
mishaps that befall railroadmen in their duty. They are transcribed here—although they
might also have been placed in chapter 11, "Working on the Railroad," with other
occupational songs and ballads.
    The earlier of the two songs, version I-A, was copyrighted by Bob Miller in 1928
(Mar. 22, 1928, E unp. 687070; renewed Mar. 24, 1955, R 146580) and recorded by him
two years later. It is a touching tale of tragedy that probably had no basis in fact, but was
entirely the creation of its very prolific author. Miller, born in Memphis in 1895, studied

classical music with the intention of becoming a concert pianist, but during the 1920s he turned to writing topical songs and ballads that proved very popular among hillbilly artists and fans. His biggest hit was the 1942 patriotic piece "There's a Star Spangled Banner Waving Somewhere."[1]

Version I-B is completely unrelated. Credited to John Lair and copyrighted in 1935 (Dec. 14, 1935, AA 191331; renewed Jan. 30, 1963, R 311110), this ballad has the earmarks of a tale based on a true event. In the 1930s the L & N Railroad did have a train Number 51 that left Corbin, Kentucky, late at night southbound for Atlanta. However, I have been unable to secure further details.[2]

The text of Miller's song is transcribed from his 1930 recording for Columbia. The Lair text is copied from the WLS folio cited in the bibliography, to my knowledge its first appearance. Since the tune in both cases is the same as that of "Little Red Caboose (III)," transcribed in chapter 11, it is not given here.

NOTES

1. Bob Miller's career has yet to be studied. Brief notes are given in Linnell Gentry, *A History and Encyclopedia of Country, Western, and Gospel Music*, 2d ed. (Nashville: Clairmont Publishing Corp., 1969), p. 490. Also useful is Doron K. Antrim, "Whoop-and-Holler Opera," *Collier's*, Jan. 26, 1946, pp. 18, 85, reprinted in Gentry, *History and Encyclopedia*, pp. 43–47.

2. At my request (relayed to him by Ivan M. Tribe), Reuben Powell asked John Lair what he could recall about the song. Lair remembered no details or dates, though he thought he had written it in the 1910s (Powell to Tribe, July 24, 1974).

REFERENCES

A. "Little Red Caboose," by Bob Ferguson (Bob Miller pseudonym) and his Scalawaggers. Recorded ca. Jan. 30, 1930 (Columbia master 149948), in New York City. Released on Columbia 15616-D on Dec. 15, 1930. First recording of Miller's song; the text is transcribed here.
"The Little Red Caboose," by John Lair. Published in *100 WLS Barn Dance Favorites* (Chicago: M. M. Cole, 1935), pp. 22–23. First appearance of Lair's song; the text is given here.

B. Botkin & Harlow, 455 (transcribed from the singing of Pick Temple) (I-A)
Pack, 12 (I-A)

C. COHEN COLLECTION:
Laura Affolter (letter, June, 1968) (I-A)
Ruth Butcher (letter, June 18, 1968) (I-A)

D. Barney Burnett and Bob Miller's Hinky Dinkers—Brunswick 446, Supertone 2074 (I-A)
Vernon Dalhart—Diva 2893-G, Harmony 893-H (as by Mack Allen), Velvetone 1893-V "Little Red Caboose" (I-A)
Bob Miller—Victor 23693, Montgomery Ward M-4337 (I-A)
—Grey Gull 4286, Van Dyke 74286 (I-A)
Red River Dave (McEnery)—Musicraft 285 (in album 60) (I-A)
Rocky Mountaineers—Columbia (England) FB 1249 (I-A)

The Wreck of the C & O *Sportsman*

THE WRECK OF THE C & O *SPORTSMAN*

Far away on the banks of New River,
While the deep shades of twilight hung low;
In the mountains of ol' West Virginia,
On the line of the old C and O
Down the valley the ol' Forty-seven
Was winding her way 'long the stream;
The drivers were rapidly pounding,
While the engine was trembling with steam.

Haskell held firm to the throttle,
Poor Anderson's fire glowed with red;
And they thought of no local so danger
Down the line on a curve just ahead.
In the dusk of a fair crimson sunset,
Near the path of the old Midland Trail,
'Twas there that the fast flying *Sportsman*
Was wrecked as she swung from the rail.

It was there in the dark shades of twilight,
While the bright crimson sky was aglow,
That Haskell and Anderson of the *Sportsman*
Gave their lives to the old C and O.
Just west of the station called Hawk's Nest,
The engine turned over the fill;
The boys were found down near the river,
By the engine they loved, lying still.

That night there were loved ones awaiting
In Huntington for those boys—in vain;
For God, the supreme crew-caller,
Had called them for another train.
Though the years full of tears may be many,
And the sad broken hearts ever burn,
While they think of the wreck of the *Sportsman*
And the loved ones who'll never return.

John Martin (Roy Harvey)

The C & O Railway may not actually have had a disproportionate number of accidents on its various lines, but it surely holds a record for the number of train-wreck songs it has inspired that have made some recoverable imprint on the hillbilly and folk traditions. The accident described in this ballad was possibly the last to be memorialized in song; it occurred on June 21, 1930, less than three months after the new "name" train, the *Sportsman*, was first inaugurated.

The details recounted in this sad tale are mostly factually correct, as we might expect from a song written less than a year after the event. At nine o'clock on Saturday evening, engineer Homer E. Haskell and fireman Henry C. Anderson, both of Huntington, West Virginia, were bringing the *Sportsman* into Hawk's Nest, a small station in Fayette County, West Virginia. There, the engineer failed to obey a "slow" order issued on account of rough track on a sharp "S" curve, and the engine, pulling several cars with it, flew off the track, to the horror of some spectators who had gathered at the depot to see the train on its way through. By the time rescuers could get to the cab, the engineer was dead; the fireman, badly burned and unconscious, died four and a half hours later. (Both men were found in the cab, contrary to the implication of the third stanza that they were thrown out in the wreck.) Three other persons were injured, but none fatally.[1] Haskell had completed thirty-five years of service that spring.

The ballad was composed by Bernice "Si" Coleman of Princeton, West Virginia, a lifelong railroad employee who also enjoyed a second career as fiddler and hillbilly recording artist. Born in 1898 in Page, West Virginia, not many miles from Hawk's Nest, Coleman's first job was as a brakeman on a dinky that ran from a coal mine two miles to the tipple. He loved the job: "That's how I got railroading in my blood."[2] In the course of forty-four years of service on the N & W Railway, Coleman worked his way up from telegraph operator to station agent to train dispatcher and finally to assistant train-master.

Coleman's musical career began around 1915, when he learned to play guitar, fiddle, and tenor banjo. In about 1928 he headed a band called Si Coleman and His Railroad Ramblers, which played every weekend at dances in the area. In 1931, he recorded eight numbers with his banjo-playing partner, Ernest Branch, for the OKeh label, and twenty-two selections for the Starr Piano Company, with Branch, Roy Harvey, and Jess Johnson. He made no recordings after that year, but has continued his musical activity until the present.[3]

Coleman and another telegraph operator, J. W. Cline, heard about the *Sportsman*'s wreck from other railroadmen and also from newspaper accounts. Coleman, who had for several years admired Vernon Dalhart as a singer and was impressed by his very popular train-wreck recordings, wanted to write a similar song himself. The ballad was recorded on June 4, 1931, the very last song that Coleman and his group recorded.

Although for many years the Starr Piano Company issued their choice material on the Gennett label, that name was discontinued in December, 1930, because of the deepening impact of the Depression. Material in the next few years was issued on two less expensive labels, Champion and Superior, the latter being sold exclusively through chain stores. "The Wreck of the C & O *Sportsman*" was released only on the Superior label under the pseudonym John Martin. The lead singer was Roy Harvey, another musician/railroader who has contributed several selections to this book; more information on his career can be found in the discussion of "The Virginian Strike of '23" (chap. 11). The Superior disc was available from the end of August, 1931, through the end of June, 1932, and then it was withdrawn from sale. During that brief ten-month period, 370 copies of the disc were shipped out for sale. How many actually found their way into listeners' homes, and how many were returned to the factory, or lay forgotten in dealers' warehouses, we do not know. Even if all 370 were sold, its success would not be considered very impressive—but then, nothing was selling well during the depths of the Depression. Under the constraint of such limited circulation, not even the normally profitable combination of popular theme, excellent text, and good singer could catapult the ballad into lasting popularity.

NOTES

1. Ron Lane has discussed this ballad and the accident that gave rise to it in his series "Folk Music of the C & O," in the *C & O Historical Newsletter*, 2 (Mar., 1970), [4]; 4 (Oct., 1972), 8–9; and 4 (Nov., 1972), 8–9. I have drawn on his account to supplement information in the ICC *Summary of Accident Investigation Reports*; facts related to me by Bernice Coleman, the author of the ballad; and the *Huntington* (W.Va.) *Herald-Advertiser*, June 22, 1930.

2. Bernice Coleman, interviewed by Guthrie T. Meade and Norm Cohen in Princeton, W. Va., Sept. 18, 1971.

3. For more details on Coleman's musical career, see Norm Cohen, "Notes on Some Old Time Musicians from Princeton, West Virginia," *JEMFQ*, 8 (Summer, 1972), 94–104.

REFERENCES

A. "The Wreck of the C & O *Sportsman*," by John Martin (pseudonym). Roy Harvey, vocal and guitar; Jess Johnson and Bernice Coleman, violins; Ernest Branch, banjo. Recorded June 4, 1931 (Starr master N-17803), in Richmond, Ind. Released on Superior 2701 in Aug., 1931.

The Wreck of Number Nine

ON A COLD WINTER NIGHT

*One of the musicians on the recording is sounding a low C here.

On a cold winter night not a star was in sight,
And the north wind kept howling down the line;
With a sweetheart so dear stood a brave engineer,
With his orders to pull old Number Nine.
He kissed her goodbye with a tear in her eye,
For the joy in his heart he could not hide;
And the whole world seemed bright when she told him that night,
On tomorrow she'd be his blushing bride.

As the train rolled along and the wheels hummed a song,
And the black smoke came pourin' from the stack,
His headlight a-gleam seemed to brighten his dream,
Of tomorrow, he'd be coming back.
Round the corner of the hill, that his brave heart stood still,
And the headlight was shining in his face.
He whispered a prayer as he threw on the air,
For he knew that would be his final race.

> In the wreck he was found laying there on the ground,
> And he asked them to raise his weary head;
> And his breath slowly went 'twas a message he sent,
> To a maiden who thought that she'd be wed.
> "There's a little white home that I bought for our own,
> Where I knew we'd be happy by and by;
> Oh, I('ll) leave it to you, for I know you'll be true,
> Till we meet at the Golden Gates, goodbye."

J. E. Mainer's Mountaineers

Of the train-wreck ballads given in this chapter, only "Old 97" and "Engine 143" exceeded in popularity this fictional account from the pen of Carson J. Robison. Robison copyrighted the ballad on January 13, 1927 (E 653129; renewed Feb. 15, 1954, R 125710). The following day Vernon Dalhart recorded it for Columbia, and typically, he made several more recordings for different companies in the following months.

The story, set to a remarkably lilting air, considering the gravity of the tragedy, is unlike the other train-wreck ballads of this chapter in one significant respect. The engineer has just become engaged to his sweetheart when he leaves on the fatal run; dying after the wreck, he tells his comrades that he leaves her the home he had bought in anticipation of their marriage. The motif of the departing fiancé who is to be married upon his return is a familiar one in late nineteenth-century popular song, as W. K. McNeil has pointed out in his discussion of songs about the 1898 sinking of the *Maine*.[1]

The two men responsible for the popularity of this song, composer Carson J. Robison and singer Vernon Dalhart, were giants who towered over the landscape of hillbilly and folk music in the 1920s. Because their contributions to the subject matter of this book are so significant, a few words on their careers are in order here.

Robison was born in the southeast corner of Kansas in 1890, the son of a country fiddler. In 1920 he moved to Kansas City and began his professional career in music as a singer over the radio. He wrote his first song in 1921. In 1924 he went to New York and soon formed a partnership with Dalhart. In addition to providing Dalhart with many of his best songs, Robison accompanied him on banjo, guitar, or ukulele. After the success of Dalhart's "Wreck of the Old 97"/"Prisoner's Song," their efforts turned to hillbilly music primarily, and Robison demonstrated a real genius for composing the type of balladry that made a lasting impression on the hill folk of the southern Appalachians and entered oral tradition. Among his better-known compositions, besides "The Wreck of Number Nine" and "The Wreck of the 1256," were "Sydney Allen," "Santa Barbara Earthquake," "Kinnie Wagner's Fate," and "Zeb Turney's Gal," all composed between 1925 and 1927. He was also not above rewriting older folksongs, such as "Naomi Wise" and "Pearl Bryan," often adding a moral that was almost a Robison signature on his disaster ballads. Finally, Robison evidently was sent many poems by his and Dalhart's fans, which he set to music and published. His relationship with C. C. Meeks was of that sort, as shown in the discussion of "Billy Richardson's Last Ride." After working with Dalhart for three years, Robison severed the partnership and began to work with Frank Luther. He continued to write and record songs through the 1930s and 1940s, and by the time of his death in New York in 1957 he had more than three hundred compositions to his credit.[2]

Vernon Dalhart was born in Jefferson, Texas, in 1883; his real name was Marion Try Slaughter. Before World War I he had established himself as a light-opera tenor. His recording career began in 1916, and for the next eight years he recorded numerous popular songs and light classics. His entry into the field of hillbilly music with his recording of "Wreck of the Old 97" has been discussed earlier in this chapter. His hillbilly career was at its height during the years he worked with Robison. After their partnership dissolved, Dalhart's star began to set. Several attempted comebacks in the following years were only moderately successful, and when he died in Bridgeport, Connecticut, in 1948, he was practically forgotten. His popularity for those few years in the late 1920s was so great, however, that hardly a folksinger or hillbilly performer who grew up then escaped his influence.[3]

Because Dalhart is already well represented in transcriptions in this chapter, we have chosen to transcribe a later version by J. E. Mainer's Mountaineers, titled "On a Cold Winter Night." J. E. Mainer, a fiddler and singer from Concord, North Carolina, was one of the most popular hillbilly entertainers in the southeast during the 1930s.[4]

NOTES

1. William K. McNeil, "'We'll Make the Spanish Grunt': Popular Songs about the Sinking of the *Maine,*" *Journal of Popular Culture,* 2 (Spring, 1969), 537–51.

2. An adequate biography of Robison has yet to be written. My sources include Hugh Leamy, "Now Come All You Good People," *Collier's,* Nov. 2, 1929, pp. 20, 58–59, reprinted in Linnell Gentry, *A History and Encyclopedia of Country, Western, and Gospel Music,* 2d ed. (Nashville: Clairmont Publishing Corp., 1969), pp. 6–13; *The ASCAP Biographical Dictionary of Composers, Authors and Publishers,* 3d ed., compiled and edited by the Lynn Farnol Group (New York: American Society of Composers, Authors and Publishers, 1966), pp. 610–11; and the articles by Jim Walsh referred to in n. 3 below.

3. For years the only significant source of information on Vernon Dalhart was Jim Walsh's seven-part series in *Hobbies, the Magazine for Collectors* (May–Dec., 1960). Walter Darrell Haden of the University of Tennessee at Martin is presently writing a full biography of Dalhart, portions of which have been published in "If I Had Wings like an Angel: The Life of Vernon Dalhart," in *Pictorial History of Country Music, Vol. 3,* edited by Thurston Moore (Denver: Heather Enterprises, 1970), pp. 3–7; "Vernon Dalhart: His Roots and the Beginnings of Commercial Country Music," *ARSC Journal,* 3 (Winter, 1970–71), 19–32; "Vernon Dalhart," in *Stars of Country Music: Uncle Dave Macon to Johnny Rodriguez,* edited by Bill C. Malone and Judith McCulloh (Urbana: University of Illinois Press, 1975), pp. 64–85; and "Vernon Dalhart: Commercial Country Music's First International Star," *JEMFQ,* 11 (Summer, 1975), 95–103, and 11 (Autumn, 1975), 129–36.

4. For biographical information and a discography for Mainer, see Chris A. Strachwitz, "Mainer's Mountaineers," in *American Folk Music Occasional,* edited by Chris Strachwitz and Pete Welding (Berkeley: Privately published 1964), pp. 49–60.

REFERENCES

A. "The Wreck of Number Nine," by Vernon Dalhart. Dalhart, vocal and harmonica; guitar and violin by unidentified accompanists. Recorded Jan. 14, 1927 (Columbia master 143308-3). Released on Columbia 15121-D (as by Al Craver) on Feb. 20, 1927. First recording of the song.
"On a Cold Winter Night," by J. E. Mainer's Mountaineers. Wade Mainer, vocal; J. E. Mainer, violin; Junior Misenheimer, banjo; Harold Christy and Beacham Blackweiler, guitars. Recorded June 15, 1936 (RCA Victor master 102600-1), in Charlotte, N.C. Released on Bluebird B-6629. Reissued on Montgomery Ward M-7088; Victor 27496; RCA Victor LPV 507 and Pickwick/Camden ACL-7022: *Smokey Mountain Ballads*; and Ball Mountain ALP 201: *J. E. Mainer's Crazy Mountaineers.*

B. Anderson, G., 208

Brown IV, 357
Cambiaire, 88
Campbell & Holstein, 28
Carman, 42
CFB, 2 (1963), 40
Crabtree, 118
Dalhart & Robison, 12
Davis, A. K., 293 (title and first line only)
Family Herald, 56 (references only)
Good Old Days, May, 1967, p. 18
Good Old Days, May-June, 1969, p. 20
Henry (1934), 77
Horstman, 334–35
Kincaid (1931), 23
Laws, 225 (G 26) (discussion only)
Layne, 15
Mainer, J. E., 18
Moore & Moore, 338
Randolph IV, 134
Rocky Mountain Collection, 27
RRM, 4 (Jan., 1931), 318
RRM, 9 (Nov., 1932), 545
Sing a Sad Song, 25 (2 lines only)
Whitter (Song #14)

C. COHEN COLLECTION:
Ruth Butcher (letter, June 3, 1968)
C. C. Meeks (letter, Nov. 7, 1969)
Janice Page (letter, June 22, 1968)

WKFA:
Mrs. Marvin Brunett (1955; manuscript)
Clyde Buckles (May, 1960)
Jo Ann Dent (Aug., 1954)
George Disney (Aug., 1954)
Richard Guess (May, 1948)
Lula Hamilton (July, 1960)
Jesse Haycraft (May, 1958)
Nettie Jarboe (fall, 1964)
Carlyle Johnson (Apr., 1948)
Sidney Kinley (May, 1955)
Mrs. Darwin Kreisle (Jan., 1961)
   "Wreck of 97"
Fred Long (Mar., 1960)
Vera R. Martin (1959; manuscript, dated
   May 22, 1928)
Mrs. Douglas Mattingly (fall, 1961)
Glen Pennington (Dec., 1950)
Chester Shepperson (fall, 1964)
Orin M. Snell (summer, 1949)
William Sweeny (Apr., 1959)

D. Bud Billings (Frank Luther pseudonym)
   —Victor 40021, Montgomery Ward 8054
   (as by Bud Billings trio)
Jeff Calhoun (pseudonym)—Grey Gull
   4172, Radiex 4172
Jenks "Tex" Carman—Four-Star X-6
   "Old Number 9"
Carver Boys—Paramount 3198, Broadway
   8246 (as by the Carson Boys)   "The
   Brave Engineer"
Vernon Dalhart—Brunswick 101,
   Supertone 2001, Brunswick 3470,
   Vocalion 5138
   —OKeh 45086
   —Edison 52088, Edison 5394 (cylinder);
   Mark56 794: *First Recorded Railroad
   Songs*
   —Gennett 6051, Champion 15232,
   Challenge 243, Challenge 321, Herwin
   75540, Silvertone 5005, Silvertone 25005,
   Silvertone 8139, Supertone 9236, Gaiety
   (Australia) P122, Vocalion (Australia)
   XA18019
   —Cameo 1247, Romeo 478, Lincoln 2712
   —Pathé 32257, Perfect 12336
   —Banner 1990, Regal 8322, Domino 3959,
   Paramount 3016, Broadway 8054,
   Domino (Canada) 21464, Apex (Canada)
   8596, Starr (Canada) 281032, Lucky
   Strike (Canada) 24094, Microphone
   (Canada) 22169, Minerva (Canada) M902,
   Crown (Canada) 81032, Oriole 897 (as by
   Frank Evans)
Tex Ritter—Capitol 20039
Leo Soileau and the Four Aces—Decca 5279
Swift Jewel Cowboys—Vocalion 05369
   "Raggin' the Rails"

E. Jenks "Tex" Carman—Rem LP 1007: *Jenks
   "Tex" Carman*
   —Sage LP C-9
   J. R. Hall—Bluebonnet BL 115: *Utah Sings
   Again*
   Highwoods String Band—Rounder 0023:
   Fire on the Mountain   "On a Cold
   Winter's Night"
   Cisco Houston—Folkways FA 2013 (FP 13):
   *900 Miles and Other Railroad
   Ballads*   "The Brave Engineer"
   Jim Howie—Prairie Schooner PSI-101:
   *Gooseberry Pie and Other Old Time
   Delights*

Clay Lewis—American Heritage AH
401-33: *Tall Shadows*
Jim and Jesse (McReynolds)—Old
Dominion OD 498-05: *Superior Sounds
of Bluegrass*
J. E. Mainer's Mountaineers—King 765: *A
Variety Album*   "Old Number Nine"
Bunk Pettyjohn—Arizona Friends of
Folklore AFF 33-4: *Bunk and Becky
Pettyjohn*
Randolph County String Band—Davis
Unlimited DU 33001: *Under the Weeping
Willow*
Jim Reeves—RCA Victor LPM/LSP 2284:
Tall Tales and Short Tempers; RCA Victor
LPM/LSP 3709: *Yours Sincerely*
Almeda Riddle—Vanguard 140/SD 140: *The
Sound of Folk Music, Vol. 2*
Debbie Sanders—Arkansaw Traveler ALP
109: *Echoes from the Ozarks*
Hank Snow—RCA Victor LPM/LSP 2705:
Railroad Man
Rosalie Sorrells—Folkways FH 5343:
Folksongs of Idaho and Utah
Mark Spoelstra—Verve/Folkways 9018:
Times I've Had
Ernest V. Stoneman—Folkways FA 2365:
Mountain Music Played on the Autoharp
Stoneman Family—Starday SLP 200: *The
Bluegrass Champs*
Tompall and the Glaser Brothers: Decca
DL/DL7 4041: *This Land*; Decca 4172:
Country Jubilee

Stanley G. Triggs—Folkways FG 3569:
Bunkhouse and Forecastle Songs
James Wall and group—Rural Rhythm
RR-JW-175: *Carter Family Favorites*
Doc Watson—Vanguard VSD 6576: *Ballads
from Deep Gap*

F. LC AFS:

Bess Allman and Lillian Short—AFS 5263
A2
Al Bittick—AFS 12050 A13
Clyde Bland—AFS 13125 B1
Pearl Brewer—AFS 11909 B24, AFS
12036 A20
J. R. Crymes—AFS 11894 A37
Anne Hart—AFS 12050 B6
Ruby Hughes—AFS 3174 B2   "On a
Cold Winter Night"
Rebecca Jones—AFS 3425 B2   "Old
Number Nine"
Earl Key—AFS 9641 B1
Nancy Philley—AFS 12038 B3
Hobart Ricker—AFS 3903 B1
Ernest Scott—AFS 12043 B8, AFS
13136 B7
Roy Sibert and Howard B. Spurlock
—AFS 1482 A1   "Old Number Nine"
Jim Turner— AFS 13141 A6
Hattie Wynne Williams—AFS 12044 B1
Clarence H. Wyatt—AFS 10889 A4

Appendix

Some Other Train-Wreck Ballads

The ballads in chapter 5 constitute a small sampling of songs dealing with train wrecks, both historical and imaginary. In this appendix, I have gathered references to other traditional ballads and hillbilly recordings that concern real (or probably real) occurrences. The ordering is chronological.

A. *"Henry K. Sawyer."* A ballad about an accident on the Bangor and Piscataquis Canal and Railroad Company that occurred June 8, 1848, at Stillwater, Me. This is the earliest railroad-accident ballad that was definitely in oral tradition. See *BFSSNE* #9, 17–19; also Flanders et al., 58–60.

B. *"Brush Creek Wreck."* A ballad about an accident on the Hannibal and Saint Joseph Railroad on Mar. 1, 1881, near Brevier, Macon Co., Mo. The only published version is given by Belden (1955), 421. Because no other reports have appeared, Laws considers its position in oral tradition dubious. See Laws, 271 (dG 37).

C. *"The Hartford Wreck."* A ballad about an accident on the Central Vermont Railroad on Feb. 4, 1887, near Hartford, Vt. The ballad dwells on the last exchanges between dying passenger Joseph Maigret and his young son. See Flanders et al., 156–59. Because he was aware of only this account, Laws considered the position of this ballad in oral tradition to be dubious. See Laws, 271 (dG 36). However, three other occurrences convince me that the ballad is—or at least was, for some time—traditional. See *RRManM*, 12 (Aug., 1910), 573; Marie Benson of North Waterford, Me., to Norm Cohen, July, 1968; Margaret MacArthur, Living Folk LP F-LFR-100: *Margaret MacArthur and Family*.

D. *"The Bridge Was Burned at Chatsworth."* A ballad about one of the worst train wrecks in American history—on the Toledo, Peoria and Western Railroad, Aug. 10, 1887, near Chatsworth, Ill. The song was written and composed by Thomas P. Westendorf and was widely popular for many years. See Laws, 227 (G 30), for references to collected versions. Another text, collected in 1923, is given in Peters, 242.

E. *"The Wreck at Kankakee."* A ballad or poem (I have not seen direct evidence for music) about a wreck that occurred prior to 1890 near the Kankakee River in Illinois. The ballad mentions Barker, the engineer, and Hosler, the fireman. No historical details are available. See *LEMJ*, 25 (Feb., 1891), 128; also *RRManM*, 9 (Sept., 1909), 761.

F. *"The Accident down at Wann."* A ballad about a train hitting a buggy at a railroad crossing and killing its occupants. The train is identified as a New York express, but the railroad and precise location are not known; presumably the accident occurred in May, 1888. See *RRManM*, 8 (Jan., 1909), 761; also Mrs. Xenia E. Cord to Norm Cohen, Sept. 8, 1972.

G. *"Wreck of the N & W Cannonball."* A ballad about an accident between two trains, one on the Norfolk and Western, the other on the Atlantic Coast Line, June 27, 1903, near Dunlop, Va. The poem was written by Cleburne C. Meeks and set to music by Carson Robison (under the pseudonym White). It was recorded by Vernon Dalhart on Columbia 15378-D and Edison 52533. See also Ralph Oatley to Norm Cohen, Sept. 29, 1967.

H. *"Maud Wreck."* A ballad about an accident on the Southern Railway, Dec., 23, 1904, near Maud, Ill. See Lelah Allison, *SFQ*, 5

HARPER'S WEEKLY.

A

JOURNAL OF CIVILIZATION

Vol. XVII.—No. 854.]　　　　NEW YORK, SATURDAY, MAY 10, 1873.　　　　[WITH A SUPPLEMENT.
PRICE TEN CENTS.

Entered according to Act of Congress, in the Year 1873, by Harper & Brothers, in the Office of the Librarian of Congress, at Washington.

THE MEADOW BROOK DISASTER—STICKING TO HIS POST.—DRAWN BY SOL. EYTINGE, JUN.—[SEE PAGE 388.]

Harper's Weekly, front cover, May 10, 1873. Courtesy of Donald Lee Nelson.

(1941), 37–38; see also Riddle-Abrahams, 80–82, where it is titled "Al Bowen," and McIntosh, 14–16.

I. *"Wreck of No. 3."* A ballad about an accident on a line owned by the Little River Lumber Company, June 30, 1909, near Townsend, Tenn. The engineer's name is given as Bryson. See G. Anderson, 204. A version entitled "Daddy Brison's Last Ride" was also sent to the LC AFS in June, 1970, by F. W. Schmidt.

J. *"Hamlet Wreck."* A ballad about the wreck of a special excursion train, July 27, 1911, near Hamlet, N.C. See Brown II, 674–76.

K. *"The C & O Wreck."* A ballad about a wreck on the C & O, Jan. 1, 1913, near Guyandotte, W.Va. See Laws, 214 (G 4), and numerous references therein.

L. *"The C & O Freight & Section Crew Wreck."* A broadside ballad about a wreck in the Big Sandy Valley in eastern Kentucky. Jay Thompson and Doc Compton were identified as being on the freight; no other historical details are available. The broadside, in WKFA, was originally in the possession of Mrs. Crockett of Ashland, Ky.

M. *"The Wreck of the Hunnicut Curve."* A ballad, possibly historical, about an accident near Paintsville, Ky., with Walter Burke, engineer. See Thomas, 122, where the ballad is credited to Buddy Preston.

N. *"The Wreck of the 36."* A ballad, possibly historical, about an accident in the Big Sandy Valley near Paintsville, eastern Kentucky, with an engineer named McDonney. See Thomas, 120, where the ballad is credited to Jim Dobbins.

O. *"Wreck between New Hope and Gethsemane."* A ballad about a head-on collision on the Louisville and Nashville Railroad in Kentucky with an engineer named Stergin. The song was copyrighted by Doc Hopkins, Karl Davis, and Harty Taylor and published in their *Mountain Ballads and Home Songs* (Chicago: M. M. Cole Publishing, 1936), p. 39, and also in *Dave Minor's Collection of Karl and Harty's Fireside Songs* (Chicago, Dave Minor, 1936?), p. 39. It was recorded by Doc Hopkins on Mar. 5, 1941 (Decca master 93548A), and issued on Decca 6039. (The reverse of this record, "Wreck of the Old Thirty-One," gives too few specific details to be considered as probably historical.) See also Ruth Butcher to Cohen, June 3, 1968.

P. *"Wreck of G & SI."* A recorded ballad about a wreck on the Gulf and Ship Island Railroad in southern Mississippi on Christmas Day (year unknown). Van Martin is identified as the engineer on train 64; no other details are available. Recorded by Happy Bud Harrison on Vocalion 5350 (ca. 1929).

Q. *"The Wreck of the Morning Mail."* A poem by Jake Taylor about an accident on the Pennsylvania Railroad's eastbound Number 23 near Greenup in southern Illinois. George Minnick is the engineer. The poem can be sung to the tune of "The Wreck on the C & O," on which it seems to be based. Published in *Jake Taylor and His Rail Splitters Log Book* (n.p., [1939?]), p. 10.

R. *"The Wreck of 444."* A ballad about an accident (possibly a collision between two engines) on the Norfolk and Western Railroad in the Clinch Valley of Virginia; crewmen Gillespie, Stuart, and Combs are mentioned. Words and music by Bess McReynolds, published in *WWVA Jamboree Book No. 2* (Chicago: M. M. Cole Publishing, 1948), pp. 28–29.

6

Asleep at the Switch

THIS VERY BRIEF chapter is intended to provide respite between two rather somber portions of the book: a chapter of railroad accidents, and a chapter of tragedies, embracing a variety of the more sorrowful aspects of the human condition.

Perhaps the title song, "Asleep at the Switch," could well have been placed in the following section on tragedies, but it has been saved for this chapter, since with the two other pieces included it forms a trio of songs whose unifying characteristic is that disaster has been averted by quick thinking.

In "Asleep at the Switch" the switchman, Tom, is tormented by worrying whether his sick child will recover; the mental anguish is too much for him, and he falls dead at the switch. Just as the passenger train approaches, his daughter Nell runs down to tell him that the child has rallied. She throws the switch barely in time to avert a catastrophe. It turns out that the family of the president of the railroad company is on board, and Nell is rewarded handsomely for her deed. The song focuses on the heroism and recognition of Nell rather than the role of her father, who—let us mince no words—failed in his job as switchman. It is thus fair to regard the song as a happy one—perhaps even a comedy, in the classical sense.

"Bill Mason" is more lighthearted yet, relating how the bride of one day, seeing hoodlums tampering with the tracks, flashes a lantern signal to her husband, the engineer, and saves the train.

Finally, "Papa's Billy Goat" brings us to the level of the droll minstrel stage or music hall. It is the still-remembered song of a mischievous goat who eats his master's red shirts off the clothesline, is tied to a railroad track for punishment, but saves himself at the last minute by coughing up the shirts and flagging the train.

These three tales do not require lengthy comparative analysis; they should be taken in the same light spirit in which they (two of them, at least) are delivered. However, one amusing contrast cannot escape comment. We note that Billy saves his life and receives no further reward. Maggie saves her husband's life and receives no further reward. But Nell saves the life of the family of a railroad president and receives a fat gratuity. Are we to conclude that saving the lives of wealthy moguls and their kin is *not* its own reward?

Asleep at the Switch

ASLEEP AT THE SWITCH

"The mid-night ex-press will be late here to-night, So side-track the west-bound freight." Those were the or-ders that Tom had re-ceived, As he passed through the round-house gate. Tom was the switch-man, with heart true as steel, And du-ty___ was first in his breast; But the thought of his boy___ who was dy-ing at home Crazed Tom, and he fell at his post. The shrill whis-tle blew on the freight for the West, When the rum-ble was heard on the mid-night ex-press. A-sleep at the switch,___ and no warn-ing light To sig-nal those trains that rushed through the night; When

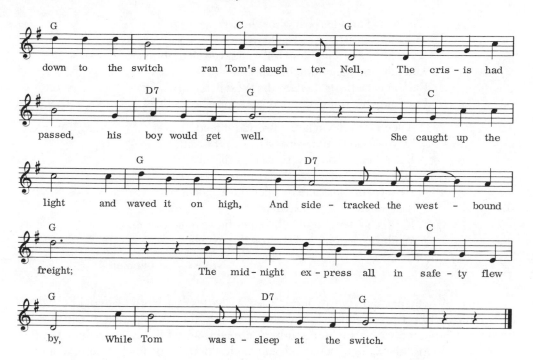

down to the switch ran Tom's daugh - ter Nell, The cris - is had

passed, his boy would get well. She caught up the

light and waved it on high, And side - tracked the west - bound

freight; The mid - night ex - press all in safe - ty flew

by, While Tom was a - sleep at the switch.

*The chord change occurs one beat earlier on the recording.
**The chord change occurs one beat later on the recording.

"The midnight express will be late here tonight,
So sidetrack the westbound freight."
Those were the orders that Tom had received
As he passed through the roundhouse gate.
Tom was the switchman, with heart true as steel,
And duty was first in his breast;
But the thought of his boy who was dying at home
Crazed Tom, and he fell at his post.
The shrill whistle blew on the freight for the West,
When the rumble was heard on the midnight express.

Asleep at the switch, and no warning light
To signal those trains that rushed through the night;
When down to the switch ran Tom's daughter Nell,
The crisis had passed, his boy would get well.
She caught up the light and waved it on high,
And sidetracked the westbound freight;
The midnight express all in safety flew by,
While Tom was asleep at the switch.

The freight slowly backed on the main track again,
The men called to Tom goodnight;
But only the sob of a girl made reply;
And they saw by the engine's light

Tom lying flat at his post where he fell,
And there with her head on his breast,
'Twas his brave daughter Nell who saved all their lives,
And those on the midnight express.
Each man on the freight for the West bared his head,
For Tom's heart had stopped, at his post he lay dead.

Asleep at the switch, the president read,
"My wife and child were on board," he said;
But as he read on, his stern face relaxed,
"This road shall reward such heroic acts."
He sat at his desk and he filled out a check,
And sent it with all dispatch,
For Tom's daughter Nell, for her brave deed that night,
While he slept his last sleep at the switch.

                                    Ernest V. Stoneman

This 1897 composition, words and music by Charles Shackford (copyright C 22880) and published by E. T. Paull, is a classic example of the combination of pathos with heroism. Compared with some of the other railroad songs of the 1890s included in this volume, "Asleep at the Switch" achieved only modest popularity; furthermore, its author has left no other pieces of lasting appeal behind.

Two completely different poems by the same title had been written prior to Shackford's composition. The better-known one was by George Hoey, author, actor, dramatist (and father of Bill Hoey of the famous vaudeville team Evans and Hoey). In this story, a switchman falls asleep at his post and is awakened by a dreadful crash. He rushes about the wreckage, hearing the moaning and shrieking of husbands, wives, and babes, and finally finds his own wife dead. In the last verse he is awakened by his wife—he had been napping, and the entire episode was just a dream. The first four lines of the poem are as follows:

The first thing I remember was Carlo tugging away
With the sleeve of my coat fast in his teeth, pulling as much as to say:
"Come master, awake, and tend to the switch—lives now depend on you,
Think of the souls in the coming train, and the graves you're sending them to."

Since this piece had appeared in 1875 in a songster, it is probable—but not certain—that it had been set to music.

The other poem titled "Asleep at the Switch" appeared in the *Railroad Trainmen's Journal*, credited mysteriously to "Will's Sister."[1] In this poem, the switchman dies just after throwing the switch. The first verse is:

In the little hut where the crossroads met
    Sat the switchman old and gray.
Who had turned the switch at his door step
    As year after year passed way;
A smile wreathes the old and wrinkled face
    That shone with a holy light.
As his memory rolled back o'er the track of time
    While he waits at the switch to night.

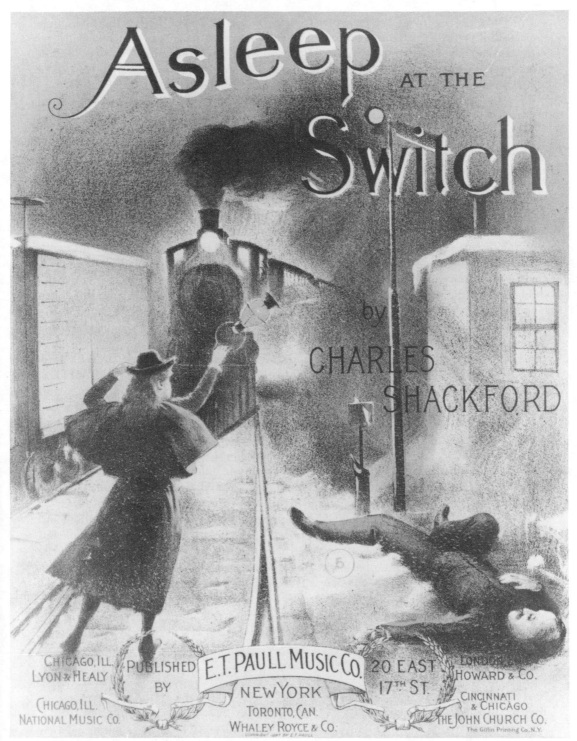

Sheet music: "Asleep at the Switch." Courtesy of Lester Levy.

Only two recordings were made of Charles Shackford's piece, both of them commercial hillbilly discs. The failure of the song to gain wider acceptance can probably be traced to the unusual stanzaic form. Shackford's verse consists of forty measures in 6/8 meter accompanying ten lines of poetry, rhymed *a b c b d e f e g g*, while the refrain consists of sixty-four measures in 3/4 meter accompanying eight lines, rhymed *a a b b c d c e*.

The earlier recording was made by Ernest V. "Pop" Stoneman for the General Phonograph Corporation in April, 1926. Pop Stoneman was born in 1893 in Carroll County, Virginia, into a family of singers and musicians. Though he was able to make his living as a carpenter, he had learned to play harmonica, autoharp, banjo, and guitar in his youth, and in 1924, when the first hillbilly recordings were hitting the market, Pop felt he could do as well as some of the others he heard. In the next five years he recorded more than two hundred selections for several companies and was one of the most popular artists of the day. In the late 1950s, now surrounded with a band of his own musically talented children, Pop began a second career, this time playing to audiences in folk festivals, coffeehouses, and television shows, that ended shortly before his death in 1968.[2] Stoneman's text is virtually identical with Shackford's, although his melody is somewhat simplified. (His tune is in fact similar to his melody for "The Orphan Girl," released on the same disc.) Lester McFarland and Robert Gardner, who recorded it in about April, 1930, sing still a different tune. Their text is the same, except for one couplet in the second verse, which they have altered to make a better rhyme, and the omission of the second chorus.

The song appeared in three of Mac and Bob's folios. In the two folios dated 1931, no credit was given for the lyrics, and the only notation was "music by Mac." In the 1941 folio, however, words and music were credited to Shackford—this even though the same plates were used as in the earlier printings, and the words and melody corresponded to Mac and Bob's version, and not Shackford's original composition.

The discography for "Asleep at the Switch" also cites a recording by Claude Moye (Pie Plant Pete), but the citation is included only because its omission might seem an oversight. Because the piece has no words, and the tune differs from Shackford's or either of the above-mentioned recordings, it cannot be considered as part of this group. I do not know what led Moye to link his particular tune with that familiar title.

Shackford's "Asleep at the Switch" has appeared in only one regional collection, and that was a 1940 recovery. No tune was reported, but on the basis of the text we can rule out the Mac and Bob version as a source. The 1962 *Renfro Valley Bugle* cited in the References mentioned receipt of a very different version of "Asleep at the Switch," much shorter than the one printed (which was Hoey's piece). Presumably this was Shackford's composition; if so, this would be the most recent recovery of the song I have found. By now, it may have dropped out of circulation entirely, although a request for the words in a 1968 issue of *Old Time Songs and Poems* indicates it is still thought about.[3]

NOTES

1. *RTJ*, Dec., 1891, p. 888.

2. For further biographical information on Stoneman, see Norm Cohen, Eugene W. Earle, and Graham Wickham, *The Early Recording Career of Ernest V. "Pop" Stoneman: A Bio-Discography*, JEMF Special Series No. 1 (Los Angeles: John Edwards Memorial Foundation, 1968); and Tony Russell, brochure notes to Rounder 1008: *Ernest V. Stoneman and the Blue Ridge Corn Shuckers*.

3. *Old Time Songs and Poems*, 2, no. 1 (Sept.-Oct., 1968), 42.

REFERENCES

A. "Asleep at the Switch," by Ernest V.
Stoneman. Vocal and guitar. Recorded
Apr., 1926 (General Phonograph Corp.
master S-74104A), in Asheville, N.C.
Released on OKeh 45044 in ca. Sept.,
1926. First recording of song; transcribed
here.
"Asleep at the Switch," sheet music. Words
and music by Charles Shackford.
Published by E. T. Paull in 1897
(copyright no. 22880).

B. Levy (1975), 87–90
Mac & Bob (1931b), 58
Mac & Bob (1931c), 57
Mac & Bob (1941), 34
Randolph IV, 136

THE FOLLOWING citations are all to the Hoey
poem:
Best Things, 75 (Song #6)
Gus Williams, 26–28
LEMJ, 22 (May, 1888), 392

RRManM, 11 (Feb., 1910), 188
RRManM, 16 (Oct., 1911), 192
RRManM, 6 (Sept., 1931), 316
RVB, 15 (May, 1962)

C. COHEN COLLECTION:
Ruth Butcher (letter, June 18, 1968)
(Hoey poem)

D. Lester McFarland and Robert Gardner—
Brunswick 461, Rex (England) U 407
J. W. Myers—(cylinder recording, probably
on his own label, number unknown)
(possibly related)
Pie Plant Pete (Claude Moye pseudonym)
—Gennett 6810, Champion 15709
(as by Asparagus Joe), Supertone
9405, Melotone (Canada) 45003

E. Slim Stuart—Arcade AR-104 (possibly
related)

Ernest V. "Pop" Stoneman. Courtesy of the John
Edwards Memorial Foundation, UCLA.

Bill Mason

BILL MASON

"Mmm. That man sure does blow a wicked whistle, don't he? Sounds like that old fellow that used to run on the Southern, between Monroe and Spencer, pulled that *Crescent Limited*. What was his name, Charlie?"

"Oh, you thinkin' about Bill Mason."

"Oh yeah. Whatever became of him?"

"Well, he got married there a while back."

"Oh, married. I thought he's sick, that's what's the matter with him, I thought."

"Yeah. Was murdered, near 'bout it, but then he got married there a while back and they made up a song about him."

"Let's play it, then."

"All right."

Bill Mason was an engineer, he'd been on the road all of his life;
I'll never forget the morning he married him a chuck of a wife;
Bill hadn't been married more'n an hour, till up came a message from Kress,
And ordered Bill to come down and bring out the night express.

While Maggie sat by the window, a-waiting for the night express,
And if she hadn't a-done so, she'd been a widow, I guess;
There was some drunken rascals that came down by the ridge,
They came down by the railroad and tore off a rail from the bridge.

While Maggie had been working, "I guess there's something wrong,
In less than fifteen minutes, Bill's train would be along."

She couldn't come near to tell him—a mile, that wouldn't have done;
She just grabbed up the lantern, and made for the bridge alone.

By Jove, Bill saw the signal, and stopped the night express,
And found his Maggie crying, on the track in her weddin' dress;
A-cryin' and a-laughin' for joy, still holdin' on to the light,
He came around the curve a-flyin'; Bill Mason's on time tonight.

North Carolina Ramblers

The song "Bill Mason" sprang from a poem attributed to Bret Harte entitled "Bill Mason's Bride." The exact date of the poem's composition is unknown; it was apparently not published in newspaper form, and Joseph Gaer, in his bibliography of Harte's works, gives no source for the piece. It does not appear in the 1912 edition of Harte's complete works or in any of the earlier collections. It does appear in the 1914 edition, in the section of volume 20 entitled "Later Poems (1871–1902)." This edition, compiled by Charles Kozlay, is apparently the first to use chronological divisions for Harte's poems, and many of the pieces included in "Later Poems" (including "Bill Mason's Bride") did not appear in the 1912 series.[1]

However, the poem was in print long before 1914. For example, it appeared in Number 6 of *100 Choice Selections* (later titled *The Speaker's Garland*), a long series of slim volumes that was published in so many editions and with such varying titles as to bewilder the bibliographer who does not have all printings at hand for examination. As far as I can tell, the poem was first included in the 1873 volume, which indicates a date of first publication no later than the early 1870s. Whatever its date of birth, "Bill Mason's Bride" makes interesting reading next to "Bill Mason"; here is the poem as attributed to Bret Harte:

BILL MASON'S BRIDE

Half an hour till train time, sir,
    An' a fearful dark time, too;
Take a look at the switch lights, Tom,
    Fetch in a stick when you're through.
On time? well, yes, I guess so—
    Left the last station all right;
She'll come round the curve a-flyin';
    Bill Mason comes up to-night.

You know Bill? No? He's engineer,
    Been on the road all his life—
I'll never forget the mornin'
    He married his chuck of a wife.
'Twas the summer the millhands struck,
    Just off work, every one;
They kicked up a row in the village
    And killed old Donevan's son.

Bill hadn't been married mor'n an hour,
    Up comes a message from Kress,

Orderin' Bill to go up there,
   And bring down the night express.
He left his gal in a hurry,
   And went up on Number One,
Thinking of nothing but Mary,
   And the train he had to run.

And Mary sat down by the window
   To wait for the night express;
And, sir, if she hadn't a' done so,
   She'd been a widow, I guess.
For it must a' been nigh midnight
   When the mill hands left the Ridge;
They come down the drunken devils,
   Tore up a rail from the bridge.
But Mary heard 'em a-workin'
   And guessed there was somethin' wrong—
And in less than fifteen minutes,
   Bill's train it would be along!

She couldn't come here to tell us,
   A mile—it wouldn't a'done;
So she jest grabbed up a lantern,
   And made for the bridge alone.
Then down came the night express, sir
   And Bill was makin' her climb!
But Mary held the lantern,
   A-swingin' it all the time.

Well, by Jove! Bill saw the signal,
   And he stopped the night express,
And he found his Mary cryin',
   On the track, in her weddin' dress;
Cryin' an' laughin' for joy, sir,
   An' holdin' on to the light—
Hello! here's the train — good-bye, sir,
   Bill Mason's on time to-night.

Harte did write several poems about railroads and railroaders: "The Ghost That Jim Saw" and "The Station-Master of Lone Prairie" both dealt with supernatural occurrences. "Guild's Signal" is perhaps better remembered by railroaders; it describes a wreck in which engineer William Guild [?Gould] on the Boston and Providence Railway was killed on April 19, 1873. "What the Engines Said" commemorated the "opening of the Pacific railroad."

Harte was attributed authorship of another railroad poem in an amusing incident related in the first issue of *Railroad Man's Magazine*. In about the 1870s, Sam Davis, then publisher of the Vallejo, California, *Open Letter*, wagered that he could imitate the style of any modern poet so closely as to defy detection. His opponent suggested Bret Harte. Within a week, Davis wrote the poem "Binley and 46" and published it in his newspaper over Harte's name, claiming that it had been found in a trunk Harte had left in a San

Francisco lodging-house years before. The hoax went undetected, until Davis finally felt compelled to reveal the truth. Many, however, refused to believe that the poem was not Harte's, and, as the article in *Railroad Man's Magazine* concluded, "There are people living who still regard 'Binley and 46' as one of Bret Harte's masterpieces."[2]

The moral is that, unless some manuscript copy of "Bill Mason's Bride," or other compelling proof, can be found, there will remain the strong possibility that Harte did not really write that poem. In fact, many poems have at one time or another been attributed to him only to be reassigned to other authors after more careful investigation. I had thought that since Kozlay, in editing his 1914 edition of Harte's works, had access to the Harte manuscripts on deposit at the Huntington Library in San Marino, perhaps the clue lay in that archive. A visit to the library, however, assured me that no trace of "Bill Mason's Bride" was to be found among Harte's papers there. Letters to the other three libraries that have large collections of Harte manuscripts (some one thousand documents among them) also brought negative results.[3] The failure to find primary sources for "Bill Mason's Bride" is indeed an unsettling puzzle.

As if to stir troubled waters yet more, there appeared in an 1871 anthology, *Romance and Humor of the Road: A Book for Railway Men and Travelers*, by Stephe R. Smith, a poem, "The Night Express," subtitled "A Station-Agent's Rhyme," which is "Bill Mason's Bride," save for a few altered words and the change of the engineer's name to Sime Murray. Since the text is so similar to the one attributed to Harte, only the first stanza is given here for comparison:

> Half an hour till train time, sir,
>   A fearful dark night, too;
> Look at the switch-lights, Tom, my boy,
>   Fetch in a stick when you're through.
> "On time!" why yes, I guess so,
>   Despatch says "left all right;"
> She'll come round the curve a-flyin',
>   Sime Murray comes up to-night. . . . [4]

Smith took no pains to inform his readers whether the stories, anecdotes, and poems in his book were from his own pen or collected from other sources. The few differences between "The Night Express" and "Bill Mason's Bride"—particularly in the name of the engineer—suggest that Smith's poem was not a rewrite of Harte's; if anything, the borrowing was in the other direction. But we cannot dismiss the possibility of an earlier poem in (oral) circulation on which both Smith and Harte (or two other, unidentified poets) built. Could the story have recounted a true incident? The possibility cannot be ruled out.

With this incomplete evidence, the following seems to me the most reasonable conclusion: By 1871 the original poem had already been in circulation, its author unknown (or at least unwilling to press claims of authorship after seeing his poem attributed to others). Smith published it in two of his books, allowing the inference to be drawn that he had written it. At about the same time, it was attributed to Bret Harte, although the absence of the poem from Harte's accepted publications and manuscripts suggests that he himself did not claim authorship. By 1914 the poem had appeared over Harte's name often enough for Kozlay to assume Harte had written it, although no positive evidence was available.

One fact does seem certain: "Bill Mason" was popular among railroaders and passen-

gers alike. It is almost impossible to deny that the piece influenced Howard Douglas's
"How an Engineer Gained His Bride," a piece of light verse published in 1877 about an
engineer who foiled his sweetheart's parents' plans for her to marry another—something
of a modern version of the old Scots ballad "Katherine Jaffray." The story, narrated by one
traveler to another as they wait at the depot for the train, concludes with this verse:

> He married her up in "Frisco,"
> And took her home as his wife.
> The fellow who was to have married her
> Then threatened to take his life.
> But nothing cared he for threatenings,
> They couldn't scare him a mite—
> Hello! the train has arrived, sir,
> Jim Hewitt's on time to-night.[5]

The song "Bill Mason" was first recorded in October, 1927, by Roy Harvey and the
North Carolina Ramblers on the Paramount label. Two years later the same band
recorded it for Columbia. Harvey, born in Greenville, West Virginia, in 1894, had been
a hogger himself before the Virginian strike of 1923 put him and other good union men
out of work, and when he went to make a living as a hillbilly musician, he took many
railroad songs—some of his own composition, some of older vintage—and immortalized
them on wax.

Although "Bill Mason" was copyrighted on February 15, 1928, with both words and
music credited to Harvey, we need not take that claim seriously, since the recording
company, Paramount, had its own publishing arm and was eager to publish any material
its artists recorded for the additional revenues the copyright would yield. According to
Thomas C. Trautman, Harvey's brother-in-law and also a railroader (he was fireman at the
same time Harvey was engineer), he himself taught Harvey the song. Trautman stated
that he learned "Bill Mason" when he was about twelve years old (in 1898) living near
Chattanooga, Tennessee. Everyone there knew it, Trautman averred. Furthermore,
Trautman believed that the story was true, and that Mason must have been an engineer
on the Southern Railway.[6] This again raises the remote possibility that the original poem
was actually based on a true incident, although there is no real evidence to that effect. We
are left with nothing more substantial than that the poem was published in the early 1870s
and by the late 1890s was firmly in oral folk tradition. Just who refashioned the poem and
set it to music, we will probably never know. Whoever it was did an excellent job of
streamlining the longer poem, stripping off the inessential details, and setting it to a tune
reminiscent of several other traditional melodies.

The version transcribed in this book was recorded by the North Carolina Ramblers
on May 6, 1929, in New York for Columbia. The vocal lead is taken by banjoist Charlie
Poole. Textually, the two Ramblers recordings are very similar, except that on the later
Columbia disc the spoken introduction has been added.

For some time I have wondered whether the song is still remembered, apart from its
survival in the collections and memories of contemporary Charlie Poole enthusiasts.
Therefore, my interest was aroused considerably by a request from a Connecticut reader
in the February, 1974, issue of *Railroad Magazine* for the words to "Bill Mason's Bride."[7]
The use of the pre–Charlie Poole/Roy Harvey title, together with the characterization of
the piece as an "old railroad song" rather than a poem, suggested that the ballad had been
sung prior to the hillbilly recordings. I sent a copy of the words to the inquirer, asking him
where and when he had learned the song, and whether he had ever heard it on radio or

phonograph recording. He responded that he had first heard the song "at the 'old swimming hole' about 40 years ago" and had not heard it since.[8] He had never heard it on radio or phonograph. He gave me the address of a man in Saint Louis County, Missouri, who had also answered his query. Warming to my task, I wrote immediately and was pleased to receive a prompt reply, but disappointed with its contents: "This song was printed in one of the late 1931 or . . . 1932 issues of the old Railroad Man's Magazine. It has appeared but once during all the years I have been reading 'Railroad.' I have never seen it appear in print elsewhere, and have never heard it sung."[9] The comments of these two rail fans convince me that "Bill Mason's Bride" made an impression on many persons forty years ago; but I am still looking for concrete evidence that the song remains alive in oral tradition.

NOTES

An earlier version of this discussion of "Bill Mason" appeared in the *JEMFQ*, 10 (Summer, 1974), 74–78.

1. In *The Writings of Bret Harte*, 19 vols. (Boston and New York: Houghton Mifflin, 1902), and other editions before 1914, all the poems appear in vol. 13, *Complete Poetical Works*. In the 1914 edition, *Harte's Complete Works* (Boston and New York: Houghton Mifflin), a twentieth volume has been added: *Songs and Poems and Other Uncollected Works by Bret Harte*, edited by Charles Meeker Kozlay; "Bill Mason" appears on p. 383 of this volume.

2. *RRManM*, 1 (Oct., 1906), 100.

3. Letters to me from Elizabeth R. Schubert, Assistant in Manuscripts, University of Virginia Library, Charlottesville, May 9, 1969; from Brooke Whiting, Literary Manuscripts Librarian, UCLA Special Collections Library, May 8, 1969; from H. H. Bancroft Library, University of California at Berkeley, May 7, 1969.

4. Stephe R. Smith, *Romance and Humor of the Road* (Chicago: Horton and Leonard, Railroad Printers, 1871 [introduction datelined Galesburg, Ill., June 1, 1871]), p. 123. Also in idem, *Romance and Humor of the Rail* (New York: G. W. Carleton, 1873), p. 134.

5. *LEMJ*, 11 (Sept., 1877), 406.

6. Thomas Trautman, interviewed by Archie Green and Gene Earle, in Beckley, W. Va., Aug. 15, 1962.

7. *RRM*, Feb., 1974, p. 54.

8. Ronald Thurlow to Cohen, Jan. 25, 1974.

9. L. K. Penningroth to Cohen, Feb. 2, 1974.

REFERENCES

A. "Bill Mason," by Charlie Poole and the North Carolina Ramblers. Poole, vocal and banjo; Roy Harvey, guitar and spoken part in introduction; Posey Rorer, fiddle. Recorded May 6, 1929 (Columbia master 148469), in New York City. Released on Columbia 15407-D on June 28, 1929. Reissued on County 509: *Charlie Poole and the North Carolina Ramblers, Vol. 2*; Columbia CS 9660: *Ballads and Breakdowns of the Golden Era*. Transcribed here.

B. IN ADDITION to the various editions of Harte's collected works, "Bill Mason's Bride" appeared in the following:

Fireman's Magazine, 7 (Jan., 1883), 56
LEMJ, 18 (Mar., 1884), 142
100 Choice Selections #6 (1873, 1875, 1895, etc.), 120
RRManM, 13 (Oct., 1910), 190
Wehman *100 Popular*, 8

D. North Carolina Ramblers—Paramount 3079, Broadway 8183 (as by the Plainsmen and Rufus Hall)

E. Peter Siegel—Elektra EKL 276: *Old Time Banjo Project*

Papa's Billy Goat/Rosenthal's Goat

PAPA'S BILLY GOAT

Papa bought him a great big billy goat,
Ma(ma) she washed most every day;
Hung our clothes out on the line,
That durned old goat he come that way.

Now he pulled down the red flanneled shirt,
You oughta hear those buttons crack;
But I'll get even with the son-of-a-gun,
Gonna tie him across the railroad track.

Tied him across the railroad track,
And the train was a-comin' at a powerful rate;
He belched up that old red shirt,
Then flagged down that durned old freight.

Then I went to the depot and I bought me a ticket,
And I walked right in and I sot right down;
Stuck my ticket in the brim of my hat,
And the doggone wind blowed it out on the ground.

The conductor come around, says, "Gimme your ticket."
Said I'll have to pay again or get left on the track;
But I'll get even with the son-of-a-gun,
Got a round-trip ticket and I ain't a-comin' back.

Then I acted an old fool, married me a widow,
And the widow had a daughter and her name was
    Maude;
Father being a widower married her daughter,
And now my daddy is my own son-in-law.

Fiddlin' John Carson

ROSENTHAL'S GOAT

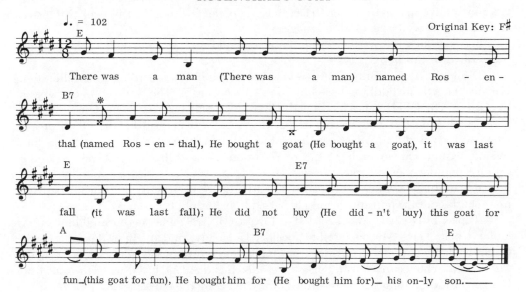

*This is more spoken than sung; the pitch is inconsistent.

There was a man named Rosenthal,
He bought a goat, it was last fall;
He did not buy this goat for fun,
He bought him for his only son.

Six red shirts hung out on a line,
When Billy saw these, says, "Now I dine."
He rolled them up in a small ball,
And swallowed shirts, clothesline, and all.

When Rosen' saw what Billy had done,
He said, "Prepare, you son-of-a-gun."
He took him to a railroad track,
And tied him down and turned his back.

When Billy saw the approaching train,
He tried to think, but all in vain;
He gave a jerk, an awful strain,
Coughed up the shirts and flagged the train.

Now Billy's stomach was lined with zinc,
He swallowed a rock, then a bottle of ink;
And then a stick of dynamite,
To satisfy his appetite.

When Rosen' got a great big stick,
And gave the goat a terrible lick;
The dynamite went off, 'tis sad to tell,
The goat went to heaven, and Rosenthal went to . . .
  [*Spoken:*] Well, that's your business.

Mac and Bob

Although its origins are still undiscovered, this song—or a close relation of it—is still vigorously alive in oral tradition; in fact, it is one of the few songs in this book that thrives as an urban as well as a rural folksong.

Because they are so different in both tune and text, two versions of the song are transcribed in full here.

The first, "Papa's Billy Goat," is taken from a hillbilly recording by Fiddlin' John Carson, the Atlanta fiddler whose June, 1923, recording of "The Little Old Log Cabin in the Lane"/"The Old Hen Cackled and the Rooster's Going to Crow" launched the hillbilly phonograph industry. The success of that disc was great enough for the OKeh people, who had recorded it in Atlanta, to bring Fiddlin' John to New York in November for a second session. On November 8 Carson recorded "Papa's Billy Goat"; it was released in OKeh's popular-music series (there was as yet no special series for hillbilly music), probably in the following month. Carson's early repertoire was divided equally between nineteenth-century pop tunes and older traditional fiddle tunes and dance songs.

"Papa's Billy Goat" was recorded in July, 1924, by Tennessee-born hillbilly entertainer Uncle Dave Macon for the Vocalion Company, and by Riley Puckett on the Columbia label in September, 1924, but the latter recording was never issued. Clayton McMichen, who recorded with Puckett, recalled that the band had learned the song from Carson.[1] Fiddlin' John's 1923 recordings were made by the old acoustical process, and a few years later OKeh had him redo some of the more successful of those early numbers; he re-recorded "Papa's Billy Goat" in March, 1927, but it was never issued. When Carson switched to Victor's Bluebird label during the Depression, he recorded the song a third time, this version in Camden, New Jersey, in 1934.

Carson's song is set to the familiar tune of "Reuben and Rachel" (now generally mistitled "Reuben, Reuben"), a ditty written by Harry Bush and William Gooch and presumably copyrighted in 1871, although Fuld has disputed that date and suggests it is a few years younger.[2] Either way, this would limit the age of Carson's version of the goat story.

Although Carson's recording was the first of that form of the song, followed within a year by Macon's and Puckett's, he was not the ultimate source of the goat story set to the "Reuben and Rachel" tune. The most recent recording of this version was made in about 1968 by J. E. Mainer of Concord, North Carolina, on the Rural Rhythm label. Mainer wrote that he learned the song, which he titled "Papa's Old Billy Goat," when he was twelve years old from a banjo player named Tom Vick.[3] That dates the song back at least as far as 1910.

Only the first three verses of "Papa's Billy Goat" deal with the goat theme. The next two relate a separate comic anecdote about a man who gets even with the train conductor by buying a round-trip ticket and riding only one way. This theme ties in neatly with another light little verse sung to the "Reuben and Rachel" tune:

> Si and I we went to the circus,
> Si got hit with a rolling pin;
> We got even with that gosh-durned circus,
> We bought two tickets and we didn't go in.[4]

Mainer's version ends there; but Carson and Macon both go on to another anecdote about a man who becomes his own father-in-law. The impression is given that this song was used as a vehicle for a series of humorous anecdotes, perhaps added or omitted at the performer's will.

A second class of variants of the goat song is represented by the transcribed text and tune of "Rosenthal's Goat." In many of these, the goat's owner is given a name, often Irish: generally, Bill Grogan; less frequently, Bill Hogan, Rosenthal, Casey, Mike Riley, William Tell, Timon Thall, Angeline, Isaac Small. The persistent Irish association suggests that the piece dates from the 1880s, when jokes and songs about immigrant ethnic groups were at their zenith (or nadir, depending on one's attitude). The version given of "Rosenthal's Goat" is transcribed from a recording by Lester McFarland and Robert Gardner, which they made for the Brunswick Company on August 15, 1928. Gardner learned the song about 1920 from Charlie Oaks, a blind minstrel from Kentucky.[5] "Bill Grogan's Goat" is the form that still survives in the city; because of its currency I give here a text from oral tradition:

> Bill Grogan's goat was feeling fine,
> Ate three red shirts right off the line.
> His master came and beat his back,
> And tied him to the railroad track.
>
> The whistle blew, the train drew nigh,
> Bill Grogan's goat knew he must die.
> He gave three bleats of mortal pain,
> Coughed up the shirts and flagged the train.
>
> The engineer looked out to see
> What in the world this thing could be.
> And when he saw 'twas but a goat,
> He drew his knife and slit its throat.
>
> When Billy got to heaven, Saint Peter said,
> "My darling Bill, where is your head?"
> "I do not know, and cannot tell,
> For all I know, it may be in . . .
> (Way down yonder in the cornfield)."[6]

The text is a little unusual because of the last two stanzas, which do not always occur and which seem clearly to be a later addition.

Although, as mentioned above, the song seems to be a piece of the 1880s, there is no concrete evidence to push it back into the nineteenth century. The version reported in the *Brown Collection* bears the headnote "Reported in 1913 by W. B. Covington as heard at Cary, Wake County (No. Carolina), 4 years ago." A version deposited in the Western Kentucky Folklore Archive at some unspecified date (probably in the late 1940s) bears this notation by the singer/contributor: "When I was a girl about 1905, the great summer amusements were real hay rides and boat rides on the Ohio River. Those who had banjoes or guitars took them and everybody sang. This was one of the songs. . . ."[7] This version was titled "Old McGall."

The earliest text that can be dated with certainty is a 1904 sheet-music version entitled "The Tale of a Shirt," words by W. W. Brackett, melody by Lottie L. Meda. Published by M. Witmark and Sons, it was not regarded as one of the firm's more successful products. While this was about the year of the song's popularity, as recalled by the WKFA informant, the sheet-music text is so different from all the other versions that I cannot accept it as an original source. It must therefore be a secondary recomposition.

The most elaborate text of this song family is the one titled "Riley's Goat" and printed by Ira W. Ford. Unfortunately, Ford, who drew from printed as well as oral sources, gave no data on the origin of the text. "Riley's Goat" clearly sounds like an Irish vaudeville song; however, the use of a green light as a clear signal suggests that that version is of twentieth-century origin (see my discussion of "The Red and Green Signal Lights" in chap. 7). "Riley's Goat" is almost too good a text; it bears many elements that appear nowhere else. Are these elements parts of the "original" that were lost in all other texts, or are they later accretions? The context of the song suggests the latter.

One version, "Billy Goat Blues," recorded by John Byrd in 1929, is particularly interesting because it indicates the wide range of musical forms in which the gastronomic excesses of Papa's goat have been acclaimed. The first verse, which gives the mood, follows:

> Oh, that Harlem Goat, mother, sure was feelin' fine,
> Oh, that Harlem Goat, honey, sure was feelin' fine;
> He eat six red shirts right off the [?clothes] line.[8]

A similar version, entitled "Harlem Goat," was deposited in the Western Kentucky Folklore Archive in 1955.

A short fragment of "Bill Grogan's Goat" appeared in Alfred Hitchcock's 1951 movie thriller *Strangers on a Train*, sung in the club car of a train by a thoroughly besotted mathematics professor.

Finally, it should be noted that the tale of the shirt-eating goat has circulated in prose form. The earliest I have seen was published in 1905, and the goat's owner was named Patrick Flanigan. Billy Golden, the immensely popular recording artist of minstrel and vaudeville material, interpolated the story in his 1917 recording "In a Bird Store," a dialogue with Billy Heins (Victor 35659, 12″ 78 rpm).

In our search for origins of this song/story, we should consider a poem by Will Hays, the successful composer of the 1860s and 1870s who gave us such popular hits as "The Little Old Cabin in the Lane," "Mollie Darling," "The Drummer Boy of Shiloh," and the forerunner to "Life's Railway to Heaven." Entitled "O'Grady's Goat" and published in 1890 (if not earlier), the poem is an Irish dialect piece relating the various troublesome deeds perpetrated by Tim O'Grady's goat. Here is the third verse, which is appropriate to the problem at hand:

> Pat Doolan's woife hung out the wash
> Upon the line to dry.
> She wint to take it in at night,
> But stopped to have a cry.
> The sleeves av two red flannel shirts,
> That once were worn by Pat,
> Were chewed off almost to the neck,
> O'Grady's goat doon that.[9]

Although it would wrap things up nicely to conclude that Hays's poem was the original source of the billy goat songs, I think such a conclusion would be too hasty.

NOTES

1. McMichen to Cohen, June 3, 1969.

2. James J. Fuld, *The Book of World-Famous Music*, rev. ed. (New York: Crown Publishers, 1971), p. 375.

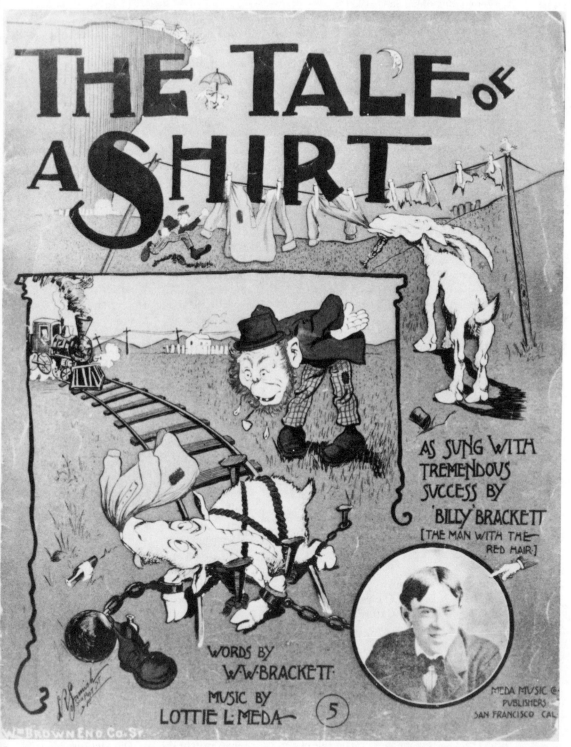

Sheet music: "The Tale of a Shirt." Courtesy of David Morton and the Archives of Popular American Music, UCLA.

3. Mainer to Cohen, Jan., 1969.

4. Sung by Yetta Pickman Cohen, who learned it in her youth (ca. 1920).

5. Dave Wylie to Cohen, Feb. 4, Oct. 14, 1969; Wylie had relayed my question to Robert Gardner.

6. From my memory; learned in Minneapolis in the early 1940s. The final line, "Way down yonder in the corn field," was both the title of a 1901 pop hit (by Will D. Cobb and Gus Edwards) and also the refrain of a much older minstrel song.

7. From Lucie Swift of Paducah, Ky., n.d.

8. "Billy Goat Blues" by John Byrd, vocal and guitar. Recorded ca. Apr., 1930, in Grafton, Wis.; released on Paramount 12997, ca. Nov., 1930.

9. "O'Grady's Goat" by Will S. Hays appears in *Shoemaker's Best Selections*, No. 18, compiled by Silas Neff (Philadelphia: Pennsylvania Publishing, 1890). For more on Hays, see the discussion of "Little Red Caboose (III)" in chap. 11.

REFERENCES

A. "Papa's Billy Goat," by Fiddlin' John
    Carson. Vocal and fiddle. Recorded Nov.
    7 or 8, 1923 (General Phonograph Corp.
    master S-72-018), in New York City.
    Released on OKeh 4994 in ca. Jan., 1924.
    Reissued on Parlophone (England)
    R3878.
    "Rosenthal's Goat," by Mac [Lester
    McFarland] and Bob [Robert Gardner].
    Vocal duet, accompanied by guitar,
    harmonica, and mandolin. Recorded Aug.
    15, 1928 (Brunswick master 28089), in
    New York City. Released on Vocalion
    5322.

B. Bain, 236   "No Harm Done" (from
    unspecified 1915 issue of *Frisco Man*)
    Botkin (1944), 453
    Brand (1961), 118–19   "This Here Goat"
    Brown III, 568   "The Billy Goat"
    Cotton Patch Rag, 7 (Mar., 1972), 4
    "The Goat That Flagged a Train" (prose
    version)
    Davis, A. K., 151   "Papa's Billy Goat"
    (title and one line only)
    Finger (1923), 28   "The Sad Goat"
    Folk Sing, 114   "This Here Goat"
    Ford, 374   "Riley's Goat"
    Gregory   "The Goat"
    Harbin, 21   "The Goat Song"
    Hurston, 148
    *Journal of the Folklore Society of Greater
    Washington*, 1 (Winter, 1969–70), 8; 1
    (Spring, 1970), 10
    Leach, M., 243–44 (prose version)
    Levy (1971), 231, 256–58   "The Tale of a
    Shirt"

Neal, 100   "Billy Goat"
Ott, 57–58 (prose version)
Peacock I, 65   "Joey Long's Goat"
Shay (1929), 78   "Angeline"
Silverman (1975) I, 310–11
Spaeth (1945), 140–41   "The Goat"
Story Parade, 27
Taylor, J. (I), 8   "Bill Goat Song"
Taylor J. (II), 10   "Billy Goat Song"
White, N. I., 231   (no title)

C. COHEN COLLECTION:
    Ruth Butcher (letter, June 3, 1968)
    Yetta Cohen (ca. 1970)
    Olive Whiteman (letter, Apr. 12, 1969)

ODUM-ARTHUR MSS:
5   "The Billy Goat"

WKFA:
Betty Brown (July 18, 1949)   "Bill
    Crogan's Goat"
Betty Green (spring, 1958)   "Bill Bailey's
    Goat"
Alpheus Hinton (Jan., 1961) (no title)
Ewing Jackson (summer, 1949)   "Sal had
    a Goat"
Jerry Martin (May, 1955)   "Harlem
    Goat"
Mary Louise Nicely (May 14, 1948)
    "One Evening Bill"
Etha Penrod (May, 1959)   "Jackson Had
    a Billy Goat"
Guy Doc Simmons, Jr. (May, 1955)
    "Bill Grogan's Goat"
Lucie Swift (n.d.)   "Old McGall"
Royal Targan (n.d.)

Eva Tarry (Spring, 1948)   "Isaac Small's
Goat," (no title), "Bill Grogin's Goat"
Mrs. J. J. Wilkey (May, 1957)   "Old
Hogan's Goat"

D. Fiddlin' John Carson—Bluebird B-5787
John Byrd—Paramount 12997; Yazoo
L-1001: *Mississippi Blues—1927–1941*
Vernon Dalhart—Gennett 3365, Challenge
313, Champion 15147, Herwin 75531,
Silvertone 3857
Uncle Dave Macon—Vocalion 14848,
Vocalion 5041

E. Sarah Ogan Gunning—Rounder 0051:
Silver Dagger
Louisiana Honeydrippers—Folk Lyric LP
122: *Bayou Bluegrass*; Arhoolie 5010:
Bayou Bluegrass   "Great Big Billy
Goat"

Group of New York children—Folkways FC
7003 (FP 703): *1, 2, 3 and a Zing Zing
Zing*   "Bill Bones"

F. ACWF:
Jack Gaffney—T7-48-1, Butte, Mont. (July
15, 1948)

LC AFS:
Ralph Alexander—AFS 11893 A
"About a Goat" (probably related)
Bob Blackstone—AFS 12042 A8
"Billy Goat Song"
Jim Howard—AFS 1376 A1   "Billy Goat
Song" (probably related)
Clarence Smith—AFS 12045 B18
"Billy Goat Song"

Fiddlin' John Carson. Courtesy of the John
Edwards Memorial Foundation, UCLA.

7

He's Coming to Us Dead

THE SONGS IN this chapter embrace a variety of pathetic situations. In the one that aptly lends its title here, "He's Coming to Us Dead," we have a vignette of an old man at the express office waiting for the corpse of his hero son who died fighting with the Boys in Blue. "Jim Blake's Message" recounts a double tragedy: the engineer, speeding home to his dying wife, receives a telegram that he is too late; barely has this message been sent over the wires when another comes in the opposite direction—the train has been derailed and the engineer also has died. "The Red and Green Signal Lights" tells of lanterns to be placed in the cabin window to inform the engineer as his train roars past whether his dying daughter is dead ("then show the red") or better ("then show the green"); in contrast to the aforementioned songs, this story ends happily. "In the Baggage Coach Ahead," probably the best-known song of the chapter, concerns a young widower and his bawling babe who ride in the Pullman car, while the dead wife rides in a casket in the baggage coach ahead. The restless passengers, at first angered by the child's crying, are all deeply moved by the father's tragic tale. "The Eastbound Train" tells of a young girl with no ticket; before the stern conductor can remove her, she unfolds her tale of a blind father in prison, on whose behalf she is going to see the governor for a pardon. Not only does the conductor allow her to remain on board, but when they reach the destination, he leads her by the hand to the governor's mansion. This account must surely have seemed incredible to listeners at a time when railroad officials were noted for their unwillingness to exchange dated tickets for another date, to accept rides in the direction opposite from that indicated on the ticket, or to make any effort to accommodate the passengers. "Please, Mr. Conductor, don't put me off the train" is the anguished cry of another child whose doleful tale melts the hearts of his listeners. This youth wants to reach his dying mother before the angels bear her away. In this case the conductor does not have to relent, for the passengers on board take up a collection to pay the boy's fare. We are not told if he reaches his mother in time. "There's a Little Box of Pine on the 7:29" tells of a plain coffin carrying home the body of a mother's darling son who died in prison. It is noteworthy that the boy had not been executed; the song leaves the distinct impression that the lost sheep was brought to justice not by Caesar's minions, but by a greater authority. "The Evening Train" concludes this chapter with some phrases reminiscent of the song that opened it. It tells of a father and son weeping uncontrollably as the dead wife/mother is being taken away in a casket in the baggage coach of the evening train.

It probably did not help the railroads' image in the public mind that the charge for transporting a corpse in the baggage coach—at least on the Virginian Railway—was not what it would have been for other baggage, but the same as the full fare that a living adult passenger would have paid for the journey, regardless of the age of the deceased. If a traveler died while on board the train, the Virginian would carry the remains to the final resting place, provided that the deceased had been holding a round-trip ticket.[1]

The songs in this chapter span some six decades—we cannot be more precise because the dates of composition of the earliest ones are uncertain. Yet they share a spirit that permits them to be juxtaposed without jarring anachronisms of style or sentiment. One cannot always select songs of professional composition over a sixty-year period and find them so alike; when this does happen, it merits comment.

The first six songs in the chapter were probably all composed in the 1890s. It was a period that had an especial fondness for the ballad. (The term *ballad* has a very special meaning to folklorists, although one not always mutually agreed upon. In the more general parlance of the pop-music world, it used to mean any slow, narrative song. In recent decades the requirement of telling a story has been dropped, and any slow song can be classified as a ballad.) The songwriter and publisher E. B. Marks expressed it from a slightly different point of view: "The public of the nineties had asked for tunes to sing. The public of the turn of the century had been content to whistle. But the public from 1910 on demanded tunes to dance to."[2]

Folksong collectors have turned up many of these nineteenth-century Tin Pan Alley ballads in their fieldwork; but all too often they have spurned them in favor of the more rural, unprofessional ballads and songs whose paternity was not quite so demonstrable. Folksongs are thus unique in the universe of collectors and things collected in that interest in them has sometimes been lost when the identity of their creators was found. This explains, for example, May Kennedy McCord's remarks about the song "He's Coming to Us Dead": "I am glad to get the old song but I do not think it is a folk ballad. I believe it was a song like 'Just Tell Them That You Saw Me' which was so popular when I was a young girl."[3] Fortunately, this attitude is becoming less prevalent among folk-song collectors.

These first six songs are now truly part of the public domain, not only by virtue of their having passed the copyright age requirement of fifty-six years, but also because they all are now in oral tradition. They are passed from parent to child, from one neighbor to another, but not necessarily on paper. They have become folksongs because their existence is no longer wholly dependent on the commercial media of sheet music, phonograph records, songbooks, or broadsides. One day, they may cease to be heard on the lips of some backwoods (or suburban) singer; then they will cease to be folksongs.

Why did these sentimental songs of Tin Pan Alley become folksongs? Why were they accepted by those who performed and listened to them, alongside the older heritage of British ballads and songs—such hoary pieces as "Lord Randall," "Scarborough Fair," or "Samuel Hall"? I think a very important factor was simply that they were ballads; they were like the older folk ballads in telling stories of human interest, dealing with common experiences, and utilizing relatively simple language. (Their musical settings were another matter, and although texts of some of these songs have been recovered in remarkably good states of preservation, the melodies often have changed or disintegrated beyond recognition.)

When the turn of the century came, as Marks observed, people were caught up first with the instrumental music of the Ragtime Era, and then with the dance music of the tango, the turkey trot, the grizzly bear, and other zoological terpsichore. Ballads fell out of favor in pop music. However, two decades later they were resuscitated and rehabilitated commercially with the dawning of the hillbilly record industry. (In many rural areas, of course, the ballads and sentimental songs of the late nineteenth century had never been forgotten.) These phonograph records were aimed at a regional market—the rural, southern, Anglo-American population, primarily—and the music was composed and performed by artists who were part of that culture group. Because the musical tastes of this populace were so well attuned to the styles of the latter nineteenth century, when hillbilly songwriters began to create their own material, naturally they echoed closely the older material that was so familiar to them and to their audiences. "Little Box of Pine" and "On the Evening Train" are hillbilly songs of 1931 and 1949, respectively, but they could easily have flowed from the pens of such great balladists of the 1890s as Charles K. Harris, Gussie Davis, or Paul Dresser.[4]

The rest of America became urbanized and urbane, and the sentimental music of the Gilded Age was an embarrassing reminder of national childhood, much as pigtails to an adolescent girl stigmatize her preteen years. Later, the young woman can look back with a more mature perspective and think fondly of those pigtail days. Similarly, when Sigmund Spaeth first published his collection of nostalgic music reminiscences,[5] his intent was a "sardonic spoofing of our naive musical past." But he found, among his public, "a truly sympathetic appreciation of how they felt and acted before the turn of the century."[6]

That characterization, of course, applied to Spaeth's audience, which was essentially urban and suburban. It is a curious sociological fact that in rural America (especially in the South) these songs were not re-accepted out of nostalgia; rather, they had never been cast aside. The explanation is part of a larger phenomenon; it is only one aspect of a rural America increasingly trying to preserve a society of log cabins and plantations in the face of irresistible tendencies toward urbanization and industrialization. Modern country music of the 1950s and 1960s (and the end does not seem to be in sight) still dwelt on the familiar themes of mother and home, still recounted tales of southerners who had moved to the big city but yearned at night for the fields of corn back home. Corn, indeed, to the smirking city-dweller whose rural roots were cut off more than three generations ago, but a symptom of an American minority desperately trying to preserve itself—much as the black nationalists want to preserve their black heritage, or as the Jewish enclaves resist assimilation to preserve their cultural identity. The South does not want to be part of the twentieth century, to forget the Civil War and agrarian society.

Let us now set aside these larger considerations and return to the songs qua railroad songs. It is curious to note that among the various themes expressed by these sentimental tone-poems we do not find unrequited or unfaithful love. Such matters are dealt with frequently in blues songs, and in lyric songs to a lesser degree (see chaps. 9 and 10, respectively). The absence of these themes from this chapter must be regarded as largely accidental, as they do appear among other sentimental songs of the 1880s and 1890s (consider, to name only a few, "After the Ball," "Two Little Girls in Blue," "There'll Come a Time," and "Broken Engagement").

Finally, dare we pass judgment on these songs as works of literature? Will they stand any enduring esthetic test of time? I think it is fruitless to assay any absolute evaluations. In this discussion, and throughout this chapter, I have tried to use the term *sentimental* without condescension; yet the very definition of the word implies a value judgment that is barely neutral at best. Furthermore, the definition of the word must be relative to some community standards, which are inevitably fickle and transient. Some future generation may well regard "In the Baggage Coach Ahead" as touchingly tender; higher-class works of literature have suffered similar oscillating valuations. Judged in the context of their peers, however, these songs rank favorably. The very fact that they are still remembered today, up to a century after their creation, testifies to their quality. After all, popular culture is unashamedly democratic in nature; and the survivors are always, by definition, the good guys.

NOTES

1. H. Reid, *The Virginian Railway* (Milwaukee: Kalmbach Publishing, 1961), p. 48.

2. E. B. Marks, *They All Sang* (New York: Viking Press, 1934), p. 156.

3. May Kennedy McCord, "Hillbilly Heartbeats," *Springfield* (Mo.) *News*, Nov. 19, 1935.

4. The development of hillbilly phonograph music and its significance for the songs in this book are discussed in chap. 2.

5. Sigmund Spaeth, *Read 'em and Weep* (Garden City, N.Y.: Doubleday, Page, 1926).

6. Ibid., 2d ed. (New York: Arco Publishing, 1945), p. vii.

He's Coming to Us Dead

HE'S COMING TO US DEAD

Original Key: F

♩ = 100

One morn-ing when the of-fice had o-pened, a
man quite old in years Stood by the ex-press
of-fice, show-ing signs of grief and tears.

*The chords on the recording are inconsistent from stanza to stanza.

One morning when the office had opened, a man quite old in years
Stood by the express office, showing signs of grief and tears.

When the clerk approached him, in trembling words did say,
"I'm waiting for my boy, sir, he's coming home today."

[*Spoken:*] Take warning from this song.

"Well, you have made a silent [?slight] mistake, and you must surely know,
That this is a telegraph office, sir, and not a town depot.

"If your boy is coming home," the clerk in smiles did say,
"You'll find him with the passengers, at the station just o'er the way."

Take warning, folks.

"You do not understand me, sir," the old man shook his head,
"He's not a-coming as a passenger, but by express instead."

Take warning, good people.

"He's coming home to mother," the old man gently said.
"He's coming home in a casket, sir, he's coming to us dead."

Then a whistle pierced their ears; "The express train," someone cried;
The old man rose in a breathless haste and quickly rushed outside.

Then a long white casket was lowered to the ground,
Showing signs of grief and tears to those who'd gathered 'round.

"Do not use him roughly, boys, it contains our darling Jack,
He went away as you boys are, this way he's coming back.

"He broke his poor old mother's heart, her sins have [?her fears have since]
    all come true,

She said this the way he'd come back, when he joined the Boys in Blue."

A lot of them come back that way, too.

Grayson and Whitter

There is nothing in the text of this song to link it unequivocally with either the Civil War or the Spanish-American War. The piece was published in 1899 with words and music credited to Gussie L. Davis, the composer of two other songs in this chapter (see "The Red and Green Signal Lights" and "In the Baggage Coach Ahead"); however, it was not uncommon for sentimental songs to be published in the 1890s that dealt with the Civil War. (Nor is it out of the question that Davis rewrote an earlier song or poem, as he did in the case of "In the Baggage Coach Ahead.")

The last line of the song is puzzling. On the face of it, the statement seems to be antiwar; but in the 1890s, national sentiment was strongly in favor of United States intervention in the Cuban struggle for independence, and many popular songs expressed that point of view.[1] There were some antiwar songs, although on a folk level—compare the widely known, humorous "Battleship of Maine."[2]

"Boys in blue" was an appropriate epithet for the United States soldiers throughout much of the nineteenth century, but during the Spanish-American War, khaki uniforms were first introduced and worn by some of the volunteer regiments. That is, although blue was being phased out at that time, the expression could still have been suitable. The vignette of a dead soldier brought home by train must have been an all-too-common scene during the Civil War: Union forces alone suffered more than 360,000 fatalities. In sharp contrast, the four-month conflict with Spain resulted in 2,500 deaths, only 400 of which were due to battle.

These general observations lead me to expect that somewhere there was a much earlier antecedent for Davis's song that predated the Spanish-American War, but I have no proof of any. The frequent appearance, during the last half of the nineteenth century, of several distinct versions of one song by different authors and composers also makes me hesitate to label a particular piece of sheet music as "the original version." Songwriters of that period evidently had a different notion from ours about originality and plagiarism; and the commonly applied argument that the existence of different versions of a song proves that the piece is a folksong may not be a sufficient proof in *that* historical period.[3]

The phrase "He's not coming as a passenger, but by express instead" is a reminder of the different meanings the work *express* has in connection with the railroads. Originally, an express train was one that went expressly to a few particular stations; by 1848 it meant a fast, nonlocal train. As early as the seventeenth century, though, the word *express* was also associated with delivery of parcels and mail, and by the time of the Civil War several express companies were thriving, the major ones being Adams and Company in the North and Southern Express Company in the South. In 1917, the federal government merged the four existing express companies (Adams, American, Southern, and Wells Fargo) into one company, the American Railway Express. Later, in an effort to blot out the image of the railway, as truck and airplane become the primary movers, the company changed its name to REA Express (which used to stand for Railway Express Agency). The point of this digression is to make clear that when the song lyrics say the soldier is coming by express, they do not mean a nonlocal train, but rather a freight train.

Apart from the 1899 sheet music referred to above, the Grayson and Whitter piece, recorded October 18, 1927, in Atlanta, is the earliest appearance of the song on disc or in print that I have found (Randolph had collected a version a few months earlier). Since the vocal lead is by Gilliam Banmon Grayson, it was undoubtedly "his" song. Ralph Peer copyrighted it January 20, 1928 (E 681402), words and music credited to G. B. Grayson. To our great misfortune, no folklorists ever interviewed the blind singer/fiddler of Laurel Bloomery, Tennessee, before his accidental death in 1930, so we will never know the sources for his wealth of beautiful ballads and tunes. His and Henry Whitter's careers are discussed in more detail in connection with "Nine Pound Hammer" (chap. 11).

Although Grayson's text follows the sheet music version rather closely (except for the notable substitution of the telegraph office for express office in the third stanza—an understandable "mistake," since the telegraph office was often situated at the train station), his tune is quite different. Davis's "original" tune is thirty-two bars long, followed by a chorus, to a different melody, of sixteen bars. Thus, Grayson's first four stanzas correspond to the first stanza of the Davis text; his fifth and sixth stanzas correspond to the chorus; and his last four stanzas, to Davis's second stanza. Grayson's eight-bar melody does not seem to be closely related to any part of Davis's more elaborate composition, nor do any of the other recorded versions. Davis wrote the melody for the thirty-two bar stanzas in 4/4 time and that for the chorus in 3/4 time—not a rare musical device in the 1890s. All subsequent folk and hillbilly versions are in one meter throughout: Grayson's, in 4/4 time; the others, in 3/4 time.

Judging by textual and musical details, the version collected by Crabtree seems to have been learned from the Grayson and Whitter recording. Wade Mainer's recording was almost certainly based on Grayson and Whitter's. The bands led by Wade Mainer and his older brother, J. E., were among the first hillbilly groups to take material extensively from other hillbilly recordings to supplement their own rich family tradition.

The three other 78 rpm recordings from the 1920s and early 1930s are all independent of the Grayson and Whitter version. The first of these was "The Boy in Blue," recorded by Stuart Hamblen in June, 1929. Hamblen learned the song in the 1910s from his grandfather, a Civil War veteran, and associated it with that war. The two recordings that followed it—by Marc Williams and by Ted Hawkins—seem to be independent of the Hamblen recording. The other collected texts cited in sections B and F of the references are all independent of any of the 78 rpm hillbilly recordings. The LP recordings by Brown, Herbert, Ledford, Nevada Slim, the New Lost City Ramblers, and the Old Hat Band all probably derive, directly or indirectly, from the Grayson and Whitter disc.

Two other versions—those by Molly O'Day and by Steve Ledford—deserve separate comment. Arranger's credit for Molly O'Day's 1947 Columbia recording was given to her husband, Lynn Davis. The song is similar to several texts, especially Hamblen's, but the final stanza is unique:

> It's broken his poor mother's heart, as partings always do,
> Thank God he died a hero's death while with the boys in blue.

This final line seems to negate any sense of antiwar sentiment in the ballad, changing it instead to a song of praise—possibly for a soldier in the Army of the Republic (O'Day is from Kentucky, a free state during the Civil War). Molly O'Day learned the song prior to her recording it from a radio show featuring Texas Ruby (Fox). I do not know if Texas Ruby's text was the same as Molly O'Day's.

The most recent recording, as of this writing, is an updated version by Steve Ledford's String Band entitled "He's Comin' from Vietnam." Though based on the Grayson and Whitter version, the song is given a new venue by the refrain:

> He's coming home to mother, he's not coming as I am;
> He's coming home in a casket, sir, he's coming from Vietnam.

NOTES

1. See William K. McNeil, "'We'll Make the Spanish Grunt': Popular Songs about the Sinking of the *Maine," Journal of Popular Culture,* 2 (Spring, 1969), 537–51.

2. See the transcription of Victor 20936 (1927) by Red Patterson's Piedmont Log Rollers in John Cohen and Mike Seeger, eds., *The New Lost City Ramblers Song Book* (New York: Oak Publications, 1964), pp. 116-17.

3. Of possible ·significance in dating the song is the report of Mary Elizabeth Buford, whose informant, Ella Miller, said (in 1940) that she had learned it in about 1894. See Buford's "Folk Songs of Florida and Texas" (Master's thesis, Southern Methodist University, 1940). If this recollection is reliable, it would place the song before the Spanish-American War. On the other hand, Bill Ellis argues for that war as the origin of the song, primarily because of its similarity to other sentimental pieces of the 1890s. See his article "'The Boys in Blue': Mother Song to Protest Song and Back Again," *Journal of the Ohio Folklore Society,* n.s., 5 (1978), 14–22.

REFERENCES

A. "He Is Coming to Us Dead," sheet music, by Gussie L. Davis. Published in New York by F. A. Mills, 1899. Copyright number 12201.

"He's Coming to Us Dead," by G. B. Grayson and Henry Whitter. Grayson, vocal and violin; Whitter, guitar. Recorded Oct. 18, 1927 (Victor master 40303), in Bristol, Tenn. Released on Victor 21139 ca. Feb., 1928. Reissued on County 513: *The Recordings of Grayson and Whitter.* First recording of the song; transcribed here.

B. *Aurora* (Mo.) *Advertiser,* Aug. 22, 1935   "The Boys in Blue"

Bronco Busters, 3   "Boys in Blue"

Buford, 181

Crabtree, 128   "He Is Coming to Us Dead"

Davis, L., 1   "Boys in Blue"

Mainer, J. E., 31

McCord, May Kennedy, "Hillbilly Heartbeats" column, *Springfield* (Mo.) *News & Leader,* Nov. 19, 1935

Owens, W., 275–77

Randolph IV, 148–50   "The Express Office," "The Boys in Blue," "The Boys in Blue"

Riddle-Abrahams, 18–20

Tribe & Morris, 29–30 (from Davis, L.) "Boys in Blue."

D. Ted Hawkins—Columbia 15752-D "Roamin' Jack"

Stuart Hamblen—Victor 40109, Electrobeam 2125, Bluebird B-5242   "The Boy in Blue"

Wade Mainer and his Mountaineers— King 585

Molly O'Day—Columbia 20441; Harmony HL 7299: *The Unforgettable Molly O'Day*   "A Hero's Death"

Marc Williams—Brunswick 564, Decca (Ireland) W4419   "The Boys in Blue"

E. Hylo Brown—Rural Rhythm 187: *Hylo Brown*

Wilma Lee and Stoney Cooper—Decca DL 4784/74784: *Wilma Lee and Stoney Cooper Sing*   "A Hero's Death"

Morris Herbert and group—Rural Rhythm RR-JEM-230: *The Legendary J. E. Mainer, Vol. 11*

Steve Ledford—Rounder 0008: *Ledford String Band*   "He's Comin' from Vietnam"

Nevada Slim (Dallas Turner pseudonym)— Rural Rhythm RR-NS-181

New Lost City Ramblers—Verve Folkways FT/FTS 3018: *Remembrance of Things to Come*

Molly O'Day, with Lynn Davis and the Cumberland Mountain Folks—Old Homestead OHCS 101: *A Sacred Collection*   "A Hero's Death"

Old Hat Band—Voyager VRLP 307S: *Concert*

F. LC AFS:

Pearl Brewer—AFS 12036 A27 "Express Office"

Nancy Philley—AFS 12038 B10   "The Boys in Blue"

Susie Wasson—AFS 11910 A   "The Boy in Blue" (possibly related)

In the Baggage Coach Ahead

IN THE BAGGAGE COACH AHEAD

Original Key: B

♩ = 168

On a dark storm-y night as the train rat-tled on, All the pas-sen-gers all gone to bed, Ex-cept a young man with a babe in his arms, who_ sat with a bowed-down head. The in-no-cent one be-gan cry-ing just then, As though its poor heart would break; An an-gry man said, "Make that child stop its noise, For it's keep-ing us all a-wake." As the train rolled on and on_ a hus-band sat in tears, Think-ing of the hap-pi-ness_ of just a few short years; For the ba-by's face brings pic-tures_ of the

cher - ished hope that's dead, But ba - by's cries can't
wak - en her___ in the bag - gage coach a - head.

On a dark stormy night as the train rattled on,
All the passengers all gone to bed,
Except a young man with a babe in his arms,
Who sat with a bowed-down head.
The innocent one began crying just then,
As though its poor heart would break;
An angry man said, "Make that child stop its noise,
For it's keeping us all awake."

"Take it out," said another, "don't keep it in here,
We've paid for our berths and want rest";
But never a word said the man with the child,
As he fondled it close to his breast.
"Oh, where is its mother? Go take it to her,"
A lady then softly said;
"I wish that I could," was the man's sad reply,
"She's dead in the coach ahead."

Every eye filled with tears as his story he told,
Of a wife who's so faithful and true;
He told how he had saved up his earnings for years,
Just to build up a home for two.
How heaven had sent them a sweet little babe,
Their young happy lives to bless;
His heart seemed to break when he mentioned her name,
And in tears tried to tell the rest.

Every woman arose to assist with the child,
There were mothers and wives on that train;
And soon the little one was sleeping in peace,
Without any thought, sorrow, or pain;
Next morning at the station he bade them goodbye,
"God bless you," he softly said;
Each one had a story to tell in their homes,
Of the baggage coach ahead.

As the train rolled on and on a husband sat in tears,
Thinking of the happiness of just a few short years;
For the baby's face brings pictures of the cherished [*pronounced
  "cheerished"*] hope that's dead,
But baby's cries can't waken her in the baggage coach ahead.

Ernest Thompson

One of the most popular pieces of Gay Nineties sentimentalia was Gussie L. Davis's composition "In the Baggage Coach Ahead," copyrighted in 1896 (E 47482) by Howley, Haviland and Company of New York, copyright assigned to E. B. Marks Music Company on July 23, 1924 (R 27800).

The popularity of this ballad was not at all hindered by the assertion that there was a touching true tale behind it. The story has been recounted by Spaeth, Geller, Marks, Gilbert, Holbrook, Randolph, Burton, Marcuse, and Ewen, each writer focusing on slightly different aspects of the story, each adding a fillip that is inconsistent with other reports.[1]

As Randolph related it in his headnotes, "Dr. James B. Watson, a Jackson County, Mo., physician, married a Pennsylvania girl in 1859. Their daughter Nellie was born in Kansas City, May 25, 1867. Mrs. [Abigail] Watson died in 1869, and Dr. Watson took the body back to [Wilkes-Barre] Pennsylvania. During the trip the little girl cried, and the doctor told complaining passengers that the child's mother was dead in the baggage coach. . . . Nellie Watson married J. M. Klapmeyer; she died May 19, 1926. . . ."

When Spaeth first wrote about this song, he concluded, "It may be surmised that Davis himself was the Pullman porter on the train. . . ." Gussie Davis had indeed been a Pullman porter for some years, after which he returned to his native Cincinnati, where he became a janitor at the Conservatory of Music. Here he picked up scraps of music; later, he became one of the top songwriters of the 1890s.

Spaeth's surmise was confirmed by E. B. Marks, who in 1934 wrote: "According to a letter I received some time ago from Heiman L. Matthews, a railroad conductor, Frank Archer of Hector, N.Y., worked the same train as Davis in the colored man's portering days. The actual incident of the mother's coffin in the baggage car ahead occurred and infused the conductor with the bardic impulse. He wrote a poem published in an upstate paper. The composer-porter of that talented train later put the lyric in song form and set it to music." The poem was entitled "Mother." Ewen added the twist that it was Davis who saw the incident and related it to Archer, another porter (according to Ewen), who wrote a poem about it.

Regardless of who actually witnessed the alleged incident, years later, after he had become a songwriter, Davis saw Archer's poem and was reminded of it. He wrote a fresh account, one considerably more pathetic than Archer's, and took it to various New York publishers. It was rejected by all, until he came to Howley, Haviland and Company, where Fred Haviland liked the song, although his business associates did not. Davis persuaded Haviland to pay him whatever he saw fit for the song, and parted with it for an insignificant sum (according to Geller) rather than take it to other publishers. Gilbert disagrees over the matter of Davis's payment, insisting he was amply recompensed for his efforts. In any case, when Imogene Comer, "Queen Regent of Song," came to Howley, Haviland looking for new material, she was shown Davis's ballad, and she liked it. She first performed it at the Howard Atheneum in Boston, to the overwhelming appreciation of her audience, and continued to sing it regularly for three years. Following the custom of the day, the song was sung while stereoscopic pictures were shown on a screen.

The accounts of all the song historians notwithstanding, there are other possible sources that may have inspired Davis to compose his ballad. The same story was told in an 1895 composition, "The Baby on the Train," words by George Cooper, music by Charles E. Pratt, published by M. Witmark and Sons. I quote one verse and chorus for comparison:

Sheet music: "In the Baggage-Coach Ahead." Courtesy of David Morton and the Archives of Popular American Music, UCLA.

The crowded train sped fast along,
Each passenger seemed light and gay,
Excepting one amid the throng,
Within whose arms a body lay.
Its feeble and complaining cries
The father tried to hush in vain,
Till "Where's its mother?" some one said,
"Do take it back to her again."

Oh, Life has scenes of gladness bright,
And Life has scenes of pain;
But ne'er will fade from out my sight,
That baby on the train.

The melody is quite different from Davis's.

I have been unable to locate the original printing of Archer's poem, "Mother." However, Marks quoted it in his discussion, and the poem also appeared in at least two hillbilly song folios of about 1940 by the singer Jack Marlow. The song is preceded by the notation "Composed by an old time railroad conductor—compliments of Dell Hildreth to Jack Marlow." The text, which differs from that quoted by Marks in only a few places, follows:

IN THE BAGGAGE CAR AHEAD

Last night we had a passenger,
He occupied a chair car seat;
With him were four small children,
Dressed very plain and neat.

Two boys of tender ages,
And two little baby girls
With blue eyes, soft and loving
And silken golden curls.

They wept, and cried, and murmured,
And tossed their little heads;
"We want to go to mamma,"
Is what they often said.

The passengers got nervous
As they heard the babies weep;
One said, "Take them to their mother
And let us go to sleep."

But a gentle little lady
Took a baby girl and said,
"Do you want to go to mamma?"
And she stroked its little head.

"Where is the children's mother?"
To the father then she said,
"The mother is in a casket
In the baggage car ahead."

Strong men's hearts began to soften,
And the women began to weep
And the man who made objection
Found he did not want to sleep.

Each of these little children's heads
Lay on a loving breast,
And soon in innocent slumber
The little ones were at rest.

But the father was heartbroken.
And this was all he said;
"Their mother is in a casket,
In the baggage car ahead."[2]

Another poem based on such an incident was published several times in the late nineteenth and early twentieth centuries under the title "The Conductor's Story." Written by Maurice E. McLoughlin in the more deliberately folksy style of a Harte or a Lowell, it makes an interesting contrast with the lyrics of Gussie Davis, who schooled himself very successfully in the Tin Pan Alley style. The following version (the differences among the printed texts are all trivial) is taken from the *Railroad Trainmen's Journal*,[3] which in turn had taken it from the *New York Sunday Mercury*.

THE CONDUCTOR'S STORY

When a man has been railroadin' twenty long years
    He gits kinder heardened an' tough
An' scenes of affliction don't trouble him much
    'Cause his natur' is coarse like an' tough.
But a scene that took place on my train one cold night
    Would a'melted the heart of a stone,
An' among the adventures which I have been through
    That night just stands out all alone.

'Twas a bitter cold night an' the train was jam full,
    Every berth in the sleeper was taken;
The people had jist turned in for the night
    An' the train for New York was a'makin',
When jist as the people to snore had begun
    An' I with a satisfied sigh
Had sat down in a chair for a short rest, I heard
    The sound of a young baby's cry.

It was one of those loud aggravatin'-like yells,
    O' the pattern that makes you jist itch
For a gun or an ax an' excites up your mind
    With wild thoughts o' murder an' sich.
It went through that car an' I needn't remark
    That the snorin' stopped right there an' then
An' that sleeper was filled with a bilin' hot crowd
    O' mad women and wild, swearin' men.

The curtain jist then that concealed berth sixteen
   Were opened an' out came a man.
As fine a young feller as ever I seen,
   But his face was all white like an' wan.
He carried the kid that was raisin' the row,
   An' commenced walkin' down through the aisle
A tryin' to stop its loud screechin'—but pshaw!
   It seemed to get wuss every mile.

An idea seemed to strike one old feller jist then,
   An' he said to the pale-faced young man,
"It seems to me, stranger, that kid could be stilled
   By a simple an' feasible plan;
The noise that it's makin' betrays what it needs—
   The child wants its mother, that's plain;
An' why don't you call her? Ten chances to one,
   She's sleepin' somewhere on the train."

A look then came over that young father's face,
   A look full of anguish an' pain;
A look that will haunt me as long as I live,
   As long as I work on a train;
An' he answered that man in a hoarse, stifled voice
   That sounded as though from afar—
"Her mother is sleeping aboard of this train
   In a box in the baggage car."

Much less widespread, although somewhat earlier, was a short piece entitled "In the Baggage Car." Its sixteen lines of unrhymed iambic pentameter told the same story in abbreviated form. The poem, published in the 1884 *Locomotive Engineers' Monthly Journal*,[4] had been reprinted from an unidentified issue of the *Boston Transcript*.

IN THE BAGGAGE CAR

The rushing train is speeding for the east
With many people hurrying to spend
Thanksgiving in the old New England homes.

The chill November night has settled down,
Enwrapping in its ever-darkening fold
The silent farms that late were whizzing by.

The father puts his little ones to sleep,
All but the baby; baby will not go.
He wails and cries; will not be comforted.

The tired folks in vain lie down to rest;
They give it o'er and try to be resigned.
At last one man breaks out, his patience gone:

"We can't stand this all night. What ails the thing?
For goodness' sake, where is its mother gone?"

The father, calm and hopeless, sadly said:
"She's in her coffin, in the baggage car."

Finally, a recitation—I have no evidence that it was set to music—that appeared in an undated songbook of about 1904. The reference to the New Orleans Exposition of 1884–86 strongly suggests a date of composition around that time.

THE NINE-FIFTEEN

The train had left Chicago—'twas the nine-fifteen;
The Pullman car was cozy, and everything serene;
We had a few aged passengers and some not in their teens,
All bound for the Exposition to be held in New Orleans.
In a corner of the Pullman a man sat with a book;
A sleeping babe was on his lap, he wore a downcast look.
He tried to read, a page he turned, then kissed the wee babe's cheek,
With such a sad expression as though he wished to speak.
The day was bright and pleasant, the scenery was grand,
But it did not interest him—he, with the book in hand.

At last we stopped for supper; while the porter dressed our bunks.
I went up to the baggage car to see about my trunks.
We pulled out quick to make up (we were thirty-eight behind),
And the man with book and baby quickly vanished from my mind,
But something soon recalled them when we slacked up with a jar,
For I plainly heard the baby's plaintive cry go through the car.

Some fellow in a lower bunk with curses low and deep
Said, "Choke the darned brat's wind off and let us get some sleep!"
Then a lady who had heard him make this forcible request.
Said, "Yes, the nasty, horrid thing won't give us any rest!"
An old gray-bearded traveler, more kindly than the other,
Said, "Mister Stranger, take the child and give it to its mother."
Then the lady in the lower and in spiteful mood, 'twas plain—
"Yes, give it to its mother; I hope she's on the train."

Then the man with baby answered, and in a sad tone said,
"She's aboard, but in her coffin, in the baggage car ahead."
What a change came o'er the travelers! Such a change I can't explain.
If I'd caught the man that cursed that child I'd heaved him off the train.
What a scene was on that Pullman—full a hundred arms were there,
All willing to caress it now and give it every care.
If on God's earth there is a word more sacred than another,
A word held dear by one and all, six letters spell it—mother.[5]

The existence of these three poems (and possibly others) well before the composition of Davis's 1896 hit raises again the question of the historicity of the incident that was supposed to have been his inspiration. One cannot deny, though, that the story captured the sentiments of the age, considering how many different forms it took in the 1880s and 1890s. To my knowledge, none of these poems has been recovered from oral tradition, although the Archer text could easily have been sung to Davis's tune.

The ballad is such that almost inevitably the story became attached to similar incidents. The liner notes to the LP *Chickie Williams Sings the Old Songs,* for instance, state that the song concerns a Reverend Jeffrey from Cattaraugus, New York, whose wife died as they and their three-day-old child were returning from a western circuit for the Wesleyan Methodist church.

The tune also attracted other railroad texts. When *Railroad Man's Magazine* printed the Davis text,[6] the editors appended a song entitled "The Hold Up of No. 9," written, they stated, to the same music, describing a train robbery on the Chicago and Northwestern near Maple Park, Illinois, "several years ago." The chorus ran:

> While the train rolled onward the robbers sat in vain,
> Thinking of the fortune that was on the flying train;
> While the train left Wells Street ten o'clock on time,
> The robbers were in the tower house waiting for No. 9.

Another parody, written and sung by Ed Coleman of Jersey City and copyrighted in 1897, combined two humorous railroad anecdotes in a loosely structured narrative. The first related a Saint Patrick's day brawl involving English and Irish:

> While the train pulled outward, McManus loudly cried:
> For insulting dear old Ireland an Englishman has died:
> Now let this be a lesson learned to all that love the red:
> Keep still, or you'll be like the mug in the baggage coach ahead![7]

The second stanza told of Grover Cleveland boarding a train and offering ten dollars for ice for his champagne; a Jew brought him a small piece, later admitting it had been used to refrigerate his brother's corpse in the baggage coach:

> While the train rolled onward, Grover stood in shame;
> Thinking of the ice he used to cool his fevered brain.
> He gave the Jew another ten, and on the quiet said:
> "Don't ever tell this story of the baggage coach ahead!"[7]

As soon as the hillbilly recording industry emerged, opening a new commercial medium for the older songs that had been thoroughly accepted by the folk, "In the Baggage Coach Ahead" was given a new and vigorous exposure.

The first hillbilly recording of the ballad was made by Ernest Thompson, a blind minstrel from Winston-Salem, North Carolina, on September 12, 1924, in New York, at Thompson's second recording session for the Columbia Phonograph Company. This is the version transcribed in this book. Three days later, George Reneau, a blind singer-guitarist from the Knoxville, Tennessee, region, recorded the song in New York for the Aeolian (Vocalion) Company. Fiddlin' John Carson recorded it in December, 1924. All three artists had simplified Davis's more elaborate Gilded Age melody; Thompson's was the closest to the original; Carson's was considerably different. Reneau's disc gave no composer credits to Davis; the Aeolian executives probably did not realize that the song was an old pop song, and doubtless took it for genuine public-domain material.

It is not unreasonable to suppose that Vernon Dalhart heard one of the above-mentioned discs and decided to use the material himself, for early in 1925 he recorded the song for seven different companies. He went back to the sheet music for Davis's original words and music. However, even Dalhart's great influence was insufficient to restore the Davis melody in the minds of traditional singers. In Charles Rose's version, recorded by

Sam Eskin in the field in 1947, all traces of the Davis tune have been lost, supplanted by a rather unmelodic but quite traditional free-flowing tune.

NOTES

1. Sigmund Spaeth, *Read 'em and Weep* (Garden City, N.Y.: Doubleday, Page, 1926), p. 174; idem, *A History of Popular Music in America* (New York: Random House, 1948), p. 268; James J. Geller, *Famous Songs and Their Stories* (New York: Macaulay, 1931), p. 173; Edward B. Marks, *They All Sang* (New York: Viking Press, 1934), p. 82; Douglas Gilbert, *Lost Chords* (Garden City, N.Y.: Doubleday, Doran, 1942), p. 268; Stewart H. Holbrook, *The Story of American Railroads* (New York: Crown Publishers, 1947), p. 432; Vance Randolph, *Ozark Folksongs*, vol. 4 (Columbia: State Historical Society of Missouri, 1950), p. 163; Jack Burton, *The Blue Book of Tin Pan Alley* (Watkins Glen, N.Y.: Century House, 1950), pp. 26–27; Maxwell F. Marcuse, *Tin Pan Alley in Gaslight* (Watkins Glen, N.Y.: Century House, 1959), p. 195; David Ewen, *American Popular Songs* (New York: Random House, 1966), p. 182.

2. The text is identical in both folios.

3. *RTJ*, Feb., 1892, p. 118.

4. *LEMJ*, 18 (Aug., 1884), 445.

5. My copy of this songbook lacks the cover; the author/compiler and title are not indicated elsewhere.

6. *RRManM*, Sept., 1908, p. 760.

7. *Delaney's Song Book*, No. 16 (New York: William W. Delaney, ca. 1898). p. 16.

REFERENCES

A. "In the Baggage Coach Ahead," sheet music. Words and music by Gussie L. Davis. Published by Howley, Haviland and Co., New York City. Copyrighted in 1896 (E 47482); copyright renewal assigned to E. B. Marks Music Co., July 23, 1924 (R 27800).

"In the Baggage Coach Ahead," by Ernest Thompson. Vocal, guitar, and harmonica. Recorded Sept. 12, 1924 (Columbia master 140035-3), in New York City. Released on Columbia 216-D on Oct. 20, 1924. Reissued on Harmony 5124-H (as by Ernest Johnson) in ca. 1928. The first hillbilly recording of the song; transcribed in this book.

B. ARCHER TEXT—all references words only:
Marlow (I), 22
Marlow (II), 5
Marks, 82
RC, 52 (Dec., 1935), 374 (credited to M. D. Nealon and localized to the Missouri, Kansas and Texas Railroad)

MCLOUGHLIN TEXT—all references words only:

LEMJ, 29 (Dec., 1895), 1043
NCLB, 26 (Mar., 1895), 42
RRManM, 7 (Nov., 1908), 382
RTJ, Feb., 1892, p. 118
Werner, 33

DAVIS TEXT (or derivatives):
Along Memory Lane, 29
Anderson, G., 97
Buford, 157
Burton, 26 (discussion only)
Century Magazine, Aug., 1908, p. 503
Cohen & Cohen (discussion only)
Compagno, 10
Crabtree, 127
Engel, 193 (words only)
Ewen (1966), 182 (discussion only)
Family Herald, 31 (references only)
Gardner & Chickering, 477 (discussion only)
Geller, 175
Gilbert (1942), 268
Good Old Days, Feb., 1969, p. 52 (words only)
Haun, 428
Holbrook, 432 (discussion only)
Horstman, 69–70

Hubbard, L., 216 (1 text quoted, 3 others reported)

Irwin, 239 (words only)

Kennedy, C. O. (1952), 261–62

Levy (1975), 94–95

Marcuse, 195 (discussion only)

Marks, 82 (discussion only)

Mountain Side Melodies, 10

Neal, 80

OTS&P, Sept.-Oct., 1967 p. 6

Pack, 44

Peters, 211

Pound (1915), 56 (discussion only)

Pound (1922), 131 (words only)

Randolph IV, 163 (words only)

RRM, 5 (June, 1931), 478

RRManM, 6 (Sept., 1908), 760

RVB, 10 (May, 1957), 3

RVB, 15 (Mar., 1962), 6

RVB, 17 (June, 1964), 6

Spaeth (1926), 174

Spaeth (1948), 268 (discussion only)

Springfield (Mo.) *News & Leader*, Sept. 30, 1934

Stout, 59 (3 texts; words only)

Turner & Miall, 157–62

C. ALL REFERENCES are to the Davis text or derivatives:

COHEN COLLECTION:

Nellie Allen (letter, Dec., 1968)

Arling R. Judd (letter, Dec., 1968)

Cora V. Wilkins (letter, Dec., 1968)

GORDON MSS:

1568—J. H. Walsh (request; 1 verse only)

ODUM-ARTHUR MSS:

14

WKFA:

A. D. Butterworth (May, 1948)

Mary E. Chelf (Apr., 1961)

Daisy Beauchamp Duggins (n.d.)

Will Gunn (May, 1960)   "Baggage Coach Express"

Thelma Coleman Hankins (May, 1959)

Nettie Jarboe (fall, 1964)   "Baggage Coach"

Bertha Kingrey (spring, 1958)

Mrs. Felix Moore (May, 1958)

Mrs. Garland Paxton (fall, 1964)

Mrs. M. L. Picard (summer, 1949)

Rebecca Sue Stovall (June, 1949) "One Dark Stormy Night"

Mrs. J. E. Yarbrough (spring, 1955)

E. A. Yeager (Apr., 1959)

D. Fiddlin' John Carson—OKeh 7006 (12″)   "The Baggage Coach Ahead"

Vernon Dalhart—Columbia 15028-D, Diva 6018-G, Velvetone 7044-V

—Victor 19627

—Edison 51557, Edison 5011 (cylinder)

—Pathé 032120, Perfect 12199 (both as by Bob Massey)

—Banner 1549, Banner 0826, Domino 3519, Domino 4643, Cameo 0426, Challenge 784, Clover 1694, Conqueror 7067, Jewel 6076, Lincoln 1520, Oriole 2076, Oriole 421 (as by Dick Morse), Pathé 32565, Perfect 12644, Regal 9847, Regal 10132, Romeo 1440, Silvertone 2701, Fossy (Australia) 9847, Sterling (Canada) 281104, Crown (Canada) 81104, Minerva (Canada) M902, Apex (Canada) 8345

—Cameo 766, Romeo 330, Lincoln 2374

—Gennett 3019, Gennett 5675, Champion 15155, Challenge 162, Challenge 311, Herwin 75563, Silvertone 5675

—Champion 15648, Champion 45031, Supertone 9241, Silvertone 8141

—Golden Olden Classics, Vol. 1, 701: *Vernon Dalhart, 1921–1927* (reissue of one of the above recordings)

Red Evans and his Orchestra—Vocalion 5173

Arthur Fields—Grey Gull 4090 (also issued as by Mr. X.), Grey Gull 4268, Van Dyke 74268 (as by Ben Litchfield), Radiex 4090

George J. Gaskin—Edison 1517 (cylinder)

—Chicago Talking Machine Company 3886 (cylinder)

—United States Phonograph Company (cylinder, no number)

Otto Gray's Oklahoma Cowboy Band —Gennett 6387

Andrew Jenkins and Carson J. Robison— OKeh 45234

Jesters—Decca 24355 (in album A-639:
  Railroad Songs)
Silas Leachman—Talking Machine
  Company 056C (cylinder)
Reg Lindsay—Rodeo (Australia) R-029
  "In the Luggage Van Ahead"
Frank Luther, Zora Layman, and
  Leonard Stokes—Decca 435 (in album
  25: *American Folk Songs*)
Jere Mahoney—Edison B 104 (cylinder)
Lester McFarland and Robert A.
  Gardner—Brunswick 200, Brunswick
  326, Vocalion 5200, Aurora (Canada)
  22013 (as by the Miller Brothers)
Metropolitan Mixed Chorus—Edison
  3175 (cylinder)   "Songs of Other
  Days #4," Edison 80596   "Songs of
  Other Days #6" (part of medley)
Tex Morton—Regal Zonophone (Australia)
  G24263   "In the Luggage Van
  Ahead"
J. W. Myers—Busy Bee 275 (cylinder)
Dennis O'Leary—Decca 12023
Steve Porter—Columbia 4543 (cylinder)
Dan Quinn—Walcutt and Leeds
  (cylinder, no number)
—United States Phonograph Company
  (cylinder, no number)
Railroad Men—Varsity 8324
George Reneau (with Gene Austin)
  —Vocalion 14918, Vocalion 5052,
  Silvertone 3047 (as by George Hobson)

Kate Smith—Columbia 2605-D
Unknown baritone—Talking Machine
  Company 4025 (cylinder)
Unknown tenor—Talking Machine
  Company 3012C (cylinder)

E. Ed McCurdy—Riverside RLP 12-807:
   Barroom Ballads
   Chickie Williams—Wheeling WLP 4001:
   Chickie Williams Sings the Old Songs
   Mac Wiseman—CMH 9001: *The Mac
   Wiseman Story*
   —Dot DLP 3213/25213: *Great Folk
   Ballads*; Dot DLP 25896: *The Golden
   Hits of Mac Wiseman*; Hamilton HLP
   130/12130: *Sincerely*; ABC ABDP-4009:
   Sixteen Great Performances

F. LC AFS:

   Bessie Atchley—AFS 13131 B24
   Pearl Brewer—AFS 12036 B9
   Mary Faulty—AFS 13129 B9
   Bessie Gordon—AFS 5006
   T. R. Hammond—AFS 11904 A16
   Della Kerr—AFS 11890 B4
   Ethel Matter—AFS 10824 A13
   Glenn H. Parker—AFS 11907 A12
   Maggie Hammons Parker—AFS 14461-9
   Nancy Philley—AFS 12038 B4
   Beckham Ritchie—AFS 12008 A11
   Charles Rose—AFS 11712 A2

Going for a Pardon/The Eastbound Train

THE EAST BOUND TRAIN

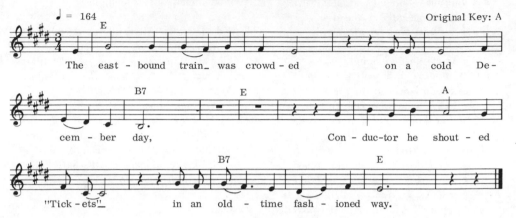

The east - bound train_ was crowd - ed on a cold De -
cem - ber day, Con - duc-tor he shout - ed
"Tick - ets"_ in an old - time fash - ioned way.

The eastbound train was crowded on a cold December day,
Conductor he shouted "Tickets" in an old-time fashioned way.

A little girl in sadness, her hair was bright as gold,
She says, "I have no ticket," just a little story told.

"My father, he's in prison, he's lost his sight, they say,
I'm going for his partner [*sic*] on a cold December day.

"My mother's daily sewing for to try to earn our bread,
While poor dear old blind father's in prison almost dead.

"My brother and my sister would both be very glad,
If I could only bring back my poor dear old blind dad."

Conductor he could not answer, he could not make reply,
By taking his rough hand wiping the teardrops from his eye.

He says, "God bless you, little one, just stay right where you are,
You'll never need no ticket while I am on this car."

Dock Walsh

"Going for a Pardon," as this ballad was originally titled, was published in 1896 by Joseph Stern and Company (copyright E 28762). The lyrics were written by James Thornton and Clara Hauenschild; the music, by James Thornton. According to the sheet music, the song was "introduced and sung with great success by Bonnie Thornton." James Thornton was one of the most popular songwriters and vaudevillians of the 1890s, but "Going for a Pardon" does not seem to be one of his better-known pieces. The copyright was renewed in 1923, assigned to E. B. Marks and Company (R 24115).

Because the original Thornton-Hauenschild lyrics are not readily available in print, and because it is interesting to compare them with later versions of the song, they are given here:

GOING FOR A PARDON

The railroad train was crowded, on a cold December day;
Conductor shouted, "Tickets!" in his old accustomed way;
When a little girl of seven, azure eyes and hair of gold,
Said, "I've got no ticket, Mister," then this little story told:
"My mother sews, to earn our bread, from early morn till night;
My father is in prison, and they say he's lost his sight."
She then told him of her mission, and how she ran away
To go and see the Governor, and for a pardon pray.

   She was going for a pardon, on that cold December day,
   A pardon for her dad, whose sight was fading fast away;
   She said her little sister and brother would be glad
   If she would only bring them back her poor blind dad.

The conductor tried to answer, but he couldn't make reply,
As with his big, rough hand he wiped a teardrop from his eye:
Softly murmuring, "God bless you, little one, stay where you are;
You will never need a ticket while I am on this car."
She told him in a whisper how her father broke the Laws,
But loved his wife and babies, and how liquor was the cause.
When the train had reached the station, he took her by the hand
And led her from the depot to the Gov'nor's mansion grand.

When the Gov'nor heard her story, he wondered at her plea;
As from her baby lips came forth, "Please set my father free,
He is getting old and feeble, and his shaven head is gray;
And besides, you know, poor Dad is blind and cannot find his way.
Just then the Gov'nor's child came in and saw Nell on her knees,
A-praying for a pardon, she said "Sign it, papa, please!"
Next day the Gov'nor led her up to a prison cell,
Unlock'd the door and sent the poor blind father home with Nell.

Thornton's ballad did not achieve the popularity of "In the Baggage Coach Ahead" (or of the following song, "Please, Mr. Conductor"), and I have found no trace of it in railroad magazines or early collections prior to the first hillbilly recording in 1925. There were, however, a few very early cylinder recordings by George J. Gaskin, Dan Quinn, and possibly others, artists who specialized in sentimental ballads around the turn of the century. On October 3, 1925, in Atlanta, Dock Walsh of Wilkes County, North Carolina, recorded the song for Columbia—his very first recording. It was released on November 30. His text and tune are transcribed in this book.

Walsh's version is sufficiently similar to most of the later hillbilly recordings, and sufficiently different from Thornton's song, to suggest the existence of a secondary ballad, composed between the turn of the century and 1925. The salient points of divergence of this secondary form, which I shall refer to as "The Eastbound Train," as distinct from "Going for a Pardon," are as follows: (1) Thornton's 4/4 tune has been replaced by a completely different waltz melody, one that could not have evolved simply by the process of gradual alteration; (2) the second half of the ballad, which relates the visit to the governor, has been discarded; (3) the opening phrase has been altered, providing the

"DOCK" WALSH

"**D**OCK" WALSH is hard to catch. So great is the demand for him at country dances and entertainments in the South, that it's mighty difficult to tell where he'll be next. However, when you do catch him, it's worth all the trouble. That's why "Dock" is recording for Columbia.

"Dock's" banjo work is as good as his singing. Consequently, he is able to play his own accompaniment. This is a big factor in making "Dock" Walsh one of the very greatest of Southern minstrels.

KNOCKING ON THE
HEN HOUSE DOOR
— Vocal with Banjo
Accomp.   15075-D
WE COURTED IN THE   10-inch
RAIN — Vocal with   75c
Banjo Accomp.

"DOCK" WALSH

Advertisement in a Columbia record catalog. Courtesy of the John Edwards Memorial Foundation, UCLA.

source for a new title; (4) significant word changes have been made, such as the new rhyme of the third couplet, and the change of *old accustomed way* in the second line to *old-time fashioned way;* (5) the chorus has been dropped, and half of it changed to a verse. The title change is logical, once the latter half of the ballad has been discarded.

The origin of the secondary ballad, "The Eastbound Train," is not known. Walsh stated that he learned the song from a left-handed banjo player named Tom Church in Lenoir, North Carolina.[1] I have no information to push the song back beyond that. A handful of other recordings followed Walsh's: in 1927, McFarland and Gardner; in 1928, Ernest V. Stoneman, Martin and Roberts, and Nelstone's Hawaiians; in 1931, Martin and Roberts again, and Riley Puckett. There are sufficient minor textual variations among these recordings to make it unlikely that all the artists learned the song from Walsh's record. Evidently, none of the research staffs of the record companies or their publishers connected "The Eastbound Train" with "Going for a Pardon," and Thornton never received credits on any of the recordings. An arrangement by Nick Manoloff was copyrighted by Calumet Publishing Company in 1935 (E 50065 and 50180).

One version, the one recorded in the fall of 1928 by Nelstone's Hawaiians, under the unique title "North Bound Train," is particularly noteworthy. Although the text is badly confused, the last two of the five verses are unmistakably taken from the last half of "Going for a Pardon."

Puckett's recording is uncommon in that the usual seven verses are followed by this moral:

> This story has one moral, and that you'll understand,
> That God guided this little one with his unseen hand.

This verse appears in no other versions.

Although "Going for a Pardon" seemed to have been generally forgotten during the first quarter of this century, the hillbilly recordings cited above injected fresh life into the secondary form, "The Eastbound Train." The long list of hillbilly song folios published mostly during the 1930s that included the song attested to its continued popularity. In most of the folios published by M. M. Cole, the song was credited to Mac and Bob (McFarland and Gardner), although they learned the song from Dock Walsh's recording.[2]

Collected versions of the song appear only in the reports of collectors who accept nineteeth-century pop songs as legitimate material for the attention of folklorists. Randolph gives two texts, one of them a manuscript version very close to Thornton's original.

NOTES

1. Dock Walsh, interviewed by Archie Green and Eugene Earle in Miller's Creek, N.C., Aug. 11, 1962. For more information on Walsh's life and career see the brochure notes to Folk-Legacy FSA 24: *The Carolina Tar Heels*.

2. Dave Wiley to Cohen, May 6, 1969. Wiley had relayed my questions to Robert Gardner.

REFERENCES

A. "Going for a Pardon," sheet music. Words by James Thornton and Clara Hauenschild; music by James Thornton. Published in 1896 by Joseph Stern and Co. Copyright E 28762; copyright renewed in 1923 and assigned to E. B. Marks and Co. (R 24115).

"The East Bound Train," by Dock Walsh. Vocal and banjo. Recorded Oct. 3, 1925 (Columbia master W141089-1), in Atlanta, Ga. Released on Columbia 15047-D on Nov. 30, 1925. First appearance of the secondary form of the ballad. Transcribed in this book.

B. *American Folk Song Folio*, 27
Anderson, G., 246
Beard, 603–5
Blue Grass Roy (1937), 28
Campbell & Holstein, 27
Cohen & Cohen (discussion only)
Davis, A. K., 115 (title and first line only of 2 variants)
Dawson (II), 35
Family Herald, 38 (reference only)
"Fiddlin' Joe's Song Corral," *Wild West Weekly*, Mar. 24, 1934, p. 136
KFBI, 20
Mac & Bob (1931a), 24
Mac & Bob (1931b), 17
Mac & Bob (1931c), 24

Mac & Bob (1941), 37
Mountain Songs, 11
OTS&P, 1 (Jan.-Feb., 1968), 9
Play and Sing, 20
Randolph IV, 186
Robison (1930), 20
Shaffer, 57
Smith, B., 58
Tiny Texan, 20
Wilson (1937a), 24
Wilson (1937b), 24

C. WKFA:
Mrs. J. W. Littleton (summer, 1948)
Mrs. Henry C. Grimes (Feb., 1956)
Melanie Price (1962)

D. Blue Sky Boys (Bolick Brothers)
—Bluebird B-8552, Montgomery Ward 8670
George J. Gaskin—Columbia 4124 (cylinder) "Going for a Pardon"
Frank Luther, with Zora Layman and Leonard Stokes—Decca 1241 (in album 25: *American Folk Songs*)
Lester McFarland and Robert A. Gardner—Brunswick 169, Supertone 2032 (as by the Kentucky Mountain Boys), Vocalion 5174
Asa Martin—Gennett 6621, Supertone 9178 (as by Emmett Davenport)

Asa Martin and Fiddlin' Doc Roberts—
    Champion 15585 (as by Jesse Coat and
    John Bishop), Champion 33045
Asa Martin and James Roberts—Banner
    32178, Conqueror 7837, Oriole 8065,
    Romeo 5065, Regal 10356, Perfect
    12711
Nelstone's Hawaiians—Victor 40065,
    Zonophone (Australia) 4232   "North
    Bound Train"
Riley Puckett—Columbia 15747-D
Dan Quinn—Chicago Talking Machine
    Company (cylinder, no number)
    "Going for a Pardon"
Ernest V. Stoneman—Edison 52299,
    Edison 5548 (cylinder); Historical HLP
    8004: *Ernest V. Stoneman and His
    Dixie Mountaineers, 1927–1928*

E. Red Allen and group—Red Clay (Japan)
    RC-104: *Red Allen*
Rex Allen—Mercury 20752/60752 and
    Mercury 12324/16324: *Rex Allen Sings
    and Tells Tales*
Beavers—Somerset 18100: *Country and
    Western Hits Made Famous by Hank
    Snow and Roy Acuff*

Lester Flatt, Earl Scruggs, and the Foggy
    Mountain Boys—Columbia CL 2686/CS
    9486: *Hear the Whistles Blow*
Jim Greer and the Mac-O-Chee Valley
    Folks—Rural Rhythm RR-133:
    Bluegrass Favorites
Kentucky Mountaineers—Folk Variety
    (West Germany) FV 12002: *Folk &
    Bluegrass at Neusuedende, 1971/2, Part 1*
Ray and Ina Patterson—County 708: *Old
    Time Ballads and Hymns*
Jimmie Williams and Red Ellis—Starday
    SLP 170: *Railroad Special;* Starday
    SEP-124
Earl Wright—Bluebonnet BL 104: *Texas
    Old Timers—Playing and Singing the
    Old Hits*

F. LC AFS:
Arlie Baker—AFS 1411 A2
Buck Buttery—AFS 11909 B24
Doney Hammontree—AFS 5364 A4 & B2
Bascom Lamar Lunsford—AFS 1795 A1
—AFS 9496 B2
Vernon Lyons—AFS 9997 B7
Nancy Philley—AFS 12038 B12
Jackie Tart—AFS 7056 A6
Marie Washam—AFS 11893 B

Please, Mr. Conductor/The *Lightning Express*

THE *LIGHTNING EXPRESS*

The *Light-ning Ex - press* from the de-pot so__ grand Had just pulled out on its way; All of the pas-sen-gers who were__ on board Seemed to be hap-py and__ gay, Ex - cept a young lad in a seat by him - self, Read-ing__ a let-ter he had; 'Twas plain to be seen by the tears in his eyes__ That the con-tents in it__ made him__ sad.

"Please, mis - ter con - duc - tor, Don't put me off of your__ train, For the best friend I have in this whole wide__ world Is wait-ing for me in vain; Ex - pect - ed to die an - y mo - ment, And

may   not   live through the   day;   I   want   to bid moth - er good-

bye,   sir,   Be - fore   God takes her a - way."

The *Lightning Express* from the depot so grand
Had just pulled out on its way;
All of the passengers who were on board
Seemed to be happy and gay,
Except a young lad in a seat by himself,
Reading a letter he had;
'Twas plain to be seen by the tears in his eyes
That the contents in it made him sad.

The stern old conductor who passed through the car,
Taking tickets from everyone there,
Finally reached the little boy's side
And gruffly demanded his fare;
"I have no ticket," the boy replied,
But I'll pay you back some day."
"I'll have to put you off the next station," he said,
But stopped when he heard the boy say:

　　"Please, mister conductor,
　　Don't put me off of your train,
　　For the best friend I have in this whole wide world
　　Is waiting for me in vain;
　　Expected to die any moment,
　　And may not live through the day;
　　I want to bid mother goodbye, sir,
　　Before God takes her away."

A little girl in a seat close by
Said, "To put that boy off, it's a shame."
So taking his hat, a collection she made,
And soon paid his way on the train.
"I'm obliged to you, miss, for your kindness to me."
"You're welcome, I'm sure, never fear."
Each time the conductor came through the car
These words seemed to ring in his ear:

　　Chorus:

                                        Blue Sky Boys

Two years after the firm of Howley, Haviland and Company published Gussie

Davis's "In the Baggage Coach Ahead," they decided to try their luck with another railroad melodrama, and accepted one written by J. Fred Helf and E. P. Moran. "Please, Mr. Conductor" was copyrighted December 17, 1898 (E 73793); the copyright was not renewed. Although the ballad achieved considerable popularity, not so much has been written about it in the pop-music histories as has been penned about Davis's piece. This is probably due to the quaint historical background of Davis's song, as well as his own renown. If there was an actual incident that inspired "Please, Mr. Conductor," it has not been reported in print.

The song has been remembered better under the title "The *Lightning Express*," the opening phrase of the first verse, and it was by that name that Triangle Music Publishing Company copyrighted it in 1925 (E 610509), with no credit to the original composers or publisher. Triangle, as was their wont with such material, credited the piece to E. V. Body, their way of saying that regardless of who originally wrote it, it had earned a secure position in the public domain.

I have found prehillbilly commercial recordings of the song by only two artists, Edward Allen and Byron G. Harlan, all on Edison cylinders; Harlan's earliest recording was made in 1899. But after 1924, the song appears frequently. The first hillbilly recording was made on March 8, 1924, in New York, by the blind singer/guitarist from Atlanta, Riley Puckett. That session was Columbia's first experience with recording hillbilly musicians. The selection was never issued. On April 26, Ernest Thompson, a blind street-singer from Winston-Salem, North Carolina, put the song on wax at his first session for Columbia, and it was released, probably in July. In the following year, most of the prominent pioneering artists (Fiddlin' John Carson, George Reneau, Ernest Stoneman, Vernon Dalhart) recorded it. When George Reneau recorded it for Vocalion, the company, evidently deciding that Reneau's untrained voice was too harsh for the sophisticated ears of its listeners, had Gene Austin sing the vocal. In company ledger sheets, officials entered the notation "no known writers." None of the earlier recordings gave composer credits either, and all were titled "(The) Lightning Express." Not until late in 1925, when Dalhart recorded the song for Victor, had the record companies discovered the composers. The only commercial recording to use the correct title was made in the early 1930s by a group called the Railroad Men who sang in barbershop-quartet style.

Numerous versions have been collected in the field ever since E. C. Perrow secured a text in North Carolina in 1913. Seventeen other versions have been deposited in the Western Kentucky Folklore Archive, and the references list other versions that have appeared in print. No important developments in words or melody have occurred; the only changes can be attributed to imperfect memory, and in no case do I consider the result to be an improvement.

REFERENCES

A. "Please, Mr. Conductor, Don't Put Me off the Train," sheet music. Words and music by J. Fred Helf and E. P. Moran. Published by Howley, Haviland and Co., New York. Copyrighted Dec. 17, 1898 (E 78793); copyright not renewed.

"The Lightning Express," by Ernest Thompson. Vocal, guitar, and harmonica. Recorded Apr. 26, 1924 (Columbia master 81743-2), in New York City. Released on Columbia 145-D in Sept., 1924. Reissued on Harmony 5121-H (as by Ernest Johnson) in ca. 1928. First hillbilly recording of this song.

"The Lightning Express," by the Blue Sky Boys. Bill Bolick, vocal and mandolin;

Earl Bolick, vocal and guitar. Recorded Aug. 21, 1939 (RCA Victor master BS-041230-1), in Atlanta, Ga. Released on Bluebird B-8369. Reissued on Montgomery Ward M-8414; RCA Camden CAL 797: *The Blue Sky Boys*; Victor (Japan) RA 5331: *The Blue Sky Boys*; and Rounder 1006: "*The Sunny Side of Life*." Transcribed in this book.

B. ALL ARE TITLED "(The) Lightning Express" unless otherwise noted.

Anderson, G., 211
Cohen & Cohen (discussion only)
Crabtree, 31
Duncan, 235
Family Herald, 45, 50 (references only)
High, 39   "The Little Boy on the Train"
Keene, 6
Odum & Johnson (1926), 44   "Please Mr. Conductor"
Randolph IV, 184, 185
RVB, 16 (Oct., 1962), 11
RVB, 37 (Nov., 1977), 11
West, C. A., 19

C. ALL ARE TITLED "(The) Lightning Express" unless otherwise noted.

WKFA:

Mrs. Roy Annis (Apr., 1959)
Annie Mae Arnol (July, 1955)   "Please Mr. Conductor"
E. N. Caldwell (E. C. Perrow Collection; 1913)
Daisy Beauchamp Duggins (n. d.) "Don't Put Me Off the Train"
Mrs. S. W. Floyd (Mar., 1948)
Nancy Frazer Jenkins (June, 1962) "The Little Boy on the Train"
Julia Keown (Jan., 1961)
Belle Kinsolving (spring, 1948)   "Mr. Conductor"
Laura Laird (May, 1948)
Mrs. W. L. Martin (May, 1957)
Nora Meisel (May, 1957)
Mrs. Garland Paxton (autumn, 1964) "Please Mr. Conductor"
Estell and Jimmy Rattliff (spring, 1964) "Please Mr. Conductor Don't Put Me Off This Train"
Sylvia Reeves (July, 1959)

Glenn and Leon Simmons (May, 1957)
Larry Spears (Nov., 1959)   "Please Mr. Conductor" or "Lightning Express"
Mrs. Floyd Sumner (summer, 1948)
Zula Williams (July, 1959)   (no title)

D. Edward Allen, Charles Hart, and chorus—Edison 3441 (cylinder)
Fiddlin' John Carson—OKeh 7008 (12" 78 rpm)
Albert Crockett and Johnny Crockett —Crown 3074, Montgomery Ward 3024 (as by the Harlan Miners Fiddlers)
Vernon Dalhart—Banner 1594, Regal 9895, Domino 3565, Oriole 473 (as by Frank Evans), Apex (Canada) 8395, Starr (Canada) 10057, Microphone (Canada) 22038, Domino (Canada) 21088, Crown (Canada) 81178
—Gennett 3129, Champion 15017, Challenge 165, Challenge 320, Herwin 75501 (as by Guy Phillips), Silvertone 3129
—Edison 51735; Mark 56 794: *First Recorded Railroad Songs*
—Victor 18937, Zonophone (Australia) EE 36
—Golden Olden Classics, Vol. 1, 701: *Vernon Dalhart, 1921–1927* (reissue of one of the above recordings)
Byron G. Harlan—Edison 7219 (cylinder), Edison B 463 (cylinder)   "Please Mr. Conductor, Don't Put Me Off the Train"
Frank Hutchison—OKeh 45144
Bradley Kincaid—Melotone 12184, Vocalion 02683, Polk 9064, Panachord (Australia) 12184, Panachord (England) 25901
Lester McFarland and Robert A. Gardner—Brunswick 200, Brunswick 326, Vocalion 5200, Aurora (Canada) 22013 (as by the Miller Brothers)
Pie Plant Pete (Claude Moye psuedonym) —Gennett 7289, Supertone 9701, Champion 16071 (as by Asparagus Joe)
Railroad Men—Varsity 8324   "Please Mr. Conductor, Don't Put Me Off the Train"
George Reneau (and Gene Austin) —Vocalion 14991, Vocalion 5056, Silvertone 3045 (as by George Hobson)
Ernest V. Stoneman—OKeh 40408

Arthur Tanner—Paramount 33160, Puritan
9160 "Lightning Express Train"

E. Everly Brothers—Cadence CLP 3016:
Songs Our Daddy Taught Us; Cadence
CLP 3059; Barnaby 511 (45 rpm)
Jim Greer and the Mac-O-Chee Valley
Folks—Rural Rhythm RR-161: *Country
Favorites*
Jim Holbert—Library of Congress Archive
of Folk Song L61: *Railroad Songs and
Ballads*
Becky Pettyjohn—Arizona Friends of
Folklore AFF 33–4: *Bunk and Becky
Pettyjohn*
Mervin Shiner—Decca 46272 (45 rpm)

F. LC AFS:
Otis Bird—AFS 12049 A37 "Please Mr.
Conductor"
Ed Burkes—AFS 12045 B33
Doney Hammontree—AFS 5365 B1
Nell Hampton—AFS 1574 A2
Mrs. H. A. Mullenix—AFS 5365 B1
"Please Mr. Conductor"
Beckham Ritchie—AFS 12008 A11
Mrs. Pete Steele—AFS 1706 B1
Fred Woodruff—AFS 5346 B2

The Blue Sky Boys, Bill and Earl Bolick. Courtesy of the John Edwards Memorial
Foundation, UCLA.

The Red and Green Signal Lights/The Engineer's Child

THE RED AND GREEN SIGNAL LIGHTS

Original Key: G

A lit - tle child on a sick - bed lay, And to death seemed ver - y near; 'Twas a par - ent's pride and the on - ly child Of a rail - road en - gin - eer. His du - ty called him from those he loved, While the light in his home burned dim; And while tears he shed, to his wife he said, "I will leave two lan - terns trimmed."

The next four lines of text are sung to the second half of the melody above, preceded by an instrumental break based on the first half of the melody.

> A little child on a sickbed lay,
> And to death seemed very near;
> 'Twas a parent's pride and the only [*pronounced "own-lie"*] child
> Of a railroad engineer.
> His duty called him from those he loved,
> While the light in his home burned dim;
> And while tears he shed, to his wife he said,
> "I will leave two lanterns trimmed.
>
> > "Just set a light as I pass tonight,
> > Set it where it may be seen;
> > If our darling's dead, then show the red,
> > If she's better, then show the green."
>
> In a cottage home by the railroad side,
> 'Twas a mother's watchful eye;

As the train went rushing by.
Just one short glance, was his only chance,
But the signal light was seen;
On the midnight air there arose a prayer,
"Thank God that light was green."

    Chorus:

        Grayson and Whitter

    Although published field collections give little clue of it, the short poem/song "The Red and the Green" enjoyed great popularity in the early decades of this century, particularly among railroaders.

    The earliest reference I have found was in the March, 1908, issue of *Railroad Man's Magazine*, in which a reader requested the words to the song "The Red and the Green." The text was supplied in the May issue, although two lines were missing, and it appeared several times in successive issues. In 1914, the editors of the magazine queried readers for their favorite railroad poems, promising to print the top five selections. "The Red and the Green" was one of them (still lacking two lines). From the time of its first printing, no author or date of first appearance could be found for the composition.

    There would be good reason—although not conclusive—to believe that the poem was written after 1898. Before that time a white light meant "clear board" and a green light meant "caution"; red meant "danger," then as now. However, after September, 1898, the New Haven Railroad changed to the green light for go-ahead; other railroads soon followed suit.[1] The symbolism of the poem would be somewhat diluted if green indicated caution rather than all clear; consequently, it would seem reasonable that the piece was written after the change in color codes. This would place the date of composition between 1898 and 1908.

    In spite of this convincing line of reasoning, it happens that the song was copyrighted in 1896. Originally titled "Just Set a Light," the words were by Henry V. Neal and the music by the redoubtable composer of Gay Nineties sentimentalia, ex–railroad porter Gussie L. Davis. It is surprising that a dozen years after its publication the song had gotten so completely out of the hands of its creators that no author could be cited. Because the original sheet-music text has not seen the light of day for many a year, I give it here:

A little child on a sick bed lay,
And to death seemed very near,
Her parents pride and the only child,
Of a railroad engineer,
His duty calls him from the ones he loved,
From this home, whose lights were dimmed,
While tears he shed, to his wife he said,
"I will leave two lanterns trimmed."

"Just set a light, when I pass tonight,
Set it where it can be seen,
If our darling's dead, then show the red,
If she's better, show the green."

In that small house, by the railroad side,
'Twas the mother's watchful eye,
Saw gleam of hope in the feeble smile,
As the train went rushing by,
Just one short look, 'twas his only chance,
But the signal light was seen,
On the midnight air, there arose a prayer,
"Thank the Lord, the light is green."

By using green as the signal color, then, perhaps the poem's author was suggesting cautious optimism, rather than unrestrained joy.

Between 1916 and 1924, the song came into the hands of three collectors. A student of E. C. Perrow at the University of Louisville turned in an untitled version in 1916. In 1922 and 1924, Robert Frothingham and Robert Gordon, respectively, each received correspondence with texts of the song titled "Red and Green Lights." Frothingham began the column "Old Songs that Men Have Sung" in *Adventure* magazine in 1922; Gordon took over in 1923 and continued until the fall of 1927. During his tenure, Gordon carried on a voluminous correspondence with readers, and gathered many fine songs.

In February, 1926, Vernon Dalhart recorded the song three times—for Gennett, Plaza, and Pathé—but under the title "The Engineer's Child." On February 4, an unpublished version of that title was copyrighted by Shapiro, Bernstein, with words credited to Henry V. Neal and music to Maggie Andrews. On March 19, a published version was copyrighted, words and music credited to Neal, Andrews, and Robert A. King. Maggie Andrews was a well-known pseudonym for Carson Robison (it was his mother's maiden name); R. A. King (1862–1932) was a staff composer for Shapiro, Bernstein during 1908–32. It is understandable why Robison took an old, popular ballad and wrote new music for it; what is puzzling is why he introduced several word changes, some distinctly inferior to the original. For example, the sixth line of the second verse reads, in the 1926 version, "To see the light a-gleam"; the sixth line of the first stanza becomes "And seeing that hope was dim." Robison's changing the title to "The Engineer's Child" was logical for the hillbilly market; it indicated the nature of the song better than the original "Just Set a Light."

The version of the song transcribed in this book is the one recorded by G. B. Grayson and Henry Whitter for Victor on July 31, 1928. They had twice recorded the song earlier that year for Gennett as "Red or Green," the title by which the song was best known before Dalhart recorded it. The recordings show no signs of influence by the Dalhart/ Robison/Neal version, although that version preceded Grayson and Whitter's on disc by two years. It is probable that Grayson, who sang lead on both recordings and had a wonderful repertoire of older traditional songs, had known the piece long before. Southern Music copyrighted the song, crediting Grayson for words and melody (June 13, 1929, E unp. 8234; renewed June 13, 1956, R 172633). Slightly in excess of 6,000 copies of the Victor recording were sold.

The Grayson and Whitter text differs in one curious respect from the original sheet music: in the fifth line of the second verse, the word *look* has been replaced by *glance* to give an added internal rhyme. This *glance/chance* couplet appears in four texts in addition to the Grayson-Whitter recording: the version collected by Perrow's student in 1916; the Frothingham manuscript of 1922, the Chuck Wagon Gang recording of 1936, and the manuscript text printed by Randolph (which, curiously, bore the subtitle "Just Set a

Sheet music: "Just Set a Light." Courtesy of Lester Levy.

Light," the only recovery of the original title). If the original sheet music were not at hand, one would conclude from these occurrences that the *glance/chance* couplet must have been part of the original text, only to be lost in most later versions. As it is, we must conclude either that some folk poet improved on the original not long after it appeared, or else that Henry V. Neal was working from an older traditional piece.

NOTE

1. Barbara Kreimer, "Information Booth," *RRM*, 79 (Apr., 1966), 36. A popular nineteenth-century poem among railroaders was Cy Warman's "Will the Lights Be White?" The second stanza identified the signal colors:

> A blue light marks the crippled car,
> The green light signals "slow,"
> The red light is a danger light,
> And the white light, "Let her go!"

In the final verses, Warman wonders about the life hereafter, using the railroaders' symbolism:

> Swift toward life's terminal I trend,
> The run seems short tonight.
> God only knows what's at the end;
> I hope the lamps are white.

In addition to being quoted in this *RRM* column, Warman's poem appears in *Songs of Cy Warman*, 2d ed. (Boston: Rand Avery, 1911), p. 69.

In a recent letter to the *RRM* editor, Roger B. Snyder states that around the turn of the century there were different meanings to the signal colors, depending on whether the signals were manual or automatic. See *RRM*, 104 (Sept., 1978), pp. 10–11.

REFERENCES

A. "Just Set a Light," sheet music. Words by Henry V. Neal, music by Gussie L. Davis. Published by Howley, Haviland and Co., New York. Copyrighted 1896.

"The Engineer's Child," sheet music, by Henry V. Neal, Maggie Andrews (Carson Robison pseudonym), and R. A. King. Published by Shapiro, Bernstein and Co., New York. Copyrighted 1926 (E 636304); renewed (R 117166).

"The Engineer's Child," by Vernon Dalhart. Dalhart, vocal; guitar and violin accompaniment. Recorded Feb. 23, 1926 (Starr master 9989), in New York City. Released on Gennett 3260. Reissued on Champion 15076, Challenge 155, Challenge 230, and Challenge 313. The first of Dalhart's three recordings, and the first recording of the Robison version.

"The Red and Green Signal Lights," by G. B. Grayson and Henry Whitter. Grayson, vocal and violin; Whitter, guitar. Recorded July 31, 1928 (Victor master 46630), in New York City. Released on Victor V-40063 ca. May 19, 1929. Reissued on RCA Victor LPV 532: *The Railroad in Folksong*. This is the version transcribed here. An earlier recording by Grayson and Whitter for the Starr Piano Co. (Gennett) on Feb. 29 differed insignificantly from the Victor version. A third recording, also for Gennett, was never issued.

B. Anderson, G., 214   "The Railroad Engineer"

Family Herald, 38 (references only)

Frothingham, *Adventure*, Nov. 30, 1922, p. 191 (request from a reader, only 1 line given)

Holbrook, 435   "The Red and the Green"

Pack & John, 15   "Just Set a Light"

Randolph IV, 135

Richardson, 43   "The Child of the Railroad Engineer"

RRM, 5 (May, 1931), 314
RRM, 74 (Oct., 1963), 31
RRM, 79 (May, 1966), 33
RRManM, 5 (Mar., 1908), 384 (request only)
RRManM, 5 (May, 1908), 763   "The Red
and the Green"
RRManM, 17 (Mar., 1912), 383
RRManM, 23 (Apr., 1914), 960
Shapiro, 20
Sherwin & McClintock, 36
Sizemore (1934), 21
Sizemore (1935), 21
Spaeth (1927), 140   "The Child of the
Railroad Engineer"

C. COHEN COLLECTION:
Laura Affolter (letter, June, 1968)
Janice Page (letter, June 22, 1968)
Dick Parman (letter, Oct., 1969)

FROTHINGHAM MSS:
J. L. Parrish (letter, Nov. 25, 1922)

GORDON MSS:
707—H. E. Burdick, letter (July 8, 1924)
with newspaper clipping containing "Red
and Green Lights"

WKFA:
Goldie Festig (E. C. Perrow Collection;
May, 1916)
Mrs. Lewis Good (1950)   "Railroad
Engineer"
Webb Hill (Mar., 1948)   "Red and Green
Lights" or "The Engineer's Child"
Fred Long (Mar., 1960)   "The
Engineer's Dying Child"
E. A. Yeager (Apr., 1959)   "The Railroad
Engineer"

D. Chuck Wagon Gang—Vocalion 04105
Al Craver (Vernon Dalhart pseudonym)
—Columbia 15060-D   "Engineer's
Dying Child"

Vernon Dalhart—Banner 1741, Conqueror
7069, Domino 3712 (some released as by
Bob White), Regal 8051, Silvertone 2706,
Apex (Canada) 8472
—Edison 51718, Edison 5135 (cylinder)
—Pathé 32171, Perfect 12250
—Victor 19983, Zonophone (England) 2748
—Vocalion 15283, Vocalion 5090
Arthur Fields—Grey Gull 4208
Jesters—Decca 24355 (in album A-639:
Railroad Songs)
Silas Leachman—Talking Machine
Company 0141C (cylinder)   "Just Set a
Light" (possibly related)
Jere Mahoney—Edison 5904, B106
(cylinders)   "Just Set a Light" (possibly
related)
Carson J. Robinson and his Pioneers—
Regal Zonophone (Australia) G21448,
Twin (India) FT 1545, Regal Zonophone
(England) MR 756 (latter two as by Bud
and Joe Billings)
Hank Snow—RCA Victor 20-4096; RCA
Camden CAL 514: *The Singing Ranger*
Henry Whitter—Gennett 6418, Challenge
397 (as by David Foley), Champion 15465
(as by Norman Gayle)   "Red or Green"
Unknown tenor—Talking Machine
Company 3071C (cylinder)   "Just Set a
Light" (possibly related)

E. Brook Benton—Mercury 20641/60641
"Child of the Engineer"
Cecil Gill—Bluebonnet BL 114
Randolph County String Band—Davis
Unlimited DU 33001: *Under the Weeping
Willow*   "The Signal Lights"
Hank Snow—RCA Victor LSP 4501: *Tracks
and Trains*

F. LC AFS:
W. J. Green—AFS 11908 B1   "Child of
the Railroad Engineer"

Jim Blake's Message

JIM BLAKE'S MESSAGE

"Jim Blake, your wife is dy-ing," _____ Went o-ver the wires to-night; The mes-sage was brought to the de-pot By a lad all trem-bling with fright. He en-tered the of-fice cry-ing, _____ His face was ter-ri-bly white; _____ "Send this mes-sage to dad and his _____ en-gine, _____ Moth-er is dy-ing to-night." _____

"Jim Blake, your wife is dying,"
Went over the wires tonight;
The message was brought to the depot
By a lad all trembling with fright.
He entered the office crying,
His face was terribly white;
"Send this message to dad and his engine,
Mother is dying tonight."

In something less than an hour
Jim's answer back to me flew;
"Tell wife I'll be there at midnight,
I'm praying for her, too."
I left my son in the office
Took a message to Jim's wife,
There found the dying woman
With scarce a breath and life.

O'er hill and dale and valley,
Plunders [*sic*] the heavy train;
Its engine is sobbing and throbbing,
And under a terrible strain.
But Jim hangs on to his throttle,
Guiding her crazy flight;
And his voice cries out in the darkness,
"God speed the express tonight!"

I telephoned the doctor,
"How is Jim's wife," I asked;
"About the hour of midnight,
Is long as she can last."
In something less than an hour,
The train will be along;
Look here, I have a message—
Oh, God, there is something wrong.

The message reads disaster,
The train is in the ditch;
The engineer is dying,
Derailed by an open switch;
And there's another message,
To Jim's wife it is addressed;
"I'll meet her at midnight in heaven,
Don't wait for the fast express."

Carter Family

The printed source of this ballad of double tragedy has so far eluded discovery. The earliest reference I have found was in a November, 1909, issue of *Railroad Man's Magazine*, when a Pennsylvania reader asked for a song entitled "Jim Blake, or the Midnight Express," the first verse of which began "Jim Blake is an engine-driver / He runs on the midnight express."[1] In the January, 1910, issue the words were supplied "in response to the request of a number of our readers."[2] Thus direct evidence can push the date of composition back only to 1909 or earlier; but the style of the song and the fact that it was evidently already in oral tradition by that time suggest an earlier date—probably the early 1890s.

I have found no prehillbilly recordings of "Jim Blake," or "The Midnight Express," as Shay titled it in his collection. The earliest recording was made by Vernon Dalhart in late April or early May of 1927 for Brunswick. The song was copyrighted (May 27, 1927, E 664950) by Carson Robison and Pete Condon. Possibly Condon had supplied the Robison song-mill with the source for Dalhart's version. Dalhart recorded the song three more times in the following twelve months—not all that often, considering his usual procedure of waxing a successful song for every company that was interested. M. F. Wheeler and M. E. Lamb also copyrighted the song (May 11, 1931, E 39796) shortly after they recorded it for Victor. The version we have transcribed was recorded by the Carter Family for Decca on June 17, 1937, in New York, and copyrighted by A. P. Carter on January 5, 1938 (E 157711).[3]

Attempts to group the various texts of the ballad into a family tree are not very successful. There are numerous small variations from one text to another, but no obvious directions of change.

Only a few of the textual variations deserve comment. Three texts (Dalhart, Pack, Carter Family) do not use the locution "the midnight express" at all, but call the train "the fast express." Only two texts have a verse about a telephone call to the doctor (Carter Family and Riddle). Most of the texts are ten to thirteen quatrains long, but Almeda Riddle's text obtained in the 1960s by Roger Abrahams is sixteen quatrains—the most complete yet recovered.[4] Furthermore, in almost every case of alternative wording, Mrs. Riddle's text seems to represent the best choice (for a nineteenth-century songwriter), and in the absence of more information, it may be tentatively assumed that her version is closest to the original. The only two exceptions are her use of the word *bedroom* where all other texts save Webb Hill's (WKFA) read *chamber*; and her following the group of versions that change the boy in the sixth verse from "his son" to "my son." Mrs. Riddle learned the song when she was ten years old, which would have been around 1908. Since this fine text is not included in her book of songs, it is printed here. At present, it stands as the paradigm to which other texts must be compared.

"Jim Blake your wife is dying,"
Come over the wires tonight,
The message was brought to the depot
By a boy all trembling with fright;
He entered the office crying,
His face was terribly white;
"Send this message to Dad on his engine,
Mother is dying tonight."

Jim Blake was our oldest driver,
Had charge of the midnight express;
He's handled the throttle and lever
The most of his life I guess;
And when I found the message
Was for my old comrade Jim,
I made no delay but hurried away
To send that message to him.

In less than an hour
Jim's answer back to me flew,
"Tell my wife I'll be there at midnight,
And I'm praying for her, too."
I left my son in my office
And went at once to Jim's wife;
I found the dying woman
With scarcely a breath of life.

And when I entered the bedroom
She took me at first to be Jim,
And fell back almost exhausted
When she found I wasn't him;

And when I read her his message,
Love shone on her face so white,
And she said in a dying whisper,
"God speed the express train tonight."

Over the hill and vale and valley
Thunders the heavy train,
Its engine is throbbing and sobbing
Under a terrible strain;
But Jim hangs on to the throttle
Guiding her crazy flight,
And his voice cries out in the darkness,
"God speed the express train tonight."

The night was dark and foggy,
The express was running on time,
Not a moment is she losing
As she thunders along the line;
Jim Blake is hoping and praying
That he may see his wife,
That he may be beside her
When she draws her last breath of life.

I telephoned the doctor,
"How is Jim's wife," I asked,
"About the hour of midnight
Is as long as she can last."
In something less than an hour
The train will be along;
But here is another message —
My God there is something wrong.

The message reads disaster,
The train is in the ditch;
The engineer is dying,
Derailed by an open switch;
And there is one more message,
To Jim's wife it is addressed:
"I meet you at midnight in heaven;
Don't wait for the midnight train."

My search of the copyright records for the source of "Jim Blake's Message" revealed several poems and songs with similar titles: "Jim's Last Ride" (1881), "The Midnight Express" (three entries—one 1888, one 1891, and one undated from the 1890s). None of these, however, is related to our song.

One early poem, of sufficient similarity in theme to "Jim Blake" to merit our attention, was titled "Happy Bill the Brakeman," by Mrs. H. A. Holcher.[5] Bill's wife is sick, but he has to make his train run anyway. She dies, and so does he on the train.

South Carolina millhand and hillbilly singer Dorsey Dixon sang a piece, which he said he had composed, titled "Bill Dawson's Last Ride"; it seems to be a recomposition of the Jim Blake story. It has not been recorded commercially, and I have not found any other versions of it.

NOTES

1. *RRManM,* 10 (Nov., 1909), 380.

2. Ibid., Jan., 1910, p. 760.

3. The available studies approach the Carter Family from different perspectives. Edward A. Kahn II takes an anthropological point of view in his doctoral dissertation, "The Carter Family: A Reflection of Changes in Society" (University of California at Los Angeles, 1970); the perspective of country music fan or collector is better served by *The Carter Family,* edited by John Atkins, Old Time Music Booklet No. 1 (London: Old Time Music, 1973). For a popular account of the Carter Family's career, see Michael Orgill, *Anchored in Love: The Carter Family Story* (Old Tappan, N.J.: Fleming H. Revell, 1975).

4. The song is cited in Almeda Riddle, *A Singer and Her Songs* (Baton Rouge: Louisiana State University Press, 1970), p. 186. I thank Roger D. Abrahams for making a copy of her text available to me.

5. *RRM,* 18 (July, 1912), 384.

REFERENCES

A. "Jim Blake," in *RRManM,* 10 (Jan., 1910), 760. Submitted in response to a reader's request published in the Nov., 1909, number. The first full text published.

"Jim Blake," collected from Almeda Riddle of Arkansas by Roger D. Abrahams. Mrs. Riddle learned the song in 1908, when she was ten years old. The fullest text that has been reported.

"Jim Blake," by Vernon Dalhart. Dalhart, vocal; guitar accompaniment. Recorded ca. May, 1927 (Brunswick masters E23284 and -85), in New York City. Released on Brunswick 173 in late 1927 or early 1928. First recording of the song.

"Jim Blake's Message," by the Carter Family. Sara and Maybelle, guitars; Sara, Maybelle, and A.P., vocals. Recorded June 17, 1937 (Decca master 62295A), in New York City. Released on Decca 5467. Reissued on Montgomery Ward 8026; Melotone (Canada) 45251; Decca DL 4557: *More Favorites by the Carter Family;* and Ace of Hearts (England) AH 112: *More Favourites by the Carter Family.* Transcribed in this book.

B. Carlisle, I., 87-89
Family Herald, 44 (references only)
"Fiddlin' Joe's Song Corral," *Wild West Weekly,* Mar. 2, 1940, p. 128

Gardner & Chickering, 479 (mentioned)
Glosson
O'Day
OTS&P, 1 (Jan.-Feb., 1968), 46
Pack, 43
Peters, 209
RRManM, 10 (Nov., 1909), 380 (request; 2 lines quoted)
RRManM, 10 (Jan., 1910), 760
RRManM, 6 (Oct., 1931), 462
RVB, 13 (Feb., 1960), 6   "The Midnight Express"
Shay (1928), 182–83   "The Midnight Express"
Spaeth (1927), 139

C. COHEN COLLECTION:
Laura Affolter (letter, June, 1968)
Mrs. Ercie Barrett (letter, Dec., 1968)
Ralph Oatley (letter, Sept. 29, 1967)

GORDON MSS:
1568—J. H. Walsh (1 verse)

WKFA:
Webb Hill (Mar., 1948)

D. Al Craver (Vernon Dalhart pseudonym)
—Columbia 15192-D
Vernon Dalhart—Champion 15546,
Supertone 9240, Silvertone 8145 ·

—Pathé 32301, Perfect 12380, Cameo 8223, Romeo 603, Lincoln 2828

Frank Wheeler and Monroe Lamb —Victor 23537, Montgomery Ward 4334   "Jim Blake, the Engineer"

E. Big Jim Griffith—Sonyatone ST-1002: *The Dixie Cowboy*

Phipps Family—Starday SLP 195: *Old Time Mountain Pickin' and Singin'* "The Engineer's Last Ride"

Jean Ritchie—Folkways FA 2427: *Precious Memories*

Arnold Keith Storm—Folk-Legacy FSA 18: *Arnold Keith Storm of Mooresville, Indiana*   "Jim Blake, Your Wife Is Dying"

Howard Vokes—Starday SLP 258: *Tragedy and Disaster in Country Songs*   "The Engineer's Last Ride"

Jane Voss—Bay 207: *An Album of Songs*

F. LC AFS:

Bessie Atchley—AFS 13132 A7   "The Midnight Express"

Noble B. Brown—AFS 8473 B1

Georgia Dunaway—AFS 10821 A8

Helen Fultz—AFS 12043 A9, AFS 13137 A3   "The Midnight Express"

Gertrude Johnson—AFS 13144 B12 "Midnight Express"

Lena B. Turbyfill—AFS 2842 B1

Unidentified singer—AFS 13162 B13

"Death on the Rail," from *Harper's Weekly*, May 10, 1893. Courtesy of Donald Lee Nelson.

There's a Little Box of Pine on the 7:29

THERE'S A LITTLE BOX OF PINE ON THE 7:29

Original Key: E♭

♩ = 152

"Dear ward-en," wrote a_ moth-er,_ "how much long-er must I wait, Be-fore_

_ you send my boy back home to me?" She_ nev-er knew the

an-gels had un-locked the pris-on gate, The one she loved_ at

last had been set free. The ward-en read her

let-ter,_ and then he soft-ly cried, As with these words of

sor-row he re-plied: "There's a lit-tle box of

pine on the Sev-en-twen-ty-nine, Bring-ing back a

lost sheep to the fold; For a par-don from a-bove has re-

turned the one you love, A sad-der sto-ry nev-er has been told.

Though he's tak-ing his last ride, nev-er more this world to roam,_

On his face there is a smile, he knows he's go-ing

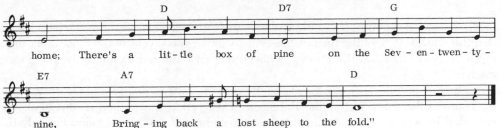

home; There's a lit-tle box of pine on the Sev-en-twen-ty-

nine, Bring-ing back a lost sheep to the fold."

"Dear warden," wrote a mother, "how much longer must I wait,
Before you send my boy back home to me?"
She never knew the angels had unlocked the prison gate,
The one she loved at last had been set free.
The warden read her letter, and then he softly cried,
As with these words of sorrow he replied:

"There's a little box of pine on the Seven-twenty-nine,
Bringing back a lost sheep to the fold;
For a pardon from above has returned the one you love,
A sadder story never has been told.
Though he's taking his last ride, never more this world to roam,
On his face there is a smile, he knows he's going home;
There's a little box of pine on the Seven-twenty-nine,
Bringing back a lost sheep to the fold."

The church was filled with music as the sermon did begin,
His brokenhearted folks were gathered there;
The preacher told the story of the boy who followed sin,
The heavy load his loved ones now must bear.
When he had preached his sermon, the organ softly played,
As on their knees the congregation prayed.

There's a little box of pine on the Seven-twenty-nine,
Bringing back a lost sheep to the fold;
In the valley there are tears as the train of sorrow nears,
The sun is gone, the world seems dark and cold.
There his lonely mother waits with the girl he left behind,
On their knees they ask in prayer why Fate's been so unkind;
There's a little box of pine on the Seven-twenty-nine,
Bringing back a lost sheep to the fold.

Martin and Roberts

Although this tragic ballad sounds very much akin to songs in this chapter that date
back to the 1890s, "Little Box of Pine" was written in 1931 by Jos. Ettlinger, George
Brown (pseudonym of Billy Hill), and De Dette Lee (pseudonym of De Dette Lee Hill). It
was copyrighted September 11, 1931 (E 25033), and again on October 21, 1932 (renewed
Oct. 21, 1959, R 221130). It seems to have been aimed specifically at the hillbilly market
rather than the larger pop-music audience, judging by the use of hillbilly singers (the
McCravy Brothers, who, in fact, did not record this song) on the sheet-music cover.
"Little Box of Pine" is typical of a large number of hillbilly songs of the late 1920s and 1930s
that echoed the spirit of the sentimental pop songs of the 1890s. The reasons for this

musical survival are complex, and involve many sociological factors; but the basic fact is that the musical style of the turn-of-the-century parlor was given, in the mountain cabins of the Appalachians and the Ozarks, a haven that far outlasted its life in the pop-music media.

The first hillbilly recording of "Little Box of Pine" was made in about October, 1931, by Tommie Reynolds and Willie Robinson. The version transcribed in this book was recorded by Asa Martin and James Roberts in February, 1933, and follows closely the original sheet music.[1]

A more recent recording by Hank Snow is noteworthy because the text departs considerably from the original. For example, the first verse reads:

> A mother wrote the warden, "How much longer must I wait
> Before you send my boy back home to me?
> Oh, my eyes are growing dim, and I'm longing for my Jim,
> Please hurry up and let my boy go free."[2]

The song has not appeared in any published folksong collection, or, to my knowledge, in any folksong archive. Because it is still being recorded commercially, however, it is too early to say for certain that the folk tradition will not pick it up after the commercial media have abandoned it.

NOTES

1. For biographical information about Asa Martin, see Guthrie T. Meade and Mark Wilson's brochure notes to Rounder 0034: *Dr. Ginger Blue, Featuring Asa Martin and the Cumberland Rangers*. Martin died in 1979.

2. From RCA Victor LPM 1861: *When Tragedy Struck*.

REFERENCES

A. "There's a Little Box of Pine on the 7:29," sheet music, by Jos. Ettlinger, George Brown (Billy Hill pseudonym), and De Dette Le (De Dette Lee Hill pseudonym). Copyrighted Sept. 11, 1931 (E 25033), and Oct. 21, 1932; renewed Oct. 21, 1959 (R 221130).

"There's a Little Box of Pine on the 7:29," by Tommy (Reynolds) and Willie (Robinson). Recorded Oct. 20, 1931 (Starr master GN 18116A), in New York City. Released on Champion 16432, Champion 45180, Montgomery Ward 4958, Superior 2935 (as by Reynolds and Robinson). First recording of the song.

"There's a Little Box of Pine on the 7:29," by Martin and Roberts. Asa Martin, guitar and vocal; Doc Roberts, violin; James Roberts, mandolin and vocal. Recorded Feb. 4, 1933 (American Record Corp. master 13031-1), in New York City. Released on Banner 32772, Melotone M12701, Oriole 8234, Romeo 5234, Perfect 12913, Conqueror 8062, Vocalion

5495 (as by Glen Fox and Joe Wilson), Melotone (Canada) 91578, Regal Zonophone (Australia) G22176 (as by Glen Fox and Joe Wilson). This version is transcribed here.

D. Bingham and Wells—Bluebird B-5154, Sunrise 3255, Elektradisc 2053, Montgomery Ward 4380, Montgomery Ward 4817

E. Pine Mountain Boys—Rural Rhythm RR-DU-2113: *The Pine Mountain Boys*
Oliver Smith—Elektra EKL 316: *Oliver Smith*
Hank Snow—RCA Victor LPM 1861: *When Tragedy Struck*
Doc Williams—Wheeling WLP 5001: *25th Anniversary Album*   "Little Box of Pine"
Mac Wiseman—Capitol T-1800: *Bluegrass Favorites*   "Ballad of the Little Box of Pine"
—CMH 9001: *The Mac Wiseman Story*

The Evening Train

THE EVENING TRAIN

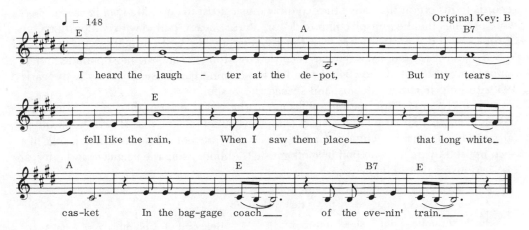

I heard the laughter at the depot,
But my tears fell like the rain,
When I saw them place that long white casket
In the baggage coach of the evenin' train.

The baby's eyes are red from weeping,
Its little heart is filled with pain;
"Oh dad," he cried, "they're takin' mama
Away from us on the evenin' train."

As I turned to walk away from the depot,
It seemed I heard her call my name;
"Take care of baby, and tell him, darlin',
That I'm goin' home on the evenin' train."

I pray that God will give me courage
To carry on till we meet again;
It's hard to know she's gone forever,
They're carryin' her home on the evenin' train.

I heard the laughter at the depot,
But my tears fell like the rain,
When I saw them place that long white casket
In the baggage coach of the evenin' train.

Molly O'Day

A relatively recent composition rounds out this casketful of tales of sorrow. "On the Evening Train," as it is properly titled, was written by Hank and Audrey Williams and published by Fred Rose Music (copyrighted June 29, 1949, EP 38092). The song is included here partly as a reminder that this style of balladry did not die out with the passing of the waltz, but lives on, transplanted from Tin Pan Alley to Tin Pan Valley.

For the last four years of his short life, Hank Williams cast a giant shadow over the world of country music. He died on New Year's Day, 1953, with more million-seller records to his credit than any other country music artist to date. Many of his recordings were of songs that he himself composed—or, at least, was credited with composing. One of those he did not record was "On the Evening Train," written jointly with his wife. Shortly after it was published, it was recorded by Molly O'Day, the most popular female country music artist of the 1940s, who left the commercial music business in the early 1950s to help her minister husband spread the gospel.

"The Evening Train" is not a folksong in the strict sense of the word; it does not have—as far as I know—any life apart from the commercial media. However, throughout this book I have included similar pieces that are not folksongs but are folk-like —composed by people steeped in a folk music tradition, using the language and musical expressions of that folk heritage.

REFERENCES

A. "On the Evening Train," sheet music, by Hank and Audrey Williams. Published by Fred Rose Music. Copyrighted June 29, 1949 (EP 38092).

"The Evening Train," by Molly O'Day and the Cumberland Mountain Folk. Recorded Apr. 4, 1949 (Columbia master C0-400662), in Nashville, Tenn.

Released on Columbia 20601 on Aug. 15, 1949. First recording of the song; transcribed in this book.

E. Wilma Lee and Stoney Cooper—Hickory LPM H-106: *Family Favorites*

Lynn Davis and Molly O'Day. Courtesy of the John Edwards Memorial Foundation, UCLA.

8

In a Boxcar around the World

THE MUSICAL FOLKLORE of hoboes, bums, and tramps is a broad field of study; the selections in this chapter are confined to those songs of vagrants in which railroads play an important role. Such widely known favorites as "Big Rock Candy Mountain" and "Down in the Lehigh Valley" are thus omitted. Interested readers are referred to Milburn's excellent collection.[1]

Although we have had tramps with us since the seventeenth century, the terms *hobo* and *bum* seem not to have come into general use in this country until the late nineteenth century; the earliest use of the word *hobo* in print cited in the *Dictionary of American English* dates from 1891, when Josiah Flynt noted that that was the tramp's name for himself.[2] Two years later, Flynt refined the term: "There are white loafers known as 'hoboes,' which is the general technical term among white tramps everywhere, and there are the 'shinies' who are negroes."[3] *Bum*, common since about 1880, at first meant any wanderer, but by 1900 came to mean a beggar. In its early usage, *tramp* referred to a transient worker, but the word took on a different meaning, and that denotation came to be reserved for *hobo*. Ben L. Reitman summarized the twentieth-century usage more than five decades ago: "The hobo works and wanders, the tramp dreams and wanders, and the bum drinks and wanders."[4] St. John Tucker phrased it somewhat differently: "A hobo is a migratory worker. A tramp is a migratory non-worker. A bum is a stationary non-worker."[5] This distinction between hobo and bum is elaborated in Howard Johnson's "Who Said I Was a Bum," often recorded in the late 1920s, which had the refrain, "I may be a hobo, but who said I was a bum?"

This evolution in the terminology for types of homeless men offers clues to the dates of composition of the songs included in this chapter, but conclusions drawn on such bases are tentative at best. "Because He Was Only a Tramp" tells of a tramp who wandered around looking for work. This, and the fact that the term is used without opprobrium in most verses, suggests a date of composition in the nineteenth century—in agreement with other evidence. "Wild and Reckless Hobo" would seem not to predate the 1880s, although "Waiting for a Train," a closely related variant, could be older, as it does not use the term *hobo*.

The literature on the hobo as a sociological problem is extensive; an important work is

343

Nels Anderson's monograph, which, though it focuses on the homeless men of Chicago, treats various aspects of hobo life.[6] Kenneth Allsop's more recent book examines many aspects of hoboing from the 1870s to the 1960s.[7] In the following paragraphs I wish to concentrate on the public attitudes toward the hobo, in particular vis-à-vis the railroads.

A widespread view around the turn of the century was that the tramps were a menace and an evil, and cost the public an enormous financial outlay as well. How long ago this attitude became well defined, I don't know; but as early as 1885 a correspondent wrote to the *Locomotive Engineers' Monthly Journal*: "There is one portion of humanity against which society is ever ready to raise its hand; for whom every well-trained dog is ever on the alert, and who barks out his suspicion at every illy dressed man that approaches the house. Now, in my belief, there is good in every one, and therefore I speak for the much abused tramp."[8] This writer spoke from personal experience. Others dealt out statistics (sometimes from the bottom of the deck). In 1908, it was estimated that there were probably more than a half-million tramps in America. This figure was arrived at by taking the ratio of the number of tramps killed annually on the railroads to the number of trainmen killed and multiplying that by the total number of trainmen employed. Tramps were taken to include all trespassers, and the number of trespassers killed has exceeded the combined number of passengers and employees killed on the railroads in every year of this century.

In 1909, Charlton Andrews catalogued the complaints against the hobo:

> Riding on trains, intimidating, often assaulting, and not infrequently murdering train-men are by no means the only offenses of the tramps. All the millions of dollars' worth of valuable goods retailed in the stores of the land must pass over the railroads before they reach the consumer, and these goods in transit are at the mercy of the tramps along the line, who are not slow to help themselves to what they want—and their wants are not modest. . . .
>
> Fifteen train robberies, accompanied by four murders, were committed in the United States last year by wandering criminals known to the unsophisticated public as "tramps." No one will ever know how many other robberies and murders were committed by the same class, . . . If such [crimes] as have been mentioned are not sufficient to show the tramp in his true character, any seeker after information can get all he wants by applying to any one who has ever been brought in contact with tramps. . . .
>
> There is a popular impression that the tramp is a downtrodden creature, whom misfortune had followed until it has deprived him of an inordinate appetite for work, but who is harmless and would soon become an ornament to society if he only had a chance. Nothing could be further from the truth.[9]

Andrews, attributing $25 million of damage to the hoboes yearly, was not alone in so vilifying tramps and hoboes.

These arguments did not go unanswered. In 1912, Frank Whiting, general claims attorney for the New York Central lines, questioned the interpretation of the data that led to the figure of 500,000 tramps in America. He reported that of 1,000 persons killed while trespassing (all of whom would have been taken as "tramps" by Kelley and Andrews), 489 resided near the place of accident, and 598 were self-supporting. His argument was that a large number of persons killed while "trespassing" were simply using the tracks to walk upon. Examining other evidence, Whiting concluded that of the 1,000 cases, fully 765 were not hoboes and 50 were, the remainder being of indeterminate status.[10]

Alice Solenberger, in her book-length study *One Thousand Homeless Men* (1911), also criticized the custom of railway officials in designating all trespassers as "tramps." She pointed out that many of the men so termed were merely seasonal and shifting workmen; while they may have been traveling the trains not as passengers, still they could not be considered confirmed wanderers. She noted that a variety of conditions, including financial failure, family difficulties, desertion or death of the wife, and inability to find employment, provided motives for men to become wanderers.[11]

"Only men with a true instinct for wandering," she observed, "can be said to be 'born tramps' and many even of these would never become confirmed in their habits of roaming if it were a little more difficult for them to indulge their abnormal propensities in this direction . . . not more than 31 percent of the chronic wanderers can plead an active desire as their excuse for being on the road. Almost 70 percent are mere drifters, men who might under different conditions have remained at home and have become useful citizens."[12]

In a poem published in 1876, Patrick Fennell, a prolific poet and railroader who was sensitive to the hardships of the common man, developed the theme that unemployment was often the reason an upstanding citizen became a tramp. His poem, "Only a Tramp," began:

> "He was only a tramp," said the papers
> When telling the news of the day,
> Of how a poor man was discover'd
> Just breathing his last by the way.

In the man's breast pocket is a letter from his wife, which reveals his sad story:

> The tale can be told by that letter,
> Denied all employment at home,
> His wretched condition to better,
> Away o'er the land did he roam;
> Repulsed by continued denials,
> He came to seek rest on this sod,
> At last there's an end to his trials,
> He rests with a merciful God![13]

Attacking another misconception of the day, Mrs. Solenberger stated, "The newspaper and stage caricatures of the tramp which invariably represent him as a dirty and idle beggar must be in large part responsible for the popular idea that he is a man who never works and who lives wholly by begging. . . . Thirty five percent of [the homeless wanderers] were found to be generally self-supporting, or at least not dependent upon the public. . . . "[14] An echo of these sentiments is heard in the version of "Because He Was Only a Tramp" transcribed in this book. The narrator is a broken-down man who searches in vain for employment; he pleads with his listeners to remember that not every poor man is a tramp. The narrator in another song, "Remember That the Poor Tramp Has to Live," is an old man, no longer fit for employment on the railroad. Now unable to support himself in a dignified manner, he is forced to go begging.

In sharp contrast, the protagonist of "Wild and Reckless Hobo" seems to be a wanderer by choice, a vagabond who cannot bring himself to settle down and who shows no regrets over his habit. The speaker in "The Railroad Boomer," on the other hand, warns his listeners that being a perennial wanderer has its distasteful side. The moribund hero of "The Dying Hobo" seems to have no regrets about his way of life; he dies looking forward to a heaven where no one has to work.

It is hard to say which of these songs better represent the sentiments of the homeless wanderers. "The Poor Tramp" and "Because He Was Only a Tramp" offer serious social commentary; "Wild and Reckless Hobo" and "Dying Hobo" romanticize somewhat the life of the hobo. The much more recent "Railroad Boomer" is a more self-conscious piece with a moral. "Milwaukee Blues" is about hoboing, but in a way that takes wandering completely for granted. Any thoughts about the virtues or vices of such a way of life are entirely outside the scope of the song.

The first six songs given in this chapter all date from the late nineteenth century, although it must be admitted that in two instances, "The Dying Hobo" and "Wild and Reckless Hobo," there is no evidence in print that they are indeed that old. The seventh song, "Milwaukee Blues," is of indeterminate age in its form given here, but it belongs to a song family that is also of the nineteenth century.

In 1935, Budd McKillips wrote in the *Railway Conductor*, "Will the depression, which has created hundreds of thousands of homeless wanderers, create a new crop and new type of 'hobo poetry'? The chances are that it will. . . ."[15] It is perhaps ironic that the best-known hobo songs of the 1930s were written not by homeless wanderers, but by a western poet and a professional New York (Kansas-born) songwriter: Waldo O'Neal's "Hobo Bill's Last Ride" and Carson Robison's "The Railroad Boomer." Both songs were actually penned in 1929, before the impact of the Depression was fully felt.

Cliff Carlisle, popular hillbilly singer of the 1930s, wrote or popularized a number of songs about boxcar-riding hoboes (the title of this chapter is the title of one of his songs), but none of them had the feeling of having been born or even sung in the hoboes' jungle camps. McKillips may have been right in his surmise, but if so, the material has yet to be adequately documented.

NOTES

1. George Milburn, *The Hobo's Hornbook* (New York: Ives Washburn, 1930).

2. See *DAE*, vol. 2, pp. 1253–54, citing Josiah Flynt, "The American Tramp," *Contemporary Review*, 60 (Aug., 1891), 255.

3. Josiah Flynt, "Tramping with Tramps," *Century*, 47 (Nov., 1893), 107.

4. Cited in Nels Anderson, *The Hobo* (1923; rpt., Chicago: University of Chicago Press, Phoenix Books, 1961), p. 12.

5. Ibid.

6. Anderson, *The Hobo*.

7. Kenneth Allsop, *Hard Travellin'* (London: Hodder and Stoughton, 1967).

8. Mrs. H. C. Lord, *LEMJ*, 19 (Sept., 1885), 525.

9. Charlton C. Andrews, "What the Hoboes Cost Yearly," *RRManM*, 10 (Nov., 1909), 357–63.

10. Frank V. Whiting, "Trespassers Killed on Railways—Who Are They?," *Railroad Trainman*, 29 (May, 1912), 442–44, reprinted from *Railway Age Gazette*.

11. Alice Willard Solenberger, *One Thousand Homeless Men* (New York: Russell Sage Foundation, 1911), chap. 12. This chapter, "Confirmed Wanderers or 'Tramps,'" was reprinted in *Railroad Trainman*, 29 (Jan., 1912), 32–39.

12. Solenberger, *One Thousand Homeless Men*, p. 231.

13. *LEMJ*, 10 (Sept., 1876), 408; also in *RRManM*, 16 (Dec., 1911), 576, and in Patrick Fennell, *Recitations, Epics, Epistles, Lyrics and Poems, Humorous and Pathetic* (Oswego, N.Y.: Published by the author, 1886), p. 158.

14. Solenberger, *One Thousand Homeless Men*, p. 222.

15. Budd L. McKillips, "Hungry Men Write Verse," *Railway Conductor*, 52 (July, 1935), 200.

Because He Was Only a Tramp

THE TRAMP

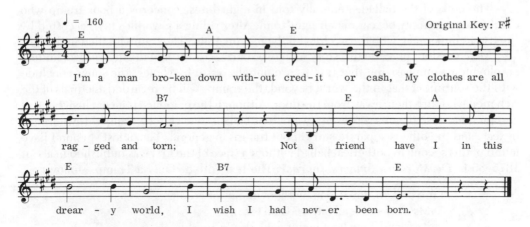

I'm a man broken down without credit or cash,
My clothes are all ragged and torn;
Not a friend have I in this dreary world,
I wish I had never been born.

In vain I search for employment,
Sleeping out on the ground cold and damp;
I'm stared [*pronounced "starred"*] in the face by starvation,
God pity the life of a tramp.

Last night down on the L and N Railroad,
There's a man most hungry and cold;
An empty boxcar stood still on the track,
He jumped in and closed up the door.

He had rode three miles in an empty boxcar,
Till a brakeman came around with his lantern;
He was thrown from the train and was killed by the rails,
Because he was only a tramp.

Kind friends, I want you all to remember,
That every poor man is not a tramp;
There's a-many true heart still beating,
Beneath the old coat of a tramp.

Poor Lazarus lay at the rich man's door,
And the dogs came and licked his sores;
But at last his spirit took its sweet flight,
Where there's room and bread for the poor.

McGee Brothers

The several texts of this song that have been preserved are so varied that it is difficult to reconstruct any meaningful evolutionary history of the composition. The title I have chosen does not appear with any of the reported texts; rather, it is the recurring line that joins together the various versions.

The core of the ballad, generally told in eight lines, concerns a poor tramp who climbs into an empty boxcar on a freight train. After riding a few miles he is accosted by the train's brakeman, who throws him off the moving train. The tramp is killed in the fall.

Most versions precede this story with two stanzas concerning the difficulty of finding employment, emphasizing that tramps are not always so by choice; the songs conclude with the sentiment that in the world beyond, the tramps will be regarded as equals of the rich men who turn them away from the door. Although the evidence is inconclusive, I feel certain that these themes represent two parent ballads: one about a tramp thrown from a boxcar, and the other a separate story about tramps in general. The oldest version I have found of this second hypothetical ballad without a trace of the first was published in about 1875–80 in *De Marsan's Singers' Journal*. The text, titled "Only a Tramp," follows:

> I'm a broken-down man, without money or credit,
> 　　My clothes are all tattered and torn;
> Not a friend have I got in this cold, dreary world—
> 　　Oh! I wish I had never been born!
> In vain I have searched for employment,
> 　　Sleeping out on the ground cold and damp;
> I am stared in the face by starvation—
> 　　Oh! Pity the fate of a tramp!
>
> 　　They tell me to work for a living,
> 　　And not through the country to stamp;
> 　　And yet, when I ask for employment,
> 　　They say I am only a tramp.
>
> Oh! the rich ones at home, by their bright, cheery firesides,
> 　　With plenty so temptingly stored,
> Have oftimes refused me, and sneered with contempt,
> 　　When I asked for the crumbs from their board;
> And if through the cravings of hunger,
> 　　With a loaf I should dare to decamp,
> They at once set the dogs loose upon me,
> 　　Because I am only a tramp.
>
> 　　Chorus:
>
> But the day will yet come when the rich man and me
> 　　Will be laid 'neath the same mother earth;
> His joys and my sorrows will then be forgotten,
> 　　When, I hope, better times will have birth;
> Yet, my friends, you should sometimes remember
> 　　That every poor man's not a scamp,
> For there's many a true heart still beating
> 　　Beneath the old coat of a tramp.
>
> 　　Chorus:

A version in the Western Kentucky Folklore Archive collected in 1948 is essentially this song with the second stanza lacking. "Broken-Down Sport," collected by Greenleaf and Mansfield in Newfoundland in 1929, links the first verse and chorus with two more verses telling how the narrator's sister married a rich squire and how his mother died brokenhearted when she heard of his awful downfall, brought on by rum. All the other items listed in the references, except the Gooley recording, include the incident in which the tramp is thrown from the boxcar and killed.

The oldest mixed version, reported by McNeil, is from an 1873–93 New York manuscript album that had belonged to Ida Harris. The song there, entitled "The Tramp," consists of seven verses and a chorus, the spelling of which clearly demonstrates an oral rather than a printed source. The texts printed by Dean and by Randolph are abridged versions of the Harris version.

The earliest recording, also titled "The Tramp," was made in June, 1926, by Al Craver (Vernon Dalhart) for Columbia. It, too, is a shorter version of the Harris text.

Four recorded versions include elements not present in Harris's manuscript. The McGee Brothers' recording of May 11, 1927, for the Brunswick-Balke-Collender Company, lacks the chorus and three of Harris's verses but has an added verse about Lazarus at the rich man's door. This recording is transcribed above.

Sam and Kirk McGee were born in 1894 and 1899, respectively, on a farm near Franklin in Williamson County, Tennessee. The boys learned to play musical instruments while in their teens, and developed a repertoire of dance tunes learned at the local dances, blues and rags picked up from black musicians, and old ballads absorbed from their mother. Sam's recording career began in April, 1926, when Uncle Dave Macon took him to New York as an accompanist. Kirk's first records were made in May of the following year. "The Tramp" was recorded on the last of that series of sessions in May.

Jack Harper's version is interesting in that it shares only two stanzas with the other texts, about throwing the tramp from the train; but to them are added five stanzas relating how the tramp had been left by his wife and was trying to find her in order to take care of his dying baby. This theme is part of Kearney's song, "The Tramp" (see the discussion of "The Poor Tramp Has to Live"). The Carter Family version, recorded for Decca in June, 1937, is unique in having a stanza that attributes the tramp's wretched condition to rum (linking it to the Newfoundland text) and warns all young men to "stick to the straight life." A. P. Carter copyrighted this version (June 23, 1938, E 169656).

The McGee Brothers' tune is generally associated with the old British ballad "George Collins" (Child 85). This is an interesting borrowing, particularly in view of the peculiar amalgamation of "George Collins" with another hobo song in this chapter, "The Dying Hobo." In 1973, Sam McGee recalled that he had learned the song in his youth from a neighbor more than sixty years earlier.[1]

NOTE

1. McGee to Cohen, Oct., 1973.

REFERENCES

A. "Only a Tramp," in *De Marsan's Singers' Journal* (ca. 1875–80). Credited to Thomas Harrington; air: "Swim Out." Earliest known printing of the version without the incident of the tramp thrown from the train.

"The Tramp," from Ida Harris manuscript autograph album, New York State,

1873–93. Printed in W. K. McNeil, "Popular Songs from New York Autograph Albums," *Journal of Popular Culture*, 3 (Summer, 1969), 46–56. Earliest known version of the full ballad with the incident of tramp thrown from train.

"The Tramp," by Al Craver (Vernon Dalhart pseudonym). Dalhart, vocal; lute accompaniment. Recorded June 25, 1926 (Columbia master 142347-2), in New York City. Released on Columbia 15086-D on July 30, 1926. Earliest recording of the song.

"The Tramp," by the McGee Brothers. Sam McGee, vocal and guitar; Kirk McGee, banjo. Recorded May 11, 1927, for the Vocalion division of Brunswick-Balke-Collender Company (master E5037) in New York City. Released on Vocalion 5171 in Sept., 1927. Reissued on Bear Family (West Germany) 15517: *Sam & Kirk McGee from Sunny Tennessee*. This version is transcribed here.

B. Dean, M. C., 71
    Edwards, R., 116   "The Tramp Song"
    Forrest, inside cover
    Greenleaf & Mansfield, 104   "Broken-Down Sport"
    Owens, T., 22
    Pack & John, 19
    Randolph IV, 368
    RRManM, 10 (Nov., 1909), 380
    RVB, 20 (June, 1967), 11

C. GORDON MSS:
    422—Mich Y. T. (Feb., 1927)

    LOMAX PAPERS:
    Text transcription by John A. Lomax from the singing of Frank DeLong of Deming, N. Mex.

    WKFA:
    Webb Hill (Mar., 1948)

D. Carter Family—Decca 5518, Coral 64019, Melotone (Canada) 45255; CMH 112: *Carter Family Original and Essential* "The Broken Down Tramp"
    Art Frazier and Hamilton's Harmonians—Herwin 75571
    Fruit Jar Guzzlers—Paramount 3099 "Pity the Tramp"
    Jack Harper—Vocalion 5494   "Tramp's Last Ride"
    Jack Kaufman—Romeo 1143, Banner 0529, Homestead 23003   "Bum Song No. 6 (The Tramp Song)"

E. Carter Family—JEMF 101: *The Carter Family on Border Radio*   "Broken Down Tramp"
    Leo Gooley—Prestige International 25014: *Ontario Ballads and Folksongs* "The Tramp"

F. LC AFS:
    Al Bittick—AFS 12050 A12
    Henry Davis—AFS 1715 B2   "The Tramp"
    Francis Sullivan—AFS 1850 A3 & B1 "Only a Tramp"

Sam McGee. Courtesy of Charles Wolfe.

The Poor Tramp Has to Live

THE POOR TRAMP

I am a poor old railroad man, once't a helping [?healthy] section hand,
And old age is slowly creeping on the way;
Now hard times is coming on, and my last gold dollar is gone,
And thps song is what I made to sing and play.

Now you ofttimes see the stamp of a poor unfortunate tramp,
Who has no home and has no place to fill;
As you see him pass along and he sings his little song,
Please remember that the poor tramp has to live.

My health broke down out on the track, with heavy loads upon my back,
Now I have to make my way the best I can;
We never know when we are young what may be our future doom,
These words is from a broke-down section hand.

Chorus:

Yes, my health is broken down, and I tramp from town to town,
Sing and play, take whatever you may give;
While I try to play and sing, just divide your little change,
And remember that the poor tramp has to live.

Ernest V. Stoneman

Two distinct songs can be recognized by the repeated line in the chorus "Remember that the poor tramp has to live." What appears to be the older was published several times in about 1880 in songsters and on broadsides, generally titled "The Tramp." The text published in Abrahams's *When the Moonbeams Gently Fall Songster* bears the notation "copyright secured 1880" but gives no author's credits. These songster texts differ slightly from all the other texts, and the rhyme scheme is somewhat more consistent. The earliest text I have found of the more usual form was published as a broadside by H. J. Wehman between 1878 and 1886. It is reproduced here.[1] On this broadside Billy Kearney is credited as author and the tune indicated is "True as Steel." Both the Wehman and the Abrahams songs consist of three verses of eight lines each and a chorus. The more familiar Wehman chorus reads:

So if you meet a tramp that bears misfortune's stamp,
If he is worthy of your aid why freely give;
Give him a hearty grip, wish him luck upon his trip,
And remember that the poor tramp has to live.

As in the chorus, the alternate lines of the verses have internal rhyme. I have found no information about Billy Kearney or when "The Tramp" was first published. Though I refer to this version as "Kearney's song," I have no proof of his authorship apart from the attribution in the Wehman broadside and some nineteenth-century songsters. "True as Steel" appeared in Ditson's *Household Melodies*, volume 2 (ca. 1880), but I have been unable to examine a copy. Kearney's song was recorded several times.

Kearney's "The Tramp" has no references to railroads. The other song with the same last line of the chorus is a recomposition of Kearney's piece, evidently by some folk poet, in which the narrator is a former railroadman. This song, at least as it has been preserved on record, shows less attention to technical poetical details, such as internal rhyme, but is also much less stilted in its use of language. Its earliest recording was Walter Morris's "The Railroad Tramp," for Columbia in April, 1926. In this book we have transcribed a later recording by Ernest Stoneman that differs only slightly from Morris's song. Stoneman, whose career is sketched briefly in connection with "Asleep at the Switch," recorded the song four times between 1927 and 1934: for Gennett in February, 1927; for Victor in May, 1927; for Edison in November, 1928 (unissued); and for the American Record Corporation in January, 1934. A copyright was taken out for the Victor disc, crediting Stoneman as author/composer (June 11, 1927, E 665387). The version given above is transcribed from the Victor recording.

[331]

THE TRAMP.

BY BILLY KEARNEY. TUNE—"TRUE AS STEEL."

How many men there are that ride in Fortune's car,
   And bolt and bar the door against the poor,
Because they have lots of gold, their hearts turn icy cold,
   They ought to be condemned for it, I'm sure.
Now speaking of the race that tramp from place to place,
   There are some of them who are men from top to toe,
So if they are in need, of this circumstance take heed,
   And remember that the poor tramp has to live.

CHORUS.

So if you meet a tramp that bears misfortune's stamp,
   If he is worthy of your aid why freely give
Give him a hearty grip, wish him luck upon his trip,
   And remember that the poor tramp has to live.

I lately saw a tramp whom people called a scamp,
   And upon him set their dogs lest he might steal;
And as he turned away, I saw him kneel and pray,
   And I know that God above heard his appeal.
For little do we know as he tramps through rain and snow,
   That once he was as happy as a king,
'Till Fortune's cruel dart had pierced his manly heart,
   And took away his home and everything.
          So if you meet a tramp that, &c.

I once heard a tramp relate the sad story of his fate,
   And how he was an outcast shunned by all;
He lived a happy life, had a loving child and wife,
   But, alas! like Eve, this woman had to fall.
For she proved weak and frail; there's no need to tell the tale
   How she turned his manly heart to sad despair;
He never since has smiled on that handsome wife or child,
   But sadly now he tramps from place to place.
          So if you meet a tramp that, &c.

H. J. Wehman, Song Publisher, 50 Chatham St., N. Y.

Broadside: Billy Kearney's "The Tramp." Courtesy of David Freeman.

In the references below, an asterisk identifies all versions of the Kearney song, as distinguished from the railroad parody. The recording by Joe Lee is a unique ballad blending Kearney's song with one about a poor boy arrested for stealing.

NOTE

1. I thank David Freeman for making a copy of this broadside available to me.

REFERENCES

A. "The Tramp," broadside. Published between 1878 and 1886 by H. J. Wehman, Song Publisher, 50 Chatham Street, New York, no. 331. Credited to Billy Kearney; tune—"True as Steel." Earliest known printing of the familiar version.
"The Railroad Tramp," by Walter Morris. Morris, vocal; guitar accompaniment. Recorded ca. Apr. 22, 1926 (Columbia master 142081), in Atlanta. Released on Columbia 15101-D on Oct. 30, 1926. Reissued on Clarion 5437-C (control no. 100584) and on Velvetone 2497-V (100584). First recording of the song.
"The Poor Tramp," by Ernest V. Stoneman. Vocal, harmonica, and guitar. Recorded May 19, 1927 (Victor master BVE-38763-2), in New York City. Released on Victor 20672 in ca. July, 1927. Copyrighted on June 11, 1927 (E 665387), with Stoneman credited as author. Reissued on Rounder 1008: *Ernest V. Stoneman and the Blue Ridge Corn Shuckers*. This recording is transcribed here; an earlier recording by Stoneman, for Gennett in Feb., 1927, differs negligibly from this one.
"The Tramp," by Joe Lee. Recorded for the Library of Congress Archive of Folk Song in 1936 (AFS 745 B2) in State Farm, Va. A unique variant.

B. *Abrahams, 54
*Brown III, 423
Davis, A. K., 280 (title and first line only)
*Delaney #1, 16
*Fagan & Fox, 58
*Foster's Songster, 18
Horstman, 327–28
*Manchester & Jennings, 58
*Pack, 75
*Pack John, 20

*RVB, 20 (June, 1967), 11
*Taylor, J. (I), 18
Wehman #2, 19
Wehman #4

C. COHEN COLLECTION:
*Laura Affolter (letter, June, 1968)

WKFA:
*Emily Irene Humphreys (Nov., 1956)
*Alvin Patterson (May, 1962)

D. *Lester McFarland and Robert Gardner—Brunswick 398 "The Tramp"
Ernest V. Stoneman—Gennett 6044, Champion 15233, Challenge 324, Challenge 398 (last three as by Uncle Jim Seaney), Herwin 75535, Challenge 244, Supertone 9255, Silvertone 5001, Silvertone 25001, Silvertone 8155 (last five as by Uncle Ben Hawkins)
—Vocalion 02655 "Broke Down Section Hand"
*Norwood Tew—Bluebird B-7950 "If You Meet a Tramp"

E. Dock Boggs—Folkways FA 2392: *Dock Boggs, Vol. 2* "Railroad Tramp"
Jimmie Skinner—Vetco 3001: *Jimmie Skinner Sings Bluegrass* "A Lonesome Railroad Man" (related piece)
*Blaine Smith—Bluebonnet BL 120: *Blaine Smith, Vol. 1* "The Tramp"
Stoneman Family—MGM E/S 4453: *Stoneman's Country* "Remember, the Poor Tramp Has to Live"

F. LC AFS:
L. Bedingfield—AFS 10824 A23 "The Broke-Down Railroad Man"
Wythe Bishop—AFS 5353 A1 "The Tramp"
Joe Lee—AFS 745 B2 "The Tramp"

Waiting for a Train/Wild and Reckless Hobo

WILD AND RECKLESS HOBOES

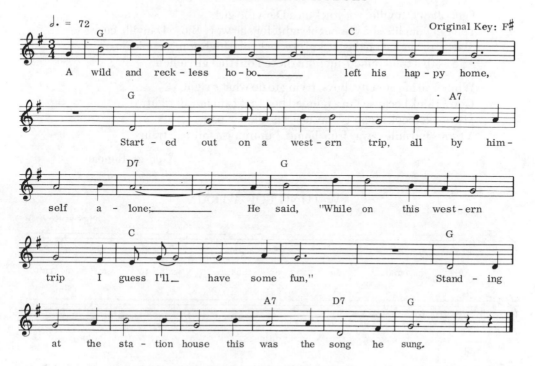

A wild and reckless hobo (he) left his happy home,
Started out on a western trip, all by himself alone;
He said, "While on this western trip I guess I'll have some fun,"
Standing at the station house this was the song he sung.

Standing on a platform, smoking a cheap cigar,
Waiting for a freight train to catch an empty car;
Thinking of those good old times and wishing they'd come again,
A thousand miles away from home, bumming a railroad train.

"Kind miss, oh, kind miss, won't you gimme a bite to eat,
A little piece of cold corn bread, a little piece of meat?"
She threw her arms around me, says, "I love you as a friend,
But if I give to you this time you'll go bumming around again."

"Kind miss, oh, kind miss, don't talk to me so rough,
You think I am a hobo because I look so tough."
She took me in her kitchen, she treated me nice and kind,
She got me in the notion of bumming all the time.

When I left the kitchen, went strolling down in town,
I heard a doubleheader blow, I thought it was western-bound;
I walked up to the railroad, up to the railroad shop,
I heard the agent tell a man that freight train would not stop.

My heart begin to roam around and I begin to sing,
If that freight train goes through this town, I'll catch it on a wing;
I pulled my cap down over my eyes and stepped up to the track,
I caught the stirrup of an empty car but never did look back.

I got off in Danville, got stuck on a Danville girl,
You bet your life she was out of sight, for she wore those Danville curls;
She wore her hat on the back of her head like high-tone people do,
And as that train pulled out from there I bid that girl adieu.

While I'm in your city, boys, trying to do what's right,
Don't think because I'm a railroad boy that I am not all right;
My pocketbook is empty, my heart is filled of pain,
A thousand miles away from home, bumming a railroad train.

George Reneau

WAITING FOR A TRAIN

All around the water tank, waitin' for a train,
A thousand miles away from home, sleeping in the rain;
I walked up to a brakeman to give him a line of talk,
He says, "If you've got money, I'll see that you don't walk."
"I haven't got a nickel, not a penny can I show."
"Get off, get off, you railroad bum," he slammed the boxcar do'.
    Yodel:

He put me off in Texas, a state I dearly love,
The wide-open spaces all around me, the moon and stars up above;
Nobody seems to want me, or lend me a helping hand,
I'm on my way from Frisco, I'm going back to Dixie land;
Though my pocketbook is empty, and my heart is full with pain,
I'm a thousand miles away from home, just waiting for a train.
    Yodel:

Jimmie Rodgers

The full-length case study that this song complex requires has been promised by D. K. Wilgus of UCLA; consequently, my discussion here is relatively brief, in view of the great quantity of material at hand. Interested readers can join me in looking forward to Dr. Wilgus's study when it is complete.

Save for two distantly related items, the history of this ballad prior to 1900 is completely unknown. The earlier of these two ancestral pieces is a mid-nineteenth-century London broadside titled "Standing on the Platform," with the subtitle "Waiting for the Train." This long ballad recounts the tale of a train traveler in England who meets a pretty girl on the train; she subsequently falsely accuses him of assaulting her. The chorus is:

Standing on the platform, waiting for the train,
There I met the girl who's been the cause of all my pain;
I often wonder whether I shall ever see again
The girl upon the platform waiting for the train.

A shorter recomposition of the ballad was evidently popular in this country in the 1860s and 1870s, for it appeared many times in print, especially in pocket songsters: *Billy Cotton's Ethiopian Songster* (1870), *Bobby Newcomb's San Francisco Minstrels' Songster* (1868), and *"Coming through the Rye" Songster* (1871), to name a few. A slightly different sheet-music version was published in 1870 by Brainard and Sons of Cleveland. This ballad tells only of the meeting and parting of the narrator and the fair maid, with no sordid tale of extortion. The chorus is different from the London broadside. No other elements of either of these pieces have been found in any of the versions of the hobo song that is our immediate concern.

Since we have no extant pre-1909 survivals of the hoboes' "Waiting for a Train," we can only speculate on its relation to these older music-hall pieces—if indeed the resemblances are other than accidental. Possibly the hobo songs were parodies, composed in the 1870s or 1880s, of some undiscovered intermediate ballad. It is unlikely that they did not see the light of day before 1890.

The earliest printed fragment I have found appeared in *Railroad Man's Magazine* in July, 1909. A reader from Missouri had requested a poem which began

While standing on the platform, waiting for the train,
Cold and hungry, I lay down, out in the cold and rain,

Thinking o'er those good old times I ne'er shall see again,
Ten thousand miles away from home, I've bummed a railroad-train.[1]

The gentleman's request was not granted, however; and it was many years before anything approaching a complete text of the song could be pieced together from fragments published in either popular or scholarly literature. In 1914 the magazine printed a request for the poem "10,000 Miles from Home," which told "of a man who bummed on a railroad train, hobnobbed with princes and kings, dined on quail, and wrote his name on every box car and gate-post."[2] This song has never turned up.

A survey of all the collected and recorded versions shows that the various texts are built up from several recurrent themes and motifs, the most widespread of which are:

A. an introductory stanza about a "wild and reckless" hobo setting off to roam;

B. an introductory stanza with the phrase "Standing on a platform, smoking a cheap cigar";

C. an introductory stanza beginning "All around the water tank, waiting for a train";

D. two or three verses about an encounter between a hobo and a woman; he asks her for something to eat; she first demurs, saying it would encourage him to continue bumming, but (usually) she finally accedes.

E. two or three stanzas about a Danville (Denver) girl who wore her hair on the back of her head "like high-tone people do";

F. two or three stanzas about an encounter with a trainman whom the hobo asks to let him ride; the trainman says he can ride if he has money; when the hobo says he is broke, the trainman orders him off the train;

G. a concluding stanza about the hoboes' paradise, borrowed from "The Dying Hobo."

These elements do not appear in random association with each other; rather, there seem to be persistent groupings that occur over and over, while other possible concatenations turn up seldom, if at all. These facts suggest strongly that we are dealing not with one epical hobo ballad, but with at least two, and possibly more, separate poems or songs that with time commingled and exchanged verses with each other. Exactly what the original pieces were is impossible to say, inasmuch as the record from the nineteenth century is completely blank. However, I would propose three hypothetical independent songs: "Wild and Reckless Hobo" (themes A and D), "Waiting for a Train" (C, F), and "Danville Girl" (B, E). "Danville Girl" would seem to have been the least stable unit, as it has been annexed by both of the other songs. "Waiting for a Train" could be the older of the other two, for it does not use the word *hobo;* this is consistent with its probable relationship with the music hall songs of about 1870. If, as suggested in the introduction to this chapter, the word *hobo* did not come into wide use until the 1880s, then "Wild and Reckless Hobo" would probably not be older than that.

More than in the case of most of the other songs discussed in this book, the role of the phonograph recordings looms very large in the history of "Waiting for a Train"/"Wild and Reckless Hobo." This is partly because we have so few examples prior to the recordings: apart from the 1909 fragment quoted above, these include only a few short fragments collected from blacks by Odum and Johnson and by White in the period 1911–16; the Burnett songbook; and the Frothingham manuscript dated 1923, which combines several verses under the title "The Wabash Cannon Ball." However, a more important reason is that various versions were recorded by several highly popular and influential hillbilly recording artists: the Carter Family, Jimmie Rodgers, Vernon Dalhart, Riley

Puckett, Jimmie Davis, Bob Miller, Gene Autry, Clayton McMichen, and Burnett and Rutherford.

The earliest recording was made by George Reneau on February 24, 1925, in New York for the Aeolian-Vocalion company; it was released in May of that year. Reneau, a blind minstrel born around the turn of the century, made his living singing on the street corners of Knoxville, Tennessee, accompanying himself on guitar and mouth-harp. One day he was heard by G. A. Nennstiel, the record manager of Sterchi Brothers, Vocalion's southern distributor. Nennstiel recommended to the Aeolian company that Reneau be brought to New York and recorded. Reneau's recording is transcribed in this book.

The Burnett songbook referred to above is an important document in connection with this song, since it includes the earliest complete text of the ballad yet recovered. Although the booklet is not dated, other evidence places the date of composition of two of the autobiographical songs at 1913; the publication date is probably that year or shortly thereafter. The text, titled "The Reckless Hobo" in the book, differs slightly from the "Ramblin' Reckless Hobo" that Richard Burnett and Leonard Rutherford recorded in

The Reckless Hobo

A rambling, reckless Hobo Left his happy home,
Started on a western trip By himself alone,
He said, upon this western trip I guess I'll have some fun;
Standing at a station hous. . This is the song he sung:
Standing on a platform Smoking a cheap cigar,
Waiting for a freight trai. To catch an empty car
Thinking of those good ole times Wishing they'd come again;
I'm a thousand miles away from home, Bumming a railroad tra

Kind Miss, kind Miss, Won't you give me a bit. to eat,
A little piece of cold corn bread A little piece of meat?
She threw her arms aroun.. me Say I'll love you as a friend,
But if I give to you this time
          You'll be bumming around again.
Kind Miss, kind Miss, Don't talk to me so rough;
You think I am a hobo Because I look so tough.
She took me in her kitche., She treated me nice and kind,
She put me in the notion Of bumming all the time.

When I left her kitchen I went strolling down in town,
I heard a double-header blow, I thought it was western bound
I walked out to the railroad, Out to the railroad shop,
I heard the agent tell a man The freight train would not stop
My heart began to rove around And I began to sing
If that freight train goes through this town
          i'll catch it on the wing
I pulled my cap down over my eyes And walked out to the track
And caught the stirrup of empty car And never did look back.

I got off in Danville, Got stuck on a Danville girl,
You bet your life she's out of sight
          She wears the Danville curl.
She wears her hair on the back of her head
          Like high toned people do,
But if a west-bound train pulls out tonight
          I'll bid that girl adieu.
Now I am in your city, boys, Trying to do what is right;
Don't think because I am a railroad boy
          That I am not all right.

My pocketbook is empty, My heart is filled with pain;
  Ten thousand miles away from home.
          Bumming a railroad train.

"The Reckless Hobo," from Richard Burnett's songbook. Reproduced in the brochure notes to Rounder 1004: *Ramblin' Reckless Hobo*.

1927. Both variants are close to the first recorded version of the song, by Reneau, but in a few instances the Burnett recording is closer to the Reneau recording than to the songbook version, suggesting that Burnett may have been influenced by Reneau's version by the time he recorded the song. Burnett stated in a 1962 interview that he "got that [song] from somebody who's been out west."[3] No one ever interviewed Reneau about his songs, so we shall never know what his sources were. Burnett claimed he sold some six thousand copies of his songbook on his travels around his native Monticello, Kentucky; and since Reneau's hometown of Knoxville, Tennessee, is not far away, it is possible that he had been influenced by Burnett's booklet before he made his records.

Vernon Dalhart recorded the song twice, once in August, 1925, and again later at an undetermined date. The two versions were different, but each consisted of five stanzas from Reneau's text. The next two recordings—by the Cofer Brothers and by Dock Boggs, both made in March, 1927—were independent versions.

The most widely known form of this song complex is Jimmie Rodgers's "Waiting for a Train." His life story, in particular his early associations with the railroads and black railroad workers of his native Mississippi, has been amply documented elsewhere.[4] He was largely responsible for the popularity of three other songs in the book: "Ben Dewberry's Final Run," "Train Whistle Blues," and "Hobo Bill's Last Ride." A brief sketch of his career and further references appear in my discussion of the latter two songs. Rodgers recorded "Waiting for a Train" on October 22, 1928; it was released on February 8 of the following year and copyrighted on March 23 (E 4483; renewed, R 167237), with Rodgers credited as author. It was one of his most popular numbers, and more than 350,000 copies were sold in the next few years. Because of its importance, it is transcribed here. Numerous field-recorded versions (e. g., Cambiaire, p. 101; Brown, p. 428; Crabtree), as well as the majority of the later commercial recordings, can be traced clearly to the Rodgers record. The earliest "covers" of Rodgers's disc were by Ed Jake West for the American Record Corporation (Mar. 22, 1929), Riley Puckett for Columbia (Apr. 10, 1929), and Hoke Rice for Gennett (April 13, 1929)—all within a couple of months of the release of the Rodgers disc.

Ralph S. Peer, Victor's A & R man who worked extensively with Jimmie Rodgers (as well as countless other white and black rural artists), recalled that someone had sent the words to "Waiting for a Train" to Jimmie. When Rodgers looked over the text, he said that he had known the song, and picked up his guitar and started playing it. He could not fit the correspondent's words to his own melody, and so changed some of the text until it was more satisfactory.[5]

Several other early hillbilly recordings are of interest because they contain elements not found either in Rodgers's song or in Reneau's "Wild and Reckless Hoboes": the Stripling Brothers' "Railroad Bum" (Aug. 19, 1929); Tim Flora and Rufus Lingo's "A Lonely Tramp" (ca. Mar., 1928); Morgan Denmon's "Wild and Reckless Hobo" (Mar., 1929)—the first to include the couplet from "The Dying Hobo" (motif G above); Darby and Tarlton's "New York Hobo" (Apr., 1929); and Prince Albert Hunt's "Waltz of the Roses" (Aug., 1929).

But without a doubt, one of the most interesting versions of this hobo song was sent to Robert Frothingham for his column in *Adventure* magazine by Herman F. Ross in 1923. The text, titled "The Wabash Cannon Ball," mixes elements of that song with "Waiting for a Train" and other fragments. Because it is so unusual, it is reprinted here:

> She rattles and she jingles,
> She rumbles and she roars,

Dashin' through the woodlands
And steamin' long the shore;
"That's a mighty engine."
Hear the merry hobo squall,
Ridin' the rods and breakbeams [sic]
On the Wabash Cannon Ball.

The railroad is completed, the boxcars on the track,
Yonder comes two hobos, with their luggage on their back;
One looks like my brother, the other my brother-in-law,
I've bummed my way from Birmingham to the State of Arkansaw.

Goin' up a street one day, as blue as I could be,
I bummed a kind old lady for a piece of bread and meat;
She gave me cake and coffee, she treated me mighty fine,
If I make another bum like this, I'll be bummin' all the time.

Standin' at a watertank, waitin' for a B & O,
Let me tell you something that I know that you don't know;
Here she comes a-runnin', almost skippin' and flyin',
They don't stop to take any water on the Pennsylvania Lines.

Standing on a platform, smokin' a cheap cigar,
Waitin' for a freight train to catch an empty boxcar;
The breakman [sic] caught my motion, said "Hobo, where you goin',
Get down, get down, you dirty bum, you can't ride no train o' mine."

I've been to Toledo, I've been to Buffalo,
I've been to St. Louie, I'm goin' to Kokomo;
I've been to Danville, a town well known to all,
By ridin' the rods and breakbeams [sic] on the Wabash Cannon Ball.[6]

NOTES

1. *RRManM*, 9 (July, 1909), 384.

2. Ibid., 23 (Mar., 1914), 719.

3. Richard Burnett, interviewed by Archie Green and Eugene Earle in Monticello, Ky., Aug. 12, 1962. For further biographical details, see the discussion of "The Dying Hobo" immediately following.

4. For the most recent and thorough documentation, see Nolan Porterfield, *Jimmie Rodgers* (Urbana: University of Illinois Press, 1979).

5. Ralph Peer, interviewed by Lillian Borgeson in Hollywood, Calif., Jan., 1958. A tape copy and tapescript of the interview were made available to me by Ed Kahn.

6. Ross, aboard the U.S.S. *Black Hawk*, to Frothingham, Jan., 1923 (Frothingham MS 42). The text was sent in response to a request printed in *Adventure* for "Wabash Cannon Ball." I have modified the punctuation and rewritten the eight-line stanzas as four-line stanzas.

REFERENCES

A. "Standing on the Platform / Waiting for the Train," broadside. Printed at the Catnach Press by W. S. Fortey, Monmouth Court, Seven Dials, London. Houghton Library, Harvard Broadside no. 25254.

"Standing on the Platform / Waiting for the Train," sheet music. "Song and Dance. As sung with Immense Success by Billy Gray." Music arranged by F. L. Martyn. Published by S. Brainard and Sons, Cleveland, 1870.

"The Reckless Hobo," in Richard Burnett

folio (ca. 1913), p. 4. Text reprinted in *Old Time Music* (London), No. 10 (Autumn, 1973), p. 11. Earliest printing of the "Wild and Reckless Hobo" form of the song.

"Wild and Reckless Hoboes," by George Reneau. Vocal and guitar. Recorded Feb. 24, 1925 (Brunswick Vocalion master 419-W), in New York City. Released on (Brunswick) Vocalion 14999 in 1925. Reissued on (Brunswick) Vocalion 5059 in ca. 1927. First recording of any form of the song; transcribed in this book.

"Waiting for a Train," by Jimmie Rodgers. Rodgers, vocal; C. L. Hutchi(n)son, cornet; James Rikard, clarinet; Dean Bryan, guitar; John Westbrook, steel guitar; and George MacMillan, string bass. Recorded Oct. 22, 1928 (Victor master BVE 47224-3), in Atlanta. Released on Victor V-40014 on Feb. 8, 1929. Reissued on RCA Bluebird B-5163, Montgomery Ward M-8109, Sunrise (Canada) 3244, Electradisk 2060, RCA Victor 21-0175 (in album P-282); Zonophone (England and Australia) E-5380, His Master's Voice (England) MH-192, Regal Zonophone (England and Australia) T 5380, Regal Zonophone (Ireland) IZ 320; RCA Victor LPM 1232: *Never No Mo' Blues*; RCA Victor LPT 3038 (10 LP); RCA Victor LPM/LSP 3315: *Best of the Legendary Jimmie Rodgers*; RCA Victor EPAT 409 (45 rpm EP); RCA Victor VPS 6091: *This Is Jimmie Rodgers*; RCA Victor 27-0101 (in 45 rpm album WPT-22); RCA Victor LPM 2094: *The Pick of the Country*; RCA Victor ANL 1-1052: *All about Trains*; RCA Victor ANS 1-1052 (8-track tape): *All about Trains*; Country Music Magazine DPL 2-0075; RCA Victor (Japan) RA-5460: *The Legendary Jimmie Rodgers 110 Collections*; RCA Victor (Japan) HP 526 (10 LP); RCA Victor (Japan) AP 3004; RCA Victor (Japan) RA 9037; RCA Victor (Japan) RA 5501; RCA Victor (England) RD 27138. Copyrighted Mar. 23, 1929, by Southern Music Publishing Company, with Rodgers credited as composer (EP 4483; renewed, R 167237). The most influential version of the song; also transcribed in this book.

"The Wabash Cannon Ball," Frothingham

MS 42. Letter sent to Robert Frothingham in Jan., 1923, by Herman F. Ross from the U.S.S. *Black Hawk*.

B. Anderson, G., 236
Best & Best, 28   "Danville Girl"
Brown III, 426, 428
Cambiaire, 3, 101
Carter Family (1935), 48
Carter Family (1937), 24
Carter Family (1941), 24
Crabtree, 201
Davis, J. (1937), 47
Davis, J. (1938), 58
Duncan, 271
Family Herald, 54 (references only)
Fuson, 128
Gordon, *Adventure*, Feb. 1, 1927, p. 204
Haun, 188
Henry (1934), 107
Horstman, 332–33
Hudson (1928), 76
Hudson (1936), 250
Laws, 230 (H 2) (discussion only)
Lomax, A. (1960), 419
Lomax & Lomax (1934), 28
Lynn, 215   "The Danville Girl"
Martin, M., 59
Milburn, 230, 249
Morton, 8
Odum, 353, 360
Odum & Johnson (1925), 210, 219
Pack, 51
Popular Cowboy Songs
Randolph IV, 360
Ridenour VI, 56
Rodgers (1934a), 14
Rodgers (1937), 48
Rodgers (1943b), 46
RRManM, 9 (July, 1909), 384
RRManM, 78 (June, 1965), 39
Stout, 113
Warner, Arthur, "Traveling with a Band," *Nation*, Apr. 27, 1932, p. 491 (reprinted in *JEMFN*, 3 [Sept., 1967], 43)
Webb (1923), 41–42   "Going to Leave the I & G"
White, N. I., 275, 374
Williams, 223

C. WKFA:
Ores Ferguson (n.d.)   "Danville Girl"

Herbert Givens (summer, 1949) "Ten Thousand Miles Away from Home"

James Jessup (May, 1948) "All around the Water Tank"

Thomas Kerr (ca. 1959) "Waiting for a Train"

Vera Reagan Martin (May, 1959) "Wild and Wreckless Hobo" [sic]

Nora Meisel (May, 1957) "Waiting for a Train"

Golden Lilburn Moore (Apr. 9, 1961) "All around the Watertank"

Permelia E. Newport (July 4, 1959) "Hobo"

Mrs. Powell (spring, 1948) "Ten Thousand Miles Away"

Jessie Richie (Nov. 19, 1959) "Rambler's Record [sic] Hobo"

Mrs. Boyd Wade (Apr. 25, 1959) "The Railroad Bum"

D. Gene Autry—Clarion 5155-C, Diva 6031-G, Velvetone 7057-V "Waiting for a Train"

Bill Baker and Bob Miller's Hinky Dinkers—Brunswick 445, Supertone 2059 "Wild and Reckless Hobo"

Dock (Moran) Boggs—Brunswick 132 "Danville Girl"

Britt and Ford—Banner 33326, Melotone 13293, Perfect 13106, Conqueror 8586, Lucky (Japan) 5051 "Free Wheeling Hobo" (derivative piece)

(Richard) Burnett and (Leonard) Rutherford—Columbia 15240-D, Clarion 5436-C, Velvetone 2496-V (last two as by Clayton and Parker); Rounder 1004: "*A Ramblin', Reckless Hobo*" "Rambling Reckless Hobo"

Jeff Calhoun (Vernon Dalhart pseudonym)—Grey Gull 4140, Radiex 4140 "Wild and Reckless Hobo"

Cliff Carlisle—Bluebird B-7094, Montgomery Ward M-7032, Montgomery Ward M-7365; Old Timey LP 103: *Cliff Carlisle, Vol. 1* "Waiting for a Ride" (derivative piece)

Carter Family—Acme 1004; Pine Mountain 206: *A.P. Carter's Clinch Mountain Ballads*

—Acme 1010 "Western Hobo" (fragment)

—Victor V-40255, Bluebird B-6223,

Montgomery Ward M-7147; RCX (England) 7102 (45 rpm EP): *The Original and Great Carter Family, Vol. 3* "Western Hobo"

Cofer Brothers—OKeh 45099 "Georgia Hobo"

Vernon Dalhart—Brunswick 2942, Supertone 2005, Aurora (Canada) 22029 "Wild and Reckless Hobo"

(Tom) Darby and (Jimmie) Tarlton— Columbia 15452-D "New York Hobo"

Jimmie Davis—Victor 23628; RCA Victor LPV 548: *Native American Ballads* "Wild and Reckless Hobo"

Morgan Denmon—OKeh 45327, Clarion 5300-C, Velvetone 2366-V (last two as by Emmett McWilliams) "Wild and Reckless Hobo"

Dixon Brothers—Bluebird B-7674, Montgomery Ward M-7337; Testament T-3301: *Babies in the Mill* "The Girl I Left in Danville"

Richard Eustis (Vernon Dalhart pseudonym)—Madison 5073, Van Dyke 75073 "Wild and Reckless Hobo"

Bob Ferguson and his Scalawaggers (Bob Miller pseudonym)—Columbia 15616-D "Wild and Reckless Hobo"

Tim Flora and Rufus Lingo—OKeh 45311 "A Lonely Tramp"

Lake Howard—Conqueror 8586 "Free Wheeling Hobo" (derivative piece)

Peg Leg Howell—Columbia 14438-D "Broke and Hungry Blues" (related)

Prince Albert Hunt's Texas Ramblers— OKeh 45375 "Waltz of Roses"

Jimson Brothers—Edison 52578, Edison 5708 (cylinder) "Waiting for a Train"

Buddy Jones—Decca 5827 "Waiting for a Train"

Clayton McMichen and his Georgia Wildcats—Varsity 5075, Continental 3086 "Free Wheelin' Hobo" (derivative piece)

Frankie Marvin—Crown 3475, Varsity 5109 "A Thousand Miles from Home"

Montana Slim (Wilf Carter)—Bluebird (Canada) 55-3201, RCA Camden CAL 527: *Montana Slim*; RCA Camden ADL2-0694: *Montana Slim's Greatest Hits* "Waiting for a Train"

Alan Moore—Crystal 174 "Waiting for a Train"

Tex Morton—Rodeo (Australia) 10-0010
"Waiting for a Train"

Bill Palmer (Bob Miller pseudonym)—
Electradisc 1908, Sunrise S-3110 (as by
the Bill Palmer Trio), Bluebird 1824,
Bluebird B-5010   "Free Wheeling
Hobo" (derivative piece)

Pie Plant Pete (Claude Moye
pseudonym)—Gennett 7167, Champion
45093, Melotone (Canada) 45093,
Supertone 9668, Superior 2577 (as by
Jerry Wallace), Champion 15970 (as by
Asparagus Joe)   "Waiting for the
Railroad Train"

Fiddlin' Powers—Edison (cylinder)
5131   "Wild and Reckless Hobo"

Jimmie Price—Cameo 9219, Romeo 1021,
Perfect 12556, Pathé 32477(?) (last two as
by Harry Wilson)   "Waiting for a
Train"

Riley Puckett—Columbia 15408-D
"Waiting for a Train"

Jim Reeves—RCA Victor 21-6749 (45 rpm);
RCA Camden CAL/CAS 686: *Country
Side*; RCA Camden CAL 793: *Country
Stars! The Country Hits!*
"Waiting for a Train"

George Reneau—Vocalion 14999, Vocalion
5059   "Wild and Reckless Hoboes"

Hoke Rice—Gennett 6839, Champion
15767 (as by Lee Landon), Supertone
9496 (as by Duke Lane), QRS R-9012
(probably same recording)   "Waiting
for a Train"

Carson Robison Trio and Frank Luther—
Crown 3083, Varsity 5079   "Waiting
for a Train"

Posey Rorer and the North Carolina
Ramblers—Edison 11009   "Wild and
Reckless Hobo"

Al Runyon—Kentucky 578

Stripling Brothers—Vocalion 5365
"Railroad Bum"

Ernest Tubb—Decca 46119, Decca
(Canada) 46119   "Waiting for a Train"

Virginia Mountain Boomers (Willie
Stoneman, Sweet Brothers, Justin
Winfield)—Gennett 6567, Supertone
9305, Champion 15610 (as by the Pine
Mountain Ramblers)   "Rambling
Reckless Hobo"

Ed "Jake" West—Banner 6370, Challenge
813, Conqueror 7348, Oriole 1561, Regal
8775, Jewel 5586, Paramount 3154,
Broadway 8109, Apex (Canada)
8951   "Waiting for a Train"

E. Lee Allen, Ralph Stanley, and the Clinch
Mountain Boys—Jalyn JLP-127: *Songs of
Love and Tragedy*   "Reckless Hobo"

Blue Sky Boys (Bill and Earl Bolick)—
Capitol ST 2483 and JEMF LP 104:
Presenting the Blue Sky Boys   "Wild
and Reckless Hobo"

Bluegrass 45—Rebel 1502   "Wild and
Reckless Hobo"

Dock Boggs—Folkways FA 2392: *Dock
Boggs, Vol. 2*   "Danville Girl"

Boys from Indiana—King Bluegrass
KB-561   "Waiting for a Train"

Walter Brennan—Liberty 53617 (45 rpm)

Elton Britt—RCA Camden CAL/CAS 2295:
The Jimmie Rodgers Blues
"Waiting for a Train"

Johnny Cash—Columbia CL 1930/CS 8730:
Blood, Sweat and Tears; Columbia GP 29:
The World of Johnny Cash; Philips
(England) CBS-BPG-62119: *Blood, Sweat
and Tears*   "Waiting for a Train"

Yodeling Slim Clark—Palomino 6352:
*Yodeling Slim Clark Sings the Legendary
Jimmie Rodgers Songs*   "Waiting for
a Train"

Jessie Clifton—Cumberland SRC 69512:
The Jimmie Rodgers Story   "Waiting
for a Train"

Stompin' Tom Conners—STC 1: *60 Oldtime
Favorites*   "Waiting for a Train"

Floyd Cramer—RCA Victor LPM/LSP
3318: *Hits from the Country Hall of
Fame*   "Waiting for a Train"

Barbara Dane—Horizon WP-1602: *When I
Was a Young Girl*   "The Danville Girl"

—Tradition 2072: *Anthology of American
Folk Songs*   "The Danville Girl"

Jim de Marcus—Rural Rhythm RR 144
"Waiting for a Train"

Roy Dorsey—Music Towne 8020 (45
rpm)   "Waiting for a Train,"

Roy Drusky—Mercury 12283   "Waiting
for a Train"

Dave Dudley—Mercury 20927/SR 60927:
Travelin' with Dave Dudley
"Waiting for a Train"

Snooks Eaglin—Folkways FA 2476: *New

Orleans Street Singer   "A Thousand
Miles from Home"
Jack Elliott—Monitor MFS 380: *Ramblin'
Jack Elliott Sings Woody Guthrie and
Jimmie Rodgers*   "Waitin' for a Train"
—Reprise RS 6284: *Young Brigham*
"Danville Girl"
—Everest Archive of Folk Music AFM 210:
Jack Elliot [sic]   "Danville Girl"
Jack Elliott and Derroll Adams—Topic
(England) 12T105: *Roll On Buddy*; Topic
(England) 10T14   "All around the
Water Tank," "Danville Girl"
Hank Ferguson—Folk-Legacy FSA 13:
Behind These Walls   "Waiting for a
Train"
Lester Flatt and the Nashville Grass—
CMH 9002: *Lester Flatt and the Nashville
Grass*   "Bummin' an Old Freight
Train"
Lester Flatt, Earl Scruggs, and the Foggy
Mountain Boys—Columbia CL 2255: *The
Fabulous Sound of Lester Flatt & Earl
Scruggs*   "Bummin' an Old Freight
Train"
Joe Glazer—Collector 1925: *Union Train*;
Collector 1924: *Singing BRAC*
"Danville Girl"
Green River Valley Boys and Glen
Campbell—Capitol ST 1810   "One
Hundred Miles Away from Home"
John Greenway—Riverside RLP 12-619:
The Great American Bum; Washington
WLP 710: *Big Rock Candy Mountain*
"All around the Water Tank"
Woody Guthrie and Cisco Houston—
Stinson SLP 44: *Folk Songs*   "Poor
Boy"; Folkways FA 2484: *Woody Guthrie
Sings Folk Songs, Vol. 2*   "Danville
Girl"; Archive of Folk Music AFM 204:
Woody Guthrie   "Poor Boy"
—Verve/Folkways FV 9007: *Bed on the
Floor*; Folkways FT 1010: *Poor Boy*;
Olympic 7101: *The Immortal Woody
Guthrie*   "Danville Girl 2"
Merle Haggard—Capitol SWBB 223:
Same Train, a Different Time
"Waitin' for a Train"
Freddie Hart and the Heart Beats—Kapp
K-765 (45 rpm); Kapp 1492/3492:
Straight from the Heart; Vocalion
VL/VL7 3929   "Waitin' for a
Train"

Cisco Houston—Folkways FA 2013 (FP 13):
900 Miles and Other Railroad Songs
"The Gambler" (related piece)
Cisco Houston (and Woody Guthrie?)—
Vanguard VRS 9107: *I Ain't Got No Home*;
Vanguard SRV 3006   "Danville Girl"
John Jackson—Arhoolie 1047: *John Jackson
in Europe*   "All around the Water
Tank"
Lil Son Jackson—Imperial 5229 (45 rpm)
"Freight Train Blues" (related piece)
Sonny James—Columbia KC 34035: *200
Years of Country Music*   "Waiting for
a Train"
John's Country Quartet—Wango LP 104:
John's Country Quartet; County 738: *The
Stanley Brothers of Virginia, Vol. 2: Long
Journey Home*   "Wild and Reckless
Hobo"
Grandpa Jones—Decca DL 4364: *Evening
with Grandpa Jones*   "Waiting for a
Train"
—Monument 8001: *Grandpa Jones
Yodeling Hits*
—Vocalion VL 73900 and MCA Coral
CB-20060: *Pickin' Time*   "Waiting for a
Train"
—RCA Victor 47-4789 (45 rpm)
"Standing in the Depot"
Jones Brothers—CMH 1776: *200 Years of
American Heritage in Song*
"Waiting for a Train"
Dickie Lee—RCA Victor LSP-4715: *Ashes
of Love*   "Waiting for a Train"
Furry Lewis—Blue Horizon (England)
7-63228   "The Dying Hobo"
Jerry Lee Lewis—Smash SRS 67128: *She
Even Woke Me Up to Say Goodbye*
"Waitin' for a Train"
—Sun 1119; Sun 121: *Ole Tyme Country
Music*   "All around the Water Tank"
New Deal String Band—Sire SES 97024:
Bluegrass   "Waiting for a Train"
New Lost City Ramblers—Folkways FA
2491: *The New Lost City Ramblers*
"Danville Girl" and "Wild and Western
Hobo"
Glenn Ohrlin—Campus Folksong Club
(University of Illinois) CFC 301: *The
Hell-Bound Train*   "Sam's 'Waiting for
a Train'"
Pine River Boys and Maybelle—Heritage 3:

Pine River Boys with Maybelle
"Danville Girl"

Obray Ramsey—Prestige International
13009: *Obray Ramsey Sings Jimmie
Rodgers Favorites*   "Waiting for a
Train"

Bud Reed—Folkways FA 2329: *All in One
Evening*   "Waiting for a Train"

Jim Reeves—RCA Victor 47–6749 (45 rpm);
RCA Victor LSP 4073(e): *When Evening
Shadows Fall: A Tribute to Jimmie
Rodgers*   "Waiting for a Train"
—Camden CXS 5-9001   "A Railroad
Bum"

Romaniuk Family—LEJ LCS 10504: *The
Romaniuk Family*   "Western Hobo"

John Sebastian—Reprise 2036: *Real
Live*   "Waiting for a Train"

Pete Seeger—Folkways FA 2003 (FP 3):
Darling Corey   "Danville Girl"

Patrick Sky—Leviathan SLIF 2000: *Two
Steps Forward—One Step Back*
"Danville Girl"

Hank Snow—RCA Victor LPM/LSP 2705:
Railroad Man   "Waiting for a Train"
—RCA Victor LSP 4708: *The Jimmie
Rodgers Story*   "Waiting for a Train"
—RCA Camden CAS-2513   "Waiting for
a Train"

Stanley Brothers. *See* John's Country
Quartet

Kenneth Threadgill—PSG Records 54:
Yesterday & Today   "Waitin' for a
Train" (2 renditions)

Billy Walker—Monument SLP 18101: *Billy
Walker Salutes the Country Music Hall of
Fame*   "Waiting for a Train"

Sammy Walker—Warner Brothers BS 3080:
Blue Ridge Mountain Skyline
"Waitin' for a Train"

Jim Wall—Rural Rhythm 1168   "The
Rambler"

Doc Watson—Vanguard VSD 79147
"Rambling Hobo"

Hedy West—Topic (England) 12T163:
Ballads   "The Girl I left in Danville"

Bob White—Front Hall FHR-011
"Ramblin' Railroad Hobo"

Buddy Williams—RCA (Australia)
MSL-10227   "Waiting for a Train"

Robin and Linda Williams—Flashlight
FLT-3003   "Danville Girl"

F. LC AFS:

Bill Atkins—AFS 1988 A & B1   "Wild
and Reckless Hobo"
—AFS 1988 B2   "Waiting for a Train"

Al Bittick—AFS 12050 A9   "Railroad
Bum"

Tilman Cadle—AFS 2027 A1   "Wabash
Sante Fe"
—AFS 2027 A2   "Wild and Reckless
Hobo"

Cameron—AFS 5149 B   "Standing on a
Corner, Smoking a Cheap Cigar"

L. D. "Jack" Franklin—AFS 11906 A
"All Around the Water Tank"

Leroy Gardner—AFS 11891 B   "All
Around the Water Tank"

John Hatcher—AFS 3003 A2   "Little
Danville Girl"

T. G. Hoskins—AFS 1461 A1   "The
Wild and Reckless Hobo"

George Lay—AFS 12050 A20   "All
around the Water Tank"

Donn O'Meara—AFS 11713 A31
"Water Tank"

Herbert Philbrock—AFS 12047 A11
"Western Water Tank"

Mamie Pridemore—AFS 12039 B7

Warren D. Walker—AFS 12044 A2

Eula Woods—AFS 13132 A18
"Denver Girl"

WKFA:

Perry Bennington—T-7-111   "Waiting
for a Train"

Vera Martin—T-7-26   "Wild and
Reckless Hobo"

The Dying Hobo

LITTLE STREAM OF WHISKEY

By a western water tank one cold No - vem - ber day, (Be-)
side an emp - ty box - car a dy - ing ho - bo lay. His
pal was stand - ing 'fore him, with a low and droop - ing head,
List- 'ning to the last words the dy - ing ho - bo said.

*This is omitted on the recording.

By a western water tank, one cold November day,
'Side an empty boxcar a dying hobo lay.
His pal was standing 'fore him, with a low and drooping head,
Listening to the last words the dying hobo said.

"So long, partner hobo, I hate to say goodbye,
[I] hear my train a-coming, I know she's getting nigh.
Tell the old conductor [?just wail off the] stops
To get a drink of whiskey come flowing down the rocks.

"To tell my girl in Danville she need not worry at all,
For I am just a-going where I will not have to work.
I will not have to work at all, nor even change my socks,
And little stream of whiskey come flowing down the rocks.

"I'm going to a better place where everything is bright,
Where handouts grow on bushes, you can sleep out every night.
Where I will not have to work at all, not even change my socks,
And little stream of whiskey come flowing down the rocks."[1]

Burnett and Rutherford

For the origins of this very familiar hobo ballad we must look back to the early nineteenth century, to the popular poem "Bingen on the Rhine" by the English poet Lady Caroline Norton (1808–77). This long piece, recounting in seven eight-line stanzas the last words of a dying soldier, began:

> A soldier of the Legion lay dying in Algiers,
> There was lack of woman's nursing, there was dearth of woman's tears;
> But a comrade stood beside him, while his lifeblood ebbed away;
> And bent, with pitying glances, to hear what he might say.

The poem was set to music in 1850 by Judson I. Hutchinson of the singing family troupe from New Hampshire that was popular in the early nineteenth century. Anthologist Helen Johnson attributed the poem's popularity partly to John Hutchinson's singing of it.[2] By twentieth-century popular-song standards, however, Hutchinson's melody is anything but catchy.

 Whatever was responsible for the popularity of "Bingen on the Rhine," it soon became the model for many parodies. A very early one, "Fair Richmond on the James," dated from the Civil War:

> A Soldier boy at Richmond lay gasping on the field,
> Fell when the fight was over, his foemen forced to yield;
> Then fell this noble hero before his foemen's aim,
> On the blood-stained field of Richmond—Fair Richmond on the James.[3]

An undated Boston broadside, probably from the 1870s, was titled "Meet Me in Heaven, or the Dying Negro": it began:

> Down in a southern valley, at quiet close of day,
> With friends all gathered round him, a dying negro lay.[4]

Probably from about the same period, from the American West, came the song "The Dying Ranger":

> The sun was sinking in the West and fell with lingering ray
> Through the branches of a forest where a wounded ranger lay;
> Beneath a tall palmetto and the sunset, silver sky,
> Far away from his home in Texas they did lay him down to die.[5]

An 1886 transportation ballad moved the setting to Australia:

> Beneath a far Australian sky an Irish exile lay;
> The sand from out his glass of life was ebbing fast away.
> The friends that stood around his bed his eyes could scarcely see;
> His thoughts which soon would be at rest, were far across the sea.[6]

A railroader's version appeared in print in 1889:

> Upon the cold and frosty ground a dying brakeman lay,
> And out of his young body life was ebbing fast away.
> The dew had moistened the dark hair that swept his boyish brow,
> His laughing eyes that shone so bright will be closed forever now.[7]

A humorous version from the Spanish-American War was titled "Bacon on the Rind, or a Soldier's Lament":

> A soldier in the cavalry lay on a canvas bunk,
> On a soap box there beside him lay a hunk of army punk;
> And as he chewed away and busy, his face turned ashen gray,
> For the soldier boy was dying in the Island far away.[8]

From about the same period came an Alaskan gold-mining parody, "The Klondike Miner":

> A Klondike City mining man lay dying on the ice,
> There was lack of women's nursing, for he didn't have the price,
> But a comrade knelt beside him as the sun sank to repose,
> To hear what he might have to say and watch him while he froze.[9]

Delaney's *Recitations* of about 1890 included this humorous parody:

> An umpire of the league nines lay dying at the plate,
> And the gory rocks about him told the story of his fate.[10]

Another railroad poem was printed in 1914, titled "The Hoghead's Dying Request"; it began:

> A hoghead on his death-bed lay, his life was ebbing fast away;
> His friends around him closely pressed to hear the hogger's last request.[11]

More recently, in 1920, the Irish Rebellion produced "Shall My Soul Pass thro' Old Ireland?":

> In a dreary Brixton prison where an Irish rebel lay,
> By his side a priest was standing ere his soul should pass away.[12]

When "The Dying Hobo" was composed, I don't know; but it probably appeared in the 1880s or 1890s. The earliest printed version I know appeared in *Railroad Magazine* in 1909. In the July issue a request was printed for a song beginning

> It was at a western water tank one cold December day,
> When in a box-car a dying hobo lay.

A text sent in was published in the September issue. This piece consisted of four eight-line stanzas and is typical of the most widely known version of the ballad. The song was first collected by folklorists in 1914 (Gray) and 1915 (Cox). These two early texts, as well as those given by Anderson, Randolph, and Spaeth, are all very similar. The ubiquity of this version suggests a spate of popularity in newspaper verse or some similar medium. Some versions (e.g., Finger, Irwin, Milburn) have extra verses recounting the paradise the dying hobo describes; these line are rich in slang, which may account for their not being more widely remembered.

"The Dying Hobo," the most famous of the progeny of "Bingen on the Rhine," itself inspired many later parodies; two were published in *Railroad Man's Magazine* in 1909. Wallrich reported several from the U.S. Air Force, some dating back to World War I. One of his early parodies is clearly modeled on "Bingen on the Rhine" directly, rather than on "The Dying Hobo."

When *Railroad Man's Magazine* printed "The Dying Hobo," the editors requested information about the author of "that classic of the weary wanderer," but none was forthcoming. Clearly, the song was an old one by 1909. The next printed version I have seen appeared in *Railroad Trainman* in 1912, credited to John Kern. Finger, on the other hand, believed that an Englishman named Bob Hughes, from whom he learned the song, actually wrote it. He also quotes a fragment that Hughes sang to the same tune as "The Dying Hobo":

> O, love, dear love, be true,
> This heart is ever thine.
> When the war is o'er
> We'll part no more
> At Ehren on the Rhine. [13]

However, this intriguing lyric has no similarity to any but the last line of Lady Norton's classic. One other claim for authorship must be reported. In 1931, *Railroad Man's Magazine* again printed "The Dying Hobo," and in the February, 1932, issue appeared a letter from Henry McNamara of Reno, Nevada, which read, "'The Dying Hobo' printed in your December issue as 'author unknown' is a poem I wrote over thirty years ago with little effort."[14] The evidence at hand is insufficient to establish the validity of any of these three claims. It may be that each of the three did indeed write some variant of "The Dying Hobo"; with a song so flexible in content—and one that obviously parodied a very popular older piece—it would not be unusual for several independent texts to have been penned. Unless some nineteenth-century texts are uncovered, it will be difficult to make any further pronouncements on this question.

"The Dying Hobo" has enjoyed an ample array of renditions on phonograph records. The earliest that can properly be regarded as a version of "The Dying Hobo" was made by Kentuckians Dick Burnett and Leonard Rutherford for Columbia in November, 1926; this recording is transcribed here. Richard Daniel Burnett was born in 1883 in Wayne County, Kentucky. He lost his eyesight in 1906, by which time he could already play guitar, banjo, violin, piano, and organ. In 1909 he started on the road to make a living as a musician. Soon he began to travel with Leonard Rutherford, who was only thirteen or fourteen at the time. The two played together for thirty-five years, traveling as far south as Florida and north to Ohio. Burnett stated that "Little Stream of Whiskey" (their title for the song) was one of Rutherford's contributions to their recorded repertoire; he himself never tried to learn the song because he didn't drink.[15]

Two unusual variants were recorded by the McMichen-Layne String Orchestra, in October, 1928, and by Roy Harvey and Earl Shirkey, in October, 1929. These two versions, as well as the one by Burnett and Rutherford, lack the usual ironic ending,

> The hobo stopped, his head fell back, he's sung his last refrain;
> His partner swiped his shoes and socks and caught the eastbound train.

Two recordings are of particular interest to students of Anglo-American balladry: by Kelly Harrell, made in November, 1926, and by Dick Justice, in May, 1929. Both begin with the usual first stanza of "The Dying Hobo" but then move to stanzas from the older traditional ballad "George Collins" (Child 85). These two variants have been transcribed and discussed elsewhere.[16]

NOTES

1. The second voice sings completely different words the last half of this line.

2. Helen K. Johnson, *Our Familiar Songs and Those Who Made Them* (New York: Henry Holt, 1907), p. 537

3. Henry W. Shoemaker, *Mountain Minstrelsy of Pennsylvania* (Philadelphia: Newman F. McGirr, 1931), p. 181. A similar song appears in *Wehman's 100 Popular Comic, Dramatic and Dialect Recitations* (New York: H. J. Wehman, n.d.), p. 10. A slightly different variant, credited to

Anne Marie Neeby, was printed in *Southern War Songs,* collected and arranged by W. L. Fagan (New York: M. T. Richardson, 1892), p. 266.

4. Printed by Horace Partridge, Boston; Wolf no. 1412.

5. Charles J. Finger, *Frontier Ballads* (Garden City, N.Y.: Doubleday, Page, 1927), p. 170. For other variants see G. Malcolm Laws, Jr., *Native American Balladry,* rev. ed. (Philadelphia: American Folklore Society, 1964), p. 125 (Laws A 14).

6. J. F. Mitchell, "The Exile's Lament," *Merchant's Gargling Oil Dream and Fate, Palmistry, &c. Songster* (Buffalo: Courier Lithography, 1888), p. 21.

7. "The Dying Brakeman," *Railroad Brakeman's Journal,* 6 (July, 1889), 308.

8. Edward Arthur Dolph, *"Sound Off!"* (New York: Cosmopolitan Book Corp., 1929), p. 191.

9. M. C. Dean, *Flying Cloud* (Virginia, Minn.: Quickprint, ca. 1922), p. 132.

10. *Delaney's Recitations,* No. 4 (New York: Wm. W. Delaney, ca. 1910), p. 11, "The Dying Umpire."

11. *RRManM,* 25 (Oct., 1914), 480.

12. Maureen Jolliffe, *The Third Book of Irish Ballads* (Cork: Mercier Press, 1970), p. 107

13. Finger, *Frontier Ballads,* p. 105

14. *RRM (Railroad Stories),* 7 (Feb., 1932), 431.

15. Biographical information on Burnett and Rutherford from an interview of Richard Burnett by Archie Green and Eugene Earle in Monticello, Ky., Aug. 12, 1962. A more recent interview by Charles K. Wolfe was published in *Old Time Music,* No. 9 (Summer, 1973), pp. 6–10, and No. 10 (Autumn, 1973), pp. 5–11.

16. See Bertrand H. Bronson, *The Traditional Tunes of the Child Ballads,* vol. 2 (Princeton, N.J.: Princeton University Press, 1962), p. 402; Judith McCulloh, "Some Child Ballads on Hillbilly Records," in *Folklore and Society,* edited by Bruce Jackson (Hatboro, Pa.: Folklore Associates, 1966), pp. 116–17; idem, "'In the Pines'" (Ph. D. diss., Indiana University, 1970), pp. 124, 173–76.

REFERENCES

A. "The Dying Hobo," in *Railroad Man's Magazine,* 9 (Sept., 1909), 760. Sent in response to a reader's inquiry published in July number. Earliest known printing of complete text.

"Little Stream of Whiskey," by (Richard Daniel) Burnett and (Leonard) Rutherford. Rutherford, vocal and fiddle; Burnett, vocal and guitar. Recorded Nov. 6, 1926 (Columbia master 143093-2), in Atlanta. Released on Columbia 15133-D on Apr. 10, 1927. Reissued on Rounder 1004: *"A Ramblin' Reckless Hobo."* Earliest recording of song; transcribed in this book.

B. Anderson, N., 212 (from *Hobo News* [June, 1917])
Bain, 218
Botkin (1951), 773
Bronson, 402
Brown III, 427; V, 247
Capt. Billy's Whiz Bang, 2 (Mar., 1921), 42
Cowboy Songs, 12
Cox (1925), 252

Finger (1927), 105
Foy, 15
Gardner & Chickering, 478 (title only)
Gray, 102
Hamlins Singing Cowboy, 51
Hubbard, L., 309
Hudson (1928), 76, 77
Hudson (1936), 251, 252
Irwin, 222
Kennedy, C. O. (1952), 17
Kennedy, C. O. (1954), 204
Laws, 231 (H 3)
Lingenfelter, 539
McCulloh (1966), 116–17
McCulloh (1970b), 173–76
Milburn, 14, 67
Peterson, 51
Porter & Bronson, 42
Randolph IV, 360
Rosenberg, 48 (title only)
RRM, 98 (Sept., 1975), 6
RRM, 104 (Aug., 1978), 4
RRManM, 9 (July, 1909), 384
RRManM 2 (May, 1930), 319
RRManM, 7 (Dec., 1931), 141

Sandburg, 186 (related piece)
Shay (1927), 61
Spaeth (1927), 131
Swan, 123
Wallrich (1954)
Webb (1923), 40–41

THE FOLLOWING are parodies of "The Dying
   Hobo":

Carlisle, C., 48   "Hobo Jack's Last Ride"
Dolph, 113   "The Passing Pilot"
Niles, 194   "Beside the Brewery at St.
   Mihiel"
RRManM, 10 (Dec., 1909), 572   "Oh
   You Ham" by James A. Crowell and
   "Twenty Years Ago" by Roy L. Nichols
Wallrich (1954)

C. GORDON COLLECTION (CALIF.):
   294—Anonymous informant

D. Arthur Fields—Grey Gull 4228, Radiex
      4228
   Travis B. Hale and E. J. Derry, Jr.—Victor
      20796; RCA Victor LPV 548: *Native
      American Ballads*
   Roy Harper (Roy Harvey pseudonym) and
      Earl Shirkey—Columbia 15535-D
      "A Hobo's Pal"
   Kelly Harrell—Victor 20527

Roy Harvey—Champion 16187, Superior
   2658   "Hobo's Pal"
Dick Justice—Brunswick 367   "One
   Cold December Day"
McMichen-Layne String Orchestra—
   Columbia 15464-D
Walker's Corbin Ramblers—Vocalion
   02678, Panachord (Australia)
   25635   "The Dying Tramp"

E. Hylo Brown—Rural Rhythm RR-HB 168:
      Hylo Brown   "Hobo's Sweetheart"
   Jim Glaser—Starday SLP 158: *Just Looking
      for a Home*; Starday SLP 170: *Railroad
      Special*
   John Greenway—Riverside RLP 12-619:
      The Great American Bum
   George Lay—Library of Congress Archive
      of Folk Song L61: *Railroad Songs and
      Ballads*
   Hermes Nye—Folkways FA 2128 (FP 47/1):
      Texas Folk Songs   "Toolie's Death"
      (related piece)
   Fields Ward—Rounder 0036: *Bury Me Not
      on the Prairie*   "The Little Stream of
      Whiskey"

F. LC AFS:
   Luvicie Beasley—AFS 11716 A26

The *Wabash Cannonball*

THE CANNON BALL

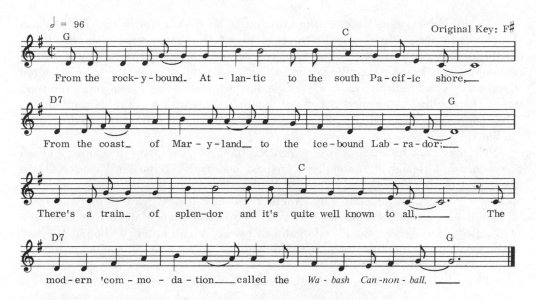

From the rocky-bound Atlantic to the south Pacific shore,
From the coast of Maryland to the ice-bound Labrador;
There's a train of splendor and it's quite well known to all,
The modern 'commodation called the *Wabash Cannonball*.

Great cities of importance, they we reach upon our way,
Chicago and Saint Louis, Rock Island so they say;
Springfield and Decatur, Peoria and them all,
We reach them by no other than the *Wabash Cannonball*.

You can hear the merry jingle and the rumble and the roar,
As she dashes through the woodland, comes creeping 'long the shore;
We hear the engine's whistle and the merry hoboes call,
As they ride the rods and brake-beams on the *Wabash Cannonball*.

There are other cities, partner, as you can easily see,
Saint Paul and Minneapolis and the famous Albert Lea;
The lakes of Minnehaha where the laughing waters fall,
We reach them by no other than the *Wabash Cannonball*.

Now here's to Daddy Claxton, may his name forever stand,
He's a brakeman that's respected by the hoboes in the land;
And when his days are over and the curtains round him fall,
May his spirit ever linger on the *Wabash Cannonball*.

You can hear the merry jingle and the rumble and the roar,
As she dashes through the woodland, comes creeping 'long the shore;

We hear the engine's whistle and the merry hoboes call,
As they ride the rods and brake-beams on the *Wabash Cannonball*.

                                                    Delmore Brothers

Of this hobo classic, George Milburn wrote in his *Hobo's Hornbook*: "The Wabash Cannonball is for the hobo what the spectral 'Flying Dutchman' is for the sailor. It is a mythical train that runs everywhere, and the ballad about it consists largely of stanzas enumerating its stops."[1] According to an anecdote printed by Lomax, the train had seven hundred cars and rode on a railroad each tie of which was made from an entire redwood tree. The conductor punched tickets by shooting holes with a .45 caliber automatic. The train went so fast that after it was brought to a stop it was still going sixty-five miles an hour.[2]

There is some uncertainty over which was the first train to use the name "*Wabash Cannonball*," although all contenders were passenger trains on the old Wabash Railroad (now part of the Norfolk and Western) in the 1880s. One *Wabash Cannonball* ran between Chicago and Kansas City. Another, in operation at least as early as 1880, operated between Saint Louis and Omaha. The fastest train of its day, it made the 415-mile trip at an average speed of almost twenty-seven miles per hour.[3] It is not inconceivable that the hobo song preceded that date, as the term *cannonball* meaning a fast train was in use by 1882.

To my knowledge, the song with the usual title first appeared in print in 1904; it was copyrighted by William Kindt (June 13, 1904, C 72630), but no author was identified in either the sheet music or the copyright entry. A second copyright the following year (Nov. 6, 1905, C 106744) by the Pioneer Music Company, credited Kindt as author and Eugene Kaeuffer as arranger. However, Kindt had based his text on an earlier song titled "The Great Rock Island Route!," which was published in 1882, words and music by J. A. Roff.[4] It is interesting to compare Roff's and Kindt's words, bearing in mind the derivative hobo versions.

THE GREAT ROCK ISLAND ROUTE	WABASH CANNON BALL
From a rocky bound Atlantic	From the Rocky bound Atlantic
To a mild Pacific shore,	To the wild Pacific shore
From a fair and sunny southland	From the sunny South bound
To an ice-bound Labrador,	To the Isle of Labrador,
There's a name of magic import	There's a name of magic splendor
And 'tis known the world through-out	That is known quite well by all
'Tis a mighty corporation	'Tis the western combination
Called the Great Rock Island Route	Called the Wabash Cannon Ball.
All great cities of importance	Great cities of importance
Can be found along its way,	Are reached along its way
There's Chicago and Peoria	Chicago and Saint Louis
And Rock Island so they say,	And Rock Island so they say,
With Davenport, and westward	And Springfield and Decatur
Still is Council Bluffs far out,	And Peoria above them all,
As a western termination	'Tis the western termination
Of this Great Rock Island Route.	Of the Wabash Cannon Ball.

Now listen to the jingle,
And the rumble, and the roar,
As she dashes thro' the woodland,
And speeds along the shore,
See the mighty rushing engine,
Hear her merry bell ring out,
As they speed along in safety
On the "Great Rock Island Route."

Then listen to the jingle,
The tumble and the roar
Of the mighty rushing engine
As she streams along the shore,
The mighty rushing engine,
Hear the bell and whistle call,
As you roll along in safety
On the Wabash Cannon Ball.

There's their "Northern Route," a daisy
As you can plainly see.
To St. Paul, and Minneapolis,
'Tis the famous "Albert Lea";
To the lakes of Minnesota,
And all points there round about,
Reached directly by no other,
Than the "Great Rock-Island Route."

To the great southwest another,
And a mighty line they run,
Reaching far famed Kansas City,
Leavenworth and Atchison,
Rich in beauty, power, and grandeur,
And they owe it all no doubt,
To the fact that they are stations
On the Great Rock Island Route.

It is difficult to say when the hobo versions sprang up; although it is possible that they came after Kindt's song, it seems probable that they preceded it. A timetable including all the cities mentioned in the various hobo versions of the song would pose an impossible route for even the most imaginative engineer. However, with Kindt's and Roff's texts at hand it becomes apparent that the 'boes' accommodation is traveling a geographically impossible amalgamation of the Rock Island (more properly, the Chicago, Rock Island, and Pacific Railroad) and Wabash routes. The cities named in stanzas 2 and 3 of Roff's song lie on the Rock Island route proper. The cities in stanza 4 were on several lines, including the Minneapolis and Saint Louis Railroad, but I have not been able to determine which, if any, had some tie-in with the Rock Island road. Kindt has changed the cities to fit the Wabash route, but with two apparent errors: Peoria and Rock Island did not lie along any spurs of the Wabash, although they were stations on the Rock Island line. Stanzas 2 and 3 of Milburn's hobo version cite, in order, Chicago, Saint Louis, Rock Island, Springfield, Decatur, Peoria, Quincy, Monroe, Mexico, Kansas City, and Denver. Monroe, like Decatur and Springfield, lies on the main route between Chicago and Kansas City; Quincy and Denver were on sidelines. Mexico was on the Wabash route between Saint Louis and Omaha. Another stanza of Milburn's text would take the train up to Saint Paul and Minneapolis—evidently a borrowing from Roff's text.

In spite of the mythical nature of the *Wabash Cannonball*, the song itself—at least in the versions that have survived—has few clues of anything but an earthly journey (albeit over an unusual route). Furthermore, although early versions had many phrases and verses that clearly identified the song as a hobo song, these hallmarks have tended to disappear from the lyrics. For example, the last line of the first verse used to contain the

Sheet music: "The Great Rock Island Route." Collection of the Lilly Library, Indiana University.

phrase "she's the 'boes' accommodation," but now it is generally rendered as "she's a regular combination" (Carter Family) or "modern combination" (Loy Bodine) or just "the combination" (Acuff). The last line of the chorus, usually sung "While she's traveling through the jungle on the *Wabash Cannonball*" in the post-Acuff renditions, used to be "As we ride the rods and brake-beams of the *Wabash Cannonball." Jungle,* of course does not refer to any dense tropical vegetation but is a slang term for a hobo camp.

The "Daddy Claxton" of Acuff's last verse has yet to be identified with any historical character. However, it should be pointed out that in many early versions the person toasted has a different name; and while "Clark" (Jack and Little Jackie folio), "Clarkston" (Bill Bundy recording), "Greenwood" (Gallarno recording) and "Cleaton" (Carter Family recording) are probably just misunderstood variants, "Boston Blackey" (Lomax) and "Long Slim Perkins" (Milburn and Frothingham) are definitely distinct.

The earliest disc recordings of "The *Wabash Cannonball*" date from 1929. Of the three made that year, the first two were by Hugh Cross, one in April for Columbia, the other in August (under the pseudonym of Ballard Cross) for Vocalion. Of greater popularity was the recording cut by the Carter Family in November for Victor. While the Victor release sold only 1,700—typical for hillbilly discs at the time—the later Montgomery Ward reissue sold 9,200 copies. However, the recordings that were most responsible for the widespread popularity of the song were made by Roy Acuff—first in October, 1936 (released in July, 1937), for the American Record Corporation and again in 1947, for Columbia. On the 1936 version, the vocal was taken by Sam "Dynamite" Hatcher, the harmonica player and frequent lead singer in Acuff's early band. For many years "The *Wabash Cannonball*" was one of Acuff's most widely requested songs; it was said by some authorities to have sold more than a million discs in 1942, at the height of its popularity.[5]

It is interesting to note the extent to which Roy Acuff's 1936 version has driven out earlier versions. The Carter Family's recording of 1929 differed from Acuff's in lacking the verse that began "She came down from Birmingham one cold December day," having instead a verse beginning "I've rode the I. C. Limited, also the royal blue." When A. P. Carter and Southern Music copyrighted the song in 1939 (Dec. 30, 1939, E 82758), however, the words were much closer to those of Acuff's recording than those of the Carter Family recording. Acuff himself copyrighted the song in 1940 (Apr. 12, 1940, E 85567), crediting the words to Kindt, with revised lyrics and arrangement by Acuff. Kindt was given composer credit on yet another copyright, that by the Calumet Music Company, with arranger credits to Bill Burns (Oct. 19, 1939, E 80352).

When Acuff re-recorded the song for Columbia in 1947, he sang it himself, omitting the chorus ("Listen to the jingle . . . "). It will be interesting to observe in years to come whether field-recorded versions follow this modification. Hatcher's earlier text was essentially the same as that recorded by Hugh Cross in 1929.

Of the other hillbilly versions preserved on disc, the one by the Delmore Brothers has the most elements from the older prehillbilly versions, and it is transcribed here.[6]

Although we can account, in general, for the origin of the text of "The *Wabash Cannonball*," the source of the tune remains a mystery. Kindt's tune is not the usual one, but is reminiscent of "The Jealous Lover" or "I'll Be All Smiles Tonight." It has been preserved, though somewhat imperfectly, on the recording by Loy Bodine. His text, which has no references to hoboes, was not used on any of the recordings. Roff's tune was different yet, and seems to have made no mark on any other versions. Burl Ives suggests that the tune is derived from a mid-nineteenth-century piece, "Uncle Sam's Farm,"[7] but an examination of the sheet music for that item reveals no noticeable similarities in melody. There are, however, a few minor textual affiliations.

"The *Wabash Cannonball*," a parody of "The Great Rock Island Route," has itself been parodized. Woody Guthrie's 1947 composition "The Farmer-Labor Train," puts the "*Wabash Cannonball*" tune and structure to use as a politcial protest song.[8] Bruce Phillips's "The Last Wabash Cannonball" commemorates the final run of the legendary train.

NOTES

1. George Milburn, *The Hobo's Hornbook* (New York: Ives Washburn, 1930), p. 189.

2. Alan Lomax, *The Folk Songs of North America* (Garden City, N.Y.: Doubleday, 1960), p. 410.

3. "'Wabash Cannonball' Not the One in Song," *Champaign-Urbana* (Ill.) *Courier*, Mar. 28, 1969; William Day, "Once More She's Roaring across the Land—Now as a Fast Detroit–to–St. Louis Diesel," *Toledo Blade*, Apr. 12, 1959.

4. I am grateful to Judith McCulloh for bringing this song to my attention.

5. Bill C. Malone, *Country Music, U.S.A.* (Austin: University of Texas Press, 1968), p. 203.

6. For biographical information on the Delmore Brothers, see the discussion of "Blow Yo' Whistle, Freight Train" in chap. 10.

7. Burl Ives, *More Burl Ives* (New York: Ballantine Books, 1966), p. 197.

8. Waldemar Hille, ed., *The People's Song Book* (1948; rpt., New York: Oak Publications, 1961), p. 85.

REFERENCES

A. "The Great Rock Island Route," sheet music. Words and music by J. A. Roff. Copyright by the J. M. W. Jones Sty. and Prtg. Co., Chicago 1882. Song on which "Wabash Cannonball" was evidently based.

"Wabash Cannon Ball," sheet music. Published by the Pioneer Music Publishing Co., credited to Wm. Kindt, arranged by Eugene Kaeuffer (copyrighted Nov. 6, 1905, C 106744). An earlier copyright was taken out by William Kindt, author unidentified, on June 13, 1904 (C 72630). First known appearance of usual form of song.

"Wabash Cannon Ball," by Hugh Cross. Cross, vocal; guitar accompaniment. Recorded ca. Apr. 9, 1929 (Columbia master 148219), in Atlanta. Released on Columbia 15439-D on Sept. 13, 1929.

"Wabash Cannonball," by the Carter Family. Sara, vocal and autoharp; Maybelle, guitar. Recorded Nov. 24, 1929 (RCA Victor master 56585-3), in Atlanta. Released on Victor 23731 in ca. Nov., 1932. Reissued on RCA Bluebird B-8350, Montgomery Ward M-7444, RCA Victor (England) 7109 (EP): *The Original and Great Carter Family, Vol. 4*; RCA Camden CAL 586: *The Original and Great Carter Family*; Regal Zonophone (Australia and New Zealand) G-24157; RCA Victor (Japan) RA-5641-50: *The Original Carter Family*: RCA (Australia and New Zealand) 20369 (EP); RCA Victor RA-5321; RCA Victor RA-5513; RCA Camden CAM 92 (Australia and New Zealand). First influential recording of the song.

"Wabash Cannon Ball," by Roy Acuff and his Smoky Mountain Boys. Vocal by Sam "Dynamite" Hatcher. Recorded Oct. 21, 1936 (American Record Corp. master C 1589), in Chicago. Released on Vocalion/Okeh 04466 in July, 1937. Reissued on Columbia 37008, Columbia 20034, and Conqueror 9121. Most popular and influential recording of song.

"Wabash Cannon Ball," by Roy Acuff and his Smoky Mountain Boys. Vocal by Roy Acuff. Recorded in Jan., 1947 (Columbia master HCO 2207), in Hollywood. Released on Columbia 37008, Columbia 20034, Columbia 37598 (in album C-143: *Songs of the Smoky Mountains*), Columbia 20197 (in album H-3: *Songs of the Smoky Mountains*), Columbia 52014, Columbia 4-33057 (45 rpm), Columbia H-2064 (45 rpm), Columbia 4-20197 (in 45 rpm album H 4-3: *Songs of the Smoky Mountains*), Columbia 6-1231 (in 45 rpm album: *Songs of the Smoky Mountains*),

Columbia B-2803 (45 rpm); Columbia HL
9004: *Songs of the Smoky Mountains*;
Columbia 3-33024: *Hall of Fame*;
Harmony HL 7082: *Great Speckle Bird
and Other Favorites*; Columbia CS 1034.
"The Cannon Ball," by the Delmore
Brothers. Alton and Rabon, vocal duet
and guitars; Chuck Mandlin, fiddle.
Recorded Sept. 29, 1938 (RCA Victor
master BS-027643-1), in Rock Hill, S.C.
Released on RCA Bluebird B-7991.
Reissued on Montgomery Ward M-7677;
RCA Victor LPV 532: *The Railroad in
Folksong*. Transcribed in this book.

B. Acuff
Alberta Slim (Song #17)
Big Slim, 17
Boni (1952), 208–9
Botkin & Harlow, 462
Casey, 24
Cheshire, 2
Clifton, 31
Cowboy Jack, 6
Cross, 11
Dean, E., 22
Donegan II, 2
Frothingham, *Adventure*, Dec. 20, 1922,
p. 192
Frothingham, *Adventure*, May 10, 1923,
p. 192
Green (1968) (discussion only)
Hillbilly Hit Parade, 46
Hit Parade, 28
Horstman, 331–32 (transcription of Acuff
recording)
Ives (1962), 242 (parody)
Ives (1966), 197
Jack & Little Jackie, 24
Jane & Carl, 10
Kreimer, *RRM*, 98 (Aug., 1975), 56–57
(from Milburn)
Leisy (1966), 341
Lomax (1960), 420
Milburn, 189
Morton, 18
Mursell (Grade 5), 100
OTS&P, July-Aug., 1968, p. 48
Pie Plant Pete, 16
Pitts (1951b), 180
Randolph IV, 363
RRM, 6 (Nov., 1931), 606
RRM, 20 (July, 1936), 69

RVB, 34 (Nov., 1977), 11
Seeger, P. (1961), 85
Silverman (1975) II, 146-47
Wakely, 24

D. Loy Bodine—Superior 2608
Bill Carlisle's Kentucky Boys—Decca 5713,
Decca 46045
Carter Family—Victor 23731, Bluebird
B-8350, Montgomery Ward M-7444,
RCA Victor (England) 7109 (EP): *The
Original and Great Carter Family, Vol. 4*;
RCA Camden CAL 586: *The Original and
Great Carter Family*; Regal Zonophone
(Australia and New Zealand) G-24157;
RCA Victor ADL2-0782(e): *50 Years of
Country Music*
Ballard Cross—Vocalion 5377
Hugh Cross—Columbia 15439-D
Denver Darling and the Cowhands
—Decca 6063   "Modern Cannon Ball"
Dizzy Dean—Colonial 2118
Delmore Brothers—Bluebird B-8404
"Wabash Cannonball Blues"
Rusty Draper—Mercury 70757
Folkcraft Square Dance Orchestra
—Folkcraft 1006
Duel Frady—Victor 20930
"Leavenworth" (derivative piece)
Roy Hall and his Blue Ridge Entertainers
—Conqueror 9230, Vocalion 04717
Charlie Monroe's Boys—Bluebird B-8118;
RCA Victor (Japan) RA 5677/81: *The
Legendary Monroe Brothers Collection
(1936–39)*   "From Shore to Shore"
Bill Mooney—Imperial 1150
Morris Brothers—Bluebird B-8252
"Wabash Cannonball #2"
Tex Morton—Rodeo (Australia) 10-0011
Bobbie Stevenson—Trophy 16
Terry Shand and his Orchestra—Decca 2,
Decca 3783, Coral 60075
Kay Starr—Capitol 15419; Capitol T-1801:
Our Best to You
Mac Wiseman—Dot 1262; Dot DLP 3408:
Fire Ball Mail; Dot 25896: *Golden Hits of
Mac Wiseman*

E. Roy Acuff—Hickory 1178 (45 rpm), Hickory
LPM 109 and HR 4504: *All Time Greatest
Hits*; Hickory LPM 114: *World Is His
Stage*; Hickory LPM 119: *Hall of Fame*;
Hickory LPM 125: *Great Train Songs*;

Hickory LPS 162: *Why Is Roy Acuff*
—Capitol 6047 (45 rpm); Capitol F1-617 (in
45 rpm album EAP 1-617: *Songs of the
Smoky Mountains*); T1-617 (in 33⅓ rpm
album LP T-617: *Songs of the Smoky
Mountains*); Capitol T/DT 1870: *The Best
of Roy Acuff*; Hilltop JS 6162: *Wabash·
Cannonball*
Roy Acuff, Jr.—Hickory 1349 (45 rpm)
Almanac Singers—Warner Brothers 1330:
Sing Along, Country Style
American Singers—Royale 18111
Andrews Sisters—Dot 3567/25567: *Great
Country Hits*
Eddy Arnold—RCA Camden CAL 471:
Eddy Arnold; RCA DPL1-0130(e):
Country Music Favorites
Uncle John Barton and the Barton
Family—Illini IR 1007 LP: *Forty Years
with Uncle John Barton and the Barton
Family*
Beavers—Somerset 18100: *Country and
Western Hits Made Famous by Hank
Snow and Roy Acuff*
Bill Black Combo—Hi 12015/32015: *Bill
Black's Combo Plays the Blues*
Ace Cannon—Hi 2220 (45 rpm); Hi
X-32080: *Country Comfort*
Judy Canova—Viking VK 802: *Featuring
Judy Canova*
Joe "Fingers" Carr—Dot 3767/25767: *Joe
"Fingers" Carr*
Maybelle Carter—Columbia KG 32436:
Mother Maybelle Carter
Carter Family—Columbia CL-2152/
CS-8952: *Keep on the Sunny Side*
—Acme LP 1: *The Carter Family*; Pine
Mountain PMR 206: *A.P. Carter's Clinch
Mountain Ballads*
Johnny Cash—Columbia CL 2537/CS 9337:
That's What You Get for Lovin' Me
Bob Chapman—Scholastic CC 0630 (45 rpm
EP): *Train Ballads*
Floyd Cramer—RCA Victor LPM/LSP
3318: *Hits from the Country Hall of Fame*;
Victor APL1/APD1-1541: *Floyd Cramer
Country*
Bing Crosby—Capitol T/ST 2346: *Great
Country Hits*
Jimmie Dale and the Western Trailsmen
—Palace M 729
Danny Davis and the Nashville Brass—

RCA Victor LSP 4494: *Best of Danny
Davis and the Nashville Brass, Country
Instrumentals, Vol. 2;* RCA Victor LSP
4232: *Movin' On;* RCA Victor APL1-0425:
*Best of Danny Davis and the Nashville
Brass*
—RCA Victor LSP 4270: *Live—In Person*
Little Jimmy Dickens—Columbia CL-1047:
Raisin' the Dickens; Columbia
CL-2551/CS-9351: *Little Jimmy Dickens'
Greatest Hits*; Harmony HL 7311: *Best of
Little Jimmy Dickens*; Harmony H 31325:
*Roy Acuff, Johnny Horton, Statler
Brothers and Lil' Jimmy Dickens
Together*
Lonnie Donegan—Mercury MG 20229: *An
Englishman Sings American Folksongs*;
Nixa (England) NPT-19012
Rusty Draper—Mercury 12274/16274:
Country Classics; Mercury 45033 (45
rpm)
Easy Riders—Epic 5-2229 (45 rpm); Epic
LN 24033
Jack Elliott—Prestige International 13045:
Country Style
Lester Flatt—RCA Victor APL1-0588: *Live
Bluegrass Festival*
Lester Flatt, Earl Scruggs, and the Foggy
Mountain Boys—Columbia CL 2354/CS
9154 and LE 10032: *Pickin', Strummin'
and Singin'*; Harmony H 30932: *Wabash
Cannonball*; Columbia KG 31964: *The
World of Flatt and Scruggs*; Columbia GP
30: *20 All-Time Great Recordings in a
Deluxe 2-Record Set*
—Columbia CL-2590/CS 9390: *Welcome to
Music City U.S.A.*
Tex Fletcher—Walden 231
Tex Fletcher and Rosalie Allen—Grand
Award 33-350: *Rodeo*
Folkswingers—World Pacific WP-1812:
Twelve String Guitar!
Connie Francis and Hank Williams, Jr.—
MGM 4251: *Great Country Favorites*
Galli Sisters—MGM 10411
Tommy Garrett—Liberty 31025/14025: *50
Guitars Go Country*
Billy Grammer—Decca 39669 (45 rpm);
Decca 74524: *Billy Grammer*
John Greenway—Riverside RLP-619: *The
Great American Bum*
Burl Ives—Decca 9-29533 (45 rpm)

Clarence Jackson and group—Rural Rhythm RR-Jack-130: *Clarence Jackson*

Wanda Jackson—Capitol T/ST 2606: *Wanda Jackson Salutes*

Bob Kames—Hollywood HLP 506

Bradley Kincaid—McMonigle BK 101A/ 102B: *The Kentucky Mountain Boy*

Pete Kirby (Bashful Brother Oswald)— Rounder 0013: *Brother Oswald*

—Rounder 0041: *That's Country*

—United Artists UAS 9801: *Will the Circle Be Unbroken*

Knoblicks—Mercury 20852/60852: *Workout*

Limeliters—RCA Victor LPM/LSP 2609: *Our Man in San Francisco*; RCA Victor LPM/LSP 2907: *Limeliters*

Living Guitars—RCA Camden CXS 9023: *Finger Lickin' Pickin'*

Hank Locklin—RCA Victor LPM/LSP 2597: *Tribute to Roy Acuff*

Louvin Brothers—Capitol ST 2827

Jim and Jesse McReynolds—Epic BN 26513: *We Like Trains*

Blind Willie McTell—Prestige BV 1040: *Last Sessions*

Marijohn and the Jacks—Harmony HL 7279

Benny Martin—CMH 1776: *200 Years of American Heritage in Song*

Merrill Jay Singers—Cabot CAB 503: *Songs of the Railroad*

Moms and Dads—Crescendo 2078: *Dance with the Moms and Dads*

Patsy Montana—Starday 8-385 (45 rpm); Starday SLP 376: *Cowboy's Sweetheart*; Sims LP 122; Rural Rhythm RRFW 2114: *Favorite Western Songs*

Moon Mullican—Guest Star GS 1497

—Starday SLP 164: *Country Music Hall of Fame*; Starday SLP 170; *Railroad Special*

Nashville String Band—RCA Victor LSP 4771: *World's Greatest Melodies*

Willie Nelson—RCA Victor LSP 4294: *Both Sides Now*

Osborne Brothers—MCA 311: *Midnight Flyer*

Jackie Phelps—Starday SLP 276: *Country Music Cannonball*

Bruce "Utah" Phillips—Philo 1004: *Good Though*

Jerry Reed—RCA Camden ACL1-0331: *Tupelo Mississippi Flash*

Edith Roberts—Rural Rhythm RR-ER-178: *Carter Family Songs*

Bob Scoby and the Frisco Jazz Band—RCA Victor LPM-1448

Pete Seeger—Folkways FA 2320: *American Favorite Ballads, Vol. 1*

Six Fat Dutchmen—Dot 3644/24644: *Hoop-Dee-Doo*

Carl Smith—Columbia CS-9870: *Tribute to Roy Acuff*

Hank Snow—RCA Victor ANL1-1052: *All about Trains*

—RCA Victor LSP 4501: *Tracks and Trains*

Pee Wee Spitelera—RCA Victor LPM/LSP 3638: *Country Clarinet*

Springfields—Philips PHM 200-076; *Folksongs from the Hills*

Billy Strange—Crescendo 94: *12 String Guitar*; Crescendo GNP 2041: *Railroad Men*

Hank Thompson—Capitol T/ST 2089: *Golden Country Hits*; Capitol T/DT 2661: *Best of Hank Thompson*

Ernest Tubb—Decca 4046/74046: *All Time Hits*

Ventures—Liberty 2023 and Dolton 2023/8023: *Country Classics*

Doc Watson—Folkways FA 2426: *Jean Ritchie and Doc Watson at Folk City*; Verve Folkways 9026: *Folk City*

—Vanguard VSD 9/10: *Doc Watson on Stage*

—United Artists UA-LA423-H2: *Memories*

Lawrence Welk—Dot 16885 (45 rpm); Dot 3725/25725: *Country Music's Great Hits*

Chubby Wise—Stoneway STY-160: *The Million Dollar Fiddle*

F.   LC AFS:

Al Bittick—AFS 12050 A3

Bill Bundy—AFS 1510A

John P. Gallarno—AFS 3400 B1

Billy Jane Thompson with group—AFS 4103 A1

Sharon Vergasons—AFS 11688 A27

Vernie Westfall—AFS 4105 B2

The Little Red Caboose behind the Train (II)

THE HOBO TRAMP

I will sing (you) a little song, won't entertain you long,
'Bout the hoboes that promenade the streets;
I will tell you how I live on what people 'cline to give
In the evening down the railroad they would be.

    They will get up on that track with a (turkey) on their back,
    Walking (with the assistance) of a cane;
    They will run around like rats, being chased by the cats,
    When they (ride the little caboose behind) the train.

On a cold winter day you will often hear them say,
"If I was only in the caboose behind the train."

    They will shiver, they will shake, while riding on the freight,
    Boxcars go mounting down the lane;
    At the station they would wait for the coming of the freight,
    In the little red caboose behind the train.

In the evening in the late, down the railroad I would wait,
Lying on some lonesome water tank;
I could hear old Number Four by her whistle and her blow,
Blowed like she never blowed before;
On the cold winter's day you could often hear them say,
"If I was only in the caboose behind the train."

    They will shiver, they will shake, while riding on the freight,
    Boxcars go mounting down the lane;
    At the station they would wait for the coming of the freight,
    And the little red caboose behind the train.

                        Darby and Tarlton

In the discussion of "The Little Red Caboose behind the Train (III)" I treat in general the many variants and songs that go by this title; here, I shall confine my remarks to one specific version that properly belongs in this chapter because the subject matter concerns hoboes. I am aware of only two independent texts of this song, one of which appeared in pulp songbooks, which means that this is another item on the fuzzy edge of the domain we call folksong. I have already outlined in chapter 3 my rather broad criteria for considering a song eligible for inclusion in a book of railroad folksongs; "Little Red Caboose (II)," by virtue of its style and its recording by a pair of hillbilly artists very close to the folk tradition, falls within these criteria.

The text transcribed above is from the recording by Tom Darby and Jimmie Tarlton, made for the Columbia Phonograph Company in Atlanta on April 12, 1928, under the title "The Hobo Tramp." Darby, born and reared around Columbus, Georgia, and Tarlton, a native South Carolinian, were a highly popular recording team between 1927 and 1933.

In that period they recorded more than seventy-five selections for Columbia, Victor, and the American Record Corporation; the most popular were "Columbus Stockade Blues" and "Birmingham Jail." Tarlton, whose career has been well documented, thanks to his rediscovery and many successful appearances in the 1960s, did a bit of hoboing and traveling himself during the 1910s and 1920s, and his repertoire included several numbers concerning tramps and/or railroads: "New York Hobo," "Lonesome Railroad," "Dixie Mail," and "Down in Florida on a Hog" ("Going Down the Road Feeling Bad").[1] "The Hobo Tramp," however, seems to have been part of Darby's repertoire rather than Tarlton's.

In some verses, Darby's singing is very indistinct, and I suspect he was mumbling because he had forgotten some of the words. For this reason, the text as it appeared in Delaney's songbook of 1892 is given below. In the transcription of Darby's singing, I have enclosed in parentheses words that are unclear on the disc and are conjectured on the basis of the Delaney text. One of Darby's elisions involved an expression that probably did not make sense to him as he learned the song, and surely needs explanation for today's readers and listeners. In line 1 of Darby's first chorus (line 5 of the first verse of the Delaney text) is the phrase "with their turkeys on their back(s)." "To have a turkey on one's back" meant, in the latter part of the nineteenth century, to be drunk.[2] Slightly later, *turkey* meant a valise, especially a canvas bag or a hobo's bindle, for carrying one's personal belongings.[3] The earliest usage with this meaning found in print dates from 1909, though the context of our song strongly suggests that the same meaning was in use at least seventeen years earlier.

LITTLE OLD CABOOSE BEHIND THE TRAIN

We're going to sing a song, we won't detain you long,
Of the bums who promenade the street;
We will tell you how they live off whatever people give,
When they leave town the railroads they do beat.
They get out upon the track with their turkeys on their backs,
They walk with the assistance of a cane;
At way stations they wait for the coming fast freight,
For they don't ride in the caboose behind the train.

   How they shiver and shake when they are riding on a freight,
   In a box car with the blind, deaf, and lame;
   On a cold winter day you can often hear them say,
   If we were only in the caboose behind the train.

When the train comes up and stops, they've got eyes, you know, like hawks,
They look out for the conductor and brakeman;
They sneak just like a rat getting chased around by cats,
And get into the best empty on the train.
When inside they spike the door, then lay down on the floor,
And go to sleep till daylight comes again;
Many capers they go through while the conductor is sleeping, too
In his little old caboose behind the train.

Since songbooks such as Delaney's usually included pieces that had already achieved a degree of popularity through previous exposure elsewhere, this version of "Little Red Caboose" probably originated prior to 1892. Because the text is so different from the original "Little Old Cabin in the Lane," it seems reasonable to conclude that this was not the first parody on that song, but followed on the heels of some of the other "Little Red Caboose" songs, such as those discussed in chapter 11.

NOTES

1. For biographical information on Darby and Tarlton, see Graham Wickham, *Darby & Tarlton* (special edition of Doug Jydstrup's *Blue Yodeler*) (Denver, 1967); Norm Cohen and Anne Cohen, "The Legendary Jimmie Tarleton [*sic*]," *Sing Out!*, 16 (Sept., 1966), 16–19.

2. J. S. Farmer and W. E. Henley, *Slang and Its Analogues* (1890–1904; rpt., New York: Arno Press, 1970), vol. 7, p. 299; Harold Wentworth and Stuart Berg Flexner, *Dictionary of American Slang* (New York: Thomas Y. Crowell, 1960), p. 566. There is an interesting parallel in the more recent usage referring to another type of drug, "to have a monkey on one's back." Both phrases involve obnoxious animals, the names of which end in *-key* (as does the name of one relevant drug, *whiskey*).

3. Wentworth and Flexner, *Dictionary of American Slang*, p. 566. This meaning seems to have been unknown to Farmer and Henley in 1904.

REFERENCES

A. "Little Old Caboose behind the Train," in Delaney's *Collection of Songs, No. 1* (Apr., 1892), p. 14. Earliest known appearance of this form of the song.

"The Hobo Tramp," by (Tom) Darby and (Jimmie) Tarlton. Vocal duet; two guitars accompaniment. Recorded Apr. 12, 1928 (Columbia master W146045-2), in Atlanta. Released on Columbia 15293-D on Sept. 20, 1928. This recording is transcribed here.

B. Wehman #3, 107

Milwaukee Blues

MILWAUKEE BLUES

Original Key: D♭

One Tuesday morning and it looked like-a rain,
Around the curve come a passenger train;
On the blinds sat old Bill Jones,
Good old hobo and he's tryin' to get home.
　　Tryin' to get home, he's tryin' to get home,
　　He's a good old hobo and he's tryin' to get home.

Way down in Georgie on a tramp,
Roads are gettin' muddy and the leaves are gettin' damp;
I got to catch a freight train and leave this town,
'Cause they don't allow no hoboes a-hangin' around.
　　Hangin' around, yes, a-hangin' around,
　　'Cause they don't 'low no hoboes a-hangin' around.

I left Atlanta one morning 'fore day,
The brakeman said, "You'll have to pay."
"Got no money, but I'll pawn my shoes,
I wanta go west, got the Milwaukee blues.
　　Got the Milwaukee blues, got the Milwaukee blues,
　　I wanta go west, I got the Milwaukee blues."

Ol' Bill Jones said before he died,
"Fix the road so the 'boes can ride;

> When they ride, they will ride the rods,
> Put all trust in the hands of God.
> > In the hands of God, in the hands of God,
> > They'll put all trust in the hands of God."
>
> Ol' Bill Jones said before he died,
> There's two more roads he'd like to ride;
> Fireman said, "What can it be?"
> "Southern Pacific and the Santa Fe [*pronounced "Fee"*].
> > Santa Fe, yes, Santa Fe,
> > Southern Pacific and the Santa Fe."

Charlie Poole and the North Carolina Ramblers

As the discussion of the ballad "Casey Jones" (chap. 4) suggests, the tangle of blues ballads and songs that are related to, but probably predate, the Casey Jones saga is difficult indeed to unravel. One strand of this material includes fragments and short ballads that deal with hoboes and wanderers. Three recurring stanzas are all we can point to that suggest any sort of unity within this group of songs; in "Milwaukee Blues" they are the first, fourth, and fifth stanzas.

The title "Milwaukee Blues" is unusual; most of the titles in this group are either (1) "Jay Gould" ("Ja-Gooze"), "Jay Gould's Daughter," or some variant; or (2) "Hobo John," "Ramblin' John," "Old John Brown," "Charlie Snyder," or (of course) "Casey Jones." In the second subgroup, the figure that is "dead and gone" is either "old Bill Jones," "Casey Jones," "Jimmie Jones," "Hobo John," "David Jones," or "ol' John Brown."

The stanza about fixing the rods so the bums can (cannot) ride is, in a half-dozen or so fragments, attached to the name of Jay Gould or Jay Gould's daughter. I have been unable to find any specific acts by Gould that could provide a historical motivation for this rhyme, notwithstanding the 1911 letter of "Kelley the Rake" to the effect that Gould's removal of platforms from baggage and mail cars on the Missouri-Pacific Railroad was the inspiration.[1] Since Gould owned the MP between 1879 and 1892, however, we can assign an approximate date to the "Jay Gould" ditties. Gould's daughter's connection in this matter is still more tenuous; Helen Gould did become a railroad buff of sorts, often riding in the locomotive attired in white silk gloves and goggles, but I have found nothing specific about her attitudes toward hoboes.[2] In any case, Helen's death did not precede that of her father, so the stanza attributing the dying wish to her was in all probability a recomposition of an older form. The same stanza has appeared with (Cornelius) Vanderbilt's daughter instead of Gould's. In her case, however, I doubt that a search for historical verification would be fruitful.

Not surprisingly, when the wish about fixing the rods (or cars) comes from the lips of some hobo or engineer, rather than from Gould or his daughter, the directive is the opposite: the fix is to be made so the 'boes *can* ride. It is difficult to discern which was the earlier—the positive or the negative plea.

The remaining two stanzas of "Milwaukee Blues" are, to my knowledge, unique in the body of recorded and published folksong, though individual phrases in them occur elsewhere. Their language convinces me that they are traditional, and of the same period as the rest of the song—the 1880s or thereabouts.

Two early recordings of "Milwaukee Blues" appeared on hillbilly records, both

North Carolina Ramblers. Courtesy of the John Edwards Memorial Foundation, UCLA.

involving the same musicians. In September of 1930, Charlie Poole and the North Carolina Ramblers recorded the song for Columbia; this is the source of the transcription given here. In December, Poole's guitarist, Roy Harvey, recorded it for the Starr Piano Company.

Charlie Poole was born in 1892 in Alamance County, North Carolina, and learned to play the banjo at an early age. In 1917, he teamed up with a West Virginia fiddler named Posey Rorer and began to play for the coal miners in that region. This was the beginning of the North Carolina Ramblers, one of the most popular bands in the Southeast during the 1920s.[3] In September, 1926, Roy Harvey joined the band as guitarist. He was born in Monroe County, West Virginia, in 1892, and spent most of his life, when he was not playing music professionally, working on the railroads. He became an engineer when he was about twenty-two—the youngest engineer on the Virginian Railway—and brought to the Ramblers' repertoire many railroading songs and ballads. Among his other contributions to this book are "Bill Mason" and "The Wreck of the Virginian Number Three" (see the discussion of those songs for more biographical information).

Either Poole, who did considerable rambling during his brief life, or Harvey, for many years a railroadman, could have provided the group with "Milwaukee Blues" (as well as other train songs). Charlie Poole, Jr., stated that his father wrote "Milwaukee Blues,"[4] and among Poole's scrapbooks was a sheet of song titles including "Milwaukee Blues," with the notation "by C. P." In one sense, then, it probably was "his" song, although he was not its author, as modern readers understand that term. More to the point, the title "Milwaukee Blues" is pencilled in alongside a crossed-out title, "Hobo Jones," which more firmly identifies the piece with its true relatives.[5]

The tune of Poole's song is also related to the group of songs with which it shares textual affinity; I have discussed it briefly in connection with "Ben Dewberry's Final Run" (chap. 4).

NOTES

1. See "Casey Jones" (chap. 4).

2. Richard O'Conner, *Gould's Millions* (Garden City, N.Y.: Doubleday, 1962), p. 205.

3. For more information on Poole and his musical career, see Clifford Kinney Rorrer, *Charlie Poole and the North Carolina Ramblers* (Eden, N.C.: Tar Heel Printing, 1968).

4. Charlie Poole, Jr., interviewed by Archie Green and Eugene Earle near Johnson City, Tenn., Aug. 13, 1962. Tapescript in *JEMFN*, 1 (June, 1966), 31–35.

5. I am grateful to Mac Benford for making copies of some of Poole's scrapbook material available to me.

REFERENCES

A. "Milwaukee Blues," by Charlie Poole and the North Carolina Ramblers. Poole, vocal and banjo; Roy Harvey, guitar; Odell Smith, fiddle. Recorded Sept. 9, 1930 (Columbia master W150779), in Johnson City, Tenn. Released on Columbia 15688-D on Aug. 15, 1931. Reissued on County 516: *The Legend of Charlie Poole*; on County 504: *Mountain Songs*; and on New World Records NW 236: *Going Down the Valley*.

B. Abbot-Swan, 42–47   "Vanderbilt's Daughter (A Railroad Song)"
Colquhoun, 43   "My Man's Gone" (New Zealand depression song; borrows one stanza)
Combs-Wilgus, 212   "John White" ("Jay Gould's Daughter")
Friedman, 317   "Joseph Mica" (from Odum)
Gordon, *Adventure*, Aug. 20, 1923, p. 192   "Charlie Snyder," "Jay Gould's Daughter"
Kansas City Star, Aug. 5, 1911   ("Jay Gould") (quoted in Cohen [1973])
Laws, 276 (dI 25) (discussion only)
Lomax & Lomax (1934), 40–41   "Ol' John Brown," "Charlie Snyder"
Martin, D.
Milburn, 250   "Hobo John"
Odum, 384   "Ja-Gooze"; 352 "Joseph Mica"

Odum & Johnson (1925), 208   "Joseph Mica"; 248   "Ja-Gooze" (both from Odum)
Perrow (1913), 167–69   "Casey Jones," "Old Jay Gould"
RRManM, 8 (Apr., 1909), 575 (no title)
Sandburg (1927), 264   "Jay Gould's Daughter" (from Lomax Collection)
Scarborough, 250   "Joseph Mica" (from Odum)
Seeger, P. (1964), 34   "Jay Gould's Daughter"
White, N. I., 374 (no title)

C. GORDON MSS:
217   "Bullfighter" ["Casey Jones"]

ODUM-ARTHUR MSS:
62   "Santa Fe Wreck"

D. Four Pickled Peppers (Norman Woodlieff, Lonnie Austin, Esmond Harris, Dal Hubbard, Hamon Newmon, Earl Taylor)—Bluebird B-8543   "Ramblin' John"
John Martin (Roy Harvey pseudonym)— Superior 2626   "Milwaukee Blues"

E. Francis H. Abbot—Library of Congress Archive of Folk Song L68: "*Folk Songs of America*": *The Robert Winslow Gordon Collection, 1922–1932* (from Gordon disc 73B)   "Casey Jones" (actually the

Abbot-Swan "Vanderbilt's Daughter" text cited in B, above)

Country Ramblers—Universe (Netherlands) UPI-24   "Milwaukee Blues"

John Greenway—Riverside RLP 12-619: *The Great American Bum*; Washington WLP 710: *Big Rock Candy Mountain* "Jay Gould's Daughter"

—Wattle (Australia) C-2   "Jay Gould's Daughter"

Buell Kazee—June Appal JA 009: *Buell Kazee*   "Jay Gould's Daughter"

J. E. Mainer and his Mountaineers —Rural Rhythm RRJE 191: *The Legendary J.E. Mainer* [Vol. 2]   "Jay Goose Is Dead"

Ed McCurdy—Classic CE 1045   "Jay Gould's Daughter"

Old Hat Band—Voyager VRLP 307S: *Concert*   "Milwaukee Blues"

Ted Prillaman and the Virginia Ramblers—Mart (no number) (45 rpm)   "Milwaukee Blues"

Red Clay Ramblers—Flying Fish FF 055: *Merchant's Lunch*   "Milwaukee Blues"

Carl Sandburg—Lyrichord LL-4 (10″ LP): *New Songs from the American Songbag*; Lyrichord LL 66: *Ballads and Songs*   "Jay Gould's Daughter"

Pete Seeger—Folkways FA 2319: *American Ballads*   "Jay Gould's Daughter"

Spark Gap Wonder Boys—Rounder 0002: *"Cluck Old Hen"*   "Milwaukee Blues"

The Railroad Boomer

THE RAILROAD BOOMER

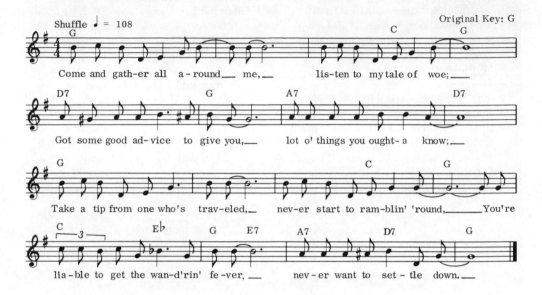

Come and gather all around me, listen to my tale of woe,
Got some good advice to give you, lot o' things you oughta know;
Take a tip from one who's traveled, never start to ramblin' 'round,
You're liable to get the wand'rin' fever, never want to settle down.

Met a little gal in Frisco, asked her if she'd be my wife,
Told her I was tired of roamin', said I'd settle down for life;
Then I heard a whistle blowin', knew it was a red-ball train,
Left her standin' by the railroad, never seen that gal again, never seen that
    gal again.

Wandered all around this country, guess I traveled everywhere,
Been on every branch-line railroad, never paid a nickel fare;
Been from Maine to Califo'nia, Canada to Mexico,
Never tried to save no money, and now I got no place to go.

Listen to a boomer's story, don't forget the things I say,
I hear another train a-comin', and I'll soon be on my way;
If you want to do a favor, when I lay me down and die,
Dig my grave beside a railroad, so I can hear the trains roll by, so I can
    hear the trains roll by.

Bud Billings and Carson Robison

The truly compulsive wanderer—the man who travels constantly, but not because of

Carson J. Robison. Courtesy of the John Edwards Memorial Foundation, UCLA.

inability to find employment or because he is fleeing the law or some woman—can strike a carefree pose that may fire the imagination of those individuals tethered more firmly to their posts. There is, of course, a tragic side to this picture—the oft-repeated tale of father and husband who periodically deserts his family because he cannot resist the urge to travel. Alice Solenberger dealt with many such individuals in the early 1900s and described her experiences in her book, *One Thousand Homeless Men*.[1]

The spritely song "The Railroad Boomer" captures the carefree mood of the railroad wanderer, with a few hints also of the tragic consequences that may be in store for him. The song was written by the prolific hillbilly songwriter Carson J. Robison in 1929 (copyrighted June 20, 1929, E 8157; renewed in 1956, R 179208). He and Frank Luther recorded it in September of that year for Victor and in November for Gennett. The Victor release, transcribed here, sold approximately 6,400 copies. Several more recordings were made in the 1930s, by them and by other artists.

The precise meaning of *boomer* in this song is uncertain; the word has meant different things at different times. Originally designating a migratory worker, the term came to be applied to railroaders who either worked for one employer far from home or changed employers frequently. At one time the word referred to settlers who joined the rush to a newly opened section of country. In 1901, *Railroad Trainmen's Journal* used it in a rather uncomplimentary way to mean a railroader who "travels the road because he likes to travel and there is not much work in it."[2] The slang dictionaries give no suggestion that the word has any etymological connection with *bum* and *bummer*, but that is an intriguing possibility; and among the recordings of the song, both professional and not, the terms *bum* and *bummer* appear in the title as frequently as *boomer*.

NOTES

1. Alice Willard Solenberger, *One Thousand Homeless Men* (New York: Charities Publication Committee, 1911).

2. "The Boomer Railroad Man," *RTJ*, 18 (Oct., 1901), 866.

REFERENCES

A. "The Railroad Boomer," by Bud Billings (Frank Luther pseudonym) and Carson Robison. Vocal duet, with accompaniment on trumpet, saxophone, violin, and guitar (Robison). Recorded Sept. 9, 1929 (RCA Victor master BVE 55680), in New York City. Released on RCA Victor V-40139 in Nov., 1929. Copyrighted by Robison on June 20, 1929 (E 8157), and renewed in 1956 (R 179208). Reissued on Zonophone (Australia) 4272. First recording of the song; transcribed here.

B. Martin, M., 20
Robison (1932), 12
Robison (1941), 50

C. COHEN COLLECTION:
Laura Affolter (2 versions)

D. Jeff Calhoun and Robert Leavett (Carson Robison and Frank Luther pseudonyms)—Grey Gull 4275, Van Dyke 74275
Frank Luther and Carson Robison—Brunswick 4648
Moonshine Kate (Rosa Lee Carson pseudonym) and her Pals—Okeh 45547   "The Poor Girl Story"
Tex Morton—Columbia (Canada) C-2338, OKeh 18020, Phillips (Australia) P24506H

—Regal Zonophone (Australia) G23166 "Railroad Bum"
Pine Ridge Boys—Bluebird B-8671
Riley Puckett—Bluebird B-8989
Goebel Reeves (the Texas Drifter)—Melotone 12242, Panachord (England) 25105, Panachord (Australia) P12242
Rice Brothers—Decca 5971
George Riley (Goebel Reeves pseudonym)—Conqueror 7707, Banner 32098, Jewel 20032, Romeo 5032, Oriole 8032, Perfect 165, Perfect 12668, Regal 10304   "Railroad Bum"
Carson Robison Trio—Romeo 1018, Cameo 9216, Conqueror 7438, Domino 4442, Regal 8885, Perfect 12560 (as by Harry "Rocky" Wilson), Pathé 32481, Broadway 4051
Carson Robison and Frank Luther—Gennett 7019, Champion 15848, Champion 45020, Supertone 9567

E. Cisco Houston—Folkways FA 2013 (FP 13): *900 Miles and Other Railroad Songs* "The Rambler"

F. LC AFS:
Buck Buttery—AFS 11909 B24 "Bummer Story"
Pauline Ramsay—AFS 5124 B1 "Freight Train Blues"
Fred Smith—AFS 13132 B25
Clarence Wyatt—AFS 10892 A4 "Bummer's Story"

Hobo Bill's Last Ride

HOBO BILL'S LAST RIDE

*Falsetto.

[*Yodel*:] Hobo Billy.
Riding on an eastbound freight train, speeding through the night,
Hobo Bill, a railroad bum, was fighting for his life;
The sadness of his eyes revealed the torture of his soul,
He raised a weak and weary hand to brush away the cold.
[*Yodel*:] Hobo Billy.

No warm lights flickered around him, no blankets there to fold,
Nothing but the howling wind and the driving rain so cold;
When he heard a whistle blowing in a dreamy kind of way,
The hobo seemed contented, for he smiled there where he lay.
[*Yodel*:] Hobo Bill.

Outside the rain was falling on that lonely boxcar door,
But the little form of Hobo Bill lay still upon the floor;
While the train sped through the darkness and the raging storm outside,
No one knew that Hobo Bill was taking his last ride.

It was early in the morning when they raised the hobo's head,
The smile still lingered on his face, but Hobo Bill was dead;

There was no mother's longing to soothe his weary soul,
For he was just a railroad bum who died out in the cold.

Jimmie Rodgers

Although this sentimental tale of "Hobohemia" has yet to appear in any published volume of folksongs collected in the field, its continued popularity on phonograph record and its occasional appearance in unpublished archives strengthen my conviction that it is securely in oral tradition at present.

The song was written by Waldo O'Neal, who was born on a ranch near Jacksboro, in east Texas, in 1908. When he was a small boy, his mother taught him western songs, and he learned to accompany himself on the guitar. At the age of fifteen, O'Neal began writing poetry, focusing on themes of his native West, and composing tunes for his poems. He published his first book of poetry in 1938. By then he had moved to Clovis, New Mexico, where he stayed with his parents for the next twenty years. He made his living at various jobs—service station operator, car salesman, carpenter—before he was stricken with arthritis, which completely disabled him in the mid-1950s.[1]

The first song O'Neal penned for publication was "Hobo Bill's Last Ride," which he had written in 1929 in the hope that the rising star Jimmie Rodgers would record it. Rodgers did, on November 13 of that year, and the song was released the following July on the RCA Victor label. In the next few years, it was also recorded by Gene Autry and Frankie Marvin, both of whom made it a practice of recording Jimmie Rodgers's hits in a style strikingly reminiscent of the "Blue Yodeler" himself.

In 1955, in a letter to Australian record collector John Edwards, O'Neal recalled some of the events subsequent to the release of "Hobo Bill":

> In 1930 he came to my home town with a traveling show, I was living in Clarendon, Texas. My mother and father met him, shook hands and had the pleasure of talking with him for several minutes. He wanted to see me, he had recorded only one of my songs at that time, "Hobo Bill," he was interested in buying two more, but we didn't know it, at the time. That night my brother attended the show; he said Jimmie came out on the stage and said, "I'm looking for a boy named Waldo O'Neal, will he please come forward, I have a check for him["]; he was holding the check in his hand. The check was only for $50.00 but it seemed very rewarding at the time. I was only 21 years old at that time.
>   . . . I would like to mention here the great pleasure I knew that day my mother came home and called me in to hear a new record. We bought all of Jimmie's records and I didn't think much about it until she placed it on the machine and it started playing. It was my song, "Hobo Bill"; you may imagine how I felt; I didn't say anything for a little while, then I was overcome with happiness; it just couldn't be true—Jimmie Rodgers, whom I had spent hours and hours listening to his records, was singing one of my very own songs.[2]

Rodgers, one of the most influential singers in the history of country music, enjoyed six years of phenomenal popularity before his untimely death in 1933. Born in Mississippi in 1897, the son of a Mobile and Ohio Railroad gang foreman, Jimmie began work at the age of fourteen as a waterboy in the Meridian railroad yards. Here it was that he learned much of his music from black workers. When tuberculosis forced him to give up the heavy work of the railroads, he turned to music to make a living.[3] He cultivated the image of the railroader—he was dubbed the "Singing Brakeman"—and his repertoire included many songs about railroaders, hoboes, and tramps, as well as other pieces that made frequent use of railroad imagery. Other songs he popularized that are included in this book are "Ben Dewberry's Final Run," "Train Whistle Blues," and "Waiting for a Train." Other railroad songs he recorded were "The Brakeman's Blues," "The Mystery of Number Five," "Southern Cannonball," and "Hobo's Meditation."

NOTES

1. Biographical information about O'Neal is taken from the introduction to his book of poems, *Star Dust of the Plains* (Clovis, N.Mex., 1957), and from Myrtle D. Constant, "Clovis Man Publishes Book of Poems," *Clovis* (N.Mex.) *Press*, Feb. 28, 1957.

2. O'Neal to Edwards, Oct. 14, 1955 (letter in the archives of the John Edwards Memorial Foundation, UCLA).

3. For further information on Rodgers, see the discussion and references for "Train Whistle Blues" (chap. 9).

REFERENCES

A. "Hobo Bill's Last Ride," by Jimmie Rodgers. Vocal and guitar. Recorded Nov. 13, 1929 (RCA Victor master BVE 56528-1), in New Orleans. Released on Victor 22421 on July 18, 1930. Reissued on Montgomery Ward M-4210, Zonophone (England) 5724, Regal Zonophone (England and Australia) T 5724, Zonophone (Australia) EE 213, Twin (India) FT 333, Twin (India) FT 1784, Regal Zonophone (Ireland) IZ 333; RCA Victor LPM 1640: *Train Whistle Blues*; RCA Victor ANLI-1052: *All about Trains*; RCA Victor ANSI-1052 (8-track tape): *All about Trains*; RCA Victor (Japan) RA 5461: *The Legendary Jimmie Rodgers 110 Collections, Vol. 3*; RCA Victor (Japan) RA 9037; RCA Victor (Japan) RA 5176; RCA Victor (Japan) RA 5510; RCA Victor (Australia) EP 20176; RCA Victor (England) RD 27110; RCA Victor (England) DPS 2021. Copyrighted by Southern Music on July 14, 1930 (EP 16752), and renewed on July 24, 1957 (R 196188), words and music by Waldo O'Neal.

B. Clifton, 30
Cowboy Jack, 22
Family Herald, 42 (references only)
Horstman, 320–21
Martin, M., 14
Pack, 6
Rodgers (1931), 22

Rodgers (1934b), 26
Rodgers (1943a), 50
RRM, 11 (July, 1933), 59
Wild West Weekly, Apr. 11, 1936, p. 124

D. Gene Autry—Gennett 7290, Champion 16073, Superior 2769, Supertone 9702
Frankie Marvin—Brunswick 474
—Challenge 691, Challenge 785 (as by Frankie Wallace)
—Crown 3026
Reg Perkins—Melotone (Canada) 93047
Sleepy Hollow Gang—Majestic 11006
Hank Snow—RCA Victor 20-4095, RCA Victor 420-0560 (in 78 rpm album); RCA Victor 447-0560 (45 rpm); RCA Victor EPA 310 (in 45 rpm EP album: *Famous Railroading Songs*); RCA Camden 722: *The One and Only Hank Snow*
Frankie Wallace (Frankie Marvin pseudonym)—Banner 0773, Cameo 0373, Conqueror 7592, Domino 4601, Jewel 6024, Oriole 2024, Perfect 12632, Regal 10079, Romeo 1388

E. Bill Clifton—Golden Guinea (Australia) GSGL 10476: *Happy Days*
John Greenway—Riverside RLP 12-619: *The Great American Bum*
Merle Haggard—Capitol SWBB-223: *Same Train, Different Time*
Cisco Houston—Folkways FA 2013 (FP 13): *900 Miles and Other Railroad Ballads* "Hobo Bill"

—Stinson SLP 12: *Folksay, Vol . 5*; Stinson
SLPX 12: *Folksay, Vols . 5 and 6*
"Hobo Bill"
Ray Hutchinson—Rich-R-Tone 8084-S: *Ray
Hutchinson*
Grandpa Jones—Monument 8001: *Yodeling
Hits*   "Hobo Bill"
Clay Lewis—American Heritage AH
401-33: *Tall Shadows*
Obray Ramsey—Prestige International
13009: *Obray Ramsey Sings Jimmie
Rodgers Favorites*
Jimmie Skinner—Mercury MG 20700:
Jimmie Skinner Sings Jimmie Rodgers
—Starday SLP 282: *Let's Say Goodbye Like
We Said Hello*

F. LCAFS:

Al Bittick—AFS 12050 A11
Troy Cambron—AFS 4140 A1

Waldo O'Neal. Courtesy of the John
Edwards Memorial Foundation, UCLA.

In a Boxcar around the World

IN A BOX CAR AROUND THE WORLD

Shuffle ♩ = 120   Original Key: C

O - de - lay - ee   ah - ee   o - lay - ee.___   I'm the man that rode the box-car   around the world,___   boys, it's a pleas-ure to me;___   South-ern Pa-cif-ic, the   C and O,___ the L and   N, and the San-ta Fe,_____   From coast to coast I've wan-dered   to the tune   of the rail - road track,   Just to hear that whis-tle   moan and   groan   to the   mu-sic of the old smoke-stack.   I nev-er wea - ry   and   I nev-er cry,___   Just let   my trou-bles   drift on   by, ___   hee - hee - hee - hee-hee,   Rid - ing   to   the east,_____   rid - ing   to   the west,__   ___   rid - ing   where the sun___   goes   down.

*Falsetto.

Yodel:
I'm the man that rode the boxcar around the world, boys, it's a pleasure
 to me;
Southern Pacific, the C and O, the L and N, and the Santa Fe,
From coast to coast I've wandered to the tune of the railroad track,
Just to hear that whistle moan and groan to the music of the old smokestack.

 I never weary and I never cry, just let my troubles drift on by,
  hee-hee-hee-hee-hee,
 Riding to the east, riding to the west, riding where the sun goes down.
 Yodel:

I've been around this cockeyed world a dozen times or more,
When I die don't you bury me, let me lay on that boxcar floor;
Roll me in that old boxcar, close the boxcar door,
Pull that throttle and step aside and let me ride forevermore.
 Yodel:

 Chorus:

                                                        Cliff Carlisle

   My sampling of songs of hoboes and wanderers concludes with a piece from the pen
of one of the most popular hillbilly performers of the 1930s, Cliff Carlisle. Born in 1904 in
Mount Eden, Spencer County, Kentucky, Clifford Raymond Carlisle was reared on a
farm and exposed early to rural music through his father's work as singing teacher for a
local church. When still quite young, Cliff purchased a Sears, Roebuck guitar and learned
to play steel-guitar style. In about 1920, Carlisle took to music more seriously, teaming up
first with a cousin, Lillian Truax, then with Wilbur Ball, and finally with his brother Bill.
His career on wax began in 1930, and in the next fifteen or so years he recorded close to
three hundred selections.[1] Many of his songs were of his own composition; a favorite
theme was hoboing, often presented in the hillybilly blues style of Jimmie Rodgers's
famous blue yodels. Although Carlisle never spent any time hoboing or bumming, his
songs in that vein are a successful blend of traditional and original elements, capturing the
flavor for the wanderer's life: "Box Car Yodel," "A Lonesome Hobo (Ramblin' Jack),"
"Hobo Jack's Last Ride," "Hobo Blues," and "I'm Glad I'm a Hobo," among others. The
opening line of Carlisle's composition transcribed here is textually reminiscent of an old
hillbilly/folk favorite, "I'm the Man That Rode the Mule around the World."[2]
   "In a Box Car around the World" was recorded in 1936 for RCA Victor. It was
copyrighted, words and melody by Cliff Carlisle, on December 11, 1936 (E unp. 136460;
renewed Dec. 11, 1963, R 327817). No other recordings of the song have been made,
and, to my knowledge, no versions have been collected anywhere. As of this writing, the
song seems bound for oblivion.

NOTES

   1. For more biographical information, see Gene Earle, "Cliff Carlisle," *Folk Style*, No. 7
(Bromley, Kent, England: Hillbilly and Folk Record Collectors Club, [1960?]), pp. 3–26.
   2. See, e.g., Uncle Dave Macon, "Man That Rode the Mule around the World,"
Vocalion 5356 (July, 1928); reissued on Folk Variety 12503: *The Gayest Old Dude in Town*.

REFERENCES

A. "In a Box Car around the World," by Cliff Carlisle. Cliff Carlisle, vocal; Bill Carlisle, vocal chorus; two guitars accompaniment. Recorded Feb. 16, 1936 (RCA Victor master 99168), in Charlotte, N.C. Released on Bluebird B-6439. Reissued on Montgomery Ward M-4772, Regal Zonophone (Ireland) IZ 783, Regal Zonophone (England) MR 2602. Copyrighted Dec. 11, 1936 (E unp. 136460), words and music by Cliff Carlisle; renewed Dec. 11, 1963 (R 327817).

Cliff Carlisle. Courtesy of the John Edwards Memorial Foundation, UCLA.

9

I've Got the Railroad Blues

IN THE LATE eighteenth century, *the blue devils* was a common expression for a fit of depression. Soon the phrase was shortened—some say first by Washington Irving—to *the blues*. Later in nineteenth-century America the word appeared often, but not always with the same meaning. In the 1850s, *blues* signified boredom; in the 1880s, unhappiness. Furthermore, since the 1830s, *blue* has also meant obscene — a meaning that, though of separate derivation, is often appropriate for the recorded blues of the 1920s and 1930s.

As applied to a genre of Afro-American folk music, the term *blues* has been defined by many writers; yet there is still not complete agreement on what constitutes a blues song. If, as is reasonable to suppose, the musical term derived from the name for an emotion, then blues songs must originally have been characterized by their emotional content: expressions of depression or unhappiness or discontent on the part of the singer. But the term has expanded considerably—otherwise, such a juxtaposition as *party blues*, a common type of bawdy music especially popular in the 1930s, would be self-contradictory.

The meaning of the blues has been discussed at length by many knowledgeable writers, to whom the interested reader is referred.[1] Here, I offer only a brief, approximate, descriptive definition. *Blues*—in particular, *folk blues* (or *country blues*)—is a type of Afro-American folk music that emerged during the last decade of the nineteenth century with the following features:

A. Each stanza consists of a rhymed couplet, the first line of which is repeated (or nearly repeated), thus forming the unusual (at least, in European-derived poetry) stanzaic pattern AAB.

B. The singing is invariably accompanied by instrument, according to a well-defined chord pattern. Each musical line tends to be longer than the singing requires, leaving a gap to be filled by an instrumental response to the vocal. In the case of a twelve-bar blues (the most usual, though not invariable, form), the chord pattern is:

A   I -   I   - I - I
A   IV -   IV   - I - I
B   V -   V or IV - I - I

400

C. Blues songs utilize a scale not found in European music; it is distinguished by a flatted third and a flatted seventh that lie, respectively, between the major and minor third and seventh of the standard European scale.

D. Blues songs do not have the narrative continuity of Anglo-American ballads. They occasionally do tell, or comment on, a story in a disjointed fashion, but more usually they consist of only loosely related stanzas that may share a common theme. In this respect they are most like those nonballad Anglo-American folksongs generally categorized as "folk lyric." Actually, it is safest to regard the stanza itself as the thematic unit.

E. Consequently, blues songs tend to be personal arrangements, although they do draw heavily on a reservoir of traditional stanzas, lines, phrases, and expressions. Of course, the impact of the phonograph record has been sufficiently great that certain blues compositions recorded by popular bluesmen have in their entirety entered oral tradition.

F. The blues singer generally regards his blues songs as "true"—if not in the literal, autobiographical sense, then in the sense of being relevant to the singer's life experience.

G. The folk blues, though a distinctly novel form of folksong at the time it emerged, nevertheless borrowed significantly from older black folksong forms, such as the spiritual, the field holler, and the minstrel song.

"City blues" (or "popular blues") emerged as a commercialized form of folk blues in the second decade of the twentieth century, largely owing to the influence of black composers like W. C. Handy. Handy's own first brush with the blues, described in his autobiography, is quoted below, in the discussion of "The Southern Blues." City blues differ principally from folk blues in being consciously composed for mass distribution (and copyrightability). Hence, city blues are metrically more regular—invariably comprised of twelve-bar stanzas—whereas folk blues often had eight- or sixteen-bar stanzas, or were even more irregular, say, following a stanza of eleven and a half bars with one of thirteen bars. City blues strive for originality of expression more than do folk blues, and are generally also marked by greater thematic continuity from stanza to stanza.

One can only speculate on the origins of the various characteristics of the blues. The singing style and the blues scale, found in the older field hollers, probably extend back to slavery days, judging from the few descriptions of slave singing that have survived in print. The interplay between vocal and instrumental can be seen as an extension of the call-and-response characteristic of much African music, though it had its parallel in the lining-out of hymns by the Anglo-Americans and the British before them.[2]

The hardest characteristic to trace is the three-line AAB stanza. It may have developed from a common form of the nineteenth-century camp-meeting spiritual, in which a stanza consisted of four lines of the form AAAB. But whether the alterations of the AAAB form to an AAB stanza demanded the introduction of the twelve-bar musical accompaniment or vice versa, is moot.

By the time race records—the commercial offshoot of black American folk music —had become well established in the early 1920s, the blues was a major song form. The first few years of the race-record industry were dominated by "classic" female blues singers, such as Ma Rainey, Bessie Smith, Ida Cox, and Clara Smith. These women generally sang the standard twelve-bar blues, mostly composed by contemporary songwriters, to the accompaniment of a small jazz combo. In the mid-1920s this format gradually was supplanted by the "country blues" of male singers—a form closer to folk blues in several respects: variety of stanzaic structures was greater; the singers sang their own compositions, frequently synthesized from traditional verses and stanzas; and the singers provided their own accompaniment (usually guitar or piano).

Also in the mid-1920s a form of blues became popular among white hillbilly artists. Often called "white blues," these songs were patterned closely after the "classic" twelve-bar AAB blues. Although there were many exceptions, on the average these white blues were lyrically drab and unimaginative compared to their black counterparts. It has often been noted that the black folksinger's capacity for improvisation was unequaled by the white folksinger's, whose strength lay more in his fidelity to centuries of oral tradition than in his own originality.

A family of favorite themes in blues of the 1920s and 1930s comprised the railroad, wandering, escape, and flight of one's sweetheart. The railroad figures in some of the earliest blues fragments preserved in print. W. C. Handy's 1903 hearing of the line "Goin' where the Southern cross' the Dog" (see "The Southern Blues") is one of our oldest train blues survivals.

An unusual railroad blues, of particular interest because of its length (eighty quatrains), was collected by W. Prescott Webb from a young black man named Floyd Canada of Beeville, Bee County, Texas, shortly before 1915. Strictly speaking, it is not a blues, and Webb was careful to note that the song consisted of four-line stanzas; but it clearly borrows from the same bag of traditional verses as do the pieces that we readily call "blues." He wrote down the song as Canada dictated it to him one day in the local railroad depot. When Webb published the song in the _Journal of American Folklore_, he dubbed it the "African Iliad" because it revealed "what the negro held to be of highest importance . . . his desires and aims, his love and hate, his ethical and chivalrous ideas, his philosophy of life, code of morals, and ideas of the future." We need not take Webb's ecstatic praise seriously to still appreciate the strengths of Canada's song, or to realize that almost every blues transcribed in this chapter has some textual connections with Canada's extended recitation—in particular, with the section that Webb subtitled "The Wanderlust and the Long Freight-Train." Since Webb himself rearranged the stanzas into five well-defined groups, I feel no reluctance to choose here only those stanzas that are particularly suited to a discussion of the railroad in blues lyrics. They offer a good sampling of railroad blues well before the influence of the phonograph could become felt.

THE RAILROAD BLUES

Every time you hear me sing this song
You may know I've caught a train and gone.
I get a letter, and this is how it read:
Stamped on the inside, "Yo lover's sick in bed."

Give me my shoes and my Carhart overalls,
Let me step over yonder and blind the Cannon Ball;
That's the long train they call the Cannon Ball,
It makes a hundred miles and do no switchin' at all.

Train I ride doan burn no coal at all,
It doan burn nothin' but Texas Beaumont oil;
That's the long train they calls the Cannon Ball,
It makes a hundred miles and do no stoppin' at all.

If you ever had the blues, you know jus' how I feel,
Puts you on the wonder, and make you want to squeal;

When you take the blues and doan know what to do,
Jus' hunt you a train and ride the whole world through.

Big Four in Dallas done burned down,
Burned all night long, burned clean to the ground;
But give me my shoes, my press overalls,
If you doan min' my goin', baby, I'll catch the Cannon Ball.

I'm worried now, but I won't be worried long,
This north-bound train will certainly take me home.
Number Nine is gone, Number Ten's switchin' in the yard,
But I'm goin' to see that girl if I have to ride the rods.

I got the railroad blues, but I haven't got the fare,
The company sho' ought to pay my way back there.
The train I ride is sixteen coaches long
Dat's de train done take yo' baby home.

I'm a goin' away, it won't be long;
When I hit Houston, I'll call it gone.
When I git to Houston I'll stop and dry;
When I hit San Tone, I'll keep on by.

How I have to hear the Monkey Motion blow,
It puts me on the wonder, and makes me want to go.
Dat passenger-train got ways jus' lak a man,
Steal away yo' girl, and doan care where she land.

I may be right an' I may be wrong,
But it takes a worried woman to sing a worry song;
When a woman's in trouble, she wring her hands and cry;
But when a man's in trouble, it's a long freight-train and ride.

I went to the depot wringin' my hands and cryin'
Everybody's bound to have trouble some time;
If I'd a listened to what my mother said,
I'd been at home lyin' in my foldin' bed.

If I feel to-morrow like I feel today,
I'm gwine to ride the last train away;
If I had all you women's hearts in my hand,
I'd show you how to treat yo' nice black man.

Red River's on the boom; Guadaloupe's standin' still;
Brown woman on the train; black one on the hill.
You brown-skin woman, let me be yo' Teddy Bear,
Put a chain on my neck, an' I'll follow you everywhere.[3]

Because of the loose, amorphous structure of many blues, a song titled "Railroad Blues" or "Box Car Blues" may have no more than a few lines that mention railroads or boxcars, and then move into other subjects. In most of the blues transcribed in this chapter, the railroad themes are more persistent, resulting in somewhat more cohesive songs than a random sampling of blues lyrics would afford. The chief exception is "How Long Blues," which is, nevertheless, included because of its great popularity and influence as a blues recording. Conversely, railroad stanzas may pop up unexpectedly under the most unpromising titles. This makes it practically impossible to offer the reader a thorough bibliography and discography of lines and themes related to the songs transcribed here.

The dozen blues in this chapter are a varied lot; though few have all the attributes of blues discussed above, all have some of them, and I suspect that most critcs would agree in labeling them all as blues.

The first two pieces are of interest in suggesting routes to the emergence of the three-line, AAB blues stanza. "KC Railroad"/"KC Moan," which may date to late in the nineteenth century, occurs in two stanza forms: AAAB and AAB. Although there is no evidence, it is convenient to assume the AAAB form, common in the nineteenth-century spirituals, to be the older. "Cannonball Blues" is of the form AA′R, where A and A′ rhyme and R is a refrain, not necessarily rhyming. This couplet/refrain stanza appeared in many blues ballads from the turn of the century or earlier; "Delia," "Railroad Bill," "Poor Lazarus," "Frankie and Albert," "Boll Weevil." (Some of these, of course, can equally well be written as quatrains followed by refrain.)

The age of the third blues, "The Train That Carried My Girl from Town," is not known. It is the only blues in this chapter that is sixteen rather than twelve bars; but since the additional four bars come from a doubling of the refrain, the form is still AA′R. It would be reasonable to speculate that it, too, dates from the turn of the century. Charlie McCoy's "That Lonesome Train Took My Baby Away" is set to a piano blues melody composed by Cow Cow Davenport probably in the 1920s, but the lyrics could well be much older. The stanzas are irregular, seldom working out to precisely twelve bars. Sleepy John Estes's "Special Agent (Railroad Police Blues)" is doubtless autobiographical and shows considerably more originality in lyrics than most of the other blues in this chapter do. It is a country, or folk, blues, but a relatively late example.

Leroy Carr and Big Bill Broonzy, major bluesmen of the 1930s, contributed the next two selections in the chapter; both exemplify the trend toward a more polished and urban blues sound immediately prior to and during the Depression years. Carr's "How Long, How Long Blues" was one of the best-known compositions of the years following its release; the railroad references in it are slight. Broonzy's "Southern Blues" is of particular interest because of one of its textual allusions.

The next selection, by Lucille Bogan, is close to the city ("Harlem" or "classic") blues idiom, but her vocal style keeps it from falling squarely into that category. There can be no reservations about labeling the following two blues by Clara Smith and Trixie Smith as city blues. They illustrate the extent to which blues had merged with jazz and pop in the mid-1920s. These city blues are generally twelve bar, AAB in structure, with the second line deviating in no more than a word or two from the first line; the vocal invariably paused a few bars for an instrumental solo, generally by horn, piano, or guitar. The text was often the work of an experienced songwriter who, though he drew to some extent on the large body of black folk verse, usually subjected it to a conformist mold that altered its shape markedly. Of course, the more enduring and influential of these city blues lyrics can themselves enter oral tradition and gradually alter the contour of what is called folksong.

To summarize the process briefly: city blues music first borrowed from the black folk tradition, then built away from it, and finally paid the loan back, with ample interest.

For this reason, city blues can be considered apart from country or folk blues for only a moment.

Such city blues seem to have provided some of the inspiration for the white blues of the 1920s. In fact, Jimmie Rodgers, the most successful of the hillbilly singers who recorded white blues, used established jazz accompanists on some of his recordings. The chapter concludes with a white blues composition by another hillbilly singer, Roy Harvey. Poetically speaking, it is impoverished verse compared to some of the striking metaphor and simile of the better country blues; but the fact that the song is a genuine outpouring of a railroader-turned-singer earns it a place of importance in this book.

NOTES

1. For good definitions and discussions of blues see Harry Oster, *Living Country Blues* (Detroit: Folklore Associates, 1969), chap. 2; Abbe Niles, introduction to W. C. Handy, *Blues: An Anthology* (New York: Albert and Charles Boni, 1926); Winthrop Sargeant, *Jazz: Hot and Hybrid* (New York: Arrow, 1938, and later editions), chap. 10 and *passim*; Marshall Stearns, *The Story of Jazz* (Oxford: Oxford University Press, 1956), chap. 10; Howard W. Odum and Guy B. Johnson, *Negro Workaday Songs* (Chapel Hill: University of North Carolina Press, 1926), chap. 2; Paul Oliver, *Blues Fell This Morning* (London: Cassell, 1960; New York: Horizon Press, 1961), introduction; Leroi Jones, *Blues People* (New York: William Morrow, 1963), chaps. 6 and 7; Jeff Titon, *Early Downhome Blues* (Urbana: University of Illinois Press, 1977), pp. xiii–xiv and *passim*.

2. For a survey of early references to such characteristics, see Dena J. Epstein, *Sinful Tunes and Spirituals* (Urbana: University of Illinois Press, 1977).

3. W. Prescott Webb, "Notes on Folk-Lore of Texas," *JAF*, 28 (July–Sept., 1915), 293–95.

KC Railroad/KC Moan

KANSAS CITY RAILROAD BLUES

♩ = 66

Original Key: C

Thought I heard old K C when it blowed, Lord, I thought I heard old K C when it blowed, Lord I thought I heard old K C when she blowed; Blowed like it nev-er blowed be-fore.

Thought I heard old KC when it blowed,
Lord, I thought I heard old KC when it blowed,
Lord, I thought I heard old KC when she blowed;
Blowed like it never blowed before.

Oh, it's comin' a time that a woman won't need no man,
Oh, it's comin' a time that a woman won't need no man,
Oh, it's comin' a time that a woman won't need no man,
Honey, I love (you), God knows I do.

Central, give me that long-distance phone,
Oh, central, give me that long-distance phone,
Oh, central, give me that long-distance phone;
Just want to talk to that brown of mine.

Andrew and Jim Baxter

KANSAS CITY RAILROAD

Don't you hear that lovin' KC blow,
Don't you hear that lovin' KC blow;
Blowed like she never blowed before.

Goin' down that road feelin' bad,
Goin' down that road feelin' bad;
Ain't gonna be treated this-a way.

Ain't got no lovin' baby now,
Ain't got no lovin' baby now;
Ain't gonna be treated this-a way.

Ought to hear that lovin' KC blow,
Ought to hear that lovin' KC blow;
Blow like she never blowed before.

My baby left me ridin' on that old KC,
My baby left me ridin' on that old KC;
I'll be ridin' if she don't come back to me.

Hand me down that long-distance phone,
Hand me down that long-distance phone;
I ain't got no lovin' baby now.

I'm goin' where the chilly winds don't blow,
I'm goin' where the chilly winds don't blow;
I ain't gonna be treated this-a way.

Ought to hear that lovin' KC blow,
Ought to hear that lovin' KC blow;
Blow like she never blowed before.

Goin' down that road feelin' bad,
Goin' down that road feelin' bad;
Ain't gonna be treated this-a way.

Ought to hear that lovin' KC blow,
Ought to hear that lovin' KC blow;
Blow like she never blowed before.

Riley Puckett

THE OLD K-C

I thought I heard that old KC blow,
I thought I heard that old KC blow,
I thought I heard that old KC blow,
And she blowed like she never blowed no more.

She was reelin' and straining every nerve,
She was reelin' and straining every nerve.
She was reelin' and straining every nerve;
She was rockin' as she come round the curve.

That KC she took my baby away,
That KC she took my baby away,
That KC she took my baby away,
And I'm sure she'll bring her back some day.

I'll be ridin' if she don't come back to me,
I'll be ridin' if she don't come back to me,

I'll be ridin' if she don't come back to me;
I'll be ridin' on that old KC.

Jess Young's Tennessee Band

While the railroad was the predominant form of passenger and freight transportation in the United States throughout the period when most of the songs in this book were born, inland waterways were also important, and they, likewise, gave birth to a substantial body of folksongs and folklore. "KC Railroad"/"KC Moan" is an example of a railroad song that has close relatives among steamboat songs; it is impossible to say at present whether one form grew out of the other, or if the two developed simultaneously.

Like most lyric folksongs and blues songs, the structure of "KC Railroad"/"KC Moan" is very fluid, and different renditions vary considerably from one another, as the three texts transcribed above illustrate. (Only one tune is given, however, as the music varies negligibly from version to version.) Jess Young's version is unusual in that it has no stanzas that do not refer to trains. Riley Puckett's and Andrew and Jim Baxter's, on the other hand, are more typical; they mention the railroad in the opening stanza only, then move on to other images of travel, imprisonment, or lost love. Puckett's second stanza introduces an element of another closely related song that shares tunes with "KC Railroad," "I'm Going down the Road Feeling Bad." Although these two texts are frequently intermingled, I have omitted from the biblio-discography any variants of the latter song that do not have some railroad references. From "Going down the Road Feeling Bad," one moves readily to such related songs with the same tune as "Way Down in Jail on My Knees" (Harkreader and Moore, Broadway 8115), "Going Where the Sugar Cane Grows" (Fiddlin' John Carson, OKeh 45338 and Bluebird 5652), "Going Where the Climate Suits My Clothes" (Carson, OKeh 45498), "Down in Florida on a Hog" (Darby and Tarlton, Columbia 15197-D), and "Going down That Lonesome Frisco Line" (Georgia Wildcats, Victor 23640).

The opening verses of "KC Railroad" are widely found and, with some variation, occur in many other blues songs set to other tunes. Mississippi Delta bluesman Charley Patton used variants on the verse in several of his blues, for instance, "Pea Vine Blues":

I think I heard the Pea Vine when she blowed
I think I heard the Pea Vine when she blowed;
Blowed just like my rider gettin' on board.[1]

In "Green River Blues":

Think I heard the Marion whistle blow,
I think I heard the Marion whistle blow;
And it blew just like my baby gettin' on board.[2]

In "Moon Goin' Down" the lines become:

Lord, I think I heard that Helena whistle, Helena whistle, Helena whistle blow,
Lord, I think I heard that Helena whistle blow;
Lord, I ain't gonna stop walking till I get in my rider's door.[3]

From other bluesmen we can hear similar lines:

> I hate to hear New York Central whistle blow,
> Ever time she whistle, to the roundhouse I got to go.[4]

and

> Lord, I hate to hear that evening train whistle when it blows,
> It gives me a feelin' that I never had before.[5]

It might be noted that although most singers perform the song to a three-line blues stanza, it is often set to a four-line stanza, with the first line repeated twice.

Of the several related steamboating songs, the most striking are those that substitute *Katy* for *KC*. The reference is to *Kate Adams*, the name of three different well-known riverboats owned by Captain James Rees and his family. The third *Kate Adams*, in service around the turn of the century, is probably the one mentioned in such lines as:

> Oh I thought I heard the *Kate Adams* when she blowed,
> She blowed jes' lak she ain't goin' to blow no mo'.[6]

A similar stanza opens Jazz Gillum's recording about the imaginary race between the *Kate Adams* and the *Jim Lee*, "Big Katy Adams":

> Well, I hate to hear, to hear big *Kate Adams* blow,
> Well, I hate to hear, to hear big *Kate Adams* blow;
> She blow just like she ain't never blowed before.[7]

In her book on riverboat life and the songs it generated, *Steamboatin' Days*, Mary Wheeler discusses this race and quotes another song fragment about it.[8] She also collected the following closely related song:

> Lawd, Lawd, seems lak I heerd the Joe Fowler blow
> Lawd, Lawd, seems lak I heerd the Joe Fowler blow.
> Blowed me lak she nevuh did befo', Lawd, Lawd, Lawd.
> Blowed me lak she nevuh did befo'.[9]

A more generalized form of the "steamship blowing" stanza has been recorded several times; compare, for example, Roy Acuff's "Steamboat Whistle Blues":

> Thought I heard that steamboat whistle blow,
> Thought I heard that steamboat whistle blow;
> Blowed like she never blowed before.[10]

Does the line "I thought I heard that KC whistle blow" refer to a specific railroad? There have been so many railroads running through Kansas City with that city as part of their name that one would be hard pressed to pick a single referent for the song lyrics. By the turn of the century the following rail lines had come into existence, some later merging with other lines: Kansas City and Santa Fe; KC and Cameron; KC and Eastern; KC, Burlington and Santa Fe; KC, Saint Joseph, and Burlington; KC and Memphis Southwestern; KC Belt; KC, Clinton and Springfield; KC, Fort Scott and Memphis; KC, Memphis and Birmingham; KC, Mexico and Orient; KC, Northwestern; KC, Rock Island; KC, Saint Louis and Chicago; KC, Shreveport and Gulf Terminal; and KC Southern Railway. According to rail historian Alvin F. Harlow, the nickname "KC" came to be associated with the Kansas City Southern.[11] Incorporated in 1900 as successor to the

Kansas City, Shreveport and Gulf Terminal Company, this was the biggest of the "KC" railroads; its relatively late appearance would seem to place the song "K.C. Railroad" in the twentieth century, probably later than the riverboat analogs. It should also be noted that "KT" or "Katy" was a popular designatiòn for the Missouri, Kansas and Texas (MK & T) Railway, which would have provided an even more obvious crossover from riverboat to railroad song. In any case, few city names are more intimately associated with railroads. This particular association, moreover, is reinforced by the common engineer's nickname, "Casey," perhaps itself a tribute to the large numbers of Irish railroaders of the 1800s.

The earliest known reference to "KC" in a traditional railroad-song fragment places it in the context of the Kentucky Central Railroad. The song was offered by the Berea College Quartette at a Chautauqua program in 1899. A reporter observed:

> And to show that the spirit of minstrelsy is not wholly dead there were one or two modern ballads, formed on the analogy of the ancient. Particularly interesting was the song of a mountaineer who had actually seen the Kentucky Central Railroad—a one-horse affair which has struggled through Berea on its way to Boone's Gap:

> > I bin, I bin,
> > And I'm goin' ter go agin,
> > A ridin' on the K. C. road.[12]

One recording of the song, the Memphis Jug Band's "KC Moan," was reissued in 1952 by Harry Smith on his influential Folkways LP anthology, *American Folk Music*, (FA 2951–2953), and made a significant impact on the folksong revival of the 1950s and 1960s. Several recordings by city singers, including Mark Spoelstra, Dave Van Ronk, and Jim Kweskin, probably derive from the Memphis Jug Band recording.

The first recording of the song was Andrew and Jim Baxter's version, transcribed in this book. The Baxters, black brothers from around Calhoun, Georgia, were taken to a Victor recording session in Charlotte, North Carolina, by hillbilly musician Bill Chitwood, who was also from Calhoun. The roots of the Baxters' small recorded repertoire lay in preblues traditional music, in a style that was readily assimilated by white folk musicians of the period. Their recording, quite successful for a blues issue at the time, sold more than 15,300 copies. Two years earlier, in July, 1925, George Walburn and Emmett Hethcox recorded an instrumental entitled "K.C. Railroad Blues" (OKeh 45004), but the tune is not the usual one. Jess Young, whose recorded version is also transcribed here, learned the song from a black guitar player named Howard Barnes, with whom he worked on a Tennessee River showboat during the years 1908–17. Young recalls that the words to the tune were written by Columbia A & R man Dan Hornsby.[13]

The earliest references to the song in print came in 1911 from folklorist Howard Odum, who obtained versions from black singers in Lafayette County, Mississippi, and Newton County, Georgia, in about 1909. Prior to this we have no knowledge of the piece.

NOTES

1. "Pea Vine Blues," Paramount 12877, recorded June 14, 1929; reissued on Yazoo L-1001: *Mississippi Blues, 1927–1936*. Ramon F. Adams, *The Language of the Railroader* (Norman: University of Oklahoma Press, 1977), p. 113, gives *peavine* as a term for a railroad.

2. Charley Patton, "Green River Blues," Paramount 12972 (master L-44-3), recorded Nov., 1929; reissued on Yazoo L-1020: *Founder of the Delta Blues*.

3. Charley Patton, "Moon Goin' Down," Paramount 13014 (master L-432-1), recorded ca. May 28, 1930; reissued on Yazoo L-1020: *Founder of the Delta Blues*.

4. Peetie Wheatstraw, "Doin' the Best I Can," Decca 7007 (master C-9443), recorded Sept. 11, 1934; reissued on Saydisc SDR191: *The Devil's Son-in-Law, Vol. 1*.

5. Milton Sparks, "Erie Train Blues," Bluebird B-6529 (RCA Victor master 91445), recorded July 28, 1935; reissued on Blues Classics BC-6: *Country Blues, Vol. 2*.

6. Mary Wheeler, *Steamboatin' Days* (Baton Rouge: Louisiana State University Press, 1944), p. 116.

7. Jazz Gillum, "Big Katy Adams," Bluebird B-8189, recorded May 17, 1939; reissued on RCA Victor LPV 548: *Native American Ballads*.

8. Wheeler, *Steamboatin' Days*, p. 19.

9. Ibid., p. 49.

10. Roy Acuff, "Steamboat Whistle Blues," Vocalion 03255 and associated labels, recorded Oct., 1936; reissued on Library of Congress LBC-6: *Songs of Migration And Immigration*.

11. Alvin F. Harlow, "Railroad Names and Nicknames," in B. A. Botkin and Alvin F. Harlow, *A Treasury of Railroad Folklore* (New York: Bonanza Books, 1953), pp. 500–505.

12. "Old English Ballads from Berea," *Berea Quarterly*, 4 (Nov., 1899), 16; reprinted from the *Springfield Republican*. The reporter's description of a one-horse Kentucky Central Railroad does not jibe with the information gleaned from Poor's *Manuals*. The Kentucky Central Association, organized in 1875, chartered the Kentucky Central Railroad Company and took possession of the former Covington and Lexington Railroad and the Maysville and Lexington Railroad in that year. The Livingston extension, completed in 1884, would probably have been the branch through Berea and Boone's Gap. The *Berea Quarterly* account suggests an older horse-powered rail route that Poor does not mention.

13. Alvin Young, Jess Young's nephew and a member of his band, was interviewed by Charles K. Wolfe in Whitwell, Tenn., on May 13, 1974. I am grateful to Wolfe for making this information available to me.

REFERENCES

A. "Kansas City Railroad Blues," by Andrew and Jim Baxter. Andrew Baxter, fiddle; Jim Baxter, vocal and guitar. Recorded Aug. 9, 1927 (Victor master 39785), in Charlotte, N.C. Released on Victor 20962. Reissued on Roots 326: *The East Coast States, Vol. 2*.

"Kansas City Railroad," by Riley Puckett. Vocal and guitar. Recorded Mar. 30, 1934 (Victor master 82711), in San Antonio, Tex. Released on Bluebird B-5471, Montgomery Ward M-7042.

"The Old K-C," by Young's Tennessee Band. Vocal, with guitar and fiddle accompaniment. Recorded ca. Apr. 18, 1929 (Columbia master W 148363), in Atlanta. Released on Columbia 15431-D on Aug. 23, 1929.

B. Asch, 102–3 (transcription of Memphis Jug Band recording)

Coffin & Cohen, 89–90 (from Odum, 361)

Odum, 287, 361–62

Odum & Johnson (1925), 221 (from Odum, 361)

White, N. I., 273

D. Four Aces and Leo Soileau—Decca 5262   "K.C. Railroad"

Fred Halliday (Lester McFarland pseudonym)—Oriole 1000   "K.C. Whistle"

Lester McFarland—Vocalion 5126 "Casey's Whistle"

Memphis Jug Band—Victor 38558; Folkways FA 2953 (FP 253): *Anthology of American Folk Music, Vol. 3*; Roots RL-337: *Memphis Jug Band, Vol. 2*   "K.C. Moan"

George Walburn and Emmett Hethcox— OKeh 45004   "K.C. Railroad Blues" (different tune)

E. Jim Kweskin and the Jug Band—

Vanguard VRS 9163; Vanguard VRS
9270/VSD 79270: *The Best of Jim Kweskin*
and the Jug Band
Maggie Valley Country Singers—Rural
Rhythm RR 134: *Maggie Valley
Singers*   "K.C. Whistle"
Don Reno and Red Smiley—King 816:
Another Day   "K.C. Railroad Blues"
Buck Ryan—Rural Rhythm RRBR 244:
Fiddling Buck Ryan   "K.C. Railroad
Blues"
Oliver Smith—Elektra EKL 316: *Oliver
Smith*   "K.C. Blow"
Mark Spoelstra—Folkways FG 3572: *Live at
the Club 47*
Dave van Ronk—Folkways FS 3818: *Dave
van Ronk Sings Ballads, Blues, and a
Spiritual*   "K.C. Moan"
—Mercury MG 20864/SR 60864: *Ragtime
Jug Stompers*   "K.C. Moan"
Chubby Wise—Stoneway STY 109:
Hoedown   "K.C. Railroad Blues"

Jess Young. Courtesy of Charles Wolfe.

Cannonball Blues/Whitehouse Blues

WHITE HOUSE BLUES

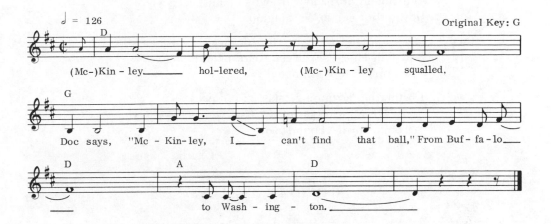

(Mc)Kinley hollered, (Mc)Kinley squalled,
Doc says, "McKinley, I can't find that ball,"
From Buffalo to Washington.

Roosevelt in the White House, he's doin' his best,
McKinley in the graveyard, he's takin' his rest,
He is gone, long long time.

Hush up, my little children, now don't you fret,
You'll draw a pension at your papa's death,
From Buffalo to Washington.

Roosevelt in the White House drinkin' out of a silver cup,
McKinley in the graveyard, he'll never wake up,
He is gone, long long time.

Ain't but one thing that grieves my mind,
That is to die and leave my poor wife behind,
I am gone, long long time.

Look-a-here, little children, don't you fret,
You'll draw a pension at your papa's death,
From Buffalo to Washington.

Standing at the station, just lookin' at the time,
See if I could run it by half past nine,
From Buffalo to Washington.

Came the train, she's just on time,
She run a thousand miles from eight o'clock to nine,
From Buffalo to Washington.

Yonder comes the train, she's comin' down the line,
Blowin' ever' station, "Mr. McKinley's a-dyin',"
It's hard times, hard times.

Look-a-here, you rascal, you see what you done,
You shot my husband with an Iver Johnston [*sic*] gun,
(It's) gettin' bad, to Washington.

[?Doc told] the horse, he's tore down his mane,
Said to that horse, "You gotta outrun this train,"
From Buffalo to Washington.

Doctor came a-running, takes off his specs,
Said, "Mr. McKinley, better pass in your checks,
You bound to die, bound to die."

Charlie Poole

CANNON BALL BLUES

Oh, listen to the train, coming down the line,
Trying to make up all of her lost time
From Buffalo to Washington.

You can wash my jumpers, starch my overhauls [*sic*],
Catch the train they call the Cannonball
From Buffalo to Washington.

My baby's left me, she even took my shoes,
Enough to give a man those doggone worried blues,
She's gone, she's solid gone.

Yonder comes the train, comin' down the track,
Carry me away but ain't gonna carry me back,
My honey babe, my blue-eyed babe.

I'm going up north, I'm going up north this fall,
If luck don't change, I won't be back at all,
My honey babe, I'm leaving you.

Carter Family

The memory of several very recent political assassinations fills the reconsideration of the assassination of President McKinley with mixed emotions: one longs to draw comparisons, but the wounds of the present make the old scars painful to contemplate. "Whitehouse Blues" deals directly with the assassination of 1901; "Cannonball Blues" is a nonnarrative blues that shares sufficient musical and lyrical characteristics with the former piece to require consideration of the two together.

Curiously, McKinley's death was in no small degree the fault of Charles Guiteau, a disappointed office-seeker who had assassinated President Garfield twenty years earlier. Garfield died as a result of the wounds because his doctors failed to decide on prompt surgery. McKinley's medical attendants, the errors of that earlier gruesome affair still fresh in their memories, opted for immediate surgery under conditions that were far from ideal.

McKinley was shot on September 6, 1901, at the Pan American Exposition in Buffalo, New York. The previous day, designated President's Day, he had given a major speech that was partly responsible for the breaking of all previous attendance records at the fair. On the sixth was to be a public reception, at which the president would shake hands with a long queue of admirers. Though there were some fifty guards, Secret Service agents, and detectives, no one took note of a young man standing in line with his hand bound up in a handkerchief. As the man, Leon Czolgosz, stepped up to the president, he fired two shots from his .32 caliber Iver Johnson pistol. He was immediately seized, pummeled, handcuffed, and hastily spirited away, lest he be lynched by the angry mob. Czolgosz was later examined and declared mentally sane; his crime was said to result from his anarchist persuasion, and he was electrocuted seven weeks later at Auburn, New York. Selig Adler, in an interesting examination of the medical aspects of McKinley's assassination and operation, cited evidence that Czolgosz had decided to murder McKinley before he became an anarchist, and three years earlier he had suffered severe mental depressions.[1]

An hour after he had been shot, McKinley underwent surgery. Dr. Matthew D. Mann, the presiding surgeon, found one of the two bullets and the track of the other into and out of the stomach, but he was unable to follow it any further. Following the then-accepted axiom that a bullet does little harm after it ceases to move, it was decided to sew the president back up and leave the bullet where it was. Mann had been handicapped not only by the president's substantial girth, but also by poor conditions. The operation had been performed in the rather makeshift emergency hospital at the fairgrounds, where lighting was inadequate and no proper surgical instruments were at hand.

For a few days it looked as though McKinley was in satisfactory condition, and the medical reports were frequently optimistic. Vice-President Roosevelt had come to Buffalo, but when it seemed McKinley would recover, he joined his family in the Adirondacks. On the afternoon of September 13, a week after the shooting, Roosevelt was climbing Mount Tahawus when a guide came into view on the trail below with news that the president had taken a distinct turn for the worse. Roosevelt was ten miles from the clubhouse, which was another thirty-five miles from the railroad station. For this occasion, the Adirondack Stage Company established relays of horses between the Tahawus clubhouse and North Creek. There a special train was waiting for the vice-president; but by the time he reached it, at dawn, after three changes of horses, and a wild drive along treacherous mountain roads, muddy from recent rains, news had already come that the President had died during the predawn hours of September 14.

Out of these facts, a folk narrative—or perhaps several—in the form of a blues ballad

PRESIDENT'S DAY

Pan-American Exposition

Thursday, **SEPTEMBER 5,** 1901.

EXCURSION RATES BY

New York Central and West Shore Railroads

For all who wish to go to Buffalo to welcome

PRESIDENT
McKinley,

*The*_____
PRESIDENT'S
CABINET,

The Justices of
the Supreme
Court of the
United States,
and Members
of the Diplo-
matic Corps.

The

Greatest

New

World's

Holiday.

A SPLENDID MILITARY PAGEANT
Including the U. S. Marine Band of 72 Pieces.

Imposing Ceremonies in the Stupendous
Stadium, including an address by the
President.

For Tickets, Time of Trains and all information, call on New York
Central or West Shore Ticket Agents.

WALTER S. RANDOLPH, Excursion Manager, Buffalo, N. Y.

GEORGE H. DANIELS, General Passenger Agent, NEW YORK.	*C. E. LAMBERT,* General Passenger Agent, NEW YORK.	*H. PARRY,* General Agent, BUFFALO, N. Y.

Form 2852.   25M.   8-24-1901.   The Matthews-Northrup Works, Buffalo and New York.   1452

Broadside: "President's Day, Pan-American Exposition." Collection of
the Chicago Historical Society.

was fashioned, probably shortly after the shooting, and almost certainly by black singers. This ballad, or group of ballads, variously titled "McKinley," "Czolgosz," or "Whitehouse Blues," achieved wide circulation by the 1920s. The blunt humor of such lines as "Mr. McKinley, you better pass in your checks / Bound to die, bound to die" stood in sharp contrast to the numerous elegaic songs and poems published by better-known names in the musical and literary establishments.

Neil Rosenberg has compiled a biblio-discography of the various printed and recorded versions of the ballad, tracing the influence of the key recorded versions.[2] Rosenberg's earliest evidence was a fascinating item in a biographical sketch of D. H. Lawrence. Writer Eleanor Farjeon, a good friend of Lawrence, recalled a Sunday evening in April, 1915, when he sang several songs, most of which were identified as Negro spirituals; but he also "set our brains jingling with an American ballad on the murder of President McKinley with words of brutal jocularity sung to an air of lilting sweetness."[3] A month later, Farjeon recalled in her autobiography, she exchanged songs with a member of the Shackleton South Pole Expedition: in return for "The Drunken Sailor," she taught him Lawrence's "Mr. McKinley." But evidently she could not recall all the words, for very shortly thereafter she asked Lawrence to write out "the six verses [which] were not so easy to remember as the tune, which, once heard, stuck like a leech."[4] Lawrence responded with the words in his next letter.

The degree to which Lawrence was taken with the McKinley ballad is also indicated by the recollection of Dr. Mary Laleeby Fisher. In 1915, when she was ten years old, Lawrence tutored her for a month. Later, she recalled, "The thing I most enjoyed about Lawrence's teaching was that he taught me some very good songs. I wish I could remember them all, but the two that stand out in my memory are the old traditional English song, 'Barbara Allen,' and a song from America about the assassination of President McKinley. Both of these he and I sang together again and again—I think I could reproduce them even now, so fond of them did I become."[5]

In his composite biography of Lawrence, Edward Nehls published one stanza of Lawrence's "McKinley."[6] As for the rest of his text, what I believe is at least part of it was published in 1924, with tune, in *The Week-End Book*. This was one of several songs and ballads declared to be, in the preface, all folksongs; but for this particular item no source was indicated. However, since one of the editors of this anthology was present that evening in April, 1915, when Lawrence sang the song, I assume that Lawrence was the source of the piece. Because it is the earliest published version, it is worth reproducing here. The melody of the first two lines is very similar to the usual tune, but the last half is significantly different.

MR. McKINLEY

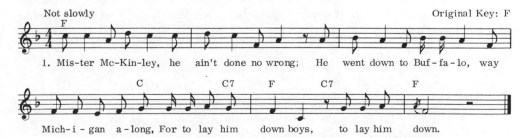

1. Mis-ter Mc-Kin-ley, he ain't done no wrong; He went down to Buf-fa-lo, way
Mich-i-gan a-long, For to lay him down boys, to lay him down.

> Mister McKinley, he ain't done no wrong;
> He went down to Buffalo, way Michigan along,
> For to lay him down boys, to lay him down.

> Mr. McKinley, he went there for fun,
> But Sholgosh he shot him with an Ivor-Johnson [*sic*] gun,
> For to lay him down boys, to lay him down.

> Mrs. McKinley, she hollered and she swore
> When they told her her good man wasn't coming home no more,
> For to lay him down boys, to lay him down.

> Sholgosh, they took him and put him in the electric chair,
> And shocked him so hard that they shocked off all his hair,
> For to lay him down boys, to lay him down.[7]

The version transcribed at the beginning of this discussion was the first commercial recording of the ballad, made by Charlie Poole and the North Carolina Ramblers in September, 1926, just two weeks after the twenty-fifth anniversary of the assassination. It is a mixture of factually correct details and blues-ballad commonplaces. For example, it is true that the doctor could not find the second ball (st. 1) and that McKinley was shot with an Iver Johnson gun (st. 10), though this last line has become in more recent versions ". . . and I've got your gun. . . . " Stanza 11, about the race between train and horse, is puzzling. It is not a commonplace; yet I have not found any historical basis for the vignette. The closest related fact I have seen was in a note sent to *Railroad Magazine*; the correspondent wrote that "a doctor specializing in police work was sent to Buffalo on a special train with a single coach. The train was so fast and swayed so much that he had to lie in the aisle on a mattress. . . ."[8] If we change the beginning of the first line from "Doctor on" to "Jumped on," then the verse makes good sense. Bill Monroe has changed "tore down his mane" to "throwed down the rein," which makes even better sense.[9]

Poole's version influenced many later ones; in particular, it was the first we know of that used the refrain "From Buffalo to Washington." In no other early versions does the city of Washington figure—as, historically, it should not. Other lines in Poole's version occur frequently in other blues ballads. For example,

> Looked old Brady right through the specs,
> He says, "There's no use in talking, Brady get your check"

is from a hillbilly version of the blues ballad "Duncan and Brady."[10] "You'll draw a pension at your papa's death" is familiar, of course, from Casey Jones ballads.

Perhaps most revealing is a comparison with the blues ballad "Delia." According to an informant of Chapman J. Milling, this ballad originated in about 1900 following the murder, in Georgia, of Delia Holmes. I quote here only the stanzas that correspond to verses of Charlie Poole's version:

> Delia, Delia, why didn't you run,
> See dat desparado had a forty fo' smokeless gun,
> Cryin' all I had done gone.

> Coonie went to Atlanta, drinkin' from a silver cup.
> Po' li'l' Delia's in the cemetary, I hope to never wake up.
> Cryin' all I had done gone.[11]

Milling's informant dates the event to within a year or so of the McKinley assassination, so there could have been borrowing from one ballad to the other, or borrowing in each case from stock commonplaces.

Riley Puckett's "McKinley," another important early recorded version, preserves some historical details not found in Poole's version. For example:

> Doctor, doctor, do all you can.
> Man shot my husband with a handkerchief over his hand,
> In Buffalo, in Buffalo.

> Jailer told Czolgosz, "What you doin' here,
> Took and shot McKinley, gonna take the electric chair,
> In Buffalo, in Buffalo."[12]

The detail about the handkerchief is correct, although Mrs. McKinley was not present during the shooting or the operation. Czolgocz did get the electric chair, although not in Buffalo. Puckett's version also has its share of blues-ballad commonplaces. In sum, though many stanzas differ from Poole's version, the mood and style are so much the same that they could have both been drawn from one, more elaborate ballad.

Even though trains are sometimes mentioned in "Whitehouse Blues," there would be insufficient cause for inclusion in this book were it not that an account of the McKinley ballads is necessary to understand the version of "Cannonball Blues" transcribed here. It was recorded by the Carter Family in 1935; they had recorded the song previously (1930), but this second recording was chosen for transcription because it contains an additional verse. The Carters' song is a traditional blues, though the tune is very similar to "Whitehouse Blues." Furthermore, the refrain, "From Buffalo to Washington," does not appear in other blues pieces related to "Cannonball Blues," and therefore may well have been borrowed from Charlie Poole's influential and popular recording.

There are several pre-1920 references to "cannonball" verses. Perhaps the earliest recovery is in the long text obtained by W. Prescott Webb prior to 1915, discussed in the introduction to this chapter. One couplet was:

> Give me my shoes and my Carhart overalls,
> Let me step over yonder and blind the Cannon Ball.[13]

Closer in language to the Carters' verse is a 1915 fragment reported from Alabama and published by Newman I. White:

> Starch my jumper and patch my overalls,
> So if I miss de local I ken ketch de cannon ball.[14]

A correspondent wrote Robert W. Gordon that he heard the following sung by miners in Kentucky in 1909–10:

> Oh de train I rides, babe, it's called the Cannon Ball,
> Oh de train I rides, babe, it's called the Cannon Ball,
> Carries fourteen coaches, got no blinds at all.[15]

In 1927, Atlanta bluesman Peg Leg Howell recorded "Hobo Blues," which opened with this stanza:

> [?Set on] my jumpers, iron my overalls,
> I'm gonna ride that train you call the cannonball.[16]

Howell's song was set to the tune of "Cow Cow's Blues," which is discussed in connection with "That Lonesome Train Took My Baby Away"—in which the same "wash my jumpers" verses appear. Pete Brown's 1942 recording "The Cannon Ball," also to the tune of "Cow Cow's Blues," likewise has a "starched his jumpers" verse, as well as an opening line that relates the song to "That Lonesome Train Took My Baby Away."[17]

The tune to the "Cannonball Blues"/"Whitehouse Blues" songs is closely related to another folksong from the turn of the century: "The Battleship of Maine," a humorous account of the tribulations of a soldier in the Spanish-American War, which also mentions McKinley.[18]

Both Poole's "Whitehouse Blues" and the Carters' "Cannon Ball Blues" were highly influential on later tradition. Ernest Stoneman learned the song from Poole, as did Charlie Poole, Jr.'s group, the Swing Billies. Bill Monroe learned "Whitehouse Blues" from an old disc belonging to his brother Charlie; this almost certainly would have been the Poole recording.[19] From Monroe the song passed through the hands of many bluegrass musicians. The Carter Family's version was transcribed in Botkin and Harlow's *Treasury of Railroad Folklore*; their recording was copied by both city (Dian James and the Greenbriar Boys, Bill Clifton) and country (Edith Roberts, Flatt and Scruggs) singers. In 1953, the Carter Sisters and Mother Maybelle recorded a derivative version under the title "He's Solid Gone," which was later covered by other artists (Tom Rush, Kings Men Five). Riley Puckett's recording, the third most influential, was the probable source of the 1938 version by Homer Brierhopper and the certain source of the recording by the Greenbriar Boys.

The North Carolina Ramblers and, later, the Carter Family, though they were worlds apart in the universe of hillbilly music, were both immensely popular and influential. The Ramblers' careers are discussed elsewhere in this book (see the discussion of "Milwaukee Blues," "The Virginian Strike of '23," and "Bill Mason"). The original Carter Family comprised Alvin Pleasant Carter, his wife, Sara, and Sara's cousin Maybelle, who married A.P.'s brother. A.P. and Maybelle Addington were born in Scott County, in the southwestern tip of Virginia, in 1891 and 1909, respectively; Sara was born in neighboring Wise County in 1898. Both Sara and Maybelle began playing banjo, guitar, and autoharp when they were very young, while A.P. played both guitar and fiddle. Soon after A.P. and Sara were married, in 1915, they began singing together. In 1926, after Maybelle married A.P.'s brother, the three began singing and playing for friends and neighbors at various local functions. In July, 1927, the trio saw an article in a local newspaper announcing that Ralph Peer of the Victor Talking Machine Company would be in Bristol, on the Tennessee-Virginia border, auditioning new talent. On the last day of the month the family loaded up the car for the twenty-five-mile trip to Bristol, and made their first recordings on the following day. The Carters were an instant success, and in the years that followed they enjoyed a series of recording sessions (totaling more than 250 songs on record between 1927 and 1941), personal appearances, and radio shows. They epitomized the wholesome and the homely in rural music—in spite of the fact that their own personal relationships were often strained and troubled; Sara and A.P. separated in 1932, though they continued to get together for professional purposes. After 1941 the trio did not record again. In the 1950s A.P. ventured a comeback: he, Sara, and their two children, Janette and Joe, recorded as the A.P. Carter Family for the small Acme company. Maybelle, meanwhile, recorded often during the 1960s, either alone or with her daughters, Helen, June, and Anita, as the Carter Sisters and Mother Maybelle.

After June Carter's marriage to Johnny Cash, the Carters became part of the Johnny Cash entourage.

The impact of the original Carter Family on both rural country music and the urban folksong revival can be measured by the number of songs that have been picked up from their repertoire, and also by the influence of Mother Maybelle's guitar picking style.

The Carters recalled learning "Cannon Ball Blues" from Leslie Riddles, a black musician and friend who accompanied A.P. on several of his trips into the mountains to collect songs to be recorded later. There is one problem with the attribution, however: while Riddles recalls that he first met the Carters in 1934, they recorded their version of "Cannonball Blues" first in 1930.[20]

NOTES

1. Selig Adler, "The Operation on President McKinley," *Scientific American*, 208 (Mar., 1963), 118–30. A somewhat different account of Czolgosz's premeditations is given in Margaret Leech, *In the Days of McKinley* (New York: Harper and Brothers, 1959), p. 593. Here it is written that Czolgosz did not decide to murder McKinley until after he had come to Buffalo to see the fair and read that the president would be attending.

2. Neil V. Rosenberg, "'Whitehouse Blues'—'McKinley'—'Cannonball Blues': A Biblio-discography," *JEMFN*, 4 (June, 1968), 45–58.

3. Eleanor Farjeon, *Edward Thomas: The Last Four Years* (London: Oxford University Press, 1958), p. 133; also quoted in Edward Nehls, ed., *D. H. Lawrence*, vol. 1., *1885-1919* (Madison: University of Wisconsin Press, 1957), p. 294.

4. Farjeon, *Edward Thomas*, p. 140.

5. Nehls, *D. H. Lawrence*, p. 304.

6. Ibid., p. 575, n. 120.

7. Vera Mendel, Frances Meynell, and John Goss, *The Week-End Book* (London: Nonesuch Press, 1924), p. 187. The page number differs in later editions.

8. Richard M. Hanschke, RRM, 95 (Apr., 1974), 4.

9. Bill Monroe, "Whitehouse Blues," Decca 29141, recorded July 1, 1953.

10. Wilmer Watts and his Lonely Eagles, "Been on the Job Too Long," Paramount 3210.

11. Chapman J. Milling, "Delia Holmes—A Neglected Negro Ballad," *SFQ*, 1 (Dec., 1937), 3–8, version by Will Winn.

12. Riley Puckett, "McKinley," Columbia 15448-D, recorded Apr. 11, 1929.

13. W. Prescott Webb, "Notes on Folk-Lore of Texas," *JAF*, 28 (July-Sept., 1915), 293.

14. Newman I. White, *American Negro Folk-Songs* (1928; rpt., Hatboro, Pa.: Folklore Associates, 1965), p. 298. Reported from Auburn, Ala., 1915–16, MS of A. L. Holloway, as heard in Monroe Co., Ala.

15. C. W. Dorris, Gordon MS 1233.

16. Peg Leg Howell and his Gang, "Hobo Blues," Columbia 14270-D, recorded Nov. 1, 1927.

17. Pete Brown and his Band, vocal by Nora Lee King, "The Cannon Ball," recorded Feb. 9, 1942 (Decca master 70302-A); released on Decca 8625, reissued on Rosetta Records PR 1301.

18. For a representative text see *New Lost City Ramblers Songbook*, edited by John Cohen and Mike Seeger (New York: Oak Publications, 1964), p. 116.

19. Quoted by Ralph Rinzler in his liner notes to Decca DL 4780: *The High Lonesome Sound*.

20. Sara Carter told Ed Kahn that Riddles was the source of the song (interview, Angels Camp, Calif., June 3, 1961). Hoping to clear up the problem of dates, Christopher (Kip) Lornell interviewed Riddles to learn his side of the story (Rochester, N.Y., in ca. June, 1975). Unfortunately, Riddles could not recall when he first met the Carters, nor could he remember the song "Cannonball Blues" itself. He first stated that he had learned it from his uncle; later in the interview he elaborated that he had learned the tune from his uncle but put the words to it himself. He thought he

probably played it in the "Sebastopol" tuning (open D). Riddles's own association with the Carters was the subject of Kip Lornell, "I Used to Go Along and Help," in *The Carter Family*, edited by John Atkins, Old Time Music Booklet No. 1 (London: Old Time Music, 1973), pp. 34–35.

REFERENCES

A. "White House Blues," by Charlie Poole with the North Carolina Ramblers. Poole, vocal and banjo; Posey Rorer, fiddle; Roy Harvey, guitar. Recorded Sept. 20, 1926 (Columbia master W 142658), in New York City. Released on Columbia 15099-D on Oct. 20, 1926. Reissued on Folkways FA 2951 (FP 251): *Anthology of American Folk Music, Vol. 1*; County 505: *Charlie Poole and the North Carolina Ramblers*; and Columbia CS 9660: *Ballads and Breakdowns of the Golden Era*. First recording of a McKinley ballad.

"White House Blues," by Bill Monroe and his Blue Grass Boys. Monroe, vocal and mandolin; Charlie Cline, fiddle; Rudy Lyle, banjo; Jimmy Martin, guitar; Ernie Newton, bass. Recorded July 1, 1953 (Decca master 85736), in Nashville. Released on Decca 29141 (10″ 78 rpm and 7″ 45 rpm). Reissued on Decca DL 4780: *The High Lonesome Sound*.

"McKinley," by Riley Puckett. Vocal and guitar. Recorded Apr. 11, 1929 (Columbia master 148243), in Atlanta. Released on Columbia 15448-D on Oct. 4, 1929.

"The Cannon Ball," by the Carter Family. A. P. Carter, vocal; Maybelle and Sara Carter, guitars. Recorded on May 24, 1930 (Victor master BVE 59979-1), in Memphis, Tenn. Released on Victor V-40317. Reissued on Bluebird B-6020; Montgomery Ward M-4742; Twin (India) FT 1962; RCX (England) 7110 (7″ 45 rpm EP): *The Original and Great Carter Family, Vol. 5*. Transcribed in B.A. Botkin and Alvin Harlow, *A Treasury of Railroad Folklore* (New York: Bonanza Books, 1953), p. 436.

"Cannon Ball Blues," by the Carter Family. A.P., Maybelle, and Sara Carter, vocal trio; Sara and Maybelle, guitars. Recorded May 10, 1935 (American Record Corp. master 17521–2), in New York City. Released on Banner, Perfect,

Oriole, Romeo, and Melotone 7–05–55, Conqueror 8816. Reissued on Harmony HL 7422: *Country Sounds of the Original Carter Family*. Transcribed in *New Lost City Ramblers Songbook*, edited by John Cohen and Mike Seeger (New York: Oak Publications, 1964), pp. 132–33.

"Mr. McKinley," in Vera Mendel, Frances Meynell, and John Goss, *The Week-End Book* (London: Nonesuch Press, 1924), p. 187. Earliest publication of the "Whitehouse Blues" subtype of this ballad. Probably based on the version sung in 1915 by D. H. Lawrence.

B. "WHITEHOUSE BLUES" VARIANTS:

Brown IV, 355   "Zolgotz"
Campbell & Holstein, 17
Davis, A. K., 263 (titles and first lines only: "Solgot Walk Up to McKinley" and "McKinley, or Oh! Roosevelt in His White House")
Duncan, 253–54   "Assassination of McKinley"
Flatt & Scruggs Picture Album Songbook, 7
Gordon, *Adventure*, Jan. 1, 1927, p. 204   "President McKinley"
Leach & Beck, 276   "McKinley"
Lomax & Lomax (1941), 256–58   "The White House Blues" (transcription of LC AFS 1523 A1)
Nehls, 294

"CANNONBALL BLUES" VARIANTS:

Silverman (1975) II, 49
Stroud, 8
Webb (1915), 293
White, N. I., 298

C. "WHITEHOUSE BLUES" VARIANTS:

GORDON COLLECTION (GA.):

518—Uncle Ben (n.d.)   "Delia"
519—L. Saunders (n.d.)   "Delia"

GORDON MSS:

778—Jackson Turner (Sept. 17, 1924) (untitled; heard in eastern Kentucky, ca. 1905)

1641—Frank L. Middleton (Mar. 13, 1926) (printed in *Adventure*; see B above)

2736—L. J. Fisher (winter, 1926–27) "Mister McKinley" (copied from print [*Week-End Book*])

"CANNONBALL BLUES" VARIANTS:

GORDON MSS:

1233—C. W. Dorris (Oct. 12, 1925) "Oh de train I rides, babe, it's called the cannon ball"

D. "WHITEHOUSE BLUES" and related pieces:

Homer Brierhopper—Decca 5588 "Mr. McKinley"

Bill Monroe and his Blue Grass Boys —Decca 29141, Decca 9-29141 (45 rpm), Brunswick (England) OE 9160 (EP); Decca DL 4780: *The High Lonesome Sound*   "White House Blues"

Sonny Osborne—Big 4 Hits 24 (78 and 45 rpm); Deresco 19 and Gateway LP 19: *Five-String Hi-Fi*; Palace 756: *Hank Hill and Stanley Alpine*; Gateway LP 31338: *The Early Recordings of Sonny Osborne, 1952–53, Vol. 2*   "White House Blues"

Pine Ridge Boys—Bluebird B-8626 "White House Blues"

Don Reno, Red Smiley, and the Tennessee Cutups—King 1360 (78 and 45 rpm); King LP 579: *Ballads and Instrumentals*   "Tally Ho" (derivative piece)

Ernest V. Stoneman—OKeh 45125 "The Road to Washington"

Ernest Stoneman and his Dixie Mountaineers—Edison 52299, Edison 5545 (cylinder); Historical HLP 8004: *Ernest Stoneman and His Dixie Mountaineers*   "Unlucky Road to Washington"

Swing Billies—Bluebird B-7121 "Buffalo to Washington"

"CANNONBALL BLUES" and related pieces:

Peg Leg Howell and his Gang—Columbia

14270-D; Swedish Blues Society EP-3 (EP)   "Hobo Blues" (related)

Charley McCoy—OKeh 8863; RBF RF-14: *Blues Roots/Mississippi*   "That Lonesome Train Took My Baby Away" (related)

Mooch Richardson—OKeh 8554; Mamlish S-3803: *Low Down Memphis Barrelhouse Blues*   "T and T Blues" (related)

E. "WHITEHOUSE BLUES" and related pieces:

Vassar Clements—Flying Fish FF 038: *The Bluegrass Session*

Bill Clifton and Hedy West—Folk Variety (West Germany) FV-12008: *Getting Folk out of the Country*

Howard DaSilva—Monitor MP 595: *Politics and Poker*   "White House Blues"

Raymond Fairchild and group—Rural Rhythm RR-146: *King of the Smokey Mountain Five String Banjo Players*   "White House Blues"

Lester Flatt, Earl Scruggs, and the Foggy Mountain Boys—Columbia CL 1830/CS 8630: *Folk Songs of Our Land*; Harmony HS 11401: *Foggy Mountain Chimes*   "McKinley's Gone"

Greenbriar Boys—Vanguard VRS 9159/ VSD 79159: *Ragged but Right* "McKinley"

Bascom Lamar Lunsford—Library of Congress Archive of Folk Song L29: *Songs and Ballads of American History and of the Assassination of Presidents* "Zolgotz" (from LC AFS 9513 A3)

Wade Mainer—Old Homestead OHTRS 4000: *From the Maple on the Hill* "McKinley"

Charlie Monroe—County 538: *Charlie Monroe on the Noonday Jamboree —1944*   "Whitehouse Blues"

Clyde Moody—Wango 102: *"The Carolina Woodchopper"—Clyde Moody Sings from the Past*   "White House Blues (Pts. 1 and 2)"

Glen Neaves and the Grayson County Boys—Kanawha 302 (Folk Promotions 12958): *28th Annual Galax Old Fiddlers Convention*   "Whitehouse Blues"

New Deal String Band—Sire SES 97024: *Bluegrass*   "White House Blues"

New Lost City Ramblers—Folkways FH 5264: *Songs of the Depression*; Aravel AN 1005: *John Cohen, Tom Paley and Mike Seeger Sing Songs of the New Lost City Ramblers*   "White House Blues" (parody)

John Renbourn—Reprise MS 2082: *Faro Annie*   "Whitehouse Blues"

Don Reno and Bill Harrell—Rural Rhythm RR-DR-171: *Don Reno & Bill Harrell with the Tennessee Cutups* "White House Blues"

Pete Rowan and others—Warner Brothers BS 2787: *Muleskinner*   "Whitehouse Blues"

Kilby Snow—Union Grove SS-3: *More Goodies from the Hills*   "White House Blues"

Earl Taylor and the Stoney Mountain Boys—Folkways FA 2318: *Mountain Music Bluegrass Style*   "White House Blues"

Virginia Mountain Boys—Folkways FA 3833   "White House Blues"

Doc Watson—Vanguard VSD 45/46: *The Essential Doc Watson*   "Whitehouse Blues"

Wilson Brothers, Larry and Joanna —MRC 1093: *Stand Tall in Bluegrass*

"CANNONBALL BLUES" and related pieces:

Eddie Boyd—GNP/Crescendo 10020: *The Legacy of the Blues, Vol. 10*; GNP/Crescendo X10010: *The Legacy of the Blues Sampler*

Mother Maybelle Carter—Briar 101: *Mother Maybelle*; Kapp KL 1413/KS 3413: *Mother Maybelle: Queen of the Autoharp*   "He's Solid Gone"

Bill Clifton and the Dixie Mountain Boys—Starday 561 (45 rpm); Starday SLP 146: *Carter Family Memorial Album*; Starday SLP 170: *Railroad Special*; Nashville NLP 2019 "Cannon Ball Blues"

Lester Flatt, Earl Scruggs, and the Foggy Mountain Boys—Columbia CL 2134/CS 8934: *Flatt & Scruggs Recorded Live at Vanderbilt University*   "Cannonball Blues"

Woody Guthrie—Verve-Folkways FV 9007/FVS 9007: *Bed on the Floor* "Baltimore to Washington": Folkways FT 1010/FTS 31010: *Poor Boy*   "Baltimore to Washington" (parody)

—Elektra EKL 271: *Library of Congress Recordings*   "Dirty Overalls" (derivative piece)

—Vanguard VSD 35/36: *The Greatest Songs of Woody Guthrie*   "Dirty Overalls" (derivative piece)

Wayne Henderson—Union Grove SS-6: *48th Union Grove Fiddlers Convention*   "Cannonball Blues"

Wayne Henderson and Ray Cline —Heritage 9: *Flat-top Guitar Pickin'*   "Cannonball Blues"

Cisco Houston—Vanguard VRS 9107: *I Ain't Got No Home*; Vanguard SRV 3006   "Hobo Blues" (derivative piece)

Dian James and the Greenbriar Boys —Elektra EKL 233/EKS 7233: *Dian and the Greenbriar Boys*   "Cannon Ball Blues"

Kings Men Five—Cuca K-1130: *The King's Men Five*   "Solid Gone"

Lucas Harmon Brothers Show—L & H 0012: *Lucas Harmon Brothers Show*

Bruce "Utah" Phillips—Philo 1004: *Good Though*   "Cannonball Blues"'

Piney Ridge Boys—King Bluegrass 553 *Flat Land Bluegrass*

Edith Roberts—Rural Rhythm RR-ER-178: *Carter Family Songs* "Cannonball Blues"

Tom Rush—Elektra EKL 288/EKS 7288: *Tom Rush*   "Solid Gone"

Seldom Scene—Rebel SLP 1511: *The Seldom Scene*   "Cannonball"

Arthur Smith—CMH 1776: *200 Years of American Heritage in Song* "Cannonball Blues"

Kilby Snow—Asch AH 3902: *Country Songs and Tunes with Autoharp* "The Cannonball"

Larry Sparks—Pine Tree PTSLP 500: *Ramblin' Guitar*   "Cannon Ball Blues"

—King Bluegrass KB 531: *Sparklin' Bluegrass*   "Cannonball Blues"

Rual Yarbrough—Old Homestead 90066:
Just Me "Cannonball"

F. "WHITEHOUSE BLUES" and related pieces:

LC AFS:

Maynard Britton—AFS 1523 A1
"White House Blues"
Luther Bryant—AFS 13718 B33

Warde H. Ford—AFS 4198 B3
"Buffalo, Buffalo"
Bascom Lamar Lunsford—AFS 1819 B
"Zolgotz"
—AFS 9513 A3 "Zolgotz"
Silas Pendleton—AFS 9059 A3 & 9060
A1 "McKinley"
Wade Ward—AFS 15055 A6

Bill Monroe (*left*). Courtesy of Dan Seeger and the John Edwards Memorial Foundation, UCLA.

The Train That Carried My Girl from Town

TRAIN THAT CARRIED THE GIRL FROM TOWN

♩ = 120

Original Key: E♭

Ten-nes - see   raised, _   Al - a - bam - a   bound, _   If my

girl leaves   me, ___   gon - na   move   from ___   town.

Chorus

Hey,   Lord, hate that   train car - ried my   girl from   town.

Alternate Chorus

Hey,   that   train ___   done carried my   girl   from

town,   Hey, ___   hey __ hey __   hey.

*Chords supplied by the music editor; on the recording, Hutchison maintains a D chord throughout or plays single notes without chords.

** ♩ = ♩

***Falsetto. The alternate chorus is transcribed from Doc Watson's singing on Vanguard VSD–79276: *Good Deal! Doc Watson in Nashville* (the original key is D).

Tennessee raised, Alabama bound,
If my girl leaves me, gonna move from town.
    Hey, Lord, hate that train carried my girl from town.

Hate that train carried my girl from town,
If I knowed her number, sure flag her down.
    Chorus:

Where was you when the train left town?
Standin' on the corner, head a-hangin' down.
    Chorus:

Wish to the Lord train would wreck,
Kill the engineer, break the fireman's neck.
    Chorus:

Hello, central, give me six-o-nine,
Want to talk to that brown of mine.
    Chorus:

Breakfast on the table, coffee's getting cold,
Some old rounder stole my jelly roll.
   Chorus:

Ashes to ashes, dust to dust,
Show me that woman (a) man can trust.
   Chorus:

Want no grease mixed in my rice,
Girl of mine took my appetite.
   Chorus:

There goes my girl, somebody call her back,
She's got her hand in my money sack.
   Chorus:

Frank Hutchison

There is no question that this beautiful bluesy song was preserved only through the recordings of Frank Hutchison, one of the best white blues guitarists of the 1920s. Only recently has information about this West Virginia musician come to light through interviews with relatives and former musical associates. Hutchison was born in Raleigh County in 1897 but spent most of his life in Logan County. As a very young boy he listened to a black railroad worker who played blues on a guitar. In his twenties he worked at various jobs, earning his living principally as a musician for a while. He made records between 1926 and 1929. For a brief period in the 1930s he was an entertainer on Ohio River steamboats, but during the Depression gave up music as a profession and ran a grocery store. He died in 1945 of cancer.[1]

According to his one-time fiddle-playing partner, Sherman Lawson, Hutchison learned to play bottleneck-style guitar from a black musician named Bill Hunt, who came into that part of West Virginia prior to 1910 looking for work entertaining the miners in the state's productive coal mines. Lawson recalled that among the several songs Hutchison learned from Hunt was "Train That Carried the Girl from Town." This, together with another Hunt song, "Worried Blues," were Hutchison's debut recordings when he went to New York in September, 1926, for the General Phonograph Corporation, owners of the OKeh record label. Although the two numbers were recorded by an inferior electrical process, they were evidently successful enough that OKeh called Hutchison back to New York in January, 1927, for another session, at which time he recorded "C & O Excursion Train," "Lightning Express," and other pieces. In November, 1926, OKeh had switched from the acoustical to the newer electrical recording process, and at Hutchison's third recording session he re-recorded "Worried Blues" and "Train That Carried the Girl from Town." He continued to make records, his last session being in September of 1929. In addition to the items already mentioned, his repertoire included such other railroad songs as "Railroad Bill," "Cannon Ball Blues," "Hell Bound Train," and "K. C. Blues." In recent years Hutchison's records have been highly prized by old-time music collectors, partly because he was one of the most exciting white blues musicians of the period to record.

In 1937, Hutchison's "Train That Carried the Girl from Town" was copied by Wade Mainer and Zeke Morris, two popular North Carolina musicians. Mainer and his associates were keen listeners to hillbilly discs, from which they learned many songs. Doc Watson was another of many musicians who were taken with the piece, and he has performed it frequently at concerts in the past decade.

In spite of its rather bluesy feel, "Train That Carried the Girl from Town" is not a blues by the usual definitions of that term: each three-line unit consists of a rhymed couplet and a chorus, rather than the AAB form characteristic of blues songs. One wonders to what extent Hutchison may have modified the piece as he learned it from Hunt. Musically, the tune is quite similar to the widely known "John Henry" tune. In both theme and structure the piece resembles bluesman Charlie McCoy's 1930 recording "That Lonesome Train Took My Baby Away," which comes next in this chapter.

The fourth couplet of Hutchison's song is similar to one stanza of Ed Bell's 1927 Paramount recording "Mean Conductor Blues":

> I pray to Lord that Southern train would wreck,
> I pray to Lord that Southern train would wreck,
> Till it kill that fireman, break that engineer's neck.[2]

The tune, however, is quite different. A much older occurrence of the same stanza is in the blues piece John and Alan Lomax published in 1934 under the title "Dink's Blues," which they said was sung by a levee-camp woman "twenty-five years ago":

> I wish to God eas'-boun' train would wreck,
> Kill de engineer, break de fireman's neck.[3]

The third couplet brings to mind such black folksong commonplaces as:

> Oh where was you when de old Titanic went down?
> I wus on de back of er mule singing "Alabama bound."[4]

And, of course, the fifth couplet is a variant of the lines from W. C. Handy's famous "Hesitating Blues":

> Hello, Central, what's the matter with the line,
> I want to talk to that high brown of mine.[5]

These related occurrences in other songs offer assurance that the composer of "Train That Carried the Girl from Town," perhaps Hutchison's acquaintance Bill Hunt, was drawing on traditional verses for his own song. One other recording is sufficiently similar that it can be considered a variant of the same text. Titled "I Wish the Train Would Wreck," it is sung in standard twelve-bar, AAB blues format. The lyrics are given here for comparison:

> When my girl leaves me, I'm gonna flag her down,
> When my girl leaves me, I'm gonna flag her down;
> I done got her number, Lord Lord, Alabama bound.
>
> I was drunk as a badger when the train left town,
> I was drunk as a badger when the train left town,
> Standing on the corner with my head hung down.
>
> I wish to the Lord the train would wreck,
> I wish to the Lord the train would wreck,
> Kill the engineer and break the fireman's neck.

Hello, central, give me six-o-nine,
Hello, central, give me six-o-nine;
I want to talk to that lovin' gal of mine.

Ashes to ashes and dust to dust,
Ashes to ashes and dust to dust;
Show me a woman, Lord Lord, that a poor man can trust.

Breakfast on the table, coffee's gettin' cold,
Breakfast on the table, coffee's gettin' cold;
Some old rounder done stole my jelly roll.[6]

The version of "Train That Carried the Girl from Town" transcribed in this book is taken from Hutchison's first, acoustical recording of the song. The later, electrical version is almost the same, except for the change in order of couplets 7, 8, and 9.

NOTES

1. The best account of Huchison's life is given by Mark Wilson in liner notes to Rounder 1007: *The Train That Carried My Girl from Town*. See also Tony Russell, "Frank Hutchison, the Pride of West Virginia," *Old Time Music*, No. 1 (Summer, 1971), pp. 4–7; and "Hutch—Sherman Lawson Interview," based on an interview by Mike Seeger as transcribed by Tony Russell, *Old Time Music*, No. 11 (Winter, 1973), pp. 7–8.

2. Ed Bell, "Mean Conductor Blues," recorded ca. Sept., 1927 (Paramount master 4820); released on Paramount 12546; reissued on Yazoo L-1006: *Alabama Blues*. The entire song is transcribed in Jeff Titon, *Early Downhome Blues* (Urbana: University of Illinois Press, 1977), p. 101.

3. John A. Lomax and Alan Lomax, *American Ballads and Folk Songs* (New York: Macmillan, 1934), p. 193.

4. Newman I. White, *American Negro Folk-Songs* (1928; rpt., Hatboro, Pa.: Folklore Associates, 1965), p. 348; cf. Dorothy Scarborough, *On the Trail of Negro Folk-Songs*, (1925; rpt., Hatboro, Pa.: Folklore Associates, 1963), pp. 214–15.

5. W. C. Handy, "The Hesitating Blues" (1915). See Handy, *Blues: An Anthology* (New York: Albert and Charles Boni, 1926), pp. 94–97.

6. Maynard Britton, "I Wish the Train Would Wreck," recorded Feb. 28, 1931 (Starr master 17512A), in Richmond, Ind.; released on Champion 16543, Champion 45051. Britton's tune bears no resemblance to Hutchison's; this is the only justification I have for assuming that Hutchison's recording was not the immediate source of his piece.

REFERENCES

A. "Train That Carried the Girl from Town," by Frank Hutchison. Recorded Sept. 28, 1926 (General Phonograph Corp. master 80144-A), in New York City. Released on OKeh 45064. Re-recorded by the OKeh Phonograph Corp. on Apr. 19, 1927 (master 80783-B), in Saint Louis, Mo. Released on OKeh 45114. On both: Hutchison, vocal and guitar. The 1927 recording was reissued on Rounder 1007: *The Train That Carried My Girl from Town*.

B. Bush (1970), 26–27
Sing Out!, 24 (Nov.-Dec., 1975), 28 (transcription from Hutchison recording)

D. Maynard Britton—Champion 16543, Champion 45051   "I Wish the Train Would Wreck"
Frank Hutchison—OKeh 45452, Velvetone 2366-V, Clarion 5300-C (last two as by Billy Adams)   "K.C.

Blues" (closely related instrumental tune)

Wade Mainer and Zeke Morris—Bluebird B-6890, Montgomery Ward M-7129 "Train Carry My Girl Back Home"

E. Bluegrass Alliance—American Heritage AH 10-30S: *Newgrass*   "Where Were You"

Lester Flatt, Earl Scruggs, and the Foggy Mountain Boys—Columbia CL 2255/ CS 9055: *Fabulous Sound of Flatt and Scruggs*

Roscoe Holcomb—Folkways FA 2374: *Close to Home*

J. E. Mainer—Rural Rhythm RRJE-222: *Vol. 6—Fiddling with His Girl Susan*

"Where Were You When the Train Left Town"

Mike Seeger and Ry Cooder—Mercury SRM-1-685: *The Second Annual Farewell Reunion*

Fields Ward—Rounder 0036: *Bury Me Not on the Prairie*

Doc Watson—Folkways FA 2366 and FTS 31021: *The Watson Family*

—Vanguard VRS 9147/79147: *Old Time Music at Newport*

—Vanguard VSD 45/46: *The Essential Doc Watson*

—Vanguard VSD 79276: *Good Deal*

Doc and Merle Watson—Poppy PP-LA210-G: *Two Days in November*

That Lonesome Train Took My Baby Away

THAT LONESOME TRAIN TOOK MY BABY AWAY

Woke up this morning, found somethin' wrong,
My lovin' babe had caught that train and gone.
Now, won't you starch my jumper, iron my overhauls [*sic*],
I'm gonna ride that train they call the *Cannonball*.

Mister depot agent, close your depot down,
The woman I'm lovin', she's fixin' to blow this town.
Now, that mean old fireman, that cruel old engineer,
Gonna take my baby and leave me lonesome here.

It ain't no telling what that train won't do,
It'll take your baby and run right over you.
Now, that engineer man, ought to be shamed o' himself,
Take women from their husbands, babies from their mothers' breast.

I walked down the track when the stars refused to shine,
Looked like every minute I was goin' to lose my mind.
Now, my knees was weak, my footsteps was all I heard,
Looked like every minute I was steppin' in another world.

Mister depot agent, close your depot down,
The girl I'm loving, she's fixing to blow this town.
Now, that mean old fireman, cruel old engineer,
Gonna take my baby and leave me lonesome here.

Charlie McCoy

For the tune to his composition "That Lonesome Train Took My Baby Away," Charlie McCoy used one of the best-known piano blues-rags, "Cow Cow's Blues." Charles "Cow Cow" Davenport, born in Anniston, Alabama, in 1894, was sent by his family to a theological college to train for the ministry, but was expelled for playing the blues.[1] He made several recordings of his piano composition; the earliest disc released was with singer Dora Carr for the OKeh label in October, 1925 (a May, 1925, recording for the Starr Piano Company was never released). The lines of McCoy's first stanza all appear in Dora Carr's vocal. The tune was recorded by numerous pianists later under a variety of titles: by Louise Johnson as "On the Wall" (Paramount 13008, 1930); by Cripple Clarence Lofton as "Streamline Train" (SA 12003, 1939); and by Meade Lux Lewis as "Riff Boogie" (Atlantic SD 7227, 1951), to name a few.

Charlie McCoy was born near Jackson, Mississippi, in 1909. Together with his brother Joe and the Chatmon family, he recorded a variety of raggy and hokum blues in several band combinations. The same day he recorded "That Lonesome Train Took My Baby Away," he also waxed, with a group called the Mississippi Mud Steppers, an instrumental version of the tune titled "Jackson Stomp." On both pieces he was backed by members of the Chatmon family.

McCoy's lyrics borrow heavily from older traditional themes. The "starch my jumper" lines were discussed in more detail in connection with "Cannonball Blues." "Mister depot agent, close your depot down" recalls both Bessie Smith's 1924 "Ticket Agent, Ease Your Window Down":

> Ticket agent, ease your window down,
> Ticket agent, ease your window down,
> 'Cause my man done quit me, tried to leave this town[2]

and also Noah Lewis's "Ticket Agent Blues":

> Ticket agent, ease your window, ease your window high, indeed, Lord,
> Ticket agent, please raise your window high,
> So I will know my train when it's passing by.
>
> Depot agent, turn your depot, turn your depot round, indeed, Lord,
> Depot agent, please turn your depot roun',
> My woman done quit me, going to leave your town.[3]

The "mean old fireman, cruel old engineer" lines also occur widely in recorded blues. In "Every Day in the Week Blues," Simmie Dooley sings:

> Slow down, mean old fireman, or cruel engineer,
> Took my good girl and left me standing here.[4]

Blind Willie McTell, in "Travelin' Blues," alters the lines to refer to a rambling hobo, rather than a fleeing lover:

> You's a cruel fireman, low down engineer,
> You's a cruel fireman, low down engineer;
> I'm trying to hobo my way and you leave me standing here.[5]

In Ed Bell's "Mean Conductor Blues" we hear:

The same train, same engineer,
That same train, same engineer
Took my woman 'way, Lord, left me standing here.[6]

Leroy Carr, in "Big Four Blues" expands the lines:

Big Four, Big Four, why should you be so mean?
Big Four, Big Four, why should you be so mean?
Why, you're the meanest old train that I've ever seen.

You've taken my baby away, and left me standing here,
Now you've taken my baby away, and left me standing here,
Well, I ain't got no one to love, and I swear I can't go nowhere.[7]

In her 1938 version of "Freight Train Blues," Trixie Smith added a verse not in her 1924 recording (compare "Freight Train Blues," discussed later in this chapter):

That's a mean old fireman, cruel old engineer,
That's a mean old fireman, cruel old engineer;
It was a mean old train that took my man away from here.[8]

More recently, when Harry Oster recorded the singing of Herman Johnson in 1961, he obtained the following lines in "C.C. Rider":

It was a great long engine and a little small engineer,
It took my woman away along and it left me standin' here.[9]

McCoy's other verses are not commonly encountered elsewhere, and may be original.

NOTES

1. For a brief biographical sketch of Davenport, see Albert McCarthy et al., *Jazz on Record* (London: Hanover Books, 1968), p. 60.

2. Bessie Smith, "Ticket Agent, Ease Your Window Down," recorded Apr. 5, 1924 (Columbia master 81670); released on Columbia 14025-D on June 10, 1924 (composer credits to Spencer Williams); reissued on Columbia G 30450: *Empty Bed Blues*.

3. Noah Lewis, "Ticket Agent Blues," recorded Nov. 26, 1930 (Victor master 64736); released on RCA Bluebird B-5675; reissued on Origin Jazz Library OJL 4: *The Great Jug Bands*.

4. Pink Anderson and Simmie Dooley, "Every Day in the Week Blues," recorded Apr. 14, 1928 (Columbia master 146064); released on Columbia 14400-D on Mar. 15, 1929.

5. Blind Willie McTell, "Travelin' Blues," recorded Oct. 30, 1929 (Columbia master 149300); released on Columbia 14484-D, on Jan. 3, 1930, as by Blind Sammie; reissued on Biograph BLP-C14: *Blind Willie McTell—1929–1933*. Transcribed in Eric Sackheim, *The Blues Line* (New York: Grossman Publishers, 1969), p. 340.

6. Ed Bell, "Mean Conductor Blues," recorded ca. Sept., 1927 (Paramount master 4820); released on Paramount 12546; reissued on Yazoo L-1006: *Alabama Blues*. For a full transcription, see Jeff Titon, *Early Downhome Blues* (Urbana: University of Illinois Press, 1977), p. 101.

7. Leroy Carr, "Big Four Blues," recorded Dec. 14, 1934 (American Record Corp. master 16416); released on Vocalion 03349; reissued on Biograph BLP-C9: *Singin' the Blues*. Transcribed in Kay Shirley, ed., *The Book of the Blues*, annotated by Frank Driggs (New York: Crown Publishers and Leeds Music Corp., 1963), p. 198.

8. Trixie Smith, "Freight Train Blues," recorded May 26, 1938 (Decca master 63866); released on Decca 7489 and associated overseas labels; reissued on Decca DL-4344: *Out Came the Blues*.

9. Harry Oster, *Living Country Blues* (Detroit: Folklore Associates, 1969), p. 421.

REFERENCES

A. "That Lonesome Train Took My Baby Away," by Charlie McCoy. McCoy, vocal; guitar, probably Bo Chatmon; banjo-mandolin. Recorded Dec. 15, 1930 (OKeh master 404726-A), in the King Edward Hotel, Jackson, Miss. Released on OKeh 8863. Reissued on RBF RF-14: *Blues Roots/Mississippi*. Transcribed in Eric Sackheim, *The Blues Line* (New York: Grossman Publishers, 1969), p. 167, and in Samuel Charters, *The Poetry of the Blues* (New York: Oak Publications, 1963), p. 137.

Special Agent/Railroad Police Blues

SPECIAL AGENT (RAILROAD POLICE BLUES)

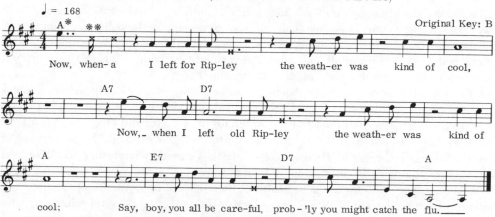

Original Key: B

*The two guitarists on this recording sometimes play different chords. The chords indicated here represent the choice of the music editor and at least one of the guitarists.
**Spoken, at approximately this pitch.

Now, when-a I left for Ripley the weather was kind of cool,
Now, when I left old Ripley the weather was kind of cool;
Say, boy, you all be careful, prob'ly you might catch the flu.

Now, I swung that Ninety-seven, I went down in the three rail bar,
Now, I swung that Ninety-seven, I went down in three rail bars;
Now, I couldn't hear the special agent when he come tippin' over the top.

Now, them special agents up the country sure is hard on a man;
Now, them special agents up the country, they sure is hard on a man;
Now, they will put him off when he hungry and won't even let him ride
    no train.

Now, I was settin' down in Centralia and I sure was feelin' bad,
Now, I was settin' down in Centralia and I sure was feelin' bad;
Now, they wouldn't let me ride no fast train, they put me off on a dog-
    gone drag.

Now, special agent, special agent, put me off close to some town,
Special agent, special agent, put me off close to some town;
Now, [I] got to do some recordin', an' I ought to be recordin' right now.

Sleepy John Estes

Special agents were railroad police—or railroad "bulls," as they were referred to in the vernacular—whose main job was to keep the trains and railroad yards clear of tramps. The need for such officials arose around the turn of the century when the number of tramps and migratory workers who tried to ride the trains for no fare began to swell to troublesome proportions. Local policemen were of little help to the railroads; their responsibility was simply to keep their towns free of undesirable persons, even if it meant ordering them to leave town on the next train. The railroad bulls were of varied sorts. The tougher of them struck terror into hoboes' hearts and acquired reputations that spread around the company accompanying warnings to all tramps and bums to stay clear of the yards and divisions that they policed. Some railroad bulls rode on the trains, working their way through the boxcars, tossing off any unpaying passengers they should encounter. A few were good enough to wait until the trains had slowed to twenty or so miles an hour before making a man jump off, but often not without first administering some corporal punishment to make the debarkation a memorable one.[1]

Sleepy John Estes's "Special Agent" is an original composition, possibly autobiographical, drawing on his knowledge of the railroad bulls. John Adam Estes was born near Brownsville, Tennessee, in 1904.[2] He recorded for RCA Victor and Decca between 1929 and 1941, and was one of the first bluesmen to be "rediscovered" in the resurgence of interest in blues in the 1960s. He died in 1977. Estes's guitar style is rather primitive, and his singing is particularly difficult to understand, even when allowance is made for the frequent tendency of bluesmen to mumble their lyrics. In numerous instances, my hearing of "Special Agent" differs considerably from that of Samuel Charters, who transcribed the song in *The Poetry of the Blues*. For example, Charters gives the second verse as follows:

> Now, I swung that 97, I went down in three rail stops,
> Now, I swung that 97, I went down in three rail stops,
> I could hear the special agent when he comes tippin' over the top.[3]

Charters interprets the "three rail stops" to mean that Estes got from Ripley, Tennessee, to Memphis, where he had made his early recordings, in three stops. I confess to being unable to interpret the words as I hear them. Dissatisfied readers are urged to listen to the LP reissue of this blues and decipher it for themselves. Ripley and Memphis are both on the Illinois Central line, about fifty miles apart; Centralia is about two hundred miles north of Ripley, situated on both IC and L & N lines.

NOTES

1. See Stewart H. Holbrook, *The Story of American Railroads* (New York: Crown Publishers, 1947), pp. 393–95.

2. For biographical information on Estes, see liner notes to Delmark DL 603: *The Legend of Sleepy John Estes*; Mike Ledbitter, ed., *Nothing but the Blues* (London: Hanover Books, 1971), pp. 237–39; and "Hammie Nixon & Sleepy John Estes," *Living Blues*, No. 19 (Jan.-Feb., 1975), pp. 13–19. For a brief musical appraisal, see Albert McCarthy et al., *Jazz on Record* (London: Hanover Books, 1968), p. 94.

3. Samuel Charters, *The Poetry of the Blues* (New York: Oak Publications, 1963), p. 77.

REFERENCES

A. "Special Agent (Railroad Police Blues)," by Sleepy John Estes. Estes, vocal and guitar; guitar, Son Bonds or Charlie Pickett. Recorded Apr. 22, 1938 (Decca master 63654-A), in New York City. Released on Decca 7491. Reissued on RBF RF-1: *The Country Blues*, and Swaggie (Australia) 1220: *The Blues of Sleepy John Estes*. Text transcribed in Samuel Charters, *Poetry of the Blues* (New York: Oak Publications, 1963), p. 77, and in *Sing Out!*, 26 (May-June 1977), 1.

How Long, How Long Blues

HOW LONG, HOW LONG BLUES

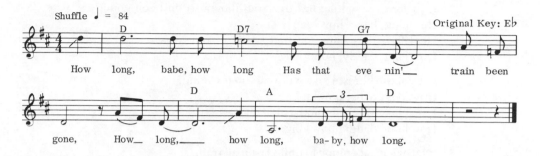

How long, babe, how long
Has that evenin' train been gone,
How long, how long, baby, how long.

(Here I stand) at the station, watch my baby leavin' town,
(Feelin') disgusted, nowhere could peace be found,
For how long, how long, baby, how long.

Now I can hear the whistle blowin', but I cannot see no train,
And it's deep down in my heart, baby, there lies an achin' pain,
For how long, how long, baby, how long.

Sometimes I feel so disgustin' [*sic*], and I feel so blue,
That I hardly know what in this world, baby, just to do,
For how long, how long, baby, how long.

And if I could holler like I was a mountain jack
I'd go up on the mountain, I'd call my baby back,
For how long, how long, baby, how long.

And if some day you're gonna be sorry that you done me wrong,
Then it'll be too late, baby, I will be gone,
For so long, so long, baby, so long.

My man gets a ramblin', I feel so bad,
Thinkin' about the bad luck that I have had,
For how long, how long, baby, how long.

Leroy Carr and Scrapper Blackwell

When the Indianapolis bluesmen Leroy Carr and Scrapper Blackwell recorded their first pair of selections for the Brunswick Phonograph and Record Corporation in June of 1928, they were inaugurating a major change in the nature of recorded blues music. Smoother, more urbane than most of the country blues that preceded them, more polished, and considerably more danceable, their style was immediately emulated by other artists as soon as their first recordings were released for sale in mid-August, 1928.

One of those first two sides was "How Long, How Long Blues," pianist Carr's recomposition of an older blues theme that had been explored by several artists. Ida Cox's recording "How Long, Daddy, How Long," credited to William Jackson, in September, 1925, may have influenced Carr; its opening stanzas follow:

> How long, how long has that southbound train been gone,
> How long, babe, how long;
> I feel like riding 'cause my blue spell has come down,
> How long, daddy, how long.
>
> I've got the blues, I've got boxcars on my mind;
> How long, babe, how long;
> I can't leave my baby and it ain't no use in tryin',
> How long, daddy, how long.
>
> It takes a good engine to pull a fast mail train,
> How long, babe, how long;
> It takes a brownskin man to run a woman insane,
> How long, daddy, how long.[1]

Although Daisy Martin's 1921 recording "How Long, How long" (OKeh 8009) and Alberta Brown's April, 1928, "How Long" (Columbia 14321-D) are listed in the Shirley and Driggs discography of "How Long, How Long Blues," they are not closely related to the Carr composition.[2]

Charlie Lincoln's 1927 recording "Chain Gang Trouble" (discussed further under "Reuben's Train"/"900 Miles") has a related, though lyrically simpler, stanza:

> How long, how long, how long, how long,
> How long 'fore I can go home?[3]

Of particular interest is Blind Lemon Jefferson's "How Long, How Long," recorded shortly after the Carr and Blackwell song was released. This is one of the few titles on which guitarist Jefferson is joined by a piano accompanist, strongly suggesting a deliberate attempt to imitate the Blackwell-Carr recording. Before the year was over, Sonny Porter (October), and Tampa Red (November) had both recorded their covers of the hit; and many more copies followed in later years.

Carr and Blackwell themselves, stimulated by the favorable reception their song was getting, recorded several sequels: "How Long, How Long Blues No. 2" and ". . . No. 3" were recorded November 6, 1928, but not issued; repeat takes made on December 19 were released. On August 13, 1929, they made "The New How Long, How Long Blues," following it with ". . . Part 2" in January, 1931. In March, 1932, they recorded "How Long Has That Evening Train Been Gone?," the last of the sequence. The extent to which the lyrics mention railroads varies. For example, in "How Long, How Long Blues No. 2" only the final stanza is pertinent:

> I haven't any money for a ticket on the train,
> But I will ride the rods, baby, be with you again.[4]

The other stanzas deal with the impecuniousness of the singer and his troubles with his woman. Likewise, other singers have taken considerable liberties with the lyrics, adapting only the tune and the refrain from the Blackwell-Carr recordings. Mama Yancey's version, transcribed by Lomax, has only the first stanza in common with the original.[5]

NOTES

1. Ida Cox, "How Long, Daddy, How Long," Paramount 12325, recorded Sept., 1925.
2. Kay Shirley, ed., *The Book of the Blues*, annotated by Frank Driggs (New York: Crown Publishers and Leeds Music Corp., 1963), pp. 72–74.
3. Charlie Lincoln, "Chain Gang Trouble," Columbia 14272-D.
4. Leroy Carr and Scrapper Blackwell, "How Long, How Long Blues No. 2," Vocalion 1241.
5. Alan Lomax, *The Folk Songs of North America* (Garden City, N.Y.: Doubleday, 1960), pp. 589–92.

REFERENCES

A. How Long, How Long Blues," by Leroy Carr and Scrapper Blackwell. Carr, vocal and piano; Blackwell, guitar. Recorded ca. June, 1928 (Vocalion master IND-623-A), in Indianapolis, Ind. Released on Vocalion 1191, Banner 32557, Oriole 8166, Perfect 0215, Romeo 5166. First recording of the song.

D. Shelley Armstrong—Champion 50008
Kokomo Arnold—Decca 7070; MCA (France) 510.116: *"Bad Luck Blues" 1934–1938*
Walter Barnes and his Royal Creolians —Brunswick 4187
Count Basie—Decca 2355, Decca (England) M-30231, Decca (Belgium) 60246, Brunswick 02762, Brunswick (Germany) A-82098, Brunswick (France) A-505224, Odeon (Argentina) 284866—Columbia 36710
Gladys Bentley—OKeh 8612
Barney Bigard and his Orchestra—Black & White 1207
Boots and his Buddies—Bluebird B-6132   "How Long—Part 1"
Leroy Carr and Scrapper Blackwell— Banner 32557, Oriole 8166, Perfect 0215, Romeo 5166, Vocalion 1241 "How Long, How Long Blues No. 2"
—Vocalion 1279   "How Long, How Long Blues—Part 3"
—Vocalion 1435   "The New How Long, How Long Blues"
—Vocalion 1585; RBF RF 202X: *Rural Blues*   "The New How Long, How Long Blues Part 2"
—Vocalion 1716   "How Long Has That Evening Train Been Gone?"
Cofer Brothers—OKeh 45486   "How Long"

Ida Cox—Paramount 12325   "How Long Daddy How Long"
Jed Davenport—Vocalion 1440, Supertone 2229; Roots RL 321: *Great Harmonica Players, Vol. 2*
Lonnie Donegan—Mercury 71026, Nixa (England) NPT 19012; Mercury MG 20229
Champion Jack Dupree—Continental 6064; Continental LP 16002
Robert Hicks (Barbecue Bob)—Columbia 14573-D; Magnolia 502: *Rough Alley Blues—Blues from Georgia, 1924–1931*   "California Blues" (related piece)
Bertha "Chippie" Hill—Circle J-1003
Skip James—Paramount 13085; Roots RL 303: *The Mississippi Blues, Vol. 2* "How Long 'Buck'"
Blind Lemon Jefferson—Paramount 12685; Biograph BLP 12015: *Blind Lemon Jefferson, 1926–29*; Roots RL 331: *Blind Lemon Jefferson, Vol. 3* "How Long How Long"
Emma Johnson—Edison 51375
Pete Johnson—Solo Art 12004, Circle J-1049
Leadbelly (Huddie Ledbetter)—Asch 343-1, Stinson 343-1; Stinson SLP 17: *Leadbelly Memorial, Vol. 1;* Allegro LEG 9025: *Goodnite, Irene;* Melodisc (England) EPM 7-63 (EP); Melodisc (England) E 1140; Fantasy 24175: *Leadbelly*
Leroy's Buddy (Bill Gaither pseudonym)— Decca 7258
William McCoy—Columbia 14393-D
Wingy Manone—Bluebird B-10749
Red Nichols and his Five Pennies —Brunswick 6160, Brunswick (England) 01213, Brunswick (France or Germany) A-9117

Sonny Porter—Columbia 14366-D

Jimmie Rushing and the Count Basie
Orchestra—Vocalion 5010

Tampa Red (Hudson Whittaker
pseudonym) and Georgia Tom (Thomas
A. Dorsey)—Vocalion 1258

Tampa Red's Hokum Jug Band—Banner
32560, Oriole 8169, Perfect 0218,
Vocalion 1228; Melodeon MLP 7324:
The Party Blues (parody)

Varsity Seven—Varsity 8173, Elite 5032
(as by the New Orleans Seven), Savoy
5544 (as by Joe Turner and his Band),
Savoy 649 (as by Joe Turner and his
Band)

Jimmy Witherspoon—Supreme 1245

E. Red Allen—Verve 1025

Bud and Travis—Liberty 3386/7386: *Bud
& Travis in Person*

Barbara Dane—World Pacific 1254
—Dot DLP 3177

Joe Darensbourg—Lark LP 331

Blind John Davis—Vogue (France) EPL
7139

John Davis—Riverside 389/390

Champion Jack Dupree—Atlantic LP
8045: *Champion Jack's Natural and
Soulful Blues*

Jack Elliott—Prestige International 13065:
Jack Elliott at the Second Fret

Doc Evans—Audiophile AP 63

Ella Fitzgerald—Verve 4062/64062: *These
Are the Blues*

Johnny Fuller—Rhythm 1779

Andy Griffith—Capitol 1105

Art Hodes and Truck Parham—Emarcy
26005/66005: *Plain Old Blues*

John Lee Hooker—Riverside RLP 12-838:
The Country Blues of John Lee Hooker;
Battle 6114: *How Long Blues*

Howlin' Wolf (Chester Burnett)—Chess

1575; Chess LP 1434   "Baby How
Long" (derivative piece)

Lil' Son Jackson—Imperial 5312

Milt Jackson and Ray Charles—Atlantic
1279

Freddy Jacobs—Westminster WP 6087

Skip James—Vanguard VRS 9219/VSD
79219: *Skip James Today*

Meade Lux Lewis—Tops LP 1533

Norman Luboff Choir—RCS Victor
LPM/LSP 3312: *Blues—Right Now*

Memphis Slim (Peter Chatman)—
Folkways FG 3535: *The Real Honky Tonk*
—United Artists UA 6137

Wilbur de Paris and Jimmy Witherspoon—
Atlantic 1266

Dan Pickett—Gotham 542; Blues Classics
BC-6: *Country Blues, Vol. 1*

Lou Rawls—Capitol T/ST 1824: *Black and
Blue*

Speckled Red (Rufus Perryman)—
Folkways FG 3555: *The Barrelhouse
Blues of Speckled Red*

Joe Turner—Atlantic LP 1234: *Boss of the
Blues*

Dave van Ronk—Folkways FS 3813:
Ballads, Blues, and a Spiritual; Verve
Folkways FV/FVS 9017: *Gambler's Blues*

T Bone Walker—Atlantic SD 7226: *Texas
Guitar from Dallas to L.A.*

Dinah Washington—Roulette 25189: *Back
to the Blues*

Josh White—Mercury MG 20203

Jimmy Yancey—Atlantic LP 525

Jimmy and Mama Yancey—Atlantic LP
1283

F. LC AFS:

Johnny Cook—AFS 3078

Flash Ridge—AFS 3561

Group of seven Negroes—AFS 1852

The Southern Blues

THE SOUTHERN BLUES

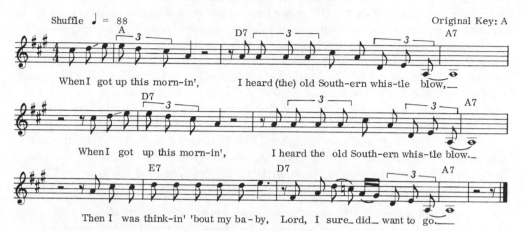

When I got up this mornin', I heard (the) old Southern whistle blow,
When I got up this mornin', I heard the old Southern whistle blow.
Then I was thinkin' 'bout my baby, Lord, I sure did want to go.

I was standin', lookin' and listenin', watchin' the Southern cross the Dog,
I was standin', lookin' and listenin', watchin' the Southern cross the Dog.
If my baby didn't catch that Southern, she must have caught that Yellow Dog.

Down at the station, looked up on the board, waitin' for the conductor just to say,
    "All aboard,"
Down at the station, Lord, I looked up on the board,
I don't know my baby left from here, ooh, but I was told.

I'm goin' to Moorhead, get me a job on the Southern line,
Said I'm goin' to Moorhead, get me a job on the Southern line;
So that I can make some money just to send for that brown of mine.

The Southern crossed the Dog in Moorhead, my my Lord, and she keeps on
    through,
The Southern crossed the Dog in Moorhead, my my Lord, and she keeps on
    through.
I say my baby's gone to Georgia, I believe I'll go to Georgia, too.

Big Bill Broonzy

Though he is better known to folk music enthusiasts for his role in the folksong
revival during the 1950s, when he appeared extensively in concerts in both the United

States and Europe, offering listeners a varied program of old folksongs, spirituals, blues, and pop songs, Big Bill Broonzy deserves recognition as one of the greatest bluesmen whose art has been preserved on disc. Born William Lee Conley Broonzy in 1893 in Scott, Mississippi, just east of the Mississippi River, Big Bill first learned to play the fiddle; in early years he had a brief stint at the pulpit before turning to music as a lasting career. He did not take up the guitar until after he left the Mississippi Delta for Chicago, where he made his first records in about 1926. He recorded prolifically, making some 250 sides before the war, and then continuing to record extensively after 1945. In the late 1940s, his audience shifted from the black consumers of R & B music to the white urban folk music connoisseurs, and Big Bill was sophisticated and skilled enough to modify his repertoire accordingly. His last recordings, like his first, were made in Chicago, in July, 1957; he died there in August, 1958.[1]

We have included Broonzy's "Southern Blues" partly because it contains one of the most celebrated of all railroad blues phrases—"where the Southern crosses the Dog." Three-quarters of a century ago, in about 1903, this line changed the course of W. C. Handy's life, and also that of the history of the blues.

> . . . one night at Tutwiler (Mississippi), as I nodded in the railroad station while waiting for a train that had been delayed nine hours, life suddenly took me by the shoulder and wakened me with a start.
>
> A lean, loose-jointed Negro had commenced plunking a guitar beside me while I slept. His clothes were rags; his feet peeped out of his shoes. His face had on it some of the sadness of the ages. As he played, he pressed a knife on the strings of the guitar in a manner popularized by Hawaiian guitarists who used steel bars. The effect was unforgettable. His song, too, struck me instantly.
>
> Goin' where the Southern cross' the Dog.
>
> The singer repeated the line three times, accompanying himself on the guitar with the weirdest music I had ever heard. The tune stayed in my mind. When the singer paused, I leaned over and asked him what the words meant. He rolled his eyes, smiled with a trace of mild amusement. Perhaps I should have known, but he didn't mind explaining. At Moorhead the eastbound and the westbound met and crossed the north and southbound trains four times a day. This fellow was going where the Southern cross' the Dog, and he didn't care who knew it. He was simply singing about Moorhead as he waited.[2]

The "Southern," of course, was the Southern railway. The "Dog" was the Yellow Dog, a vernacular name for the Yazoo Delta Railroad, and a few pages earlier in his autobiography, Handy had related an anecdote explaining how the YD acquired the name Yellow Dog. The Yazoo Delta lasted for such a brief period that we can date the verse's origin to within a couple of years. Opened in August, 1897, the Yazoo Delta first consisted of 20.5 miles of track between Moorhead and Ruelville, to the north. By 1899 it had been extended in both directions—21.5 miles to the north to Tutwiler, and 15 miles to the south to Lake Dawson. By 1903 the company was no longer in existence, having been acquired by the Yazoo and Mississippi Valley Railroad, a subsidiary of the Illinois Central Railroad. Possibly the name Yellow Dog was later applied to the Y & MV line; in any case, the incident stuck in Handy's memory, and in 1914 he wrote "Yellow Dog Blues," using the line "way down where the Southern cross' the Dog."

If the moniker "Yellow Dog" was applied to the entire Y & MV, that would help explain Handy's statement that the YD line ran from Clarksdale to Yazoo City. It never did; but the Y & MV later did, and part of that line was the old YD. If the nickname did become attached to the Y & MV, then as soon as the YD became part of the larger line, the blues verse lost its specificity, for the Y & MV crossed the Southern in several places: by 1906, crossings were to be found in Greenville, Stoneville, Elizabeth, and Moorhead, as well as a section between Webb and Minter where the two lines ran parallel. Before 1890, they crossed in Greenwood, but that section had later been taken over by the IC. In any case, after about 1902 the stanza had no informational content: it either referred to an obsolete railroad line or else designated any of several towns. Nevertheless, when Big Bill sang his "Southern Blues" in 1935, he must have had the original Yazoo Delta in mind, since he identified Moorhead as the site of crossing. Of course, Broonzy's last stanza, about the Southern continuing through to Georgia, was always correct, as several branches of the Southern crossed all of Alabama and Georgia.

Broonzy's first stanza is reminiscent of lines in other blues compositions; a very popular one was Arthur "Big Boy" Crudup's "Mean Old Frisco Blues":

Well now, I was standing, Lord, looking, watching that Southern whistle blow,
Yes, I was standing looking, watching that Southern whistle blow;
Well, she done catched that Southern, Lord, now where did the woman go.[3]

Crudup's song was in turn based on a 1931 recording by Eurreal "Little Brother" Montgomery titled "Frisco Hi-Ball Blues," with similar lines.

The third of Big Bill's stanzas is similar to the third stanza of Roy Harvey's "Railroad Blues"; for analogs, see the discussion of that latter piece at the end of this chapter.

NOTES

1. For a thumbnail biography and comments on Broonzy's stature as a bluesman, see McCarthy et al., *Jazz on Record* (London: Hanover Books, 1968), p. 28. A fuller account is found in *Big Bill Blues*, Broonzy's autobiography as told to Yannick Bruynoghe (New York: Oak Publications, 1955).

2. W. C. Handy, *Father of the Blues* (New York: Macmillan, 1941), p. 74. Handy's experience, in ca. 1903, is often cited as one of the first references to hearing the blues. But if Handy's account was precise, the singer he heard sang the same line four times—not the usual blues stanza.

3. Arthur "Big Boy" Crudup, "Mean Old Frisco Blues," recorded Apr. 15, 1942 (RCA Victor master 070863-1), in Chicago; released on RCA Bluebird 34-0704 and Victor 20-2509; reissued on RCA Victor LPV-573: *The Father of Rock and Roll*. Folk variants of Crudup's song were collected by Harry Oster; see his *Living Country Blues* (Detroit: Folklore Associates, 1969), pp. 234, 236.

REFERENCES

A. "The Southern Blues," by Big Bill (Broonzy). Broonzy, vocal and guitar; piano, probably Black Bob. Recorded Feb. 26, 1935 (RCA Victor master 85517-1), in Chicago, Ill. Released on RCA Bluebird B-5998 and B-6964. Reissued on Montgomery Ward M-4836; RCA Victor (Japan) RA 5435: *Blues, 1920–40, Vol. 3*.

I Hate That Train Called the M & O

I HATE THAT TRAIN CALLED THE M. AND O.

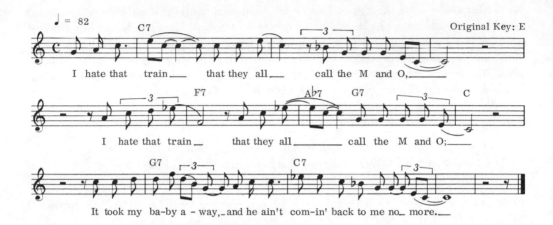

I hate that train that they all call the M and O,
I hate that train that they all call the M and O;
It took my baby away, and he ain't comin' back to me no more.

When he was leavin' I couldn't hear nothin' but that whistle blow,
When he was leavin' I couldn't hear nothin' but that whistle blow;
And the man at the throttle, Lord, he wasn't comin' back no more.

He had his head in the window, that man was watchin' those drivers roll,
He had his head in the window and he was watchin' those drivers roll;
Sayin', "I'm going away, baby, and doggone your bad-luck soul."

Now, I'm so worried, and I'm so full of gloom,
I'm so worried, and I'm so full of gloom;
And deep down in my heart, ain't nothin' but a lover's ruin.

I was sorry, I was sorry, sorry to my heart,
I was sorry, I was sorry to my heart,
To see that M and O train and me and my daddy part.

Lucille Bogan

Lucille Bogan's "I Hate That Train Called the M. and O." is another example of a railroad blues lamenting the departure of the singer's loved one, though the text suggests that the rider in question is the engineer rather than a passenger.
Lucille Bogan, also known as Bessie Jackson, was born in Amory, Mississippi, in 1897, and grew up in Birmingham, Alabama.[1] She was one of the earlier blues singers to make records, having cut her first sides for the General Phonograph Company's OKeh label early in June, 1923. Although the format of "M. and O." is, like many of her songs, in the twelve-bar, AAB blues pattern characteristic of the city blues singers, her vocal style

is somewhat rougher, and closer to the country. She was quite popular in the 1920s and 1930s, and recorded some eighty numbers between 1923 and 1935. "I Hate That Train Called the M. and O." was recorded in New York on July 30, 1934; her usual piano accompaniment was replaced on that particular selection by two guitars, in the hands of as-yet-unidentified musicians.

The M & O was the Mobile and Ohio Railroad Company, one of the older railroads of the South, having been chartered in 1848. The first section of track was opened in 1852, and by the turn of the century the company operated some one thousand miles of road. The main line ran from Mobile, Alabama, to East Cairo, Kentucky. Most of the line ran outside the state of Alabama; the closest it came to Bogan's hometown of Birmingham was about fifty miles, on a sideline from Montgomery, Alabama, to Columbus, Mississippi.

Lucille Bogan is given composer's credit on several of her recordings, but the author of "M. and O." is not known.[2]

NOTES

1. For further remarks on her style, see the liner notes to Yazoo L-1017: *Bessie Jackson & Walter Roland (1927–1935)*; see also Paul Oliver's comments in McCarthy et al., *Jazz on Record* (London: Hanover Books, 1968), p. 26. For biographical information, see Sheldon Harris, *Blues Who's Who* (New Rochelle, N.Y.: Arlington House, 1979), pp. 55-56.

2. Folklorist and blues authority David Evans tells me that this song was based on Walter Davis's very popular and much-imitated 1930 recording "M. & O. Blues," Victor V-38618 and Bluebird B-5031. The text itself is distantly related, but is part of a long cycle of blues texts inspired by the Davis record.

REFERENCES

A. "I Hate That Train Called the M. and O.," by Lucille Bogan. Bogan, vocal, accompanied by two guitars. Recorded July 31, 1934 (American Record Corp. master 15491-1), in New York City. Released on Banner 6-02-04, Oriole 6-02-04, Romeo 6-02-04, Melotone 6-02-04, Perfect 6-02-04, all in Feb., 1936. Reissued on Origin OJL-6: *The Country Girls! 1927–35*, and on Rosetta Records RR 1301: *Sorry but I Can't Take You: Women's Railroad Blues*.

Freight Train Blues

FREIGHT TRAIN BLUES

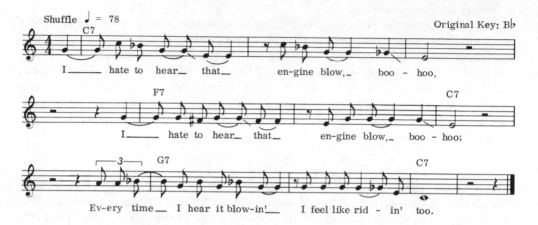

I hate to hear that engine blow, boo-hoo,
I hate to hear that engine blow, boo-hoo;
Every time I hear it blowin' I feel like ridin' too.

Got the freight train blues, I've got boxcars on my mind,
Got the freight train blues, I've got boxcars on my mind;
Gonna leave this town, because my man is so unkind.

I'm goin' away just to wear you off my mind,
I'm goin' away just to wear you off my mind,
And I may be gone for a doggone long, long time.

I asked the brakeman, "Let me ride the blinds,"
I asked the brakeman, "Please let me ride the blinds."
The brakeman said, "Clara, you know this train ain't mine."

When a woman gets the blues she goes to her room and hides,
When a woman gets the blues she goes to her room and hides;
When a man gets the blues he catches a freight train and rides.

Clara Smith

This classic city-blues piece was composed by Thomas Dorsey and Everett Murphy and copyrighted in 1924 by the Chicago Music Publishing Company. The transcription given here comes from Clara Smith's 1924 recording, though the piece had been recorded several months earlier by Trixie Smith (the two singers were not related). Trixie's version was doing well on the Paramount label, and Clara's was obviously a cover, designed to enable Columbia to offer some stiff competition. In general, however, Clara Smith was the more successful, and in fact was one of the few singers who came close to rivaling Bessie Smith (also unrelated) as the leading blues singer of the day. She recorded more than 150 selections between 1923 and 1932, typically with accompaniment by a small jazz combo. On "Freight Train Blues" she was backed by Porter Grainger, Don Redman, and Cecil Scott (piano, clarinet or goofus, and clarinet, respectively). Her rendition differs very little from the original sheet music. Trixie Smith's 1938 version, to the same tune but with some altered verses, is perhaps better known among jazz collectors because of its fine accompaniment by Charlie Shavers and Sidney Bechet.

Dorsey, the composer, was a prolific songwriter in the 1920s and 1930s. Born in Atlanta in 1899, he achieved prominence as a blues singer and pianist before devoting himself to gospel songs in 1932. His "Freight Train Blues" rests firmly on traditional verses. The fourth stanza, "let me ride the blinds," echoes various other blues recordings; King Solomon Hill, in "Gone Dead Train," sang:

> I said, "Look here, engineer, can I ride your train?"
> He said, "Look, you ought to know this train ain't mine and you asking me
> in vain."[1]

Ed Bell, in "Mean Conductor Blues," sang:

> "Hey, Mr. Conductor, let a broke man ride your blinds,
> Hey, Mr. Conductor, let a broke man ride your blinds."
> "You better buy your ticket, know this train ain't mine."[2]

Blind Willie McTell, in "Travelin' Blues":

> "Mr. Engineer, let a man ride the blind,
> Mr. Engineer, let a poor man ride the blind."
> Said, "I wouldn't mind it, fella, but you know this train ain't mine."[3]

The "boxcars on my mind" phrase also appeared in many other songs. From "T-Bone Steak Blues," by Yank Rachel:

> I got the railroad blues, got boxcars on my mind,
> I got the railroad blues, got boxcars on my mind,
> And the girl I'm loving, she sure done left this town.[4]

The last stanza of Tampa Red's "I.C. Moan Blues" is similar:

> I got the IC blues and boxcars on my mind,
> I got the IC blues and boxcars on my mind;
> I'm gonna pack my grip and beat it on down the line.[5]

White hillbilly singer Jimmie Tarlton, whose "Freight Train Ramble" was clearly patterned after Jimmie Rodgers's blue yodels, sang:

> I got the freight train rambles, I got the boxcars on my mind, hey hey hey;
> I got the freight train rambles, boxcars on my mind;
> I'm bound to see my little honey, baby, if I go some line.[6]

The last stanza, of course, has appeared in numerous songs, many predating Dorsey's 1924 composition. Such a stanza collected in 1915 appeared in "The Railroad Blues" quoted in the introduction to this chapter. Obtained in the same year, though not published until a decade later, by Robert W. Gordon, was "The Train I Ride":

> When a woman—oh, Lawd Gawd—I mean a woman—gits the blues,
> She jes' tucks her head—and she cries—
> When a woman gits the blues she cries.

When a man—oh, Lawd Gawd—I mean a man—gits the blues,
He jes' grabs a train—and he rides—
When a m-a-n gits the blues he rides. [7]

In about 1922–23 Gordon also recorded a version in California with the same title, "The Train I Ride":

When a woman gits de blues she lays down an' c-r-y-s,
When a man gits de blues he takes a freight train an' r-i-d-e-s.
Oh, de train ah ride
Oh, de train ah ride
Is sixteen coaches
Ah mean coaches—
Oh, de train I ride
Is sixteen c-o-a-c-h-e-s l-o-n-g. [8]

Clara Smith's early life has not been documented. It was reported that she was born in Spartanburg, South Carolina, in 1895. According to Derrick Stewart-Baxter, by 1918 she was a headline attraction on the TOBA circuit (Theater Owners Booking Association), and by 1921 she was filling the house at the Dream Theatre in Columbus, Georgia. [9] An effusive ad-writer for Columbia's race records catalog described her: "Every blues thinks it's full of misery until Clara Smith goes to work on it. Blues, that no ordinary mortal dare tackle, subside into a melodious melody of moans and groans when Clara gets warmed up to her work." [10] Clara Smith died in 1935 in Detroit from a heart attack.

NOTES

1. King Solomon Hill (Joe Holmes pseudonym), "Gone Dead Train," recorded ca. Jan., 1932 (Paramount master L-1254); released on Paramount 13129; reissued on Milestone 2016: *The Blues Tradition*.

2. Ed Bell, "Mean Conductor Blues," recorded ca. Sept., 1927 (Paramount master 4820); released on Paramount 12546; reissued on Yazoo L-1006: *Alabama Blues*.

3. Blind Willie McTell, "Travelin' Blues," recorded Oct. 30, 1929 (Columbia master 149300); released on Columbia 14484-D; reissued on Biograph BLP C-14: *Blind Willie McTell*.

4. Yank Rachel, "T-Bone Steak Blues," recorded Oct. 2, 1929 (Victor master 56336); released on Victor V-38595; reissued on Roots RL-310: *Missouri and Tennessee*. Transcribed in Eric Sackheim, *The Blues Line* (New York: Grossman Publishers, 1969), p. 277.

5. Tampa Red (Hudson Whittaker pseudonym), "I.C. Moan Blues," recorded mid-June, 1930 (American Record Corp. master C-5857); released on Vocalion 1538, ARC 7-03-73, Conqueror 8860.

6. Tom Darby and Jimmie Tarlton, "Freight Train Ramble," recorded Oct. 31, 1929 (Columbia master 149324); released on Columbia 15511-D.

7. *Adventure*, Nov. 10, 1925, p. 191. Gordon obtained this from R. P. Matthews, who had learned it from the singing of a black chef at Dodge City, Kans., in 1915; Gordon MS 1157.

8. Gordon Collection (Calif.) 226 (recording 126); published in *Adventure*, June 20, 1925, p. 192. For other occurrences of these lines see Newman I. White, *American Negro Folk-Songs* (1928; rpt., Hatboro, Pa.: Folklore Associates, 1965), p. 394; Peetie Wheatstraw, "C & A Blues," Vocalion 04592, recorded in 1931; John A. Lomax and Alan Lomax, *Our Singing Country* (New York: Macmillan, 1941), p. 371; Robert Duncan Bass, "Negro Songs from the Pedee Country," *JAF*, 44 (Oct.-Dec., 1931), 431; *The Frank C. Brown Collection of North Carolina Folklore*, vol. 3, *Folk Songs*, edited by Henry M. Belden and Arthur Palmer Hudson (Durham, N.C.: Duke University Press, 1952), p. 563.

9. Derrick Stewart-Baxter, *Ma Rainey and the Classic Blues Singers* (London: November Books/Studio Vista; New York: Stein and Day, 1970), p. 64. See also Sheldon Harris, *Blues Who's Who* (New Rochelle, N.Y.: Arlington House, 1979), pp. 466-67.

10. Ibid., p. 65.

REFERENCES

A. "Freight Train Blues," by Clara Smith, with her Jazz Trio. Smith, vocal; Don Redman, goofus; Porter Grainger, piano; Cecil Scott, clarinet. Recorded Sept. 30, 1924 (Columbia master 140064-3), in New York City. Released on Columbia 14041-D on Nov. 10, 1924. Reissued on VJM VLP 17: *Clara Smith, Vol. 3*, and on Rosetta Records RR 1301: *Sorry but I Can't Take You: Women's Railroad Blues*.

D. Trixie Smith—Paramount 12211; Audubon AEE; Rosetta Records RR 1301: *Sorry but I Can't Take You: Women's Railroad Blues*

E. Bill Jackson—Testament T-2201: *Long Steel Rail*   "Freight Train Blues" —Milestone MLP-3002: *Ramblin' on My Mind*

Columbia *New Process* Records

CLARA SMITH
"The World's Champion Moaner"

EVERY blues thinks it's full of misery until Clara Smith goes to work on it. Blues, that no ordinary mortal dare tackle, subside into a melodious melody of moans and groans when Clara gets warmed up to her work.

Just look at her smile. What a sight for sore eyes! Listen to her voice. A balm for tired ears! You can hear her voice, and it seems like you can almost get the smile, too, on Columbia New Process Records.

CLARA SMITH

Clara Smith is an Exclusive Columbia Artist

EASE IT . . . . PERCOLATIN' BLUES—*Piano Accompaniments by Lem Fowler*	14202-D	75c
YOU DON'T KNOW WHO'S SHAKIN' YOUR TREE—*Acc'p'd by Her Jazz Babies* CHEATIN' DADDY	14192-D	75c
GET ON BOARD—*Assisted by Sisters White and Wallace* . . . . LIVIN' HUMBLE—*Assisted by Sisters White and Wallace*	14183-D	75c
AIN'T NOTHIN' COOKIN' WHAT YOU'RE SMELLIN' . . . . SEPARATION BLUES	14160-D	75c

Viva-tonal Recording. The Records without Scratch   [9]

Advertisement in a Columbia record catalog. Author's Collection.

Railroad Blues (I)

RAILROAD BLUES

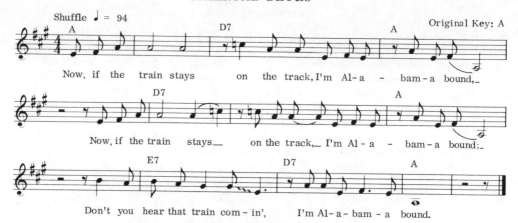

Now, if the train stays on the track, I'm Alabama bound,
Now, if the train stays on the track, I'm Alabama bound;
Don't you hear that train comin', I'm Alabama bound.

Now, the train went by with my papa on the inside,
I say the train went by with my papa on the inside;
Now, I couldn't do nothin' but hang my head and cry.

If you ever take a trip on the Seaboard and Airline,
If you ever take a trip on the Seaboard and Airline,
Now, if you ride that train, it'll satisfy your mind.

I've got the railroad blues, I wanna see my hometown,
I've got the railroad blues, I wanna see my hometown,
And if the Seaboard don't wreck, I'm Alabama bound.

Trixie Smith

Like Clara Smith, the singer of the preceding song in this chapter, Trixie Smith was an early city blues singer, more in the vaudeville blues style than the rougher country blues. She was born in Atlanta, Georgia, in 1895 and attended Selma University in Selma, Alabama. She toured frequently as a featured singer on the TOBA (Theater Owners Booking Association) circuit from about 1918 into the early 1920s and made her first recordings in 1921.[2] "Railroad Blues," for which she was given composer's credit, is one of the pieces responsible for her high reputation among jazz collectors; it was recorded in New York in March, 1925, with jazz accompaniment by several musicians from Fletcher Henderson's orchestra, including Henderson himself on piano, Louis Armstrong on cornet, Charlie Green on trombone, Buster Bailey on clarinet, and Charlie Dixon on banjo. Trixie Smith recorded some three dozen titles in five years; she made her last recording in 1939, four years before her death.

From the lyrics of the song, especially the last stanza, one might suspect that Trixie Smith was from Alabama. However, the phrase "I'm Alabama bound" was so widespread in early black folksongs as to be a commonplace and of little biographical significance. For example, Newman I. White obtained numerous fragments in 1915–16 with that phrase, such as:

> If de train goes and leaves me here,
> I got a mile to ride, I'm Alabama bound.[2]

Furthermore, "Alabama" in nineteenth-century parlance meant the South in general.[3]

In her third stanza, Trixie Smith sings of the Seaboard Air Line, a railway organized in 1900 and formed from several older companies. Its main line, nearly one thousand miles, runs from Richmond and Portsmouth, Virginia, to Tampa, Florida. Early in this century the Seaboard owned all the capital stock of the Atlanta and Birmingham Air Line Railway, a short road connecting those two cities.

NOTES

1. See Sheldon Harris, *Blues Who's Who* (New Rochelle, N.Y.: Arlington House, 1979), pp. 473-74.

2. Newman I. White, *American Negro Folk-Songs* (1928; rpt., Hatboro, Pa.: Folklore Associates, 1965), p. 306; see also pp. 307, 308, 354.

3. Harold Wentworth and Stuart Berg Flexner, *Dictionary of American Slang* (New York: Thomas Y. Crowell, 1960), p. 3.

REFERENCES

A. "Railroad Blues," by Trixie Smith and her Down Home Syncopators. Smith, vocal; Louis Armstrong, cornet; Charlie Green, trombone; Buster Bailey, clarinet; Fletcher Henderson, piano; Charlie Dixon, banjo. Recorded Mar., 1925 (Paramount masters 2064-1 and 2064-2), in New York City. Released on Paramount 12262. Reissued on United Hot Clubs of America 82, Jazz Collector (England) L102, and Rosetta Records RR 1301: *Sorry but I Can't Take You: Women's Railroad Blues*.

Train Whistle Blues

Shuffle ♩ = 104   Original Key: B

Yo-del la-ee lay-ee-o lay-ee. When a wom-an gets the blues, she
hangs her lit-tle head and cries, When a wom-an gets the blues, she
hangs her lit-tle head and cries; But when a
man gets the blues, he grabs a train and rides.

Yodel:
When a woman gets the blues, she hangs her little head and cries,
When a woman gets the blues, she hangs her little head and cries;
But when a man gets the blues, he grabs a train and rides.

Every time I see that lonesome railroad train,
Every time I see that lonesome railroad train,
It makes me wish I was going home again.
    Yodel:

Look-a yonder coming, coming down that railroad track,
Look-a yonder coming, coming down that railroad track,
With the black smoke rolling, rolling from that old smoke stack.

I got the blues so bad, till the whole round world looks blue,
I got the blues so bad, till the whole round world looks blue,
I ain't got a dime, I don't know what to do.
    Yodel:

I'm weary now, I want to leave this town,
I'm weary now and I want to leave this town;
I can't find a job, I'm tired of hanging around.

Jimmie Rodgers

    In country music's pantheon of gods and demigods, the image of Jimmie Rodgers, clothed in the striped overalls and cap of a railroad brakeman, looms large. Rodgers's biography has been sketched briefly in connection with "Hobo Bill's Last Ride." Here it is appropriate to comment further on one of his most important contributions to white country music: the white blues, particularly in the format he popularized, the "blue yodel." Bill Malone, John Greenway, and other folklorists who have written about Rodgers's songs have drawn attention to his experience as waterboy in the Meridian, Mississippi, railroad yards, where he acquired a repertoire of black folksongs and blues that served him well during the six years he was a recording artist.[1] But, interesting to note, his blues are all cast in the carefully constructed twelve-bar, AAB city blues pattern, and it is possible that he owed as much to phonograph recordings of such pieces as to the country blues he must have heard in his native Mississippi during the first decades of the century.

However much Rodgers borrowed from folk tradition—his repertoire has not been studied intensively enough to assess the extent—the debt has been amply repaid; Rodgers has left his mark not only on the dozens of professional country singers who sought to emulate him even before his death in 1933, but also on countless nonprofessional singers throughout the South. John Greenway, in one of the first articles in an academic journal to examine the impact of a professional hillbilly singer, noted that Rodgers's "Blue Yodel No. 1 (T for Texas)," "Blue Yodel No. 4 (California Blues)," "Blue Yodel No. 5," "Blue Yodel No. 8 (Mule Skinner Blues)," "Soldier's Sweetheart," "Away Out on the Mountain," and "Waiting for a Train" had all been collected and published in standard regional folksong collections. An examination of unpublished folksong collections will increase the number considerably. For example, the Western Kentucky Folklore Archive contains versions of "Blue Yodel No. 2 (My Lovin' Gal Lucille)," "Moonlight and Skies," "Hobo Bill's Last Ride," "Ben Dewberry's Final Run," and "The Soldier's Sweetheart." A single collection made in Overton County, Tennessee, in 1936, includes "Mother Was a Lady," "Peach Picking Time in Georgia," "You and My Old Guitar," "Brakeman's Blues," "Gambling Barroom Blues," "Moonlight and Skies," and "Never No Mo' Blues."[2] "Mother Was a Lady" and "Mother, the Queen of My Heart" have both also been collected in Virginia.[3]

Rodgers was listened to and admired not only by white singers: he was one of the few hillbilly artists of the 1920s whose records found their way in substantial quantity into black homes as well. David Evans, who has done extensive fieldwork in Mississippi in recent years, has related the reminiscences of several black musicians who knew Rodgers personally or were familiar with his records.[4]

Perhaps more important than the handfuls of songs learned and remembered from his discs—a statistically minuscule sampling on which to base an evaluation—is his unquestioned impact on the direction of professional country music since his heyday. Rodgers moved country music a giant step toward pop music when he recorded several pieces with trained studio musicians—Louis Armstrong, Lani McIntire, Boyd Senter— rather than with other country musicians like himself. He was the star; they were the unadvertised sidemen.

As for Rodgers's distinctive yodel, he was not the first country singer to yodel on record; that honor fell to Riley Puckett three years before Rodgers made his first recording. But Rodgers's melding of the twelve-bar blues format with the yodeling chorus was probably original—at least, original on record.[5] And to Ralph Peer, the astute talent scout, publisher, and manager who "found" Rodgers and helped build him up, goes the credit for originating the term *blue yodel* as he had earlier first applied the terms *hillbilly* and *race* to the phonograph business.

"Train Whistle Blues" is just one of the few dozen white blues pieces that Rodgers recorded and that were copyrighted in his name. It suggests the in-depth study that could profitably be undertaken of his repertoire from the perspective of traditional music of his day.

About Rodgers's blue yodels and other blues, Greenway wrote: ". . . of this great mass of song there is scarcely a word that cannot be traced to song and sung phrases of hoboes and Negro railroad workers."[6] Of course, this statement is literally true; but if one takes units of meaning larger than single words, he finds a mixture of frequently encountered commonplaces together with seldom-published (or recorded) phrases that, though perhaps original in some sense, are clearly of a piece with traditional blues lyrics. The opening stanza of Rodgers's "Train Whistle Blues," discussed earlier in connection with "Freight Train Blues," is one of the most widespread blues couplets drawing on railroad imagery. The third stanza has appeared in black tradition. Muriel Davis Longini, for instance, collected it from Chicago singers in the 1930s:

> Don't you hear the train comin' down the railroad track,
> Don't you hear the train comin' down the railroad track,
> With the black smoke rollin', comin' from the old smokestack.[7]

Rodgers himself used a variant in his own "Blue Yodel No. 5" recorded six months earlier:

> Now I can see a train comin' down the railroad track,
> I see that train comin' down the railroad track,
> And I love to hear the bark of that old smokestack.[8]

In their now-classic bluegrass instrumental, "Orange Blossom Special," the Rouse Brothers changed this couplet:

> Look-a yonder comin', comin' down the railroad track,
> Look-a yonder comin', comin' down the railroad track;
> It's the Orange Blossom Special, it's a-bringin' my baby back.[9]

Rodgers recorded "Train Whistle Blues" in Dallas on August 8, 1929, two years to the week from the date of his first recording. In time the recording was released not only in the United States, but also in England, Australia, and Japan.

NOTES

1. See John Greenway, "Jimmie Rodgers—A Folksong Catalyst," *JAF*, 70 (July-Sept., 1962), 71–76; Bill C. Malone, *Country Music, U.S.A.* (Austin: University of Texas Press, 1968), chap. 3. For the fullest treatment of this seminal artist, see Nolan Porterfield, *Jimmie Rodgers* (Urbana: University of Illinois Press, 1979).

2. Lillian Gladys Crabtree, "Songs and Ballads Sung in Overton County, Tennessee" (Master's thesis, George Peabody College for Teachers, 1936), pp. 300, 278, 305, 193, 199, 78, 194.

3. Bruce A. Rosenberg, *The Folksongs of Virginia* (Charlottesville: University Press of Virginia, 1969), pp. 83, 89. Whether "Mother Was a Lady" is traceable to the Rodgers recording or stems directly from the older sheet music is still uncertain.

4. David Evans, "Black Musicians Remember Jimmie Rodgers," *Old Time Music*, No. 7 (Winter, 1972–73), pp. 12–14.

5. Rodgers and the yodel are discussed in Robert Coltman, "Roots of the Country Yodel: Notes toward a Life History," *JEMFQ*, 12 (Summer, 1976), 91–94.

6. Greenway, "Jimmie Rodgers."

7. Muriel Davis Longini, "Folk Songs of Chicago Negroes," *JAF*, 52 (Jan.-Mar., 1939), 109. See also "S.P. Train," sung by Willie B. Thomas, transcribed in Harry Oster, *Living Country Blues* (Detroit: Folklore Associates, 1969), p. 249. It is, of course, possible that Rodgers was the source of these texts, rather than the borrower of an older tradition.

8. Jimmie Rodgers, "Blue Yodel No. 5 (Ain't No Black Headed Mama Can Make a Fool out of

Me)," recorded Feb. 23, 1929 (Victor master 49990), in New York City; released on Victor 22072; reissued on RCA Victor LPM 1640: *Train Whistle Blues*.

9. Rouse Brothers, "Orange Blossom Special," recorded June 16, 1939 (RCA Victor master BS-037358), in New York City; released on RCA Bluebird B-8218; reissued on RCA Victor LPV-532: *The Railroad in Folksong*. For an account of how this piece was composed, based on the recollections of fiddler Chubby Wise, who was present at the time, see Ivan M. Tribe, "Chubby Wise: One of the Original Bluegrass Fiddlers," *Bluegrass Unlimited*, 11 (Feb., 1977), 10–12. Wise recalled that he and Ervin Rouse put together the instrumental part of the composition one evening after seeing the Seaboard Air Line's new streamliner, the *Orange Blossom Special*. Later, Ervin and his brother Jack added lyrics and copyrighted the song.

REFERENCES

A. "Train Whistle Blues," by Jimmie Rodgers. Rodgers, vocal; Billy Burkes, guitar; Weldon Burkes, ukulele; Joe Kaipo, steel guitar. Recorded Aug. 8, 1929 (RCA Victor master BVE 55309-2), in Dallas, Tex. Released on RCA Victor 22379 on June 5, 1930. Reissued on Regal Zonophone (Australia) G23113, HMV (India) N 4345, HMV (Australia) EA 1539, Zonophone (England) E 5697, Regal Zonophone (England) T 5697, Montgomery Ward M-4223; RCA Victor LPM 1640: *Train Whistle Blues*; RCA Victor (Japan) RA 5461: *The Legendary Jimmie Rodgers Collections, Vol. 3*.

B. Horstman, 330–31
Rodgers (1967b), 49

Jimmie Rodgers's Guitar Hounds. *Left to right:* Billy Burkes, Weldon Burkes, Joe Kaipo, Rodgers. Courtesy of Billy Burkes and Nolan Porterfield.

Railroad Blues (II)

RAILROAD BLUES

[*Spoken*:] "Say, Roy, remember them old railroad days?"
"Reckon I do, boy." [*Whistles*.]
"That sure makes you feel blue, don't it?"
"Nothin' else. Boy, you want me to sing you some of them railroad blues?"
"Go ahead and sing me one."
"All right."

*The yodeling is transcribed from its second occurrence on the recording.

I hear someone a-knockin', knockin' at my front door,
Hear someone a-knockin', knockin' at my front door;
It's a doggone caller, callin' me for half past four.
　　[*Yodels chorus*:]

Went down to the roundhouse, looked up on that board,
Went down to the roundhouse, and I looked up on that board;
Get the Four-twenty-seven, but she sure gets you over the road. (Sing them
　　blues, boy.)

Back down to the depot, hook onto my train, (Lord, Lord, Lord, Lord.)
Back down to the depot, and I hook onto my train;
And read my orders, just roll them wheels again.
  [*Yodels chorus*:]

Say to the fireman, "Shovel in a little more coal," (Get 'er hot, boy.)
Say to that fireman, "Shovel in a little more coal;" (Sing them blues, boy.)
Stick your head out the window, watch the Four-twenty-seven roll.

I call(ed) for a signal, but I never look(ed) back,
I call(ed) for a signal, but I never look(ed) back;
For the Four-twenty-seven was sure ballin' the jack.

Roy Harvey and Earl Shirkey

Roy Harvey's "Railroad Blues" is the only song in this chapter that is written from the point of view of a railroad employee; in all the others, the narrator is a passenger or would-be passenger, or a bystander concerned about one of the passengers. Harvey was well suited to write a railroad blues from the engineer's perspective; he was for many years an engineer on the Virginian Railway; details about his career are given in the discussion of "The Virginian Strike of '23." The spoken interchange between Harvey and Earl Shirkey may well reflect Harvey's feelings at the time of the recording in 1929: he had gone on strike in 1923 and did not return to work for the railroads until the 1940s. The railroad was always his first love, and though he enjoyed a successful career as hillbilly musician for many years, he longed to get back in the engine cab.

Harvey built his "Railroad Blues" out of traditional elements, though the arrangement was original and unique. His opening stanza is reminiscent of the lines that appear in the Casey Jones ballads as early as 1908:

> Caller called Jones about half past four;
> He kissed his wife at the station door.[1]

A nonoccupational variant of these lines occurs in Peg Leg Howell's "Hobo Blues":

> I woke up this mornin' about half past four,
> A long tall woman knockin' on my door.[2]

The second stanza has parallels in many published and recorded blues songs. For example, the fourth stanza of Charlie Patton's "Hammer Blues" reads:

> I went to the depot, I looked up at the board,
> I went to the depot, I looked up at the board;
> If this train has left, well, it's tearin' off up the road.[3]

Or compare Lee Green's "Railroad Blues":

> I went down to the station and looked up on the board,
> I went down to the station and looked up on the board:
> I asked the depot agent, "Did my baby go down the road?"[4]

Jimmie Rodgers, in his "Brakeman's Blues," gave a different twist to the couplet:

I went to the depot and looked up on the board,
I went to the depot and looked up on the board;
It says it's good times here, but it's better down the road.[5]

Harvey's fourth stanza is again a borrowing from the Casey Jones ballads recast in twelve-bar blues format. For example, from a 1911 published text:

Just grab the shovel and heave the coal,
Put your head out the window and watch the drivers roll.[6]

Harvey and Shirkey recorded "Railroad Blues" on March 26, 1929, in New York. Harvey sang lead and played guitar; Shirkey yodeled the choruses. When it was issued, Harvey was given the pseudonym of Roy Harper, perhaps because of contractual obligations with another company. The song was later issued on Columbia's two subsidiary labels, Velvetone and Clarion, both as by Joe Fletcher and Arthur Higgins. On December 4, 1930, Roy Harvey recorded a solo version of the same song for the Starr Piano Company that was issued on Champion and Superior, the latter as by John Martin. On the Starr releases, Harvey was given composer credits, but the Columbia disc was uncredited.

NOTES

1. *RRM*, 5 (May, 1908), 764.

2. Peg Leg Howell, "Hobo Blues," recorded Nov. 1, 1927 (Columbia master 145064); released on Columbia 14270-D.

3. Charlie Patton, "Hammer Blues," recorded ca. Nov., 1929 (Paramount master L-47-2); released on Paramount 12998; reissued on Yazoo L-1020: *Charley Patton*.

4. Lee Green, "Railroad Blues," recorded ca. Aug. 21, 1929 (Vocalion master C-4098); released on Vocalion 1401. Cf. Ishman Bracey, "Woman Woman Blues," recorded ca. Mar., 1930 (Paramount master L-239-2); released on Paramount 12970; reissued on Origin Jazz Library OJL-2: *Really! The Country Blues*; Howard W. Odum and Guy B. Johnson, *Negro Workaday Songs* (Chapel Hill: University of North Carolina Press, 1926), p. 217; Harry Oster, *Living Country Blues* (Detroit: Folklore Associates, 1969), p. 226.

5. Jimmie Rodgers, "Brakeman's Blues," recorded Feb. 14, 1928 (Victor master 41738); released on Victor 21291; reissued on RCA Victor LPM 2112: *Jimmie the Kid*. An almost identical stanza appears in Sam McGee, "Railroad Blues," Champion S16804, Decca 5348; reissued on County 511: *A Collection of Mountain Blues*.

6. *Kansas City Star*, Aug. 5, 1911, Kelley the Rake to editor; reprinted in Norm Cohen, "'Casey Jones,'" *WF*, 32 (Apr., 1973), 90.

REFERENCES

A. "The Railroad Blues," by Roy Harper (Roy Harvey pseudonym). Harper, vocal and guitar; Shirkey, yodeling on choruses. Recorded Mar. 26, 1929 (Columbia master W148136), in New York City. Released on Columbia 15406-D on June 28, 1929. Reissued on Velvetone 2490-V and Clarion 5430-C, both as by Joe Fletcher and Arthur Higgins (both with control no. 100750); Arbor 201: *Charlie Poole and the Highlanders*; Vetco 103: *Songs of the Railroad*.

D. Roy Harvey—Champion 16255, Superior 2626 (as by John Martin) (Starr master GN-17348)

10

==

A Railroader for Me

UNLIKE THE OTHER chapters in this book, this one has no central, unifying theme. The songs included here are the odds and ends that seemed too good or too important not to include in a book of railroad songs, yet did not fit conveniently into the other units of the collection.

They are neither ballads (as are most of the pieces in chaps. 4 through 8, and 11) nor blues (as are those of chap. 9), nor religious compositions (chap. 12). They are often lyric as opposed to narrative folksongs (ballads). Because there is no narrative thread to impose organization on lyric folksongs, their form is often very unstable. They borrow verses from other songs, and contribute their own lines elsewhere, so that in extreme cases it is difficult to say whether a given specimen is actually an example of the "song" under consideration. Song complexes such as "Reuben's Train"/"Train 45"/"900 Miles" and "The Longest Train"/"In the Pines," for example, are difficult to deal with because of the unclear boundaries.

On the other hand, some of the pieces in this chapter are relatively well behaved, with little ambiguity in the family tree. "The Rock Island Line" is a good example, as, of course, are the relatively recent compositions included here: "Railroading on the Great Divide" and "Freight Train Blues," written in the 1930s or later.

The fact that several of the songs in this book are not, strictly speaking, folksongs, has been discussed previously (see chap. 3). This qualification applies to the two songs just mentioned. There is little, if any, evidence that they are in oral tradition (one field recording of "Freight Train Blues" does exist). However, in both lyrics and melody they are folk-like, and they could, in my opinion, easily enter oral tradition in the United States, particularly in the Southeast, as could other recent songs such as Fred Rose's "Bringing in the Georgia Mail" and "Fireball Mail."

The songs in this chapter differed greatly in popularity. The title song was never commercially significant, though it was fairly widely known. Several of the songs —Elizabeth Cotten's "Freight Train," Leadbelly's popularizations of "The Midnight Special," "The Rock Island Line," and "In the Pines," Woody Guthrie's version of "900 Miles," Hedy West's "500 Miles," and any of several versions of "New River Train" —were immensely popular during the boom of the folksong revival in the late 1950s and

459

early 1960s, as the lengthy LP discographies attest. They are also all available in numerous folksong anthologies of the same period; yet it seems unfair to exclude them from this book on those grounds. A few pieces, though they lacked popularity or wide occurrence, such as Sara Carter's "Railroading on the Great Divide" and the Delmore Brothers' "Blow Yo' Whistle, Freight Train," are simply too fine to leave out.

The songs in this chapter are arranged in approximate chronological order. The title piece, "A Railroader for Me," has slender ties with early nineteenth-century Anglo-American broadside songs and therefore deserves to head the roster. "New River Train" originated in southern Virginia, probably in the 1880s. "On the Dummy Line" and "The Midnight Special" are probably from the turn of the century, "The Rock Island Line" perhaps a bit later. The "Longest Train" complex may well be as old as Reconstruction days, but we have no written record earlier than the turn of the century. The "Reuben's Train" group may also extend back into the last decades of the nineteenth century, but again, the evidence prior to the late 1890s is nonexistent. Their placement in a chronological sequence would be wildly speculative. Elizabeth Cotten's "Freight Train" was probably composed early in this century. "Freight Train Blues" and "Blow Yo' Whistle, Freight Train" were composed in the late 1930s. Sara Carter's composition "Railroading on the Great Divide" was written in about 1952 and is thus the youngest song in the entire book.

My exclusion of later pieces does not imply that none exists, or that those that have been written are not any good. Rather, they are somewhat removed in style from the pieces of the prewar years, and it is difficult to predict a survival in oral tradition for any of them.

A Railroader for Me

RAILROAD DADDY

*This is a 4/4 measure on the recording.
The chorus follows the same melody as the verses.

As I went down to Louisville, some pleasure for to see,
I fell in love with a railroad man, and he in love with me.

I wouldn't marry a farmer, for he's always in the dirt,
I'd rather marry the railroader that wears them pretty blue shirts.

A railroader [*pronounced "railroad-aire"*], a railroader, a
railroader for me,
If ever I marry in all of my life, a railroader's bride I'll be.

I wouldn't marry a goldsmith, for he's always weighing gold,
I'd rather marry the railroader that has to shovel up coal.

Chorus:

I would not marry a merchant, for he's always pleading lies,
I'd rather marry the railroader that has them pretty blue eyes.

Chorus:

I wouldn't marry a blacksmith, for he's always dirty and black,
I'd rather marry the railroader, that works on the L and N track.

Welby Toomey

Of the many folksongs in America that deal with different aspects of courting, one popular type enumerates the various possible candidates and their virtues or shortcomings. In one subtype often found in black tradition, the song is sung from a male perspective:

> I wouldn't marry a yaller gal,
> I'll tell yo' de reason why:
> Her hair's so dad-blamed nappy
> She'd break all de combs I buy.[1]

Similar songs have been found among mountain whites:

> I wouldn't marry a pore gal,
> I'll tell you the reason why:
> She'd blow her nose on a cornbread crust
> En call it punkin pie.[2]

More closely related to "A Railroader for Me" are such pieces sung from the woman's perspective, in which the basis for selection or rejection of the suitor is occupational, as in the Virginia song "Soldier Boy for Me":

> I would not marry a blacksmith, he smuts his nose and chin,
> I'd rather marry a soldier boy
> That marches through the wind.
>   Soldier boy, soldier boy, soldier boy for me,
>   If ever I get married, a soldier's wife I'll be.[3]

In the same family is a North Carolina song, "A Farmer Boy," with this chorus:

> A farmer's boy, a farmer's boy,
> He's the one for me;
> If ever I get married
> A farmer bride I'll be.[4]

Occasionally, stanzas usually associated with "The Roving Gambler" (Laws H 4) turn up in versions of "A Railroader for Me," and vice versa. For example, H. M. Belden obtained a Missouri version entitled "The Railroader" that is in other respects similar to the one transcribed in this book; it includes the stanza standard in "The Roving Gambler":

> I took him in my little parlor
> And cooled him with my fan.
> I whispered in my mother's ear,
> "I love the railroad man."[5]

Sometimes the railroader is definitely not the favored suitor, as in "The Roving Gambler" quoted by Carl Sandburg in his folksong anthology:

> I wouldn't marry a railroad man, and this is the reason why;
> I never seen a railroad man that wouldn't tell his wife a lie.[6]

The earliest recording/publication of the song that specifies the railroader as the young girl's choice is apparently the 1907 sheet music by C. B. Ball entitled "The Railroad Boy." The song is doubtless considerably older: May Kennedy McCord, who sang it for collector Vance Randolph in 1934 (transcribed in *Ozark Folksongs*) and again in 1941 (for the Library of Congress), said she learned it in Missouri in 1897. An interesting piece of verse in the 1892 *Locomotive Engineers' Monthly Journal* suggests that "A Railroader for Me," in some form, was already familiar by that date. Titled "The Sequel," it begins:

> I would not marry a railroad man,
> Indeed, I wouldn't—no!
> For I'd never know what hour he'd come,
> Or when he'd have to go.
> Besides, one never knows where they are,
> Or what pretty girls they see;
> No! when I marry, I want a man
> That has no sweetheart but me.[7]

Needless to say, the outcome of this song is that the speaker falls in love with a railroader and marries him, as did her sister before her.

The bibliographic citations given here are confined to songs in which the railroader is the specific object of affection; references to other forms (in particular, to "The Roving Gambler" and older imported ballads) are given in Belden's headnotes[8] and in Laws's bibliography to "The Roving Gambler."[9] Whether the group of songs "A —— for me" is genetically related to the older, musically distinct "Roving Gambler"/"Roving Journeyman" songs, or only accidently shares some lines, is not obvious to me; at present I favor the latter possibility.

"A Railroader for Me" was not often recorded commercially; I have found only two titles. The version transcribed in this book, the older of the two, was made in 1925 by Welby Toomey for the Starr Piano Company. Toomey recorded a handful of ballads and songs for Starr between 1925 and 1927, then quit the music business. As one of the earliest hillbilly ballad singers to make records, he had long been a source of curiosity to me, and I longed to know more about him. My chance came in the spring of 1969, when, during a visit to Asa Martin in Irvine, Kentucky, Archie Green and I learned that Toomey had been a barber in Lexington a few years earlier. On our way home, we stopped in that city to see if we could find him, a task that proved no more difficult than locating a telephone directory. Ten minutes after we pulled off the highway into Lexington we were greeted by Welby Toomey at the front door of his suburban home.

Toomey told us that his father came to this country from England as a young boy with his parents, who settled on a farm near Winchester, in Clark County, Kentucky. Toomey himself was born in 1897 in neighboring Fayette County and has lived in central Kentucky all his life. The person primarily responsible for his becoming a recording artist was Dennis W. Taylor, a local talent scout of sorts; Taylor was evidently eager to get into the music business but was not a musician himself, and so took the role of promoter. Toomey had had a reputation as a singer in his youth, and Taylor approached him with an offer to finance a trip to Richmond, Indiana, to make records in return for a share of the royalties.

Although Toomey had long since lost all professional interest in performing, he was pleased to talk with us about those days of his youth. His career making records lasted a brief two years, and he left the hillbilly music field just as it was getting somewhere; he had married in 1925 and was beginning to raise a family, and evidently felt that the life of a music maker was not appropriate for his newly assumed domestic responsibilities. After that, he made his living either farming or barbering. But those nine songs that were released over his name still meant something to him: when he took us into his den, on the wall we saw, along with photographs of kinfolk and of the John F. Kennedy family, a 1924 photograph taken of him, Dennis Taylor, and his two instrumental accompanists, Dock Roberts and Ed Boaz, in Starr's acoustic recording studio in Richmond. Toomey still had a few of his old 78s when we visited him, and one that he played for us was "Railroad Daddy." He recalled learning the song from his sister, who played the accordion and sang. Toomey recorded one other railroad song, "The Death of John Henry." Although he recorded no religious songs then, Toomey is now very much concerned with religion, and the final moments of our visit with him were spent discussing his recent trip to the Holy Land, a journey that had meant a great deal to him.[10]

When I transcribed Welby Toomey's "Railroad Daddy" for this book and had difficulty understanding some passages, I wrote him for clarification. There are not many 1925 recordings for which this can still be done.

Toomey's tune differs only slightly from the recordings of Russell Pike and May Kennedy McCord, both from Missouri (see the references). These tunes, in turn, are quite distinct from the "Roving Gambler" tune, which is one reason for my reluctance to assert that one is derived from the other. C. B. Ball's 1907 sheet music shows still a different melody. The relative independence of the different versions is further attested by the differences in the lists of occupations cited (see the accompanying table).

	Farmer	Blacksmith	Gambler	Merchant	Preacher	Goldsmith	Miner	Town boy	Advertiser	Cowboy	Printer	Teacher	Doctor
Ball	x						x	x	x				
Randolph/McCord	x	x	x		x								
Belden	x	x	x	x									
Malone	x										x		
Pike (LC AFS)	x	x											
Lomax	x	x	x		x					x			
Toomey	x	x			x	x							
Arthur/Hatfield	x	x			x							x	x

There have been other folksongs, thematically related, on the subject of the railroader as lover. One early one, "My Ole Man's a Railroad Man," has appeared in both black and white traditions. Stanzas collected in 1891 include:

> My ole man's a railroad man, he works on Number Nine;
> Gets his fifty cents a month, and half that money's mine.

> My ole man's a railroad man, he works on Number Four;
> He's a rustlin' son of a ———, and I'm his dirty ———.[11]

NOTES

1. Newman I. White, *American Negro Folk-Songs* (1928; rpt., Hatboro, Pa.: Folklore Associates, 1965), p. 323.

2. E. C. Perrow, "Songs and Rhymes from the South," *JAF*, 28 (Apr.-June, 1915), 176.

3. Cecil J. Sharp and Maud Karpeles, *English Folk-Songs from the Southern Appalachians* (London: Oxford University Press, 1932), vol. 2, p. 381.

4. *The Frank C. Brown Collection of North Carolina Folklore*, vol. 3, *Folk Songs*, edited by Henry M. Belden and Arthur Palmer Hudson (Durham, N.C.: Duke University Press, 1952), pp. 31–32.

5. Henry M. Belden, *Ballads and Songs Collected by the Missouri Folk-Lore Society*, 2d ed. (Columbia: University of Missouri Press, 1955), p. 377.

6. Carl Sandburg, *The American Songbag* (New York: Harcourt, Brace, 1927), p. 312.

7. "The Sequel," "written for the Brotherhood of Locomotive Engineers Journal" by Mrs. A. Coffenbarger, *LEMJ*, 26 (Nov., 1892), 1022.

8. Belden, *Ballads and Songs*, p. 375.

9. G. Malcolm Laws, Jr., *Native American Balladry*, rev. ed. (Philadelphia: American Folklore Society, 1964), p. 231.

10. For further information on Toomey, see "Tapescript: Interview with Welby Toomey," *JEMFQ*, 5 (Summer, 1969), 63–65, and "Discography of Recordings by Welby Toomey," ibid., pp. 66–67.

11. Gates Thomas, "South Texas Negro Work-Songs," in *Rainbow in the Morning*, edited by J. Frank Dobie, Publications of the Texas Folklore Society, No. 5 (1926; rpt., Hatboro, Pa.: Folklore Associates, 1965), p. 169. Ellipses in the original.

REFERENCES

A. "A Railroad Boy," by C. B. Ball. Published by the George Jaberg Music Co., Cincinnati, Ohio. Copyrighted Sept. 18, 1907 (C 162220). First known published reference.
"Railroad Daddy," by Welby Toomey. Toomey, vocal; Dock Roberts, violin; Edgar Boaz, guitar. Recorded Nov. 13, 1925 (Starr master 12417A), in Richmond, Ind. Released on Gennett 3202, Challenge 159 (as by John Ferguson), and Challenge 504.

B. Belden (1955), 377
Botkin & Harlow, 465–66 (Pike version, LC AFS)
Green (1968), 26
Lomax, A. (1960), 414 (composite text)
Malone, 152–53
Randolph III, 259   "The Railroader" (from McCord)
OTS&P (Mar.-Apr., 1969), 40 (reader request, 1 stanza)
Rosenberg, 105 (title only)
Silverman (1975) I, 113

D. Emry Arthur and Della Hatfield— Paramount 3249, Broadway 8266 "A Railroader Lover for Me"

E. Logan English—Folkways FA 2136: *Kentucky Ballads*

May Kennedy McCord—Library of Congress Archive of Folk Song L61: *Railroad Songs and Ballads*   "The Railroader"
Russ Pike—Library of Congress Archive of Folk Song L20: *Anglo-American Songs and Ballads*   "A Railroader for Me"

Asa Martin. Author's Collection.

New River Train

NEW RIVER TRAIN

I am rid - ing on the New Riv - er train, I am rid - ing on the New Riv - er train; It's the same old train that has brought me here, And it's soon gon-na car-ry me a - way.

I am riding on the New River Train,
I am riding on the New River Train;
It's the same old train that has brought me here,
And it's soon gonna carry me away.

Oh darling, the time ain't long,
Oh darling, the time ain't long;
The time ain't long, till I'll be gone,
Gone away on that New River Train.

Oh darling, remember what you said,
Oh darling, remember what you said;
Remember that you said, you had rather see me dead,
Than see me in my rough and rowdy ways.

Oh darling, you can't love two,
Oh darling, you can't love two;
You can't love two and your little heart be true,
Oh darling, you can't love two.

Oh darling, come kiss me at your door,
Oh darling, come kiss me at your door;
Come and kiss me at your door, for it's time that I must go,
For I thought I heard that west-bound whistle blow.
    Chorus:

Ernest Stoneman and the Sweet Brothers

Running north-south from North Carolina across western Virginia and part of West Virginia as far as the Kanawha River, the New River, in the heart of some of the nation's richest coal veins, has been the location for several railroad lines: the C & O and the

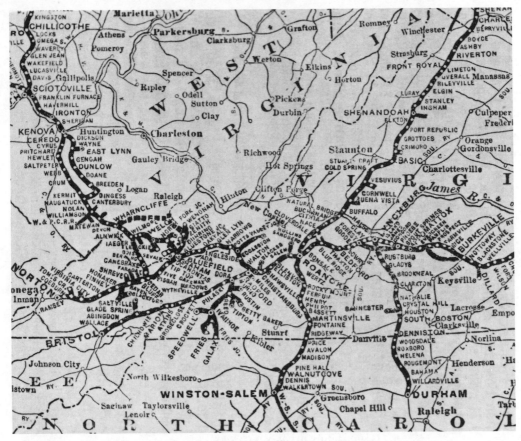

New River and neighboring railroads. Author's Collection.

Virginian in West Virginia and the N & W in Virginia all parallel it in various locations. No version of "I'm Riding on That New River Train" contains specific references to identify which railroad is being sung about, but since the earliest reports of the song all come from Virginia, that state is the likely place of origin. The Ward family of the Galax, Virginia, area claimed that the song became part of their family repertoire in about 1895.[1] According to Eric Davidson, who recorded extensively in the same area in the 1960s, local residents said the song referred to the New River Railroad branch that ran into Fries when the town was built, around the turn of the century. This cannot be quite correct. Two companies, the New River Railroad Company (of Virginia) and the New River Railroad Company of West Virginia, were chartered in 1881 by the Norfolk and Western to build extensions and branches to the N & W, and were consolidated with the N & W in May of 1882. The New River Division, a seventy-five mile stretch from New River, Virginia, to Pocahantas, West Virginia, was completed in May of 1883. But the trackage through the area of Galax and Fries was not on this New River line: it was on the Cripple Creek extension (part of which also lay alongside the New River), later called the North Carolina Division. Construction on this line began in December, 1883, and continued, with interruptions, for several years, reaching what is now Galax in the early 1890s. The song, therefore, probably refers to this extension along the New River, rather than to the New River Division itself, and probably dates to the late 1880s at the earliest.

In any case, we can assume that the song is a product of Virginia, and the earliest recordings are by residents of that area: first Henry Whitter, in about December, 1923, and then Kelly Harrell, in January, 1925. Whitter hailed from Fries, near the New River and on the N & W branch to Galax. Harrell was born near Max Meadows, a few miles north and along the same stretch of rail.

The song can be divided into two types of stanzas: verses that refer to the railroad, and an enumerative sequence of the form

> Darling, you can't love two,
> Darling, you can't love two;
> You can't love two and still be true,
> Darling, you can't love two.

Whitter's sequence went from one to four; Harrell's and others after him went as high as six. The other stanzas in the sequence are:

> You can't love one . . . and have any fun;
>
> You can't love three . . . and then love me;
>
> You can't love four . . . and love me any more;
>
> You can't love five . . . and get honey from my bee hive;
>
> You can't love six . . . that kind of love won't mix.

Almost all versions begin with or use as a chorus this familiar stanza:

> I'm riding on that New River train,
> I'm riding on that New River train;
> The same old train that brought me here
> Is soon going to carry me away.

And many conclude with Harrell's final stanza:

> Darling, remember what you said,
> Darling, remember what you said;
> Remember that you said, you'd rather see me dead
> Than see me on that New River train.

But this is the extent of train references in most versions. Ernest Stoneman's 1928 recording is one of the few with additional railroad references, and for that reason we have transcribed it here.

Harrell's version was closely copied by Tennessean Sid Harkreader in April, 1925, and then five times by Vernon Dalhart by midsummer of 1925—the first evidence that the song had left the locale that gave it birth. In November, 1925, folklorist Robert W. Gordon recorded a version from a singer in Asheville, North Carolina, noting in his transcription that he thought the song had been learned from a phonograph record.[2] The text is indeed very close to Kelly Harrell's—one of our earliest examples of the influence of hillbilly records on oral folk tradition.

After 1925, the song seemed to spread rapidly. In 1936, Bill and Charlie Monroe recorded a snappy version consisting of the enumerative stanzas (one through six), and the usual chorus, paving the way for the song's later entry into bluegrass repertoire. In the same year, Carson Robison copyrighted an arrangement under the pseudonym of

Maggie Andrews (his mother's maiden name); this version was later used by Sterling and McClintock in their collection *Railroad Songs of Yesterday*. Most versions end the enumeration at six, as did the influential recordings by Dalhart and the Monroe Brothers. But there is no reason why singers cannot, with only a little imagination, continue the sequence, as did one Ozarks singer from whom Vance Randolph collected a version that went as high as ten. Her added stanzas:

> You can't love seven . . . and meet me in heaven;
>
> You can't love eight . . . and meet me at the gate;
>
> You can't love nine . . . and our two hearts entwine;
>
> You can't love ten . . . that's too many men.[3]

In style, the song is reminiscent of several other southern mountain banjo songs, though it is difficult to say which preceded which. "My Last Old Dollar Is Gone" and "I Wish I Was a Mole in the Ground" are good examples.[4] Wade Ward's instrumental version, recorded in 1961, combines "New River Train" with "900 Miles," alternating between major and minor scales. If there were any evidence of the enumerative sequence of verses without the New River train referents, it would be easy to conclude that "New River Train" was an adaptation of an older courting song; but the two elements of the song never occur without each other.

NOTES

1. Eric Davidson, brochure notes to Folkways FA 2363: *The Music of Roscoe Holcomb and Wade Ward*, p. 8.

2. Gordon Collection (N.C.) 157; cylinder A106. Obtained from J. C. Ammons, Nov. 16, 1925.

3. "New River Train," sung by Lillian Short, LC AFS 5327 A1.

4. See, e.g., *The Frank C. Brown Collection of North Carolina Folklore*, vol. 3, *Folk Songs*, edited by Henry M. Belden and Arthur Palmer Hudson (Durham, N.C.: Duke University Press, 1952), p. 215.

REFERENCES

A. "New River Train," by Ernest Stoneman and the Sweet Brothers. Recorded July 9, 1928 (Starr master GE-14015), in Richmond, Ind. Released on Gennett 6619 in Nov., 1928 (as by Justin Winfield), and Supertone 9400 (as by Uncle Ben Hawkins). Reissued on Historical HLP 8002 (BC 2433-1): *Early Country Music, Vol. 1*.

"New River Train," by Henry Whitter. Vocal, guitar, and harmonica. Recorded ca. Dec., 1923 (General Phonograph Co. master 72341), in New York City. Released on OKeh 40143 in Oct., 1924. First recording (or publication) of the song.

"New River Train," by Kelly Harrell. Harrell, vocal; fiddle and guitar ac- companiment. Recorded Jan. 7, 1925 (Victor master 31584), in New York City. Re-recorded electrically, with fiddle, guitar, harmonica, and train whistle accompaniment, on June 8, 1926. Acoustical recording released on Victor 19596 in Apr., 1925; electrical recording released on Victor 20171 in ca. Nov., 1926. Both reissued on Bear Family (West Germany) FV 12508: *The Complete Kelly Harrell*. First influential recording of the song.

B. Britt, 32
Brown III, 137   "Darling, You Can't Love but One"
Campbell & Holstein, 8
Davis, A. K., 249 (2 versions, title and first line only)

Dykema, 48
Green (1968), 19
Gregory
Landeck (1954), 78
Leisy (1966) 239
Leisy (1973), 91
Pitts (1951a), 34–35
Pitts (1954), 16–17
Rosenberg, 90 (2 versions, title and first
    line only)
Seeger, P. (1961), 74
Silverman (1975) II, 148
Smith, J., 4
Walsh (1964)
Wolfe (1958), 76

C. GORDON COLLECTION (N.C.):
    157—John Carl Ammons, Asheville, N.C.
    (Nov. 16, 1925)

    GORDON MSS:
    2779—Foswoode Tarleton

D. Cauley Family—Banner 33146, Melotone
        13113, Perfect 13032, Oriole 8372,
        Romeo 5372
    Crazy Hillbillies Band—OKeh
        45579   "Leaving on the New River
        Train"
    Vernon Dalhart—Columbia 15032-D
    —Gennett 3084, Challenge 165,
        Challenge 321, Herwin 75506,
        Silvertone 3084
    Vernon Dalhart and Company—Edison
        51597, Edison 5032 (cylinder); Mark56
        794: First Recorded Railroad Songs
    Sid Harkreader—Vocalion 15035,
        Vocalion 5063
    Dick Hartman—Bluebird B-5871
    Hartman's Tennessee Ramblers—
        Bluebird B-6162
    Frank Luther, Zora Layman, and
        Leonard Stokes—Decca 2141
    Guy Massey (Vernon Dalhart
        pseudonym)—Pathé 032133, Perfect
        12212
    Monroe Brothers—Bluebird B-6645,
        Montgomery Ward M-4748; RCA
        Camden CAL 774: Early Blue Grass
        Music; RCA Victor (England) RCX 7103
        (EP): Country Guitar, Vol. 14; RCA

    Victor (Japan) RA 5281: Early Blue Grass
        Music
    Old Brother Charlie—Mercury 6206
    Carson Robison and his Pioneers—Regal
        Zonophone (Australia) G 40095
        "Blue River Train" (derivative piece)
    Terry Shand—Decca 3836
    Bert Shaw (Jess Hillard pseudonym)—
        Superior 2805
    South Georgia Highballers—OKeh
        45166   "Green River Train"
    Texas Rangers—Decca 5139
    Westerners—Conqueror 8204
    Henry Whitter—OKeh 40143

E. Chubby Anthony and Mike Seeger—
        Folkways FA 2318: Mountain Music
        Bluegrass Style
    Lucille Bassett—Val-Hill 1008 (45 rpm)
    Bluegrass 45—Down Home (Japan) 4501:
        Run Mountain
    Benny and Vallie Cain—Rebel 237 (45
        rpm); Rebel R-1473 (no title)
    Jack Casey—Rural Rhythm RRJC-206:
        Jack Casey
    Girls of the Golden West (Milly and
        Dolly Good)—Bluebonnet BL 106:
        Songs for You—Old and New, Vol. 1
    Billy Grammer—Decca DL 4542/74542:
        Gotta Travel On
    Bobby Helms—Vocalion 3743/73743:
        Someone Was Already There
    Iron Mountain String Band—Folkways
        FA 2477: Walkin' in the Parlor
    Kentucky Colonels—Rounder 0070: The
        Kentucky Colonels, 1965–1966,
        Featuring Roland and Clarence White
    Laurel River Valley Boys—Riverside RLP
        7504/97504: Dance All Night with a
        Bottle in My Hand; Judson J 3031:
        Music for Moonshiners
    McLain Family Band—Country Life
        CLR-6: On the Road
    Maggie Valley Boys—Rural Rhythm
        RR-MVB 170: The Maggie Valley Boys
    Alan Mills—Folkways FC 7009 (FP 709):
        More Songs to Grow On
    New River Boys—Mad Bag MB 288–289:
        Country Blue Grass Jamboree
    Professors—Beaver Fork Bflp-55: The
        Professors

Randolph County String Band—Davis
   Unlimited DU 33001: *Under the
   Weeping Willow*
Ridge Rangers—Library of Congress
   Archive of Folk Song L61: *Railroad
   Songs and Ballads*
Pete Seeger—Folkways FA 2322:
   American Favorite Ballads, Vol. 3
Glen Smith—Union Grove SS-3: *More
   Goodies from the Hills*
Smokey Mountain Boys—Starday SLP
   276: *Country Music Cannonball*
   "Smokey Mountain Train"
Ed Stoker—Voyager VRLP 313-S: *Tenino
   Old Time Music Festival, 1973–74*
Stoneman Family—Folkways FA 2315:
   Old Time Tunes of the South
Strange Creek Singers—Arhoolie 4004:
   The Strange Creek Singers
Stump Jumpers—Rural Rhythm
   RR-BE-180: *Pickin' Grinnin' 'n' Singin'*
Vandergrift Brothers—Rural Rhythm
   RR-155: *Country Greats*
Wade Ward—Folkways FA 2363: *The
   Music of Roscoe Holcomb and Wade
   Ward*
Wear Family—Rural Rhythm RR 123:
   *Country and Bluegrass with the Great
   Wear Family*
White Brothers (New Kentucky

Colonels)—Rounder 0073: *The White
   Brothers*
Lulu Belle and Scotty Wiseman—Old
   Homestead OHS 90037: *Have I Told
   You Lately That I Love You*

F. GORDON COLLECTION (N.C.):
   A106 (MS 157)—John Carl Ammons,
      Asheville, N.C. (Nov. 16, 1925)

LC AFS:
William C. Bailey—AFS 13719 29
Calvin Cole—AFS 15060 20
Carlos Gallimore—AFS 1342 A2
Leroy Gardner and Burl Langford—AFS
   11898
Dona Hammons Gum—AFS 17019 B3
Audrey Haught—AFS 11907 A
Aunt Molly Jackson—AFS 73 B3
Bascom Lamar Lunsford—AFS 1818 B1
   "I'm Riding on That New River Train"
Sidna Myers—AFS 15067 A13
Harvey Napier—AFS 9855 A2
Ridge Rangers—AFS 1693 A2
Arlene Sherman—AFS 11891 B
Lillian Short—AFS 5327 A1
Fields Ward and the Bogtrotters—AFS
   1371
Wade Ward—AFS 1371 A2
   —AFS 15066 B12
Norm Wood—AFS 13144 B9

The Rock Island Line

ROCK ISLAND LINE

Cuttin' in Arkansas. They cuttin' by axes, there's 'bout ten or twelve men on the log and they cuttin' four-foot wood, but they takin' a fly-chip out. One man on one side and one on the other, each man's got a pole-axe and this man what cut right-handed, he steps on the other side. The one that's left-handed, he's right over next to him, but he's on the other side. They cuttin' in the same chip. You can't cut your axe in there, and leave it, you got to pick it up in the rhythm with the saw as I cut down, and you bring it up. And this here's the song the boys sing:

> Oh, the Rock Island line, mighty good road,
> Oh, the Rock Island line, road to ride;
> Oh, the Rock Island line, mighty good road,
> If you want to ride, you got to ride it like you find it,
> Get your ticket at the station on the Rock Island line.

The boys swing the axes. One man he give the word and they catch him down the line, just like coaches, and all on the log:

> Jesus died to save our sins,

The old man's all down like this,

> Glory to God, we're gonna meet him again.

> On the Rock Island line, mighty good road,
> On the Rock Island line, road to ride;
> On the Rock Island line, mighty good road,
> If you want to ride, you got to ride it like you find it,
> Get your ticket at the station on the Rock Island line.

Leadbelly (Library of Congress recording, 1937)

ROCK ISLAND LINE

That Rock Island line train out of New 'leans comin' back this-a way. That depot agent gonna throw that switch board over the track. That mean that Rock Island line train's got to go in the hole. That man don't want to stop that train; he goin' to talk to the depot agent with his whistle, and this is what he gonna tell him.

I got cows, I got hors-es, I got hogs, I got sheeps, I got

*The bass pattern for the first nine measures is ♪ A ♪ G ♪ E with the A chord sustained above, struck on the second quarter-note.

goats, I got all live - stock.___ I got all live - stock.

I got cows, I got horses, I got hogs, I got sheeps, I got goats,
I got all livestock. I got all livestock.

That depot agent gonna let that train go by. When that Rock Island line train
get by, that engineerman goin' talk back to the depot agent with his whistle
and this is what he' gonna tell him.

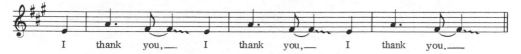

I thank you,___ I thank you,___ I thank you.___

I thank you, I thank you, I thank you.

Now that old Rock Island train is gettin' on down the road.

Oh, the Rock Is - land line,___ 'tsa might-y good road,___ Oh, the

Rock Is - land line,___ it's a road___ to ride; Oh, the

Rock Is - land line,___ it's a might-y good road, ___ If you

wants to ride you got - ta ride it like you find it, Get your

tick-et at the sta-tion on the Rock Is - land line.___

Je-sus died to save our sins; Glo-ry to God, we're gon-na meet him a-gain.___

Oh, the Rock Island line, 'tsa mighty good road,
Oh, the Rock Island line, it's a road to ride;
Oh, the Rock Island line, it's a mighty good road,
If you wants to ride you gotta ride it like you find it,
Get your ticket at the station on the Rock Island line.

Jesus died to save our sins;
Glory to God, we're gonna meet him again.
  Chorus:

I may be right an' I may be wrong,
I know you're gwine-a miss me when I'm gone.
  Chorus (2):

A-B-C double X-Y-Z,
Cats in the cupboard but they don't see me.
  Chorus:

Leadbelly (Capitol recording, 1944)

This 1950s favorite of the folksong revival has always been associated with the great black folksinger Huddie Ledbetter (Leadbelly), who, though he did not originate it, is unquestionably responsible for its popularity.

The song was first collected by John Lomax in 1934 on one of his tours of state prisons through the South searching for folksongs. He recorded it twice, first from a group of black convicts in Little Rock, Arkansas, and shortly thereafter from another group of black convicts, lead by Kelly Pace, at Cummins State Farm, Gould, Arkansas. Lomax was told it was an Arkansas song, and he did not find it elsewhere. During the trip, Leadbelly was employed as Lomax's chauffeur, and this was doubtless when he first heard "The Rock Island Line."

The words that John Lomax (and, presumably, Leadbelly) heard in 1934 were somewhat different from the text that Leadbelly later standardized. There were three stanzas and a chorus:

I said the Rock Island line is a mighty good road,
I said the Rock Island line is a road to ride;
I said the Rock Island line is a mighty good road,
If you want to ride you got to ride it like you're flyin',
Well, it made it back to Little Rock at eight-forty-nine.

Jesus died to save me in all of my sins,
Well-a glory to God, we're gonna meet him again.
  Chorus:

I said, we have engineermen, firemen, too,
We got [?as good a pullman] porters and brakemen, too.
  Chorus:

Well, the train got to Memphis just on time,
Well, it made it back to Little Rock at eight-forty-nine.
  Chorus:

Leadbelly was born on January 21, 1885, near Mooringsport, Louisiana, not far from the Texas border. The outlines of his career have been sketched repeatedly on album liner notes and magazine tributes—how he early took to music, learning to play first accordion, then harmonica, guitar, mandolin, and piano, settling down to twelve-string guitar for most of his career; how he traveled with Blind Lemon Jefferson for a period;

how he was imprisoned twice, once for murder and once for attempted murder, and both times received a pardon.

The second pardon has often been attributed to the Lomaxes' intervention on Leadbelly's behalf. However, pertinent documents indicate that (1) Leadbelly was sentenced on February 25, 1930, for a period of six to ten years, subject to commutation provided by the law; (2) in June, 1933, the Board of Pardons recommended a sentence of from three to ten years; (3) Governor O. K. Allen commuted the sentence, effective August, 1934. The Lomaxes first met Leadbelly in July, 1933. Following his release from prison, he began working for John Lomax in September, 1934, traveling with him as his chauffeur until mid-1935, when he returned to Shreveport.[1]

Leadbelly's first recordings were made for John Lomax in July, 1934. His first commercial recording sessions were with the American Record Corporation in New York in January, 1935, but of the more than forty titles recorded between January and March, only six were issued by ARC. From 1937 until his death in 1949, Leadbelly lived in New York City and became an integral part of the early folksong revival there. In addition to being a gifted musician with a powerful voice and compelling stage presence, he was intelligent and perceptive, and quick to learn what his new white city audience wanted to hear him sing. He was quick at learning new songs and adapting them to his own inimitable style.

Leadbelly first recorded "Rock Island Line" in June, 1937, for the Library of Congress in Washington, D.C. That selection, the text of which is transcribed here, has since been released on LP. His spoken introduction of the song describes the log cutting that the song accompanied when he, with Lomax, heard it in Arkansas. In June, 1940, he recorded the song for RCA Victor with the Golden Gate Quartet, this time unaccompanied and without spoken introduction. In January, 1942, he recorded it a third time for Moses Asch, who subsequently released the piece on two of his 78 rpm labels, Asch and Disc. By now Leadbelly had begun to work out the spoken introduction about livestock and pig iron that we now think of as an integral part of the song. By the time of his fourth recording, for Capitol Records in Hollywood in October, 1944 (transcribed here), the introduction was nearly complete. It still lacked the final rejoinder of the engineer who signaled to the depot agent, as his train gathered steam and disappeared from sight.

> I fooled you, I fooled you,
> I got iron,
> I got all pig iron, I got all pig iron.

This part appeared on Leadbelly's recording for Moses Asch, probably 1944–46, issued on Folkways FP 14 (subsequently renumbered FA 2014): *Rock Island Line*. During the last few years of his life, Leadbelly recorded the song again and performed it regularly at his numerous concerts and on various radio programs, thus exposing people throughout the country to what was once strictly an Arkansas worksong.

After Leadbelly's death, the song was picked up by other influential performers in the awakening folksong movement: English singer Lonnie Donegan recorded it in 1956 and had a hit on both sides of the Atlantic (it climbed to number ten on *Billboard*'s pop charts that March); and it was later recorded by such successful artists as the Weavers, Odetta, the Tarriers, the Gateway Singers, and the Rooftop Singers. In the country-and-western field it was waxed by Grandpa Jones, Johnny Horton, Johnny Cash, and others. It was parodied by Stan Freberg—a far cry from the heat and dust of the Arkansas prison farms.

"The Rock Island Line" is not a railroad song in the sense that it was sung by railroaders. It began life, to the best of our knowledge, as a worksong. If John Lomax's informants were correct that the song originated in Arkansas, that suggests that the piece dates from the early 1900s or later. In April, 1902, the Chicago, Rock Island, and Pacific Railway Company (a subsidiary of the Chicago, Rock Island, and Pacific Railroad Company, in turn a subsidiary of the Rock Island Company) first entered the state of Arkansas by acquiring controlling rights to the Choctaw, Oklahoma, and Gulf Railroad, which had a major line across the state from Mansfield, through Little Rock, to Memphis, Tennessee. (The early texts that John Lomax collected, it should be recalled, all had a stanza about a train going from Memphis to Little Rock.) On the other hand, there is no reason, based on the words of the song itself, to believe that the song could not have originated elsewhere, in which case it could have sprung up considerably earlier—the Chicago, Rock Island, and Pacific Railway Company dates back to 1880.

NOTE

1. I am grateful to John Cowley for summarizing for me the information about Leadbelly's life in the Library of Congress Archive of Folk Song files.

REFERENCES

A. "Rock Island Line," by a group of Negro convicts. Recorded by John A. Lomax in Sept., 1934, in Little Rock, Ark. Library of Congress Archive of Folk Song AFS 236 Al. Earliest known recording of the song,

"Rock Island Line," by Huddie Ledbetter (Leadbelly). Vocal and guitar. Recorded in June, 1937, in Washington, D.C. Library of Congress Archive of Folk Song AFS 995 B2. Released on Elektra EKL 301/2: *The Library of Congress Recordings*. First recording by Leadbelly; text transcribed here.

B. Brand (1961), 58–59
Donegan (1956)
Emrich (1974), 666
Landeck (1950b), 90
Leadbelly (1959a), 74
Leadbelly (1959b), 78
Leadbelly (1962), 80
Leisy (1966), 282
Leisy (1973), 116
Mursell (Grade 4), 124–25
Okun, 14, 94–96
Oliver (1957)
Reprints from Sing Out #3, 23
Silber & Silber, 102
Sing Out!, 2 (Feb., 1952), 9

Weavers (1951), 38
Weavers (1960), 12

D. Lonnie Donegan—Decca (England) F 10647, Decca (England) DFE 6345 (45 rpm); London 1650 (45 rpm); London 11008 (45 rpm); London LL-1613: *London Hit Parade*; Sire H-3711: *Roots of British Rock*

Louis M. "Grandpa" Jones—King 4918 (78 and 45 rpm); King 809: *Rollin' Along with Grandpa Jones*

Leadbelly (Huddie Ledbetter)—Victor (England) RCX-146 (7″ 45 rpm); RCA Victor LPV 505: *Midnight Special*

—Asch 102, Disc 6090 (in album 735); Stinson SLP 17: *Leadbelly Memorial, Vol. 1* (10″ LP); Melodisc (England) EPM 7-77 (EP); Melodisc (England) MLP 12-120: *The Saga of Leadbelly*; Collector's Classics CC 23: *Leadbelly*; Storyville (Denmark) A 45057 (45 rpm)

—Capitol 10021; Capitol (England) LC 6508; Capitol T 1821: *Leadbelly*; Capitol H 239

E. Chris Barber—Everest 224: *Chris Barber*

Brothers Four—Columbia CL 1828/CS 8628: *In Person*; Columbia CL 1697/CS 8497: *Brothers Four Songbook*

Johnny Cash—Sun SLP 1220: *Hot and Blue Guitar*; Sun EP 112 (45 rpm EP): *Country Boy, Vol. 1*; Sun SLP 1270: *All Aboard the Blue Train*; London (England) RE 1212 (45 rpm EP): *Country Boy, Vol. 1*; Sun 104: *Story Songs*; Sun 106: *Show Time*; Sun 127: *Original Golden Hits, Vol. 3*; Pickwick JS 6101: *Rock Island Line*

—Everest Archive of Folk Music AFM 278: *Johnny Cash*

—Columbia KC-34088: *Strawberry Cake*

—Trip X-8511: *Best of Johnny Cash Country, Vol. 2*

Coachmen—Hi Fi R420: *Subways of Boston* "Rock Island"

Don Cornell—Coral 9-61613

Country Ramblers—RCA Camden CAS 2413: *Honey Come Back/If I Were a Carpenter and Other Country Favorites*

Dick Curless—Tower T/DT 5015: *Travelin' Man*

Bobby Darin and the Jaybirds—Decca 29883 (45 rpm); Decca DL-4036: *Golden Oldies*

Jack Elliott—Prestige International 13065: *At the Second Fret*

—Prestige Folklore FL 14019: *Hootenanny with Jack Elliott*

Folk Four—Audio Fidelity 2141/6141: *Sound of Their Own*

Stan Freberg—Capitol T-2020: *Best of Stan Freberg*; Capitol T-777: *Child's Garden of Freberg*

Gateway Singers—Decca DL-8413: *Puttin' on the Style*

Goodtime Singers—Capitol T/ST 2041: *Goodtime Singers*

Honey Dreamers—RCA Camden CAL 318

Johnny Horton—Columbia 4-43228; Columbia CL-2566/CS-9366: *On the Louisiana Hayride*; Columbia CG 30884: *World of Johnny Horton*

Brian Hyland—Philips 200158/600158: *Rockin' Folk*

Leadbelly (Huddie Ledbetter)—Folkways FA 2014 (FP 14): *Rock Island Line*; Folkways FTS 31019: *Take This Hammer*; Verve/Folkways FV/FVS 9001: *Take This Hammer*

—Folkways FC 7533: *Negro Folk Songs for Young People*

—Folkways FA 2941 (FP 241): *Leadbelly's Last Sessions, Vol. 1*

—Folkways FA 2942 (FP 242): *Leadbelly's Last Sessions, Vol. 2*

—Folkways FC 7020: *Songs to Grow On, Vol. 2—School Days*

—Elektra EKL 301: *The Library of Congress Recordings*

—Playboy PB 119: *Leadbelly*

Odetta and Larry—Fantasy 3345/8345: *Odetta*; Fantasy 3252: *Odetta and Larry*; Fantasy EP 4017; Fantasy 3-15

Otis Trio—Roulette 25236: *And Now . . . the Missing Otis Trio*

Kelly Pace and group—Library of Congress Archive of Folk Song L50: *The Ballad Hunter, Parts 3 and 4*, and L8: *Negro Work Songs and Calls* (from AFS 248 A1)

Rooftop Singers—Vanguard 9134/79134: *Good Time*

Soundtrack—ABC DP 939: *Leadbelly*

Tarriers—Glory PG 1200: *The Tarriers*

Weavers—Decca 28919 (45 rpm); Decca DL-4277/74277: *Folk Songs of America*; Decca DL-4389: *Best of the Weavers*, Decca DL-5169: *The Weavers' Greatest Hits*; Decca DXB/DXSB7-173: *Best of the Weavers*

—Vanguard 9010 and VSD 6533: *Weavers at Carnegie Hall*; Vanguard VSD 15/16: *Greatest Hits*

—Vanguard 9161/79161: *Weavers Reunion*

F. LC AFS:

Group of Negro convicts—AFS 248 A1
Group of Negro convicts—AFS 2671 A1

The Midnight Special

PISTOL PETE'S MIDNIGHT SPECIAL

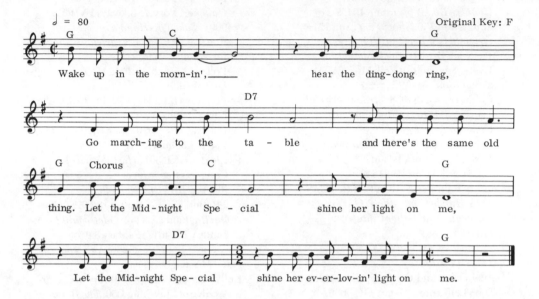

Wake up in the morn-in', _____ hear the ding-dong ring,
Go march-ing to the ta - ble and there's the same old
thing. Let the Mid-night Spe - cial shine her light on me,
Let the Mid-night Spe - cial shine her ev-er-lov-in' light on me.

Wake up in the mornin', hear the ding-dong ring,
Go marchin' to the table and there's the same old thing.
  Let the Midnight Special shine her light on me,
  Let the Midnight Special shine her ever-loving light on me.

Yonder comes my woman. How do you know?
I can tell her by her apron and the dress she wore.
Umbrella on her shoulder, piece of paper in her hand,
Marching down to the captain, she says, "I wants my man."
  Chorus:

I never had the blues so in all my life before,
Than when my baby left me, at the jailhouse door.
Oh, she left me crying, the tears rolled down her face,
Says, "I'd rather see you dead, boy, than in this place."
  Chorus:

Now, Mister McGinty is a good man,
But he's run away now with a cowboy band.
  Chorus:

Now Otto Gray, he's a Stillwater man,
But he's manager now of a cowboy band.
  Chorus:

When you go to the city, boys, you better have the [?bail],
Or the law, they'll arrest you, and they'll put you in jail.

The judge he'll fine you, they'll shake you down,
If you haven't got the money, boys, you're jailhouse bound.
  Chorus:

If you got a good man, woman, you better keep him at home,
For those city women won't leave him alone.
They'll paint and powder, they sure look swell,
And the first thing you know, woman, your man's gone to h——.
  Chorus:

Dave Cutrell

During the 1950s folksong revival, a favorite at hootenannies and concerts was this Texas prisoners' song. The Lomaxes wrote that the Midnight Special was the *Golden Gate Limited*, departing from Houston's Southern Pacific depot at midnight for San Antonio, El Paso, and points west.[1] Thirty miles out of Houston, the Midnight Special shone its light through the barred windows at the Texas state prison farm at Sugarland, reminding the inmates of the light and freedom on the other side of the prison walls.[2] In an engrossing examination titled "A Who's Who of 'The Midnight Special,'" Texas folklorist Mack McCormick traced the individuals named in some versions of the song (especially Leadbelly's) to a 1923 incident.[3] Jack Smith, a bank robber sentenced to twenty-five years' hard labor, broke out of the Houston county jail while waiting for the transfer man, Uncle Bud Russell, who was due to arrive shortly to take him to the state penitentiary. Smith was captured a few hours later by Houston sheriff T. A. Binford. Four other Houston law officers of that time were memorialized in one of Leadbelly's stanzas.

> Bason an' Brock will arrest you,
> Payton an' Boone will take you down;
> Oh, the judge will sentence you,
> Penitentiary bound.[4]

McCormick's researches do not prove that the song "The Midnight Special" originated at the time of this 1923 jailbreak. It seems more probable that Leadbelly and others set the details of that event into the framework of an earlier, well-established traditional song. The strongest evidence for this assumption is that the song appeared widely throughout the South within a very few years after 1923, and invariably in versions that did not mention any of the individuals associated with the Houston events of 1923.

That some elements of "The Midnight Special" are far older than the song as a whole is attested by verses Howard W. Odum printed in 1911:

> Get up in mornin' when ding dong rings,
> Look at table—see same damn things.[5]

The earliest reference to the song I have found was in a letter to Robert W. Gordon, then conducting the column "Old Songs That Men Have Sung" in *Adventure* magazine. Dated August 3, 1923, the letter requested additional verses of the song, and gave one verse ("If you go to the city, you better go right . . . ") and chorus. Carl Sandburg published two variants in his 1927 anthology, *American Songbag*, both without attribution. A frequent source of Sandburg's material was Robert W. Gordon's immense manuscript collection of folksongs, gathered during the several years' correspondence with readers in his column. Another of Gordon's correspondents, Terrill McKay, sent Gordon a song he called simply "Jail Song" that he had heard several years earlier, in the fall of 1923, in the Harris County Jail in Houston. Except for a few adjustments in the use of dialect, and the change of Judge Robinson's name to Judge Nelson, this song is identical with one of the two that Sandburg printed (p. 217). Gordon himself printed a fragment of the song in one of a series of columns on folksongs that he published in the *New York Times* in 1927. In McKay's version, Sheriff Binford became T. Bentley.

The first commercial recording of "The Midnight Special" was made in 1926, by Dave Cutrell, with McGinty's Oklahoma Cowboy Band, for the OKeh label; that performance is transcribed here. The first disc by a black folksinger was Mississippi bluesman Sam Collins's version, "Midnight Special Blues," recorded in September, 1927, for the Starr Piano Company. (The "Midnight Special" recorded by Sodarisa Miller in 1925 is not related.)

Billy McGinty, one-time member of Teddy Roosevelt's "Rough Riders" and an early cowboy of considerable renown in Texas, Oklahoma, and Arizona, was not himself a musician; but starting in 1925 he headed up an organization of old-time musicians from Ripley, Oklahoma. In the following months the group made numerous personal appearances and several radio broadcasts. Before long the group was joined by Dave Cutrell, an old-time musician from Drumright, Oklahoma, nicknamed "Pistol Pete." Cutrell was best known for his rendition of "The Midnight Special," and it was requested of him any time he appeared in concert.[6] In late 1925 or early 1926, Otto Gray of Stillwater took over leadership of the band. Both Gray and McGinty are mentioned in Cutrell's rendition, recorded in May, 1926. Three years later, Gray's own band (to what extent the personnel had changed I don't know) recorded "The Midnight Special" for the Vocalion label.

The person most responsible for spreading the popularity of "The Midnight Special" was doubtless Huddie Leadbetter. "Leadbelly" (see the discussion of "The Rock Island Line" for a biographical sketch and references) recorded the song several times in his career. The earliest was in July, 1934, when John Lomax recorded him for the Library of Congress in the Louisiana State Prison Farm at Angola. In early 1935, after Leadbelly's prison sentence had been commuted, the Lomaxes recorded some sixty songs from him, one of which was a second version of "The Midnight Special." The third recording was made in 1940 for RCA Victor, with the Golden Gate Quartet providing vocal accompaniment. A fourth version was waxed for Moses Asch's Disc label in 1946, and the final recording was made in 1948 and issued on the Folkways *Last Sessions* set. The first recording was reissued on the Elektra album *The Library of Congress Recordings*. A different Leadbelly text was published in the Lomaxes' 1936 collection of Leadbelly's songs, and the versions printed in several later collections by the Lomaxes are in turn different from that text. The text printed by Botkin in 1944 was transcribed by Pete Seeger from an unidentified Leadbelly recording; it is from none of those mentioned above.

The Watts and Wilson 1927 version, "Walk Right in Belmont," is of interest not only because it is fairly early, but also because it has been localized to North Carolina, as has the later piece by Roy Martin, "North Carolina Blues."[7]

In addition to the two Leadbelly recordings, the Lomaxes collected five other versions on field trips between 1933 and 1936. The first of these was obtained in July, 1933, at the Central State Farm in Sugarland, Texas, from a black prisoner nicknamed "Mexico" (probably Ernest Williams). The next, by Jesse Bradley in the state penitentiary at Huntsville, Texas, mentions Bud Russell and the undecipherable name of some judge, and changes the usual city name of Houston to Dallas. One interesting version, collected from prisoners at the state prison at Parchman, Mississippi, has this chorus:

> Let the Midnight Special shine her light on me,
> You take the Illinois Central, and come to Kankakee.[8]

The other versions contain no specific localizations. Leadbelly's recordings are, then, the only well-known early ones that specifically refer to persons involved in that 1923 Houston incident.

The "Midnight Special" tune is, in part, a variant of the 1900 ragtime pop tune "Creole Belles."

NOTES

1. John A. Lomax and Alan Lomax, *Folk Song: U.S.A.* (New York: Duell, Sloan and Pearce, 1947), p. 292.

2. An alternative explanation for what the Midnight Special meant to prison inmates was offered by Carl F. Andre of Vicksburg, Miss., in a July 27, 1955, letter to Duncan Emrich, then head of the Library of Congress Archive of Folk Song: "As I got the story, a number of years back, convicts who had been outstanding during the week were rewarded on Sunday by a visit from Memphis prostitutes who boarded a train in Memphis at Midnight Saturday; hence the title of the song."

3. Mack McCormick, "A Who's Who of 'The Midnight Special,'" *Caravan*, No. 19 (Jan., 1960), pp. 10-21.

4. From LC AFS 124 A1, reissued on Elektra EKL 301/2 (see discography).

5. "Grade Song," in Howard W. Odum, "Folk-Song and Folk-Poetry as Found in the Secular Songs of the Southern Negroes," *JAF*, 24 (Oct.-Dec., 1911), 382; reprinted in Howard W. Odum and Guy B. Johnson, *The Negro and His Songs* (1925; rpt., Hatboro, Pa.: Folklore Associates, 1964), p. 253.

6. For a brief sketch of the McGinty band and Dave Cutrell, see Leslie A. McRill, "Music in Oklahoma by the Billy McGinty Cowboy Band," *Chronicles of Oklahoma*, 38 (Spring, 1960), 66–74. An account stressing Otto Gray's role is given by Glenn Shirley, "Daddy of the Cowboy Bands," *Oklahoma Today*, 9 (Fall, 1959), 6–7, 29.

7. Watts and Wilson's recording is transcribed in Malcolm Blackard, "Wilmer Watts and the Lonely Eagles," *JEMFQ*, 5 (Winter, 1969), 126–40. Further biographical details are given in Donald Lee Nelson, "Walk Right in Belmont: The Wilmer Watts Story," ibid., 9 (Autumn, 1973), 91-96, and in the discussion of "The Night Express" in chap. 11.

8. From LC AFS 218 A1.

REFERENCES

A. "Pistol Pete's Midnight Special," by Dave Cutrell with McGinty's Oklahoma Cowboy Band. Recorded May 11, 1926 (OKeh master 9650-A), in Saint Louis, Mo. Released on OKeh 45057 ca. Sept., 1926.

B. Best & Best, 23
Boni (1952), 90–91
Botkin (1944), 908
Coleman & Bregman, 112
Delmore Brothers, 15
Dorson (1966), 16

Glazer (1964), 104–5
Gordon (1938), 51 (from his *New York Times* column, June 19, 1927)
Gregory
Hille, 28
Ives (1962), 221
Leadbelly (1959a), 52
Leadbelly (1959b), 56
Leisy (1966), 230
Lomax & Lomax (1934), 71
Lomax & Lomax (1936), 221
Lomax & Lomax (1947), 318
Lynn, 252–53

—Topic 12T134: *Move On down the Line* (part of "Railroad Worksong")

Gateway Singers — Decca 29972; Decca DL-8413: *Puttin' On the Style*

Jim Glaser—Capitol T-2009

—Starday SLP 158: *Just Looking for a Home*; Starday SLP 170: *Railroad Special*; Cumberland 29520; Smash 27028

Andy Griffith—Capitol 4052

T. Grimes Quintet—Atlantic 8013: *Dance the Rock and Roll*

Big Boy Groves—Spark 114

Woody Guthrie, Cisco Houston, and Leadbelly—Stinson SLP 6: *Folksay, Vol. 2*; Stinson SLPX 5: *Folksay, Vols. 1 and 2*

Cisco Houston—Folkways FA 2346: *Folk Songs*; Folkways FTS 31012: *Cisco Houston Sings American Folk Songs*

Burl Ives—Encyclopaedia Britannica Films EBF 6: *Songs of Expanding America*

Freddy Jacobs—Westminster WP 6087: *Swingin' Folk Tunes*

Gordon Jenkins—Decca 28272 (45 rpm)

Kingston Trio—Decca 4613/74613: *Kingston Trio*

Leadbelly (Huddie Ledbetter)—Folkways FA 2942 (FP 242): *Leadbelly's Last Sessions, Vol. 2*; Olympic 7103: *The Legendary Leadbelly*

—Elektra EKL 301: *The Library of Congress Recordings* (from LC AFS 124 A1)

Limeliters—RCA Victor LPM/LSP 2671: *Fourteen 14 Karat Folk Songs*; RCA Victor LPM/LSP 2889: *Best of the Limeliters*

John Lomax, Jr.—Folkways FG 3508: *John A. Lomax, Jr., Sings American Folk Songs*

Guy Lombardo—Decca DL-4430/74430: *Golden Folk Songs for Dancing*

Ed McCurdy—Bear Family (West Germany) 15009: *Last Night I Had the Strangest Dream*

Brownie McGhee and Sonny Terry —Prestige 1005: *Blues and Folk*

—Folkways FA 2432: *The Folk Music of the Newport Folk Festival 1959–60, Vol. 2*

McPeak Brothers—MRC 2050: *Bluegrass at Its Peak*

Maggie Valley Country Singers—Rural Rhythm RR-143

Junior Mance—Polydor 5051: *Junior Mance Touch*

Johnny Mann—Liberty 3355/7355: *Golden Folk Song Hits*

Joe Maphis and Merle Travis—Capitol T/TS 2102: *Merle Travis and Joe Maphis "Big Midnight Special"*

Jody Miller—Hilltop JM 6038: *Queen of Country*

Van Morrison—Bang 218: *Blowin' Your Mind*

Odetta—Vanguard 9137/2153: *One Grain of Sand*

—Everest Archive of Folk Music AFM 273: *Odetta*

Richard and Jim—Capitol T/ST 2058: *Folk Songs and Country Sounds*

Johnny Rivers—Imperial 66087 (45 rpm); Imperial 9274/12274: *Here We Go-Go Again*

—United Artists UA-XW103 (45 rpm); United Artists UA-LA-444-E: *The Very Best of Johnny Rivers*

Jimmie Rodgers—Paramount 2-1042: *Honeycomb*

—Roulette 25150: *Jimmie Rodgers, Folk Songs*

Pete Seeger—MDH 1: *We Sing*

—Folkways FA 2321: *American Favorite Ballads, Vol. 2*

Pete Seeger, Memphis Slim, and Wee Willie Dixon—Folkways FA 2450: *At the Village Gate*

Jean Shepard—Capitol T/ST 1525: *Got You on My Mind "Big Midnight Special"*

Skifflers—Perfect (England) PS 14015

—Columbia HL 7307: *Hootenanny!*

Jimmie Skinner—Vecto 3001: *Jimmie Skinner Sings Bluegrass*

Carl Smith—Columbia C 30548: *Carl Smith Sings Bluegrass "Big Midnight Special"*

Jimmy Smith—Bluenote 1819 (45 rpm); Bluenote 4078/84078: *Midnight Special*; Bluenote 89901: *Jimmy Smith's Greatest Hits*

Osborne Smith—Capitol T/ST 2288: *Wizardry of Smith*

Soundtrack—ABC 12184 (45 rpm); ABC DP 939: *Leadbelly*

Merle Travis—Capitol T/ST 2009: *Country Music Hootenanny*

Merle Travis and Joe Maphis—Capitol T/TS
2102: *Merle Travis and Joe Maphis*
"Big Midnight Special"
Jerry Wayne—MGM K12532
Weavers—MCA 2-4025, Decca
DL-8893/78893 and DXB/DXSB7 173:
Best of the Weavers; Decca DL-4388:
Best of the Weavers; Decca DL-5196:
The Weavers' Greatest Hits
—Vanguard VRS 9034/2030: *The Weavers at
Home*
Josh White—Elektra EKL 114: *Josh;*
Elektra EKS 75008: *The Best of Josh
White;* Elektra SMP 3: *Pops, Folk 'n Jazz
Sampler*
Hank Williams, Jr.—MGM SE 4750: *All for
the Love of Sunshine*

Mac Wiseman—Rural Rhythm 158: *Old
Time Favorites*

F. LC AFS:
Jesse Bradley—AFS 218 A1
Gant Family—AFS 647 A
Woody Guthrie—AFS 3410 A1
Gus Harper, Jim Henry, and Herman
Jackson—AFS 885 A3
Frank Jordan and group—AFS 618 A1
Huddie Ledbetter—AFS 124 A1
—AFS 133 A
"Mexico" (probably a pseudonym for Ernest
Williams)—John A. Lomax cylinder 11-5
Robert Pounds—AFS 5398 A2

Bill McGinty (*with lariat*) and Otto Gray (*with lariat and white Angora chaps*), with the bus of the original
McGinty's Oklahoma Cowboy Band. *Oklahoma Today,* Fall, 1959. Courtesy of Glenn Shirley.

On the Dummy Line

ON THE DUMMY LINE

Some folks say that the dummy won't run,
Now, let me tell you what the dummy done.
Left Saint Louis 'bout half past one,
Rolled into Memphis at the settin' of the sun.
   On the dummy, on the dummy line,
   Ride and shine on the dummy line,
   Ride and shine and pay my fine
   When I ride on the dummy line.

Got on the dummy and I had no fare,
Conductor yelled, "What you doin' in here?"
I jumped up and I made for the door,
She cracked me on the head with a two-by-four.
   Chorus:

Oh, the dummy rolled down that twenty-nine hill,
Blowed the whistle with a mighty shrill.

Stuck his head out the window, look' down the track,
You oughta seen the little dummy ball the jack.
Chorus (2):

Pickard Family

The term *dummy line* has several different meanings and likewise refers to several completely distinct songs. The *Dictionary of American Slang* glosses the term as a train carrying railroad employees.[1] In Australia, according to *A Dictionary of Slang and Unconventional English*, it meant the baggage car of a Melbourne tram.[2] *The Oxford English Dictionary* cites an 1864 usage meaning a locomotive with water condensers, from which there was no noise of escaping steam.[3] Folklorist Vance Randolph notes that in "the early days" the front part of California streetcars was open, and called the dummy.[4] The standard references on railroad, hobo, and tramp slang do not mention the term.[5]

Rail historian Archie Robertson suggested that the common version of this song originally referred to the one-mile-long Augusta Railroad of Augusta, Arkansas.[6] This company was incorporated in 1918 to take over the assets and franchises of the insolvent Augusta Tramway and Transfer Company. The latter railroad had been built in 1887 by the people of Augusta to give them a connection with the Saint Louis and Iron Mountain—under rather amusing circumstances, as Clifton E. Hull relates in his history, *Shortline Railroads of Arkansas*.[7] Hull accepts Robertson's attribution of "The Dummy Line" to the Augusta Railroad; this cannot be the origin of the verses, however, as fragments of the song were collected as early as 1913 by folklorist E. C. Perrow. An attribution to the earlier Augusta Tramway and Transfer Company would be at least chronologically possible, but the geographical references in the text (see st. 1 of the version transcribed here) lend no support to this suggestion either: the one-mile short-line is nowhere near Memphis or Saint Louis.

In the oldest text of "The Dummy Line" the word *dummy* is used in Randolph's sense—to mean part of a streetcar. Therefore it might not be considered a railroad song, although streetcars do run, literally, on rail roads. This song, obtained by Randolph in manuscript copy from an Arkansas woman who heard it sung in the 1890s, appeared frequently in pocket songsters of the 1880s. It can readily be identified by the chorus:

Riding on the dummy, glad to get a seat,
With a jolly company, all looking gay and sweet;
Riding on the dummy with the darling I adore,
Viewing hills and dales with joy I never felt before.[8]

This song was published in 1885 by George W. Hagans of San Francisco under the title "Riding on the Dummy," with words and music credited to Sam Booth and Frederick G. Carnes, respectively (copyrighted in 1885, no. 26351).

Quite different from the above are two other dummy songs. They share the same chorus, but the other stanzas are distinct. The less widely known one begins:

Across the prairie on a streak of rust,
There's something moving in a cloud of dust;
It crawls into the village with a wheeze and whine,
It's the two o'clock flyer on the dummy line.[9]

Other stanzas elaborate on the image of the slow-moving railroad train.

Sheet music: "Riding on the Dummy." Collection of the Library of Congress.

The best-known dummy song, a representative version of which is transcribed here, seems to be more common in black than in white tradition. It is invariably coupled with additional, thematically unrelated verses that differ from one text to the next. The earliest recoveries reported in print date from early in this century, but the language and style of the verses coupled with the "dummy" stanzas invariably suggest an origin on the minstrel stage thirty or forty years earlier. This is the song referred to in all the bibliographic citations other than Ford, Randolph, and the second version in Harbin.

The first two stanzas and chorus of our version are the constant part of the various texts; the final stanza, reminiscent of "Casey Jones," does not occur elsewhere. Other verses generally supplement the two-stanza-plus-chorus "dummy" fragment with stanzas that have nothing to do with the railroad. For example, the version recorded by Robert N. Page includes these verses:

> You oughta see my father's beard, how it grows,
> The other day he went to shave and cut off his nose;
> Slapped it on right upside down,
> And every time it drizzles now my father nearly drowns.

> I've got a brother by the name of Bill,
> He was in the battle at Bunker Hill;
> Fought a hard fight for a better life (?)
> It's a blame sight harder where Bill is now.

> I've got a gal down in Mobile,
> She's got a face like a lemon peel;
> She's got a wart on the end of her chin,
> She said it is a dimple, but a dimple turns in.[10]

I have found only three 78 rpm commercial recordings of the dummy song. The version transcribed here was performed by the Pickard Family in 1930 for the American Record Corporation.[11] The earliest recording, made in 1927 by Robert N. Page for the Victor Talking Machine Company, was one of two selections he recorded; it is not possible to determine from them whether he was black or white. The third item, made in 1949 by the Jesters, is a version of the song given by Ford.

The 78 rpm discography also includes Uncle Dave Macon's parody on "The Dummy Line," a song about the automobile, and Vernon Dalhart's imitation of Uncle Dave. Macon's recording made in 1926, predates both the Pickards' and Page's. One other 78 rpm hillbilly recording, "We're Riding on the Dummy Dummy Line," which Bill Cox cut in 1929 for the Starr Piano Company, was never released, and therefore it cannot be determined which dummy song it was.

A version a correspondent sent me several years ago is choice because of the inclusion of several railroad-related stanzas that are not widespread:

> Well a man was walking ahead the train,
> Oh, the whistle blew and it blew again;
> The feller hollered, "I don't care how much you blow,
> I ain't a-comin' back because you're too darned slow."

> There's a hobo got on the train one day,
> Said he'd like to ride, but he couldn't pay;

The captain said, "according to the railroad law,
I'm gonna punch your ticket, or I'll punch your jaw."

Now the Dummy train met a cow one day,
She was standing right on the right of way;
Well, shovel in the water, boys, and give the coal,
The cow she went and skinned up a signal pole.

Down in Arkansaw, where the trains go slow,
There's a big tornado began to blow;
It blew so hard it blew the Dummy off the track,
And then it turned around again and blew it back.

For the upper berth, there's a dollar due,
For a lower berth, well, they charge you two;
The upper berth is lower, and the lower's high,
We'll all be walking on our uppers by and bye. [12]

NOTES

1. Harold Wentworth and Stuart Berg Flexner, *Dictionary of American Slang* (New York; Thomas Y. Crowell, 1960), p. 165.

2. Eric Partridge, *A Dictionary of Slang and Unconventional English from the Fifteenth Century to the Present Day* (New York: Macmillan, 1961), p. 248.

3. *OED*, vol. 3, p. 713.

4. Vance Randolph, *Ozark Folksongs*, vol. 3 (Columbia: State Historical Society of Missouri, 1949), p. 277.

5. E.g., George Milburn, *The Hobo's Hornbook* (New York: Ives Washburn, 1930), and Godfrey Irwin, *American Tramp and Underworld Slang* (London: Eric Partridge, 1931).

6. Archie Robertson, *Slow Train to Yesterday* (Boston: Houghton Mifflin, 1945), p. 95.

7. Clifton E. Hull, *Shortline Railroads of Arkansas* (Norman: University of Oklahoma Press, 1969), chap. 2.

8. Randolph, *Ozark Folksongs*, vol. 3, p. 277.

9. Ira W. Ford, *Traditional Music of America* (1940; rpt., Hatboro, Pa.: Folklore Associates, 1965), p. 437.

10. Robert N. Page, "Ride and Shine on the Dummy Line," Victor 21067.

11. For a brief biographical sketch of the Pickard Family, see "The Little Red Caboose behind the Train (III)" (chap. 11).

12. Sent to me by Laura Affolter of Otis, Oreg., Aug., 1969.

REFERENCES

A. "On the Dummy Line," by the Pickard Family. Vocal trio, accompanied by harmonica, guitar, piano, and violin. Recorded Feb. 6, 1930 (American Record Corp. master 9346–2), in New York City. Released on Perfect 12625, Banner 0744, Conqueror 7574, Oriole 1995, Challenge 882, Jewel 5995, Pathé 32546, Perfect 12625, Regal 10049, Cameo 0344, Domino 4845, Romeo 1357, Paramount 3218, and Broadway 8150.

B. Beard, 457–60
Brown III, 521; V, 291
Coleman & Bregman, 70–71
Ford, 437–38
Harbin, 31, 97
Hull, 20 (1 stanza only)

The Pickard Family. *Left to right:* Mother, Ruth, Little Ann, Dad, Charlie, and Bub. Courtesy of Bob Pinson and the Country Music Foundation Library and Media Center, Nashville, Tennessee.

The Longest Train/In The Pines

IN THE PINES

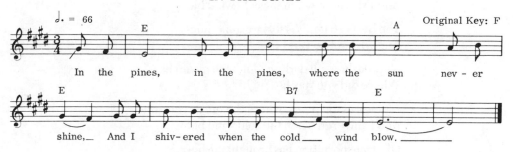

In the pines, in the pines, where the sun never shine,
And I shivered when the cold wind blow.

Oh, if I'd [?minded] what grandma said,
Oh, where would I been tonight?

I'd-a been in the pines, where the sun never shine,
And shivered when the cold wind blow.

The longest train I ever saw
Went down the Georgie line.

The engine it stopped at a six-mile post,
The cabin never left the town.

Now darling, now darling, don't tell me no lie,
Where did you stay last night?

I stayed in the pines, where the sun never shine,
And I shivered when the cold wind blow.

The prettiest little girl that I ever saw
Went walking down the line.

Her hair it was of a curly type,
Her cheeks was rosy red.

Now darling, now darling, don't tell me no lie,
Where did you stay last night?

I stayed in the pines, where the sun never shine,
And I shivered when the cold wind blow.

The train run back one mile from town
And killed my girl, you know.

Her head was caught in the driver wheel,
Her body I never could find.

Oh darling, oh darling, don't tell me no lie,
Where did you stay last night?

I stayed in the pines, where the sun never shine,
And I shivered when the cold wind blow.

The best of friends is to part sometimes,
And why not you and I?

Now darling, oh darling, don't tell me no lie,
Where did you stay last night?

I stayed in the pines, where the sun never shine,
. And I shivered when the cold wind blow.

Oh, transportation has brought me here,
Take a money for to carry me away.

Oh darling, now darling, don't tell me no lie,
Where did you stay last night?

I stayed in the pines, where the sun never shine,
And I shivered when the cold wind blow.

Dock Walsh

I have not polled enough youngsters tf the 1970s to determine whether among the sophistications of contemporary space-age life is a vaccine against the compulsion to count the cars of a passing freight train: but in my own youth I know the ailment was incurable. The popularity of "The Longest Train" suggests that the urge was not uncommon in the rural South. But any train, no matter how long, has a beginning and an end, and a sequence of cars connected one to the next in orderly fashion. Alas, the same cannot be said of the song "The Longest Train"; it is a fine example of the complex interrelationships one encounters in nonnarrative, or lyric, folksong.

Although folksong students have few tools at their disposal to facilitate the study of lyri folksongs, my burden in annotating this song is lightened immensely by being able to draw upon Judith McCulloh's study of this lyric folksong cluster.[1] She examined 160 separate versions of "In the Pines"/"The Longest Train," or other closely related folksongs, from printed, recorded, and manuscript sources dating from 1917 to 1969. In addition to the broader questions of how one studies folksongs that lack some obvious rational principle of organization, such as a ballad, which tells a story, or an alphabet song, McCulloh dealt principally with two issues: (1) what are the precise boundaries of this song complex that we refer to as "The Longest Train"/"In the Pines"; that is, what are the essential characteristics that we require musical items to have in order to be classed as the same song? and (2) can we sort out any historic or geographic development among the available texts?

In answering the first question, McCulloh noted four important identifying elements, one musical and three textual. The musical element is the "In the Pines" tune, an example of which is transcribed in this book. The textual elements are the two title-giving phrases, "in the pines, in the pines, where the sun never shines" and "the longest train I ever saw." The former occurred in 118 of the texts she examined. In the text transcribed here, it occurs five times, serving, in effect, as a chorus. The latter phrase occurred in 96 versions and could be divided into two subtypes: those specifying the location of the train, as in the version transcribed here:

> The longest train I ever saw
> Went down the Georgie line,

and those specifying the length of the train:

> The longest train I ever saw
> Was thirty coaches long.[2]

The third identifying textual element is a group of verses describing briefly an accident in which someone is beheaded (presumably by a train). It is represented by stanzas 12 and 13 of the version given here and occurred in forty versions. McCulloh concluded that any song that had (1) an "In the Pines" tune with either a "longest train" or an "in the pines" couplet, (2) a text approximating a hypothetical "Longest Train"/"In the Pines" text, or (3) a text including at least two of the three textual elements noted above could be considered a version of the song in question. Her third set of criteria opens the door to several pieces that may consist largely of other stanzas. Here I give two texts to illustrate the variety of forms the "Longest Train"/"In the Pines" family takes.

The first is Georgia bluesman Peg Leg Howell's "Rolling Mill Blues," recorded in Atlanta on April 10, 1929, and issued on Columbia 14438-D. Joshua Barnes Howell was born in 1888 in Putnam County, Georgia. He recorded several times for Columbia between 1926 and 1929, and then again for Testament in 1963, after his "rediscovery."[3]

> The rollin' mill, baby, 's done broke down,
> They ain't shipping no iron to town.
>
> The longest train I ever seen
> Run round Joe Brown's coal mine.
>
> The engine was at the four-mile hill
> And the cab hadn't never left town.
>
> Corrine, Corrine, my loving Corrine,
> Honey, let your bang grow long.
>
> The train run off the track last night
> And it killed my love Corrine.
>
> Her head was found in the driving wheel
> And her body have never been seen.
>
> I didn't bring nothing to this old world
> And I won't carry nothing away.
>
> It's late last night when my honey come home,
> I heard a rapping on her door.
>
> She got up in her stocking feet,
> Went tipping 'cross the floor.
>
> Tell me, pretty mama, what evil have I done
> That make you treat me cold?

> I've killed no man and I robbed no train
> And I've done no hanging crime.
>
> The last sweet word I heard my baby say.
> "What more, babe, can I do?"
>
> "I done more for you than I'll ever do again,
> Goodbye, my love, goodbye."

Howell's song combines the rolling mill theme, the Corrina, Corrina theme, and verses from "Late Last Night When Willie Came Home"—all elements known from the blues or white folk lyric traditions. His tune is in duple meter, closer to "How Long Blues" than to any of the tunes usually associated with the "Longest Train"/"In the Pines" family.

The other peripheral item is "Ruben," as performed by Ira Cephas, a black singer born in Madison County, Kentucky, in 1868, and living in Ohio when folklorist Bruce Buckley recorded him in 1952. The song was still fluid in Cephas's mind; a version Buckley recorded from him a year earlier was quite different. In particular, the two opening stanzas in the transcription below did not appear in the 1951 recording, thus divorcing that earlier song completely from the "Longest Train"/"In the Pines" family and placing it squarely in the "Reuben"/"900 Miles" group. The problems raised by this "lack of stability" in the repertoire of a single informant are obvious. Cephas's tune is the one usually associated with "Reuben"/"900 Miles."

> Well, the longest train that ever I seen
> Come down through Joe Brown's coal mine.
>
> Well, a man's head got hung in the driver wheel
> And his body has never been found.
>
> Is that you, Reuben a roo, that you, Reuben a roo?
> A Reuben, where you been so long?
>
> Well, the longest day I ever seen
> Was the day I left my home.
>
> And if I had a listened what mama told me
> I would not been here today.
>
> But being so hard-headed and would have my way
> Now I've got to be treated 'is a way.
>
> That you, Reuben, that you, Reuben?
> A Reuben, where you been so long?
>
> Well, I've been to the East, yes, I've been to the West,
> And I've been this whole world around.
>
> Well, I've been to the water and I've been baptized
> Now and I'm ready for my hole in the ground.[4]

As to the second question, regarding the song's development, McCulloh noted that the 157 texts she examined could be divided into approximately 40 with the "longest train" couplet but not the "in the pines" couplet and about 25 with the "in the pines" couplet but not the "longest train" one. The remainder, nearly 100 versions, include both couplets.

The accident sequence appears in all three groups. A nearly invariant association exists between the "In the Pines" tune and texts including the "in the pines" couplet, either alone or mixed with the "longest train" couplet. But texts with only the "longest train" couplet are often found set to other tunes, notably the "George Collins" tune and the "Reuben"/"900 Miles" tune. On the basis of these and other observations, McCulloh concluded that "In the Pines" and "The Longest Train" were once two separate songs or song clusters. "The Longest Train" cluster was set to various tunes in duple meter, such as that for "Reuben"/"900 Miles." The accident verses were associated with this cluster.

Two other interesting verses almost invariably associated with this cluster tie the song group to the occupation of coal mining. In seventeen texts, the location of the longest train is placed at Joe (or John) Brown's coal mine, as in stanza 2 of the Peg Leg Howell text given above. This allusion, McCulloh speculates, is to Governor Joseph Emerson Brown, who operated coal mines in Dade County, Georgia, as early as the 1870s. Although these texts come from several southern states, there is still a suggestion that Georgia is the state of origin of "The Longest Train" or at least of some elements of it, a suggestion strengthened by the frequent occurrence of the phrase "Georgia line" as the location of the train. McCulloh suggests that this phrase arose as a delocalization of "Joe Brown's coal mine" as the song spread to areas where Brown's name and mining operations were not familiar. (Alternatively, this may be an independent reference to the Georgia Railroad [and Banking Company], one of the oldest lines in the Southeast, and one referred to in other folksongs). McCulloh hypothesizes that "The Longest Train" originated in the South—whether specifically in Georgia is unclear—as early as the Reconstruction years. The place and date of origin of "In the Pines" are more difficult to pin down, but she suggests a development also in the Southeast, near the Civil War, with the two clusters coming together toward the end of the nineteenth century.

The second coal-mining reference is exemplified by stanza 19 of the text by Dock Walsh transcribed here. *Transportation* refers to free transportation offered to laborers who signed up to work in the mines (or perhaps building railroads), but who, if they wanted to leave, had to pay their own way. This verse occurs in fourteen versions, all from western North Carolina or the contiguous areas of eastern Kentucky and eastern Tennessee.

So much for the speculated early history of these songs. When one examines the nearly 160 versions that Judith McCulloh has assembled, a handful stand out as being particularly significant, either as documentary landmarks or in terms of their influence on later renditions.

The first recovery of the "In the Pines" phrase and tune was made by Cecil Sharp and Maud Karpeles, who collected the following from Lizzie Abner in Clay County, Kentucky, in 1917:

> Black girl, black girl, don't lie to me,
> Where did you stay last night?
> I stayed in the pines where the sun never shines,
> And shivered when the cold wind blows.[5]

Two years later, Newman I. White obtained four lines that a student of his had heard sung by a black railroad work gang in Buncombe County, North Carolina:

> The longest train I ever saw
> Was on the Seaboard Air Line,

> The engine pas' at a' ha' pas' one,
> And the caboose went pas' at nine.[6]

This was the first report of the "longest train" element. No tune was recorded with the text, but to the student's ear, the music was "very weird, and sudden minors are characteristic." In 1921–22, Frank C. Brown obtained a long text from Pearl Webb of Pineola, Avery County, North Carolina, that included both the "in the pines" couplet and the "longest train" couplet, as well as the "transportation" verse. It is uncertain whether this item was recorded, or only submitted in manuscript. In any case, during the years 1921–22, Brown did obtain recordings of "In the Pines"—the earliest ones to be made.

In 1925, collector Robert W. Gordon recorded on cylinder an eight-couplet version from Bertie May Moses at Morgantown, North Carolina, the first to include the accident stanzas.

The earliest commercial recording of the song was made in April, 1926, by Doctor Coble Walsh, known on records as Dock Walsh; it is transcribed here. Walsh, born in 1901 on a farm in Wilkes County, North Carolina, began to play fretless banjo when he was but four years old. Later, in his teens, he started performing at local parties and began earning money for his efforts. In 1924 he heard Henry Whitter's first hillbilly disc, "Lonesome Road Blues"/"The Wreck on the Southern Old 97" (OKeh 40015), and decided to try his hand at the new medium. When letters to both OKeh and Columbia brought no response, Walsh journeyed south to Atlanta, where both companies had been holding semiannual field-recording sessions, and eventually obtained an audition from Columbia's local manager, Bill Brown. His first recordings were made in October of 1925. The opening title was "The East Bound Train," discussed earlier in this book. At his second recording session, six months later, he recorded "In the Pines." Between 1927 and 1932 he continued to record, both as a solo artist and also with the Carolina Tar Heels and the Pine Mountain Boys. Like other young hillbilly musicians of the 1920s, Walsh gave up the professional music business when the Depression hit and turned to more traditional pursuits to support his newly acquired family. In the early 1960s he was "rediscovered" and brought before the microphone once more. He died in 1967.[7]

The first commercial recording using the "longest train" phrase in the title was the Tenneva Ramblers' "The Longest Train I Ever Saw," made for the Victor Talking Machine Company in Bristol in August, 1927. Relatively successful, the disc sold in excess of 11,100 copies. This was also the first appearance of the now-standard "six o'clock"/"nine" time sequence, as in their second couplet:

> The engine passed at six o'clock,
> And the cab it passed at nine.

When Dave Samuelson produced an LP reissue of recordings by the Tenneva Ramblers, he included in his liner notes information obtained in interviews with Claude Grant, then the only surviving member of the Ramblers. Grant told Samuelson that he had written the above couplet in Macon, Georgia, when the band was in a car waiting at a crossing for a 150-car train.[8]

Two other singers, both of whom recorded the song in the 1940s, have had particular influence on the later history of "The Longest Train"/"In the Pines." The earlier of the two was Bill Monroe, who, with his Blue Grass Boys, recorded "In the Pines" first in 1941 for RCA Victor. Because of Monroe's paramount role in the evolution and acceptance of bluegrass music, his versions have become standards in the idiom; more than two dozen recordings of "In the Pines" are based on his performances. Monroe's renditions of "In the Pines" differ from one to the next; actually, his second recording, made for Decca in 1952, seems to have had more direct influence on other bluegrass musicians than the 1941 version. Although Clayton McMichen is given composer's credits on Monroe's recordings (by virtue of his own copyright on the song in 1930), Monroe's text bears few similarities to McMichen's, which consist largely of original verses composed by McMichen mixed with a few traditional stanzas.[9] Monroe learned the song from a live 1938 radio program over a Georgia station from two artists whose names he does not recall.[10]

The other influential singer was Huddie Ledbetter (Leadbelly), who recorded the song three times in the early 1940s, each rendition noticeably different from the others. Leadbelly's influential role in the urban folksong revival in the 1940s conferred a high status on his "Black Girl," and it was learned and sung by many citybillies from the 1940s on.[11] Another effect of Leadbelly's influence was to give the impression that the song was well known in black tradition, whereas in point of fact the song is almost exclusively the provenance of white singers. In searching for an explanation of how this song got into Leadbelly's repertoire, McCulloh corresponded with Alan Lomax, who wrote her that Leadbelly "learned [the song] from someone who took it from Cecil Sharp, Volume II"—a reference to the Lizzie Abner fragment cited earlier. The Abner piece, McCulloh noted, could account for Leadbelly's tune and for seven of the ten couplets of his arrangement; the other three couplets, she speculated, could have come from the Moses recording obtained by Gordon. How could Leadbelly have had access to unpublished cylinder recordings deposited at the Library of Congress Archive of Folk Song? For a year or two after his pardon from a life sentence in the Louisiana State Prison Farm, Leadbelly served John and Alan Lomax primarily in the capacity of chauffeur. Some of his songs were almost certainly learned from informants of the Lomaxes during their field-collecting trips (see the discussion of "The Rock Island Line"); perhaps other materials were also available to him while he was in close contact with the Lomaxes.

Although the title "Black Girl" is usually associated with Leadbelly, on his other two recordings he replaced that phrase with "my girl."

NOTES

1. Judith McCulloh, "'In the Pines': The Melodic-Textual Identity of an American Lyric Folksong Cluster" (Ph.D. diss., Indiana University, 1970).

2. Sarah Gunning, recorded by Ellen Stekert in Detroit, Mich., May 1, 1965; transcribed in McCulloh, "'In the Pines,'" p. 280.

3. For additional biographical information on Howell, see Peter J. Welding, liner notes to Testament T-2204: *The Legendary Peg Leg Howell*.

4. LC AFS 11332 B5. For more information on Cephas, see Bruce Buckley, "Uncle Ira Cephas," *Midwest Folklore*, 3 (Spring, 1953), 5–18.

5. Cecil J. Sharp and Maud Karpeles, *English Folk-Songs from the Southern Appalachians* (London: Oxford University Press, 1932) vol. 2, p. 278.

6. Newman I. White, *American Negro Folk-Songs* (1928; rpt., Hatboro, Pa.: Folklore Associates, 1965), p. 274.

7. For further biographical information on Walsh, see Archie Green, brochure notes to Folk-Legacy FSA 24: *The Carolina Tar Heels*.

8. For more biographical information on the Tenneva Ramblers, see Dave Samuelson, liner notes to Puritan 2001: *The Tenneva Ramblers*.

9. Bill Monroe's career has been documented in several publications in varying depths. See, e.g., James Rooney, *Bossmen: Bill Monroe and Muddy Waters* (New York: Dial Press, 1971); Ralph Rinzler, "Bill Monroe," in *Stars of Country Music,* edited by Bill C. Malone and Judith McCulloh (Urbana: University of Illinois Press, 1975), pp. 202–21; and Neil V. Rosenberg, *Bill Monroe and His Bluegrass Boys: An Illustrated Discography* (Nashville: Country Music Foundation Press, 1974).

10. McCulloh, "'In the Pines,'" p. 451.

11. For more information on Leadbelly see the discussion of "The Rock Island Line" in this chapter.

REFERENCES

A. "Black Girl," in Cecil J. Sharp and Maud Karpeles, *English Folk-Songs from the Southern Appalachians* (London: Oxford University Press, 1932), vol. 2, p. 278. Sung by Lizzie Abner for Sharp and Karpeles on Aug. 18, 1917 at Oneida School, Clay County, Ky. Two verses and melody reported. The earliest dated text and tune reported; ultimately, the source of Leadbelly's title and text (see below).

"The Longest Train I Ever Saw," in Newman I. White, *American Negro Folk-Songs* (1928; rpt., Hatboro, Pa., 1965), p. 274. Reported to White by Alvin W. McDougle, a student at Duke University, who heard it sung by a gang of black railroad workers in Buncombe County, N.C. First appearance of the "longest train" element.

"To the Pines," Gordon recording A-124 (N.C. MS 182). Collected by Robert W. Gordon from Bertie May Moses, unaccompanied vocal, on Dec. 4, 1925, at Morganton, N.C. First appearance of the accident verses. Gordon used this version in his Folk Songs of America series in the *New York Times Magazine,* Jan. 1, 1928, p. 15, and later in his WPA collection *Folk Songs of America* (1938) in the article "Banjo Songs" (pp. 83–84). Gordon's article is probably the source of the text in Kenneth Allsop, *Hard Travellin'* (London: Hodder and Stoughton, 1967), p. 49; the Moses tune was the source of Leadbelly's (see below).

"Black Girl," by Leadbelly (Huddie Ledbetter). Vocal and guitar. Recorded ca. 1941–46. Released in 1951 on Folkways FA 2014 (FP 14): *Rock Island Line (Huddie Ledbetter Memorial Album,* *Vol. 2)*. Reissued on Folkways FTS 31019: *Take This Hammer;* Verve Folkways FV 9001: *Take This Hammer*. This version is based on the Moses tune and the Abner text. Leadbelly's several recordings of "Black Girl" were widely copied and imitated during the folksong revival of the 1950s. It is not known which of his recordings was the earliest; this version was probably the most influential. (Only the Musicraft recording—see the discography—can be accurately dated [Feb. 17, 1944].)

"In the Pines," by Bill Monroe and his Blue Grass Boys. Monroe, mandolin and tenor; Bill Westbrook, lead vocal and string bass; Pete Pyle, guitar; Art Wooten, fiddle. Recorded Oct. 2, 1941 (RCA Victor master BS 071076), in Atlanta, Ga. Released on RCA Bluebird B-8861. Reissued on RCA Camden CAL 719: *The Father of Bluegrass Music;* RCA Victor APM1-0568: *Bluegrass for Collectors*.

"In the Pines," by Dock Walsh. Vocal and banjo. Recorded Apr. 17, 1926 (Columbia master W142031-1), in Atlanta, Ga. Released on Columbia 15094-D on Sept. 20, 1926. Reissued on Columbia CS 9660: *Ballads and Breakdowns of the Golden Era*. First commercial recording; this version is transcribed here.

B. Allsop, 49
Brown III, 201, 332–34, 342, 348, 356–57
Brown IV, 201, 210, 215–16
Bush (1969), 32–33
Cumberland Mountain Folks
Duke
Fuson, 113–14
Gordon (1938), 83–84

Longest Train I Ever Saw"
—Decca 5523   "The Longest Train I
Ever Saw"
Lou Ella Robertson—Capitol 1706   "In
the Pines"
Texas Jim Robertson—RCA Victor
20-2907   "In the Pines"
Arthur Smith, and his Dixie Liners—
Bluebird B-7943, Montgomery Ward
7686   "In the Pines"
Tenneva Ramblers—Victor 20861; Puritan
3001: *The Tenneva Ramblers*   "The
Longest Train I Ever Saw"
Dock Walsh—Columbia 15094-D;
Columbia CS 9660: *Ballads and
Breakdowns of the Golden Era*   "In
the Pines"

E.   Chet Atkins—RCA Victor LM 2870: *The
"Pops" Goes Country*   "In the Pines"
Blue Sky Boys (Bill and Earl Bolick)—
Starday SLP 205: *A Treasury of Rare
Songs Gems from the Past*
"The Longest Train I Ever Saw"
—Starday SLP 257: *Together Again:* Starday
SLP 270: *The Wonderful World of
Country Music;* Starday SLP 295: *The
Country Music Hall of Fame, Vol. 4*
"In the Pines"
Elton Britt—RCA Victor 47-9503; RCA
Camden CAL/CAS 2295: *The Jimmie
Rodgers Blues*   "Singin' in the Pines"
(derivative piece)
Camp Creek Boys—County 709: *The Camp
Creek Boys*   "Fall on My Knees"
(related)
Jack Casey—Rural Rhythm RR-JC-206: *Jack
Casey*   "In the Pines"
Paul Clayton—Folkways FA 2110 (FP 47/3):
Folksongs and Ballads of Virginia   "In
the Pines"
Vassar Clements—Mercury SRM 1-1022:
Vassar Clements
Charlotte Daniels and Pat Webb
—Prestige International 13037: *Charlotte
Daniels and Pat Webb*   "In the Pines"
Gerald Duncan—Folkways FS 3812: *Music
from the Ozarks*   "In the Pines"
Easterners—Vetco LP 3003: *Echoes of the
Bonnie and Clyde Era*   "In the Pines"
Duane Eddy—Jamboree 3011: *Duane Eddy*

Plays Songs of Heritage   "In the
Pines"
Folkswingers—World Pacific 1814: *12
String Guitar*   "In the Pines"
Tennessee Ernie Ford—Capitol T/DT 700
This Lusty Land!   "In the Pines"
(derivative piece)
Connie Francis—Metro MS 538: *Connie
Francis Sings Folk Songs*   "True Love,
True Love"
Jesse Fuller—Good Time Jazz S 10039: *The
Lone Cat*   "Beat It on down the Line"
(related)
Fred Gerlach—Audio-Video Productions
A-V 102: *Gallows Pole and Other Folk
Songs;* Folkways FG 3529: *Twelve-String
Guitar: Folk Songs and Blues Sung and
Played by Fred Gerlach*   "Little Girl"
Dickson Hall, and the Wayfarers—Epic
LN-3247   "In the Pines"
Gordon Heath—Elektra EKL 119: *Songs of
the Abbaye*   "Black Girl"
Sam Hinton—Folkways FA 2400: *Sam
Hinton Sings the Songs of Men, All Sorts
and Kinds*   "In the Pines"
Roscoe Holcomb—Folkways FA 2368: *The
High Lonesome Sound*   "In the Pines"
Will Holt—Stinson SLP 64: *A Will Holt
Concert*   "Black Girl"
Cisco Houston—Vanguard VRS 9107: *I
Ain't Got No Home;* Vanguard Everyman
SRV 3006/73006: *I Ain't Got No
Home*   "My Gal"
Peg Leg Howell—Testament T-2204: *The
Legendary Peg Leg Howell*   "Blood
Red River" (related)
(LaRoy) Inman and Ira (Rogers)—Columbia
CL 1731/CS 8531: *The Exciting New Folk
Duo*   "Black Girl"
Clarence Jackson—Rural Rhythm
RR-WA-173: *Favorite Waltzes*   "In
the Pines"
—Rural Rhythm RR-CB-156: *Country
Blues Instrumentals: Hoedown,
Vol. 6*   "In the Pines"
Journeymen—Capitol T/ST 1629:
Introducing the Journeymen   "Black
Girl"
Buell Kazee—June Appal JA 009: *Buell
Kazee*   "Look Up, Look Down That
Lonesome Road"

Kossoy Sisters (Irene and Ellen)—Tradition TLP 1018: *Bowling Green and Other Folksongs from the Southern Mountains* "In the Pines"

Leadbelly (Huddie Ledbetter)—Stinson SLP 48: *Leadbelly Memorial, Vol. 3;* Storyville Special 616 003: *In the Evening When the Sun Goes Down* "Black Girl"

Louvin Brothers (Ira and Charlie)—Capitol T/DT 769: *Tragic Songs of Life;* Capitol EAP 3-769 (45 rpm) "In the Pines"

Jim McCall—Vetco LP 3010: *Pickin' & Singin'* "In the Pines"

Warner Mack—Kapp KL 1461/KS 3461: *Everybody's Country Favorites*

Wade Mainer—Old Homestead OHTRS 4000: *From the Maple on the Hill* "Don't Tell Me No Lie"

Gene Martin—Starday SLP 276: *Country Music Cannonball* "The Longest Train"

Jimmie Martin—Decca DL 4643: *Sunny Side of the Mountain* "In the Pines"

David and John Morris—Kidtown 1FR69: *Music As We Learned It* "In the Pines"

New Christy Minstrels—Columbia CL 1872/CS 8672: *Presenting the New Christy Minstrels* "In the Pines"

Osborne Brothers—Decca DL 4767: *Up This Hill and Down* "In the Pines"

Maggie Hammons Parker—Rounder 0018: *Shaking Down the Acorns* "The Lonesome Pines"

Pete Pike—Rebel LPR-1473 (no title) "In the Pines"

Possum Hunters—Takoma A1025: *In the Pines* "In the Pines"

Dale Potter—Rural Rhythm RR-DP-235: *Hoedown, Vol. 9* "In the Pines"

Jerry Reed—RCA Victor LSP-4204: *Jerry Reed Explores Guitar Country* "In the Pines"

Buck Ryan—Rural Rhythm RR-BR-244: *Fiddling Buck Ryan* "In the Pines"

Scragg Family—Sonyatone ST-1001: *The Scragg Family* "In the Pines"

Pete Seeger—Folkways FA 2321: *American Favorite Ballads, Vol. 2* "Black Girl"

—Tomato Tom 2-7003: *A Tribute to Leadbelly* "Black Girl"

Jerry Shook—Somerset SF-18300: *Country and Western Hits Made Famous by America's Greatest Singers;* Somerset SF 38300: *Country Favorites* "In the Pines"

Sir Douglas Quintet—Tribe TRS 47001: *The Best of Sir Douglas Quintet* "It Was in the Pines"

Jimmie Skinner—Vetco 3001: *Jimmie Skinner Sings Bluegrass* "In the Pines"

Red Smiley—Rural Rhythm RR-RS-160: *Red Smiley and the Blue Grass Cutups* "In the Pines"

Stanley Brothers—Wango 110 (EP) "In the Pines"

—Wango 115: *On the Air* "In the Pines"

Strange Creek Singers—Arhoolie 4004: *The Strange Creek Singers*

Earl Taylor and the Stoney Mountain Boys—United Artists UAL 3049: *Alan Lomax Presents Folk Songs from the Bluegrass* "In the Pines"

Jack Tottle—Rounder 0067: *Back Road Mandolin* "In the Pines"

Faye Tucker—Time 52108/2108: *Country and Western Soul* "In the Pines"

Two-Nineteen Skiffle Group—Esquire EP 196 (45 rpm EP) "Black Girl"

Dave Van Ronk—Verve Folkways FV/FVS 9017: *Gambler's Blues;* Folkways FS 3818: *Dave Van Ronk Sings Ballads, Blues and a Spiritual* "In the Pines"

Virginia Mountain Boys—Folkways FA 3833: *The Virginia Mountain Boys, Vol. 2*

Buck White and the Downhome Folks—County 760: *Live at the Old Time Pickin' Parlor* "In the Pines"

Josh White—Elektra EKL 701: *The Story of John Henry . . . a Musical Narrative: Ballads, Blues and Other Songs* "Black Girl"

Red White and the Dixie Blue Grass Band—Rural Rhythm RR-RW-172: *Red White and the Dixie Blue Grass Band* "In the Pines"

Chubby Wise and Howdy Forrester—Stoneway 1126 (45 rpm); Stoneway

STY-149: *Fiddle Traditions*   "In the
    Pines"
Unidentified—Folkways FS 3812: *Music*
    from the Ozarks   "In the Pines"

F. LC AFS:

William C. Bailey—AFS 13719 31
K. D. Begley—AFS 1455 A2   "Through
    the Pines Where the Sun Never Shines"
Otis Bird—AFS 12049 B14
Shorty Burks—AFS 11898 B
Ira Cephas—AFS 11332 B5   "Ruben"
June Ebbs and Laura Dixon—AFS 7925
    A1   "In the Pines"
Fuller Sisters—AFS 7883 B1   "In the
    Pines"
Leroy Gardner—AFS 11891 B
Austin Harmon—AFS 2885 A2 & B1
    "Number Nine"
Charley Jones—AFS 365 A1   "The
    Longest Train I Ever Saw"

Addie Leffew—AFS 15062 B7
Bascom Lamar Lunsford—AFS 1829 B3
    "To the Pines"
—AFS 9479 B1   "To the Pines, to the
    Pines"
Hattie McNeill—AFS 8832 B11   "The
    Lonesome Pine"
Ramona Priest—AFS 13128 A28
Ed Stillery—AFS 11902 B
Virgil Sturgill—AFS 11328 A11   "In the
    Pines"
Willie Williams—AFS 729 A3
    "Railroad Wreck"
Claude Wolfenberger—AFS 15059 B20
Unidentified group of Negro convicts—
    AFS 253 A1   "Lady, Won't You Pray
    for Me?"

GORDON COLLECTION (N.C.):

A58 (MS 37)—Bascom Lamar Lunsford
    "To the Pines"

Reuben's Train/Train 45/900 Miles

REUBEN, OH, REUBEN

Reube, Reube, oh Reube, it's Reube, Reube, oh Reube,
Reuben, where you been so long?

I've been to the East, I've been to the West,
I've been all around this old world.

I've been to the river and I've been baptized,
I'm ready for my hole in the ground.

Poor Reuben had a wreck, he broke his fireman's neck,
He can't get no letter from his home.

Reube, Reube, oh Reube, it's Reube, Reube, oh, Reube,
Reuben, where you been so long?

I've been to the East, I've been to the West,
Been all around this old world.

I've been to the river, and I've been baptized,
I'm ready for my hole in the ground.

Honey, if you just say so, I'll railroad no more,
I'll sidetrack my engine and come home.

The longest day I ever seen
Was the day that I left my home.

My mama told me and papa did, too,
That I must never roam.

Emry Arthur

NINE HUNDRED MILES FROM HOME

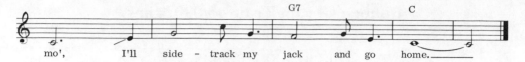

mo',   I'll   side - track my   jack   and   go   home.

In the fourth verse, the first (full) four bars are repeated.

If my baby says so, I will railroad no mo',
I'll sidetrack my jack and go home.

I will pawn you my watch, and I'll pawn you my chain,
I'll pawn you my wagon and my cane.

If my baby says so, I will railroad no mo',
I'll sidetrack my train and go home.

I got on that train and the train was a-flyin',
I looked back behind the train, saw my baby was a-cryin',
Lord, I ain't gonna be treated this-a way.

If my baby says so, I will railroad no mo',
I'll sidetrack my train and go home.

If you know the day I'm gone, you can tell the train I'm on.
You can hear the whistle blow (a) hundred mile.

If my baby says so, I will railroad no mo',
I'll sidetrack my train and go home.

If the train runs right, I'll be home tomorrow night,
For I ain't gonna be treated this-a way.

If my baby says so, I will railroad no mo',
I'll sidetrack my train and go home.

If you know the day I'm gone, you can tell the train I'm on,
You can hear the whistle blow (a) hundred mile.

You can count the days I'm gone by the train that I left on,
You can hear that whistle blow a hundred miles.

If my baby says so, I will railroad no mo',
I'll sidetrack my train and go home.

                                              Riley Puckett

I set these pieces aside as long as possible, not out of indifference to their musical charms, but out of respect for the challenge they pose to intelligent commentary. Here, the difficulties noted in the preceding discussion of "The Longest Train"/"In the Pines" return. The immediate problems are: (1) can these three songs be distinguished from each other? (2) do the three songs represent diverging branches of the same root or, conversely, merging streams of once-independent songs?

"Train 45" and "Reuben's Train" are musically the same. Apart from the earliest recordings, by Grayson and Whitter and by Mainer, Morris, and Ledford, the title "Train 45" is usually reserved for instrumental pieces. The two exceptions mentioned both lack any reference to someone named Reuben. Musically, there is no confusing "900 Miles" as it has been recorded since the 1940s and "Reuben's Train." The latter tune is invariably a one-strain melody, long enough to accommodate a two-line verse, for example, this opening stanza of Grayson and Whitter's "Train 45":

> Oh, you oughta been uptown, an' seen that train come down,
> A-heard the whistle blow a hundred miles.[1]

When the verses are written in this fashion, each line ends on the tonic. Beside the tonic, the melody uses primarily the third, fourth, and fifth degrees of the scale. In contrast, the "900 Miles" tune is twice as long. The first line is musically similar to "Reuben's Train," but the second line moves higher up the scale, to end on the dominant. The third and fourth lines are unlike "Reuben's Train."

The confusion between the two songs becomes apparent when one regards the lyrics apart from the melody; now, the overlap is considerable. The verses that occur in the various versions of the two songs can be arranged into several groups.

A. Stanzas concerning Reuben, an engineer with a drinking problem and occasionally other distasteful habits. For example:

> Oh, you ought to been up town when Reuben's train rode down,
> Lord, you could hear the whistle blow a hundred miles.[2]

> Ole Reuben went to town an' he drank that licker down,
> O Reube, Reuben, dat you, Reuben? I don' know.[3]

> Reuben he got drunk, he pawned his watch and trunk
> He was ten thousand miles from his home.[4]

> Say ol' Reuben had a wife, he's in trouble all his life.
> Den dey laid Reuben down so low.[5]

> On the first day of the year, old Reuben come up here,
> And she never has moved out since that day.

> I took my razor blade, I laid Reuben in the shade,
> And I started me a graveyard of my own, Lord knows, of my own.[6]

The first of these examples is very common. Usually the distance is 100 miles, but 1,000, 900, and 90 have also appeared. The third (or an equivalent couplet) appears in a half-dozen or so versions. The example quoted here represents one of the earliest reports of the song: it is all that Robert Duncan Bass recalled hearing sung by two Florence Country, South Carolina, blacks in 1905. The final two stanzas are unique to Wade Mainer's version and to others that can be assumed to be deliberate copies of it. Sometimes Reuben's train wrecks, as in Emry Arthur's version, transcribed above:

> Poor Reuben had a wreck, he broke his fireman's neck,
> He can't get no letter from his home.

An unusual variant ties the accident to verses from "The Longest Train":

> Reuben got killed [?on the] C & O line,
> And his poor body has never been found.

> They found his head in a driving wheel,
> 'Bout a mile and a half from town.[7]

A unique cante fable by black medicine-show man Peg Leg Sam of North Carolina outlines a story in which Reuben murders a sheriff, then, forty years later, is pursued by another sheriff and eventually caught.

B. Stanzas in which the narrator pleads with his true love for a sign of affection, or threatens to leave her.

> If my woman says so, I'll railroad no more,
> I'll sidetrack my train and go home.[8]

> My woman says so, I'll moonshine no more,
> Chop down my still and go home.[9]

> If you don't believe I'm gone, watch this train that I crawl on,
> Lord, I'm nine hundred miles away from home.[10]

> I'm a-goin' down the track, I ain't never comin' back,
> And I'll never get no letter from my home.[11]

C. Group B leads into the next cluster of stanzas, which is more characteristic of the "900 Miles" songs. Here we are told of a wanderer who wants, or is trying, to get back home to his true love:

> Said, I'm goin' down ties with these tears in my eyes,
> Tryin' to read a letter from my home.[12]

> If you say yes, I'll buy the weddin' dress,
> I'll go home on that morning train.[13]

> If the train runs right, see my woman Saturday night,
> I'm nine hundred miles away from home.[14]

> Lord, I'm one, and I'm two, lord, I'm three and I'm four,
> Lord, I'm five hundred miles from my home.[15]

The distance from home is generally 900 miles, with 500 the second most common. Ten thousand and 400 miles have also appeared. It might be noted that the last of the examples immediately preceding can be used only with the figure 500.

Stanzas characteristic of groups B and C were organized into a fairly cohesive love song lyric titled "The Midnight Dew," which Louise Rand Bascom collected in North Carolina and published in 1909.

D. Stanzas appearing in a few versions about a hobo and a tramp:

> Oh, the hobo said to the bum, "If you got any liquor I want some,
> But I can't see my mamma this-a way."

> Oh, the hobo said to the tramp, "The woods are wet an' the roads are damp,
> But I can't git back home this-a way."[16]

I have written these two fragments as if they fitted the "Reuben" tune. Actually, they were reported with refrains that suggest the longer "900 Miles" tune, although they could have been sung to a repeated "Reuben" tune. Another example:

> What did the hobo say to the bum? "Got any cornbread, save me some,
> For I never was so hungry in my life."[17]

E. A stanza beginning "If I die a railroad man," that links "Reuben" with several other songs:

> If I die a railroad man, you can bury me in the sand,
> Where I could hear old Number Nine as she goes by.[18]

F. A stanza beginning "Oh, the train's off the track," that often provides the title for another group of songs:

> Oh, the train's off the track, and I can't get it back,
> And I can't get a letter to my home.[19]

> The train is off the track and they can't get it back,
> And I'll never get back home this-a way.[20]

> Oh, the train's off the track an' I can't get it back,
> I'll meet you in the mornin' some ole day.[21]

The groupings outlined above suggest two or more separate songs. It is plausible, therefore, to suppose that there were indeed at one time two separate folksongs, the "Reuben" verses, group A, set to the "Reuben" tune; and groups B and C, set to the longer "900 Miles" tune. Groups D, E, and F could represent later accretions or readily detached portions. But the evidence for this bifurcation is scarely compelling. Furthermore, there are not very many early recoveries that point to the "900 Miles" tune and supposed accompanying text.

The earliest appearance of title use of the phrase "900 Miles" is Fiddlin' John Carson's 1924 recording, "I'm Nine Hundred Miles from Home." However, neither Carson's tune nor his text suggests anything different from the usual, sprawling "Reuben" forms, though two of his stanzas are alien to any of the songs considered in these groupings.

In October, 1925, Robert W. Gordon recorded a song titled "Old Reuben" from Julius Sutton in Dillsboro, North Carolina, that is textually suggestive of the "900 Miles" tune. On the same field trip, earlier that week, Gordon had recorded a "Reuben, or Railroad Blues" from Bascom Lamar Lunsford. Although this was not the first time a "Reuben" had been collected, the version proved interesting because Lunsford recalled singing it as a teenager, in about 1898, in Buncombe Country, North Carolina. Lunsford sang or wrote out the song three more times before his death (1935, 1949, 1968). Only four stanzas are common to all four renditions; and if we can trust these verses as being representative of what Lunsford actually did sing in 1898, then it is clear that "Reuben" and "900 Miles" were already commingled by that date:

> The wind is from the East and the snow's from the North,
> And I'm five hundred miles from my home.

> She is standing in the door, saying she hear(d) that whistle blow,
> She could hear that whistle blow a hundred miles.

> If this train sidetracks, I'll ride that freight train back,
> And I'll never leave my home any more.

> Oh, the women up in town say they chain Reuben down,
> Say they chain Reuben down so low.[22]

Of the history and development of this song—or group of songs—prior to the turn of the century, then, we can say nothing.

Although the existence of the long "900 Miles" tune prior to Woody Guthrie's handling of it is questionable, there is no doubt that he was responsible for the wide dissemination and popularity of the song from the 1940s on. According to Moses Asch, both of Guthrie's recordings of "900 Miles," one under the title "Railroad Whistle," were made in April, 1944.[23] Guthrie's two tunes differ in that one is in major, the other in minor. The minor version later became standard among folksong revival performers. Cisco Houston, who accompanied Guthrie on both of his 1944 recordings of "900 Miles," recorded the song himself twice, and it soon became associated with his name as much as with Guthrie's. In 1947 John and Alan Lomax transcribed Guthrie's version for their anthology *Folk Song: U.S.A.*, and six years later, B. A. Botkin and Alvin F. Harlow reproduced it in their own *Treasury of Railroad Folklore*.

Early in the 1960s another version of the song, titled "500 Miles," enjoyed great popularity. The source of this variant was Hedy West, a young folksinger from Cartersville, Georgia, whose repertoire drew heavily on the musical traditions of her own west Georgia family. She learned "500 Miles" from her grandmother, who had probably learned it around the turn of the century. Hedy changed the song a bit, ending up with a slow and moody love song, in sharp contrast to Guthrie's wild renditions with fiddle, harmonica, and mandolin.[24] Hedy sang the song frequently in concerts before she recorded it, and several groups put her version on disc before she did. The first was the Journeymen, one of whose members was Dick Weissman, who had heard Hedy sing the song in concert. They, followed by the Kingston Trio, and then by Peter, Paul, and Mary, all had big hits with this version in 1961–62. In October, 1963, Bobby Bare's version, "500 Miles Away from Home" climbed to number five on *Billboard*'s country chart and to number ten on the pop chart.

Two different text/tunes are transcribed in this book: one, representative of the "Reuben" group, is from a recording by Emry Arthur, whose life history was uncovered only a few years ago by hillbilly-music historian Donald Lee Nelson.[25] The "900 Miles" representative is a recording by Riley Puckett, whose career has been sketched briefly in connection with "The Freight Wreck at Altoona" (chap. 5).

Because the number of recordings is so great, I have listed those for "Reuben"/"Train 45" and "900 Miles" separately (sections D–F in the references). This distinction is not necessary for the printed references (sections B–C).

NOTES

1. G. B. Grayson and Henry Whitter, "Train 45," recorded Oct. 18, 1927 (Victor master 40307); released on Victor 21189; reissued on Old Timey X-100: *Old Time Southern Dance Music: The String Bands*.

2. Tommy Jarrell, "Reuben," Mountain 302: *June Apple*.

3. *The Frank C. Brown Collection of North Carolina Folklore*, vol. 3, *Folk Songs*, edited by Henry M. Belden and Arthur Palmer Hudson (Durham, N.C.: Duke University Press, 1952), p. 265. B text, from S.C., n.d.

4. Robert Duncan Bass, "Negro Songs from the Pedee Country," *JAF*, 44 (Oct.-Dec., 1931), 431.

5. Howard W. Odum and Guy B. Johnson, *Negro Workaday Songs* (Chapel Hill: University of North Carolina Press, 1926), p. 66.

6. Wade Mainer and the Sons of the Mountaineers, "Old Ruben," recorded ca. 1941; released on Bluebird B-8990; reissued on Old Timey LP 102: *Old-Time Southern Dance Music: Ballads and Songs*.

7. Jarrell, "Reuben."

8. Wade Mainer, Zeke Morris, and Steve Ledford, "Riding on That Train Forty-five," recorded ca. 1937; released on Bluebird B-7298 and other labels.

9. Fred Cockerham, "Reuben," Country 713: *Down to the Cider Mill*.

10. Jarrell, "Reuben."

11. Frank Proffitt, "Reuben Train," Folk-Legacy FSA 1: *Frank Proffitt of Reese, North Carolina*.

12. Mainer, Morris, and Ledford, "Riding on That Train Forty-five."

13. Phoeba Parsons, "Cherry River Line," Kanawha 303: *Old Time Music from Calhoun County, West Virginia*.

14. Grayson and Whitter, "Train 45."

15. Robert W. Gordon, *Folk-Songs of America* (New York: National Service Bureau, 1938), pp. 82–83.

16. Gordon Collection (N.C.) 118: recording A80. From Julius Sutton, Dillsboro, N.C., Oct. 28, 1925.

17. Mainer, "Old Reuben."

18. Ibid.

19. Mrs. Esco Kilgore, collected by Emory L. Hamilton, Apr. 20, 1939, in Wise, Va.; WPA (Alderman), WPA 1378 A.

20. Finley Adams, collected by James Taylor Adams, May 16, 1939, in Big Laurel, Va.; WPA (Alderman), WPA 1378 B.

21. Gordon, Sutton text.

22. The four Bascom Lamar Lunsford versions are (1) "Reuben, or Railroad Blues," Gordon recording A46 (N.C. MS 73), Asheville, N.C., Oct. 19, 1925; (2) "Reuben," LC AFS 1788 A2, recorded in New York City in 1935 by G. W. Hibbett and W. C. Greet; (3) "Rubin," LC AFS 9482 B2, recorded in Washington, D.C., Mar., 1949, by Duncan Emrich; (4) Lunsford to Judith McCulloh, Sept. 28, 1968.

23. Asch to Cohen, July, 1974.

24. Telephone conversation with Hedy West, autumn, 1974.

25. For information about Emry Arthur, see the brochure notes to JEMF LP 103: *Paramount Old-Time Tunes*.

REFERENCES

A. "Midnight Dew," in Louise Rand Bascom, "Ballads and Songs of Western North Carolina," *JAF*, 22 (Apr.-June, 1909), 244–45. Collected by Bascom; informant, date, and place not given. First publication representing the "Reuben"/"900 Miles" song cluster.

"I'm Nine Hundred Miles from Home," by Fiddlin' John Carson. Vocal and fiddle. Recorded Aug. 27, 1924 (General Phonograph Corp. master 8710-A), in Atlanta, Ga. Released on OKeh 40196 in autumn, 1924. Reissued on Vetco LP 103: *Songs of the Railroad*; Rounder 1003: *The Old Hen Cackled and the Rooster's Going to Crow*. First commercial recording of the song; first use of the phrase "900 miles" in the song cluster.

"Nine Hundred Miles from Home," by Riley Puckett. Vocal and guitar. Recorded Apr. 16, 1930 (Columbia master W150243), in Atlanta, Ga. Released on Columbia 15563-D on July 15, 1930. This version is transcribed here.

"Reuben, Oh, Reuben," by Emry Arthur. Vocal and guitar. Recorded ca. Jan., 1930 (Wisconsin Chair Co. master L-107-1), in Grafton, Wisc. Released on Paramount 3237, Paramount 3295, Broadway 8216 (as by Elroy Anderson). Reissued on JEMF 103: *Paramount Old Time Tunes*. This version is transcribed here.

"Train 45," by G. B. Grayson and Henry Whitter. Grayson, vocal and fiddle; Whitter, guitar and spoken comments. Recorded Oct. 18, 1927 (Victor master 40307), in Atlanta, Ga. Released on Victor 21189 on Mar. 16, 1928. Reissued on Bluebird B-5498; Old Timey X-100: *Old Time Southern Dance Music: The String*

Bands. These artists recorded the same
piece for Gennett a few days earlier; the
versions differ negligibly. First
appearances of the "Train 45" form of the
song cluster.

"Railroad Whistle," by Woody Guthrie,
Sonny Terry, and Cisco Houston.
Guthrie, vocal; Terry, harmonica;
Houston, guitar (?). Recorded Apr., 1944,
in New York City. Released on Stinson
627; Stinson SLP 9: *Folksay, Vol. 3*;
Stinson SLPX 9: *Folksay, Vols. 3 and 4*.
First known appearance of the minor
tune; source of most citybilly versions.

"500 Miles," by Hedy West. Vocal and
banjo. Recorded ca. 1963. Released on
Vanguard 9124: *Hedy West*, ca July,
1963. Earlier concert performances by
Hedy West were the source of the
widely popular versions under
this title.

B. Bass, 431
 Brown III, 264–65, 337–38
 Brown V, 148–50
 Buckley, 14–15
 Burton & Manning (1969), 32
 Combs (1939), 28–29   "That Lonesome
  Road"
 Gordon (1938), 82–83
 Guthrie (1942), 41
 Guthrie (1963), 30–31
 Henry (1934), 424
 Leach & Beck, 282–83
 Leisy (1966), 240
 Leisy (1973), 92
 Odum & Johnson (1926), 66
 Okun, 190
 Perrow (1913), 170–71
 Perry, 158 ("Train's offen the Track"),
  159–60
 Reprints from Sing Out #4, 33
 Roberts, 263
 Sackheim, 314 (transcription of Charlie
  Lincoln recording)
 Silverman (1975) II, 365, 382
 Sing Out!, 3 (Dec., 1952), 11
 Williams, 338

C. GORDON COLLECTION (N.C.):
 73—Bascom Lamar Lunsford
  "Reuben, or Railroad Blues"

 118—Julius Sutton   "Old Reuben"

WKFA:
 E. C. Perrow (Perrow Collection; 1961;
  T7–96)

WPA (ALDERMAN):
 Finley Adams—WPA 1378 B (Va.)
 Mrs. Esco Kilgore—WPA 1378 A (Va.)
 Etta Kilgore—WPA 1082 (Va.)

D. "REUBEN'S TRAIN"/"TRAIN 45" variants:
 Carolina Ramblers String Band
  —Melotone 13047, Oriole 8345,
  Perfect 13012, Romeo 5345
  "Ruben's Train"
 Wilma Lee and Stoney Cooper
  —Columbia 21049   "Stoney"
 Cousin Emmy (Cynthia May Carver)
  —Decca 23583   "Ruby"
  (derivative piece)
 William Francis and Richard Sowell
  —Vocalion 1090   "Roubin Blues"
 (Gilliam Banmon) Grayson and (Henry)
  Whitter—Gennett 6320, Champion
  15447 (as by Norman Gayle), Challenge
  397 (as by David Foley)   "Train 45"
 —Victor 21189, Bluebird B-5498; Old
  Timey X-100: *Old Time Southern Dance
  Music: The String Bands*
  "Train 45"
 Buell Kazee—Brunswick 217   "Poor Boy
  Long Ways from Home" (related)
 Charlie Lincoln—Columbia 14272-D; Roots
  RL-309: *Blues from Georgia (1926–1931)*;
  Historical ASC 5829: *Rare Blues of the
  Twenties, No. 4*   "Chain Gang
  Trouble"
 Wade Mainer and the Sons of the
  Mountaineers—Bluebird B-8990; Old
  Timey LP 102: *Old-Time Southern Dance
  Music: Ballads and Songs*   "Old Ruben"
 Wade Mainer, Zeke Morris, and Steve
  Ledford—Bluebird B-7298, Victor 27493
  (in album P-79: *Smoky Mountain
  Ballads*); RCA Victor LPV 507 and
  Pickwick/Camden ACL-7022: *Smoky
  Mountain Ballads*; RCA (Japan) RA 5220:
  Bluegrass Classics; Ball Mountain ALP
  201: *J. E. Mainer's Crazy Mountaineers*
  "Riding on That Train Forty-Five"

Sonny Osborne—Big 4 Hits (78 rpm and 45 rpm) 24; Gateway LP 19: *Five String Hi Fi*; Ultra Sonic LP 19: *Five String Hi Fi*; Deresco LP 19: *Five String Hi Fi*; Gateway 31388: *The Early Recordings of Sonny Osborne, Vol. 2*; Palace 756: *Bluegrass 5-String Banjo*   "Train 45"

"900 MILES" variants:

Woody Guthrie, Cisco Houston, Bess Lomax, and Baldwin Hawes—Stinson 332, Asch 432-1 (in album 432: *Folksay*); Stinson SLP 5: *Folksay, Vol. 1*; Stinson SLPX 5: *Folksay, Vols. 1 and 2*; Folkways FA 2483: *Woody Guthrie Sings Folk Songs*; Asch AA 4: *Asch Recordings 1939–1945, Vol. 2*

Brock Peters and the Four Lads—Columbia 40042   "900 Miles (from My Home)"

Riley Puckett—Columbia 15563-D "900 Miles from Home"

E. "REUBEN'S TRAIN"/"TRAIN 45" variants:

Red Allen and the Allen Brothers—King Bluegrass KB-523: *My Old Kentucky Home*   "Lonesome Ruben"

Mike Auldridge—Takoma/Devi D-1033: *Mike Auldridge: Dobro*   "Train 45½"

Blue Grass Mountain Boys—Folkways FA 2434: *The 37th Old Time Fiddler's Convention*   "Ruben"

Bluegrass Ramblers of Texas—Dane 5002: *Bluegrass from the Bluebonnet Country*   "Train 45"

Bluegrass Tarheels—United U625-S: *The Bluegrass Tarheels*   "Train 45" and "Lonesome Ruben"

Blue Ridge Mountain Boys—Time 52083/2083: *Hootenanny n' Blue Grass*   "Train 45"

Dock Boggs—Asch AH 3903: *Dock Boggs, Vol. 3*   "Ruben's Train"

Benny and Vallie Cain—Rebel SLP 1537: *More of Benny and Vallie Cain* "Train 45"

Camp Creek Boys—Mountain 302: *June Apple*   "Reuben"

Kenny Cantrell and the Green Valley Boys—SPBGMA 7601: *Home Sweet Home Revisited*   "Train 45"

Charles River Valley Boys—77 F/LEUT (England) 3: *Bringin' in the Georgia Mail*   "Old Reuben"

Bill Clifton—Bear Family (West Germany) BF 15000-2: *Going Back to Dixie* "Old Ruben"

Bill Clifton and the Dixie Mountain Boys—Nashville NLP 2018   "Old Reuben"

Fred Cockerham—County 713: *Down to the Cider Mill*   "Reuben"

Fred Cockerhan [*sic*]—County 701: *Clawhammer Banjo*   "Long Steel Rail" (related)

Randall Collins—Atteiram API 1015: *Randall Collins Stands Tall in Georgia Cotton*   "Train 45"

Elizabeth Cotten—Folkways FT 1003/ FTS 31003: *Shake Sugaree*   "Ruben"

Jenes Cottrell—Kanawha 301 (Folk Promotions FP 11567): *Old Time Music from Clay County, West Virginia* "Cherry River Line" (related)

Country Gentlemen—Folkways FA 2410: *Folk Songs and Bluegrass*   "Train 45"

—Rebel SLP 1535: *Yesterday & Today, Vol. 3*   "Train 45"

Dan Crary—American Heritage AHLP 275: *Bluegrass Guitar*   "Reuben"

Dub Crouch and the Bluegrass Rounders—Missouri Area Bluegrass Committee LP 101: *Grass Cuttin' Time in Missouri*   "Train 45"

Dub Crouch, Norman Ford, and the Bluegrass Rounders—Prof. Artist PAS 7433-22: *Next Train South*   "Ruben"

J. D. Crowe and the Kentucky Mountain Boys—Lemco 609 and King Bluegrass KB 524: *J. D. Crowe and the Kentucky Mountain Boys*   "Train 45"

J. D. Crowe and the New South—Towa (Japan) 106: *Live in Japan*   "Train 45"

Eldon Davis and Josh Graves—Kim-Pat KPL-7708: *A Touch of Grass*   "Train 45"

Hubert Davis and his Season Travelers —Stoneway STY-115: *Down Home Bluegrass*

Doug Dillard and group—Together SST-1003: *Doug Dillard's Banjo Album* "Train 4500"

Dillards—Elektra EKL 232/EKS 7232: *Back Porch Bluegrass*; Crestview CRS 7806; Legacy LEG 110: *Folk Festival* "Reuben's Train"

Raymond Fairchild and the Maggie Valley Boys—Rural Rhythm RR-146: *King of the Smokey Mountain . . .* "Train 45"

Lester Flatt, Earl Scruggs, and the Foggy Mountain Boys—Columbia CS 8364 and LE 10043: *Foggy Mountain Banjo*; Columbia KG 31964: *The World of Flatt and Scruggs* "Reuben"

—Kings of Bluegrass, Vol. 2: *Lester Flatt, Earl Scruggs, and the Foggy Mountain Boys* "Reuben"

Lester Flatt, Earl Scruggs, Doc Watson, and the Foggy Mountain Boys—Columbia CL 2643/CS 9443: *Strictly Instrumental* "Lonesome Ruben"

Flying Burrito Brothers—Philips 6641-144: *Live in Amsterdam* "Reuben's Train"

Frosty Mountain Boys—Rural Rhythm RR-FM-159: *Mamma Likes Bluegrass Music* "Pat's Train Special"

Josh Graves, Bobby Smith, and the Boys from Shiloh—Vetco 3025: *Josh Graves* "Reuben"

J. C. Hale and the Blue Fescue—Major 2207: *Down to Grass Tacks*

Halifax Three—Epic LN 24060/BN 26060: *The San Francisco Bay Blues* "Reuben Had a Train"

Hamilton County String Band—Kiwi (New Zealand) SLC-82: *Yesterday's Gone* "Reuben"

Walter Hensley—Capitol T/ST 2149: *The Five String Banjo Today* "Long Way from Home"

Joe Hickerson—Fox Hollow FH 701: *Pitter Poon the Rain Come Doon, Vol. 1*

Wade Hill and the Bluegrass Professionals—Revonah 503 "Reuben"

Smiley Hobbs—Folkways FA 2314: *American Banjo Tunes and Songs in Scruggs Style* "Train 45"

Thomas Holland and the Crossroads Boys—Prestige Folklore 14030: *Old Time Fiddling at Union Grove* "Train 45"

Holy Modal Rounders—Prestige Folklore 14031: *The Holy Modal Rounders*;

Fantasy 24711: *The Holy Modal Rounders* "Reuben's Train"

—Rounder 3004: *Alleged in Their Own Time* "New Reuben's Train" (derivative piece)

John Jackson—Arhoolie F 1035: *John Jackson, Vol. 2* "Reuben" and "Going Up North" (related)

Tommy Jarrell—County 748: *Tommy Jarrell's Banjo Album* "Old Reuben"

Tommy Jarrell and Kyle Creed—Mountain 302: *June Apple* "Reuben"

Vester Jones—Folkways FS 3811: *Traditional Music from Grayson and Carroll Counties* "Old Ruby"

Bill Keith and Jim Rooney—Prestige Folklore 14002: *Livin' on the Mountain* "Reuben's Old Train"

Kentucky Colonels—Briar BT 7202: *Livin' in the Past* "Train 45"

Kentucky Mountain Boys—Lemco LLP 609: *Bluegrass Holiday* "Train 45"

Bill Knopf and Hot Off the Press—American Heritage AH-401–524 "Train 45"

Mrs. Esco Kilgore—Library of Congress Archive of Folk Song L61: *Railroad Songs and Ballads* "The Train Is off the Track"

Knob Lick Upper 10,000—Mercury SR 60780: *The Introduction of Knob Lick Upper 10,000* "Train 45"

David Lambeth and the High Lonesome Ramblers—King Bluegrass KB 535: *A Tribute to the Stanley Brothers* "Train 45"

Laurel River Valley Boys—Judson J-303l: *Music for Moonshiners*; Riverside RLP 7504/97504: *Dance All Night with a Bottle in Your Hand* "Train 45"

Steve Ledford—Roan Mountain RM-1 (45 rpm EP) "Reuben's Train"

Bob Letterly—Weiser 1966: *National Oldtime Fiddlers Contest and Festival* "Rubens Train"

Limited Edition—Limited Edition AR 2350: *The Limited Edition* "Train 45"

Log Cabin Boys—Rural Rhythm RR-184: *Log Cabin Boys* "Train 45"

Alan Lomax and the Dupree Family
—Kapp KL-1316: *Raise a Ruckus and Have a Hootenanny* "Reuben"

Jim McCall—Vetco LP 3010: *"Pickin' and Singin'"* "Train 45"

Maggie Valley Boys—Rural Rhythm RR-170: *Maggie Valley Boys* "Reuben" and "Little Joe's Special to Maggie Valley"

Jimmie Martin—Decca 74285: *Country Music Time* "Train 45"

Mac Martin and the Dixie Travelers —Rural Rhythm RR-MM-201: *The Travelin' Blues* "Reuben's Pardon" (related)

Kenny Miller, Mrs. Miller, and Mike Seeger—Folkways FA 2314: *American Banjo Tunes and Songs in Scruggs Style* "Ruben's Train"

Bill Monroe—Decca 32245 (45 rpm)

James Monroe—MCA 2-8002: *Live at Bean Blossom* "Train 45"

Conley Mullens, Gene Cornett, and group—Pine Tree PTSLP-520 "Reuben"

New Grass Edition—Union Grove SS-10: *Fiddle & Banjo Tunes, 51st Convention*

New Lost City Ramblers—Folkways FA 2491: *Gone to the Country* "Riding on That Train 45"

—Folkways FT 1015/FTS 31015: *New Lost City Ramblers with Cousin Emmy* "Graveyard"

—Vanguard VRS 9146/VSD 79146: *Country Music and Bluegrass at Newport*

Cranford Nix—Atteiram 1503 "Evening Train"

Osborne Brothers—CMH 6202: *Number 1* "Reuben"

Don Parmley and Billy Strange— Crescendo GNP 98: *5-String Banjo* "Ruben's Train"

Phoeba Parsons—Kanawha 303 (Folk Promotions FP 41942): *Old Time Music from Calhoun County, West Virginia* "Cherry River Line" (related)

Peg Leg Sam—Trix 3302: *Medicine Show Man* "Reuben"

George Pegram and group—Rounder 0001: *George Pegram* "Reuben"

George Pegram and Walter Parham— Riverside RLP 12-610: *Banjo Songs of the Southern Mountains* "Old Reuben"

Pete Pike—Rebel R-1474 (LP, no title) "Train 45"

Piney Ridge Boys—King Bluegrass 553: *Flat Land Bluegrass* "Reuben"

Poplin Family—Folkways FA 2306: *The Poplin Family of Sumter, South Carolina* "Old Reuben"

—Melodeon MLP 7331: *The Poplin Family* "Reuben"

Potomac Valley Boys—GHP 907: *Bluegrass from Virginia* "Train 45"

Frank Proffitt—Folk-Legacy FSA 1: *Frank Proffitt of Reese, North Carolina* "Reuben Train"

Ola Belle Reed—Heritage 6: *First Annual Brandywine Mountain Music Convention* "Rueben" [*sic*]

Tony Rice—King Bluegrass KB 529: *Guitar* "Lonesome Reuben"

Buddy Rose—Dominion NR-3319: *Down Home Pickin'* "Reuben"

Art Rosenbaum—Kicking Mule KM-108: *5 String Banjo* "Old Reuben"

Scottsville Squirrel Barkers—Crown CLP 5346/CST 346: *Blue Grass Favorites* "Reuben"

Earl Scruggs—Columbia CS 1007: *Nashville's Rock* "Train Number Forty-Five"

—Columbia C 30584: *His Family and Friends* "Lonesome Reuben"

—Columbia C 32268: *Dueling Banjos* "Reuben"

Garland Shuping—Old Homestead 90038: *Garland Shuping on Banjo with the Bluegrass Alliance* "Reuben Had a Train"

Pat Sky—Vanguard VRS 9179/VSD 79179: *Patrick Sky* "Reuben"

Sloas Brothers—Rem 1023: *I'm Going Home Again* "Ruben"

Bill Smith Quartet—Contemporary M3591: *Folk Jazz* "Reuben, Reuben"

Joe Smith and the Carolina Buddies— Great Bluegrass Country Records 4045: *Joe Smith and the Carolina Buddies* "Train 45"

Ralph Stanley—Rebel SLP 1530: *A Man and His Music*   "Train 45"

Stanley Brothers—King 45-5155; King 615: *The Stanley Brothers*; King 869: *Railroad Songs*   "Train 45"

—King 45-5916; King 872: *The World's Finest Five String Banjo*   "Train 45"

—King 994: *Great, Great, Great* "Train 45" (probably one of the two recordings above)

—Rebel SLP 1495: *The Legendary Stanley Brothers, Vol. 2*   "Train 45"

—Starday SD 3003: *16 Greatest Hits* "Train 45" (one of the above King recordings)

Don Stover—Rounder 0014: *"Things in Life"*   "Old Reuben No. 1"

Stringbean—Cullman 6416 (45 rpm) "Train Special 500"

—Starday SLP 179: *Stringbean*   "Train Special 500"

Sweet Corn—Aural 9006: *All around the Mountain*   "Reuben's Train"

Gordon Tanner and the Junior Skillet-lickers—"W" MW-1038 (45 rpm EP) "Train 45"

Uncle Leroy and the Pike County Partners—Major MRLP-2195: *Star-Spangled Bluegrass*

Boyd "Shorty" Van Winkle—Monitor MF 367: *Billy Edd and Bluegrass, Too* "Ruebin" [*sic*]

Virginia Mountain Boys—Folkways FA 3833: *The Virginia Mountain Boys, Vol. 2*   "Train 45"

Cliff Waldron and the New Shades of Grass—Rebel 1502   "Reuben"

Howard Wallace—Jewel LPS 219: *When You and I Were Young*   "Train 45"

C. E. Ward, Joe Smith, and the Bluegrass Review—Bluegrass Country Recordings (no number): *Variety Album*

Wade Ward—Folkways FA 2363: *The Music of Roscoe Holcomb and Wade Ward*   "Old Reuben"

—Folkways FA 2380: *Uncle Wade* "Old Reuben"

Doc Watson and Gaither Carlton—Folkways FA 2355: *Old Time Music at Clarence Ashley's*   "Old Ruben"

Doc Watson, Gaither Carlton, and Arnold

Watson—Topic (England) 12TS336: *The Watson Family Tradition*   "Reuben's Train"

Doc Watson, Clint Howard, and Fred Price—Vanguard VSD 107/8: *Old Timey Concert*   "Reuben's Train"

Eric Weissberg—Elektra EKS 7238: *Banjo and Bluegrass*; Warner Brothers WBR 0309 (45 rpm); Warner Brothers B-2683: *Dueling Banjos from "Deliverance"* "Reuben"

Harry and Jeanie West—Stinson SLP 36: *Southern Mountain Folk Songs* "Old Ruben"

Wilson Brothers, Larry, and Joanna— MRC MRLP 1093: *Stand Tall in Bluegrass*   "Train 45"

Winnie Winston and group—Elektra EKL 276: *Old Time Banjo Project* "Reuben's Train"

Art Wooten—Homestead 104: *A Living Legend*   "Train 45"

RECORDINGS BASED on Cousin Emmy's "Ruby":

Bluegrass Blackjacks—Puritan 5004: *The Bluegrass Blackjacks*

Bonnie Lou, Buster Moore, and the Mountain Music Makers—Acme 2055 (45 rpm)

—Acme 2090 (45 rpm)   "Ruby"

Jack Casey—Rural Rhythm RRJC 206: *Jack Casey*   "Ruby"

Ray Charles—ABC ABCS 590X: *A Man and His Soul*   "Ruby"

Allan Clarke—Epic KE-31757: *My Real Name Is Arnold*   "Ruby"

Jack Clement—Hallway 45-1205 (45 rpm)   "Ruby Are You Mad"

Wilma Lee and Stoney Cooper— Columbia 21049 (45 prm)   "Stoney Are You Mad at Your Gal"

Country Pals—Rich-R-Tone ACA-568: *Your Bluegrass Favorites*   "Ruby"

Cousin Emmy (Cynthia May Carver)— Folkways FT 1015/FTS 31015: *The New Lost City Ramblers with Cousin Emmy*   "Ruby, Are You Mad at Your Man?"

Danny Davis and the Nashville Brass

—RCA Victor APL1-0565: *Bluegrass Country*

Ernie and Mack and the Bluegrass Cutups—Rural Rhythm RR-EM-140: *Blue Grass If You Please* "Ruby"

Field Brothers—Jessup MB 144: *The Field Brothers Sing of Old Kentucky and West Virginia Bluegrass* "Ruby"

Lester Flatt and Earl Scruggs—Columbia C-32244: *A Boy Named Sue* "Ruby"

Abbie Gaye, Ken, and Mel—Trac SA 101 "Ruby Are You Mad"

John Herald—Biograph BLP 12052: *You Got Magic: Fox Hollow 10th Anniversary* "Ruby"

Anita Kerr Singers—RCA Victor LPM-2581: *Vocal Stylings of "the Genius" in Harmony* "Ruby"

Kingston Trio—Capitol T/ST 1809: *New Frontier* "Honey Are You Mad at Your Man"

Kniphfers—Prestige 72-162: *The Kniphfers Play Bluegrass* "Ruby"

Mike Lattimore Show—Rural Rhythm RR-ML-169: *The Mike Lattimore Show* "Ruby, Ruby"

Curtis McPeake and Red Allen—Power Pak 218: *Bluegrass Special* "Ruby"

Roger Miller—Smash 27092/67092: *Walkin' in the Sunshine* "Ruby"

Osborne Brothers—MGM E/SE 4149: *Cuttin' Grass* "Ruby, Are You Mad"

—Decca DL 75204 and MCA 135: *Rubeeee*

Osborne Brothers and Red Allen—MGM K-12308 (45 rpm); MGM E-3734: *Country Pickin' and Hillside Singin'* "Ruby, Are You Mad"

Buck Owens—Capitol 3096 (45 rpm); Capitol ST-795: *Ruby and Other Bluegrass Specials*; Capitol ST-830: *The Best of Buck Owens, Vol. 4* "Ruby (Are You Mad)"

Russell Brothers—Jewel LPS 257: *Take Me Home, Country Roads*

Southern Strangers—PSG 53: *Kerrville Folk Festival* (1954)

Earl Taylor and the Stoney Mountain Boys—United Artists UAL 3049/UAS 6049: *Folk Songs from the Bluegrass* "Ruby"

Frank Wakefield—Kapp 2002 (45 rpm) "Ruby"

"900 MILES" variants:

Steve Alaimo—ABC Paramount 531: *Where the Action Is* "500 Miles"

Frances Archer and Beverly Giles—Disneyland WDL 3023: *Community Concert*

Hoyt Axton—World Pacific WP 1601 "500 Miles"

Kenny Ball—Jerden 776 (45 rpm)

Bobby Bare—RCA Victor 47-8238 (45 rpm); RCA Victor LPM/LSP 2835: *500 Miles Away from Home*; RCA Victor LPM/LSP 3479: *The Best of Bobby Bare*; Pickwick ACL-7003: *Five Hundred Miles Away from Home* "500 Miles Away from Home"

Leon Bibb—Liberty 3327/7327: *Leon Bibb in Concert* "500 Miles"

Bobby Bond—Time 52122 "500 Miles"

Pat Boone—Dot 45-17098 (45 rpm) "500 Miles"

Brothers Four—Columbia CL-2033/CS 8833: *Big Folk Hits* "500 Miles"

Terry Callier—Prestige 7383: *New Folk Sound of Terry Callier*

Glen Campbell—Capitol T/ST 2023: *Astounding 12-String Guitar of Glen Campbell* "500 Miles"

—Pickwick SPC 3134

Guy Carawan—Prestige 13013: *The Best of Guy Carawan*

Cayuca's Waiters—RCA Victor LPM 2929

Children of Adam—Ikon 571 F: *One More Round*

Clarence Cooper—Elektra SMP 3: *Pops, Folk, 'n' Jazz Sampler*

Country Gentlemen—Design DLP 613: *Hootenanny*; Rebel 1494: *The Best of the Early Country Gentlemen*; London (Japan) SLH 52: *Folk Hits Bluegrass Style*; Hilltop JS 6156: *Bluegrass Country* "500 Miles"

Bing Crosby—RCA Victor LSO-6070: *How the West Was Won*

Cumberland Three—Roulette R 25121: *Folk Scene USA*

Barbara Dane—Horizon WP-1602: *When I was a Young Girl*

Deaxville Trio—Jubilee JGM-1121: *On Campus with the Deaxville Trio*

Robert Decormier Singers—Command RS
  897 SD: *Folk Album*   "500 Miles"
Jackie De Shannon—Imperial 9296/12296:
  In the Wind   "500 Miles"
Dick and Deedee—Warner Brothers 1538:
  Turn Around   "500 Miles"
John Fahey and Nancy McClean—Takoma
  C 1008: *The Great San Bernadino
  Birthday Party and Other Excursions*
Raymond Fairchild—Rural Rhythm
  RR-RF-245: *Honky Tonkin' Country
  Blues*   "900 Miles Blues"
Fairmount Singers—Dot 3439/25439:
  Jimmie Rodgers Presents
Percy Faith—Columbia CL-2108/
  CS-8908: *Great Folk Themes*   "500
  Miles"
Lester Flatt, Earl Scruggs, and the Foggy
  Mountain Boys—Columbia 4-42413 (45
  rpm); Columbia CL 2686/CS 9486: *Songs
  of Rivers and Rails*   "Hear the Whistle
  Blow a Hundred Miles"
Gals and Pals—Fontana 27538/67538: *Gals
  and Pals*   "500 Miles"
Jimmy Gilmer—Dot 3668/25668:
  Folkbeat   "500 Miles"
Tom Glazer—Coral 9-61772 (45 rpm)
  "500 Miles"
Goldenaires Choir—Vox STVX 426.120:
  Songs of the Southern Mountains
Greenwoods—Decca 4496/74496:
  Greenwoods   "500 Miles"
Frank Hamilton—Concert Disc CS-54:
  Frank Hamilton   "900 Miles from
  Home"
Sam Hinton—Decca DL 8108: *Singing
  across the Land*
Roger Hopkins, Mutt Poston, and the Farm
  Hands—Rural Rhythm HO 1008:
  Country and Folk Songs   "500 Miles"
Cisco Houston—Folkways FA 2013 (FP 13):
  900 Miles and Other Railroad Songs
—Vanguard VRS 9057/VSD 2042: *The Cisco
  Special*; Vanguard VSD-35: *The Greatest
  Songs of Woody Guthrie*
Dan Isaacson—Cornell CRS-10021: *Ballads*
Clarence Jackson and group—Rural
  Rhythm RR-156: *Great Country Blues
  Instrumentals*
Journeymen—Capitol T/ST 1629: *The
  Journeymen*   "500 Miles"

Bill Justis—Smash 27047/SRS 67047:
  Dixieland Folk Style   "500 Miles Away
  from Home"
Kingston Trio—Capitol KAO/SKAO 2005:
  Sing a Song with the Kingston Trio;
  Capitol T/ST 1658: *College Concert*;
  Capitol T/ST 2614: *Best of the Kingston
  Trio*; Pickwick SPC-3323: *Where Have All
  the Pretty Flowers Gone*   "500 Miles"
—Capitol T/ST 1258: *Here We Go
  Again*   "The Wanderer" (derivative
  piece)
Norman Luboff Chorus—RCA Victor
  LPM/LSP 3312: *Blues—Right Now*
Arthur Lyman—Hi Fidelity 1024: *Midnight
  Sun*   "500 Miles"
Mary Love Singers—Power DS 402
  "500 Miles"
Mountain Dew Singers—Mountain Dew
  S 7003: *Top Country Hits of 1964*
  "500 Miles Away from Home"
Murphytown Singers—Coronet CX 257
  "500 Miles"
Johnny Nash—Jad JS 1006: *Soul Folk*
  "500 Miles"
New Christy Minstrels—Columbia CL
  1872/CS 8672: *Presenting—New Christy
  Minstrels*
Nina and Frederik—Atco 119: *Introducing
  a Fabulous Nina and Frederik*
Odetta—RCA Victor LPM/LSP 2643:
  Odetta Sings Folk Songs
Milt Okun—Elektra EKL-KIT-B: *Elektra
  Folk Song Kit*   "900 Miles"
Peter and Gordon—Capitol T/ST 2115:
  World without Love   "500 Miles"
Peter, Paul, and Mary—Warner Brothers
  WS 1449: *Peter, Paul and Mary*
  "500 Miles"
—Warner Brothers BS-2552: *Ten Years
  Together*   "500 Miles"
—Warner Brothers 2WS 1555: *Peter, Paul
  & Mary in Concert*   "500 Miles"
Vivien Richman—Bobtone FLP 2066:
  Vivien Richman Sings Folk Songs "For
  You and Me"
Johnny Rivers—Imperial LP 9293/12293:
  Johnny Rivers Rocks the Folk   "500
  Miles"
Pete Seeger—Vanguard VRS 9010: *The*

Weavers at Carnegie Hall (in medley
"Woody's Rag and 900 Miles")

Seldom Scene—Rebel SLP 1511: *Act 1*
"500 Miles"

Joe Simon—Spring 5705: *Simon Country*
"500 Miles"

Jimmie Skinner—Vetco 3001: *Jimmie
Skinner Sings Bluegrass*   "I'll Railroad
No More" (related)

Sloane Family—Old Homestead 80002:
Appalachian Bluegrass   "500 Miles"

Red Smiley and the Bluegrass Cutups—
Rural Rhythm RR-RS-160: *Red Smiley
and the Bluegrass Cutups*

Joan Sommer—Monitor MF 354: *Billy Edd:
USA*

Sonny and Cher—Atco 177: *Look at Us*
"500 Miles"

I. D. Stamper—June Appal 010: *Red
Wing*   "900 Miles"

George Stevens—Kimberly 1245

Pete Stone—Riverside RLP 12-641

Chris Terrie—Custom CS 1085: *Ode to
Billie Joe*   "900 Miles"

Villagers—Wyncote W-9010   "500
Miles"

Eric Weissberg—Elektra EKL-217: *Folk
Banjo Styles*

—Judson J-3017; Washington WLP 704: *5
String Banjo Jamboree*

Hedy West—Vanguard VRS 9124: *Hedy
West*   "500 Miles"

—Vanguard 9186/79186: *Newport Folk
Music Festival, 1964, Vol. 3*   "500
Miles"

Josh White, Jr.—Mercury MG 21022/SR
61022: *A Son's Heritage*   "500 Miles"

Roger Whittaker—RCA Victor KLP1-0078:
Travelling with Roger Whittaker
"500 Miles"

F. GORDON COLLECTION (N.C.):

A46 (MS 73)—Bascom Lamar Lunsford
"Reuben, or Railroad Blues"

A80 (MS 118)—Julius Sutton   "Old
Reuben"

LC AFS:

"REUBEN"/"TRAIN 45" variants:

Smith Brown—AFS 15067 B6

Ira Cephas—AFS 11331 B & 11332
B5   "Ruben"

Tom Chesser—AFS 7722 B1
"Hollering" (includes "Old Reuben")

Bob Bossie Clark—AFS 8487 B2   "Old
Reuben"

Fred Cockerham—AFS 14161 A5

Moss Coffman—AFS 14484 20
"Reuben's Train"

—AFS 15532 4/21   ""Reuben's Train""

Bill Cornett—AFS 11711 A18   "Old
Reuben"

Sam Davis—AFS 14651 B23

Charlie Higgins—AFS 15055 A11

Tommy Jarrell—AFS 14162 5

Addie Leffew—AFS 15062 B5   "Old
Reuben"

Bascom Lamar Lunsford—AFS 1788 A2
"Reuben"

—AFS 9482 B2   "Rubin"

Wade Mainer—AFS 17106 A7

Solomon Mains—AFS 12397 A14   "Old
Reuben"

Sid Meyer—AFS 12396 B11   "Old
Reuben"

—AFS 12396 B18   "Old Reuben"

Sid Meyer and Raymond Melton—AFS
12396 B19   "Old Reuben"

Sidna Myers—AFS 15067 A14   "Ruby"

Maggie Hammons Parker—AFS 14461 10

—AFS 14485 16

Silas Pendleton—AFS 9060 A4
"Ruby"

Frank Proffitt—AFS 12397 B38
"Whistle Blow"

George Roark—AFS 1997 B   "Crazy"

String Dusters—AFS 10504 A20
"Train 45"

David Thompson—AFS 14207 A5, A8

Fields Ward—AFS 12363 B2   "Old
Reuben Train"

Fields and Davy Crockett Ward—AFS 4080
B4   "Reuben's Train"

Wade Ward—AFS 4941   "Reuben
Train"

"900 MILES" variants:

William C. Bailey—AFS 13719 14

Lester Brooks—AFS 13032 A25   "Nine
Hundred Miles from My Home"

Lee Sexton—AFS 11710 B39   "Nine
Hundred Miles"

Emry Arthur. Courtesy of Donald Lee Nelson.

Delmore Brothers. Courtesy of the John Edwards
Memorial Foundation, UCLA.

Blow Yo' Whistle, Freight Train

This is sung as a duet on the recording, with the melody alternated between the upper and lower voices. The guitar solo has been taken by the music editor to be the melody, and the basis for deciding whether to use the upper or lower voice for each phrase.

*E-flat bass.

Blow yo' whistle, freight train, take me on down the line,
Blow yo' whistle, lay-de-he, got ramblin' on my mind.

That old freight train movin' along to Nashville,
Holds a charm that is a charm for me;
Makes me think of good old boomer days gone by,
Makes me feel so lonely, don't you see.
   Chorus:

Got a feelin' that I want to ramble,
Still I know that that can never be;
Guess I'll have to listen to that old smokestack,
Singing out this lonely song for me
   Chorus:

Delmore Brothers

The late 1920s and 1930s saw the rise to popularity of a singing style that featured several closely blending voices, moving from note to note in a perfectly timed sweet harmony that was deceptively skillful. In pop music, it was highlighted by such groups as the Boswell Sisters, the Andrews Sisters, and the Ink Spots. In the country music field, it was typified by the singing of the Blue Sky Boys (the Bolick brothers), the Callahan Brothers, and, more than any other group, the Delmore Brothers.

Alton and Rabon Delmore, born in 1908 and 1916, respectively, in Elkmont, Alabama, became professional entertainers in 1931 and enjoyed continuous popularity until 1952, when Rabon died. Their repertoire and style were basically contemporary hillbilly, but with much blues influence. They recorded and wrote many songs about railroads and hoboes, including "Midnight Special," "Freight Train Boogie," "Pan American Boogie," "Midnight Train," "Blue Railroad Train," "The [Wabash] Cannon Ball" (transcribed in chap. 8), and "I Let the Freight Train Carry Me On," in addition to "Blow Yo' Whistle, Freight Train." The brothers had deep religious convictions and would not record religious songs under their own name, doubtless in the desire to avoid mixing the sacred with the profane. Their religious output was recorded with a very popular quartet called the Brown's Ferry Four, whose other members varied from time to time, but generally consisted of Grandpa Jones and either Red Foley or Merle Travis.

"Blow Yo' Whistle, Freight Train" is a simple lyric whose beauty lies primarily in the Delmore Brothers' recorded version—mellow and wistful, a perfect blend of vocal duet, standard guitar, and four-string guitar. This was the arrangement they favored on all their recordings, although in their youth both boys played fiddle as well as guitar. The song was recorded in January of 1935 and issued a few months later. Fifteen months later, the Callahan Brothers recorded their own version, "Freight Train Blues," followed, before the end of the year, by a sequel, "Freight Train Whistle Blues No. 2." A few other versions have been recorded, but none has quite the impact of the original Delmore Brothers' version.[1]

NOTE

1. For additional information, see Alton Delmore's autobiography, *Truth Is Stranger than Publicity,* edited by Charles K. Wolfe (Nashville: Country Music Foundation Press, 1977).

REFERENCES

A. "Blow Yo' Whistle, Freight Train," by the Delmore Brothers. Alton, vocal lead and six-string guitar; Rabon, vocal harmony and four-string tenor guitar. Recorded Jan. 22, 1935 (RCA Victor master 87664), in New Orleans, La. Released on RCA Bluebird B-5925. Reissued on RCA Camden CAL 898: *Maple on the Hill and Other Old Time Country Favorites*.

B. Delmore-Vagabonds, 19
    Delmore Brothers, 25

D. Callahan Brothers—ARC 7-06-69

"Freight Train Whistle Blues No. 2"
—ARC 6-09-53, Columbia 20212, Columbia 37613, Conqueror 8731, Vocalion 03171, Okeh 03171   "Freight Train Blues"
Milo Twins—Decca 5832

E. Hank Snow—Transcription (West Germany) MLP 1003: *The Transcription Side of Hank Snow*
    Happy and Artie Traum—Rounder 3007: *Hard Times in the Country*
    Merle Travis and Johnny Bond—Capitol ST-249: *Great Songs of the Delmore Brothers*

Freight Train

FREIGHT TRAIN

Freight train, freight train, run so fast,
Freight train, freight train, run so fast;
Please don't tell what train I'm on,
An' they won't know what route I'm goin'.

When I am dead and in my grave,
No more good times here I crave;
Place the stones at my head and feet,
And tell 'em all that I'm gone to sleep.

When I die, Lord, bury me deep,
Way down on old Chestnut Street,
So I can hear old Number Nine,
As she comes rollin' by.

When I die, Lord, bury me deep,
Way down on old Chestnut Street,
Place the stones at my head and feet,
And tell 'em all that I'm gone to sleep.

Elizabeth Cotten

The musical gems that are captured for posterity through the chance encounter of a folksinger and a collector must make us wonder what countless pieces have been irrecoverably lost for want of such a contact. Elizabeth Cotten, born near Chapel Hill, North Carolina, in 1893, was one of several musically gifted children whose father supported the family by working in the mills or mines while their mother worked as a cook and midwife. Elizabeth began to hire herself out for housework when she was about twelve, and has supported herself this way for most of her life. When she was in her early forties, she moved to Washington, D.C. One day, while working in a department store there, she helped a lost child named Peggy Seeger find her mother. Elizabeth and the Seegers became good friends, and she began doing housework for them. In time, she picked up one of the Seeger guitars and surreptitiously began picking out the tunes that she had not played since her youth. Peggy and Mike Seeger, who were by then both involved with folk music, were amazed to discover her hidden talents, and encouraged her to begin performing in public.

One of Elizabeth's songs was "Freight Train," one of the few pieces she herself composed. It was inspired by a train that ran near her home: "We used to watch the freight train. We knew the fireman and the brakeman . . . and the conductor, my mother used to launder for him. They'd let us ride in the engine . . . put us in one of the coaches while they were backing up and changing . . . that was how I got my first train ride."[1]

During the 1950s, her composition was popularized by Peggy Seeger, from whom others learned it—Rusty Draper in the United States, Nancy Whiskey in England, then Peter and Gordon, and so on. Elizabeth herself recorded the song in 1958, when she was finally persuaded to cut an album for Folkways; but by that time, every young guitar picker swept up by the folksong revival had learned it. It has since become a standard, not only in the folk-revival field, but in the country music idiom as well, having been recorded by Chet Atkins, Mac Wiseman, and, more recently, Jim and Jesse McReynolds, who set new words to her tune. On too many of these recordings, Elizabeth has not been given due credit. (A law suit was necessary to give her composer credits and royalties after the song had been copyrighted in the names of other performers.)

Elizabeth Cotten's fine finger-picking style is all the more remarkable in view of the fact that she plays the guitar left-handed without restringing it (i.e., upside down, with the bass strings on the top.)

During the 1960s and 1970s, Elizabeth has appeared at many folksong festivals across the country, giving folk music audiences the chance to hear this beautiful song as performed by its creator. On stage, in her eighties, she is poised and dignified, still able to make wonderful music with either banjo or guitar. In 1974, as one of the witnesses invited to open Senate hearings on the American Folklife Preservation Act, she performed "Freight Train," and senators and audience alike, without prompting, joined in the singing.[2]

I have come across only one traditional item that is sufficiently similar to Elizabeth Cotten's lyrics to deserve mention here. This is a short piece from a Trinity College (North Carolina) student reported in 1919, with the following first stanza and refrain:

> Train, train, train, train, run so fast,
> Couldn't see nothing but de trees go past.
>
> Don't tell mama where I'm gone,
> Cause I'm on my way back home.[3]

NOTES

1. Quotation and biographical information from Mike Seeger, brochure notes to Folkways FG 3526: *Negro Folk Songs and Tunes*. See also Ed Badeaux, "'Please Don't Tell What Train I'm On,'" *Sing Out!*, 14 (Sept., 1964), 6–11; and Stephen March, "Elizabeth Cotten, Gentle Genius of the Guitar," *Southern Voices*, 1 (Aug.-Sept., 1974), 69–72.

2. See "Folk Songs Ring Out in Senate Halls," *Cleveland Press*, May 9, 1974, and Judith Martin, "An American Folklife Center?," *Washington Post*, May 9, 1974.

3. *The Frank C. Brown Collection of North Carolina Folklore*, vol. 3, *Folk Songs*, edited by Henry M. Belden and Arthur Palmer Hudson (Durham, N.C.: Duke University Press, 1952),

p. 539; also in Newman I. White, *American Negro Folk-Songs* (1928; rpt., Hatboro, Pa.: Folklore Associates, 1965), p. 402.

REFERENCES

A. "Freight Train," by Elizabeth Cotten. Vocal and guitar. Recorded in ca. 1958. Released on Folkways FG 3526: *Negro Folk Songs and Tunes*. This recording is transcribed here.

B. "Freight Train," sheet music. Credited to Jack Edwards; arranged by Walter L. Rosemont. Published by Commercial Music, New York. Copyrighted 1957. Based on Elizabeth Cotten's song; new words added.
Silverman (1975) I, 152–53
Sing Out!, 14 (Sept., 1964), 11–13

E. Chet Atkins—RCA Victor LPM/LSP 2783: *Guitar Country*; RCA Victor LPM/LSP 3558: *Best of Chet Atkins*; RCA Victor 47-8345 (45 rpm)
Norman Blake and Red Rector—County 755: *Norman Blake and Red Rector*
Guy Carawan—Folkways FG 3548: *Guy Carawan Sings, Vol. 2*
Elizabeth Cotten—Vanguard VRS 9181/VSD 79181: *The Blues at Newport, 1964, Part 2*
Jimmy Dean—Starday SLP 190: *Country Music Hall of Fame*
Delmar Delaney—Rebel F-304 (45 rpm)
Dick and Deedee—Warner Brothers 1538: *Turn Around*; Warner Brothers 1623: *Songs We've Sung on Shindig*
Rusty Draper—Mercury 12274/16274: *Country Classics*
—Monument 8005/18005: *Rusty Draper's Greatest Hits*
Dave Dudley—Mercury 20927/60927: *Travelin'*

Bill Emerson and Cliff Waldron—Rebel SLP 1485: *New Shades of Grass*
Brownie McGhee and Sonny Terry—Prestige Bluesville BV 1002: *Down Home Blues;* Fantasy 24708: *Back to New Orleans*
Raun MacKinnon—Parkway SP 7024: *American Folk Songs*
Jim and Jesse McReynolds—Capitol ST 770: *Freight Train* (new words)
Johnny Mann—Liberty 3355/7355: *Golden Folk Song Hits*
Peter and Gordon—Capitol T/ST 2220: *I Don't Want to See You Again*
Peter, Paul, and Mary—Warner Brothers 1507: *Peter, Paul & Mary*
Philo Glee and Mandoline Society—Campus Folksong Club (University of Illinois) CFC 101: *Philo Glee and Mandoline Society*
Margie Rayburn—Liberty 54506 (45 rpm)
Bob Regan and Lucille Starr—A & M 4106: *Canadian Sweethearts*
Carl Scott and Ronnie Massey—Outlet 1004: *Mountain Guitars*
Pete Seeger—Capitol W-2172: *Folk Songs by Pete Seeger*
Shady Oak Boys—Cumberland 29517/69517: *Number One Hits*
Bud Shank—Warner Brothers 1819: *Folk 'n Flute*
Sidewalk Singers—Warner Brothers 1532: *Folk Swingin' Harpsichord*
Tut Taylor—World Pacific 1829: *Dobro Country*
Jackie Washington—Vanguard 9110: *Jackie Washington*
Mac Wiseman—Capitol T/ST 1800: *Bluegrass Favorites*

Freight Train Blues

FREIGHT TRAIN BLUES

*Falsetto.

I was born in Dixie in a boomer's shack,
Just a little shanty by the railroad track;
The humming of the drivers was my lullaby,
And a freight train whistle taught me how to cry.
  I got the freight train blues,
  Lordy, Lordy, Lordy, (I) got 'em in the bottom of my ramblin' shoes;
  And when the whistle blows I gotta go,
  Oh Lordy, guess I'm never gonna lose the freight train blues.

My daddy was a foreman and my mama dear
She was the only daughter of an engineer;

Sweetie loved a brakeman, now it ain't no joke,
But it's a shame the way she kept that good man broke.
    Chorus:

I know I'm old enough to quit my runnin' around,
I've tried a hundred times to stop and settle down;
Every time I find a place I want to stay,
I hear a freight train whistle, Lord, I'm on my way.
    Chorus:

Roy Acuff

This snappy song is one of the best-known compositions of country/folk music entrepreneur John Lair. Born in Livingston, Kentucky, in 1894, Lair was involved for nearly four decades with various country music radio shows, including the WLS National Barn Dance from Chicago and the Renfro Valley Barn Dance and the Renfro Valley Gatherin' from Renfro Valley, Kentucky. His enterprises in Renfro Valley included the Pioneer Museum and the newspaper, the *Renfro Valley Bugle*, both devoted to the folk arts and crafts of that region of Kentucky. Lair also has amassed an enormous collection of early American sheet music.

"Freight Train Blues" was probably written in 1934; the first recording was by Red Foley early that year. However, the recordings most responsible for the song's popularity were those by Roy Acuff and his band. The band recorded it at their first recording session in October, 1936, with vocal lead by Acuff's harmonica player, Sam "Dynamite" Hatcher. Often the singer for the group, Hatcher also sang lead on "Wabash Cannon Ball," recorded immediately before "Freight Train Blues." The popularity of the two songs, issued back-to-back on several labels, induced Columbia to have Acuff's band record them again in January, 1947, this time with Roy singing lead on both. The transcription in this book is taken from the 1947 recording.

Hatcher, and Acuff after him, made a small but significant change in the lyrics. In Lair's original text, the second half of stanza 2 was "My Sweetie is a brake-man and that ain't no joke / It's a shame the way she keeps a good man broke." Hatcher and Acuff changed the verb to "sweetie loved," thus losing Lair's pun. In addition, Acuff omitted one stanza in his rendition. These changes enable one to determine which later versions were taken from an Acuff record rather than from the original text. The McGee recording preserves Lair's pun. A version sung for folksong collector Mary C. Parler by Christine Harvey in 1958 was probably learned from the 1947 Acuff version. This field recording suggests that Acuff's recordings will leave their mark on the folk tradition of the Southeast.

The career of Roy Acuff, for many years one of the giants of the country music field, has been traced out by other writers. Born in 1903 in Maynardsville, east Tennessee, Roy Claxton Acuff spent his early years on a farm in the foothills of the Smoky Mountains. His early ambition to become a professional baseball player was on the way to realization when he was invited by the New York Yankees to attend their summer training camp after he was graduated from high school, but a severe case of sunstroke ended his hopes. Instead, Acuff turned to music, practicing on the fiddle, which he had learned from his lawyer/minister father, and working on his singing style, which had early begun to take shape when he sang in church as a youth.

In the early 1930s he launched his long career as a professional musician by playing the fiddle with Doc Hower's medicine show. In 1933 he and his band, the Crazy Tennesseans, began performing on radio. Three years later, now called Roy Acuff and his Smoky Mountain Boys, they made their first recordings for Columbia. Roy's rise to leadership in the country music field was rapid thereafter: in 1938 he joined Nashville's Grand Ole Opry, and in 1943 "Wabash Cannon Ball" became his first million-selling hit. That same year, he and Fred Rose organized Acuff-Rose Publications, the first publishing house devoted exclusively to country music. In 1962 he was elected to the Country Music Hall of Fame. Although he has long since given over the job of fiddling to other, more talented instrumentalists in his band, Acuff can still be heard on new recordings. He continues to appear on Grand Ole Opry, where some may find his toying with a Yo-Yo, or plunking a ukulele, or balancing a fiddle bow on his nose distracting; but his singing is much the same as it was three or four decades ago when it made him famous.[1]

NOTE

1. For more biographical information about Acuff see Bill C. Malone, *Country Music, U.S.A.* (Austin: University of Texas Press, 1968), pp. 201–6; Elizabeth Schlappi, *Roy Acuff and His Smoky Mountain Boys Discography* (Cheswold, Del.: Disc Collector Publications, 1966), a bio-discography: idem, "Roy Acuff," in *Stars of Country Music,* edited by Bill C. Malone and Judith McCulloh (Urbana: University of Illinois Press, 1975), pp. 179–201; idem, *Roy Acuff: The Smoky Mountain Boy* (Gretna, La.: Pelican Publishing, 1978).

REFERENCES

A. "I Got the Freight Train Blues," by Rambling Red Foley. Vocal and guitar. Recorded ca. Mar., 1934 (American Record Corp. master CP 1016), in Chicago. Released on Conqueror 8285, Perfect 12996, Melotone 12994, Romeo 5328, Oriole 8328. First recording of the song.

"Freight Train Blues," by Roy Acuff and his Smoky Mountain Boys. Vocal by Sam "Dynamite" Hatcher. Recorded Oct. 21, 1936 (American Record Corp. master C 1590), in Chicago. Released on Vocalion/Okeh 04466, Columbia 37008, Columbia 20034, Conqueror 9121. First recording of the song by Acuff's band.

"Freight Train Blues," by Roy Acuff and his Smoky Mountain Boys. Vocal by Acuff. Recorded Jan., 1947 (Columbia master HCO 2204), in Hollywood, Calif. This replaced master C 1590 (see above) on Columbia 37008, Columbia 20034; it was also released on Columbia 37598 (in set C-143), Columbia 20197 (in set H-3), Columbia 52023, Columbia 4-20197 (in set H 4-3, 45 rpm), Columbia 6-1231 (in set 4-3, 45 rpm), Columbia 4-52023 (45 rpm); Columbia HL 9004: *Songs of the Smoky Mountains*; Harmony HL 7082: *Great Speckle Bird and Other Favorites*; Columbia CS 1034: *Roy Acuff's Greatest Hits*. This version is transcribed here.

B. Horstman, 317–18
Lair, 13

D. Pete Cassell—Decca 5954
Red Foley—Conqueror 8285, Perfect 12996, Melotone 12994, Romeo 5328   "I Got the Freight Train Blues"
Sheriff Tom Owen and his Cowboys—Mercury 6006

E. Roy Acuff—Hickory 1291; Hickory LPM 125: *Great Train Songs*
Darroll Adam—Commode (West Germany) 2000: *Live!*
—Village Thing VTS 17: *Feelin' Fine*
Hylo Brown—Rural Rhythm RRHB 200
Anita Carter—RCA Victor 48-0426
Jimmy Dean—Mercury 20786; Mercury 12292/16292: *Television Favorites*
—Starday SLP 190: *Country Music Hall of Fame, Vol.2*; Starday SLP 325: *Bummin' Around*

Tennessee Ernie Ford—Capitol T/ST 1227: *Gather'Round*.

McGee Brothers—Starday SLP 182: *Opry Old Timers*

Benny Martin—CMH 1776: *200 Years of American Heritage in Song*

Happy and Artie Traum—Rounder 3007: *Hard Times in the Country*

Joe Val and the New England Bluegrass Boys—Rounder 0025: *Joe Val and the New England Bluegrass Boys*

Frank Warner—Minstrel JD 204: *Come All You Good People*

Chubby Wise—Stoneway STY 160: *The Million Dollar Fiddle*

F. LC AFS:

Christine Harvey—AFS 11894 A46

Roy Acuff. Courtesy of the Country Music Foundation Library and Media Center, Nashville, Tennessee.

John Lair. Courtesy of John Lair.

Railroading on the Great Divide

Nineteen and sixteen I started to roam,
Out in the West, no money, no home;
I went drifting along with the tide,
I landed on the Great Divide.

Railroading on the Great Divide,
Nothing around me but Rockies and sky;
There you'll find me as years go by,
Railroading on the Great Divide.

Ask any old-timer from Old Cheyenne,
Railroad in Wyoming, the best in the land;
The long steel rails, the short crossties,
I laid across the Great Divide.

As I looked out across the breeze,
Number Three coming, the fastest on wheels;
Through old Laramie she glides with pride,
And rolls across the Great Divide.

Chorus:

A. P. Carter Family

This song, composed by Sara Carter, is probably the youngest piece in the entire book. In reply to my query concerning how she came to write the song, Sara Carter Bayes wrote: ". . . as to the song, 'Railroading On the Great Divide'—I read a book or a story about this guy in 1916, that he left his home back east somewhere and decided to just drift along, and he finally landed on the Great Divide and started working on the railroad. So as we were driving back through Wyoming, I thought about this guy, so I just wrote those few verses down, and later thought up the melody to it, and put it on record for Acme."[1]

The "original" Carter Family, consisting of A. P. Carter, his wife, Sara, and Sara's cousin, Maybelle, disbanded in 1943. Domestic difficulties had eventually led to A. P. and Sara's divorce. In 1939 Sara married Coy Bayes, a cousin of A. P., and the couple moved to California. She periodically traveled east for the next few years so that the group could continue to record and perform on radio.[2]

In 1952, A. P. Carter, Sara Carter Bayes, and their two children, Joe and Janette, began a series of recording sessions for Clifford Spurlock's Acme label. At the second of these, held in the studios of station WOPI in Bristol, Tennessee, on March 7, 1952, they recorded "Railroading on the Great Divide." The text transcribed here is from that recording, except for one word. Sara had thought that the name of the town (Laramie) was Lamar; I have taken the liberty of correcting the error in the transcription. Possibly Sara had Lamar, Colorado, in mind.

The railroad through Laramie is, of course, the Union Pacific, though it was completed many years before the date mentioned in the song.

NOTES

1. Sara Carter Bayes to Cohen, Dec. 16, 1974 (punctuation added).
2. See the discussion of "The Wreck on the C & O" (chap. 5), "Jim Blake's Message" (chap. 7), and "Cannonball Blues"/"Whitehouse Blues" (chap. 9), for further biographical information.

REFERENCES

A. "Railroading on the Great Divide," by the A. P. Carter Family. A.P., vocal; Sara Carter Bayes, vocal and autoharp; Janette Carter, guitar and vocal; Joe Carter, vocal and guitar. Recorded in Bristol, Tenn., Mar. 7, 1952. Released on Acme 992 (45 rpm); Acme DF-102; Pine Mountain PMR-206: *A. P. Carter's Clinch Mountain Ballads*.

B. *Buck's Rock*
Sing Out!, 24 (July-Aug., 1975), 10

E. Bill Clifton—Folk Variety (West Germany) FV 12003: *Folk and Bluegrass at Neusuedende*, 1971/2, Part 2
—Starday 529 (45 rpm)
New Lost City Ramblers—Folkways FTS 31041: *On the Great Divide*

11

Working on the Railroad

IN EVERY YEAR but one between 1820 and 1956, immigration to the United States from Ireland (i.e., Eire and Northern Ireland) exceeded that from the rest of Great Britain, or from any other country. In fact, during much of that period immigration from Ireland comprised 30 percent or more of the total influx to the United States. Between 1834 and 1846, Irish immigration generally varied between twenty and fifty thousand annually, but in 1846, Ireland suffered a disastrous famine. In an unlearnt lesson in ecological history that man has been doomed to repeat many times, the folly of relying on a single crop laid the country open to the devastation of a widespread potato crop failure, and more than one million deaths were recorded in the next five years. Immigration to the United States tripled; between 1847 and 1854 nearly 1.2 million Irish came to these shores. In large numbers they settled in New York, Pennsylvania, New Jersey, Ohio, Missouri, and Wisconsin.

As new immigrants mostly from lower socioeconomic backgrounds, of necessity they gravitated to jobs of an unskilled or semiskilled nature; in 1870 fully 40 percent of the Irish working force in America were unskilled laborers or domestic servants. They became road workers, steamboat stevedores, lumberjacks, canallers, whalers, and miners. They constituted 25 percent of all railroad employees (excluding clerks) in 1870. In each of these areas they left a deep mark on the musical folklore of the day. The Irish populations in the big northern cities swelled, and so did their influence on American popular culture—particularly its musical aspects. In vaudeville of the 1870s and 1880s, Irish acts predominated, followed by blackface and then Dutch and German. American Irish ballads began to take over Tin Pan Alley, from "I'll Take You Home Again, Kathleen" (1876) to "Give an Honest Irish Lad a Chance" (1880) to "When Irish Eyes Are Smiling" (1912).

A popular vaudeville song of the seventies and eighties was "The Roving Irish Gents," sung regularly by one of the early Irish teams, Needham and Kelly. It captured effectively the sentiments of the day:

> Oh we are two rollicking roving Irish gentlemen,
> In the Pennsylvania quarries we belong.

530

> For a month or so we're working out in Idaho,
> For a month or so we're strikin' rather strong.
> Oh, we helped to build the elevated railway,
> On the steamboats we ran for many a day.
> And it's divvil a hair we care the kind of work we do,
> If every Saturday night we get our pay. [1]

With the sons of Erin numbering so strong on the construction gangs and in the railroad roundhouses in the nineteenth century, it is not surprising that nearly half of this chapter's sampling of songs and ballads dealing with the occupation of railroading are pieces of Irish-American origin. The four pieces in question, "Paddy Works on the Railway," "Drill, Ye Tarriers, Drill," "Jerry, Go Ile That Car," and "Way Out in Idaho," date from the 1850s or so to the 1880s. "Paddy Works on the Railway" is not associated with any specific historical setting; in fact, it is not certain whether it originated among Irish laborers or among Irish professional entertainers. "Drill, Ye Tarriers, Drill," though copyrighted in 1888, may very well be a survival of one of the most exciting chapters in railroad history in this country: the race between the Union Pacific and Central Pacific in the late 1860s to complete the first transcontinental railroad. The two railroads were working to a common meeting point, but because the government was offering great financial rewards for each mile of track completed, the companies were in bitter competition, the CP to push as far west as possible, the UP as far east as possible. The Central Pacific hired great numbers of Chinese laborers, while the Union Pacific relied on Irish help. The UP's track-laying crews were under the direction of engineer and Civil War hero Major General Grenville M. Dodge, who treated the workers like soldiers and extracted from them marvelously efficient performance. Many were in fact, former Union or Confederate soldiers—large numbers of Irish among them. "Way Out in Idaho" dates from over a decade later, with the construction of one of the UP's many smaller lines. "Jerry, Go Ile That Car" is also from about 1880, but originated further south, with the construction of the Atlantic and Pacific Railroad (later a part of the Santa Fe). A vivid picture of the track-laying operation was quoted by William A. Bell, an English traveler in the United States in 1869:

> One can see all along the line of the now-completed road the evidence of ingenious self-protection and defence which our men learned during the war. The same curious huts and underground dwellings, which were a common sight along our army lines then, may now be seen burrowed into the sides of the hills or built up with ready adaptability in sheltered spots. The whole organisation of the force engaged in the construction of the road is, in fact, semi-military. The men who go ahead, locating the road, are the advanced guard. Following these is the second line, cutting through the gorges, grading the road and building bridges. Then comes the main line of the army, placing the sleepers, laying the track, spiking down the rails, perfecting the alignment, ballasting the rail, and dressing up and completing the road for immediate use. This army of workers has its base, to continue the figure, at Omaha, Chicago, and still further eastward, from whose markets are collected the material for constructing the road. Along the line of the completed road are construction trains constantly pushing forward "to the front" with supplies. The company's grounds and workshops at Omaha are the arsenal, where these purchases, amounting now to millions of dollars in value, are collected and held ready to be sent forward. The advanced limit of the rail is occupied by a train of long box cars, with hammocks swung under them, beds spread on top of them, bunks built within them, in which the sturdy, broad-shouldered pioneers of the great iron highway sleep at night,

Chinese camp (*above*) and Chinese construction gang (*below*) on the Central Pacific Railroad, in 1868. Both photos from the collection of the Nevada Historical Society.

Construction train (*above*) and the end of the rail in Nevada (*below*), in 1868. Both photos from the collection of the Nevada Historical Society.

and take their meals. Close behind this train come loads of ties and rails and spikes, &c., which are being thundered off upon the roadside to be ready for the track-layers. The road is graded a hundred miles in advance. The ties are laid roughly in place, then adjusted, gauged, and levelled. Then the track is laid.

Track-laying on the Union Pacific is a science, and we, pundits of the far East, stood upon that embankment, only about a thousand miles this side of sunset, and backed westward before that hurrying corps of sturdy operatives with a mingled feeling of amusement, curiosity, and profound respect. On they came. A light car, drawn by a single horse, gallops up to the front with its load of rails. Two men seize the end of a rail and start forward, the rest of the gang taking hold by twos, until it is clear of the car. They come forward at a run. At the word of command the rail is dropped in its place, right side up, with care, while the same process goes on at the other side of the car. Less than thirty seconds to a rail for each gang, and so four rails go down to the minute! Quick work, you say, but the fellows on the U.P. are tremendously in earnest. The moment the car is empty it is tipped over on the side of the track to let the next loaded car pass it, and then it is tipped back again, and it is a sight to see it go flying back for another load, propelled by a horse at full gallop at the end of sixty or eighty feet of rope, ridden by a young Jehu, who drives furiously. Close behind the first gang come the gaugers, spikers, and bolters, and a lively time they make of it. It is a grand Anvil Chorus that those sturdy sledges are playing across the plains. It is in triple time, three strokes to a spike. There are ten spikes to a rail, four hundred rails to a mile, eighteen hundred miles to San Francisco. That's the sum, what is the quotient? Twenty-one million times are those sledges to be swung—twenty-one million times are they to come down with their sharp punctuation, before the great work of modern America is completed![2]

The four songs mentioned above are but a small sampling of the Irish contribution to our musical railroad lore. Archie Green, for instance, included two other Irish-American compositions on *Railroad Songs and Ballads*, an LP edited from recordings in the Library of Congress Archive of Folk Song, "The Boss of the Section Gang" is a rarely found piece, published in 1893 but probably older than that date suggests—perhaps, like "Drill, Ye Tarriers, Drill," a song originating among Irish laborers that was later taken to the stage by Irish entertainers. "O'Shaughnessy" has been recovered more frequently; according to a 1943 *Railroad Magazine* correspondent, it was written by Tommy Miller in about 1880 and stems from work on the Saint Paul, Minneapolis, and Manitoba Railroad in the Dakota Territory. Several years ago, while casually discussing the subject of this book with some family friends, I was pleased when one of them sang for me a few lines of this latter song, sometimes also titled "I'm a Jolly Irishman Winding on the Train." My friend had moved to California in the second decade of the century, when the state was, relatively speaking, still young. The verse he contributed was all he remembered hearing sung, in about 1919–20, by a gang of contruction workers in California's Imperial Valley. Their performance had made quite an impression on him:

> They made what they call the flying switch,
> The train ran off right into the ditch;
> They call me an Irish son-of-a-bitch,
> A-winding on the train.[3]

My emphasis on the Irish contribution to occupational song should not obscure the fact that other groups did their share as well. Black American laborers, with their rich

Afro-American musical heritage, fashioned a stunning repertoire of worksongs from their New World experiences as sailors and whalers, stevedores and roustabouts, levee workers and road builders. Whether voluntarily or involuntarily, black Americans provided much-needed muscle power from the very first decades of construction on, and many of our railroads were built to the accompaniment of their track-lining and tie-tamping songs.[4] An early minstrel song dealing with railroad work comments—not very flatteringly—on their role:

> I come from Alabama,
> The other arternoon,
> I fotch'd along the banjo—
> To play the folks a tune.
>   Working on the railroad,
>   For two shillings a day,
>   Johnny keep a-picking on the banjo.
>
> The Alabama niggers
> They think they are mighty smart,
> They'd rather work a railroad,
> Than drive a hoss and cart.[5]

An even earlier fragment suggests that the treatment of baggage by black railroad porters was viewed with some suspicion:

> We're jolly rail-road porters,
> And we push for jobs with spunk,
> Bekase we fill our vittal chests
> By gettin' people's trunks.[6]

"Nine Pound Hammer" is almost surely of black origin, although it has become so widespread since its genesis, probably in the 1870s, that now it is as familiar to white folksingers as to black. It differs from the other songs in this chapter in that it is an actual "worksong"—one that is sung to accompany the act of physical labor—whereas the others are "occupational songs"—pieces that describe aspects of that labor. "Spike Driver Blues," a lyrical variant of "Nine Pound Hammer," is more an entertainment piece than an actual worksong, although their close kinship is unmistakable.

One song in this chapter, "I've Been Working on the Railroad," like the five previously mentioned, pertains to railroad construction work of one sort or another; but whether the song was actually sung by railroaders is not known. Just as likely, it began as a popular song, possibly passing briefly through the hands of railroaders before coming to rest in the present century as a favorite camp song of young city folk.

"The Night Express" brushes aside the question of the ethnic origin of the railroader and evokes his role as a family man in a vignette equally appropriate to black or white, Irish immigrant or established American.

The title "Little Red Caboose behind the Train" is doubtless as familiar as any other in this book; however, it refers to a large number of related and distinct songs, several of which are discussed either in this chapter or elsewhere in the book.

The chapter concludes with an item unusual in the annals of recorded hillbilly songs: a ballad dealing with a labor dispute on the Virginian Railway in 1923.

NOTES

1. Quoted in Douglas Gilbert, *American Vaudeville* (1940; rpt., New York: Dover Publications, 1963), p. 62.

2. William A. Bell, "The Pacific Railroads," *Fortnightly Review* (London), 11 (May, 1869), 562–78.

3. Sung to me in ca. 1975 by Bernard Glickman of Los Angeles. His tune resembled that of "Paddy Works on the Railway." A fuller version, collected by David McIntosh, appears in his "Some Representative Southern Illinois Folk-Songs" (Master's thesis, State University of Iowa, 1935), p. 53. See also MacEdward Leach, *Folk Ballads and Songs of the Lower Labrador Coast* (Ottawa: National Museum of Canada, 1965), pp. 250-51.

4. For a small sampling of such pieces, see John A. Lomax and Alan Lomax, *American Ballads and Folk Songs* (New York: Macmillan, 1934). pp. 10–20.

5. "Working on the Railroad," *Bryant's Essence of Old Virginny* (New York, 1857), p. 32; composed by William B. Donaldson, sung by Bryant's Minstrels.

6. "There'll Be a Stormy Morning," *Book of 1001 Popular Songs, or Songs for the Million* (New York: William H. Murphy, ca. 1845–46), pt. 3, p. 162.

I've Been Working on the Railroad

WORKING ON THE RAILROAD

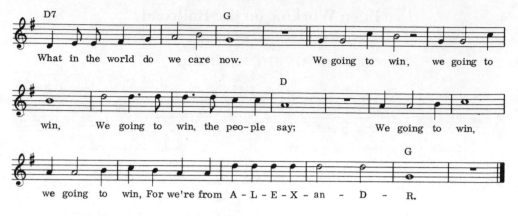

What in the world do we care now. We going to win, we going to win, We going to win, the peo-ple say; We going to win, we going to win, For we're from A - L - E - X - an - D - R.

I been working on the railroad,
I been working night and day;
I been working on the railroad,
Just to pass the time away;
Don't you hear the captain shouting,
Won't you rise up so early in the morn;
Don't you hear the captain shouting,
Dinah, blow your horn.

We are the stuff, (sure!) we are the stuff,
We are the stuff, the people say; (So they say!)
We are the stuff, (now) we are the stuff,
We're from A-L-E-X-an-D-R.

Hail, hail, the boys all here,
What in the world do we care, what in the world do we care;
Hail, hail, the boys all here,
What in the world do we care now.

We going to win, (yeah!) we going to win,
We going to win, the people say;
We going to win, we going to win,
For we're from A-L-E-X-an-D-R.

Hail, hail, the boys all here,
What in the world do we care, what in the world do we care;
Hail, hail, the boys all here,
What in the world do we care now.

Blankenship Family

In his compendium of American popular songs, Theodore Raph gives 1881 as the year "I've Been Working on the Railroad" achieved widespread popularity, having been modified from an older levee song by black railroad workers. He cites 1900 as the date of first publication of "Levee Song," of which "I've Been Working on the Railroad" was originally the second part.[1] The assumption that the railroad song was based on an older worksong from riverboating days is reasonable and attractive. However, there is no evidence for the song's currency prior to its first publication, which occurred not in 1900, but, as Fuld concluded after a thorough search of the evidence, in 1894, when it appeared in the eighth edition of *Carmina Princetonia,* one of many college songbooks published during the latter half of the nineteenth century. The song itself, under the title "Levee Song," was deposited for copyright on the same day as the book, but no copy has been found.[2] Since the song did not appear in the seventh edition (1890), it probably became widely popular in the early 1890s—at least among the college crowd. Of its assumed earlier existence in oral tradition among black laborers we know nothing. If it circulated orally before its appearance in print, then the generally accepted derivation of the railroad song from the levee song may be correct. The problems in tracing the term *levee,* which early in this century had been applied to any construction site, rather than specifically a riverbank, have been noted by Archie Green.[3]

In any case, the song was very popular early in this century. Partial evidence for its success is the parody "The Eyes of Texas," which was written to the tune of "Levee Song" in 1903, according to Fuld.[4] In 1915–16 the opening couplet was collected from black railroad workers at Auburn, Alabama, the earliest evidence for the song's currency in oral tradition. Whether it is still sung by railroad workers I do not know. In recent decades it has enjoyed immense popularity as a camp song, and probably not a child in the United States who has gone to some form of summer camp or day camp has not sung "I've Been Working on the Railroad" at the top of his lungs until his counselor was in near hysterics.

A hint of greater antiquity is suggested by a fragment sent to John A. Lomax by one of his correspondents, Ellwood Adams, probably in the 1920s or earlier. Adams was primarily concerned with a cowboy song:

> I've been out upon the round-up
> All the live-long day;
> I've been out a-punchin' cattle
> Just to pass the time away;
> Don't you hear the cattle lowing,
> We get up so early in the morn;
> Don't you hear the forman calling,
> "Cook-ee do blow your horn."

Adams followed this with "another version that I have heard":

> I've been working on the railroad
> All the live long day;
> I've been out upon the levee
> Just to pass the time away;
> Don't you hear the wistle [*sic*] blowing,
> Wake up so early in the morn;
> Don't you hear the captain calling,
> Dinah! come blow your horn.

Then he wrote: "This is, however, a corrupted version of the above. You, perhaps have heard of the second one or one similar to it or maybe you have heard this original one. If so, please send the rest, if there is any more. This fragment [i.e., the cowboy version] was sent me by a distant relative who is now traveling in the wild country on southern Utah. He said that one day he met an old-time plainesman [*sic*] who was singing this song. The fellow said it was just a few words of an old trail song that they used to sing in the Big Bend country of Texas in the 'cow days.' "[5]

Adams's opinion notwithstanding, it seems unlikely to me that the highly popular railroad song would have been a parody of a practically unknown cowboy song; I suspect the reverse to have been the case. The halcyon days of the long cattle drives were in the last three decades of the nineteenth century, which opens the possibility that both the railroad song and its cowboy parody were known in the Southwest earlier than the 1890s.

Inasmuch as this song was, as Spaeth put it, "probably the most famous standby of barbershop agonizers" next to "Sweet Adeline," one would expect it to have been recorded early in this century.[6] Yet I have found no evidence for a recording prior to 1923, when it was released by the Shannon Quartet on the Victor label. The version transcribed in this book was recorded in 1931 by the Blankenship Family. Issued in the depths of the Depression, their disc found its way into the homes of fewer than a thousand purchasers.

The Blankenship Family, from Alexander County, North Carolina, comprised William Pool Blankenship; his son, William Walter; and his daughters, Daphna and Darius. The foursome began playing together in public in 1921, when the elder Blankenship was fifty-two, and for the next decade they played at parties, dances, courthouse gatherings, and other events throughout Alexander and neighboring North Carolina counties and also in West Virginia coal towns. The family recorded two songs at their 1931 session. Victor had contracted with them for more recordings, but William Pool Blankenship died on November 17, 1931, just two months after their only record was released.[7]

"I've Been Working on the Railroad" is often followed directly by some other ditty—generally "Someone's in the Kitchen with Dinah," doubtless suggested by the last line of the chorus, "Dinah, won't you blow your horn." Fuld has discussed the sources of this song, noting that the words with a different melody from the usual one were published under the title "Old Joe, or Somebody in the House with Dinah," about 1835–48. The usual melody is probably a variation on "Goodnight Ladies."[8] The latter piece itself derives from an 1847 publication, "Farewell Ladies," but the more usual form was first printed in 1867.[9]

The Blankenships follow their "I've been working on the railroad" stanza with several verses of what seems to be a school cheer—probably from the high school of their native Alexander County. Southern Music copyrighted the song concurrent with its Victor release (Sept. 26, 1931, E unp. 47764; renewed Oct. 28, 1958, R 223774), crediting the Blankenship Family (individual members not identified) with authorship.

NOTES

1. Theodore Raph, *The Songs We Sang* (New York: A. S. Barnes, 1964), p. 195.

2. James J. Fuld, *The Book of World-Famous Music*, rev. ed. (New York: Crown Publishers, 1971), p. 309.

3. Archie Green, *Only a Miner* (Urbana: University of Illinois Press, 1972), p. 340.

4. Fuld, *World-Famous Music*, p. 309.

5. Undated letter from Ellwood Adams of St. Louis, Mo., in Lomax Papers.

6. Sigmund Spaeth, *Barber Shop Ballads* (New York: Simon and Schuster, 1925), p. 39.

7. The only available biographical information on the Blankenships appears in Bob Coltman, "We Would Have Made More Records but We Didn't Bother to Go Back: The Story of the Blankenship Family of North Carolina," *Journal of Country Music*, 7 (Dec., 1978), 42, 51–53.

8. Fuld, *World-Famous Music*, pp. 513–14.

9. Ibid. p. 255.

Blankenship Family. Courtesy of Bob Coltman and Fred Stikeleather, Jr.

REFERENCES

A. "Levee Song," in *Carmina Princetonia*,
    (Newark, N.J.: Martin R. Dennis, 1894),
    p. 24. Cited by James J. Fuld, *The Book of
    World-Famous Music*, rev. ed. (New York:
    Crown Publishers, 1971), p. 309.
    "Working on the Railroad," by the
    Blankenship Family. Vocal trio;
    accompaniment by William Pool
    Blankenship, fiddle; William Walter
    Blankenship, guitar; Daphna Blanken-
    ship, banjo-ukulele; Darius Blankenship,
    cello (not audible on record). Recorded
    May 29, 1931 (RCA Victor master 69376),
    in Charlotte, N.C. Released on Victor
    23583 in Sept., 1931.

B. Barnard, 91
    Best & Best, 28–29
    Boni (1947), 148–49
    Brand (1957), 174–77   "Levee Song"
    Brand (1961), 12

Briegel, 24
Brown III, 262; V, 147
Compagno, 45
Cowboy Songs
Dykema, 152
Ernst, 115
Everybody's, 68
Fuld (1955), 30 (discussion only)
Fuld (1971), 309 (discussion only)
Goodwin, 331
Harbin, 94
Henry (1934), 81
Kennedy, C. O. (1952), 55
Kincaid (1937), 33
Lair, 54
Landeck (1950b), 86
Leisy (1959), 32
Leisy (1973), 70
Mursell (Grade 4), 123
Pitts (1950), 35
Pitts (1953), 7–9

Raph, 195
Scarborough, 248
Shay (1927), 79 (39 in 1961 ed.)
Sherwin & McClintock, 7
Smith, G. H. 45
Spaeth (1925), 39
White, N. I., 274
Wier (1941), 242

C. LOMAX PAPERS:

E. Adams, St. Louis, Mo. (one stanza and a
parody beginning "I've been out upon the
round-up")

D. Jubileers—General 1803 (in album G-32)
Melody Boys—Montgomery Ward 7690
Missouri Pacific Diamond Jubilee
Quartet—OKeh 40868
Art Mooney and his Orchestra—Vogue
R713/R711; MGM 10298
Frank Novak and his Rootin' Tootin'
Boys—Conqueror 8834, Conqueror
9707, Perfect 20731, Vocalion 04744
Sandhill's Sixteen—Victor 20905
Terry Shand Orchestra—Decca 3714
Shannon Quartet—Victor 19059
"Levee Song—I've Been Working on
the Railroad"

E. Alley Singers—RCA Victor LPM-1629
Leon Berry—Audio Fidelity 1905/5905:
Giant Wurlitzer Pipe Organ

Maybelle Carter—Smash 27025/67025:
*Mother Maybelle Carter and Her
Autoharp;* Hilltop JS 6172: *Mother
Maybelle Carter*
Bob Chapman—Scholastic CC 0630 (7" 45
rpm EP): *Train Ballads*
Chorus—Golden GLP A19817
David Clayton-Thomas—RCA Victor
APL1–0173: *David Clayton-Thomas*
George Cook—Decca 28223 (45 rpm)
Dick Curless—Towar T/DT 5015: *Travelin'
Man*
Happy Harts—Kapp 1468/3468: *Banjos,
Banjos, Banjos*
Arthur Lyman—Hi Fi 5078 (45 rpm)
Merrill Jay Singers—Cabot CAB-503: *Songs
of the Railroad*
Rooftop Singers—Vanguard 9134/79134:
Good Time
Pete Seeger—Columbia CL 1947/CS 8747
and Harmony H 30399: *Children's
Concert at Town Hall;* Olympic 7102:
America's Balladeer
Yankovic, Frankie—Columbia CL 1738/
CS 8538: *America's Polka King*

F. LC AFS:

Lewis Coleman—AFS 1336 B3   "I've
Been Working on the Levee"
Laura Hatchmer and group—AFS 3108 A2
"Working on the Railroad"

Jerry, Go Ile That Car

JERRY, GO ILE THAT CAR

Come all ye railroad section men and listen to my song,
It is of Larry O'Sullivan, who now is dead and gone;
For twenty years a section boss, he never hired a tar,
And it's "j'int ahead and center [*pronounced "cinter"*] back, and Jerry, go
and 'il that car."

For twenty years a section boss he worked upon the track,
And be it to his credit he never had a wreck;
For he kept every j'int right up to the p'int with a tap of the tamp and bar,
And while the boys [*pronounced "buys"*] were shimmin' up the ties, it's
"Jerry, would you 'il that car."

And every Sunday morning unto the gang he'd say,
"Me boys, prepare ye be aware, the old lady goes to church today;
Now, I want every man to pump the best he can, for the distance it is far,
And we have to get in ahead of Number Ten; so Jerry, go and 'il that car."

'Twas in November in the wintertime and the ground all covered with snow,
"Come put the handcar on the track and over the section go."
With his big soldier coat buttoned up to his throat, all weathers he would
dare,
And it's "Paddy Mack, will you walk the track, and Jerry, go and 'il the car."

God rest ye, Larry O'Sullivan, to me you were kind and good,
Ye always made the section men go out and chop me wood;
And fetch me water from the well and chop me kindlin' fine,
And any man that wouldn't lend a hand, 'twas "Larry, give him his time."

"Give my respects to the road-master," poor Larry he did cry,
"And leave [*pronounced "lave"*] me up that I may see the old handcar
before I die.
Then lay the spike maul on me chest, the gauge and the old plow-bar,
And while the boys will be fillin' up the grave, oh Jerry, would you 'il
that car."

Harry "Haywire Mac" McClintock

One of California's most amazing men of letters was Charles F. Lummis (1859–1928).[1] His long list of posts and achievements included city editor of the *Los Angeles Times* (1885–87), director of the Los Angeles Public Library (1905–10), editor of *Land of Sunshine* and *Out West* magazine (1894–1909), founder of the Southwest Museum, and author of a score of books on the history of California, the Southwest, Mexico, and Peru. In addition, Lummis was a pioneer folklorist of note: as early as 1892 he published an article on New Mexico folksongs in *Cosmopolitan* magazine. In 1884, Lummis walked some thirty-five hundred miles across the continent from Cincinnati to Los Angeles, recounting his experiences in a series of letters to the *Los Angeles Times*. During that journey he first heard a fragment of "Jerry, Go an' Ile That Car," and he expended considerable effort in later years to determine the complete song and the identity of the author. In about 1904, with the help of Arthur G. Wells, general manager of the Santa Fe lines from New Mexico westward, he concluded the following:

> "Jerry" was written, I am reasonably sure, in the year 1881, and was a product of the Santa Fe route. I know that it was written by a roving Connaught man who has no other name of record than "Riley the Bum." He was a happy-go-lucky, hard-working, quick-fighting section laborer; but he was also a minstrel. Both as music and as literature the song he composed stands easily first of the "come all ye's" that have ever been made as railroad songs. It is the mother tincture of the track as it existed twenty years ago and can, by no human possibility, exist again. . . .[2]

To this account Wells appended the first printed text of "Jerry, Go Ile That Car." We do not reprint it here, as it has appeared in numerous books and articles since it first was published in 1904. In 1908 the *Santa Fe Employes' Magazine* reprinted the Lummis article. In 1910, John A. Lomax included the identical text (without attribution) in his book *Cowboy Songs*. In 1927, Sandburg used Lummis's text and tune in his influential folksong collection, *The American Songbag*. Alan Lomax borrowed text and tune for his *Folksongs of North America*, giving credit to Sandburg. Botkin and Harlow credited Sandburg for the tune they used in 1953.

The reprint of Lummis's article in the *Santa Fe Employes' Magazine* brought a response from R. W. Duncan, a foreman on the Santa Fe at Yampai, Arizona.[3] He wrote that he had learned the song in 1884, and supplied a text considerably different from the one given by Lummis. Not long afterward, Duncan sent in "The Scenic Line," written by Riley the Bum, also about an Irish immigrant who labored on the Santa Fe. This poem, published in the *Santa Fe Employes' Magazine* in 1909, began:

> My name is Teddy Ragan, I was bred on Irish soil,
> And from force of circumstances had to join the ranks of toil
> I sailed from Cork and reached New York, the finest place I'd seen
> Since I left my home far, far to roam, away in Skibbereen.[4]

Duncan's text of "Jerry, Go Ile That Car" was reprinted in *Railroad Man's Magazine* in October, 1908.

From its point of origin in the Southwest, "Jerry, Go Ile That Car" rapidly spread eastward and northward. Edith Fowke collected an unusually long version from a Captain Cates, whose father had learned the song while crossing the plains of western Canada in the 1880s. A correspondent sent Robert W. Gordon a text that he learned from someone who in turn had gotten the song from a Winnipeg hotel clerk in 1882. A section hand on the Canadian Pacific Railway was familiar with it in the mid-1880s.[5] Henry M. Belden obtained an imperfect version in Carroll County, Missouri, in 1914. Louise Pound cited a version obtained in Nebraska prior to 1915. The extent of variation exhibited over this thirty-year period was considerable. Compare, for example, the three first stanzas of the Lummis, Duncan, and Dean version—all very traditional ballad openings, yet all distinct:

(Lummis)   Come all ye railroad sectionmen an' listen to my song;
It is of Larry O'Sullivan, who now is dead and gone.
For twinty years a section boss, he niver hired a tar—
Oh, it's "j'int ahead and cinter back, an' Jerry, go an' ile that
car-r-r.

(Duncan)   My name 'tis O'Larry Sullivan, a native of the auld grane sod,
For twenty-foive long weary years I've worked upon the road;
I always made it a pint to keep up the jint be the force of the
tampin' bar-r,
And whin I am dead, O let it be said that I niver hired a tar-r-r.

(Dean)   Come, all you railroad section hands, I hope you will draw near,
And likewise pay attention to these few lines you'll hear;
Concerning one Larry Sullivan, alas, he is no more,
He sailed some forty years ago from the green old Irish shore.[6]

Until recently, "Jerry Go Ile That Car" had been recorded only once commercially. Possibly the extensive use of railroad lingo not familiar to the general public made recording company executives doubt the song's salability. That one early recording was made for Victor by Harry "Haywire Mac" McClintock in Oakland, California, in March, 1928. Mac had lived an astonishingly varied career by the time he died in 1957 at the age of seventy-four.[7] A perennial drifter, he ran away from home in his early teens and wandered all over the world. He was a railroad switchman in Africa, a civilian muleskinner in the Philippines during the Spanish-American War; a newspaper aide during the Boxer Rebellion in China; and a bum in London at the time of Edward VII's coronation. In the United States he railroaded, hoboed, herded sheep in Nevada, punched cattle in Montana. He is often credited with writing two of this country's best-loved bum songs, "Hallelujah, I'm a Bum" and "Big Rock Candy Mountain." He had a radio program in San Francisco as early as 1925, and later he had one in Los Angeles. In 1938 he began writing for *Railroad Magazine;* thirty-six of his manuscripts were published in the next twenty years. Between 1928 and 1931 he recorded twenty-seven songs and ballads for Victor, including about ten cowboy and western songs and four hobo songs. In addition to "Jerry, Go Ile That Car," his recording of "Jesse James" is transcribed in this book (chap. 4).

NOTES

1. For biographical information on Lummis, see Dudley C. Gordon, *El Alisal: The Lummis Home, Its History and Architecture* (Los Angeles: Cultural Assets Press, 1968); idem, "Charles F. Lummis: Pioneer American Folklorist," *WF*, 28 (July, 1969), 175; and Frances E. Watkins, " 'He Said It with Music'—Spanish-Californian Folk Songs Recorded by Charles F. Lummis," *CFQ*, 1 (Oct., 1942), 359–67.

2. C. F. Lummis, "An Old Song of the Rail," *Out West*, 20 (Feb., 1904), 178; reprinted in *Santa Fe Employes' Magazine*, 2 (May, 1908), 375–76.

3. "Another Version of an Old Song," letter and text by R. W. Duncan, *Santa Fe Employes' Magazine*, 2 (July, 1908), 601; reprinted in *RRManM*, 7 (Oct., 1908), 188–89.

4. *RRManM*, 3 (Mar., 1909), 375.

5. "Section Life in the West," *Cornhill Magazine* (London), Jan., 1888; reprinted in Richard Reinhardt, *Workin' on the Railroad: Reminiscences from the Age of Steam* (Palo Alto, Calif.: American West Publishing, 1970), pp. 210–17.

6. M. C. Dean, *Flying Cloud* (Virginia, Minn.: Quickprint, [1922?]) p. 26.

7. For biographical information on McClintock, see obituaries in *RRM*, 62 (Oct., 1957), 57, and *San Francisco Chronicle*, Apr. 25, 1957; also letter written by Mac to Joe Nicholas in *Disc Collector*, No. 12 (1957), pp. 1–2, and No. 13 (1959), pp. 11–13. See also Sam Eskin, brochure notes to Folkways FD 5272: *Harry K. McClintock: "Haywire Mac."*

REFERENCES

A. "Jerry, Go Ile That Car," by Harry "Mac" McClintock. Vocal and guitar. Recorded Mar. 16, 1928 (Victor master BVE-42096), in Oakland, Calif. Released on Victor 21521 in Sept., 1928. Reissued on RCA Victor LPV 532: *The Railroad in Folksong*. First recording of the song; transcribed here.

"Jerry, Go an' Ile That Car," in C. F. Lummis, "An Old Song of the Rail," *Out West*, 20 (Feb., 1904), 178. First printing of the complete song. See the discussion for references to numerous reprintings.

B. Barnes, 24 (from Sandburg)
Belden (1955), 445
Botkin & Harlow, 441 (text from *RRManM*, 1931; tune from Sandburg)
Dean, M. C., 26
Family Herald, 44 (reference only)
Fowke, 254
Fowke & Glazer, 88
Green (1968), 7 (discussion only)
Harrison, 183 (title only)
Laws, 244 (H 30) (discussion)

Lomax, A. (1960), 415 (from Sandburg)
Lomax, J. (1910, 1916, 1922), 112 (from Lummis)
Pound (1915), 59
RRManM, 7 (1908), 188–89
RRManM, 4 (Feb., 1931), 478–79
Sandburg, 360 (from Lummis)
Warman, 19 (1 stanza) "Jerry Ile the Kayre"

C. GORDON MSS:
457—R. M. MacLeod (1924, Winnipeg)

D. Shaun O'Nolan—Columbia 33476-F

E. Warde Ford—Library of Congress Archive of Folk Song L61: *Railroad Songs and Ballads*
Harry "Mac" McClintock—Folkways FC 7027 (FP 27) (10″ LP): *This Land Is My Land (American Work Songs to Grow On, Vol. 3)*
Carl Sandburg—Caedmon TC 2025: *Carl Sandburg Sings His American Songbag*

Paddy Works on the Railway

A-WORKING ON THE RAILROAD

Original Key: C**

*Chords supplied by the music editor; the original is unaccompanied.
**The singer on the recording, influenced by the natural tendency to sing progressively higher on an unaccompanied song, starts in the key of B-flat and ends on C.

Eighteen hundred and forty-one,
That's the year my troubles begun,
That's the year my troubles begun,
A-workin' on the railroad.
  Ay-re-ay-re-i-re-o,
  Ay-re-ay-re-i-re-o,
  Ay-re-ay-re-i-re-o,
  A-workin' on the railroad.

Eighteen hundred and forty-two,
That's the year I lost my shoe,
That's the year I lost my shoe,
A-workin' on the railroad.
  Chorus:

Eighteen hundred and forty-three,
That's the year I crossed the sea,
That's the year I crossed the sea
To work upon the railroad.
  Chorus:

Eighteen hundred and forty-four,
That's the year I reached the shore,

That's the year I reached the shore
To work upon the railroad.
    Chorus:

Eighteen hundred and forty-five,
I'd rather be dead than be alive,
I'd rather be dead than be alive
And work upon the railroad.
    Chorus:

Eighteen hundred and forty-six,
Picked up my shovel and picked up my picks,
Picked up my shovel and picked up my picks
To work upon the railroad.
    Chorus:

Eighteen hundred and forty-seven,
That's the year I went to heaven,
That's the year I went to heaven
To work upon the railroad.
    Chorus:

Eighteen hundred and forty-eight,
Saint Peter said I was too late,
Saint Peter said I was too late
To work upon the railroad.
    Chorus:

Eighteen hundred and forty-nine,
The devil said that I was just in time,
The devil said that I was just in time
To work upon the railroad.
    Chorus:

Ernest Bourne

The introduction to this chapter explored briefly the role of immigrant Irish comedians and singers in the development of the musical stage in the late nineteenth century; at the same time Irish tarriers, roustabouts, shantymen, jerries, and shantyboys were building the industrial underpinnings of America. An early song about the poor Irishman in the New World was "Paddy Works on the Railway," or "Poor Paddy." It seems strange now that such a song is best known as a chantey—and can be found in most collections of sailors' songs. Probably "Paddy" had followed the route of many other songs before and after it: starting life as a landlubbers' song and later shanghaied into service at sea. This is the opinion of many writers who have discussed its history, including Stan Hugill and C. Fox Smith. Some, in fact, have refused to include it among their chantey collections on the grounds that it is a Christy's Minstrels song. Richard Runciman Terry, however, was of the firm opinion that "Paddy" was based on an older capstan chantey, "The Shaver," that then became landlocked. I prefer to assume that the song originated on terra firma; but the question then arises, was it originally an occupational song of the Irish section hands, or was it first a music-hall song?

Carl Sandburg asserted the existence of sheet music for the song in the 1850s, but I have seen no precise citations. In general, opinion favors music-hall origin, although there is no firm evidence for that, either. The antiquity of the song is also unresolved, but we can date it as far back as 1864: C. Fox Smith reported a description of the song (but not a text) in a manuscript magazine of the *Young Australia*, a Black Ball clipper from London to Moreton Bay in that year: "We might mention as peculiar amongst the other strange songs which we hear, one which we think must be called 'Pat's Apprenticeship,' as it goes through the history of a number of years during which 'poor Paddy works on the railway.'"[1] This description fits the most common form of the song. Most versions begin the enumeration of years with 1841; a few start with 1861. It seems reasonable, therefore, that the song was composed in the 1850s, and possibly rewritten a decade or two later. This would make it the oldest song in this chapter—if not in the entire book.

There are two principal tunes for "Paddy Works on the Railway." The one that appears in most of the chantey collections, and that seems to be the older, is in the major (Ionian) mode with the last note of the first three lines being the dominant of the scale (the mid-cadence is the dominant below the tonic). This version has a chorus or refrain following each stanza, sung to a tune distinct from the stanzaic air, and worded generally something like:

> To work upon the railway, the railway,
> I'm weary of the railway,
> Oh, poor Paddy works on the railway.

The second form of the song owes it popularity largely to its preservation (or creation) by John and Alan Lomax in *American Ballads and Folk Songs*.[2] Set in a minor mode, the lines end on the third, seventh, third, and tonic. The chorus ("Fil-i-me-oo-re-i-re-ay") is sung to the same melody as the stanzas. Altogether, the tune is very close to that of "When Johnny Comes Marching Home" (also "Johnny, Fill Up the Bowl" and "Johnny, I Hardly Knew You"), published in 1863.[3] The Lomaxes gave the source of their version, titled "Paddy Works on the Erie," as an "old newspaper clipping"; but this does not explain the origin of their melody. A tune similar to theirs, but in the major mode, appears in *Popular College Songs*, compiled by Lockwood Honore in 1891. This text also has the "Fil-i-me-oo-re-i-re-ay" chorus, although here it is "For-o-my-or-o-my-or-o-my-ay." The Lomaxes used the same text/tune in a later volume (1947), and their version was reprinted by Botkin and Harlow, giving it still wider circulation. Unlike the 1891 text, the Lomax text includes several stanzas not in the "in eighteen hundred and forty-one" format, which are strikingly similar to a broadside, probably from the 1860s, entitled "Mick upon the Railroad."[4] For example:

PADDY (Lomax)	MICK
When we left Ireland to come here,	When furst from Limerick I come here,
And spend our latter days in cheer,	My latther days to spend and cheer,
Our bosses, they did drink strong beer,	It was to dhrink good ale and beer,
And Pat worked on the railway.	Wid the boys upon the railroad.
It's "Pat, do this" and "Pat, do that,"	Now Mick do this, and Mick do that,
Without a stocking or cravat,	Widout a stockin' or cravat,
And nothing but an old straw hat,	The divil the thing but an ould straw hat,
While Pat works on the railroad.	To work upon the railroad.

And when Pat lays him down to sleep,   When I lay me down to sleep,
The wiry bugs around him creep,   The ugly bugs around me creep,
And divil a bit can poor Pat sleep,   Bad luck to the wink that I can sleep,
While he works on the railroad.   While workin' on the railroad.

This parallel suggest that the Lomaxes' "Paddy Works on the Erie" is really an amalgamation of two songs: one, the sequence of years, beginning "In 1841," as described in the 1864 manuscript magazine, and the other, the broadside version just quoted.

"Paddy Works on the Railway" is one of a handful of songs discussed in this book for which there are no hillbilly or race record versions. The only commercial 78 I have heard is a 1941 release by the American Ballad Singers, a concert group directed by Elie Siegmeister that recorded a set for RCA Victor entitled *Two Centuries of American Folk-Songs*. Rather than transcribe that "arranged" version, we have chosen to present a noncommercial field recording made for the Library of Congress. The singer, Ernest Bourne, was recorded by Alan Lomax in Washington in 1938.

At about the same time, Lomax recorded a different version, as sung by Barbara Bell. Titled "The Great American Railway," the principal lines of text were as follows:

> In 1841 . . . The American Railway was begun . . .
> In 1842 . . . I was looking around for something to do
>   . . . Working on the railway.
> In 1843 . . . The superintendent accepted me . . .
>   To work upon the railway.
> In 1844 . . . My legs were tired, my back was sore . . .
>   From working on the railway.
> In 1845 . . . I found myself more dead than alive . . .
>   From working on the railway.
> In 1846 . . . I found myself in a hell of a fix . . .
>   From working on the railway.
> In 1847 . . . I found myself on the way to heaven . . .
>   From working on the railway.
> In 1848 . . . I picked the lock of the Golden Gate . . .
> In 1849 . . . I got my wings and my harp divine,
>   I'll sit on a cloud most all the time,
>   Overlooking the railway.[5]

Another song that circulated widely in cheap print in the latter half of the nineteenth century entitled "Paddy on the Railway" began with the line "A Paddy once in Greenock town, for Glasgow city he was bound." There is no relation between this song and the piece under discussion here.

NOTES

1. C. Fox Smith, *A Book of Shanties* (Boston and New York: Houghton Mifflin, 1927), p. 56.
2. John A. Lomax and Alan Lomax, *American Ballads and Folk Songs* (New York: Macmillan, 1934), pp. 21–22.
3. James J. Fuld, *The Book of World-Famous Music*, rev. ed. (New York: Crown Publishers, 1971), p. 639.
4. "Mick upon the Railroad" (New York: J. Wrigley no. 6770, n.d.); Wolf no. 1426.
5. Barbara Bell, "The Great American Railway," LC AFS 1631 B1 and B2.

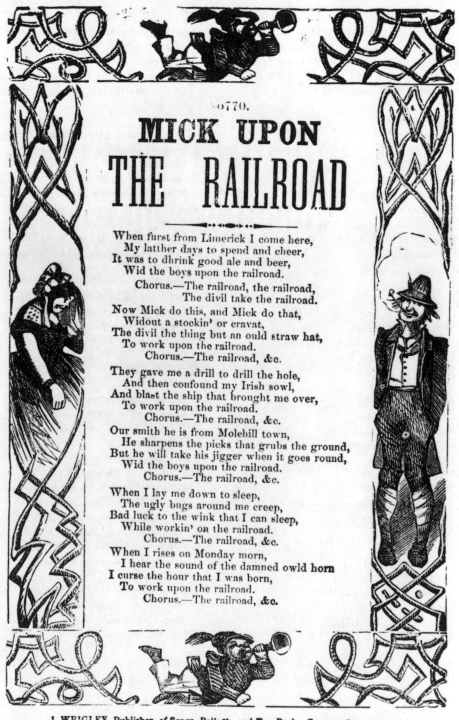

o770.

MICK UPON
THE RAILROAD

When furst from Limerick I come here,
  My latther days to spend and cheer,
It was to dhrink good ale and beer,
  Wid the boys upon the railroad.
    Chorus.—The railroad, the railroad,
        The divil take the railroad.

Now Mick do this, and Mick do that,
  Widout a stockin' or cravat,
The divil the thing but an ould straw hat,
  To work upon the railroad.
    Chorus.—The railroad, &c.

They gave me a drill to drill the hole,
  And then confound my Irish sowl,
And blast the ship that brought me over,
  To work upon the railroad.
    Chorus.—The railroad, &c.

Our smith he is from Molehill town,
  He sharpens the picks that grubs the ground,
But he will take his jigger when it goes round,
  Wid the boys upon the railroad.
    Chorus.—The railroad, &c.

When I lay me down to sleep,
  The ugly bugs around me creep,
Bad luck to the wink that I can sleep,
  While workin' on the railroad.
    Chorus.—The railroad, &c.

When I rises on Monday morn,
  I hear the sound of the damned owld **horn**
I curse the hour that I was born,
  To work upon the railroad.
    Chorus.—The railroad, &c.

J. WRIGLEY. Publisher, of Songs, Ballad's, and Toy Books. Conversation, Age, and
Small Playing Cards, Alphabet Wood Blocks, Valentines, Motto Verses, and Cut
Motto Paper, &c. No. 27 Chatham Street   (OPPOSITE CITY HALL PARK) NEW YORK

Broadside: "Mick upon the Railroad." Collection of the Library Company of Philadelphia.

REFERENCES

A. "A-Working on the Railroad," by Ernest
   Bourne. Vocal, unaccompanied.
   Recorded in Washington D.C., at Library
   of Congress, LC AFS 1637 B2, by Alan
   Lomax, 1938. Transcribed here.

B. Alden, 285
   Barnard, 78–79
   Best & Best, 11
   Boni (1947), 150–51
   Boston Evening Transcript, June 19, 1909
     (in "Notes & Queries")
   Boston Evening Transcript, June 26, 1909
     (in "Notes & Queries") (parody)
   Botkin & Harlow, 438 (from Lomax &
     Lomax [1947])
   Brand (1957), 40–41
   Brand (1961), 113
   Bullen & Arnold, 17
   Colcord, 107
   Dallas, 63, 70 (parody)
   Downes & Siegmeister (1943), 284
   Eckstorm & Smyth, 238
   Ernst, 120
   Ewen (1947), 129
   Fowke & Glazer, 84
   Glazer (1964), 114
   Harlow, 139–41
   Hille, 32
   Honore, 61
   Hood, 151
   Hugill (1966), 336
   Hugill (1969), 58 (discussion only)
   Ives (1953), 232
   Ives (1962), 168
   Kolb, 98
   Landeck (1950a), 48
   Leisy (1966), 263
   Loesser, 206
   Lomax & Lomax (1934), 20
   Lomax & Lomax (1947), 270
   MacColl, 20, 21
   Mursell (Grade 6), 108
   Pitts (1953), 60
   Sandburg, 356
   Seeger, P. (1961), 43
   Siegmeister, 72
   Smith, C. F., 56
   Sounds like Folk, 16
   Terry, 14
   Whall, 67
   Wolfe (1956), 65

D. American Ballad Singers—Victor 26723 (in
   album P-41)   "Pat Works on the
   Railway"
   Pete Seeger and Charity Bailey—Disc 5072
   (in album 604B)   "Pat Works on the
   Railway"

E. Clancy Brothers—Audio Fidelity 6255:
   Save the Land   "Paddy on the
   Railway"
   Dubliners—Epic 26337: *A Drop of the Hard
   Stuff*   "Paddy on the Railway"
   Sam Eskin—Folkways FA 2019 (FP 19): *Sea
   Shanties and Loggers' Songs*
   "Poor Paddy Works on the Railway"
   Joe Glazer—Collector 1924: *Singing BRAC;*
   Collector 1925: *Union Train*
   "Pat Works on the Railroad"
   Tom Glazer—CMS 650/4L: *The Musical
   Heritage of America, Vol. 1*   "Pat
   Works on the Railway"
   Cisco Houston—Folkways FA 2346: *Folk
   Songs*   "Pat Works on the Railway"
   Ewan MacColl—Stinson SLP 79: *British
   Industrial Folk Songs*   "Poor Paddy
   Works on the Railway"
   —Vanguard VRS 9090: *Ewan MacColl;*
   Topic 10-T-13; Topic 12-T-104: *Steam
   Whistle Ballads*   "Poor Paddy Works
   on the Railway"
   Ed McCurdy—Elektra EKL-205: *A
   Treasure Chest of American Folk Songs*
   "Paddy Works on the Railway"
   Pete Seeger—Folkways FA 2176 (FP 48/6)
   (10″ LP): *Frontier Ballads, Vol. 2;*
   Folkways FP 5003: *Frontier Ballads*
   "Paddy Works on the Railways"
   —Stinson SLP 57: *A Pete Seeger Concert;*
   Everest Archive of Folk Music AFM 201:
   Pete Seeger; Tradition 2107: *Pete Seeger
   Sings Folk Music of the World;* Sine Qua
   Non 102: *An Anthology of Folk
   Music*   "Paddy Works on the Railway"
   Weavers—Vanguard VRS 9013: *The
   Weavers on Tour*   "Fe-li-mi-oo-re-ay"

F. LC AFS:
   Barbara Bell—AFS 1631 B1 & B2
   "The Great American Railway"
   May Kennedy McCord—AFS 11875 A14
   "Workin' on the Railroad"

Drill, Ye Tarriers, Drill

DRILL, YE TARRIERS, DRILL

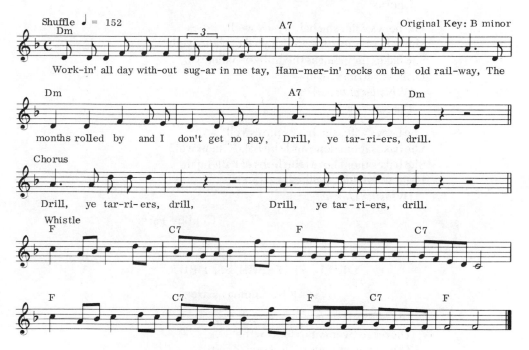

Workin' all day without sugar in me tay,
Hammerin' rocks on the old railway,
The months roll by and I don't get no pay,
Drill, ye tarriers, drill.
    Drill, ye tarriers, drill,
    Drill, ye tarriers, drill.

Workin' in the tunnel, shovelin' out the dirt,
I worked so hard that I wore out me shirt,
The tunnel caved in and we all got badly hurt,
Drill, ye tarriers, drill.
    [*Whistles chorus:*]

Standin' in the mud about six feet deep,
Workin' all night without a bite to eat,
Couldn't get to camp for the mud on me feet,
Drill, ye tarriers, drill.
    Chorus:

I went to the river to wash out my clothes,
I laid 'em on a log where the river swiftly flows,
The log rolled in, down the river went my clothes,
Drill, ye tarriers, drill.
    [*Whistles chorus:*]

Layin' in the bunkhouse, the chills o'er me creep,
The night was cold and dark, was rainin' hail and sleet,
Everybody snorin' and I couldn't go to sleep,
Drill, ye tarriers, drill.
  Chorus:

The boss's wife, she bakes pies swell,
She bakes them done and she bakes them well,
She bakes them hot as the hubs of hallelujah,
Drill, ye tarriers, drill.
  [*Whistles chorus:*]
  Chorus:

The boss's wife, she bakes pies swell,
She bakes them done and she bakes them well,
She bakes them hot as the hubs of hallelujah,
Drill, ye tarriers, drill.
  [*Whistles chorus:*]

                                        Chubby Parker

DRILL, YE TARRIERS, DRILL!

As sung by Thomas Casey

Oh! ev'ry morn at seven o'clock,
There are twenty tarriers on the rock,
The boss comes along and says "be still
And put all your power in the cast-steel drill,"
    Then drill, ye tarriers, drill,
    Drill, ye tarriers, drill,
    Oh it's work all day without sugar in your tay
    When ye work beyant on the railway,
    And drill, ye tarriers, drill.

The boss was a fine man all around
But he married a great, big, fat fardown,
She baked good bread and baked it well,
And baked it hard as the hobs of H—l.
  Chorus:

The new foreman is Dan McCann,
I'll tell you sure he's a blame mean man,
Last week a premature blast went off,
And a mile in the air went big Jim Goff.
  Chorus:

When pay day next it came around,
Poor Jim's pay a dollar short he found,
"What for?" says he, then came this reply,
"You were docked for the time you were up in the sky."

Although historians of popular music admit that the song may be older, "Drill, Ye Tarriers, Drill" is generally attributed to Thomas F. Casey. The original sheet music, published by Frank Harding's Music House in 1888, bears no claim of authorship; it simply states, "The Rousing Comic Song as sung by Mr. Thomas Casey." Because they are generally reprinted inaccurately, the original sheet-music words are given here.

I have found no incontrovertible evidence to push the song back earlier than 1888; however, a comment by John P. Davis in his 1896 history of the Union Pacific strongly suggests that it is considerably older. In a footnote to his discussion of General Dodge's organization of the work crews that laid track on the Union Pacific in the late 1860s, Davis wrote:

> Students of folk-lore will doubtless discover some substantial historical material in the refrain of a song that the author has often heard sung by an old Irish friend—evidently having seen service in more than one campaign:
>
> > Then drill, my paddies, drill,
> > Drill, my heroes, drill,
> > Drill all day, no sugar in your tay,
> > Workin' on the U. P. Railway.[1]

How tantalizingly close to a first-hand report of a mid-nineteenth-century railroad worksong!

Apparently there was no copyright claim in connection with the 1888 sheet music. However, one filed in 1930 by publisher E. B. Marks (E pub. 17779, Sept. 8, 1930) credited Casey with words, Charles Connolly with music, and Sylvester Krouse with arrangement and revision.

Even more uncertain than the origin of the song is the origin of the word *tarrier*. Whether it originally meant one who tarried, or, more probably, comes from *terrier*, the breed of dog that digs his quarry out of holes in the ground, is uncertain. In any case, the term was applied frequently toward the end of the nineteenth century to the hard-rock laborers who drilled and blasted their way across the continent paving the way for the railroad tracks.

Casey himself was such a tarrier. He also had a gift for entertaining, and gained a reputation singing in amateur theatricals in New York staged by local political clubs.[2] One of the songs performed at political rallies was "Drill, Ye Tarriers, Drill." It was exposed to a more genteel audience when playwright Charles H. Hoyt interpolated it into the second act of his musical comedy, *A Brass Monkey*, which opened at the Bijou Theater in New York on October 15, 1888. During the next few years the song was often heard on the vaudeville stage.

The song's popularity is probably due to the ironic anecdote related in the third and fourth stanzas—doubtless a joke to the upper classes who enjoyed Hoyt's stage presentation, but only a slight exaggeration to the tarriers and other workers who may have heard it sung in local taverns. In *American Vaudeville*, Douglas Gilbert quotes an interesting text from the singing of the Four Emeralds, an Irish comedy team of the 1880s. It lacks the anecdote about the explosion and differs from the usual text in other respects. For example, it has this verse, found nowhere else:

> The boardin' boss went to town one day,
> To get some sugar for to sweetin' our tay.
> He found that sugar had gone up of late,
> And forever after that we took our tea straight.[3]

Gilbert, a newspaperman for a quarter-century, was a Broadway critic and reporter. He contributed two fascinating volumes, filled with anecdotes and songs, to the literature of American popular entertainment. Unfortunately, he seldom gave precise references and sources for his recollections. Did he really recall the version of the Four Emeralds accurately, five decades after he must have heard it? If he did, that is further evidence that the song may have circulated before Casey popularized it. However, whether the above stanza preceded Casey's song or followed it, it does explain one line in the chorus, "Oh, it's work all day without sugar in your tay," which is almost always rendered in more recent versions as "Oh, it's work all day for the sugar in your tay."

It seems natural that such a song be adapted to new circumstances, should an appropriate occasion arise. A query in the *Boston Evening Transcript* in 1905 asked for the words to a song "probably composed in New York during building of the subway, the refrain of which is nearly:

> Oh, yes, work all day with no sugar in yer tay,
> Drill, Eye-tal-yuns, drill! Well!"[4]

Since the 1930s, "Drill, Ye Tarriers, Drill" has been a favorite of folksong anthologizers; during the 1950s it was very popular among the singers of the urban folksong revival. However, it has left but a weak imprint on oral tradition—only two items cited in the references pertain to versions collected in the field.

The earliest recordings of the song I have found date from before the turn of the century. These were made for Edison by Dan W. Quinn, a favorite comic singer of the times who recorded numerous dialect pieces; for the New Jersey Phonograph Company by George J. Gaskin; for the Talking Machine Company of Chicago by Silas Leachman; and for Berliner by Burt Shepard. In about 1910 it was recorded by the Peerless Quartet, a Victor ensemble headed by popular singer Billy Murray. The version transcribed here was recorded in 1931 by Chubby Parker, a popular banjo player and singer who made his reputation on the WLS Barn Dance in the late 1920s.

Parker's version is quite different from the sheet-music version, both in text and in structure. In fact, it is the only variant, apart from the text recalled by Gilbert, that differs substantively from the sheet music. While the stage version was clearly written to amuse, with but a slight suggestion of complaint, Parker's song expresses considerable dissatisfaction with the life of a tarrier.

NOTES

1. John P. Davis, *The Union Pacific Railway* (Chicago: S. C. Griggs, 1894), p. 141. This stanza is quoted in almost every account of the building of the UP, and always without attribution, e.g., by Frank P. Morse, *Cavalcade of the Rails* (New York: E. P. Dutton, 1940), p. 188; Charles Frederick Carter, *When Railroads Were New* (New York: Henry Holt, 1910), p. 252; Rupert Sargeant, *Historical Railroads* (New York: Grosset and Dunlap, 1927), p. 192; Lance Phillips, *Yonder Comes the Train* (New York: A. S. Barnes, 1965), p. 253; Adele Nathan, *The Building of the First Transcontinental Railroad* (New York: Random House, 1950), p. 99; and Charles K. Landia, *Rails over the Horizon* (Harrisburg, Pa.: Stock Pole Sons, 1938), p. 112. James McCague, *Moguls and Iron Men* (New York: Harper and Row, 1964), p. 150, quotes verses taken from a much later source (they do not appear in the Casey sheet-music version, or in Davis's stanza).

2. James J. Geller, *Famous Songs and Their Stories* (New York: Macaulay, 1931), p. 14.

3. Douglas Gilbert, *American Vaudeville* (1940; rpt., New York: Dover Publications, 1963), p. 72.

4. "Notes & Queries," *Boston Evening Transcript* Apr. 15, 1905.

Poster: "Wanted! 3,000 Laborers." Collection of the Illinois Central Gulf Railroad.

REFERENCES

A. "Drill You Tarriers Drill" [title on cover], sheet music. Title on first page of music is "Drill, Ye Tarriers, Drill!" Published by Harding's Music Office, New York, 1888.
   "Drill, Ye Tarriers, Drill," by Chubby Parker and his Little-Old-Time Banjo. Recorded Oct. 16, 1931 (American Record Corp. master 10894), probably in New York City. Released on Conqueror 7893. Transcribed in this book.

B. Barnum & Bailey, 6
   Boni (1947), 138–39
   Botkin & Harlow, 442
   Brand (1961), 144
   Delaney #1
   Dolph, 62   "Drill, Ye Engineers, Drill" (parody)
   Dykema, 153
   Engel, 171
   Ernst, 112
   Folksong Festival, 76
   Fowke & Glazer, 86
   Fowke & Johnston, 96   ("Drill, Ye Heroes, Drill," parody); 98
   Geller, 14
   Gilbert (1940), 72
   Good Old Times, 12
   Greenway, 72
   Hand, 34–36   "Drill, Ye Miners, Drill" (parody)
   Hille, 36
   Ives (1962), 170
   Landeck (1950a), 49
   Leisy (1966), 86
   Levy (1971), 326
   Lomax, A. (1960), 417
   Lomax, A. (1967), 104
   Morris, 184
   Mursell (Grade 5), 97
   Okun, 119–21
   Peacock III, 781 (derivative piece)
   Pitts (1951a), 10
   Pitts (1951b), 52–53
   Siegmeister, 80
   Smith, E. L., 17
   Weavers (1966), 76
   Wolfe (1956), 66

C. GORDON MSS:
   422—"Mich Y. T." (1927; 1 stanza)

D. Arthur Collins—Edison 1020 (cylinder) (The same release number was used for a recording by Dan W. Quinn.)
   George J. Gaskin—United States Phonograph Company (cylinder, no number)
   —Berliner 940 (7" 78 rpm), Berliner 064 (7" 78 rpm), Berliner (England) 2290 (7" 78 rpm)
   —Zon-O-Phone 5669, Zon-O-Phone 569, Zon-O-Phone 1583
   —American Talking Machine Company (cylinder, no number)
   —Chicago Talking Machine Company 3720 (cylinder)
   Silas Leachman—Talking Machine Company 016C (cylinder)
   Frank Luther with the Century Quartet —Decca 24464 (in album A-692: *Gay Nineties—Thirty-seven Grand Old Songs*)
   Chubby Parker—Conqueror 7893
   Peerless Quartet—Victor 16727   "The Railroad Section Gang Introducing 'Drill Ye Tarriers'"
   Dan W. Quinn—Edison 1020 (cylinder) —Victor 3155
   Earl Robinson—Keynote K-539 (in album 132): *Americana;* Mercury MG 20008: *Americana*
   —Timely 504, General 504
   Burt Shepard—Berliner 4 (7" single-sided disc)
   Unknown artist—Columbia XP 4004 (cylinder)
   Unknown baritone—Talking Machine Company 4009C (cylinder)

E. Bill Bonyun—Folkways FC 7402: *Who Built America?*
   Bob Chapman—Scholastic CC 0630: *Train Ballads* (7" 45 rpm EP)
   Richard Dyer-Bennet—Dyer-Bennet RD-B 4: *Richard Dyer-Bennet*
   Easy Riders—Columbia CL 1272/CS 8172: *Wanderin'*
   Warde Ford—Folkways FE 4001: *Wolfe River Songs*   "River Drivers' Song" (related)
   Bob Gibson—Riverside RLP 12-806: *I Come for to Sing*

John Greenway—Prestige International 13011: *"The Cat Came Back" and Other Fun Songs*

Cisco Houston—Folkways FA 2346: *Folk Songs;* Folkways FTS 31012: *Cisco Houston Sings American Folk Songs*

Burl Ives—Encyclopaedia Britannica Films EBF 6: *Songs of Expanding America*

Bruno Kazenas—New World NW 267: *The Hand That Holds The Bread*

Ed McCurdy—Bear Family (West Germany) 15009: *Last Night I Had the Strangest Dream*

Men of Song—Camay CA 3008: *College Folk Songs*

Ken Peacock—Folkways FG 3505: *Songs and Ballads of Newfoundland* "Drill Ye Heroes Drill" (related)

Susan Reed—Elektra EKL 116: *Susan Reed*

Walt Robertson—Folkways FA 2330: *Walt Robertson*

Dick and Jacquie Schuyler—CMH 1776: *200 Years of American Heritage in Song*

Win Stracke—Golden Records GLP 31: *Golden Treasury of Songs America Sings*

Tarriers—Glory PG 1200

Tradewinds—Diplomat DS 2278: *The Tradewinds*

Weavers—Vanguard VRS 9013: *The Weavers on Tour;* United Auto Workers UAW 2: *This Land Is Your Land: Songs of Social Justice*

F. LC AFS:

Earl Robinson—AFS 1627 A1

Gennetts of Old Time Tunes

Chubby Parker

CHUBBY PARKER

EACH week from radio station WLS, Chicago, Chubby Parker sends his messages of mirth and song to thousands of unseen admirers. These radio fans as well as his Gennett friends make him one of the country's most popular artists.

Chubby has asked us to tell everybody that he has a lot of new songs for the new year.

BIB-A-LOLLIE-BOO—*Old Time Singin'*—Banjo Acc. NICKETY NACKETY NOW NOW NOW—*Old Time Singin'*—Banjo Acc.	6077 .75
OH SUSANNA—*Old Time Vocal*—Tenor Banjo Acc. I'M A STERN OLD BACHELOR—*Old Time Vocal*—Banjo Acc.	6097 .75
WHOA MULE WHOA—*Old Time Vocal*--Tenor Banjo Acc. LITTLE BROWN JUG—*Old Time Vocal*—Banjo Acc.	6120 .75
UNCLE NED—*Old Time Singin' & Playin'*—Banjo Acc. OH—DEM GOLDEN SLIPPERS—*Old Time Singin' & Playin'*—Banjo Acc.	6287 .75

Advertisement in a Gennett record catalog. Courtesy of the John Edwards Memorial Foundation, UCLA.

Way Out in Idaho

WAY OUT IN IDAHO

*On the recording, the change to E occurs in the middle of the measure.
** On the recording, the first half of this measure is chorded B⁷.

Come all you jolly railroad men and I'll sing you if I can
Of the trials and tribulations of a godless railroad man,
Who started out from Denver, his fortunes to make grow,
And struck the Oregon Short Line way out in Idaho.

Way out in Idaho, way out in Idaho,
A-workin' on the narrow gauge, way out in Idaho.

I was roaming around in Denver one luckless rainy day,
When Kilpatrick's man-catcher stepped up to me and did say,
"I'll lay you down five dollars as quickly as I can,
And you'll hurry up and catch the train, she's starting for Cheyenne."

He laid me down five dollars, like many another man,
And I started for the depot, was happy as a clam.
When I got to Pocatello, my troubles began to grow,
A-wading through the sagebrush in frost and rain and snow.

When I got to American Falls, it was there I met Fat Jack,
They said he kept a hotel in a dirty canvas shack;
Said he, "You are a stranger and perhaps your funds are low,
Well, yonder stands my hotel tent, the best in Idaho."

I followed my conductor into his hotel tent,
And for one square and hearty meal I paid him my last cent.
Jack's a jolly fellow, and you'll always find him so,
A-working on the narrow gauge way out in Idaho.

They put me to work next morning with a cranky cuss called Bill,
And they gave me a ten-pound hammer to strike upon a drill.
They said if I didn't like it I could take my shirt and go,
And they'd keep my blankets for my board way out in Idaho.

Oh, it filled my heart with pity as I walked along the track,
To see so many old bummers with their turkeys on their backs.
They said the work was heavy and the grub they couldn't go,
Around Kilpatrick's dirty tables way out in Idaho.

But now I'm well and happy, down in the harvest camp,
And I'll—there I will continue ill I make a few more stamps.
I'll go down in New Mexico and I'll marry the girl I know,
And I'll buy me a horse and buggy and go back to Idaho.

Way out in Idaho, way out in Idaho,
A-working on the narrow gauge, way out in Idaho.

Blaine Stubblefield

Often when a folksong arises out of experiences or conditions vivid in the minds of the people who lived through them, it is framed in such a way as to be of interest only so long as the events that inspired it are remembered. Such a song dies out with the passing of the generation to whom it had a first-hand meaning. Usually, a folksong must have some universal appeal (or, lacking that, some memorable element, such as the ironic anecdote in "Drill, Ye Tarriers, Drill") to insure its survival. "Way Out in Idaho," while once well known in the Pacific Northwest, seems to have all but faded from the collective memory.

Like many another folksong (e.g., "The Wreck of Old 97" in chap. 5), "Way Out in Idaho" represents the adaptation of an older folksong (or family of songs) to new circumstances. The new setting was the construction of the Oregon Short Line, chartered in 1881 to connect the Union Pacific, which owned controlling interest in it, and the Oregon Railway and Navigation Company of the far Northwest. This would provide the UP another route to the West Coast, the primary link being with the Southern Pacific at Ogden, Utah. The ORN extended across Oregon to Huntington, almost at the Oregon-Idaho border, where it was eventually met by the OSL, which ran some 600 miles across southern Idaho and through the southwest corner of Wyoming to Granger, 156 miles east of the UP terminus at Ogden. This 600-mile linkage was completed on November 25, 1884, about three years after construction began. Another OSL line was built from Pocatello, on the main line, northward into Montana, extending through Silver Bow and eastward to Butte. A few shorter spurs were also built in Idaho. Most of this construction took place in 1882–84, which dates the ballad events—if there was any historical basis to them. Most of the OSL line was standard gauge, as would be expected of a line built by the UP as part of its own system. The only narrow-gauge section was the line from Pocatello to Silver Bow; and in 1887 work began to convert this part to standard gauge. If the phrase "workin' on the narrow gauge" in the song refers to the OSL, then we can pinpoint the events to the Pocatello–Silver Bow branch. American Falls, the other Idaho town mentioned in the text, is about twenty-two miles west of Pocatello on the OSL's main line.[1]

The family of older songs on which "Way Out in Idaho" was based includes "Buffalo Skinners" (sometimes called "Range of the Buffalo"), "Canada I O," "State of Arkansas" (or "Arkansas Traveler"), "Michigan I O," and "Hills of Mexico." All these songs deal with the hardships associated with some specific frontier occupation—railroading, buffalo skinning, lumbering, cattle driving, land draining. Four decades ago, New England folksong scholars Fannie Hardy Eckstorm and Phillips Barry discussed the relationships of some of these songs, noting their origin from a nineteenth-century English sea song, "Canada I O," which in turn was believed to be based on an eighteenth-century Scots love song, "Caledonia."[2]

This latter piece, an excellent long text of which was collected and printed by Gavin Greig more than sixty years ago, tells of a Scots lass who pays some sailors to take her home to Caledonia (Scotland). They plan to take her money and then throw her overboard; but the captain, warned by a dream, finds the girl on board bound in irons, frees her, and eventually marries her.[3] "Canada I O," the song claimed to be its immediate descendant, tells of a young lady, in love with a sailor, who asks him to take her by ship to Canada. The two songs are similar, but the latter must have been put together with extensive recomposition; even the verse form is changed. The opening stanza is:

> There was a gallant lady all in her tender youth,
> She dearly lov'd a sailor, in truth she lov'd him much
> And for to go to sea with him the way she did not know,
> She long'd to see that pretty place call'd Canada I O.[4]

More recently, other students of American folksong, Austin and Alta Fife, and later Roger Welsch, have re-examined this song complex and gathered more details pertaining to its chronological development.[5] From their studies, and other materials at hand, a fairly clear family tree merges.

In 1854, a Maine lumberman, Ephraim Braley, wrote "Canaday I O" based on his own uncomfortable experiences lumbering in Québec the previous winter. It began:

> Come all ye jolly lumbermen, and listen to my song,
> But do not get discouraged, the length it is not long;
> Concerning of some lumbermen, who did agree to go
> To spend one pleasant winter up in Canada I O.[6]

According to Mrs. Eckstorm's informant, Braley was a good singer with a comic turn, given to composing songs about local people and events. Within two decades, his song had been rewritten to fit other lumbermen's experiences in Michigan ("Michigan I O"),[7] Pennsylvania ("Colley's Run I O"),[8] North Dakota ("Shanty Teamsters' Marseillaise"),[9] and no doubt elsewhere.

Probably in the 1870s, some logger or easterner otherwise familiar with "Canada I O" or one of its progeny moved into the Southwest and recomposed it to fit events in the lives of some buffalo skinners on the frontier ("Buffalo Range" or "Buffalo Skinners"). An early printing began:

> Come all you Buffalo hunters and listen to my song
> You needn't get uneasy, for it isn't very long
> It's concerning some Buffalo hunters who all agreed to go
> And spend a summer working, among the buffalo.[10]

From there the song was adapted, probably in the early 1880s, to cattle driving in New Mexico ("The Hills of Mexico") and Arizona ("The Crooked Trail to Holbrook"):

> Come, all you jolly cowboys that follow the bronco steer,
> I'll sing to you a verse or two your spirits for to cheer,
> It's all about a trip that I did undergo
> On that crooked trail to Holbrook, in Arizona, oh.[11]

More closely related to "Way Out in Idaho" is a song of a traveler's experiences in poverty-struck Arkansas ("Arkansas Traveler" or "State of Arkansas"):

> My name it is Bill Stafford, I came from Buffalo Town;
> I've travelled this wide world over, I've travelled this wide world round;
> I've had my ups and down in life, but better days I've saw;
> I never knew what misery was till I came to Arkansaw.[12]

Dates in the various texts range from 1871 to 1896; composition in the 1870s or early 1880s is likely. The occupation offered the narrator in this song is swamp draining, but it is touched on only briefly. Of particular interest is a variant, two texts of which have been recovered, that falls between "Way Out in Idaho" and "Arkansas Traveler," sharing lines with each song. The ballad is set in Arkansas, like the latter piece, but concerns railroad work, as in the former. Its relation to "Way Out in Idaho" is sufficiently close to merit reprinting here.

THE ARKANSAW NAVVY

> Come listen to my story and I'll tell you in my chant
> It's the lamentation of an Irish emigrant,
> Who lately crossed the ocean and misfortune never saw,
> 'Till he worked upon the railroad in the State of Arkansaw.
>
> When I landed in St. Louis I'd ten dollars and no more,
> I read the daily papers until both me eyes were sore;
> I was looking for advertisements until at length I saw
> Five hundred men were wanted in the State of Arkansaw.
>
> Oh, how me heart it bounded when I read the joyful news,
> Straightway then I started for the raging Billie Hughes;
> Says he, "Hand me five dollars and a ticket you will draw
> That will take you to the railroad in the State of Arkansaw."
>
> I handed him the money, but it gave me soul a shock,
> And soon was safely landed in the city of Little Rock;
> There was not a man in all that land that would extend to me his paw,
> And say, "You're heartily welcome to the State of Arkansaw."

I wandered 'round the depot, I rambled up and down,
I fell in with a man catcher and he said his name was Brown;
He says, "You are a stranger and you're looking rather raw,
On yonder hill is me big hotel, it's the best in Arkansaw."

Then I followed my conductor up to the very place,
Where poverty was depicted in his dirty, brockey face;
His bread was corn dodger and his mate I couldn't chaw,
And fifty cents he charged for it in the State of Arkansaw.

Then I shouldered up my turkey, hungry as a shark,
Traveling along the road that leads to the Ozarks;
It would melt your heart with pity as I trudged along the track,
To see those dirty bummers with their turkeys on their backs,
Such sights of dirty bummers I'm sure you never saw
As worked upon the railroad in the State of Arkansaw.

I am sick and tired of railroading and I think I'll give it o'er,
I'll lay the pick and shovel down and I'll railroad no more;
I'll go out in the Indian nation and I'll marry me there a squaw,
And I'll bid adieu to railroading and the State of Arkansaw.[13]

This ballad probably was also composed in the 1880s, and it is difficult to tell whether it preceded or followed "Way Out in Idaho."

Folksong collectors have been able to find only a half-dozen different texts of "Way Out in Idaho" since it was first brought to Robert W. Gordon's attention in 1923. After Gordon printed a text that his informant said her father had sung in Idaho and Washington in about 1888, he received two more versions in the next three years. One correspondent, "Ben A. Ranger" of Santa Rosa, California, claimed, "This is one I know the author of, also the date, I composed the verces [*sic*] myself at the Massasoit Hotel on C and 17th St. Tacoma Wash. in August or Sep 1887. dictated by stuttering Ed Brown who had the experience and told it to me. the Foreman Bill Lowery I knew well. he and his two brothers Joe and Ed worked for Nelson Bennett. Contractor of Tacoma. I think that gives you the dope on this one."[14]

When a claimant reports such minute details surrounding the circumstances of his composing a song, he generally deserves a respectful ear. However, if Ranger did compose the song, he must have partially forgotten his own lyrics between 1887 and 1926, when he wrote Gordon, since his version lacks some of the personal names found in other texts.

I know of only two recordings of "Way Out in Idaho"—one made by Blaine Stubblefield in Washington, D.C., in 1938 for the Library of Congress, and the other by Rosalie Sorrels, copied directly from Stubblefield's recording. Stubblefield's tune is that usually associated with the western ballad "Sam Bass," and whenever "Way Out in Idaho" is printed, the music is taken either from Stubblefield's Library of Congress recording or from some version of "Sam Bass." In this book we have transcribed Stubblefield's version.

Stubblefield was born in Enterprise, Oregon, in 1896. In his youth on the Snake River he learned to play guitar and took an interest in folksongs, which he picked up from miners, cattlemen, pioneers, sheepherders, and traveling medicine men. After graduating from the University of Idaho, he took an advanced degree in journalism at the

University of Washington in 1927. While Washington, D.C., editor of McGraw-Hill's *Aviation* magazine, he was asked by a local radio station to run a weekly program of folk music. In this way he attracted the interest of Alan Lomax at the Library of Congress, and he was recorded there in 1938. In 1953 Stubblefield started the Northwest Oldtime Fiddler's Festival and Contest at Weiser, Idaho, an event that is still held annually and attracts musicians from throughout the West and Midwest. He was manager of the Weiser Chamber of Commerce from 1950 until his death in 1960.[15]

NOTES

1. Historical details of Poor's *Manual of Railroads,* various editions.

2. Fannie Hardy Eckstorm, "American Ballads," *BFSSNE,* No. 6 (1933), pp. 10–13.

3. Gavin Greig, *Folk Song of the North-East* (1909, 1914; rpt., Hatboro, Pa.: Folklore Associates, 1963), no. 77.

4. *The Forget-Me-Not Songster, Containing a Choice Selection of Old Ballad Songs as Sung by Our Grandmothers* (New York: Turner and Fisher, 1845), p. 43.

5. Austin E. Fife and Alta S. Fife, *Songs of the Cowboys, by N. Howard ("Jack") Thorp* (New York: Clarkson N. Potter, 1966), chap. 15; Roger L. Welsch, "A 'Buffalo Skinner's' Family Tree." *Journal of Popular Culture,* 4 (Summer, 1970), 107–29.

6. Eckstorm, "American Ballads."

7. See G. Malcolm Laws, Jr., *Native American Balladry* (Philadelphia: American Folklore Society, 1964), p. 155 (Laws C 17), for references.

8. Ibid.

9. G. F. Will, "Four Cowboy Songs," *JAF,* 26 (Apr.-June, 1913), 187.

10. N. Howard Thorp, *Songs of the Cowboys* (Estancia, N. Mex.: News Print Shop, 1908), pp. 31–32; reprinted in Fife and Fife, *Songs of the Cowboys,* pp. 200–201.

11. "The Crooked Trail to Holbrook," in N. Howard Thorp, *Songs of the Cowboys* (Boston and New York: Houghton Mifflin, 1921), pp. 53–54; reprinted in Fife and Fife, *Songs of the Cowboys,* pp. 207–8. Further references to this and the preceding song are in Laws, *Native American Balladry,* 137–38 (Laws B 10).

12. From J. H. Cox, *Folk-Songs of the South* (1925; rpt., Hatboro, Pa.: Folklore Associates, 1963), p. 239. See Laws, *Native American Balladry,* p. 230 (Laws H 1), for further citations. For a Canadian adaptation of this song, see Tom Brandon, "Muskoka," Folk-Legacy FSC 10: *"The Rambling Irishman."*

13. M. C. Dean, *Flying Cloud* (Virginia, Minn.: Quickprint, [1922?]), pp. 8–9. A similar text, given in Harry Lee Williams, *History of Craighead County, Arkansas* (Little Rock: Parke-Harper, 1930), pp. 337–38, is quoted in James R. Masterson, *Tall Tales of Arkansas* (Boston: Chapman and Grimes, 1943), pp. 265–66. Williams received the ballad from a Canadian who helped lay rails on the "Frisco" Railroad when it passed through Arkansas in the 1880s. It is also given in *Railroad Stories,* 19 (Apr., 1936), 112–13, in the column "The Sunny Side of the Track," where it is titled "Railroading in Arkansas."

14. Gordon MS 419 from Ben A. Ranger, Dec. 29, 1926.

15. Biographical information is from Helen Stubblefield Elliott to Archie Green, Jan. 26, 1966; I am grateful to Green for making this available to me.

REFERENCES

A. "Way Out in Idaho," by Blaine Stubblefield. Vocal and guitar. Recorded in 1938 (LC AFS 1634 B1) in Washington, D.C., by Alan Lomax. Released on Library of Congress Archive of Folk Song L61:

Railroad Songs and Ballads. Transcribed in John A. Lomax and Alan Lomax, *Our Singing Country* (New York: Macmillan, 1941), p. 269; reprinted in B. A. Botkin, "A Sampler of Western Folklore and

Songs," chap. 9 in *The Book of the American West*, edited by Jay Monaghan (New York: Julian Messner, 1962), p. 554, and B. A. Botkin and Alvin F. Harlow, *A Treasury of Railroad Folklore* (New York: Bonanza Books, 1953), p. 440.

B. Botkin (1963), 554 (from Lomax & Lomax [1941])

Botkin & Harlow, 440 (from Lomax & Lomax [1941])

Brunvand, 247 (discussion only)

Emrich (1942a), 229

Gordon, *Adventure*, Oct. 20, 1923, p. 192 (from M. E. Newson)

Gray, 37 (from Gordon) (2 stanzas only)

Green (1968), 10

Lingenfelter, 78 (from Idaho State Historical Society *Report*)

Idaho State Historical Society, *18th Bienniel Report* (1940), 72

Lomax & Lomax (1941), 269 (from Stubblefield recording)

Talley, 64   "The Old Section Boss" (related)

Welsch (1970), 124 (from Gray)

C. GORDON MSS:

287—Anon.

337—Anon.; incomplete (May, 1923)

348—Marie E. Newson (ca. July, 1923)

419—Ben A. Ranger (Dec. 29, 1926)

E. Rosalie Sorrells—Folkways FH 5343: *Folk Songs of Idaho and Utah*

The Night Express

THE NIGHT EXPRESS

From the third stanza on, each stanza uses the melody of measures 1–7 for the the first line and 24–32 for the second.

One day I met a little girl beyond the railroad bridge,
A pail of berries she had picked along the bank's high ridge.
"Where do you live, my child," I asked, "and what might be your name?"
She looked at me with eyes o'ercast, and then her answer came.

"The house beyond the bluff is ours, they call me 'Bonnie Bess,'
My father is an engineer, he runs the night express."

Ten forty-nine's on scheduled time, and 'tis a moment late,
His engine comes around the curve at quite a cheerful rate.

"Sometimes the clouds hangs overhead, his train we cannot see,
He whistles twice for mama dear, and clings the bell for me.

"The lamp in mama's window burns, placed there alone for him,
His eyes light up and then he knows that all is well within."

"And are you not afraid," I asked, "that he might wreck the train,
And there might be some sad mishap, and he nowise to blame?"

"God watches over us," she cries, "and He knows what is best,
'Tis nothing but to serve and trust, and leave to Him the rest."

So great (?) that child had faith in Him, it makes my own seem weak,
I bowed my head with sobbing heart and kissed her on the cheek,

And said to her in tendrous tones, "God bless you, Bonnie Bess,
God bless your mama and the man that runs the night express."

Watts and Wilson

This chapter, dealing with men who built or worked on the railroads, would not be complete without a representative example of the nineteenth-century parlor ballads about young children of railroaders. Such pieces are closely related to "The Red and Green Signal Lights" and "Jim Blake's Message" in chapter 7; but in those songs the emphasis is clearly on the tragic element, with occupation being of secondary importance. In "The Night Express" and similar pieces, there is no tragedy, and the fact that the child's father is employed by the railroad is necessary to the story.

Doubtless the best known of these songs was Charles Graham's hit of 1895, "My Dad's the Engineer"; in it a young lass soothes the train's passengers, worried by a nearby forest fire, with the reminder that her daddy is the engineer and will take care of everyone. In "The Night Express," a passing stranger foolishly asks the daughter of a railroad engineer if she does not worry that her father may wreck the train and suffer some mishap; the young girl, "Bonnie Bess," blanches for a moment, but then with Pollyanna cheerfulness affirms her faith that God watches over all and will do what is best.

The recording transcribed here, one of only two made of this ballad, is by a group headed by Wilmer Watts, a South Carolina textile worker and musician. It has been one of my favorite old-time hillbilly recordings ever since I first heard it; indeed, the small repertoire of recorded pieces by this group contains several outstanding musical gems. Little was known of Wilmer Watts for many years, and his recordings were extremely scarce—in some cases only a single copy being known to collectors. One evening at a gathering of folksong enthusiasts, Archie Green was enumerating research projects that had yet to be tackled, one of which was locating Wilmer Watts or his next of kin. Among those present was Donald Lee Nelson, who had just a few months earlier succeeded in locating another hillbilly musician of the 1930s who had been sought in vain for more than ten years, Lee Allen. Nelson promptly went to work, and one evening the following year he telephoned me from Belmont, South Carolina, with the triumphant news that he had located Watts's widow and children.[1]

I have found only a single printed antecedent to this recording. The poem "The Night Express" appeared in the *Locomotive Engineers' Monthly Journal* for November, 1893, without attribution, save the credit line "Div. 459." Presumably some engineer on that division either wrote the poem or, more likely, clipped it from some other source and submitted it to the *Journal*—a not uncommon practice. The poem is textually very similar to the Watts recording except for the presence of three additional stanzas. Since the periodical is not easily obtained, I reprint the full text here.

THE NIGHT EXPRESS

I met a little girl one day,
    Beyond the railroad bridge,
With pail of berries she had picked
    Along the bank's high ridge.
"Where do you live, my child?" I said,
    "And what may be your name?"
She looked at me with eyes askance,
    And then her answer came:

"The house upon the bluff is ours;
    They call me 'Bonnie Bess';
My father is an engineer,
    And runs the night express."

A sparkle came into her face,
    A dimple to her chin;
The father loved his little girl,
    And she was proud of him.

"Ten forty-nine, on schedule time,
    Scarce e'en a minute late
Around the curve his engine comes
    At quite a fearful rate.
We watch the headlight through the gloom
    Break, like the dawn of day,
A roar, a flash, and then the train
    Is miles upon its way.

"A light in mamma's window burns,
    Placed there alone for him;
His face lights up, for then he knows
    That all is well within.
Sometimes a fog o'erhangs the gorge,
    The light he cannot see;
Then twice he whistles for mamma
    And clangs the bell for me."

"Then you are not afraid?" I asked,
    "That he may wreck the train;
That there may be a sad mishap
    And he nowise to blame?"
A pallor crept into her cheek;
    Her red lips curled with pain;
They parted, then serenely smiled;
    Her heart was brave again.

"God watches over us," she said,
    "And He knows what is best,

And we have but to pray and trust
    And leave to Him the rest."
How great that childish faith of hers!
    It makes my own seem weak;
I bent my head with throbbing heart
    And kissed her on the cheek.

I said to here in cheery tones,
    "God bless you, 'Bonnie Bess!'
God bless your mother and the man
    Who runs the night express!"[2]

"The Night Express" was recorded in Chicago, in about April, 1927, for the Wisconsin Chair Company and released on Paramount 3007 and Broadway 8113. It is not known for certain who played which instrument. The three band members were Wilmer Watts, an associate known only by the last name of Wilson, and probably Charles Freshour. Since Freshour's family always believed him to have written the song, it is possible that he set the poem to music.

NOTES

1. For Donald Lee Nelson's account of the Watts band, see "'Walk Right in Belmont': The Wilmer Watts Story," *JEMFQ*, 9 (Autumn, 1973), 91–96. An earlier account was given by Malcolm Blackard, "Wilmer Watts & the Lonely Eagles," ibid., 5 (Winter, 1969), 126–40.
    2. *LEMJ*, 27 (Nov., 1893), 1014.

REFERENCES

A. "The Night Express," by (Wilmer) Watts and Wilson. Vocal with banjo, guitar, and steel guitar accompaniment. Recorded ca. Apr., 1927 (Wisconsin Chair Co. master 4433-2), in Chicago, Ill. Released on Paramount 3006 (as by Watts and Wilson) and Broadway 8113 (as by Weaver and Wiggins). First recording of the song.
"The Night Express," *LEMJ*, 27 (Nov., 1893), 1014. Only known printing.

D. Wilmer Watts and the Lonely Eagles
    —Paramount 3299   "Bonnie Bess"

Nine Pound Hammer

NINE POUND HAMMER

Well, this old__ ham-mer (Well, this old ham-mer), Just a lit-tle too heav-y (just a lit-tle too heav-y), For my size (for my size), ba-by, for my__ size (ba-by, for my size).__

*In this measure, since the two vocal parts overlap, the parenthetical text is indicated by downward stems.

Well, this old hammer, just a little too heavy,
For my size, baby, for my size.

[*Spoken*:] Drive 'er on down, boys. Break the handle off.

Oh, take this hammer, give it to the captain,
Tell him I'm gone, baby, tell him I'm gone.

If he asks you where I went to,
You don't know, baby, you don't know.

[*Spoken*:] Nine pound hammer. Just a little too heavy.

There ain't no hammer in this mountain,
Ring like mine, baby, ring like mine.

Well, this old hammer shine like silver,
Ring like gold, baby, ring like gold.

Oh, roll on, buddy, try to make your time,
For I'm broke down, and I can't make mine.

Now, this old hammer killed my buddy,
But it can't kill me, babe, it can't kill me.

Grayson and Whitter

SPIKE DRIVER BLUES

Take this ham-mer__ and car-ry it to the cap-tain,

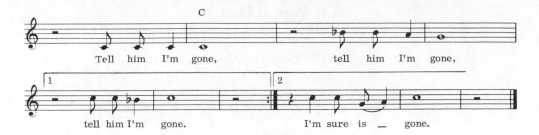

Take this hammer and carry it to my captain,
Tell him I'm gone, tell him I'm gone, tell him I'm gone.
Take this hammer and carry it to my captain,
Tell him I'm gone, just tell him I'm gone, I'm sure is gone.

This is the hammer that killed John Henry,
But it won't kill me, but it won't kill me, well, it won't kill me.
This is the hammer than killed John Henry,
But it won't kill me, but it won't kill me, ain't gon' kill me.

It's a long ways from east Colorado,
Honey, to my home, honey, to my home, honey, to my home.
It's a long ways to east Colorado,
Honey, to my home, honey, to my home, that's where [*pronounced
    "wire"*] I'm goin'.

John Henry, he left his hammer
Laying 'side the road, laying 'side the road, laying 'side the road.
John Henry, he left his hammer,
All over in red, all over in red, that's where I'm goin'.

John Henry's a steel-drivin' boy,
But he went down, but he went down, but he went down.
John Henry was a steel-driving boy,
But he went down, but he went down, that's where I'm goin'.

Mississippi John Hurt

The modern folksong scholar and enthusiast likes to set up categories whose bound-aries are often not respected by the songs and ballads themselves as they evolve and migrate. Songs of men at work, for example, are labeled according to the occupation or industry: whaling, riverboating, lumbering, mining, milling, railroading. But this classi-fication scheme cannot handle the development of the cowboys' lament "Bury Me Not on the Lone Prairie" from the older sailors' song "The Ocean Burial," or the railroading song "Way Out in Idaho" from the lumbering song "In Canada I O." Similarly, songs relating to particular physical tasks, such as digging, drilling, hammering, or hauling, move with the task itself from the coal mines to the levee camps to the road gangs.

"Nine Pound Hammer," for instance, the subject of a long chapter in Archie Green's fascinating study of coal-mining songs, *Only a Miner*,[1] is equally at home here in a collection of railroad songs because, properly speaking, it is neither a mining nor a

"Ten Pound Hammer," from *The Lithographs of Thomas Hart Benton,* copyright 1969, 1979 by Creekmore Fath. Benton described the subject of this 1967 lithograph as an "old story of my youth—before the steam hammer beat out John Henry."

railroad song, but a hammer song; it belongs wherever laborers punctuate with song the monotonous sound of steel hammer striking rock or steel spike. Of course, railroad building and mining were brought in especially close contact with the construction of the railroad lines that brought the coal cars into and out of the mines, and several songs seem to have originated specifically in this context. At least one folk musician, Merle Travis, clearly associated "Nine Pound Hammer" with the coal-mining industry, for he inserted this stanza of his own composition when he recorded the piece in 1946:

> It's a long way to Harlan, it's a long way to Hazard,
> Just to get a little brew, just to get a little brew.
> When I'm long gone, you can make my tombstone
> Out of number nine coal, out of number nine coal.[2]

Even allowing for its supraoccupational character, "Nine Pound Hammer" is a tangled complex of songs, fragments, and themes. Green (from whose research it is my pleasure to borrow extensively here) notes three frequent uses of the phrase "nine pound hammer." It may be "(1) the proper name of a fairly specific lyric folksong arising out of the hammer's many functions in railroad building, mining, and other industries; (2) a designation for a motif, significant or peripheral, in the John Henry ballad; (3) one element in an amorphous worksong complex including widely diverse titles such as 'Roll On Buddy,' 'Driving Steel,' 'Swannanoa Tunnel,' or 'Take This Hammer.'"[3]

Travis's rendition of "Nine Pound Hammer" had particularly great impact on later country and folk musicians, and in tracing the sources of this piece, Green examines its numerous versions and relatives, starting with the "Roll On, Johnnie" heard in 1891 from a Fayette County, Texas, levee-camp worker. Apart from the relevant John Henry ballads, all of Green's citations prior to 1925—the year Dorothy Scarborough's collection *On the Trail of Negro Folk-Songs* was published—lack the specific phrase "nine pound hammer." Either they dwell on the phrase "take this hammer" or "this old hammer," as in a 1915–16 manuscript variant published by Newman I. White:

> This old hammer killed John Henry,
> But it can't kill me.
> Take this old hammer, take it to the Captain,
> Tell him I'm gone, babe, tell him I'm gone.[4]

Or they are primarily based around the "roll on, buddy" phrase, a motif that comes from the tasks of hauling and rolling (wheelbarrows) rather than hammering, as in a fragment published by Robert W. Gordon in 1924:

> And it's roll on, buddy—what makes you roll so slow?
> Your buddy is almost broke—down on the K.N.O.[5]

Scarborough's short text is one of only two specific "nine pound hammer" references (apart from those in the John Henry ballads) that preceded all of the commercial recordings:

> Nine-pound hammer—kill John Henry—
> But 't won't kill me, babe—'t won't kill me.
>
> If I live—to see December—
> I'm goin' home, love—I'm goin' home.

I'm goin' back—to the red-clay country—
That's my home, babe—that's my home.[6]

Green implies that the first amalgamation of the "hammer" and "roll" elements into a single song was the 1927 commercial hillbilly recording of "Nine Pound Hammer" by Al Hopkins and his Buckle Busters (Brunswick 177). After that, this association was the rule rather than the exception. Green's discussion brings in two other types of "roll" songs, represented by Buell Kazee's 1927 "Roll On John" (Brunswick 144) and the Bowman Brothers' 1928 "Roll On Buddy" (Columbia 15357-D).

Green notes that a complete genealogy of the various songs in this complex would be difficult to construct. Nevertheless, there is an important structural key that divides the material into two distinct groups: hammer songs and "roll" songs. The "hammer" stanzas are all of the textual form A/BB—that is, nonrhyming couplets, the second line of which consists of a half-line fragment repeated (or nearly repeated). The three stanzas from Scarborough quoted above illustrate this structure. Contrast the "Roll On Buddy" quoted from Gordon: the couplet rhymes, and there is no repetitive structure to the second half of the couplet. The other "roll" songs discussed by Green also have distinctly different structures. "Take This Hammer," popularized by Leadbelly and recorded by numerous artists after him, follows the "Nine Pound Hammer" form and thus would be part of that hammer song complex. Also structurally identical is the North Carolina piece known variously as "Asheville Junction" or "Swannanoa Tunnel," a hammer song considered by some to be a local adaptation of the John Henry complex.[7]

We cannot ignore the fact that after 1927 these elements were permanently fused; but I believe the distinction is chronologically valid, and in the references I have omitted all the "roll" songs and fragments that either predate 1927 or do not have any admixture of the "hammer" elements.

Some other genealogical matters deserve mention. One concerns the connection of these hammer songs with the ballads about John Henry, a matter that was discussed briefly in chapter 4. Folklorist Guy B. Johnson, one of the first to examine the John Henry legend in depth, contended that the narrative ballads grew slowly out of the earlier, simple hammer songs. Louis Chappell, his rival on the trail of John Henry, felt the lyrical hammer songs to have played no parental role in the development of the ballads; a half-century later, Archie Green took a position sympathetic to Chappell's. Chappell and Green are probably correct in their conclusions. But another question can be asked of the relationship between the ballads and hammer songs and the John Henry story: did "Nine Pound Hammer" actually arise from the same circumstances of tunnel construction on the C & O line in the 1870s that spawned the ballad "John Henry"? Or could it have been an independent composition, possibly earlier, that some time after the John Henry incident was adapted to it? This raises another peripherally related question: how common a name was "John Henry," especially among southern blacks in the 1860s and 1870s? Could it have been like "John Doe"? Today, "John Henry" is often used as a general term for one's signature, much as "John Hancock" has been used for many years.

I cannot offer confident answers to these questions. However, the following facts stand out from the mass of materials dealing with John Henry, the nine pound hammer, and the various related songs. Almost every hammer song with the "Nine Pound Hammer" structure—whether titled "Nine Pound Hammer," "Ten Pound Hammer," "Take This Hammer," "This Old Hammer," or whatever—that does not have elements of "Roll On, Buddy" mentions John Henry. This group includes versions reported by Perrow,

White, Scarborough, Odum and Johnson, and Sandburg; two Library of Congress field recordings (1037 B2 and 6673); and Mississippi John Hurt's "Spike Driver Blues." The earliest of these texts was reported in 1913 by E. C. Perrow; he had heard it in east Tennessee in 1905. On the other hand, only those recovered by Odum and Johnson and by Scarborough include the phrase "nine pound hammer." In other words, the evidence suggests that John Henry was an integral part of this type of hammer song from the very beginning, while the particular phrase "nine pound hammer" was not, occurring in the complex only occasionally prior to those first commercial recordings of 1927.

As Green has established, the two seminal recordings of "Nine Pound Hammer" in white tradition were the 1927 Brunswick version by Al Hopkins and his Buckle Busters, the first to bear that title, and the 1946 recomposition by Merle Travis, included in his Capitol album of coal-mining songs. Since 1946, about half of all the recordings of the song show Travis's influence. Since both versions are transcribed in Green's study, I have chosen for inclusion here a recording made in 1928 by Grayson and Whitter.

Henry Whitter, born in the Sulphur Springs district of Virginia in 1892, was a cotton millhand during his early years and occasional guitar/harmonica player and singer. He played a key role in the early development of the hillbilly recording industry (see chap. 2 and the discussion of "The Wreck of the Old 97" in chap. 5). Whitter had already been making records for four years, principally for the OKeh label, both by himself and as accompanist for several other artists, when he met Gilliam Banmon Grayson at a 1927 fiddlers' convention in Mountain City, Tennessee. Grayson, a blind fiddler and singer from Laurel Bloomery, Tennessee, was several years Whitter's senior. He had traveled for many years in the company of the well-known Tennessee musician Clarence Ashley prior to meeting Whitter. In October, 1927, Whitter and Grayson made their debut on wax together for the Starr Piano Company in New York. Their first session included "Train 45," "John Henry, the Steel Driving Man," and "He's Coming to Us Dead," the last two titles remaining unissued. The following week, in Victor's temporary studio in Atlanta, they recorded "Train 45" and "He Is Coming to Us Dead" again; this time both pieces, as well as four others, were released (the latter is transcribed in chap. 7). In a February–March, 1928, session for Starr they recorded "Red or Green," made again for Victor the following July as "The Red and Green Signal Lights" (see chap. 7). At this July session they also recorded "The Nine Pound Hammer," which turned out to be one of their most successful discs: more than 10,500 copies were sold on the Victor label. The duo recorded once again, in Memphis in September–October, 1929, for RCA Victor. In 1930, this most successful musical partnership was abruptly terminated, when Grayson was killed in a truck accident. Whitter, deeply affected by the tragedy, made no records after that year. The duets by Grayson and Whitter, highlighted by Grayson's fine singing and archaic fiddle style, are among the finest specimens of early recorded hillbilly music.[8]

Two black musicians have also contributed influential commercial versions of the song: Mississippi John Hurt recorded a piece under the title "Spike Driver Blues" for OKeh in 1928, and Leadbelly recorded "Take This Hammer" several times, first for RCA Victor in 1940. Hurt's "Spike Driver Blues," a good companion piece to Grayson and Whitter's "Nine Pound Hammer," is also included in this book.[9]

John Hurt, born in Avalon, Mississippi, in 1894, represented the older style of black folk music that preceded the blues. He came to the attention of OKeh producer Tommy Rockwell through the suggestion of a white Avalon fiddler, Willie Narmour. In a fiddlers' contest Narmour had won the opportunity to record for OKeh in February, 1928, and he told Rockwell about Hurt, who was brought along for the same session. "Spike Driver

Blues" was cut at a second session, in December, 1928, in New York. The Depression brought an abrupt end to Hurt's professional career, and he lived in Avalon in poverty until 1963, when he was "rediscovered" by two blues collectors who decided to look for him there on the basis of one of his 1928 songs, "Avalon Blues."[10] In the decade after his rediscovery he regaled audiences in coffeehouses and at folk festivals with the same expert finger-picking and warm singing style that made his 1928 recordings so highly sought after by collectors. Hurt recorded "Spike Driver Blues" three times in the 1960s, each time with slightly different lyrics.

NOTES

1. Archie Green, *Only a Miner* (Urbana: University of Illinois Press, 1972), pp. 329–69.

2. Merle Travis, "Nine Pound Hammer," Capitol 48000.

3. Green, *Only a Miner*, p. 329.

4. Newman I. White, *American Negro Folk-Songs* (1928: rpt., Hatboro, Pa.: Folklore Associates, 1965), p. 261.

5. Robert W. Gordon, *Adventure*, Jan. 10, 1924, p. 191. I have rewritten his four-line stanza as two lines.

6. Dorothy Scarborough, *On the Trail of Negro Folk-Songs* (1925; rpt., Hatboro, Pa.: Folklore Associates, 1963), p. 220. Her four-line stanzas are rewritten as two-line stanzas.

7. See *The Frank C. Brown Collection of North Carolina Folklore*, vol. 2, *Folk Ballads*, edited by Henry M. Belden and Arthur Palmer Hudson (Durham, N.C.: Duke University Press, 1952), pp. 626–27.

8. An adequate biography of either of these two musicians has yet to be published. Whitter's role in the early hillbilly industry was first noted by Archie Green, "Hillbilly Music: Source and Symbol," *JAF*, 78 (July-Sept., 1965), 204–28. Grayson's career is touched on in Ralph Rinzler and Richard Rinzler, brochure notes to Folkways FA 2355: *Old-Time Music at Clarence Ashley's*, and in more detail in Joe Wilson, liner notes to County 513: *Grayson and Whitter* (second printing). For the most extensive account of Whitter's career, see Norm Cohen, "Henry Whitter," *JEMFQ*, 11 (Summer, 1975), 57–61; a complete Whitter discography follows that article (pp. 62–66).

9. "Spike Driver Blues" has been previously transcribed several times. See Moses Asch, Josh Dunson, and Ethel Raim, *Anthology of American Folk Music* (New York: Oak Publications, 1973), pp. 100–101; Alan Lomax, *The Folk Songs of North America* (Garden City, N.Y.: Doubleday, 1960), pp. 549–50, retitled "East Colorado Blues" (some new words added); Eric Sackheim, *The Blues Line* (New York: Grossman Publishers, 1969), pp. 226–27. Hurt's 1964 recording of the same song is transcribed in Stefan Grossman, Hal Grossman, and Stephen Calt, *Country Blues Songbook* (New York: Oak Publications, 1973), p. 178.

10. Information on Hurt's career can be found in Richard K. Spottswood, liner notes to Biograph BLP-C4: *Mississippi John Hurt—1928* and liner notes to Piedmont PLP-13157: *Mississippi John Hurt, 1963*; and Lawrence Cohn, "Mississippi John Hurt," *Sing Out!*, 14 (Nov., 1964), 16-17, 19-21.

REFERENCES

A. "Nine Pound Hammer," by Al Hopkins and his Buckle Busters. Recorded May, 1927 (Brunswick masters 23128–29), in New York City. Released on Brunswick 177 in Oct., 1927. First recording with the title "Nine Pound Hammer."

"Spike Driver Blues," by Mississippi John Hurt. Vocal and guitar. Recorded Dec. 28, 1928 (OKeh master 401488), in New York City. Released on OKeh 8692. Reissued on Folkways FA 2953 (FP 253): *Anthology of American Folk Music, Vol. 3*; Biograph BLP-C4: *1928: His First Recordings*. Transcribed in Moses Asch,

Josh Dunson, and Ethel Raim, *Anthology of American Folk Music* (New York: Oak Publications, 1973), pp. 100–101; in Eric Sackheim, *The Blues Line* (New York: Grossman Publishers, 1969), pp. 226–27; and in this volume.

"The Nine Pound Hammer," by G. B. Grayson and Henry Whitter. Grayson, vocal and violin; Whitter, vocal and guitar. Recorded July 31, 1928 (RCA Victor master 46633), in New York City. Released on Victor V-40105 in ca. Aug., 1929. Reissued on County 513: *The Recordings of Grayson and Whitter*. Copyrighted by Southern Music on Oct. 25, 1929 (E unp. 12532), renewed Oct. 29, 1956 (R 179741), words and melody credited to Grayson. Transcribed in this book.

"John Henry," in E. C. Perrow, "Songs and Rhymes from the South," *JAF*, 26 (Apr.-June, 1913), 163–64. Learned in east Tennessee from mountain whites in ca. 1905; recalled from memory. Four stanzas and melody. First report of a song with the "Nine Pound Hammer" structure (see discussion).

"Nine Pound Hammer," in Dorothy Scarborough, *On the Trail of Negro Folk-Songs* (1925; rpt., Hatboro, Pa.: Folklore Associates, 1963), p. 220. First published version with that title. Sent by Evelyn Cary Williams of Lynchburg; heard from singing of Charles Calloway of Bedford County, a black road-laborer.

"Nine Pound Hammer," by Merle Travis. Vocal and guitar. Recorded Aug. 8, 1946 (Capitol master 1332), in Hollywood, Calif. Released late in 1947 on Capitol 48000 (in album AD 50: *Folk Songs of the Hills*). Reissued on Capitol T 891: *Back Home* and a parallel EP, Capitol EAP-1-891: *Back Home*; Capitol T 2662: *The Best of Merle Travis*; Capitol (England) T 21020: *21 Years a Country Singer*. Transcribed and discussed in detail in Archie Green, *Only a Miner* (Urbana: University of Illinois Press, 1972), pp. 357–63. The most influential recording of the song.

B. Boni (1952), 210–11   "Take This Hammer"
Brown II, 625–27; III, 267; IV, 300–302
Chappell (1939), 179–81
Glazer (1970), 68
Gordon (1938), 16
Henry (1938), 443–44; 448–49 "Swannanoa Tunnel" (related)
Johnson, G. B., 71–83
Leisy (1966), 241
Lomax, A. (1967), 84
Lomax & Lomax (1947), 322–23
Look Away, 44   "Rocks on the Mountains"
Lunsford, 34–35   "Swannanoa Tunnel" (related)
Odum & Johnson (1926), 235–37
Perrow (1913), 163–65
Rosenberg, 62 (title only)
Sandburg, 150   "Drivin' Steel"
Scarborough, 218–21
Scott, 2   "Hammer Song"
Sharp, 42–44   "Swannanoa Tunnel" (related)
Siegmeister, 48
Taylor, J. (III)
Watson, 68   "Spikedriver Blues"
White, N. I., 261–62, 302, 409   "This Old Hammer"
Work, 233   "John Henry"

D. "NINE POUND HAMMER" variants:
Mose Andrews—Decca 7338   "Ten Pound Hammer"
Frank Blevins and his Tarheel Rattlers —Columbia 15280-D
Monroe Brothers—Bluebird B-6422, Montgomery Ward M-4747; RCA Victor (England) RCX 7103 (45 rpm): *Country Guitar, Vol. 14*; RCA Victor (Japan) RA 5281: *Early Bluegrass Music*; RCA Victor LPV 532: *The Railroad in Folksong*; RCA Victor (Japan) RA-5677: *The Legendary the Monroe Brothers Collection (1936–1939), Vol. 1*   "Nine Pound Hammer Is Too Heavy"
Ernest and Eddie Stoneman—Okeh 02655, Vocalion 02655

"TAKE THIS HAMMER" variants:
Delmore Brothers (Alton and Rabon)

—King 718; King LP 785   "Take It to
the Captain"
Leadbelly (Huddie Ledbetter)—RCA
Victor (England) RCX-146
—Asch 101 (in Disc album 735); Collectors
Classics CC 23: *Leadbelly*

E.   "NINE POUND HAMMER" variants:

Chet Atkins—RCA Victor LPM/LSP 2783:
Guitar Country
Chet Atkins and Merle Travis—RCA Victor
APLI-0479: *Atkins-Travis Traveling
Show*
Beau Brummels—Warner Brothers
WB/WS 1692: *Triangle*
Charlie Beverly—Starr 1066: *Miner's
Dobro*
Norman Blake—Takoma D-1052: *Live at
McCabe's*
Bluegrass Hillbillies—ABC Paramount
ABC/ABCS 446: *Pickin' 'n Grinnin'*
Blue Sky Boys—Starday SLP 205: *A
Treasury of Rare Song Gems from the
Past*
Dan and Louise Brock—Donerail DLP 201
and Lemco LLP 702: *Kentucky Song Bag*
Brothers Four—Columbia CL 1479: *Rally
Round*; Columbia CL-1803/CS-8603:
Brothers Four Greatest Hits
Don Brown and the Ozark Mountain
Trio—K-Ark LP 6027: *Don Brown Live*
Larry Campbell and the Country
Playboys—Union Grove SS-6: *48th Union
Grove Fiddlers' Convention*
Johnny Cash—Columbia CL-1930/
CS-8730: *Blood, Sweat and Tears*;
Columbia CL-2122/CS-8922: *All-Star
Hootenanny*; Harmony HS 11343: *Johnny
Cash*
Sanford Clark—Dot 15534 (45 rpm); Reo
(Canada) 8143
Paul Clayton—Folkways FA 2110 (FP 47/3):
*Folksongs and Ballads of
Virginia*   "Bill Dooley"
Roy Cobb—Old Homestead OHS 90057:
Traditional Sounds of Bluegrass
Country Gentlemen—Design 613:
Hootennany; Hilltop JS 6156: *Bluegrass
Country*
—Zap MLP 101: *The Country Gentlemen*

Dick Curless—Tower T/DT 50005:
Tombstone Every Mile
—Event 4274
Marcel Dadi and friends—Guitar World 4:
Marcel Dadi and Friends Country Show
Jimmy Dean—RCA Victor LPM/
LSP-3890: *Jimmy Dean Show*
Dave Dudley and the Cass County
Boys—Crown CLP 5508
Jack Elliott—Vanguard VRS 9151/VSD
71951   "Roll On Buddy"
Jack Elliott and Derroll Adams—Topic
12T105: *Roll On Buddy*   "Roll On
Buddy"
Ernie and Mack—Rural Rhythm
RR-EM-140: *Blue Grass If You Please*
Billy Faier—Riverside RLP 12-657:
Travelin' Man; Washington VM-740
Raymond Fairchild and group—Rural
Rhythm RR 146: *King of the Smokey
Mountains*
Hank Ferguson—Folk-Legacy FSA 13:
Behind These Walls
Lester Flatt—RCA Victor APL1-0588:
Live Bluegrass Festival
Lester Flatt and Earl Scruggs—Collectors
Classics 4: *Flatt and Scruggs*
—Columbia CL 1830/CS 8630: *Folk Songs
of Our Land*; Harmony HS-11401: *Foggy
Mountain Chimes*
—Columbia CL 2796/CS 9596: *Changin'
Times*   "Buddy, Don't You Roll So
Slow"
Tennessee Ernie Ford—Capitol T/DT 700:
This Lusty Land; Capitol EAP 2-700 (45
rpm); Capitol ST-833: *Folk Album*
—Capitol SVBB 11325: *25th Anniversary*
Jesse Fuller—Topic (England) 12T134:
Move On down the Line   (fragment in
"Railroad Worksong")
Harley Gabbard—Vetco 3006: *The Tall
Timber Man*
Goins Brothers—Rebel SLP 1554/55: *Ralph
Stanley & the Clinch Mountain
Boys—Live! At McClure, Virginia*
Greenbriar Boys—Vanguard VRS 9104: *The
Greenbriar Boys*; Fontana (England) TFL
6019: *The Greenbriar Boys*
Lorne Greene—RCA Victor LPM/LSP
3302: *The Man*

Smiley Hobbs—Folkways FA 2318:
  Mountain Music Bluegrass Style
Homesteaders—Riverside RM 7537:
  Railroad Bill
Mississippi John Hurt—Piedmont PLP
  13157: *Folksongs and Blues*   "Spike
  Driver Blues"
—Vanguard VRS 9148/VSD 79148: *Evening
  Concerts at Newport, Vol. 1*   "Spike
  Driver Blues"
—Vanguard VRS 9220/VSD 79220:
  Mississippi John Hurt Today   "Spike
  Driver Blues"
Aunt Molly Jackson—Library of Congress
  Archive of Folksong L61: *Railroad Songs
  and Ballads*   "Roll On Buddy"
Snuffy Jenkins and Pappy
  Sherrill—Rounder 0059: *Crazy Water
  Barn Dance*
Buffalo Johnson—Rich-R-Tone 1023 (45
  rpm)
Kentucky Colonels—World Pacific WP
  1821: *Appalachian Swing*
Last Mile Ramblers—Blue Canyon BCS
  406: *"While They Last"*
Laurel River Valley Boys—Judson J-3031:
  Music for Moonshiners; Riverside RLP
  7504: *Dance All Night with a Bottle in
  Your Hand*
Lilly Brothers—Globe (Japan) SJET 8325M:
  The Lilly Brothers at Hillbilly Ranch
Fred McKenna—Arc A 612: *Fred McKenna
  of CBC-TV Singalong Jubilee*
Jim and Jesse McReynolds and the Virginia
  Boys—Epic LN 26074: *Bluegrass
  Classics*; Columbia Special Products
  (double LP package including Epic BN
  26074)
Mac Martin—Rural Rhythm RR-232: *Just
  like Old Times*   "Swinging a Nine
  Pound Hammer" (related)
Bill Monroe and the Bluegrass Boys—
  Decca DL 4266/74266: *Bluegrass
  Ramble*; Decca DL 4485/74485: *All Time
  Hootenanny*
Odetta (Felius)—Vanguard VSD-2153: *One
  Grain of Sand*   "Roll On, Buddy"
Osborne Brothers—Decca DL 75128 and
  MCA 129: *Up to Date and Down to Earth*
Philo Glee and Mandoline Society—
  Campus Folksong Club (University of
  Illinois) CFC 101: *Philo Glee and

Mandoline Society
Piper Road Spring Band—Fiends Club
  Records (no number): *Piper Road Spring
  Band*
Malcolm Price Trio—Decca (England) KL
  4627: *Country Session*
John Prine—Atco 7274: *Sweet Revenge*
Lou Rawls—Capitol 4669
Don Reno, Bill Harrell, and the Tennessee
  Cutups—Rural Rhythm RR-DR-171: *Don
  Reno and Bill Harrell*
Tony Rice—King Bluegrass KB 529: *Guitar*
Tom Rush—Prestige Folklore FL 14003:
  Got a Mind to Ramble; Fantasy 24709:
  Tom Rush
Gary Scruggs—Columbia C-30584: *Earl
  Scruggs Performing with His Family and
  Friends*
Ralph Smith—CMH 1776: *200 Years of
  American Heritage in Song*
Stanley Brothers—Wango 104: *John's
  Country Quartet*; County 739: *The
  Stanley Brothers of Virginia, Vol. 2*
Stoneman Family—MGM SE-4578: *The
  Great Stonemans*
String Band—Nugget NRLP 102: *Me and
  My Ole Crow*
Joe Stuart—Atteiram API-L-1514: *Sittin' on
  Top of the World*
Merle Travis—United Artists UAS 9801:
  Will the Circle Be Unbroken
Dave Van Ronk—Folkways FA 2383: *Dave
  Van Ronk Sings, Vol. 2*   "Spike
  Drivers Moan"
Doc Watson—Folkways FA 2426: *Jean
  Ritchie and Doc Watson at Folk City*
  "Spike Driver Blues"
—United Artists UA-LA601-G: *Doc and the
  Boys*   "Spikedriver Blues"
Harry and Jeanie West—Riverside RLP
  12-617: *Southern Mountain Folksongs
  and Ballads*; Washington WLP 732
Roland White—Ridge Runner RRR 0005: *I
  Wasn't Born to Rock'n Roll*
Tex Williams—Liberty 3304: *Tex Williams
  in Las Vegas*
—Decca 29764, Decca 9-29764 (45 rpm);
  Decca DL 4295: *Country Music
  Time*   "New Nine Pound Hammer"
—Shasta LP 517: *The Way They Were Back
  When*

"TAKE THIS HAMMER" variants:

Leon Bibb—Vanguard 9041/S2012: *Folk Songs*

Emmett Brand—Folkways FA 2655: *Music from the South, Vol. 6*

Big Bill Broonzy—Verve MGV 3000-5: *Bill Broonzy Story*; Verve MGV 3002: *Big Bill Broonzy's Last Session*

—Storyville (Denmark) SLP 143

—Columbia (France) ESDF 1121; Columbia (France) FP 1081

Brothers Four—Columbia CL-2128/ CS-8928: *Sing of Our Times*

Hylo Brown—Starday SLP 204: *Bluegrass Goes to College*: Cumberland SRC 69520: *Bluegrass Oldies but Goodies*; Smash SRS 67028

Johnny Cash—Columbia CL 1930/CS 8730: *Blood, Sweat and Tears*   "Tell Him I'm Gone"

Easterners—Vetco 3003: *Echoes of the Bonnie and Clyde Era*

Lester Flatt, Earl Scruggs, and the Foggy Mountain Boys—Columbia CL 2045/CS 8845: *Flatt & Scruggs at Carnegie Hall*

—Columbia KG 31964: *The World of Flatt and Scruggs* (possibly same recording as above)

Walter Forbes—RCA Victor LPM/LSP 2472: *Ballads and Bluegrass*

Jesse Fuller—World Song EG-10-027 (WS-1): *Working on the Railroad*; Topic (England) 12T134: *Move On down the Line*   "Railroad Work Song"

—Good Time Jazz 10031: *Blues Jazz, Spirituals, and Folk*; Good Time Jazz L-12031: *Work Songs, Blues, Spirituals*

Gale Garnett—RCA Victor LPM/LSP 2833: *My Kind of Folk Songs*

Bob Gibson—Riverside RLP 12-806: *I Come for to Sing*

Highwaymen—United Artists UAR 3125/6125: *Highwaymen*

Clifford Jordan—Atco 1444: *These Are My Roots*

Harold Land Quintet—Imperial 9247/ 12247: *Jazz Impressions of Folk Music*

Leadbelly (Huddie Ledbetter)—Capitol EAP 1-369 (45 rpm); Capitol H-369; Capitol (England) LC 6597; Capitol T-1821: *Leadbelly*; Capitol TBO-1970: *Dimensions in Jazz*

—Folkways FA 2004 (FP 4): *Take This Hammer*; Folkways FA 2691: *Down Home Music*; Verve/Folkways FV/FVS 9001: *Take This Hammer*; Folkways FTS 31019: *Take This Hammer*

—Folkways FT 31030S: *Shout On*

—Stinson SLP 12: *Folksay, Vol. 5*; Stinson SLPX 12: *American Folksay, Vols. 5 and 6*

Maggie Valley Country Singers—Rural Rhythm RR 143

Merrill Jay Singers—Cabot CAB 503: *Songs of the Railroad*

Odetta (Felius)—Tradition TLP 1025: *Odetta at the Gate of Horn*; Tradition 2052: *Best of Odetta*

—Vanguard 9103/2109: *Odetta at Town Hall*; Vanguard VSD 43/44: *Essential Odetta*

Osborne Brothers—Decca 31546 (45 rpm); Decca DL 4602/74602: *Voices in Bluegrass*; Decca DL 4485/74485: *All Time Hootenanny*

Edith Roberts—Rural Rhythm RR-ER-178: *Edith Roberts*

Red Smiley and the Bluegrass Cutups— Rural Rhythm RR-RS-160: *Red Smiley and the Bluegrass Cutups*

Red Sovine—Starday SLP 445(S): *Who Am I?*

Horace Sprott—Folkways FA 2653 (FP 653): *Music from the South, Vol. 4*

Tarriers—Atco 8042: *Tell the World about This*

Tommy Tedesco—Everest 243: *Guitar Greats*

Sonny Terry—Storyville SLP 218: *Wizard of the Harmonica*

Sonny Terry and Brownie McGhee— Fantasy 3317: *Shouts and Blues*

—Metrojazz 2-E 1009

—Prestige Bluesville BVLP 1005: *Blues & Folk*

Johnny Tillotson—MGM 4270: *She Understands Me*

Jim Wall and group—Rural Rhythm RR-1168: *Old Time Songs*

Guitar Welsh, Hogman Maxey, and Andy Mosely—Louisiana Folklore Society (Folk Lyric) A-5: *Prison Worksongs Recorded in the Louisiana State Prison, Angola, La.*

Harry and Jeanie West—Prestige

International 13049: *Country Music in
    Blue Grass Style*
Willie Wright—Concert Disc CS 45: *I Sing
    Folk Songs*   "Take This Hammer to
    the Captain"

F. "NINE POUND HAMMER" variants:

LC AFS:

Craig Pearl and Pete Steele—AFS 1705 B1
Jimmy Strothers—AFS 745 B1   "Dis Ol'
    Hammer"
Group of Negroes—AFS 1037 B2   "Ten
    Pound Hammer"

—AFS 6673 A6   "John Henry"
    (combines "Nine Pound Hammer" and
    "Take This Hammer")
Skyline Farms group—AFS 1630 B2
    "Roll On Buddy"

"TAKE THIS HAMMER" variants:

LC AFS:

Clifton Wright and group—AFS 726 B1
Group of Negroes—AFS 6673 A6
    "John Henry" (combines "Nine Pound
    Hammer" and "Take This Hammer")

Mississippi John Hurt. From the jacket of Vanguard VSD
19/20: *The Best of Mississippi John Hurt.*

The Little Red Caboose behind the Train (III)

THE LITTLE RED CABOOSE BEHIND THE TRAIN (III-A)

*The guitar accompaniment consists of one bass note and one downward strum per measure.
The melody of the chorus corresponds to the second half of the verse.

We are jolly American railroad boys and braking is our trade,
We're always on the go both day and night;
Throwing switches, makin' flagstops, along the line we go,
And to see that all the train is made up right.
You bet we're always ready when called upon to go,
No matter whether sunshine or in rain,

And a jolly crew you'd find us if you will come and see
In the little red caboose behind the train.

    So here's success to all the boys that ride upon the cars,
    May happiness always with you remain;
    And a jolly crew you'd find us if you will come and see,
    In the little red caboose behind the train.

Two red lights we hang on each side, another one behind,
In the evening when the sun is almost gone;
You bet the lad that rides ahead will keep it in his mind
To see that all the train is coming on.
When we are near the station, how thoughtless out we go,
All a-singin' or whistlin' some refrain;
Then we climb out on the hurricane deck and leave our coats inside
Of the little red caboose behind the train.

This little car we speak of, more precious and more dear
Than all the other coaches on the line;
And the reason why we tell you, because it is our home,
We always try to keep it looking fine.
Although we have no fashion lights, no velvet cushion chairs,
Everything inside just neat and plain;
There's many an honest heart that beats beneath that rusty roof,
In the little red caboose behind the train,

    So here's success to all the boys that ride upon the cars,
    May happiness always with you remain;
    For a jolly crew you'd find us if you will come and see,
    In the little red caboose behind the train.

                                  Pickard Family

THE LITTLE RED CABOOSE BEHIND THE TRAIN (III-B)

Oh, I broke up on the L and N, and on the Southern, too,
Lord, Lord, . . . I'll never brake again;
While the only friend that's left me is that good old watch of mine
In the little red caboose behind the train.

    Don't you roll the bars (?) that tie along the cars,
    Be happy there in sunshine and in rain;
    For the only friend that's left me is that good old watch of mine
    In that little red caboose behind the train.

Now, that little car I speak of is more dear to me
Than all the rest upon the railway train;
And the reason why I say this, because it is our home,
And there'll always be . . . rain.

    Chorus:

Oh, I'm getting old and feeble and I cannot work no more,
I do not . . . the sunshine and the rain;
And the only friend that's left me is that good old watch of mine
In that little red caboose behind the train.

Marion Underwood and Sam Harris

THE LITTLE RED CABOOSE BEHIND THE TRAIN (III-C)

I am growing old and weary, and my sight is getting dim,
I've laid my links and pins away to rust;
And the only friend that's left to me in this wide world to stand
Is the little red caboose behind the train.

Oh, I'm growing old and feeble now, and my sight is getting dim,
And I cannot see those signals anymore;
I can hear those whistles blowing, and I know I'll soon be going
To a better home I know there far away.

There are young ones coming on, it is time for me to go,
They'll be pestered with the rain, the sleet, and snow;
And they'll find a heap of trouble when those hills they have to double
With the little red caboose behind the train.

Chorus:

Paul Warmack and his Gully Jumpers

Lexicographers and etymologists have not yet agreed on the origins of the word *caboose*; French, German, and Dutch sources have been suggested.[1] The term *caboose* was used in the English Navy in the eighteenth century to denote a cooking room on deck of a merchant ship, but adaptation to the railroads was purely an American inspiration. The *Dictionary of American English* and *A Dictionary of Americanisms* give 1861 as the earliest railway usage for *caboose* and 1862 as the earliest for *caboose car*. Rail historian Bill Knapke claims that in 1859 some New England traveler used the word to describe a flatcar with a shelter on it for cooking, and cites 1863 as the year the distinctive cupola top was added to the caboose.[2] All sources, then, point to the early 1860s for the introduction both of the term and of the structure as we know it. I suggest that the songs about the little red caboose came into being less than two decades later, and I shall display my evidence below. For the ultimate origins of the songs, however, we must inquire into the writings of one Will S. Hays.

William Shakespeare Hays could not have been better named. When he was born, in Louisville, Kentucky, in 1837, no one could have foreseen that he was destined to become one of America's most prominent songwriters in the 1860s and 1870s. Though his primary occupation was journalist for the *Louisville Courier-Journal*, his mark on American popular culture was made as a songwriter. Students of American folk balladry know him as the author of "The Drummer Boy of Shiloh" (Laws A 15), a Civil War composition of 1862. Between that year and 1880 he produced a steady stream of songs, mostly of the sentimental variety, dealing with parting lovers, longing for home, widows, and poor orphan children. Among his compositions that have entered oral tradition are "Take This Letter to My Mother" (1877), "I'll Remember You, Love, in My Prayers" (1869), "Mollie Darling" (1871), "We Parted by the River Side" (1866), and "The Little Old Cabin in the Lane" (1871).

Our interest here is in the last-named title, one of several pieces Hays wrote on the theme of the old rural homestead (others were "My Dear Old Sunny Home," "De Little Old Log Cabin in de Woods," "De Cabin in de Lane," and "That Cottage Home of Dan's"). Like many good songs and poems, "The Little Old Cabin in the Lane" inspired a plethora of parodies: one of the earliest was Captain Jack Crawford's "My Little New Log Cabin in the Hills," published in 1879. Under the title "The Little Old Sod Shanty (on the Claim)," Austin and Alta Fife have printed a handful of other western parodies of the same family.[3] To the same tune, or one very similar, are "Little Joe the Wrangler," "All Go Hungry Hash House," and many others. The title "Little Red Caboose behind the Train" itself indicates a trainload of songs: I know of more than ten distinct songs or poems by that name published between about 1882 and 1935.

A baker's half-dozen of these describe aspects of the life of brakemen and therefore are the proper subject of this chapter. Among these are the three oldest texts I have found, to which I shall return shortly. One "Little Red Caboose," also originating in the nineteenth century and not at all widespread, deals with hoboes and tramps primarily, and therefore more appropriately belongs in chapter 8. Two songs, written in the 1930s by John Lair and Bob Miller, deal with train wrecks and are discussed in chapter 5. Through the 1930s and 1940s, Miller's version was the one most often encountered. In the references I cite all seven of the occupational songs; annotations for the hobo version and the Lair and Miller texts are given in other chapters.

The most widespread of the occupational "Little Red Caboose" songs, designated III-A here, is also the one for which I have found the earliest printing—in a pocket songster of about 1882, one of the hundreds of pulp booklets of songs published in the latter decades of the nineteenth century. No author credit is given, but judging by the occupational slang, it is likely that the author was himself a railroadman, inspired by Will S. Hays's popular favorite or by some other parody of it. Although this version has turned up in several field collections and pulp publications, only one 78 rpm commercial recording was made, and that one is transcribed here. The song was recorded by the Pickard Family for the Plaza Record Company in 1929 and released on several labels. The Pickards included Mom and Dad Pickard and two of their children, Ruth and Bubb (Obediah, Jr.). The lead singing was by Dad Pickard, christened Obediah, who was born in Tennessee in 1874 and began his recording career in Nashville in 1927. The Pickards' musical career in the 1930s included a stint on the Grand Ole Opry and a regular program originating out of New York over the NBC network. The Pickards' recorded repertoire included two other railroad songs: "Life's Railway to Heaven" and "On the Dummy Line."[4]

The song cited in the references as III-D seems to be a localization of III-A. Both III-A and III-D were printed in early issues of *Railroad Man's Magazine*, the former in October, 1908, the latter in September of the same year. In the June, 1909, issue, a note stated that the song had been written by Edward Thelen and published in the Sedalia, Missouri, *Democrat* in 1878 or early 1879; however, the note did not specify which of the two songs was authored by Thelen. Both sound like the work of railroadmen, or of authors familiar with railroad life and lingo. "The Little Red Caboose (III-E)" was printed in

Railroad Man's Magazine in November, 1908, accompanied by a comment that it had been sung by "Slippery" Brown in Beardstown, Illinois, in 1877. This song deals specifically with the problems of keeping on time before speed recorders were invented. It is sufficiently similar to "The Little Red Caboose (III-F)," credited to James O'Connell in a 1967 issue of *Railroad Magazine,* to lead me to suspect some direct connection between the two. O'Connell's poem opens with the lines "In the year of '99, the days of 'Auld Lang Syne,' / The indicators then were still around . . . ," which suggests a composition date early in the present century.

Like III-D and III-E, versions III-B and III-C occur in only one instance each, in this case hillbilly recordings of 1927 and 1928, respectively. Both texts are transcribed here for comparison. Both are textually close to Will Hay's original, more than any others in this family. "The Little Red Caboose (III-C)" was copyrighted on November 29, 1930, with words and music credited to Paul Warmack.

To keep the record complete, I note another "Little Red Caboose behind the Train," published in 1912 by George H. Diamond, with words and music credited to Diamond. I have not found any indication that this version entered hillbilly repertoire or folk tradition. Its chorus goes:

> And at night when we'd lay down to sleep upon our humble cots,
> We would always sing some old familiar strain;
> And the angels they'd watch over us as we lay fast asleep
> In the little red caboose behind the train.

Apart from the actual dates of recovery and the suggested dates of origin of versions III-A/III-D and III-E, it is difficult to assign any chronology to this collection of parodies. If we can believe the attributions in the early *Railroad Man's Magazine* articles, 1877 or thereabout seems a good guess for the first appearance of "The Little Red Caboose." It seems unlikely that the song(s) could have originated much earlier.

There is some justification for regarding these various pieces as simply versions of a single song. Since the textual evidence, however, suggests that recomposition rather than variation better describes the relation of each song to its predecessors, I prefer to regard them as separate songs.

A final problem concerns the tune. All versions of "The Little Red Caboose," as well as other parodies such as "The Little Old Sod Shanty," are sung to the same tune as "The Little Old Cabin in the Lane." However, this is not Will Hays's original melody, but rather the tune of the hymn "Lily of the Valley." Where or when this tune first became associated with that hymn I do not know; hymnals simply state "Old English air" for its source. It is a much more singable tune than Hays's original and bears some resemblance to it, so it is easy to imagine that the one was replaced with the other, and probably early in the song's history—otherwise the parodies would not all share the same melody.

We should note here another copyrighted version of "The Old Log Cabin in the Lane." Copyrighted in 1875, with words and music credited to Grace Carlton and J.C. Chamberlain, respectively, the words show but slight similarity to Will Hays's original text, while the tune is very close to the usual "Lily of the Valley" tune. The text of this version has not, to my knowledge, gone into oral tradition; just what role its tune played is difficult to assess at present.

Nearly thirty-five years ago, another writer, Horace Reynolds, puzzled over the origins of "The Little Red Caboose behind the Train" and its various versions and relatives, although he had at his disposal only a few of the many pieces to this musical jigsaw puzzle.[5] He concluded his report by drawing together the little white church, the little red schoolhouse, and the little red caboose as a trinity of favored American institutions. Modern architectural innovations have practically made obsolete the first two of the trinity, but the red caboose is still a familiar part of our scenery.

NOTES

1. See *DAE*, vol. 1, pp. 381–82; *DA*, pp. 237–38; Alfred H. Holt, *Phrase and Word Origins*, rev. ed. (New York: Dover Publications, 1961), pp. 43–44; Joseph T. Shipley, *Dictionary of Word Origins* (Ames, Iowa: Littlefield, Adams, 1957), p. 63.

2. William F. Knapke and Freeman Hubbard, *The Railroad Caboose* (San Marino, Calif.: Golden West Books, 1968), p. 29. See also Lucius Beebe, *Highball: A Pageant of Trains* (New York: D. Appleton-Century, 1945), pp. 207–23; reprinted, with abridgement, in B. A. Botkin and Alvin F. Harlow, *A Treasury of Railroad Folklore* (New York: Bonanza Books, 1953), pp. 344–49.

3. Austin E. Fife and Alta S. Fife, *Cowboy and Western Songs* (New York: Clarkson N. Potter, 1969), pp. 67–76.

4. For further biographical information on the Pickard Family, and a complete discography, see *JEMFN*, 4 (Dec., 1968), 134–48.

5. Horace Reynolds, "The Little Red Caboose behind the Train," *Tracks*, Aug., 1946, pp. 8–10.

REFERENCES

A. "The Little Red Caboose behind the Train," by the Pickard Family (Mom, Dad, Ruth, Bubb). Vocal and accompaniment. Recorded Jan. 31, 1929 (Plaza master 8515-1), in New York City. Released on Banner 6371, Conqueror 7349, Conqueror 7736, Oriole 1562, Cameo 9278, Romeo 1080, Jewel 5590, Regal 8776, Paramount 3231, Broadway 8179 (as by the Pleasant Family), Lincoln 3305, Domino 4328, Melotone (Canada) 81037, Apex (Canada) 8916, Crown (Canada) 81057, Sterling (Canada) 281057. Reissued on Vetco LP 103: *Songs of the Railroad*. Transcribed here (version III-A).

"The Little Red Caboose behind the Train," by Marion Underwood and Sam Harris. Underwood, vocal and banjo; Harris, vocal and guitar. Recorded ca. Apr., 1927 (Starr master GE-12743A), in Richmond, Ind. Released on Gennett 6155 on Aug. 1, 1927; Champion 15297 (as by the Clinch Valley Boys) on Aug. 1, 1927; Challenge 334 (as by Borton and Thompson); and Herwin 75549. Transcribed here (version III-B).

"The Little Red Caboose behind the Train,"

by Paul Warmack and his Gully Jumpers. Warmack, vocal and mandolin; Charles Arrington, fiddle; Roy Hardison, banjo; Bert Hutcherson, guitar. Recorded Oct. 1, 1928 (Victor master 47105), in Nashville, Tenn. Released on Victor V-40067 in May, 1929. Reissued on RCA Victor LPV 532: *The Railroad in Folksong*. Copyrighted on Nov. 29, 1930 (E unp. 31498), renewed Dec. 3, 1957 (R 203824), words and music credited to Paul Warmack. Transcribed here (version III-C).

B. III-A:

Bassett
Brown III, 263
Cowboy Songs (chorus belongs to III-D)
Family Herald, 46 (references only)
Holbrook, 436 (chorus belongs to III-D)
Kreimer, *RRM*, 75 (Oct., 1964), 26 (chorus belongs to III-D)
Kreimer, *RRM*, 81 (Aug., 1967), 30 (chorus belongs to III-D)
Reynolds, 8–10
RRManM, 7 (Oct., 1908), 189–90
RRManM, 12 (June, 1910), 189–90

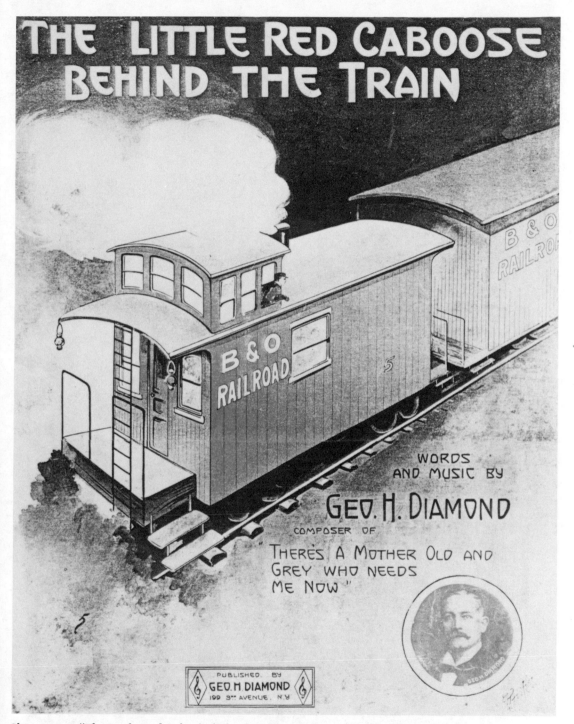

Sheet music: "The Little Red Caboose behind the Train." Courtesy of Daniel B. McCall.

III-D:
RRManM, 6 (Sept., 1908), 760–61

III-E:
RRManM, 7 (Nov., 1908), 382

III-F:
Kreimer, *RRM*, 81 (June, 1967), 36

C. III-A:

COHEN COLLECTION:
Laura Affolter (letter, June, 1968)

GORDON COLLECTION (N.C.):
12—Fred J. Lewey

WKFA:
Cordy V. Goode (handwritten ballet,
    examined 1960)

E. III-A:
Dick Unteed—Rural Rhythm RRDU-199:
*Dick Unteed and the Pine Mountain
Boys*

F. III-A:

GORDON COLLECTION (N.C.):
A12 (MS 12)—Fred J. Lewey

The Gully Jumpers. *Left to right:* Roy Hardison, Charles Arrington, Bert Hutcherson, and Paul Warmack. Courtesy of Douglas B. Green, *Country Roots.*

The Virginian Strike of '23

THE VIRGINIAN STRIKE OF '23

*Falsetto.

In the dear old town of Princeton in the year of twenty-three,
Five hundred railroad employees were as happy as could be;
Enjoying the highest prosperity and nothing to worry them at all,
But they believed in Satan and quit their jobs that fall.
    [*Yodels chorus*:]

They were told from every corner and given good advice,
But they would not listen, and now they've paid the price;
They've roamed to every country, a-waiting for a call,
To report at the Princeton roundhouse, and they've waited six years this fall.
    [*Yodels chorus*:]

The trains are moving nicely from Princeton east and west,
With men of good ability, while the poor boys takes their rest;
Their homes will ever be silent to the call boy's daily call,
Unless the Virginian railroad will call them back this fall.
  [*Yodels chorus*:]

I was one among the number that made the sad mistake,
And left my good old railroad job, my engine did forsake;
And now I'm sure downhearted, for I have no job at all,
But I'd like to run an engine on the Virginian again this fall.
  [*Yodels chorus*:]

Roy Harper and Earl Shirkey

In terms of size, the Virginia Railway was never one of the nation's major freight or passenger carriers. It began life in 1904 as the Tidewater Railway, incorporated to build a line from the West Virginia state line across Virginia to Sewall Point on the Chesapeake Bay. Two hundred and four miles had been completed by 1907, when the name was changed to the Virginian Railway. The same year, the nine-year-old Deepwater Railway of West Virginia was purchased, adding nearly sixty miles of West Virginia track to the operation. Through the 1920s the Virginia trackage totaled approximately five hundred miles, and the company operated some sixty passenger cars, and ten thousand freight cars, used mostly to haul coal.

The Virginian of the 1920s contributed four songs to this book: three ballads dealt with a 1927 two-train collision (See "The Wreck of the Virginian Number Three" in chap. 5); the fourth, with labor troubles of 1923.

The engineers' strike of 1923 came less than two years after an earlier nationwide shop strike affecting the Virginian. The engineers struck on November 8 for a variety of reasons. Complaints that boiler and mechanical deficiencies were not being corrected had gone unheeded. A principal grievance concerned doubleheader trains up Clark's Gap Hill, a steep grade with long tunnels. When two of the big engines were together, it got very hot and gassy in the tunnels, and occasionally the engineer or fireman was overcome by fumes and had to be revived. The engineers wanted the engines separated on the trains. Railroad officials estimated that four to five thousand men went on strike, or two-thirds of the crews. The strikers were threatened with dismissal if they were not back on duty by Saturday morning, the tenth. At the time of the strike, the railroad and the union had been negotiating over differences for nearly a year. The Railroad Labor Board had asked both parties to appear at a hearing on the fourteenth, and requested that the union not strike; but this request went unheeded. Within two months after the walkout, the Virginian had hired other engineers, from other roads as far away as the Union Pacific and the Wabash, to take the place of strikers. Some of the new engineers had never handled a train in mountainous country, and the company suffered financial losses for a while.[1] Within the next year, the Virginian experienced four serious accidents, in three of which the blame was placed on unqualified enginemen at the throttle.[2]

One of the Virginian's engineers at the time was Roy Harvey, a West Virginia musician who recorded several railroad songs during the 1920s: "The Brave Engineer," a variant of "The Wreck on the C & O"; "The Wreck of the Virginian Number Three"; "The Railroad Blues"; "Bill Mason"; "A Hobo's Pal," a variant of "The Dying Hobo"; "The Wreck of the C & O *Sportsman*"; "No Room for a Tramp"; and "Milwaukee Blues."

TAKE THE GREAT AMERICAN

SCAB ROUTE

C. B. & Q.

PREPARE TO MEET THY GOD.

Close Connections with the Hereafter

THROUGH TICKETS TO POINTS ON THE STYX.

N. B-Death Claims Promptly Settled.

PAUL MORTON, G. P. A. M. L.

FROM THE WYMORE DEMOCRAT.

General Prevaricator and Monumental Liar.

The strike is not off, nor will it be until the C. B. & Q. recognizes the fact that it must pay as good wages as its competitors, and then sign a treaty with its old engineers and firemen, who had worked, and been so successful in bringing it up to its former standing and standard of excellence.

The public realize the fact that a railroad like the C. B. & Q. cannot be run with threshing machine engineers and vagrants and drunkards in the places of their old reliable engineers and firemen; and the working men and their friends, or the business public of good judgment will not patronize a road which is at present a menace to life and property, and a road which seeks to crush out an organization which has done more to make traveling a safety than all the companies on this continent combined, by placing competent and sober men on the engines, and an organization which practices industry, sobriety, truth, justice, and morality.

COMMITTEE.

St. Joseph, June 8, 1888.

Broadside: "Take the Great American Scab Route C.B. & Q." Collection of the Chicago Historical Society.

Roy Cecil Harvey was born March 24, 1892, in Greenville, Monroe County, West Virginia. As a child he was always interested in trains, and he started working for the railroad in his teens. After his family moved to Princeton, he went to work for the Virginian. He loved railroading, according to his wife, and worked first as fireman, then as the youngest engineer on the Virginian. A loyal member of the Brotherhood of Locomotive Engineers, Harvey walked off his job when the union struck the Virginian in 1923. His family moved to Beckley, and he worked as a salesman in the Beckley Music Store, gradually becoming interested in phonograph records. The following year he joined Charlie Poole's North Carolina Ramblers as a guitarist, and recorded with that group from September 1926, through their last session in September, 1930. He recorded with other groups as well: with Earl Shirkey he cut "The Railroad Blues," "Hobo's Pal," and "The Virginian Strike of '23"; with the West Virginia Ramblers, "The Wreck of the C & O Sportsman" (see chap. 5).[3]

Roy's partner on his recording of "The Virginian Strike of '23" was Earl Shirkey, also a West Virginia railroader. For a few years he studied in Switzerland, which may be where he learned to yodel.

Roy Harvey's song about the strike reflects bitter disillusionment with the union. Feelings were sharply divided at the time. According to Tom Trautman, Harvey's brother-in-law, most people felt that the union leaders had deceived them; had they known the truth about the causes of the strike, they would not have agreed to walk out. Bernice "Si" Coleman, a West Virginia railroader, musician, and friend of Roy Harvey's, reported that Roy eventually turned against the strikers, and wrote the song hoping it would help him get his job as engineer back.[4] The superintendent and nearly all the other officials were willing; but Charles Hix, the president of the Virginian, was not, and Harvey's efforts came to naught. His song, one of the very few hillbilly recordings of the 1920s to deal with trade unionism, is a rare musical documentary in American railroad and labor lore.

Both Roy Harvey's widow and her brother, Tom Trautman, a railroad fireman for many years, recalled vividly an incident that took place about a year after the strike began. George Reed, a Virginian engineer, had once vowed that God should cut off his hand if he ever scabbed. But September of 1924 found him working for the Virginian as a strike-breaker, taking an eastbound run from Princeton to Roanoke. A landslide near Glen Lyn, about sixteen miles out of Princeton, caused a derailment, and the engine overturned, killing Reed. His arm was severed in the accident.[5]

Harvey set his lyrics to the familiar tune of the cowboy ballad "When the Work's All Done This Fall." That widely known piece, written in 1893 by D. J. O'Malley, was originally set to the tune of Charles K. Harris's 1892 pop hit, "After the Ball." However, the tune to which it is generally sung, and which Harvey and Shirkey used for "The Virginian Strike of '23," is very different.

Through the 1930s Harvey worked at various jobs, including policeman and newspaperman, but was not satisfied until he could get back to railroading. In 1942 he moved to Florida; some former associates on the Virginian had preceded him there, and he went to work for the Florida East Coast Railway. He remained in that company's employ until his death at New Smyrna Beach on July 11, 1958.

"The Virginian Strike of '23" cannot be classed as a folksong, as there is no evidence that it ever got away from its composer—that it entered oral tradition. But then, very few songs tied so closely to a particular historic incident do outlast the memories of those personally involved. Thus the references contain no bibliography; and the discography is confined to two entries: the original Harvey-Shirkey recording of 1929, and a deliberate copy issued in 1966.

The history of the Virginian Railway ended in December, 1956, when the line merged with the Norfolk and Western; it was, in Si Coleman's words, "the best railroad in the world to work for."

NOTES

1. H. Reid, *The Virginian Railway* (Milwaukee: Kalmbach Publishing, 1961), p. 74. See also Archie Green, brochure notes to Folkways FH 5273: *Tipple, Loom & Rail*, p. 11; *New York Times*, Nov. 9, 1923, p. 19.

2. According to the condensed statement of accidents investigated during 1924 and 1925; see *Summary of Accident Investigations Report* (Washington, D.C.: Interstate Commerce Commission, Bureau of Safety, 1926).

3. Biographical information on Roy Harvey is taken principally from interviews by Archie Green and Gene Earle with Maud Trautman, Aug. 13, 1962, and Mary Farley Harvey (Roy's widow), Aug. 14, 1962, both in Beckley, W.Va. A full study of Charlie Poole's popular and influential band, the North Carolina Ramblers, has yet to be published. Interesting accounts are contained in Clifford Kinney Rorrer, *Charlie Poole and the North Carolina Ramblers* (Eden, N.C.: Tar Heel Printing, 1968), and Chris Comber, "Charlie Poole and the North Carolina Ramblers," *Country Record Collector*, No. 8 (May, 1969), pp. 20–25, a brief biography with full discography; see also liner notes to County 505: *Charlie Poole and the North Carolina Ramblers* and brochure notes to Arbor 201: *Charlie Poole and the Highlanders*.

4. Coleman to Cohen, Mar. 14, 1974.

5. Tom Trautman, interviewed by Archie Green and Gene Earle, Aug. 15, 1962, Beckley, W.Va.

REFERENCES

A. "The Virginian Strike of '23," by Roy Harper (Roy Harvey pseudonym) and Earl Shirkey. Harvey, vocal and guitar; Shirkey, yodeling. Recorded Oct. 22, 1929 (Columbia master W149226), in Johnson City, Tenn. Released on Columbia 15535-D on Apr. 30, 1930.

E. Mike Seeger—Folkways FH 5273: *Tipple, Loom & Rail*

12

Life's Railway to Heaven

HOW DOES ONE get to heaven? In his less sophisticated moments of spiritual meditation, man has assumed that heaven has a physical, tangible existence somewhere; therefore, one would get there by the same means he would use to travel to any earthly location. The vehicles that will take us to heaven have been the same vehicles that transport us here on earth, changing only as the limits of our technology expand to include more and more highly developed machinery.

Thus, when Elijah was taken to heaven (2 Kings 2) it was assumed he was borne aloft in a chariot (although the passage does not actually state that). Because of this biblical suggestion of a heavenward ascent by chariot, many early spirituals borrowed that image: "Swing Low Sweet Chariot,"[1] "Roll de Ol' Chariot Along,"[2] "Gwineter Ride Up in de Chariot Soon-a in de Mornin,"[3] and "Good News, Chariot's Coming."[4]

Another early mode of transportation to the place of life ever after was the ship. "The Old Gospel Ship" was in print in the United States by 1853. Other songs about gospel ships in America date back to the 1820s.[5] Jackson notes some German religious songs of the fifteenth century that spoke of a sacred voyage by ship.[6]

It was inevitable that with the coming of the railroads men would envision a new means of travel to heaven. Today, with attitudes toward the railroad so different from a century ago, it is difficult to realize what impact such spiritual trains must have made. But we must also recall that when the railways were first introduced they were vilified and cursed as tools of the devil himself.[7] It must therefore have been an imaginative and venturesome soul who turned the timetables upside down and co-opted the railroad for the service of the Lord.

The ambivalent attitude toward the railroads in their early days is exemplified in the first allegorical use of railway imagery in American prose with which I am familiar: Nathaniel Hawthorne's short story "The Celestial Railroad." This modern religious satire, based on Bunyan's *Pilgrim's Progress*, was first published in 1843, although a reference in another of Hawthorne's works suggests that it was written in 1838.[8] Even if not written before 1843, that would put it a mere thirteen years after the first American railroad was put into regular use. Hawthorne's story takes the form of the dream related by the narrator. It concerns a newly installed railroad to take pilgrims to heaven, replacing the burdensome travel by foot that had previously been the custom; however, in the end the narrator finds out that the train is run by the devil's minions, and there is some question whether the passengers will ever get to the Celestial City.

The theme of the spiritual railway—the allegorical representation of our earthly sojourn as a railroad trip, the ultimate destination of which is heaven—was exploited in many nineteenth-century poems and songs. In extended metaphors such songs designated the path of piety, with the implicit warning that to stray from the route delineated by the steel rails of righteousness would lead elsewhere but heaven.

Not long after Hawthorne's "Celestial Railroad," if indeed not earlier, the broadside presses began to turn out similar railroad allegories. An early example, printed by H. Such of England, probably in the 1840s, was "The Railway to Heaven." This broadside (reproduced here) is especially interesting because of its allusions to various sectarian differences among the English Protestants.

The magazines for railroad men (and, it should be remembered, for their wives) were filled with such pieces. In 1876, the *Locomotive Engineers' Monthly Journal* printed "The Railroad Way to Glory," to be sung to the tune of "Missionary Hymn." On this railroad, the ticket was True Religion; the train, the Through-Express to Heaven:

> The Engineer is Jesus, the road in good repair;
> We hope you will go with us—
> His blood has paid the fare.
> Come in at any station!—The first is always best;
> The car of Free Salvation is better than the rest.[9]

This song is unique among those about spiritual railways in its theological message—that salvation is guaranteed by Jesus, and need not be purchased with the wages of a life of righteous toil.

"The Engine," published the following year, compared the human being himself to the engine, steaming along "the narrow track of fearless Truth":

> Oh! what am I but an Engine, shod
> With muscle and flesh by the hand of God,
> Speeding on through the deep, dark night,
> Guided alone by the soul's white light?[10]

M. A. Bigelow, in "Waiting at the Junction," dwelt on the frequent retrograde motions and pauses of a real railroad journey, noting that they all had their purpose. Likewise, in our spiritual travels:

> Thus upon the life's real journey,
> Speeding toward the sky,
> Oft we wait, or moving backward,
> Ask the reason why.
>
> In our steady vain endeavor
> After fortune's smile,
> We may see our hopes elude us
> As we wait awhile.

. . . .

> We shall end our toilsome journey,
> Reach our home of rest,
> And we feel our great Conductor
> Knoweth what is best.[11]

In April, 1881, the members of the Clinton Division of the Brotherhood of Locomotive Engineers were entertained at their sociable with an essay by Miss Rye Nelson titled "Life." It began in prose: "Life is like a train passing swiftly on its course, and dashes on like a meteor over the wide-extending plain, far beyond our sight . . ." and concluded with a poem:

> There you will engineer no longer,
> Keep on the heavenly track;
> Be faithful, then, my brother,
> Never think of turning back.
>
> Each day the road grows shorter,
> Heaven's station keep in view,
> Simple rule and safest guiding,
> Inward peace and inward light.
>
> Then when your labor is ended,
> And all your trials over,
> You will then be safely landed
> Where parting is no more.[12]

In 1885, the *Locomotive Engineers' Monthly Journal* published Clyde St. Claire's "Life on the Rail." The concluding stanzas read:

> Danger, ay, death, hovers near us—
> Not a man of us dwells on the thought;
> We shovel the diamonds, nor tremble
> That each moment with peril is fraught.
>
> One with his hand on the throttle,—
> One with his hand on the spade;—
> God bless them and keep them, brave fellows,
> Through life's checkered sunshine and shade.[13]

A few years later, the *Railroad Trainmen's Journal* published a carefully constructed allegorical poem, "Life's Railroad." In this view, each of us is the conductor on his own train of life, and many of us wreck our trains for want of proper preparation:

> All on board are lost for the want of a hand
> To turn it from the road to destruction.
> So it takes the side track, leaps over the gap
> And goes headlong to perdition.
> Too late to reverse or whistle down brakes
> Or to ring the brazen throat bell.
> While with hands on the throttle the engineer stands
> And gazes in awe at the dark gates of hell.

But if the train engineer is well equipped for the journey, the ending is happily different:

THE RAILWAY TO HEAVEN.

This Line runs from Calvary through this vain world and the Valley of
the Shadow of Death, until it lands in the kingdom of Heaven.

London :—H. Such, Printer & Publisher,
177, Union-street, Boro'. —S. E.

OH ! what a deal we hear and read,
    About Railways and Railway speed !
Of lines which are, or may be made,
And selling shares is quite a trade.

The Railway mania does extend,
From John O'Greats to the Land's End ;
Where'er you ride, where'er you walk,
The Railway is the general talk.

Allow me, as an old divine,
To point you to another line,
Which does from earth to heaven extend,
Where real pleasures never end.

Infinite wisdom sketched the plan
To save apostate, ruined man ;
And Jesus Christ, Jehovah's son,
The mighty work Himself has done.

Of truth Divine the rails are made,
And on the Rock of Ages laid ;
The rails are fixed in chairs of love,
Firm as the throne of God above.

At Calvary's cross it does commence,
And runs through all the world from thence ;
Then crosses Jordan's swelling flood,
Before the royal throne of God.

One grand first class is used for all,
For Jew and Gentile, great and small ;
There's room for all the world inside,
And kings with beggars there do ride.

In days of old, for ever past,
Men quarrelled about first and last ;
And each contended loud and long,
My church is right, and yours is wrong.

We're next the engine, some would say,
Our carriage here does lead the way ;
But oft we see the train reversed—
The first is last, the last is first.

Let no one of his carriage boast,
Nor in his outward duties trust :
Those who shall see the Saviour's face,
Must be renewed by asking grace.

About a hundred years or so,
Wesley and others said they'd go :
A carriage mercy did provide,
That Wesley and his friends might ride.

'Tis nine and thirty years, they say,
Whoever lives to see next May,
Another coach was added then,
Unto this all important train.

Linked to each other, on we pass,
Supported by the Saviour's grace ;
When to the better land we come,
We'll mix together round the throne.

Jesus is the first engineer,
He does the gospel engine steer ;
The preachers of the sacred Word,
Co-workers with their dying Lord.

We've guards who ride, while others stand
Close by the way with flag in hand,—
The flag of white, of red, and green,
At different places may be seen.

When we behold the flag that's white,
It cheers the heart, for all is right ;
But when the green we do behold,
Caution, it says, and be not bold.

Red tells us there is danger near,
Be not high-minded, rather fear ;
Place all your trust in God alone,
And in the blood which does atone.

Then let not poor nor rich despair,
He still delights to answer prayer ;
Remember he will not despise
Your humble wailings—mournful cries.

Afflictions are the tunnels drear
Through which we go while travelling here ;
But these will all be shortly past,
And heaven appear in view at last.

To cheer the dark and gloomy night,
We've lamps which give a brilliant light,
And while we urge our course along,
The cross of Christ is all our song.

We've several laws about this road,
Wrote by the finger of our God ;
Ye trespassers must all beware,
For He the guilty will not spare.

No one from his place must alight,
Until he hears the words, all right ;
And when this glorious signal's given,
You'll hear a whisper, ' This is Heaven !'

The stations are the means of grace,
The house of God, the holy place ;
No matter where that place may be,
A field, a barn, or hollow tree.

You say you will not ride with me,
Well, be it so, we still agree ;
The church of England is before
The Quakers, yea, and several more.

Baptists, and Independents too,
The Methodists both old and new ;
I can, I will, I do rejoice,
That you have such a happy choice.

CHORUS.

" My son," says God, " give me thy heart,"
Make haste, or else the train will start.

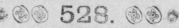 528.

> So the old train of life rolls away in the distance
> Laden with souls that are heavenward bound.
> But many a-light at the little side "stations"
> She moves slowly on, at the curve passes round
> So when at length the journey is ended
> May you on board with the passengers be,
> Who turned not aside, but attended the signals
> And alighted at last in Eternity.[14]

Another anonymous poem of the same year was entitled "The Road of Life." It began:

> A wonderful branch is this road of life;
> 'Tis built thro' the valley of fears;
> Time is the name by which it is known;
> It unites with the road called tears.
>
> There's many a grade on this road of life,
> And at times the train pulls hard;
> Then the trainmen must be firm and true,
> And never found off their guard.[15]

Eighteen ninety-two saw publication of Mrs. Frank W. Munson's "Life's Journey":

> We board the train of life with eager longing,
> The untried journey all before us lies;
> How high our hopes, how great our aspirations,
> How bright and cloudless are our morning skies!
>
> The journey, bright or sad, will soon be ended,
> And in that day our Saviour we must meet
> With empty arms, and speechless; or with gladness
> The golden grain to scatter at his feet.[16]

By the turn of the century, the ink began to run dry in this outpouring of poems of spiritual railways, although a few new ones did appear. Two such compositions were published in *Railroad Man's Magazine* in 1910. One anonymous piece, "The Right Track," began:

> Are you upon the right track, my friend?
> Are you running upon the right rail?
> The way is long and the pace is swift,
> And you want to be sure of the trail.
>
> Don't open the throttle and give her steam,
> Through the day so bright and night so black,
> Unless you are sure your way is secure,
> Unless you're upon the right track.

It ended:

> The station, Reward, is the terminal
> For the engine that never turns back;
> There is joy for you when your train is due,
> If you've made it upon the right track.[17]

William G. Hammond's "Life's Railroad" was written expressly for *Railroad Man's Magazine* and used technical language and slang familiar to railroaders. Such a poem would probably not have been published in the early brotherhood journals, since literary contributions to those periodicals were generally printed in the ladies' section, the readers of which may not have been well versed in occupational argot.

> Did you ever take time to consider
> The lives we are living each day—
> Are we helping ourselves, and our neighbors
> Along the unballasted way?
>
> Is our road-bed the best we can make it?
> Are the ties and the rails all set true?
> Are the fish-plates secure and well leveled?
> Are we always marked up, "overdue"?
>
> And when our last trip is completed,
> And we step down all covered with grime,
> The operator will send in his O.S.
> And say that we got there on time. [18]

Against this backdrop of frequent poems about spiritual railways, "Life's Railway to Heaven," the only piece of the genre to achieve wide and lasting popularity, may be put in proper perspective. While other compositions of the same period straggled off at stations along the way, the direct simplicity of M. E. Abbey's words, forceful in imagery, yet graceful in construction and devoid of any special lingo, combined with Charles Tillman's captivating melody to endow their song with a permanent seat on the musical railroad to heaven. The song seems no less popular now than three-quarters of a century ago. Possibly it was the popularity of "Life's Railway to Heaven" that inspired the Reverend Andrew Jenkins, prolific composer of hillbilly songs, to write "The Railroad of Life" in 1926.

Three of the songs in this chapter are revival spirituals. According to George Pullen Jackson, these songs developed in the nineteenth century to fill the musical needs of the camp-meeting institution. [19] Their primary requirement was that they have simple words and melodies, so that they could be sung by large outdoor gatherings of people who had no recourse to hymn books. Spirituals evolved out of the older religious folk hymns by a process of steady simplification of text. The typical form was a short stanza of four lines followed by a chorus of the same length. In its most simplified form, three of the four stanzaic lines (and sometimes even all four) were textually identical. In this chapter, "The Gospel Train Is Coming," "This Train," and "When the Train Comes Along" can be classified as spirituals. Their dates of composition have not been established, but all seem to stem from the mid-nineteenth century. "The *Gospel Cannonball*" shares with them the theme of a train that will come to take the faithful to the Master at the end of their earthly toils; but stylistically it belongs to a later period, that of the gospel song. The three spirituals included—and many others not in this book—are alike in making no moral preachments; each is predicated on the assumption that the listener/singer is going to heaven. This assertion is violated only in a metaphorical way; for example, the first stanza of Vaughan's "The Glory Train" concludes, "If you want to go get your ticket and be ready, for this train may come today." Only if "ticket" symbolizes the approved moral or religious conduct can this phrase be taken to be hortatory.

This chapter offers but a small sampling of the wealth of compositions about heaven-bound trains. Many of these songs have entered oral tradition. Others that have been collected or published and that probably date from the nineteenth century include "Git on de Evening Train,"[20] "If I Have My Tickit Lawd,"[21] "The Gospel Train,"[22] "Oh, Be Ready When the Train Comes In,"[23] "The Train Is A-Coming,"[24] "How Long de Train Been Gone,"[25] "Gospel Train,"[26] and "I'm Going Home on the Morning Train."[27]

Train imagery also figured prominently in the many sermon/song combinations recorded in the 1920s by black singing preachers. This genre (not treated here) included the Reverend A. W. Nix's "Black Diamond Express to Hell," Parts 1 and 2 (Vocalion 1098, 1927) and Parts 3 and 4 (Vocalion 1421, 1929), and "The White Flyer to Heaven," Parts 1 and 2 (Vocalion 1170, 1927); the Reverend J. C. Burnett's "The Gospel Train Is Leaving" (Columbia 14180-D, 1926); and the Reverend J. M. Gates's "Death's Black Train Is Coming" (Columbia 14145-D, 1926; Pathé 7514, 1926; Victor 20211, 1926; Domino 3872, Romeo 400, Oriole 794, and Conqueror 7080, all 1926), "Funeral Train" (Victor 20217, 1926), "Hell-Bound Express Train" (OKeh 8532, 1927), and "I'm Going Home on the Heavenbound Train" (OKeh 8827, 1930). Some of these were among the most popular releases in the race record series of the late 1920s.

In the 1930s and later, the train image was still being used by writers of gospel songs, although few of the compositions achieved great popularity. One exception is O. Mac-Leod's "That Glory Bound Train," which is widely known thanks to the 1946 recording by Roy Acuff.

Departing from the same station but headed in the opposite direction are the trains depicted in "The Hell-Bound Train" and "Little Black Train." Aside from being destined for hell rather than heaven, these songs differ from the preceding group in that they are admonitory, warning listeners that their own behavior determines which train they will ride on. Such songs can be found on English and American broadsides of the nineteenth century; a more recent example is Cliff Carlisle's "The Devil's Train."

In some allegorical railroad songs, the train comes to carry away the passengers from this world to the hereafter, but the same train goes to two destinations. For example, "The Funeral Train" concludes:

> This funeral train that I am singing about,
> It has neither whistle nor bell;
> But when you reach your station,
> It will either be Heaven or Hell.[28]

As technology advances, more modern imagery replaces the once-familiar notions of railroads to heaven or hell. Now we hear of "The Automobile of Life," recorded by Roy Acuff in 1938. Earlier, Mother McCollum sang "Jesus Is My Air-O-Plane" on a 1930 Vocalion recording. In another version of that song, the replacement of the train by the airplane is made explicit:

> Full salvation is the engine's name,
> Oil in the vessel to run just the same;
> So goodbye, Fords, and also the trains,
> We are going on to glory in the airoplane.[29]

It can be only a matter of time before some modern-day songwriter recounts an astronaut's heavenward voyage. And what will be left after that? Sci-fi enthusiasts already know about teleportation; somehow, this seems a much more appropriate way to get to heaven.

Advertisement in the *Chicago Defender*, October 1, 1927. Author's Collection.

NOTES

1. John W. Work, *American Negro Songs and Spirituals* (New York: Bonanza Books, 1940), p. 152; Gustavus D. Pike, *The Jubilee Singers, and Their Campaign for Twenty Thousand Dollars* (Boston: Lee and Shepard, 1873), p. 166; Lydia Parrish, *Slave Songs of the Georgia Sea Islands* (1942; rpt., Hatboro, Pa.: Folklore Associates, 1965), p. 166.

2. James Weldon Johnson and J. Rosamond Johnson, *The Book of American Negro Spirituals* (1925; rpt., New York: Viking Press, 1969), p. 110.

3. James Weldon Johnson and J. Rosamond Johnson, *The Second Book of American Negro Spirituals* (1926; rpt., New York: Viking Press, 1969), p. 121; Pike, *Jubilee Singers*, p. 178; recorded by Plantation Singers, Varsity 6022.

4. *Hampton and Its Students*, by Two of Its Teachers, Mrs. M. F. Armstrong and Helen W. Ludlow, with Fifty Cabin and Plantation Songs, as Sung by the Hampton Students, arranged by Thomas P. Fenner (New York: G. P. Putnam's Sons, 1874), pp. 224–25. The music section was later published separately as *Cabin and Plantation Songs as Sung by the Hampton Students,* arranged by Thomas P. Fenner, Frederic G. Rathbun, and Bessie Cleaveland (New York: G. P. Putnam's Sons, 1901); in this edition the song appears on p. 52. Later, the collection was published under the title *Religious Folk Songs of the Negro* (Hampton, Va.: Institute Press, 1909), edited by R. N. Dett; in this edition the song appears on p. 52.

5. Newman I. White, *American Negro Folk-Songs* (1928; rpt., Hatboro, Pa.: Folklore Associates, 1965), p. 93.

6. George Pullen Jackson, *Spiritual Folk-Songs of Early America* (New York, J. J. Augustin, 1937), p. 212.

7. See chap. 1.

8. "The Celestial Railroad" first appeared in the *United States Democratic Review,* 12 (May, 1843), 515–23. It was reprinted in the collection *Mosses from an Old Manse* (1846). In his introduction to the story "Rappaccini's Daughter," Hawthorne writes that the imaginary French author of that tale, M. Aubepine, wrote "Le Voyage Céleste à Chemin de Fer" in 1838.

9. *LEMJ*, 10 (Apr., 1876), 127.

10. Ibid., 11 (Apr., 1877), 107.

11. Ibid., 12 (Jan., 1878), 67.

12. Ibid., 15 (May, 1881), 225. Only three verses are given here.

13. Ibid., 19 (Aug., 1885), 475.

14. *RTJ*, 8 (Dec., 1891), 889.

15. Ibid., 8 (Apr., 1891), 251.

16. *LEMJ*, 26 (Aug., 1892), 707.

17. *RRManM*, 11 (Mar., 1910), 383.

18. Ibid., 11 (Apr., 1910), 404.

19. Jackson, *Spiritual Folk-Songs*, p. 7.

20. W. E. Barton, "Recent Negro Melodies," *New England Magazine*, 19 (Feb., 1899), 707; reprinted in *The Negro and His Folklore in Nineteenth-Century Periodicals*, edited by Bruce Jackson (Austin: University of Texas Press, 1967), pp. 302–26.

21. Mary Allen Grissom, *The Negro Sings a New Heaven* (1930, rpt., New York: Dover Publication, 1969), p. 83.

22. By C. Austin Miles, printed in *RRM*, 35 (Feb., 1918), 352.

23. Dorothy Scarborough, *On the Trail of Negro Folk-Songs* (1925; rpt., Hatboro, Pa.: Folklore Associates, 1963), p. 258; there is also a copy in WKFA.

24. Scarborough, *On the Trail*, p. 253.

25. Nicholas George Julius Ballanta(-Taylor), *Saint Helena Island Spirituals* (New York; G. Schirmer, 1925), p. 12.

26. E. A. McIlhenny, *Befo' de War Spirituals* (Boston: Christopher Publishing House, 1933), p. 107.

27. E. C. Perrow, "Songs and Rhymes from the South," *JAF*, 26 (Apr.-June, 1913), 162.

28. Scarborough, *On the Trail*, p. 262.

29. WKFA, ballet book of Walter Pearson, Alvaton, Ky., written Jan., 1929.

I'm Going Home to Die No More/The Railway Spiritualized

I'M GOING HOME TO DIE NO MORE

*On the recording, the chords in parentheses are played on a piano, on which quick changes sound more natural than on a guitar. The performer may thus wish to omit them if a guitar is being used.

The road to heaven by Christ was made,
With heavenly tools the rails were laid;
From earth to heaven the line extends,
To life eternal, where it ends.

I'm going home, I'm going home, I'm going home,
To die no more, to die no more, to die no more,
I'm going home to die no more.

Repentance is the station there,
Where passengers are taken in;
No fee for them is there to pay,
For Jesus is Himself the way.

Chorus:

Blue Ridge Gospel Singers

This brief fragment is the recorded legacy of what may very well be the oldest poetic use of railroad imagery in a religious context. Its ancestor is "The Railway Spiritualized," a poem that has appeared in print frequently—and with considerable variation from printing to printing—often with different attributions of origin. There is no evidence that it was originally a song, although it has been set to music in this century. But even before 1900 the extent of variation suggests that it may have been sung or recited from memory. H. M. Belden, who obtained a text from the manuscript ballad-book of a Missouri woman, noted two British broadside printings of the nineteenth century.[1] The UCLA Special Collections Library owns a third London broadside (reproduced here) that is of special interest.[2] Titled "The Spiritual Railway," this sheet displays two ballads side by side. One, "The Upward Line," is the poem in question; the other, "The Down Line," is a parody on its better-known companion.

In this country another version was published by Andrews, a New York broadside printer. At the head of this broadside are the instructions "can be sung to any Long Metre tune." The editors of *The New Green Mountain Songster* noted an undated print in Phillips Barry's broadside collection with the byline "Written by Tecumseh, the eldest son of Chief Maungwudaus, who is now a Missionary among the Chippeway Indians."[3] Unlike the Andrews broadside, this one does not contain the chorus, which supplies the title for the version transcribed at the head of this section. The earliest dated printing in this country I have found is from 1868, when an abridged version was published in the *Locomotive Engineers' Monthly Journal*.[4] *Railroad Man's Magazine* published a short fragment in 1918 with the headnote "The following lines were found in a railway station in England, and supposed to have been written by a gentleman while detained there, and are very old."[5] Allsop quoted excerpts from the poem, which he said "are to be found on a tombstone in Ely Cathedral, commemorating the victims of a Norfolk railway smash in 1845."[6] An answer to a 1910 request in the *Boston Evening Transcript* led me to *Chamber's Journal* for 1854, where, in a review of the book *The Voices of Our Exiles, or Stray Leaves from a Convict Ship*, the poem was quoted with this note: "A housebreaker, who had previously suffered imprisonment for another crime, furnishes 'The Railway Spiritualised'—not honestly come by we fear, though the editor is sanguine on the point."[7] This anonymous reviewer evidently assumes that the poem is older than 1854, the date of publication of *Voices*, a collection of poems by "thieves, burglars, forgers, and fire-raisers"; but I have been unable to find an earlier printing. The 1854 text follows:

> The line to heaven by Christ was made,
> With heavenly grace its rails are laid;
> From earth to heaven the way extends,
> To grace eternal, where it ends.
>
> Repentance is the station, then,
> Where passengers are taken in;
> No fee is there for them to pay,
> For Jesus heralds all the way.
>
> The Bible is the engineer,
> That points the way to heaven clear;
> Through tunnels dark, 'neath mountains high,
> It guides the pilgrim to the sky.
>
> Truth is the fire, and Love the steam
> Which moves the engine and the train.
> Hence, all who would to glory ride,
> Must come to Christ, and there abide.
>
> In the first, second, or third class.
> By faith, repentance, holiness,
> You must the prize of glory gain,
> Or you with Christ will never reign.

> Come, then, poor sinner! Now's the time,
> At any station on the line!
> If you repent and turn from sin,
> The train will stop and take you in!

The American Andrews broadside is ten stanzas in length—four more than the 1854 text or most of the others that have been printed. Yet it is impossible to state with certainty whether it is earlier or later.

The earliest musical setting I have found is in the 1901 *Gospel Gleaner*, where the song is titled "The Gospel Railroad."[8] A different tune was used in the 1916 *Golden Gospel Bells*, under the title "I'm Going Home."[9] In both of these books authorship is attributed to Mrs. Hall Booth; no source is given for the tunes. The editors of *The New Green Mountain Songster* set their manuscript text to the air of "My Heavenly Home," inasmuch as that hymn has the same "I'm going home to die no more" refrain. I have not seen their source for that hymn, J. W. Dadmun's *Aeolian Harp*, but suspect their song to be the same as "To Die No More," with the opening line "My heavenly home is bright and fair. . ." and this refrain:

> I'm going home to Christ above,
> I'm going to the Christian's rest.
> To die no more, to die no more,
> I'm going home to die no more.[10]

Since the earliest dated versions in print do not contain this refrain, it seems reasonable to conclude that it was a later addition, and did provide at least one tune. I have not seen the song in print after 1942; however, it has not been completely forgotten, inasmuch as *Old Time Songs and Poems* carried a request for it in 1968.[11]

The version transcribed in this book was recorded by the Blue Ridge Gospel Singers, a group consisting of Kentucky-born Buell Kazee, a Baptist minister, and Lester O'Keefe, an employee of the recording company, Brunswick-Balke-Collender, backed by three instrumentalists. The recording was made in New York in 1927. Kazee was one of the few hillbilly artists of the 1920s who had a clear image both of "hilllbilly" and "folk" music and of his own role in disseminating traditional music to a sophisticated city audience. A rather polished and self-conscious singing style, as well as considerable skill on the banjo, made his music acceptable to an audience much wider than that reached by many of his fellow mountain folk. In concerts, his weaving together musical examples with narrative about life in the Appalachians was as educational as it was enjoyable. In the 1960s he enjoyed a revival of popularity with college audiences, and in June, 1975, he was still appearing at folk festivals, at the age of seventy-five.[12] He died in 1976.

Buell Kazee learned "I'm Going Home to Die No More" as a child from his family; the song was traditional and current in his part of the mountains at the time of his birth.[13]

NOTES

1. Henry M. Belden, *Ballads and Songs Collected by the Missouri Folk-Lore Society*, 2d ed. (Columbia: University of Missouri Press, 1955), p. 468.
2. "The Spiritual Railway," printed by H. Such, broadside no. 734 (London, n.d.).
3. Helen Hartness Flanders et al., *The New Green Mountain Songster* (1939; rpt., Hatboro, Pa.: Folklore Associates, 1966), p. 54.
4. *LEMJ*, 2 (Apr., 1868), 101.
5. *RRManM*, 36 (Aug., 1918), 768.

THE SPIRITUAL RAILWAY.

734.   734.

THE UPWARD LINE.

THE line to Heaven by Christ is made,
   With Heavenly truth the rails are laid ;
From Earth to Heaven the line extends,
And in eternal life it ends.

Repentance is the station, then,
Where passengers are taken in—
No fee for them is there to pay,
For Jesus is himself the way.

God's word is the first Engineer,
It points the way to Heaven so clear,
Through tunnels dark and dreary there,
It does the way to glory steer.

God's love the fire, His grace the steam,
Which drives the engine and the train,
All you who would to glory ride,
Must come to Christ in him abide.

In first, second and third class—
Repentance, faith, and holiness—
You must the way to glory gain,
Or you with Christ can never reign.

Come, then poor sinner, now's the time,
At any station on the line,
If you'll repent, turn from sin,
The train will stop and take you in.

If all these trains should by you pass,
And you are found in neither class,—
When neither truth, or fire, or steam,
Can make you willing to get in.

Then sinners you will weep at last,
When Heaven is lost, and time is past—
The Heavenly train are all gone by,
The sinner must for ever die.

When all these trains at Heaven arrive,
With all who did in Christ abide,
How sweet their voices, how they sing,
And praise their great eternal King,

The King eternal on his throne,
Announces that the trains are come,
There robes are ready to put on.
And Jesus says the words " well done."

THE DOWN LINE.

THERE is a Railway downward laid,
   Which God the Father never made,
But it was laid when Adam fell—
What numbers it conveys to Hell.

Six thousand years are nearly gone,
Since first this Railway was begun,
The road is wide, and smooth, and gay,
And there are stations on the way.

Appollyon is the Engineer,
His coat of arms his servants wear,
The steam his breath, which drives the train,
The fire is sin, which feeds the flame.

The first, second, and third class,
Are full of passengers within,
The steam is up, the flag unfurled,
How quick they move to yonder world.

Her fortunes smiles, and pleasures gay,
At every station on the way,
Her dress and fashion you may find,
Of every sort and every kind.

The cheerful glass is drank with glee,
And cards and music you may see—
Both old and young, rich and poor,
All standing near the station door.

Appollyon now begins to boast,
Of numbers great—a mighty host,
Who are inclined their place to take,
To travel downward to the lake.

Oh ! think on this while yet you may,
And stop your speed without delay,
Oh ! leave the train that leads to Hell,
If you with Christ would ever dwell.

London :—H. SUCH, Machine Printer & Publisher, 177, Union Street, Boro'. S. E.

Ladies and Gentlemen it is true that some trades are flourishing, while others are in a state of starvation, the bearers are, and have been out of employment a considerable time, and being destitute, and also strangers in this part of the country, they offer these few verses for sale, (hoping that you will become purchasers of us poor tradesmen.)

Broadside printed by H. Such: "The Spiritual Railway." UCLA Special Collections Library.

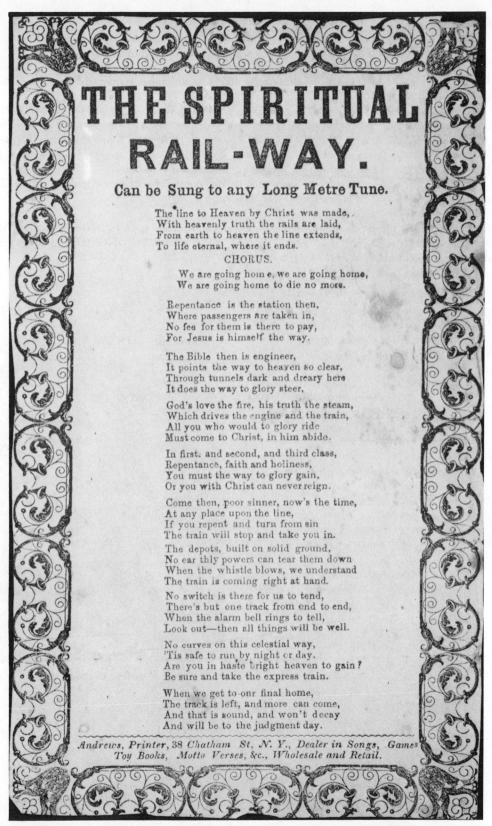

THE SPIRITUAL RAIL-WAY.

Can be Sung to any Long Metre Tune.

The line to Heaven by Christ was made,
With heavenly truth the rails are laid,
From earth to heaven the line extends,
To life eternal, where it ends.

CHORUS.

We are going home, we are going home,
We are going home to die no more.

Repentance is the station then,
Where passengers are taken in,
No fee for them is there to pay,
For Jesus is himself the way.

The Bible then is engineer,
It points the way to heaven so clear,
Through tunnels dark and dreary here
It does the way to glory steer,

God's love the fire, his truth the steam,
Which drives the engine and the train,
All you who would to glory ride
Must come to Christ, in him abide.

In first, and second, and third class,
Repentance, faith and holiness,
You must the way to glory gain,
Or you with Christ can never reign.

Come then, poor sinner, now's the time,
At any place upon the line,
If you repent and turn from sin
The train will stop and take you in.

The depots, built on solid ground,
No earthly powers can tear them down
When the whistle blows, we understand
The train is coming right at hand.

No switch is there for us to tend,
There's but one track from end to end,
When the alarm bell rings to tell,
Look out—then all things will be well.

No curves on this celestial way,
'Tis safe to run by night or day.
Are you in haste bright heaven to gain?
Be sure and take the express train.

When we get to our final home,
The track is left, and more can come,
And that is sound, and won't decay
And will be to the judgment day.

Andrews, Printer, 38 *Chatham St. N. Y., Dealer in Songs, Games Toy Books, Motto Verses, &c., Wholesale and Retail.*

Broadside printed by Andrews: "The Spiritual Rail-Way." UCLA Special Collections Library.

6. Kenneth Allsop, *Hard Travellin'* (London: Hodder and Stoughton, 1967), p. 280.

7. "Convict Literature," a review of *The Voices of Our Exiles, or Stray Leaves from a Convict Ship,* edited by Daniel Ritchie (Edinburgh, 1854), in *Chamber's Journal,* June 24, 1854, pp. 389–90.

8. F. L. Eiland et al., *The Gospel Gleaner* (Waco, Tex., and Memphis, Tenn.: Trio Music, 1901), no. 125.

9. *Golden Gospel Bells for Sunday-Schools, Conventions, etc., and General Use in Christian Work and Worship* (Lawrenceburg, Tenn.: James D. Vaughan, 1916), no. 67. I am indebted to Harlan Daniel for making this and the preceding item available to me.

10. C. H. Cayce, *The Good Old Songs,* rev. ed. (Thornton, Ark.: Cayce Publishing, 1967), pp. 214–15 (no. 363). Melody credited to E. Dumas.

11. *OTS&P,* May-June, 1968, p. 34.

12. For further biographical information on Buell Kazee, see *Sing Out!,* 20 (Sept.-Oct., 1970), 13–17, 58; and Loyal Jones, "Buell Kazee," *JEMFQ,* 14 (Summer, 1978), 57–67. A complete 78 rpm discography was published in *JEMFQ,* 6 (Spring, 1970), 19–22.

13. Kazee to Cohen, May 19, 1975.

REFERENCES

A. "I'm Going Home to Die No More," by the Blue Ridge Gospel Singers. Buell Kazee and Lester O'Keefe, vocals; Carson Robison, guitar; Bert Hirsch, violin; Bill Wirges, piano. Recorded Apr. 20, 1927 (Brunswick master E22530), in New York City. Released on Brunswick 152 in Sept., 1927.

B. Allsop, 280
   Andrews (New York printer), undated
      broadside   "The Spiritual Rail-Way"
   Belden (1955), 468
   Eiland (Song #125)
   Flanders et al. 53–54
   Glass & Singer, 18–19
   Golden Gospel Bells (Song #67)
   LEMJ, 2 (Apr., 1868), 101
   Randolph IV, 24   "The Road to Heaven"
   RRManM, 36 (Aug., 1918), 768
   Such, H. (London printer), undated
      broadside, #734   "The Spiritual
      Railway"

F. LC AFS:
   Rufus Crisp—AFS 8527 B

Buell Kazee. Courtesy of Loyal Jones.

Life's Railway to Heaven

LIFE'S RAILWAY TO HEAVEN

*This unusual meter is employed here as the waltz-time counterpart of cut time (¢ or 2/2) in order to indicate that here, as in cut time, the guitar accompaniment consists of one bass note and strum for each half-note.

**On the recording, the change to G occurs one beat later.

***On the recording, the change to G occurs one beat earlier.

Life is like a mountain railroad, with an engineer that's brave,
We must make the run successful from the cradle to the grave;
Watch the curves, the fills, the tunnels, never falter, never fail,
Keep your hand upon the throttle and your eye upon the rail.

Blessed savior, thou will guide us till we reach the blissful shore,
Where the angels wait to join us in thy praise forevermore.

As you roll up grades of trial, you will cross the bridge of strife;
See that Christ is your conductor on the lightning train of life;
Always mindful of obstruction, do your duty, never fail,
Keep your hand upon the throttle and your eye upon the rail.
    Chorus:

As you roll across the trestle look for storm or wind and rain,
On a curve or fill or trestle they will almost ditch your train;
Put your trust alone in Jesus, never falter, never fail,
Keep your hand upon the throttle and your eye upon the rail.
    Chorus:

As you roll across the trestle, spanning death's dark swelling tide,
You behold the union depot into which your train will glide;
There you'll meet the superintendent, God the Father, God the Son,
With a hearty joyous plaudit [*pronounced "plaudy-it"*], weary
    pilgrim, welcome home.

Ernest Thompson

A popular hymn for nine decades, "Life's Railway to Heaven" continues to be a favorite among bluegrass, country-and-western, gospel, folk-rock, and folk singers. In its present form the song was copyrighted January 18, 1890 (2660; renewed Dec. 29, 1917), words credited to M. E. Abbey and music to the publisher, Charles D. Tillman, a well-known figure in the field of religious music in Atlanta in the early decades of the century.

However, the song was modeled closely after an older poem written by the prominent songwriter of the 1860s and 1870s, William Shakespeare Hays, the author of such favorites as "The Little Old Cabin in the Lane," "Mollie Darling," and "The Drummer Boy of Shiloh." The piece in question, "The Faithful Engineer," was published in Hays's 1886 collection of songs and poems in the section subtitled "Poems."[1] It is reprinted here:

THE FAITHFUL ENGINEER

Life is like a crooked railroad,
    And the engineer is brave,
Who can make a trip successful
    From the cradle to the grave,
There are stations all along it,
    Where at almost any breath
You'll be "flagged" to stop your engine
    By the messenger of death.
You may run the grades of trouble,
    Many days and years of ease,
But time may have you side-tracked
    By the switchman of disease.

You may cross the bridge of manhood,
   Run the tunnel dark of strife,
Having God for your conductor
   On the lightning train of life.
Always mindful of instructions,
   Watchful duty never lack;
Keep your hand upon the throttle
   And your eye upon the track.

Name your engine "True Religion."
   When you're running day or night,
Use the coal of Faith for fuel,
   And she'll always run you right.
You need never fear of sticking
   On the up-grades 'long the road;
If you've got Hope for a fireman
   You can always pull the load.
You will often find obstructions
   By the cunning devil lain,
On a hill, or curve, or trestle,
   Where he'll try to "ditch your train."
But you needn't fear disaster;
   "Jerk her open! Let her go!"
For the General Superintendent
   All his plans will overthrow.
Put your trust in God, and fear not
   Keep a-going, don't look back;
Keep your hand upon the throttle
   And your eye upon the track.

When you've made the trip successful,
   And you're at your journey's end,
You will find the angels waiting
   To receive you as a friend.
You'll approach the Superintendent,
   Who is waiting for you now,
With a word of proud promotion
   And a crown to deck your brow.
Never falter in your duty;
   Put your faith and trust in Him,
And you'll always find your engine
   In the best of running trim.
Ring your bell and blow your whistle;
   Never let your courage slack;
Keep your hand upon the throttle
   And your eye upon the track.

Hays reprinted his poem, but with a different title, "Old Hayseed's Railroad Idea of

Life," in 1895.[2] This version was identical with the 1886 text save for two minor details: where the earlier version had "faith" for fuel (st. 3, l. 3) and "hope" for fireman (l. 7), the later text interchanged these two assignments.

Apparently Hays's poem quickly struck a responsive chord among railroad men, as it was reprinted several times in the last decades of the century. Hays's creation quickly got away from its maker, however; when his poem appeared in print, either the title was incorrect, or some changes had been made in the text, or Hays was not given due credit. Therefore, it is possible that when Maurice Abbey saw the lines that inspired him to rewrite the poem he was unaware that Hays was the author. What is difficult to understand is why Hays, who lived until 1907, did not raise some objection when he saw—as he must have—Abbey and Tillman capitalizing so richly on his theme.

Just as had happened with Hays's poem, the composition of Abbey and Tillman soon got away from its legal owners. In 1904 it was published by A. J. Showalter under a photograph of J. W. Kelly, popular singer and performer of Irish ballads in the 1890s, but with no mention of the song's true originators.[3] The Abbey-Tillman version also became a favorite in railroad magazines; I have seen it as early as 1909, at which time it appeared without any authors' credits.

"Life's Railway to Heaven" has been the model for several parodies—sure testament, if any be needed, to its continuing popularity. In 1940, journalist/folklorist George Korson collected a song titled "Miner's Lifeguard," which he dated to the first decade of this century. The first verse read:

> Miner's life is like a sailor's
> 'Board a ship to cross the wave;
> Every day his life in danger,
> Still he ventures being brave;
> Watch the rocks, they're falling daily,
> Careless miners always fail;
> Keep your hand upon the dollar
> And your eyes upon the scales.[4]

Dorsey Dixon, a cotton-mill worker as well as hillbilly musician, heard a fellow mill worker sing a verse and chorus of "Weaver's Life" in 1922. He expanded it into a full song and subsequently recorded it. The opening verse:

> Weaver's life is like an engine,
> Coming 'round a mountain steep;
> We've had our ups and downs a-plenty
> And at night we cannot sleep;
> Very often flag your fixer
> When his head is bending low;
> You may think that he is loafing,
> But he's doing all he knows.[5]

Perhaps the following poem, published in 1937 and titled "Brotherhood of Man," is also a parody:

> Life is like a placid river,
> From its source into the bay;
> Passing slowly ever onward
> Passing slowly on its way. . . .[6]

In 1970 a nonagenarian retired railroadman, William G. "Mac" MacDonald of Sekonk, Massachusetts, sent me an account of how "Life's Railway to Heaven" happened to be written. Although I have been unable to obtain corroborative evidence in support of Mac's report, I feel it is worth repeating: "The story is that at a Railway convention in Boston, the first day the music-leader found that they didn't have a suitable hymn, so that night he wrote the words and next morning a fellow member set music to it. And that night their chorus sang it and the audience just went wild over it. In 1902 I sang first tenor in our male quartette, on many occasions and it always brought great applause. . . ."[7] This account would require the existence of another version of the song between the Hays poem and the Abbey-Tillman composition, unless Abbey was the chorus leader (Tillman was not a railroadman). Perhaps this anecdote should simply be taken as more proof that a song written in the folk idiom is rapidly detached from its writers and becomes the possession of the folk themselves.

To my knowledge, the earliest recording of "Life's Railway to Heaven" was made in about 1918 on an Edison cylinder by Edward Allen and Charles Hart. The first disc recording was cut in March, 1921, by Oscar Seagle, a singer of sentimental ballads and religious pieces, on the Columbia label. The following year it was recorded for Victor by Clifford Cairns and Charles Harrison. Harrison was a popular recording artist of the day; Cairns, a producer employed by Victor, was featured on no recordings other than "Life's Railway to Heaven" and the song that backed it on the disc. Three more recordings were made in April of 1924—by Mr. and Mrs. J. Douglas Swagerty, by George Reneau, and by Ernest Thompson. Thompson, a blind minstrel from Winston-Salem, was one of the first white rural artists to be recorded by Columbia and was one of the first in that category to record "Life's Railway to Heaven." (On George Reneau's version, which may have preceded Thompson's on disc by a week or two, pop crooner Gene Austin provided the vocal. The significance of Louisiana-born Austin's southern roots on his early recordings has not been explored.) Thompson's version, waxed on April 25 at his first recording session, is transcribed here. It is very close to the original Abbey-Tillman text; the only notable difference is in the second stanza, where the third line should read, "You will always find obstructions."

It is interesting that "Life's Railway to Heaven" seems to be exclusively the property of white folksingers; to my knowledge, it has not been collected from or recorded by black artists.

A grim hint of the turn-of-the-century popularity of "Life's Railway to Heaven" occurs in Gene Fowler's account of the 1902 trial of Tom Horn in Cheyenne for the murder of Willie Nickell. Charlie and Frank Irwin, two friends of Tom, offer to sing him a last song as he waits at the gallows to be hanged. Horn requests "Keep Your Hand upon the Throttle and Your Eye upon the Rail," and the brothers oblige with two and a half stanzas, close to the original Abbey-Tillman text.[8] "Life's a Funny Proposition," a parody by A. F. Lockhart, probably stems from the same period.[9]

NOTES

1. Will S. Hays, *Songs and Poems* (Louisville, Ky.: Courier-Journal Job Printing, 1886), p. 44. See the discussion of "The Little Red Caboose (III)" for further biographical information on Hays.

2. Will S. Hays, *Poems and Songs* (Louisville, Ky.: Chas. T. Dearing, 1895), p. 91.

3. Information sent to me by Harlan Daniel of Chicago, Illinois. Hays's poem has not yet been completely forgotten; *Good Old Days*, June, 1969, p. 43, printed a request for a poem called "Life Is like a Railroad Track" or "Life Is like a Crooked Railroad."

4. George Korson, *Coal Dust on the Fiddle* (1943; rpt., Hatboro, Pa.: Folklore Associates, 1965) p. 413.

5. Dixon's song was recorded by the Dixon Brothers for RCA Victor in 1937 (Bluebird B-7802) and reissued on Testament T-3301: *Babies in the Mill*. Archie Green's brochure notes to the latter album give background information on the song. The text is transcribed in *New Lost City Ramblers Song Book*, edited by John Cohen and Mike Seeger (New York: Oak Publications, 1964), pp. 106-7.

6. *Railway Conductor*, 54 (July, 1937), 211. Written by W. R. Beard, conductor on the Great Northern Railway.

7. MacDonald to Cohen, Jan. 14, 1970.

8. Gene Fowler, *Timber Line* (New York: Covici, Friede, 1933), chap. 15; the song text appears on p. 192.

9. See Max Stein, ed., *Gems of Inspiration, Crop IV* (Chicago: Stein Publishing House, 1947).

REFERENCES

A. "The Faithful Engineer," by Will S. Hays.
In Hays, *Songs and Poems* (Louisville,
Ky.: Courier-Journal Job Printing, 1886),
p. 44. Earliest printing of the Hays song.
"Life's Railway to Heaven," sheet music.
Words by M. E. Abbey, music by Charles
D. Tillman. Published by Charles D.
Tillman, Atlanta, Ga. Copyrighted Jan.
18, 1890 (2660; renewed Dec. 29, 1917).
First publication of the Abbey-Tillman
song.
"Life's Railway to Heaven," by Ernest
Thompson. Vocal, guitar, and harmonica.
Recorded Apr. 25, 1924 (Columbia
master 81735-2), in Asheville, N.C.
Released on Columbia 158-D in
mid-1924. Reissued on Harmony 5096-H
(as by Jed Tompkins) in 1928. First
hillbilly recording; transcribed here.

B. HAYS TEXT:

Hays (1895), 91   "Old Hayseed's
Railroad Idea of Life"
LEMJ, 22 (Jan., 1888), 32   "Train Talk"
LEMJ, 22 (Sept., 1888), 809   "The
Faithful Engineer"
RTJ, July 1894, p. 640   "The Run of Life"

ABBEY-TILLMAN TEXT:

Bonar, 212
Cross, 22
Family Herald, 45 (references only)
Foley, 88
Fowler, 192

Gems
Greenway, 15
Pack
Perry, 286
Pound (1915), 56 (1 stanza only)
Railroad Evangelist, 3 (Apr., 1941), 6
RRManM, 11 (Apr., 1910), 576
RRManM, 34 (Dec., 1917), 704
Santa Fe Employes Magazine, 3 (Apr.,
1909), 520   "A Railway Song"
Wild West Weekly, June 13, 1936, p. 124

C. ABBEY-TILLMAN TEXT:

COHEN COLLECTION:

William G. MacDonald (letter, Jan. 14,
1970)

D. ALL RECORDINGS in sections D-F are of the
Abbey-Tillman song.
Allen Quartet—OKeh 45196
Blue Ridge Duo (Gene Austin and George
Reneau)—Edison 51498
Buice Brothers—Bluebird B-5613
Clifford Cairns and Charles Harrison—
Victor 18925
Calhoun Sacred Quartet—Victor 20543,
Montgomery Ward M-4350
Criterion Male Quartet—Brunswick 2931
(Sid) Harkreader and (Blythe) Poteet—
Paramount 3094, Broadway 8129 (as by
Harkins and Perry)
Bradley Kincaid—Bluebird B-8501   "Life
Is Like a Mountain Railroad"
Kirby's Carolina Ramblers—Decca 5680,

Melotone (Canada) 45307 (as by Fred Kirby's Carolina Boys)

Ed McConnell—Victor 23823, Bluebird B-8194

(John) McGhee and (Frank) Welling— Gennett 7156, Champion 15971, Champion 45125 (last two as by the Hutchens Brothers), Superior 2799, Supertone 9658 (last two as by Harper and Turner)

Montgomery Quartet—Decca 147

Pickard Family—Banner 9679, Cameo 0279, Jewel 5934, Oriole 1934, Romeo 1301

Dick Powell—Decca 3784

George Reneau (vocal by Gene Austin— Vocalion 14811, Vocalion 5030

Homer A. Rodeheaver and Virginia Asher—Columbia 165-D

John Seagle and Leonard Stokes—Victor 22060

Oscar Seagle and the Stellar Quartet— Columbia 69-M, Columbia A-3420

Smith's Sacred Singers—Columbia 15159-D, Vocalion 02921

Southern Railroad Quartet—Victor V-40002, Montgomery Ward M-8129

Mr. and Mrs. J. Douglas Swagerty—OKeh 40086

Hermes Zimmerman—Vocalion 1018

E. Roy Acuff—Hickory LPM 125: *Great Train Songs*

Harold Austin—Atteiram API-L-1519A: *Kentucky Bluegrass Preacher*

Rue Barclay, Bill Sampson, and Curly Harris—Rural Rhythm RR-Rue-145: *Hymn Time with Rue Barclay*

Curley Bradshaw—Acme 2015 (45 rpm)

Patsy Cline—Vocalion 3753: *Here's Patsy Cline*; Hilltop JM 6016: *I Can't Forget You*; Everest 5229

Country Pardners—Pine Mountain PMR 205: *Reach Out and Touch the Lord*

Jimmie Davis—Decca DL 4763: *My Altar*

Jimmy Dean—Columbia CL 1025: *Jimmy Dean's Hour of Prayer*

Evergreen Blueshoes—Amos 7002: *Ballad of the Evergreen Blueshoes*

Raymond Fairchild—Rural Rhythm RRRF 263: *Raymond Fairchild*

G. M. Farley—Rural Rhythm RR-128: *G. M. Farley*

Red Foley—Decca DL 4198/74198: *Songs of Devotion*

Tennessee Ernie Ford—Capitol T-1272: *A Friend We Have*

—Capitol ST 833: *The Folk Album*

Happy Goodman Family—Canaan CA-4613-LP: *I'm Too Near Home*

Billy Grammer—Decca DL 4212/74212: *Gospel Guitar*

Greenbriar Boys—Vanguard VRS 9104: *The Greenbriar Boys*

George Hamilton IV—RCA Camden ACL1-0242: *Singin' on the Mountain*

Harmonizing Four—Atlantic SDR-013 "Life Is Like a Mountain Railroad"

Phyllis and Billy Holmes—"X" X-0120 (45 rpm)

Burl Ives—Encyclopaedia Britannica Films EBF 6: *Songs of Expanding America* "Life Is Like a Mountain Railroad"

J. D. Jarvis—Rural Rhythm RRJD-195: *Blue Grass Gospel Songs* "Railway to Heaven"

Bradley Kincaid—Bluebonnet BL 105: *Bradley Kincaid, the Kentucky Mountain Boy, Vol. 1* "Life Is Like a Mountain Railroad"

Leverett Brothers—Birch 1947: *The Leverett Brothers*

Lewis Family—Canaan CAS 9764-LP: *Absolutely Lewis!*

Sam McGee and Bill Lowery—Davis Unlimited DU-33021: *God Be with You Until We Meet Again*

Mac Martin and the Dixie Travelers—Rural Rhythm RRMM-201: *Mac Martin and the Dixie Travelers with the Traveling Blues*

Bill Monroe and the Bluegrass Boys—Decca DL 8769: *I Saw the Light*

Oak Ridge Quartet—Starday SLP 356: *The Sensational Oak Ridge Boys*

Cathy and Lloyd Reynolds and Lyle Mayfield—Campus Folksong Club (University of Illinois) CFC 201: *Green Fields of Illinois*

Linda Ronstadt—Capitol ST 407: *Silk Purse*

Jean Shepard—Capitol ST 171: *I'll Fly Away*
Stoneman Family—Starday SLP 275: *The
  Great Old Timer at the Capital*
Carl Story—Atteiram API-L-1520A:
  Mother's Last Word
White Lightnin'—Polydor 24-4047: *Fresh
  Air*

F. LC AFS:

Willie Bledsoe and John Hensley—AFS
  1977A   "This Life Is Like a Mountain
  Railway"
Lonnie Corsbie—AFS 14157 B1
Ola Belle Reed— AFS 14105 B17

Ernest Thompson. Courtesy of the John Edwards
Memorial Foundation, UCLA.

The Gospel Train Is Coming/Get on Board

GET ON BOARD

*On the recording, the verses are sung somewhat slower than the choruses.

Oh, get on board, little children,
Get on board, little children,
Get on board, little children,
There's room for many a more.

Oh, get on board, little children,
Get on board, little children,
Get on board, little children,
There's room for many a more.

The gospel train is comin', I hear it just at hand,
I hear the car wheels running and a-rambling through the land.

   Chorus:

I hear the train a-comin', she's comin' round the curve,
She's [?whistling and a-steamin'] and straining every nerve.

   Chorus:

Tuskegee Institute Singers

THE GOSPEL TRAIN IS COMING

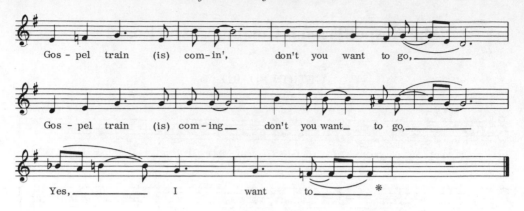

Gos - pel train (is) com-in', don't you want to go,_____

Gos - pel train (is) com-ing__ don't you want__ to go,_____

Yes,_____ I want to__ *

*At this point the guitar articulates a note that is probably meant to represent the missing word *go*.

Gospel train (is) comin', don't you want to go,
Gospel train (is) comin', don't you want to go,
Gospel train (is) comin', don't you want to go,
Yes, I want to (go).[1]

Do you want to know who's the engineer, don't you want to go,
(Do) you want to know who's the engineer, don't you want to go,
Do you want to know who's the engineer, don't you want to go?
Yes, I (want) to go.

Jesus is the engineer, don't you want to go,
Jesus is the engine(er), don't you want to go,
Jesus is the engine(er), don't you want to go?
Yes, I (want) to go.

Can't you hear the bell ring, don't you want to go,
Can't you hear the bell (ring), don't you want to go,
Can't you hear the (bell ring), don't you want to go?
Yes, (I want to go).

Can't you hear the wheel hum, don't you want to go,
Can't you hear the wheel (hum), don't you want to go,
Can't you hear the (wheel hum), don't you want to go?
Yes, I (want) to (go).

She's comin' round the curve, don't you want to go,
(She's) comin' round the (curve), don't you want to go,
She's comin' round the (curve), don't you want to go?
Yes, I want to go.

Reverend Edward Clayborn

Of the several songs known by the title "The Gospel Train Is Coming," the best known and probably oldest was popularized by the Fisk Jubilee Singers, a choir that traveled around the world in the 1870s raising money for the Fisk University in Nashville and helping to make the Negro spiritual—although in Europeanized form—better known.[2] Their version of "The Gospel Train" was first published in T. F. Seward's 1872 collection of their songs. Since then, it has been widely favored and has appeared in dozens of collections of Negro spirituals (in this regard the references are surely incomplete).

Seward's 1872 text is the one generally used in collections of spirituals. It consists of nine stanzas and this chorus:

> Get on board, children,
> Get on board, children,
> Get on board, children,
> For there's room for many a more.

Taylor, in 1882, printed a text with seven of Seward's stanzas and two different ones. Bolton (1929) printed yet two different stanzas. A text published in 1970 in *Good Old Days* included all thirteen of these verses. According to the correspondent who sent it, "It was composed many years ago by Rev. John Chamberlain who was at Northfield, N. H. one day and saw the noon train coming in. The words came to him and he went inside the depot and wrote the lines as though inspired inside of thirty minutes. . . . "[3] I have not been able to corroborate this anecdote; but its implication that the song was in print before the Fisk singers popularized it is consistent with the early appearance of stanzas other than those they apparently sang. It is also consistent with Gordon's claim (undocumented) that this song was originally a white spiritual, and in this regard, it is interesting that according to the *Good Old Days* text the chorus was originally "Get on board, get on board, / For there's room for many more." The version attributed to the Fisk Jubilee Singers reads "Get on board, little children. . . . " In another early publication the same line appears as "Git on board, little children. . . . "[4] This latter locution gives the song more the feeling of a black than of a white spiritual. Is the Fisk version the older? Or, in their desire to present a musical product that would be readily acceptable by European high-culture standards, did the Jubilee Singers "refine" the language as well as the music? I'm not sure this question can be answered.

There are, as I mentioned, several other songs that go by the title "The Gospel Train Is Coming" that differ from the piece we have been discussing. Most of these have no chorus and lack any references to little children getting on board. For comparison, we have transcribed here a representative member of this second group, offered by the Reverend Edward Clayborn at his first recording session in December, 1926, for Brunswick's Vocalion label. The format of this piece suggests a song older than the "Get on Board" variety; the AAAB stanza was typical of many spirituals sung early in the nineteenth-century by both blacks and whites in the revival camp-meeting movement.

For the standard version of "The Gospel Train Is Coming" we have transcribed one of the earliest recordings made—by the Tuskegee Institute Singers for Victor in about 1918.[5] Because that is a very short text, however, I append here the text printed in 1872 by Seward:

> The gospel train is coming,
> I hear it just at hand,
> I hear the car wheels moving,
> And rumbling thro' the land.
> > Get on board, children,
> > Get on board, children,
> > Get on board, children,
> > For there's room for many a more.

I hear the bell and whistle,
The coming round the curve;
She's playing all her steam and pow'r
And straining every nerve.
    Chorus:

No signal for another train
To follow on the line,
O, sinner, you're forever lost,
If once you're left behind.
    Chorus:

This is the Christian banner,
The motto's new and old,
Salvation and Repentance
Are burnished there in gold.
    Chorus:

She's nearing now the station,
O, sinner, don't be vain,
But come and get your ticket,
And be ready for the train.
    Chorus:

The fare is cheap and all can go,
The rich and poor are there,
No second-class on board the train,
No difference in the fare.
    Chorus:

There's Moses, Noah and Abraham,
And all the prophets, too,
Our friends in Christ are all on board,
O, what a heavenly crew.
    Chorus:

We soon shall reach the station,
O, how we then shall sing,
With all the heavenly army,
We'll make the welkin ring,
    Chorus:

We'll shout o'er all our sorrows,
And sing forever more,
With Christ and all his army,
On that celestial shore.
    Chorus:[6]

NOTES

1. In the various repetitions occasional random words and syllables (indicated by parentheses) are omitted.

2. The story of the Fisk Jubilee Singers was told in several early volumes, possibly the first of

which was Gustavus D. Pike, *The Jubilee Singers, and Their Campaign for Twenty Thousand Dollars* (Boston: Lee and Shepard; New York: Lee, Shepard and Dillingham, 1873). This volume included Theodore Freylinghuysen Seward's *Jubilee Songs* as an appendix; Seward's collection was also published separately, as *Jubilee Songs: Complete, as Sung by the Jubilee Singers of Fisk University* (New York: Biglow and Main, 1872). The best-known account of the group was J. B. T. Marsh, *The Story of the Jubilee Singers, with Their Songs* (Boston: Houghton, Mifflin, 1880), an abridgment of two histories written earlier by G. D. Pike.

3. *Good Old Days*, Aug., 1970, p. 10, submitted by Harry G. Rogers of Williamsport, Penn.

4. *Cabin and Plantation Songs as Sung by the Hampton Students*, 3d ed., arranged by Thomas P. Fenner, Frederic G. Rathbun, and Bessie Cleaveland (New York: G. P. Putnam's Sons, 1901), p. 134. The song does not appear in the 1874 edition, titled *Hampton and Its Students . . . With Fifty Cabin and Plantation Songs, as Sung by the Hampton Students*. After one more edition, the book was published under the title *Religious Folk Songs of the Negro*, edited by R. N. Dett (Hampton, Va.: Institute Press, 1909). The same plate for "Git on Board" appears on p. 134 of this edition as well.

5. I have not heard what may be the earliest recording of the song, described as follows in the *Edison Phonograph Monthly*, 3 (Mar., 1905), 9: "No. 8975. 'Parson Spencer's Discourse on Adam and Eve,' by Len Spencer, is a colored preacher's sermon to his flock with characteristic responses by enthusiastic members and singing by the choir 'De Gospel Train Am a-Coming.'"

6. Seward, *Jubilee Songs*, p. 36. The song also appears in Pike, *Jubilee Singers*, pp. 190-91.

REFERENCES

A. "The Gospel Train," in Theodore Freylinghuysen Seward, *Jubilee Songs: Complete, as Sung by the Jubilee Singers of Fisk University* (New York: Biglow and Main, 1872), p. 36. First known publication of the song; text given above.

"Get on Board," by the Tuskegee Institute Singers. Double male quartet, unaccompanied. Recorded ca. 1918. Released on Victor 18446. Part of the medley "I Want to Get Ready" and "Get on Board." This version is transcribed here.

"The Gospel Train Is Coming," by the Reverend Edward W. Clayborn, "the Guitar Evangelist." Vocal and guitar. Recorded ca. Dec. 9, 1926, probably in Chicago, Ill. Released on Vocalion 1082 and Melotone M12546. Reissued on Roots RL-328: *Southern Sanctified Singers*. (Some record labels spell the artist's name as Clayburn or Clayton; the correct spelling, according to John Godrich and Robert M. W. Dixon, *Blues & Gospel Records 1902–1942*, rev. ed. [London: Storyville Publications, 1969], p. 155, is Claiborn.) This version is transcribed here.

B. Bolton (Song #3)
Brown III, 588
Burleigh
Chambers, 21
Chappell (1939), 145
Downes & Siegmeister (1943), 204
Edwards, C. L., 26
Fenner, 134
Folk Sing, 52
Frey (1924), 38–39
Glazer (1970), 125
Good Old Days, Aug., 1970, p. 10
Gordon (1931), 211 (discussion only)
Hughes & Bontemps, 302
Johnson, H.
Johnson, J. R.
Johnson & Johnson (1925), 126
Jubilee & Plantation Songs, 19
Landeck (1950a), 56
Leisy (1966), 133
Leisy (1973), 46
Little Four Songster, 51
Marsh, 150
Minstrel Memories, 28 (1 verse and refrain)
Noble, 86
Odum & Johnson (1926), 202
Olympia Quartette Songster, 3
Pike, 190

Rodeheaver (Song #11)
Scarborough, 254
Seward, 36
Taylor, M. W.
Wheeler, O., 76–79
White, N. I., 64–65
Wier (1929), 112

D. Alphabetical Four—Decca 7594   "Get on Board Little Children"

Perry Bechtel and his Colonels—Brunswick 579   "The Gospel Train Is Coming"

Al Bernard—Grey Gull 4240   "De Gospel Train Am Comin'"

Harry C. Browne—Silvertone 3174 (probably same recording as the following)

Harry C. Browne and the Peerless Quartet—Columbia A-2255, Velvetone 7050, Diva 6024   "De Gospel Train Am Comin'"

Reverend J. C. Burnett—Columbia 14180-D   "Gospel Train Is Leaving"

Jimmie Davis—Decca 4186   "Get on Board Little Children"

Deep River Plantation Singers—Superior 2814   "Train's A Comin'" (possibly related)

Reverend Mose Doolittle and his Congregation—Victor 20295   "Get on Board"

Dunham Jubilee Singers—Columbia 14676-D   "Get on Board" (possibly related)

Kanawha Singers—Brunswick 365 "The Gospel Train"

Kansas City Gospel Singers—Castle CA-1004

Livingston College Negro Male Quartet—Victor 20949   "Gospel Train" (possibly related)

Moore Spiritual Singers—Bluebird B-8095 "Get on Board" (possibly related)

Norfolk Jubilee Quartet—Paramount 12268, Herwin 92009 (as by the Southland Jubilee Quartet)   "Get on Board, Little Children, Get on Board"

Paul Robeson—Victor 22225, HMV (England) B-3033   "Get on Board Li'l Children"

Rodeheaver and Wiseman Sextet—Silvertone 3824

Clara Smith—Columbia 14183-D   "Get on Board" (possibly related)

Southern Plantation Singers—Vocalion 1414   "Get on Board, Little Children"

Reverend Stephenson and Male Choir—Paramount 3050   "Gospel Train"

Paul Tremaine—Columbia 2302-D "Gospel Train" (possibly related)

Williams Jubilee Singers—Columbia 14457-D   "Gospel Train Is Coming"

E. Belleville A Capella Choir—Prestige International 25012   "The Gospel Train"

Martha Carson—RCA Camden CAL/CAS 906: *Martha Carson Sings*   "Get on Board Little Children"

Tennessee Ernie Ford—Capitol T/ST 818: *Spirituals*   "Get on Board Little Children"

Edwin Hawkins Singers—Buddah 5606: *Live*

Leadbelly (Huddie Ledbetter)—Elektra EKL 301/2: *The Library of Congress Recordings*   "Git on Board" (shares refrain only)

Paul Robeson—Vanguard VRS 9037/VSD 2015: *Robeson*   "Get on Board Little Children"

—Columbia ML 2038; Classics Record Library 30-5647: *Scandalize My Name*

Martha Schlamme—Vanguard VRS 7012 (10″ LP) and VSD 9019: *Folk Songs of Many Lands*   "Get on Board Little Children"

F. LC AFS:

Ernest Pettway—AFS 5067 B2 "Gospel Train Is Coming"

Mrs Horace Smith—AFS 11907 B "De Gospel Train" (possibly related)

Arthur Stitt, Robert Prosser, James Wilkinson, and William Carver—AFS 733 B3   "Git on Board" (derivative piece)

Unidentified singer—John A. Lomax cylinder 14   "The Gospel Train Is Coming"

Little Black Train

LITTLE BLACK TRAIN

Shuffle ♩ = 96
Chorus
Original Key: G

There's a lit-tle black train a-com-in', set your busi-ness right,___
___ There's a lit-tle black train a-com-in',___ and it may be here to-night.
Go tell that ball-room la-dy, all dressed in the world-ly
pride, That death's dark train is com-in',___ pre-pare to take a ride.
God said to He-ze-ki-ah, a mes-sage from on high, "You'd
bet-ter set your house in or - der, for you must sure-ly die."

*These G's are slightly flat.

There's a little black train a-comin', set your business right,
There's a little black train a-comin', and it may be here tonight.
Go tell that ballroom lady, all dressed in the worldly pride,
That death's dark train is comin', prepare to take a ride.

God said to Hezekiah, a message from on high,
"You'd better set your house in order, for you must surely die."

He turned to the wall in weeping, we see him here in tears,
He got his business fixed all right, God spared him fifteen years.

Chorus:

We see that train with engine and one small baggage car,
Your idle thoughts and wicked deeds will stop at the judgment bar.

Chorus:

That poor young man in darkness cared not for the gospel light,
Till suddenly heard the whistle blow of the little black train in sight.

"Have mercy on me, Lord, please come and set me right,"
Before he got his business fixed the train rolled in that night.

Chorus:

Carter Family

In 2 Kings 20 (also in Isaiah 38, where the same account is given), we read:

1. In those days Hezekiah fell sick unto death; and there came unto him Isaiah the son of Amoz the prophet, and said unto him, "Thus hath said the Lord, 'Give thy charge to thy house; for thou shalt die, and not live.'"
2. Then did he turn his face to the wall, and prayed unto the Lord, saying,
3. "I beseech thee, O Lord, remember now that I have walked before thee in truth, and with an undivided heart, and have done what is good in thy eyes." And Hezekiah wept aloud.
4. And it came to pass, before Isaiah was gone out into the middle court that the word of the Lord came unto him, saying,
5. "Return and say to Hezekiah the ruler of my people, 'Thus hath said the Lord, the God of David thy father, "I have heard thy prayer, I have seen thy tears; behold, I will heal thee; on the third day shalt thou go up unto the house of the Lord.
6. And I will add unto thy days fifteen years. . . . "'"

This episode from the life of Hezekiah, one of the more righteous of the kings of Israel, forms the central episode of the religious song "Little Black Train." Although it is lacking from the version transcribed here, some longer texts (e.g., those in the Scarborough and Brown collections) have an allegorical stanza based on Luke 12 : 16–21. It is indeed striking how this song combines these hoary biblical themes with such worldly images as ballroom ladies and apocalyptic trains.

When the song was composed, and by whom, I do not know, but it must have been in the late 1800s. The discographic and bibliographic references reveal that the song is equally popular among white and black singers.

The first recording of the song, to my knowledge, was made by the Reverend J. M. Gates, who waxed it four times between April and November of 1926 for various companies, and copyrighted it in August, 1926. Next to record it were the hillbilly artists Emry and Henry Arthur, who performed it for the Brunswick Company in January, 1928. The version transcribed here was made by the "original" Carter Family—Maybelle, Sara, and A.P.—for the American Record Corporation on May 7, 1935. Two copyrights were taken out in the Carters' names, in July, 1935, and November, 1937.

The Carter Family's recording career began in August, 1927, when they auditioned for Victor's traveling A & R man, Ralph Peer; but they had been making music together for local gatherings since March of 1926, when Sara's cousin Maybelle married her husband A.P.'s brother, Ezra Carter. Until the eve of World War II, Sara, Maybelle, and A.P. formed the nucleus of a group that epitomized, to southern rural listeners, the ideal in wholesome family entertainment. Their repertoire, as represented on more than 350 recordings, was rich in sentimental songs of mother, sweetheart, and home, and in religious songs; it included their own family's rich folk heritage as well as numerous songs that they learned from friends and neighbors during their travels.[1] The tune the Carters used for "Little Black Train" is similar to the melody for "Roving Gambler," another popular southern mountain folksong.

The version by hillbilly singers Emry and Henry Arthur is similar to the Carters' but contains an additional stanza:

> The rich old fool in grandeur sits, "I have no future fears,"
> My barns are overrunning, I['ve] left for many a years."
> But while he stood there planning, he got a [?fare in might],
> This rich old fool to judgment comes; your soul must be there tonight.[2]

NOTES

1. For further biographical information on the Carter Family, see "Jim Blake's Message," n. 3 (chap. 7), and the discussion of "Cannonball Blues"/"Whitehouse Blues" (chap. 9) and "Railroading on the Great Divide" (chap. 10).

2. Emry and Henry Arthur, "The Little Black Train Is Coming," recorded Jan. 17, 1928 (Brunswick master C-1551/52), in Chicago; released on Vocalion 5229 ca. Aug., 1928.

REFERENCES

A. "Death's Black Train Is Coming," by the Reverend J. M. Gates. Gates, sermon with singing; accompanied by two female voices. Recorded Apr. 24, 1926 (Columbia master 142132-2), in Atlanta, Ga. Released on Columbia 14145-D on July 20, 1926. Reissued on Conqueror 9774, Square (England) M-3 (LP); CBS 52797. Copyrighted Dec. 7, 1926 (E unp. 652310). First commercial recording of the song.

"Little Black Train," by the Carter Family. A.P., vocal; Sara, vocal and autoharp; Maybelle, vocal and guitar. Recorded May 7, 1935 (American Record Corp. master 17493-1), in New York City. Released on ARC labels (Banner, Oriole, Perfect, Melotone, Romeo) 7-07-62 in July, 1937; Conqueror 8815, Vocalion/Okeh 03112. Reissued on Harmony HL-7396: *Great Sacred Songs*; RBF RF 19: *Country Gospel Song*. Copyrighted July 17, 1935 (E unp. 108149), renewed July 19, 1962 (R 298903); and Nov. 17, 1937 (E unp. 155635), renewed Jan. 7, 1965 (R 352961). This version is transcribed here.

B. Brown III, 598
Courlander, 41
Grissom, 10
Kennedy, R. E., 17–18   "Business Affairs"

Korson, 328 (miners' parody)
Leisy (1973), 82
Lomax & Lomax (1941), 46
Scarborough, 260
Seeger, R. C., 152
White, N. I., 65–66

D. Emry and Henry Arthur—Vocalion 5229   "The Little Black Train Is Coming"
Reverend J. M. Gates—Pathé 7514, Perfect 114   "Death's Black Train Is Coming"
—Victor 20211, Bluebird B-7758; RCA (Japan) RA-5710: *Yonder Comes My Lord*   "Death's Black Train Is Coming"
—Domino 3872, Romeo 400, Oriole 794, Conqueror 7080   "Death's Black Train Is Coming"
Golden Gate Quartet—Bluebird B-7126 "Golden Gate Gospel Train"
Heavenly Gospel Singers—Bluebird 6887, RCA Victor 20-3009   "Heavenly Gospel Train"
Harmon E. Helmick—Champion 16744, Champion 45112
Royal Harmony Singers—Decca 8628 "The Gospel Train"
Seven Stars Quartette—Vocalion 05477 (possibly related)
Reverend H. R. Tomlin—OKeh 8375 "Death's Black Train Is Coming"

Wright Brothers—Okeh 05920 "Gospel Train"

E. Dock Boggs—Folkways FA 2392: *Dock Boggs, Vol. 2*

Carter Sisters and Mother Maybelle—Liberty LRP 3230/7230: *Carter Family Album*

Jesse Fuller—Good Time Jazz 12051/10051: *San Francisco Bay Blues*

Golden Gate Quartet—Vanguard VRS 8523/4: *From Spirituals to Swing* "Gospel Train Is Coming"

Woody Guthrie—Verve/Folkways FV 9007: *Bed on the Floor*; Folkways FT 1010/FTS 31010: *Poor Boy*

—Olympic 7101: *The Immortal Woody Guthrie* (probably the same recording as the preceding)

Phipps Family—Starday SLP 195: *Old Time Mountain Pickin' and Singin'*

Peggy, Barbara, and Penny Seeger—Prestige 7375: *Folk Songs with the Seegers*

Billy Ward and the Dominoes—Federal 12193 (45 rpm) (possibly related)

F. LC AFS:

Brother Elihu Trusty—AFS 1394 B1 "There's a Little Black Train A-Coming"

Advertisement in a Columbia record catalog. Author's Collection.

This Train/Same Train

THIS TRAIN IS BOUND FOR GLORY

*Chords supplied by the music editor; the original is unaccompanied.
**The higher notes are sung by the chorus beginning with this measure.

This train is bound for glory, this train (my Lord),
This train is bound for glory, this train;
This train is bound for glory, and if you ride you must be holy,
This train, my Lord, this train.

This train don't carry no liars, this train (my Lord),
This train don't carry no liars, this train;
This train don't carry no liars, no [?untrue husbands] and no [?untrue
    wives],
This train, my Lord, this train.

This train don't carry no gamblers, this train (my Lord),
This train don't carry no gamblers, this train;
This train don't carry no gamblers, hobo liars, midnight ramblers,
This train, my Lord, this train.

This train is bound for glory, this train (my Lord),
This train is bound for glory, this train;
This train is bound for glory, if you ride you must be holy,
This train, my Lord, this train.

This train don't carry no jokers, this train (no Lord),
This train don't carry no jokers, this train;
This train don't carry no jokers, no [?tough dippers], no cigaret smokers,
This train, my Lord, this train.

> This train is bound for glory, this train (my Lord),
> This train is bound for glory, this train;
> This train is bound for glory, if you ride you must be holy,
> This train, my Lord, this train.

Biddleville Quintette

I have found nothing concerning the origin of this song—or even any references to it prior to 1925, when it was first recorded. Nevertheless, by the 1920s it seems to have become relatively popular, and yet more so in the following decades. It enjoyed a thriving career during the urban folksong revival of the 1950s and early 1960s, as the LP references attest. In 1943 it suggested the title for Woody Guthrie's autobiographical novel, *Bound for Glory*. The 1951 movie *Call Me Mister* uses a parody, "This Train Is a Goin' Home Train," about taking soldiers home from World War II.

A closely related spiritual, "Same Train," appeared in print as early as 1925. Most of the published references given below from the 1920s are to this variant. The usual first stanza is:

> Same train carry my mother, same train,
> Same train carry my mother, same train;
> Same train carry my mother,
> Same train be back tomorrow, same train.

Even apart from external evidence, I would suspect that this is the older form: it is difficult to imagine the striking imagery of "this train is bound for glory" being consciously replaced by the more prosaic "same train carry my mother."

"This Train" was recorded by four different black religious singing groups between 1925 and 1931. The earliest, Wood's Blind Jubilee Singers, waxed it in August, 1925, for the Starr Piano Company for a special unnumbered Gennett release; the following month they recorded it for the Paramount label. the first regular commercial release of the song. The version transcribed here was recorded a little over a year later by the Biddleville Quintette. The first hillbilly recording was made in August, 1935, by Dick Hartman's Tennessee Ramblers; by titling it "Dis Train" they indicated that it was still considered of black provenance.

The song's later popularity among black and white singers can probably be attributed, at least in part, to the influence of John A. and Alan Lomax's 1934 anthology, *American Ballads and Folk Songs,* possibly its first appearance in print under the usual title, "This Train." The Lomaxes cited their 1933 field recording of Walter McDonald in the Parchman, Mississippi, state penitentiary as the source for their text. However, the actual recording deposited at the Library of Congress Archive of Folk Song differs considerably from the version in their anthology. Alan Lomax included "This Train" again in his 1960 anthology, *The Folk Songs of North America*, and gave the 1934 anthology as his source; but that later printing differs both from the earlier one and from the field recording. The 1934 verses not from McDonald were probably taken from a recording the Lomaxes made that year in the Bellwood prison camp, Atlanta, from the singing of an unidentified group of black convicts. The 1960 printing also seems to use some stanzas from this recording.

The 1934 field recording may shed some light on the obscure line in the next-to-last stanza in the version transcribed here. I have given the words as "no tough dippers, no cigaret smokers," assuming *dipper* is the slang term for drunkard. The 1934 recording gives "no snuff dippers, cigaret smokers." The Lomaxes' 1934 printed text reads "neither don' pull no cigar smokers," while the 1960 text reads "cigarette puffers and cigar smokers." I have also been unable to decipher the second stanza of the Biddleville Quintette recording. In later texts, the usual rhyme for "no liars" is "no high-flyers," but this is clearly not what the Biddleville Quintette sings.

Finally, I should mention Little Walter's 1955 recording "My Babe," which preserved the tune and structure of the old religious song but completely transformed it into a secular piece.[2]

NOTE

1. Little Walter, "My Babe," recorded in Chicago in 1955; issued on Checker 811, Checker 955, Checker LP 1428, and Argo LP 4025.

REFERENCES

A. "This Train Is Bound for Glory," by the Biddleville Quintette. Four male voices and one female voice, unaccompanied. Recorded ca. Jan., 1927 (Paramount master 4149-2), in Chicago, Ill. Released on Paramount 12448 in Mar., 1927. This recording is transcribed here.

B. Ballanta(-Taylor), 9   "Same Train"
Botsford
Diton, 53   "Same Train"
Faye & Cleo, 32
Folksong Festival, 30
Glosson
Guthrie (1960), 7, 11, 28
Johnson & Johnson (1926), 60   "Same Train"
Leisy (1966), 32
Lomax, A. (1960), 484
Lomax & Lomax (1934), 593
Lulu Belle & Scotty (1937), 34
Lulu Belle & Scotty (1941), 46
McIlhenny, 79   "Dat Same Train"
Mursell (Grade 6), 156
Odum & Johnson (1925), 112   "Same Train"
Parsons, 462   "Same Train"
Reprints from Sing Out #3, 27
Thurman, 21

D. Famous Garland Jubilee Singers—Banner 32267, Oriole 8098, Perfect 190, Broadway 4125, Romeo 5098   "This Train Is Bound for Glory"

Florida Normal and Industrial Institute Quartette—OKeh 40010   "Dis Train"
Hartman's Tennessee Ramblers—Bluebird B-6135   "'Dis Train"
Southern Plantation Singers—Vocalion 1250   "This Train Is Bound for Glory"
Rosetta Tharpe—Decca 2558; Decca DL-8782: *Gospel Train;* Rosetta Records RR 1301: *Sorry but I Can't Take You: Woman's Railroad Blues*
—Down Beat 104, Swing Time 104 (both as by Sister Katy Marie)
Lulu Belle and Scotty Wiseman—Vocalion 04910
Wood's Blind Jubilee Singers—Gennett (special unnumbered release)
Wood's Famous Blind Jubilee Singers—Paramount 12315, Broadway 5024 (as by Jacob's Blind Singers), Herwin 92007 (as by the Herwin Famous Jubilee Singers)   "This Train's Bound for Glory"

E. Au Go Go Singers—Roulette R/SR 25280: *They Call Us the Go Go Singers*
Anna Black—Epic 26444: *Thinking about My Man*
Big Bill Broonzy—Folkways FG 3586: *Big Bill Broonzy Story*
—Verve MGV-3000-5: *Bill Broonzy Story;* Verve MGV-3002: *Broonzy's Last Sessions*
—Storyville (Denmark) SEP 316 (EP); Storyville SLP 114

Big Bill Broonzy and Pete Seeger—
    Folkways FA 2328: *Big Bill Broonzy Sings
    Folk Songs*
—Verve Folkways FV/FVS 9008: *Big Bill
    Broonzy and Pete Seeger in Concert*
Brothers Four—Columbia CL 2122/CS
    8922: *All Star Hootenanny*
Hylo Brown—Rural Rhythm RR 176: *Hylo
    Brown Sings Folk Songs of Rural America*
Lew Childre—Starday SLP 153
Robin Christenson—Folkways 7625: *You
    Can Sing It Yourself, Vol. 2*
Wilma Lee and Stoney Cooper—Hickory
    1279 (45 rpm)
Red Cravens and the Bray Brothers—
    Rounder 0015: *419 W. Main*
Delmore Brothers—King 920 (45 rpm)
Jimmy Durante—Warner Brothers 1655:
    One of Those Songs
Blind Snooks Eaglin, Percy Randolph, and
    Lucius Bridges—Folk-Lyric FL 107 and
    Arhoolie 2014: *"Possum Up a Simmon
    Tree"*
Raymond Fairchild—Rural Rhythm RRRF
    260: *King of the 5-String Banjo*
Percy Faith—Columbia CL 2108/CS 8908:
    Great Folk Themes
Folkswingers—World Pacific 291 (45 rpm);
    World Pacific WP/ST 1812: *Twelve String
    Guitar*
Bob Gibson—Riverside RLP 1419;
    Riverside RLP 12-830
Joe Glazer—Collector 1924: *Singing
    BRAC* "This Train's a Clean Train"
    (derivative piece)
Lonnie Glosson—Rimrock RLP 156: *The
    Living Legend*
John Hammond—Vanguard VRS 9132/VSD
    2148: *John Hammond*
Cisco Houston—Vanguard VRS 9057: *The
    Cisco Special* (derivative piece)
David Houston—Epic 26482: *David*
Inman and Ira—Columbia CL 1731
Limeliters—RCA Victor LPM/LSP 2889:
    Best of the Limeliters
Alan Lomax—Kapp KL 1110: *Hootennany
    Tonight*

—Kapp KL 1343/KS 3343: *Hootenanny #2*
Trini Lopez—Reprise R/RS 6147: *Folk
    Album*
Rick Nelson and the Stone Canyon
    Band—MCA 37: *Rudy the Fifth*
Peter, Paul, and Mary—Warner Brothers
    WBR 1449: *Peter, Paul and Mary*
Edmondo Ros—London SP 44208:
    Caribbean Ros
Pete Seeger—Capitol W-2172: *Folk Songs
    by Pete Seeger*
Roberta Sherwood—Decca 9-29911 (45
    rpm); Decca DL 8319: *Introducing
    Roberta Sherwood*; Decca ED 2409
Hank Snow—RCA Victor LPM 3595
David Soul—Paramount 0021 (45 rpm)
Staples Singers—Epic LN 24132/BN 26132
Tarriers—Atco 8042: *Tell the World about
    This*
Rosetta Tharpe—Verve MGV 8439/68439:
    The Gospel Truth; Verve (England) VLP
    9008: *The Gospel Truth*; Verve (France)
    LP 3691: *The Gospel Truth*
Hank Thompson—Capitol T 618: *North of
    the Rio Grande*
Dallas Turner (Nevada Slim)—Rural
    Rhythm RR-DT-177

F. LC AFS:

Lester Adams—AFS 11870 B6   "Clean
    Train"
Dorchester Academy Boys Quartet—AFS
    3606 B
Professor Jenkins and Dorchester Academy
    Boys Quartet—AFS 3606 A
Bascom Lamar Lunsford—AFS 9503 A1
    "Same Train"
—AFS 1833 B1
Walter McDonald—AFS 1861 A1 & A2
William Milbourne ("Bill Jordan")—AFS
    5041 A1
Rebecca Tarwater—AFS 2087 A2
    "This Train Don't Carry No Gamblers"
Agnes Thorn—AFS 11907 B   "This
    Train's a Free Train"
Group of Andros Island men—AFS 502 A
    (derivative piece)
Group of Negro convicts—AFS 256 A1

When the Train Comes Along

WHEN THE TRAIN COMES ALONG

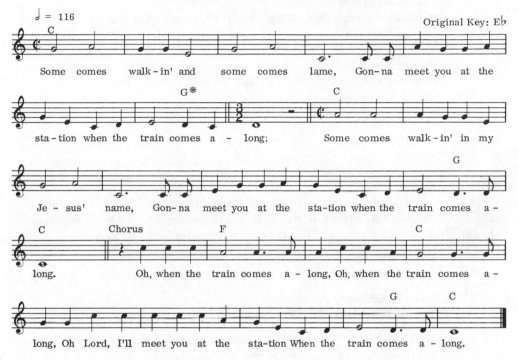

♩ = 116

Original Key: E♭

Some comes walk-in' and some comes lame, Gon-na meet you at the sta-tion when the train comes a - long; Some comes walk-in' in my Je - sus' name, Gon-na meet you at the sta-tion when the train comes a - long. Oh, when the train comes a - long, Oh, when the train comes a - long, Oh Lord, I'll meet you at the sta-tion When the train comes a - long.

*The several musicians play various chords at this point.

Some comes walkin' and some comes lame,
Gonna meet you at the station when the train comes along;
Some comes walkin' in my Jesus' name,
Gonna meet you at the station when the train comes along.

    Oh, when the train comes along,
    Oh, when the train comes along,
    Oh Lord, I'll meet you at the station
    When the train comes along.

Sins of years are washed away,
Gonna meet you at the station when the train comes along;
Darkest hour is changed to day,
Gonna meet you at the station when the train comes along.

    Chorus:

Doubts and fears are borne along,
Gonna meet you at the station when the train comes along;
Sorrow changes into song,
Gonna meet you at the station when the train comes along.

Chorus:

Ease and wealth become as dross,
Gonna meet you at the station when the train comes along;
All my boast is in the cross,
Gonna meet you at the station when the train comes along.

Chorus:

Selfishness is lost in love,
Gonna meet you at the station when the train comes along;
All my treasures are above,
Gonna meet you at the station when the train comes along.

Chorus:

Uncle Dave Macon

The beautiful rendition by Uncle Dave Macon, transcribed here, is the only evidence that this song exists in white tradition. Furthermore, Uncle Dave's text is quite different from the usual one, which consists of one chorus and two verses:

I may be blind an' cannot see,
But I'll meet you at the station when the train comes along.

I may be lame an' cannot walk,
But I'll meet you at the station when the train comes along.

When the train comes along, when the train comes along,
I'll meet you at the station when the train comes along. [1]

Another song with the same chorus and slightly different tune has verses of the form:

If my mother asks for me, tell her death done summoned me.
If my father. . . . [2]

I have found nothing in print concerning the origins of any of these variants, nor any traces prior to 1925; six separate recordings between 1926 and 1938 suggest it enjoyed wide popularity during that period.

The earliest phonograph recording was made by Odette Jackson and Ethel Grainger, who accompanied the singing preacher Reverend J. C. Burnett on many of his own recordings. Their version was made in September, 1926, in New York for Columbia. Uncle Dave waxed his version in August, 1934, in Richmond, Indiana, for the Starr Piano Company. He was accompanied by his frequent associates, Sam and Kirk McGee.

NOTES

1. John W. Work, *American Negro Songs and Spirituals* (New York: Bonanza Books, 1940), p. 94.
2. Carl Diton, *Thirty-six South Carolina Spirituals* (New York: G. Schirmer, 1928), p. 4.

REFERENCES

A. "When the Train Comes Along," by Uncle Dave Macon and the McGee Brothers. Macon, vocal and banjo; Kirk McGee, banjo; Sam McGee, guitar; one or both McGees, vocals on choruses. Recorded Aug. 14, 1934 (Starr master N-19652), in Richmond, Ind. Released on Champion 16805, Champion 45105, Decca 5373,

Decca 34317 (special limited pressing made for a Mississippi disc jockey). Reissued on RBF RF-51: *Uncle Dave Macon*. Transcribed in this book.

B. Ballanta(-Taylor), 12
   Diton, 4
   Rosenberg, 135 (title only)
   Seeger, R. C., 153
   Work, 94

D. Jubilee Gospel Team—QRS R-7058
   Norfolk Jubilee Quartet—Decca 7533
   Odette and Ethel—Columbia 14169-D
   Henry Thomas—Vocalion 1140; Origin

OJL 3: *Henry Thomas Sings the Memphis Blues*
Brother Williams Memphis Sanctified Singers—Vocalion 1482   "I Will Meet You at the Station"

E. Reverend Gary Davis—Continental CLP 16003   "I'm Gonna Meet You at the Station"
   —Stinson SLP 13: *Folksay, Vol. 6*   "When the Train Comes Along"
   —Yazoo L-1023: *Reverend Gary Davis*   "Meet Me at the Station"

F. LC AFS:
   Ray Estill—AFS 1451 A2

Uncle Dave Macon. Courtesy of Charles Wolfe.

The *Gospel Cannonball*

GOSPEL CANNON BALL

In the great and holy Bible, on the pages I do find
How God came down from heaven to redeem this soul of mine;
He's a lovin' savior and He should be known by all;
I'm headed straight for heaven on the *Gospel Cannonball*.

Listen to His story, for God is very near.
Won't you plan to meet Him, without a doubt or care?
Hear the angels singin', He's callin' one and all,
Saints will go to meet Him on the *Gospel Cannonball*.

Our churches are all dandies, and lots of people pray,
The Bible it is used more than any book today;
But there are some who shun Him and refuse to heed His call,
They'll never hear the whistle of the *Gospel Cannonball*.

Listen to His story, for God is very near,
Won't you plan to meet Him, without a doubt or care?
Hear the angels singin', He's callin' one and all,
Saints will go to meet Him on the *Gospel Cannonball*.

Listen to His story, for God is very near,
Won't you plan to meet Him, without a doubt or care?
Hear the angels singin', He's callin' one and all,
Saints will go to meet Him on the *Gospel Cannonball*.

Delmore Brothers

The discussion of "The *Wabash Cannonball*" in chapter 8 pointed out how that song was a parody of an older piece, "The Great Rock Island Route." In turn, "The *Wabash Cannonball*" has been parodized in this religious song, "The *Gospel Cannonball*." As with many of the songs in this chapter, the origin of the piece is obscure. Since the three recordings cited in the discography were all made in 1940–41, just when Roy Acuff's "Wabash Cannonball" was enjoying great popularity, it is reasonable to assume that "The *Gospel Cannonball*" was written at that time to ride on the coattails of the Acuff hit. A minor flaw with this suggestion is the fact that the earliest of the three recordings, that by Wade Mainer and the Sons of the Mountaineers, was not set to the "*Wabash Cannonball*" tune, although the words still suggest a parody of that piece. The version transcribed here, the last of the three, differs considerably from Wade Mainer's version, in both tune and text; it was recorded by the Delmore Brothers in July, 1941. The other recording, by Karl [Davis] and Harty [Taylor], made in January, 1941, differs from the Delmores' version in a few textual changes and the appearance of an extra stanza. Karl and Harty took composers' credits on their version. The most plausible explanation is that they (or someone else) rewrote an older religious parody of "The *Wabash Cannonball*" and that the Delmores learned it from them on their record. Mainer's version probably came from a printed source that did not indicate the tune to be used. It might help clarify the song's evolution if texts could be found in some printed folios.

REFERENCES

A. "The Gospel Cannonball," by Wade Mainer and the Sons of the Mountaineers. Recorded Aug. 21, 1939 (RCA Victor master BS-041203), in Atlanta, Ga. Released on Bluebird B-8349, Montgomery Ward M-8448.

"Gospel Cannon Ball," by Karl (Karl Victor Davis) and Harty (Hartford Connecticut Taylor). Vocal duet with guitar and mandolin accompaniment. Recorded Jan. 24, 1941 (American Record Corp. master C 3560), in Chicago. Released on Vocalion 06207, OKeh 06207, Conqueror 9689.

"Gospel Cannon Ball," by the Delmore Brothers (Alton and Rabon). Vocal duet with two guitars accompaniment. Recorded July 16, 1941 (Decca master 69514), in New York City. Released on Decca 5970, Decca 46049. Reissued on MCA (Japan) VIM-4017: *The Delmore Brothers*. This recording is transcribed in this book.

The Hell-Bound Train

THE HELL BOUND TRAIN

Some liberties have been taken with this transcription. The original is sung in a breathless, declamatory style, rhythmically rushed and "bunched up." Here it has been smoothed out.

*On the recording, this is spoken.

A Texas cowboy on a barroom floor
Had drank so much he could hold no more;
So he fell asleep with a troubled brain,
To dream that he rode on the hell-bound train.

The engine with murderous blood was damp,
The headlight was a big brimstone lamp;
While an imp, for fuel, was shovelin' bones,
The furnace rang with a thousand groans.

The boiler was filled full of lager beer,
And the devil himself was engineer;
The passengers were a mixed-up crew—
Church member, atheist, gentile and Jew;

Well, the train rushed on at an awful pace,
The sulfur fumes scorched their hands and face;
Wilder and wilder the country grew,
And faster and faster the engine flew.

Louder and louder the thunder crashed,
And brighter and brighter the lightning flashed;
Hotter and hotter the air became,
Till the clothes were burned from each shrinking frame.

Then out of the distance there arose a yell,
"Ha ha," said the devil, "the next stop's hell."
Then oh, how the passengers shrieked with pain
And begged the devil to stop the train.

But he capered about and he danced with glee,
And he laughed and mocked at their misery;
"My friends, you paid for your seats on this road,
The train goes through with the complete load.

"Ah, you've bullied the weak, and you've cheated the poor,
The starving brother you've turned from your door;
You've laid up your gold till your purses bust,
And given free pay [*sic*] to your beastly lust.

"You've paid full fare and I'll carry you through,
For it's only right you should have your due;
The laborer always expects his hire,
So I'll land you safe in the lake of fire.

"Your flesh will scorch in the flames that roar,
And my imps will torment you forevermore."
Then the cowboy awoke with an anguished cry,
His clothes were wet and his hair stood high.

Then he prayed as he never had prayed before,
To be saved from his sins and from hell's front door;
His prayers and his pleadings were not in vain,
For he never rode on that hell-bound train.

Smiling Ed McConnell

The relative stability of language, despite the considerable length and awkward—or, at least, unconventional—phraseology, suggests that this ballad has been perpetuated more through print than through oral transmission. Three varieties of the ballad might be distinguished, subtitled "Texas Cowboy's Dream" (I), "Drunkard's Dream" (II), and "Tom Gray's Dream" (III), according to the dreamer identified in the first line of the ballad.

The opening stanzas of representative texts of the three sub-types are as follows:

(I) A Texas cowboy lay down on a bar-room floor,
Having drunk so much he could drink no more;
So he fell asleep with a troubled brain
To dream that he rode on a hell-bound train. [1]

(II) A drunkard lay on the barroom floor,
He drunk till he could not drink no more,
He went to sleep with a troubled brain,
An' dreampt he was on the hell-bound train. [2]

(III) Tom Gray lay down on a barroom floor,
Having drunk so much he could drink no more,
And fell asleep with a troubled brain,
To dream that he rode on the hell-boud train. [3]

Some other differences seem to persist among the three forms:

  (I) The engine with murderous blood was damp
    And was brilliantly lit with a brimstone lamp.[4]

  (II) The fireman he was a crazy tramp,
    An' the headlight it was a brimstone lamp.[5]

  (III) The engine, with blood, was red and damp
    And dismally lit with a brimstone lamp.[6]

and:

  (I) While the train rushed on at an awful pace,
    The sulphurous fumes scorched their hands and face.[7]

  (II) The train it flew at an awful pace,
    The brimstone a-burnin' both hands an' face.[8]

  (III) While the train dashed on at an awful pace,
    And a hot wind scorched their hands and face.[9]

However, a full textual comparison of the three varieties suggests that these are not wholly separate and distinct ballads, but minor variants that became stabilized because of their appearance in influential collections or other printed sources.

For first bringing variant I to general notice, we have John Lomax to thank; a correspondent had mailed him the text, which he printed in his important anthology, *Cowboy Songs and Other Frontier Ballads* (1916), without attribution. In the 1938 edition, this footnote was added: "said to have been written by J. W. Pruitte, the Cowboy Preacher. Clipped from the *Ft. Gibson Post*, Apr. 8, 1909."[10] Lomax's 1910 collection, revised in 1916 and expanded in 1938, proved to be enormously popular in the West, and did much to stabilize the form of many folksongs and ballads. The texts of variant I printed by Shay (1928) and by Thorp (1921) are very similar to Lomax's. The version given by Finger (1927), who learned it as a poem in California, has enough differences to suggest another source. Also different from Lomax's text is the version in the several hillbilly and cowboy song folios published by M. M. Cole of Chicago starting in 1930. During the 1930s and early 1940s Cole produced hundreds of folios; different artists were featured on the covers, but the contents of many of the folios were drawn from the same standard plates. Thus, any song folio published by Cole with "Hell-Bound Train" on page 60 is almost sure to be identical with the three folios cited in the references (Hamlins Saddle Pals, Robison, Tiny Texan).

Variant II was collected by Vance Randolph in Missouri in 1911. It has twenty couplets (compared with Lomax's twenty-six) and differs considerably from variant I. The text printed by Alan Lomax in 1960, although credited to J. W. Pruitt [*sic*], is almost verbatim the same as Randolph's version. I have not found any other texts of II.

The earliest printing of variant III that I have located was in a 1910 *Railroad Man's Magazine;* there it was credited to F. M. Lehman. This twenty-four-couplet text was submitted by a reader in response to a request in the February issue. In October, 1914, the magazine offered a twenty-six-couplet version, which differed in a number of instances from the 1910 printing, although it, too, was attributed to F. H. [*sic*] Lehman. The mention of Tom Gray in the opening line is interesting in view of an attribution of authorship to Tom Gray in "an old copy of W. H. Fawcett's *Smoke-House Poetry*."[11]

An unusual variant of variant III was obtained by Howard W. Odum from J. D.

Arthur in 1929. This is the only printed version I have found that lacks the epilogue relating the awakening of the dreamer; it has instead an incipit and a chorus, as follows:

> Come all you good people if you want to hear,
> The story of a bad engineer,
> Who ran a train on the downward road,
> And every car held a heavy load.
> The agent stood at the station door,
> He welcomed the rich, he grabbed at the poor,
> And everybody seemed jolly and gay,
> As the hell-bound train sped on its way.

> Come, my friend, give your heart to Jesus,
> Come, my friend, join out [*sic*] happy band:
> Come today and follow the Saviour,
> He will lead you safely to the promised land.[12]

The manuscript bears instructions "to be sung to the tune of 'Casey Jones,'" as might be inferred by scansion of the poem. Frank Hutchison's 1928 recording is a considerably shortened variant of this form of the song, including the first four and last two lines of the verse cited above, the chorus (slightly changed), and two additional couplets similar to lines found in most of the versions. Hutchison uses the "Casey Jones" tune. If the text were not so abbreviated, it would be a good version to transcribe here; most other tunes cited, either in print or on record, are rather chant-like in quality.[13]

While it may be no more than coincidence, the fact that the earliest recoveries of all three variants of the ballad are in the brief span 1909–11 suggests that perhaps the song (or poem) was first composed not much earlier than that. There is the additional coincidence that "Casey Jones" was published in 1909.

A considerably older poem on the same theme—that of a train that hauls drunkards to hell—was titled "Ride on the Black Valley Railroad" and credited to I. N. Tarbox in *One Hundred Choice Selections*, No. 11 (1876). Here are some of the verses comparable to lines in "The Hell-Bound Train":

> A full supply of bad whiskey,
> For our engine is taken here;
> And a queer looking fellow from Hades,
> Steps on for our engineer.

> Our engineer chuckles and dances,
> In the wild lurid flashes he throws;
> Hotter blaze the red fires of his furnace,
> As on in the blackness he goes.

> Oh, the sounds that we hear in the darkness,
> The laughter and crying and groans;
> The ravings of anger and madness,
> The sobbings and pitiful moans.[14]

Poems such as this, and the later "Hell-Bound Train," were specialized forms of a more general theme often exploited in nineteenth-century compositions—the drunkard's dream, in which a confirmed alcoholic falls into a stupor and foresees the plight of his widow and orphaned children ten years hence, after he has been laid in the grave by Demon Rum. Except for the device of the dream, such poems and songs were similar to an even wider class of temperance songs recounting the decline and fall of the drunkard. But in the dream songs, the stern scenes of the nightmarish vision so move the sinner that upon awakening he resolves to renounce alcohol once for all; thenceforth he lives a happy and reformed man and model citizen. An early and oft-printed prototype of this ballad type is "The Drunkard's Dream."[15] Although modern readers may associate Prohibition and temperance movements with the 1920s, they were in fact products of the humanitarian awakening of the 1840s and 1850s. The crusade, which by 1861 had secured adoption of prohibition laws in many northern and midwestern states, suffered a setback during the Civil War. A growing liquor problem during the 1870s, however, induced a revival of the temperance movement; the Women's Christian Temperance Union (WCTU) was founded in 1874, the Anti-Saloon League in 1893. By 1917 two-thirds of the states had adopted prohibition laws. Homiletic pieces such as "The Hell-Bound Train" echoed popular sentiments of the times.

England, too, had its share of temperance broadsides that used the railroad to represent the alcoholic descent into decadence and dissolution; an anonymous "Railroad to Hell," which catalogs in rhythmic detail London's alehouses and grogshops, is reproduced here.

Modern country music still frequently makes use of the theme of alcohol and alcoholism, and the musical treatment of this subject in hillbilly and country music would be worth a book in itself. Suffice it to note here, however, that over the years a pronounced change in philosophy has taken place in such songs. Whereas in the nineteenth century the drunkard was seen as the author of his own downfall, more recent songs tend to blame the alcoholic beverage itself or other mitigating socioeconomic factors.

The "Hell-Bound Train" transcribed in this book was recorded in 1931 by Smiling Ed McConnell for the Starr Piano Company's Gennett Records division. The text is almost identical with that of the various Cole folios and obviously comes from the same ultimate source—if not from a folio printing directly. Recording company ledgers gave no indication of author or composer credits for McConnell's rendition. Smiling Ed recorded the song again two years later for the RCA Victor company; the release on the Bluebird label surely achieved wider circulation than Starr's Champion label had. McConnell was almost certainly not a traditional performer. He will probably be most familiar to readers for his role on "The Buster Brown Gang" radio show, starting on NBC in 1943 and broadcasting from Hollywood every Saturday morning from 11:30 A.M. to noon. Smiling Ed played piano, sang songs, and portrayed such once-familiar characters as Froggie the Gremlin.[16]

NOTES

1. John A. Lomax, *Cowboy Songs and Other Frontier Ballads* (New York: Macmillan, 1916), p. 345

2. Vance Randolph, *Ozark Folksongs*, vol. 4 (Columbia: State Historical Society of Missouri, 1950), p. 23.

3. *RRManM*, 11 (Apr., 1910), 575.

4. Lomax, *Cowboy Songs*, p. 345.

5. Randolph, *Ozark Folksongs*, vol. 4, p. 23.

6. *RRManM*, 11 (Apr., 1910), 575.

7. Lomax, *Cowboy Songs*, p. 345.

RAILROAD TO HELL.

FROM DISSIPATION TO POVERTY,

AND

FROM POVERTY TO DESPERATION.

This Line begins in the Brewery, and runs through all Public-houses, Dram-shops and Jerry-shops, in a zigzag direction, until it lands in the kingdom of Hell.

If you are determined and wishful to go,
With blind debauchees to the regions of woe,
Then go to the Tap without any delay,
And drink both your reason and money away,
But never mind care, for if you despair,
It is the first train that will carry you there.

You've nothing to do but to guzzle and swill,
As long as the Landlord is willing to fill
For this is the Line and the Railraad to Hell,
Where Drunkards and Devils for ever must dwell;
So drink all you can, it is the chief plan,
That e'er was invented by devil for man.

This Railroad it runs thro' Parlours and Snugs'
And here yau can sit round glasses and jugs,
And have what you please, such as Ale, Gin, or Rum,
To please an old friend, or an old drunken chum;
And this is the way to drink all the day,
And then stagger home wnen you've swallowed your.

Such Taverns as these arv Railroads to Hell,
Their dorrels are engines which make men rebel;
Their jugs and their glasses which furnish their Trains,
Will empty their pockees and muddle their brains
And thus drunkards ride to Hell in their pride,
With nothing but steam from the barrels inside.

We've Railroads to Heaven, and Railroads to Hell,
Where good men can ride, and where Devils can dwell;
We've Taverns for drunkards, and Churches for Saints
And quacks of all sorts to heal your complaints:
So now we can ride to Hell in our pride,
On Railroads of sin with blue Devils inside.

Old Swillsub the Doctor and guard of the Trains,
He filches your pockets and fuddles your brains;
But when he's got all from the poor silly man,
He then sends him home to do as he can,
With all his old chums, his badgers and bums,
Who sue him for money he owes in great sams.

But let us not ride on this Railroad of sin,
Nor drink either Brandy, Ale, Porter, or Gin;
And then shall we ride into Heaven with joy,
Where no drunken Quacks can our vitals destroy
With poisonous drugs, sold to us in jugs,
In either their Bars, their Parlours, or snugs.

The number of vaults which we have in town,
Have robb'd the poor lass of her bonnet and gown,
Her topknots and feathers have gone to the Pop,
And many have lost both credit and shop;
Both young men and maids of very good trades,
Have drund all they earned, and gone down to the shades.

We've plenty of signs, both Horses and Bulls,
Of Lions and Dragons, to serve drunken Trulls;
We've signs too of Angels, of Warriors and Kings—
Yes, plenty of signs of good and bad thing,
But what's their desigh? Why Gin, Rum, and Wine,
Sold here to intoxicate puppies and swine.

We've White and Black Balls and two Suns in one street,
One Swan and two Lions which never taste meat,
And here you see women with bottles and jugs,
Roll into these taverns and dram-drinking snugs,
As brazen as brass to get an odd glass,
In some of these shops where a fool cannat pass.

Na wonder that Pop-ticket woman and wags,
Are dressed up in nothing but patches and rags,
Their dresses and shawls for strong liquor they'll swop,
Yes, Tagrag and Bobatil must go to the pop;
And when this is done away they will run,
To either a Lion, a Bull, ar a Son.

Such poor sorry women who pledge their old rags,
Are known by their petticoats hanging in rags;
You'll see them at night with their heads wrapt in shalls,
Not far from the Dram-shop, or sign of Three Balls
With bonnets and hats, old dresses and brats,
Made up into dundle as you have seen Pat's.

Taylor, Printer, 92 & 93, Brick Lane.—N.E.

Broadside: "Railroad to Hell." UCLA Special Collections Library.

8. Randolph, *Ozark Folksongs*, vol. 4, p. 23.

9. *RRManM*, 25 (Oct., 1914), 479.

10. John A. Lomax, *Cowboy Songs and Other Frontier Ballads*, rev. and enl. ed. (New York: Macmillan, 1938), p. 236.

11. Cited by Randolph, *Ozark Folksongs*, vol. 4, p. 23.

12. Odum-Arthur MS 30, July 10, 1929.

13. Hutchison's recording has been reissued on Rounder 1007: *The Train That Carried My Girl from Town;* the text is transcribed in the liner notes.

14. *One Hundred Choice Selections*, No. 11 (1876), p. 181; also in *Railroad and Current Mechanics*, 22 (Dec., 1913), 67.

15. See, e.g., *The Frank C. Brown Collection of North Carolina Folklore*, vol. 3: *Folk Songs*, edited by Henry M. Belden and Arthur Palmer Hudson (Durham, N.C.: Duke University Press, 1952), p. 45. Although this song was copyrighted in 1867 in the United States, there is evidence that it is older.

16. See Frank Buxton and Bill Owen, *The Big Broadcast: 1920–1950* (1966; rpt., New York: Flare Books, 1973), p. 43.

REFERENCES

A. "The Hell Bound Train" by Smiling Ed McConnell. Vocal and piano. Recorded Jan. 3, 1931 (Starr master 17407A), in Richmond, Ind. Released on Champion 16209 in Apr., 1931, and on Champion 45137. Transcribed in this book.

"Hell Bound Train," by Frank Hutchison. Hutchison, vocal, guitar, and harmonica; Sherman Lawson, fiddle. Recorded Sept. 10, 1928 (OKeh master 401106), in New York City. Released on OKeh 45452 on July 10, 1930, and on Clarion 5300-C and Velvetone 2366-V (as by Billy Adams).

B. Beck (1942), 246–47
Beck (1948), 261–62
Cowboy Songs, 42
Fife & Fife (1969), 336–37
Fife & Fife (1970), 91–94
Finger, 110–13
Hamlins Saddle Pals, 60
Kennedy, C. O. (1952), 93–95
Kennedy, C. O. (1954), 268–70
Lomax, A. (1960), 393, 402
Lomax, J. (1916, 1922), 345–47
Lomax & Lomax (1938), 236–38
Lynn, 208–9
McCulloh & Green, 12
Ohrlin, 36–37, 254
Old Brother Charlie
OTS&P, Jan.-Feb., 1969, pp. 21, 46
Palmer, 212
Randolph IV, 23–24
Robison (1930), 60

RRManM, 11 (Apr., 1910), 575–76
RRManM, 25 (Oct., 1914), 479–80
RRManM, 3 (Aug., 1930), 160
Shay (1928), 168–70
Sherwin & Powell
Smoke-House Poetry, 175
Thorp, 79–81
Tiny Texan, 60
Wallrich, 155–57 (parody)
Wild West Weekly, Mar. 23, 1940, p. 128

D. Chuck Berry and his Combo—Chess 1615, Chess LP 1426: *After School Session*   "Downbound Train"
Reverend J. M. Gates—OKeh 8532 "Hell Bound Express Train" (related)
Smiling Ed McConnell—Bluebird 5140, Sunrise 3221, Electradisk 2046

E. Hoyt Axton—Crestview CRV 807: *The Original Hootenanny, Vol. 2* "Downbound Train"
Billy Faier—Riverside RLP 12–657: *Travellin' Man*
Hank Harral—Caprock 102 (45 rpm)
Glenn Ohrlin—Campus Folksong Club (University of Illinois) CFC 301: *The Hell-Bound Train*
Martin Yarbrough—Argo LP 4029: *The Martin Yarbrough Showcase*

F. LC AFS:

Andrew Jackson—AFS 2340

Appendix I:
Worksongs and Instrumentals
===

The omission from the main part of this book of two entire categories of musical rail-roadiana calls for either apology or some effort at redress here in these final pages. I refer to worksongs and to railroad instrumental pieces.

Folklorists distinguish between "work songs" and "occupational songs." The latter deal with labor as a subject. The cowboy sang about rounding up the cattle, fighting the Indians, or heading off stampedes. The logger sang about felling trees or untangling log jams. The railroader—to the extent that he sang about railroading (see chap. 3)—sang about rail disasters. In contrast to these occupational songs, worksongs are the musical accompaniments to physical labor itself—songs or chants used to keep the rhythm or buoy up sagging spirits. The best-known examples are the sea chanteys of the whalers and sailors of the last century, sung while anchors or sails were being raised or lowered. In the southeastern United States, black construction workers sang worksongs as they ham-mered, picked, or shoveled while constructing roads, breaking rocks, or laying railroad tracks. Between 1933 and 1942, John and Alan Lomax and other folklorists recorded more than five dozen such railroad worksongs for the Library of Congress Archive of Folk Song. John Lomax discussed this genre at some length in his autobiography, *Adventures of a Ballad Hunter* (pp. 253–62); he and his son Alan included transcriptions of some of the material they recorded in their anthologies: five selections in *American Ballads and Folk Songs;* two in *Our Singing Country;* and three, all from earlier publications, in Alan Lomax's *Folk Songs of North America*. Ben Botkin included transcriptions of some of the field recordings gathered by the Lomaxes in his anthologies: one in *A Treasury of Southern Folklore* and two in *A Treasury of Railroad Folklore;* he included three of the recordings themselves in an album edited for the Library of Congress, L8: *Negro Work Songs and Calls*. Zora Neale Hurston, who accompanied Alan Lomax on some of his 1935 recording trips, transcribed two pieces from that expedition in her own book *Mules and Men*. John Lomax included several examples in a series of lectures on American folk music that he recorded for the Library of Congress in 1941 (L52: *Adventures of a Ballad Hunter, Part 8*).

These recordings are all readily identified by any listener as musical pieces meant to accompany men engaged in physical labor. They all have strong rhythms and are sung by men, without instrumental accompaniment. With one interesting exception, such songs

645

were not recorded commercially by hillbilly and blues singers in the 78 rpm era: probably they were not deemed to have sufficient entertainment value. (One could argue, though, that some of them are musically as interesting as many a capella spirituals.) A few songs, such as "Nine Pound Hammer" and its near kin, "Take This Hammer," have been identified by informants as worksongs: yet they have been readily converted into pieces appropriate for hillbilly and blues musicians to perform and record. The list of citations below is confined to items that have not been arranged for nonwork contexts.

The exception just noted is a pair of 1927 recordings made for Paramount by a group identified on the disc as the T.C.I. Section Crew. The titles, issued on Paramount 12478, are "Track Linin'" and "Section Gang Song." Other recordings made on the same day by groups identified as the T.C.I. Women's Four and the T.C.I. Sacred Singers strongly suggest that these singers were not part of a genuine labor gang, but rather a choir— either from a commercial firm (such as the Tennessee Coal and Iron Company) or from some school—that was recreating several pieces, both sacred and secular, for commercial purposes. These sides are of interest not only because they are the only worksongs recorded commercially on 78s, but also because they are very probably the earliest recorded in any form. For these reasons it seems worthwhile to transcribe their texts here.

TRACK LININ'

[*Whistle*] All right, boys, let's go back. The whistle is blowing. I hear the captain calling. Let's go back. Haul them, boys. Let's go.

Evelina and her daughter ran a boardinghouse on the water,
Selling porkchops for a quarter, ain't it good, boys, from the slaughter.

Jack the rabbit, Jack the bear, can't you line 'em, just a hair,
Can't you line 'em, for the captain, can't you line 'em, for the straw [i.e., strawboss]
Can't you line 'em for the walker, can't you line 'em, for the boss.
Can't you line 'em, just a little bit, can't you line 'em, to the other side.

Going back to Indiana, where the section boys like to gamble.
Play dominoes, shoot dice, catch the skinnin' card, [?tie] me twice.

[*Whistle*] All right [*whistle*], all right, boys. Get out the way. Don't you see that train coming? You just dragging around with that jack; looks like it's gonna run over you. I'll bet you next time we gonna have to haul you in here on a pair of stretchers. Well, it didn't hurt nobody (?). Oh, you fellows just hanging around here, talk a whole lot of foolish talk. The captain standing, looking at you. Let's go, boys. Ain't no need of that. All right, buddy, let's line that track . . . , boy. Let's go now.

Jack the rabbit, Jack the bear, can't you line 'em, just a hair.
Mobile, Alabam', New Orleans, Birmingham.
In the morning, when I rise, cup of coffee by my side.
Captain Bill gone north, got the boys paid off.
In the morning, when he rise, cup of coffee by his side.
And I'm going back to Indiana, where the section boys got to gamble.
Play dominoes, shoot dice, play dominoes, shootin' dice.
Ain't no whistle here, ain't no [?dime], catch you gambling, boys, pay your fine.
In the morning, when I rise, cup of coffee by my side.
Going down to Indiana, where the section men like to gamble.

All right, boys, the day's work is done. Let's go get them beans.

SECTION GANG SONG

Oh captain, captain, I'm goin' away to leave you,
Oh captain, captain, I'm goin' away to leave you,
Oh captain, captain, I'm goin' away to leave you,
By next payday, oh captain, next payday.

Oh captain, captain, this is our call,
Oh captain, captain, this is our call,
Oh captain, captain, this is our call,
It's payday, captain, and you won't pay off.

Oh, captain told the poor boy, "Ain't gonna pay you off,"
Oh, captain told the poor boy, "Ain't gonna pay you off,"
Oh, captain told the poor boy, "Ain't gonna pay you off,"
But it's payday, captain, and you won't pay off.

Gonna drive this spike, boys, I'm gonna walk on down the line,
Gonna drive this spike, boys, I'm gonna walk on down the line,
Gonna drive this spike, boys, I'm gonna walk on down the line,
If the freight train pass me [*whistle*], down the road I'm gwine.

Oh, captain told the high sheriff, "Go bring me Lazarus,"
Oh, captain told the high sheriff, "Go bring me Lazarus,"
Oh, captain told the high sheriff, "Go bring me Lazarus,"
Bring him dead or alive, oh captain, bring him dead or alive.

I'm gonna make this payday, I'm gonna tip on down the line,
I'm gonna make this payday, I'm gonna tip on down the line,
I'm gonna make this payday, I'm gonna tip on down the line,
If you want me, captain, you got to come and find.

Oh captain, captain, this is our call,
Oh captain, captain, this is our call,
Oh captain, captain, this is our call,
It's payday, captain, and you won't pay off.

Below I list all the Library of Congress field recordings of railroad worksongs that I have been able to identify. There are also many recordings of worksongs by road gangs that very well could have been used in railroad building, or in other chores that black convict laborers were assigned throughout the South. An excellent sampling of these —including "Rosie," "It Makes a Long Time Man Feel Bad," "Jumpin' Judy," and "Black Woman"—is available on an LP of recordings made in 1947 by Alan Lomax, Tradition TLP 1020: *Negro Prison Songs from the Mississippi Penitentiary*.

Each song in the list is sung by blacks. To my knowledge, we have no recordings—or even transcribed texts—of worksongs by the other groups of men who built railroads in the nineteenth century. We have preserved many occupational songs by the Irish laborers who worked on the Union Pacific and other lines in the 1860s and 1870s, but no worksongs. More regrettably, we have nothing, as far as I know, from the Chinese laborers of the Central Pacific in either category. Possibly they didn't sing; more likely they did, but the tradition died out too soon to be found by song collectors, inasmuch as the Chinese laborers were relatively transitory, unlike the Irish and blacks, who remained visible in the American scene for many decades.

"Big Boy, Can't You Move 'em?" Uncle Bradley Eberhard, 1940. 3901 A3.

"Can't You Line 'em?" George Harris, 1940. 3406 A & B.

"Can't You Line 'em?" Roscoe McLean and group, 1936. 694 B1

"Can't You Line 'em?" Group of eight, 1936. 724 B1.

"Can't You Line It?" A. B. Hicks, 1935. 362 A.

"Can't You Line It?" A. B. Hicks, 1935. 363 A.

"The Dallas Railway." Will Roseborough, Will Brooks, H. Davis, and Jess Alexander, 1936. 601 B1.

"Going to See My Long-Haired Baby." A. B. Hicks, 1935. 364 A2.

"Ho, Boy, Caincha Line?" Henry Hankins, 1939. 2946 A, 2947 A1.

"I'm Goin' Home on the Mornin' Train." Group of Negro convicts, 1934. 266 B1

"I'm Going Home on the Morning Train." E. M. Martin and Pearline Johns, 1942. 6624 B2.

"L and N Mobile." Uncle Bradley Eberhard, 1940. 3901 A2.

"Laying Rail Chant." J. Wilson, R. Ramsay, G. Gorman, R. Brown, J. Kirby, L. Jones, C. Meekins, and Ed Lewis, 1936. 724 B2 & B3.

"Line It for the Captain." Manuel "Peter Hatcher" Jones, 1940. 4059 B2

"Lining Track." Luther Boyd, 1936. 599 B2

"Lining or Calling Track." Houston Bacon, 1942. 6650 A.

"Marry a Railroad Man." Henry Truvillion, 1939. 2666 A2. (Identified in the LC AFS files as a worksong, but this is not obvious from the recording.)

"Pauline." Albert Jackson, 1934. 232 B.

"Pauline." Allen Prothero, 1933. 176 B; L52.

"Pauline." Allen Prothero's quartet, 1933. 177 A1.

"Pauline." Bowlegs, 1933. 1857 A3.

"Rail Unloading." Henry Truvillion and gang, 1940. 3973 A3; L8.

"Shuffling Ties or Catching Ties." Houston Bacon and Elias Boykin, 1942. 6648 A2.

"Sinking Rails." Houston Bacon and Elias Boykin, 1942. 6647 B2.

"Spiking Down." Houston Bacon and Elias Boykin, 1942. 6648 A1.

"Steel-Calling Holler." Sam "Old Dad" Ballard, 1934. 99 A1.

"Steel-Driving Song." Henry Truvillion, 1939. 2658 A.

"Steel-Driving Song." Henry Truvillion and gang, 1940. 3973 B1

"Steel-Laying." Henry Truvillion, with Elliot Peacock and group, 1940. 3972 B3.

"Steel-Laying Holler." John "Black Sampson" Gibson, 1933. 179 B1.

"Steel-Laying Holler." Rochelle Harris, 1933. 181 A1.

"Tamp 'em up Solid." Sam "Old Dad" Ballard, 1934. 101 A4.

"Tamp 'em up Solid." Rochelle Harris, 1933. 181 A4 & B2.

"Tamp 'em up Solid." Manuel "Peter Hatcher" Jones, 1940. 4059 B1.

"Tie-Packing." Henry Truvillion and gang, 1940. 3975 B3.

"Tie-Shuffling Chant." John "Black Sampson" Gibson, 1933. 179 A1.

"Tie-Shuffling Chant." Rochelle Harris, 1933. 181 A2 & A3.

"Tie-Shuffling Chant." Group of Negro convicts, 1933. 1867 A1.

"Tie-Shuffling Song." Henry Truvillion, 1933. John A. Lomax cylinder 9.

"Tie-Tamping Chant." Richard Amerson, 1940. 4048 B1.

"Tie-Tamping Chant." James Clark, 1940. 4021 A2.

"Tie-Tamping Chant." Henry Hankins, 1939. 2947 A1 & A2.

"Tie-Tamping Chant." James Clark and Jeff Horton, 1940. 4021 B1.

"Tie-Tamping Chant." Manuel "Peter Hatcher" Jones, 1940. 4066 A3.

"Tie-Tamping Chant." Will Roseborough, Will Brooks, H. Davis, and Jess Alexander, 1936. 601 A.

"Tie-Tamping Chant." Rudolf Thompson, 1933. 1854 B.

"Tie-Tamping Chant." Henry Truvillion and gang, 1940. 3973 A2; L8.

"Tie-Tamping Song." Henry Truvillion, 1933. John A. Lomax cylinder 9.

"Tie-Tamping Song." Tudodum and K. C. Gallaway, 1933. John A. Lomax cylinder 9.

"Tie-Throwing Call." Tom Stephenson, 1940. 3976 B1.

"Tie-Toting Holler." Sam "Old Dad" Ballard, 1934. 99 A2.
"Track-Calling." Henry Truvillion, 1939. 2654 A3 & B1; L52.
"Track-Calling." Henry Truvillion, 1940. 3984 A4.
"Track-Laying Holler." Henry Truvillion and gang, 1940. 3973 A1.
"Track-Lining Holler." Richard Amerson, 1940. 4048 A2.
"Track-Lining Holler." Henry Truvillion, 1939. 2654 A1 & A2.
"Track-Lining Holler." Henry Truvillion, 1940. 3984 B.
"Track-Lining Holler." Negro convict, 1936. 599 A2.
"Track-Lining Song." James Clark and Jeff Horton, 1940. 4021 A1.
"Track-Lining Song." John "Black Sampson" Gibson, 1933. 180 B2; L8.
"Unloading Steel from Cars." Houston Bacon and Elias Boykin, 1942. 6647 B1.
"Unloading Steel Rails." Henry Truvillion, 1939. 2654 B2.
"When the Train Comes Along." Rollie Lee Johnson, 1936. 723 A2.
"Working on the Railroad." Laura Hatcher and mixed group, 1939. 3108 A2.

Instrumentals complement worksongs: the former feature instruments without voices; the latter, voices without instruments. Elsewhere in this book I have quoted Alan Lomax's theory about the influence the sounds of the locomotive and train clicking down the track have had on the nature of American blues and jazz. Without subscribing wholeheartedly to his contention that "the distinctive feeling of American hot music comes from the railroad," I would agree that those characteristic sounds of steam engine, whistle, and wheels on tracks made a lasting impression on musicians, both folk and classical. Just as Arthur Honegger's program music "Pacific 231" translates railroad sounds to the concert hall, so have such folk compositions as "Chickasaw Special," "Pan American Blues," and "Orange Blossom Special" marked the railroad's influence on blues and bluegrass. The instruments favored for train imitations are harmonica and fiddle —the latter especially among white musicians, and the former, through popular with both whites and blacks, perhaps more so among blacks. But color distinctions are not very meaningful in treating this genre of music, and several harmonica players who recorded instrumentals during the 1920s, such as Palmer McAbee and El Watson, cannot, on the basis of their music, be identified with certainty as black or white. Unlike worksongs, instrumentals have always been regarded as appropriate material by commercial record companies, and they continued to be as popular on record in the 1970s as they were in the 1920s.

The pieces vary from being extraordinarily imitative, as in "Train Imitations and the Fox Chase," to being only slightly suggestive, as in Alex Hood and his Railroad Boys' "L & N Rag," where the title seems almost an afterthought given to a nonce composition for want of anything better. "Train Imitations and the Fox Chase" gave its composer the opportunity to combine two favored themes on the harmonica. Another popular theme on that instrument was a race between a train and a Model T. In bluegrass tradition, Ervin Rouse's "Orange Blossom Special" (not strictly an instrumental, since he did write one verse with it) seems to have driven out all earlier railroad fiddle imitations. Though the originality of Rouse's composition is unquestioned, like many folk compositions, its debt to earlier pieces can easily be discerned in such recordings as Byron Parker's "Peanut Special."

Following this discussion are two lists of instrumentals that feature some railroad sound imitations: one is of Library of Congress Archive of Folk Song field recordings; the other, of commercial recordings originally issued on 78 rpm discs. These items are all primarily instrumentals, though a few have occasional incidental vocals. I have not included any of the several vocal pieces that have imitative instrumental sounds here and there, such as "CC & O Number 558" by Al Hopkins's Hill Billies (Brunswick 177) or Richard Brooks and Reuben Puckett's "Railroad Blues" (Brunswick 273), or any of the instrumental versions of titles discussed in the main part of this book. Three particularly interesting recordings deserve special mention: these are all recitatives that do little more than enumerate the stops along a particular train route, with instrumental imitative accompaniments. I refer to Henry Thomas's "Railroadin' Some" (Vocalion 1443; reissued on Yazoo L-1018: *Going Away Blues* and Herwin 209: *Henry Thomas*); Captain Apple-blossom's "Time Table Blues" (OKeh 45373); and Jimmie Davis's "The Davis Limited" (Victor 23601; reissued on RCA Victor LPV 532: *The Railroad in Folksong*).

French harp solo and imitation of train. Albert Harrison, harmonica, 1958. 11902 A.
"Honkytonk Train." Meade Lux Lewis, piano, 1938. 2495 A & B, 2496 A.
"Locomotive 1." Grant Rogers, violin, 1954. 12311 A15.
"Locomotive 2." Grant Rogers, violin, 1954. 12311 A16.
"The Lonesome Train." R. K. Moore, harmonica, 1950. 13130 A36.
"Lost Train Blues." Fred Perry, fiddle, and Glenn Carver, guitar, 1939. 3556 B.
"Orange Blossom Special." Palmer Crisp, guitar, and Sam Leslie, fiddle, 1946. 8482 B2.
"Orange Blossom Special." Harsoe and Andy Ward, 1946. 8486 A3.
"Orange Blossom Special." Hunter, Lanzo, and Espinte. 10504 A21.
"Orange Blossom Special." Uncle Charlie Higgins, fiddle. 15055 A14.
"Orange Blossom Special." Calvert, MacDonald, Jones, and Estep, 1964. 13125 A26.
"The Train." Panhandle Pete, 1941. 4794 A6.
"The Train." Chub Parham, harmonica, 1941. 4798 B1; L2.
"The Train." Daw Henson, harmonica, 1937. 1508 B1.
"Train." Ace Johnson, harmonica, 1939. 2599 B2.
"The Train." Roger Matthews, harmonica, 1935. 367 A.
"The Train." Negro, harmonica, 1935. 318 B1.
"The Train." Negro, harmonica, 1935. 340 B1.
"Train." Negro convict, harmonica, 1934. 207 A1.
"Train A-Pullin' the Crooked Hill." Pete Steele, banjo, 1938. 1704 B2.
"Train Blues." Dewey, Awilda, and Myrle Hamrick, violin, guitar, and tenor banjo, 1939. 3573 B1.
"Train Blues." Russell Wise, fiddle, and Mr. White, guitar, 1936. 3311 A3.
"Train Imitation." Richard Amerson, harmonica, 1937. 1308 A1.
"Train Imitation." Richard Amerson, harmonica, 1940. 4027 A.
"Train on the Island." Velma Nester, dulcimer, 1937. 1343 B1.

"C & NW Blues." D. H. Bilbro, harmonica. OKeh 45278; Magnolia (Sweden) 502: *Rough Alley Blues—Blues from Georgia, 1924–1931*.
"C & NW Railroad Blues." Byron Parker's Mountaineers, string band with fiddle. Bluebird B-8673; County 503: *A Collection of Mountain Fiddle Music, Vol. 2*.
"C & O Excursion." Frank Hutchison, harmonica. OKeh 45089; Vetco LP 103: *Songs of the Railroad*.
"Chickasaw Special." Noah Lewis, harmonica. Victor V-38581; Roots RL-320: *The Great Harmonica Players, Vol. 1*.
"Dixie Flyer Blues." De Ford Bailey, harmonica. Brunswick 146, Vocalion 5180.
"Donkey on the Railroad Track." Hillbillies, string band with fiddle. Vocalion 5020.
"Double Headed Train." Henry Whitter, harmonica. OKeh 40143; Vetco LP 103: *Songs of the Railroad*.

"Engineer Frank Hawk." Rainey Old Time Band, string band with fiddle. Columbia 15675-D.

"Frisco Leaving Birmingham." George "Bullet" Williams, harmonica. Paramount 12651, Broadway 5085; Yazoo L–1018: *Going Away Blues (1926–1935)*.

"Lost Train Blues." Henry Whitter, harmonica. OKeh 40029.

"Lost Train Blues." Da Costa Woltz's Southern Broadcasters, with Price Goodson, harmonica. Gennett 6187; County 524: *Da Costa Woltz's Southern Broadcasters*.

"McAbee's Railroad Piece." Palmer McAbee, harmonica. Victor 21352; RCA Victor LPV-532: *The Railroad in Folksong*.

"Mohana Blues." D. H. Bilbro, harmonica. OKeh 45278; Magnolia (Sweden) 502: *Rough Alley Blues—Blues from Georgia, 1924–1931*.

"The Moore Girl." Andrew and Jim Baxter, fiddle. Victor 21475; Roots RL-316: *The Country Fiddlers*.

"Narrow Gauge Blues." El Watson, harmonica. Victor 20951.

"New Lost Train Blues." J. E. Mainer's Mountaineers, string band with fiddle. Bluebird B-6424; County 507: *Old Time Fiddle Classics*; Old Timey 107: *J. E. Mainer's Mountaineers, Vol. 2*.

"Number 111." J. E. Mainer's Mountaineers, string band with fiddle. Bluebird B-6424; Old Timey LP 107: *J. E. Mainer's Mountaineers. Vol. 2*: Ball Mountain 202.

"One Eleven Special." Curly Fox, fiddle. Decca 5169.

"Pan American Blues." De Ford Bailey, harmonica. Brunswick 146, Vocalion 5180; County 542: *Nashville: Early String Bands, Vol. 2*.

"Peanut Special." Byron Parker and his Mountaineers, string band with fiddle. Bluebird B-8673; RCA Victor LPV-532: *The Railroad in Folksong*.

"Railroad Blues." Freeman Stowers, harmonica. Gennett 6814, Champion 14837, Supertone 9393, Supertone 9430.

"Riding the Blinds." Eddie Mapp, harmonica. QRS R7078.

"Southern No. 111." Roane Country Ramblers, string band with fiddle. Columbia 15328-D; Vetco LP 103: *Songs of the Railroad*; County 403: *Roane County Ramblers*.

"Train Imitations and the Fox Chase." William McCoy, harmonica. Columbia 15265-D, Columbia 14302-D.

"Train Special." Walter Hurdt, string band with fiddle. Bluebird B-8063.

"West Kentucky Limited." E. E. Hack String Band, string band with fiddle. Columbia 15418-D.

Appendix II:
Recommended Albums of Railroad Songs

While there have been several thousand recordings of railroad songs available at one time or another, the number of album collections of recorded material is small. Regrettably, since no album available today combines the requisites of high musical and technical quality with thorough, accurate annotation, my "recommendations" are qualified. All factors considered, however, the first three albums listed below, taken together, constitute the best introductory sampling of traditional musical railroad lore.

Undoubtedly the best general survey of traditional American railroad songs is Library of Congress Archive of Folk Song L61: *Railroad Songs and Ballads*, issued in 1968 and edited by Archie Green. This LP contains twenty-two selections drawn from Archive field recordings originally made between 1936 and 1959. An excellent thirty-five-page booklet provides a general introduction, notes, and text transcriptions for the songs. This is the only full album of railroad songs by nonprofessional traditional singers. Several other field recordings have been issued on other Archive of Folk Song albums; some of the worksongs are discussed in Appendix I. Field recordings by nonprofessional singers often have a rough quality that jars the listener not previously exposed to traditional folk music. Consequently, the following albums, though not so carefully annotated as L61, may nevertheless find broader application for demonstration purposes to nonspecialist audiences.

Three albums reissuing hillbilly recordings of the 1920s and 1930s have appeared in recent years. An outstanding anthology is RCA Victor LPV 532: *The Railroad in Folksong*, edited and well annotated by Archie Green. Issued in 1966, it is, unfortunately, out of print, but well worth searching for in specialty record shops. Vetco LP 103: *Songs of the Railroad,* with notes by Bob Hyland, is more sketchily annotated but has the advantage of still being available. A more recent album is Mark56 794: [*First Recorded*]*Railroad Songs,* featuring Vernon Dalhart. This album includes eleven songs by Dalhart and a twelfth by Gene Austin, all recorded between 1925 and 1929 for the Edison label. The liner notes are by Jim Walsh, a world-renowned authority on pioneer recording artists. Unlike the artists represented on the previous two anthological albums, Vernon Dalhart was more a shaper of folk tradition than a transmitter of it. While many of his songs were learned from the recordings of other, traditional artists, his real importance lies in the number of fresh compositions of the 1920s by such songwriters as Carson Robison,

Andrew Jenkins, and Bob Miller that he introduced to a record-buying public. Many of his recorded songs have since entered oral tradition; in fact, so great was his influence that his recorded versions of older traditional songs often practically drove out the other versions of those same songs.

Two albums of country music in a later style are Starday SLP 170: *All Aboard for the Railroad Special* and King 869: *Railroad Songs*. Issued in the 1960s, both albums reissue material originally recorded between the late 1940s and early 1960s. While perhaps half the contents of these two albums are traditional songs that are still current in the country music field, many numbers were freshly composed in the postwar years in country-and-western and bluegrass styles. Neither album has liner notes to speak of.

Among contemporary bluegrass musicians, "John Henry," "Jesse James," "Train 45," and "Cannonball Blues" are still widely popular. A few bluegrass bands have devoted substantial parts of albums to railroad songs. Columbia CL 2686/CS 9486: *Hear the Whistles Blow*, featuring Lester Flatt, Earl Scruggs, and the Foggy Mountain Boys, consists mainly of train songs, some traditional and some country-and-western composi-tions. Jim and Jesse McReynolds perform mostly country-and-western songs of the 1940s and later on Epic BN 26513: *We Like Trains*. These two albums, issued in the 1960s, represent the period when the hard-driving bluegrass style was somewhat moderated by folk-rock and country influences.

Of the major country-and-western performers of the postwar years, perhaps Hank Snow has most consistently carried on the tradition of train songs that was so successfully exploited by Jimmie Rodgers, the "Singing Brakeman," in the late 1920s and early 1930s. Snow's biggest hit was an exciting, up-tempo train song, "I'm Moving On". At least three of his many albums are built around railroad themes: RCA Victor LPM 2705/LSP 2705: *Railroad Man* (1963); RCA Victor LSP 4501: *Tracks & Trains* (1971); and RCA Camden CAS 2513: *Lonesome Whistle* (1972), a reissue from earlier Snow recordings. Roy Acuff, another major luminary in country music, made some of his biggest hits in the 1940s with train songs: "Fireball Mail," "Freight Train Blues," and "Wabash Cannonball." These and several others were re-recorded in the 1960s for the Hickory label. A dozen have been reissued on Hickory 125: *Great Train Songs: An American Legend*.

In general, albums aimed at the urban audience interested in "folk music" have been better annotated than those directed at the consumers of straight country music, though in recent years the growing serious interest in country music has often blurred this once-sharp distinction. An early album of the urban folk music revival era was Folkways FA 2013 (FP 13): *900 Miles and Other R.R. Songs*, sung by Cisco Houston (1953). Most of the eleven songs in this 10″ album were older traditional numbers, with the exception of "Hobo Bill," "The Rambler" ("Railroad Boomer"), and "The Brave Engineer" ("Wreck of the No. Nine"). The enclosed brochure included text transcriptions and general notes by Charles Edward Smith on the development of the railroads and on their place in American folklore.

A 1949 album aimed at a city audience was, to my knowledge, the first album of railroad songs issued: Decca A-639: *Railroad Songs*, a set of four 10″ 78 rpm discs (numbered individually 24353–24356), featuring the Jesters (Red Latham, Wamp Carl-son, and Guy Bonham). The material was presented as pop songs, though in fact several of the older numbers ("On the Dummy Line," "Casey Jones," "The Wreck of the Old 97," "Just Set a Light," "In the Baggage Coach Ahead") have become traditional. The album has long been out of print.

In this book I frequently have cited material that appeared in the pages of the nineteenth-century journals of the brotherhoods of firemen and locomotive engineers. The role of the railway brotherhoods has changed considerably over the past century; yet BRAC (Brotherhood of Railway and Airline Clerks), the modern descendent of the railroad employees' associations, still provides an audience for railroad songs. Joe Glazer, a well-known interpreter and writer of labor songs, has recorded two albums on the Collector Records label: Collector 1924: *Singing BRAC,* recorded for BRAC's seventy-fifth anniversary in 1975, and Collector 1925: *Union Train,* a revision of the previous album, but with some of the more specifically union-related songs replaced by more general ones.

All the material mentioned thus far has been in the white folk tradition. Blues albums tend less often to be thematically organized; three exceptions are worth nothing. Much of black folksinger Jesse Fuller's repertoire predated the blues tradition of the early twentieth century. One early 10″ album of his, World Song EG-10–027: *Working on the Railroad,* included four railroad songs. Milestone MLP 3002: *Ramblin' on My Mind—A Collection of Classic Train and Travel Blues* features a dozen contemporary bluesmen and bands performing in a variety of blues styles. All but three or four of the pieces deal with trains. Rosetta Records RR 1301: *Sorry but I Can't Take You: Women's Railroad Blues* is a collection of fifteen blues songs recorded between 1923 and 1942 that express the woman's point of view toward the train as a means of travel or, more specifically, escape.

Some of these albums may be difficult to obtain because they are out of print and available, if at all, only in specialty or secondhand record stores. Nevertheless, they are worth searching for. The following album will also be difficult to obtain, but for a different reason. Titled *Movin' On,* it is taken from the soundtrack of the film of the same name produced by Harold Mayer for the United Transportation Union and designed to tell the story of America's railroads from the 1830s through the 1930s. The music, provided by the New Lost City Ramblers and Bonnie Dobson, provides appropriate background to the narrative, though like most soundtracks the album lacks a dimension without the visual component. The album was never released for commercial distribution, but may be available to educational organizations. The album is to be recommended as much for the narrative as for the musical excerpts.

Listed below are the contents of the albums discussed:

Library of Congress Archive of Folk Song L61: *Railroad Songs and Ballads*
  "Calling Trains"—Unidentified singer
  "The Boss of the Section Gang"—Mrs. Minta Morgan
  "Jerry Will You Ile That Car"—Warde H. Ford
  "Lining Track"—Henry Hankins
  "Roll On Buddy"—Aunt Molly Jackson
  "Way Out in Idaho"—Blaine Stubblefield
  "Oh I'm a Jolly Irishman Winding on the Train"—Noble B. Brown
  "The Engineer"—Lester A. Coffee
  "George Allen"—Austin Harmon
  "The Wreck of the Royal Palm"—Clarence H. Wyatt
  "Train Blues"—Russell Wise and Mr. White
  "The New River Train"—Ridge Rangers
  "The Train Is off the Track"—Mrs. Esco Kilgore
  "Gonna Lay My Head Down on Some Railroad Line"—Will Wright
  "I Rode Southern, I Rode L. & N."—Merle Lovell

"The Lightning Express"—Jim Holbert
"Railroad Rag"—Joe Harris and Kid West
"The Railroader"—May Kennedy McCord
"The T. & P. Line"—Mrs. Mary Sulliven
"The Dying Hobo"—George Lay
"The Big Rock Candy Mountains"—Harry McClintock
"I'm Goin' Home on the Mornin' Train"—E. M. Martin and Pearline Johns

RCA Victor LPV 532: *The Railroad in Folksong*

"Orange Blossom Special"—Rouse Brothers
"The Train's Done Left Me"—Carolina Tar Heels
"Engine One-Forty-Three"—Carter Family
"Jerry Go Ile That Car— Harry "Mac" McClintock
"If I Die a Railroad Man"—Tenneva Ramblers
"The Wreck of the Virginian"—Blind Alfred Reed
"Nine Pound Hammer Is Too Heavy"—Monroe Brothers
"The Davis Limited"—Jimmie Davis
"The Cannon Ball"—Delmore Brothers
"The Longest Train"—J. E. Mainer's Mountaineers
"Wreck of the Old 97"—Vernon Dalhart
"The Red and Green Signal Lights"—G. B. Grayson and Henry Whitter
"Peanut Special"—Byron Parker and his Mountaineers
"Crime of the D'Autremont Brothers"—Johnson Brothers
"McAbee's Railroad Piece"—Palmer McAbee
"The Little Red Caboose behind the Train"—Paul Warmack and his Gully Jumpers

Vetco LP 103: *Songs of the Railroad*

"Engineer Frank Hawk"—Rainey Old Time Band
"The Engineer's Last Run"—Blue Ridge Mountain Singers
"The Nine Pound Hammer"—Al Hopkins and his Buckle Busters
"Southern Number 111"—Roane County Ramblers
"Wreck of the 1256"—Vernon Dalhart
"Double Headed Train"—Henry Whitter
"Casey Jones"—Gid Tanner and his Skillet Lickers
"Home Again Medley"—Red Mountain Trio
"Railroad Blues"—Roy Harvey and Earl Shirkey
"C. C. & O. Number 558"—Al Hopkins and his Buckle Busters
"The Engineer's Dream"—Vernon Dalhart
"I'm Nine Hundred Miles from Home"—Fiddlin' John Carson
"The Wreck of the Royal Palm Express"—Vernon Dalhart
"C. &. O. Excursion"—Frank Hutchison
"The Little Red Caboose behind the Train"—Pickard Family
"When the Train Comes Along"—Uncle Dave Macon and Sam and Kirk McGee

Mark56 794: *[First Recorded] Railroad Songs*—Vernon Dalhart

"The Runaway Train"
"The New River Train"
"Billy Richardson's Last Ride"
"The Bum Song No. 2"
"The Big Rock Candy Mountain"
"The Wreck of the Number Nine"
"The Wreck of the Norfolk & Western Cannon Ball"

"Casey Jones"
"Got the Railroad Blues" [sung by Gene Austin]
"The Wreck of the 1256"
"The Lightning Express (Please, Mr. Conductor)"
"Can I Sleep in Your Barn Tonight, Mister?"

King 869: *Railroad Songs*

"Freight Train Boogie"—Reno and Smiley
"Fast Moving Night Train"—Grandpa Jones
"Fast Express"—Stanley Brothers
"Chic-a-choo Freight"—Bob Newman
"The Wreck of 1256"—Curley Fox and Texas Ruby
"Your Daddy Is a Railroad Man"—Bill Long
"Blow That Lonesome Whistle, Casey"—Al Dexter
"Pan American"—Hawkshaw Hawkins
"Midnight Special"—Delmore Brothers
"That Memphis Train"—Grandpa Jones
"East Bound Freight Train"—Reno and Smiley
"Train 45"—Stanley Brothers
"Whistle of the Gravy Train"—Bobby Grove

Starday 170: *All Aboard for the Railroad Special*

"Casey Jones"—Jim Glaser
"Midnight Special"—Jim Glaser
"Dying Hobo"—Jim Glaser
"Railroadin' on the Great Divide"—Bill Clifton
"Cannonball Blues"—Bill Clifton
"Orange Blossom Special"—Rainbow Ranch Boys
"East Bound Train"—Williams and Ellis
"Hobo"—Benny Martin
"Wreck on the L & N Railroad"—Phipps Family
"Choo Choo Comin'"—Stanley Brothers
"Ridin' That Midnight Train"—Stanley Brothers
"Country Express"—Wayne Raney
"Train in the Hollow"—Country Gentlemen
"Wreck of Old 97"—Lew Childre
"Wabash Cannonball"—Moon Mullican
"Kentucky Hill Special"—Lonesome Pine Fiddlers

Columbia CL 2686/CS 9486: *Hear the Whistles Blow: Lester Flatt and Earl Scruggs Sing Songs of Rivers and Rails*

"Southbound"
"East Bound Train"
"Roust-a-bout"
"Bringin' in the Georgia Mail"
"Hear the Whistle Blow a Hundred Miles"
"I'm Gonna Ride That Steamboat"

"The Atlantic Coastal Line"
"Train No. 1262"
"Orange Blossom Special"
"Starlight on the Rails"
"Going across the Sea"

Epic BN 26513: *We Like Trains*—Jim and Jesse McReynolds

"I Like Trains"
"Streamlined Cannon Ball"
"Wabash Cannon Ball"
"Pan American"
"Tennessee Central (Number 9)"

"The Golden Rocket"
"A Freight Train in My Mind"
"Yonder Comes a Freight Train"
"Fire Ball Mail"
"(I Heard That) Lonesome Whistle"

RCA Camden CAS 2513: *Lonesome Whistle*—Hank Snow

"Lonesome Whistle"

"Spanish Fire Ball"

"Wabash Blues"
"The Wreck of the Number Nine"
"Big Wheels"
"El Paso"

"Waiting for a Train"
"The Streamline Cannon Ball"
"Southbound"

RCA Victor LPM 2705/LSP 2705: *Railroad Man*—Hank Snow

"Waiting for a Train"
"Big Wheels"
"The Last Ride"
"The Streamline Cannon Ball"
"Ghost Trains"
"Pan American"

"Southbound"
"Way Out There"
"Chattanooga Choo Choo"
"The Wreck of the Number Nine"
"Lonesome Whistle"
"The Crazy Engineer"

RCA Victor LSP 4501: *Tracks & Trains*—Hank Snow

"Duquesne, Pennsylvania"
"Fire Ball Mail"
"Canadian Pacific"
"I'm Movin' On"
"Folsom Prison Blues"
"That Same Old Dotted Line"

"Casey Jones Was His Name"
"Wabash Cannon Ball"
"The Train My Woman's On"
"The Engineer's Child"
"Lonely Train"

Hickory LPM 125: *Great Train Songs: An American Legend*—Roy Acuff

"Tennessee Central"
"Wabash Cannonball"
"Night Train to Memphis"
"Sunshine Special"
"That Glory Bound Train"
"Wreck of the Old 97"

"Pan American"
"Freight Train Blues"
"Fireball Mail"
"Streamlined Cannonball"
"Midnight Train"
"Life's Railway to Heaven"

Folkways FA 2013 (FP 13): *900 Miles and Other R.R. Songs*—Cisco Houston

"900 Miles"
"'Getting Up' Holler"
"The Roamer"
"Hobo Bill"
"The Great American Bum"

"The Brave Engineer"
"The Gambler"
"The Rambler"
"R. R. Bill"
"Worried Man Blues"

Collector Records 1924: *Singing BRAC*—Joe Glazer

"Talking BRAC"
"Daddy, What's a Train?"
"Casey Jones" (union version)
"Many a Man Killed on the Railroad"
"Union Train"
"Solidarity Forever"

"This Train's a Clean Train"
"Danville Girl"
"Pat Works on the Railroad"
"The Ballad of Eugene Victor Debs"
"That's BRAC"
"We Shall Not Be Moved"

Collector Records 1925: *Union Train*—Joe Glazer

"Bye Bye Black Smoke Choo Choo"
"Danville Girl"
"Pat Works on the Railroad"
"Many a Man Killed on the Railroad"
"The Ballad of Eugene Victor Debs"
"Union Train"

"Casey Jones"
"Daddy, What's a Train?"
"The Wreck of the Royal Palm"
"Casey Jones" (union version)
"Hobo's Meditation"
"This Train's a Clean Train"

World Song EG-10-027 (10″): *Working on the Railroad*—Jesse Fuller

"Railroad Work Song"   "Lining Up the Tracks"
"John Henry"   "Railroad Blues"
"San Francisco Bay Blues"   "Hangin' 'round a Skin Game"

Milestone MLP 3002: *Ramblin' on My Mind: A Collection of Classic Train and Travel Blues*

"Hear That Whistle Blow"—Johnny Young
"Standing at the Greyhound Bus Station"—Carl Hodges
"She Caught the M & O"—Leroy "Country" Dallas
"Pea Vine Whistle"—Jimmy Brewer
"Highway 61"—Honeyboy Edwards
"Ramblin' on My Mind"—Big Joe Williams
"Key to the Highway"—Blind Connie Williams
"Hobo Blues"—Dr. Isaiah Ross
"My Home Ain't Here"—John Lee Granderson
"Freight Train Blues"—Bill Jackson
"Cryin' Won't Make Me Stay"—Elijah Brown
"Mean Old Train"—W. B. "Piano Bill" Bryson

Rosetta Records RR 1301: *Sorry but I Can't Take You: Women's Railroad Blues*

"Freight Train Blues"—Trixie Smith
"Freight Train Blues"—Clara Smith
"Chicago Bound Blues"—Bessie Smith
"Choo Choo Blues"—Trixie Smith
"Railroad Blues"—Trixie Smith
"The L & N Blues"—Clara Smith
"Panama Limited Blues"—Bertha Chippie Hill
"Panama Limited Blues"—Ada Brown
"Mail Train Blues"—Sippie Wallace
"Mr. Brakeman Let Me Ride Your Train"—Martha Copeland
"TN & O Blues"—Bessie Jackson
"I Hate That Train Called the M & O"—Lucille Bogan
"He Caught That B & O"—Blue Lou Barker
"This Train"—Sister Rosetta Tharpe
"Cannon Ball"—Nora Lee King

Bibliography

The following bibliography lists all the publications and archives cited in reference sections A through C, as well as most of the publications cited in the notes. In the reference sections, abbreviations, short titles, or authors' last names are used as keywords; these are indicated in boldface at the beginning of the bibliographic entries. For articles appearing in journals, or for chapters in books, the page numbers given here are inclusive, whereas the page numbers given in the notes or references sections are limited specifically to the item or passage cited. Over the years, I have gathered materials from many second- and third-hand sources, including the personal files of various scholars, collectors, and railroad song enthusiasts. Under such circumstances, it was inevitable that occasionally a photoreproduction of some clipping or article came to me without complete bibliographic information regarding source, date, page numbers, and so on; some of these lacunae I have been unable to fill.

Early in the preparation of this book I had envisioned the bibliography as a convenient listing of all publications that contained texts of the songs discussed. As it turned out, however, the present bibliography satisfies that desideratum much as the iceberg that struck the *Titanic* satisfied Mrs. Astor's request for more ice for her cocktail. Consequently, I feel it useful to preface the full listing by citing the most important publications that have dealt with railroad folksongs—choice shavings, as it were, before the entire 'berg bursts upon the reader.

It should not take anyone more than one visit to his bookstore to be convinced of the considerable interest in railroading; each year sees the publication of yet another handful of large, lavishly illustrated books on iron horses and their riders. In view of this, it has always surprised me that there has not been more written about railroad folksongs. One of the earliest discussions was by Dorothy Scarborough, who devoted a chapter to the subject in her 1925 book, *On the Trail of Negro Folk-Songs*. Her brief comments were illustrated with blues songs, gospel pieces, and a few ballads that she and other folklorists had collected early in the 1900s. With an enthusiasm that would probably be regarded today as overly romanticized, Scarborough wrote of the influence the railroad train must have had on the Afro-American:

> [The railroad] appeals to him for various reasons. Its rhythmic turn of wheels inspires a rhythmic turn of phrase in a folk-song. Its regularly recurring noises are iambic or trochaic like the Negro's patting of foot or clapping of hand—not dactylic or anapaestic,

like some sounds in nature, the galloping of a horse, for example. The Negro's spontaneous songs are almost wholly in two-quarter or four-quarter time, rarely with the
three syllable foot. . . . The Negro has no dragon in his mythology, but he sees a modern
one in an engine and train—a fierce creature stretching across the country, breathing out
fiery smoke, ruthless of what comes in its path. It is a being diabolic and divine, or at least
a superman in force and intelligence. It gratifies his sense of the dramatic with its rushing
entrances and exits, as it feeds his craving for mystery, with its shining rails that may
lead anywhere. . . . He rides it in imagination more often than in reality. . . . He thinks
of a train as one whom he knows, sometimes a friend, sometimes as enemy, but always a
real being. . . . (p. 238)

Probably more people were introduced to the varieties of railroad folksongs through
the writings of John and Alan Lomax than through any other source. The Lomaxes were
major collectors of folksong, but they were also influential anthologizers, publishing
several volumes of folksongs, each including a sampling of railroad songs, based on their
own as well as other collectors' findings. *American Ballads and Folk Songs* (1934), their
first general anthology, opened with a chapter entitled "Working on the Railroad," an
assortment of seventeen pieces, including the well known ("John Henry," "Casey Jones,"
"The Wreck on the C & O") and the not-so-well known. At least one item, "The Gila
Monster Route," was a poem, not a song, and had probably never been reprinted since it
was first published in *Railroad Man's Magazine*. In this chapter also the Lomaxes
published a brief account of their efforts to get to the origins of "Casey Jones," and printed
several related blues ballads along with that piece. In a later anthology, *Folk Song: U.S A.*
(1947), the Lomaxes further orchestrated Scarborough's theme about the rhythms of
the rail:

It is in the texture of our popular music, however, that the railroads have left their
deepest impression. Listen to the blues, the stomps, the hot music of the last fifty years,
since most Americans have come to live within the sound of the railroad. Listen to this
music and you'll hear all the smashing, rattling, syncopated rhythms and counter-
rhythms of trains of every size and speed. Listen to boogie-woogie with its various kinds
of rolling basses. Listen to hot jazz with its steady beat. Listen to the blues with those
hundreds of silvery breaks in the treble clef. What you hear back of the notes is the drive
and thrust and moans of a locomotive . . . in our estimation, the distinctive feeling of
American hot music comes from the railroad. (p. 245)

This colorful theory makes for engaging prose, but it is as insubstantial as a whiff of smoke
from a highballing coalburner. Beside the songs in chapter 9, "Lonesome Whistles," of
Folk Song: U.S A., these authors also included relevant items in chapter 3, "Railroaders
and Hobos," of *Our Singing Country* (1941), and Alan Lomax presented a section entitled
"Railroaders and Hoboes" in *The Folk Songs of North America* (1960). Questions of
hyperbole aside, the Lomaxes' importance in preserving and disseminating American
folksong through their collecting and publishing cannot be overestimated.

Some writers have dealt intensively with particular aspects of railroad song. Guy
Johnson and Louis Chappell each devoted years of research to uncover the true story of
John Henry. Train robbers and other western badmen were the subjects of numerous
book-length accounts. Freeman Hubbard devoted whole chapters of his warmly told
Railroad Avenue (1945) to Casey Jones, John Henry, Jesse James, the Chatsworth wreck,
and Kate Shelly. "Old 97" has been subjected to as many autopsies as any other American
folksong. Hobo songs, which are practically inseparable from railroad songs, were given
full treatment by George Milburn in his *Hobo's Hornbook* (1930). Other writers devoted a

few pages to railroads in their more general anthologies: fourteen songs in Carl Sandburg's influential *American Songbag* (1927); seventeen in Botkin and Harlow's *A Treasury of Railroad Folklore* (1953); nine in Lingenfelter, Dwyer, and Cohen's *Songs of the American West* (1968).

Several books on railroad history have included digressions on songs. The most successful is "Ballads of the Rails,'" a chapter in Stewart Holbrook's well-told *Story of American Railroads* (1947).

While the literature of coal-mining songs, cowboy songs, lumbering songs, and sailor's songs grew by leaps and bounds, however, the railroader was left behind, standing at the station. Perhaps the first "book" devoted solely to railroad songs was *Railroad Songs of Yesterday*, a nine-by-twelve-inch folio compiled by Sterling Sherwin and Harry K. McClintock (1943). Of the twenty songs included, three were written for the book by Sherwin and/or McClintock, and most of the others were adapted by them from unidentified older pieces.

An early survey attempting to take into account both the sheet-music tradition and the folk tradition was Horace Reynolds's "Tin Pan Alley's Songs of the Rails" (1949), a too-brief article that suggested its author might be able to tell us a good deal more about American railroad songs.

A major milestone in the field of railroad lore was Frank P. Donovan's *The Railroad in Literature* (1940). Donovan attempted to provide a descriptive bibliography of railroad fiction, poetry, songs, biography, essays, travel, and drama in the English language—in particular, in American literature. Bibliography about a subject that has been disseminated through such ephemeral media as hillbilly song folios, pocket songsters, pulp adventure magazines, small town newspapers, college magazines, union journals, and 78 rpm phonograph records cannot hope for completeness at a first attempt; unfortunately, Donovan's successor has yet to announce himself. The chapter on songs, printed and recorded, was particularly weak—but it is easier to criticize than to improve. For a discussion of the problem, see my "Railroad Folksongs on Record—A Survey" (1970).

A few writers in recent years have tried to provide the much-needed general survey of American railroad folksongs, but none has been without shortcomings. Charles Wilson Roberts III's "The Railroad in American Folk Song" (1965) relied on the anthologies of the Lomaxes and Sandburg for fifty-two of his sixty-five quoted excerpts, with only three of the remainder quoted from recordings. Patricia L. B. Porcello's dissertation, "The Railroad in American Literature: Poetry, Folk Song, and the Novel" (1968), also fell short of providing the required overview in the folksong category, as resources were confined entirely to published collections, with, once again, the Lomaxes and Sandburg figuring heavily in the accounting. Ann Miller Carpenter's article "The Railroad in American Folk Song, 1865–1920" (1972) is somewhat more eclectic in its sources, but still rests heavily on the published researches of others. My own "Railroad Folksongs on Record—A Survey" (1970) attempted to provide a general background on songs that were commercially recorded, especially on hillbilly and race records.

Although their physical format distinguishes them from the other items mentioned, two important documents in the field of railroad folksong are Archie Green's liner notes to *The Railroad in Folksong* (1966) and his brochure notes to *Railroad Songs and Ballads* (1968), two anthological collections, the former of commercial phonograph recordings, the latter Library of Congress Archive of Folk Song field recordings. Green's commentaries rest firmly on his own considerable researches, rather than redigesting the secondhand writings of earlier authors.

Finally, two specialized articles deserve note. John T. Smith's "Rails below the Rio Grande" (1959) presents the texts of four Mexican corridos that deal with railroads. His thesis is that the hostile attitude of Mexicans toward the railroad, which they regarded as a form of foreign exploitation, militated against the rails offering the same charm and excitement for the Mexican folksinger that they do for the *norteamericano*. However, this view overlooks the fact that in many instances our own railroad songs were born out of great mistrust and hatred toward the railroads. It remains to be seen whether this situation changes as the railroads, which are considerably less advanced in Mexico than they are in the United States, become more familiar parts of the landscape there.

The special field of railroad worksongs—tie-tamping chants, hammering songs, hollers, and so on—attracted the attention of many early collectors of Afro-American folksong, including Scarborough, the Lomaxes, and Howard Odum and Guy Johnson. A more recent paper on the subject is William R. Ferris, Jr.'s "Railroad Chants: Form and Function" (1970), based largely on his interview with a sixty-seven-year-old Mississippian who worked as a railroad chanter all his life. Ferris has also written a brief overview (1974) of the various types of railroad folklore—nonmusical as well as musical.

These varied contributions constitute the main literature on American railroad folksongs. If the reader concludes that the field has not been overworked, he has received the message correctly. This book has gathered together much information that has not previously been published, but it too leaves some areas untouched, so that there is plenty of room for others—whether rail enthusiasts, folklorists, or pop music historians—to exercise their talents.

Abbot-Swan   *Eight Negro Songs from Bedford County, Virginia*. Collected by Francis H. Abbot, edited by Alfred J. Swan. New York: Enoch and Sons, 1923.

Abrahams   *"When the Moonbeams Gently Fall Songster."* New York: Edward J. Abrahams, 18–.

Acuff   *Roy Acuff Song Folio*. Nashville: Acuff Rose Publications, ca. 1943.

ACWF   Archive of California and Western Folklore. Folklore and Mythology Center, University of California, Los Angeles.

Adams, Charles Francis, Jr. *Railroads: Their Origin and Problems*. New York: G. P. Putnam's Sons, 1879.

Adams, Ramon F. *The Language of the Railroader*. Norman: University of Oklahoma Press, 1977.

AFS   *See* LC AFS.

Alabama   *Alabama*. American Guide Series, New York: R. R. Smith, 1941.

Alberta Slim   Alberta Slim. *Fifty Popular Cowboy Songs of Ranch & Range*. [Saskatoon, Canada?, 1941?].

Alden   Alden, William L. "Sailors' Songs." *Harpers Magazine*, 65 (July, 1882), 281–86.

Alderson   Alderson, William. "On the Wobbly 'Casey Jones' and Other Songs." *California Folklore Quarterly*, 1 (Oct., 1942), 373–76.

Allen   Allen, Jules Verne. *Cowboy Lore*. 1933. Rpt., San Antonio: Naylor, 1950.

Allsop   Allsop, Kenneth. *Hard Travellin': The Hobo and His History*. London: Hodder and Stoughton, 1967.

Along Memory Lane   *Along Memory Lane*. New York. E. B. Marks, 1938.

Alvarez   Alvarez, Eugene. *Travel on Southern Antebellum Railroads, 1828–1860*. University: University of Alabama Press, 1974.

American Folk Song Folio   *American Folk Song Folio*. Chicago: M. M. Cole, 1939.

Anderson, G.   Anderson, Geneva. "A Collection of Ballads and Songs from East Tennessee." Master's thesis, University of North Carolina, 1932.

Anderson, J. Q. Anderson, John Q. "Another Texas Variant of 'Cole Younger,' Ballad of a Badman." *Western Folklore,* 31 (Apr., 1972), 103–15.

Anderson, N. Anderson, Nels. *The Hobo.* 1923. Rpt., Chicago: University of Chicago Press, Phoenix Books, 1961.

Anderson, R. Anderson, Roy B. "Wreck of the 1256." *C & O Historical Newsletter,* July 1, 1969.

Appler, A. C. *The Younger Brothers.* 1892. Rpt., New York: Frederick Fell, 1955.

Asbell Asbell, Bernard, "A Man Ain't Nothing but a Man." *American Heritage,* 14 (Oct., 1963), 34–37, 95.

The ASCAP Biographical Dictionary of Composers, Authors, and Publishers. 3d ed. Compiled and edited by the Lynn Farnol Group. New York: American Society of Composers, Authors, and Publishers, 1966.

Asch Asch, Moses, Josh Dunson, and Ethel Raim, comps. and eds. *Anthology of American Folk Music.* New York: Oak Publications, 1973.

Atkins Atkins, John, ed. *The Carter Family.* Old Time Music Booklet No. 1. London: Old Time Music, 1973.

Bain Bain, William E. *Frisco Folks: Stories and Pictures of the Great Steam Days of the Frisco Road (St. Louis–San Francisco Railway Company).* Denver: Sage Books, 1961.

Ballanta(-Taylor) Ballanta(-Taylor), Nicholas George Julius. *Saint Helena Island Spirituals.* New York: G. Schirmer, 1925.

Barnard Barnard, Gloria Richman. *Ivy League Song Book.* Greenville, Del.: Rolor Publishing, 1958.

Barnes Barnes, Ruth A. *I Hear America Singing: An Anthology of Folk Poetry.* Chicago, Philadelphia, and Toronto: John C. Winston, 1937.

Barnum & Bailey *Barnum & Bailey's Concert Songster and Joker.* New York: Popular Publishing, ca. 1889.

Barry (1912) Barry, Phillips. "American Ballads." *Journal of American Folklore,* 25 (Apr.-June, 1912), 188.

Barry (1934) ———. "Reviews." *Bulletin of the Folk-Song Society of the Northeast,* No. 8 (1934), pp. 24–26.

Barton Barton, William E. "Recent Negro Melodies." *New England Magazine,* 19 (Feb., 1899), 707–19. Reprinted as William E. Barton. *Old Plantation Hymns.* Boston and New York: Lanson, Wolffe, 1899. Also reprinted (with original title) in *The Negro and His Folklore in Nineteenth-Century Periodicals,* edited by Bruce Jackson, pp. 302–26. Austin: University of Texas Press, 1967.

Bascom Bascom, Louise Rand. "Ballads and Songs of Western North Carolina." *Journal of American Folklore,* 22 (Apr.-June, 1909), 238–50.

Bass Bass, Robert Duncan. "Negro Songs from the Pedee Country." *Journal of American Folklore,* 44 (Oct.-Dec., 1931), 418–36.

Bassett *Bassett's Native Herb Songster: A Choice Collection of Comic and Sentimental Songs, as Sung by J. O'Blair.* New York: Columbus Printing Works, ca. 1882.

Beard Beard, Anne Winsmore. "The Personal Folksong Collection of Bascom Lamar Lunsford—A Thesis." Master's thesis, Miami University, 1959.

Beatty Beatty, Arthur. "Some Ballad Variants and Songs." *Journal of American Folklore,* 22 (Jan.-Mar., 1909), 63–71.

Beck (1942) Beck, Earl Clifton. *Songs of the Michigan Lumberjacks.* Ann Arbor: University of Michigan Press, 1942.

Beck (1948) ———. *Lore of the Lumber Camps.* Ann Arbor: University of Michigan Press, 1948.

Belcher *"Red" Belcher's Roundup of Favorite Hill Songs.* Book 2. N.p.: Belcher, ca. 1944.

Belden (1912)   Belden, Henry M. "Balladry in America." *Journal of American Folklore*, 25 (Jan.-Mar., 1912), 1–23.

Belden (1955)   ———. *Ballads and Songs Collected by the Missouri Folk-Lore Society*. 2d ed. Columbia: University of Missouri Press, 1955.

Best & Best   Best, Dick, and Beth Best. *The New Song Fest*. New York: Crown Publishers, 1957.

Best Things   *Best Things from Best Authors*. Vol. 2. Philadelphia: Pennsylvania Publishing, 1878.

BFSSNE   *Bulletin of the Folk-Song Society of the Northeast*. Cambridge, Mass., 1930–37. Rpt., Philadelphia: American Folklore Society, 1960.

Big Roundup   *The Big Roundup of Cowboy Songs*. N.p., n.d.

Big Slim   Big Slim [H. C. McAulife]. *Favorite Songs*. N.p., ca. 1939.

Block, Eugene B. *Great Train Robberies of the West*. New York: Coward-McCann, 1959.

Blue Grass Roy (1933)   Blue Grass Roy. *Sensational Collection of Roy's Mountain Ballads and Old Time Songs*. Chicago: M. M. Cole, 1933.

Blue Grass Roy (1937)   ———. *World's Greatest Collection of Cowboy & Mountain Ballads*. Chicago: M. M. Cole, 1937.

Boette   Boette, Marie, ed. *Singa Hipsy Doodle and Other Folk Songs of West Virginia*. Parsons, W.Va.: McClain Printing, 1971.

Bolton   Bolton, Dorothy G. *Old Songs Hymnal: Words and Melodies from the State of Georgia*. New York and London: Century, 1929.

Bonar   Bonar, Eleanor Jean. "A Collection of Ballads and Popular Songs, Iowa and Appalachian." Master's thesis, State University of Iowa, 1930.

Boni (1947)   Boni, Margaret Bradford, ed. *The Fireside Book of Folk Songs*. New York: Simon and Schuster, 1947.

Boni (1952)   ———. *The Fireside Book of Favorite American Songs*. New York: Simon and Schuster, 1952.

The Book of Navy Songs. Collected and edited by the Trident Society of the United States Naval Academy. Garden City, N.Y.: Doubleday, Doran, 1926.

Boos   Boos, Gregory D., J.D. "The Wreck of the Old '97': A Study in Copyright Protection of Folksongs for Lawyers, Folklorists, and Songwriters." *Seattle Folklore Society Journal*, 9 (Sept., 1977), 3–18.

Botkin (1944)   Botkin, B. A., ed. *A Treasury of American Folklore*. New York: Crown Publishers, 1944.

Botkin (1947)   ———, ed. *A Treasury of New England Folklore*. New York: Crown Publishers, 1947.

Botkin (1949)   ———, ed. *A Treasury of Southern Folklore*. New York: Crown Publishers, 1949.

Botkin (1951)   ———, ed. *A Treasury of Western Folklore*. New York: Crown Publishers, 1951.

Botkin (1963)   ———. "A Sampler of Western Folklore and Songs." Chap. 9 in *The Book of the American West*, edited by Jay Monaghan, pp. 501–60. New York: Julian Messner, 1963.

Botkin & Harlow   ——— and Alvin F. Harlow. *A Treasury of Railroad Folklore*. New York: Bonanza Books, 1953.

Botsford   Botsford, Florence H., comp. *Universal Folk Songster for Home, School and Community*. New York: G. Schirmer, 1937.

Bowman, Hank Wieand. *Pioneer Railroads*. New York: Arco Publishing, 1954.

Bradford   Bradford, Roark. *John Henry*. New York: Literary Guild, 1931.

Brand (1957)   Brand, Oscar. *Singing Holidays: The Calendar in Folk Song*. New York: Alfred A. Knopf, 1957.

Brand (1961)   ———, ed. *Folk Songs for Fun*. 2d ed. New York: Hollis Music, 1961.

Breihan, Carl. *The Complete and Authentic Life of Jesse James*. New York: Frederick Fell, 1953.

———. *The Day Jesse James Was Killed*. New York: Frederick Fell, 1961.

————. *The Younger Brothers*. San Antonio: Naylor Brothers, 1961.

"A Brief List of Material Relating to American Railroad Songs." Typescript. Washington, D.C.: Library of Congress Archive of Folk Song, May, 1971.

Briegel   Briegel, George F., comp. *44 Old Time Mormon and Far West Songs*. New York: George F. Briegel, 1933.

Britt   *Elton Britt's Collection of Cowboy Songs, Book 2*. New York: Bob Miller Music Publisher, 1938.

Bronaugh, W. C. *The Youngers' Fight for Freedom*. Columbia, Mo.: E. W. Stephens Publishing, 1906.

Bronco Busters   [Clements, Zeke, and his WSM Broncho Busters.] *Bronco Busters Song Album*. Birmingham: Davis Printing, n.d.

Bronson   Bronson, Bertrand. *The Traditional Tunes of the Child Ballads*. Vol. 2. Princeton, N.J.: Princeton University Press, 1962.

Brophy, John, and Eric Partridge. *The Long Trail: What the British Soldier Sang and Said in 1914–1918*. New York: London House and Maxwell, 1965.

Brown II   *The Frank C. Brown Collection of North Carolina Folklore*. Vol. 2. *Folk Ballads*. Edited by Henry M. Belden and Arthur Palmer Hudson. Durham, N.C.: Duke University Press, 1952.

Brown III   *The Frank C. Brown Collection of North Carolina Folklore*. Vol. 3. *Folk Songs*. Edited by Henry M. Belden and Arthur Palmer Hudson. Durham, N.C.: Duke University Press, 1952.

Brown IV   *The Frank C. Brown Collection of North Carolina Folklore*. Vol. 4. *The Music of the Ballads*. Edited by Jan Philip Schinhan. Durham, N.C.: Duke University Press, 1957.

Brown V   *The Frank C. Brown Collection of North Carolina Folklore*. Vol. 5. *The Music of the Songs*. Edited by Jan Philip Schinhan. Durham, N.C.: Duke University Press, 1962.

Brunvand   Brunvand, Jan Harold. "Folk Song Studies in Idaho." *Western Folklore*, 24 (Oct., 1965), 231–48.

Buckley   Buckley, Bruce R. "'Uncle' Ira Cephas—A Negro Folk Singer in Ohio." *Midwest Folklore*, 3 (Spring, 1953), 5–18.

Buck's Rock   Winston, Winnie, and Josh Rifkin, eds. *Buck's Rock Song Book*. New Milford, Conn.: Buck's Rock Work Camp, 1959.

Buel, J. W. *The Border Outlaws*. St. Louis: Dan Linahan, 1881.

Buford   Buford, Mary Elizabeth. "Folk Songs of Florida and Texas." Master's thesis, Southern Methodist University, 1940.

Bullen & Arnold   Bullen, Frank T., and W. F. Arnold. *Songs of Sea Labour (Chanties)*. London: Orpheus Music Publishing, 1914.

Burchard   Burchard, Hank. "In Quest of the Historical John Henry." *Washington Post Potomac* (magazine section), Aug. 24, 1969, pp. 11–16, 22–24.

Burleigh   Burleigh, Harry Thacker. *Album of Negro Spirituals*. New York: G. Ricordi, 1928.

Burnett   Burnett, Richard D. *Songs Sung by R. D. Burnett*. Danville, Ky.: S. N. Eads, Printer, ca. 1913.

Burt   Burt, Olive Woolley. *American Murder Ballads and Their Stories*. New York: Oxford University Press, 1958.

Burton   Burton, Jack. *The Blue Book of Tin Pan Alley*. Watkins Glen, N.Y.: Century House, 1950.

Burton & Manning (1967)   Burton, Thomas G., and Ambrose N. Manning, eds. *East Tennessee State University Collection of Folklore: Folksongs*. Johnson City: East Tennessee State University, 1967.

Burton & Manning (1969)   ————. *East Tennessee State University Collection of Folklore*. Vol. 2. *Folksongs*. Johnson City: East Tennessee State University, 1969.

Bush (1969)   Bush, Michael E. ["Jim"], ed. *Folk Songs of Central West Virginia*. Ravenswood, W.Va.: Custom Printing, 1969.

Bush (1970) ————. *Folk Songs of Central West Virginia*. Vol. 2. Ravenswood, W.Va.: Custom Printing, 1970.

Byrne Byrne, Clifford. "Jesse James: Folk Hero." *Tennessee Folklore Society Bulletin*, 20 (Sept., 1954), 47–52.

Cambiaire Cambiaire, Celestin Pierre. *East Tennessee and Western Virginia Mountain Ballads*. London: Mitre Press, 1934.

Campbell & Holstein Campbell, Aaron, and George Holstein. *Ballads of By-Gone Days: Favorite Radio Ballads of Campbell and Holstein*. Vol. 2. Kansas City: Campbell and Holstein, 1931.

Carlisle, C. Carlisle, Cliff. *World's Greatest Collection of Hobo Songs with Guitar Chords and Yodel Arrangement*. Chicago: M. M. Cole, 1932.

Carlisle, I. Carlisle, Irene Jones. "Fifty Ballads and Songs from Northwest Arkansas." Master's thesis, University of Arkansas, 1952.

Carman Carman, Jenks "Tex." *Popular Western Songs of Radio and Records*. Chicago: M. M. Cole, 1949.

Carmer (1934) Carmer, Carl. *Stars Fell on Alabama*. 1934. Rpt., New York: Hill and Wang, 1961.

Carmer (1937) ————. *The Hurricane's Children: Tales from Your Neck of the Woods*. New York and Toronto: Farrar and Rinehart, 1937.

Carpenter, Ann Miller. "The Railroad in American Folk Song, 1865–1920." In *Diamond Bessie and the Shepherds*, edited by Wilson M. Hudson, pp. 103–19. Publications of the Texas Folklore Society, No. 36. Austin: Encino Press, 1972.

Carpenter Carpenter, Charles. "Billy Richardson's Last Ride." *West Virginia Review*, 8 (Sept., 1931), 404–5.

Carter, I. G. Carter, Isabel Gordon. "Songs and Ballads from Tennessee and North Carolina." *Journal of American Folklore*, 46 (Jan.-Mar., 1933), 22–50.

Carter Family (1930?) Carter Family. *Album of Old Family Melodies*. New York: Southern Music Publishing, [1930?].

Carter Family (1935) ————. *Album of Smoky Mountain Ballads*. New York: Southern Music Publishing, 1935.

Carter Family (1937) ————. *Album of Smoky Mountain Ballads, No. 3*. New York: Southern Music Publishing, 1937.

Carter Family (1941) ————. *Album of Smoky Mountain Ballads #3*. New York: R. S. Peer, 1941.

Casey *Claude Casey's Caravan of Songs*. New York: Bourne, 1947.

Cayce, Elder C. H. *The Good Old Songs*. Rev. ed. Thornton, Ark.: Cayce Publishing, 1967. Originally published in 1913.

CFB *Colorado Folksong Bulletin*. Boulder, 1962–64.

CFQ *California Folklore Quarterly*. California Folklore Society. Berkeley and Los Angeles, 1942–46. Title later changed to *Western Folklore*; see *WF*.

Chalker Chalker, Brian. "Truth behind the Legend: Casey Jones." *Opry*, 2 (Oct., 1969), 18–19.

Chambers Chambers, H. A. *The Treasury of Negro Spirituals*. 1953. Rpt., New York: Emerson, 1963.

Chappell (1933) Chappell, Louis W. *John Henry: A Folk-Lore Study*. Jena, Germany: Frommannsche Verlag, 1933.

Chappell (1939) ————. *Folk-Songs of the Roanoke and the Albemarle*. Morgantown, W.Va.: Ballad Press, 1939.

Charters (1959) Charters, Samuel B. *The Country Blues*. New York: Rinehart, 1959.

Charters (1963) ————. *The Poetry of the Blues*. New York: Oak Publications, 1963.

Checklist *Checklist of Recorded Songs in the English Language in the Archive of American Folk Song to July, 1940*. Washington, D.C.: Library of Congress, Music Division, 1942.

Checklist Supplement   Deems, Deborah, and William Nowlin, comps. *Supplementary Listing of Recorded Songs in the English Language in the Library of Congress Archive of Folk Song through Recording No. AFS 4332 (October 1940).* Typescript. Washington, D.C.: Library of Congress Archive of Folk Song, Sept., 1974.

Cheshire   *Pappy Cheshire and His Hill Billy Champions.* Chicago: M. M. Cole, 1940.

Child, Francis James. *The English and Scottish Popular Ballads.* 5 vols. 1882–98. Rpt., New York: Cooper Square Publishers, 1965, and New York: Dover Publications, 1965.

Chimney Corner Songs   Moore, Frankie, and Cousin Emmy. *Chimney Corner Songs.* N.p., 1936.

Clifton   Clifton, Bill, ed. *150 Old Time Folk and Gospel Songs.* North Wilkesboro, N.C.: Adams Printing and Calendar, [1956].

Coffin & Cohen   Coffin, Tristram Potter, and Hennig Cohen, eds. *Folklore from the Working Folk of America.* Garden City, N.Y.: Doubleday, Anchor Press, 1973.

Cogswell, Robert. "Commercial Hillbilly Lyrics and the Folk Tradition." *Journal of Country Music,* 3 (Fall-Winter, 1973), 65–106.

Cohen (1965)   Cohen, Norm. "The Skillet Lickers: A Study of a Hillbilly String Band and Its Repertoire." *Journal of American Folklore,* 78 (July-Sept., 1965), 229–44.

Cohen (1967)   ———. Brochure notes to Testament Records T-3302: *Jimmie Tarlton: Steel Guitar Rag.* 1967.

———. "Railroad Folksongs on Record—A Survey." *New York Folklore Quarterly,* 26 (June, 1970), 91–113.

Cohen (1973)   ———. "'Casey Jones': At the Crossroad of Two Ballad Traditions." *Western Folklore,* 32 (Apr., 1973), 77–103.

Cohen (1974)   ———. "Robert W. Gordon and the Second Wreck of 'Old 97.'" *Journal of American Folklore,* 87 (Jan.-Mar., 1974), 12–38. JEMF Reprint No. 30.

———. "Bill Mason, Bret Harte, and Charlie Poole." *JEMF Quarterly,* 10 (Summer, 1974), 74–78.

———. "Fiddlin' John Carson: An Appreciation and a Discography." *JEMF Quarterly,* 10 (Winter, 1974), 138–56.

———. "Henry Whitter: His Life and Music." *JEMF Quarterly,* 11 (Summer, 1975), 57–61.

Cohen, Norm, and Anne Cohen. "The Legendary Jimmie Tarleton [*sic*]." *Sing Out!,* 16 (Sept., 1966), 16–19.

Cohen & Cohen   ———. "Tune Evolution as an Indicator of Traditional Musical Norms." *Journal of American Folklore,* 86 (Jan.-Mar., 1973), 37–47.

Cohen, Norm, Eugene W. Earle, and Graham Wickham. *The Early Recording Career of Ernest V. "Pop" Stoneman: A Bio-Discography.* JEMF Special Series, No. 1. Los Angeles: John Edwards Memorial Foundation, 1968.

Cohen Collection   Norm Cohen Collection of Folksong. Los Angeles, California.

Colcord   Colcord, Joanna C. *Songs of American Sailormen.* New York: Bramhall House, 1938.

Coleman & Bregman   Coleman, Satis N., and Adolph Bregman. *Songs of American Folks.* New York: John Day, 1942.

Coltman, Robert. "We Would Have Made More Records, but We Didn't Bother to Go Back: The Story of the Blankenship Family of North Carolina." *Journal of Country Music,* 7 (Dec., 1978), 42, 51–53.

Colquhoun   . Colquhoun, Neil. *New Zealand Folksongs.* 2d expanded ed. Wellington, Auckland, Sydney, and Melbourne: A. H. and A. W. Reed, 1972.

Combs (1925)   Combs, Josiah H. *Folk-Songs du Midi des États-Unis.* Paris: Presses Universitaires de France, 1925.

Combs (1939)   ———. *Folk-Songs from the Kentucky Highlands.* Schirmer's American Folk-Song Series, Set 1. New York: G. Schirmer, 1939.

Combs-Wilgus   ———. *Folk-Songs of the Southern United States.* Edited by D. K. Wilgus. Austin: University of Texas Press, 1967. Originally published as Combs (1925).

Comic and Sentimental Songs   *Comic and Sentimental Songs.* Kentucky, ca. 1910.

Compagno   Compagno, G. M. *Time to Sing: Folio of Community Songs for Every Occasion*. New York: E. B. Marks Music Corp., 1938.

Comstock   Comstock, Jim. *West Virginia Songbag*. Richwood, W.Va.: Jim Comstock, 1974.

"Convict Literature." Review of *The Voices of Our Exiles, or Stray Leaves from a Convict Ship*, edited by Daniel Ritchie (Edinburgh, 1854). In *Chamber's Journal*, June 24, 1854, pp. 389–90.

Cooke   Cooke, Marion. "Tracking Down a Ghost." *Tracks*, 29 (Feb., 1944), 24–27.

Corliss, Carlton J. *Main Line of Mid-America*. New York: Creative Age Press, 1950.

Courlander   Courlander, Harold. *Negro Folk Music, U.S.A*. New York: Columbia University Press, 1963.

Cousin Lee   Cousin Lee. *Album of Hill Country Ballads and Old Time Songs*. New York: Joe Davis, 1936.

Cowboy Jack   *40 Popular Songs and Mountain Ballads Sang [sic] by Cowboy Jack over Station WMMN*. Fairmont, W.Va., [1934?].

Cowboy Sings   *The Cowboy Sings*. New York: Paull-Pioneer, 1932.

Cowboy Songs   *Two Hundred Popular Cowboy Songs and Mountain Ballads*. New York: Hobo News, n.d.

Cowboy Songs #73   *Cowboy Songs*. No. 73. Derby, Conn.: American Folk Publications, ca. 1963.

Cox (1919)   Cox, John Harrington. "John Hardy." *Journal of American Folklore*, 32 (Oct.-Dec., 1919), 505–20.

Cox (1925)   ———. *Folk-Songs of the South*. 1925. Rpt., Hatboro, Pa.: Folklore Associates, 1963.

Cox (1939)   ———. *Traditional Ballads and Folk-Songs Mainly from West Virginia*. 1939. Rpt., Philadelphia: American Folklore Society, 1964.

Crabtree   Crabtree, Lillian Gladys. "Songs and Ballads Sung in Overton County, Tennessee." Master's thesis, George Peabody College for Teachers, 1936.

Cray   Cray, Ed. *The Erotic Muse*. New York: Oak Publications, 1969.

Cross   *One Hundred and One Favorite Ballads: Cowboy & Mountain Songs as Sung by Hugh Cross*. N.p., n.d.

Croy, Homer. *Jesse James Was My Neighbor*. New York: Duell, Sloan and Pearce, 1949.

———. *Last of the Great Outlaws: The Story of Cole Younger*. New York: Duell, Sloan and Pearce, 1956.

Cumberland Mountain Folks   *Cumberland Mountain Folks' Ballads of Hills and Home*. Knoxville, Tenn., 1945.

Curtis-Burlin   Curtis-Burlin, Natalie. *Negro Folk-Songs*. Book 4. New York: G. Schirmer, 1919.

DA   *A Dictionary of Americanisms on Historical Principles*. Edited by Mitford M. Mathews. Chicago: University of Chicago Press, 1951.

Dacus, J. A. *Illustrated Lives and Adventures of Frank and Jesse James and the Younger Brothers, the Noted Western Outlaws*. St. Louis: N. D. Thompson, 1882.

DAE   *A Dictionary of American English on Historical Principles*. 4 vols. Edited by Sir William A. Craigie and James R. Hulbert. Chicago: University of Chicago Press, 1938–44.

Dalhart & Robison   Dalhart, Vernon, and Carson Robison. *Album of Songs*. New York: F. B. Haviland Publishing, 1928.

Dallas   Dallas, Karl. *One Hundred Songs of Toil*. London: Wolfe Publishing, 1974.

Davis, A. K.   Davis, Arthur Kyle, Jr. *Folk-Songs of Virginia*. Durham, N.C.: Duke University Press, 1949.

Davis, J. (1937)   Davis, Jimmie. *Songs of Jimmie Davis*. New York: Southern Music Publishing, 1937.

Davis, J. (1938)   ———. *Songs of Jimmie Davis*. "Deluxe ed." New York: Southern Music Publishing, 1938.

Davis, John P. *The Union Pacific Railway: A Study in Railway Politics, History, and Economics*. Chicago: S. C. Griggs, 1894.

Davis, L. *Favorite Radio Songs of Lynn Davis and His Forty-Niners.* Beckley, W.Va., 1944.

Dawson (I) Dawson, Smoky. *First Album of Cowboy and Mountain Songs.* Melbourne: Allan, ca. 1941.

Dawson (II) ———. *Second Song Folio.* Melbourne: Allan, ca. 1942.

Dean, E. Dean, Eddie. *The "Dean" of Western Songs.* New York: Bourne, 1947.

Dean, M. C. Dean, M. C. *Flying Cloud and One Hundred and Fifty Other Old Time Songs and Ballads of Outdoor Men, Sailors, Lumber Jacks, Soldiers, Men of the Great Lakes, Railroadmen, Miners, etc.* Virginia, Minn.: Quickprint, [1922?].

Delaney *Delaney's Song Book.* Nos. 1–88. New York: William W. Delaney, 1892–1921.

Delmore-Vagabonds Poulton, Curt, and the Delmore Brothers. *Song Folio.* N.p., 1936.

Delmore Brothers *Delmore Brothers Song and Picture Album.* West Memphis, Ark.: Arkansas Publishing, n.d.

Dett Dett, R. N. *Religious Folk Songs of the Negro.* Hampton, Va.: Hampton Institute Press, 1927. An enlarged edition of T. P. Fenner, *Religious Folk Songs of the Negro,* q.v.

Dew Dew, Lee A. "The Locomotive Engineer: Folk Hero of the 19th Century." *Studies in Popular Culture,* 1 (Winter, 1977), 45–55.

Dickson Dickson, James B. "Home Grown Hero." *Tracks,* June, 1955, pp. 60–62.

Dillon, George. "The Greatest Manhunt Ever Assembled." *Startling Detective,* 64 (May, 1974), 50, 52–55, 67, 69, 71.

Diton Diton, Carl. *Thirty-six South Carolina Spirituals.* New York: G. Schirmer, 1928.

Dixon, Robert M. W., and John Godrich. *Recording the Blues.* London: Studio Vista, 1970.

Dixon Dixon, Thomas W. "Billy Richardson's Last Ride." *Railroad Magazine,* 83 (Oct., 1968), 32–33.

Dobie, J. Frank, ed. *Coffee in the Gourd.* Publications of the Texas Folklore Society, No. 2. 1923. Rpt., Austin: Texas Folklore Society, 1935.

Dolph Dolph, Edward Arthur. *"Sound Off!"* New York: Cosmopolitan Book Corp., 1929.

Donegan (1956) Donegan, Lonnie. *Album of Folk Songs.* London: Essex Music, 1956.

Donegan (1957?) ———. *The Lonnie Donegan Album of Folk Songs, Vol. 2.* London: Essex Music, [1957?]

Donovan, Frank P., Jr. *The Railroad in Literature.* Boston: Railway and Locomotive Historical Society, 1940.

———. "Hi-Fi Railroad Recordings." *Railroad Magazine,* 71 (Oct., 1960), 50–51.

Dorson (1966) Dorson, Richard M. "Negro Folksongs in Michigan from the Repertoire of J. D. Suggs." *Folklore and Folk Music Archivist,* 9 (Fall, 1966), 3–41.

Dorson (1973) ———. *America in Legend: Folkore from the Colonial Period to the Present.* New York: Pantheon Books, 1973.

Downes & Siegmeister (1940) Downes, Olin, and Elie Siegmeister. *A Treasury of American Song.* New York: Howell, Soskin, 1940.

Downes & Siegmeister (1943) ———. *A Treasury of American Song.* Rev. ed. New York: Alfred A. Knopf, 1943.

Drake Drake, Robert Y., Jr. "Casey Jones: The Man and the Song." *Tennessee Folklore Society Bulletin,* 19 (Dec., 1957), 95–101.

Duke Duke, Ray. *Songs . . . as Sung by Ray Duke and His Sugar Creek Gang.* Blytheville, Ark.: Radio Station KCLN, [1947–48?].

Duncan Duncan, Ruby. "Ballads and Folk Songs Collected in Northern Hamilton County." Master's thesis, University of Tennessee, 1939.

Dykema Dykema, Peter W., et al., eds. *Sing Out!* Evanston: Summy-Birchard Publishing, 1947.

Eckstorm & Smyth Eckstorm, Fannie Hardy, and Mary Winslow Smyth. *Minstrelsy of Maine: Folk-Songs and Ballads of the Woods and the Coast.* Boston and New York: Houghton Mifflin, 1927.

Edwards, C. L. Edwards, Charles L. *Bahama Songs and Stories.* 1895. Rpt., New York: G. E. Stechert, 1942.

Edwards, R.   Edwards, Ron. *The Overlander Songbook*. Holloways Beach, Queensland, Australia: Rams Skull Press, 1969.

Eiland   Eiland, F. L., Emmett S. Dean, J. F. Mayfield, Walter C. Mitchell, and G. H. Ramsey. *The Gospel Gleaner: A Book of Sacred Songs*. Waco, Tex., and Memphis, Tenn.: Trio Music, 1901.

Ellis   Ellis, Bill. "'The Boys in Blue': Mother Song to Protest Song and Back Again." *Journal of the Ohio Folklore Society*, n.s., 5 (1978), 14–22.

Emrich (1942a)   Emrich, Duncan. "Songs of the Western Miners." California Folklore Quarterly, 1 (July, 1942), 213–32.

Emrich (1942b)   ———. "'Casey Jones, Union Scab,'" *California Folklore Quarterly*, 1 (July, 1942), 292–93.

Emrich (1942c)   ———. "Mining Songs." *Southern Folklore Quarterly*, 6 (June, 1942), 103–6.

Emrich (1958)   ———. Brochure notes to Library of Congress Archive of Folk Song L20: *Anglo-American Songs and Ballads*. 1958.

Emrich (1974)   ———. *American Folk Poetry: An Anthology*. Boston: Little, Brown, 1974.

Engel   Engel, Lyle Kenyon. *500 Songs That Made the All Time Hit Parade*. New York: Bantam Books, 1964.

Epstein, Dena J. *Sinful Tunes and Spirituals: Black Folk Music to the Civil War*. Urbana: University of Illinois Press, 1977.

Ernst   Ernst, Karl, et al. *Birchard Music Series, Book Seven*. Evanston: Summy-Birchard Publishing, 1958.

Everybody's   *Everybody's Favorite Songs of the Gay Nineties*. New York: Amsco Music Publishing, 1943.

Ewen (1947)   Ewen, David. *Songs of America: A Cavalcade of Popular Songs*. Chicago: Ziff-Davis Publishing, 1947.

Ewen (1964)   ———. *The Life and Death of Tin Pan Alley*. New York: Funk and Wagnalls, 1964.

Ewen (1966)   ———. *American Popular Songs*. New York: Random House, 1966.

Fagan & Fox   *Fagan & Fox's International Derby Songster*. New York, 18–.

Family   *The Family Music Book*. New York: G. Schirmer, 1957.

Family Herald   Fowke, Edith. " 'Old Favorites': A Selective Index [of songs in the *Family Herald and Weekly Star*, Montreal]." *Canadian Folk Music Journal*, 7 (1979), 29–56.

Famous Old Time Songs   *Famous Old Time Songs*. New York: Padell Book, 1944.

Farjeon, Eleanor. *Memoirs of Eleanor Farjeon*. Book 1. *Edward Thomas: The Last Four Years*. London: Oxford University Press, 1958.

Farmer, J. S., and W. E. Henley. *Slang and Its Analogues*. 1890–1904. Rpt., New York: Arno Press, 1970

Fath   Fath, Creekmore, comp. and ed. *The Lithographs of Thomas Hart Benton*. Austin and London: University of Texas Press, 1969.

Faulkner   Faulkner, Harold Underwood. *American Political and Social History*. 7th ed. New York: Appleton-Century-Crofts, 1957.

Faye & Cleo   *Faye & Cleo's Home Song Favorites No. 1*. New York: Stasny Music, n.d.

Felton   Felton, Harold W. *Cowboy Jamboree: Western Songs & Lore*. New York: Alfred A. Knopf, 1951.

Fenner   *Cabin and Plantation Songs as Sung by the Hampton Students*. 3d ed. Arranged by Thomas P. Fenner, Frederic G. Rathbun, and Bessie Cleaveland. New York: G. P. Putnam's Sons, 1901. Later revised and published as *Religious Folk Songs of the Negro*. Edited by R. N. Dett. Hampton, Va.: Institute Press, 1909

Ferris (1970)   Ferris, William R., Jr. "Railroad Chants: Form and Function." *Mississippi Folklore Register*, 4 (Spring, 1970), 1–14.

———. "Railroad Folklore: An Overview." *North Carolina Folklore*, 22 (Nov., 1974), 169–76.

Fife & Fife (1969)   Fife, Austin E., and Alta S. Fife. *Cowboy and Western Songs*. New York: Clarkson N. Potter, 1969.

Fife & Fife (1970) ———. *Heaven on Horseback*. Logan: Utah State University Press, 1970.

Finger (1923) Finger, Charles J. *Sailor Chanties and Cowboy Songs*. Little Blue Book No. 301. Girard, Kans.: Haldeman-Julius, 1923.

Finger (1927) ———. *Frontier Ballads*. Garden City, N.Y.: Doubleday, Page, 1927.

Fishwick Fishwick, Marshall. "Uncle Remus vs. John Henry: Folk Tension." *Western Folklore*, 20 (Apr., 1961), 77–85.

Flanders & Brown Flanders, Helen Hartness, and George Brown. *Vermont Folk-Songs and Ballads*. 1931. Rpt., Hatboro, Pa.: Folklore Associates, 1968.

Flanders et al. Flanders, Helen Hartness, Elizabeth Flanders Ballard, George Brown, and Phillips Barry. *The New Green Mountain Songster*. 1939. Rpt., Hatboro, Pa.: Folklore Associates, 1966.

Flatt & Scruggs *Lester Flatt, Earl Scruggs and the Foggy Mountain Boys' Picture Album —Song Book*. [Nashville?, 1959?].

Flynt, Josiah. "The American Tramp." *Contemporary Review*, 60 (Aug., 1891), 253–61.

Foley (1941) *Red Foley's Cowboy Songs & Mountain Ballads*. Chicago: M. M. Cole, 1941.

Foley (1948?) *Red Foley's Keepsake Album*. N.p., [1948?].

Folk Sing Haufrecht, Herbert, ed. *Folk Sing*. New York: Hollis Music, 1959.

Folksong Festival Silber, Irwin. *Folksong Festival*. New York: Scholastic Magazine, 1967.

Ford Ford, Ira W. *Traditional Music of America*. 1940. Rpt., Hatboro, Pa.: Folklore Associates, 1965, and New York: Da Capo Press, 1978.

Forget-Me-Not Songster *The Forget-Me-Not Songster, Containing a Choice Selection of Old Ballad Songs as Sung by Our Grandmothers*. New York: Turner and Fisher, 1845.

Forrest *Original Forrest Comedy Song Book*. Chicago: Rossiter, ca. 1895.

Foster's Songster *John Foster's Great Barnum & London Circus Songster*. New York, 18–.

Fountain Fountain, Clara Garrett. *The Wreck of Old 97*. Danville, Va.: Fountain Publishers, 1976.

Fowke Fowke, Edith. "American Cowboy and Pioneer Western Songs in Canada." *Western Folklore*, 21 (Oct., 1962), 247–56.

Fowke & Glazer ——— and Joe Glazer. *Songs of Work and Freedom*. 1960. Rpt., Garden City, N.Y.: Dolphin Books, 1961.

Fowke & Johnston Fowke, Edith, and Richard Johnston. *More Folk Songs of Canada*. Waterloo, Ontario: Waterloo Music, 1967.

Fowler Fowler, Gene. *Timber Line: A Story of Bonfils and Tammen*. New York: Covici, Friede, 1933.

Fox Fox, Pat. *The Wreck of Old 97*. Danville, Va.: Fox Publishers, 1969.

Foy Foy, Jack. *Old Time Songs, Mountain Ballads and Hill-Billy Tunes*. N.p., 1931.

Frankenstein Frankenstein, Alfred. "George Alley: A Study in Modern Folk Lore." *Musical Courier*, Apr. 16, 1932, p. 6. Reprinted in *JEMF Newsletter*, 2 (June, 1967), 46–47.

Frey (1924) Frey, Hugo. *A Collection of Twenty-five Selected Famous Negro Spirituals*. New York: Robbins-Engel, 1924.

Frey (1950) ———. *Music for the Millions*. Vol. 5. New York: J. J. Robbins and Sons, 1950.

Friedman Friedman, Albert B. *The Viking Book of Folk Ballads of the English-Speaking World*. New York: Viking Press, 1956.

Frontier West *Frontier West: Stories and Songs about Wyatt Earp, Sam Bass, Davy Crockett, Billie Venero, Big Foot Wallace, Jesse James, Mike Fink, and the Texas Rangers*. New York: Lewis Music Publishing, 1958.

Frothingham MSS Letters and requests sent to Robert Frothingham, editor of "Old Songs That Men Have Sung," *Adventure*, 1922–23. In Library of Congress Archive of Folk Song.

Fuld (1955) Fuld, James J. *American Popular Music: 1875–1950*. Philadelphia: Musical Americana, 1955.

Fuld (1971) ———. *The Book of World-Famous Music*. Rev. ed. New York: Crown Publishers, 1971.

Fuson   Fuson, Harvey H. *Ballads of the Kentucky Highlands*. London: Mitre Press, 1931.

Gainer (1963)   Gainer, Patrick, Jane Cox, O. O. Kidd, et al., comps. and eds. *The West Virginia Centennial Book of 100 Songs*. West Virginia Centennial Commission on Folklore. Morgantown, W.Va.: West Virginia University, 1963.

Gainer (1975)   Gainer, Patrick. *Folk Songs from the West Virginia Hills*. Grantsville, W.Va.: Seneca Books, 1975.

Gardner & Chickering   Gardner, Emelyn Elizabeth, and Geraldine Jencks Chickering. *Ballads and Songs of Southern Michigan*. 1939. Rpt., Hatboro, Pa.: Folklore Associates, 1967.

Geller   Geller, James J. *Famous Songs and Their Stories*. New York: Macaulay, 1931.

Gems   Stein, Max, ed. *Gems of Inspiration, Crop IV*. Chicago: Stein Publishing House, 1947.

Georgia Folklore Archives   Georgia Folklore Archives. Georgia State University, Atlanta.

Gerould   Gerould, Gordon Hall. *The Ballad of Tradition*. Oxford: Oxford University Press, 1932.

Gilbert (1940)   Gilbert, Douglas. *American Vaudeville: Its Life and Times*. 1940. Rpt., New York: Dover Publications, 1963.

Gilbert (1942)   ———. *Lost Chords*. Garden City, N.Y.: Doubleday, Doran, 1942.

Glass & Singer   Glass, Paul, and Louis C. Singer, eds. *Songs of Hill and Mountain Folk*. New York: Grossett and Dunlap, 1967.

Glazer (1964)   Glazer, Tom. *A New Treasury of Folk Songs*. 2d ed. New York: Bantam Books, 1964.

Glazer (1970)   ———. *Songs of Peace, Freedom, and Protest*. New York: David McKay, 1970.

Glosson   Glosson, Lonnie. *Favorite Radio Songs*. N.p., ca. 1944.

Godrich & Dixon   Godrich, John, and Robert M. W. Dixon. *Blues and Gospel Records, 1902–1942*. Rev. ed. London: Storyville Publications, 1969.

Golden Gospel Bells   *Golden Gospel Bells for Sunday-Schools, Conventions, etc., and General Use in Christian Work and Worship*. Lawrenceburg, Tenn.: James D. Vaughan, 1916.

Good Old Days   *Good Old Days*. Seabrook, N.H. (originally Danvers, Mass.): Tower Press, 1963–.

Good Old Times   *Good Old Times Folio*. New York: Leo Feist, 1922.

Goodwin   Goodwin, George. *Song Dex Treasury of Humorous and Nostalgic Songs*. New York: Song Dex, 1956.

Gordon (1931)   Gordon, Robert Winslow. "The Negro Spiritual." In *The Carolina Low Country*, by Augustine T. Smythe et al., pp. 191–222. New York: Macmillan, 1931.

Gordon (1938)   ———. *Folk-Songs of America*. New York: National Service Bureau, 1938.

Gordon Collection (Calif.)   ———. Collection of ca. 400 songs and groups of texts acquired by Gordon while living in California, mostly dated 1922–23. Most of the recordings, and references to the manuscripts, are in the Library of Congress Archive of Folk Song; most of the manuscripts themselves have not been found.

Gordon Collection (Ga.)   ———. Collection of ca. 555 songs acquired by Gordon while residing in Darien, Ga., 1926–28 and perhaps later. Recordings in Library of Congress Archive of Folk Song.

Gordon Collection (N.C.)   ———. Collection of 374 texts acquired by Gordon during a field trip in North Carolina, Oct.–Dec., 1925. Recordings and typescripts in Library of Congress Archive of Folk Song.

Gordon MSS   ———. Letters and requests set to Gordon, editor of "Old Songs That Men Have Sung," *Adventure*, 1923–27. Also a few scattered texts dating from 1911 to 1932. In Library of Congress Archive of Folk Song.

Gray   Gray, Roland Palmer. *Songs and Ballads of the Maine Lumberjacks*. Cambridge: Harvard University Press, 1925.

Green (1966)   Green, Archie. Brochure notes to Folkways FH 5273: *Tipple, Loom & Rail*. 1966.

———. Liner notes to RCA Victor LPV 532: *The Railroad in Folksong*. 1966.

Green (1968) ————. Brochure notes to Library of Congress Archive of Folk Song L61: *Railroad Songs and Ballads*. 1968.

Green (1972) ————. *Only a Miner: Studies in Recorded Coal-Mining Songs*. Urbana: University of Illinois Press, 1972.

Green (1973) ————. "Commercial Music Graphics: Number Twenty-seven." *JEMF Quarterly*, 9 (Winter, 1973), 160–65.

Green (1978) ————. "John Henry Depicted." Graphics no. 46. *JEMF Quarterly*, 14 (Autumn, 1978), 126–43.

Greenleaf & Mansfield Greenleaf, Elizabeth Bristol, and Grace Yarrow Mansfield. *Ballads and Sea Songs of Newfoundland*. 1933. Rpt., Hatboro, Pa.: Folklore Associates, 1968.

Greenway Greenway, John. *American Folksongs of Protest*. Philadelphia: University of Pennsylvania Press, 1953.

Gregory Gregory, Bobby. *Album of Songs No. 31*. New York: American Music Publishing, 1958.

Grissom Grissom, Mary Allen. *The Negro Sings a New Heaven*. 1930. Rpt., New York: Dover Publications, 1969.

Griswold, Wesley S. *Train Wreck!* Brattleboro, Vt.: Stephen Greene Press, 1969.

Grove *Paul Grove's Roundup of Song Hits*. New York: Dixie Music, [1944?].

Gurner Gurner, Bruce. *Casey Jones and the Wreck at Vaughan*. Water Valley, Miss., 1973.

Gus Williams *Gus Williams' Olympic Songster*. New York: Robert M. DeWitt, 1875.

Guthrie (1942) Guthrie, Woody. "State Line to Skid Row." *Common Ground*, 3 (Autumn, 1942), 35–44.

Guthrie (1943) ————. *Bound for Glory*. New York: E. P. Dutton, 1943.

Guthrie (1960) ————. *California to the New York Island*. New York: Guthrie Children's Trust Fund (distributed by Oak Publications), 1960.

Guthrie (1963) ————. *The Nearly Complete Collection of Woody Guthrie Folksongs*. Edited by Pete Seeger. New York: Ludlow Music, 1963.

Haden, Walter D. *"If I Had Wings like an Angel*: The Life of Vernon Dalhart." In *Pictorial History of Country Music, Vol. 3*, edited by Thurston Moore, pp. 3–7. Denver: Heather Enterprises, 1970.

————. "Vernon Dalhart: His Roots and the Beginnings of Commercial Country Music." *ARSC Journal*, 3 (Winter, 1970–71), 19–32.

————. "Vernon Dalhart: Commercial Country Music's First International Star." *JEMF Quarterly*, 11 (Summer, 1975), 95–103; 11 (Autumn, 1975), 129–36.

————. "Vernon Dalhart." In *Stars of Country Music: Uncle Dave Macon to Johnny Rodriguez*, edited by Bill C. Malone and Judith McCulloh, pp. 64–85. Urbana: University of Illinois Press, 1975.

Hamilton Hamilton, Maxwell. "Highball to Hell." *Cavalier*, June, 1959, pp. 38–39, 80–83.

Hamlins Saddle Pals *Sensational Collection of Mountain Ballads and Old Time Songs as Sung by Jimmy and His Hamlins Saddle Pals, KFOX, KRKD*. Chicago: M. M. Cole, 1933.

Hamlins Singing Cowboy *Hamlins Singing Cowboy Sensational Collection of Mountain Ballads and Old Time Songs* [station] *KOMA* [of] *Oklahoma City, Oklahoma*. Chicago: M. M. Cole, 1933.

Hampton *Hampton and Its Students*. By Two of Its Teachers, Mrs. M. F. Armstrong and Helen Ludlow. *With Fifty Cabin and Plantation Songs, as Sung by the Hampton Students*. Arranged by Thomas P. Fenner. New York: G. P. Putnam's Sons, 1874. The music section was later published separately as *Cabin and Plantation Songs as Sung by the Hampton Students*. Arranged by Thomas P. Fenner, Frederic G. Rathbun, and Bessie Cleaveland. New York: G. P. Putnam's Sons, 1901. For other editions, *see* Fenner; Dett.

Hand Hand, Wayland D., Charles Cutts, Robert C. Wylder, and Betty Wylder. "Songs of the Butte Miners." *Western Folklore*, 9 (Jan., 1950), 1–49.

Handy   Handy, W[illiam] C[hristopher]. *Blues: An Anthology*. New York: Albert and Charles Boni, 1926. Reprinted as *A Treasury of the Blues*. New York: Charles Boni, 1949. A new edition titled *Blues: An Anthology* was edited by Jerry Silverman. New York: Macmillan, 1972.

Harbin   Harbin, E. O. *Parodology: Songs for Fun and Fellowship*. Nashville: Cokesbury Press, 1927.

Harlan   Harlan, J. B. "Railroad Bill." *L & N Employes' Magazine*, 3 (May, 1927), 30, 31, 69, 70.

Harlow   Harlow, F. *Chanteying aboard American Ships*. Barre, Mass.: Barre Gazette, 1962.

Harmonic Praises   *The Harmonic Praises: For the Song Service*. Written and compiled by H. C. Shanks et al. Morristown, Tenn.: Harmonic Publishing, 1915.

Harris, Sheldon. *Blues Who's Who*. New Rochelle, N.Y.: Arlington House, 1979.

Harrison   Harrison, Russell M. "Folk Songs from Oregon." *Western Folklore*, 11 (July, 1952), 174–84.

Hatfield Songster   Hatfield Brothers. *Pride of Mayo Songster*. New York, n.d.

Haun   Haun, Mildred. "Cocke County Ballads and Songs." Master's thesis, Vanderbilt University, 1937.

Hays (1886)   Hays, Will[iam] S[hakespeare]. *Songs and Poems*. Louisville, Ky.: Courier-Journal Job Printing, 1886.

Hays (1895)   ———. *Poems and Songs*. Louisville, Ky.: Chas. T. Dearing, 1895.

Henry (1931)   Henry, Mellinger Edward. "More Songs from the Southern Highlands." *Journal of American Folklore*, 44 (Jan.-Mar., 1931), 61–115.

Henry (1932)   ———. "Still More Ballads and Folk-Songs from the Southern Highlands." *Journal of American Folklore*, 45 (Jan.-Mar., 1932), 1–176.

Henry (1934)   ———. *Songs Sung in the Southern Appalachians*. London: Mitre Press, 1934.

Henry (1938)   ———. *Folk-Songs from the Southern Highlands*. New York: J. J. Augustin, 1938.

Henry, Robert S. "The Railroad Land Grant Legend in American History Texts." *Mississippi Valley Historical Review*, 32 (Sept., 1945), 171–94.

Herr, Kincaid A. *The L & N Railroad, 1850–1940, 1941–1959*. Enl. ed. Louisville: L & N Magazine, 1959.

High   High, Fred. *Old, Old Folk Songs*. Berryville, Ark., n.d.

Hillbilly Hit Parade   *Hillbilly Hit Parade of 1941*. New York: Southern Music Publishing, 1941.

Hille   Hille, Waldemar, ed. *The People's Song Book*. 1948. Rpt., New York: Oak Publications, 1961.

Hit Parade   *Hit Parade of Cowboy Songs*. Chicago: Chart Music Publishing House, ca. 1946.

Hodgart   Hodgart, Matthew, ed. *The Faber Book of Ballads*. 1965. Rpt., London: Faber and Faber, 1971.

Holbrook   Holbrook, Stewart H. *The Story of American Railroads*. New York: Crown Publishers, 1947.

Holt, Alfred H. *Phrase and Word Origins: A Study of Familiar Expressions*. 1936 (titled *Phrase Origins*). Rpt., New York: Dover Publications, 1961.

Honore   Honore, Lockwood, comp. *Popular College Songs*. Cincinnati: John Church, 1891.

Hood   Hood, Marguerite V., Glenn Gildersleeve, and Helen S. Leavitt, *Singing Days*. World of Music Series. Boston: Ginn, 1949.

Horstman   Horstman, Dorothy. *Sing Your Heart Out, Country Boy*. New York: E. P. Dutton, 1975.

Hough, Emerson. *The Story of the Outlaw*. New York: Outing Publishing, 1907.

Houston   *900 Miles: The Ballads, Blues and Folksongs of Cisco Houston*. Edited by Moses Asch and Irwin Silber. New York: Oak Publications, 1965.

Howse   Howse, Ruth Whitener. "Folk Music of West Tennessee." *Tennessee Folklore Society Bulletin*, 13 (Dec., 1947), 77–88.

Hubbard, F.   Hubbard, Freeman H. *Railroad Avenue*. New York: McGraw-Hill, 1945.

———. "The Real Casey Jones." *American Mercury*, 70 (June, 1950), 709–15.

Hubbard, L.   Hubbard, Lester A. *Ballads and Songs from Utah*. Salt Lake City: University of Utah Press, 1961.

Hudson (1928)   Hudson, Arthur Palmer. *Specimens of Mississippi Folklore*. Ann Arbor, Mich.: Edwards Brothers, 1928.

Hudson (1936)   ———. *Folksongs of Mississippi and Their Background*. Chapel Hill: University of North Carolina Press, 1936.

Hudson, James F. *The Railways and the Republic*. New York: Harper and Brothers, 1886.

Hughes & Bontemps   Hughes, Langston, and Arna Bontemps. *The Book of Negro Folklore*. New York: Dodd, Mead, 1958.

Hugill (1966)   Hugill, Stan. *Shanties from the Seven Seas*. 2d ed. London: Routledge and Kegan Paul, 1966.

Hugill (1969)   ———. *Shanties and Sailors' Songs*. London: Herbert Jenkins, 1969.

Hull   Hull, Clifton E. *Shortline Railroads of Arkansas*. Norman: University of Oklahoma Press, 1969.

Huntington, George. *Robber and Hero: The Story of the Raid on the First National Bank of Northfield, Minnesota, by the James-Younger Band of Robbers, in 1876*. 1895. Rpt., Minneapolis: Ross and Haines, 1962.

Hurston   Hurston, Zora Neale. *Mules and Men*. 1935. Rpt., Bloomington: Indiana University Press, 1979.

Idaho State Historical Society. *18th Biennial Report*. Boise: Board of Trustees, 1940.

Irwin   Irwin, Godfrey. *American Tramp and Underworld Slang*. London: Eric Partridge, 1931.

Ives (1953)   Ives, Burl. *Burl Ives Song Book*. New York: Ballantine Books, 1953.

Ives (1962)   ———. *Songs in America*. New York: Duell, Sloan and Pearce, 1962.

Ives (1966)   ———. *More Burl Ives*. New York: Ballantine Books, 1966.

Jack & Little Jackie   *Jack & Little Jackie Presents Songs You Love to Hear*. Sioux Falls: Radio Station KSOO, n.d.

Jackson   Jackson, George Pullen. *Spiritual Folk-Songs of Early America*. New York: J. J. Augustin, 1937.

JAF   *Journal of American Folklore*. American Folklore Society, 1888–.

Jane & Carl   Jane and Carl [J. Swanson], *The Sunshine Pals*. New York: Peer International, 1941.

JEMFN   *JEMF Newsletter*. Los Angeles, 1965–68. Continued by *JEMF Quarterly (JEMFQ)*.

JEMFQ   *JEMF Quarterly*. John Edwards Memorial Foundation at the Folklore & Mythology Center, University of California, Los Angeles. 1969–.

Johnson, G. B. (1927)   Johnson, Guy B. "John Henry—A Negro Legend." In *Ebony and Topaz*, edited by Charles S. Johnson, pp. 47–51. New York: National Urban League, 1927.

Johnson, G. B. (1929)   ———. *John Henry: Tracking Down a Negro Legend*. Chapel Hill: University of North Carolina Press, 1929.

Johnson, H.   Johnson, Hall. *30 Negro Spirituals Arranged for Voice and Piano*. New York: G. Schirmer, 1949.

Johnson, J. R.   Johnson, James R. *Radio City Edition Album of Negro Spirituals*. New York: E. B. Marks, 1940.

Johnson, M. R.   Johnson, Maynard R. "The Case of the Old 97." *People into Music / Pickin'*, 5 (Aug., 1978), 30–37.

Johnson & Johnson (1925)   Johnson, James Weldon, and J. Rosamond Johnson. *The Book of American Negro Spirituals*. 1925. Rpt. (bound with Vol. 2), New York: Viking Press, 1969.

Johnson & Johnson (1926)   ———. *The Second Book of American Negro Spirituals*. 1926. Rpt. (bound with Vol. 1), New York: Viking Press 1969.

Jones, Charles Edwin. "The Railroad to Heaven." *North Dakota Quarterly*, 40 (Autumn, 1972), 69–76.

Jones   Jones, Robert. *Comic and Sentimental Songs, Sung by Robert Jones. Also a Short Sketch of His Life*. Lost River, Ind.: Robert Jones, 1887.

Jubilee & Plantation Songs   *Jubilee & Plantation Songs: Characteristic Favorites, as sung by the Hampton Students, Jubilee Singers, Fisk University Students and Other Concert Companies.* Boston: Oliver Ditson, 1887.

Kahn Collection   Edward A. Kahn II Collection of Folksong. Santa Monica, California.

Keene   *Hank Keene's Collection of Hill Billy Songs.* South Coventry, Conn.: Keene's Music, 1932.

Kennedy, C. O. (1952)   Kennedy, Charles O'Brien. *American Ballads: Naughty, Ribald and Classic.* New York: Fawcett Publications, 1952.

Kennedy, C. O. (1954)   ———. *A Treasury of American Ballads.* New York: McBride, 1954.

Kennedy, R. E.   Kennedy, R. Emmet. *Mellows.* New York: Albert and Charles Boni, 1925.

KFBI   *KFBI Songs of the Plains.* Chicago: M. M. Cole, 1933.

Kincaid (1931)   Kincaid, Bradley. *My Favorite Old Time Songs and Mountain Ballads.* 4th ed. n.p. 1931.

Kincaid (1932)   ———. *My Favorite Mountain Ballads and Old Time Songs.* Book 5. n.p. 1932.

Kincaid (1937)   ———. *Favorite Mountain Ballads and Old Time Songs, No. 8.* New York: Southern Music Publishing, 1937.

Kirkland   Kirkland, E. C. "Collecting Ballads and Folk Songs in Tennessee." *Tennessee Folklore Society Bulletin,* 11 (Mar., 1936), 4–7.

Koehnline   Koehnline, William Angus. "A Study of Folksongs of the Western United States Reflecting Western Life." Master's thesis, University of North Carolina, 1949.

Kolb   Kolb, Sylvia, and John Kolb, eds. *A Treasury of Folk Songs.* New York: Bantam Books, 1948.

Korson   Korson, George. *Coal Dust on the Fiddle.* 1943. Rpt., Hatboro, Pa.: Folklore Associates, 1965.

Kreimer   Kreimer, Barbara. "Information Booth" column, a regular feature in *Railroad Magazine.*

Lair   Lair, John, comp. *100 WLS Barn Dance Favorites.* Chicago: M. M. Cole, 1935.

Landeck (1950a)   Landeck, Beatrice. *"Git on Board."* Rev. ed. New York: E. B. Marks, 1950.

Landeck (1950b)   ———. *Songs to Grow On.* New York: E. B. Marks, 1950.

Landeck (1954)   ———. *More Songs to Grow On.* New York: E. B. Marks, 1954.

Lane   Lane, Ron. "Folk Music of the C & O." A continuing series in the *C & O Historical Newsletter:* Pt. 1 [general introduction], 1, no. 10 (Oct., 1969), 4-5; Pt. 2 ["C & O Wreck"], 1, no. 12 (Dec., 1969), 9-10; Pt. 3 ["Wreck of C & O #5"], 2, no. 2 (Feb., 1970), n.p.; Pt. 4 ["Wreck of C & O *Sportsman*"], 2, no. 3 (Mar., 1970), n.p.; Pt. 5 ["Engine 143"], 2, no. 6 (June, 1970) "Historical Section"; pt. 6 [Billy Richardson], 2, no. 7 (July, 1970), n.p.; Pt. 7 ["Wreck of 1256"], 2, no. 8 (Aug., 1970), n.p.; Pt. 8 ["C & O Excursion"], 4, no. 8 (Aug., 1972), 7; Pt. 9 ["Wreck of C & O *Sportsman*"], 4 no. 10 (Oct., 1972), 8-9; Pt. 10 ["The Dying Engineer"], 4, no. 11 (Nov., 1972), 8-9; Pt. 11 ["The Clifftop Train"], 6, no. 3 (Mar., 1974), 6-7; Pt. 12 ["The Wreck of the C & O #5'—A Sequel"], 6, no. 4 (Apr., 1974), 14-15; Pt. 13 ["The C & O Blues"], 6 no. 10 (Oct., 1974), 10; Pt. 14 ["John Henry"], 6, no. 11 (Nov., 1974), 10-15.

Larkin   Larkin, Margaret. *Singing Cowboy.* 1931. Rpt., New York: Oak Publications, 1963.

Laws   Laws, G. Malcolm, Jr. *Native American Balladry.* Rev. ed. Philadelphia: American Folklore Society, 1964.

Layne   *Bert Layne & His Mountain Fiddlers with Riley Puckett and Richard Cox.* n.p., [1936?].

LC AFS (AAFS)   Library of Congress Archive of (American) Folk Song, Washington, D.C.

Leach, C.   Leach, Clifford. *Bottoms Up! A "Loving Cup" Filled to the Brim for All Sorts of Convivial Occasions.* New York: Paull-Pioneer Music Corp., 1933.

Leach, M.   Leach, Maria. *The Rainbow Book of American Folk Tales and Legends.* Cleveland and New York: World Publishing, 1958.

Leach, MacE. (1955)   Leach, MacEdward. *The Ballad Book.* New York: A. S. Barnes, 1955.

———. *Folk Ballads and Songs of the Lower Labrador Coast*. Ottawa: National Museum of Canada. 1965

Leach, MacE. (1966)   ———. "John Henry." In *Folklore and Society: Essays in Honor of Benj. A. Botkin*, edited by Bruce Jackson, pp. 93–106. Hatboro, Pa.: Folklore Associates, 1966.

Leach, MacE. (1967)   ———. *The [Heritage] Book of Ballads*. New York: Heritage Press, 1967.

Leach & Beck   ——— and Horace P. Beck. "Songs from Rappahannock County, Virginia." *Journal of American Folklore*, 63 (July-Sept., 1950), 257–84.

Leadbelly (1959a)   *A Collection of World-Famous Songs by Huddie Ledbetter*. Edited by John A. Lomax and Alan Lomax. New York: Folkways Music Publishers, 1959.

Leadbelly (1959b)   *The Leadbelly Legend: A Collection of World Famous Songs by Huddie Ledbetter*. Edited by John A. Lomax and Alan Lomax. New York: Folkways Music Publishers, 1959.

Leadbelly (1962)   *The Leadbelly Songbook*. Edited by Moses Asch and Alan Lomax. New York: Oak Publications, 1962.

Leamy, Hugh. "Now Come All You Good People." *Collier's*, Nov. 2, 1929, pp. 20, 58, 59. Reprinted in Linnell Gentry, *A History and Encyclopedia of Country, Western, and Gospel Music*, 2d ed., pp. 6–13. Nashville: Clairmont Publishing, 1969.

Lee   Lee, Fred J. *Casey Jones: Epic of the American Railroad*. Kingsport, Tenn.: Southern Publishers, 1939.

Leisy (1957)   Leisy, James F. *Abingdon Song Kit*. New York and Nashville: Abingdon Press, 1957.

Leisy (1959)   ———. *Let's All Sing*. Nashville: Abingdon Press, 1959.

Leisy (1966)   ———. *The Folk Song Abecedary*. New York: Bonanza Books, 1966.

Leisy (1973)   ———. *The Good Times Songbook*. Nashville: Abingdon Press, 1973.

LEMJ   *Locomotive Engineers' Monthly Journal*. Cleveland, 1867–. Published as *Locomotive Engineers' Monthly Journal*, 1867–71; *Brotherhood of Locomotive Engineers' Journal*, 1872–73; *Engineers' Monthly Journal*, 1874-82; *Brotherhood of Locomotive Engineers' Journal*, 1883–1906; *Locomotive Engineers' Journal*, 1907–59; *Locomotive Engineer*, 1960–.

Levine   Levine, Lawrence W. *Black Culture and Black Consciousness: Afro-American Folk Thought from Slavery to Freedom*. New York: Oxford University Press, 1977.

Levy (1971)   Levy, Lester S. *Flashes of Merriment: A Century of Humorous Songs in America, 1805–1905*. Norman. University of Oklahoma Press, 1971.

Levy (1975)   ———. *Give Me Yesterday: American History in Song, 1890–1920*. Norman. University of Oklahoma Press, 1975.

Life Treasury   *The Life Treasury of American Folklore*. By the Editors of *Life*. New York: Time, 1961.

Lingenfelter   Lingenfelter, Richard E., Richard A. Dwyer, and David Cohen. *Songs of the American West*. Berkeley and Los Angeles: University of California Press, 1968.

Little Four Songster   *The Little Four Songster*. New York: New York Popular Publishing, 18–.

Loesser   Loesser, Arthur. *Humor in American Song*. New York: Howell, Soskin, 1942.

Lomax, A. (1947)   Lomax, Alan. Brochure notes to Brunswick album B-1024: *Listen to Our Story*. New York: Brunswick Radio Corp., 1947.

Lomax, A. (1960)   ———. *The Folk Songs of North America*. Garden City, N.Y.: Doubleday, 1960.

Lomax, A. (1967)   ———. *Hard Hitting Songs for Hard Hit People*. New York: Oak Publications, 1967.

Lomax, J. (1910)   Lomax, John A. *Cowboy Songs and Other Frontier Ballads*. New York: Sturgis and Walton, 1910.

Lomax, J. (1915)   ———. "Some Types of American Folk-Song." *Journal of American Folklore*, 28 (Jan.-Mar., 1915), 1–17.

Lomax, J. (1916)   ———. *Cowboy Songs and Other Frontier Ballads*. [Rev. ed.] New York: Macmillan, 1916.

———. *Adventures of a Ballad Hunter*. New York: Macmillan, 1947.

Lomax & Lomax (1934)   ——— and Alan Lomax. *American Ballads and Folk Songs*. New York: Macmillan, 1934.

Lomax & Lomax (1936)   ———. *Negro Folk Songs as Sung by Lead Belly*. New York: Macmillan, 1936.

Lomax & Lomax (1938)   ——— *Cowboy Songs and Other Frontier Ballads*. Rev. ed. New York: Macmillan, 1938.

Lomax & Lomax (1941)   ———. *Our Singing Country*. New York: Macmillan, 1941.

Lomax & Lomax (1947)   ———. *Folksong: U.S.A.* (subsequently retitled *Best Loved American Folk Songs*). New York: Duell, Sloan and Pearce, 1947.

Lomax Papers   John A. Lomax Papers. Texas Historical Society, Austin.

Longini   Longini, Muriel Davis. "Folk Songs of Chicago Negroes." *Journal of American Folklore*, 52 (Jan.-Mar., 1939), 96–111.

Look Away   *Look Away: 56 Negro Folk Songs*. Rev. ed. Delaware, Ohio: Cooperative Recreation Service, 1963.

Love, Robertus. *The Rise and Fall of Jesse James*. New York: G. P. Putnam's Sons, 1926.

Lovell   Lovell, John, Jr. *Black Song: The Forge and the Flame*. New York: Macmillan, 1972.

Lowery   *Ramblin' Red Lowery's Book of Songs*. Book 1. New York: Amsco Music Sales, 1934.

Luboff & Stracke   Luboff, Norman, and Win Stracke. *Songs of Man: The International Book of Folk Songs*. Englewood Cliffs, N.J.: Prentice-Hall, 1965.

Luce   Luce, Stephen B. *Naval Songs: A Collection of Original, Selected and Traditional*. New York: Wm. A. Pond. 1883.

Lulu Belle & Scotty (1937)   *Lulu Belle's and Skyland Scotty's* [Wiseman] *Home Folk Songs*. Chicago: M. M. Cole, 1937.

Lulu Belle & Scotty (1941)   *Lulu Belle & Skyland Scotty* [Wiseman]. Chicago: M. M. Cole, 1941.

Lummis   Lummis, Charles F. "An Old Song of the Rail." *Out West*, 20 (Feb., 1904), 178–82. Reprinted in *Santa Fe Employes' Magazine*, 2 (July, 1908), 375–76.

Lunsford   Lunsford, Bascom Lamar, and Lamar Stringfield. *Thirty and One Songs*. New York: Carl Fischer, 1929.

Luther   Luther, Frank. *Americans and Their Songs*. New York: Harper and Brothers, 1942.

Lynn   Lynn, Frank. *Songs for Swingin' Housemothers*. San Francisco: Chandler Publishing, 1961.

Lyon   Lyon, Peter. *To Hell in a Day Coach: An Exasperated Look at American Railroads*. Philadelphia and New York: J. B. Lippincott, 1968.

McAfee, Broadus. "Rockmart, Georgia Site of a Tragic Train Wreck, December 23, 1926." *North West Georgia Historical and Genealogical Society*, 4 (July, 1972), 10–12.

Mac & Bob (1931a)   McFarland, Lester, and Robert Gardner. *Book of Songs*. Chicago: M. M. Cole, 1931.

Mac & Bob (1931b)   ———. *WLS Book of Songs (Old and New)*. Chicago: M. M. Cole, 1931.

Mac & Bob (1931c)   ———. *Book of Songs Old and New*. Chicago: M. M. Cole, 1931.

Mac & Bob (1941)   ———. *Mountain Songs—Western Songs—Cowboy Songs*. Chicago: M. M. Cole, 1941.

McCague, James. *Moguls and Iron Men: The Story of the First Transcontinental Railroad*. New York: Harper and Row, 1964.

McCarthy, Albert, Max Harrison, Alun Morgan, and Paul Oliver. *Jazz on Record—A Critical Guide to the First 50 Years: 1917–1967*. London: Hanover Books; New York: Oak Publications, 1968.

MacColl   MacColl, Ewan, ed. *The Shuttle and the Cage: Industrial Folk-Ballads*. New York: Hargail Music Press, 1954.

McCord   McCord, May Kennedy. "Hillbilly Heartbeats." Weekly column in *Leader-News*, 1932–38, thrice weekly in *Daily News*, 1938–42 (both Springfield, Mo.).

McCulloh (1966)   McCulloh, Judith. "Some Child Ballads on Hillbilly Records." In *Folklore and Society: Essays in Honor of Benj. A. Botkin*, edited by Bruce Jackson, pp. 107–29. Hatboro, Pa.: Folklore Associates, 1966.

McCulloh (1970a)   ———. "Indiana's Treasure Store Is a Wealth of Good Old Hoosier Lore." *Folklore Forum*, 3 (Sept.-Nov., 1970), 135–37.

McCulloh (1970b)   ———. "'In the Pines': The Melodic-Textual Identity of an American Lyric Folksong Cluster." Ph.D. diss., Indiana University, 1970.

McCulloh & Green   ——— and Archie Green. Brochure notes to Campus Folksong Club (University of Illinois) CFC 301: *The Hell-Bound Train*, by Glenn Ohrlin. Urbana, 1964.

McGuire   *Mac McGuire's Roundup of Song Hits*. New York: Dixie Music, 1944.

McIlhenny   McIlhenny, E. A. *Befo' de War Spirituals*. Boston: Christopher Publishing House, 1933.

McIntosh   McIntosh, David S. *Folk Songs and Singing Games of the Illinois Ozarks*. Carbondale and Edwardsville: Southern Illinois University Press, 1974.

———. "Some Representative Southern Illinois Folk-Songs." Master's thesis, State University of Iowa, 1935.

McNeil (1969a)   McNeil, William K. "'We'll Make the Spanish Grunt': Popular Songs about the Sinking of the *Maine*." *Journal of Popular Culture*, 2 (Spring, 1969), 537–51.

McNeil (1969b)   ———. "Popular Songs from New York Autograph Albums." *Journal of Popular Culture*, 3 (Summer, 1969), 46–56.

Mainer, J. E.   *Songs as Sung by J. E. Mainer and His Mountaineers*. n.p., [1969?].

Mainer, M. L.   Mainer, M. L. *The Epic of "Casey" Jones*. Centralia, Ill.: Privately printed, n.d.

Malone, Bill C., and Judith McCulloh, eds. *Stars of Country Music: Uncle Dave Macon to Johnny Rodriguez*. Urbana: University of Illinois Press, 1975.

Malone   Malone, Henry H. "Folksongs and Ballads, Part 1." In *Kansas Folklore*, edited by S. J. Sackett and William E. Koch, pp. 138–60. Lincoln: University of Nebraska Press, 1961.

Manchester & Jennings   *Manchester & Jennings' Eccentric Character Songster*. New York: New York Popular Publishing, 188–.

Manning, Ambrose. "Railroad Work Songs." *Tennessee Folklore Society Bulletin*, 32 (June, 1966), 41–47.

Marcuse   Marcuse, Maxwell F. *Tin Pan Alley in Gaslight*. Watkins Glen, N.Y.: Century House, 1959.

Marks   Marks, Edward B. *They All Sang*. New York: Viking Press, 1934.

Marlow (I)   *Jack & Little Jackie [Marlow] Presents Songs You Love to Hear*. N.p., [1940?].

Marlow (II)   Marlow, Jack. *Songs You Love to Hear—Book No. 3*. N.p., n.d.

Marsh   Marsh, J. B. T. *The Story of the Jubilee Singers with Their Songs*. Boston: Houghton, Mifflin, 1880.

Martin, D.   Martin, Deac. "Folk Songs or Populars?" *Music Journal*, 15 (Jan., 1957), 30, 62.

Martin, M.   Martin, Max. *Songs of the Prairie*. N.p., n.d.

Mason   Mason, Robert. "Folk-Songs and Folk-Tales of Cannon County, Tennessee." Master's thesis, George Peabody College for Teachers, 1939.

Masterson   Masterson, James R. *Tall Tales of Arkansas*. Boston: Chapman and Grimes, 1943.

Matteson   Matteson, Maurice. *American Folk-Songs for Young Singers*. American Folk-Song Series, Set 25. New York: G. Schirmer, 1947.

Maurer   Maurer, B. B., ed. *Mountain Heritage*. Ripley, W.Va.: Mountain State Art and Craft Fair, printed by Morgantown Printing and Binding, 1974.

Middleton, P. Harvey. *Railways and Public Opinion*. Chicago: Railway Business Association, 1941.

Milburn Milburn, George. *The Hobo's Hornbook*. New York: Ives Washburn, 1930.

Miller Miller, Jeffery M. "John Henry." *Laborer*, 27 (Feb., 1973), 9–14. A different version of this article was published as a pamphlet titled *John Henry*, by Jeffrey [*sic*] Miller. Clintwood, Va.: Council of the Southern Mountains.

Milling, Chapman J. "Delia Holmes—A Neglected Negro Ballad." *Southern Folklore Quarterly*, 1 (Dec., 1937), 3–8.

Minstrel Memories Reynolds, Harry. *Minstrel Memories: The Story of Burnt Cork Minstrelsy in Great Britain from 1836 to 1927*. London: Alston Rivers, [1928?].

Moody, James W., Jr. "Casey Jones Railroad Museum." *Tennessee Historical Quarterly*, 25 (Spring, 1966), 3–21.

Moore & Moore Moore, Ethel, and Chauncy O. Moore. *Ballads and Folk Songs of the Southwest*. Norman: University of Oklahoma Press, 1964.

Morison, Samuel Eliot, and Henry Steele Commager. *The Growth of the American Republic*. New York: Oxford University Press, 1950.

Morris Morris, Alton C. *Folksongs of Florida*. Gainesville: University of Florida Press, 1950.

Morse Morse, Frank P. *Cavalcade of the Rails*. New York: E. P. Dutton, 1940.

Morton *Tex Morton Sings an Album of Rodeo Favourites*. New York: Southern Music Publishing, 1951.

Mountain Side Melodies *Mountain Side Melodies*. New York: E. B. Marks, 1934.

Mountain Songs *Mountain Songs*. Chicago: Belmont Music, 1937.

Mulligan Mulligan, Peter. "Casey Jones." *Railroad Man's Magazine*, 16 (Dec., 1911), 397–402, and 17 (Apr., 1912), 494–97.

Mursell (Grade 4) Mursell, J. L., et al., eds. *Music around the World*. Music for Living, Grade 4. Morristown, N.J.: Silver Burdett, 1956.

Mursell (Grade 5) ———. *Music around the World*. Music for Living, Grade 5. Morristown, N.J.: Silver Burdett, 1956.

Mursell (Grade 6) ———. *Music around the World*. Music for Living, Grade 6. Morristown, N.J.: Silver Burdett, 1956.

Musick Musick, Ruth Ann. "Murderers and Cut-Throats in Song." *Tennessee Folklore Society Bulletin*, 19 (June, 1953), 31–35.

NCLB *National Car and Locomotive Builder*. New York, 1870–95. Published in 1870–85 as *National Car Builder*.

NCLR *New Lost City Ramblers Song Book*. Edited by John Cohen and Mike Seeger. New York: Oak Publications, 1964.

Neal Neal, Mabel Evangeline. "Brown County Songs and Ballads." Master's thesis, Indiana University, 1926.

Neely & Spargo Neely, Charles, and John W. Spargo. *Tales and Songs of Southern Illinois*. Menasha, Wis.: George Banta Publishing, 1938.

Nehls Nehls, Edward, ed. *D. H. Lawrence: A Composite Biography*. Vol. 1. *1885–1919*. Madison: University of Wisconsin Press, 1957.

Newcomb MSS (Additional) 102 texts from Kentucky sent to Robert W. Gordon at the Library of Congress Archive of Folk Song by Mary Newcomb, 1930–31.

Niles Niles, John J. "Jack," Douglas S. "Doug" Moore, and A. A. "Wally" Wallgren. *The Songs My Mother Never Taught Me*. New York: Macaulay, 1929.

Noble Noble, Gilbert Clifford. *The Most Popular Plantation Songs*. New York: Hinds, Hayden and Eldredge, 1911.

O'Conner, Richard. *Gould's Millions*. Garden City, N.Y.: Doubleday, 1962.

O'Day O'Day, Molly, Lynn Davis, and Lonnie Glosson. *Favorites of 1944*. Louisville, 1944.

Odell Odell, Mac. *Radio Song Book: 25 Outstanding Homefolk & Gospel Songs*. N.p., ca. 1949.

Odum   Odum, Howard W. "Folk-Song and Folk-Poetry as Found in the Secular Songs of the Southern Negroes." *Journal of American Folklore,* 24 (July-Sept., 1911), 255–94, and (Oct.-Dec., 1911). 351–96.

Odum & Johnson (1925)   Odum, Howard W., and Guy B. Johnson. *The Negro and His Songs.* 1925. Rpt., Hatboro, Pa.: Folklore Associates, 1964.

Odum & Johnson (1926)   ———. *Negro Workaday Songs.* Chapel Hill: University of North Carolina Press, 1926.

Odum-Arthur MSS   Manuscript obtained from J. D. Arthur, of Tennessee, and sent by Howard W. Odum to Robert W. Gordon, July 10, 1929. In Library of Congress Archive of Folk Song.

OED   *The Oxford English Dictionary.* Edited by James A. H. Murray, Henry Bradley, W. A. Craigie, and C. T. Onions. 13 vols. Oxford: Clarendon Press, 1933.

Ohrlin   Ohrlin, Glenn. *The Hell-Bound Train: A Cowboy Songbook.* Urbana: University of Illinois Press, 1973.

Okun   Okun, Milt. *Something to Sing About.* New York: Macmillan, 1968.

Old Brother Charlie   *Old Brother Charlie and Daisy Mae.* [Tampa, Fla.?], ca. 1949.

Oliver (1957)   Oliver, Paul H. "Rock Island Line." *Music Mirror,* 4 (Jan., 1957), 6–8.

Oliver (1971)   ———. "Railroad Bill." *Jazz & Blues,* 1 (May, 1971), 12–14.

Olsson, Bengt. *Memphis Blues.* London: Studio Vista, 1970.

Olympia Quartette Songster   *Olympia Quartette Songster.* New York: New York Popular Publishing, 18–.

100 Choice Selections   *One Hundred Choice Selections.* Compiled by Phineas Garrett. Nos. 1–40. Philadelphia: P. Garrett, 1866–1914. Reissued as *The Speaker's Garland and Literary Bouquet,* q.v.

O'Neal, Waldo. *Star Dust of the Plains.* Clovis, N. Mex., 1957.

Osborne   Osborne, Sonny. *Mel Bay Presents Bluegrass Banjo.* Kirkwood, Mo.: Mel Bay, 1964.

OTS&P   *Old Time Songs and Poems.* Danvers, Mass.: Tower Press, Sept.–Oct., 1967—Fall, 1971; Seabrook, N.H., winter, 1970–71–.

Ott   Ott, Irv. *On a Fast Train through Texas.* Baltimore; I. and M. Ottenheimer, 1905.

Overall   Overall, B. W. *The Story of Casey Jones, the Brave Engineer.* Jackson, Tenn.: Casey Jones Museum, 1956.

Owens, B. A. (1930)   Owens, Bess Alice. "Some Unpublished Folk-Songs of the Cumberlands." Master's thesis, George Peabody College for Teachers, 1930.

Owens, B. A. (1936)   ———. "Songs of the Cumberlands." *Journal of American Folklore,* 49 (July-Sept., 1936), 215–42.

Owens, T.   Owens, Tex. *Collection of His Own Original Songs and Old Favorites.* Chicago: Forster Music Publishing, 1934.

Owens, W.   Owens, William A. *Texas Folk Songs.* Publication of the Texas Folklore Society, No. 23. Dallas: Southern Methodist University Press, 1950.

Pack   Pack, ["Cowboy"] Loye. *Old Time Ballads and Cowboy Songs.* N.p., n.d.

Pack & John   ——— and Just Plain John. *Old Time Ballads and Cowboy Songs.* N.p., ca. 1934.

Palmer   Palmer, Edgar A., ed. *G. I. Songs.* New York: Sheridan House, 1944.

Parsons   Parsons, Elsie Clews. "Spirituals and Other Folklore from the Bahamas." *Journal of American Folklore,* 41 (Oct.-Dec., 1928), 453–524.

Partridge, Eric. *A Dictionary of Slang and Unconventional English.* 5th ed., rev. New York: Macmillan, 1961.

Peacock   Peacock, Ken. *Songs of the Newfoundland Outports.* 3 vols. Ottawa: Queen's Printer, 1965.

Perrow (1912)   Perrow, E. C. "Songs and Rhymes from the South." *Journal of American Folklore,* 25 (Jan.-Mar., 1912), 137–55.

Perrow (1913)   ———. "Songs and Rhymes from the South." *Journal of American Folklore,* 26 (Apr.-June, 1913), 123–73.

Perrow (1915) ———. "Songs and Rhymes from the South." *Journal of American Folklore*, 28 (Apr.-June, 1915), 129–90.

Perry Perry, Henry. "A Sampling of the Folklore of Carter County, Tennessee." Master's thesis, George Peabody College for Teachers, 1938.

Peters Peters, Harry B., ed. *Folk Songs out of Wisconsin*. Madison: State Historical Society of Wisconsin, 1977.

Peterson Peterson, Walter. *Sensational Collection of Mountain Ballads and Old Time Songs*. Chicago: M. M. Cole, 1931.

Pie Plant Pete *Pie Plant Pete* [Claude Moye] *and Bashful Joe's Favorite Old Time Songs, No. 3*. New York: Peer International, 1941.

Pike Pike, Gustavus. D. *The Jubilee Singers, and Their Campaign for Twenty Thousand Dollars*. Boston: Lee and Shepard; New York: Lee, Shepard and Dillingham, 1873 (copyrighted 1872).

Pitts (1950) Pitts, Lilla Belle, et al. *Singing Every Day*. Our Singing World, Grade 4. Boston: Ginn, 1950.

Pitts (1951a) ———. *Singing in Harmony*. Our Singing World, Grade 6. Boston: Ginn, 1951.

Pitts (1951b) ———. *Singing Together*. Our Singing World, Grade 5. Boston: Ginn, 1951.

Pitts (1953) Pitts, Lilla Belle. *Singing Juniors: Songs for Youth*. Our Singing World. Boston: Ginn, 1953.

Pitts (1954) ———. *Singing Teen-agers*. Our Singing World. Boston: Ginn, 1954.

Play and Sing *Play and Sing: America's Greatest Collection of Old Time Songs and Mountain Ballads*. Chicago: M. M. Cole, 1930.

Poor's Manual Poor, Henry V. *Manual of the Railroads of the United States*. Annual. New York: H. V. Poor and H. W. Poor, 1867–.

Popular Cowboy Songs *Popular Cowboy Songs of Ranch & Range*. New York: Hobo News, n.d.

Porcello Porcello, Patricia Lucille Berger. "The Railroad in American Literature: Poetry, Folk Song, and the Novel." Ph.D. diss., University of Michigan, 1968.

Porter & Bronson Porter, John E., and Bertrand H. Bronson. "Notes and Queries: Wobbly and Other Songs." *California Folklore Quarterly*, 2 (Jan., 1943), 42–44.

Porterfield, Nolan. *Jimmie Rodgers: The Life and Times of America's Blue Yodeler*. Urbana: University of Illinois Press, 1979.

Pound (1913) Pound, Louise, "Traditional Ballads in Nebraska." *Journal of American Folklore*, 26 (Oct.-Dec., 1913), 351–66.

Pound (1915) ———. *Folk-Song of Nebraska and the Central West: A Syllabus*. Nebraska Academy of Sciences Publications, 9, no. 3. Lincoln, 1915.

Pound (1922) ———. *American Ballads and Songs*. New York: Scribners, 1922.

Prince Prince, Richard E. *Steam Locomotives and Boats: Southern Railway System*. Green River, Wyo.: R. E. Prince, 1965.

Randolph (1931) Randolph, Vance. *The Ozarks: An American Survival of Primitive Society*. New York: Vanguard Press, 1931.

Randolph (1945) Kittredge, Belden [Vance Randolph]. *The Truth About Casey Jones, and Other Fabulous American Heroes, Including Johnny Appleseed, Davy Crockett, Roy Bean, and Mike Fink*. Girard, Kans.: Haldeman-Julius, 1945.

Randolph I–IV ———. *Ozark Folksongs*. 4 vols. Columbia: State Historical Society of Missouri, 1946–50.

Raph Raph, Theodore. *The Songs We Sang: A Treasury of American Popular Music*. New York: A. S. Barnes, 1964.

Ray Ray, Emick. "John Henry, the Steel Drivin' Man." *Pathway Magazine*, 2 (Mar., 1971), 15–17.

RC *Railway Conductor*. Cedar Rapids, 1884–. Published as *Railway Conductor's Monthly*, 1884–July 1889; *Railway Conductor*, Aug., 1889–July, 1954; *Conductor and Brakeman*, 1955–.

Red & Raymond   Anderson, Lonnie E., and Raymond Anderson. *Red and Raymond's Song Book Featuring the Red Headed Briarhopper and His Yodelling Son Raymond*. N.p., ca. 1934.

Redfearn   Redfearn, Susan Fort. "Songs from Georgia." *Journal of American Folklore,* 34 (Jan.-Mar., 1921), 121–24.

Reed, Robert C. *Train Wrecks: A Pictorial History of Accidents on the Main Line*. Seattle: Superior Publishing, 1968.

Reid (1961)   Reid, H. *The Virginian Railway*. Milwaukee: Kalmbach Publishing, 1961.

Reid (1964)   ———. *Extra South*. Susquehanna, Pa.: Starrucca Valley Publications, 1964.

Reprints from Sing Out! #3   *Reprints from Sing Out! The Folk Song Magazine*. Vol. 3. New York: Oak Publications, 1961.

Reprints from Sing Out! #4   *Reprints from Sing Out! The Folk Song Magazine*. Vol. 4: New York: Oak Publications, 1962.

Reynolds   Reynolds, Horace. "The Little Red Caboose behind the Train." *Tracks,* Aug., 1946, pp. 8–10.

Rhinehart   *Cowboy Slim Rhinehart Folio*. 3d ed. N.p., n.d.

Richardson   Richardson, Ethel Park. *American Mountain Songs*. New York: Greenberg, 1927.

Riddle-Abrahams   Riddle, Almeda. *A Singer and Her Songs: Almeda Riddle's Book of Ballads*. Edited by Roger D. Abrahams. Baton Rouge: Louisiana State University Press, 1970.

Ridenour   *Folk Songs of Rural Ohio*. Collected by Harry Lee Ridenour. Edited by W. Alwyn Ashburn. Berea, Ohio: Baldwin-Wallace College, 1973. Xerox. The collection is divided into books, but bound in volumes that do not always correspond to the book numbers. References are to the volume numbers.

Ripley Songster   *Thomas J. Ripley's Champion of the Day Songster*. New York: New York Popular Publishing, 188–.

RMWEJ   "Origin of Old Negro Ry. Folk Song." *Railway Maintenance of Way Employees Journal,* 40 (Sept., 1931), 13.

Roberts, Charles Wilson, III. "The Railroad in American Folk Song." *Appalachian State Teacher's College Bulletin* (Boone, N.C.), Spring, 1965, pp. 8–23.

Roberts   Roberts, Leonard. *The Tales and Songs of the Couch Family*. Lexington: University of Kentucky Press, 1959.

Robertson   Robertson, Archie. *Slow Train to Yesterday: A Last Glance at the Local*. Boston: Houghton Mifflin, 1945.

Robison (1930)   Robison, Carson J. *Carson J. Robison's World's Greatest Collection of Mountain Ballads and Old Time Songs*. Chicago: M. M. Cole, 1930.

Robison (1931)   ———. *J. Davis' Folio of Carson J. Robison Songs*. New York: Joe Davis, 1931.

Robison (1932)   ———. *The New Carson Robison Song Album*. 2d ed. New York: Southern Music Publishing, 1932.

Robison (1936)   ———. *Tip Top Album of Carson J. Robison's Songs*. New York: Tip Top Publications, 1936.

Robison (1941)   ———. *Carson Robison's "CR" Ranch Song Folio*. New York: Peer International, 1941.

Rocky Mountain Collection   *Rocky Mountain Collection*. Salt Lake City: Intermountain Folkmusic Council, 1962.

Rodeheaver   Rodeheaver, Homer. *Southland Spirituals*. Chicago and Philadelphia: Rodeheaver-Hall-Mack, 1936.

Rodgers (1931)   *Jimmie Rodgers' Album of Songs, No. 2*. New York: Southern Music Publishing, 1931.

Rodgers (1934a)   *Jimmie Rodgers' Album of Songs*. "Deluxe ed." New York: Southern Music Publishing, 1934.

Rodgers (1934b)   *Jimmie Rodgers' Album of Songs*. New York: Southern Music Publishing, 1934.

Rodgers (1934c)   *Jimmie Rodgers' Album of Songs, No. 4*. New York: Southern Music Publishing, 1934.

Rodgers (1937)   *Jimmie Rodgers' Album of Songs, No. 5.* New York: Southern Music Publishing, 1937.

Rodgers (1943a)   *Jimmie Rodgers' Album of Songs.* "Blue Yodel ed." New York: Peer International, 1943.

Rodgers (1943b)   *Jimmie Rodgers' Album of Songs.* "Supreme ed." New York: Peer International, 1943.

Rodgers (1967a)   *The Legendary Jimmie Rodgers Memorial Folio.* New York: Peer International, 1967.

Rodgers (1967b)   *The Legendary Jimmie Rodgers Memorial Folio.* Vol. 2. New York: Peer International, 1967.

Rogers   *Jesse Rogers' Favorite Songs.* New York: Joe Davis, 1938.

Rosenberg   Rosenberg, Bruce A. *The Folksongs of Virginia: A Checklist of the WPA Holdings, Alderman Library, University of Virginia.* Charlottesville: University of Virginia Press, 1969.

RRM/RRManM   *Railroad Magazine; Railroad Man's Magazine.* New York, 1906–. Published as *Railroad Man's Magazine*, Oct., 1906–June, 1913; *Railroad and Current Mechanics*, July, 1913–Dec., 1913; *Railroad Man's Magazine*, Jan., 1914–Jan., 1919; then merged with *Argosy*. Published as *Railroad Man's Magazine*, Dec., 1929 (starting again with Vol. 1)–Jan., 1932; *Railroad Stories*, Feb., 1932–Aug., 1937; *Railroad Magazine*, Sept., 1937–.

RTJ   *Railroad Trainmen's Journal.* Cleveland, then Peoria, 1883–1948. Published as *Western Railroader*, 1883–Nov., 1885; *Railroad Brakemen's Journal*, Dec., 1885–1889; *Railroad Trainmen's Journal*, 1890–1907; *Railroad Trainman*, 1908–48.

RVB   *Renfro Valley Bugle.* Renfro Valley, Ky. 1940–.

Sackheim   Sackheim, Eric. *The Blues Line: A Collection of Blues Lyrics.* New York: Grossman Publishers, 1969.

San Fernando Valley State College Archive   San Fernando Valley State College Archive. California State University, Northridge, California.

Sandburg   Sandburg, Carl. *The American Songbag.* New York: Harcourt, Brace, 1927.

Scarborough   Scarborough, Dorothy. *On the Trail of Negro Folk-Songs.* 1925. Rpt., Hatboro, Pa.: Folklore Associates, 1963.

Scardino   Scardino, Albert. "Folk Hero's Memory Lives On [John Henry]." *Columbus* (Ohio) *Dispatch,* Oct. 3, 1971.

Schlappi   Schlappi, Elizabeth. *Roy Acuff: The Smoky Mountain Boy.* Gretna, La.: Pelican Publishing, 1978.

Scott   Scott, Tom. *Sing of America.* New York: Thomas Y. Crowell, 1947.

Seeger, P. (1961)   Raim, Ethel, and Irwin Silber, eds. *American Favorite Ballads: Tunes and Songs as Sung by Pete Seeger.* New York: Oak Publications, 1961.

Seeger, P. (1964)   ———. *The Bells of Rhymney and Other Songs and Stories from the Singing of Pete Seeger.* New York: Oak Publications, 1964.

Seeger, R. C.   Seeger, Ruth Crawford. *American Folk Songs for Children in Home, School, and Nursery School: A Book for Children, Parents, and Teachers.* Garden City, N.Y.: Doubleday, 1948.

Settle, William A., Jr. *Jesse James Was His Name.* Columbia: University of Missouri Press, 1966.

Seward   Seward, Theodore Freylinghuysen. *Jubilee Songs: Complete, as Sung by the Jubilee Singers of Fisk University.* New York: Biglow and Main, 1872.

SFQ   *Southern Folklore Quarterly.* Jacksonville, Fla., 1937–.

Shaffer   Shaffer, Roy. *The Lone Star Cowboy.* Chicago: M. M. Cole, 1935.

Shapiro   Shapiro, Elliott. *Thirty-three Prison and Mountain Songs.* New York: Shapiro, Bernstein, 1932.

Sharp   Sharp, Cecil J., and Maud Karpeles. *English Folk-Songs from the Southern Appalachians.* Vol. 2. London: Oxford University Press, 1932.

Shay (1927)   Shay, Frank. *My Pious Friends and Drunken Companions.* 1927. Rpt.

(combined with *More Pious Friends and Drunken Companions*), New York: Dover Publications, 1961.

Shay (1928)   ———. *More Pious Friends and Drunken Companions*. 1928. Rpt., New York: Dover Publications, 1961.

Shay (1929)   ———. *Drawn from the Wood*. New York: Macaulay, 1929.

Shay (1930)   ———. *Here's Audacity! American Legendary Heroes*. New York: Macaulay, 1930.

Shearin & Combs   Shearin, Hubert G., and Josiah H. Combs. *A Syllabus of Kentucky Folk-Songs*. Lexington, Ky.: Transylvania Printing, 1911.

Shellans   Shellans, Herbert. *Folk Songs of the Blue Ridge Mountains*. New York: Oak Publications, 1968.

Sherwin & McClintock   Sherwin, Sterling, and Harry K. McClintock. *Railroad Songs of Yesterday*. New York: Shapiro-Bernstein, 1943.

Sherwin & Powell   Sherwin, Sterling, and Harry A. Powell. *Bad Man Songs of the Wild and Woolly West*. Cleveland: Sam Fox Publishing, 1933.

Shipley, Joseph T. *Dictionary of Word Origins*. 1945. Rpt., Ames, Iowa: Littlefield, Adams, 1957.

Shirley-Driggs   Shirley, Kay, ed. *The Book of the Blues*. Annotated by Frank Driggs. New York: Crown Publishers and Leeds Music Corp., 1963.

Siegmeister   Siegmeister, Elie. *Work and Sing*. New York: William R. Scott, 1944.

Silber   Silber, Irwin, ed. *Folksong Festival*. New York: Scholastic Book Services, 1967.

Silber & Robinson   ——— and Earl G. Robinson. *Songs of the Great American West*. New York: Macmillan, 1967.

Silber & Silber   Silber, Fred, and Irwin Silber. *Folksinger's Wordbook*. New York: Oak Publications, 1973.

Silverman (1968)   Silverman, Jerry. *Folk Blues*. Rev. ed. New York: Oak Publications, 1968.

Silverman (1975)   ———. *Folk Song Encyclopedia*. 2 vols. New York: Chappell Music, 1975.

Sing a Sad Song   Williams, Roger M. *Sing a Sad Song: The Life of Hank Williams*. 2d ed. Urbana: University of Illinois Press, 1980.

Sing 'em Cowboy   *Sing 'em Cowboy, Sing 'em: Songs of the Trail and Range*. New York: Amsco Music Sales, [1934?].

Sizemore (1934)   *Asher Sizemore & Little Jimmie's Hearth & Home Songs*. Louisville: Sizemore, 1934.

Sizemore (1935)   *Asher Sizemore & Little Jimmie's Fireside Treasures*. 1936 ed. Louisville: Sizemore, 1935.

Smith, B.   *Blaine Smith & His Boys from Iowa*. Chicago: M. M. Cole, 1937.

Smith, C. F.   Smith, C. Fox. *A Book of Shanties*. Boston and New York: Houghton Mifflin 1927.

Smith, E. L.   Smith, Elmer L., ed. *Early American Broadsides & Ballads*. Lebanon, Pa.: Applied Arts Publishers, 1969.

Smith, G. H.   Smith, George H. *Novelty Album of Old Time Favorites*. New York: Wm. J. Smith Music, 1934.

Smith, J.   Smith, Jerry. *Western Heart Throbs: A Selected Collection of Famous Copyrighted Songs—Songs You Hear on the Radio and Records*. New York: Bob Miller, 1937.

Smith, John T. "Rails below the Rio Grande." In *And Horns on the Toads*, edited by Mody C. Boatwright, Wilson M. Hudson, and Allen Maxwell, pp. 122–35. Publications of the Texas Folklore Society, No. 29. Dallas: Southern Methodist University Press, 1959.

Smith, L. A.   Smith, Laura Alexandrine. *The Music of the Waters: A Collection of the Sailors' Chanties, or Working Songs of the Sea, of all Maritime Nations. Boatsmen's, Fishermen's and Rowing Songs, and Water Legends*. 1888. Rpt., Detroit: Singing Tree Press, 1969.

Smith, N. J. H.   Smith, Nicolas Joseph Hutchinson. "Six Negro Folksongs." In *Follow de Drinkin' Gou'd*, edited by J. Frank Dobie, pp. 113–18. Publications of the Texas Folklore Society, No. 7. Austin: Texas Folklore Society, 1928.

Smith, Stephe [*sic*] R. *Romance and Humor of the Road: A Book for Railway Men and Travelers*. Chicago: Horton and Leonard, Railroad Printers, 1871.

————. *Romance and Humor of the Rail*. New York: G. W. Carleton, 1873.

Smith, W. J.   *Smith's Collection of Mountain Ballads and Cowboy Songs*. New York: Wm. J. Smith Music, 1932.

Solenberger, Alice Willard. *One Thousand Homeless Men*. New York: Charities Publication Committee, 1911.

Songs for the Rodeo   *Songs for the Rodeo*. New York: Paull-Pioneer Music Corp., 1937.

Sounds like Folk   *Sounds like Folk, No. 2: The Railways in Song*. London: E.F.D.S. Publications, 1973.

Spaeth (1925)   Spaeth, Sigmund. *Barber Shop Ballads*. New York: Simon and Schuster, 1925.

Spaeth (1926)   ————. *Read 'em and Weep: The Songs You Forgot to Remember*. 1926. Rpt., New York: Da Capo Press, 1979.

Spaeth (1927)   ————. *Weep Some More My Lady*. Garden City, N.Y.: Doubleday, Page, 1927.

Spaeth (1945)   ————. *Read 'em and Weep*. 1926. Rpt. (with revisions), New York: Arco Publishing, 1945.

Spaeth (1948)   ————. *A History of Popular Music in America*. New York: Random House, 1948.

Speaker's Garland   *The Speaker's Garland and Literary Bouquet*. Complied by Phineas Garrett. [10?] vols. Philadelphia and Chicago: P. Garrett, 1888–[1900?]. Combines *One Hundred Choice Selections*, Nos. 1–[40?], q.v.

Stambler & Landon   Stambler, Irwin, and Grelun Landon. *Encyclopedia of Folk, Country, and Western Music*. New York: St. Martin's Press, 1969.

Steckmesser, Kent L. "Robin Hood and the American Outlaw." *Journal of American Folklore*, 79 (Apr.-June, 1966), 348–55. Reprinted in *Folklore of the Great West*, edited by John Greenway, pp. 335–34. Palo Alto: American West Publishing, 1969.

Steele   Steele, Virginia. "Legends of John Henry." *Wonderful West Virginia*, 36 (Oct., 1972), 10–11, 14, and (Nov., 1972), 18–19, 21, 29.

Stein   Stein, Zonweise. "'John Brown's Coal Mine.'" *Kentucky Folklore Record*, 7 (Oct.-Dec., 1961), 147–58.

Story Parade   *Songs from Story Parade*, edited by Margaret Thorne. New York: Furrow Press, 1945.

Stout   Stout, Earl J. *Folklore from Iowa*. New York: Stechert, 1936.

Stringbean   [Akeman, Dave]. *String Bean's Song, Jokes, and Picture Book*. N.p., n.d.

Stroud   *Toby Stroud's Hill Billy Song Hits, Book Number Two*. [Wheeling, W.Va.?.], ca. 1945.

A *Study of Railroad Transportation: Teacher's Manual: Suggested Study Outlines and Source Materials*. 8th ed. "Music and Recordings," vol. 1, pp. 39–46. Washington: Association of American Railroads, 1959.

Styles   Styles, Jack. "The Man at the Throttle was Casey Jones." *Sing Out!*, 7 (Fall, 1957), 28–29.

Swan   Swan, Clara Le Grande. "A Collection of Ballads and Folk Songs from Morning Sun, Iowa." Master's thesis, State University of Iowa, 1929.

Swanberg, W. A. *Jim Fisk: The Career of an Improbable Rascal*. New York: Charles Scribner's Sons, 1959.

Talley   Talley, Thomas W. *Negro Folk Rhymes: Wise and Otherwise*. New York: Macmillan, 1922.

Taylor, J. (I)   *Jake Taylor and His Railsplitters Log Book*. N.p., [1938?.].

Taylor, J. (II)   *Jake Taylor and His Gang's Gallery*. N.p., [1938?].

Taylor, J. (III)   *Jake Taylor and His Rail Splitters Looking Glass: Intimate Glimpses into the Lives of the Rail Splitters*. N.p., [1938?].

Taylor, M. W.   Taylor, Marshall W. *A Collection of Revival Hymns & Plantation Melodies*. Cincinnati, 1883.

Tennessee   *Tennessee*. New York: Federal Writers Project, 1939.

Terry   Terry, Richard Runciman. *The Shanty Book, Part 2*. London: J. Curwen and Songs, 1926.

TFSB   *Tennessee Folklore Society Bulletin*. Maryville, Tenn., 1935–.

Thede & Preece   Thede, Marion, and Harold Preece. "The Story behind the Song: The Ballad of Jesse James." *Real West,* 16, no. 119 (Sept., 1973), 8–13, 68–69.

Thirty-one   *Thirty-one More Songs to Remember*. New York: Shapiro, Bernstein, 1959.

Thomas, Gates. "South Texas Negro Work-Songs: Collected and Uncollected." In *Rainbow in the Morning,* edited by J. Frank Dobie, pp. 154–80. Publication of the Texas Folklore Society, No. 5. 1926. Rpt., Hatboro, Pa.: Folklore Associates, 1965.

Thomas   Thomas, Jean. *Ballad Makin' in the Mountains of Kentucky*. 1939. Rpt., New York: Oak Publications, 1964.

Thorp   Thorp, N. Howard "Jack." *Songs of the Cowboys*. Boston and New York: Houghton Mifflin, 1921.

Thurman   Thurman, Howard. *The Negro Spiritual Speaks of Life and Death*. New York: Harper, 1947.

Tiny Texan   Tiny Texan. *Cowboy & Mountain Ballads*. Chicago: M. M. Cole, 1930.

Titon, Jeff Todd. *Early Downhome Blues: A Musical and Cultural Analysis*. Urbana: University of Illinois Press, 1977.

Tolman   Tolman, Albert H. "Some Songs Traditional in the United States." *Journal of American Folklore,* 29 (Apr.-June, 1916), 155–97.

Townley, Eric. "Jazz, Blues, and U.S. Railroads." *Storyville,* No. 68 (Dec., 1976–Jan., 1977), pp. 55–58.

"Transportation in American Popular Songs: A Bibliography of Items in the Grosvenor Library." *Grosvenor Library Bulletin,* 27 (June, 1945). Buffalo, 1945.

Treasure Chest   *Treasure Chest of Cowboy Songs*. New York: Treasure Chest Publishers, 1935. Also issued as *Cowboy Songs as Sung by Cowboy Joe*.

Tribe & Morris   Tribe, Ivan M., and John W. Morris. *Molly O'Day, Lynn Davis, and the Cumberland Mountain Folks: A Bio-Discography*. JEMF Special Series, No. 7. Los Angeles: John Edwards Memorial Foundation, 1975.

Triplett, Frank. *The Life, Times and Treacherous Death of Jesse James*. Edited by Joseph Snell. 1882. Rpt., New York: Promontory Press, 1970.

Turner   Nevada Slim [Dallas Turner]. *Nevada Slim's Western Gospel Roundup*. Reno: Ruby Valley Enterprises, 1972.

Turner & Miall   Turner, Michael R., and Antony Miall. *Just a Song at Twilight: The Second Parlour Song Book*. London: Michael Joseph, 1975.

Two Hundred   *Two Hundred Popular Cowboy Songs and Mountain Ballads*. New York: Hobo News, n.d.

Ulevich   Ulevich, Neal. "Wreck of the Old 97." *Washington Star Sunday Magazine,* Nov. 5, 1967, pp. 23–26.

Vagabonds   Vagabonds. *Old Cabin Songs*. Nashville: Old Cabin, n.d.

Wakely   *Jimmie Wakely's Roundup*. New York: Southern Music Publishing, 1943.

Wallrich   Wallrich, William. *Air Force Airs: Songs and Ballads of the United States Air Force, World War One through Korea*. New York: Duell, Sloan and Pearce, 1957.

Walsh (1960)   Walsh, Jim. "Vernon Dalhart." Parts 4 and 5. *Hobbies, the Magazine for Collectors,* 65 (Aug., 1960), 33–35, 60, and (Sept., 1960), 34–36, 45, 49.

Walsh (1964)   ———. "Leaving on That New River Train with a Stop-over at Foster Falls, Va." *Hobbies, the Magazine for Collectors,* 69 (Oct., 1964), 120–24.

Ward, William. *The Younger Brothers: The Border Outlaws*. Cleveland: Westbrook, 1908.

Warman   Warman, Cy. *The White Mail*. New York: Charles Scribner's Sons, 1899.

Watson   Watson, Arthel "Doc." *The Songs of Doc Watson*. New York: Oak Publications, 1971.

Weavers (1951)   *The Weavers Sing: Folksongs of America and Other Lands*. New York: Folkways Music Publishers, 1951.

Weavers (1960)   *The Weavers' Song Book*. Edited by the Weavers. New York: Harper and Row,
1960.

Weavers (1966)   *Travelin' On with the Weavers*. Edited by Ronnie Gilbert. New York and
London: Harper, Row, 1966.

Webb (1915)   Webb, W. Prescott. "Notes on Folk-Lore of Texas." *Journal of American Folklore*, 28 (July-Sept., 1915), 290–99.

Webb (1923)   ———."Miscellany of Texas Folk-lore." In *Coffee in the Gourd*, edited by
J. Frank Dobie, pp. 38–49. Publications of the Texas Folklore Society, No. 2. Austin: Texas
Folklore Society, 1923.

Webber, Bert. *Oregon's Great Train Holdup*. Fairfield, Wash.: Galleon Press, 1973.

Wehman, Henry. *Wehman's 100 Popular Comic, Dramatic and Dialect and Recitations*. New
York: H. J. Wehman, n.d.

Wehman #1   *Wehman Brothers Good Old Time Songs, No. 1, Containing a Choice Selection of
177 Songs*. New York: Wehman Brothers, 1910.

Wehman #2   *Wehman Brothers Good Old Time Songs, No. 2, Containing a Choice Selection of
174 Songs*. New York: Wehman Brothers, 1910.

Wehman #3   *Wehman Brothers Good Old Time Songs, No. 3, Containing a Choice Selection of
173 Songs*. New York: Wehman Brothers, 1914.

Wehman #4   *Wehman Brothers Good Old Time Songs, No. 4, Containing a Choice Selection of
166 Songs*. New York: Wehman Brothers, 1916.

Wehman *100 Popular*   Wehman Brothers. *100 Popular Comic, Dramatic and Dialect Recitations #2*. New York: Wehman Brothers, n.d.

Welsch (1966)   Welsch, Roger L. *A Treasury of Nebraska Pioneer Folklore*. Lincoln: University
of Nebraska Press, 1966.

Welsch (1970)   ———. "A 'Buffalo Skinner's' Family Tree." *Journal of Popular Culture*, 4
(Summer, 1970), 107–29.

Wentworth, Harold, and Stuart Berg Flexner. *Dictionary of American Slang*. New York: Thomas Y.
Crowell, 1960.

Werner   *Werner's Readings and Recitations, #7*. New York: E. S. Werner, 1892.

Wertz   Wertz, Dave. "About Wallace Saunders, Casey Jones, Simeon Webb, and a Few Other
People." *Seattle Folklore Society Journal*, 2 (June, 1971), 17–19.

West, C. A.   West, C. A., comp. *Mountain Melodies*. Vaughns Mill, Ky.: by the author, 1931.

West. J. O.   West, John Oliver. "To Die like a Man: The 'Good' Outlaw Tradition in the
American Southwest." Ph.D. diss., University of Texas, 1964.

WF   *Western Folklore*. California Folklore Society. Berkeley and Los Angeles, 1947–. Successor
to *California Folklore Quarterly*; see *CFQ*.

Whall   Whall, W. B. *Sea Songs and Shanties*. 6th ed. 1927. Rpt., Glasgow: Brown, Son and
Ferguson, 1948.

Wheeler, M.   Wheeler, Mary. *Steamboatin' Days: Folk Songs of the River Packet Era*. Baton
Rouge: Louisiana State University Press, 1944.

Wheeler, O.   Wheeler, Opal. *Sing for America*. New York: E. P. Dutton, 1944.

White, J.   *The Josh White Song Book*. Chicago: Quadrangle Books, 1963.

White, N. I.   White, Newman I. *American Negro Folk-Songs*. 1928. Rpt., Hatboro, Pa.:
Folklore Associates, 1965.

Whitey & Hogan   Grant, Roy "Whitey," and Arval A. Hogan. *Whitey and Hogan's Mountain
Memories*. New York: Bourne, 1947.

Whitter   Whitter, Henry. *Familiar Folk Songs*. N.p., ca. 1935.

Wier (1929)   Wier, Albert E. *Songs of the Sunny South*. New York: Appleton-Century, 1929.

Wier (1941)   ———. *Songs for the Leisure Hour*. New York: Longmans, Green, 1941.

Wild West Weekly. New York: Street and Smith, 1902–28.

Wilgus (1957)   Wilgus, D. K. "Folksongs of Kentucky, East and West." *Kentucky Folklore Record,* 3 (July-Sept., 1957), 89–118.

———. *Anglo-American Folksong Scholarship since 1898.* New Brunswick, N.J.: Rutgers University Press, 1959.

———. "The Rationalistic Approach." In *Folksong and Folksong Scholarship,* pp. 29–39. Dallas: Southern Methodist University Press, 1964. Also published as "Folksong Scholarship: Changing Approaches and Attitudes; 4: The Rationalistic Approach." In *A Good Tale and a Bonnie Tune,* edited by Mody C. Boatright, pp. 227–37. Publications of the Texas Folklore Society, No. 32. Dallas: Southern Methodist University Press, 1964.

Wilgus (1964?)   ———. Liner notes to Bluebonnet BL 112: *Bradley Kincaid—Album Number Four.* 1964?

Wilgus (1969)   ———. Liner notes to RCA Victor LPV 548: *Native American Ballads.* 1969.

———. "A Type Index of Anglo-American Traditional Narrative Songs." *Journal of the Folklore Institute,* 7 (Aug.-Dec., 1970), 161–76.

Williams   Williams, Cratis Dearl. *Ballads and Songs.* Lexington: Southern Atlantic Modern Language Assn., 1937

Williams, Gary. "The Case of the Siskiyou Slaying." *Frontier Times,* Mar., 1973, pp. 38–40, 46–47.

Wills   *Bob Wills' Song Book.* New York: Irving Berlin Publishing, 1942.

Wilson (1937a)   *Slim Pickens Wilson and His Prairie Playboys Folio.* Chicago: M. M. Cole, 1937.

Wilson (1937b)   Wilson, Clyde. *Finest Collection of Cowboy and Mountain Ballads.* Chicago: M. M. Cole, 1937.

WKFA   Western Kentucky Folklore Archive. University of California, Los Angeles.

WLW   *Favorite Songs of the WLW Boone County Jamboree.* Chicago: M. M. Cole, 1941.

Wolf   Wolf, Edwin, II. *American Song Sheets, Slips Ballads and Poetical Broadsides, 1850–1870: A Catalogue of the Collection of the Library Company of Philadelphia.* Philadelphia: Library Company of Philadelphia, 1963.

Wolfe (1956)   Wolfe, Irving, Beatrice Krone, and Margaret Fullerton, eds. *Proudly We Sing.* Together We Sing Series, Grade 8. Chicago: Follett Publishing, 1956.

Wolfe (1958)   ———. *Music Sounds Afar.* Together We Sing Series, Grade 7. Chicago: Follett Publishing, 1958.

Work   Work, John W. *American Negro Songs and Spirituals.* New York: Bonanza Books, 1940.

World's Best   *The World's Best Cowboy Songs.* New York: Amsco Music Sales, 1941.

WPA (Alderman)   WPA materials in the Alderman Library, University of Virginia, as cited in Rosenberg (q.v.).

WSM   *Song Favorites of WSM Grand Ole Opry.* Chicago: M. M. Cole, 1942.

Younger   *The Story of Cole Younger, by Himself, being an Autobiography of the Missouri Guerrrilla Captain and Outlaw, His Capture and Prison Life, and the Only Authentic Account of the Northfield Raid Ever Published.* 1903. Rpt. (with some changes of photos), Houston: Frontier Press, 1955.

Zanzig   Zanzig, Augustus D., comp., arr., and ed. *Singing America: Song and Chorus Book.* National Recreation Association. Boston: C. C. Birchard, 1940.

Index

Page numbers for the main discussions of songs are given in **boldface**.

NORM COHEN, born in 1936, is Executive Secretary of the John Edwards Memorial Foundation at UCLA and Editor of the *JEMF Quarterly*. He is the author of *Long Steel Rail: The Railroad in American Folksong* (1980) and of numerous articles and reviews on American folk and early hillbilly music, in *Journal of American Folklore*, *Western Folklore*, *New York Folklore Quarterly*, *JEMF Quarterly*, and other journals. Trained in chemistry and mathematics at Reed College (B. A.) and the University of California at Berkeley (M. A., Ph. D.), Cohen is Head of the Chemical Kinetics Department at the Aerospace Corporation in El Segundo, California.

DAVID COHEN, born in 1942, was co-founder and co-director of the School of Traditional Folk Music at the Ash Grove in Los Angeles, where he taught finger picking and blues guitar styles for many years. He has also taught advanced guitar classes for the Extension Division of the University of California at Los Angeles. Since 1966 he has worked as a studio guitar player. Cohen served as music editor for *Songs of the Gold Rush* (1964) and *Songs of the American West* (1968), both published by the University of California Press, and for *Long Steel Rail* (1980, University of Illinois Press).